SCANDINAVIA
DENMARK, NORWAY, SWEDEN, FINLAND, ICELAND, FAROE ISLANDS

THE ROUGH GUIDE

D1337792

ROUGH GUIDE CREDITS

Series Editor: Mark Ellingham
Editorial: Martin Dunford, John Fisher, Jack Holland, Jonathan Buckley
Production: Susanne Hillen, Gail Jammy, Kate Berens, Andy Hilliard
Typesetting and Design: Greg Ward
Series Design: Andrew Oliver

Thanks for help, ideas and encouragement to:

Denmark Britt Sander and Kurt Nielsen of the Danish Tourist Board, Ole Gram, DSB, Scandinavian Seaways, Danmarks Vandrehjem, Use-It, Gitte Sørensen.

Norway Carl P. Salicath, Odd Karsten Krogh and Capt. I. Little for sharing his specialist knowledge of Trondheim.

Sweden Barbro Hunter and Astrid Ruffhead at the Swedish Tourist Board in London and Pernilla Ullberger in Stockholm, Sylvie Kjellin of the Stockholm Information Service, Ella Brehmer at Göteborgs Turistråd, Swedish State Railways, Kristina Byström (Östergötland), Eva Ulvsbäck (Strängnäs), Peter Ericsson for help and beer in Uppsala, Anders Fernström (Vidmarkshotellet), Sofie Reutercrona (Central Hotel, Stockholm), Grand Hotel (Helsingborg), Savoy Hotel (Malmö), Hotel Linné (Uppsala) and Magnus Lagergren (Gripsholm Värdshus).

Finland Marjatta Haapio, Rytva Müller and Boris Taimitarha at the Finnish Tourist Board, Jyrki Hukka at the Helsinki Tourist Office, Suomon Retkeilymajajärestö, Saimaa Lines, Vesa Jussila, Iiris Hälli, Merja (and Tim) Carty, Marja-Leena Pietikainen, Heidi Pusa.

Iceland Hulda Jónsdóttir at Bandalag Íslenskra Farfugla, Gunnar Sveinsson and Sigurdur Arnbjörnsson at BSÍ, Arctic Experience, Scanscape Holidays, Icelandair, Ási Jónsson, HÖH, Gunni, Louise Sturgis, Maria Bienert, Dick Phillips.

Thanks, too, to all those people who have taken the trouble to write to us after the first edition of this book: Brian Barefoot, Phil Lee, Scott Ferguson, Julie Bedford, Dr. K. W. Lovel (twice!), Torcull Kennedy, Duncan Cook, Michael Pacillo, Revd. B. R. and Mrs L. M. McHugh, Marjorie Bocking, S.E.M. Whitehead, Nick Moore, M. Wilson, Julie Robinson, Joel Newman, Katie McCann, Marie Louise Kinsler and Eoin O'Sullivan, James Proctor, Mrs E. M. Sumption, Bernard Myers, Ron McLellan, Ian A. Hesford, Irene Boyle, and F. Sahlström.

And thanks, as always, to the *Rough Guides* crew and others who helped out along the way: including Greg Ward, Susanne Hillen, Mark Salter, Bridget Bouch and Helen Lee.

The publishers and authors have done their best to ensure the accuracy and currency of all the information in **The Rough Guide Scandinavia**; however, they can accept no responsibility for any loss, injury, or inconvenience sustained by any traveller as a result of information or advice contained in the guide.

Published by Harrap Columbus, Chelsea House, 26 Market Square, Bromley, Kent BR1 1NA

Typeset in Linotron Univers and Century Old Style
Icelandic typography by Jon Dear
Printed by Cox & Wyman, Reading, Berks

British Library Cataloguing in Publication Data
Brown, Jules
Scandinavia: the Rough Guide. – 2nd ed.
I. Title II. Sinclair, Mick III. Brown, Jules
914.8'0488
ISBN 0–7471–0212–0

SCANDINAVIA

DENMARK, NORWAY, SWEDEN, FINLAND, ICELAND, FAROE ISLANDS

written and researched by

JULES BROWN and MICK SINCLAIR

With additional accounts by
Helen McIlroy, Phil Lee, Dave Driscoll and Celia Woolfrey

edited by

Martin Dunford and Jack Holland

HARRAP COLUMBUS ■ LONDON

CONTENTS

Introduction

INTRODUCTION

Scandinavia – Denmark, Norway, Sweden, Finland, Iceland and the Faroe Islands – conjures resonant images: wild, untamed lands, reindeer and the Midnight Sun, peopled by wealthy, healthy, blue-eyed blondes enjoying life in a benevolent welfare state. Yet it's a picture that's only partially accurate. Certainly, by western European standards Scandinavia is affluent, with a high standard of living and the near eradication of poverty. And for travellers it holds some of Europe's most unspoilt terrain. But it's by no means paradise: there's a social conformity that can be stifling, and the problems of the other industrialised countries – drug addiction, racism, street violence – are beginning to make themselves felt. The larger part of the population clusters in the south, where there's all the culture, nightlife and action you'd expect. But no one capital fully reflects its society – nothing like it. With the exception of Denmark these are large, often physically inhospitable countries and rural traditions remain strong, not least in the great tracts of land above the Arctic Circle, where the *Same* (Lapps) survive as they have done for thousands of years – by reindeer herding, hunting and fishing.

Historically, the Scandinavian countries have been closely entwined, though in spite of this they remain strikingly individual. For visitors, the efficient and well-organised tourist infrastructure lessens the shock of getting about in what are, after all, Europe's most expensive countries. **Denmark** is the geographical and social bridge between Europe and Scandinavia – easy to reach and the best known of the Scandinavian countries. The Danes are much the most gregarious of the Nordic peoples, something manifest in the region's most relaxed and appealing capital, Copenhagen, and the decidedly more permissive attitude to alcohol.

Norway, conversely, features great mountains, a remote and bluff northern coast and the mighty western fjords: raw, inaccessible landscapes which can demand long, hard travel. Even by Scandinavian standards the country is sparsely populated, and people live in small communities along a coastline which stretches from the lower reaches of the North Sea right up to the Soviet border.

Sweden is the most "Scandinavian" country in the world's eyes: affluent and with a social system and consensus politics that are considered an enlightened model, though confidence in the country's institutions has been shaken of late with the death of Olof Palme and rising crime and unemployment. Travelling is simple enough, although Sweden has Scandinavia's least varied landscape – away from the southern cities and coastal regions an almost unbroken swathe of lakes, forests and hills, in which every Swede has a second, peaceful, weekend home.

Finland is perhaps the least known of the mainland Scandinavian countries. Ruled for hundreds of years by the Swedes and then the Russians, it became independent only this century and has grown into a vibrant, confident nation. Its vast coniferous forests and great lake systems have shaped a Finnish empathy with their country and its nature which is hard to ignore. Also, though Finland is undeniably Scandinavian and looks west for its lifestyle, there are, historically and culturally, a number of similarities between Finland and Eastern Europe; foreign policy, too, is influenced by the country's proximity to the Soviet Union.

Iceland is a severe country, dominated by a dramatic and spectacular geology, and with a language that has barely changed for a thousand years. But it's also expensive, something that may discourage casual travellers – a shame considering the uniqueness of the environment. The **Faroe Islands**, too, are pricey and practise prohibition, and with this in mind few people see them as part of a Scandinavian tour (although it is possible to reach them from Denmark, Norway or Iceland). But if you've time for a leisurely visit, their distinct, jagged beauty is well worth experiencing, and the islands are a summer breeding ground for huge numbers of birds.

Connections and costs
Travelling in Scandinavia is easy. Public transport is efficient and well co-ordinated, there are a minimum of border formalities between each country, and there are excellent connections between all the main towns and cities; indeed, on one trip it's perfectly feasible to visit several, if not all, of the mainland countries though the islands, inevitably, demand more time. From western Europe it's simplest to enter Denmark, from where you can continue northwards into Norway (by boat) or Sweden (by boat or train), the two countries separated by a long north–south border. From Sweden's east coast there are regular ferries across to Finland, as well as a land border between the two in the far north. Ferries to the Faroes and Iceland run from Hantsholm in Denmark and Bergen in Norway, ' .king in the Shetland Islands on the way.

As for **costs**, the Scandinavian countries are expensive, but not uniformly so. Denmark is the least pricey, Norway and Sweden considerably more expensive, Finland sometimes even dearer, while Iceland and the Faroes can be horrendous. Food items in supermarkets cost two to three times as much as Britain, eating out is not cheap and drink prices are unsettlingly high. It's not all bad news though. Single travellers don't lose out too much on accommodation, since hostels and the cheaper hotels usually charge by the bed. And an *ISIC* (student) card (£4), available from most student and youth travel offices, is well worth having, giving discounts and free entry to many museums and sights. If you're not eligible, the *YIEE/FIYTO* card (£3) can be a help too, especially if accompanied by the muttered word "student". In general, as a *very* rough guide, expect to pay around £15–20 a day just to get by, more like £30–40 a day to live reasonably well; for more details on costs see the relevant country's "Costs, Money and Banks" section.

When to go
Deciding **when to go** isn't easy, since, except for Denmark, Scandinavia experiences intense seasonal changes. The short summers (roughly mid-June to mid-August) can be as hot as in any southern European resort, with high temperatures regularly recorded in Denmark, southern Norway and Sweden, and the whole Baltic islands. Even the northern areas of each country are temperate, the whole of the Norwegian west coast, for example, warmed by the Gulf Stream. Rain, though, is regular, and in the far north of Norway especially, in Sweden and Finland less so, summer temperatures can plunge extremely low at night, so campers need decent equipment for extended spells of sleeping out. One bonus this far north, though not exactly a boon to sleep, is the almost constant daylight lent by the Midnight Sun.

The **summer** is celebrated everywhere with a host of outdoor events and festivities, and is the time when all the facilities for travellers (tourist offices, hotel and transport discounts, summer timetables) are functioning. However, it's also the most crowded time to visit, as all the Scandinavians are on holiday too: go either side of summer (late May/early June or September), when the weather is still reasonable, and you'll benefit from more peace and space. Autumn, especially, is a beautiful time to travel, with the trees and hillsides turning golden brown in a matter of days.

In **winter**, from November to around late May, only Denmark retains a semblance of western European weather, while the other countries suffer long, dark and extremely cold days. The cold may be severe but it is crisp and sharp, never damp, and if you're well wrapped up the cities at least needn't be off-limits – though, unless you're exceptionally hardy, the far north is best left to its own, gloomy devices. You'll find broad climatic details in each country's "Introduction"; for mean temperatures all year round, check the **temperature chart** below.

What to take

It's as well to give some thought as to **what to take** – and worth packing that bit more to stave off despair later. Expect occasional rain throughout the summer and take a waterproof jacket and a spare pullover. A small, foldaway umbrella is useful too. If camping, a warm sleeping bag is vital and good walking shoes essential (comfortable, too, in sprawling cities and the flat southern lands). Mosquitoes are a pest in summer, especially further north and in lake regions, and some form of barrier/treatment cream is necessary. For winter travel, take as many layers as you can pack. Gloves, a hat or scarf that covers your face, and thick socks are required items; thermal underwear saves you from cold legs.

	Jan	Feb	March	April	May	June	July	Aug	Sept	Oct	Nov	Dec
AVERAGE TEMPERATURES °F												
Denmark												
Copenhagen	32	32	35	44	53	60	64	63	57	49	42	36
Norway												
Oslo	23	25	30	41	52	59	63	61	52	43	34	28
Bergen	35	35	37	43	50	55	59	59	54	46	41	37
Tromsø	26	25	28	32	38	48	54	54	45	37	32	28
Sweden												
Stockholm	27	30	30	39	53	57	64	62	51	45	40	34
Östersund	18	26	22	33	50	52	59	54	44	39	30	27
Haparanda	14	21	15	30	48	56	61	55	44	36	25	22
Finland												
Helsinki	22	21	26	37	48	58	63	61	53	43	35	28
Tampere	17	17	23	35	47	56	61	59	50	40	32	25
Ivalo	8	8	16	27	39	49	56	52	42	31	21	14
Iceland												
Reykjavík	29	30	32	37	44	50	53	51	46	40	34	31

Note that these are *average temperatures*. The Gulf Stream can produce some very temperate year-round weather and, in summer, southern Scandinavia can be blisteringly hot. In winter, on the other hand, temperatures of -40°F are not unknown in the far north.

Throughout the *Guide* a geographical distinction is made between **mainland Scandinavia** (Denmark, Norway, Sweden and Finland) and the **islands** (Iceland and the Faroes), principally because most visitors to Iceland or the Faroes travel direct. The *Basics* section which follows deals only with background information on the mainland countries; for practical details on Iceland and the Faroes, see pages 547 and 621 respectively. And for more specific practical information on each of the mainland countries, see the relevant country accounts.

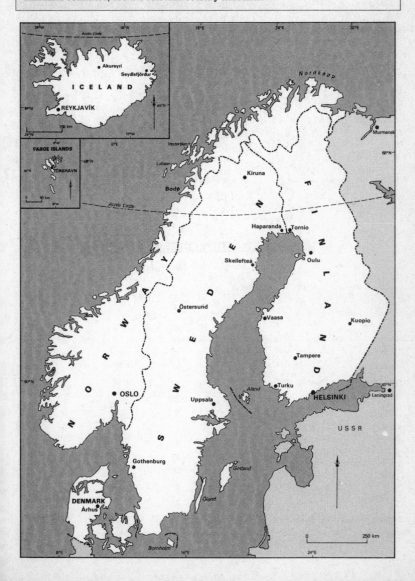

PART ONE

THE

BASICS

GETTING THERE

The details below cover routes to Denmark, Norway, Sweden and Finland from Britain, Ireland, Australia and New Zealand. For connections within Scandinavia itself, see the "Getting There" sections for each individual country. For how to get to Iceland and the Faroes, see p.548 and p.621.

BY PLANE

Flying to Scandinavia isn't especially cheap. Low-cost **charter** flights do exist, but they're few and far between and serve only limited destinations; more information below, and from the operators listed under "Packages". Often the best starting-point for the **cheapest deals** to Scandinavia is the classified sections in the Sunday newspapers (*The Sunday Times* especially), or, if you live in London, *Time Out* magazine or the *Evening Standard*. Failing that, go straight to a discount flight agent like *STA Travel* or *Campus Travel* (addresses below); they specialise in youth flights, and generally have good deals if you're under 26 or a student, as well as ordinary discounted tickets if you're not.

It's also worth trying the **major scheduled airlines** – *British Airways*, *SAS* (the airline of Denmark, Norway and Sweden) and *Finnair*. The cost of an Apex ticket is often the same as the fare you'll get from an agent. There are, however, the usual Apex restrictions: you have to book fourteen days in advance, stay at least one Saturday night abroad and you have no option to change your flight. It's not really worth shopping around the major airlines since the Apex fares at least are matched.

If you don't live in London, bear in mind that a number of smaller airlines offer good deals from different **regional airports**; full details are given below. Worth considering also is a **package deal**, particularly if you're clear on where you want to go and only intend to stay for a week or less; city breaks, particularly, can work out very good value. Again, full details below.

TO DENMARK

Between them, *British Airways* and *SAS* have nine flights a day from London to Copenhagen, a two-hour flight; from the Midlands, *Birmingham Executive Airways* fly to Copenhagen daily except Saturday. If you're keen to avoid Copenhagen, *SAS* fly around twice daily from London to Århus (1hr 40min), and it's also possible to fly from Southend to Billund in Jutland with *Maersk Air*. Apex return fares to Copenhagen and Århus are currently £150–170.

TO NORWAY

British Airways and *SAS* have several daily flights to Oslo (2hr) from London, for a fare of around £186 return; there are daily flights, too, to Bergen (£161; 2hr) and Stavanger (£153; 1hr 40min direct, up to 4hr via Copenhagen). If you're making straight for the fjords, you may find it handier (and quicker) to fly with one of the smaller airlines: *Dan-Air*, *Air Europe* and *Air UK* all offer services to Stavanger and Bergen for Apex return fares of around £140, and fly from a range of regional airports including Norwich, Humberside, Teeside, Newcastle, Edinburgh and Aberdeen. For charter fares to Oslo, try *Star Tour of Scandinavia* (address under "Package Tours", below) – they sometimes go for as little as £49 return.

TO SWEDEN

British Airways and *SAS* fly several times daily from London to Stockholm (2hr 20min) and Gothenburg (1hr 45min), for Apex return fares of £226 and £177 respectively. There's also a daily (except Sat) *SAS* service to Malmö (2hr 45min), via Århus or Copenhagen, the Apex fare £185. If you live in the north of England, or Scotland, *British Airways'* new Manchester–Stockholm service (3hr 25min), via Copenhagen, could be useful: one daily departure with an Apex fare of

AIRLINE ADDRESSES AND ROUTES

Air Europe, The Galleria, Station Road, Crawley, West Sussex (☎0293-502 671; reservations on ☎0345-444 737). Gatwick to Oslo, Edinburgh to Bergen and Stavanger; youth fares for under-25s.

Air UK, Stansted House, Stansted Airport, Essex (☎0279-755 950; reservations on ☎0345-666 777). Usually one flight daily Monday to Friday on the following routes: Aberdeen to Stavanger and Bergen, Norwich to Bergen, Edinburgh to Bergen and Stavanger, Humberside to Bergen and Stavanger, Teeside to Bergen and Stavanger.

Birmingham Executive Airways, Jetstream House, Birmingham International Airport, Coventry Road, Birmingham (☎021-782 0711). Birmingham to Copenhagen daily except Saturday; three weekly to Oslo.

British Airways, 156 Regent Street, London W1 (☎081-897 4000). London to Copenhagen, Oslo, Stockholm, Helsinki; Manchester to Stockholm and Copenhagen.

Dan-Air, Victoria Street, Horley, Surrey RH6 7QG (☎081-680 1011). Newcastle to Stavanger, Bergen and Oslo; connecting services from Gatwick and Manchester.

Finnair, 14 Clifford Street, London W1 (☎071-408 1222). London to Helsinki.

Maersk Air, Liverpool Street Station, London EC2 (☎071-623 3813). Southend to Billund (in Jutland).

SAS, 52–53 Conduit Street, London W1 (☎071-734 4020). London to Copenhagen, Oslo, Stockholm, Århus, Malmö.

DISCOUNT FLIGHT AGENTS

Campus Travel, 52 Grosvenor Gardens, London SW1 (☎071-730 3402).

STA Travel, 86 Old Brompton Road, London SW7 (☎071-937 9921).

Travel Cuts, 295 Regent Street, London W1 (☎071-255 1944).

£235 return. *Scanscape* (address under "Package Tours") run summer charters to Stockholm and Gothenburg, departing from London Stansted, around £140–150 return.

TO FINLAND

There are four daily flights between London and Helsinki, a three-hour trip; one of these is with *British Airways*, the others are *Finnair* flights. Apex return fares with both airlines are £221.

BY TRAIN

Taking a **train** can be a more relaxed way of getting there, though it doesn't work out a lot cheaper than flying, and is even more expensive if you're over 26. However, a number of deals valid for all the mainland countries make it possible to cut costs, especially if you're intending to do a lot of travelling around once there.

One of the most popular if you're under 26 is to purchase a **BIJ** ticket, which gives up to fifty percent discount on ordinary fares. Available through *Eurotrain* or *Wasteels*, these allow as many stopovers as you like and are valid for two months. You can follow a choice of routes to Scandinavia, and buy a ticket to more or less any reasonable-sized town. Tickets are available either direct from the operators themselves (addresses below), or from youth and student

travel agents. *Eurotrain* also sell something called a **Scandinavian Explorer** (from £212.50), a fixed-route ticket, valid for two months, which will get you from London and back via Copenhagen, Stockholm, Oslo and Frederikshavn. *Wasteels* will construct a similar **Mini-Tour** of Scandinavia for you: a return from London, through Denmark to Copenhagen, comes at around £122.

If you are under 26 but have no clear itinerary, the **InterRail** pass might be a better bet. At a cost of £155, it's valid for one month's unlimited rail travel throughout Europe (including the Scandinavian networks) and gives discounts on cross-Channel ferry services. There's also the **InterRail Boat Pass** (£180), which in addition gives free travel on the *Stena* line ferry services between Sweden and Denmark, and usually (it varies from year to year) on the *Silja* and *Viking* routes between Sweden and Finland. A variation on both passes is the new **InterRail Flexi-Card**, offering the same deal as the *InterRail Boat Pass* but only valid for ten days; cost £140. All these passes are available from *British Rail* stations and youth/student travel agencies, and you need to have been resident in Europe for at least six months to qualify for one.

If you're 60 or over, the **Rail Europ Senior Card** brings you thirty percent discounts in most of western Europe, including Scandinavia. To obtain it, you must first have a *Senior Citizen Rail*

Card (details from any railway station) and pay an extra £5 at any *British Rail* Travel Centre or travel agent specialising in European rail.

Anyone thinking of travelling extensively by train might be well advised to take the latest monthly copy of the *Thomas Cook European Rail Timetable* (£4.95), listing every train and ferry **timetable** in Europe.

TO DENMARK

To Copenhagen, there's a choice of three routes from London. The longest, via Harwich and Esbjerg, takes over 27hr, and cabin reservations are obligatory; the others – via either Amsterdam and Hamburg, or Ostend and Hamburg – take around 4hr less. Whichever way you go, the ordinary fare from London to Copenhagen or Århus is around £90 one-way (£174 return); the cheapest under-26 fare is currently £46.20 (£92.30 return).

TO NORWAY

There's one daily departure from London to Oslo, going via the Hook of Holland, Hamburg and Copenhagen and arriving 34hr later; the ordinary fare is £139.40 one-way (£272.20 return); £106.30 (£212.40 return) if you're under 26. Under-26s can make a considerable saving by using an alternative routing, via Harwich and Esbjerg: this only costs £166.40 return but it takes a massive sixty hours each way.

TO SWEDEN

All trains to Sweden from London go via Copenhagen, using either the Dover–Ostend or Harwich–Hook of Holland crossing; the journey takes 32hr to Stockholm, 28hr to Gothenburg and 25hr to Malmö, and ordinary one-way fares are £110–135 – around £75–85 if you're under 26; returns are exactly double the price. You could also use the Harwich–Esbjerg crossing, taking a connecting train via Copenhagen; see "To Denmark" above.

RAIL TICKET OFFICES

British Rail European Travel Centre, Victoria Station, London SW1 (☎071-834 2345).

Eurotrain, 52 Grosvenor Gardens, London SW1 (☎071-730 3402). There's also a kiosk in Victoria Station, London, and *Eurotrain* tickets can be booked at branches of *Thomas Cook, Hogg Robinson, Pickfords Travel* and *AT Mays*.

Wasteels, 121 Wilton Road, London SW1 (☎071-834 7066).

TO FINLAND

To **Finland**, all trains go to Turku and Helsinki, using the *Silja* line ferry link from Stockholm. From London an ordinary one-way ticket costs around £150, a shade over £100 if you're under 26 (around £200 return).

BY COACH

Coach services to Scandinavia can be an endurance test, but are the best option for anyone on a tight budget and over 26. To **Denmark**, the *Denmark Line* operates a weekly service from London to Copenhagen (£70 single, £95 return) and Århus (£50 single, £80 return). There's also a summer service every Saturday from London to Copenhagen, via Fredericia and Odense, operated by *JCP Sally Express* – £80 return. Journey times to Århus and Copenhagen are around 24hr and 26hr respectively. *National Express Eurolines* also operate two competitive routes to Denmark (£51 one-way, £93 return to Copenhagen), and give small discounts (around £10–15 off) to under-25s, senior citizens and students.

Eurolines are also the best bet for coaches to the other Scandinavian countries. To **Norway**, there are twice-weekly departures to Oslo, via Gothenburg, which take 45hr and cost £95 one-way, £156 return. To **Sweden**, the twice-weekly coach reaches Stockholm in about 47hr, for £90 one-way, £144 return; to Gothenburg takes 41hr (£76 one-way, £131 return); to Malmö 37hr (£68 one-way, £116 return). **Finland** is 65hr away: if you can take the journey, coaches run twice weekly to Helsinki for £112 one-way, £188 return.

BY CAR/HITCHING THE FERRIES

Ferry connections from Britain link Harwich and Newcastle with Denmark, western Sweden and southern Norway. Two main companies ply the routes; fares aren't cheap, but both offer discounts and special deals to cut costs greatly. *Scandinavian Seaways* (formerly *DFDS*) have a year-round *Midweek Super Saver* deal (cheap returns if you travel in both directions on Mon, Tues or Wed); *Seapex* fares, which have to be booked at least four weeks before departure; and a fifty percent discount for *ISIC* card holders. *Fred Olsen Lines* knock fifty percent off all routes for the over-60s and their spouses, and the registered disabled. On both lines, kids under four go free, and there's fifty percent off for those between four and sixteen years of age.

COACH COMPANIES

Denmark Line, 52 Grosvenor Gardens, London SW1 (☎071-730 8235).

JCP Sally Express, 23 Bourne End Road, Northwood, Middlesex (Mon–Fri 9–11am only; ☎0923-835696).

National Express Eurolines, 52 Grosvenor Gardens, London SW1 (☎071-730 0202); Birmingham (☎021-622 4373); Manchester (☎061-228 3881); Liverpool (☎051-709 6841).

FERRY OPERATORS

Fred Olsen Lines, Tyne Commission Quay, Albert Edward Dock, North Shields, NE29 6EA (☎091-257 9682).

Norway Line, Tyne Commission Quay, Albert Edward Dock, North Shields, NE29 6EA (☎091-296 1313).

Scandinavian Seaways, Scandinavia House, Parkeston Quay, Harwich, Essex CO12 4QG (☎0255-240 240); Tyne Commission Quay, North Shields, NE29 6EA (☎091-296 0101); London enquiries/reservations office at 15 Hanover Street, London W1 (☎071-493 6696).

United Baltic, Baltic Exchange Buildings, 21 Bury Street, London EC3 (☎071-283 1266).

Unless otherwise stated, we've quoted the cheapest possible **fares** below – for a one-way passage with a cabin or reclining-chair. Not surprisingly, all fares are usually at their lowest between January and March.

TO DENMARK

Scandinavian Seaways sail from Harwich to Esbjerg daily in summer, three times weekly in winter, and the trip takes nearly 19hr. During the summer they also make the 20hr crossing from Newcastle to Esbjerg three times a week. There's a one-way fare on both crossings of £78 in high season, though *Seapex* or *Super Saver* deals can bring the price down to about £100–110 return in high season, £74–80 return low season; at any time of year add on £40 for your car. *Scandinavian Seaways* also run a summer-only **Sea-Air** service between London and Copenhagen, travelling one way by boat, the other by plane, for £200–250.

Much less frequently (once-weekly), *Fred Olsen Lines* link Newcastle with Hirtshals, in northern Jutland, for £38–43 per person one-way, plus £17–35 for your car; journey-time around 27hr. On this route, **families** (up to five people) can get a four-berth cabin for £112–134 one-way.

TO NORWAY

There are a number of options to Norway. *Fred Olsen Lines* sail from **Newcastle to Kristiansand** once a week, a 23hr trip which costs from £38–43 one way. This service continues **to Oslo** via Hirtshals, taking 36hr and costing from £43–48 one-way. On both runs, your car goes for £17–35, motorbikes for £9, bicycles free.

There are also special deals for **families** (up to five people), who can get a four-berth cabin on both routes for £112–134 one-way. *Fred Olsen Lines* also sail once-weekly from **Newcastle to Bergen and Stavanger**, though between mid-June and mid-August only; the journey takes 24hr to Bergen and 30hr to Stavanger, and the cheapest one-way fare to either destination is £82. On this route, cars go for £26–43, motorbikes £9, bicycles free – and, again, families can occupy a cabin, this time for £230 one-way.

The other shipping line that sails direct to Norway is *Norway Line*, who sail from Newcastle to Stavanger and on to Bergen 2–3 times weekly, the trips taking 20hr and 27hr respectively. Prices on this route can be very competitive: one-way fares in spring and autumn run from £25–40 (£70–85 in the summer), £45–60 for a bed in a four-berth cabin (£90–105 in the summer). To take your car will cost £28 (though it's free if there are four paying passengers in it); motorbikes cost £7, bicycles are free. *Norway Line* also offer 25 percent discounts to students, ten percent off reclining-chair fares to *IYHF* card holders, and the usual reductions for children.

More adventurously, you can also reach Bergen in five days from Iceland via the Faroes and Shetlands with the *Smyril Line* service – see *Iceland*, "Getting There".

TO SWEDEN

To Sweden, *Scandinavian Seaways* operates two routes: from Harwich to Gothenburg 3–7 times weekly, a 24hr trip, and – July to September only – Newcastle to Gothenburg 1–2 times weekly, a

26hr journey. Prices are from £68 one-way (£94 in high season) for a couchette-bed, although a *Seapex* or *Super Saver* ticket can get you there and back for between £100 and £130 depending on the time of year. With a car you'll pay £40 on top, each way; motorbikes £18.

TO FINLAND

United Baltic run cargo ships from various British ports on a number of complex routings to the Baltic. Timetables fluctuate, but the quickest ship to Finland leaves Purfleet on Sunday, arriving after a short stop in Rotterdam in Helsinki on Tuesday. Fares, including meals, start at around £240 one-way in summer – not an especially cheap or quick way of getting there.

OTHER CROSSINGS

If you're driving or hitching, bear in mind also that there are ferry links from **West Germany** (Kiel and Travemünde) to Norway (Oslo), Sweden (Gothenburg and Trelleborg) and Finland (Helsinki), and from **Amsterdam** to Gothenburg. There are also many minor connections to the Danish islands – details from travel agents and in the relevant "Travel Details" sections.

PACKAGE TOURS

Don't be put off by the idea of taking an inclusive package. In such an expensive part of Europe, it can often be the cheapest way of working things, and can also be the only way of reaching remote parts of the region at inhospitable times of year. **City breaks**, certainly, if you just want to see one city and its surroundings, invariably work out cheaper than arranging things independently. Prices include accommodation and return travel, usually by plane, and most operators offer a range of accommodation, from hostel to luxury-class hotel. As a broad reference, four-night hotel-stays in Copenhagen start at around £200 per person; three nights in Oslo, Bergen or Stavanger will cost £200–400; the same stay in Stockholm or Gothenburg £210–380; while two nights in Helsinki will set you back about £280. Go for a week to any of these places and rates per night fall considerably.

There are also an increasing number of operators offering **special interest holidays** to Scandinavia, from camping tours to Arctic cruises. Prices for these are a good bit higher, but are generally excellent value for money. For oper-

---

SPECIALIST OPERATORS

Anglers World Holidays, 46 Knifesmith Gate, Chesterfield, Derbyshire S40 1QR (☎0246-221 717). Angling holidays in Denmark and Sweden; cottage and hotel stays.

Arctic Experience, 29 Nork Way, Banstead, Surrey SM7 1PB (☎0737-362 321). Specialist and adventure tours of Iceland, the Faroes, Spitzbergen and Greenland – from £319 for a week in Iceland to £5800 for a Pan-Arctic voyage.

Dansk Cykelferie c/o *DVL Rejser*, Kultorvet 7, DK-1175, København K (☎33-132727). Cycling holidays in Denmark from £90 for eight days.

Holiday Scandinavia Ltd, 28 Hillcrest Road, Orpington, Kent BR6 9AW (☎0689-24958). Scandinavian chalet holidays.

Norway Line, Tyne Commission Quay, North Shields, NE29 6EA (☎091-296 1313). A range of Norwegian "Flagship Holidays": bargain four-day sea breaks to fjord and coastal cruises.

Norwegian State Railways, 21 Cockspur Street, London SW1 (☎071-930 6666). City breaks, skiing holidays and cruises; not just Norwegian holidays.

Scandinavian Seaways, 15 Hanover Street, London W1 (☎071-493 6696). City breaks to

Denmark and Sweden, including two nights on board ship and two or three nights abroad – prices from around £74 out of season.

Scanscape, Hillgate House, 13 Hillgate Street, London W8 7SP (☎071-221 3244). City breaks, charter flights, fly-drive holidays and cruises.

Scantours, 8 Spring Gardens, Trafalgar Square, London SW1 (☎071-839 2927). City breaks, cruises and fly-drive holidays. Also offering budget scheduled flights to most Scandinavian destinations.

Star Tour of Scandinavia, 209 Edgware Road, London W2 (☎071-706 2520). Charter flights, cruises, city breaks and skiing holidays.

Top of Europe Tours, Sandviksgaten 53, 95132 Luleå, Sweden (☎920-94070). Dog sledding and other adventurous winter activities.

Tracks, 12 Abingdon Road, London W8 (☎071-937 3028). Group camping tours of Scandinavia and on into Eastern Europe; for 18–35 year olds; from around £665 for 31 days.

Winge of Scandinavia, 20 Pall Mall, London SW1 (☎071-839 5341). Scandinavian tours and cruises, city breaks; and worth checking for charter flights to Oslo, Copenhagen and Stockholm.

ators dealing specifically in Scandinavian **skiing** and winter sports holidays, see "Scandinavia in Winter", below.

FROM IRELAND

There are direct **flights** between Ireland and Scandinavia, most of them operated by *Aer Lingus*, although *SAS*, *British Airways* and *British Midland* also run services. There are daily flights from Dublin to **Copenhagen**, some non-stop (3hr), others via London or Manchester; Apex fares are currently IR£256 return, IR£178 if you're under 26. To **Gothenburg**, **Stockholm** and **Oslo**, flights go via London or Copenhagen and all take around 5hr; Apex returns are IR£332 (IR£240 under-26), IR£326 (IR£238) and IR£256 (IR£184) respectively. Apex fares to **Helsinki** are IR£346 return, while under-26s can only buy one-way tickets on this route, at IR£174; you'll have to book the return half in Helsinki.

It's again possible to cut costs by approaching an agent: *USIT* (address below) are one of the best for discount deals, particularly if you're under 26 or a student. Alternatively, you might find it slightly cheaper to make your own way to London and pick up one of the various routes to Scandinavia listed above.

FROM AUSTRALIA AND NEW ZEALAND

There are no **direct** flights between Australia or New Zealand and Scandinavia, though you can fly via Bangkok. However, it's not cheap. Low-season one-way fares from Auckland or

---

IRELAND ADDRESSES

Aer Lingus, 42 Grafton Street, Dublin 2 (☎01-794 764) or at Dublin airport (☎01-370 011).

British Airways, 60 Dawson Street, Dublin (☎01-610 666); The Fountain Centre, College Street, Belfast 1 (☎0232-240 522).

British Midland, 54 Grafton Street, Dublin 2; Suite 2, The Fountain Centre, College Street, Belfast 1 (☎0232-241 188).

Eurotrain, 31a Queen Street, Belfast (☎0800-269780).

SAS, Terminal Building, Dublin Airport (☎01-421 922).

Scandinavian Seaways, c/o DFDS Scanline Ltd, 72–80 North Wall Quay, Dublin 1 (☎01-726 881).

USIT, O'Connell Bridge, 19/21 Austin Quay, Dublin 2 (☎01-778 117).

Christchurch cost upwards of $NZ1194, from Sydney or Melbourne around Aus$966, to Copenhagen or Stockholm. Most people fly **to London** and move on to Scandinavia from there. Prices to London right now cost from around Aus$960 one-way from Sydney/Melbourne or $NZ1060 one-way from Auckland.

The best agent in both countries is the long-established ***STA Travel***, who have offices at 1a Lee Street, Sydney 2000, Australia (☎02/212 1255), and 64 High Street (PO Box 4156), Auckland, New Zealand (☎9/390 458), as well as in Melbourne, Canberra, Perth and Christchurch.

RED TAPE AND VISAS

EC citizens and Australian and New Zealand nationals need only a valid passport to enter Norway, Sweden and Finland for up to three months. If you want to stay longer – and you can prove you have sufficient cash to support yourself – you can often get a short extension (via the local police), although after this time you won't be allowed back to Scandinavia for a further six months.

All other nationals should consult the relevant embassies about visa requirements. For Denmark conditions are similar, though EC nationals can stay as long as they want on a valid passport.

In spite of the lack of restrictions, **checks** are frequently made on travellers at the major ports of

---

SCANDINAVIAN EMBASSIES AND CONSULATES

UK: Denmark (55 Sloane Street, London SW1; ☎071-235 1255); Norway (25 Belgrave Square, London SW1, ☎071-235 7151; 86 George Street, Edinburgh, ☎031-226 5701); Sweden (11 Montague Place, London W1; ☎071-724 2101); Finland (38 Chesham Place, London SW1; ☎071-235 9531).

EIRE: Denmark (121–122 St Stephen's Green, Dublin 2; ☎01-756 404); Norway (Hainault House, 69–71 St Stephen's Green, Dublin 2; ☎01-783 133); Sweden (Sun Alliance House, 13–17 Dawson Street, Dublin 2; ☎01-715 822); Finland (Russell House, Stokes Place, St Stephen's Green, Dublin 2; ☎01-781 344/348/831).

AUSTRALIA: Denmark (15 Hunter Street, Yarralumla, Canberra, ACT 2600; ☎062-732 195); Norway (3 Zeehan Street, Red Hill, Canberra ACT 2603; ☎062/956 000); Sweden (5 Turrana Street, Yarralumla, Canberra ACT 2600; ☎062/733 033); Finland (10 Darwin Avenue, Yarralumla, Canberra ACT 2600; ☎062/733 800).

NEW ZEALAND: Denmark (CG, 18th Floor, Marrac House, 105–109 The Terrace, PO Box 10035, Wellington 1; ☎04/720 020); Norway (see Australia); Sweden (Greenock House, 8th Floor, 39 The Terrace, Wellington 1; ☎04/720 909); Finland (see Australia).

---

entry. If you are young and have a rucksack, be prepared to prove that you have enough money to support yourself during your stay. You may also be asked how long you intend to stay and what you are there for. Be polite. It's the only check that will be made, since once you get into Scandinavia there are few passport controls between the individual countries. For another view of Scandinavian entrance policy, see *Contexts* (p.643).

MONEY AND BANKS

Of Scandinavia's currencies, Denmark and Norway use *kroner*, Sweden *kronor* – abbreviated as DKr, NKr and SKr respectively.

Although they share a broadly similar exchange rate (currently 10–12kr to the £1), the currencies are not interchangeable. We've abbreviated each as "kr", except where it's not clear which country's money we're referring to. Finland uses the markka, abbreviated as Fmk or just mk, and the rate right now is around 6.5mk to the £1.

TRAVELLERS CHEQUES & CREDIT CARDS

It's easiest and safest to carry money as **travellers cheques**, available for a small commission (usually one percent of the amount ordered) from any British bank and some building societies, whether or not you have an account. Most banks also issue current account holders with a **Eurocheque card** and chequebook, with which you can get cash from most banks in Scandinavia; you'll pay a few pounds service charge a year but usually no commission on transactions. The major **credit cards** – *Visa*, *Access* (*Mastercard*) and *American Express* – are accepted almost everywhere in return for goods or cash.

EXCHANGING MONEY

Exchanging money is easy but usually expensive. Banks have standard exchange rates, but commissions can vary enormously and it's always worth shopping around. Some places charge per transaction, others per cheque – up to £1 per cheque – so it's common sense to carry large denomination cheques (£20 or £50 instead of £10), and to try to change several people's money at once.

Banking hours vary from country to country – check each country under "Costs, Money and Banks". Outside those times, and especially in the more remote areas, you'll often find that hostels, hotels, campsites, tourist offices, airports, ferry terminals and ferries will also change money – though usually at lower rates than the banks.

COMMUNICATIONS: POST AND PHONES

Post office opening hours are given under each individual country's section on "Communications". Postal charges are not particularly high, but the cost of stamps and postcards can soon take a chunk out of the daily budget. It's cheaper to buy an aerogramme letter with the stamp included and send that, or get free postcards from the Postal Museums in Oslo and Helsinki.

You can have letters sent **poste restante** to any post office in Scandinavia by addressing them "Poste Restante" followed by the name of the town and country. When picking mail up take your passport, and make sure they check under middle names and initials, as letters often get misfiled.

Phone boxes are plentiful and almost invariably work; English instructions are normally posted up inside. To reverse the charges phone the operator, who will speak English, and ask to make a "collect call".

To make a direct call to Britain, dial the country code, wait for the tone and then omit the first 0 in the area code. For more information, see each individual country's section on "Communications".

DIALLING CODES TO BRITAIN

from Denmark ☎009-44
from Norway ☎095-44
from Sweden ☎009-44
from Finland ☎990-44

HEALTH AND INSURANCE

EC nationals can take advantage of Denmark's health services under the same terms as residents of the country. For this you'll need form E111, which in theory you can obtain by applying on form SA30 by post, one month in advance, to any DSS office in Britain. In practice, it can often be issued over the counter at a main DSS office (though not an Unemployment Benefit office).

The other mainland countries, Sweden, Norway and Finland, have reciprocal health agreements with Britain (see details given on the following page).

HEALTH PROBLEMS

In **Denmark**, tourist offices and health offices (*kommunes social og sundhedforvaltning*) have lists of doctors. If the doctor decides you need hospital treatment, it'll be arranged for free but always take your E111 with you. For doctors' consultations, dental treatment, and prescriptions (available from an *Apotek*) you will have to pay the full cost on the spot, but keep a receipt and take both it and your E111 and passport to the local health office for a refund – a sometimes long and frustrating process.

In **Norway**, hotels and tourist offices have lists of local GPs and dentists, and there'll usually be a casualty ward you can go to outside surgery hours. You'll pay 50–80kr for an appointment but will be reimbursed for part of the cost of any treatment; hospital stays are free. Get a receipt (*Legeregning*) at the time of payment, and take it and your passport to the social insurance office (*Trygdekasse*) of the district where treatment was obtained.

In **Sweden** there is no GP system: go to the nearest hospital with your passport and for 60kr they'll treat you. If you need medicine you'll get a prescription to take to a chemist (*Apotek*), maxi-mum charge 65kr. Hospital stays are free; the casualty department is the *Akutmottagning*. For dental treatment you'll pay sixty percent of the cost up to 2500kr and 25 percent above that. For dental surgeries, look for the sign *Tandläkare*.

In **Finland**, treatment at a doctor's surgery (*Terveyskeskus*), found in all towns and villages, is free, but medicines have to be paid for at a pharmacy (*Apteekki*) – although, provided you have your passport, you won't be charged more than Finns. Hospitals have a charge of 60Fmk per day.

INSURANCE

For all the Scandinavian countries it's worth taking out some kind of comprehensive insurance, especially if you're not an EC citizen. Ask about **travel insurance** policies at any bank or travel agency, or use a specialist, low-priced firm like *Endsleigh* (97 Southampton Row, London WC1; ☎071-436 4451), who offer two weeks' cover for around £12. For medical treatment and drugs, keep all the bills and claim the money back later. If you have anything stolen (including money), register the loss immediately with the local police – without their report you won't be able to claim.

INFORMATION AND MAPS

Before you leave, it's worth doing the rounds of the tourist boards and picking up a selection of free maps and brochures – though don't go mad: much of it can easily be obtained later in Scandinavia.

The rail/ferry/bus **timetables** for the most popular tourist routes are worth taking, as are the **accommodation** listings booklets available. Addresses of the various national tourist boards are given below, but if you can't find what you want from them, try the **Norwegian State Railways Travel Bureau** (21 Cockspur Street, London SW1; ☎071-930 6666), who are also agents for Swedish State Railways (*SJ*) and have brochures, timetables, maps and endless information.

TOURIST OFFICES

Once in Scandinavia, every town and some villages have a **tourist office**, from where you can pick up free town plans and information, brochures and other bumph. Many book private rooms, (sometimes hostel beds), rent bikes, sell local discount cards and change money. During summer, opening times run daily until late evening; out of high season, shop hours are more

NATIONAL TOURIST BOARDS

BRITAIN: Denmark (Sceptre House, 169–173 Regent Street, London W1; ☎071-734 2637/8); Norway (Charles House, 5–11 Regent St, London W1; ☎071-839 2650); Sweden (29–31 Oxford Street, London W1; ☎071-437 5816); Finland (66–68 Haymarket, London SW1; ☎071-930 5871).

EIRE: No tourist boards as such, but the embassies handle tourist information (see p.000).

AUSTRALIA: Denmark (60 Market Street, PO Box 4531, Melbourne, Victoria 3001). For other countries consult the embassies.

NEW ZEALAND: Again, embassies and consulates supply tourist information.

usual, and in winter they're normally closed at weekends. You'll find full details of individual offices throughout the text.

MAPS

The **maps and plans** we've printed should be fine for reference, but drivers, cyclists and hikers may require something more detailed. Tourist offices often give out reasonable road maps and town plans but anything better you'll have to buy. For really detailed plans of the capital cities, the *Falk* maps are excellent and easy to use (£4.50 each).

The best map of Scandinavia as a whole is the *Michelin* 1:1,500,000 chart (£2.65), which is perfectly adequate on all the mainland countries. As for the individual countries, the *Terrac* 1:1,000,000 is the best general map of Norway (£4.95); for Sweden and Denmark there are *Hallwag* maps (£3.95 each); for Finland there's the *Daily Telegraph* map (£3.95).

If you're staying in one area for a long time, or are **hiking** or **walking** you'll need something more detailed still – a minimum scale of 1:400,000, much larger if you're doing any serious trekking. For Norway, the 1:400,000 *Cappelens Kart* regional maps are good (£7.45 each); for Sweden there is the 1:300,000 *Esselte Kartor* series (£7.95 each); the provinces of Denmark are covered by the 1:200,000 *Kort og Matrykelstyren* series; and *Kummerley & Frey* produce a number of regional Finnish maps at a scale of 1:400,000. Also, the larger tourist offices sometimes have decent hiking maps of the surrounding area, and in Norway, Sweden and Finland the national hiking organisations have a good stock of maps and guides. Their addresses are *DNT*, Stortingsgate 28, Oslo; *STF*, Vasagatan 48, Stockholm; and *Suomen Latu*, Fabianinkatu 7, Helsinki.

All of the above maps and plans are available from *Stanford's*, 12 Long Acre, London WC2 (☎071-836 1321); What they don't have in stock, they'll order for you.

GETTING AROUND

Public transport systems are good throughout Scandinavia. Denmark, Norway, Sweden and Finland have a fairly comprehensive rail network which runs as far north as it dares before plentiful buses take over. Fjords and inordinate amounts of water – lakes, rivers and open sea – make ferries a major form of transport too. For more details see each country's "Getting Around" section, and "Travel Details" at the end of every chapter.

RAIL PASSES

Nowhere does travel come cheap, but a number of **passes** can ease the burden. If you're travelling by train there is, of course, the *InterRail* pass (see "Getting There", above). But if you don't qualify for one of these it's well worth considering a *Nordturist* pass, which is available to anyone. It costs just £115 (£173 first class), and gives gives unlimited train travel in all four mainland Scandinavian countries for 21 days: it also includes free travel (or fifty percent discounts) on many Scandinavian ferry crossings and bus routes, and free entry to Scandinavia's four railway museums. The pass comes even cheaper for under 25s (£86, £130 first class), making it a fairly serious rival to *InterRail*; kids between four and eleven pay only £57 (£86.50 first class). It's available in London from the *Norwegian State Railways* office (address above) and other travel agencies.

FLIGHTS

Internal Scandinavian **flights**, surprisingly, can also work out to be a good bargain. During the summer – usually July and the early part of August – *SAS* generally have cheap set-price tickets (one-way and return) to anywhere in mainland Scandinavia except Finland; plus other discounts for families and young people. Also, until recently, under-26s could pick up flights between the Scandinavian capitals for as little as 500kr return; check with travel agencies for up-to-date information.

CAR HIRE

Car hire is pricey, although some tourist offices do arrange summer deals which can bring the cost down a little. On the whole, expect to pay around £200–300 a week for a *VW Golf* plus petrol; see each country's "Getting Around" section for specific prices and details of rules of the road and documentation – and note that a stern attitude to drinking and driving is held everywhere.

SLEEPING

Unless you're aiming to camp rough, sleeping is going to be *the* major daily expense in Scandinavia. If you plan ahead, however, there are a number of ways you can avoid paying over the (already high) odds. Using youth hostels, camping cabins and campsites are the obvious options – popular with Scandinavians, too, and not just for tourists. There's also a series of hotel cheques and discount passes available, for use in hotels all over mainland Scandinavia.

HOTELS

Scandinavian **hotels** aren't as expensive as you might think; certainly not if you compare them with equivalent accommodation in London, say, or New York. Lots of Scandinavian hotels, usually dependent on business travellers, drop their prices drastically during the summer holiday period and at weekends year-round, so it's always worth asking in the tourist office about special local deals. Also, the capitals and other major cities feature cheap packages, usually involving a night's hotel accommodation and a free city discount card. More details, and a guide to prices, are given under each country's "Sleeping" section, as well as under the specific town and city accounts.

In addition, some Scandinavia-wide hotel chains operate a discount or **hotel cheque system** which you can organise before you leave. Either you purchase cheques in advance, redeemable against a night's accommodation in any hotel belonging to the particular chain; or you buy a **hotel pass** which entitles you to a hefty discount on normal room rates.

There are a bewildering amount of schemes available, but most only operate from June to September and they all offer basically the same deal: consult your travel agent, or one of the national tourist boards. Look out for the *Scandinavian Bonus Pass* and the *Scandinavian*

Passepartout. The main hotel chains participating are *Best Western Hotels*, *Sweden Hotels*, *Scandic Hotels*, *RESO Hotels*, *Cumulus* (in Finland) and *SARA Hotels*.

YOUTH HOSTELS

Joining the **International Youth Hostel Federation** (*IYHF*) gives you access to what is sometimes the only budget accommodation available in Scandinavia. Non-members can use most of the hostels but will pay around an extra £1.50 a night for the privilege – a sizeable sum over a couple of weeks considering the cost of annual membership (under-21s £4, over-21s £7.60). Another thing you'll need is a **sheet sleeping bag**, the only kind allowed in *IYHF* hostels, either rentable for around another £1.50 extra a night or on sale at the *YHA* shop in London (£9.95–11.95); alternatively, you can simply stitch a couple of old sheets together and take a pillowcase. You can join on the spot at the *YHA* office/shop at 14 Southampton Street, London WC2 (membership enquiries ☎071-836 1036; shop ☎071-836 8541) and at several other *YHA* shops throughout Britain, or by post.

The hostel card also provides various discounts to the holder – on museum entry, ferry crossings and sightseeing trips. See each country's "Sleeping" section for the addresses of Scandinavian national organisations, and the text for details of the hostels themselves. It's worth noting that every youth hostel in Scandinavia is listed in the *IYHF*'s *Guide to Youth Hostels Around the World* (£3.95).

In conjunction with the *InterRail* programme, the **YMCA/YWCA** has a string of **hostels** – *InterRail Points* – throughout Scandinavia, open in summer to anyone with a membership card. These have kitchens and laundry facilities, and, although much less luxurious, are often cheaper than the *IYHF* hostels. All the mainland capitals and some of the larger cities have one. Membership cards (£2) and information are available from *YMCA Inter-Point Co-ordinator*, Y Training Services, Crown House, 550 Mauldeth Road West, Manchester M21 2SJ (☎061-881 5321). Or you can join on your first night's stay at any hostel.

CAMPING

Camping is hugely popular in all Scandinavian countries and covered in more detail in each country's "Sleeping" section. But a number of points common to all the countries are worth noting. In order to use certain sites you may need a camping carnet, which you can buy at the first site you visit; camping rough is, with certain exceptions, legal in Norway and Sweden; and most campsites have furnished **cabins**, though if you intend to use these take a sleeping bag as bedding is not usually provided.

POLICE AND THIEVES

Scandinavia is one of the least troublesome corners of Europe. You will find that most public places are well lit and secure, most people genuinely friendly and helpful, and street crime and street hassle have a relatively low profile.

PETTY CRIME AND MINOR OFFENCES

However, it would be foolish to assume that problems don't exist. The capital cities have their share of **petty crime**, fuelled – as elsewhere – by a growing number of drug addicts and alcoholics after easy money. But keep tabs on your cash and passport and you should have little reason to visit the **police**. If you do, you'll find them courteous, concerned, and, most importantly, usually able to speak English. If you have something stolen, make sure you get a **police report** – essential if you are to make a claim against insurance.

As for **offences** *you* might commit, **topless sunbathing** is universally accepted in all the major resorts (elsewhere there'll be no one around to care); and **camping rough** is a tradition enshrined in law in Norway and Sweden, and tolerated in Finland, though in Denmark it's more difficult. Being **drunk** on the streets, however, can get you arrested, and drinking and driving is treated especially rigorously. **Drugs** offences, too, meet with the same harsh attitude that prevails throughout the rest of Europe.

SEXUAL HARASSMENT & THE WOMEN'S MOVEMENT

In general, the social and economic position of women in Scandinavia is more advanced than in almost all other European countries – something which becomes obvious after a short time there. Many women are in traditionally male occupations, and sexual harassment is less of a problem than elsewhere in Europe.

You can walk almost everywhere in comparative comfort and safety, and although in the capital cities you can expect to receive unwelcome attention occasionally, it's very rarely with any kind of violent intent. As always, travelling alone on the underground systems in Copenhagen, Oslo, Stockholm and Helsinki late at night is unwise. If you do have problems, the fact that almost everyone understands English makes it easy to get across an unambiguous response.

WOMEN'S ORGANISATIONS

Denmark's women's movement is in a state of flux: the once prominent *Rødstrømper* (Red Stockings) – the Radical Feminists – are now less active. But there are lots of feminist groups around the country, and in Copenhagen a couple of active women's centres: *Dannerhuset*, Gyldenslovesgade (☎33-141676), and *Kvindehuset*, Gothersgade 37 (☎33-142804). **Norway**'s women's movement is highly developed, assisted by progressive government and a 1986–1989 Labour administration led by a woman, Dr Gro Brundtland, which endeavoured to even out parliamentary representation by promoting women into the cabinet. Contacts in Oslo can be made through the *Norsk Kvinnessaksforening*, Kvinnehuset, Rådhusgate 2 (☎02-149779). In **Sweden**, the women's movement is also strongly developed, riding on the back of the social welfare reforms introduced by the Social Democratic governments of the last forty years. You'll find women's centres in most major towns, contacts in Stockholm including *Grupp 8* (Snickarbacken 10), an active socialist-feminist group, *Frederika Bremer Forbundet* (Biblioteksgatan 12), a domestic campaigning organisation and *RIFFI* (Vanadisvägen 7), set up to help immigrant women in Sweden. Women in **Finland** were the first to achieve suffrage, but in spite of that its women's movement is currently lagging behind the rest of Scandinavia, and there have been fewer further reforms to benefit the lot of women over the years. The major feminist organisation, *Unioni*, first established in 1892, in Helsinki, is the best place for up-to-date information (Bulevardi 11A; ☎90-643158, Mon–Fri 10am–1pm & 2–5pm).

GAY LIFE

Scandinavia comprises some of the most liberated and tolerant countries in Europe. Gays are rarely discriminated against in law, and the age of consent is almost uniformly the same as for heterosexuals – usually fifteen. However, in all four mainland countries you'll not find much of a scene outside the capitals.

ATTITUDES AND THE LAW

Denmark used to have a reputation for being the gay pornography capital of the world, and although this is no longer so, there is a very good gay scene in Copenhagen – for details see Chapter One. As far as the law goes, the Danish parliament recently voted to make a form of homosexual marriage legal – the first "wedding" took place on October 1, 1989, in Copenhagen – and is currently studying other ways of eliminating discrimination against gays. For more information contact the *Landsforeningen for bøsser og lebiske*, Knabro-stræde 3, Copenhagen.

Norway was the first country in the world – in 1981 – to pass a law making discrimination against homosexuals illegal, though this has not yet been fully tested in the courts. Society is reasonably tolerant of homosexuality, and gays can be quite open about their sexuality if they wish. There is a strong and effective gay organisation, with a national HQ in Oslo (*DNF-48*, Postbox 1305, Vika, N-0112, Oslo 1) and branches throughout the country.

In **Sweden** there are no laws against homosexuality and Swedish opinion is, again, reasonably liberal. However, there are very few gay bars, and gay saunas and video shops with cubicles have been outlawed since mid-1987. The national organisation, the *RFSL*, can be contacted at PO Box 350, S-10124, Stockholm, and provides a free gay guide to Sweden – though if you send for a copy, you should at least cover the postage.

From a legal point of view, there is some discrimination against gays in **Finland**. The country's penal code forbids the public encouragement of homosexuality, and unlike the other Scandinavian countries the homosexual age of consent is 18. Also, there remains a very real taboo against homosexuality in the country: even in Helsinki it's unheard of for a gay couple to embrace in a bar, let alone outside; and out of the capital gays are often ostracised and "queer-bashing" not uncommon. However, nobody has been convicted for breaking the anti-gay laws, nor – as yet – have there been any attempts to censor or confiscate gay publications. *SETA* (Org-anisation for Sexual Equality in Finland), at Mäkelänkatu 36 A 5, Helsinki, can provide further information – on Helsinki and elsewhere – and publishes a bimonthly nationwide magazine; during the summer they also print useful pages of information in English for foreign visitors to Helsinki.

DISABLED TRAVELLERS

Scandinavia is, in many ways, a model of concern for the disabled traveller: wheelchair access, other facilities and help is generally available at hotels, hostels, museums and public places.

FACILITIES AND INFORMATION

In **Denmark**, facilities are generally outstanding. The Danish Tourist Board publishes a comprehensive hundred-page brochure called *Access in Denmark – a Travel Guide for the Disabled*, which covers everything from airports to zoos. Pick up a free copy at their office in London.

For disabled travellers in **Norway**, the Norwegian Tourist Board in London issues a *Travel Guide for the Disabled* (send £1 for p&p) which lists transport, public toilets and accommodation accessible to people with disabilities. *Norwegian State Railways* have special carriages on most main routes with wheelchair space,

hydraulic lifts and a disabled toilet; and according to Norwegian law, all public buildings must be accessible to disabled people.

In **Sweden**, many hotels are provided with specially adapted rooms, and camping-cabin holidays are not beyond wheelchair users either, as some chalet-villages have cabins with wheelchair access: more information on holidays for the disabled from *Holiday Scandinavia Ltd*, 28 Hillcrest Road, Orpington, Kent BR6 9AW (☎0689-24958). There's more information, too, in the free, annual *Hotels in Sweden* guide, available from the Swedish Tourist Board in London.

Despite lagging behind the other Nordic nations, **Finland** is by no means hostile territory to the disabled traveller. However, despite attempts to adapt new buildings, little has actually been achieved; there's no one source of information for disabled travellers, although the Finnish tourist board and tourist offices inside the country will do their best to advise on facilities.

THE COUNTRYSIDE: SOME GROUND RULES

If you're going to do any hiking/camping in the Scandinavian countryside you should be aware of some specific ground rules. The landscape is there for everyone's use – camping rough, for example, is perfectly legal much of the time – but the Scandinavians are concerned to protect the environment both from the damage caused by excessive tourism and the potential disasters that can result from ignorance or thoughtlessness.

RULES AND ADVICE

Don't **light fires** anywhere other than at designated spots – and even these shouldn't be used in times of drought.

Tents may only be placed on marked sites or, on some hikes, in other designated areas – but not for more than one night. When camping, do not **break tree branches** or leave rubbish; and try not to disturb nesting **birds**, especially in the spring.

In the northern reaches of Scandinavia, be wary of frightening **reindeer herds**, since if they scatter it can mean several extra days work for the herder; also, avoid tramping over the moss-covered stretches of moorland – the reindeer's staple· diet. **Picking flowers, berries and mushrooms** is also usually prohibited in the north (though it's fine elsewhere). If you are going to pick and eat anything, however, it's a wise idea, post-Chernobyl, to check on the latest advice from the authorities – tourist offices should know the score.

As you might expect, any kind of **hunting** is forbidden without a permit, and **fishing** usually requires a special licence, available from local tourist offices. **National Parks** have special regulations on all these issues, posted on huts and at entrances, which are worth reading and remembering.

WINTER IN SCANDINAVIA

Scandinavia is by no means the summer-only destination that most travel brochures would have you believe. For a start, it's cheaper to get there by ferry or plane during the winter months; city breaks, particularly, at this time can be very good value (see "Packages" in the "Getting There" section, above). The sub-zero temperatures and snow cause surprisingly little inconvenience: the transport system remains as highly efficient and reliable as ever; most hotels and lots of youth hostels stay open; buildings (public and private) are well-insulated and heated to oven-like temperatures. And as long as you're properly equipped for going outside (thermal undies, hat, scarf, gloves, and as many layers of clothes as you can get on), you'll have few problems.

WINTER SPORTS AND CHRISTMAS

Aside from the cities, which maintain their usual roster of activities and attractions, though sometimes with reduced opening hours, the big incentive for coming at this time of year is the range of participant **winter sports** available – from ice-fishing to dog-sledging. Although you're not likely to come on a skiing package to Scandinavia (it's nearly always cheaper to go to other European resorts), it's easy to arrange a few days **cross-country skiing** wherever you end up: even in Oslo and Stockholm there are ski runs within the city boundaries, and plenty of places to hire equipment.

Even if you're not sporty – but can't face one more **Christmas** TV re-run of *The Wizard of Oz* – remember that Finland (and Norway, and Sweden, if they're to be believed) is the home of Santa Claus. His hut is just outside Rovaniemi on the edge of Finnish Lappland and, if you have a spare £500 or so, you can whip out and visit him from London on one of the many Christmas package trips laid on by *British Airways* and *Finnair*.

For this, and all other winter activities, see the list of specialist operators over the page.

WINTER OPERATORS

Norwegian State Railways, 21–24 Cockspur Street, London SW1 (☎071-930 6666). Ski packages in Lillehammer, Voss, Geilo; winter coastal voyages; Finnmark visits to *Same* towns.

Norwegian Travel Service, Church Gate, Church Street West, Woking, Surrey GU21 1DJ (☎0483-756876). Norwegian ski packages from around £250 for a five-night B&B break; half-board from around £300.

Scantours, 8 Spring Gardens, London SW1 (☎071-839 2927). Finnish Santa Claus trips, husky expeditions, reindeer farm visits, snowmobile safaris and icebreaker voyages.

Star Tour of Scandinavia, 209 Edgware Road, London W2 (☎071-706 2520). Downhill and cross-country skiing in Åre, Sweden.

WORK

Most Scandinavian countries, but particularly Norway, Sweden and Finland, are extremely suspicious of potential foreign workers, and you may have to prove on entry that you are not there to seek work (by showing return tickets, sufficient cash, etc). The chances of coming across casual work are, anyhow, slim to say the least.

THE PAPERWORK

If you're serious about **working**, though, and an EC citizen, **Denmark** is the best option, though for other than relatively low-paid bar/restaurant/hotel work you really need to speak Danish. You can stay for up to three months while you look for work, and, if you find it, a residence permit will be granted automatically. Fast-food restaurants and larger hotels have a fairly high turnover of foreign staff, and private employment agencies can occasionally place unskilled foreign workers; two Copenhagen agencies are *Manpower* (Vester-

brogade 1A) and *Royal Service Appointments* (Nørregade 28B). Once you've got a job, *Use It*, the youth info centre in Copenhagen (see the *Zealand* chapter), can help unravel the legal intricacies, but bear in mind that it's vital to get a personal registration number and social security certificate within *five days*: take ID and a statement from your employer to the nearest *Folkeregisteret* – in Copenhagen at Dahlerupsgade 6, Monday to Friday 9am–2pm.

For the rest of mainland Scandinavia the outlook is pretty bleak: the paperwork alone can be a formidable obstacle. **Norway**, **Sweden** and **Finland** all require that you have an offer of employment and a work permit before you arrive in the country – you can't apply once in the country, and if you enter before the permit is granted it will be refused. It can take anything up to three months to process your application, and it's as well to know, anyway, that jobs are very difficult to obtain unless you have a particular and needed skill, and a knowledge of the language.

OTHER OPTIONS

Other than some teaching or voluntary work, the best paid opportunity to live and work in Scandinavia for a short period is by **working on a farm**. You live with a farming family, work incredibly hard and receive board and lodging and pocket money in return. Vacancies are usually for the spring and summer although some jobs stay open for a full year. You still need to sort out all the paperwork before you arrive, however. Serious vacancies (ie for young farmers and/or people with experience) are dealt with by the *International Farm Experience Programme*, YFC Centre, National Agricultural Centre, Kenilworth,

Warwickshire CV8 2LG. For summer farm work (no experience neccessary), 18–30-year-olds should contact the *Norwegian Youth Council* (*Landsradet for Norske Ungdomsorganisasjoner*), Working Guest Programme, Rolf Hofmosgate 18, Oslo 6, Norway (apply by April 15).

If you would like to do **voluntary work** in mainland Scandinavia, send an sae to *International Voluntary Service*, Ceresole House, 53 Regent Road, Leicester LE1 6YL. They organise international workcamps two to three weeks long,

with food and accommodation provided. You must be at least 18 and pay your own travel expenses.

INFORMATION

For more information about working in Scandinavia – paid or voluntary – consult the series of books published by *Vacation Work*, which all have sections on the Scandinavian countries: *The International Directory of Voluntary Work* (£6.95), *Summer Jobs Abroad* (£5.95) and *Work Your Way Around the World* (£7.95).

DIRECTORY

ADDRESSES In Scandinavia addresses are always written with the number after the street-name. In multi-floored buildings the ground floor is always counted as the first floor; ie the fifth floor is actually the fourth floor.

ALPHABET The letters Å, Æ, Ø, Ä and Ö come at the end of the relevant alphabets, after Z.

ALCOHOL With the exception of Denmark, this is very expensive throughout Scandinavia. You'll find it's cheaper to exceed your duty-free limit and pay the duty than buying when you get there. See the relevant country section for more details.

ARCTIC CIRCLE This, an imaginary line drawn at 66° 33' latitude, stretches across three mainland Scandinavian countries – Norway, Sweden and Finland – and denotes the limit beyond which there is at least one day in the year on which the sun never sets, and one on which it never rises.

BOOKS You'll find English-language books and paperbacks in almost every bookshop, though at about twice the English price. Libraries, too, stock foreign-language books.

BRING Coffee, teabags, spirits, tinned food, film, spare batteries, tampons – all much more expensive in Scandinavia. An alarm clock/watch is useful for early morning buses and ferries, mosquito repellent and antiseptic cream handy (but vital in the far north), and a raincoat or folda-way umbrella more or less essential.

CAMPING *Camping Gaz* is only available from selected outlets in Scandinavia – details from national tourist boards – so take your own can. For hiking campers, a plastic survival bag keeps you and your pack dry. And take a torch.

DEPARTURE TAX There is none in any of the mainland countries.

GLACIERS These slow-moving masses of ice are in constant, if imperceptible, motion, and are therefore potentially dangerous. People, often tourists, die on them nearly every year. Never climb a glacier without a guide, never walk under one and always heed the instructions at the site. Guided crossings can be terrific; local tourist offices and hiking organisations have details.

LUGGAGE In most railway stations, ferry termi-nals and long-distance bus stations there are lockers. Also, tourist offices will often watch your stuff – though sometimes they charge.

MUSEUMS AND GALLERIES As often as not a charge to get in, though other than for the really major collections it's rarely more than a pound or so; *ISIC* cards are valid for reductions at most. Opening times vary greatly: in winter they are always reduced; the likely closing day is Monday.

NEWSPAPERS You'll find English newspapers on sale in every capital city – often on the day of issue – as well as in many other large towns. Your only other choices are likely to be the dire *International Herald Tribune* or (worse) *USA Today*.

NORTHERN LIGHTS (*Aurora Borealis*) These are a shifting coloured glow visible during winter in the northern parts of Scandinavia, thought to be of electrical origin. Best viewing-points are from the Norwegian *Hurtigrute* coastal steamer – though you'll need to be in luck.

TAMPONS These are available throughout Scandinavia in pharmacies and supermarkets, though at considerably greater cost than at home.

TIME Denmark, Sweden and Norway are one hour ahead of the UK, except for one month (from late Sept) when they are the same; Finland is two hours ahead, except for a similar autumn period, when it's one hour ahead.

VITAMINS If you're travelling for any length of time on a tight budget it's worth packing a jar of multivitamins. The same is true if you're a vegetarian/vegan, as neither diet is easy or cheap to uphold in Scandinavia. Failing that, a large jar of peanut butter packs the necessary proteins.

WORLD SERVICE You can keep in touch with British and world events by listening to the World Service of the BBC, which is broadcast to all of mainland Scandinavia. Frequencies vary according to area and usually change every few months. For the latest details write for the free *Programme Guide* to BBC External Services Publicity, Bush House, PO Box 76, Strand, London WC2.

PART TWO

DENMARK

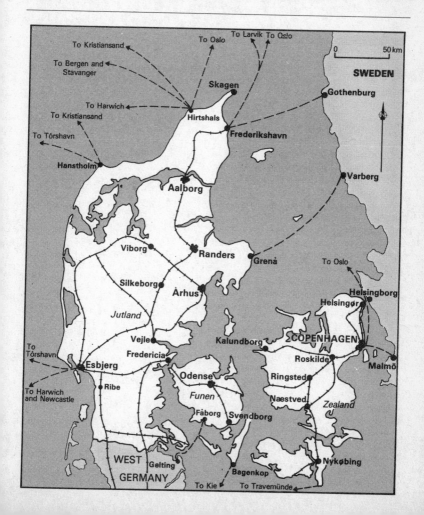

Introduction

Delicately balanced between Scandinavia proper and mainland Europe, Denmark is a difficult country to pin down. In many ways it shares the characteristics of both regions: it's an EC member, and has prices and drinking laws that are broadly in line with the rest of Europe. But Danish social policies and style of government are distinctly Scandinavian: social benefits and the standard of living are high, and – though these days leaning to the right – its politics are very much that of the consensus.

It may seem hard to believe, but it wasn't so long ago that tiny Denmark ruled a good chunk of Northern Europe. Since imperialist times, however, the country's energies have been turned inwards, towards the development of a well-organised but rarely over-bureaucratic society that does much to foster a pride in Danish arts and culture and uphold the freedoms of the individual. Indeed once here, it becomes easy to share the Danes' puzzlement over why other small, ex-empire owning nations haven't followed their example.

■ Where to go

While Denmark is the easiest Scandinavian country in which to travel – both in terms of cost and distance – the landscape itself is the region's least dramatic: very green, flat and rural, largely farmland interrupted by innumerable fairy-tale half-timbered villages. There are surprisingly few urban settlements. Apart from a scattering of small islands, three main land masses make up the country – the islands of Zealand and Funen and the peninsula of Jutland, which extends northwards from West Germany.

The vast majority of visitors make for **Zealand** (*Sjælland*), and, more specifically, **Copenhagen**: the country's one large city and an atmospheric and exciting focal point. The compact capital really has everything: a beautiful old centre, a good array of museums – both national collections and smaller oddball establishments – and a boisterous nightlife. But Copenhagen has little in common with the rest of

Zealand, which, out of the city, is largely quiet and rural – much like the rest of the country. Zealand's smaller neighbour, **Funen** (*Fyn*), has only one positive urban draw in **Odense**, and otherwise is sedate, renowned for the cuteness of its villages, and the sandy beaches of its southern coast – a major holiday destination – and numerous explorable small islands.

Only **Jutland** (*Jylland*) is far enough away from Copenhagen to enjoy a truly individual flavour, as well as Denmark's most varied scenery, ranging from soft green hills to desolate heathlands. In **Århus**, Jutland also has the most lively and enjoyable city outside the capital.

■ When to go

Copenhagen attracts visitors all year round, but the intake peaks during July and August – which means May, early June and September are probably the most pleasant times to be there, although there's plenty happening in the city throughout the year. Anywhere else is enjoyably crowd-free all year round except for July, the Danish vacation month, when the population heads *en masse* to fill the countryside and the coastal strips – though, even then, only the most popular parts are uncomfortably crowded. Many outdoor events, from big rock festivals to local folkdance displays in town squares, take place from mid-June to mid-August, when all tourist facilities and transport services (especially the more minor ferry links) are operating in full. In more isolated areas things begin to slacken off in September.

Denmark has the least extreme **climate** of the Scandinavian countries, but due to the proximity of the sea the weather can fluctuate rapidly. A wet day will as likely be followed by a sunny one and vice versa, and stiff breezes are common, especially along Jutland's west coast, where they can be particularly strong. **Summer** is on the whole sunny and clear: throughout July the temperature averages 68°F, often reaching 78°F. **Winter** conditions are cold but not severe: there's usually a snow covering from December to early February, and the temperature can at times drop as low as 5°F; but generally it hovers around or just below freezing point.

Getting There

One look at a map will show you there'll be few problems getting to Denmark from the other Scandinavian countries. Links by rail, sea and air are quick and frequent all year round, and, generally speaking, the travelling can be a rewarding part of your trip rather than a chore.

■ Trains

Copenhagen is a major junction for **trains** between Europe and the rest of Scandinavia. There are usually several daily services to Copenhagen from the major Scandinavian cities – Stockholm, Gothenburg, Oslo, Bergen, Turku and Helsinki – and less frequent links (usually one a day in summer) with remoter spots in the far north such as Narvik (in Norway) and Kiruna (in Sweden). Prices vary from around 500kr from Oslo or Stockholm to just over 900Fmk from Helsinki, though *Inter/EurRail*, *BIJ* and *Nordtourist* cards are valid on all the international routes into Denmark.

■ Buses

Several **buses** also offer direct links between the rest of Scandinavia and the major Danish cities, using the ferry routes outlined below. To Copenhagen from Sweden there are usually two buses per day from Halmstad (90SKr), via Rønne, and nine a day from Malmö (40SKr) and Lund (45SKr), using the Limhamn–Dragør ferry. For long distance enthusiasts, there's also a bus from Helsinki (305Fmk) twice a week in summer, travelling via Stockholm to Copenhagen.

■ Ferries

Precise details of the numerous **ferries** into Zealand and Jutland from Norway and Sweden are best checked in the ferry companies' latest brochures or at any Scandinavian tourist office, since timetables and prices fluctuate from year to year. There are sometimes reductions for holders of railcards (see *Basics*), and fares are usually a lot cheaper out of the end of June–early August period – though bear in mind that services are likely to be less frequent outside of peak season, and possibly non-existent in winter. Even if you're making ultimately for Copenhagen, don't disregard the possiblity of a quicker, and cheaper, crossing into north Jutland – an interesting part of Denmark, and with easy rail links to the capi-

tal; or, from Sweden, reaching Denmark by way of the very explorable island of Bornholm.

From Sweden

The quickest route **from Sweden** to Denmark is the twenty-minute *DSB* crossing from Helsingborg to Helsingør (around 12SKr), which runs around-the-clock; walk or cycle directly on board. Stockholm–Copenhagen trains also use this ferry, running straight on and off, completing the trip to Copenhagen fifty minutes later. Two other operators make the same crossing – see "Helsingør" for details.

Another inexpensive link is the *Scandinavian Ferry Lines* service from Limhamn to Dragør (28SKr), which takes just under an hour and leaves you a half-hour bus ride from central Copenhagen. The most direct link to Copenhagen, however, is the 45-minute hovercraft journey from Malmö, though this is comparatively expensive (70SKr) and doesn't run when the sea is frozen – quite likely between mid-November and mid-March.

With time to spare, you could reach Denmark proper by way of Bornholm, a sizeable Danish island that's actually nearer to Sweden. There's a daily ferry (87SKr) from Ystad to Rønne, and several daily hydrofoil crossings from Malmö to Allinge (130SKr). From Rønne, you can take the twice-daily (once-daily in winter) ferry to Copenhagen (264SKr).

Into Jutland, *Stena* sail several times a day in summer from Gothenburg to Frederikshavn (85SKr), while *Lion* sail daily from Helsingborg, Halmstad and Varberg to Grenå (for Århus), for a basic fare of 75SKr. See "Travel Details" at the end of the *Jutland* chapter for the full picture.

From Norway

The only direct connection **from Norway** to Copenhagen is the daily *Scandinavian Seaways* overnight crossing from Oslo (from 430NKr), though you'll save a lot of money by taking one of the numerous routes to either Frederikshavn or Hirtshals in Jutland. From Oslo to Frederikshavn there are 4–7 weekly crossings with *Stena* (155NKr) or, slightly more costly, *Da-No*, and – to Hirtshals – *Fred Olsen Lines*. There are also comprehensive connections from Frederikstad, Larvik and Moss to Frederikshavn (with *Da-No*, *Stena* and *Larvik Lines*), and from Kristiansand, Stavanger and Bergen to Hirtshals with *Fred Olsen Lines* – any of which should save a few kroner off the fare from Oslo. Again, for fuller facts, see "Travel Details".

■ Planes

SAS have nine **flights** daily into Copenhagen from Oslo and Stockholm, five daily from Helsinki. *Finnair* fly three or four times daily to Copenhagen from Helsinki, and *Icelandair* fly once a day from Reykjavík. Check at a tourist office or travel agent for special reduced fare deals between the Scandinavian capitals – of which there are usually several each summer. Copenhagen is very much the Danish hub of the *SAS* network (Århus is a poor second) and international arrivals often dovetail with domestic flights to other Danish cities, to which travel onwards costs little extra on top of the international fare.

A smaller Scandinavian airline, *North Flying*, have daily flights from Bergen and Stavanger to Aalborg and Århus, usual one-way fares are upwards of 1500NKr but under-26s can travel for 500NKr.

Costs, Money and Banks

Costs for virtually everything – eating, sleeping, travelling and just enjoying yourself – are far lower in Denmark than they are in any other Scandinavian country. Most British visitors will find Denmark only slightly more costly than what they're used to at home.

If you come for just a few days, stay in youth hostels or on campsites and don't eat out, it's possible to survive on £10 a day. Otherwise, moving around the country, combining campsites or hostels with cheap hotel accommodation, visiting museums, eating a full meal each day plus a few snacks and going for a drink in the evening, you can expect to spend a minimum of £20–25 per day.

■ Money and banks

Danish currency is the *krone* (plural *kroner*), made up of 100 øre, and it comes in notes worth 1000kr, 500kr, 100kr, 50kr and 20kr, and coins worth 10kr, 5kr, 1kr, 50øre, 25øre.

Banks are the best places to change travellers cheques and foreign cash; there's a uniform commission of 18kr per transaction – so change as much as is feasible in one go. Banking hours are Mon–Fri 9.30am–4.30pm, Thurs until 6.30pm. Most international airports and ferry ports have late opening exchange facilities.

Communications

As a geographically close-knit country, it's no surprise that communications in Denmark are safe and speedy. Whether you're sending a postcard home or phoning a ferry office at the other end of the country, you'll have few difficulties. Furthermore, for a country of its size, Denmark has an impressive number of newspapers and free-sheets, all of which help to keep people in touch with international, national and local events.

■ Post

Like most other public bodies in the country, the Danish **post office** runs an exceedingly tight ship. Anything you post is almost certain to arrive quickly. Mail to other parts of Europe weighing under 20g costs 3kr. You can buy **stamps** from post offices, most of which open Mon–Fri 9am–6pm, Sat 9am–1pm, with reduced hours in smaller communities, and from most newsagents. If you're more worried about receiving mail than sending it, **poste restante** is available at any named post office, and many hotels, youth hostels, and campsites will hold mail ahead of your arrival.

■ Phones

The old-style Danish **public telephones** frustratingly keep your money even if the number is engaged, which obviously means you should only insert the minimum amount to start with – a 50øre coin. The newer machines (recognise them by their yellow front-plates) give refunds and change – don't insert any money until the call is answered. Most hotels have phones in the rooms although calls from these are much more expensive than using the public phone at reception. Most youth hostels and campsites have public phones; if they don't, the warden will probably let you use the house one for a pay-phone fee. **Directory enquiries** (☎0033) are free and you'll be unlucky if the operator doesn't speak English. One thing to remember when dialling Danish numbers is to *always*, even if you're already within the area concerned, use the **area code** – a two-figure number which precedes the six-figure subscribers' number. To confuse matters, all Danish area codes were changed in May 1989 – if you come across a number that starts with 0, it's out of date. Direct dial **international codes** from Denmark are given in *Basics*. For **reverse charge international calls** call the overseas operator: ☎0015 for Europe; ☎0016 for elsewhere.

■ Media

By the lowest-common-denominator standards of the modern global media, the **Danish press**, with its predominantly serious and in-depth coverage of worthy issues, can't help but seem a little anachronistic. The main newspapers, each costing 4–7.50kr, are *Politiken*, a reasonably impartial newsheet with strong arts features, *Berlingske Tidende*, conservative/centrist, *Aktuelt*, a trade union paper, and *Kristeligt Dagblad*, a Christian paper. The best sports coverage can be found in the two tabloids – *B.T.*, which has a conservative bias, and *Ekstra Bladet*, akin to Britain's *Daily Mirror*. In Jutland, you'll also find the well-respected *Jyllands-Posten*, in morning and evening editions.

If you don't understand Danish, of course, you won't be buying the papers for their news stories as much as for their excellent **entertainment listings**, particularly *Ekstra Bladet*'s giveaway *Neon Guiden* section, and the Friday edition of *Jyllands-Posten*. The free Danish **rock music** paper, the monthly *Gaffa*, lists most of the bigger rock shows, and innumerable similar regional papers do the same for their areas – find them in cafés, record shops and the like. You can keep in touch with global current affairs with the **overseas newspapers** sold in all the main towns: most UK weekday titles cost 12kr and are available the day after publication at railway stations and the bigger newsagents. There's also a very short "News In English" at 8.30am Monday to Saturday on the Danish radio station DR3 – 93.85khz.

Danish television on first aquaintance seems as out-moded as the national press. There are two national channels, the non-commercial Channel 1, and the commercial Channel 2 – though, other than the ads, you'll struggle to spot the difference between the two. The third station, Channel 3, a cable channel, is shared with Sweden and Norway. None of these start up until the early evening, and all close down before midnight; the evening news programmes begin at 7pm and 7.30pm. If you're staying in a hotel, or a youth hostel with a TV room, you may also have the option of German and Swedish channels – plus a hatful of cable and satellite shows.

Getting Around

Despite being largely made up of islands, Denmark is a swift and easy country in which to travel. All types of public transport – trains, buses and the essential ferries – are punctual and efficient, and where you need to switch from one type to another, you'll find the timetables impressively well-integrated. Also, in such a small country, you can get from one end of Denmark to the other in half a day; even if, as is more likely, you're planning to see it all at leisure, you'll rarely need to do more than an hour's daily travelling. Besides being small, Denmark is also very flat, with scores of villages linked by country roads – ideal ingredients for effortless, problem-free cycling.

■ Trains

Trains are easily the best way to get about. *Danske Statsbaner* (*DSB*) – Danish State Railways – run an exhaustive and highly reliable network. *Inter/EurRail*, *BIJ* and the *Nordtourist Ticket* are valid on all routes except the few private lines that operate in some rural areas. There are just a few out-of-the-way regions which railways fail to penetrate, though these can be easily crossed by buses, which often run in conjunction with the trains, connecting with trains from the local railway station. Some of these buses are operated privately, some by *DSB*, on which railcards are valid (for more about buses, see below).

Train types range from the large intercity expresses (*ICs*), which have six-seat compartments and a buffet car, to the smaller, local trains (*persontog*), with larger, open-plan carriages. Departure times are listed on notices both on station concourses and on the platforms themselves (departures in yellow, arrivals in white), and by loudspeaker announcements. On the train, each station is usually announced a few minutes before you arrive. When boarding an *IC*, glance at the plan by the door that shows which seats, if any, are reserved, and when. Watch out also for *stillekupé* – quiet compartments designed for travellers desiring silence for which you pay 12kr (unless you have a first class ticket) on top of the normal fare.

Tickets should be bought in advance from the station, although they can also be bought on board. One-way tickets allow you to break your journey once, but travel must be completed on a single day. All trains have an inspector who sells and checks tickets. He or she is almost certain to speak English and is normally willing to answer your questions about routes and times. **Fares** are calculated on a zonal system: Copenhagen–Odense, for example, costs 90kr one-way, Copenhagen–Århus 143kr – probably the longest single trip you'll make. Buying a return offers no savings over two singles, but avoiding travel on a Sunday, Monday or Friday can save 20–30kr over a long trip; it's the off-peak fares we've listed above. If you don't have a railcard but are a student, there are various **train travel discounts** of up to fifty percent available through *DIS*, the Danish student travel organisation, and those **over 65** can qualify for thirty to fifty percent discounts on certain routes (details from any Danish tourist office). Those travelling in a group of three or more are also entitled to discounts of up to fifty percent – again, details from a tourist office.

Seat reservations, costing 15kr from the station ticket office, can be a good idea, especially if you've luggage to hump, on busy routes – typically those to and from ferry terminals, and in and out of major cities at holiday times; ask at a tourist or station office for advice. Reservations are compulsory on crossings of the Store Bælt, the sea dividing Zealand from Funen and Jutland. If you don't have one on this route, you can buy one on the train from the inspector; in the unlikely event of there being no spare seats, you'll be turfed off at the ferry port and will have to wait for the next train.

As for **timings**, *DSB*'s *Køreplan* (25kr from any newsagent), details all *DSB* train, bus and ferry services inside (and long distance routes outside) the country, including the local Copenhagen S-train system and all private services, and is a sound investment if you're planning a lot of travelling within the country. If you're not, smaller **timetables** detailing specific routes can be picked up for free at tourist offices and station booking counters.

■ Buses

There are only a handful of **long distance bus** services in Denmark: Copenhagen–Århus (120kr), Copenhagen–Aalborg (150kr), Copenhagen–Hantsholm (199kr), Esbjerg–Frederikshavn (160kr) and Odense–Nykøbing F. (138kr). These fares represent quite a saving over full train fares, but,

while just as efficient, long distance buses are much less comfortable than trains. Where buses really come into their own, however, is in the few areas where trains are scarce or the connections complicated. Much of Funen and northeast Jutland are barely touched by trains, for example, and if you're travelling from Esbjerg to Frederikshavn or Aalborg you save several hours – and a lot of timetable reading – by taking the bus.

■ Ferries

Ferries link all the Danish islands, and vary in size from the train-carrying *DSB* ferries between Zealand, Funen and Jutland, to raft-like affairs connecting tiny, isolated settlements a few minutes off the (so-called) mainland. Where applicable, train and bus fares include the cost of ferry crossings (although you can also pay at the terminal and walk on), while the smaller ferries commonly charge 10–40kr for foot passengers. Get the full picture from the nearest tourist office, and check "Travel Details" at the end of each chapter for frequencies and journey-times.

■ Planes

Domestic flights, operated by *SAS* under their *DanAir* arm, are hardly essential in a country of Denmark's size, but can be handy if you're in a rush: from Copenhagen, it's less than an hour's flying time to anywhere in the nation. There are three kinds of fare: "red departures" are returns valid on weekdays; "green departures" are weekend returns and slightly pricier; "blue departures" are the most expensive, valid for travel any time, with returns costing double that of a single. To give an idea of the differences, a blue single ticket costs the same as a red return. If you're **under 26** or **over 60**, regular airfares can be cut with the 300kr **standby ticket**; get details from an *SAS* desk or tourist office. Remember, too, that continuing on a domestic flight after arriving in Denmark on an international one will rarely cost more than the international fare.

■ Cycling

Cycling is the best way to appreciate Denmark's pastoral, and mostly flat, landscape, as well as being a good method of getting about in the towns. Most country roads have sparse vehicle traffic and all large towns have cycle tracks – though watch out for sometimes less-than-careful drivers on main roads. Bikes can be **hired** at nearly all youth hostels and tourist offices, at most bike shops, and some railway stations, for around 25–40kr per day, 75–180kr per week, although there's often a 100kr deposit. For more than local cycling, **plan your route** taking into account the frequent westerly winds – it's better to pedal facing east than west.

If the wind gets too strong, or your legs get too tired, you can take your bike on all types of public transport except city buses. By train, however, unless you're travelling more than 100km, an *IC* can't be used, and you'll need to take the slower local trains – and pay 12–30kr for your machine. A brochure, *Cykler i tog*, lists rates and rules in full and is free from railway stations. For a similar fee to the trains, long distance buses have limited cycle space, while ferries let bikes on for free or a few kroner. Domestic flights charge 65kr for airlifting your bike.

■ Driving and hitching

Given the excellent public transport system, the size of the country, and the comparatively high price of petrol, **driving** isn't really economical unless you're in a group. So too **car hire**, which starts at around 3300kr a week for a *VW Golf* with unlimited mileage – though it's worth checking the cut-price deals offered by some ferry lines. You'll need an international driving licence and must be aged at least twenty to take to the roads, although many car hire firms won't rent vehicles to anyone under 25. Danes drive on the right, and there's a speed limit in towns of 50kph, 80kph in open country and 100kph on motorways. Unlike Sweden and Finland, headlights need only be used after dusk. There are also random breath tests for suspected drunken drivers, and the penalties are severe. When parked in a town, not on a meter, a parking-time disc must be displayed; get one from a tourist office, police station or bank. As for **hitching**, this is illegal on motorways and difficult anywhere – not worth the bother off the main international routes: Copenhagen–Helsingør–Sweden, and from Jutland into northern Germany.

■ Local transport

Local transport in towns is by bus, or in Copenhagen by bus and *S-Train*. Single fares are 6–8kr, and tickets are usually valid for any number of journeys in an hour. If you're in one town for a while and using the buses a lot, either get a *klipperkort*, which is a coupon usually equivalent to ten single tickets and slightly cheaper, or a discounted pass from the tourist office, valid for transport in the surrounding area as well as the immediate vicinity – usually for 24 hours. Generally, unless several people are sharing, **taxis** are a raw deal. Expect to pay around 15kr plus 5–8kr per kilometre, inclusive of tip.

Sleeping

While much less costly in Denmark than in other Nordic countries, accommodation is still going to be your major daily expense and you should plan it carefully. Hotels, however, are by no means off-limits if you seek out the better offers, and both youth hostels and campsites are plentiful – and of a uniformly high standard.

■ Hotels and private rooms

Coming to Denmark on a standard package trip (see *Basics*) is one way to stay in a **hotel** without spending a fortune. Another way is to simply be selective. Most Danish hotel rooms include phone, TV and bathroom, for which you'll pay around 500kr for a double (singles from around 350kr), but going without the luxuries can result in big savings. In most large towns you'll find several hotels offering rooms without bathrooms for as little as 290kr for a double (190kr for a single), and some **inns** (or *Kro*) in country areas match this price even including full facilities. Another advantage of staying in a hotel or inn is the lack of a curfew (common in hostels in big cities) and an inclusive all-you-can-eat breakfast – so large you won't need to buy lunch.

Only in peak season will you need to **book** in advance, although obviously for the cheaper places you should make a reservation as early as you can. Danish tourist offices overseas will provide you with a free list of hotels (and approximate prices) throughout the country, though much more accurate and extensive information can, not surprisingly, be found at local tourist offices inside the country. We detail the most attractive deals and prices in the guide but often the best way to locate what's currently on offer is to simply phone the local office and ask – then phone the hotel and book. The tourist office gets no commission so has no bias. The local tourist office can also supply details of **private rooms** in someone's home, vaguely akin to – and just as variable as – British-style bed & breakfast. Reckon paying about 300–500kr a double for this.

■ Youth hostels

Youth hostels (*Vandrerhjem*) are the cheapest option under a roof. Every town has one, they're much less pricey than hotels, and they have a high degree of comfort thanks to a campaign by the Danish YHA (*Danmarks Vandrerhjem*) to raise their profile and attract families. Most hostels offer a choice between private rooms, often with toilets and showers, and dormitory accommodation, and nearly all have cooking facilities. Rates range from 51kr per person in a private room to 35kr for a dormitory bed. It's rare for hostels other than those in major towns or ferry ports ever to be full, but during the summer it's still wise to phone ahead to make a reservation, and to check on the hostel's location – some are several kilometres outside town centres.

As with all Scandinavian hostels, sleeping bags are not allowed, so you either need to carry a sheet sleeping bag or hire hostel linen – which can become expensive over a long stay. It's a good idea, too, to get an **IYHF card**, since without one you'll be lumbered with the cost of either an overnight card (18kr) or a year-long Danish YHA card (90kr). If you're intent on doing a lot of hostelling, it's worth contacting *Danmarks Vandrerhjem*, Vesterbrogade 39, DK-1620, Copenhagen V. (☎31/313612), for their guide to Danish hostels (*Vandrerhjem i Danmark*, 25kr) – in Danish but self-explanatory.

Sometimes cheaper still, and occasionally free, are **Sleep-Ins**, run by local authorities and usually open for a two-week period during the summer (normally early August). Copenhagen has a well-established one which runs all summer, offering a bed, shower and breakfast for 65kr, and most other towns have downmarket versions, often no more than a mattress on the floor. You need your own sleeping bag, sometimes only one night's stay is permitted and there may be an age restriction (typically 16–24 year olds only, although this may not be strictly enforced). Sleep-ins also come and go, so check the current situation at a local tourist office, or with *Use-It* in Copenhagen.

■ Camping

If you don't already have an International Camping Card from a camping organisation in your own country, you'll need a Visitor's Pass to camp in Denmark, which costs 30kr from any campsite and is valid on all official sites until the end of the year.

Camping rough without the landowner's permission is illegal, but possible if you stay out of sight; a dim view is taken of rough camping on beaches and an on-the-spot fine may well be imposed.

In any case, **campsites** (*campingplads*) are virtually everywhere. All sites open through the three summer months, many from April to September, while a few stay open all year. There's a rigid grading system: one-star sites have drinking water and toilets, two-star sites have, in addition, kitchen, showers, laundry and a food shop within a kilometre, while three-star sites, by far the majority, have all the above plus a TV-room, on-site shop, cafeteria, etc. Prices vary only slightly, three-star sites charging 26–36kr per person, others a few kroner less. Many sites also have **cabin accommodation**, usually with cooking facilities, which at 40–60kr, represent massive nightly savings for several people sharing, although on busy sites cabins are often booked up throughout the summer. Any Danish tourist office will give you a free leaflet listing all the sites and the basic rules. For further information, contact *Dansk Camping Union*, Gl. Kongevej 74D, DK-1850 Frederiksberg C (☎31/210600).

Food and Drink

Although good food can cost a lot, there are plenty of ways to eat affordably and healthily in Denmark, and with plenty of variety too. Much the same applies to drink: the only Scandinavian country free of social drinking taboos, Denmark is an imbibers delight – both for its great choice of tipples, and for the great number of places where they can be sampled.

■ Food

Traditional Danish **food** is centred on meat and fish: beef, veal, chicken and pork are frequent menu items – though rarely bacon, which is mainly exported – along with various forms of salmon, herring, eel, plaice and cod. Combinations of these are served with potatoes and another, usually boiled, vegetable. Ordinary restaurant meals can be expensive, especially in the evening, and are often no-go areas for vegetarians who don't eat fish – but there are many other ways to eat Danish food that won't destroy your budget or your diet.

Breakfast

Breakfast (*morgenmad*) can be the tastiest and is certainly the healthiest (and most meat-free) Danish meal: almost all hotels offer a sumptuous breakfast as a matter of course, and if you're staying in a rural youth hostel you can often attack a help-yourself table laden with cereals, bread, cheese, boiled eggs (sometimes), fruit juice, milk and tea for around a mere 30kr – though city hostels' breakfasts tend to be less exciting. Breakfast elsewhere will be far less substantial: many cafés offer a very basic one for around 20kr, but you're well-advised to hold out until lunchtime.

Lunch and snacks

You can track down an excellent-value **lunch** (*frokost*) simply by walking around and reading the signs chalked up outside a café, restaurant or *bodega* (a kind of bar which also sells no-frills food). On these notices, put out between 11.30am and 2.30pm, you'll often see the word *tilbud*, which refers to the "special"priced dish, or *dagens ret*, meaning "dish of the day" – a plate of chili con carne or lasagne for around 38kr, or a two-course set lunch for about 50kr. Some restaurants offer the **Dan Menu** – designed to make ordering and eating Danish food easy for tourists – comprising a two-course meal for 75kr, while many more carry a fixed price (75–90kr) three-course lunch in which you pick from a selection of several dishes. A variation on this idea is a choice of *smørrebrød*, or open sandwiches: slices of rye bread heaped with meat (commonly either ham, beef or liver pate), fish (salmon, eel, caviar, cod-roe, shrimp or herring) or cheese, and generously plied with assorted trimmings (mushrooms, cucumber, pickles or slices of lemon). A selection of three or four of these costs about 75kr.

Elsewhere, the American **burger** franchises are as commonplace and as popular as you'd expect, as are **pizzerias**, which are dependable and affordable at any time of day, many offering specials deals such as all-you-can-eat-salad with a basic pizza for 42kr, or a more exotic filling or dish for 45–70kr. You can also get a very ordinary self-service meat, fish or omelette lunch in a **supermarket cafeteria** for 40–75kr.

Most Danes buy **snacks** from the immensely well-patronised fast-food stands (*pølsevogn*) found in all main streets and at railways stations. These serve various types of **hot sausage** (*pølser*) for 12–18kr: the long thin *weiner*, the shorter, fatter *frankfurter*, or the *franske*, a sausage inside a cylindrical piece of bread. Alternatives include a **toasted ham and cheese sandwich** (*parisertoast*) for 13kr – vegetarians can ask for the ham to be left out – and **chips** (*pomme frites*), which come in two forms: big (*store*) and small (*lille*). The size refers to the actual chips and not the portion: the former are like fat English chips, the latter American french-fry matchsticks; they cost 15.50kr and 10.50kr respectively for a serving. All of the above come with various types of ketchup and mustard to order.

If you just want a cup of **coffee** (always fresh) or **tea** (usually a fairly exotic teabag brew), drop into the nearest café, where either will be 6–10kr. You help it down with a **Danish pastry** (*wienerbrød*), tastier and much less sweet than the imitations sold under the name elsewhere in the world.

Shops and markets

An especially tight budget may well leave you dependent on **shopping** for food. *Brugsen* and *Irma* are the most commonly found **supermarkets** (usually open Mon–Fri 9am–5pm with later hours on Thurs & Fri, Sat 9am–1pm or 2pm), and there's little difference in price, although you'll also come across *Netto*, which can be slightly cheaper but is mostly filled with freezer food. In shops, prices will be 10–40 percent higher than you're used to at home but something to look out for is *drikkeyoghurt*, a fortifying drinkable yoghurt available in a variety of fruit flavours; half a litre costs 6kr. Late-night shopping is generally impossible, although in bigger towns, the *DSB* supermarket at the railway station is likely to be open until midnight.

The best spots for fresh fruit and veg are the Saturday and (sometimes) Wednesday **markets** held in most towns, and you can buy *smørrebrød* (see above) for 5–15kr a piece from the special *smørrebrød* shops, at least one of which will be open until 10pm.

Dinner

Dinner (*aftensmad*) in Denmark presents as much choice as does lunch, but the cost is likely to be much higher. The staples such as pizzerias (see above) keep their prices unchanged from lunchtime, and many youth hostels serve simple but filling evening meals for 45–50kr – though

GLOSSARY OF DANISH FOOD AND DRINK TERMS

Basics

Brød	Bread	Nogle pølser	Frankfurter	Sukker	Sugar
Bøfsandwich	Hamburger	Nogle	Biscuits	Sødmælk	Full cream milk
Chokolade	Chocolate	småkager		Te	Tea
(Varm)	(Hot)	Ostebord	Cheese board	Wienerbrød	Pastry
Det kolde bord	Help yourself	Sildebord	A selection of		
	cold buffet		spiced and	**Egg (æg) dishes**	
Is	Ice Cream		pickled herring	Kogt æg	Boiled egg
Kaffe (med	Coffee (with	Skummetmælk	Skimmed milk	Omelet	Omelette
fløde)	cream)	Smør	Butter	Røræg	Scrambled
Letmælk	Low fat milk	Smørrebrød	Open		eggs
Mælk	Milk		sandwiches	Spejlæg	Fried eggs

Fish (*Fisk*)

Forel	Trout	Krebs	Crayfish	Sardiner	Sardines
Gedde	Pike	Laks	Salmon	Sild	Herring
Helleflynder	Halibut	Makrel	Mackerel	Store rejer	Prawns
Hummer	Lobster	Rejer	Shrimp	Søtunge	Sole
Karpe	Carp	Rogn	Roe	Stør	Sturgeon
Klipfisk	Salt Cod	Rødspætte	Plaice	Torsk	Cod
Krabbe	Crab	Røget Sild	Kipper	Ål	Eel

Meat (*Kød*)

And(ung)	Duck(ling)	Hare	Hare	Lever	Liver
Bøf	Beef	Kalkun	Turkey	Pølser	Sausages
Dyresteg	Venison	Kanin	Rabbit	Rensdyr	Reindeer
Fasan	Pheasant	Kylling	Chicken	Skinke	Ham
Gås	Goose	Lam	Lamb	Svinekød	Pork

Vegetables (*Grønsager*)

Artiskokker	Artichokes	Kartofler	Potatoes	Ris	Rice
Asparges	Asparagus	Linser	Lentils	Rosenkål	Sprouts
Blomkål	Cauliflower	Løg	Onions	Rødbeder	Beetroot
Champignons	Mushrooms	Majs	Sweet corn	Rødkål	Red cabbage
Grønne bønner	Runner beans	Majskolbe	Corn on the cob	Salat	Lettuce, salad
Gulerødder	Carrots	Nudler	Noodles	Salatgurk	Cucumber
Hvide bønner	Kidney beans	Peberfrugt	Peppers	Selleri	Celery
Hvidløg	Garlic	Persille	Parsley	Spinat	Spinach
Julesalat	Chicory	Porrer	Leeks	Turnips	Turnips

Fruit (*Frugt*)

Abrikoser	Apricots	Ferskner	Peaches	Rabarber	Rhubarb
Ananas	Pineapple	Grapefrugt	Grapefruit	Rosiner	Raisins
Appelsiner	Orange	Hindbær	Raspberries	Solbær	Blackcurrants
Bananer	Bananas	Jordbær	Strawberries	Stikkelsbær	Gooseberries
Blommer	Plums	Kirsebær	Cherries	Svesker	Prunes
Blåbær	Blueberries	Mandariner	Tangerines	Vindruer	Grapes
Brombær	Blackberries	Melon	Melon	Æbler	Apples
Citron	Lemon	Pærer	Pears		

Danish Specialities

Boller i karry	Meatballs in curry sauce served with rice	Sild røget	Smoked herring on rye bread garnished with a raw egg yolk, radishes and chives
Flæskesteg	A hunk of pork with red cabbage, potatoes and brown sauce	Skidne æg	Poached or hard boiled eggs in a cream sauce, spiced with fish mustard and served with rye bread, decorated with sliced bacon and chives
Frikadeller	Pork rissoles		
Hakkebøf	Minced beef rolled into balls and fried with onions		
Hvid labskovs	Danish stew: small squares of beef boiled with potatoes, peppercorn and bay leaves.	Ålesuppe	Sweet and sour eel soup
		Ål stegt med stuvede kartofler	Fried eel with diced potatoes and white sauce
Kalvebryst i frikasseé	Veal boiled with vegetables and served in a white sauce with peas and carrots	Æbleflæsk	Smoked bacon with onions and sautéed apple rings
Kylling grillstegt	Grilled chicken with salad	Æggekage	Scrambled eggs with onions, chives, potatoes and bacon pieces
Medisterpølse	A spiced pork sausage, usually served with boiled potatoes or stewed vegetables	Torsk kogt	Poached cod in mustard sauce with boiled potatoes
Sild i karry	Herring in curry sauce		

Drink (*Drikke*)

Appelsinvand	Orangeade	Vin	Wine	Øl	Beer
Citronvand	Lemonade	Husets vin	House wine	Eksport-Øl	Export beer (very strong lager)
Kærnemælk	Buttermilk	Rødvin	Red wine		
Mineralvand	Soda water	Hvidvin	White wine	Fadøl	Draught beer
Tomatjuice	Tomato juice	Åblemost	Apple juice	Guldøl	Strong beer

you have to order it in advance, and, as with breakfast, the best tend to be in rural areas. The most cost-effective dinners (80–100kr), however, are usually found in **ethnic restaurants** (most commonly Chinese and Middle Eastern, with a smaller number of Indian, Indonesian and Thai), which, besides à la carte dishes, often have a help-yourself table – ideal for gluttonous over-indulgence – and you usually get soup and a dessert thrown in as well. Often the same **Danish restaurants** which are promising for lunch turn into expense-account affairs at night, offering an atmospheric, candle-lit setting for the slow devouring of immaculately prepared meat or fish, where you'll be hard pushed to spend less than 200kr each; although a few serve the 75kr Dan Menu (see above) into the evening.

■ Drink

If you've arrived from near teetotal Norway or Sweden, you're in for a shock. Not only is alcoholic **drink** entirely accepted in Denmark, it's unusual *not* to see people strolling along the pedestrianised streets swigging from a bottle of beer. Although extreme drunkeness is frowned upon, alcohol is widely consumed throughout the day in Denmark by most types of people. Even at business meetings, there'll usually be a crate of beer or a bottle of *Akvavit* on hand.

Although you can **buy** booze more cheaply from supermarkets, the most sociable **places to drink** are the *pubs* and *cafés*, where the emphasis is on beer – although you can also get spirits and wine (or tea and coffee). There are also *bars* and *bodegas* (see "Food"), in which, as a very general rule, the mood tends to favour wines and spirits, and the customers are a bit older than café patrons.

The cheapest **type of beer** is **draught beer** (*Fadøl*), half a litre of which costs around 12kr. Draught beer is a touch weaker than **bottled beer**, which costs 17–18kr for a third of a litre, and a great deal less potent than the **export beers** (*Guldøl* or *Eksport-Øl*) costing 25–30kr per bottle. All Danish beer is actually lager, the most common brands being *Carlsberg* and *Tuborg*, and although a number of towns have their own locally-brewed rivals, you'll need a finely-tuned palate to spot much difference between them. One you will notice the taste of is *Lys Pilsner*, which is a very low alcohol lager – more like a soft drink.

Most international **wines and spirits** are widely available, a shot of the hard stuff costing 12–18kr in a bar, a glass of wine upwards of 15kr. While in the country you should investigate the many varieties of the schnapps-like *Akvavit*, which Danes consume as eagerly as beer, especially with meals, although most non-Danes turn pale after more than two or three. A tasty relative is the gloriously hot and strong *Gammel Dansk Bitter Dram* – Akvavit-based but made with bitters and never drunk with meals.

Directory

CONTRACEPTIVES Condoms from pharmacies, most big supermarkets and barbers, the Pill from chemists with a prescription.

EMERGENCIES ☎0-0-0. Ask for fire, police or ambulance.

FESTIVALS A wide range of music festivals – rock, folk, jazz and various combinations – take place all over Denmark throughout the summer. Some feature leading names and require tickets, but many are cheap or free. Get the details from the free music monthly, *Gaffa*, or one of the many regional freesheets from record shops, cafés, etc.

FISHING Well-stocked with bream, dace, roach, pike, trout, zander and much more, Denmark's lakes and rivers are a fishing enthusiast's dream. The only problem is bringing enough bait (much more expensive in Denmark than in the UK) to cope with the inevitably large catch. The time to come is in early or late summer, and the prime areas are in central Jutland, around Randers and Viborg, and slightly further north around Silkeborg and Skanderborg. For specialist angling trips see "Package Tours" in *Basics*.

FOOTBALL In recent years, the success of Denmark's national football team (for more on which see *Contexts*) has stimulated interest in the country's domestic soccer scene. In general, the standard is roughly on a par with the English second or third division, although teams espe-

cially worth watching are Brøndby (Copenhagen), AGF Århus, and the 1989 champions, OB Odense. The season divides into two halves, from April to early June (*Forår*) and from August to October (*Efterår*), with most matches played on Sunday afternoon; admission is 40–60kr and the local newspapers (look under *Fodbold*) and tourist office will have details.

MARKETS Virtually every town has a market, usually on Wednesday and Saturday mornings.

NUDE BATHING Trying for an all-over tan is accepted practice throughout Denmark, although you'll be arrested if you try it anywhere except at the designated beaches – which exist in most popular bathing areas. Details from the local tourist office.

PUBLIC HOLIDAYS All shops and banks are closed on the following days, and public transport and many museums run to Sunday schedules: January 1, the afternoon of June 5 (Constitution Day), December 24 (afternoon only), December 25, Maundy Thursday, Good Friday, Easter Monday, Prayer Day (fourth Friday after Easter, Ascension Day (around mid-May) and Whit Monday.

SALES TAX A tax of 22 percent is added to almost everything you'll buy – but it's always included in the marked price.

SAILING Experienced sailors can rent sailing and motorboats in many parts of the Danish coast; Kerteminde and Svenborg, on Funen's northeast and south coast respectively, are particularly well-established sailing centres. The Danish Tourist Board in London can supply full details; Danish marine charts can be bought from Søkortafdelingen, Esplanaden 19, DK-1263 Copenhagen K.

SHOPS Shop hours are Mon–Thurs 9am–5pm, Fri 9am–7pm or 8pm, Sat 9am–1pm or 2pm, Sun closed.

TAMPONS Available from pharmacies and supermarkets.

TIPS Unless you're in the habit of having porters carry your luggage, you'll never be expected to tip – restaurant bills include a 15 percent service charge.

History

Spending much time at all in Denmark soon makes you realise that its history is entirely disproportionate to its size. Nowadays a small – and often overlooked – nation, Denmark has nonetheless played an important role in key periods of European history, firstly as home-base of the Vikings, and later as a medieval superpower. Markers to the past, from prehistory to the wartime resistance movement, are never hard to find. Equally easy to spot are the benefits stemming from one of the earliest welfare state systems and some of Western Europe's most liberal social policies.

■ Early settlements

Traces of human habitation, such as deer bones prised open for marrow, have been found in central Jutland and dated at 50,000 BC, but it is unlikely that any settlements of this time were permanent, as much of the land was still covered by ice. From 14,000 BC tribes from more southerly parts of Europe arrived during the summer to hunt reindeer for meat and antlers, which provided a raw material for axes and other tools. The melting ice caused the shape of the land to change, the warmer climate enabled vast forests to grow in Jutland. From about 4000 BC, settlers arrived with agricultural knowledge: they lived in villages, grew wheat and barley and kept animals, and buried their dead in **dolmens** or megalithic graves.

The earliest metal and bronze finds are from 1800 BC, the result of trade with southern Europe. The richness of some pieces indicates an awareness of the cultures of Crete and Mycenae. By this time the country was widely cultivated and densely populated. Battles for control over individual areas saw the emergence of a ruling warrior class, and, around AD 500, a tribe from Sweden calling themselves **Danes** migrated southwards and wrested control of what became known as Denmark (Danmark).

■ The Viking era

Around AD 800, under **King Godfred**, the Danish boundaries were marked out. However, following Charlemagne's conquest of the Saxons in Germany, the Franks began to threaten the Danes' territory and they had to prepare an opposing force. They built fast seaworthy vessels and defeated Charlemagne easily. Then, with the Norwegians, they attacked Spanish ports and eventually invaded Britain. By 1033, the Danes controlled the whole of England and Normandy and dominated trade in the Baltic.

In Denmark itself, which then included much of what is now southern Sweden, the majority of people were farmers: the less wealthy paid taxes to the king and those who owned large tracts of land provided the monarch with military forces. In time, a noble class emerged, expecting and receiving privileges from the king in return for their support. Law-making was the responsibility of the *tings*, which consisted of district noblemen. Above the district *tings* was a tier of provincial *tings*, which were charged with the election of the king. The successful candidate could be any member of the royal family, which led to a high level of feuding and bloodshed.

In 960, with the baptism of King **Harald** (**"Bluetooth"**), Denmark became officially Christian – principally, it's thought, to stave off imminent invasion by the German emperor. Nonetheless, Harald gave permission to a Frankish monk, **Ansgar**, to build the **first Danish church**, and Ansgar went on to take control of missionary activity throughout Scandinavia. Harald was succeeded by his son **Sweyn I** (**"Forkbeard"**). Sweyn was a pagan but he tolerated Christianity, even though he suspected the missionaries of bringing a German influence to bear in Danish affairs. In 990, he joined with the Norwegians in attacking Britain, where Alfred had been succeeded by the well-named Ethelred "the Unready". Sweyn's son, **Knud I** (**"the Great"**) (King Canute of England), married Ethelred's widow, took the British throne and soon controlled a sizeable empire around the North Sea – the zenith of Viking power.

■ The rise of the church

During the eleventh and twelfth centuries, Denmark was weakened by violent internal struggles, not only between different would-be rulers but also between the Church, nobility and monarchy. Following the death of **Sweyn II** in 1074, two of his four sons, Knud and Harald, fought for the throne – Harald, supported by the peasantry and the Church, emerging victorious. Harald was a mild and introspective individual, though he was a competent monarch and introduced the first real Danish currency. He was constantly derided by Knud and his allies, and after his death in 1080 his brother became **Knud II**. He made generous donations to the Church, but his introduction of higher taxes and the absorption of all unclaimed land into the realm enraged the nobility. The farmers of North Jutland revolted in 1086, forcing Knud to flee to Odense, where he was slain on the high altar of Skt. Alban's Kirke. The ten year period of poor harvests which ensued was taken by many to be divine wrath, and there were reports of miracles occurring in Knud's tomb, leading to the murdered king's canonisation in 1101.

The battles for power continued, and eventually, in 1131, a **civil war** broke out that was to simmer for two decades, various claimants to the throne and their offspring slugging it out with the support of either the Church or nobility. During this time the power of the clergy escalated dramatically by way of **Bishop Eskil**, who enjoyed a persuasive influence on the eventual successor, Erik III. Following Erik's death in 1143, the disputes went on, leading to the division of the kingdom between two potential rulers, Sweyn and Knud. Sweyn's repeated acts of tyranny resulted in the death of Knud in Roskilde, but Knud's wounded aide, Valdemar, managed to escape and raise the Jutlanders in revolt at the battle of Grathe Heath, south of Viborg.

■ The Valdemar era

Valdemar I ("the Great") assumed the throne in 1157, strengthening the Crown by ending the elective function of the *tings*, and shifting the power to choose the monarch to the Church. Technically the *tings* still influenced the choice of king, but in practice hereditary succession became the rule.

After Bishop Eskil's retirement, **Absalon** became Archbishop, erecting a fortress at the fishing village of **Havn** (later to become København – Copenhagen). Besides being a zealous churchman, Absalon possessed a sharp military mind and came to dominate the monarch and his successor, Knud IV. Through him Denmark saw some of its best years, expanding to the south and east, and taking advantage of internal strife within Germany. In time, after Absalon's death and the succession of **Valdemar II**, Denmark controlled all trade along the south coast of the Baltic and in the North Sea east of the Ejder. Valdemar was also responsible for subjugating Norway, and in 1219 he set out to conquer Estonia and take charge of Russian trade

routes through the Gulf of Finland. But in 1223 he was kidnapped by Count Henry of Schwerin (a Danish vassal) and forced to give up many Danish possessions. There was also a re-drawing of the southern boundary of Jutland which caused the Danish population of the region to be joined by a large number of Saxons from Holstein.

Within Denmark, the years of expansion had brought great prosperity. The laws of the *tings* were written as the **Jutish Code**, signifying a shift toward law-making being carried out by the king rather than by the *tings*. The increasingly affluent nobles demanded greater rights if they were to be counted on to support the new king. The Church was envious of the growing power of the nobles and much bickering ensued in the following years, resulting in the eventual installation of Valdemar II's son, Christoffer I, as monarch.

Christoffer died suddenly in Ribe when his only son Erik was two years old; Queen Margrethe took the role of Regent until **Erik V** came of age. Erik's overbearing manner and penchant for German bodyguards annoyed the nobles, and they forced him to a meeting at Nyborg in 1282 where his powers were limited by *håndfæstning*, or charter, that included an undertaking for annual consultation with a *Danehof*, or forum of nobles. In 1319 **Christoffer II** became king, after agreeing an even sterner charter, which allowed for daily consultations with a *Råd* – a council of nobles. In 1326, in lieu of a debt which Christoffer had no hope of repaying, Count Gerd of Holstein occupied a large portion of Jutland. Christoffer fled to Mecklenburg and Gerd installed the twelve-year-old Valdemar, Duke of Schleswig, as a puppet king.

As they proceeded to divide the country among themselves, the Danish nobles became increasingly unpopular with both the Church and the peasantry. Christoffer attempted to take advantage of the internal discord to regain the Crown in 1329 but he was defeated in battle by Gerd. Under the peace terms Gerd was given Jutland and Funen while his cousin, Count Johan of Plön, was granted Zealand, Skåne and Lolland-Falster. In 1332 Skåne, the richest Danish province, inflicted a final insult on Christoffer when its inhabitants revolted against Johan and transferred their allegiance to the Swedish king, Magnus.

Gerd was murdered in 1340. The years of turmoil had taken their toll on all sections of Danish society: from Christoffer's death in 1332, the country had been without a monarch and it was felt that a re-establishment of the Crown was essential to restore stability. The throne was given to **Valdemar IV**. The monarchy was strengthened by the taking back of former Crown land which had been given to nobles, and within twenty years Denmark had regained its former lands, with German forces driven back across the Ejder. The only loss, Estonia, was sold.

In 1361, the buoyant king attacked and conquered Gotland, much to the annoyance of the Hanseatic League, who were using it as a Baltic trading base. A number of anti-Danish alliances sprang up and the country was slowly plundered until peace was agreed in 1370 under the **Treaty of Stralsund**. This guaranteed trade for the Hanseatic partners by granting them control of castles along the west coast of Skåne for fifteen years. It also laid down that the election of the Danish monarch had to be approved by the Hanseatic League – the peak of their power.

■ The Kalmar Union

Valdemar's daughter, Margrethe, forced the election of her five-year-old son, Olav, as king in 1380, installing herself as Regent. After his untimely death after only a seven-year reign, Margrethe became queen of Denmark and Norway, and later of Sweden as well – the first ruler of a united Scandinavia. In 1397, a formal document, the **Kalmar Union**, set out the rules of the union of the countries, which allowed for a Scandinavian federation under the same monarch and foreign policy, within which each country had its own internal legislation. It became evident that Denmark was to be the dominant partner within the union when Margrethe placed Danish nobles in civic positions in Norway and Sweden but failed to reciprocate with Swedes and Norwegians in Denmark.

Erik VII ("of Pomerania") became king in 1396, determined to remove the Counts of Holstein who had taken possession of Schleswig. In 1413 he persuaded a meeting of the *Danehof* to declare the whole of Schleswig to be Crown property, and three years later war broke out with the German-influenced nobility of the region. Initially the Hanseatic League supported the king, unhappy with the Holstein privateers who were interfering with their trade. But Erik also introduced important economic reforms within Denmark, ensuring that foreign goods reached Danish people through Danish merchants instead

of coming directly from Hanseatic traders. This led to a war with the League, after which, in 1429, Erik imposed the **Sound toll** on shipping passing through the narrow strip of sea off the coast of Helsingør.

The conflicts with the Holsteiners and the Hanseatic League had, however, badly drained financial resources. Denmark still relied on hired armies to do its fighting, and the burden of taxation had caused widespread dissatisfaction, particularly in Sweden. With the Holstein forces gaining ground in Jutland, Erik fled to Gotland and in 1439 Swedish and Danish nobles elected in his place **Christoffer III**, who acquiesced in the nobles' demands and ensured peace with the Hanseatics by granting them exemption from the Sound toll.

His sudden death in 1448 left – after internal struggle – **Christian I** to take the Danish throne. After the death of his uncle and ally, the Count of Holstein, he united Schleswig and Holstein at Ribe in 1460 and became Count of Holstein and Duke of Schleswig. In Denmark itself he also instigated the *stændermøde*: a council of merchants, clergy, freehold peasants and nobility in place of the exclusively noble *Danehof*, thereby maintaining his pledge to work in close liaison with the nobles, and forging a powerful position for the Crown – a policy which was continued by his successor, Hans.

Hans died in 1513 and **Christian II** came to the throne seeking to re-establish the power of the Kalmar Union and reduce the trading dominance of the Hanseatic League. He invaded Sweden in 1520 under the guise of protecting the Church, but soon crowned himself King of Sweden at a ceremony attended by the cream of Swedish nobility, clergy and merchant class – an amnesty being granted to those who had been in opposition to Christian. It was, however, a trick. Once inside the castle, 82 of the "guests" were arrested on charges of heresy, sentenced to death, and executed – an event which became known as the **Stockholm Bloodbath**. This was supposed to subdue Swedish hostility to the Danish monarch but in fact had the opposite effect. Gustavus Vasa, previously one of six Swedish hostages held by Christian in Denmark, became the leader of a revolt which ended Christian's reign in Sweden and finished the Kalmar Union.

Internally, too, Christian faced a revolt, to which he responded with more brutality. At the end of 1522, a group of Jutish nobles banded together with the intention of overthrowing him, joining up with Duke Frederik of Holstein-Gottorp (heir to half of Schleswig-Holstein), who also regarded the Danish king with disfavour. The following January, the nobles renounced their royal oaths and, with the support of forces from Holstein, gained control of all of Jutland and Funen. As they prepared to invade Zealand, Christian fled to Holland, hoping to assemble an army and return. In his absence, Frederik of Holstein-Gottorp became **Frederik I**.

■ The Reformation

At the time of Frederik's acquisition of the crown there was a growing unease with the role of the Church in Denmark, especially with the power – and wealth – of the bishops. Frederik was a Catholic but refused to take sides in religious disputes and did nothing to prevent the destruction of churches, well aware of the groundswell of peasant support for Lutheranism. Frederik I died the following year and the fate of the Reformation hinged on which of his two sons would succeed him. The eldest and most obvious choice was Christian, but his open support for Lutheranism was opposed by the bishops and nobles. The younger son, Hans, was just twelve-years-old but was favoured by the Church and the nobility. The civil war which ensued became known as the **Count's War**, ending in 1536 with **Christian II** on the throne, and the establishment of the new Danish Lutheran Church, with a constitution placing the king at its head.

■ Danish-Swedish conflicts

New trading routes across the Atlantic had reduced the power of the Hanseatic League, and the young and ambitious successor to Christian, **Frederik II**, saw this as a chance for expansion. Sweden, however, was also seeking to expand, with the result that the **Seven Years' War** was fought between the two countries from 1563 to 1570. The conflict caused widespread devastation and plunged the Danish economy into crisis – though this was short-lived: price rises in the south of Europe enabled Danish wealth to grow, and the increasing affluence of the time was marked by the building of the elaborate castle of Kronborg in Helsingør.

By the time **Christian IV** came to the throne in 1596, Denmark was a solvent and powerful nation. His reign was to be characterised by bold

new town layouts and great architectural works. Copenhagen became acknowledged as a major European capital, gaining both a large increase in population and much of today's skyline, including Rosenborg, Børsen and Rundetårnet. To stem the rise of Swedish power after the Seven Years' War, Christian IV took Denmark into the abortive **Thirty Years' War** in 1625, in which Danish defeat was total, and the king was widely condemned for his lack of foresight. The war led to increased taxes, inflation became rampant, and a number of merchants displayed their anger by petitioning the king over tax exemptions and other privileges enjoyed by nobles.

In 1657 Sweden occupied Jutland, and soon after marched across the frozen sea to Funen with the intention of continuing to Zealand. Hostilities ceased with the signing of the **Treaty of Roskilde**, under which Denmark finally lost her Swedish provinces. Sweden, however, was still suspicious of possible Danish involvement in Germany, and broke the terms of the treaty, commencing an advance through Zealand towards Copenhagen. The Dutch, to whom the Swedes had been allied, regarded this as a precursor to total Swedish control of commercial traffic through the Sound and sent a fleet to protect Copenhagen. This, plus a number of local uprisings within Denmark and attacks by Polish and Brandenburg forces on Sweden, halted the Swedes' advance and forced them to seek peace. The **Treaty of Copenhagen**, signed in 1660, acknowledged Swedish defeat but allowed the country to retain the Sound provinces acquired under the Treaty of Roskilde, so preventing either country from monopolising Sound trade.

■ Absolute monarchy

In Denmark, the financial power of the nobles was fading as towns became established and the new merchant class grew. The advent of firearms caused the king to become less dependent on the foot-soldiers provided by the nobles, and there was a general unease about the privileges – such as exemption from tax – which the nobles continued to enjoy. Equally, few monarchs were content with their powers being limited by *håndfæstning*.

During the Swedish siege of Copenhagen, the king had promised special concessions to the city and its people, in the hope of encouraging them to withstand the assault. Among these were a right to determine their own rate of tax. A meeting of the city's burghers decided that everyone, including the nobility, should pay taxes. The nobles had little option but to submit. The citizens, sensing their power, went on to suggest that the Crown become hereditary and end the *håndfæstning* system. Frederik III accepted and, with a full-scale ceremony in Copenhagen, was declared hereditary monarch. The task of writing a new constitution was left to the king and its publication, in 1665, revealed that he had made himself absolute monarch, bound only to uphold the Lutheran faith and ensure the unity of the kingdom. The king proceeded to rule, aided by a Privy Council in which seats were drawn mainly from the top posts within the civil service. The noble influence on royal decision-making had been drastically cut.

Christian V, king from 1670, instigated a broad system of royal honours, creating a new class of land-owners who enjoyed exemptions from tax, and whose lack of concern for their tenants led Danish peasants into virtual serfdom. In 1699 **Frederik IV** set about creating a Danish militia to make the country less dependent on foreign mercenaries. With Sweden changing its allegiance towards Britain and Holland, Denmark re-established its relations with the French, the culmination of which was the **Great Northern War**, from 1709 to 1720. This resulted in the emergence of Russia as a dominant force in the region, while Denmark emerged with a strong position in Schleswig, and Sweden's exemption from the Sound Toll was ended.

The two decades of peace which followed saw the arrival of **Pietism**, a form of Lutheranism which strove to renew the devotional ideal. Frederik embraced the doctrine towards the end of his life, and it was adopted in full by his son, **Christian VI**, who took the throne in 1730. He prohibited entertainment on Sunday, closed down the Royal Theatre, and made Court life a sombre affair: attendance at church on Sundays became compulsory and Confirmation was made obligatory.

■ The Enlightenment

Despite the beliefs of the monarch, Pietism was never widely popular, and by the 1740s its influence had waned considerably. The reign of **Frederik V**, from 1746, saw a great cultural awakening: grand buildings such as Amalienborg and Frederikskirke were erected in Copenhagen (though the latter's completion was delayed for twenty years), and there was a new flourishing of the arts. The king, perhaps as a reaction to the puritanism of his father, devoted himself to a life of pleasure and allowed control of the nation effectively to pass to the civil service. **Neutrality** was maintained through several international conflicts and the economy benefited as a consequence.

In 1766 Frederik's heir, **Christian VII**, who had scarcely more credibility as a ruler, took the Crown. His mental state was unstable, his moods ranging from deep lethargy to rage and drunkenness. By 1771 he had become incapable of carrying out even a minimum of official duties. The king's council, filled by a fresh generation of ambitious young men, insisted that the king effect his own will – under guidance from them – and disregard the suggestions of his older advisers.

Decision-making became dominated by a German Court physician, **Johann Freidrich Struensee**, who had accompanied the king on a tour of England and had gained much of the credit for the good behaviour of the unpredictable monarch. Struensee combined personal arrogance with a sympathy for many of the ideas then fashionable elsewhere in Europe; he spoke no Danish (German was the Court language) and had no concern for Danish traditions. Through him a number of sweeping **reforms** were executed: the Privy Council was abolished, the Treasury became the supreme administrative organ, the death penalty was abolished, the moral code lost many of its legal sanctions, and the press was freed from censorship.

There was opposition from several quarters. Merchants complained about the freeing of trade, and the burghers of Copenhagen were unhappy about their city losing its autonomy. In addition, there were well-founded rumours about the relationship between Struensee and the queen. Since nothing was known outside the Court of the king's mental state, it was assumed that the monarch was being held prisoner. Struensee was forced to reintroduce censorship of the press as their editorials began to mount attacks on him. The Royal Guards mutinied when their disbandment was ordered, and simultaneously a coup was being plotted by Frederik V's second wife, Juliane Marie of Brunswick and her son, Frederik. After a masked ball at the palace in 1772,

Struensee was arrested and tried, and soon after beheaded. The dazed king was paraded before his cheering subjects.

The Court came under the control – in ascending order of influence – of Frederik, Juliana and a minister, Ove Høegh-Guldberg. All those who had been appointed to office by Struensee were dismissed, and while Høegh-Guldberg eventually incurred the wrath of officials by operating in much the same arrogant fashion as Struensee had, he recognised – and exploited – the anti-German feelings which had been growing for some time. Danish became the language of command in the army and later the Court language, and in 1776 it was declared that no foreigner should be given a position in royal office.

In the wider sphere, the country prospered through dealings in the Far East, and Copenhagen confirmed its place as the new centre of Baltic trade. The outbreak of the American War of Independence provided neutral Denmark with fresh commercial opportunities. In 1780 Denmark joined the League of Armed Neutrality with Russia, Prussia and Sweden, which had the effect of maintaining trading links across the Atlantic until the end of the war.

Faced with the subsequent conflict between Britain and revolutionary France, Denmark joined the second armed neutrality league with Russia and Sweden, until a British naval venture into the Baltic during 1801 obliged withdrawal. British fears that Denmark would join Napoleon's continental blockade resulted in a British attack led by Admiral Nelson which destroyed the Danish fleet in Copenhagen. The pact between France and Russia left Denmark in a difficult situation. To oppose this alliance would leave them exposed to a French invasion of Jutland. To oppose the British and join with the French would adversely affect trade. As the Danes tried to stall for time, the British lost patience, occupying Zealand and commencing a three-day bombardment of Copenhagen. On their inevitable surrender, the Danes had little option but to join with Napoleon, although it was becoming clear that his was to be the losing side. Sweden had aligned herself with the British and was demanding the ceding of Norway if Denmark were to be defeated – which, under the **Treaty of Kiel**, is what happened.

■ The age of liberalism

The Napoleonic Wars destroyed Denmark's international prestige and left the country bankrupt, and the period up until 1830 was spent in recovery. But the king remained popular, believed to have the welfare of his subjects at heart.

Meanwhile, in the arts, a **national romantic movement** was gaining pace. The sculptor Thorvaldsen and the writer/philosopher Kierkegaard are perhaps the best known figures to emerge from the era, but the most influential domestically was a theologian called **N.F.S. Grundtvig**, who, in 1810, developed a new form of Christianity – one which was free of dogma and drew on the virtues espoused by the heroes of Norse mythology. In 1825 he left the intellectual circles of Copenhagen and travelled the rural areas to guide a religious revival, eventually modifying his earlier ideas in favour of a new faith in the wisdom of "the people" – something which was to colour the future liberal movement.

On the political front, there was trouble brewing in Danish-speaking Schleswig and German-tongued Holstein. The Treaty of Kiel had compelled the king to relinquish Holstein to the Confederation of German States – although, confusingly, he remained duke of the province. He promised the setting up of a consultative assembly for the region, while within Holstein a campaign sought to pressure the king into granting the duchy its own constitution. The campaign was stamped on hard, but the problems of the region still weren't resolved. Further demands called for a complete separation from Denmark, with the duchies being brought together as a single independent state. The establishment of consultative assemblies in both Holstein and Schleswig eventually came about in 1831, though they lacked any real political muscle.

Although absolutism had been far more benevolent toward the ordinary people in Denmark than to their counterparts elsewhere in Europe, interest was growing in the liberalism which was sweeping through the continent. In Copenhagen a group of scholars proffered the idea that Schleswig be brought closer into Danish affairs, and in pursuit of this they formed the Liberal Party and brought pressure to bear for a new liberal constitution. As the government wavered in its response, the liberal movement grew and its first newspaper, *Fædrelandet*, appeared in 1834.

In 1837 the Crown agreed to the introduction of elected town councils, and, four years later, to elected bodies in parishes and counties. Although the franchise was restricted, many small farmers gained political awareness through their participation in the local councils.

Frederik IV died in 1839 and was replaced by **Christian VIII**. As Crown Prince of Norway, Christian had approved a liberal constitution in that country but surprised Danish liberals by not agreeing a similar constitution at home. In 1848 he was succeeded by his son **Frederik VII**. Meanwhile, the liberals had organised themselves into the **National Liberal Party**, and the king signed a **new constitution** which made Denmark the most democratic country in Europe, guaranteeing freedom of speech, freedom of religious worship, and many civil liberties. Legislation was to be put in the hands of a *Rigsdag* elected by popular vote and consisting of two chambers — the lower *folketing* and upper *landsting*. The king gave the powers of an absolute monarch, but his signature was still required before bills approved by the *Rigsdag* could become law. And he could select his own ministers.

Within Schleswig-Holstein, however, there was little faith that the equality granted to them in the constitution would be upheld. A delegation from the duchies went to Copenhagen to call for Schleswig to be combined with Holstein within the German Confederation. A Danish compromise suggested a free constitution for Holstein with Schleswig remaining as part of Denmark, albeit with its own legislature and autonomy in its internal administration. The Schleswig-Holsteiners rejected this and formed a provisional government in Kiel.

The inevitable war which followed was to last for three years and, once Prussia's support was withdrawn, it ended in defeat for the duchies. The Danish Prime Minister, C.C. Hall, drew up a fresh constitution which included Schleswig as part of Denmark but totally excluded Holstein. Despite widespread misgivings within the *Rigsdag*, the constitution was narrowly voted through. Frederik died before he could give the royal assent and it fell to **Christian IX** to put his name to the document which would almost certainly trigger another war.

It did, and under the peace terms Denmark ceded both Schleswig and Holstein to Germany, leaving the country smaller than it had been for centuries. The blame was laid firmly on the National Liberals, and the new government, appointed by the king and drawn from the affluent landowners, saw its initial task as replacing the constitution, drawn up to deal with the Schleswig-Holstein crisis, with one far less liberal in content. The election of 1866 resulted in a narrow majority in the *Rigsdag* favouring a new constitution. When this came to be implemented, it retained the procedure for election to the *folketing*, but made the *landsting* franchise dependent on land and money and allowed 12 of the 64 members to be selected by the king.

The landowners worked in limited co-operation with the National Liberals and the Centre Party (a less conservative version of the National Liberals). In opposition a number of interests, encompassing everything from leftist radicals to followers of Grundtvig, were shortly combined into the **United Left**, which put forward the first political manifesto seen in Denmark. It called for equal taxation, universal suffrage in local elections, more freedom for the farmers, and contained a vague demand for closer links with the other Scandinavian countries. The United Left became the majority within the *folketing* in 1872.

The ideas of **revolutionary socialism** had begun percolating through the country around 1871 via a series of pamphlets edited by Louis Pio, who attempted to organise a Danish Internationale. In April 1872, Pio led 1200 bricklayers into a strike, announcing a mass meeting on May 5. The government banned the meeting and had Pio arrested, and he was sentenced to five years in prison and the Danish Internationale was also banned. The workers began forming trade unions and workers' associations.

The intellectual left also became active. A series of lectures delivered by Georg Brandes in Copenhagen cited Danish culture, in particular its literature, as dull and lifeless compared to that of other countries. He called for fresh works that questioned and examined society, instigating a bout of literary attacks on institutions such as marriage, chastity and the family. As a backlash, conservative groups in the government formed themselves into the **United Right** under the Prime Ministership of **J.B.S. Estrup**.

The Left did their best to obstruct the government but, as time went on, they lost seats while the strength of the Right grew. In 1889, the Left issued a manifesto calling for reductions in military expenditure, a declaration of neutrality, the provision of old age pensions, sick pay, a limit to hours of work, and votes for women. The election of 1890 improved the Left's position in the *folketing*, and also saw the election of two **Social Democrats**. With this, the left moved further towards moderation, and compromise with the right. The trade unions, whose membership escalated in proportion to the numbers employed in the new industries, grew in stature, and were united as the Association of Trade Unions in 1898. The Social Democratic Party grew stronger with the support of the industrial workers although it had no direct connection with the trade unions.

■ Parliamentary democracy and World War I

By the end of the century the power of the Right was in severe decline. The election of 1901, under new conditions of a secret ballot, saw them reduced to the smallest group within the *folketing* and heralded the beginning of **parliamentary democracy**.

The government of 1901 was the first real democratic government, assembled with the intention of balancing differing political tendencies – and it brought in a number of reforms. Income tax was introduced on a sliding scale, and free schooling beyond the primary level began. As years went by, Social Democrat support increased, and the Left, such as they were, became increasingly conservative; indeed they were barely left-wing at all and are better referred to under their Danish name, *Venstre*. In 1905 a breakaway group formed the **Radical Left** (politically similar to the English Liberals), calling for the reduction of the armed forces to the status of coastal and border guards, greater social equality and votes for women.

An alliance between the Radicals and Social Democrats enabled the two parties to gain a large majority in the *folketing* in the election of 1913, and a year later the conservative control of the *landsting* was ended. Social advances were made, but further domestic progress was halted by international events as Europe prepared for war.

Denmark had enjoyed good trading relations with both Germany and Britain in the year preceding **World War I** and was keen not to be seen to favour either side in the hostilities. On the announcement of the German mobilization, the now Radical-led cabinet, with the support of all the other parties, issued a **statement of neutrality** and was able to remain clear of direct involvement in the conflict.

At the conclusion of the war, attention was turned again towards Schleswig-Holstein, and under the Treaty of Versailles it was decided that Schleswig should be divided into two zones for a referendum. In the northern zone a return to unification with Denmark was favoured by a large percentage, while the southern zone elected to remain part of Germany. A new German-Danish border was drawn up just north of Flensburg.

High rates of unemployment and the success of the Russian Bolsheviks led to a series of strikes and demonstrations, the unrest coming to a head with the **Easter crisis** of 1920. During March of that year, a change in the electoral system toward greater proportional representation was agreed in the *folketing* but the Prime Minister, **C. Th. Zahle**, whose Radicals stood to lose support through the change, refused to implement it. The king, Christian X, responded by dismissing him and asking **Otto Liebe** to form a caretaker government to oversee the changes. The royal intervention, while technically legal, incensed the Social Democrats and the trade unions, who were already facing a national lockout by employers in reply to demands for improved pay rates. The unions, perceiving the threat of a right-wing coup, began organising a general strike to begin after the Easter holiday. There was a large republican demonstration outside Amalienborg.

On Easter Saturday, urgent negotiations beween the king and the existing government concluded with an agreement that a mutually acceptable caretaker government would oversee the electoral change and a fresh election would immediately follow. Employers, fearful of the power the workers had shown, met many of the demands for higher wages.

The next government was dominated by the *Venstre*. They fortified existing social policies, and increased State contributions to union unemployment funds. But a general depression of the economy continued, and there was widespread industrial unrest as the *krone* declined in value and living standards fell. A **general strike** lasted for a month and a workers' demonstration in Randers was subdued by the army.

Venstre and the Social Democrats jostled for position over the next decade, though under the new electoral system no one party could achieve enough power to undertake major reform. The economy did improve, however, and state influence spread further through Danish society than ever before. Enlightened reforms were put on the agenda too, making a deliberately clean break with the moral standpoints of the past – notably on abortion and illegitimacy. Major public works were funded, such as the bridge between Funen and Jutland over the *Lille Bælt*, and the *Stormstrømsbro*, linking Zealand to Falstar.

■ The Nazi occupation

While Denmark had little military significance for the Nazis, the sea off Norway was being used for the supply of iron ore from Sweden to Britain, and the fjords offered good shelter for a fleet engaged in a naval war in the Atlantic. To get to Norway, the Nazis planned an invasion of Denmark. At 4am on April 9, 1940, the German ambassador in Copenhagen informed Prime Minister Stauning that German troops were preparing to cross the Danish border and issued the ultimatum that unless Denmark agreed that the country could be used as a German military base – keeping control of its own affairs – Copenhagen would be bombed. To reject the demand was considered a postponement of the inevitable, and to save Danish bloodshed the government acquiesced at 6am. "They took us by telephone" said a Danish minister.

A national coalition government was formed which behaved according to protocol but gave no unnecessary concessions to the Germans. Censorship of the press and a ban on demonstrations were imposed, ostensibly intended to prevent the Danish Nazis spreading propaganda. But these measures, like the swiftness of the initial agreement, were viewed by some Danes as capitulation and were to be a thorn in the side of the Social Democrats for years to come.

The government was reshuffled and changed to include non-parliamentary experts, one of whom, **Erik Scavenius**, a former Foreign Minister, conceived an ill-fated plan to gain the confidence of the Germans. He issued a statement outlining the government's friendly attitude to the occupying power, and even praised the German military victory – which upset the Danish public and astonished the Germans, who asked whether Denmark would like to enter into commercial agreement immediately rather than wait until the end of the war. Scavenius was powerless to do anything other than agree, and a deal was signed within days. Under its terms, the *krone* was to be phased out and German currency made legal tender.

Public reaction was naturally hostile, and Scavenius was, not surprisingly, regarded as a traitor. Groups of Danes began a systematic display of antipathy to the Germans. Children wore red white and blue "RAF caps", Danish customers walked out of cafés when Germans entered, and the ban on demonstrations was flouted by groups who gathered to sing patriotic songs. On September 1, 1940, an estimated 739,000 Danes gathered around the country to sing the same song simultaneously. The king demonstrated his continued presence by riding on horseback each morning through Copenhagen.

Meanwhile the Danish government continued its balancing act, knowing that failure to cooperate at least to some degree would lead to a complete Nazi takeover. It was with this in mind that Denmark signed the Anti-Comintern Pact making communism illegal, but insisted on the insertion of a clause which allowed only Danish police to arrest Danish communists.

Vilhelm Buhl was appointed Prime Minister. Buhl had been an outspoken opponent of the signing of the Anti-Comintern Pact and it was thought he might end the apparent appeasement. Instead, the tension between occupiers and occupied were to climax with Hitler's anger at the curt note received from Christian X in response to the Fuhrer's birthday telegram. Although it was the king's standard reply, Hitler took the mere "thank you" as an insult and immediately replaced his functionaries in Denmark with hardliners who demanded a new pro-German government.

Scavenius took control, and, in 1943, with the idea of showing that free elections could take place under a German occupation, elections were called. The government asked the public to demonstrate faith in national unity by voting for any one of the four parties in the coalition, and received overwhelming support from the largest ever turnout in a Danish election.

Awareness that German defeat was becoming inevitable stimulated a wave of strikes throughout the country. Berlin declared a state of emergency in Denmark, and demanded that the Danish government comply – which it refused to do. Germany took over administration of the country, interning many politicians. The king was asked to appoint a cabinet from outside the *folketing*, and Germans were free for the first time to round up

Danish Jews. Resistance was organised under the leadership of the **Danish Freedom Council**. Sabotage was carefully coordinated, and an underground army, soon comprising over 43,000, prepared to assist in the Allied invasion. In June 1944, rising anti-Nazi violence led to a curfew being imposed in Copenhagen and assemblies of more than five people banned, to which workers responded with a spontaneous general strike. German plans to starve the city had to be abandoned after five days.

■ The postwar period

After the German surrender in May 1945, a **liberation government** was created, composed equally of pre-war politicians and members of the Danish Freedom Council, with Vilhelm Buhl as Prime Minister. Its internal differences earned the administration the nickname of "the debating club".

While the country had been spared the devastation seen elsewhere in Europe, it still found itself with massive economic problems and it soon became apparent that the liberation government could not function. In the ensuing election there was a swing to the Communists, and a minority *Venstre* government was formed. The immediate concern was to strengthen the economy, although the resurfacing of the southern Schleswig issue began to dominate the *Rigsdag*.

Domestic issues soon came to be overshadowed by the **international situation** as the Cold War began. Denmark had unreservedly joined the United Nations in 1945, and had joined the IMF and World Bank to gain financial help in restoring its economy. In 1947 the Marshall Plan aid brought further assistance. As world power became polarised between East and West, the Danish government at first tried to remain impartial, but in 1947 agreed to join NATO – a total break with the established concept of Danish neutrality (though, to this day, the Danes remain opposed to nuclear weapons).

The years after the war were marked by much political manoeuvering among the Radicals, Social Democrats and Conservatives, resulting in many hastily called elections and a number of ineffectual compromise coalitions distinguished mainly by the level of their infighting. Working-class support for the Social Democrats steadily eroded, and much Communist support was later transferred to the new, more revisionist, Socialist People's Party.

Social reforms, however, continued apace, not least with the Sixties' abandoning of all forms of censorship and institution of free abortion on demand. Such measures are typical of recent social policy, though Denmark's odd position between Scandinavia and the rest of mainland Europe still persists. A referendum held in 1973 to determine whether Denmark should join the EC resulted in a substantial majority in favour, making Denmark the only Scandinavian country in the community (which it still is, with no visible ill-effects on its relations with its Nordic neighbours). Otherwise, though, public enthusiasm for the EC was, and remains, notoriously lukewarm, and the prospect of European monetary union is cooling it still further.

■ The current political scene

Perhaps the biggest change in the Seventies was the foundation – and subsequent influence – of the new **Progress Party**, founded by Mogens Glistrup, who came to national attention on TV, claiming to have an income of over a million *kroner*, but through manipulation of the tax laws paid no income tax at all. The Progress Party stood on a ticket of drastic tax cuts and Glistrup went on to compare tax avoidance with the sabotaging of Nazi rail lines during the war. He also announced that if elected he would replace the Danish defence force with an answering machine saying "we surrender" in Russian. Eventually he was imprisoned after an investigation by the Danish tax office; released in 1985, he set himself up as a tax consultant.

What the success of the Progress Party pointed to was dissatisfaction with both the economy and the established parties' ways of dealing with its problems. In September 1982, after yet more *Venstre*/Social Democrat/Socialist coalitions, **Poul Schlüter** became Denmark's first Conservative Prime Minister of the twentieth century, leading the widest ranging coalition yet seen – the Conservatives joined by the *Venstre*, Centre Democrats, and Christian People's Party.

As with the political climate over the rest of Europe, the prescription for Denmark's economic malaise was seen in drastic spending cuts, not sparing the social services, and an extension of taxation into previously untapped areas such as pension funds. A four percent ceiling was set on wage increases. The government failed to win a sufficient majority in the *folketing* and an early election was called for January 1984. The goverment was returned, and felt the public had given it a mandate to continue its policies, which it did until the call for a snap election in 1987.

A total of sixteen parties contested the election, each needing at least two percent of the vote to gain a seat. The result was a significant swing to the left. The centre-right coalition lost seven seats and the Social Democrats, despite losing two seats, became by far the largest party in the *folketing*. The People's Socialists fared extremely well, finishing with 27 MPs. Schlüter resigned as Prime Minister but was then asked to form a new government after being nominated to do so by six of the nine party leaders within the *folketing*. His failure to consult non-government parties in seeking a majority was regarded as highly irregular but not unconstitutional. He made an informal agreement with the Progress Party in order to gain a single-seat working majority in the *folketing*. Three of the four seats lost by the Conservatives had gone to the Progress Party, who espoused tax cuts and immigration curbs. Their former leader, Mogens Glistrup, was returned to the *folketing* and announced his intention to be Prime Minister in "five to ten years".

The main surprise was the emergence of a new party, the **Common Course**, led by a former leader of the Seamen's Union **Prabber Hansen**. The Common Course gained four seats with policies claimed to be leftist but actually encompassing a strange left-right mix. While opposing membership of NATO, they are also pledged to tax-cuts and "keeping Denmark for the Danes". Hansen had been imprisoned for a short time following a strike in 1956; ironically, the lawyer instrumental in bringing about his release was Mogens Glistrup. It seems that the Progress Party and the Common Course, although both with limited support, now hold the balance of power on the right and the left respectively.

The election result was intensely unpopular among NATO chiefs (who already held Denmark in suspicious regard due to its "nuclear-free" status) but, despite international speculation about Denmark leaving the alliance, domestically few outside the fringe parties considered this a realistic possibility. Indeed, a further election, in May 1988, largely served to affirm the new Schüter-led government, if only, perhaps, because of the apparent lack of any workable alternative.

A BRIEF GUIDE TO DANISH

Danish in some ways is similar to German, but there are significant differences in pronunciation, Danes tending to swallow the ending of many words and leave certain letters silent. English is widely understood, as is German; young people especially often speak both fluently. And if you can speak Swedish or Norwegian then you should have little problem making yourself understood – all three languages share the same root. A handy phrasebook to take is *Traveller's Scandinavia* (Pan £2.50) – which, as well as Danish, covers Norwegian and Swedish.

PRONUNCIATION

In **pronunciation**, unfamiliar **vowels** include:

æ when long between **ai**r and ta**i**lor. When short like g**e**t. When next to "r" sounds more like h**a**t.

å when long like s**aw**, when short like **o**n.

ø like f**u**r but with the lips rounded.

e, when long, is similar to pl**a**te, when short somewhere between pl**a**te and h**i**t; when unstressed it's like **a**bove

Consonants are pronounced as in English, except:

d at the end of a word after a vowel, or between a vowel and an unstressed "e" or "i", like **th**is. Sometimes silent at the end of a word.

g at the beginning of a word or syllable as in **g**o. At the end of a word or long vowel, or before an unstressed e, usually like **y**et but sometimes like the Scottish lo**ch**. Sometimes mute after an a, e, or o.

hv like **v**iew

hj like **y**et

k as English except between vowels, when it's as in **g**o.

p as English except between vowels, when it's as in **b**it.

r pronounced as in French from the back of the throat but often silent

sj as in **sh**eet

t as English except between vowels, when it's as in **d**o. Often mute when at the end of a word.

y between b**ee** and p**oo**l

BASICS

Do you speak English?	*Taler De engelsk?*	Goodnight	*Godnat*
Yes	*Ja*	Goodbye	*Farvel*
No	*Nej*	Yesterday	*I går*
I don't understand	*Jeg forstår det ikke*	Today	*I dag*
I understand	*Jeg forstår*	Tomorrow	*I morgen*
Please	*Værså venlig*	Day after	*I overmorgen*
Thank you	*Tak*	tomorrow	
Excuse me	*Undskyld*	In the morning	*Om morgenen*
Good morning	*Godmorgen*	In the afternoon	*Om eftermiddagen*
Good afternoon	*Goddag*	In the evening	*Om aftenen*

SOME SIGNS

Entrance	*Indgang*	Arrival	*Ankomst*
Exit	*Udgang*	Departure	*Afgang*
Push/pull	*Skub/træk*	Police	*Politi*
Danger	*Fare*	No Smoking	*Rygning forbudt/Ikke rygere*
Gentlemen	*Herrer*	No Entry	*Ingen adgang*
Ladies	*Damer*	No Camping	*Campering forbudt*
Open	*Åben*	No Trespassing	*Adgang forbudt for*
Closed	*Lukket*		*uvedkommende*

QUESTIONS AND DIRECTIONS

Where is?	Hvor er?	Near/far	Er det nær/fjern
When?	Hvornår?	Left/right	Venstre/højre
What?	Hvad?	Straight ahead	Ligeud
Why?	Hvorfor?	I'd like...	Jeg vil gerne ha...
Who?	Hvem?	Where is the youth	Hvor er vandrerhjemmet?
How much?	Hvor meget?	hostel?	
How much does it	Hvad koster det?	Can we camp here?	Må vi campere her?
cost?		It's too expensive	Det er for dyrt
Here	Her	Where are the toilets?	Hvor er toiletterne?
There	Der	How far is it to...?	Hvor langt er der til...?
Good/bad	God/dårlig	Where can I get a	Hvor kan jeg tage/
Cheap/expensive	Billig/dyr	train/bus/ferry to...?	bussen/færgen til...?
Hot/cold	Varm/kold	At what time does...?	Hvornår går...?
Better/bigger/cheaper	Bedre/større/billigere	Ticket	Billet

NUMBERS

0	Nul	9	Ni	18	Atten	80	Firs
1	En	10	Ti	19	Nitten	90	Halvfems
2	To	11	Elleve	20	Tyve	100	Hundrede
3	Tre	12	Tolv	21	Enogtyve	101	Hundrede og et
4	Fire	13	Tretten	30	Tredive	151	Hundrede og
5	Fem	14	Fjorten	40	Fyrre		enoghalvtreds
6	Seks	15	Femten	50	Halvtreds	200	To hundrede
7	Syv	16	Seksten	60	Tres	1000	Tusind
8	Otte	17	Sytten	70	Halvfjerds		

DAYS AND MONTHS

Monday	mandag	January	januar	July	juli
Tuesday	tirsdag	February	februar	August	august
Wednesday	onsdag	March	marts	September	september
Thursday	torsdag	April	april	October	oktober
Friday	fredag	May	maj	November	november
Saturday	lørdag	June	juni	December	december
Sunday	søndag				

· (Days and months are never capitalised)

GLOSSARY OF DANISH TERMS AND WORDS

Banegård	Railway station	Herregård	Manor house	Rutebilstation	Bus station
Bakke	Hill or ridge	Jernebane	Railway	Rådhus	Town hall
Domkirke	Cathedral	Kirke	Church	Skov	Wood or forest
Gammel or	Old	Klint	Cliff	Stue	Room
Gamle		Kloster	Monastery	Sø	Lake
Hav	Sea	Kro	Inn	Torvet	Market square
Havn	Harbour	Plads	Square	Tårn	Tower
				Vand	Water

CHAPTER ONE

ZEALAND

As home to Copenhagen, **Zealand** (*Sjælland*) is Denmark's most important – and most visited – region. Tucked away on the east coast of the biggest Danish island, the nation's capital, though not an especially large city, dominates much of Zealand, and the nearby towns, though far from being drab suburbia, tend inevitably to be dormitory territory. Only much further away, towards the west and south, are the country manners strong and the pace more provincial.

It would be perverse to come to Zealand and not visit **Copenhagen** – easily the most extrovert and cosmopolitan place in the country, and as lively by night as it is by day. But once there you should at least make a brief journey out to see how different the rest of Denmark can be. Woods and expansive parklands appear almost as soon as you leave the city – and even if you don't like what you find, the swiftness of the metropolitan transport network, which covers almost half the island, means you can be back in the capital in easy time for an evening drink.

North of Copenhagen, the coastal road passes the outstanding modern art museum of **Louisiana** before reaching **Helsingør**. This is the only place to cross by rail into Sweden and site of the renowned **Kronborg Slot** – an impressive fortification though quite unfairly stealing the spotlight from **Frederiksberg Slot**, at nearby **Hillerød**. West of Copenhagen, and on the main route to Funen, is **Roskilde**, a former capital with an extravagant cathedral that's still the last resting place for Danish monarchs, and with a gorgeous location on the Roskilde fjord – from where five Viking boats were salvaged and are now restored and displayed in a specially-built museum. South of Copenhagen, at the end of the urban S-train system, is **Køge**, which – beyond the industrial sites that flank it – has a well-preserved medieval centre and long, sandy beaches lining its bay.

Further out from the sway of Copenhagen, Zealand's towns are appreciably smaller, more scattered, and far less full of either commuters or day-trippers. **Ringsted**, plumb in the heart of the island, is another one-time capital, a fact marked by the twelfth- and thirteenth-century royal tombs in its church. Further south, **Næstved** is surrounded by lush countryside, but is of most interest for its position on the broad route south to three smaller islands just off the coast: **Lolland**, **Falster** and **Møn**. Each of these is busy during the summer, but outside of high season you'll find them green and peaceful, and Lolland forms a leisurely backdoor route, via Langeland, to Funen.

Not part of Zealand, but reachable by ferry from Copenhagen, is the island of **Bornholm**. A huge slab of granite in the Baltic, it houses a few small fishing communities, and has some fine beaches and an unusual history, making for a stimulating detour if you're heading for Sweden – to which it's nearer than Denmark and connected by ferry.

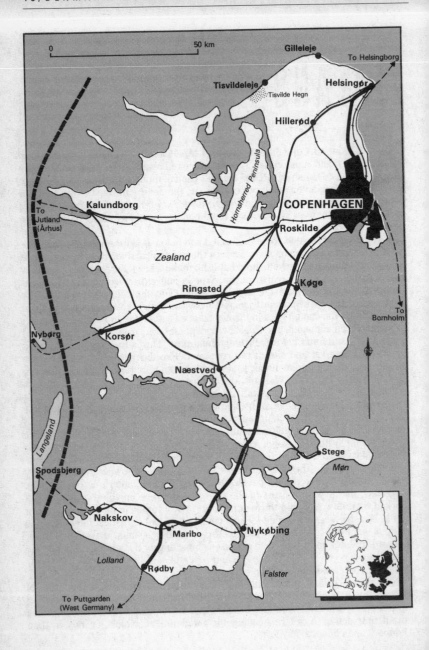

COPENHAGEN

COPENHAGEN, as any Dane will tell you, is no introduction to Denmark; indeed, a greater contrast with the sleepy provincialism of the rest of the country would be hard to find. Despite that, the city completely dominates Denmark: it is the seat of all the nation's institutions – politics, finance, the arts – and provides the driving force for the country's social reforms. Copenhagen is also easily Scandinavia's most affordable capital, and one of Europe's most user-friendly cities: small and welcoming, where people, rather than motor traffic, set the pace, as evidenced by the multitude of outside café tables and a small, strollable centre largely given over to pedestrians. In summer especially there's a varied range of lively street entertainment, while at night there's a plethora of cosy bars and an intimate club and live music network that can hardly be bettered. Not to mention, for daytime sights, the city's beckoning collections of history and of Danish and international art, as well as a worthy batch of smaller museums. If you're intent on heading north into Scandinavia's less populated (and pricier) reaches, you'd certainly be wise to spend a few days' living it up in Copenhagen first.

There was no more than a tiny fishing settlement here until the twelfth century, when Bishop Absalon oversaw the building of a castle on the site of the present Christiansborg. The settlement's prosperity grew after Erik of Pomerania granted special privileges and imposed the Sound Toll on vessels passing through the Øresund, then under Danish control – which gave the expanding city tidy profits and enabled a self-confident trading centre to flourish. Following the demise of the Hanseatic ports, the city became the Baltic's principal harbour, earning the name København ("merchant's port"), and in 1443 it was made the Danish capital. A century later, Christian IV began the building programme that was the basis of the modern city: up went Rosenborg Slot, Børsen, Rundetårnet, and the districts of Nyboder and Christianshavn; and, in 1669, Frederik III graced the city with its first royal palace, Amalienborg, for his queen, Sophie Amalie.

Like much of the Copenhagen of that time, these structures still exist, and the taller of them remain the major protruberances on what is a refreshingly low skyline. It's easy to get around: you're unlikely to find much need to venture far from the central section, which is still largely hemmed in by the medieval ramparts (now a series of parks), and is where most of the activity and sights are contained.

Arrival, information and getting around

However you get to Copenhagen you'll find yourself within easy reach of the centre. Trains pull into the **Central Station** (*Hovedbanegården*), near Vesterbrogade, on the concourse of which is *Kiosk P* (May–Sept daily 9am–midnight; April & Oct Mon–Sat 9am–5pm; rest of the year Mon–Fri 9am–5pm, Sat 9am–noon): good for free maps of the city and, for a 14kr fee, booking hotel accommodation and rooms in private homes. The *InterRail Centre* (July–mid-Sept daily 7–1am) downstairs can also be useful: restricted to *InterRail* or *EurRail* pass holders, it has large left-luggage lockers, free showers, cooking facilities, a rest area and a message board. **Long distance buses** from other parts of Denmark each stop a short bus- or S-train-ride from the centre: buses from Århus stop at

Valby; from Aalborg at Harlev; and those from Hantsholm on Hans Knudsen Plads. **Ferries** from Norway and Sweden dock close to Nyhavn, a few minutes' walk from the inner city. **Planes** use Kastrup Airport, 8km from the city and connect with the Central Station every fifteen minutes by *SAS* coach (twenty minutes; 24kr), and with Rådhuspladsen by (slower but cheaper) city bus #32.

Information

Once here, your first stop in the city should be **Use-It**, centrally placed in the *Huset* complex at Rådhusstræde 13 (mid-June to mid-Sept daily 9am–7pm; rest of the year Mon–Fri 10am–4pm; ☎33/156518), who'll provide a full rundown on budget accommodation, eating, drinking and entertainment, will hold mail and store luggage, and, in summer, issue a small but vital free newspaper called *Playtime*. There's also a regular **tourist office** (July & Aug Mon–Sat 9am–8pm, Sun 9am–1pm; May, June & Sept Mon–Sat 9am–6pm, Sun 9am–1pm; rest of the year Mon–Fri 9am–5pm; ☎33/111325), at H.C. Andersen Boulevard 22, opposite the Rådhus, with fairly ordinary tourist fare (for anything more fringe, they'll probably direct you to *Use-It*), although you can stock up on brochures and free maps of the rest of the country.

If you plan on visiting many museums, either in Copenhagen itself or nearby towns like Helsingør, Roskilde and Køge, think about purchasing a **Copenhagen Card** – valid for transport on the entire metropolitan system (which includes the towns mentioned above) and giving entry to virtually every museum in the area. Obviously its worth depends on your itinerary, but the three-day card (180kr), certainly, can save money if well used. The card is available from the tourist office, *Kiosk P*, travel agents, hotels and most railway stations in the metropolitan region.

City transport

The best way to see most of Copenhagen is simply to **walk**: the central city is compact and much of the inner area pedestrianised. To complement feet, however, an integrated network of **buses** and electric **S-trains** (*S-tog*) covers a zonal system over Copenhagen and the surrounding areas, running on average every 10–15 minutes between 5am and 3am, after which a **Night Bus** (*Natbusserne*) system comes into operation – less frequent but still running every 30–60 minutes. You can use *InterRail* or *EurRail* cards on the S-trains, but otherwise the best option is a *Rabatkort* (70kr), a yellow **ticket** which has ten stamps that you cancel individually according to the length of your journey: one stamp gives unlimited transfers within one hour in one zone (ie around the central city), two stamps are good for ninety minutes and three stamps give two hours – and two or more people can use a *Rabatkort* simultaneously. For a short single journey of less than an hour, use a *Grundbillet* (8kr) which is valid for unlimited transfers within two zones in that time. Tickets can be bought on board buses or at railway stations and should be stamped when boarding the bus or in the machines on station platforms. Except on buses, it's rare to be asked to show your ticket, but a passenger without a valid one faces an instant fine of 150kr. **Route maps** cost 5kr from stations, but most free maps of the city include bus lines and a diagram of the S-train network.

Bikes, too, can be a good way to get around the city, and are also handy for exploring the immediate countryside. The best place to hire one from is *Københavns Cyklebørs*, Gothersgade 159 (☎33/140717), for 20kr a day plus a deposit of 100kr, or try any of the other outlets included in "Listings". The basic **taxi** fare is 12kr plus 6.25 per kilometre – only worthwhile if several people are sharing; phone *Taxa* (☎31/353535) if you need a cab, hail one in the street if it's showing the "Fri" sign, or go to the rank outside the central station.

Finding a place to stay

Whether it's a hostel bed or a luxury hotel suite, **accommodation** of all kinds is easy to come by in Copenhagen, and almost all of it is located centrally. Only if you're going to be arriving late, or during July and August – much the busiest time of year – is it wise, especially if you're looking for a cheap place, to book in advance, if only for the first night. Otherwise, just turn up.

Hotels

You won't find a grotty **hotel** in Copenhagen, but the cheaper ones often (though not always) forgo the pleasures of private bathroom, phone and TV – although prices almost always include breakfast. Most of the least expensive hotels are just outside the inner centre, around Istedgade – a slightly seedy (though rarely dangerous) area on the far side of the railway station. Typical rates here are 200–250kr for a single, 350–500kr for a double. The area is also home to a number of mid-range hotels (reckon on 500kr upwards for a double), and there is also good range of mid-priced hotels around Nyhavn, on the opposite side of the Indre By.

Absalon Hotel, Helgolandsgade 19 (☎31/242211). Clean and modern, with soundproofing that makes it extremely quiet and relaxing. 500kr.

Admiral Hotel, Toldbodgade 24 (☎33/118282). A two-hundred-year-old granary beside the harbour converted into comfortable woodbeamed rooms. 595kr.

Ansgar Hotel, Colbjørnsensgade 29 (☎31/212196). Compact and tidy, this place actually lowers its prices in high season, to 408kr.

Jørgensens Hotel, Rømersgade 11 (☎33/139743). North of Istedgade, just across the Peblinge Sø from the inner centre, and the cheapest hotel in town, with doubles for 210kr. Though not exclusively gay, it's popular with gay travellers; it also offers hostel-type accommodation in summer (see below).

Mayfair Hotel, Helgolandsgade 3 (☎31/384801). Old-Danish style elegance coupled to every modern convenience. 980kr.

Missionhotellet Nebo, Istedgade 6 (☎31/211217). Small and friendly, and one of the best deals in this part of the city; you pay extra for radio and TV, otherwise 344kr.

Sophie Amalie, Skt. Annæ Plads 21 (☎33/133400). Large luxurious rooms, right by the harbour. 600kr.

Hotel Triton, Helgolandsgade 7–11 (☎31/313266). If you're a wealthy sci-fi fan look no further: futuristic style mated with modern Scandinavian design. 885kr.

Hotel Viking, Bredgade 65 (☎33/124550). Slightly faded, with an English bed & breakfast air, but quite serviceable. 540kr.

Hotel Weber, Vesterbrogade 11b (☎31/311432). Plush, cosy, and full of charm. Good value at 650kr.

COPENHAGEN

0   100 m

JAGTVEJ
NØRREBROGADE
Assistens
Kirkegård
GRIFFENFELDSGADE

GODTHÅBSVEJ

AGADE ABOULEVARD
RANTZAUSGADE

ROLIGHEDSVEJ

ROSENØRNS ALLÉ

THORVALDSENSVEJ

BÜLOWSVEJ

BRAV. H.C. ØRSTEDSVEJ

DANASVEJ

Skt. Jør

ALLÉGADE

Frederiksberg
Have

GAMMEL KONGEVEJ

MADVIGS

Storm P.
Museum

FREDERIKSBERG ALLÉ

PILE ALLÉ

PLANTANVEJ

Frederiksberg
Palace

City
Museu

ROSKILDEVEJ

ÅBOULEVARD

VESTERBROGADE

ISTE

ENGHAVEVEJ

Carlsberg Brewery

NY. CARLSBERG VEJ

SØNDER BOULEVARD

INGERSLEVSG

INGERSLEVSG

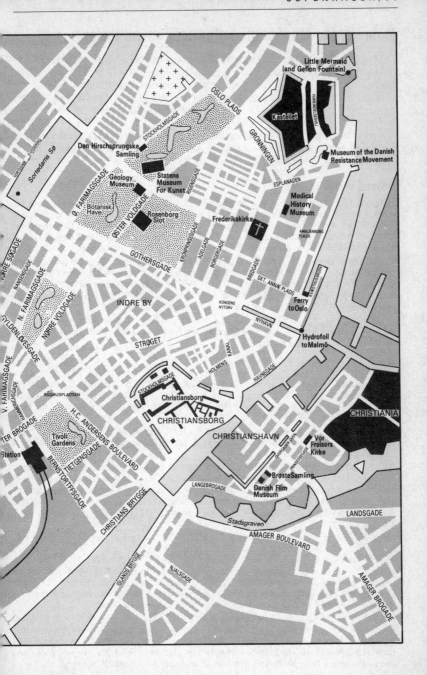

Hostels, pensions and student accommodation

Less costly, Copenhagen has a great selection of **hostel accommodation**, where a dormitory bed costs around 60kr (less in the official *YHA* hostels). Space is only likely to be a problem in the peak summer months, and during this time you should phone ahead or turn up as early as possible to be sure of a place. For the most up-to-date information ask at *Use-It*, and check the accommodation reviews in *Playtime*.

One other point. If you're staying for more than couple of weeks, **pensions** can save a lot of money over hotels, as can **subletting a room** in a student hall or shared flat. For the latest on either, ask at *Use-It*.

Official youth hostels

Bellahøj, Herbergsvejen 8, in the Brønshøj district (☎31/289715). Larger shared rooms, but more homely than its rivals, and situated in a residential part of the city. Simple to reach too: about fifteen minutes from the city centre on bus #2 (nightbus #902) to Herbergsvejen. Buses #8, #63 and #68 also stop close by. Open all year except December. Reception closed 10am–noon, and the hostel locks up at 1.30am.

Copenhagen Hostel, Sjællandsbroen (☎32/522908). A new hostel with frugal two- and four-bedded rooms. Tends to be crowded and noisy, and while there's a laundry, there's no kitchen. If you're undeterred, get to it on bus #46 (during daytime only), or on the C line S-train to Valby or Sjælør (line A or E), then a #37 bus towards Holmens Bro – all of which takes about half an hour. Open February to December; no curfew.

Lyngby, Rådvad 1 (☎42/803074). The distance from the city and an early lock-up (11pm) makes this a poor base for exploring Copenhagen. S-train to Lyngby (line A), then bus #187 to Rådvad. Open mid-May to August.

Other hostels

International University Centre, Olfert Fischersgade 40 (☎33/ 156175). At just 40kr per person, the cheapest and best-located hostel in town, between Rosenborg Have and Kastellet – though it fills quickly. Bus #10 in the direction of Emdrup. Open through most of the year; closed 11am–5pm; 1am curfew.

Jørgensens Hotel, Rømersgade 11 (☎33/139743). A regular hotel which offers summer dormitory accommodation for 65kr per person, not including breakfast. Those without a sleeping bag can hire blankets for 30kr.

KFUK/KFUM/InterRail Points, Skt. Kannikestræde (☎33/113031). About fifteen minutes' walk from the Central Station, this is the Danish *YMCA/YWCA*, with dormitory beds for 55kr (70kr with breakfast) and a 5kr reduction to railcard holders. Open July to mid-August, 8am–12.30pm & 2.30pm–12.30am. From mid-July to mid-August, there's a second *InterRail Point* a similar distance from the station at Valdersgade 15 (☎31/311574), with the same daily opening hours and prices.

Sleep-In, Per Henriks Lings Allé 6 (☎31/265059). Open mid-June to August, this is one vast hall divided into four-bedded compartments. Nice, if busy, atmosphere, with a young and friendly staff and sporadic free gigs by local bands. Beds 65kr (including breakfast) and if you don't have a sleeping bag you can hire blankets for 15kr (plus 40kr deposit). About ten minutes' from the city centre on S-train A, B or C towards Nordhavn, or by buses #1 towards Hellerup or Charlottenlund, #14 towards Svanemøllen or #6 towards Ryvang or Østrebro – get off at Idrætsparken. Closed between noon and 4pm; no curfew.

Vesterbro Ungdomsgård, Absalonsgade 8 (☎31/312070). Only open May to August, but handily-placed, ten minutes' walk from the railway station between Vesterbrogade and Istedgade. There's a noisy sixty-bed dormitory on the lower floor, but less crowded conditions (12–20 beds) on other levels. Reports vary, but the atmosphere is easy-going and there's no curfew: 80kr per person, breakfast 20kr. Buses #6, #8 and #10 stop close by.

Campsites

Of Copenhagen's four **campsites**, only one is close to the city centre, although the others are within fairly easy reach by public transport. There's little difference in price between any of them.

Absalon, 132 Korsdalsvej, Rødovre (☎31/410600). About 9km to the southwest of the city and open all year. Take S-train line B to Brøndby.

Bellahøj, on Hvidkildevej, near the Bellahøj youth hostel (☎31/101150). Central but grim, with long queues for the showers and cooking facilities. Reachable on buses #2, #8, #63 and #68. Open June to August.

Nærum on Ravnebakken (☎42/801957). Quite a way from the centre but very pleasant: take a train to Jægersborg, then private train (*InterRail* and *EurRail* not valid) to Nærum. The site has cabins and is open mid-April to mid-September.

Strandmøllen Strandøllenvej 2 (☎42/803883). Around 14km north of the city, a twenty-minute ride away on line C of the S-train (to Klampenborg). Open mid-May to September.

The City

Seeing Copenhagen is a doddle. Most of what you're likely to want to see can be found in the city's relatively small – and effortlessly walkable – centre, between the long scythe of the harbour and a semi-circular series of lakes. Within this area the divisions are well-defined. **Indre By** forms the city's inner core, an intricate maze of streets, squares and alleys whose pleasure is as much in joining their daily bustle as viewing specific sights. **North of Gothersgade** is quite different, boldly proportioned grid-pattern streets and avenues built to accommodate the Danish nobility in the seventeenth century, reaching a pinnacle of affluence with the palaces of Amalienborg and Rosenborg. The far end of this stretch is guarded, now as three hundred years ago, by the Kastellet, which lies within the fetching open spaces of the Churchill Park. Separated by moat from Indre By, **Christiansborg** is the administrative base for the whole country, housing the parliament and government offices as well as a number of museums and the ruins of Bishop Absalon's original castle. **Christianshavn**, across Inder Havnen – the inner harbour – provides further contrast, a tightly proportioned and traditionally working-class quarter, with a pretty waterfront lined by Dutch-style dwellings. A few blocks away lies **Christiania**, colonised by the young and homeless in the early Seventies, whose "alternative society" is an enduring controversy in Danish life – and merits at least a look. **Vesterbrogade** is the prime route out of the city centre to the southern suburbs, but its course begins with the carefree delights of the Tivoli Gardens and leads on to the slightly less wholesome goings-on around Istedgade, before reaching the city fringes at Frederiksberg Have.

Indre By

While not actually part of **INDRE BY**, the main way into the inner city is from the buzzing open space of Rådhuspladsen. Here, the **Rådhus** (Mon–Fri 10am–3pm; free) has a spacious and elegant main hall which retains many of its original turn-of-the-century features, not least the highly-polished sculptured bannisters leading from the ground floor. There's a lift up to the belltower (at 11am and 2pm) for a not madly impressive view over the city, but more interesting is the

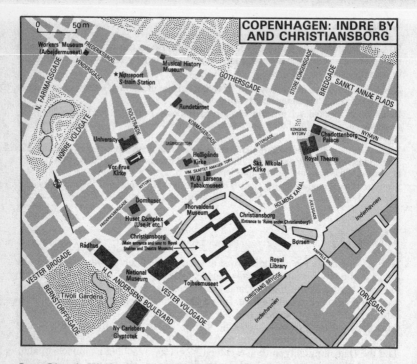

Jens Olsen's World Clock (Mon–Fri 10am–4pm, Sat 10am–1pm; 5kr), in a side-room close to the entrance. What looks like a mass of inscrutable dials is an astronomical timepiece which took 27 years to perfect and contains a 570,000-year calendar plotting moon and sun eclipses, solar time, local time and various planetary orbits – all with incredible accuracy.

Indre By proper begins with **Strøget** (literally "level measure"), a series of streets lined by pricey stores and graceless fast-food dives whose appeal is in the walkers, cyclists, roller-skaters and, even during the freezing winters, street entertainers, who parade along it. You'll find most of Indre By's charm and historic sights in the streets **west** of Strøget.

Along Strøget

Very much the public face of Copenhagen, it's hard to imagine anything unpleasant ever happening on Strøget, and the strip is perfectly suited to stress-free ambling. Often the most active part is around Gammeltorv and Nytorv, two squares ("old" and "new") on either side of Strøget, where there's a morning fruit and vegetable market, handmade jewellery and bric-a-brac stalls – and frequent political rallies. It was between these squares that the fifteenth-century Rådhus stood before being destroyed by fire in 1795. A new Rådhus was erected on Nytorv a century later, and this is now the city's **Domhuset**, or Law Courts, marked by a suitably forbidding grille of Neoclassical columns.

A few minutes' further is the **Helligånds Kirke** (daily 11am–4pm), one of the oldest churches in the city, founded in the fourteenth century though largely rebuilt from 1728. While still in use as a place of worship, there are often art shows and other exhibitions inside which provide a good excuse for a peek at the church's vaulted ceiling and its slender granite columns. Of equally low-key appeal is the tobacco shop directly across Strøget, which holds the **W.Ø. Larsens Tobaksmuseet** (Mon–Fri 9am–5pm, Sat 9am–1pm; free), and its briefly diverting clutter of vintage pipes, ornate cigar holders and every conceivable smoking accessory, plus paintings and drawings satirising the deadly habit's rituals. Just beyond, a path leads east off Strøget, through Højbro Plads and on to the grandiose **Skt. Nikolai Kirke**, where religion really takes a back pew. The upper floors of the church are used primarily as an exhibition space for contemporary artists, while at ground level there's a daytime café.

The final section of Strøget is Østergade, which flows past the swish and chic *Hotel D'Angleterre* into the biggest of the city squares, **Kongens Nytorv**. Built on what was the edge of the city in medieval times, the square has an equestrian statue of its creator, Christian V, in its centre and a couple of grandly ageing structures around two of its shallow angles. One of these, the **Royal Theatre**, dates from 1874, but the other, **Charlottenborg**, next door, was finished in 1683, at the same time as the square itself, for a son of Frederik III. It was later sold to Queen Charlotte Amalie but since 1754 has been the home of the Royal Academy of Art, which uses some of the spacious rooms for very eclectic art exhibitions. Drop in, if the building's open, just to glimpse the elegant interior.

West of Strøget

Don't think that by walking the length of Strøget, you've exhausted Indre By. There's much more to see among the tangle of buildings and streets **west of Strøget** (to the left as you walk from Rådhuspladsen). Crossing Gammeltorv and following Nørregade leads to the old university area, sometimes called the Latin Quarter, parts of which still have an academic function which accounts for the book-carrying students milling around. The old university building is overlooked by **Vor Frue Kirke** (Mon–Sat 9am–5pm, Sun noon–5pm), the cathedral of Copenhagen. Built on the site of a twelfth-century church, this dates only from 1829, rising from the devastation caused by the British bombardment in 1807. The weighty figure of Christ behind the altar and the solemn statues of the apostles, some crafted by Bertel Thorvaldsen (for more on whom, see "Christiansborg" below), others by his pupils, merit a quick call. From the cathedral, dodge across Skindergade into Gråbrødretorv, a cobbled square often crowded with buskers, best enjoyed from a table at one of the terraced cafés, on the way to **Rundetårnet** (June–Aug Mon–Sat 10am–8pm, Sun noon–8pm; April, May, Sept & Oct Mon–Sat 10am–5pm, Sun noon–4pm; Nov–March Mon–Sat 11am–4pm, Sun noon–4pm, Wed also 7–10pm; 10kr), the summit reached by a gradually-ascending spiral ramp. The tower was built by Christian IV as an observatory, and perhaps also to provide a vantage point for his subjects to admire his additions to the city. Today the best views are of the more immediate hive of medieval streets and the pedestrian processions filling them. Legend has it that Tsar Peter the Great sped to the top on horseback in 1715, pursued by the Tsarina in a six-horse carriage – a smoother technique than descending the cobbles on a skateboard, a short-lived fad in more recent times.

After leaving Rundetårnet, you could easily spend half an hour browsing the bookstores of Købmagergade; alternatively, if you have more time and a musical inclination, a more definite target is the **Musical History Museum**, just off

Kultorvet at Åbenrå 30 (Tues & Wed 10am–1pm, Fri–Sun 1–4pm; 10kr), a deceptively large place holding an impressive quantity of musical instruments and sound-making devices, spanning the globe and the last thousand years. Naturally the bulk come from Denmark and there are some subtle comments on the social fabric of the nation to be gleaned from the yellowing photos of the country dances and other get-togethers, hung alongside the instruments. Many musical recordings can be listened to through headphones, and guided tours take place every Wednesday at 11am.

Less musical sounds are provided by the cars hurtling along Nørre Voldgade, at the top of Kultorvet, marking the edge of the pedestrianised streets of the old city. There are two reasons to queue up at the traffic-lights and cross over: the first is the fruit and vegetable **market** – and Saturday fleamarket – on Israel Plads; the second is the **Workers Museum** at Rømmersgade 22 (Tues, Thurs & Fri 10am–3pm, Wed 10am–8pm, Sat & Sun 11am–4pm; 10kr), an engrossing and thoughtful guide to working-class life in Copenhagen from the Thirties to the Fifties using reconstructions and authentic period materials. Entering the museum, you can walk down a bygone Copenhagen street complete with passing tram and a shopwindow hawking the consumer durables of the day; continue, via a backyard where the washing hangs drying, through a printing works subsidised by the Marshall Plan, and into the coffeeshop, which sells an old-fashioned coffee and chicory blend by the cup. Elsewhere, mock-up house interiors contain family photos, newspapers and TVs showing newsreels of the time. The fixed exhibits are backed-up by some outstanding temporary exhibitions from labour movements around the world.

North of Gothersgade

There's a profound change of mood once you cross **Gothersgade**, the road marking the northern perimeter of Indre By. The congenial alleyways and early medieval markers of the old city give way to long, broad streets and a number of proud, aristocratic structures. A whole group of these are in the harbour area near **Nyhavn**, the obvious route if you're walking from Indre By, although perhaps the most impressive building of all is Rosenborg Slot, a short way to the west, **away from the harbour**, and close to several major museums.

Nyhavn and the harbour area

Running from Kongens Nytorv, a slender canal divides the two sides of **Nyhavn**, a wide but quite short street until recently frequented by docked sailors – who earned the area a racy reputation – but now in the advanced stages of gentrification. One or two of the old tattoo shops remain, but they're mostly here to artificially flavour the atmosphere and are outnumbered by small but expensive restaurants and a growing band of refined antique shops. The canalside is quite picturesque, however, with preserved eighteenth-century houses (three of which, incidentally, were lived in at different times by Hans Christian Andersen: nos. 18, 20 and 67) and yachts moored on the water. The far end of Nyhavn is also the departure point for the hydrofoil to Malmö, boats to Rønne – and, a block away at the end of Skt. Annæ Plads, ferries for Oslo.

From Skt. Annæ Plads, Amaliegade leads under a colonnade into the cobbled **Amalienborg Plads**, with a statue of Frederik V in its centre that was reputedly more expensive than the total construction cost of the four identical Rococo palaces which flank it. Dating from the mid-eighteenth century, the quartet of imposing buildings provides a sudden burst of welcome symmetry into the city's generally haphazard layout. Two of them now serve as royal residences and there's a changing of the guard each day at noon when the monarch is at home – generally attended by gangs of camera-toting tourists.

Between the square and the harbour are the lavish gardens of **Amaliehaven**, while in the opposite direction looms the great marble dome of **Frederikskirke**, also known as "Marmorkirken" (Mon–Fri 11am–3pm, Sat 11am–1pm, Sun noon–1pm; free guided tours Sat 11am). Modelled on – and intended to rival – St Peter's in Rome, the church was begun in 1749, but because of its enormous cost lay unfinished until a century and a half later, when its most prominent feature (one of Europe's largest domes) was completed with Danish rather than the more expensive Norwegian marble. If you can coincide with the guided tour, the reward is the chance to climb first to the whispering gallery and then out onto the rim of the dome itself. From here there's a stunning, and usually blustery, view over the sharp geometry of Amalienborg and across the sea to the factories of Malmö, in Sweden.

Further along Bredgade, at number 22, the former Danish Surgical Academy now stores the **Medical History Museum** (guided tours only; in English on Tues, Thurs & Sat at 2pm; free) – not a place to visit if you've spent the morning on a brewery binge. The enthusiastically presented (hour-long) tour features aborted foetuses, straitjackets, methods of syphilis treatment, amputated feet, eyeballs and a dissected head.

Bredgade concludes at Esplanaden, facing the green space of the Churchill Park. To the right, the German armoured car which was commandeered by Danes and used to bring news of the Nazi surrender marks the entrance to the **Museum of the Danish Resistance Movement** (May to mid-Sept Tues–Sat 10am–4pm, Sun 10am–5pm; rest of the year Tues–Sat 11am–3pm, Sun 11am–4pm; free). Initially, the Danes put up little resistance to the German invasion, but later the Nazis were given a systematically wretched time. The museum records the growth of the organised response and has a special section on the youths from Aalborg who formed themselves into the "Churchill Club". Feeling the adults weren't doing enough, this gang of fifteen-year-olds set about destroying German telegraph cables, blowing up cars and trains and stealing weapons. There's also a small, but inevitably moving, collection of artworks and handicrafts made by concentration camp inmates.

The road behind the museum crosses into the grounds of the **Kastellet** (daily 6am–10pm; free): a fortress built by Christian IV and expanded by his successors through the seventeenth century after the loss of Danish possessions in Skåne had put the city within range of Swedish cannonballs. It's now occupied by the Danish army and closed to the public. The tall arches and gateways, however, are an enjoyable setting for a stroll, as are the grassy slopes beside the moat. On a corner of the park, the **Little Mermaid** exerts an inexplicable magnetism on tourists, perched on some rocks just off the harbour bank. Since its unveiling in 1913, this bronze statue of a Hans Christian Andersen character, sculpted by Edvard Erichsen and paid for by the boss of the Carlsberg brewery, has become the best-known emblem of the city – a fact which has led to it being the victim of several subversive pranks: the original head disappeared in 1964, a cow's head was forced over the replacement in 1986, and more recently one of its arms was stolen. But it's worth enduring the crowds gawping at the mermaid for the spectacular **Gefion Fountain**, just a few yards away. The fountain's sculptured figure is by Anders Bundgaard and shows the goddess Gefion with her four sons, whom she's turned into oxen having been promised, in return, as much land as she can plough in a single night. The legend goes that she ploughed a chunk of Sweden, then picked up the piece of land (creating Lake Vänern) and tossed it into the sea – where it became Zealand.

Away from the harbour: Rosenborg Slot and the museums

Still north of Gothersgade, but away from the harbour across Store Kongensgade, lies **NYBODER**, a curious area of short, straight and narrow streets lined with rows of compact yellow dwellings. Although some of these are recently erected apartment blocks, the original houses, on which the newer constructions are modelled, were built by Christian IV to encourage his sailors to live in the city. The area had at one time declined into a slum, but a recent vigorous revamping has made the district increasingly sought-after. The oldest (and cutest) houses can be found along Skt. Pauls Gade.

Across Sølvgade from Nyboder is the main entrance to **Rosenborg Slot** (May to late Sept daily 10am–4pm; late Sept to late Oct daily 11am–3pm; rest of the year Tues, Fri & Sun 11am–1pm; 20kr, students 10kr), a Dutch Renaissance palace and one of the most elegant buildings bequeathed by Christian IV to the city. Though intended as a country residence, Rosenborg served as the main domicile of Christian IV (he died here in 1648) and, until the end of the nineteenth century, the monarchs who succeeded him. It became a museum as early as 1830 and the main building still displays the rooms and furnishings used by the regal occupants. The highlights, though, are in the downstairs treasury (separate entrance; hours as castle except late Oct–April Tues–Sun 11am–3pm), displaying the rich accessories worn by Christian IV (and his horse), the crown of absolute monarchs and the present crown jewels. Outside, the splendidly neat squares of Rosenborg Have can be reached by leaving Rosenborg itself and using the park's main entrance on the corner of Østervoldgade and Sølvgade.

Opposite the castle, marked by a few runic stones, is the **Geology Museum** (Tues–Sun 1–4pm; free), which has a great meteorite section but is otherwise quite missable unless you're a mineral freak (although the microscopic fragment of moon rock brought back by an Apollo mission and presented by Richard Nixon to the Danish people in the name of "world peace" is one of Copenhagen's greater ironies). Only slightly more worthwhile is the neighbouring **Statens Museum for Kunst** (Tues–Sun 10am–5pm; free), a mammoth collection of art, too large to take in on a short visit and too dull to warrant a longer one. While all the big cheeses have their patch – there are some minor Picassos and more major works by Matisse and Braque, Modigliani, Dürer and El Greco – it's Emil Nolde, with his gross pieces showing bloated ravens, hunched figures and manic children, who best captures the mood of the place.

Art fans will find greater things across the park behind the museum, in the **Den Hirschsprungske Samling** (May–Sept Wed–Sun 1–4pm; rest of the year Wed–Sun 1–4pm; Wed also 7–10pm; free) on Stockholmsgade. Heinrich Hirschsprung was a late-nineteenth-century tobacco baron who sunk some of the industry's profits into patronage of emergent Danish artists, including the Skagen artists (see *Jutland*) and a batch of others later to become significant. It was Hirschsprung's wish that on his death the collection – which also features Eckersburg, Købke, and lesser names from the Danish mid-nineteenth-century

Golden Age – would be given to the nation, but the government of the day vetoed the plan and Hirschsprung eventually set up his own gallery. Despite a lack of masterpieces, you can easily spend an hour on this fine collection.

Christiansborg

CHRISTIANSBORG sits on the island of Slotsholmen, tenuously connected to Indre By by several short bridges: a mundane part of the city, but administratively – and historically – an important one. It was here, in the twelfth century, that Bishop Absalon built the castle which instigated the city, and the drab royal palace that occupies the site, completed in 1916, is nowadays primarily given over to government offices and the state parliament or **Folketing** (guided tours on the hour every Sun 10am–4pm; free). Close to the bus stop on Christiansborg Slotsplads is the doorway to the **Ruins under Christiansborg** (May–Sept daily 9.30am–4pm; rest of the year Sun–Fri 9.30am–4pm; 8kr), where a staircase leads down to the remains of Absalon's original building. The first fortress suffered repeated mutilations by the Hanseatic League and Erik of Pomerania had a replacement erected in 1390, into which he moved the royal court. This in turn was pulled down by Christian IV and another castle built between 1731 and 1745. The stone and brick walls which comprise the ruins, and the articles from the castles stored in an adjoining room, are surprisingly absorbing, the mood enhanced by the semi-darkness and lack of external noise.

In and around Christiansborg's courtyard there are a number of other, less captivating museums, to which the information office close to the ruins' entrance can provide directions – the confusing array of buildings makes it easy to get lost. That said, you could probably sniff your way to the **Royal Stables** (May–Sept Fri–Sun 2–4pm; rest of the year Sat & Sun 2–4pm; 5kr) – though, unsurprisingly, it's among the country's least essential collections. Nearby, the **Theatre Museum** (June–Sept Wed, Fri & Sun 2–4pm; rest of the year Wed & Sun 2–4pm; 10kr) is better, housed in what was the eighteenth-century Court Theatre and displaying original costumes, set-models and the old dressing rooms and boxes. Exiting the courtyard and walking through Tøjhusgade takes you past the **Armoury Museum** (May–Sept Tues–Sat 1–4pm, Sun 10am–4pm; rest of the year Tues–Sat 1–3pm, Sun 11am–4pm; free), where you can view weaponry from Christian IV's arsenal and a host of crests and coats of arms. A few strides further on, a small gateway leads into the gorgeous tree-lined grounds of the **Royal Library** – an excellent venue for a picnic. The library itself (Mon–Fri 9am–6pm, Sat 9am–6pm) contains original manuscripts by Hans Christian Andersen, Karen Blixen and Søren Kierkegaard (of whom there's a statue in the gardens), though the manuscripts can be seen only by convincing those at reception that you're a bona fide scholar (a student card should suffice). Adjacent to Slotsplads is the low, long form of the seventeenth-century **Børsen**, or Stock Exchange – with its spire of four entwined dragons' tails, one of the most distinctive buildings in the city.

On the far side of Slotsholmen, the **Thorvaldsens Museum** (Tues–Sun 10am–5pm; free) is the home of an enormous collection of work and memorabilia (and the body) of Denmark's most famous sculptor. Bertel Thorvaldsen lived from 1770 to 1844 and despite negligible schooling drew his way into the Danish Academy of Fine Arts, from there moving on to Rome where he perfected the heroic, classical figures for which he became known. He's not a big name now outside Denmark, although in his day he enjoyed international renown and won commissions from all over Europe. Other than a selection of early works in the basement, the labels of the great, hulking statues read like a roll call of the famous and infamous: Vulcan, Adonis, John Russell, Gutenberg, Pius VII and Maximilian; and the Christ Hall contains the huge casts of the Christ and Apostles statues which can be seen in Vor Frue Kirke (see "Indre By"). A prolific and gifted sculptor, Thorvaldsen was something of a wit too. Asked by the Swedish artist J.T. Sergel how he managed to make such beautiful figures, he held up the scraper with which he was working and replied, "With this."

There's another major collection a short walk away over the Slotsholmen moat, the **National Museum** (mid-June to mid-Sept Tues–Sun 10am–4pm; rest of the year Tues–Fri 11am–3pm, Sat & Sun noon–4pm; free), which has an ethnographic section in a separate wing at Ny Vestergade 10, but is really strongest – as you'd expect – on Danish history; if you've any interest at all in the subject you could spend a good couple of hours here. Much of the early stuff, ranging from prehistory to the Viking days, comes from Jutland – jewellery, bones and even bodies, all of it remarkably well-preserved and much only discovered after wartime fuel shortages led to large scale digging of the Danish peat bogs. Informative explanatory texts help clarify the Viking section, the best of which – apart from the infamous horned helmets – are the sacrificial gifts, among them the Sun Chariot: a model horse carrying a sun disc with adornments of gold and bronze. Further floors store a massive collection of almost anything and everything which featured in Christian-age Denmark up to the nineteenth century – finely engraved wooden altarpieces, furniture, clothing and more – as well as a good section on peasant life.

Christianshavn

From Christiansborg, a bridge crosses the Inder Havnen to the island of Amager and into **CHRISTIANSHAVN**, built by Christian IV as an autonomous new town in the early sixteenth century to provide housing for workers in the shipbuilding industry. It was given features more common to Dutch port towns of the time, even down to a small canal (Wilders Kanal), and in parts the area is more redolent of Amsterdam than Copenhagen. Although its present inhabitants are fairly well-off, Christianshavn still has the mood of a working-class quarter, with a grouping of secondhand shops along Torvegade that are good for rummaging and, along Overgaden oven Vandet on the canalside, some immaculately preserved houses. Besides the houses, take a walk down here for the *Filmhuset*, on the corner of Store Søndervoldstræde, a small building but one which is the base of the national film industry and holds the **Danish Film Museum** (June & Aug Mon–Fri noon–4pm; rest of the year Mon–Fri noon–4pm, also Tues & Thurs 6.30–9pm; free). Here the dust is kept off the cameras, props and other remnants of an early film industry that before Hollywood and the talkies was among the world's best.

Poking skywards through the trees on the other side of Torvegade is the blue and gold spire of **Vor Frelsers Kirke** (June–Aug Mon–Sat 9am–4.30pm, Sun noon–4.30pm; mid-March to May, Sept & Oct Mon–Sat 9am–3.30pm, Sun noon–3.30pm; rest of the year Mon–Sat 10am–1.30pm, Sun noon–1.30pm; spire 10kr), on the corner of Prinsessegade and Skt. Annægade. The spire, with its helter-skelter-like outside staircase, was added to the otherwise plain church in the mid-eighteenth century, instantly becoming one of the more recognisable features on the city's horizon. Climbing the spire is fun, but not entirely without risk (though the rumour that the builder fell off it and died, while believable, is untrue). To get to the spire, go through the church and up to a trapdoor which opens onto the platform where the external steps begin: there are 400 of them, slanted and slippery (especially after rain) and gradually becoming smaller. The reward for reaching the top is a great view of Copenhagen and beyond.

Christiania

A few streets from Vor Frelsers Kirke, **CHRISTIANIA** occupies an area that was for centuries used as a barracks, but which, after the soldiers moved out, was colonised by young and homeless people. It was declared a "free city" on September 24, 1971, with a view to its operating autonomously from Copenhagen proper, and its continued existence has fuelled one of the longest-running debates in Danish (and Scandinavian) society. One by-product of its idealism and the freedoms assumed by its residents (and, despite recent lapses, tolerated by successive governments and the police) was to make Christiania a refuge for petty criminals and shady individuals from all over the city. But the problems have inevitably been overplayed by Christiania's critics, and a surprising number of Danes – of all ages and from all walks of life – do support the place, not least because Christiania has performed usefully, and altruistically, when established bodies have been found wanting. One way has been in the weaning of heroin addicts off their habits. Once, a 24-hour cordon was thrown around the area to prevent dealers reaching the addicts inside: reputedly the screams – of deprived junkies and suppliers being "dealt with" – could be heard all night. And Christiania residents have stepped in to provide free shelter and dinner for the homeless at Christmas when the city administration declined to.

The population is around 1000, swelled in summer by the curious and the sympathetic – although the residents ask people not to camp here, and tourists not to point cameras at the weirder-looking inhabitants. The craftshops and restaurants are – partly because of their refusal to pay any kind of tax – fairly cheap, and nearly all are good, and there are a couple of innovative music and performance art venues. These, and the many imaginative dwellings, including some built on stilts in a small lake, make a visit worthwhile. Additionally, there are a number of alternative political and arts groups based in Christiania, for information on whom – and on the free city generally – you should call in to *Galopperiet* (noon–5pm), to the left of the main entrance on the corner of Bødsmandsstræde and Prinsessegade.

Along Vesterbrogade

Hectic **Vesterbrogade** begins on the far side of Rådhuspladsen from Strøget, and its first attraction is, after the Little Mermaid, Copenhagen's most famous – the **Tivoli Gardens** (May to mid-Sept daily 10am–midnight; 25kr). This park of many bland amusements first flung open its gates in 1843, modelled on the soon-to-be-defunct Vauxhall Gardens in London, and in turn becoming the model for the Festival Gardens in Battersea Park. The name is now synonymous with Copenhagen at its most innocently pleasurable, and the opening of the gardens each year on (or around) May 1 is taken to mark the beginning of summer. There are fairground rides, fireworks, fountains, and nightly entertainment in the central arena which includes everything from acrobats and jugglers to the mid-Atlantic tones of various fixed-grin crooners. Naturally, it's over-rated and over-priced, but an evening spent wandering among the revellers of all ages indulging in the mass-consumption of ice cream is an experience worth having – once. Close to the H.C. Andersens Boulevard entrance is the predictable **Holography Museum** (May–Aug daily 11am–midnight; rest of the year daily 10am–8pm; 26kr) – once you've seen through one hologram you've seen through them all – and the abysmal **Louis Tussaud's Wax Museum** (May to mid-Sept daily 10am–11pm; April & mid-Sept to late Oct daily 10am–7pm; rest of the year daily 10am–4pm; 37kr).

On the other side of Tietgensgade from Tivoli is the dazzling **Ny Carlsberg Glyptotek** (May–Aug Tues–Sun 10am–4pm; rest of the year Tues–Sat noon–3pm, Sun 10am–4pm; 15kr, free to art students and *ISIC* or *FIYTO* cardholders), opened in 1897 by brewer Carl Jacobsen as a venue for ordinary people to see classical art exhibited in classical style. Centrepiece is the conservatory. "Being Danes," said Jacobsen, "we know more about flowers than art, and during the winter this greenery will make people pay a visit; and then, looking at the palms, they might find a moment for the statues." It's an idea which caught on, and even now the gallery is well-used – and not just by art lovers: there's a programme of electronic music daily at 1pm, as well as a seasonal roster of other free events; pick up a schedule on entry.

As for the contents, this is by far Copenhagen's finest gallery, with a stirring array of Greek, Roman and Egyptian art and artefacts, as well as what is reckoned to be the biggest (and best) collection of Etruscan art outside Italy. There are, too, excellent examples of nineteenth-century European art, including a complete collection of Degas casts made from the fragile working sculptures he left on his death, Manet's *Absinthe Drinker* and two small cases containing tiny caricatured heads by Honore Daumier. Easily missed, but actually the most startling room in the place, is an ante-chamber with just a few pieces – early work by Man Ray, some Chagall sketches and a Picasso pottery plate.

In complete contrast, the streets on the other side of the railway station, between Vesterbrogade and Istedgade, contain a small, token **red light area**, which comprises a few tawdry sex-clubs and suffers a little half-hearted violence from the few junkies and hookers who might be seen on the pavements after nightfall. It's not a place to linger, but it's not unduly threatening and the hotels here are perfectly safe.

At Vesterbrogade 59 is the **City Museum** (May–Sept Tues–Sun 10am–4pm; Oct–April Tues–Sun 1–4pm; free), which has reconstructed ramshackle house exteriors and tradesmen's signs from early Copenhagen. Looking at these makes the impact of Christian IV resoundingly apparent. There's a large room recording the form and cohesion which this monarch and amateur architect gave the city, even including a few of his own drawings. The rest of the city's history is told by paintings – far too many paintings in fact – and you should head straight upstairs for the room devoted to **Søren Kierkegaard**, filled by bits and bobs that form an intriguing footnote to the life of the nineteenth-century Danish writer and philosopher, and much the most interesting part of the museum. Kierkegaard is inextricably linked with Copenhagen, yet his championing of individual will over social conventions, and his rejection of materialism, did little to endear him to his fellow Danes. Born in 1813, Kierkegaard believed himself set on an "evil destiny" – partly the fault of his father who is best remembered for having cursed God on a Jutland heath. Kierkegaard's first book, *Either/Or*, published in 1843, was inspired by his love affair with one Regine Olsen; she failed to understand it, however, and married someone else. Few other people understood *Either/Or* either, and Kierkegaard, though devasted by the broken romance, came to revel in the enigma he had created, becoming a "walking mystery in the streets of Copenhagen" (he lived in a house on Nytorv). He was a prolific author, sometimes publishing two books on the same day and often writing under pseudonyms. His greatest philosophical works were written by 1846 and are generally claimed to have laid the foundations of existentialism.

Further along Vesterbrogade, down Enghavevej and along Ny Carlsberg Vej, is the **Carlsberg Brewery** (guided tours Mon–Fri 11am & 2.30pm; free); the tours, beginning from the hut to the left, are well worth joining if only for the free booze provided at the end. If you're in the vicinity pass by anytime to admire the **Elephant Gate** – four elephants carved in granite supporting the building that spans the road.

Vesterbrogade finishes up opposite the **Frederiksberg Have**, which contains the Frederiksberg Palace, now used as a military academy and closed to the public. Throughout the eighteenth century, the city's top nobs came here to mess about in boats along the network of canals which dissect the copious lime-tree groves, and its pleasant surrounds are now a popular weekend picnic spot for locals, and refreshingly free of tourists. While here, you might call in at the entertaining **Storm P. Museum** (May–Aug Tues–Sun 10am–4pm; rest of the year Wed, Sat & Sun 10am–4pm; 8kr), by the gate facing Frederiksberg Allé, packed with the satirical cartoons that made "Storm P." (Robert Storm Petersen) one of the most popular bylines in Danish newspapers from the 1920s. Even if you don't understand the Danish captions, you'll leave the museum with an insight into the national sense of humour.

Out from the centre

Unlike many other major European cities, Copenhagen has only a few miles of drab housing estates on its periphery before the countryside begins. A number of things are worth venturing out from the centre to see, although none of them need keep you away from the main action for long.

Assistens Kirkegård

Only a few minutes on foot from Indre By is **Assistens Kirkegård**: a cemetery built to cope with the dead from the 1711–12 plague. More interestingly, it contains the graves of Hans Christian Andersen and Søren Kierkegaard – both well signposted, although not from the same entrance. If lost, look at the handy catalogue by the gate on Kapelvej. The cemetery is off Nørrebrogade in the district of Nørrebro: walk from the Nørreport station along Frederiksborggade and over the lake. Alternatively buses #5, #7, #16 and #18 run along the graveyard's edge.

Grundtvigs Kirke

Slightly further out is **Grundtvigs Kirke** (June to mid-Sept Mon–Sat 9am–4.45pm, Sun noon–4pm; rest of the year Mon–Sat 9am–4.45pm, Sun noon–1pm), an astonishing yellow-brick creation whose gabled front resembles a massive church organ which rises upwards and completely dwarfs the row of terraced houses that share the street. The church, named after and dedicated to the founder of the Danish folk high schools, was designed by Jensens Klint and his son in 1913, but was not finished until 1926. To reach it takes about twenty minutes from the city centre on buses #10, #16, #19 or #21. Get off in the small square of Bispetorv soon after passing the Bispebjerg Hospital; the church itself is in På Bjerget.

Amager and Dragør

If the weather's good, take a trip to the Amager **beaches**, reachable on bus #12 along Øresundsvej (ask for Helgoland). On the other side of the airport from the beaches lies the village of **DRAGØR**, an atmospheric cobbled fishing village from where **ferries** leave for Limhamn in Sweden, and which has good local history collections in the **Dragør Museum** (May–Sept Tues–Fri 2–5pm, Sat & Sun noon–6pm; 5kr), by the harbour, and the **Amager Museum** (June–Aug Wed–Sun 11am–3pm; rest of the year Wed & Sun 11am–3pm; 5kr), a few minutes' walk away. From the city, take buses #30 or #33.

Bakken

If you're in the mood for an amusement park but can't face (or afford) Tivoli, venture out to **BAKKEN** (late March to late Aug daily 2pm–midnight; free), close to the Klampenborg stop at the end of line C on the S-train network. Set in a corner of Kongens Dyrehave (the Royal Deer Park), it's a lot more fun than its city counterpart, and besides the usual swings and rollercoasters, offers easy walks through woods of sturdy oaks and beeches. Strolling back towards Klampenborg along Christiansholmsvej, turning left at *Peter Lieps Hus* (a restaurant), gives superb views over the Øresund.

Lyngby: the open-air museum

Also to the north is the village of **LYNGBY**, and its **Open-Air Museum** (mid-April–Sept daily 10am–5pm; early Oct daily 10am–3pm; rest of the year Sun 10am–3pm; 10kr), set inside a large park and comprising restored seventeenth- to mid-nineteenth-century buildings, drawn from all over Denmark and some of its former possessions. A walk through the park leads to the **Sorgenfri Palace**, one-time home of Frederik V, though with no public admittance. Take S-train lines A or Cc to Sorgenfri.

The Tuborg Brewery

Finally, if you tire of history, culture and the arts, there's the **Tuborg Brewery** (guided tours Mon–Fri 8.30am & 2.30pm; free), the other major Danish brewer, who like Carlsberg offer a guided tour and a free drinking session to complete it. Take buses #1 or #21 northwards from the city to Hellerup; the brewery is at Strandvejen 54.

Eating

Whether you want a quick coffee and croissant, or to sit down to a five-course gourmet dinner, you'll find more choice – and lower prices – in Copenhagen than in any other Scandinavian capital. Many of the city's innumerable **cafés** offer good-value, highly-filling, **lunches**, and there are plenty of **pizzerias**, again many with daily specials and all-you-can-eat salad deals. With a little more money, try one of the many **Danish restaurants** which knock out affordable (around 80kr) and very high quality lunches, either from a set-menu or from an open-table –

though dinner will always be more expensive. Blow-out **dinners** can also be enjoyed in one of Copenhagen's growing band of **ethnic restaurants**, many of which have adopted the Scandinavian open-table idea, offering all-you-can-eat meals for around 90kr. These are seldom less than excellent value, but don't plan a night's dancing after wading through one. A useful guide to cafés and restaurants, with details of the latest special offers and buffets, is *Neon Guiden*, a free monthly supplement to the *Ekstra Bladet* newspaper, on sale all over the city. The listings are in Danish but fairly easy to decipher.

If you're stocking up for a **picnic** – or a trip to Sweden or Norway – take advantage of the numerous *smørrebrød* outlets. *Smørrebrødskunsten*, on the corner of Magstræde at Rådhusstræde, and *Centrum Smørrebrød*, Vesterbrogade 6c, are two of the most central. For more general food shopping, use one of the **supermarkets**. Of these, *Brugsen*, Axeltorv 2, and *Irma*, Vesterbrogade 1 and Borgergade 28, are cheaper than their counterparts along Strøget.

Cafés and pizzerias

Alexanders Pizza House, Lille Kannikestræde. Worth checking for its all-you-can-eat deals.

Ambrosius, Niels Hemmingsensgade 32. A studenty café, good for a quick lunch or just a refreshing coffee or beer.

Café Adagio, Rømersgade 11. Adjoinng *Jørgensens Hotel* (see "Sleeping") and serving some excellently priced no-frills lunches.

Café au lait, Nørre Voldgade 27. Opposite the Nørreport S-train station, a pleasantly unflustered place for a coffee or snack.

Caféen i Nikolaj, Nikolaj Plads. Nibble a light lunch or pastry and then tour the rest of this former church, which now houses an art gallery.

Café Santos, Vesterbrogade 53. Down-to-earth eatery with a good range of cheap basics.

Hit House Café, Nørregade 10. In moments of gastronomic and economic desperation come here – a tacky café on the ground floor of a rock venue, which serves the cheapest croissant in northern Europe for just 1kr.

Klaptræet, Kultorvet 13. Very cheap breakfasts and good value throughout the day.

La Maison d'Italiano, Fiolstræde 2. Centrally-placed and serving basic pizza with all you-can-eat salad for 38kr. Also at Nyhavn 51.

Vagabondo's Cantina, Vesterbrogade 70. The most central of several branches of this dependable pizza-chain, where hunger will be sated for less than 50kr.

Danish restaurants

DSB Bistro, Banegårdspladsen 7. Believe it or not, it's here at the railway station restaurant that you'll get a broad, comparatively low-cost, introduction to Danish food. Allow a couple of hours to explore the massive buffet – and do it from 3pm to 5pm, when it costs 98kr; otherwise it's 138kr.

LATE-NIGHT FOOD

For **late-night eating** besides *Pasta Basta*, listed under "Ethnic restaurants", and the late-opening cafés mentioned under "Nightlife", you might try the high-class and rather posey *Brønum*, Tordenskjoldsgade 1, open on weekends until 5am. Or join the thespians munching fresh bread and rolls in *Herluf Trolle*, on Herluf Trolles Gade, just behind the Royal Theatre.

Els, Store Strandstræde 3. Very plush, with a game-orientated menu and walls lined with elegant mid-nineteenth-century Danish art.

Nyhavns Færgekro, Nyhavn 5. Unpretentious and thoroughly tasty traditional food, either from the lunchtime fish-laden open-table, or the à la carte restaurant upstairs.

Peder Ox, Gråbrødretorv 11. Especially worthwhile at lunchtime when you can get three hunks of *smørrebrød* for 69kr.

Spisehuset, Rådhusstræde 13. In the *Huset* building, with a varied but always wholesome and fairly cheap menu, including a 58kr daily special.

Skt. Gertruds Kloster, Hauser Plads. In the vaults of a medieval cloister and smoulderingly romantic – though you'll spend a fortune.

Ethnic restaurants

Bali, Lille Kongensgade 4. Tread carefully around the bamboo plants and you'll find a fine Indonesian restaurant; the house special is rice tafel, costing 110kr.

Karachi, Øster Farimagsgade 12. Has a large buffet spread of Indian food for 89kr.

Koh I Nor, Vesterbrogade 33. A mix of Indian, Pakistani and Halal, and worth hitting for the daily buffet (until 10pm), which includes a bit of everything and costs 98kr.

Pasta Basta, Valknesdorf 22. An array of fish and meat pasta dishes, plus nine cold pasta bowls from which you can help-yourself for 69kr. Open until 5am, this is a favourite final stop for late-night groovers.

The Pyramids, Gothersgade 15. Gloriously over-the-top Egyptian restaurant – the food comes with belly dancers.

Rama, Bredgade 29. Top class Thai food, best from the 89kr open-table.

Zorba, Fiolstrøde 21. A dependable Egyptian diner, worth a call for its open-table: 98kr for dinner, 58kr at lunchtime.

Vegetarian restaurants

The Golden Temple, Blågådsgade 27. The best vegetarian Indian restaurant in the city, cheap and delicious; bring your own booze.

Green World, Blågådgade 4. The only vegan eatery in Copenhagen, serving small but highly nutritious meals.

Greens, Grønnegade 12–14. Just a carrot's throw from Strøget with carefully-prepared wholefood meals and snacks, which can be washed down by invigorating fruit juices. Has wonderful all-you-can-eat specials on Saturday afternoons for 98kr.

Nightlife

An almost unchartable network of **cafés and bars** covers Copenhagen. You can get a drink – and usually a snack too – in any of them, although some are especially noted for their congeniality and youthful ambience, and it's these we've listed below. Almost all the better cafés and bars are in – or close to – Indre By, and it's no hardship to sample several on the same night, though bear in mind that Fridays and Saturdays are very busy, and you'll probably need to queue before getting in.

The city is no less attractive for its **live music**. Major international names visit regularly but it's with small-scale shows that Copenhagen really excels. Minor gigs early in the week in cafés and bars will often be free, making it a cheap and simple affair to take in several places until you find something to your liking – though later in the week smaller venues may have a modest cover charge. There are also a number of medium-sized halls that host the best of Danish and overseas rock, jazz, hip-hop and funk. Things normally kick-off around 10pm and, if not free, admission is 25–75kr. Throughout the summer, there are many **free concerts** in the city parks, some featuring the leading Danish bands. You can get the latest gen on who's playing where by reading *Neon Guiden* (see "Eating"); the latest copy of *Gaffa*, free from music and record shops; or *Huset*, a monthly magazine available from the *Huset* building at Rådhusstræde 13, which lists what's on at its own three music venues.

With the plethora of late-opening cafés and bars, you'll never have to choose between going to a **disco** and going to bed. If you do get a craving for a dance-floor fling, however, you'll find the discos much like those in any major city – and always more preoccupied with providing entertainment than defining the cutting edge of fashion. You'll be dancing alone if you turn up much before midnight, although after that time, especially on Fridays and Saturdays, they fill rapidly – and stay open until 5am. There are dress codes but these are fairly easy-going – anything casual and clean will usually suffice. Another plus is that drink prices are seldom hiked-up and admission is fairly cheap: 25–45kr.

Cafés and bars

Café Dan Turrell, Skt. Regnegade 3. Something of an institution with the artier student crowd and a fine place for a sociable tipple. Spot it by the rows of bicycles parked outside.

Hånd i Hanke, Griffenfeldtsgade 20. Delectably murky, candlelit basement bar. Often has live music (see below).

Krasnapolsky, Vestergade 10. The Danish avant-garde art hanging on the wall reflects the trendsetting reputation of this ultra-modern watering hole. Come here at least once.

Peder Hvitfeldt, P. Hvitfeldtsstræde. Spit-and-sawdust-type place and immensely popular, drawing a youthful crowd. Come early if you want to sit down.

Café Sommersko, Kronprinsensgade 6. Sizeable, but crowded most nights, and with free live music on Sunday afternoons to soothe away hangovers.

Universitetscaféen, Fiolstræde 2. A prime central location and long hours (open until 5am) make this a good spot to hit, early or late, for a leisurely beer.

Live music

Bar Bue, Rådhusstræde 13 (☎33/320066). Small and smoky, regularly showcasing the pick of the Danish indie bands, interspersed with choice international acts. See also "Discos".

Ben Webster Jazz Restaurant, Vestergade 7 (☎33/938845). An eating house that's best visited for its free (at least, for the price of a drink) classy, modern jazz; Mon–Sat from 9pm, Sun from 5pm.

Caféen Funke, Skt. Hans Torv (☎31/351741). As the name suggests, a place to hear well-played funk, and often jazz too. Mon, Wed & Sat only.

Foyerscenen Jazz, Rådhusstræde 13 (☎33/320066). A part of *Huset* with some of the premier new Danish jazz combos on show each Fri & Sat evening.

Hånd i Hanke, Griffenfeldtsgade 20 (☎31/372070). Often free or cheap entry to see local or other Scandinavian bands performing in a marvellously gloomy cellar (See also "Cafés and Bars").

Hit House, Nørregade 1 (☎33/155102). The latest venue for bigger Danish names and also some modest attractions from overseas. See also "Eating".

Loppen, in Christiania. On the edge of the "free city" and a sympathetic setting for both established and experimental Danish rock, jazz and performance artists, and quite a few British and American ones too.

Montmartre, Nørregade 41 (☎33/127836). The city's major jazz venue, with big names but many free nights with local talent. See also "Discos".

Musikcaféen, Rådhusstræde 13 (☎33/320066). The mainstream rock part of *Huset*, a sizeable hall but small enough to have plenty of atmosphere on good nights – of which there are several most weeks.

Pumpehuset, Studiestræde (☎33/320066). Not part of *Huset* but run by the same people, offering a broad sweep of middle-strata rock, hip-hop and funk groups from Denmark and around the world about three times a month.

Stengade 30, Stengade 30. Brilliant youth-clubby venue in Nørrebro, across the lakes from the city centre, boasting low-priced, eclectic monthly bills of the best yet-to-be-discovered Copenhagen bands. Also has the cheapest beer prices of any city music venue.

De Tre Musketerer, Nikolaj Plads 25 (☎33/125067). A long-established and well-respected jazz venue, with a traditional leaning.

Discos

Annabell's, Lille Kongensgade 16. Comparatively upmarket but worth a fling on Fridays and Saturdays when there's a younger, brasher crowd.

Bar Bue, Rådhusstræde 13. Mixtures of punk, funk and hip-hop burst out in this compact and sweaty room (see also "Live music") usually Fri & Sat only.

Daddy's, Axeltorv 5. A bit staid, with an older age-range, but fine if you're looking to tango until dawn.

Montmartre, Nørregade 41. After the jazz (see "Live music") finishes, a vibrant and enjoyable disco takes over. One of the better spots to shake a leg.

U-matic, Vestergade 10. In the basement of *Krasnapolsky* (see "Cafés and Bars"). With the trendiest sounds and the weirdest dressed people, this is the nearest thing to a poseurs' paradise that the city has – though sociable enough to make anyone feel part of the scene. Closed Mon & Sun.

Woodstock, Vestergade 12 (☎33/112071). Pulls a large, fun-loving crowd eager to dance to anything with a beat – though the music is predominantly Sixties.

Cinemas

If drinking and dancing don't tempt, you can pass an evening in one of the many **cinemas**. New releases, often British or American with subtitles, are shown all over the city; more esoteric fare is on tap at *Foyerscenen* in *Huset*, the *Delta Bio*, Kompagnistræde 19, or the *Park Bio*, on Østergade. You can get full listings in any newspaper. For **kids**, there's special cinema, *Tivoli Bio for Børn*, by the main entrance to Tivoli Gardens.

Gay Copenhagen

Copenhagen has a lively **gay** scene, which includes a good sprinkling of gay bars and discos, a bookshop and a sauna, as well as a couple of hotels at which gays are especially welcome. For **contacts and information**, ignore the misleadingly named "Copenhagen Gay Centre" (no more than a glorified sex emporium) and get in touch with the **National Organisation for Gay Men And Women** (*Landsforeningen for bøsser og lesbiske*), which is based at Knabrostræde 3 (☎33/

131948). They offer information, advice and have a bookshop, travel agency, a café (Mon & Tues 1pm–2am, Thur & Sun 1pm–3am, Fri & Sat 1pm–5am), as well as the *Pan Club* disco, see below. There's also a **gay switchboard** (☎33/130112) and further information can be gleaned from *Pan* magazine, which doesn't have listings but does have adverts announcing the latest happenings – in Danish but easily understood. Also, the **Gay Liberation Movement** (*BBF*) meets each week on Mondays at 8pm in Bøssehuset, Karlsvognen in Christiania.

For **accommodation**, two hotels cater to gay visitors although neither is exclusively gay: *Jørgensen's*, Rømersgade 11 (☎33/139743), is the city's best-priced hotel, with rooms for 210kr per person, detailed under "Sleeping"; *Hotel Windsor*, Frederiksborggade 30 (☎33/110830), has one wing reserved for gay men and is more expensive, 280kr for a single, around 375kr for a double. Both hotels are near Israel Plads about a fifteen-minute walk from the city centre, a few minutes from the Nørreport S-train station. Both dispense handy maps showing the main gay spots in the city.

Gay bars and clubs

Amigo Bar, Schønbergsgade 4. Serves snacks and is frequented by gay men of all ages.

Club Amigo, Studiestræde 31A. Enormous club with bar, cinemas, sauna and solarium, pool room, video room and much more.

Cosy Bar, Studiestræde 24. Gets busy late, mainly with clones and motorbike boys.

Kake's Bar, Vestergade 4. Established in 1929, this is probably the oldest gay bar in the city, slightly difficult to find but worth the effort: down the passageway and through an unmarked door. Upstairs, the **Fortuna Bar** has a variety of music on offer.

Madame Arthur, Lavendelstræde 15. Elegant nightclub serving food; transvestite shows most evenings.

Masken Bar, Studiestræde 33. Relatively staid bar popular with an older clientele.

Pan Club, Knabrostræde 3. Part of the biggest and most popular gay centre in the country, see above. The disco is also big – and very enjoyable. Wed, Thurs & Sun 10pm–3am, Fri & Sat 10pm–5am.

Pink Club, Favergade 10. Fairly cruisy but enjoyable, if only for a quick look. Free entry; daily 4pm–4am.

Stable Bar, Teglgårdsstræde 3. The most masculine bar, popular with leather and motorbike types. Daily 4pm–2am.

Listings

Baby Sitters *Minerva-Studenternes Baby Sitters*, Smallegade 52A (☎31/190090). Mon–Thurs 7–9am & 3–6pm, Fri 3–6pm, Sat 3–5pm.

Banks Central branches include *Det Danske Bank*, Amagertorv 12, and *Handelsbanken* Østergade 16. Hours are Mon–Fri 9.30am–4pm, until 6pm on Thurs. There's also an *American Express* office at Amagertorv 18, and a *Bank of Tivoli* at Vesterbrogade 3, open 10am–11pm between May and mid-Sept. See also "Exchange" below.

Bike Hire *Jet-Cycles*, Istedgade 71 (☎31/231760); *Københavns Cyklebørs*, Gothersgade 157–159 (☎33/140717); *Dan Wheel*, Colbjørnsensgade 3 (☎31/212227); *Cykeltanken* Godthåbsvej 247 (☎31/871423). Also, between April and October, from the railway stations at Klampenborg and Lyngby.

Boat Tours Leave frequently from Gammel Strand and sail around the canals and harbour. Prices from 120kr per person; just turn up.

Books Most of the city's bookshops are in the area around Fiolstræde and Købmagergade. *The Book Trader*, Skindergade 23, has a varied selection of old and new books in English; *Steve's Books and Records*, Ved Stranden 10, keeps a stock of secondhand English books and assorted jazz discs; *Kupeen DIS Rejser*, Skindergade 28, has guidebooks and maps for budget travellers. Chief places for new books are *G.E.C. Gad*, Vimmelskaftet 32; *Arnold Busck* Købmagergade 49; and *Boghallen i Politikens Hus*, Rådhuspladsen 37.

Car Hire *Avis*, Kampmannsgade 1 (☎33/152299); *Hertz*, Vesterbrogade 6 (☎33/144222); *InterRent*, Jernebanegade 6 (☎33/116200); *Hire A Car*, Studiestræde 61 (☎33/120643).

Chemists 24-hour pharmacies: *Steno Apotek*, Vesterbrogade 6, and *Søndererbro Apotek*, Amagerbrogade 158.

Dental Problems *Tandlægevagten*, Oslo Plads 14, open nightly 8–10pm, Sat & Sun also 10am–noon. Turn up and be prepared to pay at least 150kr on the spot.

Doctor Emergencies ☎0041, weekdays 4–7pm. You'll be given the name of a doctor in your area. There's a night fee of around 300kr to be paid in cash. For non-urgent treatment get a list of doctors from the tourist office, *Use-It*, or a local health department (*Kommunens social og sundhedsforvaltning*).

Embassies *UK* Kastelsvej 40 (☎31/264600); *Ireland* Østerbanegard 21 (☎31/423233); *USA* Dag Hammerskjölds Allé 24 (☎31/423144); *Canada* Kristen Bernikows Gade 1 (☎33/122299); *Australia* Kristianiasgade 21 (☎31/262244); *New Zealand* (use UK).

Emergencies ☎0-0-0

Exchange Outside bank hours – and for the same rates – at the Central Station daily 7am–10pm, and the airport arrival hall, 6.30am–10pm, and departure hall, 6.30am–8.30pm.

Flea Markets There's a good, rummageable flea market at Israel Plads on Saturday mornings from May to September, and a Salvation Army market, selling bric-a-brac and old clothes, at Hørhusvej, Tues–Thurs 1–5pm, Fri 1–6pm & Sat 9am–1pm; take bus #30, #3 or #4 to Brydes Allé. Try also the Saturday morning market held in summer behind Frederiksberg Rådhus; buses #1 or #12.

Football The city has four first division football teams, by far the most successful of which is Brøndby. Take S-train line A to Brøndbyøster and follow the crowds. Big matches, and other league games, are played closer to the centre in Idrætsparken: take bus #6, #7 or #14. Fixture details from *Use-It*, the tourist magazines, newspapers, etc.

Health Shops *Helios* Åbrenå 31; *Urtekræmmeren* Larsbjønsstræde 20; *Saftbaren* Larsbjønsstræde 18; *Sæbehuset* Studiestræde 18; *City Helsekost* Linnégade 14.

Hitching First check the car-share notices on *Use-It* noticeboards. If they don't deliver anything use the following routes. Heading south to Germany, take S-train line A to Ellebjerg, which leaves you by the ring road, near the start of motorway E20. North to Helsingør and Sweden, take the S-train lines B or F to Ryparken (or bus #6, #24 or #84 to Hans Knudsen Plads) and hitch along Lyngbyvej (for the E4). West for Funen and Jutland take the S-train to Tåstrup line Bb, then walk along Køgevej and hitch from Roskildevej (A1).

Hospitals Casualty: *Righsospitalet*, Blegdamsvej 9 (☎31/396633); *Kommunehospitalet*, Østre Farimagsgade 5 (☎33/158500). Free treatment for EC and Scandinavian nationals, though others are unlikely to have to pay. See also *Doctor* above.

Late Shops The supermarket at the Central Station is open daily until midnight.

Launderettes Central ones are *Vascomat*, Borgergade 2, and *Møntvask*, Nansensgade 39; an average wash costs about 40kr.

Left Luggage Lockers on the Central Station concourse and larger ones in the *InterRail Centre* and at *Use-It*.

Library *Hovedbiblioteket*, Kultorvet 2 (Mon–Thurs 11am–7pm, Fri 11am–5pm, Sat 10am–4pm). *Huset* has a very well-stocked reading room, with international magazines and newspapers.

Lost Property The general lost property office is at Carl Jacobsvej 20, Valby (☎31/161406). Otherwise, for things lost on a bus, contact the *HT* office on Vester Voldgade (☎33/147448); lost on a train, the *DSB* office at the Central Station (call in person only); lost on a plane (☎31/503211 Mon–Fri 8am–noon & 1–4pm).

Media *Playtime* and its updates throughout the summer are essential reading, free from *Use-It*, and many cafés. The alternative radio station, *Radio Sokkelund*, broadcasts on 101.7mhz: all programmes are in Danish but contain up-to-the-minute news of events in the city. Overseas newspapers are on sale from the stall in Rådhuspladsen and some of the newsagents along Strøget.

Parking Meters Meters are colour coded in declining order of expense: blue, white, yellow. Parking is limited to three hours at the following times: Mon–Fri 9am–6pm, Sat 9am–1pm.

Post Office Main office: Tietgensgade 35 (Mon–Fri 9am–6pm, Sat 9am–1pm). Also at the Central Station (Mon–Fri 9am–9pm, Sat 9am–6pm, Sun 10am–4pm). Post office information on ☎33/146298. Poste restante at *Use-It* or any named post office.

Public Saunas At Borgergade 12, Sjællandsgade 12, and Sofiegade 15. Both open Mon–Fri 8am–6.30pm, Sat 8am–2pm; 18kr per person.

Student Travel Service *DIS*, Skindergade 28 (☎33/110044), can give advice on travelling around Denmark, and on the rest of Scandinavia and Europe.

Venereal Disease *København Venereal Klinik* in Rudolph Berghs Hospital, Tietgensgade 31 (Mon–Fri 9am–2pm & 3–7pm).

What's On Listings in the free monthly tourist magazines, *Copenhagen This Week* and *Cope City Guide*, available from tourist offices, hotels, etc. Also scrutinise the notices in *Use-It* and city cafés.

Women's Movement These days Copenhagen's main women's centre is *Dannerhuset* (☎33/141676), on Gyldenlovesgade, a decaying building which was recently taken over by a group of feminists and renovated. There's a café (Mon–Wed 5–8pm), and a bookshop (Mon–Fri 5–10.30pm), and a range of activities including a film club, counselling and self-defence courses – though these shut down during summer. *Kvindehuset*, Gothersgade 37 (☎33/142804), is another, rather less organised, centre which has a cheap café (Mon–Thurs) and a bookshop, again only open afternoons.

AROUND ZEALAND

It's easy to see more of Zealand simply by making day trips out from the capital, although, depending on where you're heading next, it's often a better idea to pack your bags and leave the city altogether. Transport links are excellent throughout the region, making much of northern and central Zealand Copenhagen commuter territory; but that's hardly something you'd notice as you pass through dozens of tiny villages and large forests on the way to historic centres such as **Helsingør**, **Køge** and – an essential call if you're interested in Denmark's past – **Roskilde**. Except for the memorable vistas of the **northern coast**, and the explorable smaller **islands** off southern Zealand and **Bornholm** to the east, however, you'll find the soft green terrain varies little; and, unless you're a true nature lover, you'll soon feel the need to push on (which is easily done) to the bigger cities of Funen and Jutland.

North Zealand: Helsingør and the coast

The **coast** north of Copenhagen, as far as Helsingør, rejoices under the tag of the "Danish Riviera"; a handy label to describe its line of tiny one-time fishing hamlets now inhabited almost exclusively by the extremely rich. It's best seen by bus (#188) from Klampenborg, last stop on line C of the S-train system, but although the views are nice and the beaches beckon, more often than not the sands are private and guarded by Alsatian dogs. A frequent train service, slightly quicker than the bus, also makes the journey from Copenhagen to Helsingør, but, unless you break the trip, you'll see much less – the views from the railway are obscured by trees.

Rungstedlund, Humlebæk and Louisiana

There are a couple – and only a couple – of reasons to stop before Helsingør. Near the turning for HØRSHOLM, off the coastal road, lies **Rungstedlund**, the former manor-house home of Karen Blixen, the grounds of which, partly turned into a bird sanctuary, are open to the public. The actual house is closed to visitors although there are well-advanced plans to open a museum, devoted to the writer's life – ask at any tourist office for the latest news. There's a much more noteworthy, and established, attraction in **HUMLEBÆK**, the next community of any size, where you'll find **Louisiana** (daily 10am–5pm, Wed until 10pm; 30kr, student reductions): a modern art museum on the northern edge of the village at Gammel Strandvej 13, a short walk from Humlebæk railway station. Even if you go nowhere else outside Copenhagen, it would be a shame to miss this: the setting alone is worth the journey, harmoniously combining art, architecture and the natural landscape. The entrance is in a nineteenth-century villa, off which two carefully – and subtly – designed modern corridors contain the indoor collection, and whose windows allow views of the outside sculpture park and the Øresund.

It seems churlish to mention individual items, but the museum's American section, in the south corridor, sticks in the mind. It includes some devastating pieces by Edward Kienholz, Malcolm Morley's scintillatingly gross *Pacific Telephone Los Angeles Yellow Pages*, in which the telephone directory cover expands to monstrous proportions and coffee stains rib the city skyline like a weird metallic grid, and (in the reading room) Jim Dines' powerful series, *The Desire*. You'll also find some of Giacometti's strange gangly figures haunting a room of their own off the north corridor, and an equally-affecting handful of sculptures by Max Ernst, squatting outside the windows and leering inwards. Except for some collages by Arthur Køpcke, and paintings by various Danish luminaries of the COBRA group, homegrown artists have a rather low profile, although their work is often shown in temporary exhibitions.

Helsingør

First impressions of **HELSINGØR** are none too enticing. The **bus** stops outside the noisy **railway station**, which is connected to the equally hectic **ferry terminal** by an ugly pedestrian bridge; beneath the bridge, Havnepladsen is usually full of transit passengers loitering around fast-food stalls. But away from the hustle, Helsingør is really a quiet and likeable town. Its position on the 4-kilometre strip of water linking the North Sea and the Baltic brought the town prosperity when, in 1429, the Sound Toll was imposed on passing vessels – an upturn only matched in magnitude by the severe decline following the abolition of the toll in the nineteenth century. Shipbuilding brought back some of the town's self-assurance, but today it's once again the whisker of water between Denmark and Sweden, and the ferries across it to Helsingborg, which account for most of Helsingør's through-traffic.

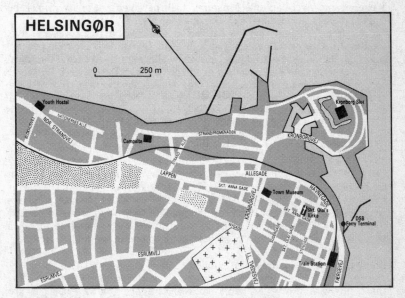

The Town

The town's other great draw, on a sandy curl of land extending seawards, is **Kronborg Slot** (May–Sept daily 10am–5pm; April & Oct daily 11am–4pm; Nov–March daily 11am–3pm; 14kr), principally because of its literary association as Elsinore Castle, whose ramparts Shakespeare's Prince Hamlet supposedly strode. Actually, the playwright never visited Helsingør, and his hero was based on Amleth (aka Amled), a tenth-century character shrouded in the fogs of Danish mythology and certainly predating the castle. Nevertheless, there are still hundreds of requests each year for the whereabouts of "Hamlet's bedroom" and a thriving Hamlet souvenir business. During the winter, guided tours leave from the entrance every half-hour; summer numbers make these impossible and, instead, a well-informed attendant hovers in every room ready to answer questions.

During the sixteenth century, Frederik II instigated construction of the present castle on the site of Erik of Pomerania's fortress, commissioning the Dutch architects, van Opbergen and van Paaschen, who took their ideas from the buildings of Antwerp. Various bits have been destroyed and rebuilt since, but it remains a grand affair, enhanced immeasurably by its setting and with an interior, particularly the royal chapel, that is spectacularly ornate – though appreciation is hampered by the steady flow of tourist traffic. Crowds are less of a problem in the labyrinthine cellars, which can be seen on a half-hourly guided tour (departing from the cellar entrance). The guide delivers the details then lets visitors wind their way around the cold, damp corridors, dimly lit by oil lamps. The body of Holger Danske, a mythical hero from the legends of Charlemagne, is said to lie beneath the castle ready to wake again when Denmark needs him, although the tacky stock-Viking style statue, which marks the legend, is well out of synch with the cellars' authentic decay. The castle also houses the national **Maritime Museum** and **Architectural Museum**, both of which are pretty dismal, but entry to them is included in the castle admission fee.

Away from Kronborg and the harbour area, Helsingør has a well-preserved **medieval quarter** worth taking a walk through. **Stengade** is the main pedestrianised street, linked by a number of narrow alleyways to **Axeltorv**, the town's small market square and usually a good spot to linger over a beer (for an ice cream, stroll into nearby Brostræde, long famous for the old-fashioned ingredients and immense size of the ices sold along it). Near the corner of Stengade and Skt. Annagade, the spired **Skt. Olai's Kirke** is connected to the Karmeliter Klosteret, which was built by monks as a hospital, became the local poorhouse in 1630, and now contains the **Town Museum** (daily noon–4pm; free). While a hospital, the place prided itself on brain operations, and the unnerving tools of this craft are still here, together with diagrams of the corrective insertions made into patients' heads. These, combined with various dark remnants from the poorhouse times, evoke a sadness not entirely alleviated by the more upbeat memories from the town's prosperous days. If after this you feel the need to lighten your mood, seek out the oddball **Journeymen's Club** (*Naverhulen*), in a nearby courtyard, cluttered with souvenirs of world travel, such as crab puppets and armadillo lampshades. Act interested and you might get a free guided tour.

Practical details ... and on to Sweden

You can pick up a free map and information on Helsingør from the **tourist office** (June, July & Aug Mon–Fri 9am–8pm, Sat 9am–5pm, Sun 9am–noon; shorter hours rest of the year; ☎49/211333) across Strandgade from the railway station, or from the tourist counter in the station itself. However, due to the tourist trade, the closest thing to a cheap **hotel** in the town is *Hotel Hamlet*, Bramstræde 5 (☎49/210591), where you'll be lucky to find a double for under 600kr. More affordably, there is a **youth hostel** (☎49/211640), open all year except December and January, literally on the beach, a twenty-minute walk to the north along the coastal road (Ndr. Strandvej); or take bus #340 from the station and get out just after the sports stadium. The **campsite**, at Sundtoldvej 9 (☎49/215856), is closer to town and also by a beach, between the main road Lappen (which begins where Skt. Annagade ends) and the sea. The usual pizza and fast-food outlets are two-a-penny around Stengade, but for healthier **eating**, *Kloster Caféen*, Skt. Annagade 35, is the prime lunchtime spot for its set menu and sizeable sandwiches. A little more expensively, there's fine Danish food in the atmospheric *Hos Anker*, Bramstræde 1, or *Færgegården*, Stengade 81b. Given the proximity of the capital, nightlife of note is a rare commodity in Helsingør, but for an evening **drink**, stroll the streets on either side of Stengade, where there are several decent bodegas. Rowdier boozing goes on at the top end of Axeltorv, the bar here popular with Swedes taking advantage of Denmark's more liberal licensing laws.

Three **ferry lines** cross from Helsingør to Helsingborg in Sweden. The main one, and probably the best option, is the *DSB* boat leaving from the main terminal by the railway station (see above) and costing 35kr; slightly more expensive – and a bit more awkward to get to – is the ferry run by *Scandinavian Ferry Lines* from Ndr. Mole, near Kronborg. The cheapest crossing, although only by a few øre, is with *Sundbusserne*, who operate a small craft often heavily buffeted by the choppy waters. It's perfectly feasible, and on a sunny day very enjoyable, to rent a **bike** from the Helsingør railway station tourist counter and cross to Helsingborg for a day's cycling along the Swedish coast. But take food and drink with you – both are much more expensive in Sweden than in Denmark.

Onwards from Helsingør: the North Zealand coast

Some of the best **beaches** in Zealand are within easy reach of Helsingør, either by bike, local buses or the small private train (*InterRail* and *EurRail* not valid) which links the main coastal communities. A whole string of highly-rated sands can be found simply by following Ndr. Strandvej (an easy task if you're based at the youth hostel) towards the village of **HELLEBÆK**. Close to Hellebæk is a well-known, if unofficial, venue for **nude bathing**. Further along the coast is **HORNBÆK**, a busy spot in the summer, but at heart a fishing village and with excellent beaches and fine views over the sea towards "Kullen", the rocky promontory jutting out from the Swedish coast. This makes a lovely spot to stay over, and there's a **campsite** (☎42/200223), open from mid-April to mid-September, at Planetvej 4.

Another fishing village, **GILLELEJE**, also makes a good short-term stop-over. While here, you should negotiate at least some of the **footpath** which runs along the top of the dunes, where, in 1835, Søren Kierkegaard took lengthy contemplative walks, later recalling: "I often stood there and reflected over my past life. The force of the sea and the struggle of the elements made me realise how unimportant I was." Ironically, so important was Kierkegaard to become, that a monument to him now stands on the path, bearing his maxim: "Truth in life is to live for an idea." There's a **campsite** (☎49/719755), open all year, just outside the village at Bregnerødvej 21.

Having got this far, you ought to carry on along the coast to **TISVILDELEJE**, and the neighbouring **Tisvildelje Hegn**, possibly the most scenically beautiful spot in the country. Besides the excellent beaches, and an official nude bathing area, the sight of the "Hegn" itself is one to remember: it was put up during the eighteenth century to stop sand drifts and the result is a variety of distorted and twisted trees. Additionally, a number of high points give rewarding views over the nearby Arresø, the largest Danish lake. Close to Tisvildeleje, between it and Rågeleje, is a **campsite** (☎42/115640) open mid-April to mid-October, on Hostrupsvej.

Inland from the North Zealand coast is forest and lake country. The western side of Esrum Sø is taken up by **Gripskov**, a dense proliferation of ancient oaks and beeches. Close by is **Fredensborg Slot** (July only daily 1–5pm; 5kr), an eighteenth-century castle built by Frederik IV to commemorate the 1720 Peace Treaty with Sweden that's a summer residence of the current Danish royals, with grand, statue-lined gardens (open all year) reaching down to the lakeside. On the north bank of Esrum Sø is a **campsite** (☎42/290323), also open all year. Once here, it's simple to reach Hillerød and Frederiksborg (see below), only a nine-minute train-ride from Fredensborg.

Hillerød: Frederiksborg Slot

HILLERØD, half an hour by train from Helsingør, and a similar distance from Copenhagen (last stop on line E of the S-train network), has a castle which pushes the more famous Kronborg well into second place, **Frederiksborg Slot** (May–Sept daily 10am–5pm; April daily 11am–4pm; Oct daily 10am–4pm; Nov–March daily 11am–3pm; 20kr), which lies decorously across three small islands within an artificial lake. Buses #701 and #703 run from the railway station to the castle but walking to it only takes about twenty minutes, following the signs (*Slottet*) through the town centre.

The castle was the home of Frederik II and birthplace of his son Christian IV. At the turn of the seventeenth century, under the auspices of Christian, rebuilding began in an unorthodox Dutch Renaissance style. It's the unusual aspects of the monarch's design – prolific use of towers and spires, pointed Gothic arches and flowery window ornamentation – which still stand out, despite the changes wrought by fire and restoration.

You can see the exterior of the castle for free simply by walking through the main gates, across the seventeenth-century S-shaped bridge, and into the central courtyard. Since 1882, the **interior** has functioned as a museum of Danish history, largely funded by the Carlsberg brewery magnate Carl Jacobsen in an attempt to create a Danish Versailles, and heighten the nation's sense of history and cultural development. It's a good idea to buy (25kr), or at least try and borrow, the illustrated guide to the museum, since without it the contents of the sixty-odd rooms are barely comprehensible. Many of the rooms are surprisingly free of furniture and household objects, and attention is drawn to the ranks of portraits along the walls – a motley crew of nobility, statesmen and royalty, who between them ruled and misruled Denmark for centuries. A succession of flat-faced kings and thin consorts gives way in the later rooms to politicians, scientists and writers.

Two rooms deserve special mention. The **chapel**, where monarchs were annointed between 1671 and 1840, is exquisite, its vaults, pillars and arches gilded and embellished, and the contrasting black marble of the gallery riddled with gold lettering. The shields, in tiered rows around the chapel, are those of the knights of the Order of the Elephant, who sat with the king in the late seventeenth century. The **Great Hall**, above the chapel, is a reconstruction, but this doesn't detract from its beauty. It's bare but for the staggering wall and ceiling decorations: tapestries, wall-reliefs, portraits and a glistening black marble fireplace. In Christian IV's day the hall was a ballroom, and the polished floor still calls up some fancy footwork as you slide up and down its length.

Away from the often crowded interior, the **gardens**, on the far side of the lake, have some photogenic views of the castle from their stepped terraces and are a good spot for a rest. The quickest way to them is through the narrow Mint Gate to the left of the main castle building, which adjoins a roofed-in bridge leading to the King's Wing.

While in Hillerød, you should also visit the **Money Historical Museum** (open during banking hours; free) at Slotsgade 16–18. During the reigns of Frederik II and Christian IV all Danish coins were minted in Hillerød. Besides samples of these, the place displays a stash of currencies from all over the world.

Some practical details

Few of Hillerød's **hotels** can match the prices you might find in Copenhagen, but usefully, if you're on a tight budget, the town has a hotel run by the Danish *YMCA*, at Slotsgade 5 (☎49/260189), with beds from 150kr. The only other budget accommodation is the **campsite** (☎42/264854), open from Easter to mid-September, at Dyrskuepladsen.

West from Copenhagen: Roskilde and around

There's very little between Copenhagen and the west Zealand coast in the way of things to see and explore, except for the ancient former Danish capital of **ROSKILDE**, less than half an hour by train from the big city. There's been a community here since prehistoric times and later the Roskilde fjord provided a route to the open sea utilised by the Vikings. But it was the arrival of Bishop Absalon in the twelfth century which made the place the base of the Danish church – and, as a consequence, the national capital. Importance waned after the Reformation and Roskilde came to function mainly as a market for the neighbouring rural communities – which it still does, as well as being dormitory territory for Copenhagen commuters. In high season, especially, it can be crammed with day-trippers seeking the dual blasts from the past supplied by its royal tombs and Viking boats; and the town sees a massive influx every July, when it hosts the Roskilde Festival – northern Europe's biggest open-air rock event. Yet at any other time, or for more than a swift visit, the ancient centre is one of Denmark's most appealing towns, and the surrounding countryside quiet and unspoilt.

The Town

The major pointer to the town's former status is the fabulous **Roskilde Domkirke** (April–Sept Mon–Sat 9am–5.45pm, Sun 12.30–5.45pm; rest of the year Mon–Sat 10–3.45pm Sun 12.30–3.45pm; 3kr), founded by Bishop Absalon in 1170, on the site of a tenth-century church erected by Harald Bluetooth, and finished

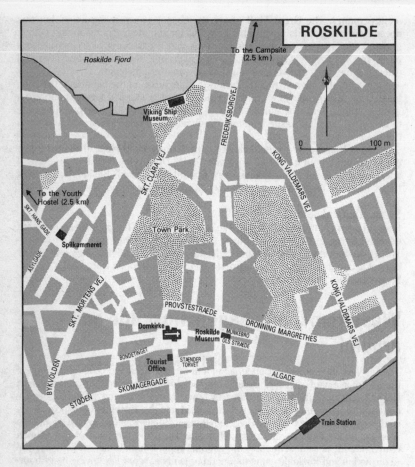

during the fourteenth century – although portions have been added up to the twentieth century. The result is a mish-mash of architectural styles, though one which hangs together with surprising neatness; every square inch seems adorned by some curious mark or etching. But it's the claustrophobic collection of coffins containing the regal remains of twenty kings and seventeen queens in four large royal chapels that really catch the eye. The most richly endowed chapel is that of Christian IV, a previously austere resting place jazzed-up – in typically early-nineteenth-century Romantic style – with bronze statues, wall-length frescoes and vast paintings of scenes from his reign. A striking contrast is provided by the simple redbricked chapel just outside the cathedral, into which Frederik IX was laid in 1972. Try to be in the cathedral just before the hour to see and hear the animated medieval clock above the main entrance: a model of Saint Jørgen gallops forward on his horse to wallop the dragon and the hour is marked by the creature's squeal of death.

From one end of the cathedral, a roofed passageway, the **Arch of Absalon**, feeds into the **Bishop's Palace**. It's in the yellow buildings of the palace that current royalty install themselves when attending ceremonies at the cathedral, and the only part open to mere commoners is the room holding the **Palace Collections** (daily May–Sept 11am–4pm, Oct–April Sat & Sun 1–3pm; 2kr). These are made up of paintings, furniture and other artefacts belonging to the wealthiest Roskilde families of the eighteenth and nineteenth centuries, though it would have to be raining very hard outside for anyone to derive much pleasure from seeing them.

The history of the town recorded in the **Roskilde Museum** at Skt. Ols Gade 18 (June–Aug daily 11am–5pm; Sept–May Mon–Fri & Sun 2–5pm; 5kr) is a little more enticing, with strong sections on medieval pottery and toys, although time is really better spent at **Spilkammeret** at Skt. Hans Gade 20 (June–Aug Sun–Wed 1–8pm, other times call ☎42/351808; 10kr) – a collection of playing cards and games crammed into two rooms of a private house with the underlying aim of "examining connections between game playing and ritual". Besides location, it doesn't have much to do with Roskilde, but it's fascinating and so vast that only a small selection of the full stock can be displayed at any one time.

Just as absorbing, and far better known, is the **Viking Ship Museum** (April–Oct 9am–5pm; Nov–March 10am–4pm; 18kr), in Strandengen on the banks of the fjord. Here, five excellent specimens of Viking shipbuilding are given the space they deserve: there's a deep sea trader, a merchant ship, a warship, a ferry and a longship, each one retrieved from the fjord where they had been sunk to block invading forces. Together, they give an impressive indication of the Vikings' nautical versatility . . . and their skill in boat-building.

Practical details . . . and the Roskilde Festival

The gabled building near the Domkirke's main entrance houses the Roskilde **tourist office** (summer Mon–Fri 9am–7pm, Sat 9am–5pm; shorter hours rest of the year; ☎42/352700). The banks of the fjord make for pleasant walks, and in the **evening**, apart from the sprinkling of bars around the town centre and some free events in the town park, there's little else to do. Serious revellers make for Copenhagen, but if you're heading towards Funen or further south in Zealand it's not really worth returning to the city just for a night. If you do decide to stay, there's a **campsite** (☎46/757996) on the wooded edge of the fjord – an appealing setting which makes it very crowded at peak times; it's open from mid-April to mid-September, and is linked to the town centre by bus #602. The **youth hostel** is further out, set amid countryside about 3km from the middle of Roskilde at Hørhusene 61 (☎42/352184). It's open all year and buses #601 and #604 from the railway station pass close; get off after the hospital and take a less-than-obvious walk along a footpath through a field.

Neither the hostel nor campsite are worth bothering with if you're going to the **Roskilde Festival**, which has grown from humble beginnings to attract around 50,000 people annually to its weekend of live rock. The festival takes place in early July and there's a special camping ground beside the festival site, to which shuttle buses run from the railway station every ten minutes. Tens of thousands of tickets are sold in advance but the organisers claim never to turn anybody away who arrives without one.

Around West Zealand

Beyond Roskilde, west Zealand is flat and bland. You might, however, be journeying through to **KALUNDBORG** to pick up ferries to Århus in Jutland or to the island of Samsø; and you can also take ferries from **KORSØR**, the other main town of the western coast, to the island of Langeland or Nyborg, on Funen. Apart from these, the only real interest lies in the **Hornsherred Peninsula**, which divides the Roskilde fjord and Isefjord. There are long, quiet beaches along the peninsula's western coast, though the lack of a railway and a skeletal local bus service means it's a place best toured by bike. Make for the medieval frescoes in the eleventh-century churches at SKIBBEY or DRÅBY, or keep on northward for **JÆGERSPRIS** and its **castle** (May–Sept daily 10am–noon & 1–5pm; 10kr), built during the fifteenth century as a royal hunting seat and last used by the eccentric Frederik VII, who lived here during the mid-1800s with his third wife. She inherited the castle after the king's death and turned it into an institution for "poor and unfortunate girls".

South from Copenhagen: Køge and around

Not so long ago, **KØGE** was best known for the pollution caused by the rubber factory and chemical works on its outskirts. Despite the town's fine sandy beaches, few ventured here to sample the waters of Køge Bay. Recently, though, the place has been considerably cleaned up, an achievement acknowledged by the extension of the southern end of line E of the Copenhagen S-train network to the town, which has put its evocatively preserved medieval centre and the bay's beaches within easy reach of the capital. It's also a good base for touring around the Stevns Peninsula, which bulges into the sea just south of the town.

Saturday is the best day to visit: a variety of free entertainment sweeps through the main streets until early afternoon and there are lively goings-on in the numerous harbourside bars. Walk from the **railway station** along Jernbanegade and turn left into Nørregade for Torvet, which is the hub of the early action. On a corner of the square is the **tourist office** (Mon–Sat 9am–1pm; ☎53/655800), while nearby, at Nørregade 4, the **Køge Museum** (June–Aug daily 10am–5pm; rest of the year Mon–Fri 2–5pm, Sat & Sun 1–5pm; 10kr) contains many remnants from Køge's bloody past, not least the local executioner's sword. If the tales are to be believed, the beheading tool was wielded fairly frequently on Torvet, a place which, perhaps not surprisingly, has also been the scene of several incidences of witchcraft and haunting. On the site of the present *Andelsbank*, the Devil is said to have appeared in the forms of a clergyman, a frog, a dog and a pig, to have thrown a boy from his bed out into the yard, and caused hands to swell – among other unwholesome ailments.

Once its market stalls are cleared away, a suitably spooky stillness falls over Torvet and the narrow cobbled streets that run off it. One of these streets, Kirkestræde, is lined with sixteenth-century half-timbered houses and leads to **Skt. Nikolai Kirke** (Sun–Fri 10am–noon & 2–4pm), where, in the heyday of sea piracy, plunderers captured in Køge Bay were hung from the tower. Along the nave, some of the carved angel faces on the pew ends lack noses, the wooden snouts having been sliced off by drunken Swedish soldiers during the mid-seventeenth century, while the font, an unattractive item in black marble and pine, replaced an earlier one defiled by a woman who performed "an unspeakable act" in it. On a more aesthetic level, Brogade, one of the narrow passageways off Nørregade, contains the **Køge Gallery and Collection** (daily 11am–5pm; free). Besides hosting temporary exhibitions by new artists, the gallery keeps examples of works-in-progress bequeathed by established Danish artists.

Beaches and accommodation

The town's **beaches**, which draw many jaded Copenhagenites on weekends, stretch along the Bay to the north and south of the town. To take full advantage of the sands, stay at one of the two **campsites** beside the southerly beach: *Søndre Strand* (☎53/ 650769) is virtually on the beach, and *Vallø* (☎53/652851) is across Strandvej, close to a pine wood. Both sites are open from April to September. Further away, 2km from the town centre along Ølbyvej, is the Køge **youth hostel** (☎53/651474), open from mid-May to August. There's no bus service to the hostel but the walk there is straightforward.

Around Køge: Stevns Peninsula

Stevns Peninsula, easily reached from Køge, is a fairly neglected part of Zealand, mainly because its coastline is more rugged and less suited to sunbathing than that immediately around Køge or in north Zealand. The town of **STORE HEDDINGE** is the obvious starting point for explorations, and you can get there by private train (*InterRail* and *Eurail* cards not valid) from Køge. In Store Heddinge you'll find a **youth hostel**, open mid-May to September, at Ved Munkevænget 1 (☎53/702022), while there are several **campsites** in the wooded areas around STRØBY.

Central Zealand: Ringsted

Though now little more than a small farming town, **RINGSTED**'s central location made it one of the most important settlements in Zealand from the end of the Viking days until the Reformation. It was the burial place of medieval Danish monarchs as well as being site of a regional *ting*, the open-air court where prominent merchants and nobles determined the administrative decisions for the province.

The Town

The three *ting* stones around which the nobles gathered remain in Ringsted's market square, but they're often concealed by the market itself or the backsides of tired shoppers. The sturdy **Skt. Bendt's Kirke** (May–mid-Sept Mon–Fri 10am–noon & 1–5pm; rest of the year Mon–Fri 10am–noon) is more dominant, and has been for 800 years. Erected in 1170 under the direction of Valdemar I, the church was the final resting place for all Danish monarchs until 1341. Four thousand people are said to have been present for the church's consecration, and although these days it receives a mere trickle of visitors compared to those flocking to the more ornate and recent royal tombs at Roskilde, it represents a substantial chunk of Danish history. Many of the most affluent Zealanders also had themselves buried here, presumably so that their souls could spend eternity mingling with those of the royals. During the seventeenth century, a number of the coffins were opened and the finds are collected in the **Museum Chapel** within the church. Besides the lead slab found inside Valdemar I's coffin, there are plaster casts of the skulls of Queen Bengård and Queen Sofia, a collection of coins found in the church and, unfortunately, only a replica of the **Dagmar Cross**, discovered when Queen Dagmar's tomb was opened in 1697 – the original is in the National Museum in Copenhagen.

Once you've seen the church you've more or less exhausted Ringsted. The town's only other attraction is the **Agricultural Museum** (Mon–Fri 11am–4pm, Sun 1–4pm; 12kr), off Skt. Bendtsgade to the rear of the church, an unexpectedly interesting documentation of the local farming community – but seeing it won't take up more than half an hour.

For stopping overnight, the **youth hostel** (☎53/611526) is handily situated across the road from the church and is open from mid-May to August. The **tourist office** (summer Mon–Fri 10am–5pm, Sat 10am–noon; winter Mon–Fri 9am–noon; ☎53/613400) is a few doors along, between the hostel and Torvet.

Southern Zealand ... and the islands

Southern Zealand is seriously rural, almost solely made up of rich rolling farmland and villages. South from Ringsted, most routes lead to **NÆSTVED**, by far the largest town in the area. Aside from a smartly restored medieval centre and a couple of minor museums, however, Næstved has little in its favour except proximity to unspoilt countryside and the river Suså, which makes it a good base for novice **canoe trips**. The river's lack of rapids and negligible current enables simple manoeuvring in either direction, and, although busy at weekends, it's free of crowds at other times. Canoes can be hired at *Slusehuset* (☎53/646144), down one of the numerous little alleys between Slagelsevej and the harbour, and rates are around 20kr for an hour and 200kr for a day. Off the river, time in the town is best spent by strolling amid the half-timbered buildings and dropping into the **Næstved Museum** at Ringstedgade 4 (Tues–Sun 9am–4pm; 5kr) for its jumble of (mainly religious) oddments and fairly ordinary selection of arts and crafts from the town's past.

The local **tourist office** (May–Oct Mon–Fri 10am–5pm, Sat 9am–noon; rest of the year Mon–Fri 10am–5pm; ☎53/721122) at Købmagergade 20a, just off Skt. Peders Kirkeplads, can fill you in on practical details, and offer suggestions for staying over in Næstved, although the only really cheap spot is the **youth hostel** at Frehasevej 8 (☎53/722091), open from mid-May to mid-September; from the railway station (which is about 1km from the centre on Jernbanegade), turn left into Imagesvej and left again along Præstøvej. There's also a **campsite** (☎53/721122) beside the hostel.

If you have the opportunity, take a trip to the island of **GAVNØ**, a few miles south of Næstved, to see its eponymous eighteenth-century Rococo palace (daily May–Aug 10am–5pm; 10kr), an imposing structure, enhanced by a delightful leafy setting. Parts of the building are still lived in by the descendants of the original owners, but it has a small viewable collection of books and paintings. Bus #85 runs about four times a day during the summer between Næstved town centre and the palace.

Falster, Lolland and Møn

Off the south coast of Zealand are three sizeable islands – **Falster**, **Lolland** and **Møn**. Connected to the mainland by road, all three islands are relatively easy to reach, but once there you'll need your own transport – bikes can be hired from virtually all tourist offices and campsites – to do any serious exploration outside the larger communities, since local buses are either rare or non-existent.

Falster

FALSTER is much the least interesting of the trio. There are some nice woods on the eastern side and some good, but very crowded, beaches along its western coast, particularly around MARIELYST. If you're ultimately making for the ferry port of GEDSER (and West or East Germany*), to the south of Falster, simply stay on the train. The island's main town, **NYKØBING** – usually written Nykøbing F. – has a major sugar industry and a quaint medieval centre, and is of practical use for its **tourist office** at Østerågade 2 (☎53/851301), which handles enquiries for all three islands. There's also a **youth hostel** (☎54/854545) at Østre Allé 112, about 2km from the Nykøbing railway station, with an adjoining **campsite** (☎54/854545), both open from May to mid-September.

Lolland

A private railway (*Inter/EurRail* cards not valid) runs to **LOLLAND** from Nykøbing, taking in SAKSKØBING, MARIBO and finally NAKSKOV, at the western extremity of the island, near to where ferries cross to Langeland. Larger and less crowded than Falster, Lolland is otherwise much the same: wooded, with excellent beaches and lots of quiet explorable corners. Each town has a tourist office, youth hostel and campsite, and **MARIBO**, delectably positioned on the Søndersø, is the most scenic setting for a short stay. The Maribo **youth hostel** is at Skelstrupsvej 19 (☎53/883318), open from March to mid-December, and you'll find the **campsite** at Bangshavevej 25 (☎53/880071), open from Easter to early September.

Møn

Not having a railway, **MØN** is the most difficult of the three islands to get to, though it's well worth the effort (take bus #64 from Vordingborg in Zealand). It's known nationally for its white chalk cliffs – the only cliffs in Denmark – but what really sets Møn apart are its Neolithic burial places, which litter the island by the score, and its unique whitewashed churches, many of which feature fourteenth-century frescoes depicting rural life – the work, apparently, of one peasant painter. The main town, **STEGE**, is, without personal transport, the most feasible base, since it's the hub of the island's (minimal) bus service and has a **campsite**, open May to August, on Falckvej.

---

* The relatively obscure ferry link between Gedser and Warnemünde, in East Germany, which for years has been used almost exclusively by local Danes on cheap shopping expeditions and booze-ups, became overrun by East Germans after the sudden lifting of travel restrictions in November 1989, tiny Gedser becoming many East Germans' first experience of the West.

The best of the Neolithic barrows is **Kong Asker's Høj**, about 20km from
Stege near SPROVE, while the foremost frescoes can be admired at
ELMELUNDE (bus #51 from Stege) and at **FANEFJORD** (take the
Vordingborg bus from Stege and get out at STORE DAMME, then walk), which
also has a Neolithic barrow in the churchyard. As for the cliffs (*Møn Klint*),
they're at the eastern end of the island and stretch for about 8km. Bus #51 runs
between the cliffs and Stege four or five times a day depending on the season.
Fifteen minutes' walk from the cliffs, at Langebjergvej 1, is a **youth hostel** (☎53/
812030), open all year except December.

Bornholm

Although much nearer to Sweden, **BORNHOLM** has been a Danish possession
since 1522. Once an important Baltic trading post, its population now live by fishing, farming and, increasingly, tourism. The coastline is blessed with great
beaches in the south, some invitingly rugged cliffs and hilly landscapes on the
northern side, while the island's centre is marked by some very walkable woods.
It's no wonder that holidaymaking Scandinavian and German families fill
Bornholm each summer.

Despite the crowds, Bornholm is an intriguing and unusual place to visit, and
quite feasible as a stopover if you're going from Denmark to Sweden or West
Germany (or even Poland), to which there are several ferry crossings (see
"Travel Details"). To get the most out of the island, you really need to travel
around the whole coast – not difficult since the island is only about 30km across
from east to west – and spend three or four days doing it. Getting around is easy,
best by bike but simple enough by bus (and all buses are equipped to carry
bikes). Accommodation is straightforward too: there's a youth hostel in each of
the main settlements and campsites are sprinkled fairly liberally around the
coast. The peak weeks of the summer are very busy, and you should phone
ahead to check space. But at any other time of year there'll be little difficulty. The
nightlife on the island can also be surprisingly lively, although often limited to
one spot in each town – invariably the café in the main square.

Ferries from Copenhagen sail to **RØNNE**, the main town on the island, where
a **tourist office** (late June–Aug Fri–Mon 8am–9pm, Tues–Thurs 8am–5pm; rest
of the year daily 9am–5pm; ☎54/950810) can fill you in on accommodation and
transport details, and give you a copy of *Bornholm Denne Uge*, a free weekly listings magazine. If you've arrived on the 6.30am boat, you can celebrate your arrival with breakfast at *Det Røde Pakhus*, at Snellemark 30, or freshly baked bread
from the bakery opposite. Otherwise, though, it's best to move on immediately:
Rønne lacks the character of many of the other island settlements. If you do need
to stay over, there's a **youth hostel**, open April to November, at Søndre Allé 22
(☎53/951340), and a **campsite**, open from mid-May to August, at Strandvejen 4
(☎53/952320).

If you're eager for beaches, make for **DUEODDE**, where there's nothing but
sands, a **youth hostel**, open from May to September, at Skrokkegårdsvej 17
(☎53/988119), and a string of **campsites**. At the other corner of the eastern
coast, **SVANEKE** is quiet, favoured by Danish retirees, but has more spectacular
scenery and the beaches are, once again, superb. There's a **youth hostel** here,
open from mid-April to October, at Reberbanevej 5 (☎53/996242), and two
campsites.

Halfway along the north coast, **GUDHJEM** is pretty too, its tiny streets winding their way around the foot of a hill, and is a good jumping-off point for the 6km trip inland to **ØSTERLARS**, site of the largest and most impressive of the island's fortified Round Churches, which date from the twelfth and thirteenth centuries. **SANDVIG**, on Bornholm's northwest corner, is also the start of a worthwhile walk, along **Hammeren**, the massive granite headland which juts out towards Sweden. Just south of Sandvig are the remains of the thirteenth-century **Hammershus**, not much in themselves but worth a visit for the views from the tall crag which the castle occupied.

If Bornholm suddenly seems too big, and the weather's good, take one of the daily ferries (from Svaneke, Gudhjem or Sandvig; any tourist office will have full details) to the tiny island of **CHRISTIANSØ**, some 25km away, a speck in the Baltic that served as a naval base during the seventeenth century, and later as a prison, though these days the minuscule population prides itself on its spiced herring...

As for **leaving Bornholm**, if you're not going back to Denmark, ferries to Sweden depart from Rønne for Ystad, and from ALLINGE, close to Sandvig, there's a hydrofoil link to Malmö. There's are also crossings from Rønne to Travemünde in West Germany, and, more adventurously, to Sassnitz in Poland.

travel details

Trains

From Copenhagen to Roskilde (25 daily; 26min); Ringsted (20 daily; 55min); Helsingør (30 daily; 50min); Næstved (20 daily; 1hr 30min); Århus (6 daily; 5hr); Odense (25 daily; 3hr) Esbjerg (20 daily; 4hr 30min); Nykøbing (20 daily; 2hr).

From Helsingør to Hellebæk (17 daily; 12min); Hornbæk (17 daily; 24min); Gilleleje (17 daily; 41min); Hillerød (23 daily; 30min).

From Roskilde to Kalundborg (5 daily, connects with ferry to Jutland; 1hr 15min); Korsør (25 daily, connects with ferry to Funen; 54min).

From Køge to Store Heddinge (19 daily; 31min); Fakse (16 daily; 38min).

From Nykøbing to Sakskøbing (21 daily; 16min); Nakskov (21 daily; 49min); Rødby (20 daily; 29min).

Buses

From Copenhagen to Helsingør (30 daily; 1hr); Århus (2 daily; 4hr 45min); Aalborg (2 daily; 6hr); Hantsholm (1 daily; 8hr 45min).

Ferries

From Copenhagen to Rønne (daily during summer, two a day in peak season; 7hr).

From Hundested to Grenå (3 daily in summer; 2hr 40min).

From Kalundborg to Århus via Samsø (8 daily; 3hr).

From Korsør to Lohals (5 daily; 1hr 30min); Nyborg (25 daily; 50min).

From Tårs to Spodsbjerg (16–18 daily; 45min).

International Trains

From Copenhagen to Stockholm (3 daily; 10hr); Helsinki (2 daily; 25hr); Turku (1 daily; 21hr); Oslo (3 daily; 9hr 30min); Bergen (2 daily; 19hr); Narvik (1 daily; 29hr); Kiruna (1 daily; 26hr); Gothenborg (4 daily; 4hr 30min).

International Ferries

From Copenhagen to Malmö (Hydrofoil: 18 daily; 45min. Boat: 2 daily; 1hr 30min); Oslo (1 daily; 16hr).

From Dragør to Limhamn (20 daily; 55min).

From Helsingør Helsingborg (*DSB* 45–60 daily; 25min. *Sundbusserne* 25–30 daily; 20min. *Scandinavian Ferry Lines* (40 daily in summer; 25min).

From Gedser to Warnemünde (4 daily in summer, otherwise 2 daily; 25min); Travemünde (4 daily; 3hr 30min).

From Rødby to Puttgarden (35–40 daily in summer; 1hr).

From Rønne to Ystad (2–5 daily; 2hr 30min); Sassnitz (2 weekly in summer; 4hr).

From Allinge: to Malmö (1 daily in summer; 4hr).

CHAPTER TWO

FUNEN

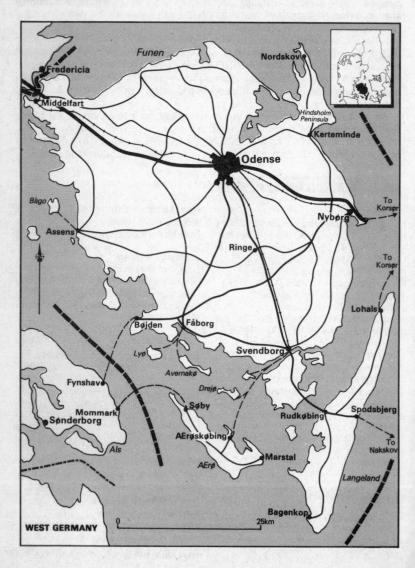

K nown as "the Garden of Denmark", partly for the lawn-like neatness of its fields and partly for the immense amounts of fruit and veg which come from them, **Funen** (*Fyn*) is the smallest of the two main Danish islands and it's true you wouldn't be missing a lot by passing quickly through it on your way between Zealand and Jutland. The pastoral outlook of the place and the coastline draw many, but its attractions are mainly worthy but low-profile cultural things, such as the various collections of the "Funen painters" and the birthplaces of writer Hans Christian Andersen and composer Carl Nielsen, who eulogised the distinctive singsong Funen accent and claimed it inspired his music. If you are keen, the island's best seen by cycling; if the saddle doesn't appeal, you'll be getting around on buses more often than trains, which are relatively scarce here.

Arriving from Zealand brings you through **Nyborg**, a town with a heavily restored twelfth-century castle, though there's really little reason to linger long on the **east coast**, and it's preferable to stick to the cross-country railway which continues to **Odense**, Denmark's third largest city and the obvious base if you're intent on picking through the small surrounding communities by day but want something other than rural quiet to fill the evenings. Close by, the former fishing town of **Kerteminde** retains some faded charm, and is near the **Ladby Boat**, an important Viking relic, and the isolated **Hindsholm peninsula**. To the **south**, Funen's coastal-life centres on **Svendborg** – connected by train to Odense, the island's only other rail line – which has good beaches and a fragmented archipelago of **islands**: vacation territory for the most part, and all served by ferries. The **west** of Funen has just one sizeable town, **Assens**, the surroundings of which hold probably the thickest gathering of manor houses in the country; few of them, however, open to the public, and you'd do well to skim through, either to the offshore islands or to Jutland.

Odense

Funen's sole industrial centre and one of the oldest settlements in the country, named after Odin, the chief of the pagan gods, **ODENSE** gained prominence in the early nineteenth century when the opening of the Odense canal linked the city to the sea and made it the major transit point for the produce of the island's farms. Nowadays it's a pleasant provincial town, with a large manufacturing sector hugging the canal bank on the northern side of the city, well out of sight of the compact old centre – which houses some fine museums and a surprisingly vigorous nightlife. Odense is also known, throughout Denmark at least, as the birthplace of Hans Christian Andersen, and, although it's all done quite discreetly, the fact is as celebrated as you might expect: souvenir shops and new hotels cater for travellers lured by the prospect of a romantic Andersen experience – something they (almost inevitably) won't find.

Information, transport and accommodation

Long distance **buses** terminate at the **railway station**, a ten-minute walk from the city centre, where you'll find the **tourist office** (mid-June–Aug Mon–Sat 9am–7pm, Sun 11am–7pm; rest of the year Mon–Fri 9am–5pm, Sat 9am–noon;

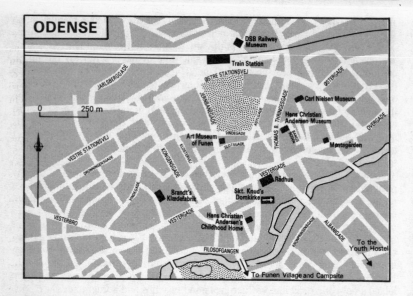

$\square$66/127520), on the ground floor of the nineteenth-century **Rådhus**. Odense has the only **public transport** in Denmark where passengers pay at the end of the trip. If you have to use more than one bus, ask the driver for a "change ticket" (in Danish *omstigning*). Better value if you're seeing Odense's museums is the **Adventure Pass**, which gets you into all of them, and gives unlimited travel on local buses for 60kr (30kr in winter) for its two-day duration; buy it from any tourist office, or most railway stations, youth hostels, campsites and hotels on Funen. If you can't face the buses, you can **rent a bike** at *Cykelcentret*, Allegade 72, or at the tourist office or youth hostel.

Hans Christian Andersen may well be to be blame for Odense's lack of **cheap hotels**. The best bets are the *Ansgarhus Motel*, Kirkegård Allé 17–19 ($\square$66/128800), and the small *Kahema*, Dronningensgade 5 ($\square$66/122821), each of which has doubles for 300–350kr. If this is too much, there's a **youth hostel** at Kragsbjergvej 121 ($\square$66/130425), open all year save for December and early January; take a #6 bus going south to Holluf Pile/Fraugade or Hjallese and get out along Munkebjergvej at the junction with Vissenbjergvej. There's also a *KFUK/KFUM* **InterRail Point** at Rødegårdsvej 91 ($\square$66/142314), open from mid-June to mid-August, and sometimes a free **Sleep-In** in summer – check at the tourist office for the latest information.

The only **campsite** actually in Odense is at Odensevej 102 ($\square$66/114702), near the Funen Village, and is open from late April to mid-September: take bus #1 from the Rådhus or railway station and get out when the bus turns off Hjallesevej into Niels Bohr Vej. The next closest site is *Blommenslyst*, about 10km from Odense at Middelfartvej 494 ($\square$66/967641), which has a few cabins and is open June to August; reach it with buses #830 or #832 – which leave once-hourly from the railway station, taking twenty minutes.

The Town

Save for two outlying museums, Odense is easily seen on foot, and you may as well start with the city's major collection: the **Hans Christian Andersen Museum** at Hans Jensen Stræde 39–43 (June–Aug daily 9am–6pm; April, May & Sept daily 10am–5pm; rest of the year daily 10am–3pm; 15kr), in the house where the writer was born in 1805. Oddly enough, Andersen was only really accepted in his own country towards the end of his life; his real admirers were abroad, which was perhaps why he travelled widely and often, and left Odense at the first opportunity. The son of a hard-up cobbler, Hans Christian Andersen's first home was a single room which doubled as a workshop in what was then one of Odense's slum quarters. It was a rough upbringing: Hans' ill-tempered mother was fifteen years older than his father, whom she married when seven months pregnant with Hans (she also had an illegitimate daughter by another man); his grandfather was insane; and descriptions of his grandmother, often given charge of the young Hans, range from "mildly eccentric" to "a pathological liar". Andersen wrote novels and a few – best-forgotten – plays, but since his death it's his fairy tales which have gained the most renown, partly-autobiographical tales (not least *The Ugly Duckling*) that were influenced by *The Arabian Nights*, German folk stories, and the traditional Danish folktales passed on by the inmates of the Odense workhouse – where Andersen's grandmother was in charge of the garden.

Few of the less-than-fairy-tale aspects of Andersen's life are touched upon in the museum, which was founded on the centenary of Andersen's birth, when Odense began to cash in on their famous ex-citizen. There's a nagging falseness about some aspects of the collection, but since Andersen was a first-rate hoarder it is stuffed with intriguing items: bits of school reports, his certificate from Copenhagen University, early notes and manuscripts of his books, chunks of furniture, his umbrella, and paraphernalia from his travels, including the piece of rope he carried to facilitate escape from hotel rooms in the event of fire. A separate gallery has headphones for listening to some of Andersen's best-known tales, read by the likes of Lawrence Olivier and Michael Redgrave, and a sloppy slide-show which purports to tell the life story of Andersen, to the accompaniment of a warped pianola soundtrack.

The area around the museum, all half-timbered houses and spotlessly clean, car-free cobbled streets, lacks character; indeed, if Andersen was around he'd hardly recognise the neighbourhood, which is now one of Odense's most expensive. For far more realistic local history, head to **Møntergården**, a few streets away at Overgade 48–50 (daily 10am–4pm; 5kr), where there's an engrossing assemblage of artefacts dating from the city's earliest settlements to the Nazi occupation, plus an immense coin collection – from as long ago and far afield as England under Danelaw and Danish rule in Estonia – which might engage you for twice as long as the Andersen museum.

There's more, but not much more, about Andersen at Monkemollestræde 3–5, between Skt. Knud Plads and Klosterbakken, in the tiny **Hans Christian Andersen's Childhood Home** (April–Sept daily 10am–5pm; Oct–March daily noon–3pm; 2kr), where Andersen lived from 1807 to 1819. More interesting, though, is the nearby **Skt. Knud's Domkirke** (May–Aug Mon–Sat 10am–5pm; June–Aug also Sun 11.30am–4pm; April, Sept & Oct Mon–Sat 10am–4pm; Nov–

March Mon–Fri 10am–4pm), whose crypt holds one of the most unusual and ancient finds Denmark has to offer: the **skeleton of Knud II** (King Canute of England). Knud was slain in 1086 by Jutish farmers, angry at the taxes he imposed on them, in the original Skt. Albani Kirke – the barest remains of which were found a couple of years ago in the city park. The king was laid to rest here in 1101, and the miracles and other events of proceeding years (see "History", for more), resulted in his canonisation as Knud the Holy. Close to Knud's is another coffin, thought to hold the remains of Knud's brother, Benedict (though some claim them to be Saint Alban, whose body was brought to Denmark by Knud); displayed alongside is the fading, but impressive, Byzantium-style silk tapestry, sent as a shroud by Knud's widow, Edele. The cathedral itself is noteworthy too. Mostly late-thirteenth-century, it's the only example of pure Gothic church architecture in the country, set-off by a finely-detailed sixteenth-century wooden altarpiece that's rightly regarded as one of the greatest works of the Lübeck mastercraftsman, Claus Berg.

While it doesn't specialise in the paintings of the best-known Funen artists (for which see "Kerteminde" and "Southern Funen"), it's in the **Art Museum of Funen**, at Jernbanegade 13 (daily 10am–4pm, Wed also 7–10pm; 5kr), a few minutes' walk from the cathedral, that you can get an idea of the region's importance to Danish art during the late nineteenth century, when a number of Funen-based painters forsook portraiture of the rich in favour of impressionistic landscapes, nature studies, and recording the lives of the peasantry. The collection also contains some stirring works by many Nordic greats, among them Vilhelm Hammershøi, P.S. Krøyer, and Michael and Anne Ancher, but most striking of all is H.A. Benedekilke's enormously emotive *The Cry*. The modern era isn't forgotten, with a selections from Asger Jorn, Richard Mortensen and Egill Jacobsen, among many others, drawn from the museums' large stock and shown in rotation.

For more modern art, walk along Vestergade to *Brandt's Klædefabrik*, a large former textile factory now given over to a number of creative endeavours (and a popular café). The **Art Exhibition Hall** here (Tues–Sun 10am–5pm; 20kr) is an increasingly prestigious spot for high-flying new talent in art and design to show off; close by are the varied displays of the **Museum of Photographic Art** (same hours; 15kr), taken from the cream of modern (and some not so modern) art photography and almost always worth a view. There's also the more down-to-earth **Danish Graphic Museum** (Mon–Fri 10am–4pm, Sat & Sun 11am–5pm; 10kr), with its bulky machines and other devices chronicling the development of printing, bookbinding and illustrating from the Middle Ages to the present day. You can buy a combined ticket for all three museums for 30kr; for the art and photography shows only 25kr.

Odense's newest museum, and one that might be considered long overdue given the importance of the man it celebrates, is the **Carl Nielsen Museum** inside the concert hall at Carls Bergs Gade 11 (daily 10am–4pm, Thurs until 8pm; 10kr). Though remembered in Denmark mostly for his popular songs, it was Nielsen's opera scores, choral-pieces and symphonies which established him as a major international composer over the turn of the century. Born in a village just outside Odense, Nielsen displayed prodigious musical gifts from an early age and joined the Odense military band as a cornet player when just fourteen (wearing a specially shortened uniform). From there he studied at the Copenhagen conservatoire and went on to worldwide acclaim, the musical cognoscenti in his own country regarding him as having salvaged Danish music from a period of decline. Despite his travels, and long period of residence in Copenhagen, Nielsen continually praised the inspirational qualities of Funen's nature and the island's tuneful dialect, even writing a somewhat sentimental essay in its praise, romanticising the landscape in which "even trees dream and talk in their sleep with a Funen lilt". If you've never heard of Nielsen, be assured that his music is nowhere near as half-baked as his prose: in the museum you can listen to some of his work on headphones, including excerpts from his major pieces and the polka he wrote when still a child. The actual exhibits, detailing Nielsen's life and achievements, are enlivened by the accomplished sculptures of his wife, Anne Marie, many of them being early studies for her equestrian statue of Christian IX, which now stands outside the Royal Stables in Copenhagen.

The final museum in central Odense is hardly essential viewing but anyone impressed with the comfort and efficiency of modern Danish trains may regard a visit to it as a pilgrimage. The **DSB Railway Museum**, immediately behind the railway station (May–Sept daily 10am–4pm; rest of the year daily 10am–3pm; 15kr), houses some of *DSB*'s most treasured artefacts, which include royal and double-decker carriages and an entire reconstructed early-1900s station, as well as a feast of otherwise forgotten facts pertaining to the rise and rise of Danish railways.

Outside the centre: the Funen Village and Funen Prehistoric Museum

South of Odense's centre, the **Funen Village** (June–Aug daily 9am–6.30pm; April, May, Sept & Oct daily 9am–4pm; Nov–March Sun 10am–4pm; 10kr) is an open-air museum, a reconstructed nineteenth-century country village lent an air of authenticity by its wandering geese, and gardens planted and maintained in the style of the time. From the farmhouse to the poorhouse, all the buildings are originals from other parts of Funen with their exteriors painstakingly reassembled and interiors carefully refurnished. In summer, the old trades are revived in the former workshops and crafthouses, and there are free shows at the open-air theatre. Though often crowded, the village is well worth a call, and you should watch out for the village-brewed beer – it tastes rather disgusting but is handed-out free on special occasions. Bus #2 runs to the village from the city centre (get out at the *Den Fynske Landsby* sign), or do what the locals do and hire a boat to float here along the river through Hunderup Skov.

Also easily accessible from the town centre, on bus #6, is the **Funen Prehistoric Museum** (Tues–Sun noon–5pm; 5kr), one of many prehistoric collections in Denmark, but one that at least makes an effort to be different, describing the displays and finds in a more accessible way than is usual. There is, for example, a simulated Bronze Age TV news broadcast, alongside displays describing how ancient symbols are used in modern times. The museum (quite new and still growing) occupies several buildings in the grounds of a sixteenth-century manor house, the very walkable landscaped gardens of which (open from dawn to dusk), are decorated by sculptures from the Danish Academy of Fine Arts.

Eating, drinking and nightlife

Most of Odense's **restaurants and snackbars** are squeezed into the central section, which means there's a lot of competition and potentially some very good bargains during the day. Simply stroll the streets looking for the signs. Failing that, a couple of the city's bodegas *Franck-A*, Vestergade 19, and *Eventyr*, Overgade 18, are reliable spots for sandwiches and speedy refills. For more substantial **eating**, the best of the many pizzerias is *Pizzeria Ristorante Italiano*, Vesterbrogade 9; more exotically, you might try the Thai food of the *Asia House*, Østre Stationsvej 40, or the Mediterranean specialities of *1001 Nats*, Vindegade 57. If you've the money, splurge in style at the seventeenth-century *Den Gamle Kro*, Overgade 23.

For evening **drinking**, the no-frills *On-off*, Ny Vstergade 19, is the place for a game of darts and cheap draught beer; otherwise, and more fashionably, drop into *Café Biografen*, Brandts Passage 39–41, decorated by a dazzling display of movie posters, or the bubbly *Café Klejn*, Vestergade 75.

There's an active **nightlife** in Odense, centred on several downbeat music venues and some swish nightclubs. For local rock music and fringe events, the place for information is the radical art/politics centre *Badstuen*, Østre Stationsvej 26 (☎66/134866), which itself often has live music – as does *Rytmeposten*, across the road at Østre Stationsvej 27a. There's bluesier and jazzier fare to be found in the likeably scruffy *Musikkælderen*, Dronningsgengade 2B, and *Hansens Værtshus*, Asylgade 7, while a more upmarket jazz venue is the *Cotton Club*, Pantheonsgade 5a. *Pakhuset*, Vestergade 75 – adjoining *Café Klejn* – has live bands on Fridays and weekends, and a free rock **disco** on Thursdays; bigger and more mainstream discos include *Grand Palace*, Benedicktsgade 46, and *Atlantic*, Overgade 45–47.

Kerteminde and around

A half-hour bus ride (#890) northeast from Odense, past the huge cranes and construction platforms at MUNKEBO – until recently a tiny fishing hamlet but now the home of Denmark's biggest shipyard – lies **KERTEMINDE**, itself having firm links with the sea: originally in fishing and now, increasingly, in tourism. The town is a sailing and holiday centre and can get oppressively busy during the peak weeks of the summer. At any other time of year, though, it makes for a well-spent day, split between the town itself and the Viking-age Ladby Boat, just outside.

The heart of the town, around the fifteenth-century Skt. Laurentius Kirke and along Langegade and Strandgade, is a neatly, and prettily, preserved nucleus of shops and houses. On Strandgade itself, the **Town Museum** (daily 10am–4pm; 5kr) has five reconstructed craft workshops and a collection of fishing equipment gathered locally. On a grander note, Kerteminde was home to the "birdman of Funen", the painter Johannes Larsen, and a fairly lengthy stroll around the marina and on along Møllebakken brings you to his one-time house, now the **Johannes Larsen Museum** (June–Oct Tues–Sun 10am–4pm; 15kr). During the late nineteenth century, Larsen produced etchings of rural locale and ornithology, going against the grain of prevailing art world trends in much the same way as the Skagen artists (see "Jutland"). The house is kept as it was when Larsen lived there, with his furnishings, knick-knacks, many of his canvases and, in the dining room, his astonishing wall-paintings. To the chagrin of the pious locals, the house in its day became a haunt of the country's more bacchanalian artists and writers. In the garden is a sculpted female figure by Kai Neilsen, a frequent visitor to the house. A story goes that during one particularly drunken party the piece was dropped and the legs broke off; someone called the local *falck*. Despite much inebriated pleading, the (sober) officer who rushed to the scene refused to take the sculpture to hospital.

Practical details

The **tourist office** is opposite the Skt. Laurentius Kirke, across a small alleyway (May–Sept Mon–Fri 9am–5pm, Sat 9am–1pm; Oct–April Mon–Fri 9am–1pm; ☎65/321121), where you can pick up details on Kerteminde's winter hotel accommodation bargains. If you want to stay over at any other time, the only low-cost option is the **youth hostel** (☎65/323929), open all year except mid-December to mid-January, at Tyveleddet 70, in the woods beside Skovvej, a twenty-minute walk from the centre (cross the Kerteminde fjord by the road bridge, take the first left and then turn almost immediately right to reach it). There's also a **campsite** (☎65/321971), open from late April to August, at Hindsholmvej 80, not far from the Larsen museum, on the main road running along the seafront – a thirty-minute walk from the centre.

Around Kerteminde: the Ladby Boat . . . and Hindsholm Peninsula

About 4km from Kerteminde, along the banks of the fjord at Vikingvej 123, is the **Ladby Boat** (May–Oct Tues–Sun 10am–6pm; rest of the year Tues–Sun 10am–3pm; 10kr), a vessel dredged up from the fjord and found to be the burial ship of a Viking chieftain. The craft, along with the remains of weapons, hunting dogs and horses, which accompanied the deceased on his journey to Valhalla, is kept in a tiny purpose-built museum. It's an interesting find, but you'll need only half an hour for a close inspection. Motor boats run from Kerteminde to the exhibit in summer, but it's a pleasant alternative to hire a bicycle and pedal there.

Cycling is also the best way to explore the **Hindsholm Peninsula**, north of Kerteminde, since it's quite small and not easy to visit by public transport. There's not actually much to see, save perhaps the ancient **underground burial chamber** (*Mårhøj Jættestue*) near MARTOFTE, which can be entered (though the bodies, of course, are long gone), but – outside of high season – the area is an unparalleled spot to pitch a tent and revel in the quiet seclusion. Further into the peninsula are two **campsites**: *Bøgebjerg Strand* (☎65/341052), on the shore opposite the island of Romsø, open mid-April to September; and, on the northernmost tip just past Nordskov at Fynshovedvej 694, *Fyns Hoved* (☎65/341014), open from May to mid-September.

Southern Funen: Svendborg, Fåborg, and the islands

Southern Funen is noted, above all, for its many miles of sandy beaches, which are filled by a near shoulder-to-shoulder tourist crush during the peak season. In July and August, the islands of the southern archipelago are more enticing:

connected by an efficient network of ferries, they range from larger chunks of
land such as Tåsinge, Langeland and Ærø – the latter two certainly worth spending a few nights on – to minute and sparsely populated places like Lyø, Avernakø,
Drejø or Skarø, which are a pleasure to explore, if only for a few hours. From
Odense, the simplest plan is to take the train to Svendborg, very much the hub of
south coast activity, although you might well find the smaller Fåborg, an hour's
bus-ride (#960 or #962) from Odense, a better south coast base.

Svendborg

Principal hangout of the Danish yachting fraternity, **SVENDBORG** is unexciting
in itself, but a good place to plot your travels around the archipelago. Ferries sail
from here to Skarø, Drejø and Ærøskøbing. The **tourist office** (July–mid-Aug
Mon–Fri 9am–5pm, Sat 9am–3pm, Sun 9am–noon; mid-March–June & mid-Aug
to mid-Sept Mon–Fri 9am–5pm, Sat 9am–noon; rest of the year Mon–Fri 9am–
5pm; ☎62/210980), opposite the harbour at Møllegade 20, can keep you up-to-
date on ferry sailings and accommodation details for the islands. In Svendborg,
there's a **youth hostel** at Christiansmindevej 6 (☎62/212616), open from mid-
March to October, nicely perched on Svendborg Sund, the strip of water between
the mainland and Tåsinge, and a **campsite** at Ryttervej 21 (☎62/22542), open
from mid-May to the end of August.

Fåborg

FÅBORG is an alternative base for the south coast, a likeably small and sedate
place, rarely as ravished by holiday-makers as Svendborg and with equally good
connections to the archipelago (ferries sail to Søby on Ærø, to Lyø and Avernakø,
and to Gelting in West Germany). If you've an interest in Danish art, the town's
other big attraction is the **Museum of Funen Painting** (April–Oct daily 10am–
4pm; Nov–March Sat & Sun 11am–3pm; 10kr), at Grønnegade 75. The museum
opened in 1910 and quickly became the major showcase for the "Funen artists",
particularly the work of Fritz Syborg and Peter Hansen, both of whom studied
under the influential Kristian Zhartmann in Copenhagen and typically filled their
canvases with richly-coloured depictions of the Funen landscapes. Apart from the
chance to admire the skills of the painters, it's interesting to view the works and
see how little the Funen countryside has changed since their completion.

Almost next door to the museum, at Grønnegade 72–73 just 200m from the
harbour, is the country's quaintest **youth hostel** (☎62/611203), open April to
October; and there's a **campsite** with cabins, open mid-May to August, at
Odensevej 54 (☎62/619004). You can check local travel details at the **tourist
office** at Havnegade 2 (June–mid-Sept Mon–Fri 9am–5pm, Sat 9am–noon; rest of
the year Mon–Fri 9am–noon & 2–5pm; ☎62/610707).

Langeland and Ærø ... and the smaller islands

You don't need to catch a ferry to reach the largest of the southern islands,
LANGELAND, which lies off the southeast coast of Funen and is connected to it
by roadbridge. A long, thin, fertile island, Langland is peaceful and has fine sea
views. Buses run from Svendborg to **RUDKØBING**, the island's main town,
where there's a **youth hostel** at Bagvejen 8 (☎62/511830), open all year, and two
campsites, at Spodsbjergvej 277 (☎62/501092), and Spodsbjergvej 182 (☎62/
501006). There are ferry links to Lolland from Spodsbjerg, about 6km east of
Rudkøbing.

For a more varied few days, however, make for the more westerly **ÆRØ**, where there are ancient burial sites, a peach of a medieval town in **ÆRØSKØBING**, and abundant stretches of sandy beach. In the town, if it's raining, drop into the **Bottle Ship Collection** and the **Memorial Rooms** (both May–Sept daily 9am–5pm; rest of the year daily 10am–4pm; 10kr), at Smedgade 22, for an eye-straining collection of ships in bottles in the former, and a riot of wood carvings, furnishings and timepieces from bygone days in the latter. The **tourist office** (June–Aug Mon–Fri 9am–5pm, Sat 9am–1pm, Sun 9am–noon; rest of the year Mon–Fri 9am–4pm; ☎62/521300), on Torvet, can give information on the island's burial places and numerous secluded spots. For sleeping, there's a **youth hostel** at Smedevejen 13 (☎62/521944), open from April to September, and a cabin-equipped **campsite** at Sygehusvej 40b (☎62/521854), open mid-May to mid-September, appealingly appendaged to the beach.

The **smaller islands** are good strolling and sunbathing country, but offer little else besides. Of them **LYØ**, population forty, is perhaps the most worthwhile for a short visit: the name, roughly translated, means "sheltered from daily life".

travel details

Trains
From Odense to Århus (30 daily; 2hr); Copenhagen (32 daily; 3hr); Esbjerg (30 daily; 2hr); Nyborg (32 daily, linking with the *DSB* ferry to Korsør; 19min); Svendborg (20 daily; 1hr).

Buses
From Odense to Assens (14 daily; 1hr); Fåborg (30 daily; 55min–1hr 18min); Kerteminde (42 daily; 30min); Nyborg (14 daily; 1hr 5min); Svendborg (18 daily; 1hr 24min).
From Kerteminde to Nyborg (17 daily; 33min).
From Svendborg to Fåborg (29 daily; 43mins); Rudkøbing (27 daily; 30min).
From Rudkøbing to Lohals (23 daily; 44min); Spodsbjerg (5 daily; 15min).

Ferries
From Nyborg to Korsør (21 daily; 50min).

South Coast Ferries
There's a mass of connections around the **south coast archipelago** and it's best to check the fine details locally. Some sailings continue year-round, others only operate during the summer. Fares are 20–35kr per person. Frequencies given below are for weekdays; often there are fewer sailings on weekends and public holidays:

From Assens to Bågø (6 daily; 30min).
From Bøjden to Fynshav (8 daily; 50min).
From Fåborg to Søby (6 daily; 1hr); Lyø (6 daily via Avernakø; 2hr).
From Lohals to Korsør (5 daily; 1hr 30min).
From Marstal to Rudkøbing (5 daily; 1hr).
From Spodsbjerg to Tårs (9 daily; 45min). .
From Svendborg to Ærøskøbing (5 daily; 1hr 15min); Drejø (4 daily via Skarø; 1hr 30min).

International Trains
From Odense to Hamburg (6 daily; 4hr 40min).

International Ferries
From Bagenkop to Kiel (3 daily; 2hr 30min).
From Fåborg to Gelting (8 daily; 2hr).

CHAPTER THREE

JUTLAND

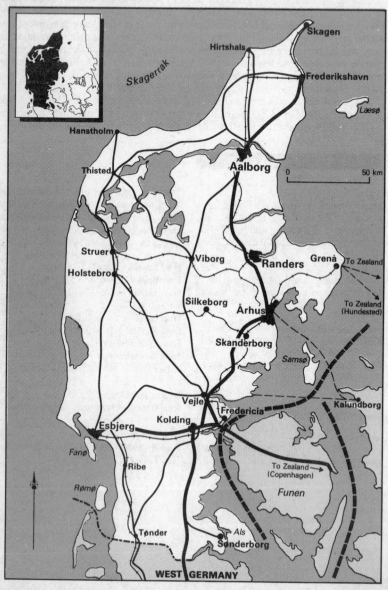

Skagen

Hirtshals

Skagerrak

Frederikshavn

Læsø

Hanstholm

Thisted

Aalborg

0   50 km

Struer

Viborg

Grenå

To Zealand

Holstebro

Randers

Silkeborg

To Zealand
(Hundested)

Århus

Skanderborg

Samsø

Vejle

Fredericia

Kalundborg

Esbjerg

Kolding

Fanø

To Zealand
(Copenhagen)

Ribe

Funen

Rømø

Als

Tønder

Sønderborg

WEST GERMANY

L ong ago, the people of **Jutland** (*Jylland*), the Jutes, were a quite separate tribe from the more warlike Danes who occupied the eastern islands. In pagan times, the peninsula had its own rulers and much power, and it was here that the legendary ninth-century monarch Harald Bluetooth began the process that turned the two tribes into a unified Christian nation. By the dawn of the Viking era, however, the battling Danes had spread west, absorbing the Jutes, and real power in Denmark gradually shifted towards Zealand.

This is where it has largely stayed, making unhurried lifestyles and rural calm (except for a couple of very likeable cities) the overriding impression of Jutland for most visitors. Yet there's much to enjoy in the unspoilt towns and villages, and Jutland's comparative large size and distance from Copenhagen – and the fact that most locals still like to consider themselves to be a cut above the Danes to the east – make it perhaps the most distinct and interesting area in the country.

There are also more regional variations in Jutland than you'll find elsewhere in Denmark. In the south, **Schleswig** is a territory long battled over by Denmark and Germany, though beyond the immaculately restored town of **Ribe**, it holds little of abiding interest. **Esbjerg**, further north, is fairly dull too, but as a major ferry port you might well arrive (or depart) here, and it gives easy access to the hills, meadows and woodlands of eastern Jutland, and to some of the peninsula's better known sights – from the old military stronghold of **Fredericia** to the ancient runic stones at **Jelling** and the modern bricks of **Legoland**.

Århus, halfway up the eastern coast, is Jutland's main urban centre and Denmark's second city, and here, besides a wealth of history and cultural pursuits, you'll encounter the region's best nightlife. It's handy, too, for the optimistically titled "Lake District", a small but appealing area of inland water between **Skanderborg** and **Silkeborg**. Further inland, the retreat of the ice-sheets during the last Ice Age has bequeathed a sharp clash of terrain: stark heather-clad moors break suddenly into dense forests with swooping gorges and wide rivers – contrasts epitomised by the wild memorial park at **Kongenshus** and the grassy vistas of the **Hald Ege**. Ancient **Viborg** is a better base for seeing all this than dour **Randers**, and from here you can head north, either to the blustery beaches of **Limfjordslandet**, or to vibrant **Aalborg**, which sits on the Limfjord's southern bank.

Across the Limfjord is Jutland at its most dramatic: a sandy semi-wilderness which reaches a crescendo of storm-lashed savagery around **Skagen**, at the very tip of the peninsula. **Frederikshavn**, on the way, is the port for boats to Norway and Sweden, and is usually full of those countries' nationals stocking up with (for them) cheap liquor . . .

South Jutland: Esbjerg, Ribe and around

Best known as an entry and exit point (to the UK by sea, to West Germany overland), more people pass through **south Jutland** than probably any other part of the country. Few of them stop here longer than they have to, however, and most head straight for the bright lights of Copenhagen or the holiday areas of the northwest coast. This might seem strange for an area that, as Schleswig, was at the heart of prolonged and bitter international bickering, but it becomes clearer once you've passed through. South Jutland's landscape and run-of-the-mill villages, while pleasant enough, are not exactly diverting.

Esbjerg

The area's only city (though not technically part of Schleswig) is **ESBJERG**, home to the world's biggest fish oil factory, the stench from which matches the gloomy tenor of what must rank as Denmark's least appealing place. If this is your first view of the country, bear in mind it's an entirely untypical one. Esbjerg is a baby by Danish standards, purpose-built as a deep-water harbour during the nineteenth century with none of the older remnants that are a feature of most communities. That said, there are a few places worth a visit and since the *Scandinavian Seaways* ferries from the UK berth here, you may well have the time to see them.

The Town

The best way to get a sense of the city's newness is by dropping into the **Esbjerg Museum** (Tues–Sun 10am–4pm; 10kr) at Nørregade 25, where the meatiest of the few displays recalls the so-called "American period" from the 1890s, when Esbjerg's rapid growth matched that of the US gold-rush towns; here the massive population influx was caused by herring fishing. Also within easy reach of the centre is the **Museum of Art** (daily 10am–5pm; 10kr), although its modern Danish artworks are fairly limp affairs; better to call in for the temporary shows which often give insights into current trends. If your tastes are more technical, miss out the art in favour of the **Museum of Printing** (May–Sept Mon–Fri 2–5pm; 5kr), at Borgergade 6, just off the pedestrianised strip, Kongensgade, which has an entertaining assortment of hand-, foot- and steam-operated presses as well as more recent, still functioning, printing machines (demonstrations on Tuesdays).

With more time to spare, take a bus (#21, #23 or #30 from Skolegade) to the large **Fisheries and Maritime Museum and Sealarium** on Tarphagevej (mid-June to mid-Aug daily 10am–8pm; rest of the year Mon–Fri 10am–5pm, Sat & Sun 10am–6pm; 25kr), where you can cast an eye over the vestiges of the early Esbjerg fishing fleet, see a representative of every type of fish found in Danish waters, and clamber around inside a dark and spooky wartime bunker built by the Germans. The Sealarium is part of a seal research centre, which often rescues seal pups marooned on sandbanks: you can see them swimming and, at 11am and 2.30pm daily, being fed. Just a few minutes' walk from the museum – follow the main road up the hill – is another of Esbjerg's more notable features, the **Sædden Kirke** (Mon–Fri 9am–1pm, Sat 9am–noon, Sun 3–5pm), whose completely redbrick interior is almost hypnotic, especially when the hundreds of hanging lightbulbs are lit – a modern reworking of traditional church architecture which is made even more unusual by its location, inside a shopping centre.

Practical details

The Esbjerg **tourist office** is at Skolegade 33 (Mon–Fri 9am–5pm, Sat 9am–noon; ☎75/125599), on a corner of the main square, and can give you all the practical information you might need, as well as a leaflet describing a short, self-guided walking tour of the city's turn-of-the-century buildings. The **passenger harbour** is a 15–20-minute well-signposted walk from the city centre, and trains to and from Copenhagen connect directly with the ferries, using the harbour station. Otherwise, there are frequent departures to all Danish cities from the main **railway station**, at the end of Skolegade.

If you're staying, you'll find the cheapest **hotel** is the *Sømandshjemmet* at Auktionsgade 3 (☎75/120688), by the harbour. The **youth hostel** is at Gammel Vardevej 80 (☎75/124258), open all year save for late December and January, 25 minutes' walk, or buses #1, #9, #11, #12 or #31, from Skolegade. Adjacent to the hostel is a **campsite** (☎75/125816) with cabins, open from mid-May to mid-September.

The Esbjerg **eating** options are fairly limited if you're on a tight budget, although you can get a decent two-course lunch for 52kr at the *Park Hotel*, on Torvegade, around the corner from the tourist office, and there are a couple of dependable and affordable Italian eateries: *Italiano Pizzeria Ristorante*, at Skolegade 20, and *La Scala*, at Kongensgade 9. More expensively, for around 120kr each, you can sample Esbjerg-style nouvelle cuisine (basically well-prepared fresh fish with everything) at *Pakhuset*, Dokvej 3, in the dock area.

A good place for an early-evening beer or coffee is the popular *Café Christian IX*, overlooking Torvet and named after the monarch commemorated by the square's equestrian statue. What little **nightlife** Esbjerg has is also based around Torvet, chiefly at *La Bonne*, a combined bar, restaurant and disco, and *5 Eifel*, a jazz pub. As you'd guess by their names, the *Andy Capp Pub* and *John Wayne Saloon*, both at Skolegade 17, are more tourist-orientated, although they do serve half-litres of draught beer for 12kr.

Ribe

Just under an hour by train south from Esbjerg (change trains at Bramming), or a 40km cycle-ride, lies the exquisitely preserved town of **RIBE**. In 856 Ansgar built one of the first Danish churches here as a base for his missionaries arriving from Germany; a hundred years later the town was a major stopover point for pilgrims making their way south to Rome. Proximity to the sea allowed Ribe to evolve into a significant trading port, but continued expansion was thwarted by the dual blows of the Reformation and the sanding-up of the harbour. Since then, not much appears to have changed. The surrounding marshlands, which have prevented the development of any large-scale industry, and a long-standing house-preservation programme, have enabled Ribe to keep the appearance and size of medieval times and the old town is a delight to wander in.

The Town

From Ribe's railway station, Dagmarsgade leads to Torvet and the towering **Domkirke** (guided tours in English, German and Danish in summer Mon–Fri 11.30am–12.30pm; 3kr), begun in 1117 on the site of Ansgar's church. Only the "Cat's Head Door" on the south side remains from the original construction, and the church's interior is not as spectacular as either its size or long history might suggest. One item of interest, though, on a pulpit pillar, is a flood-marking from 1634, a year in which Ribe was struck by flooding of such severity that the towns-folk were exempted from taxes for three years. Also, you can normally (it may be closed if the winds are strong) climb the redbrick tower and peer out over the town.

Over the road from the rear of the cathedral, the **tourist office** (☎75/421500) faces the **Weis' Stue**, a tiny inn built around 1600. It's from the inn, at 10pm each evening between May and mid-September, that the **Nightwatchman of Ribe** makes his rounds. Before the advent of gas lighting, the nightwatchman patrolled Danish towns looking through windows for unattended candles which might cause fires. The last real nightwatchman in Ribe made his final tour around the turn-of-the-century, but the custom has recently been re-introduced. The watch-man, dressed in a replica of the original uniform and carrying an original lantern (the sharp tip doubling as a weapon), walks the narrow alleys of Ribe singing songs written by Hans Adolf Brorson (bishop of Ribe in the mid-eighteenth century, whose statue you may have noticed outside the cathedral), and talking about the town's history while stopping at points of interest. It's obviously laid on for tourists, but the tour is free and can be fun. Present yourself outside the Weis' Stue a few minutes before 10pm and wait for the distinctive figure to emerge from the bar.

That's more or less all there is to Ribe, save for the paltry remains of **Riberhus Slot**, a twenty-minute walk away on the northern side of the town. The twelfth-century castle which stood here was a popular haunt with the Danish royals for a couple of centuries but was already fairly dilapidated when it was demolished by Swedish bombardment in the mid-seventeenth century. The statue of Queen Dagmar, a recent addition to the site standing in bewitching isolation, makes the trek worthwhile.

Practical details

If you stick around for the nightwatchman's tour, you'll probably need to spend the night in the town. There's a **youth hostel** (☎75/420620), open from May to mid-September, on the opposite side of the river from Skibbroen: cross the river bridge and turn left into Skt. Peders Gade. Failing that, the atmospheric *Hotel Dagmar* (☎75/420033), opposite the Weis' Stue and just as old, has double rooms for around 400kr, and a cellar bar which is the best and most crowded spot for an **evening drink**. The nearest **campsite** (☎75/420887) is 2km from Ribe, along Farupvej: it has cabins and opens from April to mid-September.

Rømø and Tønder

From SKÆRBÆK, a few kilometres south of Ribe, you can take a bus (#29) across 12km of tidal flats to the island of **RØMØ**. The action of sea and wind has given the island a wild and unkempt appearance, as well as causing a wide beach to form along the eastern side and allowing wildlife to flourish all over. There's a good chance of seeing seals basking during the spring while, on the other side of the summer, many migratory wading birds can be found, dodging the island's plentiful sheep. Besides enjoying the sands, and the fact that Rømø is a noted **nude bathing** spot, it's possible to **cross the border** without returning to the Danish mainland by using the ferry which sails from Havneby to List, on the West German island of Sylt. There are several spots on Rømø to stay overnight: in Havneby there's a **youth hostel** at Lyngvejen 7 (☎74/755188), open from mid-March to October, and just to the north of the town at Havnebyvey 201, on the #29 bus route, is a **campsite** (☎74/755122) with cabins.

On the mainland, the chief town on the Danish side, close to the border, is **TØNDER**. Founded in the thirteenth century, the town's cobbled streets still contain many ancient gabled buildings and it makes an attractive low-key base for a day or two, especially if you're here around the end of August, when the annual **jazz and blues festival** features many free street events. Details of the festival and other local matters can be obtained from the **tourist office** at Østergade 2A (☎74/721220). Otherwise call into the **Tønder Museum**, in the gatehouse of the sixteenth-century castle, and the adjoining **South Jutland Art Museum** (closed Mon) for its changing exhibitions of twentieth-century Danish works. Tønder has the charm to make you want to stay at least a night before moving on. To this end, there's a **youth hostel** at Sønderport 4 (☎74/723500), a kilometre from the railway station and open all year except December and January, and a **campsite** at Holmevej 2a (☎74/721849), open from April to September.

East from Tønder: Haderslev and Sønderborg

The eastern coast of southern Jutland has fewer spots of interest. KOLDING is a travel hub but not much more; **HADERSLEV**, once a favourite royal residence, enjoys a picturesque position on the edge of a lengthy fjord, and sports some decent, if slender, beaches and a generous sprinkling of campsites. The **tourist office** at Apotekergade 1 (☎74/525550), can provide travel and camping details for the vicinity, but while you're in the town drop into the **Haderslev Museum** (May–Sept Tues–Fri 10am–5pm; rest of the year Tues–Fri noon–4.30pm, Sat & Sun noon–5pm; free) for its regional history collection and the room devoted to the Wassner brothers – painters Valentin, Berhard and Eduard. For staying in Haderslev itself, there's a **youth hostel** at Erlevvej 34 (☎74/521347), open from February to November. The hostel is 2km from the railway station: walk through the town centre and turn right off Mølleplads. The **campsite** (☎74/527880), with cabins and open from May to August, is at Christiansfeldvej – easily spotted by the tall white watertower which sprouts above the trees.

Further to the south, **SØNDERBORG**, which straddles Jutland and the island of Als, is at the centre of an area almost claustrophobically laden with **campsites**, most of them packed in summer. While here, visit **Sønderborg Slot**, which may not be the grandest but is certainly one of Denmark's oldest castles – thought to have been built by Valdemar I during the twelfth century – where you can get the lowdown on south Jutland's history and the Schleswig wars. Also in the town is a **tourist office** at Rådhustorvet 7 (☎74/423555), and you can stay overnight at the **youth hostel** (☎74/423112), open all year and situated at Kærvej 70, a kilometre from the railway station. There's a **campsite** (☎74/424189), open from May to mid-September, on Ringgade in a tree-studded area very close to the best local beaches.

East Jutland: Fredericia, Vejle and around

There's little that's unique about **east Jutland**, although its thick forests are a welcome change if you're coming directly from the windswept western side of the peninsula. As the main route between Funen and the big Jutland cities, it's a busy region with good transport links, but the area has only two sizeable towns: **Fredericia** is the more unusual, **Vejle** the more appealing – though neither justify a lengthy stay.

Fredericia

FREDERICIA – junction of all the rail routes in east Jutland and those connecting the peninsula with Funen – has one of the oddest histories (and layouts) in Denmark. It was founded in 1650 by Frederik III who envisaged a strategically-placed reserve capital and a base to defend Jutland. Three nearby villages were demolished and their inhabitants forced to assist in the building of the new town – which afterwards they had no option but to live in. Military criteria resulted in wide streets that followed a strict grid system and low buildings enclosed by high earthen ramparts, making the town invisible to approaching armies. The railway age made Fredericia a transport centre and its harbour expanded as a consequence. But it still retains a soldiering air, full of memorials to heroes and victories, and is the venue of the only military tattoo in Denmark – an event which failed elsewhere due to lack of interest.

The Town

The half-hour walk from the **railway station** along Vesterbrogade toward the town centre, takes you through Danmarks Port, and the most impressive section of the old ramparts. They stretch for 4km and rise 15m above the streets, and walking along the top gives a good view of the layout of the town. But it's the **Landsoldaten** statue, opposite Princes Port, which best exemplifies the local spirit. The bronze figure holds a rifle in its left hand, a sprig of leaves in the right, and its left foot rests on a captured cannon. The inscription on the statue reads "6 Juli 1849", the day the town's battalion made a momentous sortie against German troops in the first Schleswig war – an anniversary celebrated as **Fredericia Day**. The downside of the battle was the 500 Danes who were killed and lie in a mass grave in the grounds of **Trinitatis Kirke** in Kongensgade.

Predictably, 300 years of armed conflict form the core of the displays at the **Fredericia Museum** at Jernbanegade 10 (mid-June to mid-Aug daily 10am–5pm; rest of the year Tues–Sat noon–4pm, Sun 10am–4pm; 10kr). There are also typical local house interiors from the seventeenth and eighteenth centuries, and a dreary selection of archaeological finds only offset by the glittering cache of silverware in the crafts department.

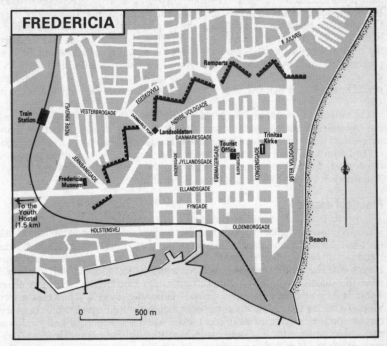

Practical details

Unless you want to laze on Fredericia's fine **beaches**, which begin at the eastern end of the ramparts, there's little reason to hang around the town very long. If you do want to stay, however, there's a **youth hostel** at Skovløbervænget 9 (☎75/921287), open from mid-February to November. The hostel's slightly awkward to reach, 2km from the railway station and further still from the town centre (bus #3 covers the town route, but only once an hour). Alternatively, use the **campsite** (☎75/957183), open from April to October, on the Vejle fjord, adjacent to a public beach and very crowded during fine weather and at holiday times. You can get other practical information from the centrally-placed **tourist office** (☎75/921377), on the corner of Dale Gade and Jyllandsgade.

Vejle

A short train-ride north of Fredericia, **VEJLE**, a compact harbour town on the mouth of the Vejle fjord, is home to the *Tulip* factory, from where 400 million sausages a year begin their journey to British breakfast tables. It's also the best base for exploring the contrasting pleasures of the Viking burial mounds at Jelling and – rather more famously – the Legoland complex at Billund, both within easy reach by bus or train.

The Town

Chief attraction in Vejle itself is **Skt. Nicolai Kirke** (Mon–Fri 9am–5pm, Sat 9am–noon, Sun 9am–11.30am) in Kirke Torvet, in which a glass-topped coffin holds the peat-preserved torso of a woman found in the Haraldskær bog. Originally the body was thought to be the corpse of the Viking queen, Gunhilde of Norway, but the claim was disputed and carbon tests carried out in 1977 dated the body at around 490 BC – too old to be a Viking but nonetheless still the best preserved "bog body" in the country. Another macabre feature of the church, though you can't actually see it, are 23 skulls in sealed holes in the northern transept. Legend has it that the skulls belong to 23 thieves who were executed in 1630.

The **Museum of Art** and **Vejle Museum** (both Tues–Sun 11am–4pm; free) are conveniently placed next to each other at Flegborg 16 and 18, but are more time-killers than collections of importance. The art museum specialises in graphics and drawings, has a collection of twentieth-century painting and sculpture and often stages innovative temporary exhibitions from around the world; the Vejle Museum has a small collection of local historical and archaeological finds.

Practical details

The **youth hostel**, on Gammel Landevej (☎75/825188), closed only for a month over Christmas, is a gleaming new building set in woods on one of the hills above the town. From the bus station, take bus #1 – or, on weekdays, #9 – which runs roughly half-hourly, bound for Mølholm, and get out at the stop just after Hestehavn. The local **campsite** is at Nørremarksvej 18 (☎75/823335): to reach it from the town centre, follow Nørrebrogade into Horsensvej, turn right along Roms Hule and then follow the signs. Additionally, there's sometimes a free **Sleep-In** during the summer at the Sports Hall on Vestre Engvej, details of which can be checked at the **tourist office**, tucked into a small courtyard off the lower end of the pedestrianised Søndergade(July Mon–Fri 9am–6pm, Sat 9am–1pm; rest of the year Mon–Fri 9am–5pm, Sat 9am–noon; ☎75/821955). The office also sells **tourist tickets** for bus travel in the surrounding area, including Jelling and Billund.

Around Vejle: Jelling and Billund

About 12km from Vejle, around twenty minutes by train, the village of **JELLING** is known to have been the site of pagan festivals and celebrations, and it has two **burial mounds** thought to have contained King Gorm, Jutland's tenth-century ruler, and his queen, Thyra. The graves were found early this century and, although only one coffin was actually recovered, there is evidence to suggest that the body of Gorm was removed by his son, Harald Bluetooth, and placed in the adjacent church – which Bluetooth himself built around 960 after his conversion to Christianity. Excavations carried out on the site of the church revealed a skeleton and items similar to ones discovered in the empty mound, backing up the theory that Harald exhumed his pagan father to give him a Christian burial. In the grounds of the present church are two big **runic stones**, one erected by Gorm to the memory of Thyra, the other raised by Harald Bluetooth in honour of Gorm. The texts, hewn into the granite, record the era when Denmark began the transition to Christianity.

Train services from Vejle to STRUER and HERNING stop at Jelling: both run about once an hour on weekdays and less frequently at weekends. If you can stomach such things, a **vintage train** operates between Vejle to Jelling and back every Sunday in July and the first Sunday in August. By **bike**, the most direct route from Vejle is the A18, although a more scenic choice is through the hamlet of Uhre and along the shores of Fårup Sø. There's a **campsite** (☎75/871653) with cabins about a kilometre west of Jelling church, on Mølvangsvej, open from mid-April to mid-September,

BILLUND, 20km or so west from Vejle, has two claims to fame, both wildly disproportionate to its size: an international airport, and Denmark's top kiddies' attraction in **Legoland**, a cornucopia of model buildings, animals, aeroplanes and other things assembled from the toy bricks – which were, in case you didn't know, invented by a Dane. Bus #912 leaves Vejle about once an hour on most days, stopping at Legoland after about 55 minutes. Children love the place; if you don't have any, avoid it like the plague.

The Lake District: Skanderborg and Silkeborg

North of Vejle is the small, rather grandly titled, Danish **Lake District**, which consists of a handful of small lakes surrounded by low hills dotted with several dozen campsites. **SKANDERBORG**, on the area's eastern fringe, gives access to Denmark's highest point, **Ejer Baunehøj**, 171m high and with several steep footpaths leading up to its summit. But **SILKEBORG** is perhaps the area's most lively centre, handsomely spread across several tongues of water. Here, the **tourist office**, at Torvet 9 (Mon–Fri 9am–5pm, Sat 9am–noon; ☎86/821911), can supply a map of the nearby **nature walks**, and when the limbs start to ache you can invigorate yourself by visiting the excellent collection of abstract art by Asger Jorn and others inside the **Museum of Art** at Gudenåvej 7–9 (April–Oct daily 10am–5pm; rest of the year Sat & Sun noon–4pm; 20kr). It was to Silkeborg that Jorn, Denmark's leading modern painter and founder of the influential COBRA group, came to recuperate from tuberculosis and, from the 1950s to his death in 1973, he donated an enormous amount of his work – and that of other artists – to the town, now displayed in this purpose-built museum. Modest by comparison is the local **Cultural Museum** (mid-April to Oct 10am–5pm; rest of the year Wed, Sat & Sun noon–4pm; 15kr), where the only really notable exhibits are the "Tollund Man" and the "Elling Girl" – 2000-year-old peat bodies.

If you want to stay over in the region, there are a number of affordable **hotels** secreted about the countryside; the Silkeborg tourist office will advise on prices and how to get to them. In Silkeborg itself the *Linå Kro*, Linåvej 17 (☎86/841443), and *Hotel Silkeborgsøerne*, on Søpladsen (☎86/841201), have doubles for around 300kr. The town also has a **youth hostel**, only closed over Christmas, at Åhavevej 55 (☎86/823642), a ten-minute walk from the town centre. There are also a couple of nearby **campsites**, both with cabins and lakeside locations: *Indelukkets* (☎86/822201), open from May to mid-September, on Vejlsøvej, a short way south of the town, and *Århusbakkens* (☎86/822824), open from April to mid-September, on Århusvej, to the north.

Århus

Geographically at the heart of the country and often regarded as Denmark's cultural capital, ÅRHUS typifies all that's good about Danish cities: it's small enough to get to know in a few hours, yet big and lively enough to have plenty to fill both days and nights; indeed you can even socialise around the clock if you want to. More unusually, it's also something of an architectural showcase, with several notable buildings spanning a century of top Danish and international design. A number of these buildings form the city's university campus, whose many students – the most radical in the country during the Sixties – contribute to a nightlife that's on a par with that of Copenhagen; it's no fluke, either, that the city is the home of the Danish rock music scene.

Despite Viking-era origins, the city's present-day prosperity is due to its long, sheltered bay, on which the first harbour was constructed during the fifteenth century, and the more recent advent of railways, which made Århus a nationally important trade and transport centre. Easily reached by train from all the country's bigger towns, and at one end of the only direct ferry link between Jutland and Zealand, Århus also receives non-stop flights from London. There's certainly no better place for a first taste of Denmark.

Arrival, information and getting around

Trains and buses stop on the southern edge of the city centre, close to the main points of interest and hotels. From the railway station it's a short walk along Park Allé, from the bus station a similar distance along Sønder Allé, to the **tourist office** (mid-June to Aug daily 9am–9pm; rest of the year Mon–Fri 9am–4.30pm, Sat 9am–noon; ☎86/121600), on the ground floor of the city's Rådhus (see below). **Airport buses** from Tirstrup arrive at (and leave from) the railway station; the one-way fare for the fifty-minute journey is 45kr.

Getting around is best done on foot: the city centre is compact and you'll seldom need to use the **buses** at all unless you're venturing out of the city to the beaches or woods on the outskirts. If you do, the transport system divides into four zones: one and two cover all the central area, three and four reach into the country. The basic ticket is the so-called **"cash ticket"**, which costs 10.50kr from the machine at the rear of the bus and is valid for any number of journeys during the time stamped on it (usually about an hour from the time of buying). If you're around for several days and doing a lot of bus hopping (or using local trains, on which these tickets are valid), it's best to buy either a **tourist ticket**, which costs 25kr for 24 hours, or a **multi-ride ticket**, which can be used 12 times and costs 80kr for rides within the immediate city area; it can also be used by more than one person at once. These tickets can be bought at newstands, campsites and shops displaying the *Århus Sporveje* sign. The driver won't check your ticket but a roving inspector might, and there's an instant fine of 150kr for travelling without one. The **bus information office** (8am–6pm) is at H.H. Seedorffs Stræde 8, on the other side of Sønder Allé from the Rådhus.

Cycling is another viable way to get around, particularly if you're heading out along the coast to Moesgård. Although there are the usual number of outlets around the city, it's cheapest to **hire a bike** from the tourist office or youth hostel.

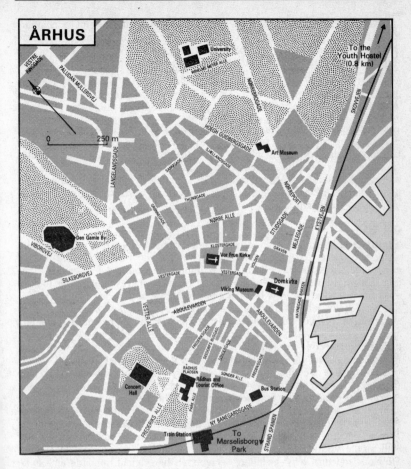

Sleeping: hotels, hostels and camping

Århus is fairly well-served by cheap accommodation. If you don't mind going without a private bathroom, the following are the two best-priced and best-located **hotels**: *Eriksens Hotel Garni*, at Banegårdsplads 6 (☎86/136296), and the *Park Hotel*, Sønder Allé 3 (☎86/123231), both of which have doubles for 295kr excluding breakfast. Slightly more expensive, but just as usefully placed, the *Århus Sømandshjem og hotel*, at Havnegade 20 (☎86/121599), has doubles for 330kr, including breakfast. If you want something more luxurious, there are plenty of mid-range hotels in the 400–500kr bracket; the tourist office has a long list.

For seeing the city, you might well find a cheap central hotel preferable to the Århus **youth hostel** on Østre Skovvej (☎86/167298), which is rather out on a limb – though at least its wooded location is close to a beach. It's a 4km-ride on bus #1, #2 or #8 from the bus or railway stations; get off at Marienlands, where the #1 and #2 turn around. The hostel's open all year except mid-December to mid-January.

Of a number of **campsites** in the Århus area, two are most useful for commuting to the city: *Blommehaven* (☎86/270207), overlooking the bay about 7km from the city centre, open from late April to August, and reached with bus #19 or less directly bus #6; and *Århus Nord* (☎86/231113), with cabins and open all year, 8km north of the city and accessible with bus #117 or #118 from the bus station.

The City

For reasons of simple chronology, Århus divides into two clearly-defined parts: even combined, these fill a small and easily walkable area. The old section, close to the cathedral, is a tight cluster of medieval streets with several viewable churches and a couple of museums, as well as the bulk of the city's nightlife. The more recent sections of Århus form a collar around the old centre, inevitably with less character, but nonetheless holding plenty that's worth seeing, not least the city's major architectural works.

Old Århus

Søndergade is Århus's main street, a pedestrianised strip lined with the major shops and overpriced snackbars that leads down into Bispetorvet and the old centre, the streets of which form a web around the **Domkirke** (Mon–Sat May–Sept 9.30am–4pm; rest of the year Mon–Sat 10am–3pm). Take the trouble to push open the cathedral's sturdy doors, not just to marvel at the soccer-pitch-length – this is easily the longest church in Denmark – but for a couple of features which spruce-up the plain Gothic interior, most of which is a fifteenth-century rebuilding after the original twelfth-century structure was destroyed by fire. At the eastern end, the altarpiece is a grand triptych by the noted Bernt Notke, one of few pre-Reformation survivors. Look also at the painted – as opposed to stained – glass window behind the altar, the work of the Norwegian Emmanuel Vigeland (brother of Gustav), most effective when the sunlight is directly on it.

From the time of the first settlement here, in the tenth century, the area around the cathedral has been the core of Århus life. A number of Viking-age remains have been discovered beneath the present *Andelsbank*, on Clements Torv across the road from the cathedral, some of which are now displayed in the bank as the **Viking Museum** (Mon–Fri 8am–4pm, Thurs until 6pm; free; enter the bank and turn left), including sections of the original ramparts and some Viking craftsmans' tools, alongside some informative accounts of early Århus. Also within a few strides of the cathedral, at Domkirkeplads 5, the **Women's Museum** (*Kvindemuseumforeningen*) (Tues–Sun; 10kr) is one of Denmark's most innovative museums, staging temporary exhibitions on many aspects of women's lives and lifestyles past and present.

After seeing the museums, venture into the small, very strollable streets close by, lined by innumerable preserved buildings, many of them housing antique shops, record stores or chic boutiques and all good for a browse. *Elka Petersen Antiques*, at Studsgade 12, is particularly worth a look, stuffed with gems and junk, at prices that will sometimes be marked down for foreigners. The area is also home to some of the city's most enjoyable cafés, and is popular drinking territory after dark (see "Nightlife", below).

West of here, along Vestergade, the thirteenth-century **Vor Frue Kirke** (May–Aug Mon–Fri 10am–4pm, Sat 10am–2pm; rest of the year Mon–Fri 10am–2pm, Sat 10am–noon) is actually the site of three churches, most notable of which is the eleventh-century **crypt church** (go in through the main church entrance and walk straight ahead), which was discovered, buried beneath several centuries-worth of rubbish, during restoration work on the main church in the 1950s. There's not exactly a lot to see, but the tiny, rough-stone church – resembling a hollowed-out cave – is strong on atmosphere, especially during the candle-lit Sunday services. Except for Claus Berg's detailed altarpiece, there's not much to warrant a look in the main church, but you should make your way through the cloister (to the left of the entrance) remaining from the pre-Reformation monastery, now an old folks' home – for the medieval frescoes inside the third church, which depict local working people rather than the more commonly found biblical scenes.

Modern Århus

If you've visited the tourist office, you've already been inside one of the modern city's major sights: the functional-style **Århus Rådhus**, built in the 1940s and as capable of inciting high passions – for and against – today as it was when it opened. From the outside, it's easy to see why opinions should be so polarised: the coating of Norwegian marble lends a sickly pallor to the building and the main block has the shape of a bloated Nissen hut. But on the inside, the finer points of architects Arne Jacobsen and Erik Møller's vision make themselves plain, amid the harmonious open-plan corridors and the extravagantly-used glass. You're free to walk in and look for yourself, but consider taking a **guided tour** – they're free, are conducted in English at 4pm on weekdays during the summer, and reveal a mass of fascinating details. Above the entrance hangs Hagedorn Olsen's huge mural, *A Human Society*, symbolically depicting the city emerging from the last war to face the future with optimism. In the council chamber, the lamps appear to hang suspended in mid-air (in fact they're held by almost invisible threads), and the shape of the council leader's chair is a distinctive curvy form mirrored in numerous smaller features throughout the building, notably by the ashtrays in the lifts – though many of these have been pilfered by tourists. Perhaps most interesting of all, however, if only for the background story, are the walls of the small civic room, covered by the intricate floral designs of the artist Albert Naur: the work took place under the Nazi occupation and in it Naur concealed various allied insignia. Finally, a lift (opened for the public at noon and 2pm during the summer; free) climbs to the bell tower and a view over the city and across the bay.

A more recent example of Århus' municipal architecture is the glass-fronted **Concert Hall**, a short walk behind the Rådhus, which has been the main venue for opera and serious music in the city since it opened in 1982. It's worth dropping into, if only for the small café (open noon–2pm) where you might be entertained for free by a string quartet or a lone fiddler.

It's just a few minutes' walk from the Concert Hall to the city's best-known attraction, **Den Gamle By**, on Viborgvej (June–Aug daily 9am–5pm, May & Sept daily 10am–5pm; shorter hours during the rest of the year; 25–30kr depending on season), an open-air museum of traditional Danish life, with sixty-odd half-timbered houses from all over the country, dismantled and moved here piece by piece. With many of the craftsmans' buildings used for their original purpose, the overall aim of the place is to give an impression of an old Danish market town. This is done very effectively, although sunny summer days bring big crowds here, and the period flavour is strongest outside of high season, when visitors are fewer.

If you're at all interested in Danish art, you may as well miss out Den Gamle By in favour of the **Århus Art Museum** (Tues–Sun 10am–5pm; 20kr) in Vennelystparken, a little way north. There's enough in the museum to give a good overview of the main national trends, from the late-eighteenth-century formal portraits and landscapes by Jens Juel, and the finely-etched scenes of domestic tension by Jørgen Somme, through to the more internationally renowned names, particularly Vilhelm Hammershoi, represented here by some of his moody interiors. There's lots of viewable modern stuff too. Besides the radiant canvases of Asger Jorn and Richard Mortensen, don't miss Bjørn Nørgård's sculptured version of Christian IV's tomb: the original, in Roskilde Cathedral, is stacked with riches; this one features a coffee-cup, an egg and a ballpoint pen.

Though so plain you'd barely notice it, the Art Museum building is often on the itinerary of architects visiting the city. It's reckoned to be a prime example of the modern Danish style, using *de rigueur* redbricks and white-framed rectangular windows, with no decoration at all. There's much more of this look on the **university campus**, a short way up Høegh Guldbergs Gade, sprawling across the hillside and overlooking the rest of the city. Most of it was built to the plans of C.F. Møller and completed just after the last war.

Out from the centre

On Sundays Århus resembles a ghost town, with most locals spending the day in the parks, woodlands or beaches on the city's outskirts. If you are around on a Sunday – or, for that matter, any sunny day in the week – you could do much worse than join them. The closest beaches (and woods) are just north of the city at **Riis Skov**, near the youth hostel, easily reached with buses #1, #2 or #8.

South of the city: Marselisborg Skov and Dyrehaven

For a more varied day, head **south** through the thick Marselisborg Skov and on to the prehistoric museum at Moesgård. Bus #6 runs directly to the museum, while bus #19 takes a more scenic route along the edge of Århus Bay, leaving you with a 2-kilometre walk to the museum. If you don't fancy the buses, be advised that this is ideal territory for cycling, or gentle hiking.

The **Marselisborg Skov** is a large park which contains the city's football and horse-trotting stadiums and sees a regular procession of people exercising their dogs. It also holds the diminutive **Marselisborg Slot**, summer home of the Danish royals, the landscaped grounds of which can be visited (between dawn and dusk) when the monarch isn't staying. Further south, across Carl Nielson Vej, the park turns into a dense forest, criss-crossed with footpaths but in which it's easy to get lost.

A simpler route to navigate, and one with better views, is along Strandvejen which runs between the eastern side of the forest and the shore. Unbroken footpaths run along this part of the coast and give many opportunities to scamper down to rarely-crowded (though often pebbley) beaches. Also on this route, near the junction of Ørnerdevej and Thormsøllervej, is the **Dyrehaven**, or Deer Park – as the name suggests, a protected section of the wood that's home to many deer. The animals can be seen (if you're lucky, they're not the most gregarious of creatures) from the marked paths running through the park from the gate on the main road. A short way on from the Dyrehaven entrance is the *Blommehaven* campsite (see "Sleeping"), and, several kilometres further, part of the prehistoric trackway belonging to the Moesgård prehistoric museum.

Moesgård Prehistoric Museum

Occupying the buildings and grounds of an old manor house, **Moesgård Prehistoric Museum** (April to mid-Sept daily 10am–5pm; rest of the year Tues–Sun 10am–5pm; 20kr, students 8kr), details Danish civilisations from the Stone Age onwards with copious finds and easy-to-follow illustrations, though it's the Iron Age which is most comprehensively covered and holds the most dramatic single exhibit – the "Grauballe Man", a skeleton dated at 80 BC discovered to the west of Århus. Found in a peat bog, which kept the carcass in amazingly good condition, it was even possible to discover what the deceased had eaten for breakfast (burnt porridge made from rye and barley) on the day of death. Only a roomful of imposing runic stones, further on, capture the imagination as powerfully as does the peat body, and you'll fully exhaust the museum in an hour.

The rest of your time should be spent following the "prehistoric tramway", which runs from the grounds of the museum (from the far corner of the courtyard) to the sea and back again. The 3-kilometre long path leads through fields and woods, past a scattering of reassembled prehistoric dwellings, monuments and burial places. On a fine day, the walk itself is as enjoyable as the actual sights, and you could easily linger for a picnic when you reach the coast. If you don't have the energy for any more walking, you can take a #19 bus back to the city from here; the stop is a hundred metres to the north.

Eating

You'll find the best **lunch** bargains simply by cruising the cafés and restaurants of the old city and reading the notices chalked up outside them. *Café Basilika* (address below) is just one which has frequent lunchtime specials for under 45kr. Two streets in this area, Skolegade and Skolegyde, are particularly worth a look, each with a number of unpretentious eateries (so unpretentious, they often look closed when they're open). Two are *Lille Karin*, at Skolegade 4–6, noted for its pancakes, and *Pinds Café*, Skolegade 11, which does excellent smørrebrød and set-lunches for 58kr. Further afield, and ideal for vegetarians with a bit of spare cash, is the wholefood of *Den Grønne Gren*, Vestergade 7, or *Kokken*, the restaurant section of the cultural centre *Huset* (address below), which has a selection of mouthwatering snacks for around 25kr. If it's Saturday, make for the all-you-can-eat smørrebrød, costing just 10kr, at *Fru Jensen*, Mejlgade 20.

Dinner is going to be much more pricey unless you stick to one of the many pizzerias. *Roma*, Frederiksgade 78, is about the best in the cheaper price-range; if you have a bit more money, try *Italia*, at Åboulevarden 9. Equally good value are the Mediterranean specialities of *Kasba*, at Vestergade 50, or, ideal for an exotic blow-out, the Mongolian food at *Ulaan Bator*, Vestergade 36, where you eat as much as you want for 98kr.

If finances are tight, or you just want to stock up for a **picnic**, use one of the *Special Smørrebrød* outlets, at Sønder Allé 2 and Ny Banegårdsgade 53. For more general food shopping, there's a branch of *Brugsen* on Søndergade, and a **late-opening supermarket** (8am–midnight) at the railway station.

Nightlife

Århus is the only place in Denmark with a **nightlife** to match that of Copenhagen. There's a diverse assortment of ways to be entertained, enlightened, or just inebriated, almost every night of the week. And while things sparkle socially all year round, if you visit during the **Århus Festival**, a week-long orgy of arts events held annually at the start of September, you'll find even more to occupy your time.

Cafés

The city has a wonderful endowment of **cafés**, many situated in the medieval streets close to the cathedral, an area which sprang to life a few years ago following a clean-up and restoration campaign. There's little to choose between the cafés themselves, each pulls a lively cosmopolitan crowd, roughly in the 23–35 age bracket, and gets crowded on Fridays and Saturdays, less so earlier in the week. The best technique is really to wander around and try a few. A likely starter is the movie-themed *Casablanca*, at Rosensgade 12, from where you could continue to either *Carlton*, Rosensgade 23, *Drudenfuss*, Graven 30, *Englen*, Studsgade 3, *Kindrødt*, Studsgade 8, or *Jorden*, Badstuegade 3. Slightly more upmarket are the jazz-based *Café Basilika* at Klostertorvet 7, or the classical music-orientated, *Café Mozart*, just outside the old centre at Vesterport 10.

All of the above close at midnight or 2am depending on the day of the week and, if they're not heading for a club, revellers with stamina aim for one of the city's two **late-night cafés**, each open until 5am: *Den Sidste Café* (literally, "the Last Café"), at Paradisgade 9, or *Café Nono*, at Klostergade 36.

Live music

There's plenty of **live music** in Århus. You can get basic details of all events from the tourist office, but better for rock music news is the *Århus Billet Bureau*, at Studsgade 46, where you can pick up a variety of free local magazines and flyers advertising forthcoming gigs.

The cream of Danish and international independent **rock** acts can be found at either *Huset*, Vester Allé 15 (☎86/122677) – which has a restaurant and cinema as well – or *58*, Vestergade 58 (☎86/130217). Gigs take place at both three or four nights a week; admission will be 20–70kr, with doors opening at 10pm and the main band on at midnight. More run-of-the-mill Danish bar bands turn up at *Fatter Eskil*, Skolegade 25 (☎86/1279545), *Fru Jensen*, Meljgade 20 (☎86/121000), and *Gyngen*, Fronthuset, Mejlgade 53 (☎86/192255). Only the latter ever charges for entry. If you're looking for more radical, and anarchic, rock music, check out the small, squat-like café, *Æsken*, at Anholtsgade 4 (☎86/138561), on a Saturday night.

The leading **jazz** venue is the smoky, atmospheric pub, *Bent J*, at Nørre Allé 66 (☎86/120492). There are jam sessions here several nights a week with free admission; for a name band expect to pay 50–90kr. For **classical and opera** , check out the regular performances at the *Concert Hall* (☎86/134344).

Clubs and discos

Both *Huset* and *58* (addresses above) host rock and new wave **discos** on nights without live bands, although the city's coolest club right now is *Club Fisk*, at

Klostergade 34 (☎86/191099). More mainstream discos are plentiful, the best of which are *Alexis*, Frederiksgade 72 (☎86/127755), *Don Quijote*, Mejlgade 14 (☎86/130234) or *Down Town*, Store Torv 4 (☎86/139577) –which has the advantage of having freshly-made pizza available from midnight. If you fancy a night of Fifties and Sixties nostalgia, the place to go is *Locomotion*, at M.P.Bruuns Gade 15 (☎86/124333).

Early in the week, admission to any disco is likely to be free; on Thursday, Friday or Saturday, you'll pay 20–40kr.

Gay life

While Århus lacks the wide network of **gay** clubs you'll find in the Danish capital, there is the long established *Pan Klubben*, at Jægergårdsgade 42, a gay social centre with a café and disco, which has lesbian-only nights on Fridays. For details of other events which may of special interest to **women**, drop into *Kvindehuset*, at Havnegade 22b.

Listings

Airport Tirstrup (☎86/363611), 44km northeast of the city. Airport buses, linking with all flights, leave from outside the railway station; the fare is 45kr and the journey takes fifty minutes.

Airlines *SAS/DanAir* domestic ☎86/131288; international ☎86/131211.

Bike Hire Cheapest from the tourist office, see "Arrival, information and getting around".

Car Hire *Avis*, Østergarde 25 (☎86/133699); *InterRent/Europecar*, Sønder Allé 35 (☎86/123500); *PS*, Thorvaldsensgade 25 (☎86/135454).

Chemist There's a 24-hour pharmacy, *Jernbaneapoteket*, at Baneårdpladsen, by the railway station.

Dental Problems Phone Dr Sahlerz (☎86/127211), Mon–Sat 8–9pm, Sun and holidays 9–10am & 8–9pm. Be prepared to pay 150kr in cash.

Doctor Call out between 7.30am and 4pm, ☎86/127211; between 4pm and 7.30am, ☎86/192122. There's a night call-out fee of 300kr, payable in cash only.

Hospitals Casualty: Århus Kommunehospital, on Nørrebrogade.

Late Shopping The *DSB* supermarket at the railway station is open daily 8am–midnight.

Market There's a fruit, veg and flower market every Wednesday and Saturday on Bispetorv, beside the cathedral.

Police Århus Politisation, Ridderstræde (☎86/133000).

Post Office On Banegardpladsen, by the railway station, open Mon–Fri 9am–5.30pm, Sat 9am–noon.

Transport Information Local buses and trains, ☎86/125211. Long-distance trains and *DSB* ferries, ☎86/131700. Århus–Copenhagen coach reservations, ☎86/341600. Other long-distance coaches, ☎86/128622.

Central Jutland: Randers, Viborg and around

From rugged windswept heathlands to lush valleys and thick belts of forest, **central Jutland** boasts some of the most varied landscapes in Denmark, which, together with the area's historical remnants, are sufficient ingredients for a couple of days of pleasurable rambling. The region is easily accessed by rail, although, if coming from Århus, you'll need to change trains at Langå to get straight into the best of it – the patch around Viborg. Failing that, stay on the train and base yourself instead in the countryside close to Randers, seeing the rest by bike or local buses.

Randers and around

A trading and manufacturing base since the thirteenth century, **RANDERS** is not a promising introduction to central Jutland. Its growth has continued apace over the years, leaving a tiny medieval centre miserably coralled by a bleak new industrial one. Even the town's major sight is bogus: the house at Storegade 13 is said to be the place where Danish nobleman Niels Ebbeson killed the German, Count Gerd of Holstein, in 1340, and a shutter on the upper storey is always left open to allow the Count's ghost to escape, lest the malevolent spirit should cause the house to burn down. But the building wasn't erected until the seventeenth century, and the slaying most likely took place somewhere near it. For advice on how to escape Randers and reach the countryside (and the budget accommodation) around it, use the **tourist office** (Mon–Fri 9am–5pm, Sat 9am–noon; ☎86/424477) inside the sixteenth-century *Helligåndshuset* on Erik Menveds Plads, in the medieval quarter.

Around Randers ... and accommodation

East from Randers is the ferry port of **GRENÅ**, from where there are sailings to HUNDESTED (in Zealand), the island of ANHOLT, and Varberg and Helsingborg in Sweden. Grenå is reachable by train from Århus (1hr 22min), though buses from Randers (#214) run roughly hourly through the day from the bus station, the journey taking about ninety minutes. In the other direction, **west** towards Viborg, the gorgeous tree-clad valley of **Nørreådalen** is a perfect setting for Randers' **youth hostel** and **campsite** (☎86/429361), both open April to mid-October and reached with bus #10 from the railway station or town centre – watch for the youth hostel sign after the bus has turned around at Fladbro Kro. Both hostel and campsite are feasible bases for seeing Viborg, just under 40km away, though if you're not equipped with car or bike, you'll need to make an early start on one of the two **buses to Viborg** from Randers, #61 and #62. The latter passes close to the hostel and the journey takes just over an hour.

Viborg and around

For a long time at the junction of the major roads across Jutland, **VIBORG** was once one of the most important communities in the country. From Knud in 1027 to Christian V in 1655, all Danish kings were crowned here, and until the early nineteenth century the town was the seat of a provincial assembly. As the national administrative axis shifted towards Zealand, however, so Viborg's importance waned, and although it still has the high court of West Denmark, it's now primarily a market town for the local farming community.

The Town

Viborg's centre is concentrated in a small area and most parts of the old town are within a few minutes' walk of each other. The twin towers of the **Domkirke** (June–Aug Mon–Fri 9am–5pm; April, May & Sept Mon–Fri 9am–5pm; Mon–Fri 9am–4pm; Oct–April 9am–3pm; every Sun 1–3pm) are the most visible feature; indeed the cathedral – instigated by Bishop Eskil in 1130 – is the most compelling reminder of the town's former glories. The cathedral was decimated by fire in 1726 and rebuilt in Baroque style by one Claus Stallknecht, though so badly that it had to be closed for two years and the work begun again. The interior is now dominated by the brilliant frescoes of Joakim Skovgaard, an artist commemorated by the **Skovgaard Museum** (May–Sept daily 10am–5pm; rest of the year daily 1.30–5pm; free), inside the former Rådhus across Gammel Torve – a neat building with which Claus Stallknecht made amends for his botching of the cathedral. There's a good selection of Skovgaard's paintings in the museum – although they can't fail to be a little anti-climactic after viewing the works in the cathedral – along with those of other members of his family.

For a broader perspective of Viborg's past, keep an hour spare for exploring the **District Museum** (June–Aug daily 11am–5pm; rest of the year Tues–Fri 2–5pm Sat & Sun 11am–5pm; free), on the northern side of Hjultorvet between Vestergade and Skt. Mathias Gade. The museum's three well-stocked floors hold everything from prehistoric and archaeological artefacts to the clothes, furniture, and household appliances, which help record the social and cultural changes in Viborg over more recent decades.

Practical details

The **tourist office** (☎86/621617), at Nytorv 5, can supply a handy map for exploring old Viborg and advise on **accommodation** if you want to stay over – more or less unavoidable for exploring the countryside around. You may be able to find a double for 400kr at the small *Hotel Viborg*, Gravene 18–20 (☎86/622722). However, the only really cheap options, as usual, are the **youth hostel** (☎86/621481), open from March to November, and the neighbouring **campsite** (☎86/611111), with cabins, both across the lake (Viborg Sø) from the town centre, along Vinkelvej.

Around Viborg: the Hald Area

Leaving Viborg and heading south on Koldingvej (an alternative minor route to the A13), you come to **Hald Ege**, a beautiful area of soft hills and meadows on the shores of Hald Sø. For all its peace, though, the district's history is a violent one. This is where Neils Bugge led a rebellion of Jutland squires against the King in 1351, and where the Catholic bishop, Jorgen Friis, was besieged by Viborgers at the time of the Reformation. Much of the action took place around the manor houses, or *Halds*, which stood here, the sites and ruins of which can be reached by following a **footpath** marked by yellow arrows. The path starts close to **Hald Laden**, a restored barn by the side of the road, where an exhibition (June–Aug daily noon–6pm; rest of the year Sat & Sun noon–6pm; free) details the history and geology of the area, and the battle against the pollution which is killing Hald Sø.

Just to the south, a road leads from the village of DOLLERUP to **LYSGÅRD** and **E.Bindstouw** (mid-April to mid-Sept Tues–Sun 9am–5pm; 5kr), the old school house where **Steen Steensen Blicher**'s nineteenth-century short stories, named after the school, have their origins. Blicher would sit here in the evenings while the local poor wove socks beside the stove and told folktales, which Blicher noted down for posterity. The small building is still in its original location and contains the fixtures and fittings of Blicher's time, including his writing board, stove, and even a few socks.

About 9km west of Viborg, beside the A-16 between **MØNSTED** and RAUNSTRUP, the **Jutland Stone** marks the precise geographical centre of Jutland. There's not much to see, just a big·inscribed rock and lots of cigarette ends. A few kilometres further, and markedly more interesting, are the **Mønsted Limestone Mines** (mid-June to mid-Aug 9am–6pm; late March to mid-June & mid-Aug to late Oct daily 10am–4pm; 20kr), which wind 35km into the earth and have a temperature which remains constant regardless of external weather. Wandering around in their cool, damp innards can be magically atmospheric, although a century ago conditions for the mineworkers here were horrific, so much so that when Frederik IV visited the place he was sufficiently appalled to bring about reforms – which led to the mines becoming known as *Frederik's Quarries* or, more venomously, *The King's Graves*. The mines are no longer

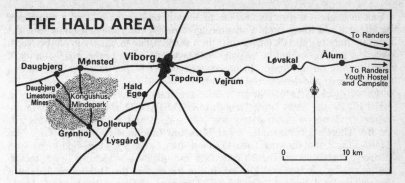

worked and are owned by a businessman who also happens to be a celebrated violinist; occasionally he appears, fiddle and bow in hand, to entertain visitors.

There's another set of **limestone mines** (hours and price as Mønsted mines) near **DAUGBJERG**, unlit and narrower than the Mønsted mines, with an elderly guide who accompanies visitors with an oil-lamp. The entrance to the mines was found by chance fifty years ago and no one has yet charted the full extent of the passages; it's said that work began here at the time of Gorm, the tenth-century King of Jutland, and that the tunnels were used as hideouts by bandits.

A few kilometres south of Daugbjerg is **Kongeshus Mindepark** (mid-April to mid-Oct 10am–6pm; 5kr for cars, walkers free) – three thousand acres of protected moorland on which there have been attempts at agriculture since the mid-eighteenth century, when an officer from Mecklenburg began keeping sheep there. For his troubles, the would-be shepherd received a grant from the king, Frederik V, and built a house which gives the park its name: *Kongeshus* ("the King's House"). A few years later, a thousand or so German migrants (the so-called "potato Germans") also tried to cultivate the place but to little avail. In the centre of the park is a memorial to the early pioneers; standing here, as the wind howls in your ears and you look around the stark and inhospitable heath, you can only marvel at their determination.

If you're not put off, there are several **campsites** around Kongeshus: *Hessellund-Sø* (☎97/101604), open from April to September, to the south near Karup, and *Haderup* (☎97/452188), also open April to September, off Jens Jensenvej to the west, are just two.

Northwest Jutland: Limfjordslandet and around

Limfjordslandet is the land around the western portion of the Limfjord, the body of water which splits northern Jutland from the rest of the peninsula. In the north-western half, both the North Sea coast and the coast of the Limfjord itself – which here resembles a large inland lake – attract legions of holidaying northern Europeans during the summer months, at which time it's a smart move to arrange accommodation in advance. At other times they are a rarely-visited quarter of the country. There are fine beaches and plenty of opportunities to mess about in boats – and to catch them to Norway and beyond – and a number of small, neat old towns with a smattering of mildly diverting museums. But the weather here is unpredictable, with sharp winds prone to bluster in off the North Sea, and getting around is difficult – railways only reach to the fringes so you'll need to rely on the buses. In other words, don't bother to come here unless you're a hardy and determined traveller.

For a quick taste of the area, take the train from Viborg and change at STRUER for the short journey south to **HOLSTEBRO**, the largest town in the region, and one with an easy-going atmosphere and a small, walker-friendly centre. There's a commendable **Art Museum** (mid-June to mid-Aug Tues–Sun 11am–5pm; rest of the year Tues–Fri noon–4pm, Sat & Sun 11am–5pm) here with a strong contemporary Danish collection and quality international items, including works by Matisse and Picasso. In the town park, the **Holstebro Museum** has a fair local history collection. The **tourist office** at Brostræde 2 (☎97/425700), can supply information for travelling deeper into Limfjordslandet. For staying overnight, there's a **youth hostel** at Søvej 2 (☎97/420693), 2.5km from the centre, off Ringevejen, open from mid-March to mid-November, and a **campsite** at Birkevej 25 (☎97/422068), equipped with cabins and open April to mid-October.

Also reachable from Struer, **THISTED**, at the end of the local railway, has access to good beaches and a youth hostel and campsite, but little else of interest beyond providing a link (by bus #40) to **HANSTHOLM**, where ferries leave for Kristiansund and Egersund in Norway, and the *Symril* boat departs for Torshavn, Lerwick, Bergen and Seyðisfjörður.

Northeast Jutland: Aalborg, Frederikshavn and Skagen

Much easier to get to and travel in than Limfjordslandet, **northeast Jutland** is nonetheless another portion of Denmark often missed by foreigners. This is a shame. The region has a highly convivial major city in Aalborg, as well as ferries to Sweden and Norway. It also, once you cross the Limfjord, boasts a landscape wilder than anywhere else on the peninsula: lush green pastures giving way to strangely compelling views of bleak moorland and windswept dunes.

Aalborg and around

The main city of north Jutland and the fourth largest in Denmark, **AALBORG***, hugging the south bank of the Limfjord, is the obvious place to spend a night or two before venturing into the wilder countryside further on. It's the main transport terminus for the region, and boasts a notable modern art museum, a well-preserved old section and the brightest (indeed only) nightlife for miles around.

---

* A few years ago, it was officially decreed that the Danish double "A" would be written as Å. The mayor of Aalborg, and many locals, resisted this change and eventually forced a return to the previous spelling of their city's name – though you will see some recent maps and a few roadsigns using the "Å" form.

Information and accommodation

The **tourist office** is centrally placed at Østerå 8 (mid-June to mid-Aug Mon–Fri 9am–8pm, Sat 9am–2pm, Sun 10am–1pm; rest of the year Mon–Fri 9am–4.30pm, Sat 9am–noon; ☎98/126022) and has information on the town, though if you're staying in Aalborg, bargain-priced hotels are hard to find. The three cheapest, with doubles from 425kr, are the *Aalborg Sømandshjem*, Østerbro 27 (☎98/121900), the *Hotel Hafnia*, J.F. Kennedys Plads (☎98/131900), and *Missionshotellet Krogen*, Skibstedvej 4 (☎98/121705). If these are too costly, make for the large, *Butlins*-like **youth hostel** (☎98/116044), open from March to mid-December. This is to the west of the town on the Limfjord bank beside the marina – take bus #2 or #12 from the centre to the end of its route. The same buses take you to the **campsite**, *Strandparken* (☎98/127629), about 300m from the youth hostel, and open from mid-May to September.

The Town

Since its beginnings, Aalborg has been known as a trading centre, and the profits from the seventeenth-century herring boom made it the biggest and wealthiest Danish town outside Copenhagen. Much of what remains of **old Aalborg** – chiefly the area within Østerågade (commonly abbreviated to (Østerå), Bispensgade, Gravensgade and Algade – dates from that era, and stands in stark contrast to the new roads which slice through it to accommodate the traffic using the Limfjord bridge.

The tourist office is as good a place as any to start exploring, with one of the major seventeenth-century structures standing directly opposite. The **Jens Bangs Stenhus** is a grandiose five storeys in Dutch Renaissance style, which, incredibly, has functioned as a pharmacy since it was built. Jens Bang himself was Aalborg's wealthiest merchant but was not popular with the governing elite, who conspired to keep him off the local council. The host of goblin-like figures carved on the walls allegedly represent the councillors of the time, while another figure, said to be Bang himself, pokes out his tongue towards the former Rådhus, next door.

The commercial roots of the city are further evidenced by portaits of the town's merchants (rather than the more customary portraits of nobles) inside **Budolfi Domkirke** (Mon–Fri 9am–3pm, Sat 9am–noon), easily located by its bulbous spire, just a few steps behind the Jens Bangs Stenhus. The cathedral, a small but elegant specimen of sixteenth-century Gothic, is built on the site of a eleventh-century wooden church, only a few tombs from which remain, embedded in the walls close to the altar. Actually, beyond the old tombs, there's little to see inside the cathedral but plenty to hear when the electronically-driven bells ring out each hour – sending a cacophonous racket across the old square of **Gammel Torv**, on which the cathedral stands.

After viewing the cathedral, drop into the **Aalborg Historical Museum**, across the square at Aldgade 42 (Tues–Sun 10am–5pm; free). The first exhibit here is a dramatic one: the skeleton of a forty-year-woman who died around AD 400, preserved by a peat bog. In comparison, the rest of the prehistoric section is fairly routine; make instead for the local collections, which provide a good record of Aalborg's early prosperity. The museum also has an impressive, if somewhat incongruous, glassworks collection showing the different designs from the various Danish glassworking centres – look out for the armadillo-shaped bottle.

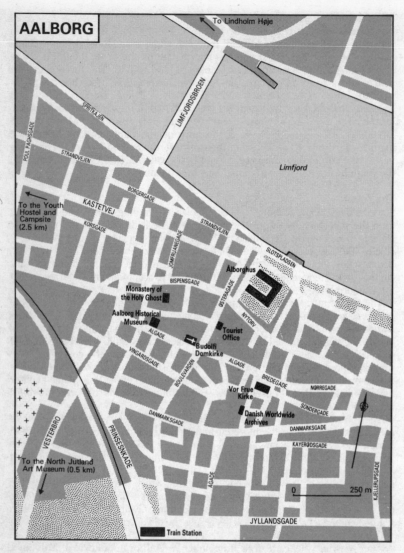

AALBORG

To Lindholm Høje

LIMFJORDSBROEN

SPRITKAJEN

POUL PAGHSGADE

STRANDVEJEN

BORGERGADE

Limfjord

To the Youth
Hostel and
Campsite
(2.5 km)

KASTETVEJ

KORSGADE

STRANDVEJEN

JOMFRUANEGADE

SLOTSPLADSEN

BISPENSGADE

Ålborghus

Monastery of
the Holy Ghost

ØSTERAGADE

Aalborg Historical
Museum

NYTORV

Tourist
Office

ALGADE

Budolfi
Domkirke

VINGÅRDSGADE

ALGADE

BOULEVARDEN

BREDEGADE

NØRREGADE

Vor Frue
Kirke

SØNDERGADE

+ +
+ + +
+ +
+ + +
+ +
+ + +
+ +

DANMARKSGADE

Danish Worldwide
Archives

DANMARKSGADE

VESTERBRO

PRINSESNKADE

KAYERODSGADE

To the North Jutland
Art Museum (0.5 km)

AGADE

0   250 m

KJELLERUPSGADE

JYLLANDSGADE

■ Train Station

Just off Gammel Torv is another significant feature of old Aalborg, the
fifteenth-century **Monastery of the Holy Ghost**, viewable by way of daily guided
tours in summer (Mon–Fri 2pm; 10kr). Tours take in the monks' refectory, kept
largely unchanged since the last monk left, and the small Friar's room, the only
part of the monastery into which nuns (from the adjoining nunnery) were permitted entry. Indeed, this was one of the few monasteries where monks and nuns
were allowed any contact at all, a fact which accounts for the reported hauntings
of the Friar's room – reputedly by the ghost of a nun who got too friendly with a

monk, and as a punishment was buried alive in a basement column (the monk was beheaded). Most interesting, however, are the **frescoes** which cover the entire ceiling of the chapel. In more recent times, the corridor outside the chapel was used for shooting-practice by the so-called "Churchill Gang", a group of local schoolboys who organised resistance to the Nazis (for more on them, see "History"); and much of the monastery now serves as an old folks' home.

The rest of old Aalborg lies on the other side of Østerågade, and is a mainly residential area – with a few exceptions. The sixteenth-century **Aalborghus** (grounds 8am–dusk) is technically a castle but looks much more like a country manor house, and always with an administrative, rather than a military, role. Aside from the free theatrical productions staged here in summer, the castle is only worth visiting for the severely gloomy **dungeon** (Mon–Fri 8am–4pm; free), to the right from the gateway, and the underground passageways which lead off it. From the castle, Slotsgade leads to the maze of narrow streets around **Vor Frue Kirke**, a dull church but with some meticulously **preserved houses** surrounding it, many of which have been turned into upmarket craft shops. The best are along the oddly L-shaped Hjelmerstald: notice no. 2, whose ungainly bulge around its midriff has earned it the nickname "the pregnant house".

If you're of Danish descent, or just keenly interested in Danish social history, visit the the **Danish Worldwide Archives**, nearby at Peder Brekesgade 5 (Mon–Thur 9am–4pm, Fri 9am–2pm; free). The story of Danish migration overseas is recorded here, through immense stacks of files and books; given enough background facts, details of individual migrants can be traced.

The old centre sets the pleasant tone of the city, but just outside it are a couple of other notable targets. One where you could easily spend an hour or two is the **North Jutland Art Museum** (mid-June to mid-Sept daily 10am–5pm; rest of the year Tues–Sun 10am–5pm; 10kr; free on Tues), on Kong Christians Allé, close to the junction with Vesterbro (bus #14 or a fifteen-minute walk from the centre). Housed in a building designed by the Finnish architect Alvar Aalto, this is one of the country's better modern art collections, strikingly contemporary in both form and content, and featuring – alongside numerous Danish contributions – works by Max Ernst, Andy Warhol, Le Corbusier and, imposingly stationed next to the entrance, Claes Oldenburg's wonderful *Fag-ends in a Colossal Ashtray*. After leaving the museum, you can get a grand, if pricey, view over the city and the Limfjord by ascending the **Aalborg Tower** (April–Sept daily 10am–6pm; 10kr), which is on the hill just behind.

From the tower, you may be able to spot what looks like a set of large concrete bunkers on a hill to the southeast of the city. These, in fact, are the **Gug Kirke** (Mon–Fri 9am–4pm), designed by Inger and Johannes Exner and opened in the early Seventies. It's one of the most unusual churches in the country. Except for the iron crucifix and the wooden belltower, the whole thing, including the font, pulpit and altar – decorated by a collage of newspapers – is made of concrete. The idea was to blend the church into the mostly high-rise parish it serves, and also to function as a community centre: the perfectly square interior can be turned into a theatre, while the crypt doubles as a café and youth club. It's unique enough to merit a close look; take bus #5 from the city centre.

Food, drink and nightlife

In pursuit of **food, drink and nightlife** almost everybody heads for Jomfru Ane Gade, a small street close to the harbour between Bispensgade and Borgergade.

Jomfru Ane (literally "young maiden Ann") was a noblewoman and reputedly a witch who, because of her social standing, was beheaded rather than burnt at the stake – though the street nowadays, at least by night, is more synonymous with getting legless than headless. Around midday, the restaurants crammed together here advertise their daily specials with signs: the most reliable are *Fyrtøjet*, at no. 19, or *Regensens*, no. 16, both of which generally have three-course lunches for 75–90kr. If it's Saturday, make a beeline for *Fru Jensen* at no. 13, where the help-yourself herring buffet costs just 5kr.

In the evening, *Fru Jensen* also has **live music**, as do several bars along the street; just walk along, listen, and decide what appeals. The better-known Danish rock acts appear at *Skråen*, Strandvejen 19 (☎98/122189), which also holds a café and multi-screened **cinema**. For less mainstream rock music, make for *Café Tusindfryd*, at Kattesundet 10. For a quiet evening drink, descend into the cellar of the Jens Bangs Stenhus for the *Duus* wine bar (closed Sundays).

Around Aalborg: Lindolm Høje and Rebild Bakker

On the north side of the Limfjord, **Lindolm Høje** was a major Viking and Iron Age burial ground, and is a captivating place, especially so in the stillness of dawn or dusk. There are a number of very rare Viking "ship monuments" here – burial places with stones arranged in the outline of a ship – plus over 600 cremation graves from the German Iron Age period, probably used by a settlement which was abandoned during the eleventh century. Get to the site from Aalborg with buses #4 or #11, each running twice an hour through most of the day, or make the 45–60-minute walk over the Limfjord bridge, along Vesterbrogade into Thistedvej, right into Viaduktvej, and straight on until Vikingvej appears to the left.

About 30km south of Aalborg is **Rebild Bakker**, a heather-covered hill in close proximity to some scattered beech woods and Rold Skov's dense proliferation of conifers. The area is prime territory for hiking, and has been a **national park** since a group of American ex-patriot Danes purchased the land and presented it to the Danish government. Nowadays it's the site of the largest American Independence Day celebration outside the USA – a good reason not to be around on July 4 – and is home to the tacky **Lincoln's Log Cabin** (May–Sept daily 10am–5pm; 10kr), a recreation of Abraham Lincoln's log cabin, filled with mundane articles from 49 American states and facts about Danish migration to them. None of the Americana disturbs the natural beauty of the area, however, and it can provide a couple of relaxing days. From Aalborg, take a train to SKØRPING or a bus (#104) to REBILD village, where there's a **youth hostel** at Rebildvej 23 (☎98/391340), only closed for a month over Christmas; the adjacent **campsite** (☎98/391110) is open all year.

Frederikshavn

FREDERIKSHAVN is neither pretty nor particularly interesting, and as a major ferry port it's usually full of Swedes and Norwegians taking full advantage of Denmark's liberal boozing laws. But the town is virtually unavoidable if you're heading north, being at the end of the rail route from Aalborg (if you've an international sailing to meet at HIRTSHALS, change trains at Hjørring). If you're not catching a boat, speed straight on to Skagen (see below); if you are, practical details are liable to be your main concern.

Arriving, information and sleeping

Buses and **trains** into Frederikshavn both finish up at the railway station; crossing Skippergade and walking along Denmarksgade brings you from the station to the town centre in a few minutes. **Arriving ferries** dock near Havnepladsen, also close to the centre, and to the **tourist office** at Brotorvet 1, on the corner of Rådhus Allé and Havnepladsen (mid-June to mid-Aug Mon–Sat 8.30am–8.30pm, Sun 8.30–11.30am & 4–8.30pm; April to mid-June & mid-Aug to Oct Mon–Fri 9am–5pm, Sat 9am–noon; rest of the year Mon–Fri 9am–5pm; ☎98/423266).

If you're forced to stay, the cheapest **hotels** are both on Tordenskjoldsgade: *Hoffmans Hotel* at number 14 (☎98/412166), and *Sømandshjemmet* at 15b (☎98/420977) are the best options, though a double in either is likely to cost at least 350kr. More cost-consciously, there's a **youth hostel** at Buhlsvej 6 (☎98/421475), 1500m from the railway station (from which turn right), closed only in January; and a cabin-equipped **campsite**, *Nordstrand*, at Apholmenvej 40 (☎98/429350 & ☎98/422982), 3km north of the town centre, just off Skagensvej, open from April to September.

The town

There are only a couple of things worth seeing in Frederikshavn. If you only have half an hour, visit the squat, white tower near the station: **Krudttårnet** (April–Oct daily 10am–12.30pm & 1–5pm; 5kr), which has maps detailing the harbour's seventeenth-century fortifications (of which the tower was a part) and a collection of weaponry, uniforms and military paraphernalia from the seventeenth to the nineteenth centuries.

With more time on your hands, take bus #1 or #2 to Møllehuset, the end of both bus routes, and walk on through Bangsboparken to the **Bangsbo-Museet** (April–Oct daily 10am–5pm; rest of the year Tues–Sun 10am–5pm; 10kr). Here, comprehensive displays chart the development of Frederikshavn from the 1600s, alongside the slightly grotesque, but very engrossing, Collection of Human Hairwork. The museum's outbuildings store an assortment of maritime articles, distinguished only by the twelfth-century Ellingå Ship, and a worthwhile exhibition covering the German occupation during World War II and the rise of the Danish Resistance movement.

Skagen

If you have the option, skip Frederikshavn altogether in favour of **SKAGEN**, which perches almost at the very top of Jutland amid a desolate landscape of heather-topped sand dunes, its houses painted a distinctively bright shade of yellow. Forty kilometres north of Frederikshavn, Skagen can be reached by private bus or train (*EurRail* and *InterRail* cards not valid), both of which leave from Frederikshavn railway station roughly once an hour – the bus is the best choice if you're planning to stay at the Skagen youth hostel as it stops outside.

The Town

Sunlight seems to gain extra brightness as it bounces off the two seas which collide off Skagen's coast, something which attracted the **Skagen artists** in the late nineteenth century. Painters Michael Ancher, Peder Severin (P.S.) Krøyer and writer Holger Drachmann arrived in the small fishing community during 1873 and 1874, and were later joined by Lauritz Tuxen, Carl Locher, Viggo

Johansen, Christian Krogh and Oscar Björck. The painters often met in the bar of *Brøndum's Hotel*, off Brøndumsvej, and the owner's step-sister, Anna, herself a skilful painter, married Michael Ancher. The grounds of the hotel now house the **Skagen Museum** (June, July & Aug daily 10am–6pm; May & Sept daily 10am–5pm; April & Oct daily 11am–3pm; rest of the year Sat & Sun 11am–3pm; 25kr), which comprises the most comprehensive collection of the artists' work. It's an impressive place, not least because so many of the canvases depict local scenes, using the town's strong natural light to capture subtleties of colour; the light, no less powerful today, streams in through the museum's windows. Many of the works, particularly those of Michael Ancher and Krøyer, are outstanding, although the paintings of Anna Ancher, while perhaps the least technically accomplished, often come closest to achieving the naturalism which the artists sought.

A few strides away, at Markvej 2, the **Anchers' Hus** (mid-June–mid-Aug daily 10am-6pm; May to mid-June & mid-Aug to Sept daily 9am-5pm; Oct & Jan–April daily 11am–3pm; Nov & Dec Sat & Sun 11am–3pm; 20kr), home of Michael and Anna, has been restored with the intention of evoking the atmosphere of their time – which, through an assortment of squeezed tubes of paint, sketches, paintings, piles of canvases, books and ornaments, it does remarkably well. Less essential, and a bit overpriced, is **Drachmanns' Hus** (June to mid-Sept daily 10am–4pm; 15kr), at Hans Baghsvej 21 on the junction with Skt. Laurentii Vej, where Holger Drachmann lived from 1902. Inside the house is a large collection of Drachmann's paintings and sketchbooks, although it was for his lyrical poems, at the forefront of the turn-of-the-century Danish neo-Romantic movement, that he was best known. Such was Drachmann's cultural importance that, on his death, the major Danish newspaper, *Politiken*, devoted most of their front page to him – facsimilies of which can be seen here.

The arrival and subsequent success of the artists inadvertently made Skagen fashionable, and the town continues to be a popular holiday destination. But it still bears many marks of its tough past as a fishing community, the history of which is excellently documented in **Skagen Fortidsminder** (May–Sept daily 10am–5pm; rest of the year daily 10am–4pm; 20kr), on P.K. Nielsenvej, a fifteen-minute walk south along Skt. Laurentii Vej (or the much nicer Vesterbyvej) from the town centre. The museum – built on the tall dune where townswomen would watch for their menfolk to return from the sea during storms – examines local fishing techniques in its main displays, reinforced by photos showing the millions of fish that would be strewn along the quay waiting to go the auction hall. Among the auxiliary buildings are reconstructions of the houses of both rich fishermen and their far poorer employees: the rich fisherman's house includes a macabre guest room kept cool to facilitate the storage of bodies washed ashore from wrecks, while the poor fisherman's dwelling makes plain the contrast in lifestyles – just two rooms to accommodate the parents and their fourteen offspring.

Around Skagen: the buried church . . . and Grenen

Amid the dunes to the south of town, about twenty minutes' walk along Skt. Laurentii Vej and Gammel Kirkestræde and onto a signposted footpath, is **Den Tilsandede Kirke**, or "the Buried Church" (June–Aug 11am–5pm; 3kr). The name is misleading since all that's here is the tower of a fourteenth-century church built in what was then a minor agricultural area. The church was assaulted by vicious sandstorms during the eighteenth century: by 1775 the entrance could only be reached with the aid of shovels, and in 1810 the nave and most of the fittings were sold, leaving just the tower as a marker to shipping – while not especially tall, the tower's white walls and red roof are easily visible from the sea. Still under the sands are the original church floor and cemetery. Although part of the tower is open to the public, the great fascination is simply looking at the thing from outside, and comprehending the incredible severity of the storms.

The forces of nature can be further appreciated at **Grenen**, 4km north of Skagen, along Skt Laurentii Vej and straight ahead along the beach. This is the actual meeting point of two seas – the Kattegat and Skagerrak – the spectacle of their clashing waves (the seas flow in opposing directions) is a powerful draw, although only truly dramatic if the winds are strong. On the way back, spare a thought for Holger Drachmann (see above), a man so enchanted by the thrashing seas that he chose to be buried in a dune close to them. His tomb is signposted from the car park.

Practical details

In Skagen, the **railway station** is on Skt. Laurentii Vej, a short walk from the **tourist office** at Skt. Laurentii Vej 18 (Mon–Sat 9am–5pm; ☎98/441377). **Staying overnight** in Skagen is infinitely preferable to going back to Frederikshavn any sooner than you have to. For its artistic associations, *Brøndum's Hotel*, Anchervej 3 (☎98/441555), is by far the most atmospheric spot; the fact that few of the rooms have bathrooms and all are far from luxurious keeps the price of doubles down to around 450kr – but book well ahead in summer. A little cheaper is *Sømandshjem*, Østre Strandvej 2 (☎98/442110), with doubles for under 400kr. The budget options are further out. The **youth hostel**, open from mid-March to October, is at Højensvej 32 (☎98/441356), in GAMMEL SKAGEN, about 3km from Skagen proper (the only bus service there is the #78 to Frederikshavn). Of a number of **campsites**, the most accessible are *Grenen*, (☎98/441470) to the north along Fyrvej, which has cabins, and *Poul Eeg's* (☎98/442546), on Batterivej, left off Frederikshavnvej just before the town centre; both sites are open from April to September.

travel details

Trains

From Esbjerg to Copenhagen (20 daily; 5hr); Århus (16 daily; 3hr 15min); Ribe (14 daily; 36min); Fredericia (27 daily; 1hr 23min).

From Ribe to Tønder (12 daily; 45min).

From Fredericia to Vejle (23 daily; 20min); Århus (25 daily; 1hr 22min).

From Århus to Copenhagen (5–6 daily; 5hr); Randers (20 daily; 40min); Aalborg (20 daily; 1hr 40min); Viborg via Langå (18 daily; 1hr); Frederikshavn (20 daily; 3hr).

From Skanderborg to Silkeborg (18 daily; 30min); Århus (25 daily; 15min).

From Viborg to Struer (17 daily; 45min).

From Struer to Holstebro (28 daily; 15min); Thisted (25 daily; 1hr 30min).

From Frederikshavn to Skagen (12 daily; 40min).

Buses

From Skærbæk to Havneby (6–8 daily; 25min)

From Sønderborg to Fynshav (7–8 daily; 30min).

From Århus to Copenhagen (2 daily; 4hr).

From Randers to Viborg (19 daily; 1hr 15min); Grenå (12 daily; 1hr 15min)

From Thisted to Hanstholm (14 daily; 45min); Aalborg (14 daily; 2hr 30min).

From Frederikshavn to Skagen (11 daily; 1hr).

Ferries

From Fynshav to Bøjden (8 daily; 50min).
From Århus to Kalundborg (8 daily; 3hr 10min).
From Grenå to Hundested (3 daily summer only; 2hr 40min); Anholt (1 daily summer only; 2hr 45min).

International Trains

From Fredericia to Flensburg (8 daily; 1hr 45min).

International Ferries

From Esbjerg to Harwich (1 daily in summer; 19hr 45min); Newcastle (3 weekly in summer; 21hr).

From Havneby to List (7–12 daily June–Oct; 55min).

From Grenå to Varberg (1 daily summer only; 4hr); Helsingborg (1 daily summer only; 4hr 30min).

From Hanstholm to Kristiansand (1 daily summer only; 4hr); Egersund (1 daily; 6hr 30min); Torshavn/Lerwick/Bergen/Lerwick/Seyðisfjörður (1 weekly; 11hr/27hr/36hr/77hr/96hr).

From Hirtshals to Harwich (1 weekly; 23hr); Stavanger and Bergen (2 weekly; 11hr 15min and 18hr); Egersund (1 weekly; 6hr 30min); Kristiansand (3 daily; 4hr 30min); Oslo (4 weekly; 9hr).

From Frederikshavn to Gothenburg (8 daily; 3hr 15min); Frederikstad (5 weekly; 5hr); Oslo (*Stena Line* 1 daily; 10hr; *Dano Linjen* 5 weekly; 13hr 30min); Larvik (1 daily; 6hr); Moss (1 daily; 7hr).

PART THREE

NORWAY

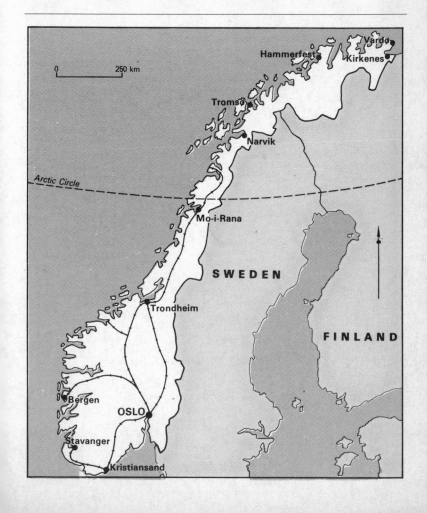

Introduction

In many ways Norway is still a land of unknowns. Quiet for a thousand years since the Vikings stamped their distinctive mark on Europe, the country nowadays often seems more than just geographically distant. Beyond Oslo and the famous fjords the rest of the country might as well be blank for all many visitors know – and, in a manner of speaking, large parts of it are. Vast stretches in the north and east are sparsely populated and starkly vegetated, and it is, at times, possible to travel for hours without seeing a soul.

Despite this isolation, Norway has had a pervasive influence. Traditionally its inhabitants were explorers, from the Vikings – the first western European discoverers of Greenland and North America – to more recent figures like Amundsen, Nansen and Heyerdahl; while Norse language and traditions are common to many other isolated fishing communities, not least northwest Scotland and the Shetlands. At home, too, the Norwegian people have striven to escape the charge of national provincialism, touting the disproportionate number of acclaimed artists, writers and musicians (most notably Munch, Ibsen and Grieg) who have made their mark on the wider European scene. It's also a pleasing discovery that the great outdoors – great though it is – harbours some lively historical towns.

■ Where to go

Beyond **Oslo**, one of the world's most prettily sited capitals, the major cities of interest – in roughly descending order – are medieval **Trondheim**, **Bergen** in the heart of the fjords and hilly, northern **Tromsø**. None is exactly swinging, but they are nonetheless likeable, walkable cities worth time for themselves, as well as being on top of startlingly handsome countryside. The perennial draw, though, is the **western fjords** – a must, and every bit as scenically stunning as they're cracked up to be. Dip into the region from Bergen or Åndalsnes, both accessible direct by train from Oslo, or take more time and appreciate the subtleties of the innumerable waterside towns and villages. The **south** of Norway, and in particular the long southern coast, is popular with holidaying Norwegians, with its beaches and white-washed wooden towns; the central, more remote regions are ideal for hiking and camping.

Far to the north of here Norway grows increasingly barren, and what tourist trail there is peters out altogether. The vast lands of **Troms** and **Finnmark** were once the home of outlaws and still boast wild and untamed tracts. There are also the *Same* tribes and their herds of reindeer, which you'll see on the thin, exposed road up to the North Cape, or **Nordkapp** – the northernmost accessible point of mainland Europe. The Cape is the natural end to the long trek north, although there are still several hundred kilometres further east which could claim that distinction. In fact, right the way to the Soviet border.

■ When to go

Norway is still regarded as a remote, cold country – spectacular enough but climatically inhospitable. **When to go**, however, is not as clear-cut a choice as you'd imagine. There are advantages to travelling during the long, dark **winters** with their reduced everything: daylight, opening times and transport services. Winter sports facilities are excellent and many youth hostels stay open for skiing; and, if you are equipped and hardy enough to reach the far north, seeing the phenomenal **Northern Lights** (*Aurora Borealis*) is a distinct possibility. **Easter**, too, is the time of the great and colourful *Same* festivals. But it is cold, often bitterly so, and this guide has been deliberately weighted towards the **summer** season, when most people travel and when it is possible to camp and hitch to keep costs down. This is the time of the **Midnight Sun**: the further north you go, the longer the day becomes, until at Nordkapp the sun is continually visible from mid-May to the end of July. The table below lists the dates between which the Midnight Sun is visible in different parts of the country. As regards **temperatures**, roughly speaking January and February are the coldest months, July and August the warmest; the Gulf Stream makes the north surprisingly temperate during summer.

THE MIDNIGHT SUN

(whole sun above the horizon)

Alta: May 18–July 27.
Bodø: June 4–July 8.
Hammerfest: May 16–July 27.
Nordkapp: May 13–July 29.
Tromsø: May 20–July 20.

N.B. These dates may vary by 24 hours either way.

Getting There

There's no problem in reaching Norway from the rest of Scandinavia. There are very regular train services from Sweden, year-round ferry connections from Denmark and flights from all the mainland countries. More longwindedly, you can also reach Norway from Iceland, via the Faroes and the Shetland Islands; for full details of this see *Iceland*, "Getting There".

■ Trains

By **train** you can reach **Oslo** from Stockholm (2–3 daily) or from Copenhagen/Gothenburg (3–4 daily); and there are regular services to **Trondheim** (2 daily) and **Narvik** (2–3 daily), again from Stockholm. Anyone under 26 can buy a *BIJ* ticket on these routes and *InterRail/Nordturist* passes are valid – for full details see *Basics*.

■ Ferries

Consider using one of the many ferry services **from Denmark** to Norway. There are connections from **Copenhagen** to Oslo with *Scandinavian Seaways*, from **Frederikshavn** to Oslo with *Da-No Linjen*, to Moss with *Stena Line*, and Fredrikstad and Larvik with the *Larvik Line*. You can also sail from **Hirtshals** to Oslo, Kristiansand, Egersund, Stavanger and Bergen with *Fred Olsen Lines*, and, summer only from **Hantsholm** to Kristiansand and Egersund. Schedules depend on time of year, but on most routes crossings are made several times daily during summer and once daily during winter; a few services stop altogether in low season. **Prices** tend to rise sharply during the summer: one-way deck-passenger fares can vary from around 100Dkr for the shorter crossings to upwards of 400Dkr for the Copenhagen–Oslo crossing. All ferries take cars, and on the Copenhagen–Oslo run, for example, you pay an extra 200–600Dkr per car, depending on size.

For fuller details contact the local tourist offices in the relevant Danish towns, or the appropriate ferry companies; and see the Norway and Denmark chapters' "Travel Details" sections.

There's also a year-round ferry service **from Sweden**, linking Strömstad, north of Gothenburg, with Sandefjord, north of Larvik. It's operated by *Scandi-Line* (Strömstad; ☎0526-11 151), and runs twice daily, taking two and a half hours, the one-way fare costing around 80–95kr.

■ Planes

Norway has international airports at Oslo, Bergen, Stavanger, Trondheim and Tromsø; most flights from elsewhere in Scandinavia are with *SAS*. A variety of discounts (family/group/student) can make internal Scandinavian flights realistic, though most are only available in summer. Tourist offices will have the latest information.

One small operator worth considering is *North Flying*, who run services from Denmark (Aalborg to Bergen and Stavanger, Århus to Bergen). There is one daily flight on each route, and tickets cost from 1485Dkr one way; under 26s 525Dkr.

Costs, Money and Banks

Norway does not come cheap. Spells of camping, youth hostelling and self-catering are the only way of sticking to any kind of budget, and even then it's tight.

It'll cost from £5–9 a night for a **bed** in a youth hostel, for a private room in a house around double that; hotels cost upwards of £20 a night per person. **Eating**, too, can be extortionate. Apart from hostel breakfasts, which for £4 or so are usually excellent, and the occasional £4–5 set lunch, you may have to depend on junk food; supermarket food costs about twice as much as in Britain. **Alcohol** is similarly unaffordable – a half litre of beer in a bar costs about £3, though beer from a supermarket is more reasonable, as is wine bought from a state-licensed store. **Getting around** is better news. Most travellers use some kind of rail pass, there are a fistful of discounts and internal deals and the state subsidises the more remote and longer bus hauls.

A **daily average** is difficult to pinpoint. You could exist for a short time – hitching, camping rough, one large picnic meal a day but *nothing* else – on £5–7; using hostels and local transport, sightseeing, the occasional meal out, and the (very) occasional drink, it's more likely to be anything from £15 to 25 a day, plus whatever rail pass you use. If you're staying in hotels and eating decently, you're looking at a minimum of £50 a day. You'll have to be really disciplined – cut down on coffee, snacks, walk when you can – to avoid spending a fortune.

■ Money and banks

Norwegian currency is the *krone*, one of which is divided into 100 øre. Denominations are 10, 50, 100, 500 and 1000kr. There are no **currency**

restrictions on entering the country, though you can't take out more than 5000kr in Norwegian notes and coins.

Banks open Monday–Friday 8am–4pm, generally staying open an hour later on Thursday, but closing an hour earlier during the summer (June–Aug). Some airports, railway stations and campsites have **exchange offices** open in the evenings and at weekends – they're detailed in the text. Two banks that give cash advances on **credit cards** are *Den Norske Creditkassen* and *ABC Bank*.

Communications

Norwegian communications are excellent, and things are made even easier by the fact that post and telephone office staff nearly all speak good English. You needn't miss out on TV or newspapers either, since it's easy to track down foreign papers and the television networks carry imported British and American programmes, subtitled for the home audience.

■ Post and phones

Post office opening hours are usually Monday–Friday 8am–5pm, Saturday 8am–1pm. **Stamps** for letters and postcards from Norway to Europe currently cost 3.80kr and are available from post offices, kiosks and stationers. **Telephone** boxes take 1kr and 5kr coins (some take 10kr coins, too) and there is a minimum 2kr charge – which, for international calls (made from any public callbox), can mean a ridiculous conveyor-belt feeding of cash. However, in Oslo and some of the larger cities there are **telephone offices**, open until late evening; addresses are detailed in the text. **Directory enquiries** can be called on ☎0180 for Scandinavian countries, ☎0181 otherwise. To make a **reverse-charge call** from Norway, phone ☎0118 (inland) or ☎0115 (abroad).

■ Media

Most British and some American daily **newspapers**, and the odd established periodical, are on sale in most towns from *Narvesen* kiosks, large railway stations and at airports. As for the **Norwegian media**, state advertising, loans and subsidised production costs keep a wealth of smaller papers going that would bite the dust elsewhere. Most are closely linked with political parties, although the bigger city-based papers

tend to be independent. Highest circulations are claimed by the independent *Verdens Gang* and the independent-conservative *Aftenposten*.

The **television** network has expanded over the last few years, in line with the rest of Europe. Alongside the state channel, there's a new private one, *TV Norge*, while *TV3* is a channel common to Norway, Denmark and Sweden. In most of Norway, too, you can pick up Swedish TV broadcasts, while *MTV* and *Superchannel* are the mainstay of most hotel TV services. It's unadventurous stuff on the whole: much is imported, so there is invariably something on that you'll understand (*Dallas* and *Miami Vice* are big) – one reason why lots of Norwegian youth speak English with an American accent. The British programmes shown are usually worthy series (*The Forsyte Saga*) and right-on comedies (*The Young Ones*).

Getting Around

Norway's transport system – a huge mesh of trains, buses and ferries – is comprehensive and reliable. In the winter (especially in the north), services can be cut back severely, but no part of the country is isolated for long.

All the main air, train, bus and ferry services are detailed in the invaluable (and free) *Rutehefte for Turister* (**tourist timetables**), available from most Norwegian tourist offices or in advance from the National Tourist Board in London – for the address of which see *Basics*. Or check the more hefty *Rutebok for Norge* (94kr from large Norwegian bookshops) which contains every schedule in the country, and which most tourist offices and all travel agents hold; ask for photocopies of the relevant pages. Also, train schedules are included in the free pamphlet, the *NSB Togruter*, available at most stations.

■ Trains

Train services are run by *Norges Statsbaner* (*NSB*) – Norwegian State Railways – and work, apart from a few branch lines, on four main routes which link Oslo to Stavanger in the south, to Bergen in the west and to Trondheim and on to Bodø in the north. The nature of the country makes most of the routes engineering feats of some magnitude and worth a trip in their own right – the tiny **Flåm line** and sweeping **Rauma line** to Åndalsnes are exciting examples.

Prices are steep, the popular Oslo to Bergen run, for example, costing 390kr one-way.

However, if you don't already have a rail pass there are a number of special **discounts** and deals which can cut costs. The *Midtukebillet* (Midweek ticket; 340kr, valid seven days), covers a one-way journey of any length with stopovers, the only restriction being that you mustn't begin your travels on a Friday or Sunday; the *Minigrupperabatt* (Mini-group discount on minimum journeys of 100km one-way) gives 25 percent discount on normal fares to groups of at least two people; the *Kundekort* (Season ticket; 250kr, valid one year) gets half-price tickets on Monday, Wednesday, Thursday and Saturday, and thirty percent discounts on Friday and Sunday. **Senior Citizens** (ie those over 67), their spouses, the **blind** and **kids** between four and fifteen are all also entitled to half-price tickets; children under four go free as long as they don't occupy a seat. Details of these and other seasonal deals can be had from any railway station, where you can also pick up *NSB*'s free leaflets on each of the lines, detailing what there is to see as you go.

It's worth noting that most express trains (*Ekspress* or *Hurtigtog*), and all overnight trains, require an advance **seat reservation** (13kr) whether you have a rail pass or not. In high season it's wise to make a seat reservation anyway as trains can be packed. **Sleepers** are reasonably priced, certainly in view of the fact that if you use them you'll save a night's hotel accommodation: a bed in a three-berth cabin costs 80kr, two-berth 160kr and one-berth 320kr.

■ Buses

Where the train network won't take you, buses will – and at no great cost either: a typical fjord journey, like the Åndalsnes to Geiranger trip, costs around 80kr, while the eleven-hour bus ride between Narvik and Alta is a reasonable 346kr. You'll need to use buses principally in the western fjords and the far north, though there are also a series of long-distance **express buses** which connect major towns throughout Norway. As a rough guide most longer-distance routes tend to operate once daily, usually early; shorter hauls, although more frequent, often tail off in the late afternoon. **Tickets** are usually bought on board, but travel agents sell advance tickets on the more popular routes. Information on specific routes, and timetables, is available from the local tourist offices or from *Nor-Way Bussekspress*, Jernbanetorget 2, N–0154 Oslo 1 (☎02/33 08 62).

As far as **discounts** go, students and *Nordturist/InterRail* pass holders pull in a fifty percent discount on bus travel between the two rail termini of Fauske/Bodø and Narvik, and those with *Nordturist* can also go free on the bus service between Storlien (in Sweden) and Trondheim. Students can try for discounts on bus lines further north: though sometimes only open to Norwegian students, it's still worth flashing your card at every opportunity. Otherwise, as usual, children between four and sixteen travel for half price, under-fours go free provided they don't take up a seat.

If you're going to do lots of travelling, or intend to return to Norway within the year, consider *Nor-way Bussekspress*'s **Buss Pass**, which costs 1000kr and is valid for twelve months. It gets 33 percent discounts on express bus journeys over 100km long (ie 1500kr worth of travel for the money); the driver just punches the value of your journey on your pass as you board. It can also be used on journeys to Europe, provided the journey goes from Oslo, via Gothenburg in Sweden. Buy the pass in travel agents, main post offices and *Nor-Way Bussekspress* offices – the main office address is given above.

The Nord-Norge Bussen

A long-distance coach, the **Nord-Norge Bussen**, runs between Fauske, the northernmost reach of the railway, and Kirkenes, close to the Soviet border – a 48-hour journey involving at least one stopover. The route is operated by several bus companies who combine to provide one bus daily, which runs all year as far as Alta, and two daily from there to Kirkenes – though on the second leg of the journey snow can play havoc with the schedules between October and May. It can be a thrilling ride, though it has a less-than-thrilling hostess commentary on some of the more spectacular bits. Buy tickets as you go or one all-inclusive ticket in advance: details from travel agents and the Fauske tourist office; see also "Travel Details" in Chapters Seven and Eight.

■ Ferries

It would be difficult to avoid using a **ferry** in Norway. In the western fjords, the northern coastal reaches, even in Oslo, they are a vital transport link. You'll rarely pay very much to use them – say 10–20kr – and on shorter hops the ride may well be included in the bus fare. Otherwise, just walk on and pay the conductor on board. Where the ferries are part of a longer road route, they either connect with the relevant buses or there are constant daily services. Nearly all are car-ferries, roll-on, roll-off, which also means that hitch hikers have a captive audience on the more isolated stretches. Several inland **lakes** and waterways have ferry services, too, including Lake Mjøsa, near Oslo and the Telemark Canal.

The Hurtigrute

There's a rather grander ferry service, too, the **Hurtigrute** (the word literally means "rapid route"), a daily coastal steamer which links Bergen with Kirkenes, and stops off on the way. It's really a delivery service for the remote towns of northern Norway, but has of late been marketed to tourists, and you may find the lounges full of elderly English and American travellers.

Tickets for short jumps up the coast are quite expensive, certainly compared with the comparable bus fares, and the full eleven-day return cruise (including meals) goes for anything from 4100–11,350kr. But prices are reduced outside the period June to September, kids aged between four and fifteen go for half price, and under 26s can buy a special **coastal pass**, which costs 1300kr for 21 days' unlimited travel. Get it on board on your first trip or at the *Hurtigrute* company offices in Trondheim (☎07/52 05 00), Narvik (☎082/44 090) or Tromsø (☎083/86 088). Most travel agents and local tourist offices have copies of the sailing schedule.

As for specifics, although it's a cruise ship you don't need to have a cabin: sleeping in the lounges or on deck is allowed. But plan carefully before buying your ticket, since single tickets only allow one overnight stop; visiting the Lofoten Islands, for example, Stamsund is the better stop-over place. The older ships are the nicest, and tend to have showers you can use on the lower corridors; newer models have fully self-contained cabins. Car drivers should use the new ships as the old ones only have room for five or six vehicles which have to be winched – expensively – on and off. Bikes travel free. A 24-hour cafeteria supplies coffee and snacks, and there's a good value restaurant which does a reasonable breakfast (45kr) and dinner for around 120kr.

■ Planes

Internal flights can prove a surprisingly cheap way of hopping about the country, especially if you're short on time and want to reach, say, the far north. Tromsø to Kirkenes takes the best part of two days by bus; it's an hour by plane. Domestic air routes are serviced by four main **companies** – *SAS*, *Braathens SAFE*, *NorskAIR* and *Widerøe* – and there are several **discounts** available. Under 25s can buy standby tickets to anywhere at half-price; families, too, travelling together pay half-price; while so-called *Mini-pris* tickets are available on return flights on certain routes and days. Details vary year to year, but as a broad reference you can fly from Oslo to Bergen for around 790kr one-way (870kr *Mini-pris* return), to Tromsø for around 1560kr one-way (1850kr *Mini-pris* return).

A couple of **air passes** are worth noting. *Braathens SAFE's Visit Norway Pass* is valid on all the company's routes during the summer period: two-flight coupons cost around 600kr, four-flight coupons around 1110kr. *Widerøe* have a fourteen-day air pass which costs 1900kr (mid-June to mid-Aug only); or, during roughly the same period, you can travel on selected one-way flights for just 350kr. Ask at the Norwegian Tourist Board in London for details, or at any tourist office in Norway. Or contact *Widerøe* (☎02/50 91 30) and *Braathens SAFE* (☎02/59 70 00) in Oslo.

■ Driving and hitching

Driving, in the north especially, can be a positive adventure. On the whole, roads are good, although you'll need to take care on the winding mountain passes and in the enormous tunnels of the hillier regions. In winter – if they're open (see the box below) roads like the E6 Arctic Highway, which runs to Kirkenes, branching off into the Finnmarksvidda and up to Nordkapp, are not for the inexperienced or ill-equipped. **Fuel** is readily available, even in the north, and, if anything, is a few pence cheaper than in Britain: current prices are around 5kr a litre, slightly cheaper for lead-free petrol. Remember to carry an extra can if you're heading for Nordkapp and beyond.

Documentation is straightforward: your driving licence and vehicle registration papers are all that's needed, and it's recommended that you carry the international green card of insurance (compulsory for motorcyclists). **Rules of the road** are strict: you drive on the right, with dipped headlights required at all times, there's a speed limit of

50kph in built-up areas, 80kph on open roads (90kph on some), seatbelts are compulsory for drivers and front seat passengers (back seat passengers, too, if fitted) and drunken driving is severely frowned upon. You can be asked to take a breath test on a routine traffic-check; if over the limit, you will have your licence confiscated and may face 28 days in prison.

If you **break down**, the *Norges Automobil-Forbund* (*NAF*) patrols all mountain passes between mid-June and mid-August, and there are emergency telephones along roads and motorways; pick-up service numbers are given under city listings in the text. Basic breakdown help is free to *AA*/*RAC* members.

Car hire is expensive. Expect to pay around 3000kr a week for a *VW Golf* or similar-sized car with unlimited mileage. However, some tourist offices come up with special summer deals in conjunction with local outfits, so keep an eye out. You'll need to be 21 or over, too: look for car hire firms in the telephone directory under *Bilutleie*.

Try and steer clear of **taxis** (*Drosje*) in towns and cities, as they are uniformly expensive, with a minimum fare of over 20kr. The only time it's worth hiring one is if you're in a group in one of the more remote places – at Nordkapp, for instance – when special excursion rates apply.

Hitching is a thorny subject. In general, Norwegians don't queue up to offer lifts to hitchers, and most young Norwegians don't hitch at all. Short distances – the western fjords, the south coast – are your best bet for lifts, but wherever you are you'll have to be prepared for some long waits. Use signs for longer trips so that drivers know in advance how long they are going to have to put up with you; and, during June and from September onwards, be sure to check that any mountain passes you may have to cross are open.

**MAJOR MOUNTAIN PASSES:
OPENING DATES**

Highway 7: Hardangervidda. Open all year.

Highway 55: Sognefjellsvegen. Closed late Dec–early May.

Highway 58: Geiranger. Closed early Dec–mid-May.

Highway 63: Trollstigen. Closed mid-Nov–mid-May.

Highway 95: Skarsvåg–Nordkapp. Closed mid-Nov–late May.

■ Cycling

Cycling is not as ludicrous as it sounds, and is a great way of taking in the scenery – just be sure to wrap up warm and dry and take extra care on the more precipitous routes. Check your journey thoroughly, too, as cyclists aren't allowed through some tunnels; you'll need good lights to ride through the ones that aren't prohibited. Bikes nearly always go free on ferries, sometimes on buses; there's a 25kr fee to take them on trains, and express trains don't take bikes at all.

Throughout Norway it's possible to **rent bikes** at between 25kr and 50kr a day – ask at tourist offices, youth hostels and campsites, and check the guide. Specific cycle routes and advice can be obtained from the *Norwegian Youth Hostel Association* in Oslo – see below for address – or from the Norwegian cycling organisation, **Syklistenes Landsforening**, Majorstuveien 20, N–0367 Oslo 3 (☎02/44 27 31). They publish a book, *Sykkelferie i Norge* ("Cycling Holidays in Norway"), and a map which indicates which roads and tunnels are inaccessible to cyclists.

Sleeping

There's no way around it: accommodation in Norway is a major expense, and you need to excercise both thought and patience to find anwhere even halfway reasonable.

■ Youth hostels

Youth hostels (*Vandrerjhem*) provide the accommodation mainstay: about eighty in all, spread right across the country (except east of Nordkapp), with handy concentrations in the western fjords, the central hiking regions and around Oslo. The hostels are invariably excellent and the Norwegian hostelling association, **Norske Vandrerhjem**, Dronningensgate 26, Oslo (☎02/42 14 10), puts out a free pamphlet, *Vandrerhjem i Norge*, which details locations, opening dates, prices and telephone numbers.

Prices vary greatly, anything from 55kr to 90kr (115–130kr in Oslo), although the more expensive ones nearly always include a good breakfast. On average, reckon on paying 50–60kr a night for a bed, 40–45kr for breakfast and 60–65kr for a hot meal. Bear in mind also that almost all hostels have a few regular doubles and family rooms on offer: if you're lucky enough to find one vacant, they are, at around 150–200kr a time, the cheapest rooms you'll find in Norway.

Incidentally, non-members can use the hostels, too, though you'll pay an extra 20kr a night for the privilege – so join the *IYHF* before you leave home to save money.

It cannot be stressed too strongly that **ringing ahead** to reserve a hostel bed in peak season, summer or winter, will save you lots of unnecessary legwork. Most hostels close between 11am and 4pm, and – though less of a drawback in a country where carousing is so expensive – there's normally an 11pm/midnight curfew. Where breakfast is included, ask for a breakfast packet if you have to leave early to catch transport; otherwise note that hostel **meals** are not always a good buy (exceptions are mentioned in the text). Most, not all, hostels have small kitchens but usually no pots, pans or crockery, so self-caterers should take their own.

■ Campsites, cabins and mountain huts

Camping is the only other way of keeping accommodation costs right down. There are hundreds of official sites throughout the country, most listed by the **Norges Automobil-Forbund** (*NAF*), the Norwegian Automobile Club, whose office is at Storgaten 2, Oslo (☎02/42 94 00). Sites are of a high standard, and prices are usually around 30kr a tent, plus a small charge per person. The Norwegian Tourist Board in London publishes an annual list, *Camping Sites in Norway*, which should be sufficient, but for complete listings the *NAF* publish a yearly book, *Camping Norge*, which you can buy in some bookshops in Britain (or write to *NAF* Distribusjonsavd, Postboks 494 Sentrum, N–0105 Oslo 1, sending £8 by international postgiro to account no. 5 12 84 00).

Camping rough in Norway is more than tolerated; indeed, as in Sweden, it is a tradition enshrined in law. You can camp anywhere in open areas as long as you are at least 150m away from any houses or cabins. As a courtesy, ask farmers for permission to use their land – it is rarely refused. Fires are not permitted in woodland areas or in fields between April 15 and September 15, and camper vans are not allowed (ever) to overnight on lay-bys. For other countryside restrictions, see *Basics*, "The Countryside". A good sleeping bag is, not surprisingly, essential, since even in summer it can get very cold, and, in the north at least, a mosquito repellent and sun-protection cream are vital.

Cabins and mountain huts

Where campsites score for the non-camper, too, is as a source of **cabins** Almost every campsite has them, usually four-bedded affairs with kitchen facilities and sometimes a bathroom, and the prices – from 150kr per cabin – make it the cheapest way for a group, or a couple, to see the country in some comfort. In the fish-rich Lofoten and Vesterålen Islands, the chalets are called **rorbuer** and nearly always have fishing facilities, so that you can fend for yourself.

One further option for hikers is the chain of **mountain huts**, or *hytter*, on hiking routes countrywide, run by **Den Norske Turistforening** (*DNT*), the Norwegian Mountain Hiking Association. You have to be a member to use these, and they range from staffed lodges serving meals (55–110kr a night) to unstaffed huts where you leave the money for your stay in a box provided (from 45kr a night). Membership is 185kr a year (120kr for under-21s and over-67s); details from *DNT*, Stortingsgate 28, Postboks 1963 Vika, N–0125 Oslo 1 (☎02/41 80 20); or, in England, from *Mountain & Wildlife Venture*, Brow Foot, High Wray, Ambleside, Cumbria (☎05394–33285).

■ Hotels, pensions and private rooms

Hotels are, for the most part, way out of the reckoning for budget travellers – the cheapest double room in Oslo, without bath, will set you back around 400kr a night. Still, if you're not pressed quite so hard for cash, or simply want a night of comparative luxury, there are plenty of bargains to be found. Oslo, in particular, has some relatively cheap summer deals, as do the other towns and cities – for details contact the local tourist office and check the text. Remember, too, that the price of a hotel room always includes breakfast and that central hotels can save on transport out to the more distant hostels and campsites.

Slightly cheaper are the rarer **pensions**, called *pensjonater* or *hospits*: small, intimate boarding houses usually available in the more touristy towns, which go for about 120–160kr single, 200–300kr double; breakfast is usually extra. Failing that, tourist offices in larger towns can sometimes fix you up with a **private room** in someone's house, which may include kitchen facilities. Prices are competitive – around 80–100kr single, 130–180kr double – though there's a booking fee (10–15kr) on top, and the rooms themselves can be some way out of the centre.

Food and Drink

Norwegian food can, at its best, be excellent: fish is plentiful, and carnivores can have a field day trying meats like reindeer steak or elk. But once again all this costs money, and those on a tight budget may have problems varying their diet. Vegetarians, too, won't find much to tempt them. Be prepared to cater for yourself and shop in supermarkets for the consistently healthiest and cheapest eating. The same can be said of drinking, too: buying from the supermarkets and state off-licenses is often the only way you'll afford a tipple.

■ Food

Many travellers exist almost entirely on a mixture of picnic food and hot meals that they rustle up themselves, with the odd snack and café meal thrown in to boost morale. However, there are a number of ways to eat out reasonably: a good self-service breakfast goes some way to solving the problem, served in almost every hostel and hotel; special lunch deals will get you a hot meal for around 50kr; while alongside the regular restaurants – which *are* expensive – there's the usual array of budget pizzerias and caféterias in most towns.

Breakfast, picnics and snacks

Breakfast (*frokost*) in Norway is a huge self-service affair of bread, crackers, cheese, eggs, preserves, cold meat and fish, washed down by unlimited tea and coffee: it's usually excellent at youth hostels, and memorable in hotels, filling you up for the day for around 50kr.

If you're buying your own **picnic food**, bread, cheese, yoghurt and fruit are all good value, while other staple foodstuffs – rice, pasta, canned fish and vegetables – are roughly twice the price of British equivalents. Anything tinned is dear: baked beans at around 7kr a can, ravioli 16kr, while coffee and tea are also very expensive – take your own. Beware of a cheapish sandwich spread called *Kaviar*, bright pink, sold in tubes and packed full of additives. Real caviar, on the other hand – from lump-fish rather than sturgeon – is widely available and relatively inexpensive.

Fast food probably offers the best chance of a hot and filling snack. The indigenous

Norwegian stuff, served up from a **Gatekjøkken** – a street kiosk or stall – in every town and village, consists mainly of rubbery hotdogs (*varm pølse*), pizza slices and chicken pieces and chips. American-style burger bars are also creeping in. Oslo has its first *McDonalds* and other towns often feature the Scandinavian *Clockburger* – hardly health food but at least the standard is consistent and they nearly always have the cheapest coffee in town. A better choice, and often no more expensive, is simply to get a sandwich, normally a huge open affair called a **smørbrød** (pronounced "smurrbrur"), heaped with a variety of garnishes. You'll see them groaning with shrimps, salad and mayonnaise in the windows of **cafés**, or in the newer and trendier sandwich bars in the larger towns.

Ice cream is almost a Norwegian hobby. As well as selling numerous varieties of the stuff – not at all bad on the whole – ice-cream bars are popular hangouts with the young and, with burger joints, often the only place you'll find any life on a Saturday night in the more rural centres. **Cakes and biscuits** are good too: watch for doughnuts, Danish pastries (*Wienerbrød*), butter biscuits (*kjeks*) and waffles (*Vafler*).

Good **coffee** is available everywhere, served black or with cream, rich, strong, and, in many places, particularly at breakfast, free after the first cup. **Tea**, too, is ubiquitous, but the local preference is for lemon tea or a variety of flavoured infusions; if you want milk, ask for it. All the familiar brands of **soft drinks** are available as well.

Lunch and dinner

For the best deals, you're going to have to adjust your body clock throughout your stay and eat the main meal of the day at lunchtime (*lunsj*), when **kafeterias** (usually self-service restaurants) lay on daily specials, the **dagens rett**. This is a fish or meat dish served with potatoes and a vegetable or salad, often including a drink, sometimes bread, and occasionally coffee too; it should go for around 50kr. Dipping into the menu is more expensive, but not cripplingly so if you stick to omelettes or cheap cutlets of meat. Most department stores and large supermarkets have surprisingly good *kafeterias*, as does every main railway station. You'll also find them above more traditional restaurants in larger towns, where they might be called *Kaffistovas*.

Restaurants, serving dinner (*middag*) and real Norwegian food, are out the range of many budgets. Seafood is good, as are the more obscure meats, but both can be wildly expensive – and the cheapest bottle of plonk will set you back at least 90kr. If someone else is paying, smoked salmon comes highly recommended and, in the north especially, watch out for elk (*elg*) and reindeer steaks (*reinsdyrstek*) – a taste sensation for the curious. Again, the best deals are at lunchtime, when many restaurants put out a **koldtbord** (the Norwegian *smörgåsbord*), where for a fixed price of around 80–100kr you can get through as much as possible during the three or four hours it's served. Highlights include vast arrays of pickled herring, salmon (*laks*), cold cuts of meat, dried reindeer, a feast of breads and crackers and usually a few hot dishes too – meatballs, soup and scrambled eggs.

There are a growing number of **ethnic restaurants**, the most affordable of which are the pizza joints in most towns – though two people sharing a huge pizza and a couple of small beers won't get away for less than 130–170kr.

Vegetarians are in for a hard time. Apart from a couple of specialist restaurants in Oslo there is little you can do except make do with salads, look out for egg dishes in *kafeterias* and supplement your diet from supermarkets. If you are a **vegan** the problem is greater: when the Norwegians are not eating meat and fish, they are attacking a fantastic selection of milks, cheeses and yoghurts. At least you'll know what's in every dish you eat, since everyone speaks English.

■ Drink

On the surface, there's little difference between Norway and Britain when it comes to drinking: everything you'll want is available, although if it's alcoholic, the money that you hand over is closer to the debt of a Third World country than the price of a drink. There are subtler differences, though, not least the paternalistic attitude that only lets you buy takeouts from a state off-license and views social drinking as a curse.

What to drink

A historic temperance movement and the machinations of tax politics mean that Norwegian alcohol prices are amongst the highest in Europe. **Beer** is lager-like and comes in three strengths (class I, II or III), of which the strongest and most expensive is class III. **Wine** (all imported) and **spirits**, too, are both way over the top in price, so it's best to bring your duty-free allowance in with you (one litre of spirits and one litre of wine for everyone over twenty). One local brew worth experimenting with at least once is *akevitt*, served ice-cold in little glasses and at forty percent proof, real headache material – though more palatable with beer chasers.

Where to drink

Beer is sold in supermarkets and shops all over Norway, though some local communities, particularly in the west, have their own rules and restrictions; it's about half the price you'd pay in a bar. Wines and spirits can only be purchased from the state-controlled shops, known as **Vinmonopol**. There's generally one in each small town, though there are more branches in the cities (twenty in Oslo): opening hours are Monday–Wednesday 10am–4pm, Thursday 10am–5pm, Friday 9am–4pm, Saturday 9am–1pm, though times can vary depending on the area; they'll be closed the day before a public holiday. Wine is quite a bargain, from around 30kr a bottle.

Going out for a drink is a different proposition. Wherever you go, a half-litre of beer costs between 30kr and 40kr. You can get a drink at most **outdoor café's** and at an increasing number of **bars**, **pubs** and **cocktail bars**. Only in the cities is there any kind of "European" bar life, and even then – at least outside the capital – things tend to close down at around 11pm, although licensed discos and clubs stay open later. Only in Oslo will you be able to keep going until at least 1am, and 4am in some places.

As for conventions, despite the obstacles to drinking, the Norwegians take it all very seriously. Like many Scandinavians they are not social drinkers – asking someone out for a drink during the week labels you an alcoholic – but weekends can be riotous, especially in remoter regions. Incidentally, **buying a round** is virtually unheard of in Norway and people normally pay for their own – something which, considering the prices, is worth remembering.

The country is still littered with people making their own illicit brews in illegal **stills**. If you are invited over "for a drink", be very careful about what you think you are drinking. Swigging something akin to aviation fuel in any sort of quantity can leave you, quite literally, speechless.

GLOSSARY OF NORWEGIAN FOOD AND DRINK TERMS

Basics and snacks

Appelsin-marmelade	Marmalade	Kaviar	Caviar	Pommes-frites	Chips
		Kjeks	Biscuits	Potetchips	Crisps
Brød	Bread	Krem	Double cream	Ris	Rice
Eddik	Vinegar		(for desserts)	Rundstykker	Roll
Egg	Egg	Marmelade	Jam	Salat	Salad
Eggerøre	Scrambled	Melk	Milk	Salt	Salt
	eggs	Mineralvann	Mineral water	Sennep	Mustard
Flatbrød	Crispbread	Nøtter	Nuts	Smør	Butter
Fløte	Single cream	Olje	Oil	Smørbrød	Sandwich
	(for coffee)	Omelett	Omelette	Sukker	Sugar
Grøt	Porridge	Ost	Cheese	Suppe	Soup
Iskrem	Ice Cream	Pannekake	Pancakes	Varm pølse	Hot-dog
Kake	Cake	Pepper	Pepper	Yoghurt	Yoghurt

Meat (Kjøtt) and Game (Vilt)

Dyrestek	Venison	Lever	Liver	Skinke	Ham
Elg	Elk	Oksekjøtt	Beef	Spekemat	Dried meat
Kalkun	Turkey	Postei	Paté	Stek	Steak
Kjøttboller	Meatball	Pølser	Sausages	Svinekjøtt	Pork
Kylling	Chicken	Reinsdyr	Reindeer	Varm pølse	Frankfurter
Lammekjøtt	Lamb	Ribbe	Pork rib		/Hot-dog

Fish (Fisk) and Shellfish (Skalldyr)

Ansjos	Anchovies	Laks	Salmon	Sild	Herring
Blåskjell	Mussels	Makrell	Mackerel	Sjøtunge	Sole
Brisling	Sprats	Piggvar	Turbot	Småfisk	Whitebait
Hummer	Lobster	Reker	Shrimps	Torsk	Cod
Hvitting	Whiting	Rødspette	Plaice	Tunfisk	Tuna
Kaviar	Caviar	Sardiner	Sardines	Ål	Eel
Krabbe	Crab	Sei	Coalfish	Ørret	Trout
Kreps	Crayfish				

Vegetables (Grønsaker)

Agurk	Cucumber/gherkin/pickle	Hvitløk	Garlic	Poteter	Potatoes
		Kål	Cabbage	Rosenkøl	Brussel
Blomkål	Cauliflower	Linser	Lentils		sprouts
Bønner	Beans	Løk	Onion	Selleri	Celery
Erter	Peas	Mais	Sweetcorn	Sopp	Mushrooms
Gulrøtter	Carrots	Nepe	Turnip	Spinat	Spinach
Hodesalat	Lettuce	Paprika	Peppers	Tomater	Tomatoes

Fruit (Frukt)

Ananas	Pineapple	Eple	Apple	Plommer	Plums
Appelsin	Orange	Fersken	Peach	Pærer	Pears
Aprikos	Apricot	Fruktsalat	Fruit salad	Sitron	Lemon
Banan	Banana	Grapefrukt	Grapefruit	Solbær	Blackcurrants
Blåbær	Blueberries	Jordbær	Strawberries	Tyttbær	Cranberries
Druer	Grapes	Multer	Cloudberries		

Terms

Blodig	Rare, underdone	*Marinert*	Marinated	*Stekt*	Fried
Godt stekt	Well done	*Ovnstekt*	Baked/roasted	*Stuet*	Stewed
Grillet	Grilled	*Røkt*	Smoked	*Sur*	Sour/pickled
Grytestekt	Braised	*Saltet*	Cured	*Syltet*	Pickled
Kokt	Boiled				

Norwegian Specialities

Brun saus Brown sauce served with most meats.

Fiskeboller Fish balls, served under a white sauce or on open sandwiches.

Fiskesuppe Fish soup.

Flatbrød A flat unleavened cracker, half barley, half wheat.

Gammelost A hard, strong smelling, blue-veined cheese.

Geitost/ Gjetost Goat's cheese, slightly sweet and fudge- coloured. Similar cheeses have different ratios of goats milk/ cows milk, *mysost* one of the "goatiest".

Kjøttkaker med surkål Homemade burgers with cabbage and a sweet & sour sauce.

Koldtbord A midday buffet with cold meats, herrings, salads, bread and perhaps soup, eggs or hot meats.

Lapskaus Pork and vegetable stew, common in the south and east.

Lutefisk Fish (usually cod) preserved in an alkali solution and flavoured; an acquired taste.

Multer Cloudberries – wild berries, found north of the Arctic Circle and served with cream (*med krem*).

Pinnekjøtt Western Norwegian Christmas dish of smoked mutton steamed over shredded birch bark, served with cabbage.

Reinsdyrstek Reindeer steak, usually served with boiled potatoes and cran- berry sauce.

Rekesalat Shrimp salad in mayonnaise.

Ribbe, julepølse, medisterkake Eastern Norwegian Christmas dish of pork ribs, sausage and dumplings.

Trondhjemsuppe Fruit porridge with barley, dried fruit and blackberry juice.

Drinks

Appelsin saft	Orange juice	*Sitronbrus*	Lemonade	*Vin*	Wine
Fruksaft	Fruit juice	*Vann*	Water	*Søt*	Sweet
Kaffe	Coffee	*Varm*	Hot chocolate	*Tørr*	Dry
Te med melk/ sitron	Tea with milk/lemon	*sjokolade* *Akevitt*	Aquavit	*Rød*	Red
Melk	Milk	*Eplesider*	Cider	*Hvit*	White
Mineralvann	Mineral water	*Øl*	Beer	*Rosé* *Skål*	Rosé Cheers

Directory

BORDERS There is little formality at the Norway/Sweden border, slightly more between Norway and Finland. However, the northern border with the Soviet Union is a different story. There are ornithological reasons why you might want to poke around the area to the east of Kirkenes, but border patrols (from both sides) won't be overjoyed at the prospect. If you have a genuine wish to explore the region, it's best to inform the Norwegian authorities.

CANOEING Lots of opportunities on Norway's coast, lakes and rivers: contact *Norges*

Kajakkforbund, Hauger Skolevei 1, N–1351 Oslo (☎02/51 88 00) for a list of regional canoeing centres and rental possibilities. Local tourist offices have information, too.

CUSTOMS RESTRICTIONS Over and above the duty-free allowance (one litre of spirits and one litre of wine per person over twenty), you're allowed to take in another four litres of either, though you'll pay 80kr and 29kr respectively a litre in duty. If you're driving/camping, you can't import eggs and potatoes, or milk and cream from countries other than Scandinavian ones.

FISHING Fishing licences are available from hotels, campsites and tourist offices, valid for a day, a week or a season. You'll also need fishing insurance (60kr) if you're fishing for salmon, sea char or fresh water fish, payable in any post office. If you take your own fishing tackle, you must have it disinfected before use. There's more information in the book *Angling in Norway* (£4.50), published by the Norwegian Tourist Board and available from *BAS Overseas Publications*, BAS House, 48–50 Sheen Lane, London SW14 8LQ (☎01-876 2131).

KIDS No real problems with taking children to Norway. They go for half-price on most forms of transport, and get the same discount on an extra bed in their parent's hotel room. Family rooms are widely available in youth hostels, while many of the summer activities detailed in this book – events in folk parks, water sports and the like – are geared towards kids anyway. There are also baby-compartments (with their own toilet and changing-room) for kids under two and their escorts on most trains, and baby-changing rooms at Oslo, Bergen Trondheim and Bodø railway stations.

LEFT LUGGAGE In most railway stations and ferry terminals there are lockers. Also, tourist offices will often watch your stuff – though sometimes they charge.

NATURISM Nude bathing is perfectly legal, though be considerate of other people. Details on nude bathing from *Norsk Naturistforbund*, Postboks 189 Sentrum, N–0102 Oslo 1.

PUBLIC HOLIDAYS Everything will be closed on the following days: January 1, Maundy Thursday, Good Friday, Easter Monday, May 1 (May Day), May 17 (Constitution Day), Ascension Day (also in May), Whit Monday, Whit Tuesday, Christmas Day and Boxing Day.

SHOPS Opening hours are Monday–Friday 9am–5pm, Thursday 9am–6/7pm, Saturday 9am–2/3pm. Newspaper kiosks (*Narvesen*) and takeaway food stalls are open in the evenings until 10pm or 11pm (weekends, too).

SMOKING Since July 1988, smoking has been prohibited in all public buildings, including railway stations, and it's forbidden on all domestic flights.

SOCIETIES Contact the *Anglo-Norse Society*, c/o the Royal Norwegian Embassy, 25 Belgrave Square, London SW1. They'll put you in touch with regional friendship groups based in the UK, who organise a variety of cultural and social events throughout the year.

SUMMER SKIING For information on slalom or cross-country skiing on the fjells between mid-May and August, contact *Stryn Sommarskisenter*, Stryn Reiselivslag, Postboks 18, N–6880 Stryn (☎057/71 995); *Finse Skisenter*, Postboks 12, N–3590 Finse (☎05/52 67 11); or for summer glacier skiing *Rana Turistkontor*, N–8600 Mo-i-Rana (☎087/50 421).

History

Despite its low profile these days, Norway has a fascinating history, its people past explorers and conquerors of northern Europe and its islands, as well as North America. Though at first an independent state, from the fourteenth century onwards Norway came under the sway of first Denmark and then Sweden. Independent again since 1905, it's only recently that Norway has emerged fully onto the international stage, playing a leading part in the increasingly important environmental movement.

■ Early civilisations

The earliest signs of human habitation in Norway date from around 10,000 BC. This, the **Kosma** culture from Finnmark, relied upon seal-fishing for its livelihood. By 8000 BC reindeer-hunters were living in northern Norway, essentially a static people dependent upon flint and bone implements. As the edges of the ice cap retreated from the western coastline (earlier than in Sweden and Finland), these regions began to support a hunting and fishing population. Carvings and **rock drawings** – naturalistic representations of birds, animals and fish – found at Alta in Finnmark have been dated to around 5000 BC.

These Norwegian tribes remained a migratory people for a long time and it took immigrants from the east, most notably the **Boat Axe people** – so-called because of the distinctive shape of their weapons/tools – to bring about real agricultural development.

Around 1700 BC Germanic settlers began to move into Norway from Jutland and southern Sweden. Depictions of **Bronze Age** life (1500–500 BC) are revealed in the rock carvings which became prevalent in southern Norway during this period: pictures of men ploughing with oxen, riding horses, carrying arms and using boats to navigate the coastal water passages. Generally, though, the implements used by the ordinary people continued to be of stone. Bronze articles were almost entirely imported, found mostly in areas settled by the Boat Axe people, who were essentially an aristocratic culture.

Around 500 BC two adverse changes affected Norway. The country suffered with the rest of Scandinavia from a marked deterioration in climate, and the central European advance of the Celts interrupted trade relations with the Mediterranean world. The poor climate encouraged the development of settled, communal farming in an attempt to improve winter shelter and storage. The early **Iron Age**, though, all but passed Norway by,

The **classical world** knew little of Norway. The Greek geographer, Pytheas of Marseilles, went far enough north to note the short summer nights and probably visited southern Norway, but otherwise what lay beyond was inhospitable and unexplored. Pliny the Elder mentions "Nerigon" as the great island south of the legendary "Ultima Thule", the outermost region of the earth.

Following the collapse of the Roman Empire, Norwegian warriors took full advantage of the **Great Migration period** (fifth to sixth century AD), when whole peoples benefited from the temporary power vacuum. Hoards of appropriated spoils from all over the Mediterranean have been found in Norway. The emphasis on settlement and trade shifted from the west coast to the eastern regions and Trøndelag – areas with easy access to Sweden and its ruling tribe, the *Svear*. Throughout the country, bogs rich in iron ore were exploited and domestic iron-smelting (with its concomitant technical advances) flourished. A farmer class developed, based on a wealth in fields and animals. As all early farms were fundamentally similar, these communities were fairly democratic, although certainly patriarchal. Rural districts evolved with central markets and places of worship.

By the eighth century Norway was a country of **small, independent kingships**, the country's geography preventing any real unity. Only in southeastern Norway, where communication was easier, was there a dynastic grouping whose Swedish connections earned it a place in the **Ynglingatal** – a dynastic list compiled in the late eighth century by the Norwegian *skald* (court poet) Tjodolv. Although the country as a whole remained almost entirely outside the civilised world, advances were being made. There was a specific Merovingian influence on western Norway, which was the only region (apart from northern France) to adopt the short one-edged Saxon sword. And there was an expansion in shipbuilding and seafaring: the iron axe meant that planks could be hewn, and thus it was possible to build vessels fit for the open seas.

■ The Vikings

Overpopulation, internal dissension and the obvious mercantile attractions were all factors in the rapid expansionism that saw Scandinavians suddenly explode upon Europe and the Mediterranean in the ninth century. The patterns of attack and eventual settlement were dictated by the geographical position of the various Scandinavian countries: much as the Swedish Vikings turned eastwards and the Danes south and southwest, so the Norwegians headed west. Norwegian pirates or **Vikings** (from the Norse word *vik*, meaning creek or bay) fell upon the Hebrides, Shetland, Orkney, the Scottish mainland and western Ireland. The Hebrides were quickly overrun, the Pictish population able to offer little resistance, and, with the Isle of Man, formed the basis of a Norse kingdom, providing a base for future attacks upon Scotland and Ireland.

The Norwegians founded Dublin in 836, and from Ireland launched attacks eastwards across the northeast of England. By the end of the century, Norwegian Vikings had also landed and settled in the Faroe Islands and Iceland, while to the south Norwegians were encountering the Muslim power – records indicating attacks by Vikings upon Seville as early as 844.

The raiders soon became settlers, establishing a merchant class at home in Norway. Slave markets in Dublin and elsewhere assisted labour-intensive land clearance schemes; cereal and dairy farming extended into new areas in eastern Norway; and the fishing/hunting economy found new ground in the far north. Othere, a Norwegian chieftain, told Alfred the Great about his home in Finnmark where he kept reindeer and took tribute from the *Same*.

Pagan culture reached its peak in the Viking period. Western Norway adopted the Germanic "wergild" system of compensation: every free man was entitled to attend the local *Thing* or parliament, while a regional *Lagthing* made laws and settled disputes. Viking craftsmanship is seen at its best in the **ship burials** of Oseberg and Gokstad, which reveal detailed ornamentation and expert carving – both are on display in Oslo's Viking Ship Museum. The Oseberg ship is thought to be the burial ship of Åse, wife of the *Yngling* king Gudrød Storlatnes and mother of Halvan the Black.

It was from this dynastic family that Norway's first king, **Harald Håfrage** (the Fair-Haired), king of the tiny Vestfold region, claimed descent.

During the ninth century Norway was still a land of petty rulers, much of its south under Danish influence. Shortly before 900 (the date is unclear) Harald won a decisive victory at Hafrsfjord (near modern Stavanger) which gave him control of the coastal region as far north as Trøndelag. It sparked an exodus of minor rulers, most of whom left to settle in Iceland. Harald managed to maintain his conquests to the north and, before he died, named his son as his successor.

Erik Bloodaxe held on to his father's throne only briefly before fleeing to Northumbria in 945 (where he had a second short reign in the Viking kingdom of York). His youngest brother, later **Håkon the Good** (raised by the English King Athelstan in Wessex), returned to take the throne and, initially, was well received. Confirmed in England, his attempts to introduce Christianity to Norway failed. But he did carry out a number of reforms, establishing a common legal code for the whole of Vestlandet and Trøndelag, as well as introducing the system of *Leidang*, the division of the coastal districts into areas responsible for maintaining and manning a warship. His rule was punctuated by struggles against Erik's heirs, who were backed by Harald Bluetooth (the Danish king). Killed in battle in 960, Håkon was succeeded by Harald Eriksson (one of Bloodaxe's sons), whom Bluetooth killed ten years later in an attempt to halt his growing independence from Denmark. A Danish "appointee" to the throne, Håkon Sigurdsson, was to be the last genuine heathen to rule Norway. He based his rule at Trøndelag, still staunchly pagan.

In 995 **Olav Tryggvesson**, a Viking chieftain confirmed in England, sailed to Norway to challenge Håkon, who was fortuitously murdered by one of his own servants. Claiming descent from Harald Håfrage, Olav founded Nidaros (now Trondheim) as his base in an attempt to force Christianity onto the pagan north. However, his real problem remained the enmity of the Danish-controlled southeastern regions of Norway, and of Bluetooth's son Sweyn, who regarded Norway as his rightful inheritance. In alliance with the Swedish king, Sweyn defeated Olav at the sea battle of Svolder, and Norway was divided up amongst the victors.

Meanwhile, outside Norway, expansionism was underway. Norwegian settlers in **Iceland** established a parliament, the *Althing* in 930, based on Norwegian law. There were further Norwegian Viking discoveries too. Erik the Red, exiled from Norway and then banished from Iceland for three years for murder, set out in 985 with 25 ships, fourteen of which arrived in **Greenland**, where two communities developed. The **North American** shore had already been sighted by ships blown off course on the way from Norway to Greenland. In 1000 Erik's son, Leif, sailed to Labrador and then south to a region he called "Vinland" where grapes and corn were found growing wild. Both places, although never settled, marked a now accepted Norwegian "discovery" of North America.

■ The arrival of Christianity

Olav Haraldsson sailed for Norway in 1015, taking advantage of the problems caused by the death of the Danish King Sweyn Forkbeard. Sweyn's son Knud – king (Canute) of England – wasn't able to muster much support from his subordinate Norwegian earls and Olav soon gained recognition as king of Norway. For the first time the king's supporters were powerful inland farmers, a clear indication of how Norwegian society was moving away from its sea-based Viking past. Olav was severe in his attempts to convert Norway into a Christian land and his methods caused bitter opposition, yet during his reign the western coast of Norway adopted a system of church law. However, by 1028 disaffection was at its height and a combined Danish and English fleet led by Knud forced Olav to flee, first to Sweden and then to Russia. Knud's son Sweyn (and his mother, the English Queen Aelfgifu) took the Norwegian crown, only to be faced soon after – in 1030 – by the sensational return of Olav at the head of a scratch army. Olav, however, was defeated by an alliance of local farmers and land-owners at **Stiklestad**, the first major Norwegian land-battle.

Olav was killed by those who had most to fear from him, those who had already lost influence to a growing royal power. But they were to fare even worse under Sweyn and reaction against him and Aelfgifu soon grew. In 1035, Olav's young son, Magnus, returned from exile and was made king. People began to look back to Olav as a champion: there was talk of miracles and with the rising Norwegian church looking for a saint to improve its appeal, Olav was canonised. The remains of **St Olav** were reinterred ceremoniously at Nidaros, today's Trondheim, where his memory and alleged miracles hastened the conversion of much of Norway.

On Magnus' death, **Harald Hardråda** (Olav's half-brother) became king and consolidated his grip on the eastern uplands, establishing the boundaries of Norway. Then, turning his attention southwards, he sailed on England. In 1066, the Norwegian army marched on York but Harald was defeated and killed at Stamford Bridge by the English King Harold Godwinesson. Harald's son, **Olav Kyrre** – the Peaceful – agreed never to attack England again, and he reigned as king of Norway for the next 25 years. Peace engendered economic prosperity and treaties with Denmark ensured Norwegian independence. Three native bishoprics were established and cathedrals built at Nidaros, Bergen and Oslo. It's from this period, too, that Norway's surviving **stave churches** date: wooden structures resembling an upturned keel, they were lavishly decorated with dragon heads and scenes from heathen mythology, proof that the traditions of the pagan world were slow to disappear.

■ The Age of Greatness

Although Norway was confirmed as an independent power, the twelfth century saw a long period of internal disorder as the descendants of Olav Kyrre struggled to maintain their influence. Civil war ceased only when **Håkon IV** took the throne in 1240. He strengthened the Norwegian hold on the Faroe and Shetland Islands (which now paid tax and accepted a royal governor), and, in 1262, both Iceland and Greenland accepted Norwegian sovereignty. When his claim to the Hebrides was disputed by Alexander III of Scotland, Håkon assembled an intimidatory fleet but died in 1263 in the Orkneys. Three years later the Hebrides and the Isle of Man (always the weakest links in the Norse Empire) were sold to the Scottish crown by Håkon's successor, **Magnus the Lawmender**. Under Magnus, Norway prospered, achieving her greatest medieval success. The nobility began to assume greater power and were exempted from taxes in the 1270s, but they never became independent feudal lords – scattered farms were difficult to control and castles were rare.

It was in this period that Norwegian **Gothic art** reached its full maturity. Construction of the nave at Nidaros Cathedral began, as did work on Håkon's Hall in Bergen. **Håkon V** was to recover some of the ground lost to the nobility by reducing his Council in numbers and status. New castles were built (especially in Oslo, which became his capital), endowed with royal castellans and garrisons, and all officials were brought under Håkon's immediate control.

Norway, however, was in danger of losing her independence from two quarters. The **Hanseatic League** and its merchants had steadily increased their influence, holding a monopoly of imports and controlling inland trade too. With strongholds in Bergen and Oslo, the League came to dominate the economy. Secondly, when Håkon died in 1319 he left no male heir and was succeeded by his grandson, the three-year-old son of a Swedish duke. The boy, Magnus Eriksson, was elected Swedish king two months later, marking the virtual end of Norway as an independent country until 1905.

Magnus assumed full power over both countries in 1332, but his reign was a difficult one and when the nobility rebelled he agreed that the monarchy should again be split: his three-year-old son, Håkon, would become Norwegian king when he came of age, while the Swedes agreed to elect his eldest son Erik to the Swedish throne. It was then that the **Black Death** struck (1349), spreading quickly along the coast and up the valleys, and killing almost two-thirds of the population.

Håkon VI acceded to the Norwegian throne in 1355 and, despite opposition in Sweden, the idea of union persisted. Håkon married Margaret, daughter of Valdemar (king of Denmark), and when Valdemar died Margaret's son Olav took the Danish throne. And on Håkon's death in 1380, Olav inherited the Norwegian throne too, uniting the crowns of Denmark and Norway in a union that was to last 400 years.

■ The Kalmar Union

Despite Olav's early death in 1387, Margaret persevered with the union. Proclaimed "First Lady" by both the Danish and Norwegian nobility, she made a treaty with the Swedish nobles in 1388 which recognised her as regent of Sweden and agreed to accept any king she should nominate. Her chosen heir, **Erik of Pomerania**, was accepted by the Norwegian Council in 1389 as their hereditary sovereign, and in 1397 he was crowned at a diet in Sweden, known as the Kalmar Union.

After Margaret's death in 1412 Norway suffered. All power was concentrated in Denmark, foreigners were preferred in both state and church, and the country became impoverished by paying for Erik's wars against the Counts of Holstein. When Denmark and Sweden formally withdrew their allegiance from Erik in 1439, Norway ceased to take any meaningful part in Scandinavian affairs. Successive monarchs continued to appoint foreigners to important positions, appropriating Norwegian funds for Danish purposes and even mortgaging Orkney and Shetland (1469) to the Scots. Literature languished as the Old Norse language was displaced by the dominant Danish tongue, and only the Norwegian church retained any power.

Briefly, it looked as if Norway might recover some influence. In 1501–2, a Swedish-Norwegian nobleman, **Knut Alvsson**, crossed the border and soon overcame southern Norway as far as Bergen. But he was resisted by the Danish heir to the throne (later Christian II) and treacherously murdered as he sued for peace. Ibsen, for one, later saw this as a terrible blow for Norway, and the country remained neglected and outside the developments that led to the secession of Sweden and the **break up of the union** in 1523.

■ Union with Denmark

Norway had undergone a vigorous "Danicization" during the years of the Kalmar Union, but with the fall of Christian II in 1523, there seemed to be some hope for the country. The nobility rallied under the archbishop of Nidaros, Olav Engelbrektsson, in order to gain terms from the new king Frederick I. They failed, as they did again on Frederick's death, the ensuing Danish civil war producing victory for Christian III and **the Reformation**. In 1536 Christian, a Protestant, declared that Norway should cease to be a separate country and that the Lutheran faith should be established. Norway's national identity was thus further eroded: there was no written Norwegian literature and Danish gradually became the official language; the spoken tongue changed from Old Norse to the bastardised Middle Norwegian; the nobility declined, there was no effective leadership, and even the church lost power and influence – the only notable church construction was the rebuilding of Nidaros Cathedral.

Lutheranism was slow to take root among the conservative Norwegian peasantry, but it served as a powerful instrument in establishing Danish influence in Norway. The Bible, catechism and hymnal were all in Danish, the bishops were all Danes and, after 1537, so were all the most important provincial Norwegian governors. Also,

Frederick II embroiled Norway in the disastrous and inconclusive Northern Seven Years' War (1563–70) with Sweden, after which the tax burden on the country increased again.

During the reign of Frederick's son, **Christian IV**, Norway began to regain some of her former wealth and status. The most active of the Danish kings in Norway, he visited the country often, founding new towns and promulgating the first real national Norwegian Law. The first half of the seventeenth century saw economic advance too, due to a rapid population growth, marked increases in trade, copper and silver mining, the development of a Norwegian-controlled herring industry and, most importantly, a decline in the power of the Hanseatic League. But the tendency for Danish kings to drag Norway into their wars continued, Norway losing her eastern provinces (Jämtland and Härjedalen) to Sweden in 1645.

Frederick III, already acknowledged as absolute ruler in Denmark, called together the Norwegian Estates in 1661 to acclaim him similarly. The so-called "Twin Kingdoms" (of Denmark-Norway) came into being: Norway was incorporated into the administrative structure of Denmark and granted a *Stattholder* (governor-general) who ruled in Norway through a strict bureaucratic system. There were positive advantages for Norway: the country acquired better defences, simpler taxes, a separate High Court and further doses of Norwegian law.

Despite the full establishment of the Lutheran church in Norway by the end of the seventeenth century, the Reformation brought none of the intellectual stimulus it produced elsewhere. The **Renaissance** followed on late with little to show: the first printing press wasn't established until 1643, and despite the efforts of a small group of Norwegian humanists who completed a set of nostalgic writings about the past, the reading public remained insignificant. The only real expression of the Renaissance spirit was in the towns and buildings put up by Danish king Christian IV (notably Kongsberg, Kristiansand and Christiania – later Oslo): grid-built towns of great elegance.

Under Frederick II's successors, the disputes with Sweden which had beset the century came to a head. The Swedish king, Karl XII, invaded Norway in 1716 only to be repulsed initially by the Norwegian naval hero **Peter Torkenskiold** who destroyed his fleet. Karl was killed in Norway in 1718 and the **Peace of Frederiks-borg** (1720) left Norway in peace for the rest of the eighteenth century.

The **absolute monarchy** of the eighteenth century concerned itself with every aspect of Norwegian life. Missionaries were sent into Finnmark to introduce Christianity to the *Same*, a similar mission was sent to long-neglected Greenland in 1721. Peace favoured the growth of trade and the period saw comparatively little exploitation of the peasantry as tenants – there were still few large estates and no aristocracy on the land. **Culturally** the period saw the emergence of Norway's first modern poet, Peter Dass, whose verses and descriptions of Nordland (in his *Nordland's Trumpet*) were immensely popular; also of Ludwig Holberg, born in Bergen and best known for the 26 comedies he wrote for the Copenhagen Theatre between 1722 and 1727. The Trondheim Scientific Academy was founded in 1760 and a Norwegian Society established in Copenhagen in 1772. With trade monopolies abolished and the number of smallholders increasing, the emergence of a middle class helped shift the mood in Norway towards rejecting the union with Denmark. They wanted the same privileges as the Danes – their own bank, university and treasury.

Despite this, Norway was one of the few countries little affected by the French Revolution. Instead of political action there was a **religious revival**, with Hans Nielson Hauge emerging as an evangelical leader. His movement, characterised by a marked hostility to officialdom, caused concern and he was imprisoned; yet he provided the nucleus of a fundamentalist layman's movement, still a puritanical force to be reckoned with in parts of west and southwest Norway.

The period leading up to the **Napoleonic Wars** was a boom time for Norway: overseas trade, especially with England, flourished. The demand for Norwegian timber, iron and cargo-space heralded a period of unparalleled prosperity. Denmark-Norway had remained neutral throughout the Seven Years' War (1756–63) between England and France, and renewed that neutrality in 1792. However, when Napoleon forced Denmark into his Continental System in 1807, the British fleet bombarded Copenhagen and forced the surrender of the entire Dano-Norwegian fleet. Denmark, in retaliation, declared war on England and Sweden. The move was disastrous for the Norwegian economy, which had suffered bad harvests in 1807 and

1808, and the English blockade of its seaports ruined trade and caused starvation in the country.

Union on an equal footing with Sweden became an increasingly attractive idea to many Norwegians: it offered the best opportunity of restoring the lost trade with England. With Crown Prince Bernadotte (formerly one of Napoleon's generals) made heir to the Swedish throne, the idea became a possibility, and following his part in the defeat of Napoleon at Leipzig in 1813, Bernadotte (later Karl Johan XIV) claimed Norway on behalf of Sweden. At the **Peace of Kiel** in 1814 the defeated Danes were forced to cede all their rights in Norway to Sweden (although they did keep the dependencies – Iceland, Greenland and the Faroes). Four hundred years of union had ended.

■ Union with Sweden: 1814–1905

Norwegian feeling was that a mere transfer of the union to Sweden did nothing for the country's independence. A Constituent Assembly was summoned to Eidsvoll in April 1814 and produced a **constitution**. Issued on May 17, 1814 (still a national holiday), this declared Norway to be a "free, independent and indivisible realm." However, pressure grew on Norway from the signatories of the Kiel treaty to accept the union and it took a short war with Sweden before the Moss Convention of August 1814 recognised the Norwegian constitution and *Storting* (parliament). Although Bernadotte, as heir and crown prince in Sweden, didn't accede to the throne until 1818, he became regent and virtual ruler of both Sweden and Norway immediately.

The ensuing period was marred by struggles between the *Storting* and the crown over the nature of the union. Although the constitution emphasised the independence of Norway, she remained an inferior partner: the king had a suspensive veto over the *Storting*'s actions; the post of *Stattholder* in Norway could be held by a Swede; while foreign and diplomatic matters concerning Norway remained entirely in Swedish hands. Despite this, **Karl XIV** (as Bernadotte became in 1818) proved a popular king in Norway, and during his reign the country enjoyed a fair amount of independence. From 1836 all the highest offices in Norway were filled exclusively by Norwegians, new penal codes were introduced and democratic local councils established – something, in part, due to the rise of the peasant farmers as a political force in Norway.

The layout and buildings of modern Oslo – the Royal Palace, Karl Johans Gate, the university – date from the same post-union period, and the gradual increase in prosperity had important **cultural implications**. J.C. Dahl, Norway's great nature painter, was instrumental in the moves to establish the National Gallery in Oslo in 1836, and Henrik Wergeland, poet, prose writer and propagandist of major talent, remained passionate in his championing of the Norwegian national cause. The important **temperance movement**, too, gained a foothold in Norway. Acquiring government patronage in 1844, it was instrumental in forcing laws to prohibit the use of small stills – once found on every farm. By the mid-nineteenth century consumption of spirits had dropped drastically and coffee rivalled beer as the national drink.

Under Oscar I and Karl XV, **pan-Scandinavianism** flourished and then failed, as elsewhere in Scandinavia. This belief in a natural solidarity between Denmark, Norway and Sweden was espoused most loudly by artists and intellectuals, most notably Ibsen and Bjørnson. Oscar, a liberal monarch, found himself in some sympathy with the prevailing views, and in 1848 promised aid to Denmark when their troops were forced to withdraw from Schleswig-Holstein in the face of a Prussian advance. Though there was little enthusiasm anywhere for an actual engagement, the gesture was seen as a victory for pan-Scandinavianism. Not so in 1864, though, when Austria and Prussia declared war on Denmark. Karl wanted to help, but Swedish public opinion and the Norwegian *Storting* were unenthusiastic about the prospect, and pan-Scandinavianism died a toothless death. Little more than an academic movement even in its heyday, the loudest cries of treachery came from **Henrik Ibsen**, whose poetic drama, *Brand*, was a spirited indictment of Norwegian authority, and made his name in Norway.

Domestic politics changed, too, with the rise to power in the 1850s of **Johan Sverdrup**. Realising that independence would only come about if the *Storting* assumed real executive power, his new Reform Society propounded many of his views. Initial success came when a bill was passed to allow annual sessions of parliament. That the *Storting* was increasingly determined to rule emerged in the later struggle over whether the king's ministers should be answerable to parliament. Sverdrup's efforts ensured that a bill was passed to that effect in 1872 and again in 1874 and 1877. Each time, the new king, **Oscar II**, used his suspensive veto until, in 1880, the bill was passed for the third time in an unchanged form. It no longer required royal assent but Oscar claimed an absolute veto in constitutional matters. Sverdrup rallied Norwegian support and the 1882 *Storting* elections returned a formidable *Venstre* (Left) Party which, in 1884, impeached the supporters of the veto as well as the Prime Minister. Sverdrup headed a new ministry which was to take its authority from the *Storting*, not the crown – in effect a straight transition to full parliamentary government.

Economic growth continued and by 1880 Norway had the world's third-largest merchant navy (after the USA and Britain), while whaling expanded with the Norwegian invention of the harpoon. Considerable overpopulation in rural areas at this time was solved to some degree by widespread **emigration** to North America: in 1910 a US census recorded 800,000 of its inhabitants as either Norwegian or natives of Norwegian parents.

The *Venstre* Party scored another huge parliamentary majority in 1885. However, the party split over rows concerning the foreign ministry of the two countries (solely in Swedish hands since 1814) and 1891 saw victory for a Radical Left Party under Johannes Steen, demanding a separate foreign ministry for Norway. Initial demands were for a separate Norwegian consular service, reasonable enough given the extent of the country's merchant shipping interests. But the king refused to agree and the matter was referred to a Union Committee, which sat inconclusively until Steen assumed power again in 1898 with a new majority government. That year the Flag Law, removing the Union sign from the Norwegian mercantile marine flag, became operational and further attempts at compromise failed. When the *Storting* finally voted to establish a separate Norwegian consular service in 1905, Oscar again refused to sanction the move. The government resigned, claiming that as the king no longer exercised his constitutional functions the union should be dissolved. A plebiscite in August 1905 returned an overwhelming vote for **dissolution of the union**, which was duly confirmed by the Treaty of Karlstad. A second plebiscite determined that independent Norway should be a monarchy rather than a republic and, in November 1905, Prince Karl of Denmark (Edward

VII's son-in-law) was elected to the throne as **Håkon VII**.

Dissolution came at a time of further economic advance, engendered by the introduction of hydro-electric power. Social reforms also saw funds available for unemployment relief, accident insurance schemes and a Factory Act (1909). An extension to the franchise gave the vote to all men over 25 and, in 1913, to women too. The education system was reorganised, and higher sums spent on new arms and defence matters. This pre-war period also saw the emergence of a strong Trades' Union movement and that of a Labour Party committed to revolutionary change.

Culturally, the last years of the nineteenth century were fruitful for Norway. Alexander Kielland, a popular author outside Norway too, wrote most of his works between 1880 and 1891; while Knut Hamsen published his most characteristic novel, *Hunger*, in 1890. Slightly earlier, **Edvard Grieg** (1843–1907) had been inspired by old Norwegian folk melodies, and composed some of his most famous suites for Ibsen's *Peer Gynt*. Grieg was at the centre of Oslo musical life between 1866 and 1874, his debut concert the first to consist entirely of works by Norwegian composers. The artist **Edvard Munch** was also active during this period, completing many of his major works in the 1880s and 1890s.

■ Between the wars

Since 1814 Norway had had little to do with European affairs and at the outbreak of **World War I** declared herself strictly neutral. Sympathy, though, lay largely with the Western Allies, and the Norwegian economy boomed since its ships and timber were in great demand. By 1916, however, Norway began to feel the pinch, as German submarine action hit both enemy and neutral shipping, and by 1918 Norway had lost half its chartered tonnage and 2000 crew. When the USA entered the war, strict trade agreements were enforced to prevent supplies getting to Germany, and rationing had to be introduced. The price of neutrality was a rise in state expenditure, a soaring cost of living and, at the end of the war, no seat at the conference table. In spite of its losses Norway got no share of the confiscated German shipping, although it was compensated in part by gaining sovereignty of **Spitzbergen** and its coal deposits – the first extension of the Norwegian frontiers for 500 years. In 1920 Norway also entered the new League of Nations.

The decline in world trade, though, led to a decreased demand for Norway's shipping. Bank failure and currency fluctuation were rife, and, as unemployment and industrial strife increased, a developing Norwegian **Labour Party** took advantage. With the franchise extended to all those over 23 and the introduction of larger constituencies, it had a chance, for the first time, to win seats outside the large towns. At the 1927 election the Labour Party, together with the Social Democrats from whom they'd split, were the biggest grouping in the *Storting*. Because they had no overall majority and because many feared their revolutionary rhetoric, they were manoeuvred out of office after only fourteen days. Trade disputes and lockouts continued and troops had to be used to protect scabs.

Prohibition was adopted in 1919 following its wartime introduction but it did little to quell – and even exacerbated – drunkenness. It was abandoned in 1932 and replaced by the government sales monopoly of wines and spirits still in force today. The 1933 election gave the Labour Party more seats than ever. Having shed its revolutionary image, a campaigning reformist Labour Party benefited from the increasing conviction that state control and a centrally planned economy was the only answer to Norway's economic problems. In 1935 the Labour Party, in alliance with the Agrarian Party, took power – an unlikely combination since the Agrarians had boasted **Vidkun Quisling** as their defence spokesperson, a staunch anti-communist and virulent opponent of the Labour Party. In 1933 he'd left to found *Nasjonal Samling* ("National Unification"), a fascist movement which proposed, among other things, that both Hitler and Mussolini should be nominated for the Nobel Peace Prize. Quisling had good contacts with Nazi Germany but little support in Norway – local elections in 1937 reduced his local representation to a mere seven and party membership fell to 1500.

The Labour government under **Johan Nygaardsvold** presided over an improving economy. By 1938 industrial production was 75 percent higher than it had been in 1914; unemployment had dropped as expenditure on roads, rail and public works increased. Social welfare reforms were implemented and trade union membership increased. When war broke out in 1939, Norway was only lacking one thing – adequate defence. A vigorous member of the League of Nations, the country had pursued disarmament and peace policies since the end of World War I and was determined to remain neutral.

World War II

As **World War II** broke – and despite the warning signs from Germany – Norway again emphasised her neutrality. In early 1940, with Hitler preparing an invasion force, the Norwegians were more interested in the Allied mine-laying off the Norwegian coast – an attempt to prevent Swedish iron ore being shipped from Narvik to Germany. On the same day that they protested to Britain, the **German invasion** of Norway took place: the south and central regions of the country were quickly overrun, the Germans declaring that they were there to protect Norway from the British. King Håkon and the *Storting* left for Elverum, where the government was granted full powers to take whatever decisions were necessary in the interests of Norway – a mandate which later formed the basis of the Norwegian government-in-exile in Britain. The Germans demanded that Quisling be accepted as Prime Minister but this was rejected outright, and for two months a resistance campaign was fought by the Norwegians. They were no match for the organised German troops and in June both king and government fled to Britain from Tromsø (northern Norway). The country was rapidly brought under Nazi control, Hitler sending **Josef Terboven** to take full charge of Norwegian affairs.

The fascist *NS* was declared the only legal party in Norway and the media, civil servants and teachers brought under party control. As **civil resistance** grew, a state of emergency was declared: two trade union leaders were shot, arrests increased and a concentration camp was set up outside Oslo. In February 1942 Quisling was installed as "Minister President" of Norway, but it was soon clear that Quisling's government didn't have the support of the Norwegian people. The church refused to co-operate, schoolteachers protested and trade union members and officials resigned *en masse*. In response, deportations increased, death sentences were announced and a compulsory labour scheme was introduced.

Military resistance escalated. A military organisation (*MILORG*) was established as a branch of the armed forces under the control of the High Command in London. By May 1941 it had enlisted 20,000 men (32,000 by 1944) in clandestine groups all over the country. Arms and instructors came from Britain, radio stations were set up and a continuous flow of intelligence about Nazi movements sent back. Sabotage operations were legion, the most notable the destruction of the heavy-water plant at **Rjukan**, foiling a German attempt to produce an atomic bomb. Reprisals against the resistance were severe, but active collaboration with the enemy attracted only a comparative handful of Norwegians.

The **government-in-exile** in London continued to represent free Norway to the world, mobilising support on behalf of the Allies. Most of the Norwegian merchant fleet was abroad when the Nazis invaded and by 1943 the Norwegian navy had seventy ships fighting on the Allied side. In Sweden, Norwegian exiles assembled in "health camps" at the end of 1943 to train as police troops in readiness for liberation.

When the Allies landed in Normandy in June 1944, overt action against the Nazis in Norway by the resistance was discouraged, since the Allies couldn't safeguard against reprisals. By late October, the Russians had crossed the border in the north and forced the Germans to retreat — which they did, burning everything in their path and forcing the local population into hiding. To prevent the Germans reinforcing, the resistance planned a campaign of mass railway sabotage, stopping three-quarters of the troop movements overnight. As their control of Norway crumbled, the Germans finally **surrendered** on May 7, 1945, King Håkon returning to Norway on June 7 — five years to the day since he'd left for exile.

Terboven committed suicide and the *NS* collaborators were rounded up. A caretaker government took office, staffed by resistance leaders, and was replaced in October 1945 by a majority **Labour government**. The Communists won eleven seats, reflecting the efforts of Communist saboteurs in the war and the prestige that the Soviet Union enjoyed in Norway after liberation. Quisling was shot, along with 24 other high-ranking traitors, and thousands of collaborators were punished.

■ Post-war reconstruction

At the end of the war Norway was on its knees: the north had been laid waste, half the mercantile fleet lost, and production was at a standstill. Recovery, though, fostered by a sense of national unity, was quick and it took only three years for GNP to return to its pre-war level. Norway's part

in the war had increased her prestige in the world, a situation acknowledged as Norway became one of the founding members of the **United Nations** in 1945: its first Secretary-General, Tryggve Lie, was Norwegian Foreign Minister. With the failure of discussions to promote a Scandinavian defence union, the *Storting* also voted to enter **NATO** in 1949.

Domestically, there was general agreement about the form that social reconstruction should take. The laws that introduced the Welfare State in 1948 were passed virtually unanimously by the *Storting*. The 1949 election saw the government returned with a larger majority and Labour governments continued to be returned throughout the following decade, the premiership for most of this time held by **Einar Gerhardsen**. As national prosperity increased, society became ever more egalitarian, levelling up rather than down. Subsidies were paid to the agricultural and fishing industries, wages increased and a comprehensive social security system helped to eradicate poverty. The state ran the important mining industry, was the largest shareholder in the hydroelectric company and built an enormous steel works at Mo-i-Rana to help develop the economy of the devastated northern counties. Rationing ended in 1952 and, as the demand for higher-level education grew, new universities were approved at Bergen, Trondheim and Tromsø.

■ Beyond consensus: modern Norway

The political consensus in favour of Labour began to turn in the early 1960s. Following changes in the constitution concerning the rural constituencies, the centre had realigned itself in the 1950s, the outmoded Agrarian Party becoming the **Centre Party**. Defence squabbles within the Labour Party led to the formation of the **Socialist People's Party** (*SF*), which wanted Norway out of NATO and sought a renunciation of nuclear weapons. The Labour Party's 1961 declaration that no nuclear weapons would be stationed in Norway except under an immediate threat of war did not placate the *SF* who, unexpectedly, took two seats at the election that year. Holding the balance of power, the *SF* voted with the Labour Party until 1963 when it helped bring down the government over the mismanagement of state industries. A replacement coalition collapsed after only one month, but the writing was on the wall. Rising prices, dissatisfaction with high taxation and a continuing housing shortage meant that the 1965 election put a **non-socialist coalition** in power for the first time in twenty years.

Under the leadership of **Per Borten** of the Centre Party, the coalition's programme was unambitious. However, living standards continued to rise and although the 1969 election saw a marked increase in Labour Party support, the coalition hung on to power. Norway had applied twice previously for membership of the **European Economic Community** (EEC) – in 1962 and 1967 – and with de Gaulle's fall in France, 1970 saw a fresh application. There was great concern, though, about the effect of membership on Norwegian agriculture and fisheries, and in 1971 Per Borten was forced to resign following his indiscreet handling of the negotiations. The Labour Party, the majority of its representatives in favour of EEC membership, formed a minority administration. And when the 1972 referendum narrowly voted "No" to joining the EEC the government resigned.

With the 1973 election producing another minority Labour government, the uncertain pattern of the previous ten years continued. Even the post-war consensus on **Norwegian security policy** broke down on various issues – the question of a northern European nuclear-free zone, the stocking of Allied material in Norway – although there remained strong agreement for continued NATO membership. Indeed, most Norwegians continue to believe in the existence of a Soviet threat. In the biggest spy case since World War II, a senior official in the Ministry of Foreign Affairs was exposed as a Soviet spy in 1984.

In 1983, the Christian Democrats and the Centre Party joined together in a non-socialist coalition, which lasted only two years. It was replaced in 1986 by a minority Labour administration, led by **Dr Gro Harlem Brundtland**, Norway's first woman Prime Minister. She made ringing changes to the way the country was run, introducing seven women into her eighteen-member cabinet – a world record. However, her government was beset by problems for the three years of its life: tumbling oil prices led to a recession, unemployment rose (though only to four percent) and there was widespread dissatisfaction with Labour's high taxation policies.

At the **general election in September 1989** Labour lost eight seats and was forced out of office, but more surprising was the success of the extremist parties on both political wings – the anti-NATO Left Socialist Party and the right-wing anti-immigrant Progress Party both scored spectacular results, increasing their representation in the *Storting* many times over. This deprived the Conservative Party (one of whose leaders, bizarrely, is Gro Harlem Brundtland's husband) of a majority it might have expected, the result yet another shaky minority administration. This time it is a **centre-right coalition** between the Conservatives, the Centre Party and the Christian Democrats, led by Mr. Jan Syse.

The new government faces problems familiar to the last Labour administration. There's continuing conflict over joining the European Community, a policy flatly rejected by the Centre Party. Race is back on the agenda, too. The success of the Progress Party (up from two to 22 seats in Parliament) has alarmed many people: its policy (all too familar in Britain) is to slash welfare spending, cut taxes and stop immigration and, for the first time in years, it has an audience in Norway. Also, despite relative Norwegian wealth and an advanced social policy, the late 1970s and 1980s have seen a development of the **social problems** that have plagued other European countries: drug addiction, violent crime and public drunkenness have all increased. As in Sweden, the reasons are not immediately obvious nor obviously economic, with unemployment (despite its recent rise) still manageable and an overall shortage of skilled labour.

Other problems, too, have whipped up public fervour, most notably that of the threat of **acid rain** to the Norwegian countryside. Norway is one of the highest net recipients of sulphurous waste products in the world (much of it from the UK) and records acid pollution levels comparable to the most heavily polluted industrial regions of Europe. The country plays an active role in international campaigning against acid rain, the visit of Mrs Thatcher to Oslo in 1987 seeing the riot police out for the first time to quell the angry demonstrations.

Politically, Norway is in for a stormy time for the next two or three years. The constitution rules out new elections until 1993 and if the present coalition falls, the Labour Party could find itself back in power by default. Whoever rules, though, without a majority it's unlikely that there will be a distinct upturn in the unsteady economy, or a satisfactory compromise on the question of EC membership – both burning issues at present.

A BRIEF GUIDE TO NORWEGIAN

There are two official Norwegian languages: *Riksmål* or *Bokmål* (book language), a modification of the old Dano-Norwegian tongue left over from the days of Danish dominance; and *Landsmål* or *Nynorsk*, which was developed with the nineteenth-century upsurge of Norwegian nationalism and is based on the Old Norse dialects that came before. You'll see both on your travels but of the two, *Bokmål* is the most common – and is the language we use here.

As elsewhere in Scandinavia, you don't really need to know any Norwegian to get by in Norway. Almost everyone, especially younger people, speaks some English, and in any case many words are not too far removed from their English equivalents; there's also plenty of English (or American) on billboards, the TV and at the cinema. Mastering a hello or a thank you will, however, be greatly appreciated, while if you speak either Danish or Swedish you should have few problems being understood. If you don't, and can't master the Norwegian, a basic knowledge of German is a help too. Of the **phrasebooks**, much the most useful is *Norwegian for Travellers* (Berlitz £2.25), though if you intend to visit Denmark and/or Sweden on the same trip, *Traveller's Scandinavia* (Pan £2.50) covers all three languages.

PRONUNCIATION

Pronunciation can be tricky. A **vowel** is usually long when it's the final syllable or followed by only one consonant; followed by two it's generally short. Unfamiliar ones are:

ae before an r, as in b**a**d; otherwise as in s**a**y

ø as in f**u**r but without pronouncing the r

å usually as in s**a**w

øy between the ø sound and b**oy**

ei as in s**a**y

Consonants are pronounced as in English except:

c, q, w, z found only in foreign words and pronounced as in the original

g before i, y or ei, as in **y**et; otherwise hard

hv as in **v**iew

j, gj, hj, lj as in **y**et

rs usually as in **sh**ut

k before i, y or j, like the Scottish lo**ch**; otherwise hard

BASICS

Do you speak English ?	*Snakker De engelsk ?*	Good morning	*God morgen*
Yes	*Ja*	Good afternoon	*God dag*
No	*Nei*	Good night	*God natt*
Do you understand ?	*Forstår De ?*	Goodbye	*Adjø*
I don't understand	*Jeg forstår ikke*	Today	*I dag*
I understand	*Jeg forstår*	Tomorrow	*I morgen*
Please	*Vær så god*	Day after tomorrow	*I overmorgen*
Thank you (very much)	*Takk (tusen takk)*	In the morning	*Om morgenen*
You're welcome	*Vær så god*	In the afternoon	*Om ettermiddagen*
Excuse me	*Unnskyld*	In the evening	*Om kvelden*

SOME SIGNS

Entrance	*Inngang*	Police	*Politi*
Exit	*Utgang*	Hospital	*Sykehus*
Gentlemen	*Herrer*	Cycle path	*Sykkelsti*
Ladies	*Damer*	No Smoking	*Røyking forbudt*
Open	*Åpen*	No Camping	*Camping Forbudt*
Closed	*Stengt*	No Trespassing	*Uvedkommende Forbudt*
Arrival	*Ankomst*	No Entry	*Ingen adgang*
Departure	*Avgang*	Pull/push	*Trekk/trykk*

QUESTIONS AND DIRECTIONS

Where ? (where is/are ?)	*Hvor ? (hvor er ?)*	Near/far	*i nærheten/langt borte*
When ?	*Når ?*	Good/bad	*God/dårlig*
What ?	*Hva ?*	Vacant/occupied	*Ledig/opptatt*
How much/many ?	*Hvor mye/hvor mange*	A little/a lot	*Litt/mye*
Why ?	*Hvorfor ?*	More/less	*Mer/mindre*
Which ?	*Hvilket ?*	Can we camp here ?	*Kan vi campe her ?*
What's that called in Norwegian ?	*Hva kaller man det på norsk ?*	Is there a youth hostel near here ?	*Er det et ungdomsherberge i nærheten ?*
Can you direct me to . . . ?	*Kan De vise meg veien til . . . ?*	How do I get to . . . ?	*Hvordan kommer jeg til . . . ?*
It is/there is (is it/is there)	*Det er (er det)*	How far is it to . . . ?	*Hvor langt er det til . . . ?*
What time is it ?	*Hvor mange er klokken ?*	Ticket	*Billett*
Big/small	*Stor/liten*	Single/return	*en vei/tur-retur*
Cheap/expensive	*Billig/dyrt*	Can you give me a lift to . . . ?	*Kan jeg få sitte på til . . . ?*
Early/late	*Tidlig/sent*	Left/right	*Venstre/høyre*
Hot/cold	*Varm/kald*	Go straight ahead	*Kjør rett frem*

NUMBERS

0	*null*	9	*ni*	18	*atten*	70	*sytti*
1	*en*	10	*ti*	19	*nitten*	80	*åtti*
2	*to*	11	*elleve*	20	*tjue*	90	*nitti*
3	*tre*	12	*tolv*	21	*tjueen*	100	*hundre*
4	*fire*	13	*tretten*	22	*tjueto*	101	*hundreogen*
5	*fem*	14	*fjorten*	30	*tretti*	200	*to hundre*
6	*seks*	15	*femten*	40	*førti*	1000	*tusen*
7	*sju*	16	*seksten*	50	*femti*		
8	*åtte*	17	*sytten*	60	*seksti*		

DAYS AND MONTHS

Sunday	*søndag*	January	*januar*	July	*juli*
Monday	*mandag*	February	*februar*	August	*august*
Tuesday	*tirsdag*	March	*mars*	September	*september*
Wednesday	*onsdag*	April	*april*	October	*oktober*
Thursday	*torsdag*	May	*mai*	November	*november*
Friday	*fredag*	June	*juni*	December	*desember*
Saturday	*lørdag*				

(Days and months are never capitalised)

GLOSSARY OF NORWEGIAN TERMS AND WORDS

Apotek	Chemist	*Havn*	Harbour	*NRK*	Norwegian State TV
Bakke	Hill	*Hytte*	Cottage, cabin	*Rådhus*	Town hall
Bokhandel	Bookshop	*Innsjø*	Lake	*Sentrum*	City centre
Bro/bru	Bridge	*Jernbanestasjon*	Railway station	*Sjø*	Lake
Dal	Valley	*Kirke/kjerke*	Church	*Skog*	Forest
Domkirke	Cathedral	*KFUM/KFUK*	Norwegian YMCA/YWCA	*Slott*	Castle, palace
Drosje	Taxi			*Storting*	Parliament
E.Kr	AD	*Klokken/kl.*	o'clock	*Tilbud*	Special offer
Elv	Stream	*KNA*	Norwegian equivalent of the RAC	*Torget*	The main town square, often home to an outdoor market
Ferje/ferge	Ferry				
Fjell/berg	Mountain	*MOMS*	Value Added Tax		
F.Kr	BC	*Museet*	Museum	*Vann/vatn*	Water or lake
Foss	Waterfall	*NAF*	Norwegian Automobile Association	*Vei/veg/vn.*	Road
Gate (gt.)	Street			*Å*	River
Hav	Sea				

CHAPTER FOUR

OSLO AND AROUND

D espite tourist office endeavours, **Oslo** retains a decidedly low profile among European cities. Even comparisons with other Scandinavian capitals are less than favourable, and critics have it marked down as a sort of cultural poor relation. You'll inevitably pass through – from Oslo the main train routes head out west to the fjords, south to the coast and east to Sweden – but take heart: Oslo is definitely worth seeing. The city notches up some of Europe's best museums, fields a cosmopolitan street-life that surprises most visitors, and helps revive travellers weary of the quiet northern wilderness.

Seeing Oslo takes – and deserves – time. Its half a million inhabitants have room to spare in a city whose vast boundaries (453 square kilometres) encompass huge areas of wood, sand and water. There's a less hectic feel to Oslo than most capitals: getting around the sights becomes a different proposition when you're as likely to be swimming or trail-walking as strolling the city centre. **Island beaches** in the Oslo Fjord and open forest and ski-jumps at **Holmenkollen** are all targets for a longer stay within the city limits, while just beyond Oslo's borders is the modern art centre at leafy **Høvikodden**.

Further afield, and on the train routes out, there are several towns of passing interest. **Fredrikstad**, a preserved seventeenth-century fortified town, is good for an outdoor historical ramble, either as a day-trip or – more feasibly – en route to Sweden or Denmark. To the north, the shores of **Lake Mjøsa** are a peaceful stop, its major towns – Lillehammer, Hamar, Eidsvoll and Gjøvik – connected by an ancient paddle steamer. And to the west there's the old royal postal route to the fjords, which runs through **Fagernes** before climbing over the barren mountains.

OSLO

OSLO is the oldest of the Scandinavian capital cities, founded, according to the Norse chronicler Snorre Sturlason, around 1048 by Harold Hardråde. Several decimating fires and 600 years later, Oslo upped sticks and shifted west to its present site, abandoning its old name (*os*, settlement at the mouth of the *Lo* river) in favour of Christiania – after the seventeenth-century Danish king Christian IV responsible for the move. The new city prospered and by the time of the break with Denmark in 1814, Christiania (indeed Norway as a whole) was clamouring for independence, something it achieved in 1905 – though the city didn't revert to its original name for another twenty years. The modern city centre reflects the era well: wide streets, dignified parks and gardens, solid nineteenth-century buildings and long, consciously classical vistas combine to lend it a self-satisfied, respectable air. In Oslo, you get the feeling, the inhabitants are proud of their wealthy city and of the rapid changes that are underway today – notably an ambitious construction programme and a fast-growing cultural life.

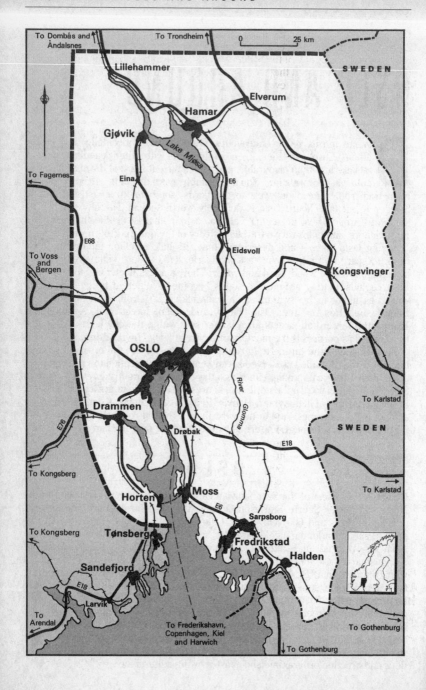

Oslo's biggest draw is its **museums**. The city has a huge variety: Thor Heyerdahl's Kon-Tiki Museum, fabulous Viking ships, the Munch Museum ablaze with a good chunk of the painter's work, the bronze and granite sculptures of Gustav Vigeland, and the moving historical documents of the Resistance Museum. Enough to keep even the most battle-weary museum-goer busy for a few days. And there's a decent **outdoor life**, too, much of the city sporting a good range of cafés, buskers and bars. Indeed in summer the whole city virtually lives outdoors, making Oslo perhaps the country's most agreeable place simply to idle away time. During winter, too, the city's prime location amid hills and forests makes it a lively and affordable ski centre.

Arrival, information and getting around

All trains and buses arrive bang in the centre of Oslo. Following a lengthy refurbishment, international and domestic **trains** now use **Oslo Sentralstasjonen**, known as Oslo S (☎02/42 19 19), at the eastern end of the city centre; the old Oslo Vestbane station (Oslo V), which used to handle departures to Stavanger and Larvik/Skien, has closed down. There's a new central **bus terminal**, *Galleri Oslo* (or Oslo M), handily placed in Jernbanetorget, outside Oslo S under a shopping centre: this handles most of the bus services within the city and out from Oslo. Express bus travellers, and those arriving with *National Express Eurolines*, will be dropped instead at another terminal, the *Nor-Way Bussterminal* (☎02/33 01 91) on Havnegata, on the harbour side of Oslo S.

Ferries from Copenhagen, Fredrikshavn and Hirtshals/Harwich arrive at the quays east of Akershus Castle, a short walk from Oslo S. From Kiel you'll arrive at Hjortneskaia, some way west of Oslo V; tram #9 and buses #21 or #27 run into the centre. Ferries from Arendal, in southern Norway, dock at Akershus pier in front of the castle.

Two **airports** serve Oslo, the largest of which, handling mainly scheduled flights, is at Fornebu, about 9km from the centre and connected with the centre by regular *SAS* bus (*Flybussen*; daily 7.30am–11.30pm; 25kr), a 25-minute journey; it's cheaper to walk from the airport to the main road and catch local bus #31 (every 30min until midnight) to the National Theatre or Jernbanetorget. The other airport, Gardermoen, 50km from Oslo, is used principally by charter traffic and is also linked with the centre by *Flybussen* (50min; 50kr). For **departures**, the *Flybussen* terminal is in Galleri Oslo at Jernbanetorget: buses run every fifteen minutes to Fornebu (daily 6am–9.45pm) and two hours before flight departures to Gardermoen.

Arriving **by car**, there are eighteen video-controlled toll-points on the way into the city: you pay 10kr each time you enter and there are 250kr spot-fines for those who avoid the tolls. Not surprisingly, the introduction of these caused some opposition: recently one toll site was destroyed in a bomb attack.

Information

There's a **tourist kiosk** inside Oslo S (daily 8am–11pm; Oct–May Fri–Sun closed 3–4.30pm; ☎02/41 62 21), which can book rooms for you (see below), and a main, more helpful, **tourist office** in the Rådhus (waterfront entrance: mid-May to mid-Sept Mon–Sat 8.30am–7pm, Sun 9am–5pm; mid-Sept to mid-May Mon–Fri

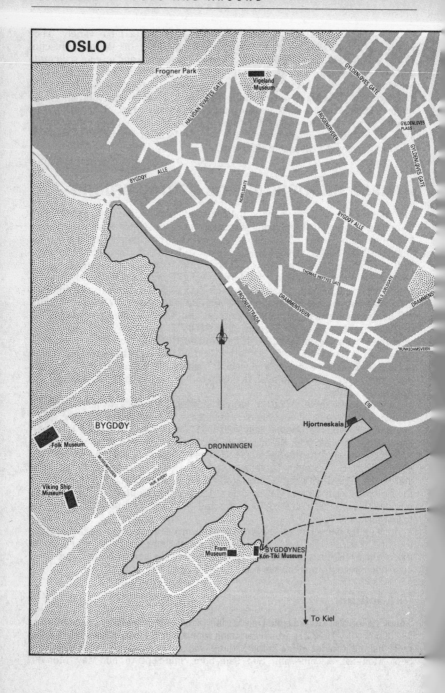

OSLO

Frogner Park

Vigeland
Museum

GYLDENLØVES GATE

GYLDENLØVES
PLASS

HALVDAN SVARTES GATE

FROGNERVEIEN

BYGDØY ALLE

NOBELS GATE

GYLDENLØVES GATE

BYGDØY ALLE

THOMAS HEFTYES GATE

DRAMMENSVEIEN

NIELS JUELS GATE

DRAMMENS

FROGNERSTRADA

MUNKEDAMSVEIEN

BYGDØY

Folk Museum

MUSEUMSVEIEN

HUK AVENY

Viking Ship
Museum

DRONNINGEN

Hjortneskaia

E18

Fram
Museum

BYGDØYNES
Kon-Tiki Museum

↓ To Kiel

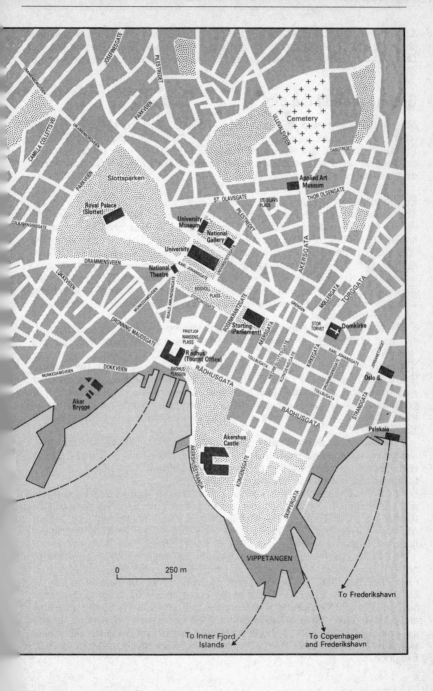

Cemetery

Applied Art
Museum

Slottsparken

ST. OLAVSGATE

ST. OLAVS
PLASS

THOR OLSENGATE

Royal Palace
(Slottet)

University
Museum

National
Gallery

University

KARL JOHANSGATE

National
Theatre

DRAMMENSVEIEN

BISØVOLL
PLASS

DRONNING MAUDSGATE

FRIDTJOF
NANSENS
PLASS

Storting
(Parliament)

STOR
TORVET

Domkirke

Rådhus
(Tourist Office)

RÅDHUS
PLASSEN

RADHUSGATA

Oslo S.

Aker
Brygge

DOKKVEIEN

MUNKEDAMSVEIEN

RADHUSGATA

Palekaia

Akershus
Castle

VIPPETANGEN

0   250 m

To Frederikshavn

To Inner Fjord
Islands

To Copenhagen
and Frederikshavn

8.30am–4pm, Sat 8.30am–2.30pm; ☎02/42 71 70). Both hand out a city plan and also have free copies of various booklets: the *Oslo Guide*, *What's On in Oslo*, the *Oslo Museum Guide* – invaluable listings brochures for events and services in the city.

Getting around the city

Most of the **city transport** is operated by *AS Oslo Sporveier*, whose information office, *Trafikanten*, is in Jernbanetorget, beneath the tower outside Oslo S (Mon–Fri 7am–8pm, Sat & Sun 8am–6pm; ☎02/41 70 30). Apart from a useful transport map, they'll also hand over a **timetable** booklet called *Rutebok for Oslo*, which details every transport schedule in the city.

Public transport

The public transport choice is between buses, trams, a small underground rail system (the *Tunnelbanen*), local trains and ferries. City **bus** travel has become a bit simpler with the opening of the Galleri Oslo terminal. There are twenty routes operating strictly within the city limits, and other services head out of Oslo, too, but the vast majority pass through Jernbanetorget; another common stop is outside the National Theatre (*Nationaltheatret*). Details of which bus to take where are given in the text throughout. Most buses stop running at around midnight, when **night buses** take over on certain routes – full details in the time-table, *Rutebok for Oslo*.

The fewer, slower **trams** run on five lines through the city, from east to west, and tend to duplicate the bus routes. Major terminals are Jernbanetorget and Stortorvet.

The Tunnelbanen – **T-bane** – has eight lines, all of which converge at Stortinget, right in the city centre. From here, four run westbound (*Vest*) and four eastbound (*Øst*). The system mainly serves commuters living in the suburbs, but you'll find it useful for trips out to Holmenkollen and around – where the trains travel above ground. The system runs from around 6am; last trains around 12.30am.

A series of **local commuter trains**, run by *NSB*, link Oslo with Moss, Drammen and the outlying towns; departures are from Oslo S. A useful link to remember is the service to Jaren/Gjøvik which makes its first stop in Grefsen – handy for Oslo's main youth hostel.

Numerous **ferries** cross the fjord to connect the city with its outlying districts and archipelago: to Bygdøy and the museums they leave from the piers outside the Rådhus (April–Sept); for the islands, they go from Vippetangen quay, behind Akershus Castle (bus #29 from Jernbanetorget to the quay); to Nesodden, in the fjord, and Drøbak (see "Around Oslo") they leave from the Aker Brygge pier.

At 13kr for a flat-fare **ticket** (bought from the bus/tram driver/ferry conductor, or at T-bane stations), with which you can't transfer, the transport system is expensive. But there are several ways you can **cut costs**. Best is to buy an *Oslokortet* or **Oslo Card** – available at the tourist offices, most hotels and camp-sites in Oslo and *Trafikanten* – which gives free admission to all the museums and unlimited free travel on the whole transport system and free parking, as well as some useful discounts in shops, hotels and restaurants. Valid for either one, two or three days, it costs 80kr, 120kr and 150kr respectively, children up to 15 half-price.

If you're not into museums, then a straight **travel pass** might be a better buy. A twenty-four-hour pass costs 40kr, valid for unlimited travel. There are also the *Minikort* (five rides; 60kr) and *Maxikort* (twelve rides; 135kr) passes, along with passes for longer stays, available from *Oslo Sporveier*. On buses, the driver will check your ticket; on trams you're trusted to have one; *Mini/Maxikort* tickets should be cancelled in the machine. Though the practice might seem widespread, bear in mind that **fare-dodging** is punished by some pretty hefty spotfines.

If you've got an *InterRail/Nordturist* pass it's worth knowing that they – like the Oslo Card – are valid on *NSB*'s local commuter trains.

Taxis, bicycles and cars

You should feel safe enough on all the public transport in Oslo and, on the whole, women on their own will have an easier time of it than in most European capitals. If you do feel threatened, it's little comfort to know that **taxis** are luxurious but dear – around 60kr for up to a ten-minute, five-kilometre ride; to call one ring *Oslo Taxicentral* ☎02/38 80 90.

If you want to get about under your own steam, **bicycle hire** is the nicest option: 60kr a day plus 500kr deposit from *Den Rustne Eike*, Oscarsgata 32 (☎02/ 44 18 80). **Car hire** is considerably more pricey, though if you have an Oslo Card there's a ten to twenty percent discount with *Hertz*; car-hire company addresses are detailed under "Listings" on p.184. Incidentally, the Oslo Card also gets you **free parking** at the city's municipal carparks (the "P-lots"), a saving worth having. Pick up the leaflet "How to Park in Oslo" from petrol stations, hotels or the tourist office.

Finding a place to stay

In summer, July especially, the scramble for **budget beds** in Oslo's hostels becomes acute, and it is always worth ringing ahead to check on space. Certainly, for peace of mind, reserving a bed for your first night is recommended. Otherwise, the **Accommodation Centre** at Oslo S (daily 8am–11pm; ☎02/41 62 21) can give you full accommodation lists, or make bookings for you if you're looking for a private room, pension or a hotel; there's a 15kr booking fee per person.

Hostels

There are three hostels in Oslo itself, all very popular and open to people of any age, though you'll need to be a member of the respective organisations (nonmembers will pay around 20kr more than the prices listed below). If space is tight, there are two other hostels situated just outside Oslo, worth considering as commuting in each day is easy.

City hostels

KFUM InterRail Point, Møllergata 1 (☎02/42 10 66). The cheapest and most central bed in Oslo, five minutes' walk from Oslo S, near the Domkirke (entrance on Grubbegata). 65kr a bed, showers and cooking facilities; but only open mid-July to mid-August 8–11am and 5pm–midnight.

Oslo Haraldsheim, Haraldsheimveien 4, Grefsen (☎02/22 29 65). Best of the two *IYHF* youth hostels, 5km out of the centre, but open all year except Christmas week and with spectacular views over the Oslo Fjord. Take trams #1 or #7 from Storgata, near the Domkirke, to Sinsen (the end of the line) or any local train to Grefsen, from where you turn right out of the station and look for the path leading up the hill from the tram terminus. The 115kr price (140–150kr Nov–April) includes breakfast and there's a small kitchen; and there are also single rooms (195kr) and double rooms (290kr) available.

Oslo 2, Sognsveien 218, Pan (☎02/23 76 40). The other *IYHF* Oslo hostel, but much smaller than Haraldsheim and only open mid-June to mid-August; kitchen facilities. Again, the 130kr price includes breakfast, and there are rooms from 270kr. Take T-bane line #13 west to Kringsjå.

Hostels outside the city centre

Drammen Vandrerhjem, Korsvegen 62, Drammen (☎03/82 21 89). Outside the city, but numerous daily trains run to Drammen, a thirty-minute ride (then take bus to Lijordet); open end-June to mid-August and closed from 11am–4pm; 70kr a bed, single rooms 105kr, doubles 140kr.

Vansjøheimen, Nesparken, Moss (☎09/23 53 34). A little further out, but worth considering if Oslo's full. There are several trains daily to Moss, an hour's ride; the hostel is in the Nesparken park, two kilometres from the station. It's open June to August (closed from 10am–5pm) and costs 65kr a bed.

Rooms and pensjonater

The Accommodation Centre at Oslo S can book you into **private rooms** from 100kr single and 180kr double – and the supply rarely dries up. This is something of a bargain as some have cooking facilities too; however, they tend to be out of the city centre, and there is a minimum two-night stay.

Slightly more upmarket, **pensjonater** (or pensions), which cost from 150kr single, 300kr double, can also be booked through the Accommodation Centre – though if you want to avoid the booking fee, try the ones on the following list (*always* ring ahead first).

Pensjonater

Bella Vista, Årrundveien 11b (☎02/65 45 88). Only eighteen beds, 200kr single, 300kr double, 350kr with bath. Kitchen facilities, too; open June to August.

Cochs Pensjonat, Parkveien 25 (☎02/60 48 36). Recently refurbished, in a nice position behind the Royal Palace. The rooms have a kitchen unit and go from 300kr single, 400kr double; triples and quadruples get the price down to around 130kr per person.

Ellingsens Pensjonat, Holtegate 25 (☎02/60 03 50). Basic, but clean, and about the best value there is; singles from 150kr, doubles from 250kr. Tram #1 (direction Majorstuen) to Uranienborg.

Lindes Pensjonat, Ths. Heftyesgate 41 (☎02/55 37 82). Handy for the Vigeland sculptures, but it's used more as a long-term residential place and is fairly grotty to boot. Singles 200kr, doubles 250kr. Tram #2 to Frogner Plass.

St Katarinahjemmet, Majorstuveien 21b (☎02/60 13 70). Open mid-June to mid-August only; singles 175kr, doubles 275kr. Tram #1 (direction Majorstuen) to Valkyrie Plass.

Sjømannshjemmet, Tollbugata 4 (☎02/41 20 05); entrance on Fred Olsen's Gate. Very central and popular with seamen as the port is nearby. Scruffy, but good value doubles at 270kr (singles 210kr); the rooms have showers.

Hotels

There *are* cheapish hotels in central Oslo, though at the bottom end of the market – a minimum of 300kr single, 450kr double – you're not going to get anything more than a box room. Prices given below are standard room rates for the cheaper hotels, but several **deals** make some other hotels affordable, too: most offer fifty percent discounts at weekends between October and June, while in **July** – when Norwegians leave town for the holidays – prices in the bigger hotels tend to drop radically. It's always worth checking with the Accommodation Centre in Oslo S for the latest offers. Also, nearly every room rate is at least mildly softened by the inclusion of a good buffet breakfast.

Budget hotels

Anker Hotel, Storgaten 55 (☎02/11 40 05). A big hotel in a good location; singles with bath from around 400kr, doubles with bath from 540kr; breakfast included.

Ansgar Hotel, Møllergate 26 (☎02/20 47 35); at Youngstorget. 470kr single, 620kr double, breakfast included.

City Hotel, Skippergata 19; entrance on Prinsensgate (☎02/41 36 10). Dead central and a popular standby; singles 300kr, basic doubles 440kr (with shower 550kr); breakfast included.

Hotel Fønix, Dronningensgate 19 (☎02/42 59 57). Again, very centrally located, just around the corner from the main post office; singles from 270kr, doubles from 450kr; breakfast included.

Munch Hotel, Munchsgate 5 (☎02/42 42 75). Well-appointed, central hotel; 585kr single with shower, doubles with shower 685kr, though weekend rates bring these prices down around 200kr; all rooms with TV and breakfast included.

Standard Hotel, Pilestredet 27 (☎02/20 35 55); the street runs northwest of the University. On the shabby side but competitive with singles from 390kr, doubles from 540kr, breakfast included.

Camping and cabins

Camping is a fairly easy proposition in a city with plenty of space, the nearest site just three kilometres from the centre. If you're out of luck with rooms in town, some sites also offer both **cabin** and regular room space. You could also ring one of the following cabin rental agencies and ask about availability: *Hytteuleien*, Youngstorget 4 (Wed–Fri 10am–4pm, Sat 10am–1pm; ☎02/42 87 20), and *Den Norske Hytteformidling*, Kierschowsgate 7 (Mon–Fri 9am–5pm; ☎02/35 67 10).

For **sleeping rough**, the concourse of Oslo S is open all night but can get rowdy. If it's warm enough you'd do better to use Oslo's numerous parks and forests. The Sognsvann T-bane route (line #13) to the end of the line takes you to accessible woodland; the Holmenkollen route to Frognersteteren (line #15) is high and deserted and has great, if windy, views; while the islands of the inner archipelago have beaches and quasi-legal camping sites. Some islands carry "No Camping" signs but this doesn't seem to be too rigorously enforced.

Campsites

Ekeberg, Ekebergveien 65 (☎02/19 85 68). Just three kilometres from the city centre and open June to August; bus #72 from the National Theatre or #24 from Jernbanetorget goes past.

Bogstad Camp, Ankerveien 117 (☎02/50 76 80). Larger, better equipped, with free showers, and with rooms and cabins available (around 450kr). It's open all year, nine kilometres out, bus #41 from the National Theatre. It gets crowded, though, so ring ahead first.

Stubljan at Hvervenbukta (☎02/61 27 06). Way out on the Oslo Fjord; open June to August; bus #75 to Ingierstrand from Oslo S.

The City

If you've come to Oslo for the showpiece museums and galleries you're not going to spend a great deal of time in the city centre proper – most of them are way outside in the suburbs. But the city itself is a humming, good-natured kind of place, easy and pleasant to walk around, and with plenty of alternative sights, mostly free and underrated. Not that walking around is always straightforward. Clanking trams, the odd hill and a succession of roadworks and obtrusive construction programmes make the whole exercise an assault course at times. The transport system is good, though, so you shouldn't have too many problems getting around quickly if time is short.

Despite the awesome proportions of Greater Oslo, it's difficult to get lost in the city centre: just remember a few simple landmarks. From **Oslo Sentralstasjonen** (Oslo S) the main street and city artery, **Karl Johans Gate**, heads directly up the hill, pedestrianised until it reaches the **Storting** (parliament building) at the top. From here it sweeps down past the **University** to the **Royal Palace**, which sits in parkland at the western end of the city. Away from the palace, on the waterfront, is the distinctive twin-towered **Rådhus**, while back towards Oslo S, on the peninsula overlooking the harbour, is **Akershus Castle**. Between the castle, the Storting and Oslo S, and up as far as the **Domkirke**, is a tight, slightly gloomy grid of streets and high buildings, snaked by trams and buses, laid out by Christian IV in the seventeenth century and nowadays the city's commercial hub.

Away from the centre, Oslo's layout becomes less formal and more residential. You could walk to the museums at **Bygdøy**, but public transport is easier and much quicker. Any further out and the city's enormous reach becomes only too obvious. **Holmenkollen**, for example, whose ski-jump makes a crooked finger on Oslo's skyline, is still within the city boundaries, but its forest and lakes feel anything but urban.

> It's as well to note again that buying an **Oslo Card** gets you free entrance to all the museums and sights detailed below, as well as free transport between them – a saving well worth considering, even if you're only going to see a couple of things.

Central Oslo

The best, and easiest, starting point for exploring **CENTRAL OSLO** is Oslo S railway station, on the eastern side of the city centre. From here, **Karl Johans Gate** cuts westwards through the heart of the city, Oslo's most varied street, ranging from the bars and buskers around the station to the dignified calm of the Royal Palace at the other end. In between, on either side, the narrower streets – still largely conforming to their original seventeenth-century grid-plan – conceal a dozen churches, museums, squares and gardens.

Along Karl Johans Gate

The first section of Karl Johans Gate, heading west and uphill from the station, is pedestrianised, leading past pavement cafés and sporadic T-shirt and jewellery stalls to the **Domkirke** on the right (Sept–May Mon–Fri 10am–1pm; June–Aug Mon–Fri 10am–3pm, Sat 10am–1pm) – not a vital sight, by any means – heavily restored and with few of its original late-seventeenth and early-eighteenth century fittings remaining – though with stained glass by Emmanuel Vigeland (see below). Outside, **Stortorvet** is the main city square, though not the central focus of city life, most of which centres on Karl Johans Gate itself. Guarded by a stout nineteenth-century statue of Christian IV, Stortorvet is instead the site of a flower market conducted from the backs of delivery vans. More rewarding is a browse around the curious circular cloistered building nearby, the **Basarhallene**. Now beleaguered by almost continuous circles of traffic, it was the city's provincial food market in the last century and has since been revived as a complex of trendy art and handicraft shops.

At the top of the hill, the **Storting** or parliament building looks down with classical clarity to the far end of Karl Johans Gate, an imposing chunk of neo-Romanesque architecture .at was completed in 1866. It's open to the public (July & Aug only Mon–Sat 11am–2pm; free) but the (obligatory) guided tour takes in little that can't be gleaned from the outside. The park space in front, **Eidsvolls Plass**, flanks Karl Johans Gate, and – along with the university gardens further down – is one of the busiest centres of night-time Oslo. It's usually full of jewellery hawkers, ice-cream kiosks and milling people carefully sipping overpriced drinks from the swish pavement cafés (though most young Oslonians are content to see and be seen around the fountain and on the grass). In summer there are occasional festivals here – live bands and music – as well as the more usual punks and winos stretched out in the sun.

On the far side, the **National Theatre** café is the nicest, if most expensive, place to watch the world go by, though the neo-Classical theatre itself, built in 1899 and flanked by two pompous statues of Ibsen and Bjørnson, is of most interest as a transport terminus – around the back and facing the palace, the two tunnels in front of you are for the westbound T-bane (on the right) and the local trains and eastbound T-bane (on the left). Inside the theatre, whose red and gold main hall has been recently restored, you can take a **guided tour** (Mon at 6pm all year and daily from mid-June to first week in Aug; 15kr), the cheapest way to see the impressive building; performance prices tend towards the astronomical, and in any case most productions are in Norwegian.

The **Royal Palace** (*Slottet*), beyond the theatre, is a monument to Norwegian openness. Built between 1825 and 1848, at a time when other monarchies were nervously counting their friends, it still stands without railings and walls, the grounds (*Slottsparken* and *Dronningparken*) open to the public. You can't actually go into the palace, but there's quite a snappy changing of the guard, daily at 1.30pm. In front, right at the end of Karl Johans Gate, the statue is of Karl XIV Johan himself. Formerly the French General Bernadotte, he abandoned Napoleon and, elected as king of Sweden, assumed the Norwegian throne after the Treaty of Kiel (1814), when Norway passed from Denmark to Sweden. Seemingly not content with the terms of his motto (inscribed on the statue), "The people's love is my reward", Karl Johan had this whopping palace built, only – and soberingly – to die before its completion.

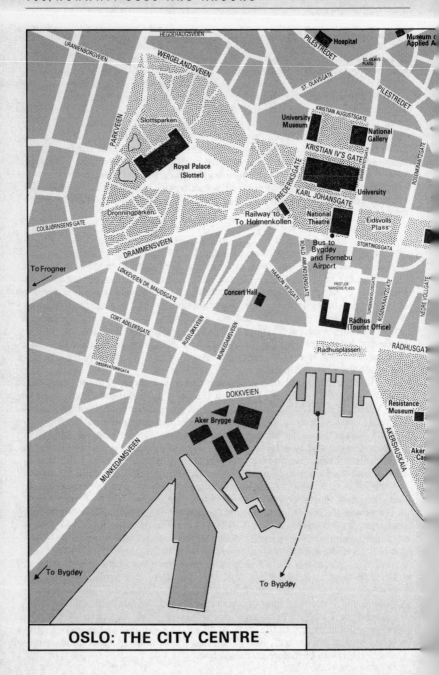

OSLO: THE CITY CENTRE

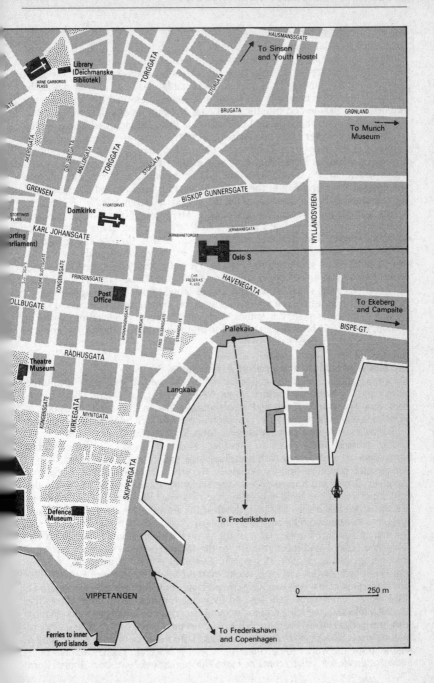

The University and its museums

Back along Karl Johans Gate, the nineteenth-century buildings of the **University**, all classical columns and sweeping steps, fit well in this monumental end of the city centre. The university **Aula** (July only Mon–Fri noon–2pm; free), the main hall between the university's two symmetrical wings, has huge interior murals by Edvard Munch, the controversial result of a competition held by the university authorities in 1909 to decorate their hall on the cheap (though they weren't actually unveiled, after much heated debate, until 1916). Munch had just emerged (cured) from a winter in a Copenhagen psychiatric clinic when he started on the murals, and the major parts of his work, *The History, Sun* and *Alma Mater*, reflect a new mood in his work: confident and in tune with his beloved Norwegian nature. Back outside, during term-time, the university steps are usually full with students; at the beginning of the university year (around August 20) you'll find them spreading their old textbooks out for sale on the pavements.

Just around the corner, the **University Museums** (Tues–Sun 11am–3pm; winter open at noon; free), at Frederiksgate 2, are excellent. There are two main collections here, Historical and Ethnographical, and of the two the **historical** section on the ground floor is much the best: extensive Viking finds – weapons, coins and clothes – that are a required stop if you intend to visit the Viking Ship Museum at Bygdøy (see below). There's also a medieval room that's rich in detail (a typical piece the small ornamental knight proud on his bronze horse) and an eclectic collection of church art (including some quite outstanding carved stave-church porches), medieval games and runic stones. The **ethnographical** section, upstairs, is basically an exhibition of African and Asiatic art and culture: more colourful, but pretty standard stuff.

The National Gallery and Applied Art Museum

Norway's largest and best collection of art is only a step away from the University: the **National Gallery** (Mon, Wed & Fri–Sat 10am–4pm, Thurs 10am–8pm, Sun 11am–3pm; free), at Universitetsgata 13. An accessible collection of works, it's made more so by the provision of free and well-informed guided tours during July and August (usually at noon, Mon, Tues & Thurs).

The **ground floor** used to combine a showy display of contemporary Norwegian art and design with a curious side gallery full of casts from Italian Renaissance sculpture (mostly Donatello, the odd Michelangelo) and a horde of Egyptian, Greek and Roman copies. The sculpture should still be there, but the contemporary art has been shifted to a new National Museum of Contemporary Art, for which see below. Upstairs, the **first floor** divides between sixteenth- and seventeenth-century religious and modern European art on the left, and Norwegian painting on the right. In the former section, gloomy icons from the Novgorod School lead incongruously to the Impressionists – assorted bursts of colour from Manet, Monet, Degas, and Cezanne, as well as a distant, piercing Van Gogh self-portrait and later works by the likes of Picasso and Braque. The Norwegian masters aren't much by comparison – only the romantic works of J.C. Dahl merit a close look. But beyond here lies the museum's centrepiece, the Munch collection, which gathers together some representative works (dating from the 1880s and 1890s up to 1916) in one central room, with a side gallery of minor pieces. This is what most visitors gravitate towards, though it would be a shame to see the works (by no means his best) in isolation. There's another floor above, often closed, which contains more Norwegian and Nordic-art Anders Zorn the most notable name – and a small collection of original Greek and Roman sculpture.

Still on the museum circuit, you may as well continue to the far end of the Universitetsgata and, to the right at St Olav's Gate 1, the **Museum of Applied Art** (Tues–Fri 11am–3pm, Tues also 7–9pm, Sat & Sun noon–4pm; 15kr, students 8kr). This has a claim to be the Norwegian national museum, with a multi-faceted collection of period furniture, clothes and modern design. The protected and intricate thirteenth-century *Baldishol* tapestry is still top exhibit – probably the finest, certainly the oldest, woven tapestry in Europe. A lesser-known contender is the display of Crown Princess Sonja's collected costumes (dresses is too prosaic a word) – breathtaking in their opulence.

Damstredet and around

Continue north from the Museum of Applied Art, past St Olav's Kirke, and Akersveien runs along the side of Vår Frelsers cemetery, with **Damstredet** running off it to the east, down the hill. A residential suburb in the nineteenth century, the wooden houses here, built at all kinds of odd angles, now mostly contain graphics studios and clothes shops for fashion-conscious under-fives. Back up the main road, Akersveien, it's not far to the **Gamle Aker Kirke** (Mon–Thurs noon–2pm; free), built in 1100 and touted as the oldest stone church in Scandinavia still being used as a parish church. From here, if you've the legs for a walk, it's worth doubling back to Damstredet and then following Møllerveien over the bridge over the river into eastern Oslo. A working-class district, this is where **Edvard Munch** lived and worked between 1885 and 1889 and a blue plaque marks his first floor flat, over what's now a china shop, on the corner of Nordre Gate and Thorvald Meyers Gate. Across the road, a conglomeration of offices and studios used by Oslo's jazz industry has a good café if you're feeling peckish (11am–4pm). A zig-zag walk through a grid of down-at-heel, formerly grand, apartment blocks takes you past Sofienberg church onto Langgata, where a clump of white, wooden houses spreads on either side of the street – not much to look at now, but interesting to see how Oslo once appeared, when it was, according to Munch, very much a "Siberian town".

To the water: the Rådhus and Aker Brygge

Back towards the centre, down Universitetsgata from the Museum of Applied Art and across the gardens, you won't want to miss the **Rådhus** (April–Sept Mon–Sat 10am–3pm, Sun noon–3pm; Oct–March Mon–Sat 11am–2pm, Sun noon–3pm; free), Oslo's modern and controversial City Hall. Constructed of bright red brick, and opened in 1950 after nearly twenty years in the making to celebrate Oslo's 900th anniversary, few people initially had a good word for the building: it was, most claimed, an ugly and strikingly un-Norwegian addition the the city. Nonetheless, its twin towers are a grandiose statement of civic pride, and nowadays rank as the most distinctive part of waterfront Oslo. The interior, entered from Fridtjof Nansen's Plass, was equally contentious, much of it a pictorial – and for some, completely over-the-top – record of all things Norwegian. Great swabs of stylised murals depict *Work*, *Administration* and *Leisure* in Oslo, with an equally vivid set portraying different historical and domestic phases throughout the country. It's a self-congratulatory work, but as a free and overwhelming art display it is difficult to beat. There are **guided tours** around the building two to three times a day, between 11am and 2pm.

Outside the Rådhus, the central **harbour** is always busy with ferries and boats, Bygdøy and the little archipelago shimmering in the distance. Underneath the Rådhus's towers, right on the waterfront, are some chunky bronze and granite sculptures, including six powerful figures representing the people who worked on the building. Cast your eyes to the right, from the City Hall steps, and you'll see the old **Oslo V railway station**, now mostly closed down, although part of it is used as a café and as the site of a Christmas market. Beyond lie the old warehouses of Oslo's shipyard. Set back from the harbour, they are nowadays given over to the cavernous hi-tech shopping halls of the **Aker Brygge** development, reached by tubular walkway from Vestbane Plassen. The shops are fairly mainstream and as financially crippling as everywhere else in Oslo. But the place itself is definitely worth the effort, a futuristic concoction of walkways, circular staircases and glass lifts, all dressed up in neon, plastic and primary colour. And hungry souls can eat quite cheaply in one of several ethnic kitchen-bars while watching the street performers out on the wharf.

Along Rådhusgata: older buildings and some museums

Rådhusgata, running east, cuts off the splash of land holding Akershus Castle and leads down to the other harbour, where the Danish ferries dock, the layout of gridded streets on either side a legacy of seventeenth-century Oslo. It's a familiar pattern, repeated in all Christian IV's new towns, although in Oslo, sadly, it's really only the layout that still survives. There are a couple of buildings of interest in these streets, though, particularly the **Theatre Museum** (Wed 11am–3pm, Sun noon–4pm; 5kr) at Nedre Slottsgate 1, housed in what's left of the *Gamle Rådhus* (1641), Oslo's old town hall. Inside, the city's first theatre performance took place in 1667, commemorated today by a crowded display of theatre trivia – posters, models and costumes. Further up, at Bankplassen 4, the brand new **National Museum of Contemporary Art** (Tues–Fri 10am–7pm, Sat & Sun 10am–4pm; free) sits in another grand building, the old *Bank of Norway*, erected at the turn of this century. It's based on the collections that once stood jumbled together in the National Gallery and is, reputedly, very good indeed.

If you're into offbeat museums there's one more, close by, in the grid of streets to the north. The **Post Museum** at Dronningensgate 15, on the third floor of the post office building (Mon–Fri 10am–3pm; free), isn't exactly a must-see but is more entertaining than you might think: much more than just stamps, and with free postcards to the discerning punter . . .

Akershus Castle and its museums

Though very much part of central Oslo by location, the jutting thumb of land that holds **Akershus Castle**, much the most significant memorial to medieval Oslo, is quite separate from the city centre in feel. Built on a plateau overlooking the harbour in around 1300, the castle was already the veteran of several unsuccessful sieges when it assumed the role of city protector in 1624. After the latest in a series of destructive fires, Christian IV simply ordered the whole town to be moved over the bay from Ekeberg and it was eventually rebuilt north of the Akershus walls in its present position. The king had the castle modernised as a Renaissance palace and, in an attempt to change the town's luck, called his new creation, predictably enough, Christiania – a name which stuck until 1925. What remains of the fortress has been extensively rebuilt and is now the home of the

Royal Mausoleum. However, despite a clinical restoration job, the castle retains a separate significance for all Norwegians – as the Nazi HQ during the last war.

The main entrance is from Festningsplassen, over the road from the city hall and up and across the small park underneath the walls. Both **park and ramparts** (daily 6am–10pm; free) have some heady views of the harbour and the Bygdøy peninsula. The **castle** itself (mid- to end April & mid-Sept to Oct Sun only 12.30–4pm; May to mid-Sept Mon–Sat 10am–4pm, Sun 12.30–4pm; 10kr, free guided tour at 11am, 1pm & 3pm, Sun at 1pm & 3pm) is used mainly for state receptions these days, though the tour shows you various empty rooms and the chapel. The labyrinthine structure, restored and refined, is antiseptic, but exploring the underground passages and dungeons is fun. There's a new exhibition, too, the **Christiania Bymodell** (June to mid-Sept Tues–Sun 11am–5pm; 30kr, students 10kr), tracing the development of Christian's city and including a scale model of Oslo as it appeared in 1838 – worth popping into to get a fuller idea of what the gridded city looked like when it was protected by the fortress.

Time is better spent, however, in the **Resistance Museum** (mid-April to Sept Mon–Sat 10am–4pm, Sun 11am–4pm, Oct to mid-April Mon–Sat 10am–3pm, Sun 11am–4pm; 10kr, family ticket 20kr, students free), a separate building in the grounds of the fortress – and signposted as the *Hjemmefrontmuseum*. Akershus was a German headquarters during the Nazi occupation of Norway, and the site of executions of captured Resistance fighters. Some excellent, mostly pictorial, displays document the building's past role as well as presenting a moving and factual story of occupation, resistance and eventual victory. Pressing buttons brings up extracts of Quisling's announcement of his assumption of puppet power in April 1940, while photographs show the defeated Nazis handing over their weapons. All in all, a moving, stoical display which says much about the importance of the Norwegian Resistance to the Allied cause.

There's one other thing to see while you're in the grounds. But the **Defence Museum**, also known as the Armed Forces Museum (Mon–Fri 10am–3pm, Sat 10am–4pm, Sun 11am–4pm, plus April–Sept Tues & Thurs till 8pm; free), over the drawbridge on the far side of the parade ground, is a poor foil to the quiet heroics of the Resistance collection – a depressing array of guns, tanks, bombs and planes, presumably used more for attack than defence.

The Bygdøy peninsula

Other than the city centre, the place you're likely to spend most time in Oslo is the **Bygdøy peninsula**, across the bay to the west of the city, where five separate museums make up an absorbing cultural and historical display; indeed, it's well worth devoting a full day – or, less wearyingly, two half-days – here. On foot it's a long hike around the edge of the bay, but **bus #30** runs regularly from Jernbanetorget and the National Theatre to the Folk Museum and Huk; and in summer (May to Aug) regular **ferries** ply between the Rådhus (from pier 3 every 30min from 7.45am–5.15pm) and Dronningen and Bygdøynes piers, from where lengthy but well signposted walks run between the museums.

The Folk Museum and Viking Ships

A few minutes' walk uphill from Dronningen Pier, the **Norwegian Folk Museum** on Museumsveien (Jan to mid-May Mon–Sat 11am–4pm, Sun noon–3pm; mid-May to Aug Mon–Sat 10am–6pm, Sun 11am–6pm; Sept Mon–Sat 11am–

6pm, Sun noon–5pm; 25kr, students 10kr, winter 10kr, students 4kr) combines vast indoor collections of furniture, china and silverware with an open-air display of reassembled period farms, houses and other buildings. Notable inside is the reconstructed nineteenth-century Norwegian parliament chamber complete with ink-wells and quills at the members' seats, and Ibsen's study, preserved from his last home in Oslo. The rest of the exhibits – the silverware and furniture in partic- ular – reveal convincingly that, alongside the poverty and starvation that forced mass emigration from Norway during the last century, there was a wealthy stratum of society in the country; certainly, for some at least, Norway wasn't simply a poor country full of peasant farmers.

However, it's the open-air collections that demand most attention. The recon- structed buildings – farms, a stave church, houses and workplaces – are arranged geographically to emphasise the idea of variety and development in rural architec- ture. Nearly all are open for viewing (except in winter) and multilingual guides roam the site to explain the vagaries of the collection. It's better to wander the dusty paths aimlessly than follow the confusing signs, though it's worth a special effort to track down the stave church (from Gol), particularly if you don't plan to travel elsewhere in Norway.

Only a few minutes away, on Huk Aveny, the **Viking Ship Museum** (Nov– March daily 11am–3pm; April & Oct daily 11am–4pm; May–Aug daily 10am–6pm; Sept daily 11am–5pm; 10kr, students 5kr) contains a hoard of loot retrieved from three ritual ship burials (for more on which see *Contexts*). The star exhibits, the *Oseberg* (a royal barge) and *Gokstad* (a Viking longboat), have been spectacularly restored following their late-nineteenth-century discovery in fragments on farms in Vestfold. Lavishly decorated and carrying bodies buried a thousand years ago, the ships were equipped with grave-furniture, textiles, solid jewellery and other implements, all of it now on display. It's a marvellously preserved mixture of decorative items, like the ceremonial sleighs to be used in a glorious afterlife, and smaller, more mundane pieces – buttons, combs, cups and needles and suchlike; and the display as a whole shows an attention to detail not usually associated with the Vikings. The ships themselves, also, were much more than glorified coffins, and are a good example of just how skilled the Vikings were as boat-builders. A copy of the *Gokstad* ship sailed across the Atlantic in 1893, and special viewing towers enable you to see inside the hulls, the mere size of which is impressive – enough room for 32 crew.

Around the rest of the peninsula

The bus continues on to the rest of the museums; or you can double back and pick up the ferry onto Bygdøynes pier. Best, though, is a stroll through the posh, leafy residential **streets** in between – where, amongst other members of the Oslo élite, the former Labour Prime Minister, Gro Brundtland, lives. Walk down, also, to **Huk** and **Paradisbukta** beaches, just behind the museums on the western side of the peninsula – some of Oslo's best, and most exclusive, swimming places.

The **Kon-Tiki Museum** (Sept–Oct & April to mid-May daily 10.30am–5pm; Nov–March daily 10.30am–4pm; mid-May–Aug daily 10am–6pm; 12kr, students 6kr) is something special. On display inside is the balsawood raft on which, in 1947, Thor Heyerdahl made his now legendary journey across the Pacific from Peru to Polynesia. Heyerdahl wanted to prove the trip could be done: he was convinced that the first Polynesian settlers had sailed from pre-Inca Peru, and rejected prevailing opinions that South American balsa rafts were unseaworthy.

Looking at the flimsy raft, *Kon-Tiki*, and the later one of papyrus, *Ra II*, on which he crossed the Atlantic in 1970, you could be forgiven for agreeing with Heyerdahl's critics – and for wondering how the crew didn't murder each other after a week in such a confined space. Easter Island statues and secret cave graves give further weight to Heyerdahl's ethnological theories; if you're especially interested, his story is thrillingly told in his books *The Kon-Tiki Expeditions* and *The Ra Expeditions* – a good read for the beach outside the museum.

Just over the road, the mammoth triangular display hall is the **Fram Museum** (beginning to mid-May daily 11am–3.45pm; mid-May to Aug daily 10am–5.45pm; Sept daily 11am–4.45pm; Oct & mid-March to April daily 11am–2.45pm; 10kr, students 5kr), protecting the beached Polar vessel *Fram* – designed by Colin Archer, a Norwegian shipbuilder of Scots ancestry, and launched in 1893. The ship's design was unique, its sides made smooth to prevent the ice from getting a firm grip on the hull, while inside a veritable maze of beams, braces and stanchions held it all together. A veteran of three expeditions, the vessel's finest hour came in 1911 when it carried Roald Amundsen to within striking distance of the South Pole, a feat he achieved a month before Scott of the Antarctic, who died on his way back. Inside the ship, the living quarters will horrify claustrophobics; yet it was in conditions like these that people went further north and south than ever before.

Lastly, next door, the **Norwegian Maritime Museum** (Jan–April & Oct–Dec Mon–Sat 10.30am–4pm, Sun 10.30am–5pm, Tues & Thurs till 8pm; May–Sept daily 10am–8pm; 12kr, students 6kr) is a sparkling new building housing a fairly pedestrian – though thorough – collection of maritime artefacts. The Boat Hall has its moments if you are into Norwegian fishing craft through the ages; otherwise, you'll probably be more taken with the café, a handy vantage point from which to overlook the bay, beach and city.

The Munch Museum

The **Munch Museum**, Tøyengata 53 (May–Sept Tues–Sat 10am–8pm, Sun noon–8pm; Oct–April Tues, Thurs & Sun 10am–8pm, Wed & Fri–Sat 10am–4pm; 20kr, students 10kr), is reachable on bus #29 from Jernbanetorget (get off at Tøyen skole) or by T-bane from Stortinget to Tøyen. From Haraldsheim youth hostel it's easier to take tram #1 or #7 to Carl Berner Plass, from where it's a ten-minute walk down Finnmarkgata or a short ride on bus #20.

Some background

Born in 1863, **Edvard Munch** had a melancholy childhood, overshadowed by the early deaths of both his mother and sister. After some early works, including several self-portraits, he went on to study in Paris – a city he returned to again and again, and where he fell (fleetingly) under the sway of the Impressionists. In 1892 he went to Berlin, where his style developed and he produced some of his best and most famous work, though his first exhibition was considered so outrageous it was closed after only a week: his work was, a critic wrote, "an insult to art". Generally considered the initiator of the Expressionist movement, for much of his life Munch wandered Europe, prolifically producing and exhibiting. However, it wasn't until well into his career that he was fully accepted in his own country. After a nervous breakdown, induced by drink and overwork, he did eventually return to Norway, continuing to paint until his death in 1944. In his will he donated all the works in his possession to Oslo city council – a mighty bequest of several thousand paintings, prints, drawings, engravings and photographs which took nearly twenty years to catalogue and organise for display in this purpose-built gallery.

The museum

The collection is huge, and only a small part of it can be shown at any one time – an advantage, since you don't feel daunted by what's on display. Visiting exhibitions limit the Munch collection to one long gallery, which can appear cluttered, but most of the more highly praised works are usually present.

His **lithographs and woodcuts** are shown in one half of the gallery, a dark catalogue of swirls and fogs – technically brilliant pieces of work and much more than simple copies of his paintings; indeed they're often developments of them. In these he pioneered a new medium of expression, experimenting with colour schemes and a huge variety of materials, which enhance the works' rawness: wood blocks show a heavy, distinct grain, while there are colours like rust and blue drawn from the Norwegian landscape. As well as the stark woodcuts on display, there are also sensuous, hand-coloured lithographs, many focusing on the theme of love (in the form of a woman) bringing death.

In the main gallery, the **early paintings** are typically Munch: deeply, and personally, pessimistic – *The Sick Child*, first of a series of studies on the same theme, a good example. More interesting are the great works of the **1890s**, which form the core of the collection and are considered among Munch's finest achievements. Among many, there's *Dagny Juell*, a portrait of the Berlin socialite, Ducha, with whom both Munch and Strindberg were infatuated; the chilling *Virginia Creeper*, a house being consumed by the plant; and, of course, *The Scream* – though this is in such demand internationally you'll be lucky to catch it on display. If you do, consider Munch's words as you view it:

> *I was walking along a road with two friends. The sun set. I felt a tinge of melancholy. Suddenly the sky became blood red. I stopped and leaned against a railing dead tired, and I looked at the flaming clouds that hung like blood and a sword over the blue-black fjord and the city. My friends walked on. I stood there trembling with fright. And I felt a loud unending scream piercing nature.*

Munch's style was never static, however. After recovery from his breakdown and retirement to the secluded Oslo fjord region, **later paintings** reflect a renewed interest in nature and physical work, as in the 1913 *Workers Returning Home*. His technique changed in these later paintings, using streaks of colour to represent points of light, as in the *Death of Marat II*, painted in 1907. Later still, his paintings absorb entirely the landscape, himself and people around him. The light *Children in the Street*, Kragerø and *Model by the Wicker Chair*, with skin tones of pink, green and blue, reveal at last a happier, if rather idealised, attitude to his surroundings, most evident notably in works like *Ploughing*, painted in 1919.

The exhibition is punctuated by **self-portraits**, a graphic way of representing Munch's state of mind at various points in his career. *The Night Wanderer* (1923), a gaunt figure lit by luminous green light, suggests that he was still restless, even in the latter half of his life.

The Botanical Gardens ... and more museums

If you need a break from Munch's neuroses, the large park just around the corner holds the University's **Botanical Gardens**, on Trondheimsveien (greenhouses Tues–Fri 7am–8pm, Sat & Sun 10am–8pm; gardens open all day every day; free), a pleasant and quiet spot. In the same park you'll also find a series of university-sponsored **museums** (Tues–Sun noon–3pm; free) containing extensive geological, zoological and paleontological collections. A good one for the kids when it's wet.

Frogner: the Vigeland Sculpture Park and Museum

On the other side of the city and reachable direct from the Munch Museum on bus #20, or tram #2 from the centre, **Frogner Park** holds more of Oslo's better cultural targets – in particular the Vigeland Sculpture Park and Museum, which commemorate another modern Norwegian artist of world renown, **Gustav Vigeland**. Between them, they hold the artist's life's work, presented to the city in return for favours received, in the shape of a studio and apartment, during the years 1921–30.

Vigeland began his career as a wood-carver but later, heavily influenced by Rodin, turned to stone and bronze as a medium. He started work on the **sculpture park** (always open; free) in 1924, and was still working on it when he died in 1943. It's a literally fantastic work. Here he had the chance to let his imagination run riot and, when unveiled, the place wasn't without its critics. From its monumental wrought iron gates the central path takes you into a world of frowning, fighting and posing bronze figures which flank the bridge in front. The **central fountain**, part of a separate commission begun in 1907, is an enormous bowl representing the burden of life, supported by straining sinewy bronze Goliaths while, underneath, water tumbles out around clusters of playing and standing figures.

But it's the twenty-metre high **obelisk** up on the stepped embankment, and the grouped granite sculptures around that, which caused much of the controversy when first erected. It's a humanistic work, a writhing mass of sculpture which depicts the cycle of life as Vigeland saw it: a vision of humanity teaching, playing, fighting, loving, eating and sleeping – and clambering on and over each other to reach the top. The granite children scattered around the steps are perfect: little pot-bellied figures who tumble over muscled adults, and provide an ideal counterpoint to the real Oslo toddlers who splash around in the fountain, naked and undeterred.

At the southern corner of the park – at Nobelsgate 32 – the **Vigeland Museum** (Nov–April Tues–Sun 1–7pm; May–Oct Tues–Sun noon–7pm; free) was the artist's studio during the 1920s and traces the development of his work through a series of monumental plaster casts, drawings and woodcuts. Some of his early pieces are disturbing, not least a wall relief of emaciated figures – a far remove from the chubby characters outside. In the summer, concerts and recitals are held in the museum's courtyard. *

Other museums . . . and a couple of cafés
If you've energy to spare, the Frogner Park has a couple of other museums, neither worth a special trip but of mildly diverting interest. The **City Museum** (June–Aug Tues–Fri 10am–6pm, Sat & Sun 11am–5pm; rest of the year Tues–Fri 10am–4pm, Sat & Sun 11am–4pm; 10kr, students 5kr) is housed in the long, low

---

* Vigeland fanatics should note that there's an exhibition of the work of the sculptor's younger and lesser known brother, Emmanuel, a respected artist in his own right, in the **Emmanuel Vigeland Museum** (Sun only noon–3pm; free). The address is Grimelundsveien 8 (T-bane line #15 to Slendal).

late-eighteenth-century Frogner Manor, though its largely Norwegian-labelled mass of photographs and articles detailing city history are unlikely to appeal to everyone. If you're thirsty, though, the café here is fairly cheap. Not far away is the **Skating Museum** (*Skøytemuset*), in the Frogner Stadion on Majorstua (open all year by appointment; call ☎02/61 11 10; free), which documents the history of Norwegian skating.

You may perhaps be more enticed by the park's **cafés**, open-air and fancy places to sit and drink in the summer. Nurse a beer at either the *Frognerparken Kafe* – "Bru" to the locals – or *Herregårds Kroa*, both to the left of the bridge as you approach the obelisk.

Old Oslo: views, runic stones and ruins

Despite its mid-eleventh-century foundation, virtually nothing of Harald Hardråde's Oslo remains, principally because the original medieval city, built to the east on the **Ekeberg** heights, was wooden and subject to repeated obliterating fires – after which it was abandoned entirely for a safer site beneath Akershus. There are pitifully few fragments left, and they're worth seeking out if only for the spectacular views and the chance to poke around in the less visited end of town.

It's about a ten minute tram ride (#9; Ljabru direction) from Jernbanetorget to the **Merchant Marine Academy** (*Sjømannsskolen*), high on a hill overlooking the fjord and city. The tram stops outside the building and the views from the fjord-facing terrace are some of the most extensive in Oslo, stretching all the way to the Holmenkollen ski-jump and beyond. Back on the main road, follow the sign pointing into the park (marked *Fortidsminne*) downhill into a quiet grassy reach, to a tiny fenced-off section below to the left, anonymous and overlooked. On the rocks inside, a group of ochre **carvings** of animals and matchstick people, 5000 years old, are the earliest evidence of settlement along the Oslo fjord.

To have any chance of glimpsing the patchy ruins of the early medieval settlement of Oslo, you need to walk back down the hill from the academy. On the left, in between the railway sidings and industrial clutter, is the **Sørenga ruinpark**, through which a marked path leads from Bispegata to the disappointing remnants of the eleventh-century Royal Palace and the Maria Church. Further up Oslogata, at St Halvard's Plass, at the heart of the *Gamlebyen* or old town, are the excavations of St Olav's cloister and a couple of churches – St Halvard's Church and the Cross Church – abandoned after the 1624 fire led Christian IV to move Oslo from here for good. The **Ladegården** (guided tours May–Sept Wed 6–7pm, Sun 1–2pm; free), on the far side of Oslogata, gives, by way of scale models, a good idea of how it all looked. It is, in itself, a rather grand residence, built in 1725 and resting on the site (which includes the foundations) of the thirteenth-century Bishop's Palace, once the most fortified building in the city.

Holmenkollen and Sognsvann

Holmenkollen, a forested range of hills just twenty minutes' T-bane ride from the National Theatre (route #15 to the end of the line) is about the best place to get away from central Oslo's noise and traffic without actually leaving the city limits. It's classic Norwegian countryside, lush and peaceful; there's not much to do except tramp the forest paths – invigorating enough after a morning in the city centre – but if it's clear, follow the signs to the **Tryvannstårnet TV Tower** (May & Sept daily 10am–5pm; June daily 10am–7pm; July daily 9am–10pm; Aug daily 9am–8pm; Oct & April Mon–Fri 10am–3pm, Sat & Sun 11am–4pm; 13kr, students 7kr). A lift shoots you up to a viewing room from which you can see the Swedish border – though even a light mist makes this a pointless exercise. There are more views (free this time) if you follow the road from the tower, via Voksenkollen station, to the **Krag statue** nearby.

Otherwise, it's a fifteen-minute walk downhill, following the main road, to the combined **Holmenkollen Ski Museum and Ski Jump** (Jan–April & Oct–Dec Mon–Fri 10am–3pm, Sat & Sun 11am–4pm; May & Sept daily 10am–5pm; June daily 10am–7pm; July daily 9am–10pm; Aug daily 10am–8pm; 15kr for either, students 10kr; or 21kr for both, students 14kr; for TV tower, too, 25kr, students 20kr) – a more entertaining display than the name promises. As well as skis through the ages the museum has clothes and equipment, from the latest in competition ski-wear to the seemingly makeshift garb of early Polar explorers, Nansen and Amundsen included. Afterwards, climb to the top of the adjacent international ski-jump and hang on as you look straight down. It's a horrifying descent, almost vertical, and it seems impossible that the tiny bowl at the bottom could pull the skier up in time – or that anyone could possibly want to jump off in the first place. The bowl is the finishing point for the 8000-strong *Homenkollen March*, a cross-country skiing race which forms part of the Holmenkollen Ski Festival every March.

A kilometre or so further down the road is the Holmenkollen T-bane station, signposted to the right after the Homenkollen restaurant (see "Eating and Drinking"). Regular trains run back into the centre.

Sognsvann

The other escape into the forested hills around Oslo is to **Sognsvann**, reached on T-bane line #13 which you take to the end of the line. There's a lake, **Sognsvannet**, a short walk away from here with good swimming on its eastern side, and there are plenty of signposted **walks** in the surrounding area. One heads along the road from the station, turns left onto Ankerveien and continues to an old farm building known as *Løkka*. If you wanted to stay in these peaceful surroundings, it's worth noting that the *Oslo 2* youth hostel at Pan is only one stop back down the line from Sognsvann at Kringsjå.

The islands of the inner fjord and city beaches

Oslo's small archipelago of **islands** in the inner fjord is the city's summer playground, and makes going to the beach a viable – if unusual – option for a European capital. Jumping a ferry, attractive enough in the heat of the day, is also one of the pleasanter forms of entertainment at night, and the islands are popular party venues for Oslo's preening youth. **Ferries** (13kr each way, Oslo Card valid) leave from the Vippetangen quay, behind Akershus Castle: departures in summer are roughly every half-hour until around 11pm; in winter, the services are reduced to hourly between 7am and around 4pm.

Hovedøya, the nearest and most popular island, contains the overgrown ruins of a twelfth-century Cistercian monastery built by English monks. There's a café in summer, swimming from a rocky shore and lots of shady places to lie. Nearby **Lindøya** is packed full of holiday homes and summer houses but has a few pictu-

resque small harbours and paths scattered around. The ferry here goes on to
Nakholmen, just west of Lindøya, too. The best beaches are probably those on
Gressholmen and **Langøyene**, further south, a 10–20-minute ride from
Vippetangen; those on the southern side of Langøyene are officially designated
naturist. These islands have free **camping** during the summer and at night the
ferries are full of people with sleeping bags and bottles on their way to join swimming parties. The other place you can get to by ferry (from the Aker Brygge ferry
pier) is the tip of the peninsula that reaches into the fjord, **Nesodden**, which is
accessible year-round.

City beaches

For more swimming, though less frenetic carousing, there are plenty more
beaches within easy travelling distance of the city centre.

On the **western** side of the fjord, the closest, popular choices are the beaches at
the Bygdøy peninsula, **Huk** and **Paradisbukta**, reached on bus #30 from the
National Theatre (see above for more details). **Rolfstangen** is a sandy beach near
Fornebu airport (bus #31 from the National Theatre), while further afield is the
island of **Langåra**, 16km west of the city. There's good swimming here, and you
can camp, too; either take the local train to SANDVIKA and a ferry from there, or
use the ferry to Nesodden from Aker Brygge and pick up a connecting ferry there.

On the **eastern** side of Oslo's fjord, there are a whole string of beaches accessible on bus #75B from Jernbanetorget, which leaves roughly hourly (two-hourly at
the weekend). Ulvøya is closest, a ten-minute ride away, followed by Katten,
Hvervenbukta and Ingierstrand at roughly five-minute intervals. If you're with
children, the first – **Ulvøya** – is best. If you want to swim nude, go on to
Strandskogen, 2km south of Ingierstrand beach.

Eating and drinking

Oslo isn't the cheapest place to survive in, but one advantage of the capital is that
there's a great deal more choice here than anywhere else in the country. Those
counting the *kroner* will find it fairly easy to buy snacks and sandwiches from
stalls and markets throughout the city; and if your budget is more generous,
eating in some good-value restaurants is a possibility. **Drinking** is uniformly
expensive, but alongside the usual bars and pubs, the summer sees the opening
of some pleasant outdoor cafés, which give Oslo a holiday air. Many bars, too,
stay open until around 3–4am, and often don't fill up until around midnight.

Markets, supermarkets and snacks

Markets are always good for fruit and vegetables, especially towards the end of
the day. Try the few stalls outside the Aker Brygge development or in
Jernbanetorget; or one of the grander affairs at Youngstorget or Grønlands Torg
(Mon–Sat 7am–2pm). For determined self-caterers, **supermarkets** are thick on
the ground and many department stores have food halls. Cheapest, good for
basic foods and bulk-buying though poor on choice, is *Rimi 500* on
Rosenkrantzgate, near the City Hall. The bigger stores, like *Bonus* on Storgata,
have "pick and mix" salad bars (around 5kr per 100g). For late-night food, *Jens
Evesen*, in the T-bane station at Grønland, is open until 11pm.

Snacks and sandwiches

Stand-up snacks – burgers, *varme pølser*, chips, etc – are on sale from kiosks and stalls on virtually every street corner. **Burger joints**, too, have multiplied in the last few years. *McDonalds* now have three branches, the two most central at Nedre Slottsgate 21 and Storgaten 15, both open until 11.30pm. If you don't want to eat here, they do at least serve the cheapest coffee in Oslo.

More healthily, there's *Wenches* **sandwich bar**, on Rådhusgata just below Christiania Torv, which has monstrous open sandwiches from 17kr (Mon–Sat 10am–5pm). Pricier is *Helios* **health and wholefood shop** on Universitetsgata, opposite the National Gallery. If you fancy tea and **cakes**, try the *City Conditori* on Tollbugata, an old fashioned bakery with a frieze around the walls of cherubs sowing, reaping and baking; a pot of tea and a cake costs 18kr.

Cafés and restaurants

For sit-down food, best value, as ever, are *kafeterias*, where the most favourable buys are usually at **lunch** time. However, you can afford to eat out **at night**, if you stick to the growing band of ethnic restaurants and watch what you drink. Check the list of café-bars below, many of which serve good-value food despite being primarily drinking and meeting joints.

Avocado, Thor Olsens Gate, near the Museum of Applied Art. A vegan restaurant where 45kr buys you unlimited stabs at a choice of five hot dishes, numerous salads and fruit salads; smaller platefuls of food can be had for 15–35kr. Sun–Thurs noon–6pm.

Clodion, Krysset Thomas Heftyesgate; just up from Bygdøy Allé. An arty café with oil paintings and a candelabra and good food: soups at around 38kr, bowls of pasta for 56kr. Food served 10am–11pm, drinks until 3am.

Coco Chalet, Ovre Slottsgate 8. Stylish, with potted palms and occasional live music. The service is famed for being slow and off-hand, though compensated for by the good food – ask for the daily specials, which go for around 69kr. Mon–Thurs & Sun until 1am, Fri & Sat until 4am.

Caroline Café, Oslo Sentralstasjon. A good, cheap cafeteria, offering daily lunch deals and a basic menu: it opens early and usually has some sort of inclusive breakfast offer, too. Daily 7.30am–10pm.

Ekebergrestauranten, Kongsveien 15. Daily, help-yourself buffet lunches in the summer from 11.30am–3pm for 135kr; or a cheaper version (80kr) served between 3–6pm. And a ten percent discount with the Oslo Card. Tram #9 to Sjømannsskolen

Grei Kafeteria, Skippergata 3. A dockside café, with meals from 38kr, daily lunches around 45–50kr. Mon–Fri 6am–7pm, Sat & Sun 9am–3pm

Holmenkollen, Holmenkollveien 119; a short walk down the hill from Frognerseteren T-bane station. Excellent Norwegian specialities well worth the fairly high prices.

Kafé Celsius, Rådhusgata 19; hidden through an unlikely looking gateway. Plenty of seating and an open courtyard in the summer, log fires in the winter; popular on Sunday afternoon. Mediterranean-inspired food, like Greek meat stew (68kr) and soup with pesto and cheese (42kr). Open until 2am, Sun until 11pm.

Krølle Kro, Uranienborgveien 13. A good, cheap place to eat Norwegian food. Recommended.

Malik's; a chain with branches on Karl Johans Gate and on Trondheimsveien. A varied menu including Wienerschnitzel for around 60kr or cheaper burger meals.

Nelly's Wunderbar, Thorvald Meyers Gate 70. High-priced, tiny restaurant serving gourmet food that's worth splashing out on, not least for the impromptu five-minute drag shows on the kitchen steps by Nelly herself who then returns to wait on the tables.

Peppe's Pizza. A chain of American-style pizza restaurants with branches at Stortingsgata 4 and Frognerveien 54, near Frogner Park, among others. Share their huge pizzas – 55kr plus each – or eat from the help-yourself salad bar for around 40kr a head.

Postcaféen, Dronningensgate 19; next to the *Hotel Fønix*. Decent, hearty and averagely-priced meals. Mon–Fri 8am–7.30pm, Sat 8am–6pm, Sun noon–7.30pm

Storyville, Universitetsgata 26. New Orleans-style bistro-bar with reasonably priced Creole cooking. Handy for *Barock*, see below. Closed Sun.

Vegeta Vertshus, Munkedamsveien 3b, at its junction with Stortingsgata. More upmarket than *Avocado* and open at night, this vegetarian restaurant has a help-yourself buffet with fine salads, mixed vegetables, pizza, potatoes and rice. Small platefuls go for around 40kr; the 90kr meal includes dessert, a drink and coffee. Daily 10am–10pm.

Café-bars and pubs

Oslo has an impressive **café life**, with a lot of new places opened up in the last couple of years, all of which serve coffee, alchoholic drinks and, most of the time, good-value food. Many of the café-bars stay open until well after midnight, until 3–4am in some cases; a half-litre of beer will set you back around 30–35kr everywhere, a light beer or cappuccino around 15–20kr.

Barbeint, Drammensveien 20; near the Royal Palace. If you know Scandinavian bands and cult films then you may spot a few faces in this fashionable bar. Open until 3am.

Café de Paris, Akersgata 16. Extravagant decor and a children's area; decent food, too. Open until 3.30am, 2am on Sun.

Café Sjakk Matt, Haakon VII's Gate 5. Open all day, it's worth dropping in this café for a snack: the food is reasonably priced at around 40–45kr a plate. Open until 2am, Fri & Sat 3am.

Café de Stijl, Dronningensgate. One of the few cafés with a spirits license; background jazz music, occasional theatre performances downstairs while upstairs there's an eclectic decor old tram seats, plants and mirrors. Open until 4am, closed Mon.

Café Stravinsky, Rosenkrantz Gate. A music bar which was once one of the most fashionable venues in Oslo; still busy from midnight right up until 4am.

Lorry, on the corner of Parkveien and Hegdehaugsveien, by the Royal Palace. A boisterous pub with a piano, frequented mostly by drunk artists and would-be artists. There's a wide choice of beers and, at Christmas, a special Norwegian set meal for around 110kr.

Oslo Mikrobryggeri, on Holtegata, at the junction with Bogstadveien, behind the Royal Palace. A male-orientated pub with home-brewed dark beer, popular with English drinkers.

Palace Grill, Solligata 2, off Drammensveien. A small American bar with a Fifties jukebox; open late and popular with everyone from yuppies to winos. The short menu includes a chilli for 36kr.

Queen's Café, Hegdehaugsveien, close to the junction with Oscarsgate and just up from the Royal Palace. Half-litres of beer here go for 25kr, making it the cheapest place to drink in Oslo. They sell small pizzas, too, for around 40kr, if you get hungry.

Rockall, Rosenkrantz Gate. On a street of cafés, this place has beer at 24kr a half-litre before 9pm.

The Scotsman, Karl Johans Gate 17. A decidedly odd place to drink, swathed in tartan and selling traditional Scottish pizzas to the accompaniment of country and western songs sung by two Englishmen. Whatever you think of this, the coffee and sandwich deal for 22kr between noon and 4pm is worth checking out. Open until 11.30pm.

Theatercaféen, in the *Hotel Continental*, Stortingsgata 24–26 (open until midnight). A glittering brasserie, popular with the well-heeled of Oslo – hence the prices – but a magnificent place for an indulgent drink.

Tiffani, at the Colbjørnsens Gate end of Skoveien, behind the Royal Palace. A bar where the imaginative decor – furniture like art gallery exhibits – is the attraction.

Tut-ankh-Amon, Rosenkrantz Gate. Another good, late bar on this street, open until 4am.

Nightlife

For **entertainment listings**, it's always worth checking *Natt & Dag*, available free from cafés, bars and shops, or *What's On in Oslo*, which contains a day-by-day account of all that is cultural and entertaining, free or otherwise. Obviously, summer is the best time to be in Oslo, although a student presence keeps things active right throughout the year.

Discos and clubs

Entrance to a **disco** will set you back around 50kr – though, amazingly, drink prices are the same as anywhere else; closing times are generally around 3am. Most Oslo discos are, however, rather staid. Of the few that exist outside the larger hotels, **Barock**, Universitetsgate 26 (daily 6pm–3am; food until 1am), is one of the best, a restaurant, bar and disco place, currently favoured by record industry types. **Cat's Disco**, Storgata 25, is a mixed disco with gay nights on Wednesday and Saturday; **Den Sorte Enke** – now that the *Metropol* has closed down – is the most popular gay club in Oslo. The **Waterfront**, Munkedamsveien 53b (daily noon–4am), is also worth a look, a former Goths hangout that has whitewashed its walls but still attracts fans of leather and the Cure.

Live music: rock, jazz and classical

Tracking down **live music** isn't too difficult, though the live music scene is less developed than in Copenhagen or even Stockholm. Classical music fans are better served, with several important venues in the city centre. **Tickets** for most events can be bought direct from the concert halls, or from *Teatersentralen*, Youngstorget 5 (Mon–Fri 9am–4pm) and *Bilettsentralen*, Roald Admunsensgate.

Rock venues
More and more bands are including Oslo in their tours, and there are a few venues that host regular gigs – at least weekly. **Rockefeller**, Torggata 16 (☎02/20 32 32), stages big-name acts, mostly from abroad; **Sardines**, Munkedamsveien 15 (☎02/83 00 75), mixes Norwegian bands with the international talent. **Smuget**, Kirkegata 34, has live Norwegian jazz, rock and blues every night; open 8pm–4am.

Jazz venues
The most regular jazz performances are at **Guldfisken**, Rådhusgate 2 (☎02/41 14 89), the **Rosenkrantz Hothouse**, Pilestredet 15b (☎02/20 39 89), **Oslo Jazzhus**, Toftesgate 69 (☎02/38 37 65), and the **New Orleans Workshop**, Christiesgate 5, where there's trad jazz on Thursdays at 7.30pm. There's also the Oslo International **Jazz Festival** in August.

Classical music
The main venues for classical music are the newly restored **Gamle Logen**, the city's old Assembly Rooms, Grev Wedels Plass 2 (☎02/33 22 60) and Oslo's **Concert Hall**, Munkedamsveien 14 (*Konserthuset*; ☎02/20 93 33). **Free summer concerts** are given in the courtyard of the Vigeland Museum; watch out also for good classical programmes at a variety of other venues – Oslo Domkirke, the

Munch Museum, the University Aula – in which the works of Grieg feature heavily.

The cinema, theatre and opera . . . and folk dancing

Cinemas are a good bet as all films are shown in their original language with Norwegian subtitles. They're also surprisingly cheap to get into, especially matinees and early-evening showings (from around 40kr). The main central screens are *Saga*, Stortingsgata 28, *Eldorado*, Torggata 9, and *Sentrum*, Arbeidersamfunnets Plass 1. *Sentrum* and *Klingenberg*, Roald Amundsens Gate 4 (close to the Rådhus), have late-night screenings on Friday and Saturday; listings in the local press or from the tourist office.

All **theatre** productions are in Norwegian, making them of limited interest to tourists, though the Oslo Card gives you a twenty-percent discount on tickets. There's a full list of theatres, mainstream and fringe, in the *Oslo Guide*. The card also gets you a 25-percent discount on tickets for the **opera**: *Den Norske Opera* is based at Storgata 23 (☎02/42 94 75), and the season runs from September to June.

For a really different evening (or for when you get really bored) there are **folk dancing** displays at the open-air theatre in the Folk Museum at Bygdøy, and in the Oslo Concert Hall, Munkedamsveien, on Monday and Thursday (at 9pm) – both during July and August only.

Sport, kids and daytime amusements

Oslo is above all an outdoor city, and when you've tired of the museums and cafés, it offers any number of ways to work off excess energies in various sports and active pastimes, in its hinterland of forests, parks, beaches and lakes. During winter, especially, the focus shifts to the city outskirts, when you can do everything from skating to sleigh-riding, making Oslo a great city for kids. When the weather's bad, children can also enjoy themselves in a variety of youth-orientated museums.

Sport and daytime amusements

One sport (if it is a sport) that is popular with Oslo inhabitants is **fishing**. To take advantage of the teeming fjord and forest lakes you'll need a permit (75kr; kids 30kr), available from sports shops; you also have to pay a state fee of 30kr, at any post office. In the winter, ice fishing is popular, too, but follow what the locals do as it can be dangerous on weak ice.

Tennis is also possible on the courts at Valle Hovin (daily 8am–9pm); take the T-bane to Helsfyr. The more central courts in Frogner park are usually hired out for the season, although cancellations mean that there's often a vacant court if you ask at the kiosk there. On rainy days settle for **ten-pin bowling** at *Solli Bowlinghall*, Drammensveien 40 (Mon–Fri 9am–12.30am, Sat & Sun 11am–12.30am), or *Strøms Bowling*, Torgata 16 (Mon–Thurs 11am–11pm, Fri & Sat 11am–midnight, Sun 1pm–midnight).

Winter sports

For **skating**, there is an artificial rink open to the public at Valle Hovin (T-bane line #3, #4 or #6 to Helsfyr) from mid-October to mid-March; skate hire is available. Otherwise admission is free to Oslo's natural ice rinks, dotted around the city, though you pay to use the cloakrooms.

As for **skiing**, skis and equipment can be hired from *Skiservice A/S* Voksenkollen T-bane station (☎02/14 21 24), on the Holmenkollen line. Cross-country enthusiasts should call in at the Ski Society (*Skiforeningen*) office, 2nd floor, Storgaten 20 (☎02/17 05 78): they can tell you more about Oslo's floodlit trails, downhill and slalom slopes, ski schools (including a children's ski school) and weekend ski buses to Norefjell – the city's nearest mountain resort. For spectators, March sees the annual *Holmenkollen Ski Festival*, which includes the world championships in cross-country and ski-jumping – tickets and information from the Ski Society.

Kids' attractions

The city beaches (see above) are perhaps the best place to take the kids if the weather's up to it; there are also open-air **swimming pools** at Frogner Park, *Frognerbadet*, Middlethunsgate 28 (Mon–Fri 7am–7pm, weekends 10am–5pm; 27kr, kids 11kr), and at *Tøyenbadet*, Helgesensgate 90, near the Munch Museum (same times, same prices). Both are free with the Oslo Card. In winter, use *Tøyenbadet*'s indoor pools, sauna, solarium and water-slides.

A winter activity which kids always enjoy is **sleigh riding** in the Oslo forest. This can be arranged through *Vangen Skistue*, c/o Knut Brøndelsbo, PO Box 29, Klemmensrud Oslo 12 (☎02/86 54 81) and *Sørbråten Gård*, c/o Helge Torp, Mariadalen Oslo 8 (☎02/42 35 79).

Museums for Kids

Failing that, there are a number of **museums** that are directed at kids as much as adults, and are good reserves for winter afternoons. Most obviously, the **Children's Art Museum** (*Barnekunstmuseet*), Lille Frøensveien 4 (Jan–June Tues–Thurs 9.30am–2pm, Sun noon–5pm; July–Aug Tues–Fri 11am–5pm, Sun noon–5pm; 20kr, kids and students 15kr; T-bane to Frøen), is an international collection of children's art – drawings, paintings, sculpture and handicrafts – along with a children's workshop with painting, music and dancing.

The **Technical Museum** (*Norsk Teknisk Museum*), Kjelsåsveien 143 (mid-May to mid-Sept Tues–Sun 10am–7pm; mid-Sept to mid-May Tues 10am–9pm, Wed–Sun 10am–4pm; 20kr, students 10kr; tram # 11 to Kjelsås), out to the north of the city close to the Maridal lake, is a new inter-active museum, equipped with working models and a galaxy of things to push and touch, as well as a café and picnic area.

Similarly, the **Transport Museum** (*Sporveismuseet*), Slemdalsveien 1–3, entrance in Gardeveien (April–Sept Sat & Sun noon–3pm; Oct–March Sun noon–3pm; 10kr, families 20kr; T-bane to Majorstua), will appeal to children especially, an early-nineteenth-century tram hall housing old trams and trolley buses, alongside an illustrated history of Oslo's efficient public transport system.

Listings

Airlines *Air France*, Fridtjof Nansens Plass 6 (☎02/42 10 45); *British Airways*, Karl Johans Gate 16b (☎02/33 16 00); *Lufthansa*, Haakon VII's Gate 6 (☎02/20 08 36); *North West Airlines*, Tollbugata 28 (☎02/33 59 00); *SAS*, Ruseløkkveien 6 (☎02/42 99 70).

Banks and exchange Banks are open Mon–Fri 8.15am–3.30pm (June–Aug 8.15am–3pm), Thurs till 5pm. Out of these hours Oslo S has an exchange office open June to Sept daily 7am–11pm; Oct–May Mon–Fri 8am–8.30pm, Sat 8am–2pm. There are exchange facilities at the two airports: Fornebu (Mon–Fri 6.30am–9pm, Sat 7.30–7pm, Sun 7am–10pm) and Gardermoen (Mon–Fri 6am–9pm, Sat 6am–8pm, Sun 6am–6.30pm); you can also change money and travellers cheques at the Ekeberg and Bogstad campsites, the main post office and the *Oslo 2* hostel at Pan.

Books and newspapers The *International Bookshop*, Prinsengate 21, carries a large selection of English and American books, magazines and newspapers, as do the kiosks at Oslo S. The *Travel Bookshop*, Hegdehaugsveien 34, has a comprehensive selection of maps and guides; *Syklistens Landsforening*, Mariadalsveien 60 (☎02-71 92 93), the Norwegian Cyclist Association, has specific cycling books and maps.

British Council Office and reference library at Fridtjof Nansens Plass 5 (☎02/42 68 48).

Car rental *Avis*, Munkedamsveien 27 (☎02/84 90 60) and at Fornebu airport (☎02/53 05 57); *Hertz*, c/o *SAS Scandinavia Hotel*, Holbergsgate 30 (☎02/20 01 21) and at Fornebu airport (☎02/53 36 47); *Bislet Bilutleie*, Pilestredet 70 (☎02/60 27 70).

Car breakdown For pick-up services, call *NAF Alarm* (24-hr service; ☎02/42 94 00); *Falken Redningskorps* (☎02/23 25 85); or *Viking Redningstjeneste* (24-hr service; ☎02/60 60 90).

Chemist There is a 24-hour service at *Jernbanetorgets Apotek*, Jernbanetorvet 4b (☎02/41 24 82). Also, all chemists carry a rota in the window advising of the nearest open shop.

Dentist *Oslo Kommunale Tannlegevakt*, Tøyen Senter, Kolstadgata 18; Mon–Fri 8–11pm, Sat & Sun 11am–2pm & 8–11pm (☎02/67 48 46).

Embassies *UK*, Ths. Heftyesgate 8 (☎02/55 24 00); *Ireland* (use UK embassy); *USA*, Drammensveien 18 (☎02/44 85 50); *Canada*, Oscarsgate 20 (☎02/46 69 55); *Australia* (information office at Jerbanetorget 2; ☎02/41 44 43; more serious matters are dealt with by UK embassy); *New Zealand* (use UK embassy).

Emergencies Police ☎002; Fire ☎001; Ambulance ☎003. *Oslo Kommunale Legevakt* (☎02/20 10 90), Storgaten 40, has a 24-hour medical/rape/psychological counselling service, as well as a casualty and out-patient service; or look in the telephone directory under *Leger* for private doctors.

Ferry companies *Da-No Linjen* (to Frederikshavn) Palékaia, Bjørnvika (☎02/41 68 70); *Scandinavian Seaways* (to Copenhagen) Karl Johans Gate 1 (☎02/42 93 50); *Fred Olsen Lines* (to Harwich/Hirtshals) Fred Olsensgate 2 (☎02/67 76 35); *Stena* (to Frederikshavn) Storgaten 5 (☎02/33 50 00); *Jahre* (to Kiel) Karl Johans Gate 31 (☎02/42 20 99).

Gay life Not much of a scene as such, but advice is available and activities and events organised by *Det Norske Forbundet av. 1948*, Øvre Slottsgate 15 (☎02/42 98 54). Gay switchboard on ☎02/36 00 90/1 or ☎02/42 98 54.

Hitchhiking A lift service, whereby you share petrol costs and pay a small administration charge for international lifts, is operated by *Haikocar* (☎02/42 66 67); for more details check with the Youth Information Centre (see below). On your own, for Stavanger and Bergen, take the local train to Skøyen and hitch from Drammensveien; for Trondheim and the north, take the T-bane to Carl Berners Plass and hitch from Trondheimsveien; for Gothenburg and Sweden, make for Bispegata and hitch from the road south to Svinesund (E6), or – signposted – for Sarpsborg.

Laundrettes *Bislett Vask og Rens*, Theresesgate 25 (Mon–Fri 9am–7pm, Sat 9am–3pm); *Majorstua Myntvaskeri*, Vibesgate 15 (Mon–Fri 8am–8pm, Sat 8am–5pm); *Myntvask*, Ullevålsveien 15 (daily 7am–11pm). The *Haraldsheim* Youth Hostel also has washing and drying facilities.

Left Luggage Lockers and luggage office at Oslo S.

Library Read foreign newspapers and periodicals for free at the *Deichmanske Bibliotek*, Henrik Ibsengate 1.

Mountain hiking *Den Norske Turistforening*, Stortingsgatan 28 (Mon–Fri 8.30am–4pm, Thurs until 6pm; ☎02/41 80 20), has free maps and gives hiking advice and information on route planning – an invaluable first call before a walking trip elsewhere in Norway. Join here to use their network of mountain huts; they also run a weekly summer bus to the Jotunheimen area.

Police Emergencies, ring ☎002. Otherwise, in case of trouble or lost property (*Hittengodskontoret*) go to *Oslo Politikammer* Grønlandsleiret 44 (☎02/66 99 66), bus #72 from the National Theatre.

Post Office Main office at Dronningensgate 15 (Mon–Fri 8am–8pm, Sat 9am–3pm). Poste Restante at counters 37–41; exchange cash or American Express travellers' cheques only.

Telephones Kongensgate 21 (8am–9pm), entrance on Prinsensgate. International phone-calls can also be made from any city phone box.

Travel agents For discount flights, *BIJ* tickets, *ISIC* cards, etc, try the *Universitetenes Reisebyrå*, Universitetssenteret, Blindern (Mon–Fri 8.15am–3.45pm; ☎02/45 32 00); T-bane line #13 to Blindernveien. More centrally, there's also *Terra Nova*, Dronningensgate 26 (Mon–Fri 9.30am–4pm). Tickets for *National Express Eurolines* services from *Tourbroker Reisebyrå*, Drammensveien 4 (☎02/42 10 19).

Women's Movement The *Norsk Kvinnessaksforening*, Kvinnehuset, Rådhusgate 2 (Mon–Fri 5–10pm, Sat 11am–5pm; closed in summer; ☎02/41 28 64) can put you in touch with women's groups in Oslo and the rest of Norway, and provide information on events and activities.

Youth Hostel Association *Norske Vandrerhjem* has a travel bureau at Dronningensgate 26 (☎02/42 14 10) which sells *BIJ* tickets, *FIYTO* cards and provides up-to-date hostelling information on the rest of the country.

Youth Information Centre Akersgata 57 (☎02/11 04 09). For both Norwegians and foreigners who want to stay in Norway for some time, this organisation can advise on work permits, residence laws, summer jobs, permanent accommodation, health and social security matters, organised groups and other issues. It's open Mon–Fri 11am–6pm (4pm during school holidays).

AROUND OSLO

Oslo is an enormous city, and even the most avid sightseer would take several days to exhaust all the possibilities within its sprawling limits – especially since some of the major city sights tend to come under the category of day or half-day trips, Bygdøy, Frogner Park and Holmenkollen being good examples. Given this, the area around Oslo – and in particular the towns of the **Oslo Fjord** – tend to get short shrift from travellers. And frankly, it's more attractive to stay within the city if your time is at all limited. For the most part, both eastern and western sides of the fjord feature characterless industrial towns, former whaling ports, naval bases, and only the odd castle ruin to add any colour.

But if you have more time there are several places on train and bus routes out of the city that do warrant a stop. A couple are easy trips that should be high on your list anyway. **Southwest**, only just out of Oslo city proper, the **Henie-Onstad Art Centre** is a fine collection of modern art that demands an afternoon at least; to the south, down the **eastern side** of the fjord, **Drøbak** is a lively summer resort with good swimming.

Further out, on the train route south to Sweden, you'll pass through **Moss** to reach seventeenth-century **Fredrikstad**, an interesting contrast to the capital, and **Halden**, hard by the border and defended by a glorious castle. Oslo Fjord's **western side** is less attractive, at least until you reach the resort towns south of Tønsberg – covered in the following chapter.

North of Oslo, **Lake Mjøsa** and its towns are convenient if you're heading to, say, Trondheim – though if you're only taking in part of the lake, a day trip is also feasible. And from the lake extends the once-arduous **postal route** over the mountains to the western fjords, an easier ride today by bus from Oslo to **Fagernes**.

Southwest: the Henie-Onstad Art Centre and the Oslo fjord

Barely out of the city at all, the **Henie-Onstad Art Centre** (Mon–Fri 9am–9.30pm, Sat & Sun 11am–9.30pm; 20kr, students 10kr, half-price with Oslo Card; ☎02/54 30 50), in a beautiful location overlooking the fjord at **HØVIKODDEN**, is Norway's biggest international modern art centre, and one that most cities would move mountains to possess. The foundation of the Olympic skater Sonja Henie (whose world championship and Olympic medals form an incongruous side-exhibition) and her shipowner/art collector husband Niels Onstad, their collection of twentieth-century painting and sculpture is extensive. Matisse and Picasso, post-war French abstract painters, Expressionists and modern Norwegians all figure highly, and are exhibited alongside regular changing exhibitions by local contemporary artists. The centre also hosts regular concert and theatre programmes. When you've seen the exhibits, there's a **café** at the centre and access to a nearby **beach** on the fjord.

You can **get here** by bus from Universitetsplassen; #151, #153, #161, #162, #251, #252 and #261, stopping at Høvikodden; free with the Oslo Card.

The western side of the fjord: Drammen and Horten

Oslo's suburbs extend a long way south, past the art centre, the houses with carved, wooden verandahs and gabled porches eventually giving way to a series of largely industrial towns. **DRAMMEN**, built on an arm of the fjord, is one of the largest, station and apartment blocks on one side of the water, a mixture of turn-of-the-century buildings and modern office blocks on the other – buses plying the bridge between the two. There's no reason to get off (though you might be staying here in the hostel if Oslo is full) and, anyway, once out of Drammen, the scenery becomes more rural – with frequent farms and small settlements – as the train heads into summer holiday country. **HORTEN** is the only real stop, a popular place in summer, with a **campsite** (*Rørestrand Camping*; ☎033/73 340), open from May to August, 1500m outside town, and an hourly **ferry** connection with Moss (19kr), across the fjord.

Southeast: Drøbak, Fredrikstad and Halden

The **eastern side of Oslo Fjord** is prettier than the west, with beaches running almost from the city for the first few kilometres down the fjord (see "Oslo"). The bus to **DRØBAK** (#541, hourly from Roald Amunsensgate in Oslo; 36kr), 40km south of the city, takes you along the coast right next to the water, past the small archipelago of islands and several inland lakes. Many of the coastal stretches are good for swimming and have been taken up by wooden bathing huts, and you'll pass the occasional patch of rock and grass where it's worth jumping off the bus. There are more formal facilities at Drøbak itself – a tiny, dark sand beach and concrete jetties past the old, wooden church. Plenty of people come here to swim in summer and there are a couple of restaurants and a pub-disco to cater for them. It's nice to wander around, too. The small lanes of white houses, one of them sporting a ship's figurehead, cover the headland above the marina. From Oslo, you can reach the offshore island of **Håøya** direct by way of a weekend summer ferry service from the Aker Brygge pier – a good way to see some of the fjord.

Moss, Fredrikstad and Halden

If you're keener to see the towns of the Oslo area than the countryside, **trains** run roughly every two hours from Oslo to Fredrikstad, passing through **MOSS**, another industrial and forgettable town, though again with a hostel and ferry connections across the fjord to Horten. Half an hour on, the old town at **FREDRIKSTAD** is unique in Scandinavia: a complete fortified town where the seventeenth-century cobbled streets and buildings have been preserved intact. It sounds faintly twee and certainly overcrowded, but is (incredibly) neither. In fact, if you're in Oslo for any time at all, Fredrikstad's old centre is well worth the journey. Fredrikstad is also a good place to see on your way in or out of the country: it's on the Gothenburg–Copenhagen–Hamburg train run, and a summer ferry runs daily from Frederikshavn in Denmark.

Beyond the **Domkirke** (tours in July Mon–Fri 10am–4pm), which was decorated by Emmanuel Vigeland, there's little reason to linger in the new town on the train station side of the river: the old town is only a two-minute (2kr) ferry-ride away from Ferjestedsveien, a little way downriver. The main gate through the high stone walls gives onto the central square: uncannily, and authentically, old and peaceful on a quiet or wet day, when the streets echo with nothing but the sound of your own footsteps. Turfed ramparts and a moat surround the town on three sides, and about the only signs of the times are the small shops and cafés installed in the ground floors of some of the old houses. There are guided tours from June to August but you shouldn't need someone else to point out the obvious and powerful atmosphere here.

If you want to know more, a **museum** (June–Aug Mon–Sat 10am–4pm, Sun noon–5pm; rest of the year weekends only noon–5pm; 5kr), housed in the old *Gamle Slaveri* where prisoners once did hard labour, gives the lowdown. Other than that, though, it's best to just browse. If you need to stay, there is a **campsite** (June–Aug only) in the grounds of Kongsten Fort behind the old town.

Another place many people break their journey to or from Sweden is at **HALDEN**, forty minutes from Fredrikstad and the last major town before the border. There's a fine seventeenth-century **castle** here overlooking the town, which you can visit.

North of Oslo: Lake Mjøsa . . . and on to the fjords

Lake Mjøsa is Norway's biggest lake, and its 2000-odd square kilometres are a favourite haunt of Norwegian families after the solitude of its surrounding fields, woods and pastures. It's halfway country: the quiet towns around the lake – Eidsvoll, Hamar, Gjøvik and Lillehammer – give a taste of the rural experience to come in the rest of the country, before routes head onwards north and west into wilder parts. Approaches by **train** are easy, the closest point to Oslo only an hour away. And once there, a 130-year-old **paddle steamer**, *Skibladner*, connects all four main towns on the lake's shores: currently, it runs once daily except Sunday, between mid-June and mid-August, starting in Gjøvik; check the text below and "Travel Details" at the end of the chapter for details. Tickets range from 70kr per person to Hamar, to 110kr to Eidsvoll, and are bought on board.

Eidsvoll

EIDSVOLL, at the bottom end of the lake – and closest to Oslo – has a particular place in Norway's recent history. It was here that the National Council gathered on May 17, 1814 to proclaim a new constitution following the break with Denmark. The **Council Hall**, originally a farmhouse, has been preserved as it was then and is visited by almost every Norwegian child at some stage in their school career – though for non-Norwegians the interest is limited.

Trains from Oslo to Eidsvoll are fairly frequent and take just an hour. You could use the town as a starting point for an extended trip around the lake since the **paddle-steamer** leaves Eidsvoll at 2pm on Monday, Wednesday and Friday, travelling (one-way only) to Hamar in three hours and Gjøvik in four hours.

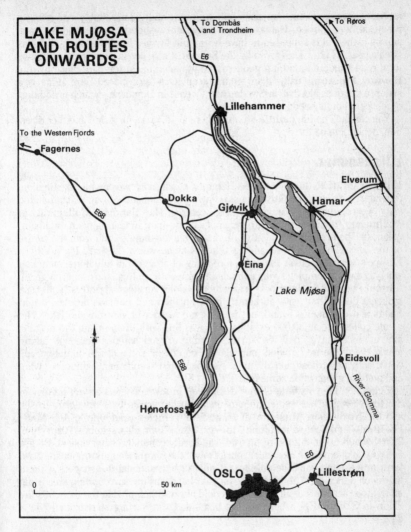

**LAKE MJØSA
AND ROUTES
ONWARDS**

To Dombås
and Trondheim

To Røros

E6

Lillehammer

To the Western Fjords

Fagernes

Elverum

Dokka

Gjøvik

Hamar

E68

Eina

Lake Mjøsa

Eidsvoll

River Glomma

Hønefoss

E68

E6

OSLO

Lillestrøm

0   50 km

Hamar

If you are looking for somewhere to spend the night there's a **youth hostel** at
Finstadsgate 11 (June–Aug; 80kr; ☎065/23 641), 2km from the station, but otherwise **HAMAR** has nothing particular to recommend it other than the route out,
north by train to RØROS (see Chapter Eight): a fine four-hour ride over the hills
and through huge forests. If you have to wait for connections, in town there's the
Hedmark Folk Museum and Cathedral Ruins (May–Sept) at Strandveien
100, which combines the remains of the town's twelfth-century cathedral, an

archaeological museum, open-air folk museum and – improbably enough – a medieval herb garden. Hamar was an important bishopric in the Middle Ages, and its cathedral is supposed to have been built by the "English Pope", Nicholas Breakspear, in 1157. Destroyed by the Swedes, it now lies in ruins, partly because local road-builders found it a good source of materials. In the park close by, the **Railway Museum** (daily 10am–4pm, except Oct–April closed Sun; 10kr) is a sister to the ones at Gävle in Sweden and Odense in Denmark – which is about as much as rail-buffs need know.

You can pick up the **paddle-steamer** here at 10.45am, for a ride in either direction, depending on the day.

Lillehammer

LILLEHAMMER (literally "Little Hammer") is a more worthwhile destination. In winter, it's one of *the* European ski-centres, a young and vibrant place founded sixty years ago as a major tourist centre. The **Sandvig Collection at Maihaugen** (hours vary, but are generally 10am–4pm; June–Aug open until later; 25kr, 20kr before June 8 and after August 17), a ten-minute walk from the centre of the town along Anders Sandvig Gate, is alone worth the halt. It's northern Europe's largest open-air museum, a re-siting of around 120 buildings, including working farms complete with animals, a thirteenth-century stave church (from Garmo), workshop interiors (carpenters, violin makers, printers and pipe makers) decked out with authentic tools, finished and unmade articles, order-books and documents – and, not least, some wonderful views of the lake. The whole collection, all 30,000 exhibits of it, was the work of one man, the magpie-ish Anders Sandvig, and it's worth spending a good half-day here and taking advantage of the free guided tour. Have a go, too, at some of the homely, traditional activities (these and the tour summer only) – spinning, baking, weaving and pottery: good, wholesome fun.

Culturally, there is little else to detain you in town. There's an **art gallery** in Stortorget which has some monumentally boring works by Norwegian artists, and the **Norwegian Museum of Historical Vehicles** (mid-June to Aug Mon–Fri 10am–6pm; Sept to mid-June Mon–Fri 10am–2pm; all weekends 10am–4pm; 20kr), which is quite good but, again, can hardly command mass appeal. Better, and as you'd expect in a premier tourist town, the **shops** along Storgata are good for a browse and you'll be able to get hold of international newspapers without too much difficulty. With more time on your hands, as the surrounding area is big on outdoor activities of all kinds, you could always hitch or ride the daily bus the 22km to **SJUSJØEN**, where rowing boats and windsurfing start from 100kr a day.

Some practical details

Lillehammer's **tourist office** (mid-June to mid-Aug Mon–Sat 9am–7pm, Sun noon–5pm; rest of the year Mon–Fri 9am–4am, Sat 9am–1pm; ☎062/51 098), which has free town-plans, is a two-minute walk up Jernbanegata from the **railway station**. To get to *Birkebeiner's* **youth hostel** (☎062/51 994), walk up Storgaten, turn left, walk to the river and follow the signs that point up the steep road ahead – a 2-kilometre walk but worth it. The hostel, open June to August, costs 115kr a night, including a large buffet breakfast, and has double rooms for 260kr. Also, **campers** can stick up a tent outside.

There are loads of **cafés and restaurants** in Lillehammer, though they're often more flashy than functional: two relatively cheap haunts are the *Din Café*, Storgata 73, and *Bøndernes Hus*, next to the post office on Kirkegata, which has a salad bar and good-sized snacks. For evening liaisons, *Brenneriet* off Storgata is the most popular disco in town.

Gjøvik

GJØVIK, in the other direction, back towards Oslo, is actually the starting-point for the paddle-steamer service: boats leave at 9.30am daily except Sunday, calling at Hamar, Eidsvoll and back to Gjøvik (on Mon, Wed & Fri); and Hamar, Lillehammer and back (on Tues, Thurs & Sat). Given that Gjøvik is also connected directly to Oslo by train (a two-hour ride), it's also a possible day trip – though you'd have to stay overnight if you wanted to make the 9.30am boat trip the next day. There's a **youth hostel** (☎061/71 011) on Parveien, which is open all year and costs 107kr (double rooms 200kr), including breakfast.

Once, bizarrely, the world's leading producer of fishhooks, Gjøvik's contemporary attractions can't compete with those heady days, but there's another **Rural Museum** for addicts of the reconstructed Norwegian farmhouse.

On to the fjords: the royal postal route

Gjøvik used to give access to the western fjord region by way of a train link with **FAGERNES**. Although this no longer exists, it's still possible to travel on the old **Royal Postal Route**, which stretched from Oslo to Bergen, by doubling back to the capital and taking the bus. This gives you hours of marvellous views, riding high above the forests and through rolling green countryside.

From Fagernes there are **buses** across the barren *Fillefjell* – apart from the occasional campsite and motel, a vast slice of nothing far above the tree line. The route continues, down into the fertile **Laerdal valley**, alongside a winding river which gets ever wilder and faster until reaching the comparative serenity of **LAERDAL** itself, a small community where you might be tempted to break the journey (direct buses from Oslo, too). There's a small **youth hostel** (☎056/66 101) at the *Offerdal Hotel*, open May to September, which costs 75kr a night.

At Laerdal you're only a short bus-ride from REVSNES, from where you can catch a **ferry** across the Sognefjord to KAUPANGER, FLÅM or GUDVANGEN – for all of which see "Bergen and the Western Fjords".

travel details

Trains
From Oslo to Myrdal/Voss/Bergen (4–5 daily; 4hr 30min/5hr 15min/6hr 30min); Røros/Trondheim (2 daily; 6hr/8hr 30min, plus one extra train daily to Røros via Hamar); Gjøvik (4–5 daily; 2hr); Eidsvoll/Hamar/Lillehammer (5–8 daily; 1hr/1hr 30min/2hr 15min, 3 continuing to Trondheim via Dombås in 6hr 40min); Lillehammer/Dombås/Åndalsnes (4 daily; 2hr 15min/4hr 10 min/5hr 50min); Kristiansand (3–4 daily; 5hr); Stavanger (3 daily; 8hr); Tønsberg/Larvik (8–10 daily; 1hr 30min/2hr 10min); Moss/Fredrikstad/Halden (11 daily; 1hr/1hr 30min/2hr 10min).

Buses
From Oslo to Drøbak (hourly; 1hr); Bergen via Aurland, Gudvangen and Voss (1 daily; 13hr); Haugesund via Kongsberg and Odda (1 daily;

10hr); Laerdal/Sogndal/Balestrand (1 daily; 6hr/ 7hr/8hr 30min); Fagernes (4–5 daily; 3hr 30min, 1 continuing to Laerdal in 7hr); Hamar/ Lillehammer/Stryn (1 daily; 2hr/3hr/8hr); Gjøvik (1 weekly; 2hr 30min); Alta/Hammerfest via Sweden (3 weekly; 27hr/30hr; reservations obligatory).

From Gjøvik to Lillehammer (Mon–Sat 2 daily; 1hr 15min).

From Lillehammer to Otta/Dombås (Mon–Sat 2 daily; 2hr 30min/3hr 30min).

Ferries

From Oslo to Hovedøya/Lindøya/Nakholmen (half-hourly; 5min/10min/15min); Gressholmen (half-hourly; 10min); Dronningen/Bygdøynes (half-hourly; 10min/15min).

From Moss to Horten (continual crossings daily 6am–10.30pm; 35min).

International Trains

From Oslo to London, via Hamburg (2 daily); Paris (2 daily); Rome (1 daily); Copenhagen via Gothenburg (3–4 daily); Stockholm (2–3 daily).

International Buses

From Oslo to Gothenburg (3 daily; 5hr 30min).

International Ferries

From Oslo to Copenhagen (1 daily; 16hr); Frederikshavn (2 daily; 10–14hr); Hirtshals (4 weekly; 9hr); Kiel (1 daily June–Aug, otherwise 6 weekly; 19hr 30min); Harwich via Hirtshals (1 weekly; 36hr).

From Moss to Frederikshavn (1 daily; 7hr 30min).

From Fredrikstad to Frederikshavn (1–2 daily; 7hr).

CHAPTER FIVE

SOUTHERN NORWAY

T he half-moon bulge that is **southern Norway** is an immediately appealing region: flatlands and fells topped with a tempting coastal concentration of islands and long beaches. It's a combination not lost on the Norwegians, who have made the south coast their principal domestic holiday choice. Everyone else, though, tends to pass quickly through. Those arriving on **ferries** from Harwich or Newcastle, and Hirtshals or Hantsholm (in Denmark) are usually intent upon seeing Oslo, the western fjords and little else – a prejudice often confirmed by the railway journey east or west, which tunnels its way through long stretches of countryside.

Part of the problem with the area is **access**. The railway runs just inland for most of its journey across southern Norway, only dipping down to the coast at the major resorts – a disappointing ride, the views shielded much of the time behind undulating hills. To travel any further inland – not that there's much more than a few isolated villages dotted around the valleys – you have to rely on infrequent and expensive buses, and unless you're a committed hiker and camper, you may find it not worth the bother. A better plan, if time is limited, is to stay with the railway, taking a couple of days to see the coast and afterwards either heading north on one long bus-ride through the central southern fells to Bergen and the fjords, or staying on the eastbound train to Oslo.

The region may, of course, be your first view of Norway and it's worth spending at least some time at your point of arrival. International ferries put in to the western port of **Stavanger**, the region's major town, and central **Kristiansand**, a lively resort. Both are attractive centres in their own right, Stavanger with its medieval cathedral and – albeit small – preserved old town, and its direct ferry and express boat connections with Bergen to the north. To the east, the coastline changes for the better and the numerous **islands and beaches** are an obvious draw. On the way to or from Oslo, **Kongsberg** and **Tønsberg** were once important centres, the former with a grand church that suitably reflects the town's eighteenth-century importance as a centre of silver production.

Stavanger

STAVANGER is something of a survivor. While other Norwegian coastal towns have fallen foul of the precarious fortunes of fishing, Stavanger has over the years grown into one of Norway's most dynamic economic power-bases. Fish canning and its own merchant fleet brought initial prosperity, which shipbuilding and, more recently, the oil industry have since sustained: the port builds the rigs for the offshore oilfields and afterwards refines the oil before dispatch. None of which sounds terribly enticing, and Stavanger, certainly, isn't one of Norway's most alluring cities. But if you have arrived here from abroad by ferry or plane, or find yourself at the end of the Sørland railway line, it is worth sparing at least a little time to

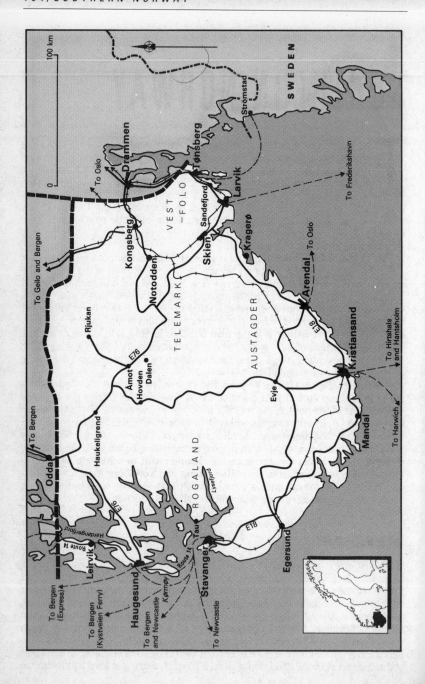

see the elegant old town before heading for the fjords or Oslo. In any case, Stavanger is a brash, international place, not totally unlikeable: foreign oil-workers have made English virtually the first language, and there's even a weekly English-language newspaper, *Saga* – useful for reviews of the week's TV if little else.

Arrival and information

Ferries from Hirtshals and Newcastle arrive at the harbour, *Vågen*, a short walk from the main square, Torget; the *Kystveien* ferry from Bergen docks a little further up at Sandvigå. **Express boat** (*Hurtigbåt*) arrivals from Bergen alight at the terminal at the bottom of Kirkegata, at the top of which is the lake and the cathedral. The **airport** is 14km south of the city at SOLA: there's an *SAS* bus (25kr) into Stavanger, which stops at the major hotels; or local buses #143 or #152 run into the centre (from around 6am–midnight), every half an hour, dropping you at the **bus and railway station** on the western side of the town's central lake. All the **local ferries**, out to the islands and fjords around Stavanger, arrive at and depart from the Fiskepiren terminal, east along the harbour from the express boat terminal.

Just up from the railway station is the **tourist office** (June–Aug Mon–Fri 9am–6pm, Sat & Sun 9am–4pm; Sept–May Mon–Fri 9am–4pm, Sat 9am–1pm; ☎04/53 51 00), in a two-storey pavilion building. They'll give you the free *Stavanger Guide*, a listings booklet, and also the **Stavanger Card**, which is free and entitles you to fifty-percent discounts on local buses and museum entry, and gives other deals on car hire, boat services, sightseeing and the like. The tourist office also rents out **bikes** in summer, though just about everywhere is walkable, even the youth hostel.

Finding a place to stay

If you need to **stay over**, there's plenty of choice in Stavanger. The town sees a high turnover of business people and tourists, and in summer you'll be able to get a good deal on hotel rooms.

Hostels

The cheapest option, at 50kr per night, is the **YMCA hostel** and *InterRail Point* (*KFUM*; ☎04/53 28 88) at Rektor Berntsensggate 7, which has showers, a kitchen and laundry facilities but is only open during July and the first week of August (7–10am & 4–11pm). The official *Mosvangen* **youth hostel** (☎04/52 75 60), Henrik Ibsensgate 21, is comparatively expensive (120kr; double rooms 170kr), but prices include a fine breakfast and lakeside surroundings. Open all year except Christmas week, it's a thirty-minute walk from the centre: from Madlaveien, turn left on to the E18, from which a cycle-path leads around a lake to the hostel. After dark it's easier to take the blue *NSB* bus #28 from outside the railway station, or yellow bus #78, #97 or #99 from *Rogalandsbanken*, near the tourist office.

Guest houses and hotels

There are a few **guest houses** in central Stavanger which won't completely wreck the budget either. *Bergeland Gjestgiveri*, Vikedalsgata 1a (☎04/53 41 10), charges 200kr per person including breakfast: it's east of the railway station,

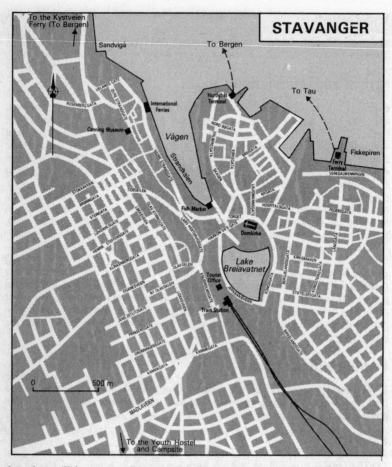

though you'll have to walk around the lake to reach it. The *City Gjestehuset*, Madlaveien 20 (☎04/52 04 37), is slightly more expensive – around 430kr for a double room with bath. Some of the **hotels** have summer deals, too, between June and August; check with the tourist office. As a pointer, the *Grand Hotel*, Klubbgata 3, off Hospitalsgata (☎04/53 30 20), lets its double rooms, with bath and TV, for around 210kr per person during summer (including breakfast); the *Commandør Hotel*, Valberggata 9, right in the centre, is even cheaper – from 125kr per person in July and at the beginning of August.

Camping

For **camping**, there's a site next to the *Mosvangen* youth hostel (☎04/53 29 71), open June to August only and with cabins for rent. If you want to be nearer the sea, camp out at ØLBERG (☎04/65 43 75), 6km west of the airport. This is again open June to August only; take bus #40 from the centre, or bus #149 every hour or so from the airport.

The Town

Much of central Stavanger is modern, built with oil money, and of little interest to the casual visitor, the shipyards and their offices displaying a showy, transient prosperity. It's the town's old centre, **Gamle Stavanger**, above the international ferry terminals, which is of greatest appeal – and the least changed part of town. Though a far cry from the modern structures back towards the harbour, the buildings here are a product of their own wealthy age. Tall wooden warehouses flank the western quayside, split by a succession of narrow lanes: walk up any of them and you're in the heart of the residential quarter, once home for local seamen and visiting merchants. The long rows of white-painted houses, gas lamps, picket fences and tiny terraced gardens, most dating from the late eighteenth century, make for engaging, if over zealously preserved walks along the cobbled streets. A note of realism is brought to bear by the **Canning Museum**, right in Gamle Stavanger at Øvre Strandgate 88 (June–Aug Tues–Sun 11am–3pm; rest of the year except Dec Sun 11am–4pm; 10kr) – a reconstructed sardine-canning factory which gives a glimpse of the industry that saved Stavanger from decay in the nineteenth century. As Stavanger comes to terms with the current decline in the oil industry, it's an instructive lesson in diversification.

Walk back through the old town towards the centre and you'll pass the **Maritime Museum** (June–Aug Tues–Sun 11am–3pm, rest of the year except Dec Sun 11am–4pm; 10kr) at Nedre Strandgate 17, which gives another useful insight into the particular history of Stavanger. The exhibits are as much to do with the trade that the shipping industry engendered as the sea itself and there are nice touches here – like the old sailmaker's room and various reconstructed shop and office interiors.

Along the length of the harbour, on **Torget**, there's a daily market, flowers, fruit and veg filling the square, while for fresh fish you should check out the teeming watertanks on the quayside. The streets around **Skagen**, on the jut of land forming the eastern side of the harbour, make up the town's shopping area, a bright mix of spidery lanes, pedestrianised streets and white-timbered houses, that covers the area where the original settlement of medieval Stavanger lay – though little remains of the layout, or the atmosphere. The spikey **Valberg Tower** (Mon–Fri 10am–4pm, Sat 9am–1pm; free) was a nineteenth-century fire-watch and, along with some distinctly unthrilling ceramics and textile displays, gives sweeping views of the city and its industry from the top. Take a look, too, inside the **Kulturhus**, close by at Sølvberggaten 2 (Mon–Sat 10am–10pm, Sun 1–10pm), where there's usually something going on: the complex holds a cinema, library, art gallery, bookshop and café.

The only relic of medieval Stavanger is on the fringes of Torget close to **Breiavatnet** lake, which sits in the middle of the city – the twelfth-century **Domkirke** (mid-May to mid-Sept Mon–Sat 9am–6pm, Sun 1–6pm; mid-Sept to mid-May Mon–Sat 9am–2pm), whose pointed-hat towers signal a Romanesque church altered irredeemably by modern renovation. The classically simple interior, built by English craftsmen, has been spoilt by ornate seventeenth-century additions, including an intricate pulpit and five huge memorial tablets adorning the walls of the aisles: all a swirling jumble of richly carved angels, crucifixes, death's heads, animals and apostles.

Around from the cathedral, in the grid of streets to the east of the lake, the **Norwegian Emigration Centre**, Bergjelandsgata 30 (Mon–Fri 10am–2pm & 5–

8pm, Sat 9am–1pm), might be of interest if you have Norwegian ancestors. The archives here are extensive and the staff will help you trace your descendants (180kr for each written request): it helps to go equipped with the name, birthplace, birthdate and – if you know it – year of emigration of the person you're seeking.

Eating and drinking

With many tourists just passing through, and what restaurants there are aimed squarely at the expense account oil business, Stavanger isn't a great place to **eat** on any kind of budget. If you're staying at the youth hostel you may as well avail yourself of the meals served up there – reasonable and filling for the most part. Otherwise, the café in the *Kulturhus* (see above) is always a good bet; there's a *Wimpy* (open until 2.30am Fri & Sat) at Skagen 6; and a branch of *Peppe's Pizza* at Kirkegata. Several Chinese restaurants in town serve up fixed-price lunches (around 50kr), among them the *Hong Kong Garden*, Østervåg 9, and the *Shanghai*, Nytorget 8.

Drinking, too, isn't exactly loaded with thrilling possibilities, though you'll be able at least to slake your thirst in one of the several mundane places along Skagenkaien and Strandkaien. If you're determined to make the most of Stavanger then you can finish the night at one of a couple of licensed **discos** – *Mr Jones* on Strandkaien and *New York* on Skagenkaien both open daily from 9pm until 2am.

Listings

Airlines *Braathens SAFE*, Strandkaien 2 (☎04/53 60 70); *British Airways*, at Sola airport (☎04/65 15 33); *Dan Air*, Strandkaien 2 (☎04/53 60 70); *SAS*, Rosenkildetorget 1 (☎04/52 15 66).

Car rental *Avis*, Kongsgaten 50 (☎04/52 85 65); *Europcar*, Lagårdsveien 125 (☎04/52 21 33); *Hertz*, Hillevågsveien 33 (☎04/58 17 00); *Interrent*, Hillevågsveien 21–23 (☎04/58 97 02); *Stavanger Bilutleie*, Kong Karls Gate 71 (☎04/52 03 52).

Consulates *United Kingdom*, Haakon VII's Gate 8 (☎04/52 58 01).

Ferries *Det Stavangerske Dampskibsselskap* (local ferry lines; ☎04/52 00 65); *Fred Olsen Lines*, Strandkaien (☎04/53 01 49); *Norway Line*, Strandkaien (☎04/52 45 45); *Kystveien*, (☎05/14 11 00).

Left luggage In the express boat terminal (daily 7.15am–9pm) and the railway station (daily 7am–10pm).

Shops Open until 7pm on Thursday and Friday.

Telephone office Nygaten 15 (Mon–Wed & Fri 8.30am–4pm, Thurs 8.30am–7pm, Sat 8.30am–2pm).

Around Stavanger: Rogaland County

Stavanger can get uncomfortably crowded in the summer, but fortunately there is some excellent **hiking** close by in **Rogaland County**, which roughly covers the area south of Haugesund and down to Flekkefjord on the southern coast. There are easy trips, too, out from Stavanger on a wide variety of local **ferries** and boats.

Hiking routes

The local **hiking association**, *Stavanger Turistforening* (Mon–Fri 9am–4pm; ☎04/52 75 66), Muségata 8, has full details on the 900km of local trails they administer, route planning information and weather conditions. They also run thirty mountain cabins in the area for association members – join at the office – as well as organising a ski-school (in English) on winter weekends. The nearest **cabins** are accessible by ferry and bus from Stavanger, most easily at ÅDNERAM or VIGLESDALEN, from where you can join an extensive circular trail that has cabins every few hours. The busiest time is at Easter; in summer there should be no problem finding room to sleep.

Fjord trips: Tau and the Lysefjord

If you're going to see a little of the **fjord region** around Stavanger you'll need to pick up the full ferry and express boat timetable from the *DSD* terminal on the harbour front. Boats are fairly frequent and from most places there are bus connections on to local points of interest, so you shouldn't get stuck.

The most popular trip, within fairly easy reach of Stavanger, is the pretty **Lysefjord** and its dramatic **Pulpit Rock**, a 600m-high sheer cliff to which the tourist office runs expensive (around 200kr) return speedboat/coach trips from June to August. You can do the same trip independently, catching a local ferry from Fiskepiren in Stavanger to **TAU** (a 45-minute journey), and an hourly bus from there to JØRPELAND. Hitching from there to the start of the Pulpit path is easy enough, from where it's a two-hour hike to the top. Alternatively, there's an express boat which runs directly to Jørpeland from Stavanger, though it's less frequent and more expensive. Things are, of course, easier still if you stay at one of the two **campsites** at **BJØRHEIMSBYGD**, near Tau: as well as camping, *Wathne Camping* (☎04/44 64 17) has eight cabins for rent; *Hamrane Hyttefelt* (☎04/44 64 20) has seven four-bed cabins, at 340kr a night.

There are **other ferries**, if you only have time for a short tour of the waterways around Stavanger. The ferry to Vikevåg on the island of **Rennesøy** only takes an hour or so and calls at a couple of other islands on the way – including Askje at **Mosterøy**, from where buses (June–Aug) run to the medieval **Utstein cloister**.

The Route North: Stavanger to Bergen

If you're a train fanatic, or already committed to a rail pass, you need to go back to Oslo to travel on to Bergen. If not, you can, despite the fragmented nature of the coast, get there more directly by bus and ferry. In fact, the **direct routes** will save you time and are for the most part more spectacular.

By express boat and ferry

For speed if not economy, best bet is the *Hurtigbåt* or **express boat**, which runs all year. This requires advance seat reservations (☎04/52 20 90) and costs around 326kr one-way – though students, youth hostel members and rail pass holders qualify for a thirty-percent discount. The trip takes four and a half hours and departures are from the terminal on Stavanger's harbour front.

Cheaper (currently 150kr one-way; children, students and senior citizens 100kr), but slower, the *Kystveien* **ferry** is usually an overnight journey, and leaves from Sandvigå, the harbour beyond the old town. Another option is the **ferry from Newcastle**, which during summer continues on to Bergen and charges about 200kr (25-percent student discount available) for the one-way hop. Tickets for all alternatives are available from the terminal offices or travel agents in the city; also see "Travel Details" at the end of this chapter.

By bus and ferry: via Haugesund

If you've time to spare, **Route 14** or the *Kystvegen*, which cuts across the western archipelago on a succession of connecting buses and ferries, is more interesting: a scenic trip, and with several good jumping-off points on the way to Bergen. You can do this as quickly, or as slowly, as you like: services (on which you should pay as you go) vary, but in summer the first bus usually departs Stavanger at 9am, arriving – if you want to make it in one day – in Bergen at around 6pm. The tourist office can provide exact timetables.

First stop on Route 14 is **Karmøy**, the largest island in the area, dotted with a host of Viking sites and finds. If you want to stop over there is usually room at the cheap **youth hostel** (☎04/82 01 91) in **SANDVE**: it's open all year except Christmas week, and charges 70kr (double rooms 140–180kr).

The northern end of the island is connected by bridge to the mainland at **HAUGESUND**, a small and lively port at which the regular express boats from Stavanger also call. It was here that the first ruler of Norway as one kingdom, Harald Håfagre (Harald the Fair-Haired), was buried, and a curious obelisk 3km out of the centre marks his alleged resting place. He gained sovereignty over these coastal districts at a decisive sea-battle in 872, an achievement which, according to legend, released him from a ten-year vow not to cut his hair until he became king of all Norway – hence his nickname. Although there's no real reason to stay other than for the quiet surroundings, you could make Haugesund your overnight stop if you wished: the **youth hostel** at Skeisvannsvegen 20 (☎047/71 21 46) is open from June to August and its steep prices (120kr; double rooms 350kr) include breakfast. From Haugesund, Route 14 continues on to Bergen via the island of **Stord**, where there's another hostel at **LITLABØ** (☎054/94 310) – also open June to August and a bargain at 60kr a bed, 110kr a double.

If you're impatient for the fjords, there is an alternative **route inland** and then north from Haugesund. One daily bus (at 9am; 133kr) makes the two-hour journey to **ODDA**, situated on a long finger of the Hardangerfjord, which also has a youth hostel (address on p.220), from where it's only a ferry and bus ride to Bergen.

Along the coast: Egersund, Mandal and Kristiansand

Trains out of Stavanger run south down the coast, through long flat plains with the sea on one side and distant hills away to the east. **EGERSUND** is the first notable stop, a Norwegian "white town" with characteristic white-painted wooden houses – and, during summer, **ferry connections** to Hantsholm and Hirtshals in

Denmark. Egersund marks the start of the south coast proper. From here, almost the entire shoreline is interrupted by a series of great valleys running north to south, through which the train tunnels eastward – technically wonderful but inevitably monotonous. There are stops at the odd small station in the hills, but unless you're camping or take a fancy to somewhere specific, there is no real reason to get off before MARNADAL, from where bus connections from the railway station jog you down to the coast at **MANDAL**. This is Norway's southernmost town, and it's a popular tourist spot with a fine beach and more white houses. There's a couple of **hotels**, one – the *Mandalitten Hotell* (☎043/61 422) – at Store Elvegata 23a, which has basic doubles from around 360kr, and a **campsite** (☎043/63 416). From Mandal there are daily buses to Kristiansand, or you can nip back to Marnadal and the train line.

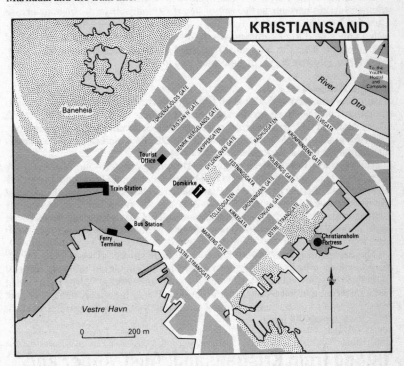

Kristiansand

Like so many other Scandinavian towns founded by and named after Christian IV, **KRISTIANSAND** is the closest thing to a resort there is in Norway – a bright, energetic place which thrives on its ferry connections with England and Denmark, and its excellent (though crowded) beaches. The seafront and its adjoining streets are a most un-Norwegian – and not at all unpleasant – bustle of cocktail bars, fast-food joints, souvenir shops, ice-cream vendors and signs in English.

The town has retained the seventeenth-century quadrant plan that characterised all Christian's projects and is, in the main, worth a quick skirt around – especially when everyone else has gone to the beach and left the central pedestrianised streets relatively uncluttered. Of specific sights, though, there are few. The Domkirke is modern and mock-Gothic, while the squat **Christiansholm Fortress**, overlooking the colourful marina at the east harbour, never saw real service, and these days hosts arts and crafts displays. Marginally more interesting, there's the *Baneheia* **recreational area**, a large cool park with lakes, swimming and endless trails that can be a good place to camp (although not quite legally); to reach it, turn left out of the railway station and walk up Vestre Strandgate.

One of the better moves you can make is to catch a boat, *M/S Maarten* (from the fish market harbour at the end of Vestre Strandgate) for a two-hour **cruise** through the offshore waters. It stops at several islands which have been designated public (and free) **camping** areas, so you can doss down and catch the boat back the next day. The boat runs from mid-June to the beginning of September, Monday to Saturday at 9.30am and costs around 50kr.

Practical details

Train, **bus** and **ferry** arrivals are all fairly close to each other, by Vestre Havn, on the edge of the town grid. The **tourist office** is a step up at Henrik Wergelandsgata 17 (mid-June to mid-Aug Mon–Sat 8am–7pm, Sun noon–7pm; mid-Aug to mid-June Mon–Fri 8am–4pm; ☎042/26 065), and can provide a handy map and information on accessible beaches and islands.

The cheapest **hotels** are a couple on Dronningensgate, – the *Norge* and the *Rica Fregotten* – though they're no real bargain at around 520kr a double including breakfast; the tourist office may have better suggestions. The **youth hostel** at Kongsgård Allé 33 (☎042/95 369) costs 90kr a night and is 2km from the railway station; cross the large bridge, Lundsbroen, walk up Østerveien and it's off to the right in the *Badminton Senteret* (open mid-June to mid-Aug; closed between 10am and 4pm).

The **campsite** (☎042/94 759) has a good, small stretch of beach close by. It's on Marvikveien in Roligheden, open from June to August, in the same general direction as the youth hostel: once across the bridge, turn right along Kuholmsveien and left along Tegelverksveien. The swimming is good here and, out of season at least, there's nothing to prevent you from throwing a sleeping bag down among the trees.

Inland from Kristiansand: Aust-Agder and Telemark Counties

The whole of the region **north and inland** of Kristiansand is much tougher to see on any kind of fleeting visit. This was for many years bandit country: its villages are isolated and the bus network fairly limited, making it a good region for keen outdoor-types but hard work for less specialised travellers. There are few facilities and **accommodation** is mostly in youth hostels, campsites and camping cabins – and even those are few and far between.

Aust-Agder

One daily **bus** leaves Kristiansand to travel due north to **HOVDEN** in **Aust-Agder County**, a hiking base served by a selection of country hotels and cabins, as well as a **youth hostel** – the *Triangel Feriesenter* (☎043/39 501). This costs 80kr a night (double rooms from 250kr), and is open from mid-June to mid-September. Hovden is a useful stop, even if you're not equipped for the country-side, since the same bus continues northwest to Odda and on to Voss – an ideal way to jump from the south coast to the western fjords without having to detour to either Bergen or Oslo. Equally, if you're coming from the fjords, making for Hovden lets you pick up the very early (5.50am) once-daily (not Sat) bus from there to **ARENDAL**, on the southeastern coast of Aust-Agder – from where there's a summer **ferry** up the Oslo Fjord to Oslo (around 360kr return, students half-price). The Arendal **tourist office**, at Torvgata 6, has more details. (Incidentally, Arendal is also reachable on a branch rail-line, off the main route from Kristiansand, changing at Nelaug.)

Telemark

The more easterly county, **Telemark**, is trickier to reach, at least from Kristiansand. It's worth the effort, though, for a sight of some heavily rural parts of the country that most tourists never come near. Without your own transport, you'll have to approach from Oslo, not a bad move as twice a week from the capital you can catch the direct bus to **RJUKAN** in the dead centre of southern Norway. With the country under occupation by the Nazis in World War II, this was the site of a German laboratory racing to produce heavy water, with which they could have produced a nuclear bomb. The Norwegian resistance, in one of the most spectacular escapades of the war, blew the whole place sky high – a story recounted in the fine film *The Heroes of Telemark*, starring Kirk Douglas. There's a **youth hostel** in Rjukan, open May to October (70kr a bed, double rooms 300kr). The other approach to Telemark is less direct but perhaps more enjoyable, taking the daily **ferry** from SKIEN to **DALEN**, a ten-hour ride north-west up the inland waterways that costs around 150kr. There's a **campsite** (☎036/77 191) in Dalen, open June to mid-August, and if you can pick up a lift – or hike – the 22km north to ÅMOT, there's a daily bus (at 2.30pm) from there to either Oslo or Odda/Haugesund.

Routes to Oslo: Vestfold County

Telemark's short coastline continues to the north with **Vestfold County**, which runs down the western bank of the Oslo Fjord, the whole coast teeming with small, bright fishing villages, holiday islands and thousands of summer (mainly Norwegian) tourists. Local buses make connections between most of the villages and the main railway line, but you should have no trouble hitching short distances on the busy roads: the E18 runs south and close to the coast all the way from Oslo.

One of the nicest places to stay on this stretch of coast isn't actually in Vestfold at all, but close by in Telemark. **KRAGERØ** is a pretty town whose scenery inspired Edvard Munch – who used to spend his summers here – to some of his jollier paintings. There's a **youth hostel** here, at Lovisenbergveien 20 (☎03/98 21 52), open all year, costing 125kr including breakfast; double rooms at 250kr. Further up the coast, the larger towns of **LARVIK** and **SANDEFJORD** are really only worth seeing if you're catching a ferry; see "Travel Details" for the possibilities.

Tønsberg

With Oslo so close, though, few people bother to stop in Vestfold at all, and if you're not a beach-fiend there's not a great deal to see. **TØNSBERG**, a few kilo-metres north of Sandefjord, is a case in point. Allegedly founded by the son of Harald Håfagre in the ninth century, the town rose to prominence in the Middle Ages as *the* ecclesiastical and trading centre in Norway. The sheltered sound made a safe harbour, the flat plain was ideal for settlement, and the town's palace and fortress assured it the patronage of successive monarchs. All of which sounds exciting, and you might expect Tønsberg to be one of the country's more important historical attractions. Sadly, though, there's little of the period left.

The castle, **Slottsfjellet**, on a hill directly ahead of the railway station, remains in ruins, touted by the local tourist office as "Tønsberg's Acropolis" – a claim which is obviously absurd, though it takes little imagination to appreciate the castle's defensive and strategic position. The Swedes burned it down in 1503 and the place has never been rebuilt: what you come for now are mainly the views – not much enhanced, incidentally, by paying to climb the viewing tower.

Apart from its medieval importance, Tønsberg was known for whaling, an industry common to the whole coast, and the **Vestfold County Museum**, on Farmannsveien (July & Aug Mon–Sat 10am–5pm, Sun 1–5pm; rest of the year Mon–Fri 10am–2pm; 5kr) turn right out of the station – has a rather sad array of whale carcasses on show. Outside on the slopes of the Slottsfjell are collections of farmhouses, barns and workshops, all carefully preserved and open for a poke around the decorated rooms and fire-blackened kitchens.

Practical details

During the summer there is a small **tourist office** (July daily & Aug Mon–Sat 10am–6pm) down on the quayside, or in winter try at Storgaten 55. In town, the **youth hostel** (☎033/12 848), nestling directly underneath the hill and open June to August, is a nice base: 110kr including breakfast (doubles 290kr). If you need something **to eat**, *Kafe Diva* on Rådhusgata can oblige: bands frequently play here and the café is open until 2.30am.

Kongsberg

Just out of Vestfold county, in Buskerud, and only an hour or so from Oslo, there is a more vital stop. A local story claims that the silver responsible for the exis-tence of **KONGSBERG** was discovered by two goatherds, who stumbled across a vein of the metal laid bare by the scratchings of an ox. True or not, Christian IV, his eye to the main chance, was quick to exploit the find, and with the rise of this, his mining centre, so the seventeenth-century silver rush began. It turned out that Kongsberg was the only place in the world where silver was to be found in a pure form, and by the following century the town was the largest in Norway – half of its 8000 inhabitants employed in and around the 300-odd mine shafts that were sunk in the area. The silver works closed in 1805, when Kongsberg began to make money out of its Royal Mint, and, a few years later, the armaments factory opened which employs people to this day.

Statues on the town's bridge commemorate various, often foolhardy, attempts to locate new finds of silver (including using divining rods), but of more interest are the **silver mines** themselves (open for tours mid-May to Aug; 10kr), 7km out of town at SØLVVERKET – though these are a bit of a struggle to get to without your own wheels. There are buses to NOTODDEN (June to mid-Aug Mon–Fri 3–4 daily), from the bus terminus outside the railway station or, failing that, it's possible to hitch along the E76 in the Larvik direction, from which the mines are signposted off to the right. It's well worth the effort, since the informative tour includes a ride on a train through black tunnels to the shafts, a thrilling way to spend the afternoon.

To understand the enormous political power that the mines engendered it's necessary to visit **Kongsberg Kirke** (mid-May to Aug Mon–Fri 10am–4pm, Sat 10am–1pm, Sun open after service until 1pm; rest of the year Tues–Fri 10am–noon), the largest and arguably most beautiful Baroque church in Norway. It dates from the most prosperous mining period at the end of the eighteenth century and sits, impressively, in a square surrounded on three sides by period wooden buildings. Inside, too, it's a grand affair, its enormous and showily mock-marbled western wall unusually comprising altar, pulpit and organ: a reverse order which had a political significance – the priest over the altar would exhort the assembled workers to be more industrious in the pursuit of profit. The plush seating arrangements were rigidly, and hierarchically, defined, and determined the church's principal fixtures. On the opposite wall is the "King's Box" and boxes for the silver-works managers, while other officials sat in the glass-enclosed "cases". The pews on the ground floor were reserved for women, while the sweeping three-tiered balcony was the domain of the Kongsberg workers and petit bourgeoisie.

As for the rest of Kongsberg, it's an agreeable, if quiet, place in summer, with plenty of green spaces and a river that tumbles through the centre in three wide waterfalls. Enthusiasts (or thwarted mine-visitors) might enjoy the **Mining Museum** (mid-May to Aug daily 10am–4pm; 2kr, students free), housed in the old smelting-works at the river's edge, but merely pottering around is much the most enjoyable way of spending time here.

Practical details

Given Kongsberg's choice of accommodation you might well want to stop over. The **tourist office** (Jan to mid-June & mid-Aug to Dec Mon–Fri 9am–4pm; mid-June to mid-Aug Mon–Sat 9am–7pm, Sun noon–4pm; ☎03/73 15 26) is outside the **railway station**, at the top of Storgaten, and can direct you to a **campsite** (*Lågdalsmuseet Camping*; ☎03/73 22 28) down by the river which has cabins for rent. Over the bridge and further up the main road towards the church is the **youth hostel** (☎03/73 20 24), open all year (105kr including breakfast; doubles from 320kr); while at Hyttegate 4 there is a cheaper **YMCA hostel** (☎03/73 60 26), though this is only open from the first week in July to the first week in August.

travel details

Trains
From Stavanger to Egersund/Marnadal/Kristiansand (3–4 daily; 1hr/2hr 40min/3hr); Oslo (3 daily; 9hr).
From Kristiansand to Kongsberg/Drammen/Oslo (5 daily; 3hr 30min/4hr/5hr).
From Kongsberg to Oslo (7–8 daily; 1hr 30min).
From Skien to Larvik/Sandefjord/Tønsberg/Oslo (9–10 daily; 45min/1hr/1hr 25min/3hr).
From Nelaug to Arendal (4–5 daily; 40min).

Buses
From Stavanger to Mandal/Kristiansand (1–2 daily; 4hr/5hr).
From Kristiansand to Hovden/Odda/Voss (1 daily; 4hr 30min/7hr 30min/10hr).
From Hovden to Arendal (1 daily; 5hr); Odda/Voss (1 daily; 3hr/5hr 30min).
From Haugesund to Odda/Åmot/Kongsberg/Oslo (1 daily; 2hr/5hr/8hr/10hr).
From Kongsberg to Rjukan (Fri at 8.10pm & Sun at 10.10pm only; 2hr); Drammen/Oslo (1 daily; 1hr/1hr 45min); Odda/Haugesund (1 daily; 6hr 30min/8hr 30min).

Ferries
From Stavanger to Bergen (*Kystveien*: Jan to mid-June & mid-Aug to Dec Mon–Sat 1 daily; mid-June to mid-Aug, via Krokeide, with a connecting bus service to Bergen, Mon–Fri 2

daily, Sat & Sun 1 daily; 7hr); Tau (hourly; 45min); Askje/Vikevåg (6–11 daily; 45min/1hr 10min).
From Arendal to Oslo (July & Aug 1 daily; 6hr).
From Skien to Dalen (June, July & Aug 1 daily; 10hr).

Express boats
From Stavanger to Haugesund/Bergen (*Hurtibåt* service 2–3 daily; 1hr 30min/4hr 30min); Haugesund (3 daily; 1hr 30min); Tau (Mon–Fri 3 daily; 20min); Jørpeland (Mon–Fri 2 daily; 30min); Vikevåg (4 daily except Sat; 30min).

International Ferries
All frequencies below, except those from Stavanger to Newcastle/Hirtshals, and Sandefjord to Strömstad, apply to the period mid-June to August only.

From Stavanger to Newcastle (end of May to mid-Oct 2–3 weekly; 18hr); Hirtshals (2 weekly; 11hr).
From Egersund to Hantsholm (3–4 weekly; 7hr 30min); Hirtshals (1 weekly; 10hr).
From Kristiansand to Hirtshals (1–2; 4hr); Hantsholm (4 weekly; 4hr); Harwich (1 weekly; 23hr).
From Larvik to Frederikshavn (1–2 daily, rest of the year 6 weekly; 6–8hr).
From Sandefjord to Strömstad (1–2 daily; 2hr 30min).

CHAPTER SIX

BERGEN AND THE WESTERN FJORDS

I f there's one familiar – and enticing – image of Norway it's the fjords: huge clefts in the landscape which occur throughout the country right up to the Soviet border, but which are most easily, and impressively, seen on the western coast. Wild, rugged and peaceful, these water-filled wedges of space are visually stunning; indeed, the entire fjord region elicits inordinate amounts of purple prose from tourist office handouts, and for once it's rarely overstated. The fjords are undeniably beautiful.

Under the circumstances it seems churlish to complain of the thousands of summer visitors who tramp through the picturesque villages – quiet and isolated places the other nine months of the year. The rolling mountains are relentlessly roamed by walkers, the fjords cruised by steady flotillas of white ferries. But if it all smacks too much of package holiday nightmare don't be put off: there's been little development and what there is is still not intrusive. Even in the most popular regions it's possible to find lots of spots not yet penetrated by the coach parties.

As for specific destinations, **Bergen**, Norway's second-largest city and so-called "Capital of the Fjords", is a welcoming place boasting some good museums – the best located in an atmospheric old warehouse quarter, dating from the city's days as the northernmost port of the Hanseatic trade alliance. As its tourist title suggests, Bergen is also a handy springboard for the western fjords. Easily

THE FJORDS: APPROACHES AND TRAVEL DETAILS

Norway's western fjords comprise perhaps the most confusing region to tour by **public transport**, though this is not due to a poor service. Bus and ferry connections are good, albeit expensive, and on the roads you'll find hitching short distances is generally easy. The problem is more one of **access**. By rail, you can only reach Bergen in the south and Åndalsnes in the very north. For everything in between – the Nordfjord, Jostedalsbreen glacier and Sognefjord – you're confined to buses and ferries, and although they virtually all connect up with each other, it means that there is no set way to approach the fjord region. We've covered the fjords **south to north** – from the major city Bergen, via the Sognefjord, Nordfjord, Geirangerfjord and Romsdalfjord, to Åndalsnes. There are certain obvious connections – from Bergen to Voss and Flåm, and from Åndalsnes over the Trollstigen to Geiranger, for example – but routes are really a matter of personal choice; the text details the alternatives. It's a good idea to pick up full **bus and ferry timetables** from the local tourist offices whenever you can, and be aware that shorter bus routes are often part of a longer routing on which the buses and ferries link up – meaning that you shouldn't get stranded anywhere.

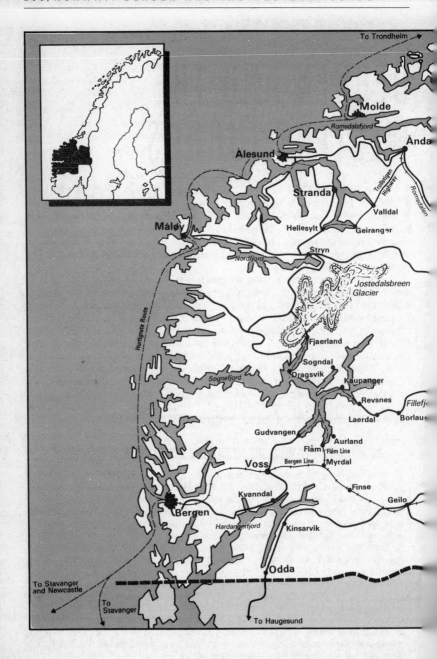

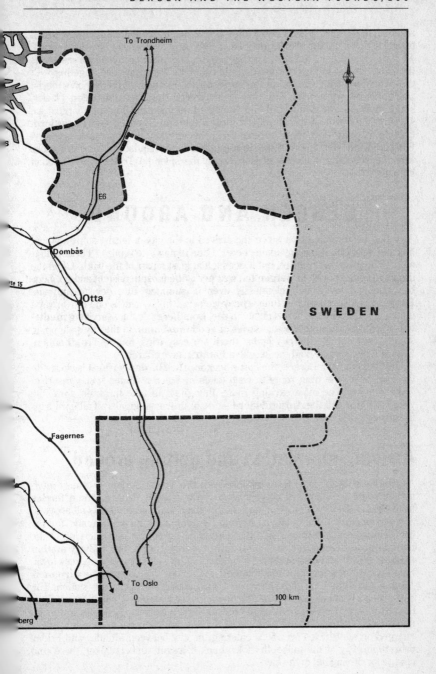

reached, to the east, is the **Flåm Valley** and its inspiring mountain railway, which trundles down to the **Aurlandsfjord**, a tiny arm of the mighty **Sognefjord**, Norway's longest and deepest. The Sognefjord, lined with pretty village resorts, is the most famous and over-exposed of the country's waterways and, together with the **Nordfjord** lying parallel to the north, soaks up much of the region's tourist traffic. There are several less congested targets: the **Jostedalsbreen** glacier, sitting between the Sognefjord and Nordfjord, is mainland Europe's largest ice sheet; while north of the Nordfjord there's the tiny S-shaped **Geirangerfjord**, holding perhaps the most spectacular concentration of impressive scenery. Further north still, towards the **Romsdalfjord**, the landscape becomes more extreme, reaching pinnacles of isolation in the splendid **Trollstigen** mountain highway.

BERGEN AND AROUND

As it had been raining ever since she arrived in the city, a tourist stops a young boy and asks him if it always rains here. "I don't know" he replies, "I'm only thirteen." The joke isn't brilliant, but it does tell at least a part of the truth. Of all the things to contend with in **Bergen** the weather is the most persistent and predictable, raining heavily and relentlessly even in summer. But, despite the rain, Bergen has a spectacular setting – between seven hills – and is one of Norway's most enjoyable cities. There's plenty to see, from Bergen's fine, surviving **medieval buildings**, through a whole series of good **museums**, to the city's shopping streets. Just outside the city limits, there are easy trips, too, to **Troldhaugen**, Edvard Grieg's home, and the excellent **Fantoft** stave church.

Heading out from Bergen, the fjords beckon. The **Hardangerfjord** is closest to the city, while the train route to Oslo takes in **Voss**, a winter sports resort of some renown. The most exciting route, though, is to take the train down the valley to **Flåm** and the **Aurlandsfjord** – one of the most popular of all fjord trips in Norway.

Arrival, information and getting around

As well as a local centre for ferry-links with the fjords, Bergen is a busy international port and may well be your first stop in Norway. **International ferries** from Britain, Denmark, Iceland and the Shetland and Faroe Islands all arrive at *Skolltegrunnskaien*, the quay just beyond Bergenhus fortress; **domestic ferries** from Haugesund, Stavanger and the fjords line up on the opposite side of the harbour at separate quays stretching down towards Torget. The **railway station** (☎05/31 96 40) and **bus station** (☎05/32 67 80) are close together across town, both facing Strømgaten, a few minutes' walk from the centre. The **airport** is 19km south of the city and *SAS* buses (35kr) connect with the bus station. The city is also a terminal port for the *Hurtigrute* **coastal steamer**, which leaves from the harbour (*Frieleneskaien*) behind the university daily for Kirkenes in the far north (see "Getting Around"). If you're **driving** into Bergen, note that a **toll** is charged on all vehicles over 50cc entering the city between Monday and Friday 6am–10pm. Pay at the tollbooths (5kr; book of twenty tickets 90kr); there's no charge for driving *out* of the city.

Information and getting around

The **tourist office** is in Torgalmenning (May–Sept Mon–Sat 8.30am–9pm, Sun 10am–7pm; Oct–April Mon–Sat 10am–3pm; ☎05/32 14 80) and has free copies of the *Bergen Guide*, an exhaustive consumer's guide to the city, a city transport plan, and the useful **tourist ticket** (45kr), a 48-hour unlimited pass for use on the city's buses. Otherwise, each flat-fare ticket is 11kr, bought on the bus and valid for an hour – though tell the first driver if you intend to change buses. For 50kr you can buy a 24-hour ticket valid on all the buses which run into Bergen's surroundings. Another useful link to be aware of is the **ferry** (Mon–Fri 7.15am–4.15pm; 6kr) across the harbour, from Carl Sundsgate to a point near Bryggen. Should you need a **taxi**, ring ☎05/99 09 90.

Finding a place to stay

Budget accommodation is no great problem. There's a couple of good youth hostels, a choice of private rooms and guest houses, and plenty of campsites in the vicinity.

Youth hostels

The **YMCA hostel** (*InterRail Point*) at Kalfarveien 8 (☎05/31 06 70), up behind the station and open mid-July to mid-August, is the city's cheapest option and has free showers, kitchen and laundry facilities. It can get full, though, in which case the enormous *Montana* **youth hostel** (☎05/29 29 00), 5km from the centre, is a good standby – though this too can fill quickly in summer. It's open from May to mid-October, costs 85kr a night, and is reached in twenty minutes on bus #4 (stop Laegdene), which runs from outside the main post office.

Private rooms and guest houses

The tourist office books **private rooms**, which are usually more central than the hostels, at 130kr for a single, 200–240kr for a double, with triples from 260–300kr, plus a 15–20kr booking fee.

Slightly more expensively, there are several **guest houses** in the centre, all of which are listed in the *Bergen Guide*. *Mrs Berntsen's*, at Klosteret 16 (☎05/23 35 02) is by far the best of the bunch, at 150kr per person: it's halfway down the peninsula, heading towards the aquarium (follow Klostergate); look for the white, wooden house, set back from the square. Otherwise, the *Fagerheim* (☎05/31 01 72), at Kalvedalsveien 49a (a continuation of Kalfarveien, beyond the railway station), charges from 170kr a single, 250–300kr a double, 360kr triple; the *Shalom Pensjonat* (☎05/32 69 93), Parveien 22, has doubles for around 370kr.

Camping

The nearest **campsite** to the city centre is *Bergenshallens Camping* (☎05/28 28 40), though it isn't a wonderful choice for those with just a tent and it gets full very quickly – ten minutes away on bus #3 from the main post office; it's open mid-June to mid-August. Instead, you might try the other summer-only campsite, the *Tennis Paradis Centre* (☎05/91 01 13) is on the E68, close to the Fantoft stave church (see below). Out of season there's *Lone Camping* (☎05/24 08 20), 20km from the centre on the E68, but this is only really practical for those with their own transport – though it does have **cabins** available for rent.

Penniless travellers can always head for the hills and **sleep rough**: the funicular railway up Mount Fløyen leads to the top of a wooded mountain laced with paths and lakes, where there's plenty of places to throw down a sleeping bag; see below for details.

The City Centre

Founded in 1070 by King Olav Kyrre ("the Peaceful"), Bergen was the largest and most important town in medieval Norway, capital city by 1240, and later a Hanseatic League port and religious centre which supported thirty churches and monasteries. Little of that era survives, although the medieval fortress – **Bergenhus** – still commands the entrance to the harbour. The city divides into several distinct parts: the wharf area, **Bryggen**, under the shadow of the fortress, once the working centre of the Hanseatic merchants and now the oldest part of Bergen; on and around adjacent **Torget**, home to a colourful fish market; and the **modern city centre**, which stretches from behind the main square down the long central Nordnes peninsula, taking in some of the best of Bergen's museums and shops.

Torget and the modern city centre

Lilian Leland, writing about Bergen in 1890, complained that "Everything is fishy. You eat fish and drink fish and smell fish and breathe fish." And almost a hundred years on not much has changed, as a wander around Bergen's **fish market** at **Torget** (daily except Sun 8am–3pm) will testify. Vats of ice overspill onto the already slippery surface, while under every stall sit huge mounds of prawns and crab-claws, buckets of herring and a thousand other varieties of marine life on slabs, in tanks and under the knife. Fruit, vegetables and flowers have a place in today's market but it's still the fish that make their mark.

From Torget, central Bergen spears right and left around the harbour. To the left, the **modern city centre** is, on the whole, a soulless nineteenth-century grid, and hasn't much (beyond a few good museums, see below) worth trudging around to see. Other than the compact sixteenth-century **Rådhus** in Rådstuplass, close to the post office, once a private residence and still closed to the public, the buildings and municipal edifices – theatre, university, library – are uninspiring, solidly built with turn-of-the-century money and nascent nationalist feeling. **Marken**, a hilly cobbled street of leaning wooden houses, now for the most part converted into craft and clothes shops, comes as a pleasant surprise, and not far beyond, at the end of Kong Oscars Gate, stands the only surviving **town gate**. Built in 1628, farmers entering town through the stone arch had to pay a toll – as do, 360 years later, car drivers on the way into Bergen.

Back in the centre, it's about a twenty-minute stroll (or take bus #4) to the end of the peninsula and **Nordnesparken**, which has a summer open-air swimming pool and a marvellous **Aquarium** (May–Sept daily 9am–8pm, Oct–April daily 10am–6pm; 22kr, children and students 10kr). The aquarium is the best in Norway, with daft-looking penguins, roly-poly seals, and aquatic life from prawns to piranhas.

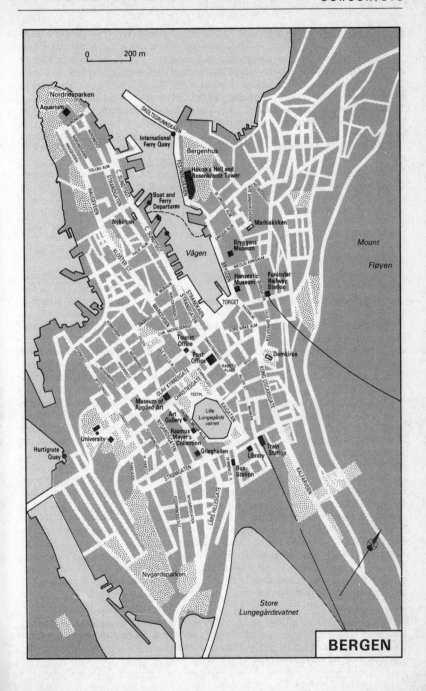

BERGEN

Bryggen and around

The real interest though – historically and culturally – is on the eastern side of the harbour. **Bryggen** was the site of the original settlement at Bergen, and is its best-preserved quarter containing, among other things, the distinctive wooden gabled warehouses that front the wharf. The area was once known as **Tyskebryggen**, or "German Quay", so named after the Hanseatic merchants who dominated life in Bergen from the early fifteenth century onwards. Their influence, based on an ability to trade grain and beer in return for the fish that came down from northern Norway, led them to settle in Bergen and shape the town to their own ends. Relations with the locals, as in other places where the Hanseatic League operated, were sometimes strained – on one occasion the entire Hansa-dominated town council was put to flight by axe-wielding malcontents. But by the mid-sixteenth century the League's power had waned, and the warehouses were destroyed by fire in 1702. Today's colourful line of buildings is eighteenth-century, and nowadays houses shops, restaurants and craft stores. The name Tyskebryggen, too, was dropped after the 1945 Liberation, when nationalist feeling against the occupying German force swayed a decision to revert to the original Bryggen.

One of the best preserved of the warehouses doubles as the **Hanseatic Museum** (June–Aug daily 10am–5pm; May & Sept daily 11am–2pm; rest of the year Sun, Mon, Wed & Fri 11am–2pm; 10kr, children and students 5kr), a memorial to merchant life in the Hanseatic period and containing the possessions and documents of contemporary families. Inside it is dark and dingy, with a warren-like layout that was not entirely accidental. The League's employees were forbidden to fraternise with the locals, even the League's own cleaning staff, and the houses were built with celibacy in mind, keeping the living quarters well away from the bedrooms, and constructing the rooms so that the beds could be made up from outside.

Good though this is, it's the **Bryggens Museum** (May–Aug Mon–Fri 10am–4pm, Tues & Thurs until 8pm, Sat & Sun 11am–3pm; Sept–April Mon–Fri 11am–3pm, Sat noon–3pm, Sun noon–4pm; 10kr, children free), next to the *SAS Royal Hotel*, that is Bergen's showpiece, containing a cultural muddle of things dug up here through the ages. The imaginative exhibitions attempt a complete reassembly of medieval life, put into context by the reconstruction *in situ* of the twelfth-century foundations of some of Bryggen's original boathouses and warehouses – and, outside through the window, by the scant thirteenth-century ruins of the **Lavranskirken** and **Mariagildeskålen** or guildhall.

More complete is the building behind the museum, the **Mariakirken** (May–Aug Mon–Fri 11am–4pm; rest of the year Tues–Fri noon–1.30pm; June–Sept 5kr entry), which is Bergen's oldest extant building, a delightfully decorated twelfth-century treasure. Not surprisingly it attracted the attention of the Hanseatic League merchants, who secured ownership of the church in 1408, later adding the fine Baroque pulpit and altar. Services were in German until 1868 and some of the traders are still here, buried under headstones in the graveyard.

The English-speaking **guided tours** of Bryggen are warmly recommended. Daily between June and August, they take roughly an hour and a half, and cost 40kr; the tickets are on sale from Bryggens Museum – and you can then re-use the ticket to get back into all the museums later in the day.

Further up the quayside, past the warehouses and their narrow squeezed passages, is the **Rosenkrantz Tower** (mid-May to mid-Sept daily 10am–4pm; rest of the year Sun noon–3pm; 6kr, children and students 3kr), enlarged in 1565 from its thirteenth-century foundations and used as a fortified residence by the lord of Bergenhus, Erik Rosenkrantz. There are **guided tours** around here every hour, and the winding spiral staircases, medieval rooms, a dungeon and low rough corridors make it an exhilarating half-hour's scramble. Behind the tower in the grounds of the old fortress (park and grounds open 7am–11pm) the **Håkonshallen** (same times as the Tower, also Thurs 3–6pm; 6kr, children and students 3kr), is a dull reconstruction of the Gothic ceremonial hall built for King Håkon in the mid-thirteenth century. Both buildings were wrecked by the explosion of a German ammunition ship in 1944, and the newness of their rebuilding shows.

Øvregaten, the Domkirke and Mount Fløyen

Bryggen is – and has been for 800 years – bounded by **Øvregaten**, the street which used to mark the extent of the rows of tenements and warehouses that reach back from the quayside. Walking along it from the Mariakirken, it's easy to see the old layout of houses – a warren of tiny passages separating warped and crooked buidings. At Øvregaten 50, the building known as the **Schøtstuene** (June–Aug daily 10am–4pm, May & Sept daily 11am–2pm; rest of the year Sun, Tues, Thurs & Sat 11am–2pm; 10kr, children and students 5kr) comprised the old Hanseatic Assembly Rooms, and exhibitions inside shed a little more light on daily life in the period.

Beyond, and good for a browse, **Lilla Øvregaten** is Bergen's antique shopping street, its far end marking the edge of Bryggen, where stands the **Domkirke** (summer Mon–Fri 11am–2pm) – though this has been restored and rebuilt almost beyond interest.

If you've got the time, it's far better to head up the hill behind the houses, for a bird's eye view of the layout of Bryggen and its surroundings. From here you can continue up to the summit of **Mount Fløyen** ("The Vane"), 320m above sea level – though an awesomely steep **funicular railway** does the job much quicker. It runs every half-hour until 11pm, the return fare 24kr (children 12kr).

Bergen's other museums and galleries

University Museums

Sydneshaugen, at the top of Olav Kyrres Gate, within a couple of minutes' walk of each other in the university grounds. *Daily 11am–2pm; and see below.*

Three collections – maritime, historical and natural historical all well laid out and exhaustive. The *Maritime Museum* (closed Sat; 5kr, children and students free) is of limited interest, a huge glasshouse stuffed with a fairly predictable set of things nautical, from Viking times to the present day. The *Historical Museum* (closed Fri; free), on the other hand, is much more than its name suggests: especially strong on the region's cultural history – furniture and folk art in particular – and with some outstanding displays of medieval church art and architecture, including a whole room full of sculpted pulpits and thirteenth-century altar-pieces. The *Natural History Museum*, at the front of the university buildings (closed Thurs; free) is probably worth missing altogether, much of it a veritable graveyard of birds, beasts and fish – vastly depressing and occasionally disgusting.

Rasmus Meyer's Collection

Rasmus Meyers Allé. *Mid-May to mid-Sept Mon–Sat 11am–4pm, Sun noon–3pm; rest of the year daily except Tues noon–3pm; 5kr, students and winter free.*

A rambling townhouse featuring Norwegian art with an upper floor almost entirely devoted to Munch. For a thoroughly civilised afternoon take in the daily piano recital, usually Grieg, and the introduction to the gallery's Munch collection (daily June to Aug, at 4pm; 35kr).

Municipal Art Museum

Rasmus Meyers Allé; next door to the Meyers gallery.*Mid-May to mid-Sept Mon–Sat 11am–4pm, Sun noon–3pm; rest of the year daily except Mon noon–3pm; 5kr, students free.*

This museum covers the last 150 years of Norwegian painting and is dominated – like the period itself – by the uninspired landscapes of J.C. Dahl. However, the "Stenersen's Collection" (same times; 5kr), in an adjacent gallery, pulls the place up from the ranks of the mediocre: an impressive cache of moderns with large patches of work by Picasso, Munch and Klee.

Leprosy Museum,

Kong Oscars Gate 59.*Mid-May to Aug daily 11am–3pm; 15kr, students and children 4kr.*

Located in an eighteenth-century hospital, this purports to tell the tale of the Norwegian fight against leprosy, a serious problem in earlier times. The disease was particularly endemic during the Middle Ages, but cases of leprosy were still being reported by Danish travellers in the eighteenth century. Of interest to medics and ghouls alike.

Fishery Museum

Permanenten building, Nordahl Brunsgate; between Olav Kyrres Gate and Christies Gate.*Mid-May to Aug Mon–Sat 10am–3pm, Sun noon–3pm; rest of the year Wed & Sun only noon–3pm; 4kr.*

This fills in the gaps left by the maritime collections at the university. Unless you're an enthusiast, its boats, harpoons and maps are not wildly exciting. It may still be closed for restoration.

Applied Art Museum

Permanenten building; same address as the Fishery Museum. *Mid-May–Aug Mon–Sat 10am–3pm, Sun noon–3pm; rest of the year daily except Mon noon–3pm; 5kr, students 2.50kr.*

European arts and craft, antique and contemporary, but unimaginatively displayed, its large rooms filled with old, cold furniture. Again, it may still be closed for restoration.

Eating, drinking and nightlife

As you'd expect, there's lots of choice for **eating** in Bergen and you shouldn't have any difficulty in filling up fairly cheaply. Bergen's **nightlife** tends to revolve around the city's students and is at its most active during term-time.

Eating

For **breakfast**, *Baker Brun* on Torget does coffee for 4kr and sells the city's speciality, the *shillingsboller* – a spiral, sugar-strewn bun. If you're around between the end of August and mid-June, the *Student Centre* canteen, Parkveien 1, does **snacks** and coffee, as well as full meals for under 30kr – and you don't need student ID.

Otherwise, for **meals** you're best off at one of Bergen's numerous *kafeterias*, found all over the centre. *Mekka*, a dive on Skostredet (off Kong Oscars Gate, near the Domkirke), is the cheapest, with 40kr meals and a local clientele. More touristy, though not much more expensive, are the assembly-line *Kaffistovas*, generally good for fish dishes. There are branches at Torget 1 (*Kaffistova BUL*) and Strandkaien 2 (*Ervingen*). You might also try the *Norske Burger*, at Hessel Stuen on Ole Bulls Plass, not as bad as the name suggests – a plateful of pork, sauerkraut and pickles goes for around 50kr. There's a branch of *Peppe's Pizza* at Finnegården 2, while the *Taj Mahal*, an Indian restaurant on Marken, near the railway station, does some **vegetarian** meals, a main dish with rice costing about 50kr. A little more upmarket, though also suitable for vegetarians, are the **lunch buffets** operated by several of the larger hotels. The *Grand Hotel Terminus*, Kong Oscars Gate 71, near the railway station, is just one – a grand help-yourself between noon and 3pm (Sun 1–4pm) for 150kr.

Drinking

The *Student Centre* proper, unlike its canteen, is open most of the year and has noticeboards full of events and entertainment. During the academic year the hottest place in town is *Hulen*, a club in an old air-raid shelter under Nygårdsparken, which has cheap beer and hosts live bands midweek, discos at the weekends. You'll need a student ID but should be able to get signed in without too much trouble.

Otherwise, try *Theatercafeen*, Chr. Michelsensgate 10, a popular pub – expect to queue to get in – or *Café Galleri*, on Kong Oscars Gate (just up from the Domkirke). Women may feel more comfortable at the busy *Café Opera*, Engen 24, near Ole Bulls Plass.

Other entertainment

Bergen is pretty big on **folk events** – singing, dancing and costumed goings-on of all kinds. The *Bergen Festival* is the biggest annual jamboree, usually held during the last twelve days of May. Principal venue is the monstrous glass and concrete Grieghallen, where you can pick up tickets and information. Otherwise, there's **folk dancing** at Bryggens Museum (mid-June to mid-Aug; Wed & Sun at 8.30pm; 60kr).

Cinemas, as usual, show films in their original language. A central screen is at *Engen* on Engen. The *Bergen Philharmonic* give **concerts** from September to June in Grieghallen. On very dull days you can catch Bergen's **brass band** playing in the city park most summer afternoons, as well as outside Håkonshallen at noon every Thursday.

Listings

Airlines *Braathens SAFE, British Airways* and *Dan-Air* all at Ole Bulls Plass 4 (☎05/23 23 25); *KLM*, Vågsalmenning 10 (☎05/32 00 90); *Lufthansa*, Torgalmenning 9 (☎05/31 12 30); *SAS*, Torgalmenning 1 (☎05/23 63 00).

British Consulate, Strandgaten 18 (☎05/32 70 11).

Cable Car For larger views of the city from Mount Ulriken (643m) 20kr up and 10kr down. Bus #2 or #4 to Haukeland Hospital, or from the youth hostel save yourself the fare and scramble up the mountain directly above you.

Car rental *Budget*, Carl Sundsgate 57 (☎05/31 14 13); *Hertz*, Nygårdsgaten 89 (☎05/32 79 20).

Car trouble *Viking Salvage Corps* is a breakdown service; Edvard Griegsveien 3 (☎05/29 22 22). The *NAF* is at Torgalmenning 3 (☎05/31 17 90).

Chemist 24-hour service at *Apoteket Nordstjernen*, at the bus station.

Emergencies Police ☎002; Ambulance ☎003; Fire ☎001. Casualty (24-hour) and emergency dental care (daily 10–11am & 7–9pm) at Lars Hillesgate 30 (☎05/32 11 20).

Exchange The tourist office will change money when the banks are closed but the rates are poor; the big hotels offer a rate in between the two.

Garages Indoor car parks include: *Bygarasjen* at the bus station (open 24hr; 45kr a day); *Citypark*, Markeveien 7 (Mon–Sat 7am–11pm; short-time parking); *Parkeringshuset*, Rosenkrantzgaten 4 (Mon–Fri 8am–5pm, Thurs until 7pm, Sat until 3pm; short-time parking).

Launderette *Jarlens Vaskoteque*, Lille Øvregate 17; near the funicular (Mon–Fri 10am–8pm, Sat 9am–3pm). Coffee bar here, too.

Library Strømgaten 6 (Mon–Fri 9am–8pm, Sat 9am–2pm; July & Aug weekdays until 3pm, Mon & Thurs until 7pm, Sat until 1pm); for foreign newspapers and the Edvard Grieg manuscript collection.

Post Office *see map*; open Mon–Wed & Fri 8am–5pm, Thurs 8am–7pm, Sat 9am–1pm.

Shopping Bergen has more varied hours than elsewhere, usually Mon–Fri 9am–5pm, Thurs until 7pm, Sat 9am–2pm. Some food shops stay open later, for example the *Nye Fosse* supermarket, opposite the *SAS Royal Hotel*, which opens Mon–Fri 9am–8pm, Sat 9am–6pm. And the shopping centres, *Galleriet* and *Bystasjonen* are open Mon–Fri 9am–8pm, Sat 9am–4pm.

Student Centre Parkveien 1. A wealth of handy services – English books, bank, health centre, travel agency, *ISIC* cards, etc; closed July & Aug.

Swimming There's an outdoor, heated pool near the Aquarium (bus #4) and an indoor pool, *Sentralbadet*, at Teatergaten (25kr, children 8kr), off Håkonsgaten.

Telephones For international calls use the Telegraph Building at Byparken; Mon–Sat 8am–9pm, Sun 2–7pm.

Travel Agents The *Norske Vandrerhjem* travel office, at Strandgaten 4 (☎05/32 68 80), is open Mon–Fri 8.30am–4pm and sells *BIJ* and discount ferry tickets, cheap flights and *FIYTO* cards.

Women's organisation *Zonta* is an international women's organisation; contact Berit Wollan, St Hanshaugen 56, 5033 Fyllingsdalen (☎05/16 19 92).

Around Bergen

Having seen the city centre, most people head immediately for the fjords. Before you do that, however, bear in mind three slightly more low-key attractions worth making the trip out for. Two of them, **Edvard Grieg's home** and the twelfth-century **Fantoft stave church**, south of the centre, are accessible on organised excursions (ask at the tourist office; around 100kr), but it's cheaper, and almost as easy, to find your own way. You could see both in an afternoon, and the stave church, certainly, is Norway's most handily placed. The other draw, an open-air **museum**, is just to the north of the city.

Troldhaugen

Grieg's home is reached by regular bus from the bus station (platform 14/15) to Hopsbroen, a fifteen-minute journey, from where the house is a twenty-minute walk: turn right from the stop, left at Hopsvegen, and follow the signs. Edvard Grieg, probably Norway's only composer of world renown, has a good share of commemorative monuments in Bergen – a statue in the city park, the *Grieghallen* concert hall and, most tangibly, **Troldhaugen** (May–Sept daily 10.30am–1pm & 2.30–5.30pm; 10kr) – his home for 22 years on the nearby Nordås Lake. Built in 1885, it was at this house that he composed many of his best-known works, and where he and his wife – the singer, Nina Hagerup – are buried in a curious tomb blasted into a rock face and sealed with a memorial stone. The house is virtually as he left it, a jumble of photos, manuscripts and period furniture; if you can bear the hagiographical atmosphere the obligatory conducted tour is quite entertaining – especially the discovery that Grieg was only five feet tall and bore an uncanny resemblance to Einstein. There are also summer **music recitals** here throughout July, usually on Wednesday and Sunday; tickets and information at the entrance.

The Fantoft Stave Church

To get to the **Fantoft stave church** from Troldhaugen, walk back to Hopsbroen, turn left, and follow the main E68 road to the Paradis crossroads, where you should take the right turn to Birkelundsbakken, walk up the hill to the car park and follow the signs. If you're coming direct from the city centre, take bus #2 from the post office, get off at the last stop and walk down the hill, Birlundsbakken. Buses run back into Bergen from Paradis.

The church (mid-May to mid-Sept daily 10.30am–1.30pm & 2.30–5.30pm; 5kr), regarded as one of the finest examples of its kind, is a less cosmetic attempt to present Norwegian history to the tourist, though you still have to join a guided tour. Built in the twelfth century, it was brought from Fortun in the Sognefjord region in 1883 and restored to its present pristine condition, bulging with lattice-work rafters and carved wooden detail. Some of its features are a little bizarre for a Christian church – the Viking-style dragon's head decorations adorning the roof and the fact that the building resembles a Chinese pagoda. But on the whole the place is steeped in familiar Christian prejudices: there's a separate women's entrance in the north wall, where they were forced to kneel in what is still the coldest part of the church, and lepers and other unfortunates heard the service from outside through a flap cut in the wood.

The Old Bergen Museum

Bus #1 or #9 from the city centre runs to SANDVIKEN and the **Old Bergen Museum** (May to mid-June daily noon–6pm; mid-June to mid-Aug daily 11am–7pm; mid-Aug to mid-Sept daily noon–6pm; 20kr, children 10kr, families 40kr). Set in the open air, this is a collection of around forty wooden houses, representative of eighteenth- and nineteenth-century Norwegian architecture, their interiors dressed up to give you an idea of small-town life. If you're not going on to Oslo and the excellent Folk Museum there, it's as good as any of the other open-air constructions that dot the country. There are guided tours around the site every hour.

The Hardangerfjord

Bergen advertises itself, rather sharply, as "Capital of the Fjords", and the tourist office does organise a barrage of round-trips (bus and ferry) from the city. However, since most can be done independently, they're an expensive option. The most popular excursion, to the Flåm valley, is, for example, better seen on the way to or from Bergen by rail (see below). If anywhere, it's VOSS (accessible direct from Bergen by train) – a little way north and still within the Hardangerfjord system – that's the better base for the southern fjords. For the other fjords, though there are direct boats from Bergen which are less long-winded, it is cheaper to either head on north by bus from Voss or approach from the other rail terminus, Åndalsnes (see p.229) or even Fagernes (see p.191).

Only the 120km-long **Hardangerfjord** is easily and cheaply accessible from Bergen – by bus. It's the first of many rattling trips to be made in the fjord region: the road twists up the valley past thundering waterfalls and around tight bends before chasing down the other side to **NORHEIMSUND**, sheltered in a bay of the fjord. There is precious little to the town – one main street and a tiny harbour – and the time it takes to change transport is all the time you'll need. Like many fjord settlements, it's the travel in between that is the real attraction.

Given Norheimsund's usefulness as a transport junction, southbound travellers may want to pick up the twice-daily ferry to **ODDA** (see also p.200), a two-hour jaunt up the fjord and then down one of its slender arms (the ferry originates in Bergen). At Odda there's a **youth hostel** (☎054/41 411) at Bustetungate 2, open from June to August (80kr a night). Or you can take the bus north on up the Hardangerfjord, a pleasant ride, through KVANNDAL and GRANVIN to Voss.

Voss

All the right ingredients are there – snow-capped hills and a lakeside town with a thirteenth-century church – so it's difficult to say why **VOSS** is so dull. Essentially a winter-sports haven, the industrious tourist office does its best to promote the town as a touring centre, but it's hard to escape the conclusion that the season is artificially extended to include summer. Nevertheless, the town is much the most convenient base for the best of the southern fjords and is ideal for making day-trips to the Flåm valley – including the much vaunted "Norway in a Nutshell" tour (see below).

Buses stop outside the **railway station** which, if you're just passing through, has luggage lockers on the platform. A right turn and a ten-minute walk along the lake brings you to the excellent **youth hostel** (☎05/51 20 17), a spanking new building overlooking the water which serves cheap meals and is open all year, except November and December (85kr a night). The **campsite** (☎05/51 15 97), open all year round and with a few cabins, bicycle-hire and washing machines, is at the other end of town by the lake – turn left from the station and take the right fork past the church. As you might expect, there are plenty of cheapish (400–500kr double) **pensjonater** in Voss and though they'll be fully booked during winter, you should have little trouble in the summer – ask at the tourist office.

Central Voss is thoroughly modern. Apart from the octagonally spired **kirke**, whose walls are up to two metres thick in places, most was destroyed by German bombs during World War II. The **tourist office** (in the *Tinghus*, left off Prestegardsalleen beyond the church: June–Aug Mon–Sat 9am–7pm, Sun 2–6pm; rest of the year Mon–Fri 9am–4pm; ☎05/51 17 16) concerns itself more with hiking and touring in the surrounding area, but pick up a free *Voss Guide*, which has useful listings, and any amount of handy information and timetables. If you plan to go to Flåm via Myrdal (see below), and don't intend stopping over anywhere, consider buying a "**Norway in a Nutshell**" ticket, an inclusive train/bus/ferry ticket for the Voss–Myrdal–Flåm–Gudvangen–Voss route.

Winter in Voss

Skiing starts in January and though there's nothing fancy here, you should be able to get in a few enjoyable days' winter sports. One main lift, a little way up between the station and the youth hostel, gives access to several short runs, from where you can take more lifts up to **Slettafjell** (918m). A long run circles back to the valley from here. More lifts operate from BAVALLEN, near the town.

Full **equipment**, for both downhill and cross-country skiing, will set you back around 120kr per day. Lift passes are 135kr per day. On Wednesday and Friday, some trails are lit for night-skiing (25kr). More information on all these options is available from the tourist office.

The train to Flåm

From Voss **buses** run to the Sognefjord via VINJE, either heading over the Vik mountains to VIK or east to GUDVANGEN – the most direct routes to Norway's longest fjord. But more popular, and infinitely more exciting, is the **train journey** eastwards from Bergen, through Voss, along the main railway line as far as barren MYRDAL. From here a twelve-mile branch line plummets 900m down into the **Flåm valley** – a ride not to be missed under any circumstances. The track, which took four years to lay, spirals down the mountainside through hand-dug tunnels, at one point travelling through a reverse tunnel to drop nearly a thousand feet. The gradient of the line is one of the steepest anywhere in the world, and as the train screeches its way down the mountain, past cascading waterfalls, it's worth remembering that it has five separate sets of brakes, each capable of bringing it to a stop.

FLÅM village, the train's destination, lies alongside meadows and orchards on the **Aurlandsfjord** – a matchstick-thin branch of the Sognefjord. People in the past have risen to the challenge and **walked from Myrdal** down the old road into the valley instead of taking the train – an enthralling five-hour hike through changing mountain scenery. The only advice that the tourist office gives about this route is not to walk the other way, *up* to Myrdal, which would take forever. The tiny **train**, on the other hand, runs all the year round, a local lifeline during the deep winter months.

Having made the exciting journey to **FLÅM**, you could be excused for wondering why you bothered. It's a tiny village that on summer days can be packed with tourists who pour off the train, eat lunch in one of the few hotels and then head out by bus and ferry, having captured the stunning valley on film. Out of season, though, or in bad weather, or even in the early evening when the day-trippers have all moved on, Flåm can be wonderful – and one of the most restful places on earth to spend the night. If you are prepared to risk the weather, September is probably the best time to visit. The peaks already have snow on them and the vegetation is just turning from green to its autumnal golden brown.

If you do stay, there are a couple of small **hotels**, the *Fretheim Hotell* (☎056/32 200) and *Heimly Lodge* (☎056/32 241), where you should be able to get a double room for around 500kr. Or head instead for *Flåm Camping* (☎056/32 121) and the nearby *pensjonat*, which has beds for 90kr and a kitchen – both are only a few minutes' (signposted) walk from the railway station.

The **tourist office** (May–Sept daily 8.30am–7pm; ☎056/32 106) is in a small wooden hut on the station platform: they are strong on local transport information and hiking in the area but most handy for advance inclusive ferry/bus tickets back to Voss (60kr).

Around Flåm: the Aurlandsfjord

In summer there are daily (except Sat) **ferries** from Flåm to **GUDVANGEN**, a two-hour cruise away, up the **Aurlandsfjord** and down the narrower Nærøyfjord, whose high rock faces keep out the sun throughout the winter. Connecting buses wait at Gudvangen for onward-travel to Voss and then it's your choice: east or west along the Bergen railway line. Failing that, you could stick around in Gudvangen if you haven't tired of the tranquillity: there's a small **hotel**, the *Gudvangen Motell* (☎05/52 39 29), with doubles for 420kr, and a **campsite**, *Vang Camping* (☎05/53 19 26), open mid-May to mid-September.

The route back to Oslo

The **railway route back to Oslo** is one of the most impressive rail rides in the country, taking in a good number of forests, waterfalls, windswept mountains and wild valleys. It's good hiking country too, and there are a couple of well-placed **youth hostels** – at MJØLFJELL (☎05/51 81 11), 6km from the station (75kr a night; doubles 200kr), and at **GEILO** (75kr; doubles 250kr; ☎067/85 300) – around which you can base a hike. You can ski at Geilo in the winter, though staying at the hostel then will be much more expensive than in summer. There's also, surprisingly, a cycle path, a resurfaced construction road dating from the building of the Bergen line at the turn of the century. The hostels will have information on the path, but for advance planning and bike-hire speak to *Norske Vandrerhjem* in Oslo before leaving.

The higher reaches of the railway line are desolate places even in good weather – and at **FINSE**, the railway's highest point, snow in early August isn't unusual.

THE WESTERN FJORDS

Although you can get close to some pretty fair scenery around Bergen, the fjord region proper only really begins to pay dividends once you head north – up the western coast or across the inland mountains and plateaux. It's here that you see the **western fjords** in all their grand splendour.

During the Ice Age, around three million years ago, Scandinavia was wholly covered in ice, which was extremely thick inland but thinner towards the coast. Under the weight of the ice the river valleys grew deeper, leaving basins when the ice retreated that filled with sea water and became the fjords. Due to the salt-water and the warm Gulf Stream, the fjords remained largely ice-free, and, because the ice had been thinner (ie less heavy) at the coast, were often deeper than the sea itself. The Sognefjord, for example, reaches depths of 1250m, ten times that of most of the North Sea.

The **Sognefjord**, cutting 180km inland, is the most strident of Norway's great fjords. Flåm, at the southern end of one of its tiny arms (see p.221), is its most touted tourist spot, but its wider stretches, running east–west to the coast, are just as impressive. Further north, and running parallel to it, there is the **Nordfjord**, smaller at ninety kilometres long, but more varied in its scenery, with patches of the Jostedalsbreen glacier visible beyond. The **Geirangerfjord**, further north again, is a marked contrast – tiny, sheer and rugged; while the northernmost **Romsdalfjord** and its many branches and inlets show signs of splintering into the scattered archipelagos which characterise the northern Norwegian coast.

The Sognefjord

Apart from Flåm, you'd do best to approach the **Sognefjord** from the north: it's on that bank that most of its appealing spots lie, and in any case transport connections on the south side (from Vinje) are, at best, sketchy.

Balestrand and around

BALESTRAND is a good first stop, a tourist destination since the mid-nineteenth century when it was discovered by European travellers in search of cool, clear air and picturesque mountain scenery. Kaiser Wilhelm II was a frequent visitor, as were the British, and these days, as the battery of small hotels and restaurants above the quay testify, the village is used as a touring base for the immediate area – though farming remains the villagers' principal livelihood.

Buses arrive on the quayside, where you'll also find the **tourist office** (May–Sept daily 8.30am–12.30pm & 3–6pm; ☎056/91 255) – good for maps showing local hiking routes. A hundred metres away, in the comfortable *Kringsjå Hotel*, the **youth hostel** (☎056/91 303) is open mid-June to August. If you stay here you can take advantage of the excellent-value dinner – 60kr for a candlelit two-course meal in the hostel. There are a couple of other reasonably priced hotels in the village, too, and a **campsite**, (*Sjøtun Camping*; ☎056/91 223), a kilometre or so past the English Church, which has cheap cabins for rent.

Beyond two marked **Viking burial mounds** on the way out to the campsite, supposed to be the tomb of King Bele, there's not too much to see in Balestrand

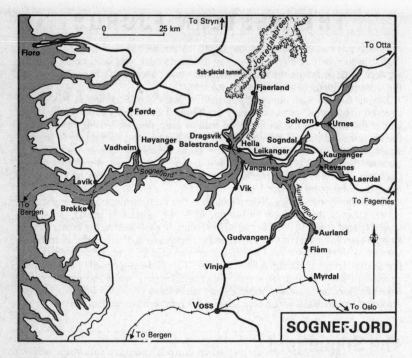

itself. But on the southern side of the fjord, in **VIK** (reachable by ferry from nearby HELLA or DRAGSVIK to **VANGSNES** and then a bus) is one of the Sognefjord's several **stave churches**. This one, *Hoprekstad* (15kr), is twelfth century and famed for the sculpted heads on its Gothic altar canopy, though it's very dark inside. Otherwise, you can pick up the daily **express boat** service from Balestrand to Flåm and Gudvangen.

The Fjærlandsfjord

If you're travelling north from Balestrand it's worth remembering that for years traffic had first to travel west and then north, via FØRDE, rounding the Jostedalsbreen glacier to reach STRYN and the Nordfjord. Buses still make that journey, although a more direct route is now possible, using a new 6km-long **subglacial tunnel** starting at **FJÆRLAND**. This was formerly one of the most isolated spots on the Sognefjord, and Fjærland is still only accessible from Balestrand by ferry (several daily; 27kr). It's a trip worth making, whether or not you continue to the Nordfjord through the tunnel. The **Fjærlandsfjord** – at the far end of which Fjærland lies – is wild and isolated: the mountainsides aren't as steep as usual but blanketed with a thick covering of trees down to the water's edge, while vast vertical clefts in the rock accommodate a succession of tumbling waterfalls.

You can visit two arms of the nearby **Jostedalsbreen glacier** (for more on this, see the Nordfjord, below) from Fjærland, and it is in fact the cheapest place from which to do so. One bus daily (mid-May to mid-Sept; 50kr return) leaves the village for combined visits to the Flatbreen and Bøyabreen arms – the latter the one you see as you enter the southern end of the tunnel.

East: Sogndal and Kaupanger

Before reaching Fjærland, the ferry from Balestrand also calls at HELLA, from where it's possible to pick up the eastbound bus to **SOGNDAL** – bigger and livelier than Balestrand and a much better place to overnight. Its **tourist office** (June–Aug Mon–Fri 9am–6pm, Sat 9am–1pm; rest of the year Mon–Fri 9am–2pm; ☎056/71 161) is opposite the bus terminal and has free hiking maps of the area and **bikes** for rent – a good idea as getting to nearby sights necessitates some form of transport. There is a comfortable **youth hostel** (☎056/72 033), open July and August, in the Folkehøyskolen (70kr a night), though the *Loftesnes Pensjonat* (☎056/71 577) is a good deal, too, at under 400kr double. It's at Fjørevegen 17, right in the centre, and serves some good food as well.

Sogndal is a good place to base yourself for a few days' rambling around. Twenty-odd kilometres away, the early-twelfth-century **stave church** at **URNES** is the oldest and best preserved of its kind in the country, with wooden carved decorations and a location that's worth the considerable effort involved in reaching it. There are irregular buses (or you can hitch) to SOLVORN, 15km to the north, off Route 55, from where ferries depart to Urnes twice daily on Friday, Saturday and Sunday.

Kaupanger
KAUPANGER, 12km southeast of Sogndal, is easier to get to, and as well as a heavily restored thirteenth-century **stave church** also has a **folk museum**, with the usual open-air buildings and an indoor collection of children's toys. Regular buses drop you at either, just outside Kaupanger's centre, or simply follow the old Sogndal–Kaupanger road which skirts the fjord – a lovely three-hour hike. Kaupanger also has some important **ferry connections**, with boats leaving regularly to Gudvangen (one starting-point for ferries to the **Aurlandsfjord** and Flåm valley; see above) and REVSNES, from where buses make the long haul over the mountains to Oslo via Fagernes – the old postal route, covered in Chapter Four.

The Nordfjord and the Jostedalsbreen Glacier

Emerge from the Fjærland tunnel, heading north, and you've just journeyed right the way under the Jostedalsbreen glacier. Buses go this way round the eastern reaches of the **Nordfjord** to end their run at **STRYN**, a busy, small town set amid green slopes. It's an important transport junction – for buses to the rest of the fjords and to the glacier, and for fjord ferries – and may need an overnight stop. If so, from the **bus station** walk to the right along Route 15 (Grotli direction) to the **youth hostel** (☎057/71 106), which has 70kr dormitory-beds (doubles 150kr) and is open June to August. It's signposted off to the left – a ten-minute walk up the hill. There's also a **campsite** (☎057/71 136), back down the hill by the main road.

West to Måløy and Bergen

Several inter-connected stretches of water make up the Nordfjord, all with different names but characterised by the same high surrounding mountains and deep green reflective water. With your own transport it's perhaps the most accessible of the fjords: unlike the Sognefjord, roads run along both banks and flank each branch.

Without wheels, however, **travelling west** along the fjord from Stryn is tricky without the occasional stretch of hitchhiking: there is a bus, but only one a day. Nonetheless it's an impressive route, much of the road running alongside the fjord until it reaches the small fishing town of **MÅLØY**, stuck on an island at the fjord's mouth. Perhaps a better way of making the trip is to use the **coastal ferry service** to Bergen, which operates from Stryn twice weekly all year, a leisurely cruise along the fjord and then south down the coast.

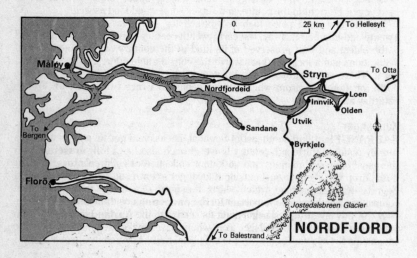

East: Loen, Olden, Innvik and Utvik

Eastbound possibilities from Stryn are more encouraging. The nearby cluster of villages – **LOEN, OLDEN, INNVIK** and **UTVIK** – each lie at the head of a bulbous nodule off the main fjord and are easily accessible by bus, or feasibly on foot. They're all noted centres for hiking in the lush valleys that radiate out from the fjord, and from Loen and Olden you're within striking distance of their respective – and tranquil – glacial lakes.

Tourist offices in Stryn, Loen and Olden can help with specific routes for anyone not content with a mere ramble, and each village has at least one **campsite**, usually with cabins, that are rarely full. If you want more comfort, Loen is your best bet – there's a choice of local **guest houses** with rooms at around 300kr.

The Jostedalsbreen Glacier

You can't help but notice the nearby, lurking presence of the **Jostedalsbreen glacier** at some stage of your wanderings: the 800-square-kilometre ice plateau dominates the whole of the inner Nordfjord region. Lying between the eastern ends of the Nordfjord and Sognefjord, its 24 arms flowing down into the nearby valleys, it's Jostedalsbreen that gives the local rivers and glacial lakes their distinctive blue-green colouring. Catching sight of the ice, nestling between peaks and ridges and licking its way downwards, can be unnerving: the overbearing feeling is that it shouldn't really be there. As the poet Norman Nicholson wrote of the glacier . . .

> *A malevolent, rock-crystal*
> *Precipitate of lava,*
> *Corroded with acid,*
> *Inch by inch erupting*
> *From volcanoes of cold*

Which is an evocative and accurate description of a phenomenon that, for centuries, presented an impenetrable north–south barrier, crossed only at certain points by determined farmers and adventurers. **From Stryn** a daily bus (1hr; 65kr return) leaves for the most accessible arm at **BRIKSDAL**, calling at both Loen and Olden (see above). At Briksdal, it's an easy 45-minute walk to the glacier, passing waterfalls and rivers on the way, and once there it's a simple matter to get close to the ice itself: there's a very flimsy rope barricade and a small warning sign – be careful. If you've lacked photo-opportunities thus far, you can hire a pony and trap at the souvenir/café area for the short ride to the glacier, something that will cost you around 100kr.

With your own transport it's an easy matter to follow the road from Loen through the valley to within 45 minutes' walk of *Kjenndal*'s glacier. Note, though, that you have to pay a toll on the last few kilometres of the road. For other views of the glacier by public transport use the excursion bus from Fjærland (see p.224); **buses south** to the Sognefjord also skirt the glacier, the Fjærlund tunnel exit heralded by a vast river of ice.

The Geirangerfjord

The **Geirangerfjord** is one of the region's smallest fjords, but also one of its most breathtaking. A convoluted branch of the Storfjord, it cuts well inland, marked by impressive waterfalls and with a tiny village at either end of the fjord's snake-like profile. You can reach the Geirangerfjord from the north or south; indeed, from Stryn and the Nordfjord, the westernmost village, HELLESYLT, lies right on the bus route to ÅLESUND (see p.231). But you'd do best to approach **from the north** if you can: GEIRANGER, the other village, and the whole of the rest of the fjord are accessible on a long day-trip from ÅNDALSNES (see p.229), via the wonderful Trollstigen highway. Coming this way, the bus thunders down a final set of switchbacks and stops high up on the *Ørnevegen*, the Eagle's Highway, for a first view of the fjord and the village glinting in the distance. There is little as stunning anywhere in western Norway.

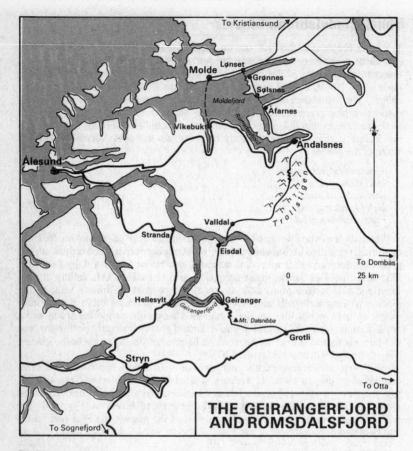

THE GEIRANGERFJORD AND ROMSDALSFJORD

Geiranger

GEIRANGER village enjoys a commanding position at one end of the 16km S-shaped fjord, and, despite a couple of large new hotels, remains almost absurdly picturesque. Hills roll away behind the houses, the fjord hemmed in by sheer rock walls scattered with wisps of hairline waterfalls. Most people arrive only to take a cruise on the fjord, afterwards returning to Åndalsnes or continuing south to the Nordfjord. But you may find it difficult to tear yourself away. The **hotels** are uniformly expensive, though there is a **campsite** bang at the foot of the fjord in the village. This understandably gets full in summer, in which case there's another, with cabins, 4km away and also at the water's edge (☎071/63 068); get the Åndalsnes bus to drop you off if that's where you've arrived from.

The Geiranger **tourist office** (June–Aug daily 9am–7pm; ☎071/63 099) pushes expensive sightseeing boat-tours of the fjord. But you'd be better off taking the car ferry (23kr), which leaves outside, to Hellesylt, the obvious – and only – stop, an hour's ride away through the double bend of the fjord.

Hellesylt and around

In Viking times **HELLESYLT** was an important and well-protected port. From the village, waterways took traders and warriors to England, France and Russia, and many old Viking names survive in the area. Nowadays it's primarily a stop-off on tourist itineraries – though few stay, and by nightfall the village is quiet and peaceful. The **tourist office** is on the quayside (June–Aug daily 9am–5.30pm; ☎071/65 052), and besides giving out local hiking routes and information sells English newspapers and changes money.

The **youth hostel** (☎071/65 128), set in a hill on the right of the village (up the winding road, or a short-cut path to the right of the waterfall) gets mixed reviews. It does have fjord-facing rooms and cabins for rent, but showers cost 10kr and the warden is rather grumpy. It's open June to August, and costs 60kr a night. You might want to splash out instead on the *Grand Hotel* (☎071/65 100), which is a reasonable 460kr for a double room with bath, breakfast included.

The nearest **campsite** is 2km away at STADHEIMFOSSEN (☎071/65 079), though if you hike into the surroundings camping is free and unlimited. For entertainment, there is a tiny **beach** by the ferry quay, the prelude to some very cold swimming. Or you could splash about (as many do) in the waterfall in the centre of the village. The youth hostel sells **fishing cards** (15kr a day) and the tourist office rents out **rowing boats** for days spent on rather than in the water.

A century ago, pony and trap took cruise-ship tourists from Hellesylt to ØYE, through the sweeping **Norangdal Valley**. Hikers can follow the route today, a 25-kilometre walk beside a bubbling river. From Øye, buses continue another eight kilometres to LEKNES, where there is a **campsite** with cabins, or they return to Hellesylt (daily except Sat mid-June to mid-Aug). If you're only looking for a day's ramble, a good climb is up the zigzag road near the youth hostel to RINGDAL farm, from where the whole valley opens out, Shangri-La like, before you.

The Romsdalsfjord and around

Travelling from Oslo by rail to Åndalsnes, the line splits at **DOMBÅS**, a regional hiking centre, with a **youth hostel** (70kr; doubles 150kr; ☎062/41 045) that's open from mid-June to mid-August and for winter skiing. However, you might prefer to push straight on. There are two lines to choose from, both impressive: the **Dovre line** continues northwards over the fells to OPPDAL, and ultimately to Trondheim, while the **Rauma line** begins a thrilling two-hour roller-coaster rattle down through the alpine mountains of the **Romsdal valley** to the **Romsdalsfjord** – a journey which, to appreciate the increasingly spectacular scenery and engineering, should really be made in daylight. Apart from the Hardangerfjord, reached from Bergen, the Romsdalsfjord is the only other Norwegian fjord accessible by train – which explains the number of backpackers wandering its principal town of Åndalsnes. Easy bus and ferry connections make the short links to more interesting towns nearby.

Åndalsnes

For many travellers **ÅNDALSNES**, connected by fast train with Oslo, is often the first – and sometimes only – contact with the fjord country, a distinction it doesn't really warrant. Despite a wonderful setting between lofty peaks and looking-glass water, the town is unexciting: small, modern and industrial. You'd do best to get out into the surroundings as soon as possible. The best and most logical route onwards is south to the Geirangerfjord, and the extraordinary trip there, over the Trollstigen, is covered below.

Night-train arrivals should have no difficulty in catching bus connections south or west on the same day. But if you need to stay, there's a comfortable **youth hostel** (☎072/21 382), open all year (advance booking essential in winter), a 2-kilometre hike along the E69 towards Ålesund, through the tunnel and over the bridge. It costs 65kr (doubles from 180kr), the breakfasts are excellent, and the hostel also rents out **bikes** – much the best form of transport for exploring the immediate area. There's also a **campsite** with cabins (☎072/21 629) back down the road and first left before the hostel, open mid-May to mid-September. The **tourist office** in town (mid-June to mid-Aug Mon–Sat 9am–9pm, Sun 2–9pm; rest of the year Mon–Sat 9am–4pm, Sun 9am–1pm; ☎072/21 622) also rents out **bikes**, and **rowing boats** on the fjord. Otherwise, stock up in the small daily market and climb the local **mountain**, the huge shadowy mass that lurks behind the town. It's a steep, sometimes very steep, two-hour climb through the trees to the top, but the views over the fjord and valley are very fine indeed.

West to Molde

There are two **bus routes** from Åndalsnes to Molde. One, via VIKEBUKT, skirts the length of the Romsdalsfjord (49kr; includes 1 ferry-crossing); the other, via ÅFARNES is slightly quicker and more frequent (58kr; includes two ferry-crossings), the last bus back connecting in Åndalsnes with the night train to Oslo. On a day trip, it's a good idea to go one way and return the other; **hitching** either way is also perfectly feasible.

The trip is superb whichever route you take – and much the best reason for making the journey. Though prettily situated on the northern bank of the Moldefjord, **MOLDE** itself, sheltered beneath a weighty range of snow-capped mountains, and with a climate temperate enough for it to be known (by the tourist office at least) as the "Town of Roses", has little to offer. Much of its original features were laid waste by fire in 1916 and German bombs in 1940, and to make a visit really pay dividends you should contrive to be here during the **international jazz festival**, held annually in the last week of July. Tickets are relatively cheap (80–120kr) and easy to come by, and there's often a smattering of big names among the homegrown talent. You can get advance information from *Norsk Musikkforlag* (Karl Johans Gate 39, Oslo) or from the festival office in Molde at Øvrevei 13 (☎072/55 267); tickets are available from the festival office or the *Alexandra Hotel* in town.

For more general enquiries, the **tourist office** is next to the hotel at Storgata 1 (June–Aug daily 8am–8pm; rest of the year Mon–Fri 9am–4pm; ☎072/57 133). The only cheap accommodation is at the **youth hostel** (☎072/54 330), a student hall 500m from the bus station at Fabrikkveien 4–8, open mid-June to August and – be warned – booked up well in advance during the festival; it costs 90kr, a double room 180kr. Alternatives during the festival – though not at other times of the year – are the intriguingly titled *Jazzcampen*, a **campsite** 2km west of Molde along Julsundvegen, or, for originality, the *Orion* ship – moored at the pier in front of the hotel. This hires out berths for 50kr a night.

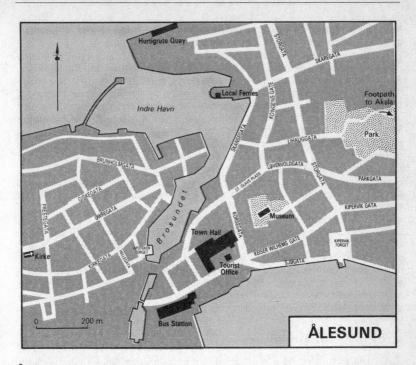

Ålesund and around

Norway's biggest fishing port, **ÅLESUND** is immediately – and distinctively – different from the functional stone and brick of other modern Norwegian town centres: a conglomeration of proud grey and white facades, lavishly decorated and topped with a forest of turrets and pinnacles. The town's buildings look as if they were stuffed into any available space and embellished by manically competitive architects – an observation which contains an element of truth. In 1904, a disastrous fire left 10,000 people homeless and the town centre destroyed. A hectic reconstruction programme saw almost the entire area rebuilt by 1907 in a bizarre Art Nouveau style which borrowed heavily from the German *Jugendstil* movement. Kaiser Wilhelm II, who used to holiday around Ålesund, gave assistance, and the architects, most of whom had learnt their craft abroad, built in a style which ended up a strange hybrid of up-to-date foreign influences and folksy local elements – the buildings showing off decorative flowers, dragons, human faces and fairytale turrets.

A stroll down **Kongens Gate** reveals many of the best features of Ålesund, but most of the central streets are as decorative as each other – and well worth a studied stroll. The **tourist office** in the Rådhuset (June to mid-Aug Mon–Fri 8.30am–5pm, Sat 8.30am–2pm; rest of the year Mon–Fri 9am–4pm; ☎071/21 202) sells the *Ålesund Pass* which, for 40kr per day (60kr for two days), gives free bus-travel, museum-entry and an hour's free bike-rental – though it's probably not worth shelling out for unless you are staying at the campsites, a few kilometres out of town. A better move is to pick up the free *Ålesund Guide* and *On foot in Ålesund* – a guided walking tour around the most interesting bits of town.

Not that – besides the architecture – there are many. There's a **park**, beneath *Aksla* mountain, which has a wide vantage point over the town and the harbours. And a **museum** at Rasmus Rønnebergsgate 16 (Mon–Sat 11am–3pm, Sun noon–3pm; 10kr) which records the devastation caused by the 1904 fire in a series of gloomy photographs and models. Otherwise, if you're staying overnight, you may just as well get out of town altogether and make a trip to the neighbouring **islands**, which have a variety of attractions including a thirteenth-century marble church (a rarity in Norway) and some Viking necropoli. Or take the ferry voyage through the nearby **Hjørundfjord** – only 40km-long but one of the most visually impressive in the country, high mountains rising sheer on either side. Apocryphally, the fjord takes its name from the days when the Black Death swept through the Norwegian valleys, leaving just one woman, called Hjørund, alive in the area.

There is no youth hostel in town but the *Aarsæthergården Pensjonat* at Hellegate 6 (☎071/23 203) has rooms at around 300kr. Or there are two local **campsites**, one of which (☎071/35 204), 5km from the centre on the #10/22 bus routes, has good double rooms at around 110kr, open all year. For **eating**, *Skateflua Kafeteria* on the ferry quay is probably the cheapest place for **lunches** and large sandwiches; *Cafena* at Kongens Gate 25 has a similar menu and prices and the same extensive watery views; while *Peppermøllen*, on Kirkegate by the bridge, swings until 3am at the weekends, though it's not a place to eat on a budget.

Over the Trollstigen

Buses run from Ålesund down to Hellesylt and the marvellous Geirangerfjord, but to travel this way would be to miss experiencing the alarming heights of the **Trollstigen** or "Troll's Path" – a trans-mountain route **between Åndalsnes and Geiranger** that's equally compelling in either direction, although drivers and cyclists should be very careful in wet weather.

The trip from Åndalsnes starts gently enough, running up into a valley surrounded by some of the more famous mountain peaks in Norway: *Kongen* and *Bispen*, the King and the Bishop, are the highest. Soon, though, the sheer audacity of the road becomes apparent, climbing its way across the face of the mountain in eleven huge zig-zags, halfway up running directly in front of the tumultuous **Stigfossen Falls** – where the bus stops for photographs. On a clear day the views from here are heart-stopping, the water dropping away 180m under the bridge into the valley. Back on the bus, ask the driver to point out the tall vertical face of the **Trollvegen cliff**. As you might expect, this is a haunt of experienced mountaineers (who, incidentally, didn't conquer it until 1966) but it has also recently been attracting parachutists in search of the ultimate thrill, as well as a number of suicides. In an attempt to curb the deaths, jumping off has been made illegal, but it hasn't stopped the committed – or cut the death toll.

There is nothing at the top except a bare expanse of mountain and a lodge where the bus makes a stop. You can hike around up here to your heart's content but watch out for quick weather changes, and be aware of the bus schedules on to Geiranger. It's not a good place to get stranded.

The road soon descends into the Valldal valley, a lush place known for its strawberries. The water in the fjord at **VALLDAL** is a gorgeous deep blue and the tiny village has a huge **campsite** and a smaller **youth hostel** (☎071/57 511), 100m from the harbour (June–Aug; 60kr a night, doubles 160kr). But it's a silent, shadowy village, and unless you intend walking in the hills, it's better to press on to Geiranger, only a short ferry-bus ride away.

travel details

Trains

From Bergen to Voss/Myrdal/Oslo (3–4 daily; 1hr 10min/2hr/6hr 30min–8hr 30min); plus extra daily trains to Voss.

From Myrdal to Flåm (June–Sept 7–8 daily; 50min; rest of the year 6 daily, 4 at weekends).

From Åndalsnes to Dombås/Oslo (3 daily; 2hr/ 6–8hr).

From Dombås to Oppdal/Trondheim (3 daily; 1hr/2hr 30min).

Buses

From Bergen to Voss/Gudvangen/Gol/Oslo (1 daily; 2hr 15min/4hr/8hr/11hr); Norheimsund/ Voss (3–4 daily; 2hr/4hr); Ålesund via Nordfjord (Mon–Fri 1 daily; 10hr); Loen/Stryn/Dombås/ Trondheim (1 daily; 7hr/7hr 30min/12hr/15hr).

From Voss to Vinje/Gudvangen (4–9 daily; 30min/1hr 20min); Norheimsund/Bergen (3–4 daily; 2hr/4hr); Sogndal (2–4 daily; 3hr–4hr 30min); Odda/Hovden (1 daily; 2hr 30min/6hr).

From Stryn to Loen/Olden/Innvik/Utvik/ Balestrand (1 daily; 10min/20min/40min/50min/ 6hr); Nordfjordeid/Måløy (1 daily; 1hr/2hr); Bergen (1 daily; 7hr); Oslo (1 daily; 8hr 30min).

From Balestrand to Sogndal (3 daily; 1hr 30min, 2 continuing to Kaupanger in 2hr); Stryn (Mon– Sat 1 daily; 4hr 30min).

From Sogndal to Otta, on the Oslo-Åndalsnes railway line (June to mid-Aug 1 daily; 5hr 30min).

From Otta to Geiranger (June–Aug 1 daily; 4hr); Fagernes (1 daily; 4hr).

From Flåm to Aurland/Laerdal (Mon–Sat 1 daily; 30min/2hr).

From Geiranger to Åndalsnes (2 daily; 3hr); Dalsnibba/Grotli (1 daily; 1hr/1hr 30min).

From Åndalsnes to Geiranger (June–Aug 2 daily; 3–4hr); Ålesund (3–4 daily; 2hr 20min); Molde (Mon–Sat 4 daily, Sun 2 daily; 1hr 30min).

From Ålesund to Hellesylt/Stryn (1–2 daily except Sat; 2hr 40min/4hr); Molde (1–2 daily; 2hr 15min); Trondheim (1–2 daily; 8hr 10min); Bergen (1 daily except Sat; 11hr).

Coastal Ferries and Express Boats

From Bergen to Stavanger (2–3 daily; 4hr 30min); Måløy/Stryn (3 weekly; 11hr/19hr); Balestrand/Flåm (2 daily; 4hr/6hr 30min).

Fjord Ferries

Just about all of the fjord settlements are connected by ferry. Services are frequent and regular, running many times daily up until about 10pm on most routes. Less frequent services include:

From Geiranger to Hellesylt (May–Sept 5 daily; 1hr 10min).

From Aurland to Gudvangen (May–Sept 2–3 daily; 1hr 30min); Flåm (May–Sept 2 daily; 30min).

From Balestrand to Hella/Fjærland (May–Sept 4 daily; 25min/1hr 30min).

From Gudvangen to Revsnes/Kaupanger (mid- May to mid-Sept 3–4 daily; 2hr/2hr 20min); Flåm (June–Aug 1 daily; 1hr), Bergen (June–Aug 1 daily; 6hr).

International Ferries

From Bergen to Shetlands/Faroes/Iceland (1 weekly June to mid-Sept; 11hr/24hr/41hr); Newcastle (2–3 weekly May–Oct; 21hr).

CHAPTER SEVEN

TRØNDELAG AND NORDLAND

T røndelag and Nordland – two long, thin counties standing top to toe above the western fjords – mark the real transition from rural southern to blusterous northern Norway. **Trøndelag**, the forested southern part of the region, is a gentle introduction, its main town, **Trondheim**, easily accessible from Oslo by train. But travel north of here and you begin to feel very far removed from the capital: the express trains which thunder northwards leave the leafy south very quickly behind, and travelling becomes more of a slog as the distances between places grow ever greater. In **Nordland** things get increasingly wild – "Arthurian", thought Evelyn Waugh – though, save the scenery you can see from the train, there is little of delaying interest between Trondheim and the handsomely sited steel town of **Mo-i-Rana**.

Just north of here you cross the **Arctic Circle**. The land becomes ever more spectacular – craggy coastal country – and even the major industrial towns here have a feral quality about them, while the offshore chains of the **Lofoten and Vesterålen Islands** are almost separate lands: rugged landscapes, idyllic fishing villages and cheap accommodation make the islands a vital stop. Back on the mainland, the settlement furthest north is **Narvik**, scene of some of the fiercest fighting by the Allies and Norwegian Resistance in World War II, and now a modern port handling vast quantities of iron-ore amid some startling rocky surroundings.

Transport is good, which is just as well given the isolated nature of much of the region. The **E6** is the major road route north of Mo-i-Rana, known as the Arctic Highway. With a sign and patience it's possible to hitch it. The **train** network reaches as far north as Fauske, **buses** making the link to Narvik, from where a separate rail-line runs the few kilometres to the border and then south through Sweden. The only real problem is likely to be **time**. It's a day's journey from Trondheim to Fauske, another day to Narvik, and without time to spare you should think twice before venturing further: the travelling can be arduous and in any case it's pointless if done at a hectic pace. If you do have time, remember that a thick book and plenty of sandwiches are essential on the longer bus-runs.

Southern Trøndelag: Trondheim and Røros

Friendly, medieval **Trondheim** is hardly remote – an easy, if lengthy, train run from Oslo – but from here the long trek to Nordkapp begins in earnest. Small, scarcely credible as Norway's third city, Trondheim guards the huge Trondheimsfjord and is dominated by its grand cathedral. And to the south, in the heart of Sør-Trøndelag, the ghostly eighteenth-century mining town of **Røros**, high on a mountain plateau, is a worthy stop.

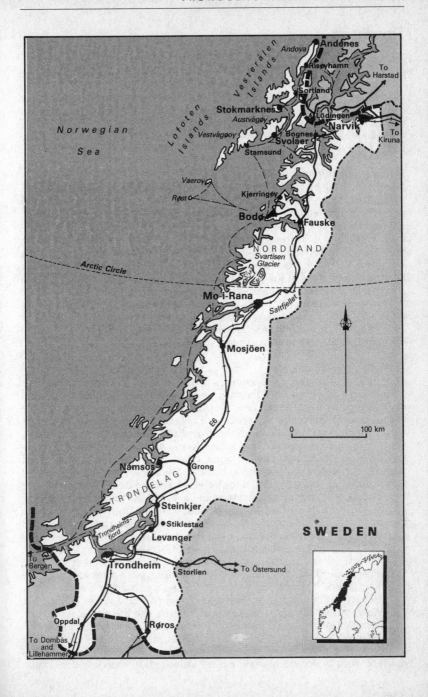

Trondheim

Though you might not think so now, **TRONDHEIM**, an atmospheric city with much of its medieval heart intact, has been an important Norwegian power-base for centuries. The early Norse parliament, or *Ting*, met here, and the city was a major pilgrimage centre at the end of a route stretching back to Oslo. Today, the city centre sits compactly on a small triangle of land, bordered by fields and water. It's a manageable and likeable place where even the main sights – bar the marvellous cathedral – have a low-key quality about them. Despite the university and the lure of its city streets, the pace of Trondheim is slow and provincial.

Arriving and getting around

Trondheim is the first major northbound stop of the *Hurtigrute* **coastal steamer**, which docks at the harbour behind the **railway station**, from where you simply cross the bridge onto the triangular island that holds all of central Trondheim. Express **buses** stop at the bus station, close to Torvet in the city centre. The **tourist office** is in Torvet (June–Aug Mon–Fri 8.30am–8pm, Sat 8.30am–6pm, Sun 10am–6pm; Sept–May Mon–Fri 9am–4pm, Sat 9am–1pm; ☎07/51 14 66) and can provide the free *Trondheim Guide* (also available on arrival at the station information office and at the youth hostel) and a transport route plan. They will also change money outside banking hours, though at dodgy rates.

Transport in town is by buses and trams, but in most cases you can just as easily walk. Only if you're going outside town, to one of the outlying museums or the campsite, is it worth buying the unlimited 24-hour tourist ticket – 30kr from the tourist office, valid on all local buses and trams.

The City

The goal of Trondheim's pilgrims was the colossal **Nidaros Domkirke**, Scandinavia's largest medieval building. Gloriously restored following the ravages of the Reformation and several fires, it's still the focal point of any visit to the city and the inspirational centre of Trondheim. The building, tagged after Trondheim's former name, Nidaros ("mouth of the river Nid"), is dedicated to King Olav. Baptised in England, he was forced to flee Norway after his countrymen, disgruntled by his zealous, evangelical reforms, called upon the English king, Knud (Canute), for assistance in dislodging him from the throne. Olav returned in 1030 to reclaim his inheritance but fell at the battle of Stiklestad (near Trondheim) – see below – and, following a posthumous return to favour, his body was moved here and its resting place marked by the erection of a church. Over the years the church was altered and enlarged to accommodate the growing bands of medieval tourists, achieving cathedral status when the town became an archbishopric in 1152 and becoming the traditional burial place of Norwegian royalty. Since 1814, the cathedral has also been the place where Norwegian monarchs are crowned.

The best time to see the church is in late afternoon, when it's comfortably free from tour groups. The magnificent blue-grey soapstone building is a true hodge-podge of styles: the original eleventh-century church was a simple basilica, but subsequent alterations added Romanesque features, and the nineteenth-century reconstruction sports a combination of Norman and English Gothic influences. The stonework on the west entrance is marvellous, massed ranks of carvings and figures peering down upon a quiet square. Inside, the gloomy half light hides much of the lofty decorative work, but the stained glass, especially the circular

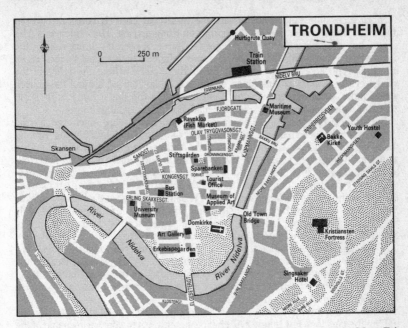

window above the main portal, is superb. (Opening hours: summer Mon–Fri 9.30am–5.30pm, Sat 9.30am–2pm, Sun 1.30–4pm; winter Mon–Fri noon–2.30pm, Sat 11.30am–2pm, Sun 1.30–3pm; 5kr; 2kr to climb the tower, which is only open in the summer.)

The grounds, riverbanks and churchyard, are eminently strollable. Behind the Domkirke, overlooking the river, the heavily restored **Erkebispegården** (mid-June to mid-Aug Mon–Fri 10am–3pm; guided tours 7kr) was the archbishop's palace, built in the twelfth century for the third archbishop, Øystein, and for years doubling as the city armoury. It's been thoroughly cleaned up since then, and many of the old weapons are now displayed in a separate building (June–Aug Mon–Fri 9am–3pm, Sat 9am–2pm, Sun 10am–2pm; 3kr), along with a Resistance museum. Following the river around, it's a short walk to the **old town bridge** (*Bybrua*), an elegant wooden reach with splendid views over early-eighteenth-century gabled and timbered warehouses, most of which have since been converted to restaurants and offices.

The broad avenues of Trondheim's centre date back to the seventeenth century. Designed to lessen the damage caused by frequent fires, they and their pavement cafés, benches and flowerbeds surround a tangle of narrow alleys and wooden frontages that forms the nucleus of Trondheim. The most conspicuous survivor of the town's many fires is **Stiftsgården** (mid-May to Aug Mon–Sat 11am–2pm; 5kr), the towering yellow creation half-way up Munkegate. Built in 1774–78, this claims to be the largest wooden building in northern Europe (no big deal really) and these days is an official royal residence – a role which represents a considerable upgrading from the original one of home to a mere royal adviser. A glance into the spacious courtyard is about as much as you need – inside is just a lot of rooms and some faded furniture.

More accessible (and spookier) are the **medieval church ruins** discovered under the *Sparebanken*, around the corner on Kongensgate. The evidence is a bit shaky, but it is believed to be St Gregory's church, a twelfth-century relic of the days when Trondheim had fifteen or more religious buildings. Clamber down into the crypt, a semi-circular cellar under the chancel where the relics of the saint were kept. Excavations found nearly 500 bodies buried around the church walls, and a small exhibition is on hand to explain the finds. Entry is free and access is from Søndregate, through the bank during its opening hours.

Back along Kongensgate, **Torvet** is the main city square, anchored by the statue of St Olav perched on a tall stone pillar like some medieval Nelson. Among the sculptures and buskers, there's a daily fruit and veg market, and the occasional local flogging hand-made jewellery. From the square you can see right along Munkegate, up to the Domkirke and down towards the water, before which Olav Tryggvasonsgate cuts a wide swathe through the centre of town. At its western end is the compact **Ravnkloa** (Mon–Fri 8am–4.30pm, Sat 8am–2pm), a lively fish market, usually with cheap mussels and prawns on sale in its cold and smelly fish hall. The market looks out over the water to the fortress island of **Munkholmen**, where there's a Benedictine abbey that was converted to a fortress after the Reformation to hold eighteenth-century Norwegian political prisoners (tours; 6kr). Today the island's a bathing spot, popular with the local youth, who avoid the day-tripper crowds by scrambling around the rocks on the side of the island farthest from the harbour. Ferries run between June and August, 10am–5pm, from Ravnkloa, 17kr return.

Finally, a word about **cruises** in the Trondheimsfjord, a good way to escape the milling throngs for a few hours. The cheapest method is to take a trip on one of the boats run by *Fosen Trafikklag A/S*, whose office is at *Fosenkaia* by the railway station. Full day excursions run from 120kr but they also operate an overnight cruise, leaving Trondheim at 3pm and returning at 9am the next day, stopping at up to fifteen places between Trondheim and FRØYA. This costs 90kr, or 130kr including dinner and breakfast (cabins extra, forty percent student discount).

Trondheim's museums

Art Gallery

Bispegata 7B. *Tues–Sun 11am–4pm; winter opening an hour later; 10kr, art students free.*

A good assortment of Norwegian and European eighteenth- and nineteenth-century works, but let down by shoddy labelling and an unimaginative layout.

Maritime Museum

Fjordgate 6. *Mid-June to Aug daily 10am–3pm, Sun all year noon–3pm; 10kr, students 5kr.*

Crowded display of model ships and navigational equipment. Nautical enthusiasts only.

Museum of Applied Art

Munkegata 5. *Mon–Sat 10am–3pm, Thurs 10am–7pm, Sun noon–4pm; 10kr, students 5kr.*

Glorious exhibition of furniture, tapestries, clothes and precious metals, arranged chronologically from the Renaissance to the 1950s. Two rooms display a treasury of Art Nouveau work, complete with Munch woodcuts and a Vigeland sculpture. Cheap café inside too.

Museum of Musical History

Ringve Manor at Lade. *Mid-May to Sept daily tours in English at noon, 2pm & 3pm; Oct daily at noon, Sun at noon & 2pm; rest of the year Sun only at 1pm & 2pm; 20kr, students and youth hostel members 10kr.*

Housed in a beautifully sited seventeenth-century manor house out of town on the Lade peninsula, a spectacular collection of old musical instruments, demonstrated and explained by a lengthy – and obligatory – guided tour. Tram #1 or bus #4 (from Dronningensgate) to Lade.

Trøndelag Folk Museum

At Sverresborg. *Mid-May to August, conducted tours four times a day; admission 15kr.*

Indoor and outdoor collections in reconstructed and restored houses, highlighting the region's life and culture. Take bus #8 or #12 from Dronningensgate to Wullumsgården.

University Museum

Erling Skakkesgate 47. *May & Sept Mon–Sat noon–3pm; June–Aug Mon–Sat 11am–3pm, Wed 6–8pm, Sun all year noon–3pm; 2kr, students 1kr.*

Excellent and extensive collection of stuffed animals, birds, insects and *Same* bits and pieces. Pick of the lot, though, is the new church art exhibition in the separate *Schøninghuset*, around the corner – pulpits, processional crosses, triptychs and fonts by the barrowload.

Sleeping, eating and nightlife

Beds are plentiful in Trondheim. The tourist office books **private rooms** for 140–150kr a double, plus a 10kr fee, and there's a **youth hostel** at Weidemannsveien 41 (☎07/53 04 90), open all year except Christmas and Easter, a twenty-minute hike from the centre out past the Bakke church and straight uphill; bus #9 (5kr) also runs there. It's expensive (120kr) but the price includes breakfast and there are a few double rooms available, too, for around 390kr. Other choices include a selection of **hotels and pensjonater**, all around the 500kr double mark: try the *Singsaker Sommerhotell* Rogertsgate 1 (☎07/52 00 92), on the other side of the Kristiansten fortress, which has basic doubles from 390kr. The nearest **campsite**, *Sandmoen Camping* (☎07/88 61 35), is 9km out of town, near Heimdal on the E6, but it does have a selection of cabins and rooms if everywhere is full – and it's open all year. Take bus #44 from the bus station, get off at the last stop, walk under the bridge and follow the signs.

For **eating**, the *IMI Hotel* on Kongensgate does very cheap daily lunches, the *Skipperstua* cafeteria at Ravnkloa good omelettes and fish. Insomniacs and homeless travellers can eat Mexican food – from around 30kr – at *Tønnes Taco Bar*, off Olav Tryggvasonsgate at Gjelvangveita 2, which is open daily until 6am. There's also a *Peppe's Pizza* at Kjøpmannsgate 25. **Snacks** – coffee and cake – can be had most cheaply, and atmospherically, at *Brygge Bakeri* outside the fish hall, plus there is a cluster of fast food joints, most notably *Clock Burger*, on Olav Tryggvassonsgate.

Due to the town's large student population, **nightlife** in Trondheim can be quite lively. *Studentersamfunnet*, just over Elgeseter bridge, has cheap drinks, music and dancing and is fun during term-time – though you may need student ID to get in. *The Ritz* at Skansen (Wed–Sun 9pm–2.30am) features British bands and a cheap bar, and is hot and bluesy on Friday nights: expect to pay a cover charge of around 50kr.

Røros

If you're heading into Sweden, and don't want to send postcards from HELL just before the border – a desperate place with little other than its name to recommend it – **RØROS** (and the journey to it) is the other main target of southern Trøndelag. Norway's highest mountain town, it's an airy, blustery place even on a summer's afternoon – unspoilt and quiet and, despite a trickle of tourists, little changed since its money-spinning days as a copper mining town.

Until the mining company went bust a decade or so ago, the copper mines had been the basis of life here for over 300 years. The dirty and dangerous work was supplemented by a little farming and hunting, and life for the average villager can't have been anything but hard. Things have perked up a little since: Røros is now on UNESCO's World Heritage list, and there are firm stylistic controls on its dainty grass-roofed cottages. Film companies regularly use the town as an authentic backdrop for their productions – among them, as the labour camp in *One Day in the Life of Ivan Denisovich*, a choice which says a lot about Røros.

In the town centre, **Røros kirke** (June–Sept Mon–Fri 10am–2pm, Sat 10am–12.30pm; 7.50kr) is the most obvious target for a stroll, a dominant reminder of the economic power fostered by the mines in the eighteenth century. Built in 1784, and once the only stone building in the town, it's more like a theatre than a religious edifice: a huge structure, capable of seating 2000 people, and like Kongsberg's church (see Chapter Five) designed to overawe rather than inspire. The pulpit is built directly over the altar, a psychological gambit to emphasise the importance of the priest's word. A two-tiered gallery runs around the church with separate boxes for the rich (who paid for the privilege of sitting screened by curtains), while a royal box holds commanding views from the back.

Immediately below the church, alongside the river, lies the oldest part of Røros. Grass-thatched miners' cottages, storehouses and workshops squat in the shadow of the mountainous slagheap – more tourist attraction than eyesore, and providing fine views over the town and beyond. Two parallel streets, Bergmannsgata and Kjerkgata, lead into **Malmplassen** (literally "ore-place"), heart of the old mining and working area: there's an obvious division between the bigger houses at the bottom end of town, where the owners and overseers lived, and the smaller artisans' dwellings further up, many of which have become art and craft shops. It was in Malmplassen that the ore drivers arrived from their journey across the mountains to have their cartloads of ore weighed on the outdoor scales. Outside the main works, which are currently being converted into a new museum, the smelter's bell signalled the start of each shift. Until completion the only indoor museum in town is the small **Copper Company's Collection**, in the early-nineteenth-century *Hyttstuggen* building (guided tours only, at specific times, May 31–August 10; 8kr).

Out of town, the **mines** themselves (guided tours only: up to 6 daily mid-June to mid-Aug; 1–3 daily rest of June, rest of Aug & Sept; 30kr), 13km away, are reachable by taxis, which will wait and take you back for around 200kr. Get a group together to share costs by asking at the tourist office; or simply hitch – take Route 31 towards Sweden for 6km and then follow the signs to *Olavsgruva*.

Practical details

The **railway station** is at the foot of the town, a couple of minutes' walk from the **tourist office** (mid-June to mid-Aug Mon–Fri 10am–6pm, Sat 10am–1pm; rest of the year Mon–Fri 10am–4pm, Sat 10am–1pm; ☎074/11 165), where you can pick up a free booklet and town plan.

The infrequent train service north and south will probably mean a night's stay in Røros. The **youth hostel** (☎074/11 089), Øraveien 25, behind the railway lines next to the sports ground, is cheap and cheerful (50kr a bed), open from mid-May to mid-September. The **campsite** is next door and has a row of cabins available for rent. **Bikes** can be rented from the *Røros Turisthotell*, as can cross-country skiing gear.

Northern Trøndelag: Levanger, Stiklestad and St Olav

From Trondheim, unless you've bags of time, there's little reason to tarry before MO-I-RANA in Nordland, about 400km north and reachable by frequent express train. Much of northern Trøndelag, though scenic enough, is best sped through. Levanger, an hour and a half out of the city, isn't worth a stop for itself, certainly, but if you're around in July you may want to drop in on the St Olav's Day celebrations at **STIKLESTAD**, fifteen kilometres away.

A descendant of Harald Hafågre (the Fair-Haired), **Olav II** was one of Norway's greatest medieval heroes, a fiercely evangelical Christian king who was dislodged from the throne and banished from the country. Having got together an army, he returned in 1030, but was defeated and killed here in Stiklestad by locals suspicious of his reformist (and Christian) intentions. Though too late for Olav, Christianity took firmer root within years of his death, and it wasn't long before the dead king was canonised and his battered remains transferred to the cathedral in Trondheim, later to become a crowded pilgrimage centre. He's now remembered on the site of his final defeat by the colourful **St Olav Pageant**, a costume drama performed in an open-air amphitheatre in Stiklestad on July 29 each year.

You can get more information from the Stiklestad Association (☎076/78 500) or, in summer, from the **tourist office** in LEVANGER. **Staying over** will have to be at Levanger's youth hostel, open June to mid-August (☎076/81 638; 55kr a night). If this is full, the only other reasonable option is the *Levanger Vertshus* (☎076/81 144), Petter Nyengetsveien 1; doubles from around 350kr.

Into Nordland: Mo-i-Rana, Fauske and Bodø

The last and only worthwhile stop before the Arctic Circle is **MO-I-RANA** or "Mo", a cosy little town at the end of the Rana fjord. There's nothing much to Mo, and the town is dominated by an enormous steel plant. But it's an ideal base for trips to the **Svartisen ice cap**, one of whose tongues reaches down to a lake 32km north of the town. Boats run across the lake (*Svartisvatn*) hourly between mid-June and August and cost 30kr return, dropping you a 3km-hike away from the glacier, whose name means, graphically, "Black Ice" – strong shoes are essential. Getting to the lake, though, is more difficult: you really need a car.

Without one you can either catch a bus to RØSSVOLL airport and hitch the 20km from there on, or if you're feeling energetic, rent a bike (50kr a day) in town from *Mo Sykkel & Sport* (☎087/50 436).

With your own wheels it's also no problem to reach the underground caves at **Grønnligrotten**, where guided tours (mid-June to mid-Aug daily, on the hour; 10kr) take you through a series of passages and marble caves formed some five million years ago, complete with waterfalls, lakes and weird rock formations.

Full details of both trips are available at Mo's **tourist office** (mid-June to mid-Aug Mon–Fri 9am–8pm, Sat 9am–2pm & 5–8pm, Sun 5–8pm; ☎087/50 421), immediately opposite the **railway station**. And once you've done them there's nothing to prevent you leaving. *Top Deck* tour buses, on their way up to Nordkapp, have been known to pick up stray travellers from the **youth hostel** (May–Sept; ☎087/50 963) – a kilometre out of town on the E6 at Finsetveien 1; 70kr a night, double rooms 140kr. Otherwise it's a short train trip up to FAUSKE, which is as far north as the rail system goes.

The Arctic Circle and Fauske

Given its appeal as one of the last great wildernesses, crossing the **Arctic Circle** is a grave disappointment. For drivers and bus travellers, there's a monument to mark the spot and a café with Jack Frost certificates on the main road. But that aside, the landscape, uninhabited for the most part, is undeniably bleak. Train travellers, unlike those on the northbound train in Sweden which stops for a photocall (p.428), will probably cross the line without even realising it – though you may hear a special toot on the whistle.

But for a brief stretch of line into Sweden further north, **FAUSKE** marks the northernmost point of the Norwegian rail network and is, consequently, an important transport hub. Northbound travellers will almost certainly have to spend the night here unless they make a quick change onto the connecting bus to NARVIK. The comfortable **youth hostel** (☎081/44 706), open mid-June to mid-August, is right in the centre of town, a ten-minute walk from the **railway station** – down the hill, left and right at the junction (78kr a night; doubles 210kr). The *Lundhøgda* **campsite** (☎081/43 966) though, open June to mid-September, is a fifty-minute walk away, along Route 80.

Fauske is also the departure point of the *Nord-Norge Bussen* (see "Getting Around"), the express **bus** service which complements the railway by carrying passengers as far as KIRKENES, close to the Soviet border. Get tickets from the travel agency in Fauske or buy them on the buses, which leave twice daily from the **bus station** next to the *Shell* garage on the main road. There is a fifty percent discount for *InterRail/Nordturist* pass holders on the first step of the route, to Narvik, a five-hour trip which is a gorgeous run past fjords, peaks and snow.

Bodø

Consider also, if you have time on your hands, travelling the hour it takes to get to **BODØ** – west and slightly south of Fauske – either by bus or on the Nordland train which terminates there. (If you decide to continue north afterwards, the same half-price bus deal to Narvik operates from Bodø too.) There's precious little to Bodø itself: it's a bright, largely modern town. But there's a mixture of things to see and do in the surroundings, and the town is a regular stop on the

Hurtigrute steamer route and also much the best place from which to hop over to the Lofoten islands (see below).

In town, the only real diversion is the two-kilometre walk to the **Bodin kirke** (June–Aug daily 10am–8pm). The thirteenth-century church contains a colourful set of seventeenth-century fixtures, including a lovingly carved altarboard and pulpit, both painted a century later by Gottfried Ezechiel, (whose work crops up again and again throughout the region). You could also make the short climb up *Rønvik*, the **mountain** on the outskirts of town, from where (June to mid-July) you can see the Midnight Sun; indeed it's one of the few decent places from which to view it uninterrupted by obscuring mountains.

Bodø practicals

Back in Bodø, practical details are straightforward. The *Hurtigrute* **coastal steamer** docks behind the **railway station**, from where it's a short walk along Sjøgata to the **tourist office** at Tollbugata 10 (June–Aug Mon–Fri 9am–4.30pm, Sat 10am–1.30pm; rest of the year Mon–Fri 9am–4pm; ☎081/21 240), which is good for information on connections to the Lofoten Islands. The **bus station** is in the car park behind the tourist office.

If you have to spend the night there's plenty of accommodation. The **youth hostel** (☎081/25 666), open mid-June to mid-August, is ten minutes' walk from the railway station (to the left), a large and luxurious place with singles and doubles (for 80kr a head) and immaculate kitchens (but lousy breakfasts). Alternatively, the tourist office books **private rooms** in town for 75kr (no booking fee) per person. Up the accommodation scale, there are a few small **hotels** which won't break the bank: *Opsahl Hospits* (☎081/20 704), Prinsensgate 131, *Gunda Johnsens Pensjonat* (☎081/24 250), Prinssensgate 80 and *Kristensens Pensjonat* (☎081/21 699), Rensåsgate 45 all go for around 300kr double. You can **camp** three kilometres from the centre at *Bodøsjøen Camping* (☎081/22 902), on the way to the Bodin kirke – walk left out of the railway station and follow the signs. For **eating**, the *Neptun Café*, behind the bus station, is a good bet, as is the café in the cheap central supermarket, *Koch*.

Out from Bodø: Saltstraumen and Kjerringjøy

Most of the excursions from Bodø are least harrowingly seen with your own transport. **Saltstraumen**, 33km from town, is a favourite place for fishing: a literal *maelstrom*, through which billions of gallons of water are forced several times daily, making a headlong rush between inner and outer fjord. Fishing is popular here since the fish get trapped between the conflicting currents – cheating really, since catching them is like shooting at them in a barrel. The whirling creamy water is at its most impressive at high tide, and its most violent when the moon is new or full. Sadly, though, the bus (#819) rarely coincides with either and it might be easier to hitch out and then **camp** overnight at *Saltstraumen Camping* (☎081/87 560), which has cabins for rent (around 300kr) at the water's edge.

It isn't any easier to get to the old **trading station** at **KJERRINGJØY**, a restored collection of nineteenth-century buildings and interiors which was the last stop for Lofoten-bound fishermen. There are guided tours around the place in summer (daily at 11.30am, 1.30pm & 3.30pm; 20kr) but, again, the ill-timed late-afternoon bus means you really have to stay if you want to see anything. If you decide to do this, the *Kjerringjøy Prestgård* (☎081/11 204) **hostel** has 50kr beds, though bear in mind the bus back to Bodø leaves at the crack of dawn each morning.

The Northern Islands: Lofoten and Vesterålen

A raggle-taggle collection of islands in the Norwegian Sea, the Lofoten and Vesterålen archipelagos are like Norway in miniature: their inhabitants are tough but welcoming, the terrain hard and unyielding, and the main – really the only – industry is fishing. The weather is temperate but wet, and there is a cultural tradition that goes back hundreds of years.

The **Lofoten Islands** are the best known, a string of six mountainous, almost alpine, land masses that have everything from puffin colonies in the south to beaches and fjords in the north. The chugging boat from Bodø, which is the traditional approach, brings you face to face with the peaks of the Lofoten Wall, a hundred-kilometre stretch of mountain which, due to the proximity of the islands to each other, appears unbroken – a towering set of jagged teeth biting into the skyline.

The **Vesterålen Islands** have been overshadowed as a tourist destination. The landscape is gentler, the ground richer than in the Lofotens, the villages well off the beaten track, and it takes time to explore the cluster of islands properly. But a quick visit is possible as the two largest towns, Sortland and Stokmarknes, are on the coastal steamer route.

Island practicals

As far as **accommodation** goes, *rorbuer* (or fisherman's shacks), rented out to tourists during the summer, are the islands' speciality, particularly on the Lofotens. King Øystein ordered them to be built at the harbours in the twelfth century so that visiting fishermen could rest easy instead of sleeping under the upturned hulls of their boats. Nowadays the word – made up of *ror*, to row and *buer*, referring to the actual house – retains its traditional meaning, and locals still ask "will you row this winter?" meaning "will you go fishing this winter?" The huts themselves are simple, with bunk beds and wood-fired stoves and, shared between four people, work out at around 40kr a head, sometimes much cheaper. Full lists are available from local tourist offices. Otherwise there are two **youth hostels** in the Vesterålen Islands, five in the Lofotens and enough places to pitch a tent to exhaust even the most dedicated camper.

Transport might be the only headache. A bus service connects most places but is sketchy: to avoid getting stuck, pick up a bus and ferry timetable from any major town beforehand. Walking/hitching is one way to speed things up and short distances are easy enough. But really you solve all your problems by either arriving with or hiring a **bike**, which you can do from the Stamsund youth hostel on Lofoten.

Details on **getting there** – from the mainland – are listed below. But if you intend to visit both chains, note that there is a **ferry** link between Lofoten and Vesterålen (between FISKEBOL and MELBU) – cutting out a time-wasting trip back to the mainland.

The Lofoten Islands

Stretched out in a skeletal curve across the Norwegian Sea, the **Lofoten Islands** are the hub of the northern winter fishing. At the turn of every year cod migrate from the Arctic Ocean to spawn here, where the waters are tempered by the Gulf Stream. The fishing months are January to April, but at other times, too, it's impossible to ignore the fishing, which impinges totally upon all aspects of the islands' life. At every harbour stand massed ranks of wooden racks used for drying the catch (to produce dried cod for export), full and odiferous in winter, empty in summer like so many abandoned climbing frames.

The Lofotens have their own relaxed pace, and are perfect for a simple, unclut-tered few days. For somewhere so far north, the weather is exceptionally mild: summer days can be spent sunbathing on the rocks and hiking around the superb coastline, or scrambling across the mossy hills. And when it rains, as it does frequently, life focuses on the *rorbuer*, cooking freshly caught fish over wood-burning stoves, singing, telling stories and gently wasting time. It sounds rather contrived, and in a sense it is – the way of life here is to some extent preserved like this for tourists. But it's rare to find anyone who isn't less than completely enthralled by it all.

GETTING TO THE LOFOTENS

1). The *Hurtigrute* **coastal steamer** – the only service to carry cars – calls at two ports in the Lofotens, Stamsund and Svolvær, of which Stamsund is preferable, espe-cially for a short stay. The steamer leaves Bodø at 3pm daily and tickets are 188kr to Stamsund, slightly more to Svolvær, free with a Coastal Pass (see "Getting Around").

2). There are also passenger **express boats**, which work out slightly cheaper than the coastal steamer: one linking Bodø with Svolvaer, another linking Narvik with Svolvaer (see *Travel Details*).

3). By **bus** you can leave the main E6 road at ULVSVÅG, take a connecting bus to SKUTVIK (21kr) and the **ferry** (41kr) from there to Svolvær. **Coming from Narvik** buses run to SORTLAND, main town of the adjacent Vesterålen Islands, from where it's a quick bus-ride and ferry crossing south to the Lofotens and Svolvær.

4). If you are under 26, **flying** standby from Bodø to Svolvær is a distinct – and economic – possibility, as it is to the southern islands in the group, Værøy and Røst; ask at Bodø tourist office for details. Getting to these more southerly islands direct by boat (see below), on the other hand, is not recommended unless you have plenty of time.

Austvågøy

SVOLVÆR, on **Austvågøy**, the largest and northernmost island of the group, is a disappointing introduction to the islands. Though you may find it one of the easier centres in which to stay (it is the administrative and transport centre of the Lofoten Islands), it has all the bustle but little of the charm of the other fishing towns.

Still, this is where you may well arrive. The **tourist office**, in the main town square, has fairly useless maps and the informative *Lofoten Tourist Guide* (10kr), but little else. For **accommodation**, the youth hostel (☎088/70 777) in the *Nye*

Polar Hotel, open all year, is expensive (120kr including breakfast; doubles 240kr) and not to everyone's taste – though it's smart enough and has decent facilities. For a more intimate experience, try instead the lovely wooden *Svolvær Sjøhuscamping* (☎088/70 336), at Parkveien N. – from the square, turn right at the *Radio-TV* shop and it's on the right past the library (*bibliotek*). Open May to September, it's a snug fishing house with views over the water: around 90kr a night gives a bed, use of the well-equipped kitchen, free showers and cheap bike rentals.

Svolvær's surroundings are, however, delightful – so much so that Svolvær has become a haven for **foreign artists**, who live in a small colony within the town's boundaries, their work usually on show at one of two galleries. It's easy enough to walk to **KABELVÅG**, 5km away, (although there are several daily buses, too) and to the **Lofoten Island Museum** (summer Mon–Fri 9am–3pm, Sat & Sun 11am–3pm; 10kr) – the definitive collection of fishing and other cultural paraphernalia on the islands. Kabelvåg itself is the oldest fishing village in the Lofotens, and it was here that King Øystein ordered the original *rorbuer* to be built in 1120.

Svolvaer is also a good centre for **hiking** and **climbing**. The tourist office has details of routes, the most famous of which is the climb up the *Svolværgeita* ("Svolvær goat"), right above the town. Daring mountaineers jump between the horns of the adjacent peaks, and the town's cemetery 2000 feet below is full of those who missed. You may also be cajoled into taking a **cruise** down the **Trollfjord**, an impossibly narrow stretch of water up and down which countless excursion boats inch a careful way, wringing gasps from camera-crazy tourists. Unless you're a fjord fanatic, though, the pricey cruises are a bit of a con, even more so when you realise that the fjord was actually appropriated by the Lofotens from the Vesterålen Islands, at the other end of the sound; see p.248.

Vestvågøy

It's the second island of the group, **Vestvågøy**, that captivates most travellers to the Lofotens. This is due in no small part to the immediate beauty of **STAMSUND**, which strings around its bay in a colourful jumble of wooden houses and chalets. This is the other port at which the coastal steamer docks and is much the best base for touring the rest of the island.

First place to head for is the **youth hostel** (☎088/89 166), a little way down the road from the port, made up of several *rorbuer* perched over a pin-sized rocky bay. It's open all year and very friendly, the warden, Ruar Justad, dispensing rooms (55kr a head) and information like a benevolent wizard; there's even a washing machine and tumble-drier if the travelling's taking its toll. There's a great atmosphere here, and many travellers return time and again. The fishing, too, is fine: the hostel has free rowing boats and lines to take out on (usually still) water – and you can cook what you catch on the wood-burning stoves. Ringing ahead is advised, though persevere if the hostel is full: the sleeping arrangements are flexible to say the least, and there is often room in a couple of cottages further up the hillside.

For touring the rest of the island, the hostel also hires out **bikes and mopeds** (40kr and 70kr a day respectively), and is the best source of information on just about everything – much better, in fact, than the village's tourist information booth. If, incidentally, you don't make (or fancy) the youth hostel, there are some regular *rorbuer* in the village too, and the *Lofoten Hotel* (☎088/89 300) by Stamsund harbour – though this is naturally much more expensive; from 400kr for a double room. If you're **camping**, it's not far to nearby STEINE, where an offshore archipelago of pinprick islands conceals a **campsite** and several *rorbuer* (☎088/89 283).

Back through Stamsund, and a couple of kilometres from LEKNES (administrative centre of the islands and home to its airport), is **FYGHE**, worth a stop for an excellent **museum** (June–Aug Mon–Fri 11am–4pm, Sat & Sun noon–3pm; 10kr, 5kr students) in a restored nineteenth-century schoolhouse. Enthusiastic guides and some self-explanatory displays reveal how horribly hard life was a hundred years ago – the box-room cottage reconstructed outside just seems intimate until you realise that it slept between eight and twelve people.

Head out, too, towards the western coast. At **HAUKLAND** there is one of the most popular of the island's beaches, a long sandy stretch with deep green water. In the sunshine the swimming is fine and there is a **campsite** for longer stays. If the caravans get a bit much, hike around the coast as far as **UTAKLEIV**, a favourite spot to watch for the Midnight Sun and good for rough camping. As with everywhere here, though, watch the weather: changes can be dangerously rapid.

Real isolation can be found further north at **UNSTAD**, where a rough road winds up into the hills, through a tunnel blasted out of the rock, and down to an enormous cove, which stretches away to the sea like an oversized football field. The high hills here flank either side of a smallish beach that few, if any, tourists ever reach. In winter, the village is cut off by the snow that whisks across the tiny plain, and the wind sends the waves crashing up onto the fields. It might be blustery in the summer, but no one will object to you putting a tent up at the edge of the beach – although it'd be polite to ask first in the village.

Flakstadøya and Moskenesøya

You're going to need more time to get further south than Vestvågøy. **Flakstadøya** and **Moskenesøya** islands are served by bus, but the ferry connection from Lilleeidet (on Vestvågøy) to Napp (on Flakstadøya) is hardly frequent and once on the islands you'll probably need to walk or hitch to get around.

On Flakstadøya, **RAMBERG** is the main town, where you should ask about visiting **Flakstad kirke**, a red timber structure built of Russian driftwood in 1780: its altar-piece and pulpit are by the busy Gottfried Ezechiel. There is a **campsite** (☎088/93 140) in Ramberg, *rorbuer* too, as there are – more picturesquely – in **NUSFJORD** to the south. Unlike many of the fishermen's huts in the Lofotens which were erected more in response to tourist demand than to that of the fishing fleet, the ones in and around the curved harbour of Nusfjord are the genuine nineteenth-century article and the fishing village is regarded as one of the best-preserved in Norway.

South, over the bridge on to Moskenesøya, **SUND** is worth a stop for a quirky **museum** of old boats and engines (open all year; 10kr). **REINE**, with more views and some dominant mountains, is the occasional midway port between Bodø and the southernmost bird islands of Værøy and Røst and has more *rorbuer* (☎088/92 177) for rent. Nine kilometres further south the bus line ends abruptly at the tersely named **Å**, where there's a new **youth hostel** (☎088/91 162), open June to August and costing 80kr. You can rent bikes and rowing boats from here, but take care on the water. Beyond Å is the *Moskenestraumen* – the terrifying **maelstrom** described by Edgar Allen Poe in his short story, *A Descent into the Maelstrom*. There are easier places to see one of these in Norway (Bodø for instance), but this is the original. Of it Poe wrote:

Even while I gazed, this current acquired a monstrous velocity. Each moment added to its speed – to its headlong impetuosity. In five minutes the whole sea . . . was lashed into ungovernable fury . . . Here the vast bed of the waters seamed and scarred into a thousand conflicting channels, burst suddenly into frenzied convulsion – heaving, boiling, hissing . . .

Værøy and Røst

Værøy and **Røst** are the only islands of any size in the little archipelago that dangles south from the main chain of the Lofotens. Unless you're careful, the irregular ferry schedules can strand you on either for days, but the gist of the timetable is that **ferries** run from Bodø to both islands and back again – a circular and continuous route – once-daily; the ferries call at Reine, too, on Tuesday and Saturday. **Flights**, more simply, leave daily from either Bodø or Leknes, and on standby fares there's a fifty percent discount to those under 26, which compares well with sea crossings to the rest of the Lofotens. High summer season return fares, too, are discounted heavily if booked at least fourteen days in advance; tourist offices in Svolvær and Bodø can make sense of it all.

If you make it, the islands are internationally famous for their bird colonies, the crags supporting an incredible number of puffins (around three million), the rare sea eagle and eider ducks. The weather is uncommonly mild throughout the year, hiking trails ubiquitous, and the occasional beach glorious and deserted. Importantly, there are also two **youth hostels**, one on either island: the one at Røst (☎088/96 109) is open from May to August and costs 60kr a night; the one at Værøy (☎088/95 346) from mid-May to mid-September, again, 60kr a night. There's a **campsite**,too, on Værøy – *Sørheim Camping* (☎088/95 182) – with cabins to rent.

The Vesterålen Islands

The larger **Vesterålen Islands** lie to the north of the Lofotens, an indistinct grouping that's greener, less mountainous (except on the west coast) and more agricultural than its neighbour. Walking is the prime occupation, and it's as satisfying as you might expect, though consider also renting a bike. Bus services are infrequent, and hitching unpredictable.

The south: the Trollfjord, Stokmarknes, Melbu and Bø

The best way **to arrive** is by coastal steamer. A narrow sound separates the Lofotens from the Vesterålens, and every ship in the summer takes the opportunity to detour into the two-kilometre long **Trollfjord**. Slowing to a mere chug, the

---

GETTING TO THE VESTERALENS

The *Hurtigrute* **coastal steamer** calls at STOKMARKNES and SORTLAND in the south, RISØYHAMN in the north – of which Stokmarknes is the handiest for youth hostels and the Trollfjord.

There's also a **ferry** which connects Fiskebol in the Lofotens with MELBU, at the southern tip of the islands. Confusingly, Sortland's limits also incorporate part of Hinnøya, Norway's largest island (though nothing to do with Vesterålen); a **bridge** connects the two (providing access to the E6 via the Lødingen–Bognes ferry) while **buses** also link Sortland with Harstad, Fauske and Narvik.

vessels inch up the narrow gorge, smooth stone towering high above blocking out the light. At its head the boats effect a nautical three-point turn and then crawl back to rejoin the main waterway. It's very atmospheric, and the effect is no less grand when the weather is foul. All this is free if you have a Coastal Steamer Pass (see "Getting Around"). Everyone else has two choices: return cruises from Svolvaer are expensive (summer twice daily, around 150kr return) but last a healthy three and a half hours. A better move, if you are going to the Vesterålen Islands from the Lofotens anyway, is to buy a single ticket on the coastal steamer from Svolvaer to Stokmarknes, around 100kr.

After the ride, **STOKMARKNES** can't help but feel a bit of a letdown. There is a **tourist office** (mid-June to mid-Aug only), at the harbour, from where it's best to pick up what you need and then count on heading out of town. If you can't, *Stokmarknes* **camping** (☎088/52 022) has a few cheap cabins for rent and is open from June to mid-September; or there's a well-equipped **youth hostel** (☎088/57 106), open all year, 16km south in **MELBU** – 70kr a night, doubles 220kr. Connected by fairly regular bus, Melbu is an old trading centre, though largely modern these days and home of the largest trawler fleet on the islands. You can rent **bikes** here, or even the warden's car (200kr a day plus petrol to hostel association members).

From Stokmarknes, an **express boat** (25kr) hums across the fjord to STRAUMSNES, from where you can reach some supremely isolated spots. The nearby tiny community of RINGSTAD has **rorbuer** available (☎088/37 480), the price including rowing boats and fishing lines. From Straumsnes it's a 10km-walk or infrequent bus ride (Sortland direction) to the small **youth hostel** (☎088/35 668) at **BØ**, enticingly close to the 800m-long Fjærvoll **beach**. The hostel has its own **campsite** and is open mid-June to August; 50kr a night, doubles at just 100kr.

Sortland and around

SORTLAND, is a handy place to start and finish any exploration of the islands. It's the transport centre of Vesterålen and, with 4000 inhabitants, the only large (ish) town. The informative **tourist office** (end of June to mid-Aug 24hr; rest of the year Mon–Fri 9am–5pm, Sat 10am–2pm; ☎088/21 555), in the foyer of the *Sortland Nordic Hotel*, offers bike rental, lists of *rorbuer* and a map of town; and the **hotel** itself (☎088/21 833) does a groaning hot and cold buffet lunch for 65kr – though its rooms aren't as good value, starting at around 500kr. More realistically, Sortland's **campsite** (☎088/22 578), which has cabins for rent, is 2km out of town and open between March and November. The tourist office will also advise on staying out at **NYKSUND**, a deserted fishing village in the north currently being restored by a group of students from Berlin. It's normally possible – should you so desire – to lend a hand with the restoration and sleep in the old houses and fishing sheds.

East from Sortland, mountaineers are drawn to the shovel-shaped **Reka mountain**, 600 metres high and something of a challenge. It's a distinctive landmark in some fairly adventurous surroundings and if you want to stay in the area the warden of the Melbu youth hostel has a cottage for hire. Ask him for details and get hold of some fishing gear before you go.

North: to Andenes

Further north the going gets trickier. Vast tracts of marshland and open moors are buffeted by summer winds, and cycling can get tiring. There's a good bus service, though, between Sortland and **ANDENES**, a fishing port in the far north, and if you are not camping – in which case you can pitch a tent just about anywhere – this is the best place for which to head. Apart from RISØYHAMN, last Vesterålen call of the coastal steamer, there are few other alternatives on the way. There used to be a very small **youth hostel** in Andenes, though it may have closed down: check in Stokmarknes or Sortland and, if so, you'll have to rely on the *Viking Hotell* (☎088/41 455), Fjordgata 2, whose rooms start at 420kr, and a **campsite** (*Damsgård Camping*; ☎088/41 184), which has well-priced cabins.

For what it's worth, things to do in Andenes, apart from simply wandering the lovely coastline, include a **Polar Museum** (mid-June to mid-Aug daily 10am–1pm & 4–7pm) inside an old merchant's house and a nineteenth-century **lighthouse** (open to visitors mid-June to mid-Aug) – as well as the annual **Deep Sea Fishing Festival** (first week in July, entry 160kr includes boat hire and all charges). The **tourist office** (June to Aug only) in Andenes has all the details.

Narvik

NARVIK is a relatively modern town, established less than a century ago as an ice-free port to handle the iron ore brought by train from northern Sweden. And it makes no bones about its main function: the **iron ore docks** are immediately conspicuous upon arrival here, slap bang in the centre of town, the rust-coloured machinery overwhelming the whole waterfront. The industrial complex is strangely impressive, and it's difficult to dislike the cat's cradle of walkways, conveyor belts, cranes, funnels and drive belts, which could be one huge set from a James Bond movie.

Narvik's first modern settlers were the navvies who built the railway line to the mines in Kiruna, over the border – a Herculean task commemorated every March by a week of singing, dancing and drinking, the locals dressed in nineteenth-century costume. The town grew steadily up to the last war, when it was demolished by fierce fighting for control of the harbours and the iron ore supplies. The hulks of German destroyers still lie out in the water, the bodies of hundreds of soldiers and sailors – Nazis and Allied troops – in the cemeteries scattered around the town.

There are guided tours around the **dock areas** (daily in summer 1.30pm; 10kr), which leave from the gates of *LKAB* building, beyond the freight rail tracks – interesting if only for the opportunity to spend an hour inside such a hellish mess. Ore is brought here by rail from Sweden and carried on the various conveyor belts to the quayside where it is shipped out – around thirty million tons a year.

Otherwise the town centre is, inevitably, rather lacking in appeal, with modern stone replacing the wooden houses and buildings flattened during the war. Try and devote an hour or so to the **Krigsminne Museum** (March–Sept daily 10am–2pm; June–Aug daily 10am–10pm; 10kr), in the main town square close to the docks. Run by the Red Cross, it documents the wartime German saturation bombing of the town, and the bitter and bloody sea and air battles in which hundreds of foreign servicemen, British included, died alongside the local population. It's a thoroughly moving account, and thoughtfully done too: one display juxtaposes German bullwhips with small toys made by Russian POWs as thanks for food parcels smuggled in by locals who faced execution if discovered; another shows a mock-up Resistance hideaway with a radio operator broadcasting clandestinely – the waxwork of a man who still lives in Narvik.

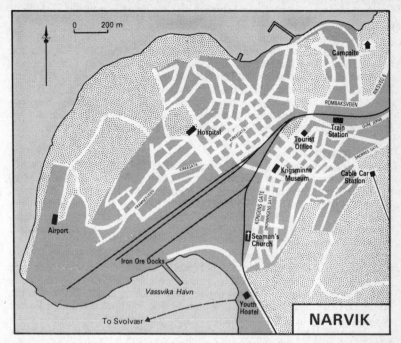

Beyond that, it's best to head for the open country. A *Gondolbaner*, or **cable car** (March–Oct; 35kr each way), from behind the bus station, whisks passengers up to the 700-metre heights of *Fagernesfjellet*, where on a clear day the Lofoten range is visible – as, if you stick around and it stays clear, is the Midnight Sun. The last cable car back returns after midnight, but avid Midnight Sun watchers leaving on the early morning train to Kiruna can leave their packs at the railway station, take a ride up and then walk down. It's possible to walk up too, the hike taking about two to three hours.

For a lesser walk and lesser views, head up the road behind the railway station and look out over town and water. Keener walkers should try the **trails and cabins** strung out in the mountains towards the Swedish border. The cabins are maintained by the *Narvik Touring Association* and the keys are kept at the fire station in town (☎082/45 100), who will want a deposit for their use.

Practical details

The **railway and bus stations** are close together, and near to the **tourist office** at Kongens Gate 66 (June to mid-Aug Mon–Sat 9am–9pm, Sun 5–8pm; Sept–May Mon–Fri 9am–3.30pm; ☎082/43 309). They book **private rooms** (around 100kr single, 170kr double, 210kr triple; 10kr fee), and for 5kr will look after your pack. There's also a popular **youth hostel**, the *Norkalotten* (☎082/42 598) at Havnegate 3, open mid-March to mid-September, whose 100kr price (double rooms 300kr) includes breakfast and showers and which has no curfew. If the hostel's full, the cheapest *pensjonat* is the *Briedablikk* (☎082/41 418) at Tore Hundsgate 41, at the top of Kinobakken, which has doubles for around 190kr. The **campsite** is two kilometres north of town at ORNESHAUGEN – turn right along the main road from the station and keep walking, or take any bus going to the airport.

For **eating**, the *Havnecafé* (closed Sun and most of July), down the road from the hostel, has the best-value meals in town. Or there's the *Café Rosa*, over the main railway bridge opposite the town square, which turns into a **nightclub** in the evenings. **Drinkers** will find booming disco music and a lively crowd at the outdoor café in the main square; the one up the road by the *Grand Royal Hotel* is more touristy and more expensive. More bizarrely, the friendly **Swedish Seamen's Church**, just up the road from the hostel, is open until 10pm and has cheap coffee and cakes, international papers – and a pool table in the aisle.

On from Narvik

There's a choice of several routes on from Narvik. The **rail link** (the *Ofotbana*), cut through the mountains a century ago, runs east and then south into Sweden. BJØRNFELL is the nearest place to the border on the Norwegian side – from where it's only a short hop to VASSIJAURE in Sweden, and a couple of hours more on to KIRUNA. The trip is popular with hikers who stop off in the mountains on both sides of the border to plug into the network of mountain cabins and trails (for more on which see p.431).

Bus travellers can travel north to ALTA along one of the most beautiful routes in the country, a succession of switchback roads, lakeside forests, high peaks and lowlands. In summer cut grass dries everywhere, stretched over wooden poles forming long lines on the hillsides like so much washing drying. Buses also run off the E6 to TROMSØ; and note that from Narvik, southwards to either Fauske or Bodø by bus, rail pass holders get a fifty-percent discount. There's also an all-year **express boat service** connecting Narvik with Svolvær in the Lofoten Islands. It leaves from the harbour next to the youth hostel.

travel details

Trains

From Trondheim to Stockholm (2 daily; 12hr); Dombås/Oslo (3 daily; 2hr 30min/6hr 45min); Røros/Oslo (1–2 daily; 3hr/8hr 30min); Levanger/Mo-i-Rana/Fauske/Bodø (2 daily; 1hr 20min/7hr 15min/10hr 20min/11hr).
From Narvik to Stockholm (2–3 daily; 21–24hr).

Buses

From Trondheim to Dombås/Stryn/Bergen (1 daily; 3hr/7hr 30min/15hr); Molde/Ålesund (1–2 daily; 6hr/8hr); Røros (1–2 daily; 3hr 10min); Stockholm (1 on Thurs at 6.30am; 13hr 30min).
From Fauske to Bodø (2 daily; 1hr 10min); Narvik (2 daily; 5hr); Sortland (1 daily; 4hr 30min); Harstad (1 daily; 6hr).
From Narvik to Tromsø (1–3 daily; 5–6hr); Alta (1 daily; 11hr); Fauske/Bodø (2 daily; 5hr).

Nord-Norge Bussen

There are 2 buses daily from Fauske to Nordkjosbotn; one daily continuing to Alta (overnight stops necessary at Narvik and Alta). Two daily continue to Karasjok, the first running on to Kirkenes the same day, the second stopping in Karasjok. See also "Travel Details" in *Troms and Finnmark* and "Getting Around".

Ferries/Express Boats

The *Hurtigrute* **coastal steamer** leaves Trondheim at noon daily (northbound) and 10.15am daily (southbound).
From Fiskebol to Melbu (7–12 daily; 30min).
From Svolvær to Skutvik (8 daily; 2hr).
From Stokmarknes to Straumsnes (Mon, Wed & Fri 2 daily, Sun 1 daily; 20min).
From Bodø to Svolvær (1 daily except Sat; 5hr); Værøy/Røst (1 daily; 5–8hr; and returning to Bodø in 13hr.
From Narvik to Svolvær (1 daily except Sat; 4hr).

CHAPTER EIGHT

TROMS AND FINNMARK

Baedeker, writing 100 years ago about Norway's far northern provinces, **Troms** and **Finnmark**, observed that they possess "attractions for the scientific traveller and the sportsman, but can hardly be recommended for the ordinary tourist." And, to be frank, this is still not too far off the mark today. These are enticing lands, no question, the natural environment they offer stunning in its extremes. But the travelling can be hard, the specific attractions well distanced and, when you reach them, subtle in their appeal.

Troms' intricate coastline has influenced its history since the days when powerful Viking lords operated a trading empire from its islands. Even today, over fifty percent of the population lives offshore, and the marvellous island countryside is great for hiking. It was from **Tromsø**, so-called "Capital of the North" and nowadays a lively university town, that the king and his government proclaimed a "Free Norway" in 1940 before fleeing into exile in Britain.

The appeal of Finnmark is less obvious. Much of it was laid waste during World War II by a combination of Russian bombs and the retreating German army's scorched-earth policy. It's now possible to drive for hours without coming across a building more than forty years old. Most travellers head straight for **Nordkapp** from where the Midnight Sun is visible between mid-May and the end of July – and then for **Kirkenes**, last town before the Soviet border, where you really feel yourself on the edge of Europe. Consider also, though, travelling inland to the intriguing *Same* towns of **Kautokeino** and **Karasjok** where, in the endless flat scrub plains (the *Finnmarksvidda*), winter temperatures plummet to - 25°C. Even more adventurously, it's becoming easier these days to reach **Spitzbergen**, an archipelago six hundred kilometres north of Norway, frozen solid for most of the year but visitable in July and August.

Approaches to the far north are limited but spectacular: trains don't run this far and access is either by **coastal steamer** (the *Hurtigrute*) or by bus. The *Hurtigrute* takes the best part of two days to circumnavigate the huge fjords between Harstad and Kirkenes; **bus** transport throughout the summer (and some of the winter) is efficient and regular, using the windswept E6 Arctic Highway as far north as Kirkenes. Branches also run off north to Nordkapp and south into the *Finnmarksvidda* and – eventually – Finland. These aren't areas you want to get stranded in so pick up full **timetables** from any local travel agent or tourist office: on the longer rides it's a good idea to buy tickets in advance. And don't count on easy **hitching** anywhere in this region. As for accommodation, there are a few **youth hostels** and **hotels** but rather more **campsites**; in any case, if you've a tent and a well-insulated sleeping bag, you can more or less bed down where you like.

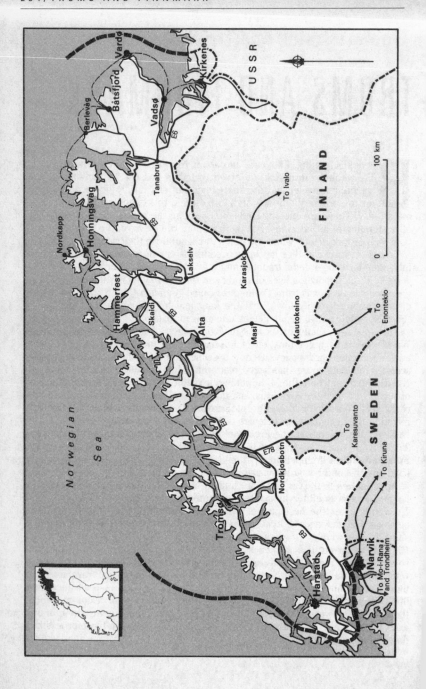

Troms: Harstad and Tromsø

Most travellers, if they make it this far, are in a hurry to forge further north to Nordkapp. But, unless you are *really* short on time, you'd do better to break the long journey at one of only two worthwhile stops in sparse Troms: either at **Harstad**, handy for some gentle hiking, or – better – **Tromsø**, northern Norway's largest town and boasting the region's only significant nightlife.

Harstad

Leaving the Nordland railway at Fauske it's a dramatic bus ride north to **HARSTAD**, which sits surrounded by craggy, snow-topped mountains on the island of **Hinnøy**. The journey and the surroundings are, however, more enticing than the town itself, which is home to much of northern Norway's engineering industry, its docks an unseemly tangle of supply ships, repair yards and cold storage plants. Thankfully, moving on quickly is possible: Harstad is a *Hurtigrute* port, and daily buses run out to the Lofoten Islands.

The main item of interest, the **Trondenes kirke** (summer only: Mon–Fri 9am–2pm, Tues & Thurs 6–8pm, Sat 9am–noon, Sun 9am–noon & 5–7pm; free), is outside the town centre, a short two-kilometre walk beyond the harbour. In medieval times this was the northernmost church in Christendom. The thirteenth-century building is an intriguing example of a fortress church, its walls in parts over two metres thick – though apart from some badly faded murals most of the original decoration has gone. The old church *ell*, for checking measures in parish disputes, hangs from the massive medieval iron-clad door.

After wandering central Harstad's hilly streets with their rainbow-coloured wooden houses, terraces and clear views of the mountains, there are few other reasons to hang around. The **North Norwegian Annual Arts Festival** (concerts, theatre and dance) provides a spark of interest (and hotels full to bursting) in late June. As does the **International Fishing Festival**, usually held during the first weekend in July, when the angler landing the biggest fish becomes the winner of the improbable *Order of the Giant Fisherman*.

Practical details: arriving and sleeping

The **tourist office**, at Strandgata 20b (June–Aug Mon–Fri 8am–3pm, Sat 8am–1pm; rest of the year Mon–Fri 8am–3pm; ☎082/63 235) has details of all the local events, as well as information on summer hiking trails, mountain huts and bicycles for hire (at around 20kr a day).

To stay, there's a **youth hostel** (☎082/64 154), open June to mid-August, in the *Trondames Folkehøgskole*. It costs 100kr a night (doubles 230kr) and is closed during the day from 11am to 6pm. For a change, though, there are also several fairly cheap **guest houses** in town: *Høiland Hospits* (☎082/64 690) and *Sentrum Hospits* (☎082/62 938) are both on Magnusgate and have singles from 200kr, doubles from 250kr. Failing that, there's a **campsite** (☎082/73 662), 5km from the centre and open all year – it has cabins for around 120kr and swimming from the nearby beach. Take any of the buses to SØROVER and get off at KANEBOGEN.

Moving on: the offshore islands

Regular buses and ferries run to **Bjarkøy**, a pretty island and an accessible spot for a day trip. Historically important, Bjarkøy was the home of Tore Hund, Viking lord and one-time liegeman of King Olav, who converted Norway to Christianity. Their relationship cooled when Olav had Tore Hund's nephew executed; according to the *Sagas*, Hund was one of the men who struck down the king at Stiklestad in 1030. There are several more islands in the group and the mishmash of mountains, coral sands and bird colonies make for excellent hiking and camping. The tourist office has full timetables for all local transport.

Afterwards, the most obvious journey north is to TROMSØ, a fine journey to make by coastal steamer (six hours) although the quickest connection is by express boat (*Hurtigbåt*), which runs there in half the time.

Tromsø

TROMSØ was once known, rather preposterously, as the "Paris of the North", and though even the tourist office doesn't make any pretence to such grandiose titles now, the city still likes to think of itself as the capital of northern Norway. Which in a way is fair enough. It's a likeable small city, with an above-average and affordable nightlife lent by a high-profile student population, two cathedrals and some surprisingly good museums. Certainly, as a base for this part of the country it's hard to beat.

Arriving and finding a place to stay

The *Hurtigrute* **coastal steamer** docks in the centre of town at the quay at the bottom of Kirkegata; **buses** arrive and leave from the adjacent car park. The **tourist office** (June to mid-Aug Mon–Fri 9am–8.30pm, Sat 9am–6pm, Sun 2–5pm; rest of the year Mon–Fri 9am–4pm; ☎083/84 776) is on Storgata, near the Domkirke, and sells a 24-hour **tourist ticket** (25kr) valid for unlimited city bus travel, though most places can easily be reached on foot. The tourist office might store packs, but if not there is a **left luggage** (*Bagasje*) on the harbour front, which is open from Monday to Friday until midnight; 12kr per day.

The massive and very comfortable **youth hostel** (☎083/85 319), open mid-June to mid-August, demands a key-deposit of 50kr but has no curfew: it costs 80kr a night (doubles 215kr) and is a couple of kilometres from the quay – bus #24 goes from outside the *Sparebank* on Fr. Langes Gata to ELVERHØY or else it's a steep twenty-minute walk.

Alternatively, the tourist office books **private rooms** (100kr single, 150kr double; 15kr fee) in town, or try one of two reasonable **pensjonater**: *Skipperhuset Pensjonat* (☎083/81 660), Storgata 112, or *Park Pensjonat* (☎083/82 208), Skolegaten 24. Both charge around 250kr single, 300kr double. It's also worth checking the larger **hotels**, whose summer discounts (*Minipris*), though more expensive – around 200kr each in a double – include a huge breakfast. The tourist office will have details; one generally cheapish place is *Polar Hotell* (☎083/86 480), Grønnegate 45, whose double rooms start at around 475kr. The nearest **campsite**, with cabins, is over the bridge on the mainland at *Tromsdalen Camping* (☎083/35 157) and is open all year; take bus #36 from Storgata.

The Town

You can best orientate yourself by way of Tromsø's cathedrals. The **Domkirke** (Tues–Sat 1–4pm; free) serves to emphasise how prosperous the town was by the nineteenth century, the result of its substantial barter trade with Russia. Completed in 1861, it's one of Norway's largest wooden churches, with some

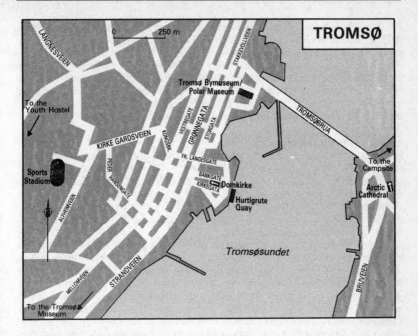

imposing fixtures in a solemn salmon-pink interior. On the other side of the water, over the rickety Tromsø Bridge, the white and desperately modern **Arctic Cathedral** (Mon–Sat 10am–2pm & 4–6pm, Sun 1–7pm; 4kr) is spectacularly different: eleven immense triangular concrete sections form the church, representing the eleven Apostles left after the betrayal, while the entire east wall is made up of one huge stained glass window. A further nice touch is the organ, built to represent a ship (when viewed from underneath) in place of the usual hanging votive ship.

Back in the centre of town, on Stortorget, there's a daily fruit and veg **market** and a *Domus* supermarket with a good café overlooking the harbour. In summer, fresh fish and prawns are sold from boats down on the waterfront here. Follow the harbour round and you're in the heart of old Tromsø: the raised ground at the water's edge made this area a natural site for fortification in the thirteenth century, though a fire in 1969 left few buildings of any interest. One that did survive is the Customs House, built in 1789 and now housing the **Tromsø Bymuseum** (June–Aug daily 11am–3pm; Sept–May Mon–Fri 11am–3pm; 5kr), the town museum, whose collection – mainly nineteenth-century – includes a Heath Robinson-style mousetrap. The **Polar Museum** (June–Aug daily 11am–3pm; 5kr), close by, is better, covering trading, industrial and scientific activity throughout the ages in the Polar region by way of good photographs and some realistic reconstructions – though its enthusiasm for seal clubbing and polar bear shooting (graphic shots and reconstructions of both) is offensive.

Perhaps more rewarding is the **Tromsø Museum** (June–Aug daily 9am–6pm; Sept–May Mon–Fri 9am–3pm, Wed 7–10pm, Sat noon–3pm, Sun 10am–3pm; 5kr, students 2kr), a 25-minute walk from the centre along Strandveien; or take bus

#21. It's a thoughtful collection, consisting of zoology and botany displays, a *Same* exhibit, and an ecclesiastical art section of note, including some lovely pieces, mostly medieval and post-Reformation, which have been rescued from northern churches, notably the eighteenth-century "pastor boards" – a pictorial roll-call of local clerics. The nearby **Aquarium** (June–Aug daily 10am–5pm; entry included in museum admission charge), a quick walk through the trees down to the water, is, apparently, the world's northernmost public aquarium – really its only justifiable claim to fame, since the largest thing in it is a catfish.

Eating, drinking and nightlife

For **eating**, the areas around the tourist office and along Storgata are good hunting grounds. Budget meals are available in the *Maritim* cafeteria opposite the tourist office, or just up the road at the *Sagatun* in Richard Withs Plass. For pizza and salads, *Tromsøpalmen*, at Storgata 45, is popular. Look in, too, on the *Ungdommens Hus* (Tues–Sun noon–midnight), on the waterfront along from *Domus*, which has a cheap café/restaurant, occasional discos and gigs and is home to the local radio station.

Places to drink are also remarkably thick on the ground. *Samfunnskafeen* at Storgata 95 is the cheapest, teeming with local drunks. Trendier and more expensive is the *Teaterkafeen*, in the Kulturhus above Stortorget, an arts centre which stays open until 1am most days. *Prelaten*, at Sjøgata 12, is popular and a good place to hear jazz, and finally there is the noisy *Ølhallen Pub*, at Storgata 4. If you want to continue your carousing, during term-time the Students Union (*Studenthuset*) at Skippergata 44 could help with ideas, but specific places include *Fun Club*, Grønnegata 81, a student bar with a disco upstairs, and *Paletten*, Storgata 51, which maintains its arty name by hosting occasional exhibitions. Cover charges at both run to 40kr and upwards.

Into Finnmark: Alta and around

Strung out across a number of scattered settlements, **ALTA** is not the kind of place anyone would want to spend much time. It was interesting enough once – for decades not Norwegian at all but Finnish and *Same*, and host to an old and much visited *Same* fair. But the fair stopped at the end of the last war – which, together with recurring fires, destroyed all the old buildings except the church – and these days Alta is in the grip of a comprehensive new development that has no real centre, and little soul.

For all that, it's an important transport junction and hard to avoid: heading to Nordkapp by road almost certainly means an overnight stop in Alta in order to catch the connecting bus to Honningsvåg the next day; and buses also head east from here along the E6 to Kirkenes and south to Kautokeino. But the town does have one remarkable feature, almost worth spending another night for, the **rock carvings at Hjemmeluft** – the most extensive area of prehistoric rock carvings in northern Europe.

The site is officially open during summer (mid-June to mid-Aug) from 8am until 8pm, and entrance costs 10kr, but you can usually get in all year round and very nearly around the clock in summer. To get there, walk a kilometre or so further on from the campsite (see below) and onto the wooden walkways that you see as you drive into Alta. The carvings themselves make up an extraordinarily complex tableau of ships, animals and people. They were executed, it's estimated, between 2500 and 6000 years ago, and although the colours have been retouched by scientists they are indisputably impressive: clear, stylish, and ultimately rather touching in their simplicity.

Once you've seen the carvings you've really seen Alta. **Buses** call at Bossekop ("whale bay"), the original settlement by the water of the Altafjord, and if you're **not staying** you may as well jump off here. There's a **tourist office** (June–Aug Mon–Fri 9am–7pm, Sat 9am–4pm, Sun noon–7pm; ☎084/35 041) and other facilities (a café, bank, post office), and you can normally leave your bag here if you just want to walk down to the carvings.

If you're **staying**, you need to keep on the bus as far as Sentrum, the newest and least likeable part of Alta, close to which there's a **youth hostel** (☎084/34 409) – five minutes' walk further up the E6 at Midtbakkveien 50. It's open from mid-June to mid-August, costs 85kr a night and has excellent facilities: it's *always* worth reserving a bed here in advance, so popular is the route up to Nordkapp. If it's full, Alta has a couple of more expensive places that you might be thankful for: the *Alta Sommerhotell*, Løkkeveien 2 (☎084/35 000), is about the cheapest, at around 400kr for a double room. There are also three or four **campsites** in the area, one with cabins (☎084/35 226) on the southern side of Bossekop (next door to the rock carvings).

Eating is most cheaply done at the *Alta Gjestestue* (Mon–Fri 7am–10pm, Sat 8am–9pm, Sun 9am–9pm), opposite the petrol station in Bossekop – breakfast at around 40kr and dinner from 60kr.

Around Alta

There are a couple of side-trips that can be made from Alta for anyone intent upon a spot of serious walking. Southbound buses go past **KÅFJORD**, whose nineteenth-century church, a relic of the copper-mining period which ended in 1878 when the English-owned company abandoned the workings, signals the path up to **Hallde** peak (907m). Here there are the remains of the first **Northern Lights Observatory**, burnt down by the Germans in 1944 but now partially restored for visitors. In summer, it's a three- to four-hour hike up to the top, and even then it's wise to check the weather reports and connecting buses from Kåfjord before setting off.

What was once northern Europe's biggest **canyon** at **SAUTSO** – a good target for some serious walking beyond Alta – is now reported to have been dammed, which rather spoils any chances you might have had of adventurous deeds. Check with the tourist office in Alta for the latest information.

The Finnmarksvidda: Kautokeino and Karasjok

From Alta there are two routes into the vast plain of the **Finnmarksvidda**: immediately south to KAUTOKEINO, or east across the peninsula to LAKSELV and then south to KARASJOK. But for the steady encroachment of tourism over recent years, lifestyles have remained much the same here for centuries. The main occupations are reindeer-herding, hunting and fishing: the few thousand semi-nomadic **Same** who live here have continued a largely unaltered, traditional lifestyle dictated by their animals. They remain in the flat plains and shallow valleys during the winter, migrating towards the coast in early May as the snow begins to melt – hard to believe, but it can get exceptionally hot here in summer. By October, both people and deer are journeying back from their temporary summer quarters and preparing for the great Easter festivals, when weddings and baptisms are celebrated. This is without question the best time to be in Finnmark and when the famed reindeer races are run. Summer visits, on the other hand, when most families and their deer are at pasture grounds in the north, can be disappointing, with little of the colour and activity you'll find during winter. For more on the *Same*, see *Contexts*.

Kautokeino

The easiest town to reach from Alta, **KAUTOKEINO**, is a bumpy bus-ride south along Route 93, following a long stretch of scrub, trees, rock and telegraph wires. It is, strangely enough, something of a tourist draw, principally due to the preponderance of pseudo-ethnic jewellers from the south who have set up here in search of closer contact with nature and a fast buck. During the summer, the town's main street is lined with souvenir booths which attract the travellers to and from Finland like flies. They are not, however, selling tourist tack: stores like *Juhl's Silvergallery* (summer daily 8.30am–10pm, winter daily 9am–8pm), a two-kilometre walk from the centre following the signs, is a complex of workshops and showrooms making and selling high-quality silver work – worth buying. It's hard to take the half-baked spiritual nonsense that accompanies it all seriously, but the work itself is fine. Back in town, the **Kautokeino kirke** is a delightful red wooden building decorated inside in bright, typically *Same* colours – seen again on Sunday in the costumes which turn out for the occasion. Nearby there is a small **open-air museum** featuring a few draughty-looking dwellings: you'll see the same little turf huts and skin tents all over Finnmark – usually housing summer souvenir stalls.

Now that the youth hostel has closed down, regular **accommodation** in Kautokeino is expensive, confined to the *Kautokeino Turisthotell* (☎084/56 205), where double rooms cost around 900Kr. There are, though, a couple of **campsites**, one with cabins available for rent, or if you can time the buses right, you could move on to Karasjok (see below) where there is a youth hostel and more reasonably-priced accommodation. Failing that, simply head for the open spaces and camp on the plains, though take care not to go too far – it's wild country. Incidentally, if you want to eat fried **reindeer**, then this – Chernobyl permitting – is the place to do it.

Karasjok

The only other settlement of any size on the plain, **KARASJOK**, known as the "Capital of the Lapps", is even more popular with tourists – though it's not greatly different to Kautokeino. The **Same Museum** (June–Aug daily 9am–6pm, rest of the year Mon–Fri 9am–3pm, weekends 10am–3pm; 10kr, students 5kr), near the bus station, is the last word on the *Same*, with a mass of cultural and applied art. The infrequent bus services might force you to spend the night in Karasjok – no great hardship. There's a **youth hostel** (☎084/66 446), the *Karakroa* at

Kautokeinoveien 9, open June to August, which will put you up for 60kr a night – and they have a selection of single and double rooms, too.

From Karasjok, **route 92** is a popular way to enter Finland, while the same road links Karasjok directly with Kautokeino (several buses weekly). Karasjok is also a stop for the *Nord-Norge Bussen* which continues up the E6 to Kirkenes; or conversely, returns to Alta and points south via LAKSELV (see p.264).

Hammerfest

As the tourist office takes great pains to point out, **HAMMERFEST** is the world's northernmost town; it was also, they add, the first town in Europe to have its streets lit by electric light. Hardly fascinating facts, but both give a glimpse of the pride that the locals take in having made the most of what is, indisputably, an inhospitable region. The harsh elements aside, the town was burnt to the ground in 1891 and, having been rebuilt, was promptly razed again, this time by retreating Germans at the end of World War II. Instead of being abandoned, Hammerfest was stubbornly rebuilt a second time and, rather than the grim industrial town you might expect, it is today a bright and rather elegant port. What really dominates Hammerfest, though, is fish: the *Findus* fish-processing plant is the town's main employer.

The town's main street, **Strandgatan**, runs parallel to the harbour, a bustling run of supermarkets, cafés and some rather chic clothes and souvenir shops – inspired by the town's function as a stopoff on the way to Nordkapp. Most action takes place down on the main quay, where the **coastal steamer** docks and the ship's tourists usually spend their hour or so on shore eating shellfish straight from the stalls along the wharf or buying souvenirs from the small summer *Same* market. The **tourist office** (open all year; ☎084/12 185) is a short walk left from the quay on Sjøgata and, if you are going to stay, can provide a map and information sheet.

Beyond that there isn't a great deal to see. Have a quick look inside the **Royal and Ancient Polar Bear Society** (Mon–Fri 8am–6pm, Sat & Sun 10am–3pm; free), in the basement of the town hall, which is full of stuffed specimens of the majestic animals. The society's museum tells the story of Hammerfest as a trapping centre and of its own dubious history as an organisation that hunted and trapped polar bears, eagles and arctic foxes. They'll try and cajole you into supporting the organisation by making you join . . . Honestly, you can live without the certificate.

Some practical details

Buses arrive (from Alta) and leave from down by the quay, and there are regular, if infrequent, connections back to the E6 for Nordkapp (north) and Alta (south). If you need **to stay**, the only cheap accommodation is at one of two **campsites** where you can rent cabins: the *NAF Camping Storvannet* (☎084/11 010), a fifteen-minute walk from the centre out by the sports stadium (mid-June to mid-Aug; four-bedded cabins for 150kr); and *Hammerfest Motell og Camping* (☎084/111 26), 1500m from the centre and open May to September. With more disposable income, try the *Brassica Hotel* (☎084/11 822), Storgata 9–11, whose double **rooms** go from around 550kr.

Honningsvåg and Nordkapp

A good 80km nearer the North Pole than Hammerfest (bus from Alta/ Hammerfest), **HONNINGSVÅG**'s official designation as a village has robbed it of the title of the world's northernmost town – though it is hardly any smaller, nor less hardy in the face of adversity, sitting as it does in the middle of a treeless windswept terrain surrounded by snow fences to protect it from avalanches. It's a fishing village primarily, but to travellers it's of more interest for its proximity to Nordkapp, 34km away – which, given the hit-and-miss nature of transport in these parts, may mean an overnight stay.

If it does, there's a **youth hostel/campsite/cabin** complex (☎084/75 113), open June to mid-August, 8km out on the road to Nordkapp and accessible by the same bus. It's beautifully situated on the Skipsfjord, costs just 50kr a night for a bed and serves superb meals – usually fish fresh from the fjord – as well as all-day life-saving breakfasts. In the village itself, the *Rogers Inn* at Norkappveien 79 (☎084/72 465) costs around 450kr double. If you need to **eat** in the village, there are several take-away kiosks along Storgata and a couple of cafés back near the hotel – one on the harbour front, the other the inspiringly named *Café Ritz* over the road.

If you do stay out at the hostel, be aware of the early departure times of **onward transport**: the southbound coastal steamer leaves at 6.45am, the first bus to Lakselv at 7am – you may need to book an early taxi (number from the youth hostel) to take you into town to pick these up. The **tourist office** (open all year; ☎084/72 894), in *Nordkapphuset*, a community and exhibition centre next to the bus station in Honningsvåg, has full details on all routes.

Getting To Nordkapp

Rounding Nordkapp **by coastal steamer** is still the most impressive way to see Nordkapp, but this can only be done from April to mid-May. The rest of the **summer**, the steamer puts in at Honningsvåg, from where you catch a special hire-coach which gets you there and back within the two-hour stop (130kr return).

If you're not travelling by *Hurtigrute*, or this seems pricey, there's enough tourist traffic in summer to make **hitching** a possibility. Better, though, is the **bus**, which runs there and back from Honningsvåg at least a couple of times daily throughout the summer (first one to Nordkapp at 12.20pm, the last one arriving back in Honningsvøg at 1.15am; 75kr return).

As for **winter**, it's not really on: the *Hurtigrute* steamer doesn't round the Cape, and even when the road is open there's no public transport link. Assuming the road is open, the only option is a **taxi**. These leave from the quayside and charge around 400kr plus 15kr per person for the return trip.

Nordkapp – Europe's northernmost point

Although **Nordkapp** is the real goal, walking at least some of the winding road out there is rewarding. The road slowly twists its way up from Honningsvåg and then runs for the Cape across the tundra, mountains stretching away on either side. From June to October this is pastureland for reindeer, and there are herds of them grazing right up to the road. Traffic tends to frighten them away but on foot you will be able to get quite close. The *Same* who bring them here every summer set up camp at the roadside in full costume, selling clothes, jewellery and antler sets, which many travellers attach to the front of their cars. The feeling of complete isolation hits quickly. There are snow-patches still around as the road ascends to the plateau, and a coat is a good idea even in high summer. In winter the road is closed, blocked by snow, and some years doesn't open until the beginning of June.

Nordkapp itself might be expected to be a bit of a disappointment. It is, after all, only a cliff with an arguable claim to being the northernmost point of Europe. (Nearby, but inaccessible, Knivskjellodden actually stretches about 1500m further north.) But there is something about this bleak, wind-battered promontory that excites the senses. The nineteenth-century traveller Richard Acerbi in his *Travels to the North Cape* was one of many who got carried away by it all. "The northern sun", he wrote, "creeping at midnight along the horizon, and the immeasurable ocean in apparent contact with the skies, form the grand outlines in the sublime picture presented to the astonished spectator." Quite.

Originally a *Same* sacrificial site, Nordkapp was named (the "North Cape") by the English explorer Richard Chancellor in 1553, as he drifted along the Norwegian coast in an attempt to find the Northeast Passage. He failed, but the trade route he opened to Russia brought the Cape to the attention of others. Louis Philippe of Orleans, later king of France, visited during his Scandinavian exile and was followed in 1873 by Oscar II, whose visit opened the tourist floodgates. These days **North Cape Hall** contains a post office (where you get your letters specially stamped), souvenir shop and cafeteria, though it's all really only busy when the tour buses arrive – and even then, a few minutes' walk can take you somewhere completely isolated. Francesco Negri, who visited Nordkapp in 1664 probably summed it up best: "I am now standing at North Cape, on the utmost point of Finnmark – on the very edge of the world. Here the world ends, as does my curiosity, and I shall now turn homewards, God willing . . ."

East to Kirkenes and the Soviet border

Beyond Nordkapp the landscape is more of the same, a bleak and relentless expanse of barren plateaux and ocean. Occasionally the picture is relieved by a determined fishing village commanding sweeping views over the fjords that slice into the mainland. But there is little here for the eyes of a tourist, nothing to do in what are predominantly fishing and industrial towns, and few tangible attractions beyond the sheer impossibility of the landscape. This in itself can be fascinating, however: it's difficult to feel further estranged from regular western comforts than here, and after a while the alien scenery becomes strangely compelling.

The most spectacular way to travel is by the **coastal steamer** as far as KIRKENES (which then returns to Bergen). This also saves on accommodation problems: there's only one youth hostel (at Lakselv) on the way, and very limited budget accommodation, which means a tent can also come in handy. **Camping** space is plentiful and official campsites often have cabins for rent, but the sites are geared towards car travellers and are often some way out of town. **Buses** run regularly although generally only once a day and not at all overnight, so be prepared to spend the night somewhere. Consider **standby flights** as a way to get at least one way quickly – Tromsø to Kirkenes is perhaps the most useful connection, from where you can slowly make your way back west.

The land route east: Skaidi, Lakselv and Tana Bru

The land route east is via the E6 Arctic Highway, which you pick up in **SKAIDI** – also the nearest stop for the *Nord-Norge Bussen*, which continues on to Karasjok in Finnmark, and east to Kirkenes. The road follows the western side of the Porsangerfjord and its occasional fishing villages to **LAKSELV**, whose main interest is good fishing on the river (*Lakselv* means salmon river) and its **youth hostel** (☎084/61 476), open June to August only. Beds here cost 90kr (doubles 250kr) and you can swim nearby as well as rent rowing boats – the only drawback being that the hostel is 7km from the village itself, a long walk but not unpleasant. As well as being on the *Nord-Norge Bussen* route, Lakselv is linked directly with Honningsvåg by bus (two daily), so even if you don't have a great deal of time, you can still take in a little of the country beyond Nordkapp quite easily.

The bus then continues south to Karasjok before moving on to **TANA BRU** (several local campsites), a *Same* settlement around the suspension bridge over the River Tana, which sweeps down to the Tanafjord and the Arctic Ocean. (Twice weekly during summer a **bus** also runs north from Lakselv across the peninsula to IFJORD, and then south to rejoin the main road at Tana Bru.) From here, the main road runs along the southern side of the Varangerfjord. It's a bleak, weather-beaten run, all colour and vegetation confined to the northern side, with its scattered farms and painted fishing boats. As the road swings inland, it's something of a relief to arrive in Kirkenes (see below).

The sea route east: by Hurtigrute

Few people travel to the towns on the far eastern **Varanger peninsula**, north of Kirkenes and, frankly, unless you are travelling by ship, it is a long ride just to say you have been there. The *Hurtigrute*, on the other hand, steers a fine route into the deep blue water of the Varangerfjord, edging its way between islands and rock bluffs. There's snow on the mainland even in July, which makes for a picturesque run across the fjord, the odd fishing boat the only thing in sight. The steamer stops at the fishing villages of BÅTSFJORD and BERLEVÅG, which sit amid a landscape of eerie green and grey rock and cliff, splashes of colour in a land otherwise stripped by the elements.

It's more attractive to press on to **VARDØ**, Norway's most easterly town. The star-shaped **fortress** raised here by Christian V in 1738 has remained virtually unchanged over the years – something explained by the fact that it has never seen active service. Scrambling around the ramparts is good fun, and there is a small **museum** within the walls (2kr) which contains a surviving beam from an earlier medieval fortress, signed by a later succession of Norwegian kings. If you haven't already worked out what's missing from the flat and barren landscape, it becomes obvious when you see Vardø's one and only **tree**, a rowan sheltered inside the fortress.

The **tourist office** is inside the only hotel in town – the *Norten Hotel Barents* – and can direct you to the *Gjestegården* pension, Strandgate 72 (☎085/87 529), which has double rooms at 380kr, including breakfast. Other than that, there's plenty of room to **camp rough**. Bear in mind, though, that Vardø is the only Norwegian town within the arctic climatic zone, obvious when you can see your breath on a bright July afternoon. There is no through road west of Vardø, and if travelling by bus you will have to return the way you came – to Vadsø.

VADSØ used to be Finnish speaking, and even now half the population claims Finnish origin. On the island of Vadsøya, where the original town stood, is the mast to which Roald Amundsen's airship, *Norge*, was moored in 1926 – about the only thing to survive the war intact, Russian bomber attacks adding to the destruction caused by German fires. There is nothing to do in today's town, although there is a **tourist office** (June–Aug Mon–Fri 10am–5pm, Sat 10am–3pm). If you need **to stay**, *Lailas Gjestehus* (☎085/53 335), Brugate 2, has doubles for around 300–400kr including breakfast, and there's a **campsite** (☎085/51 622), 500m from the church – open all year and with cabins to rent. There are daily **buses**, too, from Vadsø to Kirkenes, but note that the *Hurtigrute* doesn't always stop here – see "Travel Details".

Kirkenes and the Soviet border

During World War II the mining town of **KIRKENES** suffered more bomb attacks than any other place in Europe apart from Malta. What was left was torched by the German army retreating in the face of the liberating Russian troops, who found 3500 local people hiding in the nearby iron-ore mines. The mines are still working and provide the obvious prosperity in what is a brand new town, with rows of uniform wooden houses arranged around a central grid behind the harbour.

If it sounds grim, it's not to slight Kirkenes, which has certainly suffered. In fact, it's rather an intriguing town, with some pleasant gardens and residential areas, its surroundings best seen as you edge in by steamer. It's also, perhaps, one of the few towns in the world which it seems almost churlish to leave quickly, given the effort involved in reaching it.

The *Hurtigrute* **coastal steamer** docks down at the busy harbour and spends two hours here every morning preparing for the return journey to Bergen. It won't take any longer than this to see the town. The **bus station** is also down at the harbour and the *Nord-Norge Bussen* leaves daily at 10am for Fauske. Other buses leave for Vadsø (daily; 125kr), and the airport (connects with flights; 30kr). The **tourist office** (June Mon–Fri 8am–8pm, Sat noon–6pm; July & Aug same hours plus Sun noon–6pm; ☎085/92 544) is behind the *Rica Hotel* in a little wooden hut just off the E6.

There are a couple of **campsites** in the vicinity: one, *Kirkenes Camping* (☎085/98 028), is 7km out of town on the E6, and has cabins available, though you may well have to walk there as buses are at best infrequent and non-existent on Sundays. The only other budget alternative is to try *Storby's Overnatting*, at Riiser Larsensgate 10, which has a few **beds** available from 125kr each. Or grit your teeth and pay up for the *Rica Hotel* (☎085/91 159), whose regular prices are expensive (around 700kr double) but can sometimes be cut by taking up one of their more reasonable summer price deals.

The Soviet border
The **Soviet border**, to which the tourist office runs trips, is only 16km away from Kirkenes. In these *glasnost* days, you can now take photographs of the frontier, provided you don't snap any Soviet personnel or military installations – which rather limits you as there's little else there. At the moment, there is no road or any other crossing over the border from here unless you're on a tour – in which case you'll have to get off the Norwegian bus and cross the border on foot. There

are moves afoot, though, to re-open the route to Murmansk, which – if it ever happens – would be a ride well worth making. In the meantime, you'll have to be content with the reflection that if you have made it to Kirkenes and the border, you are further east than Istanbul and as far north as central Greenland . . .

Spitzbergen

Named after its "needle-like" mountains by Barents in 1596, the archipelago of **Spitzbergen** (Svalbard to the Norwegians) must be one of the most inhospitable places on earth. Six hundred and forty kilometres north of the Norwegian mainland, it's largely covered with ice, the soil frozen down to five hundred metres in places. Certainly, it's hard to believe that it was once covered with lush, tropical forest – the remains of which account for a continuing Norwegian presence there, alongside a substantial Russian mining community, around 4000 people in all. Yet there are convincing reasons to make a trip to this oddly fertile land. Between April and August there's continuous daylight; the snow virtually all melts by July, leaving the valleys covered in flowers; and there's an abundance of wildlife – arctic foxes, polar bears and reindeer on land, and seals, walrus, even whales offshore.

The Norwegian tourist board does its best to put you off going: its literature states that there is "no accommodation, cafeteria or restaurants or provision stores at Spitzbergen", and without doubt, it's not a trip to be undertaken lightly. That said, there is a year-round *Braathens SAFE/SAS* **flight**, operating out of Tromsø, up to four times weekly; it takes an hour and a half, and standard fares are from 1360kr one-way. You'll land at **LONGYEARBYEN**, roughly in the middle of the main island and the only real settlement of any size. Despite the dire warnings, there is one shop, reputedly a restaurant, and it is even apparently possible to find **rooms** in Longyearbyen, though you'd be well advised to check before setting out: the tourist office in Tromsø should be able to help, or write to The Governor's Office, N-9170 Longyearbyen, Norway for more information. Permission is usually given, too, to visit the Russian settlement, home to around twice as many people as live in Longyearbyen.

The real difficulties lie in getting around and finding anywhere to stay, and it's normally better to travel to Spitzbergen on an **organised tour**. Expensive adventure "cruises" (polar bear spotting and the like) again depart from Tromsø (and some other places), and again you should contact the Tromsø tourist office or the Norwegian tourist board for more information. It's also possible to go on a tour from Britain: *Arctic Experience* (see *Basics* for address and details) run complete fifteen-day camping excursions to Spitzbergen in July and August, for around £1400 all-in. If this tempts anyone, we would be very interested to receive accounts of any kind of trips made to Spitzbergen for inclusion in the next edition.

travel details

Nord-Norge Bussen
From Nordkojsbotn, reached from Narvik and Tromsø, to Alta (1 daily; 11hr).
From Alta to Skaidi/Lakselv/Karasjok/Tana Bru/ Kirkenes (2 daily; 2hr/4hr 30min/6hr/9hr/12hr). See also "Travel Details", Chapter Seven.

Buses
From Tromsø to Nordkjosbotn (3–5 daily; 1hr 30min); Narvik (2–3 daily; 5hr 30min); Alta (1 daily; 7hr).
From Alta to Skaidi/Honningsvåg (Mon–Sat 2 daily, Sun 1; 2hr/5hr); Hammerfest (Mon–Sat 2

daily, Sun 1; 2hr/3hr); Kautokeino (1 daily; 3hr); Tromsø (1 daily; 7hr).

From Hammerfest to Skaidi/Honningsvåg (Mon–Sat 2 daily, Sun 1; 1hr 15min/4hr 20min); Alta/Oslo (April to Sept 3 weekly; 3hr 30min/ 29hr).

From Honningsvåg to Lakselv (2 daily; 4hr); Nordkapp (1st week June to 1st week Aug 4 daily; 10 days either side 1–2 daily; 50min).

From Kautokeino to Karasjok (Mon, Wed, Fri & Sun 1 daily; 2hr); Alta (3 weekly; 1hr 40min).

From Karasjok to Inari/Ivalo/Rovaniemi in Finland (1 daily; 9hr 30min).

From Lakselv to Honningsvåg (2 daily; 4hr); Tana Bru (summer 2 weekly; 4hr 20min).

From Kirkenes to Vadsø (1–2 daily; 3hr 30min).

From Vadsø to Vardø (1–3 daily; 1hr 30min).

Hurtigrute Coastal Steamer

Northbound 1 daily from Harstad to Kirkenes via Tromsø, Hammerfest, Honningsvåg, Vardø, Vadsø (Sun & Thurs only) in 39hr.

Southbound 1 daily from Kirkenes to Harstad via Vadsø (Mon, Tues, Wed, Fri & Sat only), Vardø, Honningsvåg, Hammerfest, Tromsø in 39hr.

PART FOUR

SWEDEN

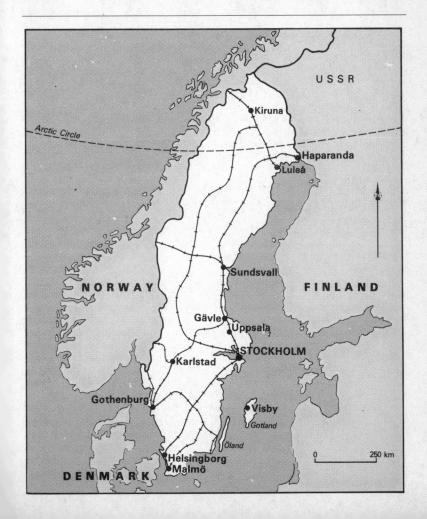

Introduction

Sweden lolls contentedly within an endless natural beauty. Remote, expensive, cold – all of these generalisations may be true, but none are exact. However, Sweden *is* large, clean and efficient and, as it boasts no single concentration of sights (other than in Stockholm), you're as likely to fetch up on a sunny Baltic beach as camp in the forest or hike through national parks.

One aspect of the country most likely to impinge on the cluttered eye of Europeans is the sense of space. Away from the relatively densely-populated south, travelling without seeing a soul is not uncommon and taking these vast, unpopulated stretches in a limited time can be exhausting – and unrewarding. Better, on a short trip, to delve into one or two regions and feel the atmosphere, to get to know the pervasive nature which shapes the Swedes' attitude to life: once you have broken through the oft-quoted reserve of the people there is a definite emotive feel to the country. And initial contact is easy, as almost everyone speaks functional, often perfect, English.

■ Where to go

The **south and southwest** of the country are flat holiday lands. For so long disputed Danish territory (which the landscape certainly resembles), the provinces now harbour a host of historic ports (including **Gothenburg**, **Helsingborg** and **Malmö**) and less frenetic beach towns – all old and mostly fortified. Off the **southeast** coast, the Baltic islands of **Öland** and **Gotland** are the country's most hyped resorts – and with good reason, supporting a lazy beach-life to match that of the best southern European spots – but without the hotel blocks, crowds and tat.

Central and northern Sweden is the country of tourist brochures: great swathes of forest, inexhaustible (around 96,000) lakes and some of the best wilderness hiking in Europe. Two train routes link north with south. The eastern run, close to the **Bothnian coast**, passes old wood-built towns and planned new ones, and ferry ports for connections to Finland. In the centre, the trains of the **Inland Railway** strike off through some remarkably changing nature, lakelands to mountains, clearing reindeer off the track as they go. Both routes meet in Sweden's **far north** – home of the *Same*, oldest indigenous Scandinavian people. Here, the Midnight Sun keeps the days long and bright; and in high summer, the sun never sets.

Of the cities, **Stockholm** is supreme. A bundle of islands housing regal and monumental architecture, fine museums and the country's most active culture and nightlife: it is a likely point of arrival and a vital stop-off. Two university towns, **Uppsala** and **Lund**, demand a visit, too, while nearly all of the other major cities can make some sort of cultural claim on your attention; chiefly Gävle, Umeå, Gällivare and Kiruna. Time is rarely wasted in humbler towns either, the immediate beauty of the local surroundings adequately compensating for any lack of specific sights.

■ When to go

Summer in Sweden is short and hectic. From rowdy Midsummer's Night onwards, accommodation is scarce and trains packed as Swedes head out to the country and onto the beaches. Outside the peak, **July**, things are noticeably quieter. To avoid the rush, September and late May are both usually bright and warm. The **Midnight Sun** extends the days in June and July, and above the Arctic Circle it virtually never gets dark. Elsewhere it stays light until very late, up to midnight and beyond. Thanks to the Gulf Stream, temperatures in Sweden are surprisingly high – see the temperature chart in *Basics* – and, on the south coast, can be as hot as any southern European resort.

Winter, on the other hand, can be a miserable experience without the proper clothing. It lasts long (November to April solid) and gets very cold indeed, temperatures of -15°C and below are not unusual even in Stockholm. Further north it is positively arctic. The days are short and dark (in the far north the sun barely rises at all) and biting winds cut through the most elaborate of padded coats. On the plus side, the snow stays crisp and white, the air is clean, the water everywhere frozen solid; a paradise for skaters and skiers. Stockholm, too, is particularly beautiful with its winter covering of snow and ice.

Getting There

The cheapest Scandinavian connection with Sweden is from Denmark, by bus and ferry, and regular trains and ferries connect other mainland countries. Getting there by plane is inevitably more expensive, but for details of special internal deals, see under *Basics*, "Getting Around".

■ Trains

There are four possible **train** routes into Sweden **from Norway**. Cheapest is the five-hour run from Oslo to Gothenburg (313Nkr) and the slightly longer route from Oslo to Stockholm (450Nkr); the twelve-hour ride from Trondheim to Stockholm and the day-long (23-hr) haul from Narvik to the capital are both reasonable at around 500Nkr.

Trains **from Denmark** (Copenhagen) to Gothenburg (around 200Dkr) or Stockholm (around 900Dkr) use the Helsingør–Helsingborg ferry crossing, the whole train taken on board – a four-and-a-half and eight-and-a-half hour journey respectively.

Anyone under 26 can buy a *BIJ* **ticket** for these routes and all **rail passes** are valid too. Note that a *Nordturist* or *InterRail* train pass gives free or discounted travel on various ferry lines between Denmark or Finland and Sweden – see below for more details.

■ Buses

There are several useful **bus** routes into Sweden from other Scandinavian cities, though the frequent services **from Denmark** are the only ones that will get you there quickly. Easiest connection is on one of the several daily buses from Copenhagen to Malmö/Lund (45Dkr/50Dkr), using the Dragör–Limhamn ferry. The *Kystlinien* service (around 100Dkr) links Kastrup airport and Copenhagen with Helsingborg, using the ferry from Helsingør, the bus continuing up the south-western coast of Sweden to Halmstad to connect with trains to Gothenburg. If you're heading for Stockholm, then daily buses (around 100Dkr) from Kastrup/Copenhagen also run via Helsingør to Ängelholm airport in Sweden to connect with regular flights to the capital.

It's a longer haul **from Norway**, and much more expensive, too: there are several daily buses from Oslo to Gothenburg, the journey taking five or six hours; and one daily bus from Oslo to Stockholm, a nine-hour ride. **From Finland** most routes converge upon Helsinki or Turku and then use the ferry crossings to Stockholm: departures are at least once-daily and cost from 150Fmk.

■ Ferries and hydrofoils

Ferry or hydrofoil services to Sweden are plentiful, and to make any sense of the timetables and prices which change from year to year, check the companies' brochures and ask at any local tourist office. You'll find other details – frequencies and journey times – in the **Travel Details** at the end of each chapter. **Prices** range from under 20DKr for the short Helsingør–Helsingborg crossing to around 125Fmk for a deck-class ticket from Helsinki; more prices are given below. In addition, a couple of rail passes give **discounts and free travel** on some of the ferry routes. The **Nordturist** pass currently gives free passage on the *SJ* and *DSB* ferries between Helsingør and Helsingborg, the Turku–Stockholm (*Silja Line* only) and Fredrikshavn–Gothenburg (*Stena Line*) crossings; as well as a 50 percent discount on the routes Helsinki–Stockholm (*Silja Line*), Copenhagen–Malmö (*DS* hydrofoil only) and Vasa–Umeå (*Vaasanlaivat*). And an **InterRail plus Boat** pass gives free travel on a'l *Silja* and *Stena Line* ferries.

From Denmark

Shortest and cheapest ferry crossings are Helsingør–Helsingborg (25min) and Dragör–Limhamn near Malmö (55min); just walk on board on both ferries. There are also year-round ferry connections to Gothenburg from Fredrikshavn, which cost around 50Dkr, a three-and-a-half-hour journey. And from Grenå, *Lion* sail daily to Varberg, Halmstad and Helsingborg for a fare of around 70Dkr. Quicker (45min), are the more expensive hydrofoil services to Malmö and Helsingborg from Copenhagen (70Dkr) – though these crossings are often disrupted by frozen sea between November and March. The other approach from Denmark is to come via the Danish island of Bornholm. Ferries from Copenhagen run to Rønne, from where you can cross daily to Ystad, on the southern Swedish coast (around 90Dkr).

From Finland

Longer ferry journeys link Sweden with Finland, the major crossing the Helsinki–Stockholm route, a fourteen-hour trip with either *Silja* or *Viking* that costs from 125Fmk. There are regular crossings from Turku (54Fmk) and from Mariehamn (33Fmk) in the Finnish Åland Islands to Stockholm. If you're aiming for the north of Sweden then you might be better crossing from Vaasa: there are year-round services to Umeå, Sundsvall and Örnsköldsvik, journeys of between four to eight hours and costing from around 65–80Fmk. There is also a crossing from Kaskinen, south of Vaasa, to Gävle (95–120Fmk), a ten-hour ride.

From Norway

There's one crossing from Norway to Sweden, from Sandefjord to Strömstad, north of Gothenburg: it operates twice daily all year, takes two and a half hours and costs 75–90Nkr one-way.

Costs, Money and Banks

Sweden _is_ expensive, but certain bargains make it a better deal than neighbouring Norway and Finland. If you don't already have a rail pass, flying standby (around £15 anywhere for under 26s) is a fast and affordable option in cutting travel costs. Elsewhere, regional and city discount travel passes ease what could otherwise be a burden. Accommodation, too, can be good value: youth hostels are all around £6 a night, or less, and of exceptional quality; campsites are plentiful and cheap. Eating is made bearable by the daily lunch offers found throughout the country – around £4 for a big, all-inclusive meal plus drink.

Put all this together and you'll find you can exist – camping, self-catering, hitching, no drinking – on around £6–8 a day, though hardly for any length of time. Stay in hostels, eat lunch, get out and see the sights and this will rise to anything from £15–25. And to these figures add on £3 for every drink in a bar, around £1.50 for coffee and cake and £15 minimum a night in a hotel. Remember, though, that the countryside (and much of your camping) is free, museums usually have low (or no) admission charges and that everything everywhere is clean, bright and works.

■ Money and banks

Swedish **currency** is the _krona_ (plural _kronor_), made up of 100 öre. It comes in coins of 10öre and 50öre, 1kr and 5kr; and notes of 10kr, 50kr, 100kr, 500kr, 1000kr and 10,000kr.

You can change money in **banks** all over Sweden, which are open Mon–Fri 9.30am–3pm, though branches in Stockholm and Gothenburg have longer summer hours (see the various city "Listings" sections). Outside normal banking hours you'll also be able to change money in exchange offices at airports and ferry terminals, and in post offices (look for the "PK Exchange" sign); as well as at _Forex_ exchange offices – again, see the relevant "Listings" sections.

Communications

Communications – post and phones – within Sweden are good, and as most people speak at least some English you won't go far wrong in the post or telephone office. You'll be able to keep in touch with home by tuning into the TV – which relies heavily on English and American programmes – and listening in to one of the English-language radio stations.

■ Post

Post offices are open Mon–Fri 9am–6pm, Sat 10am–1pm, with some branches closed on Saturday throughout July, Sweden's holiday month. You can buy **stamps** at post offices, most newspaper kiosks, tobacconists and hotels: letters and cards within Europe cost 3.30kr, to the other Nordic countries 2.30kr. **Poste restante** is available at all main post offices; take your passport along to claim mail.

■ Phones

For international **telephone calls** either head for the (rare) **telephone office** (_Tele_ or _Telebutik_), usually open outside normal shopping hours until around 9pm daily, or dial direct from public **payphones**. This is very easy: the phones take 2kr and 5kr coins and the operators all speak English. A new service, the **Turist Telefon**, offers half-price calls from pay-phones in the major cities between mid-June and mid-August; the kiosks are clearly marked.

International codes **from Sweden** are given in _Basics_. For reverse charge international calls ring the **overseas operator** ☎0018. The **directory enquiries** number in Sweden is ☎07975.

■ Media

Assuming that you don't read Swedish, you can keep in touch with world events by buying **foreign newspapers** in the major towns and cities, sometimes on the day of issue, more usually the day after.

Swedish **TV**, as in the rest of Scandinavia, is fairly unchallenging stuff. On top of the two Swedish state channels, _Kanal 1_ and _TV2_, there's a new commercial station, _TV3_, shared with Denmark and Norway, and a whole host of satellite and cable channels – all of which you'll end up glued to if you've blown all your money on a hotel and can't afford to go out. The good news is that imported foreign programmes are in their original language, so you don't have to miss *Miami Vice* and *Minder*.

On the **radio** there's national (ie Swedish) news in English on *Radio Sweden International*, daily in summer at 1pm, 2.30pm, 4pm, 6pm, 8.30pm, 11pm, 1am and 4.30am (throughout the country on 1179kHz MW; in Greater Stockholm on 89.5FM). Gothenburg local radio also has a daily half-hour programme in English, covering the latest news and giving sightseeing tips. The BBC *World Service* can be heard on 61.95MHz.

Getting Around

Sweden's internal transport system is quick and efficient and runs through all weathers. Services are often reduced in the winter (especially on northern bus routes), but it's unlikely you'll ever get stranded anywhere. In summer, when everyone is on holiday, trains and (less so) buses are packed: on long journeys making seat reservations is a good idea.

All train, bus, ferry and plane schedules are contained within the giant **Restider** (timetable), of which every tourist office and travel agent has a copy. It's not worth buying (it's 30kr) or carrying around; just ask for photocopies of the relevant pages.

Watch, too, for city and regional **discount cards**. One payment gets a card valid for anything from a day to a week and usually includes **unlimited local travel** (bus, tram, ferry, sometimes train), museum entry and other discounts and freebies. Often on sale during the summer only (valuable exceptions are those in Stockholm and Gothenburg), where useful they are detailed in the text. Otherwise it's worth asking at tourist offices as schemes change frequently. Other cities/regions that currently have discount cards are Malmö, Helsingborg, Norrköping, Östersund, Småland region (including Öland), Gotland, Västerbotten and Norrbotten.

■ Trains

Swedish State Railways (**SJ** – *Statens Järnvägar*) has an extensive network, running right into the north of the country above the Arctic Circle and on into Norway (to Narvik). Other than flying, it's the quickest way to get around Sweden's vast expanses. The service is

excellent, especially on the main routes: Stockholm and Gothenburg, for example, are now linked by fast, hourly trains.

Tickets are expensive but, happily, it's almost never neccessary to pay the full rate. Full second-class **fares** only apply on Friday and Sunday; on all other days there's a 25 percent discount. Other deals include: *InterRail/Nordturist* passes valid for unlimited travel, fifty percent discounts for Senior Citizens and under-16s, and a top one-way second class fare of 430kr for all journeys of 881km or over. Also, from mid-June to mid-August a supplement of 50kr lets you travel first class on most trains. More details from any railway station in Sweden, or Norwegian State Railways (SJ's agents) in London (21–24 Cockspur Street, SW1; ☎071-930 6666). You'll find that nearly all railway staff speak good English, which means you've got more than a sporting chance of buying the right ticket every time: conversely, it's difficult to be convincing if you're caught by the conductor in possession of an invalid or wrong ticket.

To ensure a seat, you might want to make a **reservation**: on some trains – indicated by an "R" or "IC" in the timetable – it's compulsory and costs 15kr. One booklet worth picking up is the free *SJ Tågtider* **timetable** from any railway station. Published twice yearly, this is an accurate and comprehensive list of the most useful train services in the country, except for those of the Inlandsbanan and Pågatågen (see below). Otherwise, each train route has its own timetable leaflet, available free from the local station.

The Inlandsbanan

If you're in Sweden for any length of time at all, then travelling at least a section of the **Inlandsbanan** (Inland Railway) is a must: a single track route which runs for over 1300km from Kristinehamn to arctic Gällivare. Although part of the SJ network, the *Inlandsbanan* operates largely as a tourist venture in the summer and is accessible on a very cheap inclusive ticket (around 440kr for 14 days, 495kr for 21 days, unlimited travel). Details, again, from most large railway stations and see the "Central and Northern Sweden" chapter for a full user's guide.

Pågatågen

In southern Sweden, in Skåne, a local private company, **Pågatågen**, operates trains between

Helsingborg, Lund and Malmö. They're fully auto-
mated and you buy your tickets from a machine
on the platform which accepts coins and notes.
Railcards aren't valid on these trains, but prices
on the short hops are low.

■ Buses

Long distance buses (*Expressbussar*) tend to be
operated by *SJ* (most bus stations are adjacent to
the railway station) on express routes between
large towns, and to and from Stockholm.
Complementing rather than competing with the
rail system, you'll find that the *Expressbuss* often
only runs at weekends (usually Friday and
Sunday), and tends to be cheaper than the equivalent train-ride: Helsingborg to Stockholm, for
example, costs just 160kr. In the north, buses are
more frequent since they're used to carry mail to
isolated regions. Several companies operate daily
services, and fares are broadly similar. Major
routes are listed in the "Travel Details" at the
end of each chapter and you can pick up a
comprehensive **timetable** at any *Expressbuss*
terminal.

    Local buses, too, are frequent and regular.
Count on using them, as many hostels and campsites are a fair distance from town centres. Flat
fares cost 6–9kr, the ticket usually valid for an
hour. Most large towns operate some sort of
discount system where you can buy cheaper
books of tickets – details from the local tourist
office and in the text.

■ Planes

The **plane** network is operated by *SAS* and
Linjeflyg and various deals can make flying a real
steal, especially those long slogs north. **Mini-
pris** family fares mean the first passenger pays
the full fare, but an accompanying spouse and
children pay only 200kr each for travel to or from
Stockholm; certain routes on certain days carry
25–65 percent reductions on normal fares;
Senior Citizens pay a flat rate of 200kr or 300kr,
depending on distance, for one-way fares (400kr
if the journey involves changing in Stockholm);
and **under 26s** can fly standby anywhere in
Sweden for 150kr or 200kr, depending on
distance, one-way – 250kr if you have to change
in Stockholm. **Children** under two travel free.
Most of these fares have to be booked in
advance; more details from local travel agents
and tourist offices.

■ Ferries

Unlike Norway and Finland, domestic **ferry**
services in Sweden are few. The various archipelagos on the southeast coast are served by small
ferries, the most comprehensive network being
within the **Stockholm archipelago**, for which
you can buy an island-hopping boat pass – see
"Stockholm and Around" for more details. The
other major link is between the Baltic island of
Gotland and the mainland (at Nynäshamn,
Oskarshamn and Västervik), very popular routes in
summer for which you should really book ahead –
all the relevant details are covered in Chapter
Eleven. With your own boat it's possible to cross
Sweden between Stockholm and Gothenburg on
the **Göta Canal** or, alternatively, you can take an
expensive cruise along the same route; ticket and
journey details are given on p.355

■ Cars, hitching and taxis

Driving presents few problems since roads are
good and generally reliable. The only real danger
are the reindeer (in the north) and elk (north and
further south) which wander onto roads. Watch
out in bad light particularly – if you hit one, you'll
know about it. As for **documentation**, you need
a full licence and the vehicle registration document; an international driving licence and
insurance "green card" are not essential. **Speed
limits** are 110kph on motorways, 90kph and
70kph on other roads, 50kph in built-up areas –
although between mid-June and mid-August the
110kph limit drops to 90kph on most roads. It's
compulsory to use **dipped headlights** during
daylight hours; and, if you are taking your own
car, remember to get the beam of your headlights
adjusted to suit **driving on the right**. If you're
motoring into northern Sweden then it's recommended that you fit mud flaps to your wheels and
stone guards on the front of caravans. Swedish
drink/driving laws are among the toughest in
Europe and random breath-tests the norm. Even
the smallest amount of alcohol can lead to lost
licences (always), fines (often) and prison
sentences (not infrequently).

    Despite the amount of holiday traffic and the
number of young Swedes with cars, **hitching** is
rarely worth the effort as long-distance lifts are
few and far between. Shorter hops are easier to
find, especially when travelling along the coasts
and in the north, but not having to rely upon
hitching as your main means of transport is the

best bet. If you do try it, always use a sign and be prepared for long waits.

Taxis are no bargain anywhere. A three-kilometre ride will set you back around 60kr and there's a minimum charge of around 15kr. If you order a taxi by phone, that adds another 30kr to the total – all in all, taxis are worth avoiding in cities where the public transport systems are excellent.

Car hire and petrol prices

Car hire is uniformly expensive, though most hire companies have special weekend tourist rates – from around 400kr, Friday to Monday, for a small car. It's worth checking out local tourist offices in the summer which sometimes recommend or operate cheapish weekly deals; otherwise, expect to pay around 2500kr a week, unlimited mileage, for a *VW Golf* or similar-sized car in the summer months. The major international companies are represented in all the large towns and cities – details under the various city "Listings".

Petrol currently costs around 5kr per litre; lead-free petrol is widely available and slightly cheaper. Most petrol stations are self-service (*Tanka Själv*) and lots of them have automatic pumps (*Sedel Automat*) where you fill up at any time using 10kr and 100kr notes.

■ Cycling

A much better way to get around independently is to **cycle**. Some parts of the country were made for it; the southern provinces (and Gotland in particular) are ideal for a leisurely pedal. Many towns are best explored by bike and tourist offices, campsites and youth hostels often rent out machines from around 50kr a day, 200kr a week. If touring, be prepared for long-distance hauls in the north and for rain in summer. Taking a bike on a train counts as luggage and will cost you 50kr.

The *Svenska Cykelsällskapet* (cycling association; Box 6006, S-164 06 Kista, Stockholm; ☎08/751 62 04) signposts **cycle routes** in central and northern Sweden; and there's an English-language **guidebook** to cycling in Sweden, available from *Cykelfrämjandet*, Box 6027, S-102 31 Stockholm (☎08/32 16 80). Also, contact the *STF* (see below) for details of cycling package holidays in Sweden, which include youth hostel accommodation, meals and cycle hire.

Sleeping

Surprisingly, finding somewhere cheap to sleep is not the hassle that might be expected in an otherwise expensive country – provided you're prepared to do some advance planning. There's an excellent network of youth hostels and campsites, while in the cities private rooms and bed and breakfast places are common. Year-round discounts even make hotels affordable, an option certainly worth considering in the large cities where a city discount card is thrown in as part of the package.

■ Hotels

Hotels come cheaper than you'd think in Sweden. Although there's little chance of a room under 200kr a night anywhere, you may fall lucky in Stockholm and the bigger cities during the summer, especially July, when the Swedes all head south out of the country. The rest of the year, rooms at weekends are much cheaper than midweek, when business travellers push up prices. On average, for a room with TV and bathroom you can expect to pay from 350kr single, 500kr double. Nearly all hotels include breakfast in the price – which, given its size, can form a useful saving.

The best **package deals** are those operated in Malmö, Stockholm and Gothenburg, where 185–220kr (minimum) gets you a hotel bed for one night, breakfast and the relevant city discount card thrown in. These schemes are generally valid from mid-June to mid-August and at weekends throughout the year, but see the accommodation details under the city accounts for more exact information.

The other option to consider is buying into a **hotel pass** scheme, where you pay in advance for a series of vouchers or cheques which then allow discounts or free accommodation in various hotel chains throughout the country. Further details about this are found in the free booklet *Hotels in Sweden*, available from the National Tourist Board in London, which also lists every hotel in the country.

■ Youth Hostels

The biggest choice (indeed, quite often the only choice) lies with the country's huge chain of **youth hostels** (*Vandrarhem*), operated by the *Svenska Turistföreningen* (*STF*: Vasagatan 48,

Stockholm; ☎08/790 31 00). There are 280 hostels in the country, mainly in southern and central Sweden, but also at regular and handy intervals throughout the north. Forget any preconceptions about youth hostelling: in Sweden rooms are family orientated, modern, clean and hotel-like, existing in the unlikeliest places in old castles, schoolrooms, country manors, even boats. Virtually all have well equipped self-catering kitchens and serve a buffet breakfast.

Prices are low (40–70kr plus a 10kr heating supplement in winter; non-members pay an extra 25kr a night) and correspond to one of three grades. It would be impossible to list every hostel in this guide, so consult the *International Youth Hostel Handbook* (Volume 1) or the handbook published by the *STF* – 45kr from hostels, tourist offices and large bookshops (or available from *STF*, Box 25, S-101 20 Stockholm).

Some tips: hostels are used by Swedish families as cheap hotel-standard accommodation and can fill quickly, so *always* ring ahead in the summer; family rooms are often available for couples; hostels are usually closed between 10am and 5pm, curfews around 11pm/midnight.

■ Private rooms and B&B

A further option are the **private rooms** in people's houses that most tourist offices can book for you in any reasonable sized town. Around 70kr single, 100–150kr double, they are an affordable and pleasant option: all have access to showers and/or baths, sometimes a kitchen too, and hosts are rarely intrusive; where rooms are available they are mentioned in the text, or look for the word *Rum*.

Farms throughout Sweden offer **B&B** accommodation and self-catering facilities, lists available from *Land-Resor*, Vasagatan 12, 105 33 Stockholm (☎08/787 55 90). Or book your B&B accommodation before you leave through *Biltur Logi*: their representative in England is S. Hawthorne, Bingley Cottage, Bingley Lane, Rivelin, Sheffield S6 6GA, to whom you send £5 for their handbook and pass which lets you into the scheme. The accommodation (in small hotels rather than private houses) costs roughly between 140kr and 200kr a night per person, with discounts for children.

■ Campsites

Practically every town or village has at least one **campsite** and these are generally of a high stan-dard, something which is reflected in the price: pitching a tent costs around 35kr a night, sometimes a small charge per person too. Most are open June to September, some (around 200, in winter sports areas) throughout the year. The bulk of the sites are approved and classified by the Swedish Tourist Board and a comprehensive listings book, *Camping Sverige*, is available at larger sites and most Swedish bookshops (or, in advance, from *Stanfords*, 12–14 Long Acre, London WC2; ☎071/836 1321). The Swedish National Tourist Board in London also puts out a short free list.

Note that you'll need a **camping carnet** (22kr from your first stop) at most sites and that **camping gaz** is tricky to get hold of in Sweden – take your own if possible.

Thanks to a tradition known as *Allemansrätt* (Everyman's Right), it's perfectly possible to **camp rough** throughout the country. This gives you the right to camp anywhere for one night without asking permission, provided you stay a reasonable distance (100m) away from other dwellings. In practice (and especially if you're in the north) no-one will object to discreet camping for longer periods although it's always as well, and polite, to ask first. The wide open spaces within most town and city borders make free camping a distinct possibility in built-up areas, too.

■ Cabins and mountain huts

Many campsites also boast **cabins**, usually decked out with bunk beds, kitchen and equipment, but not sheets. It's an excellent alternative to camping for a group or couple; cabins go for around 150–250kr for a 4-bedded affair. Again, it's wise to ring ahead to secure one. Sweden also has a whole series of **chalet villages**, which – on the whole – offer high-standard accommodation at prices to match. If you're interested in a package along these lines, contact the Swedish Tourist Board for more details.

In the more out-of-the-way places, *STF* operates a system of **mountain huts** strung along hiking trails and in national parks. Usually staffed by a warden, and with cooking facilities, the huts cost around 80kr a night for members (90kr in winter). More information and membership details from the *STF* travel shop/info offices at Vasagatan 48, Stockholm and at Öster Larmgatan 15-21, Gothenburg.

Food and Drink

Eating and drinking is going to take up a large slice of your daily budget in Sweden, though you'll always get good value for your money. At its best, Swedish food is excellent, largely meat, fish and potato based, but varied for all that, and generally tasty and filling. Unusual foods are the northern Swedish delicacies – reindeer and elk meat, and wild berries – while herring comes in so many different guises, in restaurants and supermarkets, that fish fiends will always be content. Drinking is more uniform, the lager-type beer and imported wine providing no surprises; the local spirit, aquavit, however, is worth trying at least once – it comes in dozens of different flavours.

■ Food

Eating well and cheaply in Sweden are often mutually exclusive aims, at least as far as a sit-down restaurant meal is concerned. Real Swedish food is liable to be expensive, while cheaper foreign restaurants (principally pizzerias and Chinese) are hardly ubiquitous. Yet it's not impossible to eat good, hot meals cheaply: best strategy is to fuel up on breakfast and lunch, both of which offer good-value options.

Breakfast, snacks and self-catering

Breakfast (frukost) is almost invariably a help-yourself buffet served in most youth hostels and some restaurants for around 30–40kr, free in hotels. If you can eat vast amounts between 7am and 10am it's nearly always good value. Juice, milk, cereals, bread, boiled eggs, jams, salami, tea and coffee appear on even the most limited tables. Swankier venues will also add herring, porridge, yoghurt, paté and fruit. Something to watch out for is the jug of filmjölk next to the ordinary milk – it's thicker, sour milk for pouring on cereals. **Coffee** in Sweden is always freshly-brewed and very good; often, after paying for the first cup it's free, or at least available for a greatly reduced price – look for the word Påtår. **Tea** is less exciting – weak Liptons as a rule – but costs around the same; 6–10kr a go.

For **snacks** and lighter meals the choice expands, although their availability is inversely related to their health value. A Gatukök (street kitchen) or Korvstånd (hot-dog stall) will serve a selection of hot-dogs, burgers, pizza slices,

chicken bits, chips, ice cream, coke, crisps and ketchup – something and chips will cost around 20–25kr. These stalls and stands are on every street in every town and village. More upmarket (if that's the word) **burger bars** are spreading like wildfire and a hefty burger and chips meal will set you back a shade over 30kr: the local Clockburger is cheaper than McDonalds and Wimpy, but all are generally the source of the cheapest coffee in town.

It's often nicer to hit the **konditori**, a coffee shop with succulent pastries and cakes. They're not particularly cheap (coffee and cake for around 15–20kr) but are generally as good as they look; and the coffee is often free after you've paid for the first cup. This is also where you come across smörgåsar, open **sandwiches** piled high with an elaborate variety of toppings. Favourites include shrimps, smoked salmon, eggs, cheese, paté and mixed salad; again, around 15–20kr a time.

For the cheapest eating, it's hard to beat the **supermarkets** and **markets**. Buy the heavier "black" bread (around 15kr a loaf) rather than the fluffy cheaper white stuff – it's much more filling. A tube of kaviar (12kr), made from cod roe, is a sort of concentrated Thousand Island spread and good for crispbread (which, itself, is the cheapest thing to buy). Anything tinned is very expensive except mackerel and mussels. Yoghurt and milk are good value, and bananas, apples and oranges the cheapest fruits. For those actually **cooking**, pasta, rice, tinned tomatoes, onions, peppers (capsicums) and tinned mushrooms provide filling cheap meals; but tea, coffee and anything frozen or packeted will be twice the British price. Biscuits are around 10kr a packet except for the universal Marie brand – small Rich Tea types. Stores to watch for are Åhlens and Domus, national chains with big food-halls, weigh-your-own fruit and veg, and "pick and mix" salads.

Restaurants: lunch and dinner

Eating in a **restaurant** (restaurang) needn't be out of your price range as long as the meal you eat is **lunch**. Most restaurants offer something called the **Dagens Rätt** (daily dish) at around 35–50kr – often the only affordable way to sample real Swedish cooking (Husmanskost – "home cooking"). Served between 11am and 2pm this is simply a choice of main meal (usually one meat, one fish dish) which comes with bread/crispbread and salad, sometimes a soft drink or light beer, usually coffee too. Some Swedish dishes – like *pytt i panna* and *köttbullar* (see the "Food Listings", below) – are standards. On the whole, though, more likely offerings in the big cities are pizzas, basic Chinese meals and meat/fish salads. Other cheapish places for lunch are **cafeterias**, usually self-service with cheaper snacks and hot meals which won't be of a thrilling quality but at least will fill you up: large department stores and railway stations are good places to look. If you're travelling **with kids**, watch for the word *Barnmatsedal*, or "Children's menu".

More expensive, but good for a blow out, are restaurants and hotels that put out the **Smörgåsbord** at lunchtime for around 100–150kr. Following the breakfast theme, you help yourself to unlimited portions of herring, hot and cold meats, eggs, fried and boiled potatoes, salad, cheese, desserts and fruit. To follow local custom you should start with aquavit, drink beer throughout and finish with coffee; but this will add to the bill unless it is a fancier and dearer inclusive spread (usually found on Sunday). A variation on the buffet theme is the **Sillbricka**, a specialist buffet where the dishes are all based on cured and marinaded herring – it might simply be called the "herring table" on the menu. This, too, is excellent and runs to about the same price as the *Smörgåsbord*; it's often found in country inns and restaurants.

If you don't eat the set lunch, meals in restaurants, especially at **dinner** (*middag*), can be dazzlingly expensive. Expect to pay at least 150–200kr for a three course affair, to which you can add 30–40kr for a beer, 90–100kr for the cheapest bottle of house plonk. The food in Swedish restaurants will either be *Husmanskost*, in which case it will generally be marvellous, or French-style nouvelle cuisine – a pricey way to eat carrot shavings and one brussel sprout.

Swedes eat early and lunch in most restaurants is served from around 11am, dinner from around 6pm.

Ethnic restaurants

For years the only **ethnic** choice in Sweden was between the pizzeria and the odd Chinese restaurant and – where you can find them – these still offer the best value dinners. In **pizzerias** you'll get a large, if not strictly authentic, pizza for around 30–35kr, usually with free coleslaw and bread, and the price generally stays the same at lunch or dinner. As well as the local restaurants, the *Pizza Hut* chain has recently made its mark in

Sweden, though these are a little more expensive. **Chinese** restaurants nearly always offer a set lunch for around 50kr and though pricier in the evenings (from around 60–80kr a dish), a group of people can usually put quite a good-value meal together. In recent years the choice has expanded to include a barrage of **Middle Eastern** kebab takeaways and cafés, where you'll get something fairly substantial in pitta bread for around 25–30kr. Other ethnic options, however, are exclusive and expensive. **Japanese** and **Indonesian** food (increasingly common) is expense account stuff.

Vegetarians

It's not too tough being **vegetarian** in Sweden given the preponderance of buffet-type meals available, most of which are heavy with salads, cheeses, eggs and soups. The cities, too, have salad bars and sandwich shops where you'll have no trouble feeding. And if all else fails, the local pizzeria will always deliver the non-meaty goods. At lunchtime you'll find that the *Dagens Rätt* in many places has a vegetarian option; don't be afraid to ask.

■ Drinking

Drinking is notoriously pricey and there is no way of softening the blow – unless you're prepared to forgo bars and buy exclusively in the state liquor shops. Content yourself with the fact that Swedes, too, think it's expensive: you won't find yourself stuck in rounds at the bar that demand a second mortgage to pay them off, and it's perfectly acceptable to nurse your drink as long as you like.

What to drink

If you drink anything alcoholic in Sweden, a good choice is **beer**, which – while expensive – at least costs the same almost everywhere, be it café, bar or restaurant; around 35kr for a half litre of lager-type drink. It's actually very good: unless you specify, it will be *starköl*, the strongest Class III beer; cheaper will be *folköl*, the Class II and weaker brew; whilst cheapest (around half price) is *lättöl*, a Class I concoction notable only for its virtual absence of alcohol. Classes I and II are available in supermarkets at 7–8kr a can, although the real stuff is only on sale in the state licensed liquor stores – see below – where it's around a third of the price you'll pay in a bar. *Pripps* and *Spendrups* are the two main brands.

GLOSSARY OF SWEDISH FOOD AND DRINK TERMS

Basics and snacks

Bröd	Bread	*Olja*	Oil	*Småkakor*	Biscuits
Frukt Juice	Fruit juice	*Omelett*	Omelette	*Smör*	Butter
Glass	Ice cream	*Ost*	Cheese	*Smörgås*	Sandwich
Grädde	Cream	*Pastej*	Paté	*Socker*	Sugar
Gräddfil	Sour cream	*Peppar*	Pepper	*Soppa*	Soup
Gröt	Porridge	*Pommes*	Chips	*Sylt*	Jam
Kaffe	Coffee	*frites*		*Te*	Tea
Knäckebröd	Crispbread	*Ris*	Rice	*Vinäger*	Vinegar
Mineralvatten	Mineral water	*Salt*	Salt	*Våffla*	Waffle
Mjölk	Milk	*Senap*	Mustard	*Ägg*	Eggs

Meat (*Kött*)

Biff	Beef steak	*Köttbullar*	Meatballs	*Oxstek*	Roast beef
Fläsk	Pork	*Kyckling*	Chicken	*Renstek*	Roast reindeer
Kalvkött	Veal	*Lammkött*	Lamb	*Skinka*	Ham
Korv	Sausage	*Lever*	Liver	*Älg*	Elk
Kotlett	Cutlet/chop				

Fish (*Fisk*)

Ansjovis	Anchovies	*Kräftor*	Freshwater	*Sardiner*	Sardines
Blåmusslor	Mussels		crayfish	*Sik*	Whitefish
Fiskbullar	Fishballs	*Lax*	Salmon	*Sill*	Herring
Forell	Trout	*Makrill*	Mackerel	*Strömming*	Baltic
Hummer	Lobster	*Räkor*	Shrimps/		herring
Kaviar	Caviar		prawns	*Torsk*	Cod
Krabba	Crab	*Rödspätta*	Plaice	*Ål*	Eel

Vegetables(*Grönsaker*)

Blomkål	Cauliflower	*Morötter*	Carrots	*Svamp*	Mushrooms
Brysselkål	Brussel sprouts	*Potatis*	Potatoes	*Tomater*	Tomatoes
Bönor	Beans	*Rödkål*	Red cabbage	*Vitkål*	White cabbage
Gurka	Cucumber	*Sallad*	Salad	*Vitlök*	Garlic
Lök	Onion	*Spenat*	Spinach	*Ärtor*	Peas

Fruit (*Frukt*)

Ananas	Pineapple	*Hallon*	Raspberry	*Persika*	Peach
Apelsin	Orange	*Hjortron*	Cloudberry	*Päron*	Pear
Aprikos	Apricot	*Jordgrubbar*	Strawberries	*Vindruvor*	Grapes
Banan	Banana	*Lingon*	Cranberries	*Äpple*	Apple
Citron	Lemon				

Terms

Blodig	Rare	*Grillat/Halstrad*	Grilled	*Rökt*	Smoked
Filé	Fillet	*Kall*	Cold	*Stekt*	Fried
Friterad	Deep fried	*Kokt*	Boiled	*Ugnstekt*	Roasted/baked
Genomstekt	Well-done	*Lagom*	Medium	*Varm*	Hot
Gravad	Cured	*Pocherad*	Poached	*Ångkokt*	Steamed

Swedish Specialities

Björnstek	Roast bear meat; fairly rare but served at Orsa, see p.000.	Pytt i panna	Cubes of meat and fried potatoes with a fried egg.
Bruna bönor	Baked, vinegared brown beans, usually served with bacon.	Potatissallad	Potato salad.
Fisksoppa	Fish soup.	Sillbricka	Various cured and marinaded herring dishes; often appears as a first course at lunchtime in restaurants.
Getost	Goat's cheese.		
Gravad lax	Salmon marinaded in dill, sugar, and seasoning; served with mustard sauce.	Sjömansbiff	Beef, onions and potato stewed in beer.
Hjortron	A wild, northern berry, served with fresh cream and/or ice-cream	Ärtsoppa	Yellow pea soup with pork; a winter dish served traditionally on Thursdays.
Kryddost	Hard cheese with caraway seeds.		
Köttbullar	Meatballs served with a brown sauce and cranberries.	Ål	Eel, smoked and served with creamed potatoes or scrambled eggs (äggröra).
Lövbiff	Sliced, fried beef with onions.		
Mesost	Brown, sweet cheese; a breakfast favourite.		

Drinks

Apelsin juice	Orange juice	Mineralvatten	Mineral water	Te	Tea
Choklad	Hot chocolate	Mjölk	Milk	Vatten	Water
Citron	Lemon	Öl	Beer	Vin	Wine
Frukt juice	Fruit juice	Saft	Squash	Skål	Cheers!
Kaffe	Coffee				

Wine is pricey, too, especially in restaurants where you end up paying vintage prices for Chateau de Rubbish; a glass of wine in a bar or restaurant costs around 30kr. And even the Swedish Tourist Board recommend taking in your duty-free quota of **spirits**, though if you do buy them in bars, they are all known by their generic English names.

For experimental drinking, **aquavit** is a good bet. Served ice-cold in tiny shots, it's washed down with beer – and hold onto your hat. There are various different "flavours", too, spices and herbs added to the finished brew to produce some unusual headaches. Or try **glögg**: served at Christmas, it's a mulled red wine with cloves, cinnamon, sugar and more than a dash of aquavit.

Where to drink

You'll find **bars** in all towns and cities and most villages. In Stockholm and the larger cities the move is towards brasserie-type places – smart and flash and, for rucksack-toting travellers, sometimes intimidating. Elsewhere, you still come across more down-to-earth drinking dens, often sponsored by the local union/welfare authority, but the drink's no cheaper and the clientele heavily male and drunk. Either way, the bar is not the centre of Swedish social activity –

if you really want to meet people, you'd be better off heading for the campsite or the beach . . .

In the summer, **café-bars** spread out onto the pavement, better for kids and handy for just a coffee. In out of the way places, when you want a drink and can't find a bar, head for the nearest hotel. Wherever you drink you'll find that things close down around 11pm/midnight, though not in Gothenburg and Stockholm where – if your wallet is bottomless – you can keep drinking all night.

The Systemsbolaget

Venturing into a **Systemsbolaget** (the state off-licence) is a move into a twilight world. Buying alchohol is made as unattractive as possible, everything behind glass and grilles and served by dour, disapproving faces. There is still a real stigma attached to alcohol and its (public) consumption, and punters sneaking out with a brown paper bag full of the hard stuff are not a rare sight. Buying from the Systemsbolaget is, however, the only option for many budget travellers, and apart from strong beer (10kr for a third-litre) the only bargain is the imported wine – at 30–35kr a bottle. The shops are open Monday to Friday only (9am–6pm), closed weekends and the day before a public holiday; minimum age for being served is 20, and you may need to show ID.

Directory

ANGLING Sweden's 96,000 lakes make for a lot of fishing. It's free along the coast or in the larger lakes, but for anywhere else get a fishing permit from the local tourist office. A leaflet is available from the Swedish National Tourist Office in London (for address see "Basics").

CHEMISTS *Apotek* in Swedish are generally open shopping hours, although Stockholm has a 24-hr chemist. Larger towns operate a rota system of late opening, rota and addresses posted on the doors of each apotek.

CONTRACEPTION Condoms are available in every *apotek*, in various department stores and supermarkets, and occasionally from dispensers in the street. Anything else on prescription.

CUSTOMS Your duty-free limit is one litre of spirits, one litre of wine and two litres of beer (or two litres of wine if no spirits are taken in). Other restrictions, if you're taking in a car/caravan are: no potatoes (seriously), fresh, smoked or frozen meat and a limit of 5kg of fruit and veg.

EMERGENCIES Dial ☎90 000 for police (*Polis*), fire brigade (*Brandkår*) or ambulance (*Ambulans*) free of charge from any phone-box.

HOLIDAYS Banks, offices and shops close on the following days and may close earlier on the preceding day: January 1, January 6 (Epiphany), Good Friday, Easter Monday, May 1 (Labour Day), Ascension Day, Whit Monday, Midsummer's Day, All Saint's Day, Christmas Day, Boxing Day.

SHOPS Open Mon–Fri 9am–6pm, Sat 9am–1pm. Some department stores stay open until 8–10pm in cities, and open on Sunday afternoons as well.

TIPPING Hotels and restaurants include their service charge in the bill, usually 13–15 percent. Where you will frequently have to hand over cash is to cloakroom attendants in bars and discos – 5–6kr a time.

History

Sweden has one of Europe's longest documented histories, but for all the upheavals of the Viking times and the warring of the Middle Ages, during modern times the country has seemed to delight in taking an historical back seat. For one brief period, when Prime Minister Olof Palme was shot dead in 1986, Sweden was thrust into the international limelight. Since then, however, it's regained its poise, even though the current situation is fraught: political infighting and domestic disharmony is threatening the one thing that the Swedes have always been proud of – and that other countries look up to; the politics of consensus, the passing of which, arguably, is of far greater importance even than the assassination of their Prime Minister.

■ Early Civilisations

It was not until around 6000 BC that the **first settlers** roamed north and east into Sweden, living as nomadic reindeer hunters and herders. By 3000 BC people had settled in the south of the country and were established as farmers; and from 2000 BC there are indications of a development in burial practices, with **dolmens** and **passage graves** found throughout the southern Swedish provinces. Traces remain, too, of the **Boat Axe People**, so called because of their characteristic tool/weapon shaped like a boat. The earliest Scandinavian horse riders, they quickly held sway over the whole of southern Sweden.

During the **Bronze Age** (1500–500 BC) the Boat Axe People traded furs and amber for southern European copper and tin. Large finds of finished ornaments and weapons show a comparatively rich culture. This was emphasised by elaborate burial rites, as their dead were laid in single graves under mounds of earth and stone.

The deterioration of the Scandinavian climate in the last millenium before Christ coincided with the advance across Europe of the Celts, which halted the flourishing trade of the Swedish settlers. With the new millenium, Sweden made its first mark upon the classical world. Pliny the Elder (23–79 AD) in the *Historia Naturalis* mentioned the "island of Scatinavia" far to the north. Tacitus was more specific: in 98 AD he referred to a powerful people, the *Suinoes*, who

were strong in men, weapons and ships; a reference to the **Svear** who were to form the nucleus of an emergent Swedish kingdom by the sixth century.

The Svear settled in the rich land around Lake Mälaren, rulers of the whole country except the south. They gave Sweden its modern name: *Sverige* in Swedish or *Svear rike*, the kingdom of the Svear. More importantly, they gave their first dynastic leaders a taste for expansion, trading with Gotland and holding suzerainty over the Åland islands.

■ The Viking period

The Vikings – raiders and warriors who dominated the political and economic life of Europe and beyond from the ninth to the eleventh century – came from all parts of southern Scandinavia. But there is evidence that the **Swedish Vikings** were among the first to leave home, the impetus being a rapid population growth, domestic unrest and a desire for new lands. The raiders turned their attention largely eastwards, in line with Sweden's geographical position and knowing that the Svear had already reached the Baltic. By the ninth century the trade routes were well established, Swedes reaching the Black and Caspian Seas and making valuable trading contact with the **Byzantine Empire**. Although more commercially inclined than their Danish and Norwegian counterparts, Swedish Vikings were quick to use force if profits were slow to materialise. From 860 onwards Greek and Muslim records relate a series of raids across the Black Sea against Byzantium; and across the Caspian into northeast Iran.

But the Vikings were settlers as well as traders and exploiters, and their long-term influence was marked. Embattled Slavs to the east gave them the name **Rus**, and a creeping colonisation gave the area the Vikings settled in its modern name, Russia. Russian names today – Oleg, Igor, Vladimir – can be derived from the Swedish – Helgi, Ingvar, Valdemar. For more on the Rus, see p.646.

Domestically, **paganism** was at its height. Freyr was "God of the World", a physically potent God of Fertility through whom dynastic leaders would trace their descent. It was a bloody time. Nine **human sacrifices** were offered at the celebrations held every nine years at Uppsala. Adam of Bremen recorded that the great shrine there was adjoined by a sacred grove where "every tree is believed divine because of the death and putre-faction of the victims hanging there".

Viking **law** was based on the *Thing*, an assembly of free men to which the king's power was subject. Each largely autonomous province had its own assembly and its own leaders: where several provinces united, the approval of each *Thing* was needed for any choice of leader. For centuries in Sweden the new king had to make a formal tour to receive the homage of each province.

■ The arrival of Christianity

Christianity was slow to take root in Sweden. Whereas Denmark and Norway had accepted the faith by the turn of the eleventh century, Swedish contact was still in the east and the people remained largely heathen. Missionaries met with limited success and no Swedish king was converted until 1008, when **Olof Skättonung** was baptised. He was the first known king of both Swedes and Goths (that is, ruler of the two major provinces of Västergotland and Östergotland) and his successors were all Christians. Nevertheless, paganism retained a grip on Swedish affairs, and as late as the 1080s the Svear banished their Christian king, Inge, when he refused to take part in the pagan celebrations at Uppsala. By the end of the eleventh century, though, the temple at Uppsala had gone and a Christian church was built on its site. In the 1130s Uppsala replaced Sigtuna – original centre of the Swedish Christian faith – as the main episcopal seat and, in 1164, Stephen (an English monk) was made the first archbishop.

■ The warring dynasties

The whole of the early Middle Ages in Sweden was characterised by a succession of struggles for control of a growing central power. Principally two families, the Sverkers and the Eriks, waged battle throughout the twelfth century. **King Erik** was the first Sverker king to make his mark: in 1157 he led a crusade to heathen Finland, but was killed in 1160 at Uppsala by a Danish pretender to his throne. Within 100 years he was to be recognised as patron saint of Sweden, and his remains interred in the new Uppsala Cathedral.

Erik was succeeded by his son **Knut**, whose stable reign lasted until 1196 and was marked by commercial treaties and strengthened defences. Following his death, virtual civil war weakened

the royal power with the result that the king's chief ministers, or **Jarls**, assumed much of the executive responsibilty for running the country. So much so that when Erik Eriksson (last of the Eriks) was deposed in 1229, his administrator **Birger Jarl** assumed power. With papal support for his crusading policies he confirmed the Swedish grip on the southwest of Finland. His son, Valdemar, succeeded him but proved a weak ruler and didn't survive the family feuding after Birger Jarl's death. Valdemar's brother Magnus assumed power in 1275.

Magnus Ladulås represented a peak of Swedish royal power not to be repeated for 300 years. His enemies dissipated, he forbade the nobility to meet without his consent and began to issue his own authoritative decrees. Preventing the nobility from claiming maintenance at the expense of the peasantry as they travelled from estate to estate earned him his nickname; Ladulås or "Barn-lock". He also began to reap the benefits of conversion – the clergy became an educated class upon whom the monarch could rely for diplomatic and administrative duties. By the thirteenth century, ambitious Swedish clerics were in Paris and Bologna, while the first stone churches appeared in Sweden. The most monu-mental is the early Gothic **cathedral** built at Uppsala.

Meanwhile the nobility had come to form a military class, exempted from taxation on the understanding that they would defend the Crown. In the country the standard of living was still low although an increasing population stimulated new cultivation. The forests of Norrland were pushed back, more southern heathland turned into pasture, and crop rotation introduced. Noticeable, too, was the increasing **German influence** within Sweden as the Hansa traders spread. Their first merchants settled in Visby and, by the mid-thirteenth century, in Stockholm.

■ The fourteenth century – towards unity

Magnus died in 1290, power shifting to a cabal of magnates led by **Torgil Knutsson**. As Marshal of Sweden, he pursued an energetic foreign policy, conquering western Karelia to gain control of the Gulf of Finland; and building the fortress at Viborg, lost only with the collapse of the Swedish Empire in the eighteenth century.

Magnus' son Birger came of age in 1302 but soon quarrelled with his brothers Erik and

Valdemar. They had Torgil Knutsson executed and rounded on Birger who was forced to divide up Sweden between the three of them. An unhappy arrangement, it lasted until 1317 when Birger had his brothers arrested and starved to death in prison – an act which prompted a shocked nobility to rise against Birger and force his exile to Denmark. The Swedish nobles restored the principle of elective monarchy by calling on the three-year-old **Magnus** (son of a Swedish duke and already declared Norwegian king) to take the Swedish Crown. During his minority a treaty was concluded with Novgorod (1323) to fix the frontiers in eastern and northern Finland. This left virtually the whole of the Scandinavian peninsula (except the Danish provinces in the south) under one ruler.

Yet Sweden was still anything but prosperous. The **Black Death** reached the country in 1350, wiping out whole parishes and killing perhaps a third of the population. Subsequent labour shortages and troubled estates meant that the nobility found it difficult to maintain their positions. German merchants had driven the Swedes from their most lucrative trade routes: even the copper and iron-ore **mining** that began around this time in Bergslagen and Dalarna relied on German capital.

Magnus soon ran into trouble, threatened further by the accession of Valdemar Atterdag to the Danish throne in 1340. Squabbles over sovereignty of the Danish provinces of Skåne and Blekinge led to Danish incursions into Sweden and, in 1361, Valdemar landed in Gotland and sacked **Visby**. The Gotlanders were massacred outside the city walls, refused refuge by the Hansa merchants.

Magnus was forced to negotiate and his son **Håkon** – now King of Norway – was married to Valdemar's daughter Margaret. With Magnus later deposed, power fell into the hands of the magnates who shared out the country. Chief of the ruling nobles was the Steward, **Bo Jonsson**, who controlled virtually all Finland, and central and southeast Sweden. Yet on his death, the nobility turned to Håkon's wife **Margaret**, already regent in Norway (for her son Olof) and in Denmark since the death of her father, Valdemar. In 1388 she was proclaimed "First Lady" of Sweden and, in return, confirmed all the privileges of the Swedish nobility. They were anxious for union, to safeguard those who owned frontier estates and strengthen the Crown against any

further German influence. Called upon to choose a male king, Margaret nominated her nephew, **Erik of Pomerania**, who was duly elected king of Sweden in 1396. And as he had already been elected to the Danish and Norwegian thrones, Scandinavian unity seemed assured.

■ The Kalmar Union

Erik was crowned king of Denmark, Norway and Sweden in 1397 at a ceremony in **Kalmar**. Nominally, the three kingdoms were now in union: but, despite Erik, real power remained in the hands of Margaret until her death in 1412.

Erik was at war throughout his reign with the Hanseatic League. Villified in popular Swedish history as an evil and grasping ruler, the taxes he raised went on a war that was never fought on Swedish soil. He spent his time instead in Denmark directing operations, leaving his queen Philippa (sister to Henry V of England) behind. Erik was deposed in 1439 and the nobility turned to **Christopher of Bavaria**, whose early death in 1448 led to the first major breach in the union.

No one candidate could fill the three kingships satisfactorily, and separate elections in Denmark and Sweden signalled a renewal of the infighting that had plagued the previous century. Within Sweden, unionists and nationalists skirmished, the powerful **Oxenstierna** (unionist) family opposing the claims of the **Sture** (nationalist) family; until 1470 when **Sten Sture** (the Elder) became "Guardian of the Realm". His victory over the unionists at the **Battle of Brunkenberg** (1471) – in the middle of modern Stockholm – was complete. It was a victory that gained symbolic artistic expression in the **statue of George and the Dragon** which still adorns the Great Church in Stockholm.

Sten Sture's primacy fostered a new cultural atmosphere. The first **university** in Scandinavia was founded in Uppsala in 1477, the first printing press appearing in Sweden six years later. Artistically, German and Dutch influence was great, traits seen in the decorative art of the great Swedish medieval churches. Only remote **Dalarna** kept alive a native folk art tradition.

Belief in the union still existed though, particularly outside Sweden, and successive kings had to fend off almost constant attacks and blockades emanating from Denmark. With the accession of **Christian II** to the Danish throne in 1513, the unionist movement found a leader capable of turning the tide. Under the guise of a crusade to free Sweden's imprisoned archbishop Gustav Trolle, Christian attacked Sweden and killed Sture. After Christian's coronation, Trolle urged the prosecution of his Swedish adversaries (gathered together under an amnesty) and they were found guilty of heresy. Eightytwo nobles and burghers of Stockholm were executed and their bodies burned in what became known as the **Stockholm Blood Bath**. A vicious persecution of Sture's followers throughout Sweden ensued, a move that led to widespread reaction and, ultimately, the downfall of the union.

■ Gustav Vasa and his sons

Opposition to Christian II was vague and unorganised until the appearance of the young **Gustav Vasa**. Initially unable to stir the locals of the Dalecarlia region into open revolt, he left for exile in Norway but was chased on skis and recalled after the people had had a change of heart. The chase is celebrated still in the **Vassalopet** race, run each year by thousands of Swedish skiers.

Gustav Vasa's army grew rapidly and in 1521 he was elected regent and, with the capture of Stockholm in 1523, king. Christian had been deposed in Denmark and the new Danish king, Frederick I, recognised Sweden's *de facto* withdrawal from the union. Short of cash, Gustav found it prudent to support the movement towards religious reform propagated by Swedish Lutherans. More of a political than a religious **Reformation**, the result was a handover of church lands to the Crown and the subordination of church to state. It's a relationship that is still largely in force today, the clergy being civil servants paid by the state.

In 1541 the first edition of the Bible in the vernacular appeared. Suppressing revolt at home, Gustav Vasa strengthened his hand with a centralisation of trade and government. On his death in 1560 Sweden was united, prosperous and independent.

Gustav Vasa's heir, his eldest son **Erik**, faced a difficult time; not least because the Vasa lands and wealth had been split between him and his brothers, Johan, Magnus and Karl (an atypically imprudent action of Gustav's before his death). The Danes, too, pressed hard, reasserting their claim to the Swedish throne in the inconclusive **Northern Seven Years' War** which began in 1563. Erik was deposed in 1569 by his brother who became **Johan III**, his first act to end the war at the **Peace of Stettin**. At home Johan

ruled more or less with the goodwill of the nobility, but upset matters with his Catholic sympathies. He introduced the liturgy and Catholic-influenced *Red Book*, and his son and heir Sigismund was the Catholic King of Poland. On Johan's death in 1592, Sigismund agreed to rule Sweden in accordance with Lutheran practice but failed to do so. When Sigismund returned to Poland the way was clear for Duke Karl (Johan's brother) to assume the regency, a role he filled until declared king **Karl IX** in 1603.

Karl had ambitions eastwards but, routed by the Poles and staved off by the Russians, he suffered a stroke in 1610 and died the year after. The last of Vasa's sons, his heir was the seventeen-year-old Gustav II, better known as Gustavus Adolfus.

The rule of Vasa and his sons made Sweden a nation, culturally as well as politically. The courts were filled and influenced by men of learning; art and sculpture flourished. The **Renaissance** style appeared for the first time in Sweden with royal castles remodelled – Kalmar a fine example. Economically, Sweden remained mostly self-sufficient, its few imports luxuries like cloth, wine and spices. With around 8000 inhabitants, Stockholm was its most important city, although **Gothenburg** was founded in 1607 to promote trade to the west.

■ Gustavus Adolfus: the rise of the Swedish Empire

During the reign of **Gustavas II Adolfus** Sweden became a European power. Though still in his youth he was considered able enough to rule, and proved so by concluding peace treaties with Denmark (1613) and Russia (1617), the latter isolating Russia from the Baltic and allowing the Swedes control of the eastern trade routes into Europe.

In 1618 the **Thirty Years' War** broke out in Germany. It was vital for Gustavus that Germany should not become Catholic, given the Polish king's continuing pretensions to the Swedish Crown, and the possible threat it could pose to Sweden's growing influence in the Baltic. A treaty with a defeated Poland in 1628 gave Gustavus control of Livonia and four Prussian seaports, and the income this generated financed his entry into the war in 1630 on the Protestant side. After several convincing victories Gustavus pushed through Germany, delaying an assault upon undefended Vienna. It cost him his life. At the **Battle of Lützen** in 1632 Gustavus was killed, his body stripped and battered by the enemy's soldiers. The war dragged on until 1648 and the **Peace of Westphalia**.

With Gustavus away at war for much of his reign, Sweden ran smoothly under the guidance of his friend and Chancellor, **Axel Oxenstierna**. Together they founded a new Supreme Court in Stockholm (and ones too for Finland and the conquered Baltic provinces); reorganised the national assembly into four Estates of nobility, clergy, burghers and peasantry (1626); extended the university at Uppsala (and founded one at Åbo – modern Turku); and fostered the mining and other industries that provided much of the country's wealth. Gustavus had many other accomplishments too: he spoke five languages and designed a new light cannon which assisted in his routs of the enemy.

■ The Caroleans

The Swedish Empire reached its territorial peak under the **Caroleans**. Yet the reign of the last of them was to see Sweden crumble.

Following Gustavus Adolfus' death and the later abdication of his daughter, Christina, **Karl X** succeeded to the throne. War against Poland (1655) led to some early successes and, with Denmark espousing the Polish cause, gave Karl the opportunity to march into Jutland (1657). From there his armies marched across the frozen sea to threaten Copenhagen; the subsequent **Treaty of Roskilde** (1658) broke Denmark and gave the Swedish Empire its widest territorial extent.

However, the long regency of his son and heir, **Karl XI**, did little to enhance Sweden's vulnerable position, so extensive were its borders. On his assumption of power in 1672 Karl was almost immediately dragged into war: beaten by a smaller Prussian army at Brandenberg in 1675, Sweden was suddenly faced with war against both the Danes and Dutch. Karl rallied, though, to drive out the Danish invaders, the war ending in 1679 with the reconquest of Skåne and the restoration of most of Sweden's German provinces.

In 1682 Karl XI became **absolute monarch** and was given full control over legislation and *reduktion* – the resumption of estates previously alienated by the Crown to the nobility. The armed forces were reorganised too and by 1700 the Swedish army had 25,000 soldiers and twelve regiments of cavalry; the naval fleet was expanded to 38 ships and a new base built at Karlskrona (nearer than Stockholm to the probable trouble spots).

Culturally, Sweden began to benefit from the innovations of Gustavus Adolfus. *Gymnasia* (grammar schools) continued to expand and a second university was established at **Lund** in 1668. A national literature emerged, helped by the efforts of **George Stiernhielm**, "father" of modern Swedish poetry. **Olof Rudbeck** (1630–1702) was a Nordic polymath whose scientific reputation lasted longer than his attempt to identify the ancient Goth settlement at Uppsala as Atlantis. Architecturally, this was the age of **Tessin**, both father and son. Tessin the Elder was responsible for the glorious palace at **Drottningholm**, work on which began in 1662, as well as the cathedral at **Kalmar**. His son, Tessin the Younger, succeeded him as royal architect and was to create the new royal palace at Stockholm.

In 1697 the fifteen-year-old **Karl XII** succeeded to the throne and under him the Empire collapsed. Faced with a defensive alliance of Saxony, Denmark and Russia there was little the king could have done to avoid eventual defeat. However, he remains a revered figure for his valiant (often suicidal) efforts to prove Europe wrong. Initial victories against Peter the Great and Saxony led him to march on Russia where he was defeated and the bulk of his army destroyed. Escaping to Turkey, where he remained as guest and then prisoner for four years, Karl watched the Empire disintegrate. With Poland reconquered by Augustus of Saxony, and Finland by Peter the Great, he returned to Sweden only to have England declare war on him.

Eventually, splits in the enemy's joint alliance led Swedish diplomats to attempt peace talks with Russia. Karl, though, was keen to exploit these differences in a more direct fashion. In order to strike at Denmark, but lacking a fleet, he besieged Fredrikshald in Norway in 1718 and was killed by a sniper's bullet. In the power vacuum thus created, Russia became the leading Baltic force, receiving Livonia, Estonia, Ingria and most of Karelia from Sweden.

■ The Age of Freedom

The eighteenth century saw absolutism discredited in Sweden. A new constitution vested power in the Estates, who reduced the new king **Frederick I**'s role to that of nominal Head of State. The Chancellor wielded the real power and under **Arvid Horn** the country found a period of stability. His party, nicknamed the "Caps", was opposed by the hawkish "Hats", who forced war with Russia in 1741; a disaster in which Sweden lost all of Finland and had its whole east coast burned and bombed. Most of Finland was returned with the agreement to elect **Adolphus Frederick** (a relation of the Crown Prince of Russia) to the Swedish throne on Frederick I's death, which duly occurred in 1751.

During his reign Adolphus repeatedly tried to reassert royal power, although he found that the constitution was only strengthened against him. The Estates' power was such that they issued a stamp with his name when Adolphus refused to sign any bills. The resurrected "Hats" forced entry into the **Seven Years' War** in 1757 on the French side, another disastrous venture as the Prussians repelled every Swedish attack.

The aristocratic parties were in a state of constant flux. Although elections of sorts were held to provide delegates for the *Riksdag* (parliament), foreign sympathies, bribery and bickering were hardly conducive to a democratic administration. Cabals continued to rule Sweden, the economy was stagnant, reform delayed. It was, however, an age of intellectual and scientific advance, surprising in a country that had lost much of its cultural impetus. **Carl von Linné**, the botanist whose classification of plants is still used, was professor at Uppsala from 1741–78. **Anders Celsius** initiated the use of the centigrade temperature scale; **Carl Scheele** discovered chlorine. A royal decree of 1748 organised Europe's first full-scale census, a five-yearly event by 1775. Other fields flourished too. **Emmanuel Swedenborg**, the philosopher, died in 1772, his mystical works encouraging new theological sects. And the period encapsulated the life of **Carl Michael Bellman** (1740–95), the celebrated Swedish poet, whose work did much to identify and foster a popular nationalism.

With the accession of **Gustav III** in 1771, the Crown began to regain the ascendancy. A new constitution was forced upon a divided *Riksdag* and proved a balance between earlier absolutism and the later aristocratic squabbles. A popular king, Gustav founded hospitals, granted freedom of worship and removed many of the state controls over the economy. His determination, too, to conduct a successful foreign policy led to further conflict with Russia (1788–90) in which,

to everyone's surprise, Gustav managed to more than hold his own. But with the French Revolution polarising opposition throughout Europe, the Swedish nobility began to entertain thoughts of conspiracy against a king whose growing powers they now saw as those of a tyrant. In 1792, at a masked ball in Stockholm Opera House, the king was shot by an assassin hired by the disaffected aristocracy. Gustav died two weeks later and was succeeded by his son **Gustav IV**, the country led by a regency for the years of his minority.

The wars waged by revolutionary France were at first studiously avoided in Sweden but, pulled into the conflict by the British, Gustav IV entered the **Napoleonic Wars** in 1805. However, Napoleon's victory at Austerlitz two years later broke the Coalition and Sweden found itself isolated. Attacked by Russia the following year, Gustav was later arrested and deposed, his uncle elected king.

A constitution of 1809 established a liberal monarchy in Sweden, responsible to the elected *Riksdag*. Under the constitution **Karl XIII** was a mere caretaker, his heir, a Danish prince, who would bring Norway back to Sweden – some compensation for finally losing Finland and the Åland Islands to Russia (1809) after 500 years of Swedish rule. On the prince's sudden death, however, Marshal Bernadotte (one of Napoleon's generals) was invited to become heir. Taking the name of **Karl Johan**, he took his chance in 1812 and joined Britain and Russia to fight Napoleon. Following Napoleon's first defeat at the Battle of Leipzig in 1813, Sweden compelled Denmark (France's ally) to exchange Norway for Swedish Pomerania.

By 1814 Sweden and Norway had formed an uneasy union. Norway retained its own government and certain autonomous measures. Sweden decided foreign policy, appointed a viceroy and retained a suspensive (but not absolute) veto over the Norwegian parliament's legislation.

■ The nineteenth century

Union under Karl Johan, or **Karl XIV** as he became in 1818, could have been disastrous. He spoke no Swedish and a few years previously had never been to either kingdom. However, with Karl and his successor, **Oscar I**, prosperity ensued. The **Göta Canal** (1832) helped commercially, and liberal measures by both monarchs helped politically. In 1845 daughters were given an equal right of inheritance. A Poor Law was introduced (1847), restrictive craft guilds reformed, and an Education Act passed.

The 1848 revolution throughout Europe cooled Oscar's reforming ardour, and his attention turned to reviving **Scandinavianism**. It was still a hope, in certain quarters, that closer co-operation between Denmark and Sweden-Norway could lead to some sort of revived Kalmar Union. Expectations were raised with the **Crimean War** of 1854; Russia could be neutralised as a future threat. But peace was declared too quickly (at least for Sweden) and there was still no real guarantee that Sweden was sufficiently protected from future Russian threats. With Oscar's death, talk of political union faded.

His son **Karl XV** presided over the reform of the *Riksdag* which put an end to the Swedish system of personal monarchy. The Four Estates were replaced by a representative two- house parliament along European lines. This, together with the end of political Scandi-navianism (following the Prussian attack on Denmark in 1864 in which Sweden stood by), marked Sweden's entry into modern Europe.

Industrialisation was slow to take root in Sweden. No real industrial revolution occurred and developments – mechanisation, introduction of railways etc. – were piecemeal. One result was widespread **emigration** amongst the rural poor, who had been hard hit by famine in 1867 and 1868. Between 1860 and 1910 over one million people left for America (in 1860 the Swedish population was only four million). Given huge farms to settle, the emigrants headed for land similar to their own in Sweden; to the mid-West, Kansas and Nebraska.

At home, Swedish **trade unionism** emerged to campaign for better conditions. Dealt with severely, the unions formed a confederation (1898) but largely failed to make headway. Even peaceful picketing carried a two year prison sentence. Hand in hand with the fight for workers' rights went the **temperance movement**. The level of spirit consumption was alarming and various abstinence programmes attempted to educate the drinkers and, if neccessary, eradicate the stills. Some towns made the selling of spirits a municipal monopoly; not a long step from the state monopoly that exists today.

With the accession of **Oscar II** in 1872, Sweden continued on an even, if uneventful,

keel. Keeping out of further European conflict (the Austro-Prussian War, Franco-Prussian War and various Balkan crises), the country's only worry was a growing dissatisfaction in Norway with the union. Demanding a separate consular service, and objecting to the Swedish king's veto on constitutional matters, the Norwegians brought things to a head – and in 1905 declared the union invalid. The Karlstad Convention confirmed the break and Norway became independent for the first time since 1380.

The late-nineteenth century was a happier time for Swedish culture. **Strindberg** enjoyed great critical success and artists like **Anders Zorn** and **Prince Eugene** made their mark abroad. The historian **Artur Hazelius** founded the Nordic and Skansen museums in Stockholm; and the chemist, industrialist and dynamite inventor, **Alfred Nobel**, left his fortune to finance the Nobel Prizes. An instructive tale, Nobel hoped that the knowledge of his invention would help eradicate war – optimistically believing that mankind would never dare unleash the destructive forces of dynamite.

▓ Two World Wars

Sweden declared a strict neutrality on the outbreak of **World War I**, tempered by much sympathy within the country for Germany, sponsored by the long standing language, trade and cultural links. It was a policy agreed with the other Scandinavian monarchs too – but a difficult one to pursue. Faced with British demands to enforce a blockade of Germany and the blacklisting and eventual seizure of Swedish goods at sea, the economy suffered grievously; rationing and inflation mushroomed. The **Russian Revolution** in 1917 brought further problems to Sweden. The Finns immediately declared independence, waging civil war against the Bolsheviks, and Swedish volunteers enlisted in the White army. But a conflict of interest arose when the Åland Islands – Swedish-speaking – wanted a return to Swedish rule rather than stay with the victorious Finns. The League of Nations overturned this claim, granting the islands to Finland.

After the war, a Liberal/Socialist coalition remained in power until 1920, when **Branting** became the first socialist prime minister. By the time of his death, in 1924, the franchise had been extended to all men and women over 23 and the state-controlled alcohol system (*Systembolaget*) set up. Following the Depression of the late 1920s and early 1930s, conditions began to improve after a Social Democratic government took office for the fourth time in 1932. A **Welfare State** was rapidly established – unemployment benefit, higher old-age pensions, family allowances and paid holidays. The **Saltsjöbaden Agreement** of 1938 drew up a contract between trade unions and employers to help eliminate strikes and lockouts. With war again looming, all parties agreed that Sweden should remain neutral in any struggle and rearmament was negligible, despite Hitler's apparent intentions.

World War II was slow to affect Sweden. Unlike 1914, there was little sympathy for Germany, but neutrality was again declared. The Russian invasion of Finland in 1939 (see *Finland: History*, p.456) brought Sweden into the picture, providing weapons, volunteers and refuge for the Finns. Regular Swedish troops were refused though, fearing intervention from either the Germans (then Russia's ally) or the Allies. Economically, the country remained sound – less dependent on imports than in World War I and with no serious shortages. The position became stickier in 1940 when the Nazis marched into Denmark and Norway, isolating Sweden. Concessions were made – German troop transit allowed, iron ore exports continued – until 1943/44 when Allied threats were more convincing than the failing German war machine. Sweden became the recipient of countless refugees from the rest of Scandinavia and the Baltic. Instrumental, too, in rescuing Hungarian Jews from the SS, was **Raoul Wallenberg**, who persuaded the Swedish government to give him diplomatic status in 1944. Unknown thousands (anything up to 35,000) of Jews in Hungary were sheltered in "neutral houses" (flying the Swedish flag), fed and clothed by Wallenberg. But when Soviet troops liberated Budapest in 1945, Wallenberg was arrested as a suspected spy and disappeared – later reported to have died in prison in Moscow in 1947. However, unconfirmed accounts had him alive in a Soviet prison as late as 1975, and in 1989 some of his surviving relatives flew to Moscow in an attempt to discover the truth about his fate. They came away empty handed, though it only seems a matter of time until the Soviet authorities, in these days of *glasnost*, reveal what really happened.

The end of the war was to provide the country with a serious crisis of conscience. Physically unscathed, Sweden was now vulnerable to Cold War politics. Proximity to Finland and, ultimately, to the Soviet Union meant that Sweden refused to follow the other Scandinavian countries into **NATO** in 1949. The country did, however, much to Conservative disquiet, return most of the Baltic and German refugees who had fought against Russia during the war into Stalin's hands – their fate not difficult to guess.

■ Post-war politics

The wartime coalition quickly gave way to a purely **Social Democratic** government committed to welfare provision and increased defence expenditure – non-participation in military alliances didn't mean a throwing down of weapons.

Tax increases and a trade slump lost the Social Democrats seats in the 1948 general election and by 1951 they needed to enter a coalition with the Agrarian (later the Centre) Party to survive. The coalition lasted until 1957, when disputes over the form of a proposed extension to the pension system brought it down. An inconclusive referendum and the withdrawal of the Centre Party from government forced an election which saw no change. Although the Centre gained seats and the Conservatives replaced the Liberals as the main opposition party, the Social Democrats still had a (thin) majority.

Sweden regained much of its international moral respect (lost directly after World War II) through the election of **Dag Hammarskjöld** as Secretary-General of the United Nations in 1953. His strong leadership greatly enhanced the prestige (and effectiveness) of the organisation, participating in solving the Suez crisis (1956) and the 1958 Lebanon-Jordan affair. He was killed in an air crash in 1961 towards the end of his second five-year term.

Throughout the 1950s and 1960s, domestic reform continued unabated. It was in these years that the country laid the foundations of its much-vaunted social security system, although at the time it didn't always bear close scrutiny. A **National Health Service** gave free hospital treatment, but only allowed for a small refund of doctor's fees, medicines and dental treatment – hardly as far-reaching as the British system introduced immediately after the war.

The Social Democrats stayed in power until 1976, when a **non-Socialist coalition** (Centre/Liberal/Moderate) finally unseated them. In the 44 years since 1932, the Socialists had been an integral part of government in Sweden, tempered only by periods of war and coalition. It was a remarkable record, made more so by the fact that modern politics in Sweden has never been about ideology, so much as detail. Socialists and non-Socialists alike share a broad consensus on foreign policy and defence matters, even on the need for the social welfare system. The argument instead has been economic, and a manifestation of this is the **nuclear issue**. A second non-Socialist coalition formed in 1979 presided over a referendum on nuclear power (1980), the pro-nuclear lobby securing victory; the result, the immediate expansion of the nuclear reactor programme.

■ Present day affairs

The Social Democrats regained power in 1982, subsequently devaluing the *krona*, introducing a price freeze and cutting back on public expenditure. They lost their majority in 1985, having to rely on Communist support to get their bills through. Presiding over the party since 1969, and Prime Minister for nearly as long, was **Olof Palme**, probably now the most famous least-known foreign leader. Assassinated in February 1986, his death threw Sweden into modern European politics like no other event. Proud of their open society (Palme was returning home unguarded from the cinema), the Swedes were shocked by the gunning down of a respected politician, diplomat and pacifist. The country's social system was placed in the limelight, and shock turned to anger and then ridicule as the months passed without his killer being caught. Police bungling was criticised and despite the theories – Kurdish extremists, right-wing terror groups – no-one was charged with the murder.

Then the police came up with **Christer Pettersson**, who – despite having no apparent motive – was identified by Palme's wife as the man who had fired the shot that night. Despite pleading his innocence, claiming he was elsewhere at the time of the murder, Pettersson was convicted of Palme's murder and jailed. However, there was great disquiet about the verdict, both at home and abroad: the three legal representatives in the original jury had voted for acquittal at

the time; it was thought that Palme's wife couldn't possibly be sure that the man who fired the shot was Pettersson, since by her own admission she had only seen him once, on the dark night in question and then only very briefly. On appeal, Christer Pettersson was acquitted and released in 1989 and the mystery is now no closer to being solved, though the Swedish police still appear to believe that they had the right man but not enough evidence to convict.

Ingvar Carlsson was elected the new Prime Minister after Palme's murder, a position confirmed by the **1988 General Election** when the Social Democrats – for the first time in years – scored more seats than the three non-socialist parties combined. However, at the time of writing, the country is facing a very uncertain political future. Carlsson's was a minority government, the Social Democrats requiring the support of the Communists to command an overall majority – support that was usually forthcoming but that, with the arrival of the **Green Party** into Parliament in 1988, could no longer be taken for granted. The Greens and Communists are jockeying for position as protectors of the Swedish environment, and any Social Democrat measure seen to be anti-environment could cost them Communist support. The real problem for the Social Democrats, though, is the state of the economy. With a background of rising inflation (nine percent the projected figure for 1990) and slow economic growth, the government announced an austerity package in January 1990, which included a two-year ban on strike action, and a wage, price and rent freeze – strong measures which astounded most Swedes, used to living in a liberal, consensus-style society. The Greens and Communists would have none of it and the Social Democrat government resigned a month later. At the time of writing, the Social Democrats were back in charge of a minority government, having agreed to drop the most draconian measures of their programme. But whatever happens over the next couple of years, many think that the model concensus has finally broken down.

Perhaps more worryingly for the government, a series of **scandals** has recently swept the country, leading to open speculation about a marked decline in public morality. The Bofors arms company was discovered to be involved in illegal sales to the Middle East, and early in 1990 the Indian police charged the company with paying kickbacks to politicians to secure arms contracts. There's been insider dealing at the stock exchange and the country's Ombudsman resigned over charges of personal corruption. Swedes are having to come to terms with their new position in the eyes of Europe and are finding that it's a painful process. Possible membership of the European Community is being mooted for the first time in a decade, teenagers rioted in central Stockholm throughout the summer of 1987 and the Swedish legal system is being held up to some close and critical scrutiny. Certainly, moral and political transformation is afoot.

A BRIEF GUIDE TO SWEDISH

Nearly everyone, everywhere in Sweden speaks English, the tourist offices often staffed with what appear to be native Americans (most pick up the accent from films and TV). Still, knowing the essentials of Swedish is useful, and making an effort with the language certainly impresses. If you already speak either Danish or Norwegian you should have few problems being understood; if not, then a basic knowledge of German is a help too. Of the phrasebooks, most useful is *Swedish for Travellers* (Berlitz; £2.25), or use the section in *Travellers' Scandinavia* (Pan £2.50).

PRONUNCIATION

Pronunciation is even more difficult than Danish or Norwegian.

A **vowel** sound is usually long when it's the final syllable or followed by only one consonant; followed by two it's generally short. Unfamiliar combinations are:

ej as in m**a**te.

y as in **ewe**.

å when short as in h**o**t; when long as in r**a**w.

ä when before r as in m**a**n; otherwise as in g**e**t.

ö as in f**u**r but without the r sound.

Consonants are pronounced as in English except:

g usually as in **y**et; occasionally as in **sh**ut.

j, dj, gj, lj as in **y**et.

k before i, e y, ä, or ö, like the Scottish lo**ch**; otherwise hard.

qu as **kv**.

sch, skj, stj as in **sh**ut; otherwise hard.

tj like lo**ch**.

z as in **s**o.

BASICS

Hello	*Hej*	Yes	*Ja*	Today	*i dag*
Good morning	*God morgon*	No	*Nej*	Tomorrow	*i morgon*
Good afternoon	*God middag*	I don't understand	*Jag förstår inte*	Day after tomorrow	*i övermorgon*
Good night	*God natt*	Please	*Var så god*	In the morning	*på morgonen*
Goodbye	*Adjö*	Thank you (very much)	*Tack (så mycket)*	In the afternoon	*på eftermiddagen*
Do you speak English ?	*Talar ni Engelska*	You're welcome	*Var så god*	In the evening	*på kvällen*

SOME SIGNS

Entrance	*Ingång*	Closed	*Stängt*	No smoking	*Rökning förbjuden*
Exit	*Utgång*	Push	*Skjut*	No camping	*Tältning förbjuden*
Men	*Herrar*	Pull	*Drag*	No trespassing	*Tillträde förbjudet*
Women	*Damer*	Arrival	*Ankomst*	No entry	*Ingen ingång*
Open	*Öppen, öppet*	Departure	*Avgång*	Police	*Polis*

QUESTIONS AND DIRECTIONS

Where is . . . ?	*Var är . . .*	Good/bad	*Bra/dålig*
When ?	*När*	Left/right	*Vänster/höger*
What ?	*Vad*	Vacant/occupied	*Ledig/upptagen*
Can you direct me to . . .	*Skulle ni kunna visa mig vägen till . . .*	A little/a lot	*Lite/en mängd*
		I'd like	*Jag skulle vilja ha . . . ett*
It is/There is (is it/is there)	*Det är/det finns (är det/finns det)*	A single room	*enkelrum*
What time is it ?	*Hur mycket är klockan*	A double room	*ett dubbelrum*
Big/small	*Stor/liten*	How much is it ?	*Vad kostar det*
Cheap/expensive	*Billig/dyr*	Can we camp here ?	*Kan vi tälta här*
Early/late	*Tidig/sen*	Campsite	*Campingplats*
Hot/cold	*Varm/kall*	Tent	*Tält*
Near/far	*Nära/avlägsen*	Is there a youth hostel near here ?	*Finns det något vandrarhem i närheten*

NUMBERS

0	*noll*	9	*nio*	18	*arton*	70	*sjuttio*
1	*ett*	10	*tio*	19	*nitton*	80	*åttio*
2	*två*	11	*elva*	20	*tjugo*	90	*nittio*
3	*tre*	12	*tolv*	21	*tjugoett*	100	*hundra*
4	*fyra*	13	*tretton*	22	*tjugotvå*	101	*hundraett*
5	*fem*	14	*fjorton*	30	*trettio*	200	*tvåhundra*
6	*sex*	15	*femton*	40	*fyrtio*	500	*femhundra*
7	*sju*	16	*sexton*	50	*femtio*	1000	*tusen*
8	*åtta*	17	*sjutton*	60	*sextio*		

DAYS AND MONTHS

Sunday	*söndag*	January	*januari*	July	*juli*
Monday	*måndag*	February	*februari*	August	*augusti*
Tuesday	*tisdag*	March	*mars*	September	*september*
Wednesday	*onsdag*	April	*april*	October	*oktober*
Thursday	*torsdag*	May	*maj*	November	*november*
Friday	*fredag*	June	*juni*	December	*december*
Saturday	*lördag*				

Days and months are never capitalised

GLOSSARY OF SWEDISH TERMS AND WORDS

Berg	Mountain	*Muséet*	Museum
Bokhandel	Bookshop	*Pressbyrå*	Newsagent
Bro	Bridge	*Rabatt*	Rebate/discount
Cykelstig	Cycle path	*Rea*	Sales (and Vrakpriser, bargain)
Dal	Valley	*Riksdagshus*	Parliament building
Domkyrka	Cathedral	*Sjö*	Lake
Drottning	Queen (as in Drottninggatan, Queen Street)	*Skog*	Forest
		Slott	Castle
		Spår	Platform (at railway station)
Färja	Ferry	*Stadshus*	Town hall
Gamla	Old (as in Gamla Stan, old town)	*Stora*	Great/big (as in Storatorget, main square)
Gata (gt)	Street	*Strand*	Beach
Hamnen	Harbour	*Stugor*	Chalet, cottage
Järnvägsstation	Railway station	*Torg*	Central town square, usually the scene of daily/weekly markets
Klockan (kl)	O'clock		
Kyrka	Church		
Lilla	Little (as in Lilla Torget, small square)	*Universitet*	University
		Väg (v)	Road

CHAPTER NINE

STOCKHOLM AND AROUND

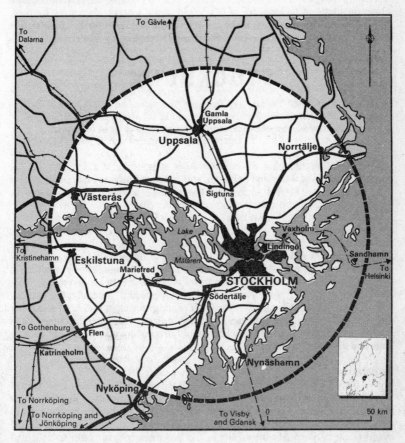

Stockholm comes lauded as Sweden's – and Scandinavia's – most beautiful city and, apart from a couple of sticky modern developments and a tangled road junction or two, it lives up to its own propaganda. Straddling several small islands the capital is a delightful place in which to spend time; not least as a contrast to the apparently endless lakes and forests of the rest of the country. And if, as is likely, you arrived in Sweden at one of the southwestern ports then Stockholm is attractive and accessible – good for a few days spent amid regal monuments, hi-tech high-cost consumerism and its stylish inhabitants.

Move away from Stockholm and it's not difficult to appreciate its unique geographical position. Water surrounds the city, and though you can travel by train and bus it's worth making the effort to follow the serene lakes, canals and rivers by boat. The eastern **archipelago** is within easy reach, 24,000 Baltic islands and a summer playground for holidaying Stockholmers. Then, close by and to the west of the city, there's **Drottningholm**, the seventeenth-century royal residence which gains nothing from its description as Sweden's Versailles and everything from a glorious lakeside location. Another simple trip is to the equally important castle of **Gripsholm** at Mariefred, again just an hour away by boat. And still within day-trip reach is the ancient capital and quiet medieval university town of **Uppsala**, a distinctive foil to Stockholm's burgeoning modern air.

STOCKHOLM

"It is not a city at all," he said with intensity. "It is ridiculous of it to think of itself as a city. It is simply a rather large village, set in the middle of some forests and some lakes. You wonder what it thinks it is doing there, looking so important."
Ingmar Bergman, interviewed by James Baldwin.

Self-important possibly, but **STOCKHOLM** is without doubt a disparate capital, one whose tracts of water and parkland, and range of monumental buildings give it an ageing, lived-in feel – an atmosphere that's at odds with its status as Sweden's most contemporary and forward-looking city.

Gamla Stan, the old town quarter and site of the original settlement, is an atmospheric mixture of pomp and historical accuracy; ceremonial buildings surrounded on all sides by a latticework of medieval lanes. Further afield and into the surrounding **modern city**, Stockholm trades tradition for a thoroughly up-to-date feel – wide boulevards, shopping malls and conspicuous, showy wealth. Yet the city isn't glitzy: you're never far from water or greenery, a reminder that Stockholm is one of Europe's more rural, saner capitals. Culturally, the city has few peers in Scandinavia and there are rich pickings for most tastes. Of some fifty different **museums and galleries**, the extraordinary seventeenth-century **Vasa** warship and **Skansen**, oldest – and best – of Europe's open-air museums, receive loud, and deserved, acclaim.

Orientation

Three small islands at the mouth of Lake Mälaren constitute the oldest part of Stockholm, and on them most of the city's national and historical buildings fight for breathing space. **Gamla Stan**, the original heart of the city, is the web of streets criss-crossing the centre of this island mass. Immediately east and next island along is **Skeppsholmen**, site of the two most central youth hostels, and with the best views of Stockholm's proud curving waterfront – from the Royal Palace round to the National Museum.

The modern city has moved just to the north and is split into two main sections: **Norrmalm**, north and east of the railway station, contains most of the fancier hotels, shopping streets and Kungsträdgården, the lively central park;

while, further east, **Östermalm** is more residential – a mix of grand avenues and smart houses that also boasts a succession of museums. Just to the north is the port for the *Silja* line ferries to Finland.

Out of the centre proper are **Djurgården**, the huge park to the east, and **Södermalm**, the striking island a few steps south of Gamla Stan. Gently rolling Djurgården contains Skansen, the Vasa ship, a host of other museums and Gröna Lund Tivoli amusement park. And for all purposes the parkland to the north, though separated by an expanse of water, is also considered part of Djurgården. Radiating out from beyond Slussen (the sluice separating the fresh waters of Mälaren from the salty Baltic), rocky Södermalm hides a couple of offbeat museums and some cheap places to sleep and eat. It's from down here, too, that the *Viking* line ferries leave for Finland. Connected by bridge to the western end of Södermalm, **Långholmen** Island is the target for summer swimming at its good beach. You can stay at the old prison, now converted to a youth hostel and hotel.

Arriving and information

All planes – international and domestic – arrive at **Arlanda airport**, 45km north of Stockholm. Buses (*Flygbussarna*: 6.10am–11pm; 35kr) run every ten minutes from the airport into the city, dropping at Cityterminalen (see below), journey time roughly fifty minutes.

By **train**, you'll arrive at and depart from **Central Station**, a cavernous structure on Vasagatan in Norrmalm. Inside, there's a useful money exchange and a room booking service, *Hotellcentrallen* (see below, "Finding a place to stay"); while all branches of the Tunnelbana, Stockholm's underground system, meet at T-Centralen, the station directly below Central Station. **Cityterminalen**, a hi-tech terminal adjacent to Central Station (and connected by escalators and walkways), handles all the **bus** services: airport bus, domestic and international services all arrive and depart from here; again, there's an exchange office, and the bus ticket office is here too – see "Listings".

Ferries connect the city with Helsinki and Turku in **Finland**, and with Mariehamn in the Finnish Åland Islands. There are four ferry lines: for *Viking Line* arrivals at Tegelvikshamnen, in the south of the city (in Södermalm), it's a thirty-minute walk across Gamla Stan to the modern centre; or take a connecting bus from outside the ferry terminal to Slussen and then the Tunnelbana to T-Centralen. *Åland Line* and *Birka Line* services dock in Södermalm, too, just up the quayside and close to Slussen at Stadsgården. From the *Silja Line* terminal in the northeastern reaches of the city, it's a short walk to Gärdet or Ropsten and then take the Tunnelbana into the centre. When leaving Stockholm by ferry, note the Swedish name for your Finnish destination: Helsinki is *Helsingfors* and Turku is *Åbo*. The boats which ply the **Göta Canal**, between Stockholm and Gothenburg (see "Gothenburg and the South"), dock at the quay on the island of Riddarholmen, just a couple of minutes' walk from Gamla Stan.

Information: the tourist centres

You should be able to pick up a map of the city at most points of arrival, but it's worth making your way to one of the **tourist centres** run by the *Stockholm Information Service* (*SIS*). Each hands out fistfuls of free information and you'll find a functional **map** in most of the brochures and booklets – though it's probably worth shelling out 10kr for the decent and larger plan of Stockholm and the surrounding area. You'll also be able to buy the valuable Stockholm Card (see below) from any of the tourist information centres.

The **main office** is in Norrmalm, on the ground floor of *Sverigehuset* (Sweden House: mid-June to Aug Mon–Fri 8.30am–6pm, Sat & Sun 8am–5pm; Sept to mid-June Mon–Fri 9am–5pm, Sat & Sun 9am–2pm; ☎08/789 20 00), at the northwestern corner of Kungsträdgården (off Hamngatan). Pick up *Stockholm This Week*, a free listings and entertainment guide, as well as any number of brochures and timetables. Upstairs, the **Swedish Institute** maintains an English-language library; free fact sheets are available on national matters as well as info on studying and working in Sweden; well worth a raid.

There are **other tourist centres** too: in the Stadshuset (May & Sept daily 9am–1pm; June–Aug daily 9am–5pm; ☎08/51 21 12); at the Kaknäs TV tower at Djurgården (Jan–March & Oct–Dec daily 9am–6pm; April & Sept daily 9am–10pm; May–Aug daily 9am–midnight; ☎08/667 80 30); and at Arlanda airport (daily 24hr; ☎08/797 61 00).

For youth-orientated information visit the **International Youth Centre** (see "Finding a place to stay", below) at Valhallavägen 142 or consult the **information desk** (mid-June to mid-Aug Mon–Fri 11am–5pm) in the *Hantverkshuset* hostel on Skeppsholmen. Lastly **Kulturhuset**, the monster cultural centre at Sergels Torg in Norrmalm, has a city information desk on the ground floor (Mon–Thurs 11am–8pm, Tues until 10pm, Fri–Sun 11am–6pm).

Left luggage

If you need to **leave luggage** anywhere on arrival, avoid the lockers at Central Station which are notoriously unsafe. Better to use the left luggage proper on the lower level (daily 7am–11.30pm) and bear in mind that there are safe lockers, too, at the *Hantverkshuset* youth hostel and the *Silja* and *Viking* ferry terminals.

Getting around

Stockholm winds and twists its way across islands, over water and through parkland, a thoroughly confusing place. To find your way around, best bet is to equip yourself with one of the tourist **maps** and walk: it takes about twenty-five minutes to cross central Stockholm on foot, east–west or north–south. Sooner or later, though, you'll have to use some form of **transport** to reach the more distant sights and, while routes are easy enough to master, there's a bewildering array of passes and discount cards available; the brief rundown below should help. One thing to try and **avoid**, though, is paying as you go on the city's transport system – an expensive business. The city is zoned, a trip within one zone costing 10kr (5kr for children and off-peak), with single tickets valid within that zone for one hour; cross a zone and it's another 5kr.

Public transport

Storstockholms Lokaltrafik (*SL*) operates a comprehensive system of buses and trains (underground and local) reaching well out of the city centre. There's an information office, the **SL-Center** inside T-Centralen station at Sergels Torg

(Mon–Thurs 9am–6pm, Fri 9am–5.30pm), which doles out timetables; and you can buy a useful **transport map** (27.50kr) from the office, or from *Pressbyrå* newspaper kiosks.

Quickest and most used of the transport systems is the **Tunnelbana** (T-bana), Stockholm's underground railway, based on three main lines with a smattering of branches. Entrances are marked by a blue **T** on a white background. It's the swiftest way to travel between Norrmalm and Södermalm, via Gamla Stan, and it's also handy for trips out of the centre into the suburbs – to ferry docks and distant youth hostels and museums. The T-bana is something of an artistic venture too, many of the stations like functional sculptures: for example, most centrally, T-Centralen is one huge papier-mâché cave; and Kungsträdgården is littered with statues and spotlights.

Buses can be less direct due to the nature of Stockholm's islands and central pedestrianisation – for help, consult the tourist centres' free bus route maps. If you still find the standard lines too complex, the *Turistlinjen* (Tourist Route) buses make a continuous and convoluted loop through the city, stopping at most points of interest on the way. There are regular daily departures between mid-June and mid-August on this service (Oct–April Sun only); one day's unlimited travel costs around 35kr (free with Stockholm Card, see below); and central pick-up points include *Sverigehuset*, Central Station and the National Art Museum.

Ferries provide access to the sprawling archipelago (for details of which see "Around Stockholm"), but they also link some of the central islands: Djurgården is connected with Nybroplan in Norrmalm (summer only) and Skeppsbron in Gamla Stan (all year); while there's a summer service from Stadshuset (Stadshusbron) to Långholmen. These trips all cost 12kr one-way. For longer water trips, **cruises** on Lake Mälaren and city boat tours also leave from Stadshusbron, from Nybroplan and from the quays in front of the *Grand Hotel* – the Stockholm Card is valid for a discounted tour on most of them.

Travel passes and tickets

The best pass to have, certainly if you're planning to do any sightseeing at all, is the *Stockholmskortet* or **Stockholm Card** – giving unlimited travel on city buses, ferries, underground and local trains, free museum entry, discounts on boat trips and tours, plus free parking and other surprises. Cards are sold undated and stamped on first use, then valid for 24 hours (125kr), 48hours (190kr) or 72 hours (285kr): one card will cover one adult and two children. They are **not valid** on the direct buses to the airport or on the connecting night-bus to the Nynäshamn ferry terminal (for Gotland) – although there's nothing to stop you using your card to go by local train to Nynäshamn.

Of other options, the *Turistkort* or **tourist card** is valid for 24 hours (central Stockholm, 22kr; or the whole county, 40kr) or 72 hours (whole county only, 76kr), and gives unlimited travel on public transport and rides on the ferries to Djurgården. In addition, the 72-hr card gives you admission to Skansen, Gröna Lund Tivoli and the Kaknäs TV tower. Under 18s and OAPs qualify for a fifty percent discount on either card.

Alternatively, you can buy a strip of fifteen *SL* **ticket coupons** (45kr, 22.50kr for off-peak travel), using two for each city journey; while the *SL* **monthly card** (225kr) is often worth considering even for stays of only a week or fortnight. And with a monthly card, another 120kr (200kr otherwise) buys a **Waxholmbolaget supplementary card** which gives one month's free boat travel in the archipel-

STOCKHOLM

SVEAVAGEN

VALLHALLAVAGEN

SOLNABRON

S.T.ERIKSGATAN

Vanadislunden

BIRGER JARLSGATAN

NORRTULSGATAN

UPPLANDSGATAN

SVEAVAGEN

ODENGATAN

KARLBERGSVAGEN

ODENPLAN

ODENGATAN

UPPLANDSGATAN

KUNGSTENSGATAN

BIRGER JARLSGATAN

SVEAVAGEN

Vasaparken

N O R R M A L M

Hospital

Adolf Fred.
Kyrkä

BRUNNSGATAN

BIRGER

TORSGATAN

KAMMAKARGATAN

Concert
House

KUNGSGATAN

KUNGSGATAN

OLOF PALMESGATAN

SVEAVAGEN

JAKOBSBERGSGATAN

MASTER SAMUELSGATAN

0   500 m

GAMLA BROGATAN

Cityterminalen

VASAGATAN

Post
Office

Kulturhuset

SERGELS TORG

HAMNGATAN

FLEMINGGATAN

KLARABERGSGATAN

Sverigehuset
(Tourist Office)

KUNGSHOLMGATAN

Klara
Kyrka

Kungsträd
Opera
House

GUST
AD TORG

STRONG

VASAGATAN

K U N G S H O L M E N

Central
Station

Riksdagshuset

Helgeandsho

BACKERSGATAN

NORR MALARSTRAND

Stadshuset

Riddarhuset

Sto

Ferry to
Gripsholm

RIDDARHOLMEN

GAMLA
STAN

M ä l a r e n

Riddarholms
Kyrkan

SODERM
TORG

LÅNGHOLMEN

Långholmen
Youth Hostel

SÖDER MÄLARSTRAND

SÖDERMALM

Maria Magdalena Kyrka

KOSTERGATAN

HORNSGATAN

SANKT PAULSGATAN

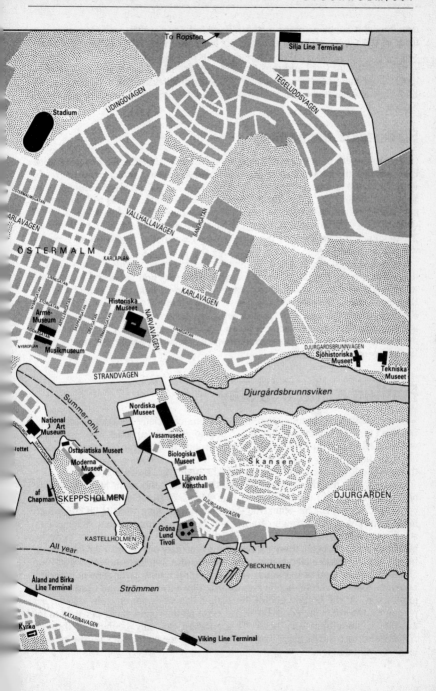

ago. Buy the supplementary card at *Waxholmbolaget*'s office at Strömkajen (in front of the *Grand Hotel*). Otherwise an **Inter-skerries card** (150kr) from the same office buys sixteen days' travel on the archipelago boats.

The Stockholm Card and tourist tickets are on sale in *Sverigehuset*, the other tourist information centres, *Pressbyrå* (newspaper) kiosks and *Hotellcentralen*; the *SL* tickets and cards are available from the *SL* office inside T-Centralen or Central Station.

Bikes, taxis and parking

Given this wealth of help, other transport seems a bit superfluous. For the record **bike rentals** (roughly 25kr per hour) are available from *Cykelspecialisten Hoj In* (☎08/34 57 58) at Karlsbergsvägen 55 (Odenplan T-bana) or *Skepp o Hoj* (April to Sept only; ☎08/60 57 57) at Djurgårdsbron, the bridge that leads to Djurgården; and **taxis**, either hailed in the street or summoned by ringing ☎08/15 00 00 (☎08/15 04 00 for advance booking). If you ring, it will cost 25kr for the taxi to get to you, and then 29–40kr per nine kilometres: driving across the city centre will cost around 80kr.

Drivers should watch where they park. In the centre, parking is not allowed one night a week (midnight–6am) for street cleaning, and signs and meters say which night on which block. If your car is towed away (and they are) it will go to Ropsten, north of the city, and you'll have to pay (hugely) to get it back (T-bana to Ropsten, ring ☎08/54 21 20). Stockholm Card holders, though, can park freely and safely in all metered spaces between June and August, except on street cleaning nights – look for the words *Gatukontoret* or *Parkeringsbolaget* for valid spaces. For **car rentals** see "Listings".

Finding a place to stay

There's plenty of accommodation in Stockholm, especially for budget travellers, but don't turn up late in summer and expect to get a **cheap bed**. They exist, but will take effort and some walking/ringing around to find. For this reason, booking your first night's accommodation in advance is always a good idea, either through the *Sverigehuset* tourist centre or the hotels and hostels direct.

Alternatively, use the services of **Hotellcentralen**, the room booking service on the lower level of Central Station (Jan–March & Oct–Dec Mon–Fri 8.30am–5pm; April Mon–Fri 8am–5pm; May–Sept daily 8am–9pm; ☎08/24 08 80), which holds comprehensive listings of hotel and hostel accommodation. Where they score over ringing yourself is by having the latest special offers direct from the hotels trying to fill beds: there's a booking fee of 20kr per room, 10kr for a youth hostel. *Hotelcentrallen* also features the **Stockholm Package** between mid-June and mid-August (and at weekends all year round), a nifty arrangement whereby bookings made at certain hotels are rewarded by a free Stockholm Card for each night's stay. At the bottom end of the scale it can work out cheaply – 260kr per person in twin room including breakfast; right up to around 450kr per person for a room in something very posh. This package can only be booked through *Hotellcentralen* (who'll charge you a 20kr booking fee on top); it's no use turning up at individual hotels.

Hostels

It's no real loss if you can't afford Stockholm's hotels since there's a wide range of good, well-run hostel accommodation, costing from around 60–70kr a night per person. There are no less than four official *STF/IYHF* hostels in the city, two of which – *af Chapman* and *Långholmen* – number amongst the best youth hostels in Scandinavia, if not Europe. You'll have to plan ahead if you want to stay at most of the places listed below: a phone call on arrival is the least that you should do; for other places you'll need to have booked weeks in advance.

STF hostels

Af Chapman, Skeppsholmen (☎08/10 37 15). This square-rigged ship moored at Skeppsholmen has unsurpassed (at least at this price) views over the old town. Without an advance written reservation (try a fortnight before you arrive) the chances of a space in summer are negligible, although queuing from around 7am has been known to yield a bed: the drawbacks of a nautical night's accommodation are no kitchen and a midday lockout. Open April to mid-December; 72kr a bed.

Hantverkshuset, Skeppsholmen (☎08/20 25 06). A dead central hostel, at the foot of the *af Chapman*'s gangplank. Immensely popular, it's little better for speculative arrivals, although at least it's open all year. Again, there's no kitchen or washing/drying facilities and the same midday lockout; 72kr a bed.

Långholmen, Kronohäktet, Långholmen (☎08/668 05 10). Stockholm's newest and grandest *STF* hostel is situated inside the old prison buildings on the island of Långholmen – the cells converted into smart hotel and hostel rooms. Between June and August and at weekends year-round, the 272 beds go for around 70kr each (85kr non-members), breakfast 40kr; at other times there are just 26 hostel beds so always ring ahead first. If you want to use the hotel room facilities (TV, video and phone) then there's an extra charge, but it's still the best deal you'll get in Stockholm. There's a summer ferry service (10kr) from Stadshusbron to the island, a ten-minute ride; or take the T-bana to Hornstull and follow the signs.

Zinken, Zinkens väg 20, Södermalm (☎08/68 57 86); T-bana Zinkensdamm. Huge and open all year, with kitchen facilities; 72kr a bed.

Other hostels

Columbus Hotell & Vandrarhem, Tjärhovsgatan 11, Södermalm (☎08/ 44 17 17); T-bana Medborgarplatsen. Open all year, this friendly hostel has dorm beds at 70kr, doubles at 190kr.

Dansakademien, Döbelnsgatan 56 (☎08/31 31 18); T-bana Rådmandgatan. A dance academy with cheap summer dorms (55kr per person); open July and August only.

Frescati Hostel, Professorsslingen 13–15 (☎08/15 79 96); T-bana Universitet. A large hostel with 120 beds; rooms from 140kr; open June to August.

Fryshuset, Tegelviksgatan 19–23, Södermalm (☎08/714 52 40); T-bana to Slussen and then bus #46 to the end of the line. A *YMCA*-run venture with a gym and café. For a couple of years it put mattresses on the floors in July and August only. That side of it seems to have folded, but check with the tourist centre who will know if the facility exists.

International Youth Centre, Valhallavägen 142 (☎08/663 43 89); T-bana line #13 or #14 to Karlaplan, Valhallavägen exit. By far the cheapest bed in town; mid-June to August a dorm bed costs 30kr (plus 10kr compulsory annual membership), breakfast 10kr, and there's a maximum five-night stay. The free showers, laundry, and kitchen are open to non-residents too, and other goodies include foreign newspapers, sewing machinés, luggage storage and a cheap café. The info desk is open Mon–Sat 1–9pm, while the hostel is closed between 10am and 1pm and during the winter (when it's strictly café and info only).

Kista InterRail Point, Jyllandsgatan 16 (☎08/752 64 56); T-bana line #11 to Kista, exit Sorögatan. A fair distance out from the centre, but with beds at 50kr, breakfast 15kr, plus kitchen and laundry facilities. Open mid-July to mid-August only, 7am–midnight.

Sundyberg InterRail Point, Vackravägen 4–6, Sundyberg (☎08/98 47 53); T-bana line #11 to Näckrosen, exit Storskogstorget. To the north of Stockholm, beds 50kr, kitchen facilities available. Open mid-July to mid-August, 7–10am & 5–10pm.

Hotels and pensions

In summer, it's a buyer's market in Stockholm as the business trade declines, but don't count on anything less than 150–200kr a night per person. The cheapest choices, on the whole, are found to the north of Cityterminalen, in the streets to the west of Adolf Fredriks Kyrka. But don't rule out the more expensive places either: there are some attractive "weekend prices" and other offers, which make a spot of luxury a little more affordable.

Budget hotels and pensions

Hotell Anno 1647, Mariagränd 3 (☎08/44 04 80); near Slussen, in Södermalm; T-bana Slussen. Handy location for the old town. The very cheapest rooms go from 325kr single, 400kr double, including breakfast.

Berglunds Pensionat, Kammakargatan 40 (☎08/10 80 65); T-bana Rådmandgatan. Within walking distance of central Norrmalm, this tiny pension has just five rooms; single 250kr, double 350kr.

Hotel Danielson, Wallingatan 31 (☎08/11 10 76). A small place, off Drottninggatan, north of Central Station; from 250kr single, 350kr double.

Hotel Gamla Stan, Lilla Nygatan 25 (☎08/24 44 50). Really the only half-way affordable old-town hotel, though it's no gift at around 840kr double including breakfast; save it for a special occasion.

Gustav af Klint, Stadsgårdskajen 153, Södermalm (☎08/40 40 77). One of several floating hotels, this homely boat moored off Södermalm is where those who can't get onto the *af Chapman* (see below) end up; 260kr single and 360kr double make it a bargain; you can walk from Gamla Stan in a few minutes.

Hotell Gustav Vasa, Västmannagatan 61 (☎08/34 38 01); T-bana Odenplan. Not a bad location, in the northern part of Norrmalm, and cheap enough; singles from 250kr, doubles from 320kr, breakfast included.

Gustavsvikshemmet, Västmannagatan 15 (☎08/21 44 50); T-bana Odenplan. Same street and same prices as above, but much smaller (only nine rooms) and breakfast not included.

Karelia Hotell, Birger Jarlsgatan 35, Norrmalm (☎08/24 76 60). Finnish-owned, this pleasant and central hotel has basement "cabins" at around 400kr double (often a lot cheaper if still available late in the day) and weekend suites from around 450kr – all including breakfast. See also "Entertainment".

Hotell Långholmen, Kronohäktet, Långholmen (☎08/668 05 00). A beautiful conversion, this was once a prison, the rooms fashioned from the former cells. Singles 520kr, doubles 660kr, extra bed 100kr; weekend and summer price down to 350kr single and 550kr double, all including breakfast – a real bargain. See also "Hostels", above.

Pensionat Oden, Odengatan 38 (☎08/30 63 49); T-bana Odenplan. Another Norrmalm location; singles around 300kr, doubles 395kr, including breakfast. It's small, so ring first.

Hotell Örnsköld, Nybrogatan 6 (☎08/667 02 85); T-bana Östermalmstorg. Cheap Östermalm location; singles from 295kr, doubles from 575kr.

Östermalms Pensionat, Sibyllegatan 19, Östermalm (☎08/660 30 89); T-bana Östermalmstorg. Fairly central and handy for Djurgården; singles 375kr, doubles 495kr, breakfast included.

Camping

With the nearest campsite 10km away, camping in Stockholm can prove a bit of a burden. It's easier with a **campervan** since there are two special sites in the city centre. The tourist centres have free camping maps available, detailing facilities at all Stockholm's campsites.

As a last resort, **sleeping rough** is a tricky proposition in central Stockholm and not really advised. Though not illegal to sleep in a park there are few places where you won't draw attention to yourself, long summer nights not helping matters. The open spaces of Djurgården offer the best opportunity while there's generally a posse of homeless travellers whiling away the night outside the *af Chapman* on Skeppsholmen.

Campsites

Bredäng (☎08/97 70 71). Southwest of the centre and near the beach; open all year, 65kr per tent site. T-bana line #13 and #15 to Bredäng.

Flaten (☎08/773 01 00). Fifteen kilometres southeast and open May to September; 20kr per site. Bus #401 from Slussen.

Östermalms Husvagncamping (☎08/10 29 03). Behind the Stockholm Stadium, this is for campervans only; mid-June to the end of July, a maximum two night stay.

Södermalms Husvagncamping (☎08/43 91 18). Close to Eriksdalsbadet swimming pool; for campervans only; open mid-June to the end of July; a maximum stay of two nights.

Ängby (☎08/37 04 20). West of the city and also near a beach, open June to August, 30kr per site. T-bana line #17 or #18 to Ängbyplan.

The City

Seeing the sights is a straightforward business in Stockholm: everything is easy to get to, opening hours are long, the city pleasant and presentable. And though the sights and museums have changed, visitors for 150 years have noted Stockholm's aesthetic qualities. Once, in the centre, there were country lanes, great orchards, grazing cows, even windmills. The downside then was no pavements (until the 1840s) and no water system (until 1858), open sewers, squalid streets and crowded slums. But Stockholm today is one of Europe's brightest, cleanest, most sanitary cities, with a waterfront skyline that has few equals. Yet, apart from the spruced up old town, which is getting more chic and pricey each year, the city has little soul. Unless you're very into museums (of which there's an indiscriminate abundance), Stockholm's fabled beauty palls after a few days spent tramping past expensive shops and restaurants. It's all been a bit too much for the city's middle class bratpack, and dozens are arrested every summer for livening things up with a spot of window smashing in central Norrmalm. More shockingly, though, for all Swedes, a Norrmalm street saw the murder of their Prime Minister, Olof Palme, in 1986.

Old Stockholm: Gamla Stan and Riddarholmen

Three islands make up **Old Stockholm** – Riddarholmen, Staden and Helgeandsholmen – the whole history-riddled mass a clutter of seventeenth- and eighteenth-century Renaissance buildings backed by hairline medieval alleys.

Here, on the three adjoining polyps of land, Birger Jarl erected the first fortifications in 1255 and for centuries this was the city of Stockholm.

Although strictly speaking only the largest island, Staden, contains **Gamla Stan** (the old town), it's a name that is usually attached to the buildings and streets of all three islands. Once Stockholm's working centre, nowadays Gamla Stan is primarily a tourist city, an eminently strollable concentration of royal palace, parliament and cathedral, and one which represents an extraordinary tableau of cultural history. The central spider's web, especially approaching across Norrbro or Riksbron into its old heart, invokes potent images of the past: sprawling monumental buildings and high, airy churches form a protective girdle around the narrow streets. The tall, dark houses in the centre were mostly those of wealthy merchants, still picked out today by intricate doorways and portals bearing coats of arms. Some of the alleys in between are the skinniest thoroughfares possible, steeply stepped between battered walls; while others are dead ends, covered passageways linking leaning buildings. It's easy to spend hours wandering around here, although the atmosphere these days is not so much medieval as mercenary: there's a dense concentration of antique shops, art showrooms and pricey cellar restaurants, though to be fair, the frontages don't often intrude upon the otherwise light-starved streets.

The Riksdagshuset and the Medeltidsmuseum

You'll walk past the **Riksdagshuset** (Jan–May & Sept Sat & Sun noon–2pm; June–Aug Mon–Fri noon–3.30pm; free), the Swedish parliament building, almost every time you enter and leave the old town. Completely restored in the 1970s (though only seventy years old then), it's a deceptive place as the columned, stately and original front (seen to best effect from Norrbro) is hardly ever used. The business end is the new glassy bulge at the back and it's around here that **free guided tours** perambulate. Being Sweden rather than Westminster the seating for members is in healthy non-adversarial rows, grouped by constituency and not by party.

In front of the Riksdagshuset, accessible by a set of steps leading down from Norrbro, the **Medeltidsmuseum** (Jan–May & Sept–Dec Tues–Sun 11am–5pm, Wed until 9pm; June–Aug Tues–Thurs 11am–7pm, Fri–Sun 11am–5pm; 20kr, children 5kr) is the best city-related historical collection in Stockholm. Medieval ruins, tunnels and walls, were discovered during excavations under the parliament building and they've been incorporated into a walk-through underground exhibition. There are reconstructed houses to poke around, models and pictures, boats, skeletons and street scenes. With the detailed English labelling that goes with it, it's a splendid display; good for the kids, too.

The Kungliga Slottet

Cross over a second set of bridges and up rears the most distinctive monumental building in Stockholm, the **Kungliga Slottet** (Royal Palace) – a low, pinky-brown square building whose two front arms stretch down towards the water. The old *Tre Kronor* (Three Crowns) castle of Stockholm burned down at the beginning of King Karl XII's reign, leaving his architect, Tessin the Younger (see *Around Stockholm*, "Drottningholm"), with a free hand to design a simple and beautiful Renaissance successor. Finished in 1760 the Palace is a striking achievement: uniform, almost sombre, outside, the magnificent Baroque and Rococo interior is a swirl of state rooms and museums, usually open to the public. The sheer size and

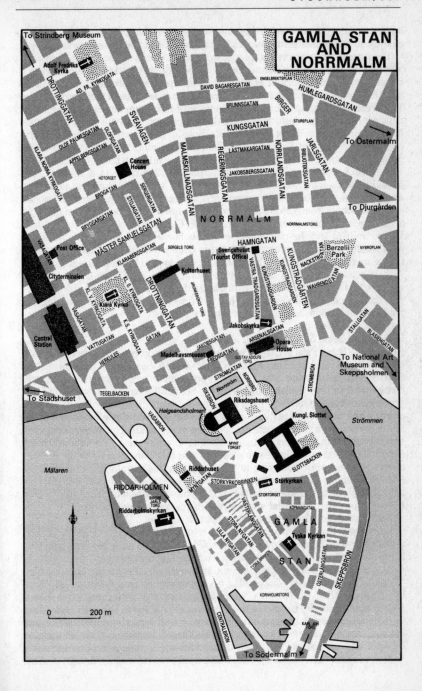

GAMLA STAN
AND
NORRMALM

limited opening hours conspire against seeing everything at once, which would anyway be an expensive business without a Stockholm Card and some discretion.

The **Apartments** (Jan to mid-May & mid-Aug to Dec Tues–Sun noon–3pm; mid-May to mid-Aug Tues–Sat 10am–3pm, Sun noon–3pm; 15kr, students 5kr) form a relentlessly linear collection of furniture and tapestries. All basic Rent-a-Palace stuff, too sumptuous to take in and inspirational only in terms of their colossal size. The **Treasury** (Jan–April & Oct–Dec Mon–Sat 11am–3pm, Sun noon–4pm; May–Sept Mon–Sat 10am–4pm, Sun noon–4pm; 15kr, students 10kr), on the other hand, is for once worthy of the name. Its ranks of jewel-studded crowns grab the eye, the oldest that of Karl X (1650), the most charming those belonging to the princesses Eugène (1860) and Sofia (1771). Also worth catching is the **Armoury** (Jan–April & Sept–Dec Tues–Fri 10am–4pm, Sat & Sun 11am–4pm; May–Aug Mon–Fri 10am–4pm, Sat & Sun 11am–4pm; 15kr, students 10kr), less to do with weapons and more to do with ceremony – suits of armour, costumes and horse-drawn coaches from the sixteenth century onwards. It certainly couldn't be accused of skipping over historical detail. King Gustav II Adolf died in the Battle of Lützen in 1632 and the museum displays his horse (stuffed) and the blood and mud spattered garments retrieved after the enemy had stripped him down to his undies on the battlefield. For those with the energy, the **Palace Museum** (June–Aug daily noon–3pm; 3kr) contains parts of the older *Tre Kronor* castle, its ruins underneath the present building. And there's the **Museum of Antiquities** (June–Aug daily noon–3pm; 3kr) and the **Hall of State** (May–Sept daily noon–3pm; Oct Sat & Sun only noon–3pm; 2kr) for real palace junkies.

Into Gamla Stan: Stortorget and around

Beyond the Royal Palace and you're into Gamla Stan proper, the streets suddenly narrower and darker. The highest point of old Stockholm is crowned by **Storkyrkan**, almost the first building you stumble upon: the Great Church, consecrated in 1306. Pedantically-speaking, Stockholm has no cathedral, but this rectangular brick church is now accepted as such, the monarchs of Sweden married and crowned here. Storkyrkan gained its present shape at the end of the fifteenth century, with a Baroque remodelling in the 1730s. The interior is marvellous. Twentieth-century restoration removed the white plaster from the red brick columns and, although there's no evidence that this was intended in the original church, it gives warm colouring to the rest of the building. Much is made of the fifteenth-century Gothic sculpture of *St George and the Dragon*, certainly an animated piece but easily overshadowed by the royal pews – more like golden billowing thrones – and the monumental black and silver altar-piece. If you're around, organ recitals take place every Saturday at 1pm.

Stortorget, Gamla Stan's main square, is still handsome and elegantly proportioned. Crowded by eighteenth-century buildings, whose walls bear wrought iron lamps, it's well placed for access to the surrounding narrow shopping streets. In 1520 Christian II used the square as an execution site during the so-called "Stockholm Blood Bath", dispatching his opposition en masse with bloody finality. Now, as then, the streets **Västerlånggatan** and **Österlånggatan**, **Stora Nygatan** and **Lilla Nygatan** run the length of the old town, although today their time-worn buildings harbour a succession of art and craft shops, restaurants and discreet fast food outlets. It's commercial but largely unobtrusive, and in summer buskers and evening strollers clog the narrow ways, making it an entertaining area to wander – and to eat and drink. There are few real targets, though at some stage you'll probably pass the copy of the George and Dragon statue in **Köpmantorget** (off Österlånggatan). Take every opportunity, too, to scuttle up side streets, where you'll find fading coats of arms, covered alleyways and worn cobbles at every turn.

Just off Västerlånggatan, on Tyska Brinken, the **Tyska kyrkan**, or "German Church" (Sat & Sun noon–4pm), belonged to Stockholm's medieval German merchants, the meeting place of their Guild of St Gertrude. A copper-topped red-brick church atop a rise, it abandoned its secular role and assumed a religious aspect in the seventeenth century, when the Baroque decorators got hold of it: the result, a richly fashioned interior with the pulpit dominating the nave, is outstanding. Sporting a curious royal gallery in one corner, designed by Tessin the Elder, it came complete with mini palace roof, angels and the three crowns of Swedish kingship.

If you want lighter relief, then a final call in Gamla Stan might be at the **Postal Museum** (Tues & Thurs–Sat 11am–3pm, Wed 11am–8pm, Sun 11am–4pm; free), at Lilla Nygatan 6 – though you'd have to be a real fan of Swedish stamp design to get much out of it.

Riddarhuset and Riddarholmen

If the history has gripped you, it's better to keep right on as far as the handsome Baroque **Riddarhuset** (Mon–Fri 11.30am–12.30pm; 10kr, students 5kr), the seventeenth-century "House of Nobles". In its *Great Hall* the Swedish aristocracy met during the Parliament of the Four Estates (1668–1865) and their coats of arms – around 2500 of them – are splattered across the walls. Some 600 of the families survive, the last ennoblement in 1974. Take a look downstairs, too, in the *Chancery* which stocks heraldic bone china by the shelfload and rackfulls of fancy signet rings – essential accessories for the eighteenth-century noble-about-town.

Riddarhuset shouldn't really be seen in isolation. It's a matter of seconds across the bridge onto **Riddarholmen** ("Island of the Knights") proper, and to **Riddarholmskyrkan** (May–Aug Mon–Sat 10am–3pm, Sun 1–3pm; Sept Mon–Sat noon–3pm; 5kr). Originally a Franciscan monastery, for over six centuries the church has been established as the burial place of Swedish royalty. Since Magnus Ladulås was sealed up here in 1290, his successors have rallied round to create a Swedish pantheon and, amongst others, you'll find the tombs of Gustav II Adolf (in the green marble sarcophagus), Karl XII, Gustav III and Karl Johan XIV, plus other innumerable and unmemorable descendants. Walk around the back of the church for views of the Stadshuset and Lake Mälaren, given piquancy in winter when the water freezes solid right up to the bridge, Västerbron, in the distance.

Skeppsholmen

Off Gamla Stan's eastern reaches, but annoyingly unconnected by bridge or boat, lies the island of **Skeppsholmen**; home to most younger travellers in Stockholm who end up at one of the island's two youth hostels. Other than this convenience, the reason for being here is an eclectic clutch of museums, the nearest to the hostels being the **Moderna Museet** (Tues–Fri 11am–9pm, Sat & Sun 11am–5pm, 20kr, students 10kr, under 16s free & free for all each Thurs), one of the better modern art museums in Europe. The roomy, well-designed layout alone is encouraging, while the collection is surprisingly comprehensive, representing many of the twentieth century's greatest artists. Dali's monumental *Enigma of William Tell* shows the artist at his most conventionally unconventional, while Matisse's *Apollo* (1953) also stands out, a broad and confident work. Look too for Picasso's *Guitar Player* and a whole stream of Warhol, Lichtenstein, Man Ray and Francis Bacon. It's a pleasing place to idle away time, with outdoor tables and jazz/rock concerts in the summer, a decent café inside and temporary exhibitions held all year.

A steep climb up the nearby hill, to the northern tip of the island, leads to the **Östasiatiska Museet**, the Museum of Far Eastern Antiquities (Tues 11am–9pm, Wed–Sun 11am–5pm; 20kr, students 10kr, free on Wed). The reward is an array of objects which display incredible craftsmanship – fifth-century Chinese tomb figures, delicate jade amulets, an awesome assembly of sixth-century Buddhas, Indian watercolours and gleaming bronze Krishna figures. But it seems redundant to mention a few particular favourites when one roomful of treasures leads unfailingly into another. Half a day well spent.

Other than this, there's little to detain you on Skeppsholmen or on adjacent, microscopic **Kastellholmen**, connected by a bridge to the south. Both islands are in the Baltic, attractive enough to have induced the Swedish Navy to settle there in the nineteenth century, and some of the old barracks are still visible. If you're taking a turn around the islands though, be aware of Skeppsholmen's other diversion – the Architecture Museum, for which see "Stockholm's Other Museums", below.

The National Art Museum

On the way to Skeppsholmen, as you approach the bridge, Skeppsholmbron, you'll pass the striking waterfront **National Art Museum** (Jan–June & Sept–Dec Tues 10am–9pm, Wed–Sun 10am–5pm; July & Aug Tues–Sun 10am–5pm; 30kr, students 20kr), looking right out over the Royal Palace. The impressive collection is contained on three floors: the **ground floor** is taken up by changing exhibitions of prints and drawings; and this is where you'll have to leave your bags (in the refundable lockers provided). There's a museum shop and a café here, too.

The **first floor** is devoted to applied art and if it's curios you're after, this museum has the lot – beds slept in by kings, cabinets leaned on by queens, plates eaten off by nobles – mainly from the centuries when Sweden was a great power. There's modern work alongside the ageing tapestries and furniture, including Art Nouveau coffee pots and vases, and the intelligent simplicity of Swedish wooden chair design.

It's the **second floor**, though, that's of more engaging interest. There's a plethora of European and Mediterranean sculpture and some mesmerising sixteenth- and seventeenth-century Russian Orthodox icons. The paintings are equally wide ranging and of a similar high quality. Something of a coup for the museum is their display of Rembrandt's *Conspiracy of Claudius Civilis*, one of his largest monumental paintings, in room 33. Picturing a scene from Tacitus' *History*, the bold work shows a gathering of well-armed chieftains. There are minor works by other, later masters (most notably Renoir), and some fine sixteenth- to eighteenth-century works by **Swedish artists**. One, by Carl Gustav Pilo, a late-eighteenth-century painting, depicts the coronation of Gustav III in the Storkyrkan in Gamla Stan – the detail interesting since it shows the church with white plaster columns and not the red-brick of today.

So much is packed into this museum that it can quickly become confusing and overwhelming. To wade through all this, splash out 5kr on the guidebook; money well spent.

Norrmalm

Modern Stockholm, its wide streets, shops, office blocks and small parks, lies immediately to the north and east of Gamla Stan; and it's split into two distinct sections. You'll either arrive at or be set down in **Norrmalm**, and can't avoid passing through this central area on your wanderings around the city. East of here, the streets begin to widen out into classier, residential Östermalm (for which, see below).

Around Gustav Adolfs Torg

Down on the waterfront, at the foot of Norrbro, is **Gustav Adolfs Torg**, more a traffic island than a square these days, with the eighteenth-century **Opera House** (*Operan*) its proudest and most notable building. It was here at a masked ball in 1792 that King Gustav III was shot by one Captain Ankarström, an admirer of Rousseau and member of the aristocratic opposition. The story is recorded in Verdi's opera *Un Ballo in Maschera*, and you'll find Gustav's ball costume, as well as the assassin's pistols and mask, displayed in the palace armoury in Gamla Stan. The opera's famous restaurant, *Operakällaren*, which faces the water, is hellishly expensive, the trendy café less, but not invitingly, so. Gustav's statue marks the centre of the square where, apart from the views, the only affordable entertainment is to rent a fishing rod and try to pull salmon out of **Strömmen**, the waters flowing through the centre of the city. Stockholmers have had the right to fish this outlet from Lake Mälaren to the Baltic since the seventeenth century – it's not as difficult as it sounds and there's usually someone standing on one of the bridges nearby trying their luck.

Just off the square, at Fredsgatan 2, is the **Medelhavsmuseet**, a museum devoted to Mediterranean and Near Eastern Antiquities (Tues 11am–9pm, Wed– Sun 11am–4pm; 15kr, students 5kr). Its enormous *Egyptian* display shows just about every aspect of Egyptian life up to the Christian era. As well as several whopping great mummies, the most attractive pieces are the bronze weapons, tools and domestic objects from the time before the Pharaohs. The *Cyprus* collections are also huge, the largest such gathering outside Cyprus itself, depicting life through a period spanning 6000 years. Additionally the museum contains strong Greek displays and, comprehensively, Etruscan and Roman art. A couple of rooms examine Islamic culture through pottery, glass and metal work as well as portraying decorative elements from architecture, Arabian calligraphy and Persian miniature painting. A sparkling museum all round.

From Central Station east to Kungsträdgården

Head up **Vasagatan** and it's only a few minutes to **Central Station** and the brand new **Cityterminalen**, hub of virtually all Stockholm's transport. Just when Stockholm threatens to get all modern and showy, though, ducking down Klarabergsgatan to the right reveals **Klara kyrka** (Mon–Fri 10am–6pm, Sat 10am–7pm, Sun 8.30am–6pm): it's typical of Stockholm's hidden churches, only the spires visible as you negotiate the surrounding streets. Hemmed in on all sides, the church is particularly delicate, with a light and flowery eighteenth-century painted interior and an impressive, golden pulpit. If you needed another reason to call in, a room inside (10am–6pm) serves free coffee and biscuits and has English newspapers to look over. Out in the churchyard a memorial stone commemorates the eighteenth-century Swedish poet Carl Michael Bellman, whose popular, lengthy ballads are said to have been composed extempore: his unmarked grave is somewhere in the churchyard.

Head back down towards Gustav Adolfs Torg and the water and Norrmalm's eastern boundary is marked by **Kungsträdgården**, most fashionable and central of the city's numerous parks. Once a royal kitchen garden, it's now Stockholm's main meeting place, especially in summer when there's almost always something going on: free evening gigs, live theatre, dance schools and cafés – along with decorative guardsmen who march past the park on their way to the Royal Palace (July & Aug weekdays at noon, weekends at 1pm). In the winter, the *Isbanen*, open-air ice rink at the top end, hires out skates (daily 9am–4pm; 10kr) so that five-year-old Swedish kids can humiliate inept ice-crazed tourists. The main tourist office, **Sverigehuset**, is here, too, at the corner with Hamngatan, while the bottom, west, side of the park holds **Jakobs kyrka** (daily 11am–5pm), another of the city's overlooked churches. It's the pulpit again that draws the attention, a great, golden affair, while the date of the church – 1642 – is stamped high up on the ceiling in gold figures. There are weekly concerts here as well; organ and choir recitals on Saturday at 3pm.

Nybroplan

The water's edge square just to the east is **Nybroplan**, marked by the white-stone, relief-studded **Kungliga Teatern**, Stockholm's showpiece theatre. The curved harbour in front is the departure point for all kinds of archipelago ferries and tours. And in the mid-distance you can see the Nordiska and Vasa museums over on Djurgården, also reached by ferries from Nybroplan. Birger Jarlsgatan strikes north from Nybroplan, now a major shopping street but until 1855 the site of two pillories and largely rural.

Segels Torg to Hötorget

Kungsträdgården reaches from the water northwards as far as **Hamngatan** and, at the western end of this, past the enormous *NK* department store, lies **Sergels Torg**, modern Stockholm at its most blatant. It's an unending free show centred around the five seething floors of the **Kulturhuset** (Mon ground floor only 10am–8pm; otherwise Tues 11am–10pm, Wed–Fri 11am–6pm, Sat & Sun 11am–5pm; reading room Mon–Fri from 9am, Sat & Sun from noon) whose windows look down upon the milling square. Inside the building, devoted to contemporary Swedish culture, are temporary art and craft exhibitions which combine with workshops open to anyone willing to get their hands dirty. The reading room (*Läsesalongen*) on the ground level is stuffed with foreign newspapers, books, records and magazines; and people when it's wet. Check the information desk on the ground floor for details of poetry readings, concerts and theatre performances – these and everything else, including admission, are free. And the café on the top floor has the best views of central Stockholm you'll find.

A spewing fountain, around a tall, wire-like column, dominates the massive space outside, while one level down in **Sergels Arkaden** buskers, brass bands and the odd demonstration interfere with shoppers and browsers. There's an entrance into **T-Centralen**, the central T-bana station, on this level, too. With money to spend, the shopping area around Sergels Torg is where consumption in Stockholm becomes most conspicuous. But heading north, it's difficult to get excited by the city's grid of pedestrianised shopping streets. In summer, the odd jewellery stall and busker add a bit of variety but basically it's a glut of Nordic consumerism – expensive clothes for expansive wallets. As far as **Hötorget** that is. Outside in the square you'll find an open-air fruit and veg market and below, the wonderful indoor **Hötorgshallen**; rambling, gluttonous food halls with ethnic snacks. Pick up a falafel and some fruit and munch on the crowded steps of the **Konserthuset**, one venue for the presentation of the Nobel Prizes.

North: Strindberg and Palme

From Hötorget parallel streets run uphill and north as far as Odengatan and the City Library in its little park. Continuing on foot gives you glances of the odd bit of greenery, tucked away here and there: and along the way, diversions include an excellent museum and a notable church. The **Strindbergsmuséet** (Tues–Fri 10am–4pm, Sat & Sun noon–4pm; 15kr) is housed in the last building in which the writer lived in Stockholm, the so-called "Blue Tower" at Drottninggatan 85. August Strindberg's home between 1908 and 1912, the house has been preserved to the extent that you must put plastic bags on your feet to protect the floors and furnishings. The study is as he left it on his death, a dark and gloomy place – he wrote with venetian blinds and heavy curtains closed against the sunlight. Upstairs is his library, a musty room with all the books firmly behind glass. Which is a shame because Strindberg was not a passive reader: he underlined heavily and criticised in the margins as he read, though rather less eruditely than you'd expect. "Lies!", "Shit!", "Idiot!" and "Bloody Hell!" tended to be his favourite comments. Good English notes are supplied free, and the nearest T-bana stop is Rådmansgatan.

Close by, set in secluded gardens between Drottninggatan and Sveagatan, sits **Adolf Fredrik's kyrka**, which would have remained an almost unnoticed eighteenth-century church, the yard full of picnicking office workers, were it not for one of the most tragic, and unexplained – events in recent Swedish history.

The church has a noteworthy past: the cemetery was the original burial place of the French philosopher Descartes who died of pneumonia in Stockholm in 1650. His body went back to France in 1661, and a monument records his brief (mortal) stay. But the church is of far greater significance to modern Stockholmers still reeling from the assassination of their Prime Minister, **Olof Palme**, who is buried here. Shot on the way home from a nearby cinema, his death sent shock waves through a society unused to political extremism of any kind. Like most Scandinavian leaders his fame was his security, and he died unprotected, gunned down in front of his wife in February 1986. A politically instructive end, it has sadly led to a radical and negative rethink of the open government policy pursued in Sweden for decades. When Christer Pettersson was jailed for the murder (see "History"; p.291), most Stockholmers thought that was the end of the story, but his eventual release after a successful appeal has only re-opened the debate. There have been recriminations and resignations amongst a derided police force and though, in the past, immigrant Kurdish extremists and right-wing terror groups were the popular suspects, theories have even suggested the assassin came from within, or was hired by, the police force itself . . .

Kungsholmen: the Stadshuset

Take the T-bana back to the centre, get off at T-Centralen and it's only a matter of minutes from there, across the small Stadshusbron bridge, to the island of **Kungsholmen**. Here, the **Stadshuset** (guided tours Mon–Fri at 10am, Sat & Sun at 10am & noon: tower open May to Sept daily 10am–3pm; 10kr) is an obvious attraction; and, to be honest, the only real reason to set foot on the island.

Finished in 1932, it's one of the landmarks of modern Stockholm, and the Stadshuset's simple, if drab, exterior brickwork doesn't prepare you for the intriguing details inside. If you're a visiting Head of State you'll be escorted from your boat up the elegant waterside steps. If you're not, the only way to view the innards is on one of the guided tours, which reveal the kitschy Viking-style legislative chamber and the impressively echoey Golden Hall.

It's hardly worth venturing beyond the Stadshuset and further into Kungsholmen, the largish island being a conglomeration of all the public buildings that had to go somewhere – law courts, hospital, sports ground and police headquarters. But Stadshusbron is the departure point for a couple of the city's best **cruises**, around Lake Mälaren and under Stockholm's bridges: tickets from the kiosk, discounts with a Stockholm Card.

Östermalm

East of Birger Jarlsgatan the streets get noticeably broader, a uniform grid as far as Karlaplan. Beyond, the greenery of Djurgården begins to make itself felt, the impressive residences as likely to be consulates and embassies as fashionable houses. **Östermalm** was one of the last areas of central Stockholm to be developed and the chief feature of this end of the city was once the barracks: it's a link continued today by the presence of the **Armémuseum** (Tues–Sun 11am–4pm; 5kr) at Riddargatan 13. Hardly anyone comes to visit its three floors, packed from top to bottom with precision killing machines, uniforms, swords and medals. Indeed, you tend to be outnumbered by museum attendants who seem to consider an interest in the exhibits as proof of social deviancy, and who stay keenly alert and omnipresent.

Directly across Riddargatan is the innovative **Musikmuseet** (Tues–Sun 11am–4pm; 15kr, students 8kr) at Sibyllegatan 2, containing a range of instruments which visitors can play ("carefully" pleads the notice). The museum charts the history of music in Sweden using photographs, instruments and sound recordings: best are the sections that deal with the late-nineteenth century, a time when folk music had been given a fresh impetus by the growing labour movement. The concluding parts on "progressive" and "disco" music are very brief and uninteresting with the merest mention of punk and, astonishingly, nothing on *ABBA**.

Just back from the museums, **Östermalmstorg** has its own **market hall**, very similar to Norrmalm's Hötorgshallen; a tempting place for a wander if you're feeling peckish.

The Historiska Museet

If you're trailing around Östermalm's gridded streets, you're bound to end up at circular **Karlaplan** sooner or later, if only because many of the city's buses head

---

*It seems pertinent to mention Sweden's Fab Four here, who rocketed to international fame after winning the Eurovision Song Contest in 1974. At one time the country's biggest export after Volvo cars, *ABBA* spawned a series of imitators, none as good or as enduring. A talented bunch, they've now gone their separate ways and onto new projects (the stage show *Chess* the most obvious success) but their old records still sell well – indeed, in Australia sales of their *Greatest Hits* albums are reported to have reached statistical saturation point.

this way. If you do, jump on a bus (#44) heading for Djurgården (or walk the few hundred metres down Narvavägen) as far as the important **Historiska Museet** (Tues–Sun 11am–4pm, Thurs until 8pm; 20kr, students 15kr, free on Thurs), the most wide-ranging historical display in Stockholm. It's really two large collections, museums of *National Antiquity* and *Monetary History*. Ground floor highlights include the ideal Stone Age household – flaxen-haired youth, stripped pine benches and rows of neatly labelled herbs – and a mass of Viking weapons, coins and boats. Upstairs there's a worthy collection of medieval church art and architecture, with odds and ends turned up from all over the country and evocatively housed in massive vaulted rooms. If you're heading to Gotland, be sure to take in the reassembled bits of stave churches, uncovered on the Baltic island – some of the few examples that survive in Sweden.

Djurgården

When you tire of the streets, it's time to utilise Stockholm's parkland mass, just to the east of the centre. Originally a royal hunting park throughout the sixteenth to eighteenth centuries, **Djurgården** is actually two distinct park areas separated by the water of Djurgårdsbrunnsviken, which freezes over in winter to provide some central skating. You could walk to the park from Central Station, but it's quite a hike: take the **bus** instead (#44 from Karlaplan or #47 from Nybroplan); or the **ferry** from Nybroplan (summer only) or Skeppsbron (all year).

The TV Tower
The transport detailed above will take you to the most famous of Stockholm's museums, which lie in the southern patch of parkland, but roaming **northwards** in the park is equally rewarding, principally for the excellent views from the 160-metre-high **Kaknäs TV tower** (Jan–March & Oct–Dec daily 9am–6pm; April & Sept daily 9am–10pm; May–Aug daily 9am–midnight; 12kr) over at the eastern end. Not that it means much, but it's the highest building in Scandinavia: you can see over the city and archipelago and there's a restaurant about 120m up if you want an airborne cup of coffee. Bus #69 goes all the way there from Sergels Torg, passing a gaggle of sundry museums – Dance, Maritime, Technical and Ethnographical – each listed on p.318. And beyond Ladugårdsgärdet, north of the tower and where windmills used to pierce the skyline, lies Värtahamnen and the *Silja* line ferry terminal.

Nordiska Museet, Skansen and Gröna Lund Tivoli
South, over Djurgårdsbron, a full day isn't enough to see everything. Starting with the palatial **Nordiska Museet** or Nordic Museum (Jan–May & Sept–Dec Mon–Thurs 10am–4pm, Tues until 8pm, Sat & Sun noon–5pm; June–Aug Mon–Fri 10am–4pm, Tues until 8pm, Sat & Sun noon–5pm; 15kr, students 10kr) is useful if only because the same cultural themes pop up repeatedly throughout the rest of the park's exhibits. The displays are a decent attempt to represent Swedish cultural history in an accessible fashion, and the *Same* section is particularly good. On the ground floor of the cathedral-like interior is Carl Milles' phenomenal statue of Gustav Vasa, the sixteenth-century king who drove out the Danes, and an inspirational figure who wrought the best from the sculptor (for more of whom, see p.327).

But it's for **Skansen** (Jan–April & Sept–Dec daily 9am–5pm; May–Aug daily 9am–10pm; 20kr, 12kr winter) that most people come: a great open-air museum with 150 reconstructed buildings, from a whole town to windmills and farms laid out on a region-by-region basis, with each section boasting its own daily activities – traditional handicrafts, games and displays – that anyone can join in. Best of the buildings are the small *Same* dwellings, warm and functional, and the craftsmen's workshops in the old town quarter; and you can also potter around a small zoo and a bizarre **aquarium** (20kr), fish cheek by jowl with crocs, monkeys and snakes. Partly because of the attention paid to accuracy, partly due to the admirable lack of commercialism, Skansen manages to avoid the tackiness associated with similar ventures elsewhere. Even the snack bars dole out traditional foods and, in winter, great bowls of warming soup.

Immediately opposite Skansen's main gates **Gröna Lund Tivoli** (May to mid-Sept Mon–Sat 1pm–midnight, Sun 1–10pm; restricted hours in winter; 30kr) is not a patch on its more famous namesake in Copenhagen, though it's decidedly cleaner and less seedy. Definitely, it's more of a place to stroll than indulge in rides (none included in the entrance fee), which are frankly tame. At night the emphasis shifts as the park becomes the stomping ground of Stockholm's youth – disco music, cafés and some enterprising chat-up lines.

The Vasa Museum

In a brand new building, close to the Nordiska Museet, the **Vasa Museum** (mid-June to mid-Aug daily 9.30am–7pm; rest of the year daily 10am–5pm, Wed also until 8pm; 25kr, children 5kr) is, without question, head and shoulders above anything else that Stockholm has to offer in the way of museums. Built on the orders of King Gustav II Adolf, the *Vasa* warship sank in Stockholm harbour on her maiden voyage in 1628. Preserved in mud for over 300 years, the ship was raised along with 12,000 objects in 1961 and, after display in a temporary museum for the last few years, now forms the centrepiece of a startling, purpose-built hall on the waters's edge. The museum itself is built over a part of the old naval dockyard, and was designed to give the impression of a large, soft copper tent, the materials used supposed to relate to navy colours and designs: stone and ochre, tarred and black beams mixed with whites, reds and the green of Djurgården.

Impressive though the building is, nothing prepares you for the sheer size of the **ship**: 62m long, the main mast originally 50m over the keel, it sits virtually complete in a cradle of supporting mechanical tackle. Surrounding walkways bring you nose to nose with the cannon hatches and restored decorative relief, the gilded wooden sculptures on the soaring prow designed to intimidate the enemy and proclaim Swedish might. With the humid atmosphere (as the ship takes literally years to dry out) and the immediacy of its frightening bulk, it's not difficult to understand the terror that such ships must have generated. Adjacent **exhibition halls** and presentations on several levels take care of all the retrieved bits and pieces. There are reconstructions of life on board ship, detailed models of the *Vasa*, displays relating to contemporary social and political life, films and videos and excellent English notes. In short, a must.

Södermalm

An area largely neglected by most visitors to the city, it's worth venturing beyond Slussen's traffic interchange for the heights of **Södermalm**'s crags. As you look over from Gamla Stan, you'll see turrets and towers ahead of you, the skyline punctured by church spires and a wall of rocks to the right. The perched buildings are vaguely forbidding, but get beyond the speeding main roads skirting the island and a lively, and surprisingly green, area unfolds – one that's still, at heart, emphatically working class. By bus, take the #48 or #53 from Tegelbacken, or use the T-bana and get off at either Slussen or Medborgarplatsen.

Walking, you reach the island over a double bridge from Gamla Stan, and just to the south of the square (Södermalmstorg) is the rewarding **Stadsmuseet** (Tues–Thurs 11am–7pm, Fri–Sun 11am–5pm; 10kr), hidden in a basement courtyard. The Baroque building, designed by Tessin the Elder and finished by his son in 1685, was once the town hall for this part of Stockholm; now it houses a set of collections relating to the city's history as a sea port and industrial centre. Nearby, take a look at the **Katarina kyrka**, rebuilt in Renaissance style in the eighteenth century. On this site the victims of the so-called "Stockholm Blood Bath" were buried in 1520, the betrayed nobility of Sweden who had opposed King Christian II's Danish invasion. Their bodies were burned as heretics outside the city walls and it proved a vicious and effective coup, Christian disposing of the opposition at one fell swoop.

That's about as far as specific sights go in Södermalm, although you might as well wander westwards towards Mariatorget, a spacious square where the Art Nouveau influence on its buildings hasn't quite been eradicated. One of the finest examples now houses a **Museum of Toys** (Tues–Fri 10am–4pm, Sat & Sun noon–4pm; 15kr). Everything from tin soldiers to space guns, it's of rather more interest to big than little kids, there not being a lot you can actually play with.

You might be staying in Södermalm, or end up here at night since there are some good bars and restaurants in this quarter of the city. **Götagatan**, particularly, has a broad choice of cheapish restaurants, some "pubs" (see "Drinking" below) and a few well-stocked bookshops.

Långholmen

Whether you stop in Södermalm or not, the buses and T-bana trains come this way for the island of **Långholmen**, just off its western side. There's a popular **beach** here, which gets packed in the summer, a chance to swim and plenty of shady walks through the island's trees. One of the better places to stay in the city is the newly-converted youth hostel/hotel (see "Finding a place to stay"), sited in what used to be Långholmen's large prison building. There's a café here in the summer, where you can sit outside and have a drink – worth doing since the tables and chairs take up space in the former exercise yard, narrow, bricked-up runs with iron gates at one end.

You don't have to come through Södermalm to reach Långholmen – though if you do, get off the T-bana at Hornstull and follow the signs (or bus #54 to Högalidsgatan). In summer there's a more direct **ferry** from Stadshuset, which drops you right by the hostel.

More parks and gardens

Given Stockholm's sense of space and pleasant aspect, there isn't the same urge as in some cities to head for a park and escape the bustle: even the most built-up parts of Norrmalm and Södermalm have a stack of quiet gardens and squares tucked away if you search hard enough. If you're spending only a couple of days in the city, then you'll probably visit **Djurgården** anyway – its excellent range of museums interspersed by rolling parkland and one of them, Skansen, open-air itself; see above for more details. But there are a few other outdoor destinations worth seeking out, especially if you have **children** in tow, or if you're keen to see the less frequented northern parts of Stockholm.

Best place to take the kids is **Vanadisbadet** (mid-May to mid-Sept daily 10am–6pm; 30kr), a water-sports and activity park in Vanadislunden, at Sveavägen 142; T-bana to Odenplan. More genteel, and further north of the city centre, at Frescati, is the **Bergianska Botaniska Trädgården** (May–Sept noon–4pm), a botanical garden and park whose greenhouse holds the world's largest water lily: if that's something you'd go a long way to see, take the T-bana to Universitet and then bus #540. Back towards the city, the **Fjärilshuset** (Tues–Sun 11am–3pm; 15kr) is a butterfly house, where you can walk between free-flying tropical butterflies. It's in Hagaparken; T-bana to Odenplan.

Stockholm's other museums

Stockholm has fifty-odd museums scattered within its limits, and while you'd have to be very keen to want to see the lot, some of the minor collections are worth seeking out: what follows is a brief and biased rundown of the best – and worst. Full details are given in the booklet that comes with the Stockholm Card and in *Stockholm This Week*, both available from tourist information centres. Also, the Stockholm Card will get you into nearly all the museums listed below for free; note that most of them are closed on Monday.

Arkitektur Museet

Skeppsholmen (close to Hantsverkhuset hostel). *Tues 11am–9pm, Wed–Sun 11am–5pm; 15kr, students 10kr.*

Stages temporary exhibitions on various aspects of architecture and urban planning within Sweden. Small but rarely uninteresting.

Biologiska Museet

Djurgården; bus #44 or #47. *Daily except Mon noon–4pm; 6kr.*

A tired panorama of stuffed animals and birds, it's ever so pointless, but housed in a rather pleasing copy of a Norwegian stave church.

Dansmuseet

Laboratoriegatan 10, off Strandvägen; bus #68. *Daily except Mon noon–4pm; 10kr.*

Housed in an Art-Nouveau house near Djurgården, this is a push-button film archive of world dance, with costume and mask displays.

Eldh Studio Museum

Lögebodavägen 10; bus #43 or #53 to Roslagstull. *May–Sept Tues–Sun noon–4pm closed; 15kr.*

The collected works of Swedish sculptor Carl Eldh in an art studio designed by the architect responsible for the Stadshuset. Neat gardens in pleasant surroundings.

Etnografiska Museet

Djurgårdsbrunnsvägen 34; bus #69. *Tues–Fri 11am–4pm, Sat & Sun noon–4pm; 15kr.*
More plundered Asian ethnographical gear that wouldn't fit in any of the other museums.

Hallwylska Museet

Hamngatan 4, Norrmalm. *June–Aug daily 11am–4pm, Jan–May & Sept–Dec Tues–Fri noon–3pm, Sat & Sun noon–4pm; 20kr, students 10kr..*
Guided tours only (in English at 1pm on Sunday, otherwise Swedish) around this private collection of the Countess von Hallwyl, whose middle name was not discrimination. Eclectic is hardly the word – paintings, silver, porcelain, weapons, furniture, tapestries and the kitchen sink.

Hologram Museum

Drottninggatan 100, Norrmalm. *Jan–June & Sept–Dec Tues–Fri 11am–5pm, Sat & Sun 11am–4pm; July & Aug Mon–Fri 11am–5pm, Sat & Sun 11am–4pm; 20kr.*
Far less remarkable than you might hope, this steeply priced private gallery is a disappointment. Disembodied limbs and faces loom out of the wall as you move from one hologram to the next, but it's unsettling only the first time, unimpressive the twentieth.

Liljevalch Konsthall

Djurgårdsvägen 60, Djurgården. *Tues–Sun 11am–5pm, also Tues & Thurs until 9pm; 20kr.*
A difficult one to pigeonhole. Constantly changing exhibitions revolve around modern art and sculpture displays, Swedish and international. The most rewarding time to visit is in February and March when the Spring Salon selects and displays the winners of the annual art competition. Consistently good, you may have to queue to get in.

Marionettmuseet

Brunnsgatan 6, Norrmalm; T-bana Hötorget. *Daily 1–4pm; closed July; 15kr.*
A collection of 4000 puppets, marionettes and associated paraphernalia, mainly from Asia. Central and diverting; English guided tours on Saturday at 3pm.

Sjöhistoriska Museet

Djurgårdsbrunnsvägen 24, bus #69. *Daily 10am–5pm, Oct, Nov & March also Tues 6–8.30pm; 15kr, students 5kr.*
A glance into the Swedish relationship with the sea at this excellent Maritime Museum. Much is revealed of early boat-building; there's a selection of scale models, some from the seventeenth century; and a perfunctory look at the modern Swedish navy who are evidently proud of their torpedoes.

Spårvägsmuseet

platform of Odenplan T-bana. *Mon–Fri 10am–5pm, Jan–May & Sept–Dec also Sat 10am–5pm; 4kr..*
SL's transport museum, and a good one for kids. An old tram, uniforms and machinery to poke at as the trains rattle away overhead.

Tekniska Museet

Museivägen 7, off Djurgårdsbrunnsvägen, bus #69. *Mon–Fri 10am–4pm, Sat & Sun noon–4pm; 20kr, students 10kr.*

Contains everything you'd expect – and lots of it. If you drool at the prospect of bulky displays on iron production, the history of electricity and Swedish building technology you'll be in seventh heaven. The same museum contains the *Teknorama* (daily noon–4pm) and the Telemuseum, which deals with telecommunications – both a veritable haven of buttons to push and things to touch.

Vin & Sprithistoriska Museet

Dalagatan 100; T-bana Sankt Eriksplan. *April–Dec Tues–Fri 10am–4pm, Sun 1–4pm; 10kr.*

An unexpectedly fascinating place covering all aspects of the wine making and distilling processes. Worth visiting just for the mechanical sniffing cabinet, whereby you sniff one of fifty spices used to flavour aquavit, guess what it is and press the button for confirmation. No free samples though.

Eating

Consumption of any kind is expensive in Sweden and its capital city offers few bargains. But observe a few rules, accept a few facts, and you should manage a reasonable existence. As far as **eating out** goes, one option is to shift your main meal of the day to lunchtime, when almost every café and restaurant offers a good value set menu (the *Dagens Rätt*) for around 35–50kr – usually Monday to Friday only. Ethnic food, particularly pizzas and Chinese meals, can be reasonably priced, too. Or stick to cheaper (but not much) burgers, kebabs and market food. There is no such thing as a cheap evening restaurant meal in Stockholm, certainly not if you're going to drink alcohol with your food as well.

Breakfast and snacks

If your hostel or hotel doesn't do **breakfast**, the restaurant at Central Station lays out a large buffet between 6.30am and 10am daily; 45kr per person and good value at that. For **burgers**, the choice is between *MacDonalds*, the *Clock Burger* chain and the occasional *Wimpy*, including one in the arcade at Sergels Torg. Prices are dearer than in Britain although the burger restaurants are usually the cheapest place to get a cup of coffee. And just about everywhere you'll be able to buy ice cream, hot dogs and other calorific junk from kiosks and street vendors.

Markets and supermarkets

Of the indoor **markets**, *Hötorgshallen* in Hötorget is cheaper and more varied than *Östermalmshallen* in Östermalmstorget. The former is awash with small cafés and ethnic snacks, although buy your fruit and veg outside where it's less expensive. The latter is posher and quieter; pleasant for a wander but you'll find most things cheaper in the *Åhlens* store over the other side of the square.

Elsewhere, there's a small **fruit and veg** stall outside the *Gallerian* shopping centre on Hamngatan (by Sergels Torg); and more stalls outside Brommaplan T-bana. For central **supermarkets**, try *KSF* in Järntorget, Gamla Stan (Mon–Fri 8am–9pm, Sat & Sun 10am–9pm) and *Metro* (Mon–Fri 9am–8pm, Sat 9am–6pm, Sun 11am–6pm) in the underground arcade at Sergels Torg.

Cafés and restaurants

The three main areas for decent eating, day or night, are Norrmalm, Gamla Stan and Södermalm: as you might expect, it's most expensive to eat in the old town, but **set lunch** deals make even that affordable. Lots of the places listed below also appear in the "Entertainment" section, as there's a fairly fine line between cafés, restaurants and bars in Stockholm, many offering music and entertainment in the evening as well as food throughout the day. **Vegetarians** shouldn't have too much difficulty in finding something to eat, either: some of the possibilities are detailed below.

Norrmalm

Daily News Café, Kungsträgården, by *Sverigehuset* tourist centre. A swish bar/restaurant with disco, the lunch here (11.30am–3pm; 42kr) is generally tasty Swedish food, and there's a special late-night menu (11.30pm–1.45am; 50–80kr a dish) for party-goers.

Hard Rock Café, Sveavägen 75. Loud rock music, all-American fun, and hefty burger meals from around 60kr; generally a queue to get in.

Hotell Karelia, Birger Jarlsgatan 35. Dress up (no jeans) and the excellent hotel restaurant has a "Happy Hour" (Mon & Wed 5–8pm). All food and drinks are half price – unheard of elsewhere – while a wild Finnish band whips up a dancing frenzy. If you want to drink, you'll be expected to eat (sumptuous Finnish food from around 50kr) although early on a Monday you should be able to get way with just a beer or two.

Operakällaren, Operan, Gustav Adolfs Torg. A bill at the famous Opera House restaurant could seriously damage your wallet (starters from 130kr!) but the daily *smörgåsbord* (Mon–Sat 11.30am–3pm, Sun noon–6pm) is fabulous and (just about) affordable – 160kr per person for a spread beyond compare. Otherwise, the daily lunch in the *Café Opera*, around the back, is 85kr.

Pizza Hut, branches at Sveavägen 8 and Klarabergsgatan 56. Hitting Scandinavia in a big way, at least you know what you're getting at *Pizza Hut* even if it isn't that good. Pizzas go for around 50kr a head.

Sergels Pärla Pizzeria, Sergels Torg, in the underground arcade. Big pizzas, a daily salad or lasagne, all with bread and coleslaw for around 40kr; one of the city's best budget bargains and served all day. Open daily 11am–9pm.

Teatercafeet, Stadsteater, Sergels Torg. A daily 38kr lunch, always including a vegetarian dish; and a reasonably priced à la carte menu, too (Mon–Fri 10.30am–3pm).

Wärdshuset Markurells, Vasagatan 26; opposite the *Royal Viking Hotel*. Popular and cheapish, mainly Swedish menu – lunch around 43kr.

Gamla Stan

Café Art, Västerlånggatan, Gamla Stan. Down the steps between nos. 60 and 62 into a fifteenth-century cellar-café; quiet and gloomy, with massive sandwiches (35kr), good coffee (16kr; free refills) and cakes. Open daily 11am–11pm.

Café Old Town, Västerlånggatan 34. Nothing special, but the daily "Happy Hour" (11am–6pm) offers cut-price pizzas (29kr) as well as drinks.

Dragon Palace, Kornholmstorg 55. For a bit more cash than usual you could have a good meal here: vegetable dishes 75kr, a large set lunch at 100kr per person, and smaller three-dish meals at 65kr.

Fisherman's Inn, Stora Nygatan 25. A fish restaurant with a steeply-priced menu, but the daily lunch goes for 43kr, so worth a whirl.

Den Gyldene Freden, Österlånggatan 51. Stockholm's oldest restaurant, "The Golden Peace", open since 1772 and now owned by the Swedish Academy, who dine here every week. It certainly isn't cheap – expect to pay around 230–250kr for just two courses, without drinks – but the atmosphere, food and style unparalleled in the city.

Kafegillet, Trångsund; to the side of Storkyrkan. A fourteenth-century cellar-restaurant dealing in traditional Swedish food. Lunches around the 40kr mark.

Lilla Karachi, Lilla Nygatan 12. Pakistani restaurant with a 38kr vegetarian meal; an interesting change for Stockholm.

Pariserbullen, Skräddergränd, a tiny alley off Västerlånggatan. Pizzas, pasta, Mexican food and vegetarian dishes – up to and around 40kr.

Pizza al Taglio, Storkyrkobrinken 11. Tiny take-away with a few tables; pizza and pasta from 30kr.

Samborombon, Stora Nygatan 28. A sweet little Italian restaurant with a good '42kr lunch and a daily pasta at only 27kr. Not bad at all for the area.

Slinger Bulten, Stora Nygatan 24. Traditional Swedish food and good lunches from 45kr.

Södermalm

Café Pan, Götagatan 11. A New Age joint with a vegetarian café, which has a nice line in snacks.

Lassa i Parken, Högalidsgatan 56; T-bana Hornstull. Café housed in an eighteenth-century house with a pleasant garden; daily lunch (11am–3pm) basic but good.

Lilla Budapest, Götagatan 27. A good stop for weighty, set menu Hungarian lunches. Also has a bar whose drinks are a few crowns cheaper than most other places.

Österns Pärla, Götagatan 62. Reasonable Far Eastern food, around 60–65kr a dish; and a three-course lunch for 68kr.

Pelikan, Blekingegatan 40. Atmospheric, working class Swedish pub, with excellent traditional food; the *pytt i panna* is good.

Pizzeria, Sankt Paulsgatan 3; corner of Götagatan. Cheap pizza take-aways.

Drinking, nightlife and entertainment

There's plenty to keep you occupied in Stockholm, from pubs and clubs to the cinema, live music and theatre: the only drawback is the price, but you'll just have to grit your teeth and bear it if you don't want to spend every night in front of the hostel/hotel TV.

Alcohol in pubs, bars and cafés is uniformly expensive, though **Happy Hour** at various establishments throws up some bargains; see below. Wherever there's **live music** at one of these places you'll generally have to pay a cover charge, too, of around 30–50kr. Also, if you don't want to feel very scruffy, wear something other than jeans and training shoes – many places won't let you in dressed like that anyway. Be prepared, too, to cough up five or six crowns to leave your coat at the cloakroom; a requirement at many bars as well as at discos and clubs. Apart from the weekend, Wednesday night is an active time in Stockholm; usually plenty going on and queues to get in the more popular places.

Other **entertainment** – gigs, theatre and cinema – is pretty varied though; and quite often, especially in the summer, it can be free.

Bars, brasseries and pubs

Brasserie Vau de Ville, Hamngatan 17, Kungsträdgården, Norrmalm. Posh and popular brasserie with snacks and drinks, as well as a regular menu; open until 12.30am, 1.30am Friday and Saturday.

Café Opera, Opera House, Gustav Adolfs Torg, Norrmalm. If your Katherine Hamnett gear isn't too crushed, and you can stand just one more martini, then join the queue outside; open until 3am daily.

Fenix, Götagatan 40, Södermalm; just up from Slussen. American-style bar that's trendy, noisy and lively. Good selection of beers and cheapish food.

Gråmunken, Västerlånggatan 18, Gamla Stan. Cosy café/pub, usually busy and with live jazz several nights a week.

Kristina, Västerlånggatan 68, Gamla Stan. Café by day (with a 38kr lunch); Happy Hour 4–8pm when beer is only 27kr, a bottle of wine 75kr; and live jazz after 8pm, free entry.

Söders Hjärta, Bellmansgatan 22, Södermalm. Swanky restaurant with a less intimidating and friendly bar on the mezzanine floor; generally crowded and lively. You'll have to check your coat on the way in.

Stortorgskällaren, Stortorget, Gamla Stan. The restaurant is expensive (not surprising given its position) but between 3pm and 8pm (Fri & Sat 7pm) the Happy Hour drinks make it an attractive stop; beer 29kr, wine 75kr a bottle. Open until 1am daily.

Live music: rock and jazz

Apart from the cafés and bars already listed, there's no shortage of specific venues which put on **live music**; see the list below. Most of these will be local bands, for which you'll pay around 50kr entrance, but nearly all the big names make it to Stockholm as well these days, playing at a variety of seated halls and stadiums – prices for these are, of course, much more expensive.

Main large venues are the new *Stockholm Globe Arena*, Johanneshov, T-bana Gullmarsplan (☎08/600 34 00); *Konserthuset* in Hötorget, Norrmalm (☎08/10 21 10); and the *Isstadion* (☎08/600 34 00) – ring for programme details or ask at the tourist centre.

Café Pan, Götagan 11, Södermalm. Regular evening music programme as well as hippy healing sessions and all manner of things "green".

Cityhallen, Drottninggatan 28, Norrmalm. A big, bright bar/restaurant with live Scandinavian rock and R&B nightly; cheapish food and drink, too.

Engelen, Kornhamnstorg 59, Gamla Stan. Live music – jazz, rock and blues – nightly until 3am, but arrive early to get in.

Fryshuset, Tegelviksgatan 19–23, Södermalm; T-bana to Medborgarplatsen then bus #46. A youth centre-cum-musicians' collective, currently sporting a lively line-up of local punk, hardcore and trash metal. Ring ☎08/714 52 40 for details.

Hard Rock Café, Sveavägen 75, Norrmalm. R&B bands (often American) every Tuesday and Saturday.

Kaos, Stora Nygatan 21, Gamla Stan. Live music from 9pm nightly; rock bands on Friday and Saturday in the cellar; and reasonable late night food.

Stampen, Stora Nygatan 5, Gamla Stan. Long-established and rowdy jazz club, both trad and mainstream; occasional foreign names too.

Tre Backar, Tegnergatan 12–14, Norrmalm; T-bana Rådmansgatan. Good, cheap pub with a live cellar venue. Music every night; open until midnight (closed Sunday).

Discos . . . and gay clubs

Club Timmy, Timmermansgatan 24, Södermalm. A gay club with a café/bar next door (*The Pink Room*); T-bana to Mariatorget, open Monday to Thursday 8–11pm, weekends till 1.30am.

Daily News Café, Kungsträdgården, Norrmalm. There are two discos inside this café/restaurant, both doing good business; a fairly young crowd.

Fylkingen, Munchenbryggeriet, Söder Mälarstrand 27, Södermalm. Trendy club which hosts regular live concerts, particularly avant-garde and electronic stuff.

Heinz Pub, Hornsgatan 90, Södermalm. A gay bar, open until midnight, and with a cheapish restaurant.

Culture: classical music, theatre, cinema

For up-to-date **info** about what's on where, check the special Saturday supplement of the *Dagens Nyheter* newspaper. Also, the latest issue of *Stockholm This Week*, free from the tourist centre, is indispensable for **arts listings**. It contains day-by-day information about a whole range of events – gigs, theatre, festivals, dance – sponsored by the city, many of which are free and based around Stockholm's many parks. Popular venues in the summer are Kungsträdgården and Skansen, where there's always something going on. If your Swedish is up to it, there's a free monthly paper, *Nöjesguiden*, which details all manner of things cultural – from the latest films to a club guide. You'll see it in bars and restaurants; pick up a copy and get someone to translate.

Classical music

Classical music is always easy to find. Many museums – particularly the Historiska Museet and the Musikmuseet – have regular programmes; there's generally something on at *Konserthuset* in Hötorget, Norrmalm (☎08/10 21 10) and *Berwaldhallen*, Strandvägen 69, Östermalm (☎08/784 18 00); and check the *Kungliga Musikaliska Akadamien*, Stallgatan 9, near the National Art Museum (☎08/20 86 18).

If you're after **church music**, you'll find it in Adolf Fredriks kyrka, Norrmalm (lunchtime); St Jakobs kyrka, Norrmalm (Sat at 3pm); Johannes kyrka, Norrmalm; and Storkyrkan, Gamla Stan. More details from *Stockholm This Week*.

Theatre and cinema

There are dozens of **theatres** in Stockholm, but only one has regular performances of **English-language productions**: the *Regina* (Drottninggatan 71; ☎08/20 70 00). It features touring plays and visiting actors – tickets and more information from the theatre. If you want tickets for anything else theatrical, it's often worth waiting for reduced-price standby tickets, available from the kiosk in Norrmalmstorg.

Cinemas are incredibly popular, new releases nearly always full. Largest venues are on Kungsgatan, a lively street on a Saturday night, and you can get full listings from the local press or the tourist information centres. Tickets cost around 50kr and films are never dubbed into Swedish.

Finally, **Kulturhuset** in Sergels Torg has a full range of artistic and cultural events – mostly free – and the information desk on the ground floor has programmes to give away.

Listings

Airlines *British Airways* (Norrmalmstorg 1; ☎08/23 39 00); *Finnair* (Norrmalmstorg 1; ☎08/24 43 30); *KLM* (Sveavägen 24–26; ☎08/23 13 50); *Lufthansa* (Norrmalmstorg 1; ☎08/23 05 05); *Pan Am* (Jakobstorg 1; ☎08/23 19 20); *SAS* (Sveavägen 22; ☎08/780 10 00).

Airport Bus From Cityterminalen every ten minutes between 5am and 10.15pm; tickets 35kr from the automatic machines or the kiosk, *not* on the bus.

American Express Birger Jarlsgatan 1 (☎08/814 39 80); Mon–Fri 8.30am–5pm, Sat 10am–1pm.

Banks Generally open later in central Stockholm than the rest of the country; Mon–Fri 9am–5.30pm; bank at Arlanda airport open daily 7am–10pm. Commission on exchanging travellers' cheques at banks varies between 10kr and 20kr per cheque. Use the railway station exchange office instead (see "Exchange" below) – it's far cheaper.

Buses *SJ Buss* office, Cityterminalen (Mon–Fri 8.30am–6pm, Sat 9am–3pm, Sun 11am–6pm); for tickets and timetables, national and international departures.

Car Rental *Ansa International* (Klarabergsgatan 33; ☎08/24 26 55); *Avis* (Sveavägen 61; ☎08/34 99 10); *Europcar* (Birger Jarlsgatan 59; ☎08/23 10 70); *Hertz* (Mäster Samuelsgatan 67; ☎08/24 07 20); *InterRent* (*Sheraton Stockholm*, Tegelbacken 6; ☎08/21 06 50).

Chemist 24-hr service from *C.W Scheele*, Klarabergsgatan 64 (☎08/21 89 34).

Credit Cards Cash advances with *American Express* (*Resespecialisterna*, Sturegatan 8), *Access/Mastercard* (at *Handelsbanken* and *S-E Banken*) and *Visa* (at *PK-Banken* and *Fösta Sparbanken*).

Dental Problems Emergency dental care from Regeringsgatan 20 (☎08-23 58 45/20 06 17), daily 8am–6pm.

Doctor Tourists can get emergency outpatient care at the hospital for the district they are staying in; check with the *Medical Care Information* (☎08/44 92 00).

Embassies and Consulates *UK* (Skarpögatan 6–8; ☎08/667 01 40); *Eire* (Östermalmsgatan 97; ☎08/661 80 05); *USA* (Strandvägen 101; ☎08/783 53 00); *Canada* (Tegelbakken 4; ☎08/462 379 20); *Australia* (Sergels Torg 12; ☎08/24 46 60); New Zealand citizens should use the Australian Embassy.

Exchange *Forex* money exchange office at Central Station (daily 8am–9pm) and Cityterminalen (daily 9am–6pm).

Emergencies Ring ☎90 000 for Police, Ambulance or Fire services.

Ferries Tickets for Finland from *Silja Line*, Kungsgatan 2 at Stureplan (☎08/22 21 40); *Viking Line*, Stureplan 8 (☎08/714 56 00); *Birka Line*, Södermalmstorg 2 (☎08/714 55 20).

Gay info The *Gay Community Centre* (Sveavägen 59; T-bana Rådmansgatan) has a restaurant, café, bar, disco, bookshop, as well as counselling services and meeting facilities. It also houses the Swedish Federation for Lesbian and Gay Rights (*RFSL.* ☎08/736 02 13) who sponsor various events – Gay Pride week is second week of August.

International newspapers Buy them at kiosks in Central Station, Cityterminalen or at the *Press Center*, Regerinsgatan 12. Read them for free at the *Stadsbiblioteket* (City Library), Sveavägen 73, or at *Kulturhuset*, Sergels Torg.

Laundry Self-service laundromats at Sturegatan 4 and St Eriksgatan 97.

Police Main HQ (*Polishuset*) at Agnegatan 33–37 (☎08/769 30 00); a local office in the Central Station. Police Lost & Found Office, Tjärhovsgatan 21, Södermalm (☎08/41 04 32).

Post Office Main Post Office, Vasagatan 28–34; Mon–Fri 8am–8pm, Sat 8am–3pm; for poste restante, take your passport.

Saunas *Hotel Karelia*, Birger Jarlsgatan 35 (3–10pm; 35kr, closed Sun); *Sergel Plaza*, Brunkebergstorg 9 (9am–10pm; 50kr, closed Sun).

Skiing There are thirty downhill ski slopes in the county, most reached easily by public transport. More info from the tourist centres.

Swedish Touring Club *STF*, Vasagatan 48. Info about Swedish youth hostels, mountain huts, hiking trails, maps and membership; *FIYTO* cards available.

Swimming Pools Outdoors at *Vanadisbadet*, Vanadislunden, Sveavägen and at *Eriksdalsbadet*, Eriksdalslunden, Södermalm; indoors at *Forsgrenska badet*, Medborgarplatsen 2–4 and *GIH-badet*, Drottning Sofias väg 20, Östermalm.

Telephones Skeppsbron 2, Gamla Stan; daily, 8am–midnight. Also an office at Central Station, Mon–Fri 8am–8pm, Sat 9am–1pm.

Toilets Central public toilets in Gallerian shopping centre, T-Centralen and Cityterminalen.

Travel Agency *SFS-Resor*, Kungsgatan 4 and out at the university in Frescati; discounted rail and air tickets, *ISIC* cards.

AROUND STOCKHOLM

Such are Stockholm's attractions, it's easy to overlook the city's surroundings. And, although the rural picture isn't that different, after only a few kilometres the countryside becomes noticeably leafier, the islands less congested, the water brighter. As further temptation, some of the country's most fascinating sights are within easy commuting distance of the city, like the spectacular **Millesgården** sculpture museum and **Drottningholm**, Sweden's greatest royal palace. Further out is the the little village of **Mariefred**, containing Sweden's other great castle, **Gripsholm** – and, like Drottningholm, it's accessible by a fine boat ride. Other trips, into the labyrinthine **archipelago** or to gentle **Uppsala**, really merit a longer stay, although if you're pressed for time it's possible to get in and out within a day.

The only drawback, if you're planning to do much scuttling back and forth, is likely to be high **travel expenses** – which it's possible to lessen by some preliminary planning. A **Stockholm Card** (see p.298) is good for travel and entry to Millesgården and entry to Drottningholm. You could also travel to Drottningholm by bus free with the card, though the ferry (half-price with the card) is more fun. To get the most out of the archipelago, you're best off with some form of **boat pass** that allows you to island hop – see p.299 for ticket details. For Uppsala, the quickest route is by regular **trains**, on which all rail passes are valid. A meandering alternative is to take the **boat** from Stockholm (Stadshusbron) at 9.45am (June to mid-Aug daily except Mon and Fri), arriving in Uppsala at 5.30pm and calling at Sigtuna and Skokloster on the way. It costs 100kr one way, 140kr return (next day); and 140kr if you go by boat and return by train the same day.

Lidingö and Millesgården

Lindingö is a residential, commuter island, just northeast of the city centre, which you'll have already glimpsed if you arrived from Finland on the *Silja* line ferries, which dock immediately opposite. It's worth a second look, though: eagle eyes may have spotted, across the water, the tallest of the statues from the startling **Millesgården** – the outdoor sculpture collection of **Carl Milles** (1875–1955), one of Sweden's greatest sculptors and collectors.

The statues sit on terraces carved from the island's steep cliffs, and many of Milles' animated, classical figures perch precariously on soaring pillars, overlooking the distant harbour: ranked terraces of gods, angels and beasts. A huge *Poseidon* rears over the army of sculptures, the most remarkable of which, *God's Hand*, has a small boy delicately balanced on the outstretched finger of a monumental hand. If you've been elsewhere in Sweden much of the work may seem familiar, copies and casts of the originals adorning countless provincial towns. If this collection inspires, it's worth tracking down two other pieces by Milles in the capital – his statue of *Gustav Vasa* in the Nordic Museum at Djurgården and the *Orpheus Fountain* in Norrmalm's Hötorget. Millesgården was the sculptor's home and studio, and the house now forms a museum commemorating his work and displaying his staggeringly rich collection of Greek and Roman art.

Millesgården is at Carl Milles väg 2 (Jan–March and Oct–Dec Tues–Fri 11am–3pm, Sat & Sun 11am–4pm; April–Sept daily 11am–5pm; 15kr). To **get there**, take the T-bana to Ropsten then the local train one stop to Torvikstorg.

The Lidingöloppet

The island is also the venue for the world's biggest cross-country running race, the **Lidingöloppet**, held on the first Sunday in October. It's been going since 1965, the 30km course attracting an international field of around 30,000 runners – quite a sight as they skip, or crawl, up and down the island's hills. For more information or, God forbid, if you want to take part, ask at the tourist centre in Stockholm or ring ☎08/765 26 15.

Drottningholm

It's worth making the effort to visit the harmonious royal palace of **Drottningholm** (May–Aug daily 11am–4.30pm; Sept Mon–Fri 1–3.30pm, Sat & Sun noon–3.30pm; 15kr, students 10kr), pushing it well up the list even if your time in Stockholm is limited. Beautifully located on the shores of leafy Lovön island, eleven kilometres west of the centre, it's a lovely fifty-minute boat trip there (see below).

Drottningholm is perhaps the greatest achievement of the architects **Tessin** – father and son. Work began in 1662 on the orders of King Karl X's widow, Eleonora, and Tessin the Elder modelled the new palace in a thoroughly French style – leading to the usual tedious descriptions of a "Swedish Versailles". Apart from anything else, it's considerably smaller than its French contemporary, utilising false perspective and *trompe l'oeil* to bolster the elegant, though rather narrow, interior. On Tessin the Elder's death, in 1681, the palace was completed by his son, already at work on Stockholm's Royal Palace. Inside, good English notes are available to sort out each room's detail, a riot of Rococo decoration largely dating from the time when Drottningholm was bestowed as a wedding gift on Princess Louisa Ulrika (a sister of Frederick the Great of Prussia). No hints, however, are needed to spot the influence in the Baroque "French" and later "English" **gardens** that back onto the palace.

Since 1981 the Swedish royal family has slummed it at Drottningholm, using the palace as a permanent home, a move that has accelerated recent efforts to restore parts of the palace to their original appearance – so that the monumental **Grand Staircase** is now exactly as envisaged by Tessin the Elder.

Though it's an expensive extra, try not to miss the **Court Theatre** (May–Aug Mon–Sat 11.30am–4.30pm, Sun 12.30–4.30pm; Sept daily 12.30–3pm; guided tours only, hourly in English 17kr, students 8kr) in the grounds of the Palace. It dates from 1766, its heyday a decade later when Gustav III imported French plays and acting troupes, making Drottningholm the centre of Swedish artistic life. Stick with the (English) guided tour and you'll get a flowery though accurate account of the theatre's decoration: money to complete the building ran out in the eighteenth century, which means that things are not what they seem, painted papier-mâché frontages penny-pinching substitutes for the real thing. The original backdrops and stage machinery are still in place though, and the tour comes complete with a display of the eighteenth-century special effects – wind and thunder machines, trapdoors and simulated lightning. If you're in luck you might catch a **performance** here (usually June–Aug; drama, ballet and opera), the cheapest **tickets** for which run from around 40–60kr, though decent seats are more likely to be at least double that: check the schedule at Drottningholm or ask at the tourist centres in the city. You can also book from abroad by writing to *Drottningholms teatermuseum*, *Föeställningar*, Box 27050, S-102 51 Stockholm (☎08/660 82 25/660 82 81).

With time to spare, the extensive palace grounds also yield the **Chinese Pavilion** (April & Sept daily 1–3.30pm; May–Aug daily 11am–4.30pm; 10kr), a sort of eighteenth-century royal summer house. In a small village nearby, in the 1760s, silk farming was attempted with specially imported silk-worms. Sadly the Swedish winter proved too much for the poor beasts, who all froze to death.

Getting there

The finest way to reach Drottningholm is by **ferry**, which takes just under an hour each way and cost 25kr one-way, 45kr return. They leave every thirty minutes from Stadshusbron to coincide with the opening times. Or take the T-bana to Brommaplan and bus #301 from there – a less thrilling ride, but free with the Stockholm Card.

The Archipelago

Stockholm's **archipelago** is real summer holiday material, literally thousands of islands harbouring beaches, great swimming and some worthy historical sights. With a boat pass, island-hopping is simple and relatively cheap: even without one, many places are close enough to visit on a day trip from Stockholm.

Transport

For access to the archipelago, the **Inter-skerries Card** (June–Aug, valid 16 days; 125kr) is a good buy as it allows unlimited travel on *Waxholmsbolaget*'s boats; and a

25 percent discount on tickets for the *Kustlinje* service that operates up and down the whole of the Swedish east coast archipelago – from NORRTÄLJE to NYNÄSHAMN. You can buy the card at *Sverigehuset* tourist centre, or from the *Waxholmbolaget* office at Strömkajen (Mon–Fri 7am–5.15pm, Sat 7am–2.30pm, Sun 7am–6pm), below the *Grand Hotel*. The boats to the archipelago leave from the adjacent numbered berths on the quayside. (Holders of the *SL* Monthly Card can simply buy a **supplementary boat card** instead – see p.302.)

Some ideas

VAXHOLM is only an hour away, an atmospheric wooden harbour town with an imposing fortress. This structure superseded the fortifications at Riddarholmen in Stockholm and guarded the waterways into the city, successfully staving off attacks from the Danes and Russians in the seventeenth and eighteenth centuries: nowadays it's an unremarkable museum (daily noon–4pm) of military bits and pieces. Incidentally, you can also reach Vaxholm by bus, from Vallhallavägen in Stockholm (#670, #671, #672, #673). Or, if you have a bike, head to **Utö** island: cycle trails, beaches and a twelfth-century iron mine.

Way to the north, **NORRTÄLJE** (tourist office: mid-June to mid-Aug Mon–Sat 9am–8pm, Sun 1–8pm) is an old spa town and capital of the Roslagen region. There's a quirky Cartoon Museum here, and the regional Roslagen Museum (summer daily noon–4pm; 5kr) is housed in an old gun factory in the centre of town. Norrtälje is a handy jumping off point for trips to **GRISSLEHAMN** in the north, a small fishing village with the pretty studio home of early twentieth-century writer and artist Albert Engström, paintings and nick-nacks displayed inside. Note, too, that there are **ferry** connections (2–3 daily; 30–40kr) to Eckerö, on the Finnish Åland Islands, from Grisslehamn – a two-hour crossing.

On the island of Björkö (Birch Island), **BIRKA** is Sweden's oldest city. A Viking trading centre at its height during the tenth century, a few obvious remains lie scattered about (including the remnants of houses and a vast cemetery), along with some good beaches and swimming. In the outer archipelago, **Sandhamn** island is a summer sailing centre with a homely little village; and **Bullerö** a nature reserve with trails and an exhibition of the archipelago's plenteous flora and fauna.

Accommodation

Accommodation is widely available throughout the archipelago. Numerous **youth hostels** exist on the islands and along the coast; notably at FJÄRDLÅNG (near ORNÖ), MÖJA (and nearby ST. KARLSHOLMEN), NORRTÄLJE, DALARÖ, GÄLLNÖ, BJÖRKÖ and ADELSÖ. All are open June to mid/end of August only – full information from the *STF* office in central Stockholm. Or rent a **cottage** in the heart of the archipelago on the island of **Ingmarsö**. A small village of holiday cottages here offers accommodation from around 2000kr a week for four people in high season, in May down to around 1200kr, and from September onwards well under 1000kr. Book these at the tourist centre in *Sverigehuset* in Stockholm, which has a catalogue of other cottages scattered throughout the archipelago. **Campsites** are surprisingly hard to find – at least the official variety. There are few sites as such, although a tent and a little imagination will pose no problems for a night's stay at most places. Open fires are prohibited all over the archipelago.

Mariefred and Gripsholm

If you've only got time for one boat trip around Stockholm, make it to **MARIEFRED**, a tiny village about an hour west of the city, whose own peaceful attractions are bolstered by one of Sweden's most enjoyable castles. There's a choice of **water transport**, grandest the *M/S Mariefred* **steamboat**, which leaves from Klara Mälarstrand near the Stadshuset. It runs daily from mid-June to mid-August at 10am (weekends only a month either side) and costs 95kr return (65kr one-way); buy your tickets on board for the three-and-a-half-hour trip. Or, much quicker, is the *Pendelbåtarna* **catamaran**, which leaves from the other side of the Stadshuset, on Norra Mälarstrand; departures are three times daily, 60kr one-way (kids half-price), for the hour's whizz through the waters.

Mariefred itself – the Swedish name derived from an old monastery, Pax Mariae, or Mary's Peace – is as quiet, and quintessentially Swedish, as such villages come. Surrounded by clear water, a few minutes up from the quayside and you're strolling through narrow streets whose well-kept wooden houses and little squares haven't changed much in decades. The water and enveloping greenery make for a leisurely amble around: if you call in at the central **Rådhus**, a fine eighteenth-century timber building, you can pick up a map, with a walking tour marked on it, from the **tourist office** inside (June & Aug Mon–Fri 10am–7pm, Sat & Sun 10am–6pm; July daily 10am–8pm). You could ask here, too, about **bike hire**, or try *Emils Krukor* at Långgatan 20, the road that runs north from near the church.

One stop should be at the **Railway Museum** in the village: you'll probably have noticed the narrow gauge tracks running all the way to the quayside. There's an exhibition, old rolling stock and workshops, but it's a collection given added interest by the fact that the steam trains still run to and from Mariefred; all the details below, under "Leaving Mariefred".

Gripsholm Castle

Lovely though the village is, touring around it is really only a preface to seeing **Gripsholm** (Nov–Feb Sat & Sun noon–3pm; March–April & Sept–Oct Tues–Fri 10am–3pm, Sat & Sun noon–3pm; May–Aug daily 10am–4pm), the imposing red-brick castle built on a round island just to the south of the village: walk up the quayside and you'll be able to see the path there running across the fields.

In the late fourteenth century, Bo Johnsson Grip, the Swedish High Chancellor, began to build a fortified castle at Mariefred, although the present building owes more to two Gustavs – Gustav Vasa, who started rebuilding in the sixteenth century, and Gustav III, who was responsible for major restructuring a couple of centuries later. Rather than the hybrid that might be expected, the result is rather pleasing – a textbook castle, whose turrets, great halls, corridors and battlements provide an engaging tour. The guide will point out most of the important bits and pieces as you go: there's a vast portrait collection, which includes recently commissioned works of political and cultural figures as well as assorted royalty and nobility; some fine decorative and architectural work; and like Drottningholm, a private theatre built for Gustav III. It's too delicate to use for performances these days, but in summer there are plays and events which take place out in the castle grounds; more information from the tourist office in Mariefred.

Some practicalities ... and leaving Mariefred

Mariefred warrants a night, if not for the sights which you can exhaust in half a day, then for the pretty and peaceful surroundings. There's only one **hotel** (see below), a wildly expensive option, but ask in the tourist office about **rooms** in the village, or take the bus 15km northwest to nearby STRÄNGNÄS, where there is a **youth hostel** (☎0152/168 61), open mid-June to mid-August and costing 55kr a night. With a tent, the local **campsite** is a good choice: *Mariefreds Camping* (☎0159/102 30) has a waterside location, is open May to mid-September, costs 45kr per tent and has camping cabins available, too.

The *Gripsholm Värdshus*, overlooking the water at Kyrkogatan 1, may be a pricey place to stay (around 800kr per person minimum!), but this beautifully restored inn (the oldest in Sweden) is at least worth thinking about for **lunch**. The food is excellent and around 150kr will get you a turn at the herring table, a main course, drink and coffee – all enhanced by the terrific views over to Gripsholm.

When it comes to **leaving Mariefred**, the catamaran currently departs at 7.15am, 11.15am and 3.15pm (Sat & Sun an hour later). A different method is to take the **narrow gauge steam train** from Mariefred which leaves roughly hourly (24kr return; half-price for kids and rail pass holders) between 10am and 5pm for LÄGGESTA, a twenty-minute ride away. From here it's possible to pick up the regular *SJ* train back to Stockholm; check the timetable for connections with the tourist office before you leave. Of course, you could always come to Mariefred from Stockholm this way, too: take the train from Central Station to Eskiltuna via Södertälje and get off at Läggesta; the first steam train to Mariefred is at 10.43am. Note that the steam train runs daily between June 24 and August 20, otherwise on Saturday and Sunday only down to the beginning of May and up to the end of September.

Uppsala

First impressions as the train pulls into **UPPSALA**, only an hour from Stockholm, are encouraging. The red-washed castle looms up behind the railway sidings, the cathedral in the foreground obvious and dominant. A sort of Swedish Oxford, Uppsala clings to the past through a succession of striking buildings connected with and scattered about its cathedral and university. Primarily the city is regarded as the historical and religious centre of the country, and it's as a tranquil daytime alternative to the capital (and for an active, student-geared nightlife) that Uppsala draws the traveller.

Around the city

Centre of the medieval town and a ten-minute walk from the train station is the great **Domkyrkan** (June–Aug daily 8am–8pm; Sept–May daily 8am–8pm), Scandinavia's largest cathedral. Built as a Gothic brag to the people of Trondheim that even their mighty church could be overshadowed, it loses out to its competitor by reason of the building material (local brick rather than imported stone), and only the echoey interior remains impressive: particularly the French Gothic ambulatory, sided by tiny chapels and bathed in a golden, decorative glow. One chapel contains a lively set of restored fourteenth-century wall paintings that tell the legend of St Erik, Sweden's patron saint: his coronation, crusade to Finland, eventual defeat and execution at the hands of the Danes, for which he was canonised. The Relics of Erik are zealously guarded in a chapel off the nave: poke around and you'll also find tombs of Reformation rebel Gustav Vasa and his son Johan III, and that of Linnaeus, the botanist, who lived in Uppsala. Time and fire have led the rest of the cathedral to be rebuilt, scrubbed and painted until it more resembles a historical museum than a thirteenth-century spiritual centre; even the characteristic twin spires are late-nineteenth century additions.

The rest of the buildings grouped around the Domkyrkan can all claim a cleaner historical pedigree. Opposite the towers the onion-domed **Gustavianum** (July & Aug daily 11am–3pm; rest of the year daily noon–3pm) was built in 1625 as part of the university, and is much touted by the tourist board for its tidily preserved anatomical theatre. The same building houses a couple of small collections of *Egyptian*, *Classical* and *Nordic* antiquities, with a small charge for each section (July & Aug daily 11am–3pm).

The current **University** building is the imposing nineteenth-century Renaissance edifice over the way. Originally a seminary, today it's used for lectures and seminars, and is the centre for graduation ceremonies each May. The more famous of its *alumni* include Carl von Linné (Linnaeus) and Anders Celsius, inventor of the temperature scale. No-one will mind if you stroll in for a quick look, but to see the locked rooms (including the glorious *Augsberg Art Cabinet*, an ebony treasure chest presented to Gustav II Adolf) ask in the office inside, to the right of the main entrance (*Vaktmästeri*): or catch a **guided tour** – May to August at 12.30pm and 2pm, 12kr.

A little way beyond is the **Carolina Rediviva** (Mon–Fri 9am–8.30pm, Sat 9am–5.30pm; June to mid-Sept also Sun 1–3.30pm), the university library. On April 30 each year the students meet here to celebrate the first day of Spring, all wearing the traditional student cap which gives them the appearance of disaffected sailors. It's one of Scandinavia's largest libraries, with around four million books: adopt a student pose and slip in for a wander round and a coffee in the rest room. More officially, take a look in the **manuscript room**, a collection of rare letters and other paraphernalia. The beautiful sixth-century *Silver Bible* is on permanent display, as is, oddly, Mozart's original manuscript for *The Magic Flute*.

After this, the **castle** (mid-May to mid-June & mid-Aug to mid-Sept Mon–Fri 10am–2pm, Sat & Sun 11am–4pm; mid-June to mid-Aug daily 10am–5pm; guided tours only; 10kr) up on the hill is a disappointment. In 1702 a fire that destroyed three quarters of the city did away with much of the castle, and only one side and two towers remain of what was once an opulent rectangular palace. But the facade still gives a weighty impression of what is missing, like a backless Hollywood set.

Seeing Uppsala, at least the compact older parts, won't take up much time. What does, if the weather holds out, is strolling alongside the river which runs through the centre. In the summer there are several places and cafés good for an hour or two, and enough greenery to make this stretch more than just pleasant. One beautiful spot is the **Linnaeus Gardens** (May–Aug daily 9am–9pm; free) over the river on Linnégatan. The university's first botanical gardens, they were relaid by Linnaeus in 1741, some of the species he introduced and classified still surviving.

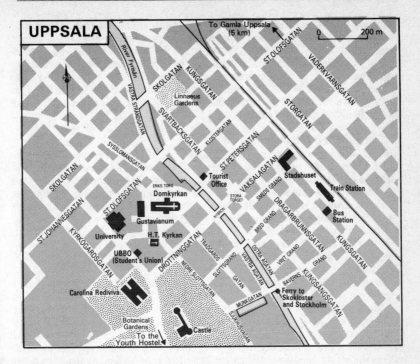

Practical details

Uppsala's **railway station** and **bus station** are adjacent to each other and it's not far to walk down to the **tourist office** (May & Sept Mon–Fri 9am–6pm, Sat 9am–2pm; June–Aug Mon–Fri 9am–7pm, Sat 9am–2pm; rest of the year Mon–Fri 10am–6pm, Sat 10am–2pm; ☎018/11 75 00) at St Persgatan 4, Gamla Torget. There's a second information desk in Uppsala Castle (for opening times see above). Both places hand out an English guide to the town, which has a useful map inside. The **boats** for Skokloster and Stockholm arrive at and depart from the pier south of the centre, at the end of Baverns Gränd. Bus #801 (45kr) runs between Uppsala and **Arlanda airport**, so if you wish you can bypass Stockholm either on arrival in or departure from Sweden: in Uppsala it leaves from the bus station, outside the railway station, every 15 to 30 minutes between 4.45am and 11.35pm.

Accommodation

Though so close to Stockholm, staying over can be an attractive idea. There are two **youth hostels**: a *YMCA InterRail Point* (☎018/ 18 85 66), 2km from the centre (bus #7 from Stora Torget) at the corner of Svartbäcksgatan and Torbjörnsgatan, open July to mid-August (8–11am & 5–10pm; 50kr a night; breakfast 20kr); and *STF*'s beautifully sited *Sunnersta Herrgård* (☎018/32 42 20), six kilometres south of Uppsala at Sunnerstavägen 24 (bus #20 from Nybron, by Stora Torget) – it's open May to August and costs 60kr a night. There are a few cheapish **hotels**, too, right in the centre, like the *Hotell Elit* (☎018/13 03 45), Bredgränd 10, while for a more expensive – though thoroughly pleasant – night's stay, try the *Hotel Linné* (☎018/10 20 00): it's at Skolgatan 45, the rooms overlooking the Linnaeus gardens. For a night's unofficial **camping**, head the few kilometres north to the open spaces of GAMLA UPPSALA (see below). Or there's a regular site (☎018/32 41 33) by Lake Mälaren at GRANEBERG, 7km out and open May to August: bus #20 from Nybron, 40kr a night per tent or 60kr per night for a two-person cabin.

Eating, drinking and nightlife

Eating and entertainment are straightforward in this university town, easier again if you have some form of student ID. For **snacks** and cheap coffee try the *Alma* café in the basement of the university building. Across the square, the *Café Ubbo* in the student union office is open all year, 9am–3/4pm; cheap set lunches. For **vegetarian** food it's difficult to beat lunch at *Barowiak*, a large wooden house immediately below the castle off Nedre Slottsgatan: jazz while you eat and plenty of students around. A similar set-up and equally popular is the *Café Katalin* on Svartbäcksgatan. The summer brings a glut of open air cafés around the town, the most popular on the river: *Åkanten* below St Erik's Torg is among the best. Many stay open until the early hours, an unusual bonus.

At **night** most of the action is generated by the students in houses called *Nations* contained within the grid of streets behind the university backing on to St Olofsgatan. Each a sort of college fraternity, they run dances, gigs and parties of all hues and, most importantly, boast a very cheap bar. The official line is that if you're not a Swedish student you won't get in to most of the things advertised around the town: in practice, being foreign and nice to the people on the door generally yields entrance; with an *ISIC* card it's even easier. As many students stay around during the summer, functions are not strictly limited to term time. A good choice to begin with is the *Uplands Nation*, off St Olofsgatan and Sysslomansgatan near the river, with a summer outdoor café open until 3am. *Barowiak* puts on live bands in the evenings (around 80kr entry), while the *Café Katalin* is open late, too, and has jazz nights. *Club Dacke* is a student-frequented disco on St Olofsgatan, near the Domkyrkan, while one of the liveliest joints is *Rackis*, a music bar out near the student residences on St Johannesgatan – there's live music here nearly every night; bus #1 to Student Staden.

Gamla Uppsala

Five kilometres to the north of the present city three huge **barrows**, royal burial mounds dating back to the sixth century, mark the original site of Uppsala, **GAMLA UPPSALA**. This was a pagan settlement – and a place of ancient sacrificial rites. Every ninth year the festival of *Fröblot* demanded the death of nine people, hanged from a nearby tree until their corpses rotted. The pagan temple where this bloody sacrifice took place is now marked by the Christian **Gamla Uppsala kyrka** (April–Aug daily 9.30am–8pm; Sept–March daily 9.30am–dusk), built over pagan remains when the Swedish kings first took baptism in the new faith. What survives is only a remnant of what was, originally, a cathedral – look in for the faded wall paintings and the tomb of Celsius, of thermometer fame. Set in the wall outside, there's an eleventh-century rune stone.

There's little else to Gamla Uppsala, and perhaps that's why the site remains mysterious and atmospheric. There's an **inn** nearby, *Odinsborg*, where – if you've got kids, or even if you haven't – you might want to sample the "Viking lunch"; a 60kr spread of soup, hunks of meat served on a board and mead, which comes complete with the horned helmet, an essential item if you're considering pillaging and plundering the afternoon away. And there's opportunity, too, if you're discreet, to **camp** beyond the inn, amid the ghosts.

To get to Gamla Uppsala, take **bus** #14 (hourly, not Sun), #24 (not Sun), #25 (not Sun) or #54 (Sun) from Dragarbrunnsgatan.

travel details

Trains

From Stockholm to Södertälje/Läggesta (3–6 daily; 30min/1hr); Helsingborg (4 daily; 7hr, 3 continuing to Copenhagen in 8hr 30min); Malmö (5–10 daily; 7hr); Gothenburg (weekdays virtually hourly, weekends less frequent; 4–4hr 45min); Uppsala/Gävle (11–16 daily; 45min/1hr 40min); Boden (3 daily; 14hr); Östersund (5 daily; 6hr 30min).

From Uppsala to Leksand/Mora (3 daily; 2hr 50min/3hr 40min); Stockholm (at least hourly; 45min).

Buses

From Stockholm to Nynäshamn (for ferry to Gotland): a connecting bus leaves 90min before ferry's departure, from Vattugatan close to Central Station (30kr single); Uppsala/Borlänge (Fri 2, Sat 1, Sun 2; 1hr/3hr 30min); Strängnäs/ Kristinehamn (3–4 at the weekend; 1hr/4hr); Gävle (Fri 3, Sat 1, Sun 2; 2hr 30min); Sveg/

Klövsjö (for Inlandsbanan; Fri, Sat & Sun 1 daily; 6hr/8hr 30min); Gothenburg (Fri & Sun 1 daily; 8hr); Helsingborg/Malmö (Fri & Sun 1 daily; 9hr/ 10hr); Umeå (Fri & Sun 1 daily; 10hr); Leksand/ Rättvik (Fri 2, Sat 1, Sun 2; 4hr 30min/5hr); Östersund (Sun 1 daily; 9hr).

International Trains

From Stockholm to Trondheim (2 daily; 11– 14hr); Oslo (1–3 daily; 6hr 30min); Narvik (2–3 daily; 21hr).

International Ferries

From Stockholm to Helsinki (1 *Viking* line and 1 *Silja* line daily; 15hr); Turku (2 *Viking* line and 2 *Silja* line daily; 1 daily on each line via the Åland Islands; 11–13hr); Eckerö (2–3 daily; 3hr; a bus leaves from Tekniska Högskolan T-bana 2hr before ferry's departure for Grisslehamn).

From Nynäshamn to Gdansk (Poland: one weekly; 19hr); Gotland (see p.391).

CHAPTER TEN

GOTHENBURG AND THE SOUTH

The **south** of Sweden is a mixed bag, a nest of coastal provinces, extensive lake and forest regions and gracefully ageing cities and towns. Much of the area is the target of Swedish holidaymakers – which means it's choc-full of clean campsites, beaches and cycle tracks, though rather thin on specific sights. Sweden's two largest splashes of water, **Vänern** and **Vättern**, dip into the region and there's little respite there from water-borne tourists; the lakes are connected to each other (and to east and west coasts) by a lengthy, popular canal and waterway system.

Still, there is a real historical interest to the southern provinces, not least in the cities that line the coast. The flatlands and fishing ports were almost constantly traded between Denmark and Sweden, counters won and lost in the fourteenth to seventeenth centuries. Several fortresses, not all forlorn, bear witness to the region's medieval buffer status. Of all the cities, grandest is **Gothenburg**, as likely a first sight of Sweden as Stockholm, especially if you're bringing a car over from Britain. Beyond the gargantuan shipyards, Sweden's second city is green and cultured and worth more time than the traditional post-ferry exodus allows. To the north of Gothenburg, the rocky **Bohuslän** coastline and the small riverside towns on the way to **Lake Vänern** are traditional escapes. And from the lake, the **Göta Canal** runs all the way to the Baltic.

The **south** is full of holidaymakers, too, though this time they're not on the water but in it, as the various counties boast some excellent beaches. Thin **Halland County**, immediately south of Gothenburg, also offers **Varberg** and the best of southern Sweden's fortresses. **Skåne County**, the southernmost region of Sweden, has been settled since the Iron Age, the plains and corn fields reminiscent of Denmark just over the sound – indeed, the county was under Danish rule until the middle of the seventeenth century. Again, though, it's Skåne's ports that attract most interest: **Helsingborg**, a stone's throw from Denmark, and **Malmö**, still solidly sixteenth-century at its centre. **Lund**, a medieval cathedral and university town, is an obvious and enjoyable stop between either place; while the coast of Skåne County stretches eastwards as far as Renaissance **Kristianstad**.

To the east, **Blekinge County** consists of a succession of small coastal resorts, culminating in the once-great naval centre of **Karlskrona**, Sweden's second city in the eighteenth century but today living strongly on its memories.

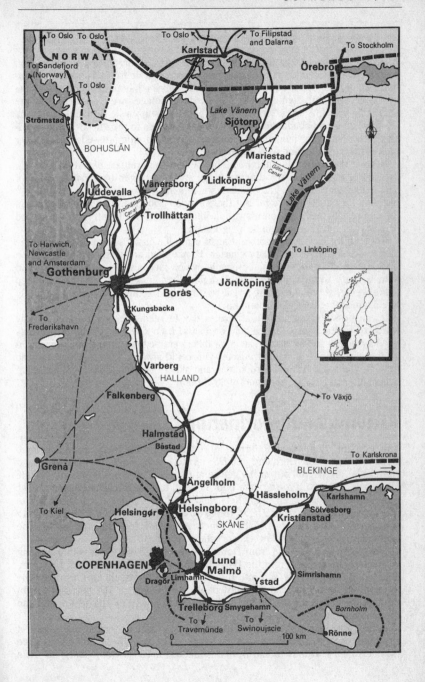

GOTHENBURG AND AROUND

Arriving in **Gothenburg** (Göteborg) by ship provides an abrupt, if misleading, introduction to Scandinavia's largest port. Ferry arrivals from Harwich are shuttled in alongside the dock-strewn river, a ride offering glimpses of colossal industrial concentration. Coming from Denmark, the images are less fleeting as the ship pulls up right in the centre of the port and shipyards. Although the occasional rusting and abandoned dry dock bears witness to the effects of the recession in the shipping industry, it's difficult to remain unimpressed by the sheer bulk of the surviving and working hardware.

Beyond the shipyards though, Gothenburg is the prettiest of Sweden's cities. Traffic-free streets and broad avenues are split and ringed by a canal system of simple elegance. Trams, gardens and squares all add to the impression that the planners for once got it right. But there's a downside too. Keeping traffic out of the centre has pushed it onto swirling interchanges on the city's outskirts, and driving in or hitching out can be a nightmare.

Gothenburg has been a sort of transit camp for business and travel since the days of its seventeenth-century charter. People tend not to stay long and those that stop at all are often businesspeople, which means that accommodation and entertainment in the centre can be flash and dear. Luckily, there's enough cheap cultural entertainment to make a visit worthwhile, and the parks, canals and lively street atmosphere are all free and fun.

If you possibly can, devote at least a day to seeing the region immediately **north of Gothenburg**. Only a boat or a short train ride away, **Trollhättan** is as good a place to aim for as any, an enjoyable riverside town. And if you're inspired by the possibilities of water transport you could always make the four day trip from Gothenburg, through Trollhättan and along the **Göta Canal** – a fine route which, ultimately, stops just short of Stockholm.

Arriving and information

You're more than likely to arrive in Gothenburg by **ferry**, from England, Denmark or West Germany. *DFDS* ferries from **England** (Harwich and Newcastle) arrive well out of the centre at Skandiahamn. Buses waiting outside fill up and then shuttle everyone into the city, to Nils Ericsons Platsen – 25kr (children 10kr), but keep the ticket (valid one hour) and use it to travel on to your accommodation. (For *DFDS* **departures**, catch the same bus, #115, from platform V at Nils Ericsons Platsen ninety minutes before the ship leaves. The Gothenburg Card – see below – is *not* valid on this bus.)

Stena line ferries to and from **Denmark** (Fredrikshavn) dock within walking distance of the centre. From the **West Germany** (Kiel) ferry drop-off it's a 3km-hike along the riverside and into the city. Several buses, though, run past the terminal on the main road (Oskarsleden), and getting on #64 takes you right through the centre and out to the *Ostkupan* youth hostel; or take #94 or #86 into the centre.

Train arrivals are all at **Central Station** which forms one side of Drottningtorget: inside there's an exchange office and the *SJ* bus ticket office (see "Listings"). **Buses** to and from destinations north of Gothenburg use **Nils**

Ericsons Platsen, immediately behind Central Station; and for destinations south of Gothenburg, the **Heden** terminal, which is behind Trädgårdsföreningen at the junction of Parkgatan and Södra Vägen. This is also where the buses from Stockholm and Malmö drop you.

From *Landvetter* **airport**, 25km east of the city, buses run roughly every twenty minutes (*Flygbuss*: daily 6am–11.30pm; 40kr) into the centre, stopping in Drottningtorget, outside Central Station; it's a thirty-five minute journey. On Friday and Saturday, there's a night bus from the airport (#691 or #692) to the centre, at 1.30am and 3am.

Tourist information

Gothenburg has two **tourist offices**. Handiest for recent arrivals is the **kiosk** in *Nordstan*, the indoor shopping centre next to Central Station. It's open all year (Mon–Fri 9.30am–6pm, Sat 9.30am–3pm), hands out free maps, sells the Gothenburg Card (see below) and books hotel and private rooms. The **main office** (Jan–April & Sept–Dec Mon–Fri 9am–5pm, Sat 10am–2pm; May Mon–Fri 9am–6pm, Sat & Sun 10am–2pm; beginning to mid-June & mid- to end Aug daily 9am–6pm; mid-June to mid-Aug daily 9am–8pm; ☎031/10 07 40) is a five-minute walk down Östra Hamngatan, on the canal front at Basargatan 10; again, free maps, room booking service, and restaurant and museum listings.

Getting around the city

Gothenburg is perhaps the most immediately attractive Swedish city around which to **walk**. Unlike Stockholm there are no forbidding central streets or distant islands, and secluded parkland is generally close at hand. Having said this, the walk from the central transport termini up and down the main boulevard, Avenyn, is a long slog, and to reach the youth hostels you can't avoid using some form of transport. To that end pick up a free **transport map** (*Linje Kartan*) from the tourist office, which details all the city routes and those for the surrounding area, too.

Public transport

Most tempting for short hops are the **trams** that clunk around the city and its outskirts. There are eight lines, all of which pass through somewhere fairly central at some stage, so you can't go too far wrong. The terminus outside the Central Station (Centralstationen) or the ranks in Kungsportplatsen are the easiest places to pick one up – just check the destination and number on the front to make sure of your direction. **Buses** use much the same routes, but central pedestrianisation can lead to some odd and lengthy detours. You shouldn't need to use them at all in the city centre; routes are detailed in the text where neccessary.

Each city journey costs two 4.5kr **tickets** (ie 9kr); 7–16 year olds go for half-price. You buy them from the bus or tram driver, who can also sell you a book of eleven discounted tickets for 35kr – worth having if you're in town for a couple of days. Validate the ticket in the machine and note that you can then continue in the same direction on the next bus or tram for free. Alternatively, a **24-hour**

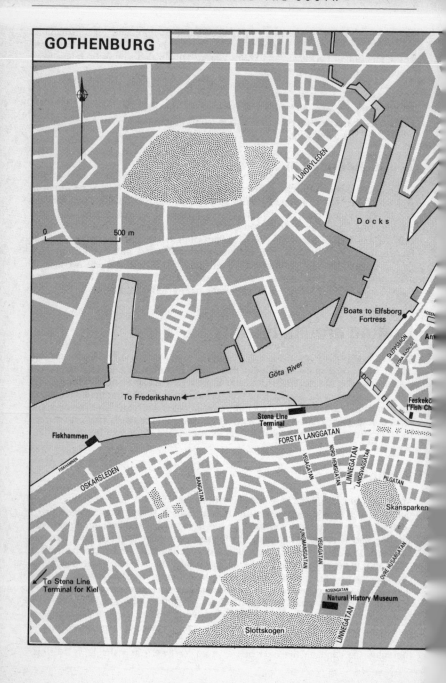

GOTHENBURG

0   500 m

LUNDBYLEDEN

Docks

Boats to Elfsborg
Fortress

ROSEN

SLEPSBRON

STORA HAMNUS

An

Göta River

To Frederikshavn

Feskekö
('Fish Ch

Stena Line
Terminal

FORSTA LANGGATAN

Fiskhammen

VEGGATAN

NORD HEMGATAN

LINNEGATAN

LANDSVAGSGATAN

PILGATAN

FISKHAMMEN

OSKARSLEDEN

BANGATAN

Skansparken

JUNGMANSGATAN

VEGGATAN

OVRE HUSARGATAN

To Stena Line
Terminal for Kiel

ROSENGATAN

Natural History Museum

LINNEGATAN

Slottskogen

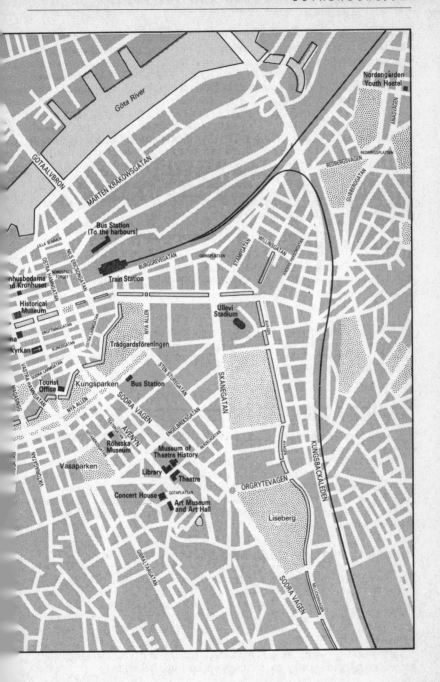

pass costs 20kr from the tourist office: it's valid on all city transport and will save a lot of money if you intend to move about a bit. Using the trams, avoiding the front carriage with the driver and getting on at the back is possible, free and illegal. However, roving inspectors hand out instant 400kr fines for **fare dodging** – and as all the ticket information is in English on boards posted at bus and tram stops, ignorance is no defence.

The Gothenburg Card

A popular move is to buy a *Göteborgskortet*, or **Gothenburg Card**, a pass which gives unlimited bus/tram travel, free museum entry and various other concessions (detailed in the text where applicable). Moreover the card also grants a free day trip to Fredrikshavn on the *Stena Line* ferry, making it a cheap way to leave Sweden for Denmark. The card is valid for 24 (70kr), 48 (120kr), 72 (165kr) or 96 (200kr) hours – children roughly half-price – and you get it from either tourist office, *Pressbyrå* kiosks or campsites and hotels in the city.

Cars, taxis and bikes

If you've brought a **car** over from Britain, then it's useful to know that the Gothenburg Card lets you use parking meters in the city free of charge, on the days that your card is valid. Ask the tourist office, or your hotel, for parking authorisation. You'll find a list of **car rental** agencies under "Listings", below. Otherwise, **taxis** can be summoned by ringing ☎20 04 00.

Gothenburg has an excellent series of cycle lanes and cycle racks throughout the city and, if you don't have your own, you can **rent bikes** from *Torpa Cykel & Sport*, Kaggeledstorget, Vidkärrsallén 8 (tram #1 to Kaggeledstorget): around 40kr per day and 200kr per week.

Finding a place to stay

As far as **accommodation** goes, central budget choices are virtually nonexistent. If it's vital to stay right in the middle of things, then it's best to take advantage of the tourist office's special hotel deal, for more on which see below. If this is beyond your budget, then the cheapest option lies in booking a private room near the centre, or staying in the youth hostels, all a good few kilometres away but of a consistently high standard. If you let either of the tourist offices book you a hotel or a room anywhere, you'll be charged a 25kr fee: ring ☎031/10 07 40 for bookings or information.

Private rooms and youth hostels

The tourist office will also find you **private rooms** in and out of the city centre. Prices are competitive – 130kr single, 90kr each in doubles and triples. For longer stays, a week or more, contact *SGS Bostäder*, Utlandgatan 24 (Mon 3–7pm, Tues–Fri 10am–4pm, Sun 4–8pm; ☎031/81 33 71) who rent out **furnished rooms** with kitchen and bathroom for around 970–1140kr per week: the price includes sheets but you'll need your own kitchen utensils.

Falling back on **youth hostels** in the Gothenburg area is no bad thing. There are several, all good-quality and relatively cheap, listed below.

Nordengården, Stockholmsgatan 14 (☎031/19 66 31); tram #1 or #3 to Stockholmsgatan, or #6 to Redbergplatsen. A private hostel which costs around 40kr a night in large dormitory rooms, 60kr each in a four-bedded room. With a kitchen and free showers, it's good value so ring ahead, or try and call in the morning before 10am to secure a bed. Open May to mid-September.

Ostkupan, Mejerigatan 2 (☎031/40 10 50). A large and busy *STF* hostel, open June to August; 55kr a night – take bus #64 from Brunnsparken to Gräddgatan, or tram #5 to St Sigfridsplan then bus #62 (Kalebäck direction) to Gräddgatan.

Partille, Landvettervägen, Partille (☎031/44 61 63). Another *STF* choice, 15km east of the city but open all year; bus #514 or #515 from Heden bus terminal (every 15min 6am–8pm, half-hourly 8pm–12.30am; a 30-min ride); 55kr a night.

M/S Seaside, Packhuskajen (☎031/13 64 67); at the harbour, by Maritima Centrum. A moored ship with thirty one- to four-bedded cabins; 100kr per person, breakfast 35kr and sheets 25kr.

Hotels and pensions

The tourist office co-ordinates the **Gothenburg Package**, where paying from 210kr to 400kr per person gets you a room in a central hotel, with breakfast and a free Gothenburg Card thrown in. For three people travelling together, adding an extra bed brings the price down a little in most hotels. It's undoubtedly a bargain and good for early morning departures or a treat. Over thirty hotels take part in the scheme, so you should find something you like. The package operates every weekend (Fri–Mon) all year, and daily from mid-June to mid-August; book it through the tourist office, *not* by turning up at individual hotels.

Otherwise, most hotels have a **weekend price**, which should be significantly lower than usual: it's always worth asking. The lists below also include some **pensions** and though there are no real bargains you might find the option useful. Hotels taking part in the Gothenburg Package scheme are marked "GP", together with their current package price per person per night.

Hotel Allén, Parkgatan 10 (☎031/10 14 50); opposite Heden bus terminal. Nothing flash; singles from 300–350kr, doubles with shower 400–450kr; breakfast included.

Hotell Eggers, Drottningtorget (☎031/80 60 70). The original railway hotel, this is a lovely building whose large rooms (some for non-smokers) are full of ageing furniture. GP 310kr.

Hotell Ekoxen, Norra Hamngatan 38 (☎031/80 50 80). Smart, new hotel bang in the centre whose price includes breakfast, sauna and evening buffet meal. GP 310kr.

Hotel Kung Karl, Nils Ericsonsgatan 23 (☎031/17 28 35); right next to Central Station. A plush, family-run hotel whose price includes sauna and Sky Channel TV. GP 280kr.

M.E. Pensionat, Chalmersgatan 27a (☎031/20 70 30); just up from the junction with Kristinelundsgatan. A small place with just ten rooms. Look for the sign that says "Rums – Pensionat"; 275kr single, 350kr double.

Hotel Onyxen, Sten Sturegatan 23 (☎031/16 01 36); opposite Scandinavium stadium. Fine old hotel whose weekend prices are 350kr single, 440kr double, including breakfast.

Hotel Örnen, 1st floor, Lorensbergsgatan 6 (☎031/18 23 80). Good location, on a street parallel to Avenyn, and – at 300kr double – cheap and popular; ring first.

Cabins and campsites

Between three or four people it's worth renting a **cabin** at a campsite. These generally have a well-equipped kitchen (but no bedding), while showers and loos are shared with the campers. *Kärralunds* **campsite** (☎031/25 27 61) is only 4km out and open all year – tram #5 to Welandergatan (Torp direction) and then follow the signs. There are excellent facilities: cabins here cost around 200kr (for three) or 250kr (sleeps four), and there's a private **hostel** on site too – 60kr a night each. Pitching a **tent** costs 60kr, no charge per person and the site encompasses forest and lakes.

For sand and beaches the two **campsites** at ASKIM are better, both 12km out. *Askims* (☎031/28 62 61) is open June to mid-August and has some cabins available; *Västervågs* (☎031/281517), May to September, doesn't. Get to both on trams #1 or #2 to Linnéplatsen and then bus #83 or #783 (Säro direction).

Sleeping rough is not a great idea in well policed Gothenberg, although with discretion and a search for the forested bits, it should be reasonably safe in Slottsskogen, the large park in the southwest of the city. Take tram #1 or #2 to Linnéplatsen.

The City

The best way to acquaint yourself with the layout of **GOTHENBURG** is to jump on a **paddan boat** (May to mid-Sept departures every 15-30min; 35kr, families 85kr, free after 2pm with Gothenburg Card), moored immediately outside the main tourist office, for an hour-long water-tour of the city. King Gustav II Adolf, looking for western trade, founded Gothenburg in the early seventeenth century as a response to the high tolls charged by the Danes for using the narrow sound between the two countries. As a Calvinist and businessman, Gustav much admired Dutch merchants, inviting them to trade and live in Gothenburg. It's their influence that shaped the city, and as the boat chugs its way under the twenty-odd low bridges of the central canal, familiar Dutch pictures emerge. Out on the open river, amongst the hulking dry docks and gaping harbours, it's difficult to reconcile the mess with the ordered houses and parks of the centre.

Back on dry land Gothenburg can be an infuriating place to try and see quickly because of the limited opening times of its places of interest – usually 11am–4pm, with most things closed on Monday. You either have to be very quick and methodical, or stay another day.

The centre: old Gothenburg and the harbour

If your time is limited, sticking within the limits defined by the central canal – roughly old and commercial Gothenburg – is a logical first choice. **Gustav Adolfs Torg**, alongside the original central canal, is a pompous, windswept square, where a statue of the swaggering Gustav himself surveys the city. The buildings which surround him are worth pausing over: the nineteenth-century **Börshuset**, or Exchange building, faces the canal, its white, double-columned facade topped with figurines and split by four intricate wooden doors; and, flanking the western side is the fine **Rådhus**, originally built in 1672 as a court house and rebuilt in 1817.

Only a few hundred metres around the corner (towards the river) the **Kronhuset**, off Kronhusgatan, is a contrasting surprise – a typical seventeenth-century Dutch design and Gothenburg's oldest building. Built in 1643, its red brick walls and green roof slates look like the backdrop to a Vermeer. Once a meeting hall and supposed site of a seventeenth-century parliament, it now houses an historical exhibition (Tues–Sat noon–4pm, Sun 11am–5pm; May–Aug Mon noon–4pm; 5kr). The rest of the cobbled courtyard outside is flanked by the mid-eighteenth-century **Kronhusbodarna** (Mon–Sat 11am–4pm), now togged up as period (nineteenth-century) craft shops selling sweets and souvenirs and nowhere near as tacky as the tourist office's description of them as *Ye Olde Shops*. The square and its buildings are supposed to convey something of Gothenburg's past, but it's hard going with no surviving old town to supply background.

For that background the **Historical Museum** (May–Aug Mon–Sat noon–4pm, Sun 11am–5pm; Jan–April & Sept–Dec Tues–Sat noon–4pm, Tues also 6–9pm, Sun 11am–5pm; 10kr) at Norra Hamngatan 12 is comprehensive and particularly strong on local matters. Housed in the eighteenth-century headquarters of the *East India Company*, the collections – rooms full of furniture and decorative art – are accessible enough, though, as with many similar museums in Sweden, the whole is rescued from repetition by complementary **ethnographical** and **archaeological** collections. These are excellent, with everything from prehistoric finds to African art, and are worth a separate visit for themselves.

The harbour

If you've taken the paddan boat tour, you'll have already seen the best views of the **harbour** – from the water. However, a new outdoor maritime museum, the **Maritima Centrum** (May & Sept Sat & Sun 11am–5pm; June–Aug daily 11am–5pm; 35kr, children 15kr) gives you a different view, and allows you to clamber aboard various types of vessels moored at the quayside – a warship, cargo boats, trawlers, a ferry and even a floating restaurant. There's an indoor museum, too, and you can either pay just to see one or two of the ships or get the 35kr ticket which gives you access to everything, including the museum. Even outside the opening hours it's worth going down to the quays to have a look around. The ship yards beyond the harbour look like a rusting meccano set, put into sharp perspective by the *IBM* building and the other new technology industries whose offices are adjacent: Lego-like structures of tubes and bricks with red and white stripes.

This part of the harbour is linked by overhead walkway to *Nordstan* shopping centre, so that you can avoid the busy road interchange below. Note that your Gothenburg Card *isn't* valid for the Maritima Centrum.

Churches and trade

In its seventeenth- and eighteenth-century heyday Gothenburg was first and foremost a trading and export centre, and its churches were always decidedly low key. The **Domkyrkan** (Mon–Fri 9.30–11.30am, Thurs also 5.30–6pm, Sat 8am–3pm, Sun 10am–3pm) over the canal on Kyrkogatan is a good, though admittedly later, example: simple wooden portal, mock marble pillars and a gilt altar that today seem weary and faded. And it's no surprise to find that what seems to be the area's most notable church, the **Feskekörkan** ("Fish Church") on the canal at Rosenlundsgatan, is in fact a fish market, built in 1873. It's open Tuesday to Friday, from 9am to 5pm, Saturday 9am to 1pm, and there's an excellent fish restaurant inside too; tram #1, #3 or #4 to Järntorget. For serious fish dealing it's instructive to go down to the fish harbour, **Fiskhamnen**, a couple of kilometres west of the centre, where daily auctions take place. You'll need to be keen – the auctions start at 7am, Monday to Friday. Take tram #3 or #4 to Stigbergstorget.

For more proof of the decorative care lavished on all things commercial and secular, pop into the **Antikhallarna** (Mon–Fri 10am–6pm, Sat 10am–2pm; closed Sat May–Aug) at the top of Västra Hamngatan. A permanent antique market on two lofty floors, the collectors' items (from stamps to suits of armour) are ranged between marble walls and pillars and kept dry under the loveliest of black-leaded glass roofs.

Avenyn and around

Cross the canal from Kungsportsplatsen and, with the **Stora Teatern** straight ahead, Kungsportsavenyn runs all the way up to Götaplatsen. This wide strip, known simply as **Avenyn** or "the Avenue", is Gothenburg's showiest thoroughfare, once consisting of a line of private houses fronted by gardens. A couple of buildings at the canal end, near the theatre, still survive from those days – high and pastel-coloured, with fine balconied frontages. The side streets, too, particularly on the western side, remain handsome and neat; a grid pattern of tall buildings reminiscent of central Glasgow's neat tenement blocks. These days Avenyn itself is no longer residential, but rather a length of pavement restaurants and brasseries. Of an evening everyone takes to the streets to walk and watch – a custom that almost makes you forget you're this far north. During the day Avenyn's business is shopping, although a couple of good museums lurk in the side streets.

Gardens, arts and crafts

Avenyn crosses a green belt of land fronting the canal: **Kungsparken**, on the right, and – on the left – the **Trädgårdsföreningen** (April–Sept daily 7am–9pm, 2kr; rest of the year daily 7am–6pm, free). The latter is the better, a botanical garden with sculpture park and a beautifully-restored nineteenth-century **Palm House** (June–Aug daily 10am–8pm; Sept–May daily 10am–4pm; 10kr) containing distinctly un-Scandinavian flora. Throughout the summer, theatre and music groups perform regularly in the park at lunchtime.

A bit further up Avenyn, the **Rösska Museum of Arts and Crafts**, at Vasagatan 37–39 (May–Aug Mon–Sat noon–4pm, Sun 11am–5pm; Sept–April Tues–Sat noon–4pm, Wed also 6–9pm, Sun 11am–5pm; 10kr, architectural/craft students free), celebrates (among other things) Swedish design through the ages. Some beautiful antique furniture competes for the honours alongside modern cutlery, glass and silverware, and there's a large collection of (often very good) contemporary photographs.

Götaplatsen

If you're not shopping or eating there's nothing more on Avenyn until **Götaplatsen** at the top, the modern cultural centre of Gothenburg. Milles' muscled *Poseidon* fronts the traffic and ranged around him and the square are the Concert Hall, City Theatre and the respected **Art Museum** (May–Aug Mon–Sat noon–4pm, Sun 11am–5pm; Sept–April Tues–Sat noon–4pm, Wed also 6–9pm, Sun 11am–5pm; 10kr, art students free). The massive facade is not a jot misleading: inside are enormous collections that should be catholic enough for most tastes. Chiefly though it's the Impressionists who hold sway – Cézanne, Pissarro and Renoir all fighting for wall space. Of the Swedish artists present, the works of

Carl Kylberg are best, while downstairs modern and pop art take over, with Warhol's obligatory *Marilyn Monroe* amongst a host of other works. The modern Scandinavians get more than a look in too, a refreshing change.

Adjacent to the Art Museum, the **City Library** (Mon–Thurs 10am–8pm, Fri & Sat 10am–6pm) has a "what's on" noticeboard that's worth checking, international newspapers, chess sets and a basement café for recuperation. Less enticingly, you may want to glance at the *Tittskåpen* on the way out – cases upon cases of miniature dolls.

And, if you're so inclined, round the corner on Berzeliigatan, the old Lorensberg Theatre now houses a pedestrian **Museum of Theatrical History** (Tues–Sat noon–4pm, Sun 11am–5pm; free), black and white stills, manuscripts and posters arranged around its former changing rooms.

The rest of the city: parks and fortresses

Top of the agenda for most visitors and all kids is **Liseberg** (mid-April to mid-Sept; 20–25kr depending on season, under 7s and Gothenburg Card free), an amusement park with some high-profile rides and acres of gardens, restaurants and fast food. Even without going on anything (no rides included in the entrance fee), it's not a bad way to spend an afternoon or evening. Litter-free, there's enough amusement to be derived from the crooning MOR bands playing "Blue Spanish Eyes" over crackly tannoys for even the most devout funfair hater. At night it gets louder and its restaurants, cafés and gardens are good for some entertaining – and safe – strolling. Tram #5 goes right to the gates, but if you've made it as far as Götaplatsen it's only another five minutes by foot across the university grounds.

Skansparken, a tiny park west of the centre, is worth the walk for the views rather than for the **Military Museum** (Wed 7–9pm, Sat 1–3pm, Sun noon–3pm; free) in the seventeenth-century fortress tower at the top of the park's hill. The whole area between Järntorget and Skanstorget merits a casual browse, faintly decaying residential streets with a smattering of cheap places to eat. For real expanses of parkland and summer entertainment just keep going west towards **Slottskogen** (trams #1 and #2 to Linnéplatsen): lakes and trees, a **Natural History Museum** (May–Aug Mon–Sat noon–4pm, Sun 11am–5pm; Sept–April Tues–Sat noon–4pm, Wed also 6–9pm, Sun 11am–5pm; 10kr) and a quiet corner for a sunbathe.

Nya Elfsborg Fortress

More great views of the harbour can be had from the excursion boats that run to the **Nya Elfsborg Fortress** (mid-May to mid-Sept daily: boats every 75min from 9.45am–5.30pm; 35kr, families 85kr, free with Gothenburg Card). A seventeenth-century island defence guarding the harbour entrance, the surviving buildings have been turned into a museum and café. A tour allows just enough time to poke around the old walls and crumbling prison cells. A ship of the East India Company, the *Göteborg*, sank at the entrance to the harbour in 1745 and the island is currently being used as the base for the marine archaeology that's underway: you should be able to study the work in progress during the summer.

The boat to the fortress leaves from Stenpiren, only a few hundred metres from Lilla Torget.

All the action: eating, drinking and nightlife

There's no shortage of places to grab a good **lunch** in Gothenburg. Almost every street in the centre has a place to snack, while the indoor shopping malls are rife with cafés and restaurants all offering cheap daily menus. At night the choice is less wide, but if you've got cash to spare there are some excellent restaurants. As for **nightlife**, it's a question of what you can afford. The trendiest hangouts are the mushrooming *brasseries* where bright clothes and chromium bars are all the rage, and there are some late night cafés and **discos** to keep you out of bed later on. Gothenburg has a fairly brisk **live music** scene, too – jazz, rock and classical – as well as the usual **cinema** and theatre opportunities that you'd expect.

Eating

The details and lists below cover all the possibilities, from snacks to full meals. There's plenty of choice in the city, not least at lunchtime when most restaurants have a set price meal that commonly includes main course, a drink, bread and a coffee. The only thing you won't see much of in Gothenburg, at least at the lower end of the market, is Swedish food: the trend instead, as befitting the city's trade port status, is towards a growing number of pricey ethnic restaurants, Portuguese to Japanese, alongside the usual staples of pizza, pasta and burgers.

Markets and snacks

The *Stora Saluhallen*, the indoor **market** in Kungstorget (Mon–Fri 9.30am–6pm, Sat 9.30am–2pm) is tempting beyond words – freshly baked bread, fruit, fish and endless cheeses; and it houses the two cheapest coffee/snack bars in town. There's an open-air **fruit and veg** market (*Gröna Hallen*) just outside. And the *Domus* store on Avenyn (Mon–Sat 10am–9pm, Sun 1–9pm) contains a **supermarket** if you're self-catering.

If you want hot food, the area around Skansparken is useful for **take-aways**; *Georges* (pizza and kebabs) in Järntorget, *Pizzabutik Rimini* at Långgatan 1 and a *7-Eleven* store (burgers, drinks and supermarket) nearby, off Linnégatan. More central **street kiosks**, selling hotdogs and burgers, include the *Gatukök* opposite the *Park Avenue Hotel*, Avenyn (open daily until 3am, Fri & Sat 4am), and one on Kungsportsbron, by the canal. There are also several *McDonalds* scattered around, including a couple on Avenyn.

A nice place for a **coffee and cake** is *Jaktslottcaféet*, Otterhällegatan 16 (daily 11am–4pm), a restored hunting-lodge just off Kungsgatan in the area bounded by the central canal.

Lunch

Gothenburg is packed with places serving set price lunches, nearly all good value. The ones to avoid are those right on Avenyn, 10–20kr pricier than elsewhere, though even at this end of town there are good choices if you know where to look. Most of the places below are open at night, too, but the prices given are for the lunchtime deals – see below for full blown dinners in restaurants.

Gondoliere, Avenyn 2. Around 40–50kr gets a good lunch in this Italian restaurant on Avenyn, with covered seating on the pavement, although the pizzas are more expensive (50–60kr) if you come at night. Similar menu and prices at the *Gondola*, further up at no. 4.

Kungstorgscaféet, Kungstorget. A no-nonsense cafeteria outside the market hall with very cheap meals – meatballs and potatoes 29kr, omlettes 27kr and egg and bacon fry-ups for 31kr (Mon–Fri 6am–5pm, Sat 6am–2.30pm).

Kåren, Götabergsgatan 17; by Geijersgatan. Easily the cheapest deal in town in the city's Student Union building. Set lunches for 23kr (Mon–Fri 11am–2pm) and a café here open Mon–Fri 10am–4pm. You may need student ID.

Leony Salad Bar, Fredsgatan 1. A good-value place with the daily salad going for 35kr, including bread and a drink. Other salads and plates of pasta are around 40kr, sandwiches 30kr.

Malaysia Saté Restaurant, Östra Hamngatan 19. Far Eastern food in a new restaurant; 41kr for the set lunch.

Matkällaren, corner of Kristinelundsgatan and Lorensbergsgatan; turn off Avenyn at *Hotel Rubinen*. A basement pizzeria which turns out good 38kr lunch deals on hamburger and steak and chip meals and fine, big pizzas, including bread, coleslaw and drink (Mon–Fri 11am–9pm, Sat 1–9pm).

Peking, Fredsgatan 4. One of the better Chinese choices: a lunch buffet for 59kr is served Mon–Fri 11.30am–4pm; or there are two set lunches at 37kr and 55kr.

Sara Hotel Europa, Köpmansgatan 38. The hotel restaurant puts on an excellent buffet at the weekend; 55kr to help yourself to salads, potatoes, bread, a drink, ice cream and coffee (Fri 11.30am–2pm, Sat noon–3pm, Sun 1–4pm).

Taj India, Odinsgatan 6; close to Central Station. Indian set lunches for 55kr (Mon–Fri 11am–2.30pm).

Ättaglas; a floating restaurant moored at Kungsportsbron next to the paddan boats. Excellent daily lunch for 59kr served on the lower deck.

Evening eating

Some of the places below have already been mentioned under "Lunch", but you're more likely to want to go (or go back) to them at night.

Annorlunda, Lilla Korsgatan 2. A vegetarian restaurant reportedly adequate, if not brilliant.

Casa Portuguesa, Avenyn 10–12. A new Portuguese restaurant with terrific food, especially the fish dishes. It's not cheap, but is one of Gothenburg's better dining experiences.

Gyllene Prag, Sveagatan 25. Czech restaurant which is reasonably priced and popular with the local students.

Marco Polo, Lilla Nygatan 2; next to *Palladium* cinema. An averagely-priced pizzeria and Italian restaurant, whose main attraction is that it's open Fri & Sat until 3am. Set lunches, too.

Pizza Hut; branches on Avenyn and in *Nordstan* shopping centre. You know exactly what you'll get; 43kr for a small pizza, 77kr for something more substantial; and 45kr for a main course, help-yourself salad.

Räkan, Lorensbergsgatan 16. If you've got the cash for just one blow-out, come here. A fish and shellfish restaurant, covered with fishing gear, the centrepiece is a large indoor pool across which you navigate radio-controlled boats laden with your prawn dinner. Excellent, fresh food and a fun place to eat it; around 200–300kr a head, depending on how carried away you get. Closed Monday.

Taj India, Odinsgatan 6; see above. It's worth trying at night, too, if you can afford it since there's a good vegetarian set dinner for 175kr; or separate dishes cost from 95–110kr, vegetable dishes 65–75kr (open daily until 11pm).

Ättaglas, Kungsportsbron; see above. Upstairs the speciality is fish, which is marvellously cooked and presented, but it's a pricey spot – around 120kr for a main course; open till around 1.30am on Fri & Sat, 12.30am otherwise.

Drinking: bars and night-cafés

There's an excellent choice of places to drink in Gothenburg, with the added bonus that some places stay open until well into the small hours. Avenyn is the focal point of much of night-time Gothenburg, but wherever you are you should find somewhere to wet your whistle.

Brasserie Julien, Götaplatsen 9. Smart bar/restaurant on two floors. Seats outside in summer, and a mainly young clientele.

Brasserie Lipp, Avenyn 8. One of the trendiest hangouts, back down the avenue, with a good-sized bar up front, a restaurant at the back – generally crowded.

Fröken Olssens Kafe, Östra Larmgatan 14. Popular haunt and good for a quick cappuccino in pleasant surroundings. Reasonably priced food, too, and open very late at the weekend (Mon 8am–7pm, Tues–Fri 8am–4am, Sat 10am–3pm & 9pm–4am).

Gamle Port, Östra Larmgatan 18. British beer in the downstairs pub, restaurant and (fairly crummy) disco upstairs.

George Duwal, Kyrkogatan 32. A nightcafé open during the day and then from around midnight until 5am most days.

Musik Café Avenyn, Avenyn. No drinks license, but a young crowd in this popular café getting into ice cream and coffee. Live music (folky stuff), too; open daily until 11pm, Fri & Sat until 1am.

Tvåkanten, Avenyn, junction with Kristinelundsgatan. Amiable coffee bar with seats outside in the summer; sandwiches and the like on sale.

Entertainment: discos, live music, cinema and theatre

There's plenty of other things to do in Gothenburg besides eat and drink. The details below should give you some ideas, and pick up the free weekly newspaper *Göteborg denna Vecka* which lists restaurants, bars, concerts, discos and almost anything else you might want to know about – it's in Swedish but isn't very difficult to decipher.

Dancing

You can lay some steps down at a few **discos**, which are strangely and inordinately popular with the local youth. For current favourites ask anyone under 30 working in the tourist office, or check out the *Yaki-Da* on Nya Allén, behind the Palm House in Trädgårdsföreningen (Wed–Sat 9pm–3am). The Gothenburg Card gives free entry to three other discos in town, including the *Gamle Port* (see above) but these are all fairly duff. Also, beware flyposters advertising cheaper one-off discos in town, generally the unlicensed province of Gothenburg's seventeen-year-olds.

Live music

Rock and pop bands play at a variety of venues in town, largest the *Scandinavium*, the stadium on Skånegatan, which hosts most of the big, international acts; and *Lisebergshallen* in Liseberg. Smaller venues are *Yaki-Da* (see above), who put on local acts as well as British and American bands, and *Kåren*, the Student Union building (see "Lunch" above).

There are several good **jazz clubs** in Gothenburg, too. *Jazzhuset* at Erik Dahlbergsgatan 3 puts on trad, Dixieland and swing (Wed & Thurs 8pm–1am, Fri & Sat 8pm–2am). And there's also *Nefertitti*, Hvitfeldtsplatsen 6 (daily except Sun from 9pm), and *Jazzklubben* in Esperantoplatsen. All cost from around 50kr entrance. One place that defies categorisation is *Cafe Planken*, Vasaplatsen 3, which has classical music programmes every afternoon (2–6pm) and a choice of folk, cabaret, jazz, mediums, healers and Swedish singers at night; around 50–70kr entrance. Otherwise, there's **classical music** in the *Konserthuset*, Götaplatsen and the *Stora Teatern*, Avenyn – details from the tourist office.

Other entertainment

The major **cinemas** are on Avenyn and in *Nordstan* shopping centre. The local newspapers or the tourist office can tell you what's on; entrance around 50kr. **Theatre** productions are almost exclusively in Swedish, though in an attempt to entice you in, the Gothenburg Card gets you two tickets for the price of one at the *Stadsteatern*, Götaplatsen, and the *Folkteatern*, Olof Palmes Plats, Järntorget. There's a ticket booking office at Kungsportsplatsen 2 for theatre and sports events – or ask at the tourist office.

Football fans can catch *IFK Göteborg* (also known locally as *Blåvitt* – the "Blue and Whites") at Ullevi stadium; take trams #1, #3 or #6. They're a handy team and were the 1987 UEFA Cup champions. Other sports events take place here, too, or at *Scandinavium*.

If sports don't grab you, give the *Happy Jazz Cruise* a whirl: a weekly four-hour **cruise** during summer up the Göta Canal with a trad jazz band on board; 85kr covers the trip and the entertainment and there's a restaurant on board, too – tickets from the tourist office.

Listings

Airlines *British Airways*, at the airport (☎031/94 13 15); *Finnair*, Fredsgatan 6 (☎020/78 11 00); *KLM*, at the airport (☎031/94 16 40); *Lufthansa*, Fredsgatan 1 (☎031/17 28 40); *SAS*, Norra Hamngatan 20–22 (☎031/63 85 20). Flight information on ☎031/94 20 50 (daily 7am–10pm).

Airport Bus Departures from Central Station every 15–20min from 5am–11.30pm (Sat 10.30pm); 40kr. A nightbus (#691 or #692) from Nils Ericsons Platsen leaves at 12.45am and 2.15am on Fri & Sat only.

Banks and Exchange Open Mon–Fri 9.30am–3pm. A branch inside the *Nordstan* shopping centre stays open until 5.30pm. There's a *Forex* exchange office inside Central Station (daily 8am–9pm).

Buses Tickets for *SJ* buses running between Gothenburg and Olso from *SJ Buss Center*, inside Central Station, Drottningtorget entrance (Mon–Sat 7.30am–6pm, Sun 10.30am–6pm); and from Nils Ericsons Platsen to points north of the city, and to Kungsbacka and Varberg (office open Mon–Fri 7.30am–5.45pm, Sat 8am–2pm). For routes to Stockholm, Helsingborg and Malmö from Heden, reservations are obligatory from *G.O. Bussresebyrå*, Drottningatan 50 (☎031/80 55 30).

Car Rental *Avis*, at Central Station (☎031/17 04 10) and the airport (☎031/94 60 30); *Europcar*, Odinsgatan 19 (☎031/80 53 95) and at the airport (☎031/94 61 40); *Hertz*, Stampgatan 16 (☎031-80 37 30) and at the airport (☎031/94 60 20); *Interrent*, at the airport (☎031/94 62 10); *Vasa Biluthyrning*, Teatergatan 22–24 (☎031/20 07 00).

Chemist *Apoteket Vasen* is open 24hr; Götagatan 10, in the *Nordstan* shopping centre.

Doctor *Medical Care Information* on ☎031/41 55 00. There's a private clinic, too, *City-Akuten* (Mon–Fri 8am–6pm, Sat 9am–2pm; ☎031/10 10 10).

Newspapers Buy international newspapers from *Press Centre* in *Nordstan* shopping centre, Central Station, or *Tursiten*, Kungsportsplatsen. Or read them for free in the City Library, Götaplatsen.

Police Skånegatan 5; ☎031/80 08 00.

Post Office Main office for Poste Restante is in Drottningtorget (Mon–Fri 10am–6pm, Sat 10am–2pm).

Swimming Nearest pool is *Valhallabadet* right next to the Scandinavium sports complex.

Telephone Office Hvitfeldsplatsen 9 (Mon–Fri 9am–6pm, Sat 10am–2pm).

Travel Agency *SFS Resebyrå*, Berzeliigatan 5, for *BIJ* tickets and *ISIC* cards (Mon–Fri 9.30am–5pm).

North of Gothenburg: Bohuslän, Trollhättan and the Göta Canal

Although most people head out of Gothenburg fairly swiftly, usually south towards the port towns and Denmark or east to Stockholm, it's worth sticking around for a couple of days to see something of the distinctive countryside **north** of the city. For all the places below, you could use Gothenburg as a base, though there is good **accommodation** to be found in nearly every town and village since the region is a popular holiday destination for Swedes. **Transport** is good, too, either by regular train or local boats and ferries; and think about hiring a bike, either in Gothenburg or one of the smaller towns roundabout – one of the best ways to see this attractive region.

Bohuslän

Bohuslän county, the coastal strip north of Gothenburg, draws countless tourists onto its rocky islands and hairline fjords. It can get crowded here in July, but the traditional wooden cottages, dinky fishing villages and occasional batch of prehistoric rock carvings make the county worth at least a quick look. With your own transport, getting to the most picturesque parts is easy, and any of the smaller roads off the E6 yield myriad camping sites and beaches; and a good few youth hostels too. By **train** it's trickier although the railway line runs through industrial UDDEVALLA (from where there are buses and boats out), and terminates at STRÖMSTAD, right on the coast. If you're **camping** anywhere in Bohuslän you'll have little trouble finding a spot, though it's worth getting hold of the comprehensive *Camping Guide for the Swedish West Coast*, free from the tourist office in Gothenburg.

Possibly Sweden's oldest resort, stony **STRÖMSTAD** was first developed in the eighteenth century, Mary Wollstencroft (visiting in 1795) remarked; "The town was built on, and under [rocks]. Three or four weather-beaten trees . . .

shrinking from the wind. The steeple . . . wisely placed on a rock at some distance, not to endanger the roof of the church." The little town is busier these days, though still windy: in fact, it's a fairly trendy place to come on holiday, the Swedes drawn by the possibility of local island-hopping and by the nearby fishing villages with their good restaurants. If you're going to stay, there's a **youth hostel** (☎0526/10 193) at Norra Kyrkogatan 12, open June to August, or ask at the tourist office in town about renting a private room. Strömstad, with the E6 close, is also a handy point for hitching north to Oslo and the departure point for a year-round **ferry** service to Sandefjord, also in Norway.

Trollhättan, Vänersborg and the Göta Canal

If you don't have your own transport then the easiest places to see – and the most rewarding on a short visit – are the few small towns that lie along the river/canal that stretches from Gothenburg north to Lake Vänern. The river Göta was made navigable as far as the lake by a series of locks built last century (see below) and it's a fine day out to make the journey by **boat** up the **Trollhättan Canal**: Gothenburg's tourist office sells tickets (150kr one-way) for the route from the city to TROLLHÄTTAN, around 70km north. Alternatively, you can reach Trollhättan by **train**, several daily making the forty-minute trip. A few kilometres further north, VÄNERSBORG lies right on Lake Vänern itself, a holiday town with some elk-spotting possibilities close at hand.

Trollhättan

A delightful target for a trip, **TROLLHÄTTAN** is the kind of place you might end up staying for a couple of days without really meaning to. A small town, nevertheless it manages to pack in plenty of offbeat entertainment, mixed with some peaceful river surroundings. Built around the fast river that for a couple of hundred years powered its flourmills and sawmills, Trollhättan remained fairly isolated until 1800 when the first successful set of locks was installed to bypass the town's furious local waterfalls. River traffic took off and better and bigger locks were installed over the years, so that these days tankers up to 3500 tons use the system – an average of ten daily throughout the year, as well as around 6000 yachts and boats in the summer.

The locks and the steep sides of the falls are the main sights in town and there are **paths** along the whole system as well as orientation maps and guided tours from mid-June to mid-August (daily 11am–6pm). One footpath leads from Oskarsbron, one of the town's central bridges, down to the **hydroelectric power station**, in operation since 1910, its thirteen massive generators all computer-controlled. It's open daily from June to August for guided tours (10am–4pm), a more interesting visit than you might think since the building itself is fine, with a great arched stone frontage. Around the front, to the side of the generators, an eel ladder takes eels out of the water in early spring, as they migrate from the sea at Gothenburg, moving inland to the lake: they can't make it past the falls or the power station so they're collected here and taken by lorry to Vänern, the process reversed in September and October when they return. Further on down at the upper lock, the engaging **Kanalmuseum** (mid-June to mid-Aug daily 11am–7pm; rest of the year Sat & Sun only noon–5pm; 5kr, children free) puts the whole thing into perspective: model ships, a history of the canal and locks, old tools and fishing gear.

It's best if you can combine all this watery activity with a visit in July when the **Fallensdagar** takes place: a festival with dancing and music based around the waterfalls. The summer is the only time when the sluices are opened and you can see the falls in all their crashing splendour, so it's well worth catching – though if you miss the festival (which usually takes place in the third week of July for three or four days), the sluices are opened on a couple of weekends during May and June, and on Wednesday and Sunday in July and August (at 2.15pm).

If you want to stay in Trollhättan, as well you might, there's an excellent **youth hostel**, *Strömsberg* (☎0520/129 60), overlooking the river on the opposite side from the centre: a fifteen-minute walk from the railway station, it's the white building on the hill. It costs 65kr a night, 90kr for a room with the use of a kitchen and there are regular hotel rooms, too (from 430kr double including breakfast); open all year. Or the tourist office in the town centre can book you a **private room** all year round, some with kitchen, for 60–80kr a night each. There's a **campsite** (☎0520/30 613), open June to August, close to the centre and by the river, which rents out bikes and has a barbecue area.

Vänersborg

Around 10km north of Trollhättan, **VÄNERSBORG** isn't immediately different, a likeable little resort town on the southern tip of Lake Vänern, which means plenty of swimming and boating in the vicinity. There are buses from Trollhättan but you'll really need your own transport to see the local sights, namely the twin hills of **Hunneberg** and **Halleberg** to the east of town, which support a wide range of wildlife including a 200-strong elk population. The hills are ancient places, 500 million years old, and early human remains have been uncovered, as well as traces of an old Viking fort. It's a grand drive up to the curious flat-topped hills, which are thickly wooded, and once there you'll need to crawl the narrow roads in order to have a chance of seeing anything. The elks are a brown-grey colour, easily confused with the thick forest all around, despite weighing up to 600 kilos and being up to two metres high. In July (every Tues & Fri at 8pm), the Vänersborg tourist office in Hamnplats, down the road from the railway station by the guest harbour, run an **Elk Safari** (30kr, under 15s 15kr), a two-hour jaunt through the hills in a double-decker bus: so confident are they that they know the right places for elk-spotting, they'll give you your money back if you don't see one.

There's a **youth hostel** here, too, at Hunneberg, Bergagårdsvägen 9 (☎0521/203 40), which costs 100kr a night; and a couple of more central **hotels** whose weekend prices get down to around 300–350kr double – *Strand Hotel*, Hamngatan 7 (☎0521/138 50) and *Höglunds Pensionat*, Kyrkogatan 46 (☎0521/115 61). With transport (or a couple of kilometres' walk away), there's an excellent **place to eat** in nearby VARGÖN, between Vänersborg and the twin hills: *Ronnums Herrgård* is an eighteenth-century manor house which serves a fine 148kr set lunch – two courses, drink and coffee (11.30am–2pm).

Lake Vänern and the Göta Canal

Vänersborg lies on **Lake Vänern**, one of the two great central Swedish lakes (the other, Vättern, is covered in the next chapter). Centuries ago it was realised that these lakes, together with rivers east and west, could be used to make inland transport easier. A continuous waterway from Gothenburg across country to the Baltic would provide a vital trade route, both a means of shipping iron and timber out of central Sweden and of avoiding Danish customs charges levied on traffic through Öresund. It wasn't until 1832 that the system was completed, hand-dug canal sections connecting together navigable rivers and the two lakes, and though it's no longer an important trade route it's still in constant use – by thousands of tourists who ply the waters from mid-May to mid-September.

The **Göta Canal**, as the system is properly known, is 190km long, stretching from the Baltic to Vänern – and together with the Trollhättan Canal it links the Baltic to the North Sea. Expensive **cruises** make the whole trip in three to four days, either way, from Gothenburg or Stockholm – tickets from around 1000kr from *Rederiaktiebolaget Göta Kanal*, Hotellplatsen 2, in Gothenburg (☎031/80 63 15). However, that's not the only option. The canal is also served by a succession of **ferries** for which you just turn up and buy a ticket; either short jumps or return trips from the larger centres. Places accessible by **train**, apart from Trollhättan, include MARIESTAD and **MOTALA**, from where you can take day trips and evening cruises. And with a **bike** you can cycle the canal's towpaths in between the two lakes (Sjötorp to Vassbacken) and then east of Vättern from Motala. The *Göta kanalbolag* office in Motala has a cycling and walking guide for sale which marks the various paths.

THE SOUTH: HALLAND, SKÅNE AND BLEKINGE COUNTIES

The coast **south** of Gothenburg shows an immediate contrast with the rocks and inlets of the northern stretch. **Halland**, a finger of land facing Denmark, is a length of almost unbroken sandy shoreline, punctuated by some of the most laid-back resorts in the south. None are particularly exciting, with the exception perhaps of **Varberg**, but most offer a decent chance of finding space on a good beach; and nearly all boast, or are close to, a youth hostel.

A few kilometres down the coast, the ancient lands of **Skåne** begin, one of the earliest settled parts of Sweden and scene of constant medieval conflict over sovereignty with Denmark. Its swathes of rolling grassland and pockets of forest are fronted by characteristic, windy beaches. Although Skåne was finally ceded to Sweden in the late-seventeenth century, the Danish inheritance died hard, and is still preserved today in a local accent that's thick and often incomprehensible to other Swedes. If you've come from Denmark there's much that seems familiar: the surviving castles and architecture, even the traditional agricultural methods bear close comparison. As a first glimpse of Sweden – for arrivals at the busy ports of **Helsingborg** and **Malmö** – Skåne is hardly typical. But it rewards a few days' investigation if only to offer a contrast to the wood and water that start in earnest a little further north. You'll hardly notice that you've crossed the border from Skåne into **Blekinge**, such is the uniform nature of Sweden's southern coast. It's a thin strip of a county, with more low-key resorts and plenty of campsites, the only real interest in **Karlskrona**, a decent sized town with a marine air.

If you're going to do much in the way of roaming the area, the whole of Skåne is accessible on the useful *Sommarbiljetten* (mid-June to mid-Aug only; 140kr), a ticket giving unlimited **bus and train** travel: available, along with a full set of county timetables, from local stations and tourist offices.

Kungsbacka, Varberg and Halmstad

The train (or bus #730 from Nils Ericson Platsen) is barely out of Gothenburg before it reaches **KUNGSBACKA**, a small, quiet town with its roots in the thirteenth century. The only day really worth stopping is the first Thursday of the month when a bustling **market** sprawls around its ageing square. Otherwise Kungsbacka's gentle river and **campsite** can make it a pleasant enough alternative to continuing on to Gothenburg at night. There's also a **youth hostel** (☎0300/19 485), open mid-June to mid-August and 2km from the railway station, on the road to Sarö.

Varberg

If you like the look of the Halland coastline, then **VARBERG** is the better choice for a longer stay. A handy entry point to southern Sweden, a year round **ferry service** links GRENÄ in Denmark to the seemly harbour town. In the summer Varberg is a lively enough resort with endless opportunities for camping and lazing around, although to miss staying overnight in the thirteenth-century **fortress** would be a shame. Varberg's old moated castle now houses a **youth hostel** (☎0340/887 88) in its creaking prison building. You get a key to your own cell, two storeys of them ranged around a central gallery, spy-hole included. The hostel is open June to August and advance booking is recommended.

Even without staying there the fortress is the draw in Varberg. Won back from the Danes in 1645 and occupying a commanding position overlooking beach and harbour, it's a natural target for a stroll. The **museum** (mid-June to mid-Aug daily 10am–7pm; mid-Aug to mid-June Mon–Fri 10am–4pm, Sat & Sun noon–4pm; 5kr) inside features as its most notable occupant the *Bocksten Man*. Murdered (garrotted and drowned) in the fourteenth century, his body and clothes were preserved in a local bog for 600 years and the whole grisly specimen is now on display – his clothes (the world's only completely preserved medieval costume), pickled body and unnerving flame-red hair.

Beyond this, there's not a great deal of Varberg to wander around, but then the small central **beach** is only a few minutes' walk away, as well as another 6km of cliff-backed sand in Varberg's immediate surroundings. There are two nudist beaches too (separate ones for men and women), just to the south of the castle.

Some practical details

Regular **trains** run down the coast stopping at Varberg, or you can take the local **bus**; #732 from Nils Ericson Platsen in Gothenburg. The **tourist office** (mid-June to mid-Aug Mon–Sat 9am–8pm, Sun 4-8pm; ☎0340/887 70) is in the church square, a short walk up the hill from the railway station. If the prison hostel is full (July is the busiest month) there is a second **youth hostel** (☎0340/410 43 or 411 73) open all year but a long 8km south of the town near HIMLE. In town, try the cheap *Hotell Bergklinten* (☎0340/115 45), Västra Vallgatan 25, close to the railway station, whose double rooms go for around 250kr. Or **camp** at one of the two official sites in Varberg, the nearest a 3km stroll south along a small coastal road leading away from the fortress; the other across the bay at GETTERÖN (☎0340/168 85), open April to mid-October. Alternatively, once past the nudist beaches, you could simply throw down a sleeping bag anywhere.

Halmstad

The largest town and "capital" of Halland county, **HALMSTAD** is another hour down the line and handsome enough for a short stop. With the obligatory castle and medieval church, the town has all the trappings of importance, and you could do worse than give it a couple of hours or so between trains.

From the **railway station**, the centre is straight down the road directly ahead and over the bridge, and you'll find the **tourist office** (June & Aug Mon–Fri 9am–6pm, Sat 9am–3pm; July Mon–Sat 9am–8pm, Sun 4–8pm; ☎035/10 93 45) at Kajplan on the river front. **Storatorget**, the town's main square and market place, cocoons *Mille*'s strident fountain, *Europa and the Bull*, with the restored four-teenth-century **St Nikolai kyrka** (daily 8.30am–3pm) flanking one side. From here, the **castle** and museum are well signposted, the **museum** (Mon–Fri 10am–4pm, Wed 5–7pm, Sat & Sun noon–4pm; 5kr) particularly worth seeing, lying in parkland and remarkable for its tapestry paintings – the *Bonadsmålningar*. Typical of the region, these were eighteenth- and nineteenth-century Christmas decorations painted on old linen, tablecloths and leftover paper, then hung on the walls until Twelfth Night. As you might expect, episodes from the Bible dominate, although the number of wedding scenes indicates a flurry of such ceremonies held at Christmas. It's a colourful and humorous collection, the best tableau showing the successive ages of man; the Grim Reaper ready, at the end, with his scythe.

Staying over

Halmstad has no enormous attraction, but along with the other local towns there are plenty of **accommodation** possibilities nearby that you might need to take advantage of – certainly if you're newly arrived here on the **ferry** from Grenå, over in Denmark. The hotels in town are all pricey and you're better off at either the **campsite**, *Hagöns Camping* (☎035/12 53 63) at ÖSTRA STRANDEN, open May to August and a three-kilometre walk to the left from the station down Stationsgatan; or at one of the local **youth hostels**. There's one in Halmstad itself, at Skepparegatan 23 (☎035/12 05 00), open mid-June to mid-August, and another twenty minutes further south by train at old and shady LAHOLM – at Tivolivägen 4 (☎0430/133 18), open all year and just 500m from the railway station.

Båstad

The train takes just thirty minutes to leave Halland and enter **Skåne**, where – tucked inside the northeastern reaches of the county – is **BÅSTAD**. It's one of the least Danish-influenced towns in the county and the more interesting for it. Originally a simple harbour – Båstad means "boat place" – the sheltered settlement is besieged by summer visitors, not for the beaches, which are handsome enough, but for the **tennis**. A sort of Swedish Wimbledon, Båstad is a clutter of courts, hotels and sports facilities all in the most beautiful of settings. Both Swedish Open and Davis Cup matches are played here on a centre court overlooking the sea. **Tickets** start at 150kr (the Swedish Open is at the beginning of July) and accommodation during tournaments is impossible. And with Bjorn Borg working for the Swedish Tourist Board these days, the crush can only get worse.

However, avoid the rich and gifted and Båstad can be a delightful place for an out of (tennis) season break. The very small centre fields some rather grand, if weather-beaten, old houses, the road continuing down to the town's duned and sandy stretch. And Båstad claims 34 other tennis courts where you can hire the neccessary gear, a fifteenth-century (and much restored) church and a wealth of walks, **beaches** and greenery. All in all, worth a day or so if time isn't pressing.

The only pain is the town's distance from its **railway station**, the centre a good half an hour's walk down the hill, left along the main road and way on up to Stortorget and the **tourist office** at no. 1. You'll pass the **youth hostel** (☎0431/759 11) on the way, off to the left on Korrödsvägen; open June to August. As might be expected, there's no shortage of **hotels** in town though you'll have to start looking early in high season if you're to find anywhere reasonable: start with the tiny *Nybo Pensionat*, Köpmansgatan 81 (☎0431/701 92), with double rooms from around 270kr; and, close to the station, either the *Hotel-Pension Furuhem*, Roxmansvägen 23 (☎0431/701 09), or the *Hotel-Pension Enehall*, Stationsterrassen 10 (☎0431/750 15) – simple doubles from 350kr. **Camping** could be a good bet – Båstad's mild climate is renowned – either officially at Norravägen (☎0431/243 30), open mid-June to mid-August; or rough, out of town and among the dunes.

Helsingborg

At **HELSINGBORG** only a narrow sound separates Sweden from Denmark, and over the water the castle at Helsingør is clearly visible (see p.75). Indeed, Helsingborg was Danish for most of the Middle Ages, with a castle that controlled the southern regions of what is now Sweden. The town's enormously important strategic position meant that it bore the brunt of repeated attacks and rebellions, the Swedes conquering the town on six separate occasions, only to lose it back to the Danes each time. Finally, in 1710, a terrible battle saw off the Danes for the last time, though the battered town then lay dormant for almost two hundred years, depopulated and abandoned. Only in the nineteenth century, when the harbour was expanded and the railway built, did Helsingborg find new prosperity. Some of the central buildings reflect those times – the main square is more a boulevard, encircled by tall, solid buildings whose plain facades are decorated with fancy, carved pediments. Today, Helsingborg finds it hard to persuade people to stay for longer than it takes to make their train connections, but it's a likeable enough port town with a couple of fair cultural diversions and a decent choice of places to stay and eat.

Arriving and information

There are three different companies which operate **ferries** across the sound **to and from Helsingør**. *Sunsbussarna* are the quickest, for foot-passengers only and running every fifteen minutes, arriving at the terminal on Hamntorget. The *SFL* ferries, which can carry cars, dock opposite; while the *SJ/DSB* ferries are the ones that carry the **trains from Denmark**. They dock at **Helsingborg F** station (*Färjestationen*), on the waterfront behind Hamntorget, also where **trains** from Gothenburg, Stockholm and northern Sweden arrive. For ticket details on all these services see "Listings".

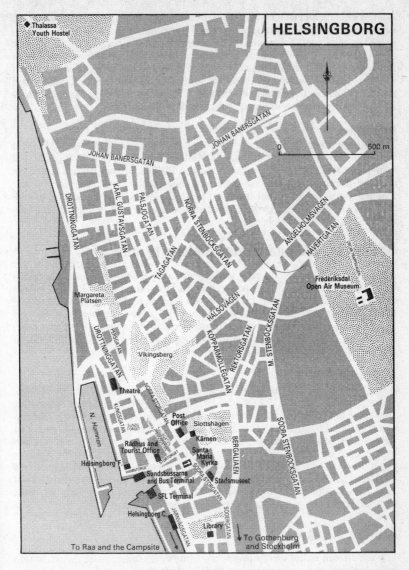

There are **other ferries from Denmark**, too, which link with Helsingborg: the ones from Grenå in Jutland dock at Sundsterminalen, which is one of the outer harbours behind Helsingborg C station (see below); and from Snekkersten, south of Helsingør, you'll arrive at Hamntorget.

Trains to and from Lund, Malmö and Landskrona are operated by a private company, *Pågatågen*, and use the station **Helsingborg C**, which is 400m along Järnvägsgatan from the harbour; again, ticket details under "Listings". **Buses**

from Stockholm and Gothenburg arrive in Hamntorget; the **Bussterminal** on the square, next to the *Sundsbussarna* terminal has information about these services, as well as about local buses, and stocks timetables for the *Pågatåg* trains.

All that said, a new **central terminal** is being built on the harbourside in Helsingborg which will eventually handle all ferry and bus arrivals/departures; it will also have an underground railway terminal, parking facilities, offices and shops. It's not due to be finished until mid-1991, so the confusing plethora of arrival and departure points outlined above should hold until then.

Information

The **tourist office** (June & Aug Mon–Sat 9am–7pm, Sun 3–7pm; July Mon–Sat 9am–8pm, Sun 3–8pm; rest of the year Mon–Fri 9am–5pm; May & Sept also Sat 9am–noon; ☎042/12 03 10) is inside the red Rådhus, just up from Hamntorget and the harbour. As well as maps and information, you can pick up the **Helsingsborgskortet** or Helsingborg Card (35kr, valid 3 days, end-May to end-Sept only): it gives free city bus travel, museum entry and swimming and half-price ferry crossings to Helsingør.

Getting around and finding a place to stay

Almost everything is within easy **walking** distance, though you'll need to take a **bus** to get to the youth hostel and to the nearby fishing village of Råå; numbers detailed in the text. Buy your ticket (6kr) on the bus; it's valid for two changes of bus within the next ninety minutes. There's also a **free bus** service (Mon–Fri 11am–6pm, Sat 10am–1pm) which runs on a circular route through the city: catch it at the top of Hamntorget or along Järnvägsgatan for its run along Södergatan and both sections of Storgatan.

Accommodation

If you need to stop for the night, cheap central **hotels** include the *City Hotellet*, Södra Storgatan 3 (☎042/13 64 35), with doubles from 350kr, and *Hotel Högvakten*, Stortorget 14 (☎042/12 03 90), from around 400kr double. Helsingborg's *Thalassa* **youth hostel** (☎042/11 03 84) is fairly plush, a villa in its own grounds and open all year – either a three-kilometre walk north along Drottninggatan or a #4 bus ride from outside the tourist office, stopping at Pålsjöbaden. There's also the *Nyckelbo* youth hostel (☎042/920 05) 7km away in LARÖD, open June to mid-August; bus #201 from Hamntorget every half an hour. For **camping**, try the waterfront site at Råå, 5km southeast of town, which has a swimming pool; bus #1 from Drottninggatan stopping at Kielergatan – and see "Råå" below.

Around the town

The **waterfront** is the most obvious place to begin explorations, though admittedly, beyond the busy harbours and freight yards, there's not a great deal to see. Carl Milles' symbolic *Shipping Monument*, a bronzed Mercury perched high on a pillar, focuses attention on the town's main business. Just up from Hamntorget and the harbours, the massive, neo-Gothic **Rådhus** looks positively church-like, with its stained glass windows, central clock tower and pointed steeples. There are guided tours around the showy interior in July (Mon–Fri at 10am). The town hall marks the bottom of **Stortorget**, the long thin square which slopes up to the lower battlements of what's left of Helsingborg's medieval castle: the **kärnan** or keep (June–Aug daily 9am–8pm; Sept–March daily 9am–3pm; April & May daily 9am–5pm; 5kr) – the first thing you'll see as you get off ferry or train. The original fortification, built by the Danish king Valdemar Atterdag, was completely destroyed in 1680 although this fourteenth-century defensive brick tower – its walls in parts four metres thick – survived. The views from the top, over the sound, are worth the entrance fee although you don't miss much from the lower (free) battlements.

Off Stortorget, **Norra Storgatan** contains Helsingborg's oldest buildings, attractive seventeenth- and eighteenth-century merchants' houses with quiet courtyards. The earliest – at no. 21, next to the *Åhlens* store – is from 1641, a red-brick house criss-crossed with beams. Walk back and on to Södra Storgatan and the Gothic **St Maria kyrka** (Mon–Sat 8am–4pm, Sun 9am–4pm, silver collection Mon–Fri noon–1pm only) occupies its own cluttered square. Built around 1450, the craftsmanship inside the huge church belies its plain, almost dowdy exterior – both pulpit and reredos positively gleam.

A step up the road at Södra Storgatan 31 the **Stadsmuseet** (May–Aug Mon–Sat 11am–6pm, Sun noon–6pm; Sept–April Tues–Sat 11am–4pm, Sun noon–4pm; 5kr, students free) is a glorious mess of bric-a-brac: dolls, clothes, paintings, tea sets, desks, frying pans and push chairs. A separate building is crammed with stuffed animals and birds – parrots to sharks – while upstairs there's an alarming array of bottled fish and intestinal creatures into whose exact nature it's wise not to enquire too closely.

With more time on your hands, walk (or take bus #3 from the Rådhus) out to **Fredriksdal** (May to mid-June & mid-Aug to Sept daily 10am–6pm; mid-June to mid-Aug daily 10am–7pm; 5kr), an eighteenth-century manor house set in its own grounds just beyond the sports stadium. It's the place to while away a hot afternoon in the botanical and rose gardens, and following the trails around its small open-air museum. There's a reconstructed old-town quarter, with workshops and store interiors on display, and usually some kind of demonstration of old crafts taking place as well.

Eating and drinking

You shouldn't have any difficulty at all in finding somewhere **to eat**, particularly at **lunchtime**. *La Pikant*, Nedre Holländeregatan (junction with Södergatan, beyond the library) serves 39kr meals all day, a popular place; and back towards the centre there's the *Tex Mex Bar*, Södra Storgatan 10 – *tacos* at around 10kr plus other Mexican and vegetarian food, open until 1am. *Graffiti Café*, Bruksgatan 17, is a baked potato joint, where you should be able to fill up for around 25–30kr. And *La Dolce Vita* on Billeplatsen, the cobbled square leading up from St Maria kyrka, serves a pizza set lunch for 38kr. Helsingborg F's restaurant serves lunches for around 30–35kr; otherwise it's open Monday to Saturday 6.30am–8.45pm, Sunday 8.30am–8.45pm.

For **evening eating**, you need a little more money to dine at *Casa Nostra*, Drottninggatan 116, the best Italian restaurant in Helsingborg. And if it's your last night in Sweden then you might want to splash out on one of the best restaurants anywhere in the country: the restaurant in the *Grand Hotel*, on Stortorget (closed Sun), is magnificent, coat-tailed waiters serving fine traditional Swedish food in an elegant dining room. A full meal, not including drinks, will set you back around 400–500kr, but it's money well spent.

Bars, discos and live music

For no-frills **drinking**, the *Charles Dickens Pub* at Södergatan 43 has an English pub menu, the cheapest beer in town and QPR pennants behind the bar. It's not as atmospheric as it sounds. Fans of the reconstructed English pub can continue their investigations at a new venue on Norra Storgatan (junction with Springpostgränden), which was due to open at the turn of 1990. Better places for a drink are the *Mollberg Brasserie*, in the hotel of the same name on Stortorget – a popular place for a beer, overlooking the square. Helsingborg's trendy set meet at the bar/restaurant inside the city theatre; called *Theatterkatten*, it's open until 2am.

The *Dag & Natt* bar on Norra Hamnen, across the railway tracks, has the most popular **disco** in town. Or take bus #7 out to the Folk Parken and *Sundspärlen*, a venue for open-air summer discos, theatre and eating. One good place to see **live music**, primarily Swedish and Danish rock bands, is *Caesar's Palace*, Bollbrogatan 6 – music every Thursday night (7pm–2am), although closed between mid-June and mid-August. In the summer you'll have to be content with the *Kul i Juli* programme put on in the park behind Kärnen: free concerts, clowns and local artists, usually on Tuesday at 8pm.

Listings

Airport Nearest airport is at Ängelholm, 30km north of town, for domestic departures (bus from the *Grand Hotel*, Stortorget, 50min before flight departure). For international services, you'll need Copenhagen's Kastrup airport: take the *Kustlinjen* bus from Hamntorget; a 2-hr journey.

Bike Rental From *GP Sports Shop* in Norra Storgatan; or at Karl Krokksgatan 60. And see Råå, below.

Buses Buses to Stockholm (160kr) and Gothenburg (80kr) leave from Hamntorget; tickets from inside Helsingborg F; departures only on Friday and Sunday.

Car Rental *Avis*, Södergatan 109 (☎042/14 53 01); *Budget*, Gustav Adolfs Gata 47 (☎042/12 50 40); *Europcar*, Kungsgatan 4 (☎042/11 53 33); *Interrent*, Muskötgatan 1 (☎042/17 01 15); *Ta'En Hybril*, Hälsovägen 29 (☎042/18 55 81).

Chemist *Björnen*, Drottninggatan 14. Open shop hours & Sun 11am–4pm.

Exchange Exchange office in Helsingborg F; Mon–Fri 8am–7pm, Sat 8am–2pm, Sun 9.15am–4pm; maximum 7kr fee.

Ferries *SFL* ferries depart every 15min, day returns 22kr, one-way 16kr, return 32kr (kids 6–11 half-price); *Sundbussarna* every 20min, 14kr one-way, 21kr return, half-price for kids 6–14 and for adults on Sun. See "Travel Details" for full schedules.

Left Luggage Lockers at Helsingborg F (10kr) and at the *Sundsbussarna* terminal.

Library Bollbrogatan 1 (*Stadsbiblioteket*: June–Aug Mon–Fri 10am–7pm, Sat 10am–2pm; Sept–May Mon–Fri 10am–7pm, Sat 10am–3pm). Read international newspapers here, listen to music or use the café.

Post Office Stortorget 17 (Mon–Fri 8am–6pm, Sat 9am–1pm). You can exchange money here but it costs 20kr per transaction.

Telephone Office Bruksgatan 24 (Mon–Fri 9.30am–6pm, Sat 9.30am–1pm).

Trains The *Pågatåg* trains from Helsingborg C require a ticket bought from an automatic machine on the platform; *InterRail* and *Nordturist* cards are not valid. The machines take 10kr notes and 5kr and 1kr coins: it's 30kr one-way to Lund and 40kr one-way to Malmö. Fare dodging invites a 400kr spot fine.

Around Helsingborg: Råå

It's only 5km south down the coast to **RÄÄ**, an old fishing village which, in recent years, has become a much sought after area in which to live. Bus #1 from outside the Rådhus runs there every fifteen minutes or so, through the horrid industrial clutter on the outskirts of Helsingborg – the chemical industries here have a reputation for local pollution. You'll be dropped right at the **harbourside**, which remains an active and attractive place; indeed Råå has escaped the development and ruin of much of the rest of the local coastline. There's a museum on the quay, devoted to fishing and the sea, and next to it a good restaurant, the *Råå Wärdshus*.

During the summer, little **ferries** (30–35kr return) leave from Råå's harbour for the nearby island of **Ven**, half an hour offshore. There are some good beaches here, small restaurants and cafés, **cabins** and **bikes** (25kr a day) to rent, a nice place for a lazy day's swimming and pottering around. During the winter, you can reach Ven from LANDSKRONA, south of Helsingborg, though few of the holiday facilities still operate then.

Lund

Just forty minutes south of Helsingborg, **LUND** is the most obvious target for a trip – though as it's actually much closer to Malmö (see below) it's better to base yourself there instead. Either way, it's a place not to be missed while you're in southern Sweden, a beautiful university town crowned by a gorgeous twelfth-century Romanesque cathedral, sitting pretty in the quiet medieval centre.

The Domkyrkan

It's only a short walk from the **railway station**, on the edge of town, to the weatherbeaten **Domkyrkan** (Mon–Fri 8am–6pm, Sat 9am–5.15pm, Sun 9.30am–6pm), its swirls of grey-white stone contrasting nicely with the mellow red-brick buildings of the university which stand all around. Consecrated in 1145, the cathedral has remained virtually unchanged since. The two square, nineteenth-century towers are the only significant alteration to what is a beautifully proportioned church – considered by many to be Scandinavia's finest medieval building. Don't go straight in. It's worth walking around the outside first to fix the attractive shape in your mind – and check the carved surround above the main door: Christ Pantocrator shown holding the Bible, his hand held out in benediction. Inside, the delicate, semi-circular apse at the eastern end of the church harbours a gleaming fifteenth-century altarpiece and a half-mosaic of Christ surrounded by angels. Otherwise, apart from the altar stalls, the cathedral is quite plain, the roof supported by ribbed arches. The object that draws most attention inside is an **astronomical clock**, a full century older than the altarpiece. It reveals its ecclesiastical Punch and Judy show – fighting knights, trumpeters and the Three Wise Men – daily at noon and 3pm.

Don't leave the Domkyrkan without seeing the **crypt**, underneath the apse. Littered with tombs and elaborately carved tombstones, it's a blaze of low pillars, some of which were sculpted with a vivid imagination. One pillar is gripped by a stone man, the giant Finn who lived near Lund when the new cathedral was being built. Hearing the new church bells, he rushed to town to destroy the church that had disturbed him, grasped the first pillar and was promptly turned to stone.

Around the rest of town

Outside the cathedral, **Kyrkogatan** is lined with staunch, solid, nineteenth-century civic buildings – the *Sparbanken* and the *Stadshuset*. Follow the street down into the main square, **Stortorget**, and you'll pass the *Universitets Apotek* which offers a marked contrast, though it dates from the same period: an inlaid wooden interior, with stone and glass jugs and bottles ranged along the walls. The first right at the bottom of the square leads you along **Kattesund**, halfway down which is an excavated set of medieval walls. The tourist office (see below) is built over part of them and viewing windows let you see down onto the walls; and adjacent is the **Drottens Kyrkoruin** (May–Aug Mon–Fri 11am–5pm; Sept–April noon–4pm; all year Sat 10am–2pm, Sun noon–4pm; 5kr), the remains of a medieval stone church in the basement of another modern building.

There are several **museums** – usual university art, historical and archaeological collections – in Lund, but the real interest is in the powerful atmosphere of the old streets behind the Domkyrkan. **Kiliansgatan**, directly behind the cathedral's apse, is a lovely cobbled street, whose fine red-brick houses sport tiny courtyards and gardens. Nearby **Adelgatan** and **Lilla Tomegatan** are appealing too, all cottages, cobbles, climbing roses and bicycles – just right for a stroll. In this web of streets you'll pass **Kulturen** (May–Sept daily 11am–5pm; Oct–April daily noon–4pm; 20kr), really the only museum you need bother with: a mixture of indoor and open-air collections, the entrance is in Tegnérplatsen, just behind the Domkyrkan.

Finish off your meanderings with a visit to the **Botaniska Trädgård** (mid-May to mid-Sept 6am–9.30pm; mid-Sept to mid-May 6am–8pm), just beyond Kulturen, five minutes' walk from the centre. It's an extensive botanical garden, with some shaded pathways, all the shrubs, plants and trees labelled and classified.

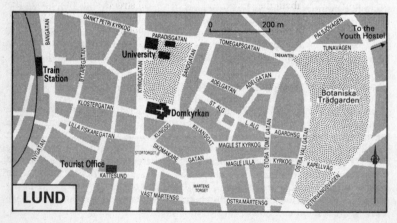

Practical details

Train arrivals are at the western edge of town, everything an easy walk from the station. The **tourist office** (June–Aug Mon–Fri 9am–6pm; Sept–May Mon–Fri 9am–5pm; ☎046/12 45 90) is on Kattesund and hands out a map and the *Dagbok Lund*, a monthly diary of events with museum and exhibitions listings. If that's closed, you'll be able to get information next door at the Drotten Kyrkoruin.

If you're on a budget there's only one place to **stay** in town, the **youth hostel** (☎046/12 40 84) at Tunavägen 39, a road that runs from the northern boundary of the botanical gardens. That the hostel is open June to August only is no real problem, since Malmö and Helsingborg both make better bases.

A couple of recommendations for **eating**. *Mellan Östern* on Kungsgatan, behind the Domkyrkan (off Stortorget) sells falafels (24kr), kebabs (35kr) and hummus (27kr) – open Monday to Friday 11am–7pm and Wednesday to Saturday also 11pm–3am. Or try the daily lunch (35kr) at *Chrougen*, the student union café in the university grounds, behind the Domkyrkan (next to the *Akademiska Föreningen*): it's served from 11am–2.30pm, the café otherwise open from 9am–4pm. There's **entertainment** here too, at night; jazz, discos and bands, watch for flyposters.

Malmö

Once the second largest city in Denmark, **MALMÖ** was won back for Sweden by Karl X, who marched his armies across the frozen belts of water to within striking distance of Copenhagen. Pinned back, the Danes signed the 1658 Treaty of Roskilde, handing over Skåne, Blekinge and Bohuslän, counties which have remained Swedish ever since. Malmö, though, had already acquired its most characteristic buildings – castle, town hall and merchants houses – and these remain today, an historical enclave within a handsome city. The oldest parts and buildings, primarily two impressive squares and a fourteenth-century church, are dead central. The whole is encircled by a canal which winds west through the castle park and then around its ramparts as a moat.

Malmö is a city that has adapted well to later restoration. There's no artificial museumy quality about the centre: the late medieval streets and cobbled squares echo to the sounds of modern commerce, the doll's-house buildings are lived and worked in, and the modern pedestrian malls are unobtrusive. If you're planning to come from Copenhagen by hydrofoil, a quick and easy crossing, then Malmö will be your first sight of Sweden; not a bad introduction at all.

Arriving, information and getting around

All the **ferries and hydrofoils** from Copenhagen dock at various terminals along Skeppsbron; ticket details under "Listings". Just up from here is **Central Station**, where all **trains** arrive and depart; the private *Pågatåg* services (to/from Helsingborg/Lund) use platforms 9–13 at the back – either walk through Central Station, or there's a separate entrance, marked *Lokalstationen*, on Centralplan.

The main **bus terminal** is outside Central Station, in Centralplan: buses to and from Lund, Kastrup airport (in Denmark), Kristianstad/Kalmar and Ystad all stop here. Buses from Stockholm, Helsingborg and Gothenburg arrive at Slussplan, east of Central Station, at the end of Norra Vallgatan. If you arrived at **Sturup**

airport, east of Malmö, the hourly *Flygbuss* (7.15am–11.15pm; 30kr) also drops you in Centralplan; or you can travel direct to Lund if you wish, again hourly (7.15am–11.15pm; 30kr).

The other possible point of arrival is via the Dragör–Limhamn **car-ferry**, which drops you at the southwestern edge of town: buses (#41B) run up nearby Strandgatan into the centre, right to Central Station.

Information

From Central Station, cross the bridge and the **tourist office** is at Hamngatan 1 (mid-June to mid-Aug Mon–Fri 10am–6pm, Sat & Sun 9am–1pm; rest of the year Mon–Fri 9am–5pm, Sat 9am–1pm; ☎040/34 12 70). From here pick up a wealth of information: good free maps, a listings/events brochure (*Malmö This Month*) and the useful **Malmökortet**, or Malmö Card – which gives free museum entry, unlimited local transport plus discounts on the crossings to Copenhagen. It costs 50kr for 24 hours and is also available for 48 hours (60kr), 72 hours (70kr) and 96 hours (100kr) – children half-price. The tourist office also sells a good-value **round trip ticket** (95kr), valid for the train to Lund and Helsingborg, the crossing to Helsingør, travel on to Copenhagen and the return by hovercraft to Malmö.

Getting around the city

Like most of the southern towns and cities, you'll be able **to walk** around Malmö fairly comfortably, though if you get tired the Malmö Card lets you travel free on the city's green **buses** which, otherwise, cost 7kr (10kr at night), the ticket valid for an hour. More importantly, the card also grants a fifty percent discount when you use the *Pågatåg* **trains** to nearby Lund or Helsingborg and gives other discounts on **car rental**, something you might consider if you intend to see a lot of the Skåne area. Car rental agencies are given under "Listings".

One other option you might pursue is to hire a **pedal boat** in which to splash up and down the city's central canal. Hire them at Södertull, Gustav Adolfs Torg (May–Sept 11am–7pm); fifty percent off with the Malmö Card.

Finding a place to stay

Malmö is one of the easier places in southern Sweden to find good, cheap accommodation. There are a couple of hostels and the tourist office can either book you a private room in someone's house or sell you a "Malmö Package" – along the lines of the similar deal that exists in Gothenburg and Stockholm.

Hotels

The **Malmö Package** provides a double room in a central hotel, breakfast and Malmö Card included: you book at the tourist office, the scheme runs daily from mid-June to mid-August, weekends only the rest of the year, and costs from 185kr per person in the cheapest category – more like 240kr for most of the hotels that take part. Not all the hotels listed below are included in the Package; those that are are marked with "MP" and show the current price per person.

Hotel Anglais, Stortorget 15 (☎040/714 50). Perfect position on the central square and a grand old hotel. MP 270kr.

Continental Hotel, Hospitalsgatan 2 (☎040/12 19 77). Fairly pricey choice but its location is worth paying for; right in the old centre, between Lilla Torg and Malmöhus. 490–590kr single and 590–690kr double in rooms with bath and TV, breakfast included.

Hotell Pallas, Norra Vallgatan 74 (☎040/11 50 77). Cheapest hotel in the Malmö Package scheme, overlooking the canal just along from the tourist office. MP 185kr, but inexpensive anyway, the regular price only 350kr single, 450kr double, breakfast an extra 30kr.

Savoy Hotel, Norra Vallgatan 62 (☎040/702 30). So you might not be able to afford to stop in this extravagantly priced old hotel overlooking the canal, but nip inside to take a look at the illustrious guest list printed on a brass name-plate by the lift: Cliff Richard, ABBA, Henry Kissinger, Judy Garland, Mel Brooks, Sammy Davis Jnr, Uncle Tom Cobley and all.

Private rooms and youth hostels

The tourist office has a list of **private rooms**, something that will cost you around 80kr each, less for subsequent nights. Or stay at either of the two **youth hostels** listed below.

InterRail Centre, Kyrkogatan 3B (☎040/ 11 85 85). The Centre is open mid-June to mid-August (daily 9am–9pm) and offers showers, luggage storage, a hitch-hiking and counselling service. They also run free buses to their hostel, *Kirsebergs Fritidsgård*, at Dalhemsgatan 5, which is open the same dates, 6pm to 9am; 50kr per night including breakfast.

STF Vandrarhem, Backavägen 18 (☎040/822 20); 5km out of the centre; bus #18 from Centralplan, get off at Vandrarhemmet, cross over the traffic lights and take the first right – the hostel is signposted 100m away to the left. Well-equipped, but a bit of a way out and not overly friendly; open all year (8–10am & 4–10pm).

Camping

Camping is at *Sibbarps Camping* (☎040/34 26 50), on Strandgatan, open all year; bus #41B from Central Station, out past the Limhamn–Dragör ferry terminal. Rough campers could take their chances in Slottsparken, although it's probably wiser to hit the beaches beyond the official campsite.

The City

You'll get most out of just walking around Malmö. The largely pedestrianised streets and squares are conducive to a leisurely stroll and, with the canals and central parks, there are few places in Sweden more enjoyable. You'll be able to see most things described below in a good day's sightseeing, but staying at least one night means you don't have to rush. For a point of reference, start with Stortorget and the surrounding streets and squares, heading west to the castle and the gardens to finish.

Stortorget and around

Most of the medieval centre was taken apart in the early sixteenth century to make way for **Stortorget**, a vast market square, as impressive today as it must have been when it first appeared. Karl X, high on his horse, gets pride of place in the centre, and the square is surrounded by a welter of grand buildings – banks and offices mostly – but the eyes are drawn to the **Rådhus**, flanking one side. Built in 1546, two nineteenth-century restorations hijacked its original style, the finicky exterior now that of the Dutch Renaissance. It's impressive enough, despite the architectural fiddling, popping with statuary, spiky accoutrements and some solid window decoration. Having feasted your eyes there are tours of the more original interior. To the right of the town·hall, the **Apoteket Lejonet** is another soaring study in red stone, gargoyled and balconied, while inside what is still only a chemist's shop, are beautiful carved wooden shelves and a counter. From here, **Södergatan** runs off south towards the canal, Malmö's main pedestri-

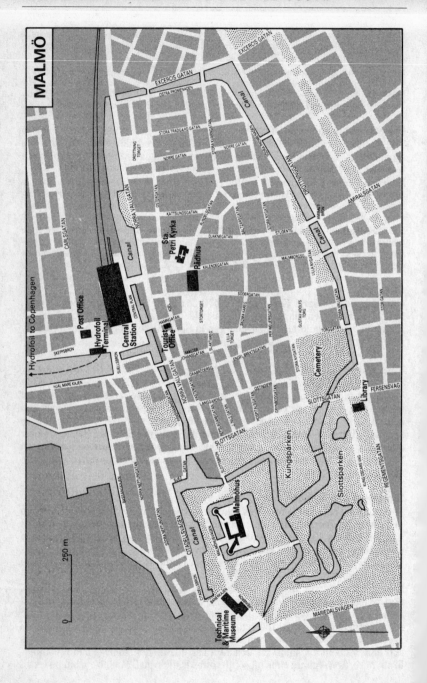

MALMÖ

EXERCIS GATAN

EXERCIS GATAN

ÖSTRA PROMENADEN

STIGA TRÄDGÅRD GATAN

DROTTNING
TORGET

NORRE GATAN

NORRE GATAN

Canal

KATTSUNDSGATAN

DJAKNEGATAN

Sta.
Petri Kyrka

Rådhus

KALENDEGATAN

SÖDERGATAN

STORTORGET

Canal

AMIRALSGATAN

Canal

CARLSGATAN

Post Office

Hydrofoil
Terminal

SKEPPSBRON

Central
Station

CENTRAL PLAN

HAMNGATAN

Tourist
Office

HJAL MARE KAJEN

SUELLSBRON

NORRA VALLGATAN

Cemetery

Library

FERSENSVAG

SLOTTSGATAN

SLOTTSGATAN

Kungsparken

Canal

Malmöhus

Slottsparken

Technical
& Maritime
Museum

MARIEDALSVAGEN

Hydrofoil to Copenhagen

250 m

0

anised shopping street. At the Stortorget end there's a line of sculptures of marching musicians; further down a rake of fashionable cafés and restaurants.

Behind the Rådhus sits **St Petri kyrka** (Mon–Sat 9am–4pm, Sun 10am–4pm), Malmö's fine Gothic church. Baltic in inspiration, the style owes much to German influence in Sweden, with more than shades of Lübeck in its final form. You have to get inside to appreciate its real proportions, as it's hemmed in by new buildings. The bright white interior means that your eyes are immediately drawn to the two most impressive decorative items: the pulpit and a four-tiered altarpiece, both of striking workmanship and elaborate embellishment.

A man who had much to do with Malmö's sixteenth-century rebuilding was **Jörgen Kock**, Mayor and Master of the Danish Mint during the time when Skåne (and Malmö) was ruled from Denmark. Danish coins were struck in Malmö on the site of the present Malmöhus castle (see below) until irate local Swedes stormed the building and destroyed it in 1534. Kock's outrage at the affront to his Mint was probably tempered by the fact that he lived in the prettiest house in the city, **Jörgen Kocks Gård**, back on the opposite side of Stortorget and fronting Västergatan. Finished in 1525, the bold stepped front is decorated with statuettes and coats of arms, few of which are originals – visit the city museum in Malmöhus for those. Just up the road, another red-brick house from the same period, **Rosenvinge Huset**, has a simpler facade, but sports the same plaque-studded coat of arms above the door.

Lilla Torget

Lilla Torget is everyone's favourite part of the city, a late-sixteenth-century spin-off from an overcrowded Stortorget. Comprising half-timbered houses, flowers and iron lamps, the small square is usually full and doing a roaring trade from jewellery stalls. Summer evenings see live music, often jazz in June, and various other cultural activities, so it's always worth a look. The southern side of the square is formed by a row of brick and timber mid-nineteenth-century ware-houses, unremarkable given the other preserved buildings around, except that they contain the **Form Design Center** (Jan–June Tues, Wed & Fri 11am–5pm; July Tues–Fri 11am–5pm, Sat 10am–4pm; Aug–Dec Thurs 11am–8pm, Sat 10am–4pm, Sun noon–4pm; free), a kind of Yuppies' Habitat Museum. Even if design doesn't thrill you, the very cheap prices in the inside café will. Other shops around here are equally arty and upmarket, selling books, antiques and gifts, though one other place that is worth dropping in on is the **Saluhallen** (Mon–Thurs 10am–6pm, Fri 10am–7pm, Sat 10am–3pm), an excellent indoor market.

Malmöhus

Take any of the streets running west from Stortorget or Lilla Torget and you soon come up against the edge of **Kungsparken**, within striking distance of **Malmöhus** (Tues–Sat noon–4pm, Thurs also 5–9pm, Sun noon–4.30pm; June–Aug only Mon noon–4pm). A low, red fortified castle, it's a sturdy construction, defended by a wide moat, two circular keeps and grassy ramparts which rise from the surrounding park. Following its destruction as Denmark's Mint, a new fortress was raised by Danish king Christian III in 1536, only to be of unforeseen benefit to the Swedes who, once back in control of Skåne, used it to repel an attacking Danish army in 1677. For a time a prison (Bothwell, third husband of Mary, Queen of Scots, its most notable occupant), the castle and its outbuildings now constitute a series of terrific museums with city-related, art, natural history, technical and military collections. Entrance, on the canal side, is 10kr (free with the Malmö Card), the ticket then valid for all Malmö's other museums for the rest of that day. There's a good café inside, too, with cheap coffee and tea, salads and sandwiches. The **grounds** are good for a stroll, peppered with small lakes and an old windmill. The paths lead all the way down to Regementsgatan and the City Library in the southeastern corner of the park – and you can continue walking through greenery as far as Gustav Adolfs Torg, across the Gamla Begravnings Platsen, an old and silent graveyard.

After your tour around Malmöhus's internal collections, nip out of the main entrance and turn left for the **Technical and Maritime Museum** (same times as Malmöhus; 10kr), both in the same building along Malmöhusvägen. Just before here, a narrow street – **Banerkajen** – leads down to the canal. There's a line of small wooden cottages which sell fish from out the front on slabs. And from mid-May to mid-September (Sat & Sun 11am–5pm; 10kr, free with Malmö Card) you can pick up a veteran **tram** here for a short tour through parts of the city.

Other attractions

Other central **museums**, like the transport and sporting collections detailed in the booklet that comes with the Malmö Card, are pretty dispensable. A couple of galleries, though, are worth looking out for. **Malmö Art Gallery** (Tues & Thurs 11am–8pm, Wed 11am–9pm, Fri–Mon 11am–5pm; 10kr), at St Johannesgatan 7, has exhibitions which change regularly: it pulls in some excellent touring collections as well as being a lively centre for theatre and film. It's in the south of the city; buses #32, #33, #36, #37 and #40 all run past it. Watch out for good exhibitions, too, at the oddly-named **Rooseum** (Tues–Thurs 11am–7pm, Fri–Sun 11am–5pm; 10kr), a private art gallery in the old city power station; guided tours on Tuesday, Wednesday and Thursday at 5.30pm, Sunday at 2pm.

Eating and drinking

Some good-value **lunches** should ensure that you don't starve in Malmö, and all the best places are right in the centre. Malmö has perked up recently, too, in terms of **bars and cafés**, with a central selection that should satisfy even those touting the sharpest haircuts.

Markets

Snacking from markets is no bad thing in Malmö given the choices. **Saluhallen** (see above), the covered market in Lilla Torget, is excellent, stuffed with fruit, veg and a wholefood caff. Or hop on a bus to the southern quarter of Möllevången: **Möllevångstorget** has a large morning market and enough Yugoslav emigrés to staff a host of delis, bakeries and cafés offering good cheap lunches, mainly kebabs, pittas and salad bars. Self-caterers should give the fish market at **Banerkajen** (Mon–Sat 6–9am) a viewing at least. From old fishermen's huts by the canal in front of Malmöhus, the produce goes to locals and not to traders, ensuring a look-in for small-time buyers.

Restaurants

Restaurant Canton, Södra Vallgatan 5; by Davidshallbron. About the cheapest Chinese joint in town, with set lunches from 45kr and a no-nonsense menu whose dishes start at around 50–60kr, soups 20–30kr.

Casa Mia, Södergatan 12. A smart Italian place with big, crispy pizzas, the best in the city, for around 50kr; pasta around 60kr and wine a not outrageous (for Sweden) 59kr a half-litre. There's a full Italian menu, too, but the pizzas are the best value.

Central Station, Centralplan. The railway station café is open from 6.30am and serves a 37kr breakfast.

Lilla Köket, Norra Vallgatan 88. A fairly meaty, mainly Swedish menu; lunches 38–40kr; cheapish wine and beer; open Mon–Thurs 11am–11pm, Fri & Sat 11am–1am.

Oporto, Södergatan 5. A Portuguese restaurant with a decent, but pricey, menu. Better value are the 38kr lunches (Mon–Fri 11.30am–3pm only) though there's nothing Portuguese about these – meat, fish or pizza choice.

Pieter's Corner, junction of Västergatan and Gråbrödersgatan. Cheap, 38kr pizzas served all day and realistically priced drinks, too; see "Bars and Cafés", below.

Pizza House No. 1, Lilla Nygatan 11; behind *Burger King* on Gustav Adolfs Torg. Averagely-priced pizzeria.

Åhlens, Södergatan. Department store restaurant open Mon–Fri 9am–5.45pm, Sat 9am–2.45pm, serving a solid 55kr daily lunch.

Bars and cafés

Le Coeur, Södergatan 7. French-style brasserie complete with wobbly French singing and *croque-monsieur*. Averagely priced beer and a pleasant atmosphere.

Jim's Bar Västergatan 16; junction with Gråbrödersgatan. Bar/café open until midnight and with cabaret perfomances on Tuesday night.

Pieter's Corner; junction of Västergatan and Gråbrödersgatan. After your pizza stick around for the beer (which is a few crowns cheaper than elsewhere), the young clientele and the disco on Saturday night.

Suck, Stortorget 25. Right on the central square, this youth café and centre hosts discos, bands and other events. Open Mon, Tues & Thurs 3–10pm, Wed 6–10pm, Fri & Sat 3pm–midnight, Sun 3–10pm.

Entertainment

It used to be that the only entertainment in Malmö was watching rich drunks become poor drunks at the blackjack table in the Central Station bar. Now, if you know where to look, there are some decent **live music** venues and **discos**, most of which are cheaper to get into than their London counterparts. And if that doesn't appeal there's one of Europe's finest **football** teams based in the city, as well as a range of other sporting and not so sporting pastimes.

Live music and discos

Apart from the bands and discos that are put on at *Suck* (see above), there are a couple of more specific **venues** to try. Best place to see live bands is *Matssons Musikpub*, Göran Olsgatan 1 (behind the Rådhus), which is open nightly from 9.30pm to 2am and puts on a variety of Scandinavian R&B and rock bands – around 50kr entry, drinks the usual price. *Fredmans*, Regementsgatan 4 (daily 9pm–2am) puts on **jazz** three or four times a week, while one night a week (usually at the weekend) it becomes *The Tin Can Club*, offering – in its own words – "Psychedelic rock 'n' wave"; 50kr entry. The *Lilla Köket* restaurant (see above) also puts bands on: look for posters in the window. •

The **Concert Hall**, Föreningsgatan 35 (☎040/34 35 00) is home of the Malmö Symphony Orchestra; information about performances from the tourist office; 25 percent discount on tickets with the Malmö Card. The *Musikhögskolan* (☎040/19 22 00), Ystadvägen 25, is the other main classical music venue.

Top soccer action ... and other sports and pastimes

Malmö FF are one of Europe's most exciting teams, Swedish league champions on several occasions and past winners of the UEFA Cup. The team plays at Malmö Stadium, John Erikssons väg; bus #34, #37 or #38 from the centre. Entrance is from around 30kr, though the Malmö Card currently gets you onto the terraces for just 10kr (☎040/10 30 20 for info).

Swimming is easy, either at *Aq-va-kul*, Regementsgatan 24 (Mon noon–9pm, Tues–Fri 9am–9pm, Sat 9am–5pm, Sun 10am–6pm; 10kr; bus #34 or #41), an adventure pool with waves and chutes; or at the beaches and pools (May–Aug Mon–Fri 7am–7pm, Sat & Sun 8am–4pm) in Sibbarp, by Limhamn; bus #41B. If you've got kids to amuse, take them to **Malmöparken** (mid-April to mid-Sept), an amusement park at Amiralsgatan 35; buses #32 and #36–38. More unusually, you can go **fishing** from the city, on boats leaving from Hjälmarekajen, opposite the hydrofoil terminal. The tourist office again has details; you'll be able to rent fishing gear; and there's a small discount with the Malmö Card.

Listings

Airlines *British Airways*, Sturup airport (☎040/50 18 06); *Finnair*, Baltzarsgatan 31 (☎040/10 09 75); *KLM*, Baltzarsgatan 25 (☎040/766 55); *Lufthansa*, Kalendegatan 11 (☎040/717 10); *SAS*, Baltzarsgatan 18 (☎040/35 70 00).

Airport Buses Hourly *Flygbuss* to Kastrup airport (#109; daily 5am–10pm; 55kr) from Centralplan; hourly *Flygbuss* to Sturup airport (#110; Mon–Fri 5.30am–8.25pm, Sat 6.15am–7.25pm, Sun 8.25am–7.25pm; 30kr).

Buses From Centralplan to Lund (#130), Kristianstad/Kalmar (#805), Ystad (#330). From Norra Vallgatan, an *Intercitybuss* (#999; 40kr) runs to Copenhagen via the Linhamn–Dragör ferry.

Car Rental *AI Vasa*, Rundelsgatan 15 (☎040/775 30); *Avis*, Stortorget 9 (☎040/778 30); *Budget*, Baltzarsgatan 21 (☎040/775 75); *Europcar*, Mäster Nilsgatan 22 (☎040/38 02 40); *Hertz*, Skeppsbron 3 (☎040/749 55). Agencies, too, inside the *SAS* hovercraft terminal on Skeppsbron and at Sturup airport.

Chemist 24-hr service at *Apoteket Gripen*, Bergsgatan 48 (☎040/19 21 13).

Consulate British Consulate at Jörgen Kocksgatan 65 (☎040/18 45 65).

Doctor Doctor on call daily 7am–10pm; ☎040/33 35 00. Also Mon–Fri 10pm–midnight; ☎040/33 10 61. And at other times ☎040/33 10 00.

Exchange *Forex*, Hamngatan 1 (June–Aug Mon–Fri 9am–7pm, Sat & Sun 9am–4pm); at the Central Station post office (Mon–Fri 8am–6pm, Sat 9.30am–1pm); and in the *Flygbåtarana* terminal (daily 7.30am–8pm; see "Ferries and Hydrofoils").

Ferries and Hydrofoils *Flygbåtarana*, Skeppsbron (hydrofoil; 70kr one-way to Copenhagen, 25 percent discount with Malmö Card; ☎040/10 39 30); *Malmoe-Copenhagen Line*, Skeppsbron (cheaper ferries; 25 percent discount with Malmö Card; ☎040/701 50); *SAS*, Skeppsbron (hovercraft direct to Kastrup airport; 475kr one-way; ☎040/35 71 00); *SFL*, Limhamn–Dragör crossing (23–28kr one-way; children half-price; car plus passengers 235–420kr return; ☎040/16 20 70).

Left Luggage Lockers in Central Station (10kr) and in the *Flybåtarna* terminal.

Post Office Skeppsbron (Mon–Fri 8am–6pm, Sat 9.30am–1pm); Central Station (Mon–Fri 5–8.30pm, Sun 2–6pm).

STF Hiking and youth hostel info, from an office inside the tourist office.
Telephone Office *Televerket*, Storgatan 23 (Mon–Fri 8am–9pm, Sat 9.30am–3pm).
Trains *Pågatåg* info office inside the *Lokalstationen* (Mon–Fri 7am–7pm, Sat & Sun 9am–5pm). Tickets to Lund, 18kr one-way.

Ystad

An hour by local train from Malmö, **YSTAD** sits at the end of a coasting ride through rolling farmland that makes up much of the southern tracts of Skåne. Arriving by train, though, is misleading since the railway station is down by Ystad's docks – a murky area that gives no hint of the cosy little town that's to come. In the nineteenth century its inhabitants made a mint from smuggling, a profitable occupation in the days of Napoleon's Continental Blockade. Quite apart from coming to see the crumbly, medieval market town, you might well be leaving Sweden from Ystad: ferries depart from here to the Danish island of Bornholm and to Poland.

From the **railway station**, cross the tracks to the square, St Knuts Torg, where you'll find the **tourist office** (mid-June to mid-Aug Mon–Fri 9am–7pm, Sat 9am–6pm, Sun 2–6pm; rest of the year Mon–Fri 9am–5pm; ☎0411/772 79). You can get a brochure about Ystad with a map of the town inside, though you're hardly likely to get lost without it: it's a very small place. The square is also where **buses** from Lund and Malmö will drop you.

The streets wind up to **Stortorget**, a well-proportioned square, at the back of which sits the grand **Sta Maria Kyrka**, a church which has been added to continually since its original foundation in the fourteenth century. The red-brick interior displays heavy, decorative tablets lining the aisle walls and enclosed wooden pews – the sculpted end-pieces showing flowers and emblems. The green box-pews at either side of the entrance were reserved for women who hadn't yet been received back into the church after childbirth. From the church, take a walk down **Lilla Västergatan**, the main street in Ystad in the seventeenth and eighteenth centuries. Its houses are pastel-coloured, chocolate-box constructions with square windows and brass name-plates: you can only assume that the inhabitants don't mind being peered in upon, since there are few net curtains up.

Walk back through Stortorget and, away to the left, it's not far down to the old **Greyfriars Monastery** and museum (Mon–Fri noon–5pm, Sun 1–5pm; free), a thirteenth-century survival which contains the usual local cultural and historical collections, given piquancy by their medieval surroundings. Outside, there's a little lake and pleasant gardens.

Practicalities

There are several **hotels** in town, but nothing that's a better bargain than in nearby Malmö. You might want to stay in the **youth hostel** (☎0411/772 97), though, which is a couple of kilometres from the station at Sandskogen; open all year although limited to groups from September to May. Sandskogen also has a campsite (☎0411/772 95), open May to mid-September, and cabins for rent (☎0411/772 79).

For **eating** while in Ystad try *Café Diana*, Stora Östergatan 31 (Mon–Fri 7am–6.30pm, Sat 7am–4pm, Sun 11am–5pm), which has cheap coffee and snacks. Or, if you're an early arrival off one of the ferries, the *Hotel Continental* on Hamngatan does a buffet breakfast for 45kr (Mon–Fri 7–10am, Sat & Sun 8–10.30am).

Leaving, the **ferry terminal** is behind the railway station: look for the sign "Till Färjorna" on the platform, turn left and walk for ten minutes along the quayside to the ticket office and departure hall. To Poland, tickets cost from 220kr one-way; to Bornholm it's around 80kr one-way, bikes 16kr. **Buses** to Malmö (#330), Lund (#335) and Smygehamn (#183) – Sweden's most southerly point – leave from the square in front of the railway station. See "Travel Details" for more information on both ferries and buses.

Kristianstad

To see the rest of the eastern side of Skåne, unless you have transport you'll have to double back to Malmö and take the train across the county, changing at HÄSSLEHOLM for **KRISTIANSTAD** – a Renaissance town of Christian IV, seventeenth-century builder-king of Denmark. It's a shining example of the king's architectural preoccupations, the central squares and broad gridded streets flanking a wide river, and dating from 1614 when Skåne County still belonged to Denmark. There are other towns in Scandinavia built by Christian (notably Kristiansand in southern Norway – see p.201), but Kristianstad is the earliest and most evocative. It's a place in which, for no particular reason, hanging around is easy: spending time amongst Kristianstad's rangy eighteenth- and nineteenth-century buildings, pausing awhile at the pavement cafés and window-shopping in the smart boutiques.

Right opposite the railway station is the town's most striking building, the **Trefaldighetskyrkan** (daily 9am–5pm). It stands as a symbol of all that was glorious about Christian's Renaissance ideas and is the largest church of its kind in northern Europe. Finished in 1628, it's simple, bright and eminently likeable. A forest of pews inside fills the cool white church from back to front, their high sides and carved gargoyles obstructing a clear view of altar and pulpit. Maybe that's as it should be, leaving the soaring ornate organ facade the most beautiful object.

Kristianstad also attracts much interest among movie enthusiasts, since the country's oldest film studio recorded Sweden's first films here between 1909 and 1911, flickering works now on video and viewable at the **Film Museum** (Tues–Fri & Sun 1–4pm; free) at Östra Strandgatan 53, a building that was itself originally a studio.

A few practicalities

The **tourist office** (June–Aug Mon–Fri 9am–8pm, Sat 9am–5pm, Sun 1–6pm; rest of the year Mon–Fri 9am–6pm; ☎044/12 19 88) down Västra Boulevarden (a straight walk to the right from the station) rents out **bikes** – a good way to idle around the attractive surroundings. A **campsite**, *Charlottsborg Camping* (☎044/11 07 67), open all year, has a small **hostel** attached to it and campers can use all the hostel facilities, like the TV and lounge room; take bus #12 to VÄ from Busstorget, close to Lilla Torget. There's another, official, **youth hostel** (Stavgatan 3; ☎044/24 85 35) in nearby ÄHUS, thirty minutes away down the coast, regular buses again from Busstorget.

Blekinge County ... and Karlskrona

East of Kristianstad, both road and rail routes follow the sea-facing shelf of land
that is **Blekinge**, the county comprising a further stretch of small resort towns in
the fashion of those on the western coast. Unlike Varberg and its neighbours,
however, none of these are terribly interesting, but most are perfectly functional
for a day's swimming. SÖLVESBORG and KARLSHAMN are both inviting and
seasidey enough for a few hours, and there are several **campsites** near either for
longer stays.

Karlskrona

If this doesn't appeal, stick with the coast until **KARLSKRONA** – a decent sized
town, the county capital – and where the coastline assumes some interest in the
shape of a small archipelago. Founded by Karl XI in the late seventeenth century,
Karlskrona was specifically designed to accommodate his Baltic fleet in its sheltered and ice-free harbour. Purposely wide streets swallowed his military parades
and the layout survives, largely intact; while the naval and military connection is
still apparent in everything that Karlskrona does. Admirals have streets named
after them, and even their own church – the 1685 timber-built **Kungliga
Amiralitetskyrkan** (June–Aug Mon–Sat 10am–5pm, Sun noon–5pm). Cadets
career around the centre on bikes and there's a graphic **Maritime Museum**
(daily noon–4pm; 2kr) at the far end of Amiralitetstorget. Some of the islands of
Karlskrona's archipelago are off-limits to foreigners, a military zone in which only
Swedes can camp and swim.

Still, it's not all obsessively or oppressively naval in town. An old fishing port,
Karlskrona's cobbled **Fisketorget** was once site of the daily fish market, the
boats tying up at the quayside. There are no fish anymore, and the boats are
more likely to be posh yachts, but it's a pretty place to sit, with the water here the
deepest blue and green. The **Blekinge County Museum** (Mon–Fri 9am–4pm,
Sat & Sun noon–3pm; free) at the back of the square is hardly full of vital stuff –
mock-ups of nineteenth-century family life, local craftwork, that kind of thing –
but it does have an unusual, if small, gallery of Swedish oils and pencil sketches.

The main square, **Stortorget**, is large enough to accommodate two churches,
both designed by Tessin the Younger. Best is the circular Romanesque
Trefaldighetskyrkan (built for the town's German merchants in 1709), rather
than the turretted and baroque **Fredrikskyrkan**, though it's tricky to get in
either, the doors often firmly shut. If they are, ask at the **tourist office** (mid-June
to mid-Aug Mon–Sat 9am–8pm, Sun 10am–8pm; rest of the year Mon–Fri 9am–
6pm, Sat 10am–1pm; ☎0455/834 90), right behind Fredrikskyrkan at Södra
Smedjegatan 6.

Karlskrona: some practicalities
To get into the centre and to Stortorget, turn right out of the **railway station** and
walk through the park, straight up the hill. The **bus station** is next to the railway, and there's a twice-weekly express coach to Stockholm. There's also a
useful **ferry** service (mid-June to mid-Aug; 20kr) to and from RONNEBY to the
west. Arrive like this and the ferry drops you at Saltö, an island connected by
bridge to Karlskrona, from where it's an easy walk to the centre.

Cheap **accommodation** is not central. The nearest **youth hostel** (☎0455/283 15) is a fair distance away on Verkö, an island to the east of town; open June to August. The nearest **campsite** isn't too close either – but with a peaceful lakeside setting, it's recommended. Take bus #1 (it stops on Ronnebygatan, down the hill and parallel to Stortorget) to the *OK* garage at MARIEDAL, a 7km ride.

Food in Karlskrona is rather easier to find. There are several pizzerias, cafés and ice cream parlours and as the town has Sweden's largest high school, hanging out in these places is a big activity. More specifically, an outdoor café to one side of the Trefaldighetskyrkan serves up grilled half chickens at reasonable prices. There's also a daily **market** (except Sunday) in the summer, sprawled across Stortorget.

travel details

Express trains

Daily express trains operate throughout the region, in particular **Oslo–Copenhagen** (via Gothenburg, Varberg, Halmstad and Helsingborg) and **Stockholm–Copenhagen** (via Helsingborg). Both routes have a branch service through to Malmö. Despite complicated timetabling, the service is frequent and regular north or south between Gothenburg and Helsingborg/Malmö.

Trains

From Gothenburg to Trollhättan (Mon–Sat roughly hourly, Sun 6; 40–50min); Vänersborg (Mon–Fri 5 daily; Sat & Sun 1; 1hr); Strömstad (9 daily, bus on some departures; 2hr 40min–3hr); Stockholm (hourly; 4hr 40min); Karlskrona/Kalmar (4–6 daily; 4hr 50min).
From Helsingborg to Lund/Malmö (hourly, Sun two-hourly; 40min/50min).
From Malmö to Lund (at least hourly; 15min); Hässleholm (hourly, with two-hourly trains on to Kristianstad; 1hr 30min); Karlskrona (5 daily; 3hr 30min); Ystad (Mon–Fri roughly hourly, Sat 4 daily, Sun 6; 1hr).

Buses

From Gothenburg to Helsingborg/Malmö (Fri & Sun 2 daily; 3hr 30min/4hr 30min); Strömstad (2–3 daily; 2hr 30min); Kungsbacka (hourly; 1hr); Jönköping (3–6 daily; 2hr 30min); Falun/Gävle (2–3 daily; 8hr/10hr); Kalmar (Fri & Sun 1 daily; 6hr); Stockholm (Fri 3 daily, Sun 2; 7–8hr); Karlskrona (Fri & Sun 1 daily; 7hr); Oslo (2–3 daily; 5hr 30min).
From Helsingborg to Båstad (6 daily; 1hr); Halmstad (9–12 daily; 1hr 50min); Malmö (Fri & Sun 3 daily; 1hr 10min); Helsingør/Copenhagen (7–10 daily; 1hr/2hr).

From Malmö to Helsingborg/Halmstad/Gothenburg (Fri & Sun 1–3 daily; 1hr 20min/3hr/5hr); Lund (at least hourly; 30min); Kristianstad/Kalmar (1 daily; 2hr/6hr); Jönköping (Fri & Sun 1 daily; 5hr); Stockholm (Fri & Sun 1 daily; 11hr).
From Ystad to Malmö (Mon–Fri 3 daily, Sat & Sun 1; 1hr); Lund (Mon–Fri 3 daily, Sat & Sun 1–2; 1hr 15min); Smygehamn (Mon–Fri 7 daily, Sat & Sun 2; 40min).
From Kristianstad to Lund/Malmö (1 daily; 1hr 30min/2hr); Kalmar (1 daily; 4hr)
From Karlskrona to Stockholm (Fri & Sun 1 daily; 7hr).

Ferries

From Gothenburg to Harwich (1 daily in summer, 3 weekly rest of the year; 24hr); Newcastle (2 weekly June to mid-Aug; 24hr); Frederikshavn (3–6 daily; 3hr 15min); Kiel (1 daily; 14hr).
From Varberg to Grenå in Denmark (1–3 daily; 4hr).
From Halmstad to Grenå (1–2 daily; 4hr).
From Malmö to Copenhagen (6 daily; 1hr 30min).
From Helsingborg to Helsingør (every 15–20min all day and night; 25min); Grenå (1–2 daily; 4hr).
From Limhamn (Malmö) to Dragör (hourly; 55min).
From Ystad to Rönne on Bornholm (mid-June to mid-Aug 4 daily; 2hr 30min); Swinoujscie in Poland (2 daily; 7–9hr).

Hydrofoils

From Malmö to Copenhagen (*Flygbåtarna* hourly 5am–midnight; 45min; no winter service if the Øresund freezes over); Kastrup airport (*SAS* hourly 8am–8pm; 45min).

CHAPTER ELEVEN

THE SOUTHEAST

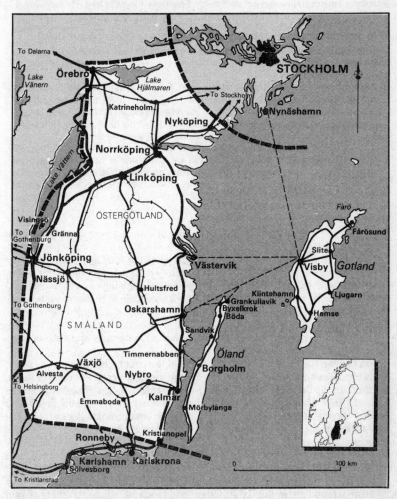

A less obvious target than the south coast resorts, Sweden's **southeast** repays a stop over on the southern routes to and from Stockholm; while the two Baltic islands deserve to be taken independently, such is their singular attraction. Train transport on the mainland, especially between the towns close to **Lake Vättern** and Stockholm, is good; speedy, regular

THE BALTIC ISLANDS: SOME PRACTICAL INFORMATION

It's easy and inexpensive to reach either **Öland** or **Gotland**. A 6km long bridge connects Öland with Kalmar on the mainland, and **buses** make the trip regularly throughout the year. **Ferries** sail to Gotland (Visby) from the Småland ports of Västervik and Oskarshamn, as well as from Nynäshamn, south of Stockholm. **Getting around** is made easier by the **Småland/Öland Card** (100kr/3 days, 150kr/8 days; from tourist offices, train stations and travel agencies), a pass that gives unlimited travel on buses throughout Öland and the Småland region, though *not* Gotland which has its own pass. Buy the Småland/Öland Card in Kalmar and the bus trip over the bridge to Öland is free. Usefully, the card also pulls in free museum entry, a return ferry ride to Öland from Oskarshamn and other concessions in the two districts.

Alternatively, there's no better terrain to **cycle** on, rented bikes available cheaply on both islands. **Campsites** are plentiful, although Öland and Gotland are probably the best places in southern Sweden to exercise *Allemans Rätt* and camp rough. Even during the manic July rush, when virtually the whole of Sweden is on holiday, there is always more than room for a tent outside the busier spots.

To avoid the hectic summer weeks altogether come in late May or September when, depending on bravado, you can still swim. Gotland is also one of the most popular places for the Swedes to celebrate **Midsummer's Night**. Beds will be at a premium but, having said that, if you get as drunk as everyone else you probably won't care about the lack of a roof over your head.

services mean that you could see some of the places on a long day trip from the capital.

Östergötland, bordering the eastern shores of the lake and reaching as far east as the Baltic, is not a county where many foreign visitors linger. Its waterways (part of the Göta Canal) and countryside, though, draw lots of Swedes and while you might not have the time to delve into its natural beauty as enthusiastically as they do, you can make breaks in your journey at a couple of fine towns, **Norrköping** and **Linköping**.

South, and **Småland County** straddles a varied geography and encompasses some stridently different towns.

Jönköping, the largest town to the north of the county, is a prosperous place, its lakeside setting handy for access to the holiday centres around Vättern. Further south, through endless forest, the so-called "Glass Kingdom" centres around **Växjö**. Abundant wood fuel serviced a glass industry already flourishing here in the eighteenth century, families living in small communities around the forest glassworks. The tradition is still strong, the art at its best in the town's museum, but easy to see *in situ* at any of the surrounding glass factories. Heading east to the sea, **Kalmar** is a likeable stop, too, an historic fortress town and jumping off point for Öland.

Outside the fragmented archipelagos of east and west coasts, Sweden's only two true **islands** are in the Baltic: **Öland** and **Gotland**, adjacent slithers of land with unusually temperate climates. Domestic tourist havens for years, an increasing number of foreigners are now finding their way there for sun, beaches and some remarkable historic (and prehistoric) sights, chiefly Gotland's medieval Hanseatic capital, **Visby**.

Östergötland

Östergötland is a strategically placed county, only a couple of hours from Stockholm, whose attractions have much to do with the connecting rivers and lakes that thread through it. East of Lake Vättern, the Göta Canal runs for the Baltic, passing and bypassing a number of towns whose original function is indicated by the suffix to their names: the word "kop" (pronounced "shurp"), meaning "market", in a town's name is a clear sign that it once stood on an important trade route, something that's true of Östergötland's two main towns, NORRKÖPING and LINKÖPING.

There's a special **tourist ticket** (1 day, 35kr; 3 days 70kr) that's valid on all the buses in Östergötland; buy it at local tourist offices, main post offices and *Pressbyrån* kiosks.

Norrköping

The trains across the country from the capital to Malmö take a shade over two hours to reach **NORRKÖPING**, a manufacturing town whose roots lie back at least as far as 1500 BC. This is the date at which **rock carvings** found at Himmelstalund, a couple of kilometres west of the centre by the river Strömen, have been estimated: the clear and animated red pictures detail ships, people, animals and weapons. It's the nineteenth century, though, that impinges upon the rest of town, a bright and pleasant place built on the river, where most of what there is to do centres around re-creations of the textile industry that made Norrköping prosperous. The **Norrköping Museum** (June–Aug Mon–Fri 10am–4pm, Thurs also 4–8pm, Sat & Sun noon–4pm; rest of the year Mon–Fri 10am–4pm, Tues & Thurs also 4–8pm, Sat & Sun noon–4pm; free), down on the river in the centre of town, at Västgötegatan 19–21, puts you in the picture by providing some interesting background information; while several of the old industrial buildings remain, too. One – an odd triangular-shaped factory building – sits on a bank in the middle of the river and is destined to become a Worker's Museum in the near future: if it's not yet open as such, you'll probably be able to get inside anyway since it already hosts temporary exhibitions and concerts.

Some practical details

Although you probably won't give Norrköping itself more than half a day, the surrounding attractions – Löfstad Manor and Kolmården Djurpark (see below) – are worth **staying over** for. The **tourist office** (June–Aug Mon–Fri 9am–7pm, Sat 9am–6pm, Sun 10am–4pm; rest of the year Mon–Thurs 10am–5pm, Fri 10am–4pm; ☎011/15 15 00) is on Drottninggatan in the Town Hall: a few minutes' walk down the main road from the railway station and over the bridge. They can sell you the **Norrköping Card** (100kr), valid for three days (between mid-June and mid-Aug) which offers various discounts and admissions – including free entry to Löfstad and a discount on entry to Kolmården.

There's a **youth hostel** (☎011/10 11 60), open all year except mid-December to mid-January, at Ingelstagatan 31, which is less than a kilometre north (behind) of the railway station. And a couple of central **hotels** aren't bad value either: there are summer deals at both *Hotell Cedric*, Gamla Rådstugugatan 18–20 (parallel to Drottninggatan; ☎011/12 90 30) and *Strand Hotell*, Drottninggatan 2 (☎011/16 99

00) which should get you a double room at around 300kr. Most central **campsite** is by the rock carvings at Himmelstalund – *Citycamping* (☎011/17 11 90), Utställningsvägen, a walk west along the river.

Around Norrköping: Löfstad Manor and Kolmården Djurpark

Either one of two easy trips from Norrköping neatly complete the rest of the day if you've decided to stay overnight in the area. Closest, ten kilometres south of town, is **Löfstad Manor** (May Sat & Sun only; June–Aug daily; tours hourly on the hour noon–4pm; 15kr, kids 5kr), a grand country house in its own grounds, whose buildings and outbuildings date from the seventeenth and eighteenth century. Its last owner, Emily Piper, died in 1940 and the house has been left exactly as it was on her death – though, surrounded by the furniture and furnishings of several generations, the impression is of a manor house at the height of its late-eighteenth- and early-nineteenth-century magnificence. It's a rich collection of artefacts with some interesting touches: the house was designed to be self-sufficient, even to the extent of the machine in the scullery that twisted metal into new bed springs. **Bus** #480 or #481 runs from Norrköping's bus terminal (at the side of the railway station) to the house, a twenty-minute ride; ask for *Löfstad Slott*.

In the other direction, 20km north of Norrköping, **Kolmården Djurpark** is one of the country's biggest attractions. A combined zoo, safari park and dolphinarium, it's understandably popular with kids, who have their own children's zoo, as well as access to a gaggle of other diversions and enclosures. If your views on zoos are negative, it's just about possible to be convinced that this one is different: there are no cages, but instead sunken enclosures, rock barriers and moats to prevent the animals from feasting on their captors. There's certainly no shortage of things to do either: there's a cable-car ride over the safari park, a tropical house, working farm, and dolphin shows; four or five hours' worth all told.

If you're interested in just one or two specific attractions in the park it might be as well to ring first (☎011/951 00; or get Norrköping tourist office to find out for you). The zoo closes for a couple of months each year, the safari park only opens when the weather is calm and the temperature doesn't drop below –10°C. Generally, though, most things are **open** daily from 10am until around 4–6pm; the dolphinarium has 1–4 shows daily for most of the year; the **price** varies according to what you want to see, but a combined ticket for everything (including the dolphin shows) runs from 75–140kr, depending on the season.

If you don't have your own transport, you can **get there** on bus #432 from Norrköping, which runs right to the park in fifty minutes, roughly hourly from the bus terminal. There's a very expensive **hotel**, the *Vidmarkshotellet* (☎011/15 71 00), at the park – though if you wanted a quiet treat, its weekend price (around 650kr double) isn't too outrageous. Alternatively, you can **camp** close by, at the water's edge and near the hotel, at *Kolmården Camping* (☎011/941 42); or the #432 bus continues past the park to KVARSEBO, another fifteen minutes beyond, where there's a **youth hostel** (☎011/960 46), open mid-June to mid-August – ring first as it only has 32 beds.

Linköping

The second of Östergötland's major towns is 46km southwest of Norrköping, just half an hour on the train. **LINKÖPING** preserves much of its late-nineteenth-century character in a remarkable open-air museum called **Gamla Linköping** (May–Aug daily 10am–5pm; Sept to April Mon–Fri 9am–4pm), which consists of an entire town of houses, shops and businesses designed to portray Swedish provincial life a century ago. The wooden buildings, street lighting, fences, signs, trees and flowers were taken from all over Linköping and rebuilt within a street pattern that was copied from the original nineteenth-century city. There are working craft shops (ceramics, gold and silversmiths and woodworkers), stores, a school and houses – which the locals join a massive waiting list to live in. The restrictions put many off, though: not least that you can't change the house in any way at all, and that you have to suffer an endless stream of tourists traipsing through what is still a living town. It's a fascinating place and throughout the year there are various events centred around Gamla Linköping and guided tours. The shops are open nearly every day, so you'll always have the opportunity to buy some home-made sweets or other homely nineteenth-century fare.

The other thing to see in town is the fine medieval **Domkyrkan** (daily 9am–6/7pm), set in a green swathe of land very close to central Stortorget. One of Sweden's most impressive cathedrals, its spire rises to 107m, a strident landmark for miles around. Stonemasons from all over Europe, including England, worked on the well-proportioned building and it shows elements from three centuries of construction, from Romanesque to Gothic.

If you wanted to stay, Linköping has a **youth hostel** (☎013/17 64 58), though it's 7km out of the town: bus #202 from the railway station to Björnkärrsgatan 14; the hostel is open from mid-June to mid-August.

Småland

If you're in **Småland County** you're most likely to be on your way elsewhere. Long train rides across the thickly forested and lake-ridden county are a familiar feature of travel from the southwestern coast to Stockholm; or of the journey east from Gothenburg to the Baltic coast and its ports. Hardly the most attractive part of Sweden, there are few vital stops within the county, though the major, and peripheral, towns – **Jönköping**, **Växjö** and **Kalmar** – are all lively enough to warrant time.

Historically, Småland has had it tough. Subsistence agriculture failed the eighteenth- and nineteenth-century peasantry, who took to mass emigration to ease their lot. Those that remained (and Småland was almost depopulated in the midnineteenth century) sought economic refuge in the traditional industries, iron, wood – and, later, glass. Established as early as the sixteenth century when Gustav Vasa brought Venetian craftsmen to Sweden, the glass industry soon prospered, moving into Småland's ailing iron foundries. And today, the glassware is world famous for its design and quality, southeast Småland known locally as the *Glasriket* (Glass Kingdom).

Jönköping

One of the oldest medieval trading centres in the country, **JÖNKÖPING** (the "k" is soft, pronounced "sh") has a more modern if prosaic claim to fame – in Sweden at least. It's lauded as the home of the matchstick, the nineteenth-century manufacture and worldwide distribution of which made Jönköping the wealthy place it is today. The wide boulevards, high office blocks and a fussily designed centre tend – unfortunately – to obscure the town's plum position on the shores of Lake Vättern. Arriving by bus or train, right on the water's edge, shows you Jönköping's best aspect. However, despite a couple of tinier lakes south of the centre and some extensive parkland, you'll probably want to stay at one of several prettier sites out of town on Vättern, though give Jönköping time enough at least to see the **Tändsticksmuseet** (June–Aug Mon–Fri 10am–6pm, Sat 11am–1pm, Sun 3–5pm) at Västra Storgatan 18; the Matchstick Museum, housed in the original match factory built in 1844. An unlikely source of interest, the "unique collection of matchbox labels and match-making machines" is nothing more or less than that.

Practicalities

Railway and **bus station** are next to each other on the lake's edge, the **tourist office** (June–Aug Mon–Fri 8am–8pm, Sat 9am–4pm, Sun 1–5pm; rest of the year Mon–Fri 8am–5pm; ☎036/16 90 50) one block up at Västra Storgatan 9. For **shops**, food and supermarkets walk east (with the water on your left), the street changing its name half way to Östra Storgatan. For decent views of the lake and a coffee while debating the next move, *Café Hackspetten* in the *Alliansmissionen* building (on the left as you leave the covered walkway from the railway station) has cheap roof garden fare.

Accommodation is surprisingly plentiful. The tourist office has a list of fairly cheap central **hotels** (around 100–150kr single, 200kr double) and books even cheaper **private rooms** (80kr single, double). The **youth hostel** (☎036/614 88) is 8km away at NORRAHAMMAR, at the top of a steep hill and surrounded by vast expanses of forest. Take bus #28 or #29 from Västra Storgatan as far as Spånhultsvägen. **Camping** is more accessible, the site at *Rosenlund* (☎036/12 28 63) right on the lakeside. Take buses #2, #3, #4 or #22 from outside the tourist office; the site is open all year.

Around Jönköping: Lake Vättern

There are much better places to spend the night around **Lake Vättern**. Common opinion favours nearby **GRÄNNA** backed by high hills, one of which (*Grännaberget*) offers sweeping views of the lake. The small town dates from the seventeenth century, its wooden houses – remarkably – never yet fallen prey to fire. There are still only a couple of thousand inhabitants here, though the **kyrka** gained its handsome Baroque alterations when the town numbered a mere ten houses. Gränna was the birthplace of **S.A. Andrée**, the man who set off to reach the North Pole by balloon in 1897: the remains of him and his ill-fated expedition were discovered thirty years later, on White Island in the Arctic. There's a museum in town devoted to Andrée, displaying some of the photographs that he and his team took. Two **youth hostels** serve Gränna, the first (☎0390/ 103 15) close to the tourist office and open mid-June to July, the second (☎0390/114 20) right on the beach close to the ferry. Slightly larger, it's also open longer, from May to August.

From Gränna a twenty-minute **ferry** crossing (half-hourly; 12kr, free with Småland/Öland Card) drops you on **Visingsö**, a tiny island in the middle of Vättern. The ruins of two castles can fill a few lazy hours before getting back. Or you could return straight to Jönköping on a second and direct **ferry** service. The *Magnus Ladulås* (30kr single, 50kr return) runs between Jönköping and Visingsö on Sunday (mid-May to the end of August) and Wednesday (end of June to the beginning of August); two ferries a day, a two-hour journey each way.

Buses (#121 or #122; 1hr) run the 40km to Gränna roughly every half-hour on weekdays, fewer at weekends from Jönköping bus station.

Växjö

One of the most unpronounceable of Swedish towns (try the "xj" as a kind of "qu" sound), **VÄXJÖ** is by far the handiest place to base yourself if you're at all interested in the distinctive glassware produced in the region. A Viking trade depot, Växjö relinquished a last hold on its medieval past when the cathedral – originally twelfth-century – was thoroughly restored in 1960. So, other than the two excellent museums (see below) there's no real reason to linger in the centre, bright as it is, and hitting the surroundings is of greater interest. Daily tours take in the local glassworks, entry to which is free. To avoid the crowds ask at the **tourist office**, Kronobergsgatan 8 (☎0470/414 10) about visits to the smaller and more traditional works – like the ones at nearby ÄLGHULT or BERGDALA.

For just looking, not buying, the glass collections in the **Smålands Museum** (Mon–Fri 9am–4pm, Sat 11am–3pm, Sun 1–5pm; 5kr) in Växjö itself are probably among the best in the world. Functional and decorative glassware from the Greek and Roman empires to present day Swedish pieces; all impressively stacked and lit and provoking fantasies of cathartic vandalism. More than just glass, look out too for the composite late-medieval chapel, all its decorative art lifted from various churches in the region.

Right next door is the **Emigrants House Museum and Research Centre** (June–Aug Mon–Fri 9am–5pm, Sat 11am–3pm, Sun 1–5pm; rest of the year Mon–Fri 9am–4pm; 5kr, day pass for the research centre 25kr). The special *Dream of America* exhibition tells brilliantly the history of nineteenth-century Swedish emigration to the empty lands of North America. Poor agricultural conditions locally, regular harvest failures and little alternative industrial employment all helped drive a starving peasantry abroad, doubly attracted by offers of great farms and a landscape similar to their own. Around a million people made the crossing between 1850 and 1925 – a quarter of the total Swedish population, a fifth of them from the Småland region. It makes moving reading, and moist-eyed American descendants are not a rare sight. The emigrants' story achieved literary and popular recognition in the works of **Vilhelm Moberg**, probably the most widely read novelist in Sweden. The museum includes a permanent exhibition of his life – he died in 1973 – with some of the original manuscripts on display. There's a research centre too, where interested parties can try to trace their family connections; apparently, not an impossible task in Europe's biggest archive library on emigration. The museum is at the head of the lake, just a couple of minutes from the tourist office and behind the railway station.

If you're just passing through, a 5km path around the **lake** in town can occupy a pleasant hour or two. Or ask at the tourist office about using the **tennis courts** for the afternoon, remembering not to challenge the locals to a game: Mats Wilander comes from Växjö.

Practicalities

Växjö, a reliable place to spend the night, has one of the country's finest **youth hostels** (☎0470/630 70). It's 6km out at EVEDAL (bus #1 or #1B from opposite the tourist office to the end of the line; last one at 6.15pm, weekends 5.15pm) and boasts its own beach; open all year. There's a large **campsite** there too, but both hostel and campsite are useless for early morning departures as the first bus back into town is at 10am. In town, you may get a decent deal in the summer at *Hotell Esplanad*, Norra Esplanaden 21 (☎0470/225 80), with doubles from around 400kr.

Ports and ferries

There's little reason to hang about anywhere else in the region (with the exception of KALMAR – see below), although it's as well to know that Småland's **ports** are handy departure points for ferries to the Baltic islands of Öland and Gotland. The two to note are **VÄSTERVIK** (for Visby) and **OSKARSHAMN** (for Visby and a summer service to Byxelkrok in Öland). Both are accessible by train unlike smaller and more southern **TIMMERNABBEN**, site of an occasional summer ferry service to Borgholm on Öland. Given the extent of the other services it's hardly worth making a special journey, but you'd probably find it easy enough to hitch the 40km or so there to or from Kalmar (down the E66).

Kalmar

Bright **KALMAR** had much to do with Sweden's medieval development. It was the scene of the first meeting of the *Riksdag* called by failing king Magnus Eriksson in the mid-fourteenth century, and played host to the formation of the Kalmar Union, the agreement of 1397 uniting Sweden, Norway and Denmark as one. All of which would only be of mild interest but for the survival in an impressively intact form of the Kremlinesque **Kalmar slott** (May to mid-June & mid-Aug to Sept Fri & Sat 10am–4pm, Sun 1–4pm; mid-June to mid-Aug Mon–Thurs 10am–7pm, Fri & Sat 10am–5pm, Sun 1–5pm; Oct–Nov & March–April daily 1–3pm; Dec–Feb Sun 1-3pm; 5kr, students 3kr).

Beautifully set on a tiny island a few minutes' walk away from the bus and railway stations, the castle is defended by a range of steep embankments and regular gun emplacements. The original fourteenth-century buildings survived eleven different sieges virtually unscathed, a record not respected by King Johan III who restored and rebuilt in the late sixteenth century to achieve the existing structure. He did a good job, and the castle is storybook accurate: turrets, ramparts, a moat and drawbridge, dungeon and (perhaps oddly) some of the finest decorative craftsmanship on display in Sweden. The painted and spruced interior repays a long dawdle (it helps if you borrow the *Kalmar Castle* guide – in English – from the reception desk): highlights include the intricately panelled *Lozenge Hall* and a dark, deep dungeon. Given such a setting, the only real disappointment is that there's no evidence that the important Kalmar Union treaty itself was signed in the castle, though it certainly was promulgated in Kalmar – somewhere.

If the castle seems to defend nothing in particular it's because the town was shifted to Kvarnholmen, an island to the north of the castle, in the mid-seventeenth century following a fire. This is modern Kalmar (though only modern compared to the castle), a graceful and straightforward grid settlement which centres on the Baroque **Domkyrkan** (daily 8am–7pm), which curiously lacks the traditional dome. Bang in the middle of Stortorget, which also features the contemporary and similarly styled *Rådhus*, both cathedral and town hall were built by (the Elder) Tessin. Neither though are particularly striking, time being better spent in wandering the streets around **Lilla Torget**. There's not a great deal left – several seventeenth-century buildings and some city walls – but what remains is authentic and atmospheric enough to be pleasing.

By now the **Kronan exhibition** should be housed in a new County Museum on Skeppsbrogatan, and it's worth seeing. The *Kronan* was once one of the three biggest ships in the world (twice the size of the *Wasa*, which sunk in Stockholm) when it went down in 1676 fully laden and crewed. Eight hundred men died and the ship lay undisturbed (apart from the retrieval of a few cannons) until 1980,

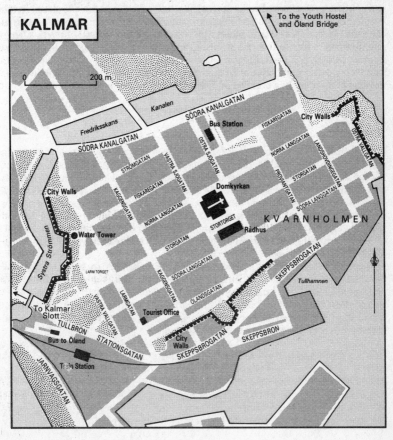

when it was salvaged for its treasures. The dramatic displays are not only of gold and silver coins but clothing, sculptures, jewellery, weapons – in fact, a complete picture of seventeenth-century maritime life and a remarkable insight into a society at the height of its political powers.

Kalmar practicalities

The **tourist office** (☎0480/153 50) is only a spit away from the **railway station** and **bus terminal**, at Larmgatan 6, at the junction with Ölandsgatan. It's useful for information about the island of Öland, and doles out a decent map of Kalmar. Options for staying overnight are also good. The tourist office arranges **private rooms** from around 80kr single, 120kr double, or stay at the *Kalmar Lågprishotell* (☎0480/255 60) at Rappegatan 1C. It's 1500m walk away on Ängo, the next island north, and costs around 260kr double, including breakfast. A **Sjöfartsklubben** (a sort of seaman's mission but open to all) on Skeppsbrogatan has doubles from around 100kr each and cheaper dorm accommodation; while **camping** happens on Stensö island, 3km from the centre, and with a few cheap cabins for rent.

For **food**, *Hamncafeet* at Skeppsbron opens at 6am for the harbour workers and continues to sell good value sandwiches and coffee until the afternoon. In the evening *Baronen* nightclub on Skeppsbrogatan has free entrance some nights, as does the disco, *Cincano*, in Koppartorget (near the water tower) – there's a lively pub downstairs too. At the end of July Kvarnholmen is closed off for the night as *Kalmar Dansar och Ler* ("Kalmar Dancing and Smiling") drinks and boogies its way through the night. Entrance is around 20kr for live bands, beer tent (very unusual in Sweden) and carnival high jinks.

Öland

Only a hundred years ago **ÖLAND** was rarely visited by tourists. Today its charms can be obscured by the hundreds of thousands who arrive each summer. It's the sort of place where a Swedish Famous Five would come on holiday: flat green cycling country and a mostly unspoilt coastline; the rest a mixture of wooden cottages with candy-striped canopies, flower boxes and ice cream parlours, windmills and tea gardens. The mainly Swedish summer invasion certainly clogs the main roads with traffic and takes over **Borgholm**, the capital. Yet there are still plenty of isolated places left, and a bike and tent will put you in touch with most of them.

Nearly 400 **windmills** dotted around the flat countryside give the island a peculiarly Dutch air, and almost as common are the enticing castles, fortresses and burial mounds that mark the landscape. Major sights start with the ruined **Borgholm Castle** and end with the reconstructed prehistoric fort at **Eketorp**. In between are the barren wastes of the **Stora Alvaret**, a vast tract of limestone soil in the south covering almost a third of the island.

Getting there and getting around

Getting to Öland is easy. **Drivers**, **cyclists** and **hitch-hikers** should take the Ängö link road to Svinö (just outside Kalmar), which, followed by the bridge (no footpath access) leads to Möllstorp on the island. From there, follow the signs and the traffic streams to Borgholm further north. **Buses** (#101 or #106) make the same journey from Kalmar's bus terminal. They depart on the hour, every hour, for the 50-minute ride to Borgholm until 4pm when services become rather more erratic, but do continue until around midnight. The only surviving **ferry services** are a summer route from Oskarshamn to Byxelkrok; from Visby to Grankullavik, and (less usefully, less certainly) Timmernabben to Borgholm.

Getting around the island is slightly more difficult. A bus network with regular if few services connects most places – picking up a free bus timetable at Kalmar tourist office should help matters. Hitch-hiking is easiest on the main road between Mörbylånga and Borgholm. Elsewhere, be prepared to wait and walk. However, Öland only really opens up to travellers with their own wheels. You can **rent bikes** for around 40kr a day, 200kr a week in both Kalmar and Borgholm. Again, ask at the tourist office for details.

Borgholm

BORGHOLM is the nearest thing Öland has to an island capital. Old holiday villas on the outskirts give it the air of a solid and respectable resort, but don't say much about the town's status as a teeming holiday centre. For decades now the locals have been swamped by the summer rush of visitors, without whose money Borgholm and the island would be in a sorry state.

During the nineteenth century, Öland was all but depopulated, a quarter of its inhabitants leaving for America after repeated bad harvests. It's a decline that has continued into the twentieth century as people have moved to the mainland in search of jobs. There's no significant industry on the island, and the tourists and the new bridge which brings them are an invaluable source of income. Borgholm is therefore touristy by design rather than by accident but, surprisingly, its small centre and pretty harbour have remained largely unspoilt.

Undoubtedly the main attraction in town is the atmospheric ruin which was **Borgholm Castle**. Situated on a hill overlooking Kalmar Sound, the original twelfth-century fortifications were easy to defend, but that didn't prevent enemies trying their luck and the castle suffered several protracted sieges. Already in a state of disrepair, it was further destroyed by fire in 1806 and the moody ruins have been a tourist attraction ever since. Massive in scale, the corridors and rooms are often open to the sky, the energetic clambering around only marginally tempered by the threat of shaky masonry. It's a brisk walk up to the castle through the trees of the **nature reserve** (follow the signs to *Borgholms slottsruin*), with excellent views to the mainland.

Arriving, sleeping and eating
Finding your way around the small grid system that constitutes central Borgholm isn't a problem. The bus from Kalmar drops you close to the **tourist office** (☎0485/123 40), at the harbour end of Storgatan, the main street that runs right through the centre of town. Campers should pick up the *Öland Camping Turistkarta*, a free camping map, while the *Ölands Kartan* (30kr) is useful for cycling or driving around the island.

The **bus station** for departures to the rest of the island is on Sandgatan, up and a few blocks to the left of the tourist office. Behind it, on a small peninsula five minutes' walk from the centre, is the **campsite**, *Kapelludden's Camping* (☎0485/101 78), while the **youth hostel** (☎0485/119 39) is even closer at Tullgatan 12A. Up Storgatan on the left, it's open from mid-May to mid-September. There is another much larger hostel at ROSENFORS (☎0485/107

56), 1km from the centre, open May to mid-September. If arriving on the Kalmar bus get the driver to stop at the *Gulf* petrol station just before Borgholm proper. The hostel is 100m away on the left, set back in the trees.

The high concentration of Swedish tourists tends to push up the price of **eating**, and even the few pizzerias are relatively expensive: but try *Borgholmsbaren* on Kyrkogatan which has a cheap daily lunch menu. If you're self-catering, note that there's no kitchen at the *Rosenfors* hostel.

Around the island

With only a little time to spare, the **north** of the island is easiest to reach, on the regular local buses. There are good beaches to be found, and an opportunity to leave Öland by **ferry** without returning to Borgholm. By way of a marked contrast, a great deal of the **south** of the island is characterised by the treeless limestone plain known as the Stora Alvaret, a haven for wildlife.

The north

First real stop is **HÖGBY** which has the only remaining church houses on the island, relics of medieval Högby Church nearby. If you have a tent and an urge to use it, then stay on the bus until it reaches **BÖDA**, a rather elongated settlement but one which marks the start of the Böda Crown Park. Bus #106 will take you right past the **youth hostel** (☎0485/220 38) at the southern end of the village, open mid-May to mid-August. Ask the driver to stop, otherwise it continues a few hundred metres further to the supermarket opposite *Kyrketorp* **campsite** (☎0485/220 43) from where begins 10km of beach bordering the park and running north. For the most part it's clean golden sand backed by dunes and forest, with the chance to camp rough almost anywhere; or at the more official *Böda Sands Camping* (☎0485/123 40) half way up.

From the northernmost bay of the island, at **GRANKULLAVIK, summer ferries** depart to Gotland (around 120kr), though not at the weekends. The bay itself has some great swimming from its small beaches.

Southwest, at the impossibly named **BYXELKROK**, there's also a summer connecting service with the mainland. Ferries leave daily for OSKARSHAMN (55kr one-way, 60kr day-return, 20kr bikes, free with Öland Card). Byxelkrok itself is quiet, with a lovely sheltered harbour and, when docked, the ferries dwarf the fishing smacks and low red-painted wooden houses which overlook them. To the south, beyond the lighthouse, the mostly rocky beaches become a little sandier. If you want to stay, the village has several campsites within easy reach.

The south

Hardly any roads cross the Stora Alvaret, the main route being down the west coast to OTTENBY and, to a lesser extent, back up the east side of the plain to GÅRDBY. With your own transport, what there is to see is fairly accessible. By bus it's a little more difficult – though by no means impossible. Services are less frequent than in the north and some timetable juggling will be necessary to avoid being stranded.

Coming over the Öland Bridge, **FÄRJESTADEN** is most people's first glimpse of the island; and a glimpse is usually all that it is as the cars and buses swing north on their way to Borgholm. Indeed there's no real reason to stop unless you need money, food or buses to the south.

The main road then skirts the limestone plain virtually all the way down to the southern tip of the island. By keeping to the smaller back roads, several coastal **campsites** and countless detached little communities come within reach. With the exception of the largely uninteresting **MÖRBYLÅNGA**, the "capital" of the south, there are few people and fewer facilities, so if you don't have a car, take what you need with you. For non-campers who want a base other than Borgholm, Mörbylånga has a cheap **hotel**, the *Pensionat Sandbergen* (☎0485/363 93), with singles for just 150kr, doubles for 240kr.

Öland has around nineteen forts dotted about, mostly built between 300 AD and 600 AD as protection against plundering raids by local tribes. Remains of walls, burial grounds and other archaeological debris can be seen throughout the island, but the best place to visit for a close look at Öland's past is the village of **EKETORP**, where an archaeological museum has been created out of the finds from a major 1970s excavation. Three separate settlements were identified on the site, the first probably a ceremonial and market place in use during the fourth century AD, the last a fortified agrarian community dating from about 1000. The reconstruction was planned to display both its Iron Age and medieval character, and the result is a remarkable achievement in imaginative popular archaeology.

The **site** is open daily between May and September, 9am to 5pm and entry is 15kr. Guided tours explain much of the intricacies behind the reconstruction, but a solitary wander around the walls and dwellings is the best way of absorbing the ancient feel of the place.

Getting there might be a problem. Four buses (#112) a day run from Mörbylånga bus station, two on Saturday and only one on Sunday. The same line continues to OTTENBY and passes the **youth hostel** there (☎0485/620 62), open from May to August. The bus is not actually scheduled to stop at the hostel but, as on the rest of the island, you can usually persuade the driver to stop almost anywhere you want. Talk to the **tourist office** (June–Aug; ☎0485/415 55) in Mörbylånga at Köpmangatan 4 to check on the latest timetables. If all else fails, you should be able to cadge a lift northwards during the high season with the crowds arriving here by car.

Gotland

The rumours about good times on **Gotland** are rife. You'll hear that the short summer season really motors like nowhere else in Sweden; that it's hot, fun and cheap. Largely, these rumours are true: the island has a youthful feel as young, mobile Stockholmers desert the capital for a boisterous summer spent on its beaches.

Gotland itself, and in particular its capital, **Visby**, has always seen frenetic activity of some kind. A temperate climate and fortuitous geographical position attracted the **Vikings** as early as the sixth century and the lucrative trade routes they opened, through to Byzantium and western Asia, guaranteed the island its prosperity. With the ending of the Viking domination a "Golden Age" followed, Gotland's inhabitants sending embassies, maintaining trading posts and signing treaties with European and Asian leaders as equals. However, by the late twelfth century their autonomy had been undermined by the growing power of the **Hanseatic League**. Under its influence Visby became one of *the* great cities of medieval Europe, as important as London or Paris, famed for its wealth and stra-

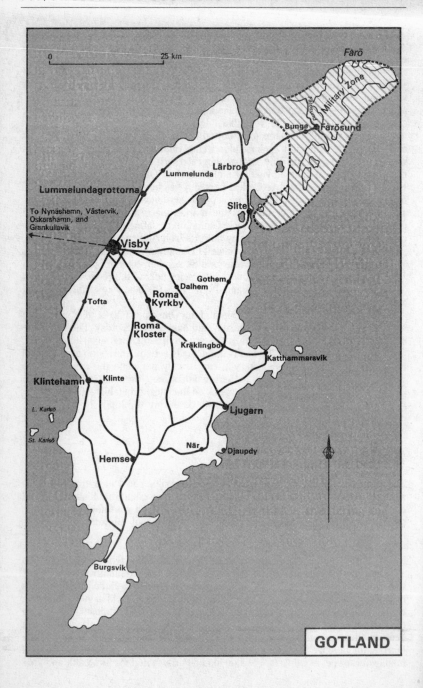

tegic power. A contemporary ballad had it that, "The Gotlanders weigh their gold with twenty pound weights. The pigs eat out of silver troughs and the women spin with golden distaffs".

This romantic notion of the island's prosperity remained popular until this century, when Gotlanders began relying on tourism to prop up the traditional industries of farming, forestry and fishing. Twentieth-century hype makes great play of the beaches and the sun, and with good reason: the roses that give Gotland its tacky *Island of Roses* tag have been known to bloom at Christmas. It's not all just tourist brochure fodder though. Nowhere else in Scandinavia is there such a concentration of unspoilt **medieval country churches**. Built before the end of the fourteenth century, 93 of them are still used, displaying a unique Baltic Gothic style and providing the most permanent reminder of Gotland's ancient wealth.

GETTING THERE: THE FERRIES

Ferries to Gotland are numerous and, in summer, packed, so try and plan well ahead. *Gotlandslinjen*, the ferry line, has booking centres in both Nynäshamn and Oskarshamn. Or, in Stockholm, call into *Gotland City* (☎08/23 61 70) at Kungsgatan 48, which can provide plenty of info and sell advance tickets. One-way **fares** cost 100–130kr during high season (mid-June to mid-Aug), 160kr on Friday, Saturday and Sunday; and there are student discounts (30 percent) on all crossings (except high season). Bicycles go for free. See *Travel Details* for schedules and frequencies.

The nearest port to Stockholm is Nynäshamn which has a useful **youth hostel** (☎0752/158 34), open all year, not far from the railway station.

Visby

Undoubtedly the finest approach to **VISBY** is by ship, seeing the old trading centre as it should be seen – from the sea. The popular summer night boats from the mainland are crammed with backpackers, and it's good to get out on deck for the early sunrise. By 5am the sun is above the city, silhouetting the towers of the cathedral and the old wall turrets. Gliding in on the morning tide, the heady experience is – much as it must have been for thirteenth-century traders – welcoming and reassuring.

Arriving and information

All the huge **ferries** serving Visby dock in the same terminal just outside the city walls and off our map. Just turn left and keep walking for the centre. Alternatively, a short way to the right along the harbour front leads to *Gotlandsresor* at Färjeleden 3, the main **tourist office** (May to mid-June Mon–Fri 8am–5pm; mid-June to mid-Aug Mon–Fri 8am–7pm, Sat & Sun 8am–11pm; rest of the year Mon–Fri 9am–5pm; ☎0498/190 10). There's a second tourist office within the city walls in the seventeenth-century *Burmeister House* in Donnersplats (mid-April to May Mon–Fri 8am–5pm, Sat & Sun noon–6pm; June to mid-Aug Mon–Fri 8am–8pm, Sat & Sun 10am–7pm; mid-Aug to mid-Sept Mon–Fri 8am–5pm, Sat & Sun 10am–4pm; ☎0498/109 82). Both sell the **Gotlands Kortet** (50kr), a pass which gives unlimited bus travel, free museum entry and indoor swimming throughout the island for three days. Otherwise pick up free and useful maps of the city and island.

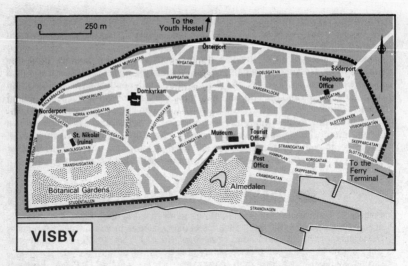

Visby is best walked around. Despite its warren-like first appearance, it's a simple matter to get the hang of the narrow criss-cross cobbled streets. The main square **Storatorget** is signposted from almost everywhere and early arrivals will be rewarded by the smell of freshly baked bread from the square's bakery (open from 5am). Modern Visby has spread beyond the limits defined by its old city walls and today the new town gently sprawls from beyond **Österport** (East Gate), a few minutes' walk up the hill from Storatorget. From here, in **Östercentrum**, the **bus terminal** serves the rest of the island; the tourist office has free timetables .

Getting around: hiring a bike

For getting around the island it's hard to resist the temptation to **hire a bicycle**. Each ferry arrival at Visby is plagued by people hustling bikes, and if you don't have one you might as well succumb here. It's hardly worth shopping around as rentals all seem to cost the same, around 25–30kr a day, cheaper by the week.

CYCLING TIPS

● Gotland is flat but even so cycling can get tiring, and it's worth hiring a slightly more expensive **3-speed** model.

● **Luggage** can usually be left at the rental office, although a few kronor more gets you baskets or bicycle trolleys.

● Most places offer **bike insurance** (around 5kr a day) and the choice is yours: the built-in rear wheel lock should be enough to deter most joyriders, but if you are worried, an extra chain and padlock will do the trick. Be warned though that if your machine goes walkabout when insured, you'll still be liable for the first 150kr. A replacement, on the other hand, will cost about 2000kr.

● Check if you can **return the bike** the morning after the rental runs out. Most rental places are down by the ferry terminals, and it's fairly standard practice to let you keep the bike overnight to ride down to the harbour the next morning. Otherwise early ferry departures mean a long walk from the youth hostel or campsites.

Around the city

Visby is much older than its medieval remnants suggest. The name derives from its status as a Stone Age sacrificial site – "the settlement", *by*, at "the sacred place", *vi* – but it's the medieval trappings that give the city its distinctly Mediterranean air. The magnificent **defensive wall** is the most obvious manifestation of Visby's previous importance, a three-kilometre circuit enclosing the entire settlement. It was hardly a new idea to fortify trading centres against outside attack, although this land wall, thrown up around the end of the thirteenth century, was actually aimed at isolating the city's foreign traders from the island's own locals. Annoyed at seeing all their old trade monopolised, the Gotlanders saw something sinister in the wall's erection and didn't have to wait long to be vindicated. In 1361, during the power struggle between Denmark and Sweden, the Danish king Valdemar III took Gotland by force and advanced on Visby. The burghers and traders, well aware of the wealth of their city, shut the gates and sat through the slaughter outside. Excavations this century revealed the remains of 2000 bodies, more than half of them women, children and invalids. **Valdemar's Cross**, a few hundred metres east of Söderport (South Gate), marks their mass grave. Erected by the survivors of the carnage, it reads factually and pathetically: "In 1361 on the third day after St James the Goths fell into the hands of the Danes. Here they lie. Pray for them."

Back inside the city, the merchants surrendered, and a section of the wall near Söderport was broken down to allow Valdemar to ride through as conqueror. **Valdemar's Breach** is recognisable by its thirteen crenellations representing, so the story goes, the thirteen knights who rode through with the Danish king. Valdemar soon left clutching booty and trade agreements, and Visby continued to prosper while the country stagnated, its people and wealth destroyed.

The old **Hanseatic harbour** at *Almeden* is now a public park and nothing is much more than a few minutes' walk from here. Pretty **Packhusplan**, the oldest square in the city, is bisected by curving Strandgatan which runs southwards to the fragmentary ruins of **Visborg Castle**, overlooking the harbour. Built in the fifteenth century by Erik of Pomerania, it was blown up by the Danes in the seventeenth century. In the opposite direction, northwest, Strandgatan runs towards the sea and the lush **Botanical Gardens**, just beyond which is the **Jungfrutornet** (Maiden's Tower) where a local goldsmith's daughter was walled up alive – reputedly for betraying the city to the Danes. Strandgatan itself is the best place to view the impressive merchants' houses looming over the narrow streets, the store-rooms above living quarters and cellars below. The **Gotlands Fornsal Museum** (mid-May to Aug daily 11am–6pm; rest of the year Tues–Sun noon–4pm; 10kr, students 5kr) is here at Strandgatan 14, and tells the sad tale of the 1361 slaughter. Along with the usual Viking and medieval relics, it also claims the largest collection of painted windows in Scandinavia.

At the height of its power Visby maintained sixteen **churches** and while only one, the Cathedral of St Mary, is still in use, the ruins of eleven others – very often only their towers or foundations – can be seen. The **Domkyrkan** (daily 10am–4pm) was built between 1190 and 1225 and as such, dates from just before the great age of Gothic church building on the island. Used as both warehouse and treasury in the past, it's been heavily restored and about the only original fixture left is the thirteenth-century sandstone font inside. Most striking are its towers, one square at the western front and two slimmer eastern ones, standing sentry over the surrounding buildings. Originally each had spires, but since an eighteenth-century fire they've been crowned with fancy Baroque cupolas, giving them the appearance of inverted ice cream cones.

Seventeenth- and eighteenth-century builders and decorators found the smaller churches in the city to be an excellent source of free limestone, tiles and fittings – which accounts for the fact that most are today in ruins. Best of what's left is the great **St Nicolai ruin**, just down the road from the Domkyrkan, once the largest church in Visby. Destroyed in 1525, its part-Gothic, part-Romanesque shell hosts a mystic pageant opera, the *Petrus de Dacia*, throughout July and the beginning of August. By all accounts, it's a spectacle well worth seeing; tickets (from around 60kr) are available from the tourist office.

As far as main sights go, that's it. Strolling around the streets and walls though, is not something that palls quickly, but when it does head for the water's edge. **Studentallén** is a popular late evening haunt and the sunsets are magnificent – brilliant fiery reds, glinting mirrored waters and bobbing sailing boats in the middle-distance.

Sleeping, eating, drinking

There's a friendly and cheap **youth hostel** (☎0498/169 33), 2km from the centre at Gråbo Torget 7 and open from the end of May to the beginning of August. It's wise to ring ahead at weekends and throughout July, though there always seems to be floor space if you insist. Buses from Östercentrum leave regularly but stop early in the evening. Alternatively, there's a **private hostel**, *Hultmans* (☎0498/184 00), at Söderväg 20 right in the centre. It's not a bad bargain at 80kr per person in two- and three-bedded rooms, 100kr single. The tourist office can book you a **private room** in town, from around 110kr single. And they can also tell you about more upmarket places: there are several **pensions** at around 300-400kr double, but most of them are some way out of town – not that it matters much if you've hired a bike.

Chiefly, though, Gotland is a place for **camping** and *Nordenstrands* (☎0498/121 57) is the closest site, 1km outside the city walls and open from May to September; follow the cycle path that runs through the Botanical Gardens along the sea front. Nearby, and on the same stretch of coast, an unofficial site seems to have appeared, full of mainland youth on extended drinking holidays. After the success of Ulf Lundell's youth culture novel *Jack* (after Kerouac), which extolled the simple pleasure of getting wasted on a beach, Gotland (handy for Stockholmers) became *the* place to go for wild summer parties: this, and other similar sites, distinguishes itself by the number of bikes and empty bottles around. Staying here, the most exercise you will get is cycling to and from the *Systembolaget*.

For **eating**, the usual *Dagens Rätt* deal applies in most restaurants and the centre is small enough to wander around and size up the options. More specifically, **Adelsgatan** is lined with cafés and snack bars and has a couple of cheap kebab take-aways. Best place for sit-down drinking is the café-terrace *Vardklockar*. Strandgatan is the focus of Visby's evening parade. Impeccably dressed Scandinavians mingle with the better off foreign tourists in the bars, restaurants and floral gardens and if you can't afford to eat and drink with them you can at least share the atmosphere. The alternative is an evening on the sea front with a cheap takeout from the liquor store. **Discos** are uniformly expensive, although the *Burmeister* on Strandgatan has free entrance on certain nights. The tourist office can tell you when and how to get to *After Beach*, a bar/club 4km north of Visby, which has free live bands most afternoons in the summer.

Gotlanders enjoy a unique license from the state to brew their own **beer**, the recipe differing from household to household. It's never for sale but summer parties are awash with the stuff – be warned, it is extremely murky and strong.

A few facts

Banks Östercentrum has the largest concentration of branches for changing money.

Cycle route A cycle route circumnavigates almost the entire island, signposted out of Visby.

Ferries Buy tickets down at the terminal buildings.

Market Fruit, veg and souvenirs in Storatorget daily (except Sunday) throughout the summer.

Post Office Main Post Office for *Poste Restante* at Norra Hansegatan 2 (Mon–Fri 9am–6pm, Sat 10am–noon).

Systembolaget In Stora Torget and at Österväg 3. The only other liquor stores on the island are at Hemse, Slite and Klintehamn.

Telephones Make international calls from the Telephone Office on Bredgatan (May–Aug Mon–Fri 8.30am–3.30pm).

Visby Carnival An annual event in the last week of June that features an exuberant Samba school amongst other noisy entertainments.

The rest of the island

There is a real charm to the rest of Gotland – rolling green countryside, forest-lined roads, fine beaches, and small fishing villages. And everywhere churches dominate the rural skyline, the remnants of medieval settlements destroyed in the Danish invasion. It's rather like a detached Cornwall, the best of it being that very few people bother to go and explore. Main roads are surprisingly free of traffic, the back roads positively deserted. Dive down a smaller track whenever possible to get the most out of touring, though if you're biking, some of the unmade tracks and private roads can be a bit hairy.

Thirteen kilometres north of Visby are the **Lummelundagrottarna** (May–Aug daily 9am–4pm; 20kr), limestone caves, stalagmites and stalactites that form a disappointingly dull and damp stop – far better to press on further into the eminently picturesque north, where many of the secluded cottages are summer holiday homes for urban Swedes. In fact so attractive is the country round here that the army has claimed it as its own, and the whole of the peninsula north of LÄRBRO is thus prohibited to foreign tourists. If you're worried about straying into forbidden territory, check with the tourist office in Visby, who arrange special day **bus trips** (from 145kr) to FÅRÖ ("Sheep Island") – its last British visitors were sailors of the Anglo-French squadron stationed during the Crimean War to defend neutral Sweden from the Russian Baltic Fleet. You can, though, go as far as **BUNGE** without special permission and it's worth making the journey to visit its bright fourteenth-century fortified *kyrka* and **open-air museum** (mid-May to mid-Sept daily 10am–6pm; 15kr). Despite (or perhaps because of) its cement factory, **SLITE**, just to the south and open to everyone, has a sandy beach and good swimming. If you want to pay for your camping then the **campsite** (☎0498/208 10), open from May to September, is right on the beach.

The island's marked cycle route heads inland and then south from Slite but stick with the coastal road as far as ÅMINNE, the little village at the mouth of the river Gothemå, where there's another coastal **campsite** (☎0498/340 11), open June to August. A few kilometres away at **DAHLEM** is perhaps the best example of a church in the Gotlandic Gothic style. Its chancel and nave date from the mid-thirteenth century, its steeple a little later; while the interior detail – like the decorative wood carvings on the fourteenth-century choirstalls – is delicate and precise.

For **beaches**, head for the east coast around **LJUGARN**, where the small village is about the closest thing to a resort in Gotland. At the end of the road and overlooking the miniscule harbour is a small **youth hostel** (☎0498/931 84), one of the most comfortable on the island, and open from June to mid-August. At **KATTHAMMARSVIK**, to the north, there's another lengthy sandy beach with jetties, swimming steps and shallow reaches; while a few kilometres away through shaded country lanes is a much bigger hostel at SANDVIKEN. In the unlikely event that either place is crowded, head south towards **NÄR** and then take any of the small private roads to the coast: once by the sea there's little problem finding a place to pitch a tent.

HEMSE is Gotland's second largest town, but still little more than its one main street. Take a quick look at the Romanesque church, and stock up in the relative abundance of shops and supermarkets. From Hemse the main road 141 runs across country to KLINTEHAMN, the last 10km or so through forest, open to the road and offering plenty of camping possibilities.

Stora and Lilla Karlsö

The two offshore islands of **Stora Karlsö** and **Lilla Karlsö** have been declared nature reserves, and both have bird sanctuaries where razorbills, falcons and eider duck breed relatively undisturbed. It's possible to reach the islands on summer cruises from **KLINTEHAMN**: tickets (from the tourist office, mid-June to mid-Aug daily 3–7pm; ☎0498/403 08) are 90kr return to Stora, 60kr return to Lilla Karlsö. The only accommodation is on Stora Karlsö in tiny fishermen's huts – as picturesque as it sounds and, at prices from 40kr a night, an economic way of escaping Gotland's throngs. Book rooms well in advance on ☎0498/ 411 31; any other kind of camping is not allowed on the islands. For beds in Klintehamn itself, the **youth hostel** (☎0498/415 58) is on the edge of the village on route 140. It's open from mid-June to the beginning of August.

travel details

Trains
From Norrköping to Linköping (hourly; 30min); Stockholm (hourly; 2hr); Malmö (two-hourly; 4hr 40min).

From Kalmar to Emmaboda (3–4 daily; 50min); Växjö (3–4 daily; 1hr 30min); Gothenburg (3–4 daily; 5hr) plus more frequent local trains to Emmaboda and Växjö; Stockholm (7 daily; 6hr 30min); Malmö (8 daily; 3hr 40min).

From Oskarshamn to Nässjö (3–4 daily; 2hr 50min); Jönköping (3–4 daily; 3hr 20min); Gothenburg (3–4 daily; 5hr 30min).

For local trains to Västervik, change at Linköping.

Buses
From Norrköping to Löfstad Manor (5–12 daily; 20min); Kolmården Djurpark (4–7 daily; 1hr); Linköping/Jönköping/Gothenburg (2–3 daily; 40min/2hr 30min/5hr); Stockholm (4–7 daily; 2hr); Kalmar (1–3 daily; 3hr 30min–4hr).

From Växjö to Linköping/Norrköping/ Stockholm/Uppsala (Fri & Sun 1 daily; 4hr/4hr 30min/7hr/8hr).

From Kalmar to Lund/Malmö (1 daily; 5hr 45min/6hr 15min); Oskarshamn/Västervik/Stockholm (3–7 daily; 1hr 30min/2hr 30min/7hr); Gothenburg (Fri & Sun 1 daily; 6hr).

Ferries
From Nynäshamn to Visby (mid-June to mid-Aug 2–3 daily; 5hr).
From Oskarshamn to Visby (mid-June to mid-Aug 2 daily; 4hr).
From Västervik to Visby (mid-June to mid-Aug 1 daily; 3hr 30min).

From Grankullavik (Öland) to Visby (1 daily; 3hr).

From May to mid-June and mid-August to mid-September, the Västervik and Grankullavik services don't operate; and the Nynäshamn and Oskarshamn routes are down to 1–2 sailings daily.

Throughout the rest of the year, the only service is between Visby and Nynäshamn or Oskarshamn – usually night boats and much less frequent.

CHAPTER TWELVE

THE BOTHNIAN COAST: GAVLE TO HAPARANDA

Sweden's eastern coast forms one edge of the **Gulf of Bothnia**, a corridor of land that, with its jumble of erstwhile fishing towns and squeaky-clean contemporary urban planning, is quite unlike the rest of the country. Almost the whole of its length is dotted with settlements that reveal a faded history. Some, like **Gävle**, **Hudiksvall** and **Skellefteå** still have their share of old wooden buildings, promoting evocative images of the past, but much was lost during the Russian incursions of the eighteenth century. Today, towns like **Umeå** and **Luleå** are more typical; bright, modern, centres for manufacturing or domestic tourism. You'll hear little about these places – even their tourist offices are decidedly low-key – but it's worth stopping over for a couple of days to sample this distinctive part of Sweden, either as you head north on the long train ride to Kiruna (see next chapter), or after arriving across the Gulf from Finland (see below). It's tempting to stay longer, too, the extensive Bothnian Coast an attractive target for Swedish holiday-makers. Though the weather isn't as reliable as further south, you're guaranteed clean beaches, crystal-clear waters and fine hiking. The only caveat, alarming proof of how far north you're holidaying, is that in 1986 Gävle received one of the highest doses of radiation outside Kiev from the Chernobyl disaster. Picking and eating wild mushrooms and berries is still not a good idea.

Some travel details

The **railway** hugs the coast until just beyond Sundsvall, then moves inland, running all the way to Kiruna and on into Norway. Still, if you're without an *InterRail/Nordtourist* pass, a couple of local **bus** tickets can ease transport costs. In **Västerbotten**, roughly south of Skellefteå to north of Umeå, the *Bussluffakort* (220kr; valid 21 days) gives unlimited county bus travel and a fifty percent discount on the ferry ride to Jakobstad in Finland; as well as being valid on some routes strictly outside the county – Skellefteå–Arvidsjaur and Umeå–Örnköldsvik, for example. A similar offer exists in **Norrbotten** (Luleå northwards) where a seven-day bus ticket costs around 100kr. Both are only available in the summer (mid-June to mid-Aug) and can be bought from bus stations and tourist offices.

One of the Bothnian ports might be your first glimpse of Sweden if you've crossed from Finland **by ferry**. There are regular, year-round, services from several Finnish towns across the Gulf: chiefly Vaasa (Vasa in Swedish) to Umeå, Sundsvall or Örnsköldsvik; Pietarsaari (Jakobstad) to Skellefteå; and Kaskinen (Kaskö) to Gävle. Crossings are most regular in the summer months, journey times between four and eight hours depending on the crossing. **Ticket** details for making the journeys the other way – ie to Finland – are given in the text.

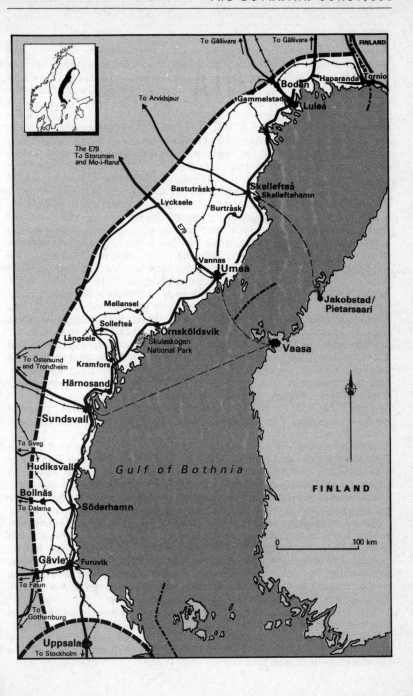

Gävle

It's only two hours north by train from Stockholm to **GÄVLE**, principal city of the county of Gästrikland and communications hub for the west and north. Gävle is an old city, its town charter granted in the mid-fifteenth century, although this knowledge doesn't prepare you for the sophisticated centre: large squares, broad avenues, proud monumental buildings and an inescapable air of solvency. Almost completely rebuilt after a fire in 1869, the layout reflects the heady success of its late-nineteenth-century industry when Gävle was the export centre for the timber and metal produced locally. Only one part of the old town remains and this is the place to head for as soon as the train arrives.

Gamle Gefle escaped much of the fire damage and now tries hard to get away with its description as the authentic old town. Roses climbing around pastel-coloured wooden cottages on narrow cobbled streets conspire to make it all thoroughly likeable, if a bit of a fraud – the juggled alleys now house artists' and craft shops and a café or two. For a more realistic glimpse of social conditions a century ago, visit the **Joe Hill-Gården** (summer daily 10am–3pm; free) at Nedre Bergsgatan 28. Joe Hill, born Joel Hägglund in the house in 1879, emigrated to the United States in 1902, Americanised his name and became a working-class hero – his songs and speeches became rallying cries to comrades in the *International Workers of the World*. But, framed for murder in Salt Lake City, he was executed in 1915. The syndicalist organisation to which he belonged runs the museum, a collection of standard memorabilia – pictures and belongings – given piquancy by the telegram announcing his execution and his last testament.

The heart of Gamle Gefle is bounded at one end by the youth hostel (see below) and at the other by the canalised river that runs through the centre of town. On the canal side at Södra Strandgatan 20 is the **Länsmuseet** (Tues, Thurs & Fri 10am–5pm, Wed 10am–9pm, Sat & Sun 1–5pm; free), a thoughtful county museum that's a cut above the usual fare. Displays concentrate on the role of the ironworks and fisheries in the locality, and the upper two floors contain art collections, in particular the work of local hero *Johan Erik Olson*, whose vivid imagination and naive technique produced some strange child-like paintings.

The modern centre lies over the river, its broad streets and tree-lined avenues designed to prevent fires from spreading. From the sculpture-spiked **Rådhus** up to the theatre, a central slice of parks, trees and fountains neatly splits the city. All the main banks, shops and stores are in the grid of streets on either side of the central avenue, while the roomy **Stortorget**, sporting a phallic monolith, has the usual open-air **market** (Mon–Sat from 9am) worth patronising for fruit and veg.

Gävle's other sights – none of them major – are out of the centre but close enough to reach on foot. Back at the river by the main double bridge **Gävle Slottet**, the seventeenth-century residence of the county governor, lost its ramparts and towers years ago and now lurks behind a row of trees like some minor country house. It's not possible to get in it for a poke around, although with an appointment you can visit the **Fängelmuseet** (Prison Museum: ☎026/ 11 75 59) on the premises; speak to the tourist office if this appeals.

Near here, a footpath along the riverfront leads to a wooden bridge, across which is Kaplansgatan and the **Heliga Trefaldighets Kyrka**, a seventeenth-century church that's a masterpiece of wood-carved decoration. Check out the pulpit, towering altarpiece and screen – each the superb and exact work of a German craftsman, Ewert Friis.

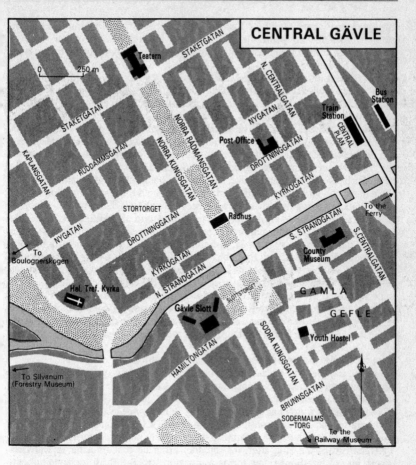

Keep to the path on the south side of the river and a fifteen-minute signposted walk leads to **Silvanum** (daily except Mon 10am–4pm; free) at Kungsbäcksvägen 32, a forestry museum at the edge of the rambling **Boulognerskogen** park. The museum is about as interesting as it sounds, but the park is the place to while away an hour or two, with its marked paths, music pavilions, mini-golf and open-air café.

The one other museum in town is the **Järnvägsmuseet** (June–Aug daily 10am–4pm; Sept–May daily except Mon 1–4pm; 10kr, families 25kr, free with *InterRail* card) at Rälsgatan 1, a #6 bus ride from outside the Rådhus on Norra Kungsgatan. A railway enthusiasts' paradise, it's stuffed to the gills with locomotives and other paraphernalia.

Some practicalities

The **railway station** and **bus station** are at the eastern end of the city and only a few minutes' walk from the centre or Gamle Gefle: if you're thinking of heading south, it's wise to buy bus tickets back to Stockholm in advance. **Ferries** from

Kaskinen in Finland (south of Vaasa) arrive at the harbour behind the railway station: crossings are with the *KG Line* and tickets back the other way, to Finland, cost from 145–175kr depending on the season; departures from Gävle usually at 8.30pm.

The **tourist office** (summer Mon–Fri 9am–8pm, Sat 10am–2pm, Sun noon–4pm; winter Mon–Fri 9am–5pm; ☎026/ 10 16 00) is at Norra Strandgatan 13, off Stortorget. Here, you can pick up free maps and information about fully furnished **apartments** in central Gävle, from 60kr a night per person (plus a 25kr fee), cheaper by the week/month. The **youth hostel** (☎026/12 17 45) is well placed in the old town at Södra Rådmansgatan 1, and is open all year except mid-December to mid-January. Or you might try for a summer price at one of the central **hotels**: the *Hotell Aveny*, Södra Kungsgatan 31 (☎026/11 55 90) should give you a double room for between 400kr and 500kr. **Camping** is not so straightforward, at least in the centre, and late arrivals and rough campers would be best off heading for the large Boulognerskogen park; otherwise, see "Around Gävle", below.

There's a reasonable choice too as far as **food and nightlife** goes. As a rule anywhere around Nygatan and Stortorget is good for basic daily **lunch** offers: for a change, *Bali Garden*, Nygatan 37, is Indonesian while the *Roma* next door does take-away pizzas from 26kr. Early birds can try the café in Centralplan, opposite the railway station (which itself has a good cheap restaurant) – open from 6am for inexpensive breakfasts and endless sandwiches. For buying your own, the *ICA* supermarket in the same square is open daily until 8pm. At **night**, *Café Fontaine*, on the central avenue, Norra Kungsgatan, is a good stop for outside tables, coffee and cheapish beer to a driving disco beat. It has a popular **disco** (Wed–Sun), too; while the *Victoria*, on Norra Strandgatan, has weekly cheap-entry nights.

Around Gävle: Limön and the Furuvik amusement park

From the harbour at Södra Skeppsbron (beyond the railway station) a summer **ferry service** (3 daily; 15kr) operates to the island of **Limön**, part of a small archipelago favoured for its swimming and hiking. The ferry calls at **ENGELTOFTA** which has a youth hostel at Bönavägen 118 (☎026/961 60), open mid-June to mid-August, and a **campsite** (☎026/990 25), open June to August. You can also reach hostel and campsite by bus: #5 to Engeltofta for the hostel and ENGESBERGS, the stop after, for the site. From here, it's not far to **BÖNAN** where an old lighthouse now forms a museum (☎026/991 10 for appointment; free), and plenty more good swimming.

In the other direction, 10km south of Gävle, is **Furuvik amusement park** (mid-May to mid-June & mid- to end Aug daily 10am–4pm; mid-June to mid-Aug daily 10am–6pm; 55kr, includes all rides), with a zoo, fairground, parks and playgrounds – probably the cheapest entertainment in Gävle. Bus #821 leaves every half-hour from the bus station. There are tales of a **campsite** out here too, open mid-May to August, although there must be a strong possibility that it's full to the brim of shrieking children and camper vans.

Söderhamn and Hudiksvall

On the first leg of the journey further into *Norrland* the railway sticks close to the coast, and as onward trains are frequent enough, it's a good idea to break the journey at some of the towns en route. Two in particular would suit a leisurely stop.

Söderhamn

It's easy to see that **SÖDERHAMN** was once much more important than the present town suggests. Founded in 1620 its glory days came several decades later, and the seventeenth-century **Ulrika Eleonora kyrka** that towers over the Rådhus gives hints of the wealth the city once had. Relics from an earlier church that stood on the same spot are kept in the **museum** (June–Aug daily noon–6pm; 5kr), half way up Oxtorgsgatan from the Rådhustorget: once a rifle manufacturing workshop when Söderhamn supplied the weapons that helped Sweden to dominate northern Europe. Look in for an engaging collection of ecclesiastical junk.

Söderhamn itself is a familiar mix of pedestrianised shopping streets and parkland, and it's inviting enough to while away some time at a pavement café. However, the wide open spaces do not give a true impression of the area, as a climb up the white **Oskarsborg tower** (June–Aug daily 9am–9pm; 2kr) will prove. From up here surrounding forests, having hemmed the town in, stretch away as far as the eye can see.

If you're attracted to the town, staying in Söderhamn is unfortunately a bit of a hassle. The *Stadshotellet*, Oxtorgsgatan 17 (☎0270/114 10), is a swanky spot: you're looking at 800kr double, though summer sees the price drop a bit. The nearest **youth hostel** (☎0270/452 33) is 12km away at MOHED, open from June to August. Fairly regular buses from the **bus station** (opposite the railway over the canal) go there – take bus #68 and get off at MOKORSET. There's a **campsite** (☎0270/452 33) at the hostel, too. It's probably best to head back to Gävle (see above) or – better – on to Hudiksvall; both are only an hour away by train.

Hudiksvall

HUDIKSVALL has had its share of excitement over the years. An important commercial and shipping centre, it bore the brunt of the Russian attacks in the early eighteenth century, and to this day its church is pockmarked with cannon holes. The old preserved buildings – the most interesting part of the city – split into two main sections. From the railway station walk to the right, crossing the small canal, and the old **harbour** is on the right. Bounded by a couple of wooden bridges the wharfside is flanked by a line of fishermen's cottages and storehouses, all leaning into the water, boats moored up outside. These days the delicately picturesque fronts hide a run of bike and boat repair shops, handicraft studios and the like. There's a **tourist office** (mid-June to mid-Aug Mon–Fri 9am–7pm, Sat 10am–6pm, Sun noon–6pm; rest of the year Mon–Fri 9am–4pm; ☎0650/139 20) close by, over the railway tracks and overlooking the water, which hands out free maps of the town.

The other part, **Fiskarstan** (Fishermen's Town), is the area beyond the *Stadshotellet*, further down Storgatan, which contains neat examples of the so-called "Imperial" wood-panel architecture of the late eighteenth and nineteenth centuries. It's a tightly knit block of streets lined with beautiful wooden houses, now privately owned by Hudiksvall's comfortably off. Take a peek inside some of the little courtyards, all window boxes and cobblestones, for an idea of what gentrification Swedish-style looks like. The history of the buildings is placed in perspective in the excellent **Hälsingland Museum** (mid-June to mid-Aug Mon–

Fri 9am–7pm, Sat & Sun 10am–4pm; rest of the year Mon–Fri 9am–4pm, Sat & Sun noon–4pm; free) on Storgatan, which traces the development of Hudiksvall as a harbour town since its foundation in 1582. Have a look at the paintings of **John Sten** upstairs – born near Hudiksvall, his work weirdly veered from Cubism to a fanciful, more decorative style.

The best time to visit Hudiksvall is the first couple of weeks in July when the town hosts the **Musik vid Dellen**, a multifarious cultural festival in and out of town, in and out of doors; information and tickets for events from the tourist office.

Hudiksvall practicalities

If you want to break the journey, Hudiksvall is as good a place as any on the coast, an enjoyable stop. There's a cheapish **hotel**, the *Hotell Hälsingegården*, Storgatan 49 (☎0650/102 65), where doubles go for around 400kr. But it's worth making every effort to stay in the **youth hostel** (☎0650/150 60), a bargain not to be bettered throughout Sweden: between mid-June and mid-August it's sited in *Stadshotellet*, the swishest hotel in town, at Storgatan 36. Those with a valid hostel card can stay in a single or double room – each has bathroom, TV, and video – for the standard youth hostel price while everyone else pays around 800kr. You can also use the swimming pool and get a gourmet breakfast for around 30kr, so – not surprisingly – it is essential to ring ahead and reserve a bed. If you are perverse enough to want to **camp** in the face of all this opulence, the nearest site is at MALNBADEN (☎0650/113 26), 3km to the east of town.

One place to **drink** is the *Bacchus* in the *Hantverksgården* building on Brunnsgatan (off Storgatan, beyond *Stadshotellet*) which has a terrace overlooking the water. Free to get in, the café is generally open until 10pm, Saturday until 3am, with a music bar on Tuesday in winter until midnight.

Sundsvall

Known as the "Stone City", **SUNDSVALL** is immediately and obviously different. Once home to a rapidly expanding nineteenth-century sawmill industry, the whole city burned down in 1888 and a new centre built completely of stone emerged within ten years. The result is a living document of turn-of-the-century urban architecture, designed and crafted by architects who were engaged in rebuilding Stockholm's residential areas at the same time. Their work – 573 residential buildings in four years – was achieved at a price. The workers who had laboured on the stone buildings were shifted from their old homes in the centre, victims of their own success in refurbishing the city. Moved out south to a poorly-serviced suburb, the glaring contrast between the wealth of the new centre and the local poverty was only too obvious. Selma Lagerlöf in *The Wonderful Adventures of Nil* remarked of Sundsvall, "Around the stone city there was an empty space, and then a wreath of wooden houses lying peacefully and happily in small gardens, but they seemed to know that they could not compete with the stone houses and did not dare to get near to them."

The sheer scale of the rebuilding is clear as you walk in from the railway station. The style is simple, uncluttered limestone and brick, the size often overwhelming. Most of the buildings were offices as well as residences and the four-

and five-storey houses are palatial structures. The **Esplanaden**, a wide central avenue, cuts the grid in two, itself crossed by **Storgatan**, the widest street, and a succession of smaller roads. The design guaranteed space in the centre of town and the area around **Stortorget** is still the roomy shopping and commercial centre that was envisaged.

Several of the buildings in the centre are worth a second look, not least the mock-Baroque exterior of the **Sundsvall Museum** (summer daily 11am–4pm; winter Mon–Fri 11am–5pm, Tues & Thurs until 8pm, Sat & Sun 11am–4pm; free) which, inside, rates not much more than a gallop through its permanent art exhibition. The **Gustav Adolfs Kyrkan** (June–Aug daily 11am–4pm; Sept–May daily 11am–2pm) marks one end of the new town, a soaring red-brick structure whose interior looks like a large Lego set. At the other end, down by the harbour, massive warehouses on either side of Magasinsgatan have been converted into a cultural centre.

Beyond the city's design, the most attractive diversion is the tiring three-kilometre climb to the heights of **Gaffelbyn** and the **Medelpads Fornminnesförening** (summer daily 9am–7pm; winter Mon–Fri 10am–4pm, Sat & Sun 11am–4pm free), an open-air handicrafts museum. Walk up Storgatan, cross over the main bridge and follow the sign to the youth hostel (see below), up a steep path on the left; the museum is just beyond the hostel. It's a throwaway though likeable collection of arts and crafts, more like a jumble sale than a museum: tropical butterflies, stuffed boa constrictors and a grass skirt or two brought back by local sailors. Head further up the road to the restaurant and the views are fantastic, both from the terrace (free) and the viewing tower (ask in the restaurant, small charge). It's this sort of aerial perspective that assists appreciation of the planned city below.

Staying on in Sundsvall

From the **railway station** the centre is five minutes' walk away, with the helpful **tourist office** (June–Aug daily 7am–7pm; rest of the year Mon–Fri 9am–5pm; ☎060/11 42 35) in the main square, Stortorget: collect a free map and plenty of advice on the surrounding area. The **bus station** is at the bottom of Esplanaden, though if you want advance tickets for the bus to Stockholm (Fri & Sun only; 90kr), visit *Y-Buss* (☎060/17 19 60) at Trädgårdsgatan 13.

The **youth hostel** (☎060/11 21 19) is a cheap and grotty camping/cabin affair at Norra Stadsberget, the mountain overlooking the city. It would be only marginally more expensive to stay at the *YMCA InterRail Point* **hostel** (☎060/11 35 35) right in town at Kyrkogatan 29 near the church, although it's only open from mid-July to mid-August. Small, it offers free showers, a kitchen, a gym and a cheap breakfast. It's more likely that you're going to have to splash out on a **hotel** if you want to stay: surprisingly, there's a fair amount of choice. The *Hotel Ritz*, Esplanaden 4 (☎060/15 08 60) has rooms from around 400kr double, and *Hotell Wega*, Tullgata 6 (☎060/11 35 27) goes for around the same price. Ask at the tourist office about special summer prices elsewhere.

For **eating**, Storgatan is lined with pizza places and restaurants, most offering daily lunch menus. The best is *Stallet*, at the harbour end, which boldly claims 85 different pizzas: at lunchtime, a huge pizza, salad, bread, beer and coffee shouldn't come to more than 40kr. *Bake-Off Brödbutik* next to the town museum has the cheapest coffee and cakes, and fresh fruit and veg is best from the **market** (Mon–Sat from 8am) in Stortorget.

Moving on

When you come to leave Sundsvall, there's a ferry service across the Gulf of Bothnia to Vaasa in Finland. Tickets run from 115–175kr one-way, depending on the season, (fifty percent student discount outside summer season) and can be bought from *Resespecialisterna* in Stortorget or from the ferry office on the harbour front. Departures are generally in the late afternoon or evening (daily at 9pm in summer).

Inland: to Sollefteå and around

From Sundsvall the train turns inland, running up the coast only as far as HÄRNÖSAND, another sixteenth-century market town with a scattering of preserved wooden houses. From here it's a slow 80km northwest to SOLLEFTEÅ, set in a beautiful position on the banks of the Ångerman River.

Sollefteå

SOLLEFTEÅ is appealingly peaceful, little more than one main pedestrianised street, Storgatan, with a park and gardens. In truth, there's nothing much to do, save wander through its pretty surroundings, but you might want to stretch your legs for an hour or two. It's an easy stroll to the single attraction, the unassuming Sollefteå kyrka (summer daily 7am–4.30pm; winter 8am–dusk), on a small hill overlooking the river just outside town. The eighteenth-century church encompasses bits of the original medieval building within its shell; the separate wedding-cake bell tower is a later addition. Across the main road, the curious Regiment Museum (Mon–Fri noon–3pm; July daily noon–3pm & Tues 6–8pm; free) contains, amongst other more mundane exhibits, a stuffed regimental horse.

If the tourist office (June to mid-Aug Mon–Fri 9am–7pm, Sat 10am–3pm, Sun noon–6pm; rest of the year Mon–Fri 8am–4pm) on Storgatan is to be believed, Father Christmas lives in Sollefteå (as well as in a thousand and one other Scandinavian towns) and you can apparently visit his workshop in REMSLE (ring ☎0620/113 79 for an appointment), just outside town.

If you're looking for somewhere to spend the night, the campsite (☎0620/173 70) right by the river is pleasant enough. It's open all year and has four-bedded cabins for 150kr.

Österås, Långsele and Bräcke

You're more likely to want to stick around if you're aiming for nearby ÖSTERÅS, 8km from Sollefteå and surrounded by foresty peace and quiet. There's a youth hostel (☎0620/231 55) here – and the trip is worthwhile, if only to stay at the hostel itself, a vegan-run haven of stripped pine, potted plants and window-boxes. There is a bus from Sollefteå, but only at noon and 4pm (Mon–Sat); other than this, walking or hitching is the most reliable method – take the Östersund road (E87) and Österås is signposted to the right after 2km. Otherwise you could get off the train at LÅNGSELE, the mainline junction, and hitch the 8km to Österås from there.

From Långsele the northern Swedish rail system opens out. Southwest, trains run to **BRÄCKE**, where there is a **youth hostel** (☎0693/105 05) in the *Hotell Jämtkrogen*, open from mid-June to mid-August, but precious little else. The choice is then west to Östersund (see p.423) and ultimately western Norway, or south to Gävle and into Dalarna.

The Coastal Route North: Örnsköldsvik and around

Northeast from Långsele the railway line still runs well inland, parallel to the **coastal (E4) road**. This is the major route north from Stockholm to Kiruna, and one which you'd do well to make a stopover on since it's a long slog: several branch lines down to the coast help break up the route.

Örnsköldsvik

At MELLANSEL the only reason to get off would be to take the local train down to the port of **ÖRNSKÖLDSVIK** (usually shortened to Övik). It's a fine base for some local hiking and camping (see below), and though there's only one thing to see in town, that alone is worth the effort. The **museum** (Tues & Wed 11am–8pm, Thurs–Sun 11am–4pm; free) is a surprising revelation for such a one-horse town. Ignore the typical collections of prehistoric finds and nineteenth-century furniture and get them to let you into the adjacent workshop, which conceals a sparkling documentation of the work of **Bror Marklund**, born locally. Most of his art was commissioned by public bodies and goes unnoticed by travellers who brush against it all the time: his *Thalia*, the goddess of the theatre, rests outside the City Theatre in Malmö, and his figures adorn the facade of the Historical Museum in Stockholm. Inside the workshop, look for the jester plaster casts, brilliantly executed and one of Marklund's most easily identifiable motifs.

From Övik, it's easy to get out into the archipelago and camp on the **islands** nearby. A **ferry** leaves three times weekly to TRYSUNDA (1hr 30min; around 50kr return) and once weekly to ULVÖN (2hr 30min; around 80kr return); on the latter rooms can be rented at the old Ulvö school in SÖRBYN (☎0660/881 22). Alternatively, the **Höga Kusten** trail runs from Övik, a 130km "High Coastline" path that takes in the magnificent **Skuleskogen** national park. You can hike out to the park, 20km from town, or cut the journey by bussing it to NÄSKE and walking from there. Once in the park you can only camp in the permitted areas.

Övik practicalities

Coming to Övik will probably mean at least a night's stay, since connections back to the main line aren't that frequent. There's a **youth hostel** (☎0660/880 00), open from the end of June to the beginning of August, a couple of kilometres up the hill beyond the white museum in the town centre. Övik's **tourist office** (June to mid-Aug Mon–Fri 9am–8pm, Sat & Sun 10am–7pm; ☎0660/125 37) in a hut on the E4 roundabout – follow the main road from the station to the centre – will supply the usual facilities and has **ferry service** details to Vaasa in Finland. Basically it runs three times a week, out of summer season, and costs 95–140kr one-way.

Vännäs and routes west and east

Back on the main train line, if Övik is a one-horse town then in **VÄNNÄS** even the horse has bolted. If it's at all avoidable, don't spend the night here in the **youth hostel** (☎0935/123 50), as there's absolutely nothing to do. The **E79 road** runs through the village, to LYCKSELE and STORUMAN in the northwest of Sweden, so hitching that way is one possibility: at Storuman you're on the Inlandsbanan route, the very scenic inland railway (see p.416). The best solution, though, is to take the branch line east to the lively university town of UMEÅ, a half-hour's journey away.

Umeå

There is a young feel to **UMEÅ**, borne out by a stroll around the airy modern centre. Those who aren't in pushchairs are pushing them, and the ice cream bars and cafés are packed with teenagers. Demographically, it's one of Sweden's most youthful towns, and the addition of the country's newest university means that there is more than usual to get to grips with. It's a town, above all, to rest up in – a couple of days would not be too long to spend here.

It's best to start your wanderings down at the river in front of the **Rådhus**. The little park and the lingering bits of turn-of-the-century timber architecture look out over the water responsible for the town's name. "Uma" means "roar" and refers to the sound of the river's rapids, now converted into hydroelectric power further upstream. If you've got a bike (see below for rental), it's a gentle day's work to cycle the river's length to NORRFORS and its 3000-year-old rock carvings. Back down the other side, the cycle path leads past the hydroelectric station. The 35km route is shown on a free *Umeåleden* map from the tourist office.

As well as the accommodating ambience in town, Umeå also has one terrific museum complex, **Gammlia**, which merits a good half-day's attention. The original attraction around which everything else developed is the **Friluftsmuseum** (daily 11am–5pm; free), an open-air group of twenty regional buildings, the oldest the seventeenth-century gatehouse on the way in. The indoor **Västerbotten Museum** (summer Mon–Fri 9am–6pm, Sat & Sun noon–6pm; winter Mon–Fri 9am–4pm, Sat & Sun noon–4pm; free) houses the main collection: three basic exhibitions which canter through regional history, from prehistory to the Industrial Revolution. It's all good stuff, well laid out and complemented by an array of videos and recordings, with a useful English guidebook available for 3kr. Linked to the Västerbotten Museum is the **Bildmuseum** (summer Tues–Sun noon–6pm; winter Tues–Sat noon–4pm, Sun noon–5pm; free) the university art collection, which highlights contemporary Swedish work and a cobbled-together set of old masters. Back outside, the regional history continues in a separate **Maritime Museum** (daily 11am–5pm; free), a small hall clogged with fishing boats.

Umeå practicalities

The **tourist office** (summer Mon–Fri 8am–8pm, Sat 9.30am–5pm, Sun noon–4pm; winter Mon–Fri 8am–5pm; ☎090/16 16 16) in Renmarkstorget is a friendly place and dishes out free maps. You can also buy a **24-hour bus ticket** (15kr), valid on all the local buses which leave from Vasaplan. Or **rent a bike** from the bicycle shop in Rådhustorget: it's very cheap. English-language **newspapers** can be found at the *Stadsbiblioteket* at Rådhusesplanaden 6, and *Telebutiken* at Rådhusesplanaden 3 is the place to make **international phone calls** (Mon–Fri 9.30am–5pm).

The **youth hostel** (☎090/19 43 00) is a 45-minute walk from the railway station, in the *Hotell Åliden* out near the student campus at ÅLIDHEM; open June to August, the facilities are excellent and buses #1, #2 and #61 go past. Ålidhems Centrum behind the hostel has a bank, supermarket, bar and take-away pizza joint. The tourist office meanwhile, will book you into more central beds in a **private room** – from 60–75kr a night. The **campsite** (☎090/16 16 60) at NYDALA is 5km out of town on the E4; open all year it has some very cheap *Trätält* (tiny four-bedded cottages; around 100kr/night), washing machines, a lake and cycle hire; bus #2 goes past.

Wining and dining possibilities are increased by the number of students in town, and there's a wide choice of venues. *Ahlens* do a good daily lunch, while *Oasen* at Kungsgatan 69 is a salad bar, and is extremely good value – salad, crispbread, beer and coffee for around 40kr. For snacks try the café in the *Stadsbiblioteket* or one of the kebab stalls all over the pedestrian centre. At the *Konditori Mekka* at Rådhusesplanaden 17 near the railway station the pastries are delicious and coffee refills are free. Market food – fruit and veg – comes from Rådhustorget in front of the Rådhus.

Nightlife is almost exclusively student orientated. The university campus hosts discos in the union building (*Universum*) at weekends in the winter, Sunday only in the summer; around 50kr entrance. In the **Ålidhem Centrum**, behind the youth hostel, the *Krogen* is inordinately popular; a pub/disco during

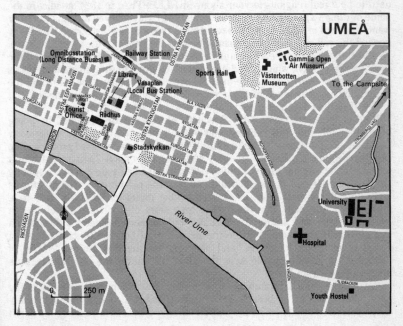

the week (free Tuesday), and a nightclub at the weekends. In town, *Scharinska Villan* on Storgatan, near the church, has a disco/pub at the weekends, free with a student card. Check all these nights and events with the university (switchboard ☎090/16 50 00) or the tourist office, which has an unusually good idea of what's going on. Locals haunt the *Kafé Pastell* in Renmarkstorget, a more expensive joint with a pavement section in summer.

Leaving Umeå

Inter-city **buses** leave from the *Omnibusstation* in Järnvägstorget. **Ferries** and **catamarans** to Vaasa in Finland depart all year from Umeå harbour. The bus marked *Vasabåta* leaves from the local bus station at Vasaplan for the harbour 45 minutes before departure. Ferry prices vary but outside high season (end of June to mid-Aug) you'll save a lot of money by travelling Monday to Thursday. Otherwise the crossing is around 95–140kr one-way, with a special discount rate valid only on the last ferry of the night, arriving in Vaasa at 2am; *InterRail/ Nordturist* and *YIEE or FIYTO* card holders qualify for a fifty percent discount on the standard price. **Tickets** and more information from *Vasabåtarna* at Renmarkstorget 7.

Skellefteå

"In the centre of the plain was Skellefteå church, the largest and most beautiful building in the entire north of Sweden, rising like a Palmyra's temple out of the desert", enthused the nineteenth-century traveller Leopold von Buch. For there used to be a real religious fervour about **SKELLEFTEÅ**. In 1324 an edict in the name of King Magnus Eriksson invited "all those who believed in Jesus Christ or wanted to turn to Him" to settle between the rivers of Skellefteå and Ule. Many heeded the call and parishes mushroomed on the banks of the river Skellefteå. By the end of the eighteenth century a devout township was centred around the monumental church, which stood out in stark contrast to the surrounding plains and wide river. Nowadays, more material occupations support the town, and the tourist office makes much of modern Skellefteå's gold and silver refineries. But it's the church and its preserved village that still attract the attention.

Both of these are part of the **Nordanå Kulturcentrum**, reached by going down the hill from the **railway station** and then a five-minute walk along Storgatan or Strandgatan. There's a theatre and café, a twee period grocer's shop (*Lånthandel*) and a **museum** (roughly May–Aug daily noon–7pm; free). It's best to come in the evening when all this is closed and the paths are clear for a solitary stroll. At the far end of the museum complex the old **church village** spreads away up a dusty main drag, overlooked by the proud **kyrka** (daily 8am–4pm; mid-June to Aug daily 8am–8pm). The long rows of wooden cottages are an evocative sight, and during the daytime you can peek inside. It's the church though that is the magnet: inside the neo-Classical building is an outstanding series of medieval sculptures, and look too for the 800-year-old "Virgin of Skellefteå", a walnut carving near the altar; it's one of the few Romanesque images of the Virgin Mary.

Beyond the church, Strandpromenaden runs away along the north side of the river, interrupted by barbecues and grassy stretches. Crossing the eighteenth-century wooden bridge below the church takes you back to town along the south bank. The path is narrow and overgrown in parts, but it snakes all the way back to Parksbron past the occasional boat and silent fisherman. On **Långholmen**, one of the tiny islands between the old bridge and Parksbron, there's a café, and it would be a splendid day out on the slow river, pulling up at one of the leafy picnic spots. Hire **rowing boats** (30kr per hr, 150kr for 6hr) down at the riverside immediately below the City Park in town – available from 11am to 6pm.

Practical details

For all its contemporary go-ahead industry, largely computers and electronics, modern Skellefteå is quiet and retiring. The small centre is plum between the railway and the river and based around a modern paved square, at the top of which is the **bus station**. One block up from the water at Storgatan 46, the **tourist office** (mid-June to mid-Aug Mon–Fri 8am–8pm, Sat 9am–6pm, Sun 10am–4pm; rest of the year Mon–Fri 8am–4pm, Sat 9am–2pm; ☎0910/588 80) has toilets and all day *MTV* broadcasts as well as the usual facilities.

The **youth hostel** (☎0910/372 83) is well worth seeking out too, large Swiss chalets in a beautiful setting, half an hour's walk from the centre. From the station, go down and left along Strandgatan, cross the bridge and walk to the left along Tubölegatan: keep to the gravel path rather than the main road and the hostel, open mid-June to mid-August, is on the left. If this is full, a second tiny **hostel** (☎0914/109 44) at BURTRÄSK might have room: it's open mid-May to August and is 45 minutes away by bus #21 (3 daily Mon–Fri, 2 at weekends). In town, the *Stiftsgården* **hotel**, Brännavägen 25 (☎0910/772 72), is a reasonable 285kr double. For **campers** *Skellefteå Campingplats* (☎0910/188 55) is 1500m north of the railway station just off the E4. Cheapest **lunch** deals are in the *Arken Café*, Stationsgatan 18 and *Rimini Hämtpizza* on Skeppargatan.

Onwards from Skellefteå

Moving on throws up several possibilities. To get back to the main **train** line north, you'll have to nip back up the line to BÅSTUTRÄSK. **Buses** run to BODØ in Norway every Monday and Friday calling at ARVIDSJAUR; while special summer deals offer return trips to Umeå or LULEÅ for around 100kr.

Ferries connect the town with Pietarsaari (Jakobstad) and Kokkola in **Finland**, services running from May to October. There are several daily crossings in high season, the fare around 120kr (cheaper before mid-June and after mid-Aug). The harbour is east of the town centre and trains run there, to **Skelleftehamns övre**, the end of the line. More information on all these services, and tickets, from *Resespecialisterna* at Torget 4.

Boden and Luleå

BODEN is a bit like Crewe: an extremely large railway junction whose station is generally full of dozing bodies and stacked rucksacks. Venture out of the station doors and the similarity ends – the town is a pleasant surprise, and worth exploring if you've time to kill.

The green and open centre lies split by the river. Over the water and to the right is the **church**, around which the town grew up, cottages, stables and streets spreading down the hill to the river. About twenty of the houses remain and are rented out as superior **hostel** accommodation during the summer. It costs 145kr

for three beds (165kr in July) and the **tourist office**, next to the church
(June–Aug Mon–Fri 9am–8pm, Sat 10am–5pm, Sun 10am–8pm) can supply you
with full details. The **campsite** is a couple of minutes' walk from the church on
the water's edge and it's here that **canoes** go cheaply – 10kr an hour – for a
paddle around the gardens and woods of town, really the best way of seeing
Boden.

Luleå

Off the main line and 25 minutes away, LULEÅ is a pleasant diversion but hardly
merits the big sell of the free city guide; ". . . the town in the north with the
medieval cathedral from where education and Christianity were spread into the
heathen darkness of an Arctic province." The medieval **Domkyrkan** went centuries ago and the latest model, built in 1893, is a modern barrage of copper chandeliers hanging like Christmas decorations. Still, there's enough elsewhere – not
least a couple of good **beaches** – to make it worth giving Luleå half a day's
attention.

Though nothing special – a standard county museum – it's worth dropping into
the **Norrbottens Museum** (Mon 1–5pm, Tues–Fri 9am–4pm, Sat & Sun noon–
4pm; free), at Storgatan 2, as it gives a first glimpse of the *Same* life and culture
that begins to predominate northwest of Luleå (see the next chapter). If the
weather's good, the next stop after the museum should be **Gültzauudden**, a
wooded promontory with a great beach – it's where the rest of Luleå will be.
When the locals have deserted the beach for the nightlife along pedestrianised
Storgatan, sleeping rough here shouldn't be too difficult either.

Luleå practicalities

From the **railway station** the centre is a few minutes' walk up Storgatan. Past the
cathedral and across the green Rådhustorget, the **tourist office** (summer Mon–
Fri 9am–5pm; winter Mon–Fri 8am–4pm; ☎0920/937 46) at Rådstugatan 9 has
maps and **bike rental** (20kr per day, 100kr deposit). They'll also have info on
Luleå's **carnival** at the end of July/beginning of August: four days of music, dancing and street theatre centred around the open-air pavilion on Storgatan.

You might want to stay in order to take in GAMMELSTAD (see below) on a
day trip, in which case there is a **youth hostel** (☎0920/932 64), 25 minutes' walk
away at Bergviken on Ytterviksvägen. It's open mid-June to mid-August and a
campsite shares the same stretch of land.

Not surprisingly Luleå is livelier in the winter when the students are around:
try the small theatre *Lillian* behind the library for concerts, café and entertainment. But plain **eating and drinking** is not bad in the summer. Storgatan has a
selection of lunch deals in its restaurants and cafés; *Två rum och kök* at number
47 does a daily vegetarian meal. Cheapest and most filling is *La Marmite* at
Magasinsgatan 5, with hefty pizzas. Summer **clubbing** is done at the *Roxy*, live
bands and disco in the *Stadshotellet* on Storgatan.

Gammelstad

The original settlement of Luleå grew up around the medieval church at
GAMMELSTAD, 10km west of the modern city. An expanding shipping trade
soon outgrew the harbour and the whole town was shifted by royal command in

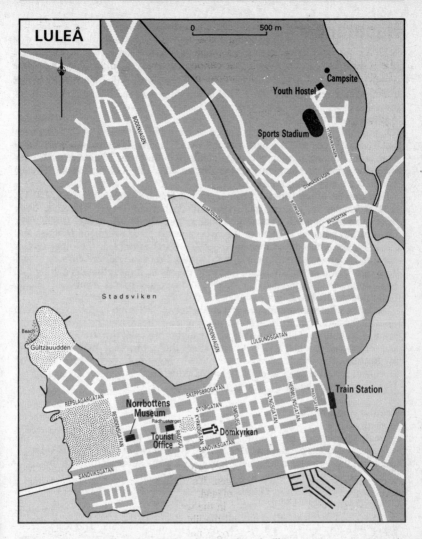

1649 to its present location. Today the abandoned village supports an **open-air museum** (mid-June to mid-Aug daily noon–4pm; free) on the land around the church. The **kyrka** itself (June & July daily 9am–8pm; Aug daily 9am–6pm) dates from the end of the fifteenth century, and its choir stalls and ornate triptych are fine medieval originals. The tourist office, located in one of the village's cottages, organises guided walks around the site.

The train speeds past Gammelstad's mostly disused station on its way in and out of Luleå, and a **bus** is the easiest approach to the village. Bus #32 leaves every hour from Rådhustorget (Storgatan), the last one back at 9.30pm (11kr; 30min).

Haparanda

Hard by the Finnish border and at the very north of the Gulf of Bothnia, **HAPARANDA**, a morgue-like town, is hard to like. The **railway station** sets the scene, a grand looking building that reflects Haparanda's aspirations to be a major trading centre after World War I. That never happened, and hiking up the streets towards Torget in the centre, the town gets less impressive.

What gives the town at least some character is its proximity to Finland. Haparanda is the main transit point for motor traffic between the two countries and TORNIO (see p.531) is just over the river. Haparanda's inhabitants are bilingual, and both sets of money change hands in both towns. There are no border formalities, and sleeping in cheaper Haparanda, and looking around livelier Tornio is a happy compromise.

The **tourist office** (Mon–Fri 8am–7pm, Sat & Sun 10am–2pm; ☎0922/150 45) is at Storgatan 92, a short walk right and up beyond Torget. They can book **private rooms** in town from around 50kr single. The **youth hostel** (☎0992/111 71) is at Strandgatan 18, next to the river, a smart place with good facilities and cheap meals; while the **campsite** (☎0992/118 01) is right at the other end of town and a fair way from the bridge to Tornio. From the railway, turn right and then right again down Storgatan, following the signs. If everything is getting full, *Simolins Rum* at Storgatan 65b (☎0992/120 68) has rooms from 80kr single, 160kr double, 180kr for four beds.

As far as **entertainment** goes you are better off in Tornio in every respect. Do what all the Swedish locals do at the weekends and head over the river where the drink is plentiful and cheaper. Late Friday nights are wild, the streets full of tired and emotional people trying to negotiate the return leg over the bridge. Meanwhile, Haparanda sleeps undisturbed. For **food**, the *Domus* store on Storgatan has the cheapest daily menu while the *Pizzeria Leilani*, Köpmansgatan 15, is that strange beast, a Chinese pizza parlour.

Around Haparanda

Haparanda is a handy base for several side trips.

Seskarö island is 24km south of town, a beachy haven for windsurfers and swimmers. There's a **campsite** (☎0992/201 50) and **cabins** (☎0992/202 15) available. The tourist office runs a **boat trip** (50kr) every summer through the archipelago and the price includes food at a grill party on an island on the way.

North of town, 15km away, **KUKKOLAFORSEN** hosts a "Whitefish Festival" (*Sikfesten*) on the last weekend of July. The whitefish, a local delicacy grilled on large open fires, are caught in nets at the end of long poles. Fishermen dredge the fast, white water, and scoop the whitefish out onto the bank. The festival celebrates a sort of fishermen's harvest, centuries old, although now largely an excuse to get plastered. Beer tent, evening gigs, dancing and heavy drinking are the order of the day. It'll cost around 50kr to get in, although if staying at the adjacent **campsite** (☎0992/310 20), which has cabins as well as cheap tent space, you can wander at will. At other times, check out the local **museum** (daily 8am–10pm; free) and freshwater aquarium; working nineteenth-century mills and enormous salmon.

More excitement is to be had out on the river. Try **river rafting** in the Kukkola rapids. 60kr hires the gear – helmet and life-jacket specifically – and pays for a short trip down river plus a certificate at the end. Ask at the tourist office in Haparanda or at Kukkolaforsen campsite.

travel details

Trains

From Gävle to Söderhamn (6–8 daily; 50min); Hudiksvall (6–8 daily; 1hr 45min); Sundsvall (6–8 daily; 2hr 50min; with 3–4 daily continuing to Sollefteå in 5hr 40min and Långsele in 5hr 50min; and 3 daily direct to Långsele in 5hr 30min); Uppsala/Stockholm (hourly; 1hr/2hr); Malmö (3–6 daily; 9–10hr); Östersund (6 daily; 4hr; with 2 daily continuing to Trondheim).

From Stockholm to Narvik via Gävle, Bräcke, Långsele, Mellansel (for Övik), Vännäs (for Umeå), Bastuträsk (for Skellefteå), Boden (for Haparanda), Gällivare and Kiruna (2–3 daily; 2hr/6hr/6hr 30min/8hr 30min/10hr 30min/12hr/14hr/26hr/33hr).

Buses

From Gävle to Gothenburg (2 daily; 9hr); Stockholm (Fri, Sat & Sun 1 daily; 2hr 20min); Sundsvall/Bräcke/Östersund (Sun 1 daily; 4hr/5hr 20min/6hr 20min); Söderhamn/Hudiksvall/Sundsvall/Sollefteå/Örnsköldsvik (Fri 2, Sat 1, Sun 1 daily; 1hr/2hr/3hr 30min/5hr 30min/6hr); Umeå/Skellefteå/Luleå (Fri & Sun 1 daily; 7hr 30min/9hr/11hr)

Coastal services: in addition, services between the major coastal towns (Sundsvall, Umeå, Skellefteå and Luleå) are good, frequent and complex. The most important ones are mentioned in the text and all the others in copious timetables that you can get from any local tourist office. For all long distance rides, it's wise to buy tickets in advance from travel agencies or the bus stations.

Other services: the east coast is also a major route into Norway (to Mo-i-Rana from Umeå) and Swedish Lappland (to Arvidsjaur from Skellefteå and to Jokkmokk from Luleå/Boden).

Ferries to Finland

From Gävle to Kaskinen (mid-June to mid-Aug 1 daily; rest of the year 5 weekly; 10hr).

From Sundsvall to Vaasa (June–Aug 1 daily; rest of the year 5 weekly; 8hr).

From Örnsköldsvik to Vaasa (May to mid-June & mid-Aug to Oct 3 weekly; 5hr).

From Umeå to Vaasa (ferry mid-June to mid-Aug 3 daily, rest of the year 1–2 daily; 4hr: catamaran 2–3 daily; 2hr 15min).

From Luleå to Jakobstad and Kokkola (May–Oct several daily; 4hr).

CENTRAL AND NORTHERN SWEDEN

n many ways, the long wedge of land that comprises **central and northern Sweden** – from the northern shores of Lake Vänern to the Norwegian border – encompasses all that is most popular and typical of the country. Rural and underpopulated counties without exception, this is Sweden as seen in the brochures: lakes, holiday cottages, forests and reindeer. And these images are true enough. The Swedes have always lived like this here, from the people of the central lands and forests who were the first to rise against the Danes in the sixteenth century; to the *Same* and their deer, earliest settlers of the wild lands further north.

Folklorish **Dalarna** county is the most intensely picturesque region. Even a quick tour around one or two of the more accessible places gives an impression of the whole: red cottages, sweeping green countryside, summer festivals and water bluer than blue. Dalarna's inhabitants maintain a cultural heritage (echoed in contemporary handicrafts and traditions) that goes back to the Middle Ages. And the county is *the* place in which to spend midsummer, particularly Midsummer's Night, when the whole region erupts in a frenzy of celebration.

The **Inlandsbanan**, the great Inland Railway, cuts right through central and northern Sweden and links virtually all the towns and villages covered in this chapter. Running from Lake Vänern to **Gällivare**, above the Arctic Circle, it ranks with the best European train journeys, an enthralling 1300km in two days. Certainly, it's a much livelier approach to the far north than the east coast run from Stockholm. **Östersund** marks the half-way point, a shimmering, modern lakeside town. From here trains head in all directions; west to Norway, south to Dalarna and Stockholm – and north.

The wild lands of the **Same** make for the most fascinating trip in northern Sweden. Buses connect the railway line to the smaller villages, no longer remote but retaining vestiges of a vastly different life. The omnipresent reindeer are a constant reminder of where you are, but the enduring *Same* culture, which once defined much of these lands, is now under threat. The problems posed by tourism are escalating, principally erosion of grazing grounds. In the last two years there has been a fundamental shift in living patterns, the result of fallout from the Chernobyl disaster: the grazing grounds have been affected and the *Same* are unable to slaughter deer as their economy requires.

For more on the *Same*, their history, lifestyle and traditions, see "The *Same* and Chernobyl" in *Contexts* p.652.

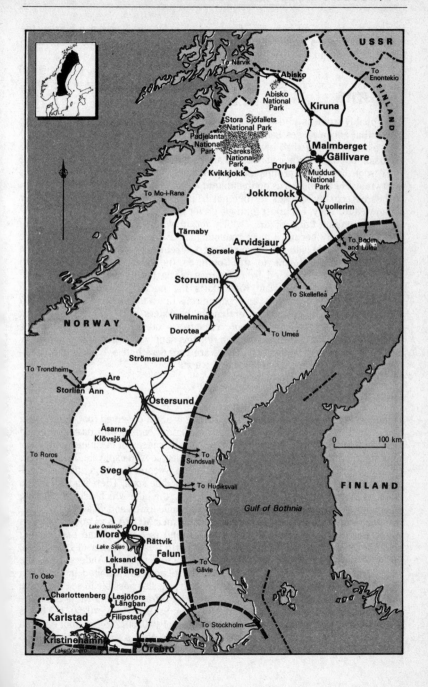

Further north, around industrial **Kiruna** and as far the Norwegian border, the rugged (sometimes dangerous) **national parks** offer some of the best wilderness hiking around.

Dalarna

It's probably fruitless to dwell too much on the agreed beauty of **Dalarna**, the region that encompasses Lake Siljan and its hinterland. It holds a special, misty-eyed place in the Swedish heart and should certainly be seen, though not to the exclusion of points further north. And anyway, despite its charms it's conceivable you'll soon tire of the prominent folksy image. One small lakeside town looks pretty much like another, as do the ubiquitous handicrafts and souvenirs.

Dalarna actually spreads further north and west than most brochures ever acknowledge. They, like most tourists, prefer to concentrate on the area immediately surrounding **Lake Siljan** – which, on the whole, isn't a bad idea. North of ORSA the county becomes more mountainous and less populous, and although it's fairly accessible with your own transport, it remains tricky for an independent trip. All the major towns to the south on the other hand, from Orsa to BORLÄNGE, are connected by rail, most only a twenty- to thirty-minute-ride apart. Alternatively, the main road skirts the northern side of the lake to RÄTTVIK, whence it diverges on separate runs down to Borlänge via LEKSAND and FALUN. Two other options: **ferries** ply the waters of the lake between Mora and Leksand, or you can hire **bicycles** from tourist offices and campsites throughout Dalarna. The happiest plan remains simply to strike off and not worry too much about accommodation. There are countless hotels, hostels and campsites around, the main ones detailed in the text.

Around Lake Siljan

Things have changed since Baedeker, writing in 1889, observed that "Lake Siljan owes much of its interest to the inhabitants of its banks, who have preserved many of their primitive characteristics . . . In their ideas of cleanliness they are somewhat behind the age." Today, it's not the people who captivate but the scenery: **Lake Siljan** is what many tourists come to Sweden for, its gentle surroundings, traditions and local handicrafts weaving a subtle spell. There's a lush feel to much of the region, the vegetation enriched by the lake which adds a pleasing dimension to what are, essentially, small, low-profile towns and villages.

If you've only got time to see part of the lake, then **MORA** is as good a place as any to head for – connected by ferry to Leksand (see below) and one starting point for the *Inlandsbanan* rail route. At the north western corner of Lake Siljan, the little town is more or less a showcase for the work of Anders Zorn, the Swedish painter who lived in Mora and whose work is exhibited in the **Zorn Museum** (open all year). More enthusiastically, it's also possible to see his home and studio throughout the summer. The **tourist office** (summer Mon–Sat 9am–8pm, Sun noon–8pm; winter Mon–Fri 9am–5pm, Sat 9am–1pm; ☎0250/151 00) is down on the quayside and there's a **youth hostel** (☎0250/265 95), too, open all year, 3km out of town. Alternatively, the *Hotell Natt o Dag*, Kyrkogatan 33 (☎0250/130 60), has rooms for around 500kr.

At **RÄTTVIK**, on the eastern bulge of the lake, there's an introductory spread of museums and craft exhibitions, an inviting chance to indulge in Dalarna's more cultural aspects.

Rättvik's Gammelgård, 2km from town, has reconstructed buildings, period furniture and traditional costumes on display: the latter you'll see worn if you catch any of the Midsummer celebrations in the region. The **tourist office** (summer Mon–Sat 9am–9pm, Sun 1–9pm; winter Mon–Fri 9am–5pm, Sat 9am–1pm; ☎0248/109 10) is in Torget across from the station; the **youth hostel** (☎0248/105 66), open June to August, in Knektplatsen a few hundred metres away at the end of Järnvägsgatan; and the **campsite** (☎0248/116 91) right on the lakeside behind the railway tracks.

LEKSAND is perhaps the most popular and traditional of the Dalarna villages and certainly worth making the effort to reach at Midsummer. Festivals then recall age-old maypole dances, accompanied by gnarled folk musicians, and the celebrations culminate in the **church boat races**, an aquatic procession of decorated longboats which the locals once rowed to church every Sunday. You can see the spectacle in nearby SILJANSNÄS (Midsummer's Day), Leksand (first Sunday in July) and TÄLLBERG (first Tuesday after Midsummer). The **tourist office** (☎0247/803 00) in Norsgatan has cycles for hire, as does the **youth hostel** (☎0247/ 101 86), 2km south of the centre at Parkgården and open all year. There are **campsites**, too, in Leksand, at ORSANDBADEN or over the bay at VÄSTANVIK.

Falun and Borlänge

The **copper mines** (May–Aug daily 10am–4.30pm; July Mon–Sat 10am–6pm; rest of the year Sat & Sun only 12.30–4.30pm) in nearby **FALUN**, were the reason for the town's unprecedented seventeenth- and eighteenth-century prosperity. Two-thirds of the world's copper ore was mined there, and Falun acquired buildings and a proud layout commensurate with its status as Sweden's second largest town. The mines were said by the botanist Carl von Linnaeus to be as dreadful as hell itself, and conditions were appalling. An unnerving element of eighteenth-century mining was the omnipresence of copper vitriol fumes, a strong preservative. One recorded case exists of a young man whose body was found in the mines in 1719. He'd died 49 years previously in an accident and the corpse was so well preserved that his erstwhile fiancée, by then an old woman, recognised him immediately.

Falun's **tourist office** (☎023/836 37) runs guided tours to the mines and is in the main square, Stora Torget. Falun would make a fairly cheap base for touring the area: try the *Pensionat Solliden*, Centralveien 36 (☎023/321 26), which has double rooms for under 300kr. There's a **youth hostel** (☎023/105 60) here, but it's a good 4km away at HARALDSBRO, open all year except for the last two weeks of December. The **campsite** (☎023/835 63) is at the National Ski Stadium (*Riksskidstadion*) at Lugnet, also open all year.

For rainy days **BORLÄNGE**, a few kilometres south of Falun, is a more attractive target; a **geological museum**, **craft village** and **Museum of the Future** all lie in the centre. The **tourist office** (☎0243/181 25) is in the green *Liljekvistska parken* not far from the railway station. A **youth hostel** (☎0243/276 15) lies 3km from the station at Kornstigen 223a.

The Inlandsbanan: from Kristinehamn to Östersund

The **Inlandsbanan** (Inland Railway) is the most charismatic of the Scandinavian rail routes, linking KRISTINEHAMN, in central Sweden, with GÄLLIVARE, 1300km further north. The section below deals with the first part of the line, which runs from Kristinehamn to the half-way point, Östersund; coverage of the second section starts on p.426.

It took over forty years to complete the **railway**, connecting up the small private sections of track that served local industry throughout the country. It opened in 1937, and remains a largely working network, in winter often providing the only link between the more isolated regions; in summer it's a tourist route, the money subsidising a line that could never make a profit from its normal traffic. There's a refreshing service element in its day-to-day operation. When you want to get off, you tell the conductor and the train stops, station or not: conversely, you can flag it down if you find yourself stranded on some of the wilder sections of the line.

INLANDSBANAN: THE PRACTICAL DETAILS

As a route, the *Inlandsbanan* provides extremely cheap access from southern to northern Sweden. An **Inlandsbanan kortet** (available June–Aug only) is valid for 14 days' (440kr) or 21 days' (495kr) unlimited travel up and down the network. The deal is co-ordinated by the twenty communities that lie along the route and also provides a map, full timetables, and a hefty wedge of discounts on campsites, meals, museums and various activities. Local county buses are half-price to ticket holders, and for onward travel the ticket also pulls in thirty percent discounts on connecting trains – eg Gällivare–Narvik – and a half-price *SAS* flight to or from Karlstad, Östersund or Kiruna. Buy the whole package from travel agents or any main Swedish railway station.

A few bits of **information** help smooth the route. Taken in one go, the whole journey lasts two days. There are no night trains, so travelling the whole line, in either direction, it's necessary to spend the night in Östersund: hostels and campsites along the route provide for other stopovers. A huge tome in each train details festivals, events and activities, and for any other tourist information the guards are helpful and forthcoming. The line is open in winter but only standard *SJ* tickets are available then. In **September**, cloudberry and mushroom season, a special ticket valid between Mora and Gällivare costs only 275kr for 14 days (21 days; 325kr); but all activities and hotels are closed. *InterRail/Nordturist* pass holders can use their tickets on the line all year, but they don't qualify for any of the discounts or activities.

Kristinehamn

The *Inlandsbanan* begins at **KRISTINEHAMN**, a pretty harbour town on the northern fringes of **Lake Vänern**. It's been an important port since the fourteenth century, when the iron ore from the Bergslagen mines was shipped out from the town. Five hundred years later one of the country's earliest railways speeded up the process when cars loaded with iron ore coasted downhill from the mines to the port. The empty cars were then pulled back to Bergslagen by horses and oxen. It's this length of railway line that today forms the first part of the inland route.

Kristinehamn is proud, and quite rightly so, of its towering fifteen-metre-high **Picasso sculpture**, a sandblasted concrete pillar standing guard over the river entrance to the town. The striking piece is one of the *Les Dames des Mougins* series based on Picasso's wife Jaqueline, and was raised and decorated by the Swedish artist Carl Nesjar. Seeing as Picasso only provided a photograph of a model of the sculpture and never actually set foot in Sweden, the "Picasso sculpture" tag seems a little unfair to Nesjar. To get there (the sculpture is 7km from the centre), follow Presterudsvägen, out along the cycle track/footpath that skirts the river, past Kristinehamn's flotilla of garish private boats – right to the statue.

Kristinehamn would hardly warrant an overnight stop but for the abundance of budget accommodation and the need to catch the morning train northwards. From the **railway station**, turn left and a five-minute walk brings you to the large main square and a river that branches its way through the centre. The **tourist office** (summer only; ☎0550/105 73) is at the far end of the square facing the *Stadshotellet* (☎0550/150 30), the most expensive place to stay in town. It's a lovely turn-of-the-century building and if you felt like splashing out anywhere en route this is the best choice: double rooms around 750kr, though quite possibly cheaper in the summer. For economy, the friendly *Hotel Svea* (☎0550/118 11), the yellow building immediately left of the station, is handiest: open mid-June to the end of August, its hostel-type accommodation costs 60kr a night, breakfast available. Even cheaper, but further out, is the *Sanna Fritidsgård* (☎0550/104 59), a church **hostel** at Djurgårdsvägen 4, which costs around 35kr a night. It's open June to mid-August, and a special daily bus runs there at 7.40pm from the railway station; otherwise bus #3 leaves from Norra Torget every half hour. Both these options rather squeeze out the official **youth hostel** (☎0550/147 71) at Kvarndammen, a tiny place 5km away. It is, however, open longer, from May to August.

Filipstad, Långban and Mora

At **FILIPSTAD**, manufacturing home of the *Wasa* crispbread that dominates every Swedish supermarket, the *Inlandsbanan* line suffers its only break, and a bus takes over for the 180km stretch north to MORA (see below). However, the railway track does still exist, and although mightily overgrown, offers one of the weirder forms of transport available in Scandinavia. *Aktiv Feries* (☎0590/360 57) hires out **tandemdressin**, tandem bikes with train wheels that you cycle up and down the disused track. There's 50km to cover and plenty of places to camp on the way (although you could cover the whole distance in a long day). Each bike costs around 300kr a day and can carry four people (two pedalling, two precariously perching) plus backpacks. Rent them from the company's office in LILJENDAL (close to OFORSEN), or ring and ask at which section of the line to pick them up. One of the best stretches is from SÅGEN northwards.

Before reaching Oforsen the bus that links the two sections of track calls at LÅNGBAN, heart of the old Värmland mining district. You can get off here for a bit of modern prospecting, bashing rocks with a pinhead hammer in a vast quarry. Reputedly, over 300 different minerals exist in this area, and the nearby museum will have a look at any interesting rocks you dig up. Unfortunately, even the golden-looking ones are usually just plain old iron ore. As another diversion, the old smelting house, shafts and buildings all still stand and are open for visits. The **Manor House** was the birthplace of the Ericsson brothers: Nils, master railway- and canal-builder, a sort of Swedish Brunel, and John, the man who invented the marine propeller and the rotating gun turret. He emigrated to America and on his death in 1889 his will vigorously declared, "Rather my remains should rest under a gravel heap on Swedish ground than under a marble monument in this country." He's buried in Filipstad, the Americans sending home the ungrateful emigré on an armoured cruiser.

At **MORA** the train picks up bus passengers and continues its now uninter-rupted run to Gällivare – though if you miss it, or fancy seeing a bit of the area, there's a **youth hostel** in town for stopovers. From Mora the whole of the Dalarna region is connected by a series of short rail hops as far as Borlänge, and for more on the town and region, see "Dalarna" above. Mora, actually, is not a bad introduction to the Dalarna theme, rural beauty and laid back lakeside villages, but without the time for a more leisurely tour it's probably better to stick with the inland train. It stops next at ORSA, fifteen minutes away, a small place lurking on the banks of Lake Orsasjön.

Orsa

There are bears in **ORSA**. Huge brown ones roam the surrounding dense forest, graceful and measured creatures most of the time. Few sightings are made in the wild, except by hunters who cull the steadily increasing numbers each year, but visit the **Grönklitt bear park** (late May–Sept; 15kr) and they are out in force. Whatever your natural reservations about such places, think again. The bears are not tamed or caged, but wander the 800 square kilometres of the forested park at will, hunting and living as normal. It's the humans that are caged, having to clam-ber up viewing towers and along protected paths. Watching the bears throws all preconceptions out of the window. They are funny, gentle and vegetarian. A **hostel** (☎0250/521 63) at the park has fine facilities; 80kr in twin-bedded rooms including breakfast, TV and kitchen. Watch what you eat in the adjacent restau-rant though – if it looks like pink roast beef it's bear meat.

The park is 13km from Orsa, an easy enough hitch, or ask about buses in the **tourist office** (mid-June to mid-Aug Mon–Sat 9am–9pm, Sun 1–9pm; mid-Aug to mid-June Mon–Fri 9am–5pm, Sat 9am–1pm; ☎0250/521 63) in Centralgatan. Orsa has an official **youth hostel** (☎0250/405 15) too, 1500m from the railway station and open from June to August. Or try *Strandvillan*, Älvgatan 6 (☎0250/408 73), 500m from the station, whose rooms go for under 400kr.

Härjedalen county

Härjedalen county is excellent walking terrain, a sparsely populated fell region stretching north and west to the Norwegian border. In **SVEG**, site of a 1273 "parliament" called to hammer out a border treaty between Sweden and Norway, you'll find a **youth hostel** (☎0680/103 38) open June to September. It's at Vallarvägen 11, a five-minute walk from the station, with a **campsite** (☎0680/108 81) nearby. Incidentally, you can reach Sveg direct from Stockholm by bus at the weekend (Fri, Sat & Sun 1 daily), but it's a seven-hour ride.

The region's ski slopes have produced their fair share of champions. At **ÅSARNA**, four of them (names that mean nothing to the average Brit) have clubbed together and run a **ski-centre**, summer as well as winter. An attached **campsite** (☎0687/302 30) has a beautiful private lake and beach, and while it's virtually impossible to stay here in winter without an advance booking, in summer you can just turn up. There's also bed and breakfast in a campsite **cabin** for around 100kr. The centre is on the main road a few minutes away from the station, and there's a **tourist office** (June–Aug daily 8am–10pm; ☎0687/301 93) inside.

Åsarna is well placed for a quick jaunt to **KLÖVSJÖ**, twenty minutes away by twice-daily bus (or by the bus on Saturday from Stockholm/Sveg). A thoroughly charming place with its log cabins set in rolling verdant pastures, it has gained the reputation of being Sweden's most beautiful village. Church bells echo over the lake and cattle wander about freely in and out of dozens of perfect holiday snaps. Besides taking a look at **Tomtangården** (July to mid-Aug daily), a preserved seventeenth-century farm estate, there's not much to do except breathe the bitingly clean air. Ask in the **tourist office** (mid-June to mid-Aug; ☎0682/212 50) about buses to the *Katrina Värdshus* if you are around and hungry on Sundays. This nearby **inn** serves traditional pasture village food between noon and 6pm; fresh milk, home-made bread and butter, goat's cheese and cloudberries and cream. And if you want to stay, multi-bedded rooms at the inn go from 65kr each a night.

The second section of the *Inlandsbanan*, Östersund to Gällivare, is covered on p.426.

Östersund and around

Halfway point on the *Inlandsbanan* is **ÖSTERSUND**, easily the largest town until Kiruna in the far north. It's a major transport junction, the E75 running through town on its way to the Norwegian border. Trains speed north and south on the *Inlandsbanan*, west to Trondheim and southeast to Gävle. **Storsjön** (the Great Lake) lends the town a holiday atmosphere, unusual this far inland, and it's a welcoming place in which to fetch up. Depending, that is, on how close you get to the water. The lake has a monster (it's even been claimed that subterranean passages link the lake with Loch Ness) and sightings are numerous if unsubstantiated. It all adds a few thrills to the otherwise tranquil **steamboat cruise** (July daily except Mon; June & first two weeks of Aug 3 weekly; 30kr) on the lake, a two-hour passage on the creaking *SS Thomee*. Buy tickets from the quayside half an hour before departure.

Otherwise, the main thing to do in town is to visit **Jamtli** (park open all year; buildings and activities mid-June to mid-Aug daily 11am–6pm; 15kr), an impressive open-air museum, a quarter of an hour's walk north along Rådhusgatan. The first few minutes are a bit bewildering, full of volunteers milling around in traditional country costume, farming and milking much as their ancestors did. They live here throughout the summer and everyone is encouraged to join in – baking, tree felling, grass cutting. For kids it's ideal, and you'd have to be pretty hard bitten not to enjoy the enthusiastic atmosphere. Some intensive work has been done on getting the settings right: the restored and working interiors are gloomy and dirty, and without a hint of the usual pristine historical travesty. In the woodman's cottage, presided over by a bearded lumberjack who makes pancakes for the tourists, shoeless and scruffy "Just William" children kip happily in the wooden cots. Outside, even the roaming

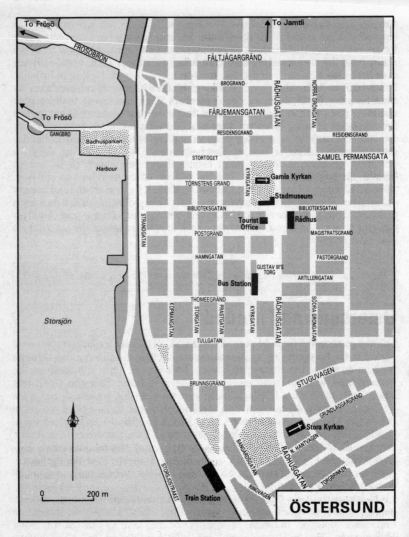

ÖSTERSUND

cattle and the planted crops are accurate for the times portrayed, while a complete "old town" has been erected near the entrance. On the way in or out, the **Länsmuseum** (summer Mon–Fri 9am–6pm, Sat & Sun noon–4pm; winter Mon–Fri 9am–4pm, Tues until 9pm, Sat & Sun noon–3pm; free) shows off the county collections: a rambling houseful of local exhibits that includes monster-catching gear devised by lakeside worthies last century.

Back in the centre, the town slopes down to the water in an intoxicated fashion and it's tiring work strolling the pedestrianised streets that run around Stortorget. Apart from the **Stadmuseum** (Tues–Fri noon–5pm, Sat 1–5pm; free) – a crowded 200 years of history in a house the size of a shoebox – next to the old church on Rådhusgatan, and the **Gamle kyrkan** (Mon–Fri 10am–2pm) itself, there's not a vast amount in the way of sights. The **harbour** is a better bet, a fleet of tiny boats and a couple of light aircraft lolling about on the clean water. Here, from Badhusparken, you can take the foot/cycle bridge over the lake to **Frösön**. This island was site of the original Viking settlement in Jämtland and takes its name from the pagan god Frör. There's plenty of hiking and a good few historical stops too. Just over the bridge in front of the red-brick office block, hunt for the eleventh-century **rune stone** which commemorates Östmadur, son of Gudfast, first missionary to the area. The main road runs west 5km to **Frösö kyrka**, an eleventh-century church with a detached bell tower.

Östersund: some facts

The **tourist office** (June to mid-Aug Mon–Sat 9am–8pm, Sun 11am–6pm; rest of the year Mon–Fri 9am–5pm; ☎063/14 40 01) is opposite the minaret-topped Rådhus at Rådhusgatan 44 and handy for a wealth of information. The **Storsjökortet** (65kr; valid mid-May to mid-Aug) is a nine-day pass giving free bus rides, museum entry and discounted bus and boat sightseeing trips. If you're only seeing Jamtli (see above) and moving on, forget it as everything else in town is free and can be walked to. Ask about **bike hire**, which used to be free from the tourist office until it got sick of replacing stolen ones. If they haven't resurrected the system *Egons Cykel* at Kyrkagatan 27 can oblige.

For a central **hotel**, try either *City Hotellet*, Artillerigatan 4 (☎063/10 84 15), or *Hotell Linden*, Storgatan 64 (☎063/11 73 35) – rooms for 400-500kr depending on the season. The **youth hostel** (☎063/12 85 61) is close to the railway station (just by the Stora kyrkan) at Tingsgatan 12 and open mid-June to mid-August. More atmospheric is a night spent in the **hostel** inside Jamtli, a newly-furnished place within the old town block in the museum. The tourist office will book rooms there for a fee and although it's slightly more expensive, staying there should guarantee free entrance to the open-air museum. **Campers** can stay either at *Östersunds Fritidsby* (☎06/11 37 06), open all year and a couple of kilometres down Rådhusgatan; or on Frösön island at *Frösön camping* (☎063/432 54), open June to mid-August, bus #3 from the centre.

Gastronomically, there's more choice in Östersund than for a very long way north. Wholefood snacks and coffee plus bookshop at the *Sol Café*, Prästgatan 31; more expensive meals in the young and trendy *Brunkullans* restaurant, Postgränd 5; and late evening music in the *Night and Day* café at Kyrkgatan 70. For **breakfast** (and the first inland train of the day leaves at 7.30am), the railway station café is good value and always busy.

West from Östersund: to the Norwegian border

The E75 pretty much follows the route trudged by medieval pilgrims on their way to Nidaros (now Trondheim) over the border. A couple of centuries later the region became a bitter battleground between Norwegian and Swedish forces disputing the border; memorial stones and decrepit defences litter the way. Pick up hiking maps and advice from the tourist office in Östersund if you aim to do some serious walking. Otherwise, there's only a couple of places that merit a stop and a ramble.

Åre

ÅRE, two hours by train from Östersund, is Sweden's most prestigious ski resort. During the snow-bound season rooms are like gold dust and prices about as high: which is to say that if you do intend to come to ski, book accommodation well in advance through the tourist office. Equipment, surprisingly, is not so dear to hire. Avoid the downhill runs (where the ski lift inflates prices) and stick to cross-country, and it could be done for 300kr a week.

In summer, though, the Alpine village is quiet, a likeable haven for ramblers. The **funicular railway** (every 30min; 10kr) runs up to the *Fjällgården Hotel* and footpaths radiate out from there through the valley. Or, for a more energetic scramble, the **Kabinbanen** (cable car; 25kr one-way, 30kr return) whisks you to the viewing platform on *Åreskutan* mountain from where it's a thirty-minute clamber to the summit. The shortest walk down takes just over two hours, although several longer trails lead back to the village. The **kyrka** (key hangs outside the door) just above the campsite is a marvellous thirteenth-century building. Inside, the smell of burning candles and the dark decoration weave a powerful spell.

The **tourist office** (mid-June to mid-Aug daily 9am–7pm, rest of the year daily 9am–5pm; closed Sat & Sun May, Sept & Oct; ☎0647/500 10) is in the square 100m above the railway station. There's plenty of **accommodation** in the village, packed in winter but with room to spare during the summer: ask about possibilities at the tourist office, or – if you want the views – give the *Fjällgården* a whirl; see above; from 450kr a night. There's a **youth hostel** (☎0647/301 38), open all year, 8km southeast of town on the E75 at UNDERSÅKER; bus #614 from Torget (not Sun) as far as BRATTLAND. **Private rooms** in town go from around 50kr and almost all have kitchen, shower and TV. The **campsite** (☎0647/511 00) is five minutes' walk from the station and open all year except September and October.

Storlien

Six kilometres from the Norwegian border, **STORLIEN** is the last place to stop if you don't intend to do any hiking (which is good and rugged around here). There's nothing except a hotel (cheap lunches), a supermarket, a railway station and mile upon mile of open countryside. At least the **youth hostel** (☎0647/700 50) is closer to the station than in Åre, a three-kilometre walk across the railway tracks to the E75 and then left down the main road; it's open from mid-July to August.

If you're merely after a bed for the night then ÅNN, halfway between Åre and Storlien, is the best bet. The **youth hostel** (☎0647/710 70) there is no distance from the station, and is open all year round.

The Inlandsbanan: north to Gällivare

Elk and reindeer are more in evidence on this section and at times the train has to slow and stop to let them clear the tracks. On the other occasions that the train calls a halt, with no station in sight, it's usually for a reason; the guard pointing out a beaver damming a nearby stream, or at the Arctic Circle where everyone piles off for photos.

The first section of the *Inlandsbanan*, Kristinehamn to Östersund, is covered on p.420–423.

Vilhelmina and Storuman

At **VILHELMINA**, you're well into the north – and you've just broached the massive tracts of land which support the *Same*. There's a **youth hostel** here (☎0940/114 50), open mid-June to mid-August, at Tallåsvägen 34; it's a kilometre or so from the railway station. Closer in, the cheap *Lilla Hotellet*, Granvägen 1, just 200m from the station, has double rooms for around 175–225kr.

However, **STORUMAN**, an hour away, is a worthier target, especially if you are keen to do some walking in the unspoilt surroundings. Trains and the E79 "Blue Way" route run east to Umeå from here, while westwards is the starting point for trips into the mountains of *Tärnafjällen*. Hiking details and maps are available from Storuman **tourist office** (June–Aug; ☎0951/105 00) at Höjdvägen 3. The **youth hostel** (☎0951/113 58) is a couple of kilometres out on the E79 (to Tärnaby), open mid-June to mid-August. Incidentally, in the middle of the local campsite there's a Lapp church – not an outstanding example but easily accessible.

Tärnaby

Regular buses make the two-hour drive to **TÄRNABY** from Storuman. Right in the hills, it's worth the effort to get well away from the tourist trail. The tiny village was the birthplace of Ingmar Stenmark, double Olympic gold medallist and Sweden's greatest skier. It's a typically gorgeous place; yellow flower-decked fields run to the edge of the mountain forests here, the trees felled to leave great swathes that accommodate World Cup ski slopes. The **Samegården** (end of June to mid-Aug daily 11am–6pm; 10kr), in the village, is a good introduction to *Same* history, culture and customs. The museum recalls older times when, after a kill in a bear hunt, the gall bladder was cut open and the fluid drunk by the hunters. If the journey is too much for one day there's a **youth hostel** (☎0954/104 20) in Tärnaby, open June to August. Or small groups can rent a four-bedded flat for around 400–550kr: ask at the *Tärnaby Fjällhotell*, Östra Strandvägen 16 (☎0954/104 20).

Walkers should note that the southern end of the 500-km "Kungsleden" trail is at HEMAVAN near Tärnaby – see *Hiking in the National Parks*, p.431.

Sorsele, Arvidsjaur and the Arctic Circle

SORSELE is the next major stop on the *Inlandsbanan*, although "major" is perhaps a misleading word to use about this pint-sized town. On the Vindel River, Sorsele became a *cause célèbre* amongst conservationists in Sweden, causing the government to abandon its plans to regulate the flow here by building a hydro-electric station. It remains wild, untouched and seething with rapids, and the **campsite** (☎0952/101 24) on the river bank, open all year, is close to all the action. There's a **youth hostel** (☎0952/100 48) too, a small place open from mid-June to mid-August.

ARVIDSJAUR contains Sweden's oldest surviving *Same* village. It dates from the late eighteenth century, a huddle of houses which was once the centre of the great winter market in Arvidsjaur. They were not meant to be permanent homes, but rather a meeting place during festivals, and the last weekend in August is still taken up by a great celebratory shindig. There's no hostel, but the **campsite** by the lake has cabins.

A couple of hours north of Arvidsjaur the *Inlandsbanan* finally crosses the **Arctic Circle** just south of JOKKMOKK (see below). This is occasion enough for a bout of whistle blowing as the train pulls up to allow everyone to take photos of the hoardings announcing the crossing. Painted white rocks curve away over the hilly ground, a crude but popular representation of the Circle: one foot on each side is the standard photographic pose. It's all a bit over the top, since the geographical Circle is not constant at all, and shifts a few metres each year towards the Pole – but for argument's sake this spot is as good as any. If the godforsaken area appeals then there's even a **campsite** (☎0971/ 111 14), actually on the Circle. Take a taxi (50kr) from the centre of Jokkmokk, an eight-kilometre ride.

Jokkmokk

In the midst of a densely forested, marshy county the size of Wales, **JOKKMOKK** is a welcome oasis. Once wintertime *Same* quarters, a market and church heralded a permanent settlement by the beginning of the seventeenth century. The town – the name means "bend in the river" – is today a renowned handicraft centre, a *Same* high school keeping language and culture alive. Jokkmokk's **museum** on Storgatan is the place to see some of the intricate work. Have a glance too at the so-called **Lapp kyrka**, in which corpses were interned in wall vaults during winter, waiting for the thaw when the *Same* could go out and dig graves. The temperatures in this part of Sweden plunge to -35°C and below in wintertime.

The great **winter market** still survives, now nearly 400 years old, held on the first Thursday, Friday and Saturday of each February, when 30,000 people gather in town. It's the best and coldest time to be in Jokkmokk, and staying means booking accommodation a good six months in advance. A smaller and less traditional autumn fair at the end of August is an easier though poorer option. Locals invite you to take a dip in the river during summer. It's very cold and I'd stick to the **salmon fishing** in the town's central lake, for which you'll need a permit. Catch anything and there's a cleaning table and fireplace laid on.

By now the **tourist office** (summer daily 9am–9pm; winter Mon–Fri 9am–5pm; ☎0971/172 27) should be installed in the museum, but if not, try at Porjusvägen 4 close to the **railway station** – walk up Stationsgatan and it's on the right. They've got all sorts of printed bumf, useful for those considering hiking in the region. In summer there should be no problem getting a place at the **youth hostel** (☎0971/ 119 77), open mid-June to mid-August; just follow the signs from the station. The **campsite** (☎0971/123 70) is open all year, 3km east of town on route 97. One winter option is the *Jokkmokk Ski Club*'s **sleep-in** (☎0971/104 37), a sleeping bag on the floor job for winter market visitors. Ring at least six months ahead to find out when bookings commence.

Vuollerim and Porjus

Forty-five kilometres southeast of Jokkmokk on route 97 (to Luleå) lies **VUOLLERIM**, site of the Lule River Project. Archaeological digs have uncovered evidence of prehistoric habitation in the area – pit houses, fires, rubbish dumps and drainage works – some of it dating back 6000 years. A small and self-explanatory **museum** (summer only; free) covers the development of the various sites and finds, but the whole thing really comes alive if you can get one of the archaeologists to show you around the site – it's a detective story of immense proportions. Don't bother walking out to the site on your own: the excavations are virtually complete and without specialist knowledge it all looks like a mudbath. Regular buses connect Vuollerim with Jokkmokk. (And on the way out watch for the military camp outside Jokkmokk. Just beyond it the road almost mysteriously widens out to airport runway size; perhaps not a coincidence.)

In the other direction, north, but up the same road 97 (or by train to Gällivare) is **PORJUS** and its waterfalls. Picked as the likeliest spot for a power station in 1910, the backbreaking work began the same year. It was an obvious choice of site, *Swedish State Railways* requiring power for electrification of the new line between Luleå and the Norwegian border. Logistically it was a disaster. The nearest railway station was 50km away at Gällivare and the two places were not linked by road. For the first year, until an inland rail stretch was complete, men carried loads of up to seventy kilos for the whole distance along planked paths – on their backs. The power station is open to the public and a museum documents its history. Opening hours generally coincide with *Inlandsbanan* train arrival times, and there are free guided tours.

Gällivare

GÄLLIVARE is one of the most important sources of iron ore in Europe. The modern mines and works are distant, dark blots down which, in the summer, the tourist office ferries relays of tourists. If you have any interest in seeing a working mine, don't wait until Kiruna (see p.432), which has a tame "tourist tour"; get down these instead. Buses (15kr) leave from the railway station and entrance to the mines is another 15kr, after which it's no time to get claustrophobic.

Gällivare is strictly two settlements: Malmberget where the mines are situated and Gällivare itself, an older village and one more pleasant than its surrounding industry suggests. Originally a *Same* village in the seventeenth century, little evidence of that remains. Only the **Lappkyrkan** (summer daily 9am–6pm) down by the river survives, a mid-eighteenth-century construction also known as the *Ettöreskyrkan* (one öre church) after the one öre subscription drive through Sweden that paid for it. Really though, the river and the surrounding mountains are the nicest part of town. The centre is a steely grey mesh of new streets best walked through quickly.

Dundret mountain overshadows the town, the target of Midnight Sun spotters. You can walk up to *Bornfällen*, about a four-kilometre hike on a well marked path and the views are magnificent. But this isn't the very top. Buses make that journey up a winding road especially for the Midnight Sun, leaving daily between June 20 and July 27 (30kr return) from the railway station at 11pm, returning at 1am.

Practicalities

The **tourist office** (June–Aug daily 9am–10.30pm; rest of the year Mon–Fri 10am–5pm; ☎0970/186 63) is at Storgatan 16 opposite a *Domus* store. Its long summer hours are aimed at late *Inlandsbanan* arrivals and the office is equally accommodating – good free maps and hiking information. The same building has a café downstairs and a museum upstairs dealing with *Same* history. The **youth hostel** (☎0970/143 80) is behind the railway station – cross the tracks by the metal bridge – and is open May to September, with accommodation in small cabins. Because of the town's strategic position (north to Kiruna, south to Stockholm) booking ahead in summer is advised. There's also a small **private hostel**, *Lapphärbärget* (☎0970/104 92), next to the Lappkyrkan with cheap beds. The *Hotell Dundret*, Per Högströsgatan 1 (☎0970/110 40), very close to the station, has double rooms for around 360kr. The **campsite** (☎0970/186 79) is by the river, open June to August; and you can hire **bikes** here too.

If accommodation is really tight, space can usually be found at Malmberget, 5km away. The *Malm Hotel* (☎0970/244 15) in Torget there has beds for hostel members at 55kr. Buses run every hour from Gällivare bus station, outside the tourist office.

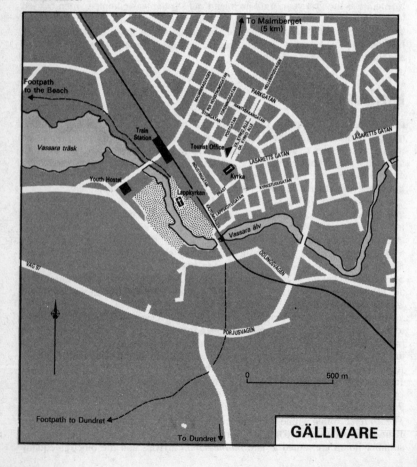

Hiking in the National Parks

It's not a good idea to go **hiking in the national parks** of northern Sweden on a whim. Even for experienced walkers, the going can be tough and uncomfortable in parts, downright treacherous in others. Mosquitoes are a real problem: it's difficult to describe the misery of being covered in a blanket of insects, your eyes, ears and nose full of the creatures. Yet there is no great outdoors quite like it in the rest of Europe. Reindeer are a common sight since the parks are breeding grounds and summer pastures, and *Same* settlements abound throughout the region; at RITSEM and VAISALUOKTA for example.

A few tips: Don't count on hiking before midsummer as snow and flood water are dangerous handicaps: the best hiking time is mid-July to the beginning of September. Take a good sleeping bag and, for longer treks, a tent as parts of some trails don't have overnight cabins. Get decent maps, boots and proper advice before setting out. And don't forget the mosquito repellent.

Kungsleden

Kungsleden (the "Royal Route") is the most famous and popular of the trails, a 500-kilometre route from ABISKO in the north to HEMAVAN, near Tärnaby, in the south. It's well marked, passing through various sections of the national parks (see below). There are no overnight cabins on some parts of the trail, and you'll need to be fit and experienced to complete the whole route. For a few days' hiking only, starting in Abisko is probably best. A *Turiststation* offers sound advice, and there's a string of cabins reaching down the trail as far as KVIKKJOKK. **Accommodation** in Abisko is at the *Gästgården Abisko* (☎0980/ 401 00), 100m from the railway station: from around 70kr a bed. You reach the trailhead by **train**: it's just before the Norwegian border on the Kiruna–Narvik run – get off at the *Abisko Turist* station. Alternatively, get to Kvikkjokk by **bus**, on the regular services between Kvikkjokk and Jokkmokk (the latter on the *Inlandsbanan*).

Other trails and parks

MUDDUS is the place recommended for beginners, a pine forested park between Jokkmokk and Gällivare. Its western edges are skirted by route 97 and the easiest approach is to leave the highway at LIGGADAMMEN and follow the small road to SKAITE. There's an easy hiking trail (50km long), cabins and a couple of campsites.

For low fells, large lakes and moors, head for **PADJELANTA**, the park adjacent to the Norwegian border. A 150-km trail runs from Kvikkjokk north to VAISALUOKTA (overnight cabins every 10–20km), and the hike and occasional spot of mountain clambering will take at least a week. Get to Kvikkjokk by bus from Jokkmokk and to Vaisaluokta from Gällivare: bus Gällivare–Ritsem, boat Ritsem–Vaisaluokta. Timetables are available in the brochure *Turist trafik i Fjällen*.

The Kungsleden also runs through **STORA SJÖFALLET**, the northernmost park. Best approach again is from Gällivare via Ritsem, where there's overnight accommodation.

The real baddie is **SAREK**, the terrain officially classed as "extremely difficult". There are no tourist facilities, trails, cabins or bridges; the fjords are dangerous, the weather rotten. Unquestionably not for anyone without Chris Bonnington-style experience. Up-to-the-minute information on this one can be had from *Fjällenheten* in Jokkmokk at Åsgatan 20, and the approach is via Kvikkjokk. Kungsleden walkers will pass through the very southeast corner, Padjelanta trail walkers through the southwest of Sarek.

Proper information, advice and encouragement for all these routes and parks is dished out by *Svenska Turistföreningen* (the Swedish Touring Club) which has offices at Vasagatan 48, Stockholm and Östra Larmgatan 15–21, Gothenburg. Or speak to any of the tourist offices at Gällivare, Jokkmokk, Kiruna or Tärnaby.

Kiruna

KIRUNA was the hub of the battle for control of the iron ore supply during World War II. From here, ore was transported north by train to the great harbour at Narvik over the border in Norway. Much German firepower was expended in an attempt to break the supply to the Allies. In the process, not surprisingly, both towns suffered considerably.

The train ride to Kiruna today rattles through sidings, slagheaps and ore works, a bitter contrast to the surrounding wilderness. The mines still dominate the town and do so much more depressingly than, say, the harbours at Narvik. They are ugly, brooding reminders of Kiruna's undoubted prosperity, and despite the new central buildings and open parks, the town retains a frontier feel. The tourist office runs daily **guided tours** around the mines during the summer, tickets 33kr from the office. (If you've brought kids along, only those over ten can go.) A coach takes visitors through the underground road network and then stops off at a "tourist" mine, part of a leviathan structure containing service stations, restaurants, computer centres, trains and crushing mills.

Even the other sights in town are firmly wedded to the all-important metal in one way or another. The tower of the **Rådhus** (summer Mon–Sat 9.45am–5pm, Sun 11am–5pm; winter Mon–Fri 9am–5pm) is obvious even from the railway station, a strident metal pillar harbouring an intricate latticework, clock face and sundry bells which chime raucously at noon. It was designed by Bror Marklund and the whole hall unbelievably won the 1964 award for the most beautiful Swedish public building. Inside there's a tolerable art collection, *Same* handicraft displays and a small tourist information stall.

Only a few minutes up the road, **Kiruna kyrka** (daily 10am–6pm) causes a few raised eyebrows. Built in the style of a *Same* hut, it's a massive origami creation of oak beams and rafters the size of a small aircraft hangar. *LKAB*, the iron ore company that paid for its construction, was also responsible for **Hjalmar Lundbohmsgården** (June–Aug daily 10am–8pm; free), a country house once used by the managing director of the company and "founder" of Kiruna. Displays inside mostly consist of turn-of-the-century photographs featuring Hjalmar Lundbohm himself and assorted *Same* in their winter gear.

The **Kiruna Samegård** (mid-June to Sept daily 10am–6pm; 5kr) at Brytaregatan 14 is the most rewarding exhibition of *Same* culture in town. The handicrafts may be familiar but what won't be is the small display of *Same* art, really very good. There's a souvenir shop and café, and a general store where visiting *Same* buy the basic handicraft materials – antler bone, reindeer skin and lasso rope sold by the metre.

Some practical details

Arriving by train, pick up a town plan from the **information booth** (mid-June to Aug daily 9am–10pm) right on the platform. If you want to stash luggage for the day use the cheaper station lockers and not the **tourist office** at Hjalmar Lundbohms Vägen 42 (10kr), who should be used instead for all practical information (May & mid- to end-Aug Mon–Fri 9am–5pm; June to mid-Aug Mon–Sat 9am–9pm, Sun noon–8pm; Sept–May Mon–Fri 10am–4pm; ☎0980/ 188 80). From the railway station, walk under the bridge, up the hill past the park and it's opposite the Rådhus. A **private room** from here costs around 110kr single, 140kr double.

The **youth hostel** (☎0980/171 95) is less than 1km from the station; turn right and follow the signs. Open mid-June to August, it's a noisy spot with trains zooming past through the night, and it does fill quickly in summer. An alternative is to try *Villa Polley* (☎0980/171 81) at Järnvägsgatan 25, which as the street name suggests is very near the railway station; beds from 65kr, singles 125kr and doubles 175kr. There's also a chance of **rooms** being found at Renstigen 1 (☎0980/114 51) on the corner of Parkgatan, around 70kr each in a double room with kitchen, TV and shower. The **campsite** is a twenty–minute walk from the centre on Campingvägen and has (expensive) cabins available.

On from Kiruna

The obvious route is north into Norway and to Narvik. Since 1984 there have been two choices; by train on the last leg of the long run from Stockholm, and now by road. The **Nordkalottvägen** (North Calotte Highway) runs parallel to the railway on the Swedish side, and along the way are the remains of several navvy camps left over from the time of the track's construction. **ABISKO** before the border is a busy stop for hikers embarking on the Kungsleden trail. (Note that there are two stations at Abisko and, if hiking, make sure you get off at the right one (see *Hiking in the National Parks* for details).

East of Kiruna, it's a twenty-five-minute bus ride to **JUKKASJÄRVI**, formerly a *Same* market place and site of a fine **folk museum** down by the river. Five buses a day leave from outside Kiruna tourist office, the last one back at 7.30pm.

travel details

Buses

From Östersund to Åre (Sun 1 daily; 1hr 30min). **From Sveg** to Stockholm (Fri, Sat & Sun 1 daily; 7hr); Klövsjö (Sat 1 daily; 2hr 45min).

Trains

From Östersund to Stockholm (4 daily; 6hr 30min); Åre/Storlien/Trondheim (3–4 daily; 2hr/3hr/5hr).
From Mora to Rättvik (3–5 daily; 30min); Leksand (3–4 daily; 1hr); Borlänge (3–5 daily; 1hr 30min); Stockholm (3–5 daily; 4hr 15min).

From Gällivare to Kiruna (2 daily; 1hr 30min); Abisko (2 daily; 3hr); Narvik (2 daily; 4hr 30min); Stockholm (2–3 daily; 16hr).

Inlandsbanan trains

June to August services below; reduced rest of year
From Kristinehamn to Östersund (2–3 daily; 11hr); although only one bus daily connects Filipstad to Mora (currently dep 11.25am, arr 2.35pm).
From Östersund to Gällivare (2 daily, although only one on the section Storuman–Arvidsjaur; 14hr).

PART FIVE

FINLAND

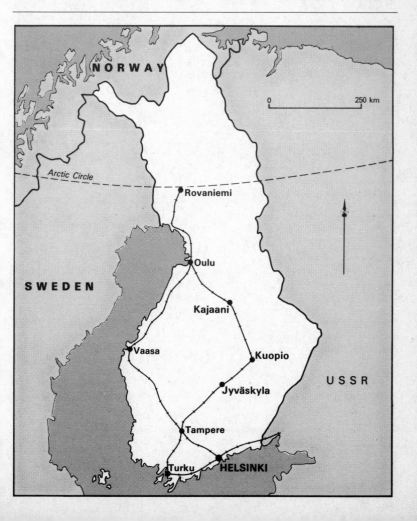

Introduction

Mainland Scandinavia's most culturally isolated and least understood country, Finland has been independent only since 1917, having been ruled for hundreds of years by Imperial powers: first the Swedes and then the Tsarist Russians. Much of its history involves a struggle simply for recognition and survival.

During the Swedish period, the Finnish language (one of the world's strangest and most difficult) was regarded as fit only for peasants – which the majority of Finns were – and later attempts were made to forcibly impose Russian. All publications were in Swedish until the *Kalevala* appeared in the early nineteenth century. A written collection of previously orally-transmitted folk tales telling of a people close to nature and living by hunting and fishing, the *Kalevala* instantly became regarded as a truly Finnish history, and formed the basis of the **National Romantic** movement in the arts which flourished from the mid-nineteenth century, stimulating political initiatives towards Finnish nationalism.

It's not surprising therefore that modern-day Finns have a well-developed sense of their own culture, and the legacy of the past is strongly felt – in the still widely popular Golden Age paintings of Gallen-Kallela, Edelfelt and others, the music of Sibelius, the National Romantic architecture (paving the way for modern greats like Alvar Aalto); or in the fact that the scars of the 1918 Civil War, which split the nation following independence, have yet to heal fully. Equally in evidence, even among city dwellers, are the deeply ingrained down-to-earth values of rural life, together with the spiritual qualities of the sauna. A small but significant proportion of Finns actually come from **Karelia** – ostensibly a large tract of land now scythed in two by the Finnish-Soviet border and sparsely inhabited, but historically a homeland distinct from Finland *and* Russia, and one whose traditional peasant culture is highly revered.

Some elderly rural dwellers are prone to suspicion of anything foreign, but in general the Finnish population is much less staid than that of its Nordic neighbours. And there is a mood of optimism, aided by the nation's uniquely subtle politics following the Scandinavian consensus model domestically, but pioneering a successful foreign policy based on the need to establish a credible neutrality next door to a superpower. It's worth noting that only a few decades ago the Soviet Union was threatening to absorb Finland just as it had the Baltic republics of Estonia, Latvia and Lithuania.

■ Where to go

Mainly flat and filled by huge forests and lakes, you'll need to travel around a lot to appreciate Finland's wide regional variations. **The South** contains the least dramatic scenery, but the capital, **Helsinki**, more than compensates, with its brilliant architecture and superb collections of national history and art. Stretching from the Soviet border in the east to the industrial city of **Tampere**, the vast waters of the **Lake Region** provide a natural means of transport for the timber industry – indeed water here is a more common sight than land. Towns lie on narrow ridges between lakes, giving even major manufacturing centres green and easily accessible surrounds. **Ostrobothnia**, the upper portion of the west coast, is characterised by near-featureless farmlands and long sandy beaches which are – to Finns at least – the regions's main draw. Here too you'll also find the clearest Swedish influence: in parts up to a third of the population are Swedish-speaking *Finland-Swedes*, and there's a rich heritage from the days of Swedish trading supremacy. **Kainuu** is the thickly-forested heart of the country, much of its small population spread among scattered villages. The land begins to rise as you head north from here, folding into a series of fells and gorges that are ripe for spectacular hiking. **Lappland**, completely devoid of large towns, contains the most alluring terrain of all, its stark and haunting landscapes able to absorb any number of visitors on numerous hiking routes. Most distinctive within this area are the *Same*, the semi-nomadic reindeer herders, whose culture remains strong and relatively untainted by modern culture.

■ When to go

The official Finnish holiday season is early July to mid-August, and during these weeks there's an exodus from the towns to the country regions. The best time to visit the rural regions is either side of these dates, when things will be less crowded and less hectic – though no cheaper.

In **summer**, regarded as being from June to early September, Helsinki and the south, and the

Lake Region, enjoy mild and sunny weather. Temperatures are usually 65–75°F, sometimes reaching 90°F in the daytime, but they drop swiftly in the evening, when you'll need a light jacket. The north is always a few degrees cooler and often quite cold at night, so carry at least a thick jumper. The **Midnight Sun** can be seen from Rovaniemi northwards for two months over midsummer; the rest of the country experiences a night-long twilight from mid-June to mid-July.

Winter, roughly from late October to early April in the south, a few weeks more on either side in the north, is painfully cold. Helsinki generally fluctuates between freezing point and 5°F, the harshest months being January and February; in the north it's even colder, with just a few hours of daylight; and in the extreme north the sun doesn't rise at all. The snow-covering generally lasts from November to March in the south, a few weeks longer in the north. On the plus side, Finland copes easily with low temperatures and transport is rarely disrupted.

The best time for **hiking** is from May to September in the south and from June to September in the north. You'll need a good quality tent, a warm sleeping bag, rainwear, spare warm clothing, thick-soled rubber boots, a compass and detailed maps. Maps and other equipment can be bought in the nearest Tourist Centre to the hiking route. (See "The Countryside" in *Scandinavia Basics*, for more on hiking.)

Getting there

How hard it is to get to Finland obviously depends on which part of Scandinavia you're coming from. From the east coast of Sweden it's easy, with regular ferry crossings from a number of points and usually good onward links once you've arrived. Further north, Sweden and Norway both have land borders with Finland and these are no fuss to cross by bus – or in one place a train – although in a few spots you may have to wait several days between connections. From Denmark, it's impossible to get to Finland without passing through Sweden unless you fly, although there is a direct bus service and fairly frequent trains.

■ From Denmark

The only direct **bus** link from Copenhagen to Finland runs once a week during the summer to Helsinki, three times weekly to Turku; one-way fares cost just under 500DKr. Services run on to Seinäjoki and Jyväskylä. Naturally, it's a fairly exhausting trek, taking 25 hours. If you're travelling with *InterRail, BIJ,* or *Nordtourist* passes, it's a much better idea to take the **train**: there are 1– 2 daily from Copenhagen to Turku (21hr) and Helsinki (25hr). Without a pass, however, the single fare is a hefty 1477DKr.

■ From Sweden's East Coast

The most frequent **ferries** from Sweden to Finland run between Stockholm and Helsinki and are operated by the *Silja* and *Viking* lines. Each company has a year-round overnight service which costs from 180SKr one way. Both lines also sail twice-daily from Stockholm to Turku (78SKr) and Mariehamn (50SKr), although between Stockholm and Mariehamn the *Birka Line* is cheaper (30–40SKr). On the same route there's also the *Anedin* service (90SKr). *Viking* run from Kapellskär to Mariehamn and Naantali (30SKr/60SKr). *Viking* also link Stockholm and Naantali (78SKr).

There are a number of other routes between Sweden and the Finnish west coast. *Eckerö* lines run from Umeå to Vaasa (115SKr); *Vasabåtarna* run from Umeå and Örnsköldsvik to Vaasa (95– 140SKr), and Sundsvall to Vaasa(115–175SKr); *Jakob* ferries connect Skellefteå and Kokkola (90–140SKr); *KG* link Gävle and Kaskinen (145– 175SKr). Bear in mind, though, that some services only run in summer.

For current details and the latest news on the numerous discounts – ranging from fifty percent reductions to free passage for holders of *Inter/ EurRail* cards – check with a travel agent or the relevant ferry office.

■ From Northern Sweden and Norway

Between the neighbouring towns of Haparanda in Sweden, and Tornio at the northern tip of the Gulf of Bothnia, there are numerous **buses** and a twice daily **train**, which continues to Helsinki. In the Arctic North, buses also connect the Norwegian/Finnish border towns of Karasjok/ Karisganiemi and Skipbotn/Kilpisjärvi, and the Finnish border villages of Polmak and Nuorgam; fares and schedules, beyond what we've included under "Travel Details" at the end of the relevant chapters, can be checked at any tourist office or bus station.

■ By plane

Finnair have non-stop **flights** from Copenhagen to Helsinki three or four times a day, from Stockholm four or five times a day and from Oslo twice a day. There are also six flights a week to Tampere from both Stockholm and Oslo, as well as a daily flight from Copenhagen, three a day from Stockholm, and five a week from Gothenburg, to Turku. Check with a travel agent for the occasional bargain reductions between Scandinavian cities.

Costs, Money and Banks

If you're arriving from Norway or Sweden, Finland's high prices will come as little surprise; if you're not, you're in for a very big shock. As in the adjoining Scandinavian countries, expenditure in Finland, on food, drink, transport or accommodation, can quickly reach astronomical proportions – and it's essential to plan with care.

There are ways to cut **costs**, and we've detailed them where relevant, but as a general rule you'll need £20–30 a day to even live fairly modestly – staying mostly at youth hostels or campsites, eating out every other day and supplementing your diet with food from supermarkets, visiting only a few selected museums and socialising fairly rarely. To live well, and see more, you'll be spending closer to £50.

■ Money and banks

Finnish **currency** is the *markka* (plural *markkaa*), which divides into 100 *penniä*. Notes are 1000mk, 500mk, 100mk, 50mk and 10mk; coins are 5mk, 1mk, 50p, 20p, 10p, and 5p. The **exchange rate** at the time of writing 6.5mk to £1.

As usual, the best way to carry money is as travellers cheques. These can be changed at most **banks** (Mon–Fri 9.15am–4.15pm), the charge for which is usually 15mk (though several people changing money together need only pay the commission charge once). You can also change money at hotels, though normally at a much worse rate than the banks offer. In a country where every markka counts, it's worth looking around for a better deal: in rural areas some banks and hotels are known not to charge any commission at all. Some banks have currency exchange desks at transport terminals which open to meet international arrivals.

Communications

In general, communications in Finland are dependable and quick, although in the far north, and in some sections of the east, minor delays arise simply because of the geographical remoteness.

■ Post and phones

Unless you're on a hiking trek through the back of beyond, you can rest assured your letter or card will arrive at its destination fairly speedily. The cost of mailing anything weighing under 20g to other parts of Europe is 2.50mk. You can buy **stamps** from a **post office** (Mon–Fri 9am–5pm; longer hours at the main post office in Helsinki), from the street stands or *R-kioski*, and at some hotels. **Post restante** is available at the main post office in every large town.

An out-of-order **public phone** is virtually unheard of in Finland, although many of them, widely found on streets and transport centres, have a dilapidated look. The minimum cost of a **local call** is 1mk. Phones take 1mk and 5mk coins, and a few older ones also accept two 50p coins, which run out rapidly so have a supply of small change to hand. **International calls** are cheapest between 10pm and 8am; to the UK, the cost is around 5mk a minute. **Hotel phones** are more expensive, though not prohibitively so on local calls.

■ Media

The biggest-selling Finnish **newspaper**, and the only one to be distributed all over the country, is the daily *Helsingin Sanomat* (5mk). Most of the others are locally-based and sponsored by a political party, except for the second most popular daily rag, *Uusi Suomi* (5mk), which is an independent paper that publishes an English-language resumé of the day's news. All newspapers carry entertainment listings; only the cinema listings – where the film titles are translated into Finnish – present problems for non-speakers. A better place for what's on information, if you're in Helsinki, Tampere or Turku, is the free *City* (appearing fortnightly in Helsinki, monthly in Turku and Tampere), which carries news, features and entertainment details on the surrounding area. For **rock music** listings, the fortnightly *Rumba* (9.80mk) has a rundown of forthcoming gigs and festivals throughout the country.

Overseas newspapers, including most British and some US titles, can be found, often on the day of issue, at the Academic Bookstore, Pohjoisesplanadi 39, in Helsinki. Most cost 10mk, with Sunday editions around 12mk. Elsewhere, foreign papers are harder to find and less up-to-date, though they often turn up at the bigger newsagents in Turku, Tampere and, to a lesser extent, Oulu.

Finnish **television**, despite its three channels (one of which is called *MTV*, but is no relation to the better-known round-the-clock rock music station), isn't exactly inspiring and certainly won't keep you off the streets for long. Moderately more interesting is the fact that, depending on where you are, you might be able to watch Swedish, Estonian and Russian programes. A few youth hostels have TV rooms, and most hotel room TVs have the regular channels plus a feast of cable and satellite alternatives.

Getting Around

Save for the fact that traffic tends to follow a north–south pattern, you'll have few headaches getting around the more populated parts of Finland. The chief forms of public transport are trains, backed-up, particularly on east–west journeys, by long-distance coaches. For the most part trains and buses integrate well, and you'll only need to plan with care when travelling through sparsely inhabited areas such as the far north and east. Feasible and often affordable variations come in the form of boats, planes, bikes, and even hitching – though car hire is strictly for the wealthy.

■ Trains

The swiftest land link between Finland's major cities is invariably the reliable **trains**, operated by the national company, *VR*. Large, comfortable express trains (and a growing number of "ICs", super-smooth state-of-the-art Inter-City trains) serve the principal **north–south** routes several times a day. Elsewhere, especially on east–west hauls through sparsely populated regions, rail services tend to be skeletal and trains are often tiny one- or two-carriage affairs. The Arctic North is not served by trains at all.

InterRail, *BIJ*, and *Nordturist* passes are valid on all trains; if you don't have one of these and are planning a lot of travelling, get a **Finnrail Pass** *before* arriving in Finland from a travel agent or Finnish Tourist Office (for addresses see *Basics*). This costs £54 for 8 days, £90 for 15 days, and £112 for 22 days.

Otherwise **fares** are steep. The 1hr 40min journey between Helsinki and Tampere costs 64mk one way; a major trek, such as the 6hr 40min from Helsinki to Oulu, works out at around 186mk. The good news is that tickets are valid for a month, and you can break your journey once, provided the ticket is stamped at the station where you stop – unless the total distance covered is under 75km. You should **buy tickets** from station ticket offices (*lippumyymälä*), although you can also pay the inspector on the train. If there are three or more of you travelling together, **group tickets**, available from a train station or travel agent, can cut the regular fares on journeys over 75km by at least twenty percent. **Senior Citizens** with *Rail Europ* cards are entitled to a thirty percent discount on regular tickets, or fifty percent if they are over 65 and buy a Finnish Senior Citizens railcard (50mk).

Seat reservations, costing 12–15mk (25mk on *ICs*), can be a good idea if you're travelling over a holiday period or a Friday or Sunday evening. **Sleeping berths** are also available on a number of routes, for upwards of 70mk. The chief advantage of these, besides comfort, is of course the possibility of avoiding a night's accommodation charge.

The complete **timetable** (*Suomen Kulkuneuvot*) for rail, bus, ferry and air travel within the country is published every two months and costs 54mk from stations and kiosks. This is essential for plotting complex routes; for simplified details of the major train services, pick up the free *Taskuaikataulu* booklet from any tourist office or railway station.

■ Buses

Buses – run by local private companies but with a common ticket system – cover the whole country, and are often quicker and more frequent than trains over the shorter east–west hops and are essential for getting around the remoter regions. In the Arctic North there are no railways, so all public transport is by road.

Fares are fixed according to distance travelled: approximately 38mk for 100km, 128mk for a 400km journey. All types of ticket can be purchased at a bus station or at most travel agents; only ordinary one-way tickets can be bought when boarding the coach, though on journeys of 75km or less there's no saving over buying a return anyway. On return trips of over 75km, expect a reduction of ten percent. To cut costs, there is a slightly bewildering array of **discounted tickets** available: three or more people travelling 75km or more qualify for a **group reduction** of twenty percent; holders of *YIEE/FIYTO* cards (but not *ISIC* cards) can get a thirty percent reduction on trips of similar length. **Students** can also buy a bus travel discount card for 25mk, which gives 35–50 percent reductions on journeys of 75km or more; these are available from bus stations, with proof of being in full-time education and a photo. Similar reductions can be claimed by those **over 65**; again you need a 25mk card, available at bus stations. If you're going to travel a lot by bus, the cheapest way of working things is to get a **Coach Holiday Ticket**, which gives 1000km of coach travel over any two-week period for 240mk; buy it from any long-distance bus station, though exactly how much money it saves will obviously depend on your itinerary. For information, the free bus **timetable**, *Suomen Pikavuorot*, which lists all the routes in the country, can be found at most coach stations.

Planes

With their range of discounts, domestic **flights** can be comparatively cheap as well as time-saving if you want to cover long distances, such as from Helsinki to the arctic north. That said, travelling by air means you'll miss many interesting parts of the country; also, the only flights from smaller towns to the bigger centres – Helsinki, Tampere and Oulu – tend to depart at around 6am. The **Finnair Holiday Ticket**, which costs around 1050mk, gives unlimited use of domestic flights for 15 days; the **Finnair Youth Holiday Ticket**, for those under 23, costs around 815mk for the same period. Under-23s also qualify for a fifty percent discount on regular fares in off-peak hours. Holiday tickets are restricted to foreigners but can be bought inside or outside Finland from *Finnair* offices or travel agents. There's also a variety of off-peak summer reductions which can be checked at travel agents and airline or tourist offices in Finland.

Ferries

Lake travel is aimed more at holidaying families than the budget-conscious traveller. **Prices** are high considering the distances, and progress is slow as the vessels chug along the great lake chains. If you have the time, money and inclination, though, it can be worth taking one of the shorter trips simply for the experience. Routings are many and details can be checked at any tourist office in the country and at Finnish Tourist Offices abroad. As an example of fares, Jyväskylä to Lahti costs about 250mk and takes just over eleven hours.

Cycling

Cycling is seldom an arduous way to see the country at close quarters since the only appreciable hills are in the far north and extreme east. Villages and towns may be separated by at least several hours' pedalling, however, and the scenery can get monotonous. Finnish **roads** are of high quality in the south and around the large towns, but are much rougher in the north and in isolated areas; beware the springtime thaw when the winter snows melt and sometimes cover roads with water and mud. All major towns have bike shops selling spares – and Finland is one of the few places in the world where you can buy bicycle snow tyres with tungsten steel studs. Most youth hostels, campsites and some hotels and tourist offices offer **bike hire** from 30mk per day, 100mk per week; usually there's also a deposit of around 120mk.

Driving and hitching

With such a good public transport network, **car hire** is only worth considering if you're travelling as a group of four or five as it's extremely expensive (as is petrol). The big international companies such as *Avis, Budget, EuropCar-InterRent* and *Hertz*, and the similarly priced Finnish company, Oy Polarpoint, have offices in most Finnish towns and at international arrival points. They all accept major credit cards; if paying by cash, you'll need to leave a substantial deposit. You'll also need (obviously) a valid driving licence, at least a year's driving experience, and to be aged at least 19–23, depending on the company you rent from.

Rates for a medium-sized car are 150–210mk per day, with reductions for longer loans, down to around 2000mk for a fortnight's use. On top of this, there's a surcharge of 1.90–2.3mk per km (which may be waived on long-term loans) and a drop-off fee of around 200mk if you leave the car somewhere other than the place from which it was hired. For more details on car hire before arriving in Finland, visit an office of one of the international companies mentioned above, or ask at a Finnish Tourist Board office.

If you **bring your own car** to Finland, it's advisable (though not compulsory) to have a Green Card as proof of insurance. If you do this and are involved in an **accident**, report it at once to the Finnish Motor Insurer's Bureau, Bulevardi 28, 00120 Helsinki (☎90/19251).

Once underway, you'll find the next financial drain is **petrol**, which costs just under 4mk a litre. **Service stations** are plentiful (except in the far north, where they are few and far between) and usually open from 7am to 9pm from Monday to Saturday, often closing all-day Sunday – although in summer in busy holiday areas, many service stations stay open round-the-clock. Though **roads** are generally in good condition there can be problems with melting snows, usually during April and May in the south and during June in the far north. The speed limit is 80kph, except where signposted otherwise, and on motorways, where it's 100kph.

Other **rules** of the road include: using **headlights** when driving outside built-up areas, as well as in fog and in poor light; the compulsory wearing of **seatbelts** by drivers and all passengers. As elsewhere in Scandinavia, penalties for **drunk driving** are severe – the police may stop and breathalyze you if they think you've been driving erratically. In some areas in the north of the country, **reindeer and elk** are liable, especially around dusk, to take a stroll across a road. Although these are sizeable creatures, damage (to the car) is unlikely to be serious, although all such collisions should be reported at the nearest police station.

Finnish **roadsigns** are similar to those throughout Europe, but be aware of bi-lingual place names (see "Language"); one useful sign to watch for is *Keskusta*, which means "town centre".

Hitching is generally easy, and sometimes the quickest means of transport between two spots. Finland's large student population has helped accustom drivers to the practice, and you shouldn't have to wait too long for a ride on the busy main roads between large towns. Make sure you have a decent road map and emergency provisions/shelter if you're passing through isolated regions. While many Finns speak English, it's still handy to memorise the Finnish equivalent of "let me out here" – *jään pois tässä*.

■ Local transport

It's only in and around very small towns and villages that you may struggle to get about by means other than foot. In cities and larger towns, **public transport** takes the form of a comprehensive bus network (together with trams in Helsinki) with fares of 7–12mk for a single journey. After midnight, **taxis** (*taksi*) may be your sole mode of conveyance. These can be hailed in the street, found at taxi-ranks or phoned for (look under *Taksiasemat* in the phone book). Taxis are cheaper in the north than the south, and most expensive of all in Helsinki. Basic charges are normally around the 9–10mk plus 5mk per kilometre, with additional charges at night and on weekends. With several people sharing, taxis can be an affordable way to travel between isolated towns when public transport is scarce.

Sleeping

Whether you're at the end of a long-distance hiking trail or in the centre of a city, you'll find at least some kind of accommodation in Finland to suit your needs. You will, however, have to pay dearly for it: prices are high and only by being aware of special offers and the cheap times in which to travel will you be able to sleep well on a budget.

■ Hotels

Finnish **hotels** (*hotelli*) are rarely other than polished and pampering: TV, phone and private bathroom are standard fixtures, breakfast is invariably included in the price, and there's often free use of the sauna and swimming pool too. Costs can be formidable – frequently in excess of 400mk for a double – but planning ahead and taking advantage of various discount schemes and seasonal reductions can cut prices, often to as little as 300mk.

In **major cities**, particularly Helsinki, there can be bargains in business-orientated hotels during July and August, and on Fridays, Saturdays and Sundays throughout the year. Exact details of these change frequently, but it's worth checking the current situation at a local tourist office. Reductions are also available to holders of Helsinki Cards and the similar card issued for Tampere. Otherwise, between July and August you won't find anything under 350mk by turning up on spec. Hotels in **country areas** are no less comfortable than those in cities, and often they're a touch less costly, typically 250–300mk. However, space is again limited during summer.

Expense can be trimmed a little under the *Finncheque* system, which offers an unlimited number of vouchers costing 150mk each per person, entitling two holders to a double room in hotels in participating chains between June and August. Even with the voucher, though, there's a surcharge of 75mk in the more expensive hotels, and a similar amount *always* levied on single rooms, effectively rendering the scheme a non-starter for those travelling alone. You can only buy the *Finncheque* outside Finland at a Finnish Tourist Board office or a specialist travel agent, who will also supply addresses of the hotels involved. Don't worry about buying more vouchers than you might need – they are refundable at the place of purchase. Another discount is that offered by the downmarket *Scanhotel* chain, who offer a year-round fifty percent discount to holders of *ISIC* cards, lowering their prices to 120–160mk for a double. The chain doesn't, however, cover much of the country.

In many towns you'll also find **tourist hotels** (*matkustajakoti*), a more basic type of hotel, broadly akin to British-style bed and breakfast (without the breakfast). They charge 140–180mk per person, but are often full throughout the summer. The facilities of **summer hotels** (*kesähotelli*), too, are more basic than regular hotels, since the accommodation is in student blocks (there are universities in all the major cities and in an impressive number of the larger towns) which are vacated from June to the end of August. Bookable in Finland from any travel agent, summer hotel prices are around 180mk per person. Bear in mind that identical accommodation – minus the bed linen and breakfast – comes a lot cheaper in the guise of a youth hostel (see below).

■ Youth hostels

Often the easiest and cheapest place to rest your head is a **youth hostel** (*retkeilymaja*). These exist throughout the country, in major cities (which will have at least one) and isolated country areas. The only time you're likely to run into problems finding hostel space is from June to August (especially mid-July to mid-August), when hostels in the bigger centres and the more popular hiking areas are often full; it's *essential* to

phone ahead to reserve a place, which many hostel wardens will do for you. If you're arriving on a late bus or train, say so when phoning and your bed will be kept for you; otherwise bookings are only held until 6pm. Things are quieter after mid-August, although a large number of hostels close soon after this date – check the one you're aiming for doesn't. Similarly, many hostels don't open until June.

Hostels are bracketed into three **grades**: A two-star hostel (26–35mk per person) has basic washing and cooking facilities and beds in dormitories, except for a few "family rooms" (ie smaller rooms with three or four beds). The three-star hostels (28–40mk), found in towns and country areas, have showers, cooking facilities, serve meals – at least breakfast – and have a larger number of family rooms. Four-star hostels, or "Fin hostels", are often identical to Summer Hotels (see above), and may even occupy part of the same building. These have two- and four-bedded rooms only, at least one washroom and toilet to every three rooms; prices are usually 34-55mk.

All youth hostels have wardens to provide general assistance and arrange **meals**: most hostels offer breakfast, usually for 24mk, and some serve dinner as well (around 40mk). Hostel breakfasts, especially those in busy city hostels, are rationed affairs and – hunger permitting – you'll generally be better off waiting until you can find a cheapish lunch somewhere else (see "Food And Drink", below). The only hostel breakfasts really worth taking advantage of are those offered at Summer Hotels, where hostellers can mingle with the hotel guests and, for 24–30mk, partake of the help-yourself spread.

All the quoted hostel prices apply to members; **non-members** face a 10mk supplement per night – very pricey over a long hostel tour (see *Basics* for how to become a member). **Sleeping bags** are not permitted, so bring a sheet sleeping bag: bedlinen can be hired but is expensive. The *IYHF* handbook won't tell you the category of a particular hostel: for this you need the Finnish YHA's guide called *Suomen Retkeilymajat*, which costs 20mk and is available directly from them (*Suomen Retkeilymajajärjestö*) at Yrjönkatu 38B, 00100 Helsinki (☎90/6940377).

■ Campsites and camping cottages

Official **campsites** (*leirintäalue*) are plentiful in Finland. Most open from May or June until August or September, although some stay open longer and a few all year. Sites are graded on a star system: one-star sites are in rural areas and are fairly basic; two-star sites have running water, toilets, and showers; three-star sites, often on the outskirts of major towns, have hot water and full cooking and laundry facilities. The cost for two people sharing is 20–57mk depending on the site's star rating. Campsites outside major towns are frequently very big (a 2000-tent capacity isn't uncommon), and they're very busy at weekends during July and August. Smaller and more remote sites (except those serving popular hiking routes) are, as you'd imagine, much less crowded.

Many three-star sites also have **camping cottages**. These range from simple sleeping accommodation for 2–5 people, to the luxury class equipped with TV, sauna, kitchen and fridge. The cabins cost 100–400mk per day, and can be attractively cheap for several people sharing. However, it's advisable to book cabins as far ahead of arrival as possible if you're coming during July or August.

Without an *International Camping Card* (see *Basics*) you'll need a *National Camping Card*, available at every site for 10mk and valid for a year. If you're considering **camping rough**, remember it's illegal without the landowner's permission – though in practice, provided you're out of sight of local communities, there shouldn't be any problems.

■ Hiking accommodation

Hiking routes invariably start and finish close to a campsite or a youth hostel. Along the way there are several types of basic accommodation. Of these, a *päivätupa* is a cabin with cooking facilities which is opened during the day for free use; an *autiotupa* is an unlocked hut which can be used by hikers to sleep in for one night only – there's no fee but often no space either during the busiest months. A *varaustupa* is a locked hut for which you can obtain a key at the Tourist Centre at the start of the hike – there's a smallish fee and you'll almost certainly be sharing. Some routes have a few *kämppä*, cabins – originally erected for forest workers but now used mainly by hikers; check their exact location with the nearest Tourist Centre. On most hikes there are also marked spots for pitching your own tent and making fires. For fuller hiking details see *Ostrobothnia, Kainuu and Lappland*.

Food and Drink

Finnish food is full of surprises and demands investigation. It's pricey but you can keep a grip on the expense by indulging most often at markets and at the many down-to-earth dining places, saving restaurant blow-outs for special occasions. Though tempered by many regulations, alcohol is more widely available than in much of the rest of Scandinavia: there are many places to drink but also many people drinking, most of them indulging moderately but some doing it to excess on a regular basis, regarding themselves as the last true Finns.

■ Food

Though it may at first seem a stodgy, rather unsophisticated cuisine, **Finnish food** is an interesting mix of western and eastern influences. Many dishes resemble those you might find elsewhere in Scandinavia – an enticing array of delicately prepared fish (herring, whitefish, salmon and crayfish), together with some exotic meats like reindeer and elk; others bear the stamp of Russian cooking – solid pastries and casseroles, strong on cabbage, pork and mutton.

All Finnish food will leave a severe dent in your budget, as will the ethnic cuisines, notably the innumerable pizzerias, that you'll come across all over the country. The golden money-saving rule is to eat **lunch** (*lounas*, usually served from 11am–2pm) rather than the much dearer **dinner** (*päivällinen*, usually from 6pm). Also, eke out your funds with stand-up snacks and by selective buying in supermarkets. If you're staying in a hotel, don't forget to load up on the inclusive **breakfast** (*aamiainen*) – often an open-table laden with herring, eggs, cereals, cheese, salami and bread.

Snacks, fast food and self-catering

Economical **snacks** can be found in the market halls (*kauppahalli*), where you can find basic foodstuffs along with local and national specialities. Adjoining these halls are cafeterias, where you will be charged by the *weight* of food on your plate. Look out for *karjalan piirakka* – oval-shaped Karelian pastries costing 4–5mk which contain a gluey amalgam of rice and potato – delicious hot but disgusting cold. Also worth trying is *kalakukko*, a chunk of bread with pork and whitefish baked inside it – legendary around

Kuopio but available almost everywhere. Expect to spend around 12mk for a chunk big enough for two. Slightly cheaper but just as filling, *lihapii-rakka* are envelopes of pastry filled with rice and meat – ask for them with mustard (*sinappi*) and/or ketchup. Most railway stations and the larger bus stations and supermarkets also have cafeterias proffering a selection of the above and other greasier nibbles.

Less exotically, the big **burger** franchises are widely found, as are the *Grilli* and *Nakkikioski* roadside fast-food stands turning out burgers, frankfurters and hot-dogs for 12–18mk; they're always well-patronised when the pubs shut.

Finnish **supermarkets** – *Sokos*, *K-Kaupat*, *Pukeva* and *Centrum* are widespread names – are fairly standard affairs. In general, a substantial oval of dark ryebread (*ruisleipä*) costs about 4mk, ten *karjalan piirakkas* 12mk, a litre of milk 4mk, and a packet of biscuits around 9mk. Unusually, Finnish tinned **soup** (*keitto*) can be an excellent investment for self-catering, a usually flavourful option with hunks of meat and vegetables that's a long way from the dribble-like liquid you may be used to at home.

Coffee (*Kahvi*) is widely drunk and costs 5–7mk per cup; in a *baari* or *kahvila* it's sometimes consumed with a *pulla* – a kind of doughy bun. Coffee is normally drunk black, although milk is always there if you want it; you'll also commonly find espresso and cappuccino, although these are more expensive. **Tea** (*tee*) costs 5–10mk, depending on where you are and whether you want to indulge in some exotic brew. In rural areas, though, drinking it is considered a bit effete. When ordering tea, it's a good idea to insist that the water is boiling before the teabag is added – and that the bag is left in for more than two seconds.

Mensas, restaurants and pizzerias

If you're in a university town, the campus cafeteria or **student mensa** is the cheapest place to get a hot dish. Theoretically you have to be a student but you are unlikely to be asked for ID. There's a choice of three meals: *Kevytlounas (KL)*, the "light menu", which usually comprises soup and bread; *Lounas (L)*, the "ordinary menu", which consists of a smallish fish or meat dish with dessert; and *Herkkulounas (HL)*, the "delicious menu" – a substantial and usually meat-based plateful. All three come with bread and coffee, and each one costs 12–15mk. Prices can be cut by half if you

borrow a Finnish Student ID Card from a friendly diner. The busiest period is lunchtime (11.30am–12.30pm); later in the day (usually 4–6pm), many mensas offer price reductions. Most universities also have cafeterias where a small cup of coffee can cost as little as 1mk.

If funds stretch to it, you should sample at least once a *ravintola*, or **restaurant**, offering a lunchtime buffet table (*voileipäpöytä* or *seisova pöytä*), which will be stacked with tasty traditional goodies that you can feast on to your heart's content for a set-price of around 65mk. Less costly Finnish food can be found in a *baari*. designed for working people and generally closed from 5pm or 6pm, a *baari* serves a range of Finnish dishes and snacks (and often the weaker beers, see "Drink", below). A good day for traditional Finnish food is Thursday, when every *baari* in the country dishes up *hernekeitto ja pannuka-kut*, thick pea soup with black rye bread, followed by oven-baked pancakes with strawberry jam, with buttermilk to wash it down; all for around 35mk. You'll get much the same fare from a *kahvila*, though a few of these, especially in the big cities, fancy themselves as being fashionable and may charge a few markkaa extra.

Although *ravintola* and *baaris* are plentiful, they're often outnumbered by **pizzerias**, as varied in quality here as they are in any other country but especially worthwhile for their "lunch specials", when a set-fee of 36–45mk buys a pizza, coffee and everything you can carry from the bread and salad bar. At other times, a simple pizza on its own will be 32–45mk. Many of the bigger pizza chains offer discounts for super-indulgence – such as a second pizza for half-price and a third for free if the eater can polish off the first two. **Vegetarians**, especially those who don't eat fish, are likely to become well-acquainted with pizzerias – specifically vegetarian restaurants are thin on the ground, even in major cities.

■ Drink

Finland's **alcohol laws** are as bizarre and almost as repressive as those of Norway and Sweden, but unlike those countries boozing is tackled enthusiastically, even regarded by some as an integral part of the national character. Some Finns, men in particular, often drink with the sole intention of getting paralytic; younger Finns are more inclined to regard the practice simply as an enjoyable social activity.

GLOSSARY OF FINNISH FOOD AND DRINK TERMS

Basics

Juusto	Cheese	*Maito*	Milk	*Piirakka*	Pie
Kakku	Cake	*Makeiset*	Sweets	*Riisi*	Rice
Keitto	Soup	*Perunat*	Potatoes	*Voi*	Butter
Keksit	Biscuits	*Piimä*	Buttermilk	*Voileipä*	Sandwich
Leipä	Bread				

Meat (*Lihaa*)

Häränfilee	Fillet of beef	*Kinkku*	Ham	*Sianliha*	Pork
Hirvenliha	Elk	*Lihapyörykat*	Meatballs	*Poro*	Reindeer
Jauheliha	Minced beef	*Nauta*	Beef	*Vasikanliha*	Veal
Kana	Chicken	*Paisti*	Steak		

Seafood (*Äyriäisiä*) and Fish (*Kala*)

Ankerias	Eel	*Rapu*	Crayfish	*Silakat*	Baltic herring
Graavilohi	Salted salmon	*Sardiini*	Sardine	*Silli*	Herring
Hauki	Pike	*Savustettu lohi*	Smoked salmon	*Suolattu*	Pickled herring
Hummeri	Lobster				
Katkaravut	Shrimps	*Savustettut silakat*	Smoked Baltic herring	*Taimen* or *forelli*	Trout
Lohi	Salmon				
Makrilli	Mackerel	*Siika*	Large, slightly oily, white fish	*Tonnikala*	Tuna
Muikku	Small whitefish			*Turska*	Cod

Egg dishes(*Munaruoat*)

Hillomunakas	Jam omelette	*Kinkkumunakas*	Ham omelette	*Pekonimunakas*	Bacon omelette
Hyydytetty muna	Poached egg	*Munakas*	Omelette	*Perunamunakas*	Potato omelette
		Munakokkeli	Scrambled eggs		
Juustomunakas	Cheese omelette			*Sienimunakas*	Mushroom omelette
Keitetty muna	Boiled eggs	*Paistettu muna*	Fried egg		

Vegetables(*Vihannekset*)

Herneet	Peas	*Paprika*	Green pepper	*Sieni*	Mushroom
Kaali	Cabbage	*Pavut*	Beans	*Sipuli*	Onion
Kurkku	Cucumber	*Peruna*	Potato	*Tilli*	Dill
Maissintähkät	Corn on the cob	*Pinaatti*	Spinach	*Tomaatti*	Tomato
		Porkkana	Carrot		

Fruit (*Hedelmä*)

Appelsiini	Orange	*Luumu*	Plums	*Pähkinä*	Nut
Aprikoosi	Apricot	*Mansikka*	Strawberry	*Persikka*	Peach
Banaani	Banana	*Meloni*	Melon	*Raparperi*	Rhubarb
Greippi	Grapefruit	*Omena*	Apple	*Sitruuna*	Lemon
Kirsikka	Cherry	*Päärynä*	Pear	*Viinirypäle*	Grape

Sandwiches (*Voileipä*)

Kappelivoileipä	Fried French bread with bacon and topped by a fried egg	*Oopperavoileipä*	Fried French bread with hamburger and egg
Muna-anjovisleipä	Dark bread with slices of hard-boiled egg, anchovy fillets and tomato	*Sillivoileipä*	Herring on dark bread, usually with egg and tomato

Finnish Specialities

Kaalikääryleet	Cabbage rolls: cabbage leaves stuffed with minced meat and rice	Piparjuuriliha	Boiled beef with horseradish sauce
Kaalipiirakka	Cabbage and mincemeat pie	Porkkanalaatikko	Carrot casserole; mashed carrots and rice
Karjalanpaisti	Karelian stew: beef and pork with onions	Poronkäristys	Sautéed reindeer stew
		Sianlihakastike	Gravy with slivers of pork
Kurpitsasalaatti	Pickled pumpkin served with meat dishes	Silakkalaatikko	Casserole with alternating layers of potato, onion and Baltic herring, with an egg and milk sauce
Lammaskaali	Mutton and cabbage stew or soup		
Lasimestarin silli	Pickled herring with spices, vinegar, carrot and onion	Stroganoff	Beef with gherkins and onions, browned in a casserole, braised in stock with tomato juice and sour cream
Lihakeitto	Soup made from meat, potatoes, carrots and onions		
Lindströmin pihvi	Beefburger made with beetroot and served with a cream sauce	Suutarinlohi	Marinated Baltic herring with onion and peppers
Lohilaatikko	Potato and salmon casserole		
Lohipiirakka	Salmon pie	Tilliliha	Boiled veal flavoured with dill sauce
Makaroonilaatikko	Macaroni casserole with milk and egg sauce		
		Venäläinen silli	Herring fillets with mayonnaise, mustard, vinegar, beetroot, gherkins and onion
Maksalaatikko	Baked liver purée with rice and raisins		
Merimiespihvi	Casserole of potato slices and meat patties or minced meat	Wieninleike	Fried veal cutlet

Drinks

Appelsiinimehu	Orange juice	Konjakki	Cognac	Tonic vesi	Tonic water
Gini	Gin	Limonaati	Lemonade	Vesi	Water
Kahvi	Coffee	Olut	Beer	Viiniä	Wine
Kalja	Dark ale	Tee	Tea	Viski	Whisky
Kivennäisvesi	Mineral water				

What to drink

Finnish spirits are much the same as you'd find in any country. **Beer** (*olut*), on the other hand, falls into three categories: "light beer" (I-Olut) – more like a soft-drink; "medium strength beer" (*Keskiolut*, III-Olut) – more perceptibly alcoholic, sold in many food shops and cafés; and "strong beer" (A-Olut or IV-Olut), which is on a par with the stronger English beers, and can only be bought at the *ALKO* shops and fully licensed (ie grade A) restaurants and nightclubs.

The main – and cheapest – outlet for alcohol of any kind is the **ALKO** shop (Mon–Thurs 10am–5pm, Fri 10am–6pm, Sat 9am–2pm). Even the smallest town will have one of these, and prices don't vary. In an ALKO shop, strong beers like *Lapin Kulta Export* – an Arctic-orginated mind blower – and the equally potent *Karjala*, *Lahden A*, *Olvi Export*, and *Koff* porter, cost 6.20–6.50mk for a 300ml bottle. Imported beers such as *Heineken*, *Carlsberg* and *Becks* go for 8.90–9.30mk a bottle. As for **spirits**, *Finlandia* vodka and *Jameson's* Irish Whiskey are 180mk and 210mk respectively per litre. There's also a very popular rough form of vodka called *koskenkorra*, ideal for assessing the strength of your stomach lining, and costing 140mk. The best bargain in **wine** is reputedly the Hungarian variety, which changes hands for around 35mk per bottle. French wines range from 45mk to 185mk a bottle.

Where to drink

Most **restaurants** have a full licence, and some are actually frequented more for drinking than eating; it's these which we've listed under "Drinking" throughout the text. They're often also called bars or pubs by Finns simply for convenience. Just to add to the confusion, some so-called "Pubs" are not licensed; neither are *Baari*, mentioned above.

Along with ordinary restaurants, there are also **dance restaurants** (*tanssiravintola*). As the name suggests, these are places to dance rather than dine, although most do serve food as well as drink. They're popular with the over-40s, and before the advent of discos were the main places for people of opposite sex to meet. Even if you're under 40, dropping into one during the (usually early evening) sessions can be quite an eye-opener. Expect to pay a 10–30mk admission charge.

Once you've found somewhere to drink, there's a fairly rigid set of **customs** to contend with. Sometimes you have to queue outside the most popular bars since entry is permitted only if a seat is free – there's no standing. Only one drink per person is allowed on the table at any one time except in the case of *porter* – a stout which most Finns mix with regular beer. There's always either a doorman (*portsari*) – whom you must tip (3–5mk) on leaving – or a cloakroom into which you must check your coat on arrival (again 3–5mk). Bars are usually open until midnight or 1am and service stops half an hour before the place shuts. This is announced by a winking of the lights – the *valomerkki.*.

Some bars and clubs have **waitress/waiter service**, whereby you order, s/he fetches, and you pay on delivery of your drinks. A common order is a *tuoppi* – a half-litre glass of draught beer, which costs 20–25mk (up to 30mk in some nightclubs). This might come slightly cheaper in **self-service** bars, where you select your tipple and queue up to pay at the till.

Wherever you buy alcohol, you'll have to be of **legal age**: at least 18 to buy beer and wine, and twenty or over to have a go at the spirits. ID will be checked if you look too young – or if the doorman's in a bad mood.

Directory

CANOEING With many lakes and rivers, Finland offers challenges to every type of canoe enthusiast, expert or beginner. There's plenty of easy-going paddling on the long lake systems, innumerable thrashing rapids to be shot, and abundant sea canoeing around the archipelagos of the south and southwest coast. Canoe hire (available wherever there are suitable waters) costs around 20mk per hour, 100mk per day, or 400mk per week. Many tourist offices have plans of local canoeing routes, and you can get general information from the Finnish Canoe Association, Radiokatu 2, 00240 Helsinki (☎90/1582363).

CONTRACEPTIVES *Kondomis* are easily available from chemists, kiosks, and machines in public toilets and some restaurant toilets.

CUSTOMS There are few, if any, border fomalities when entering Finland from another Scandinavian country by land (although the crossing from Norway at Näätämö is – at least in theory – closed to non-Scandinavians from 10pm to 7am). The same applies by sea; only by air do you usually need to show your passport. As for bringing food into Finland, up to 8kg of meat or meat products are allowed, provided the meat has undergone thermal or other heat treatment rendering it free of infection, and up to 8 litres of pasturised, heat-treated and sterilised milk or milk products. Also permitted are up to 3kg of vegetables, fruit or berries.

DENTIST Seeing a dentist can be very expensive: expect to spend around 100mk. Look under "Hammaslääkäri" in the phone book, or ask at a tourist office.

DOCTOR Provided you're insured, you'll save time by seeing a doctor at a private health centre (*Lääkäriasema*) rather than queuing at a national health centre (*Terveyskeskus*).

EMERGENCIES ☎000.

FISHING Non-Scandinavians need a General Fishing Licence if they intend to fish in Finland's waterways; this costs 25mk from post offices and is valid for one year. In certain parts of the Arctic North you'll need an additional licence, also 25mk, obtainable locally. Throughout the country you'll also need the permission of the owner of particular stretch of water, usually obtained by buying a permit on the spot. The nearest campsite or tourist office will be able to give details of this, and advise of the many regional variations on national fishing laws.

MARKETS In larger towns, these usually take place every day except Sunday from 7am to 2pm. There'll also be a market hall (*kauppahalli*) open weekdays 8am–5pm. Smaller communities have a market once or twice a week, usually including Saturday.

NUDE BATHING Sections of some Finnish beaches are designated nude bathing areas, sometimes sex-segregated and often with an admission charge of around 2mk. The local tourist office, or campsite, will have the facts.

PUBLIC HOLIDAYS Shops and banks will be closed on these days and most public transport will operate a Sunday schedule; museum opening hours may also be affected. January 1, May 1, December 6, December 24, 25 and 26. Variable dates: Epiphany (between January 6 and 12), Good Friday and Easter Weekend, the Saturday before Whit Sunday, Midsummer's Eve, All Saint's Day (the Saturday between October 31 and November 6).

SAUNAS These are cheapest at a public swimming pool, where you'll pay 10–20mk for a session. Hotel saunas, which are sometimes better equipped than public ones, are more expensive (20–30mk) but free to guests. Many Finnish people have saunas built into their homes and it's quite common for visitors to be invited to share one.

SHOPS Supermarkets are usually open Mon–Fri 9am–5pm, Sat 9am–noon. Some in cities keep longer hours. In Helsinki the shops in Tunneli are open until 10pm.

FINNISH AND SWEDISH PLACE NAMES

On most maps and many transport timetables cities and towns are given their Finnish names followed by their Swedish names in parentheses. Both Swedes and Finland-Swedes will frequently use the Swedish rather than the Finnish names. The main ones are listed below.

Finnish	Swedish
Helsinki	Helsingfors
Porvoo	Borgå
Turku	Åbo
Pori	Björneborg
Tampere	Tammerfors
Mikkeli	St. Michel
Savonlinna	Nyslott
Vaasa	Vasa
Kokkola	Gamlakarleby
Oulu	Uleåborg

History

Finland's history, inextricably bound with the medieval superpowers, Sweden and Russia, and later with the Soviet Union, is a stirring tale of a small peoples' survival – and eventual triumph – over what have often seemed impossible odds. It's also a story full of powerful contemporary resonances, as the other Baltic nations strive towards independence.

■ First settlements

As the icesheets of the last Ice Age retreated, parts of the Finnish Arctic coast became inhabited by tribes from eastern Europe. They hunted bear and reindeer, and fished the well-stocked rivers and lakes: relics of their existence have been found and dated at around 8000 BC. Pottery skills from outside were introduced around 3000 BC, and trade with Russia and the east flourished. At the same time, other races from the east were arriving and merging with the established population; the **Boat Axe** culture (1800 BC–1600 BC), which originated in Central Europe, spread as Indo-Europeans migrated, and the seafaring knowledge they possessed enabled them to begin trading with Sweden from the Finnish west coast. This is indicated by **Bronze Age** findings (around 1300 BC) concentrated in a narrow strip along the coast. The previous settlers withdrew eastwards and the advent of severe weather brought this period of occupation to an end.

■ The arrival of the Finns

The antecedents of the Finns were a primordial race based in central Russia who moved outward in two directions. One tribe went south, eventually to Hungary, and the other westward to the Baltic where it mixed with Latgals, Lithuanians and Germans. The latter, the "Baltic Finns", were migrants who crossed the Baltic around AD 400 to form an independent society in Finland. In AD 100 the Roman historian Tacitus had already described a wild and primitive people called "the Fenni". This is thought to have been a reference to the earliest **Same**, who occupied Finland before this. With their more advanced culture, the Baltic Finns absorbed this indigenous population, although some of their pre-existing customs were maintained. The new Finns worked the land, utilised the vast forests and made lengthy fishing expeditions on the lakes.

■ The pagan era

The main Finnish settlements were along the west coast facing Sweden, with whom trade was established. The cessation of this trading, caused by the Swedish Vikings' opening up of routes to the East, in turn forced these western communities into decline. Meanwhile the Finnish south coast was exposed to seaborne raiding parties and most Finns moved inland and eastwards, a large number settling around the huge Lake Ladoga in **Karelia**. Eventually the people of Karelia were able to enjoy trade in two directions – with the Varangians to the east and the Swedes to the west. Groups from Karelia and the more northern territory of Kainuu regularly ventured into Lappland to fish and hunt. At the end of the pagan era Finland was split into three regions: Varsinais-Suomi ("Finland proper") in the southwest, Häme in the western portion of the lake region, and Karelia in the east. Although they often helped one another, there was no formal cooperation between the inhabitants of these areas.

■ The Swedish era (1155–1809)

At the start of the tenth century, pagan Finland was neighboured by two opposing religions: Catholicism in Sweden on one side and the Orthodox Church of Russia on the other. The Russians wielded great influence in Karelia, but the west of Finland began to gravitate towards Catholicism on account of its high level of contact with Sweden. In 1155, King Erik of Sweden launched a Crusade into Finland, and although its real purpose was to strengthen trade routes, it swept through the southwest leaving the English **Bishop Henry** at **Turku** to establish a parish. Henry was killed by a Finnish yeoman, but became the patron saint of the Turku diocese and the region became the administrative base of the whole country. Western Finland generally acquiesced to the Swedes, but Karelia didn't, becoming a territory much sought after by both the Swedes and the Russians. In 1323, under the **Treaty of Pähkinäsaari**, an official border was drawn up, giving the western part of Karelia to Sweden while the Russian principality of Novgorod retained the eastern section around Lake Ladoga. To emphasise their claim, the Russians founded the Orthodox **Valamo Monastery** on an island in the lake.

Under the Swedish Crown, Finns still worked and controlled their own land, often living side by side with Swedes who came to the west coast to safeguard sea trade. Finnish provincial leaders were given places among the nobility. In 1362 King Håkon gave Finland the right to vote in Swedish royal elections. When the Swedish throne was given to the German, Albrecht of Mecklenburg, in 1364, there was little support for the new monarch in Finland, and violent opposition to his forces who arrived to occupy the Swedish-built castles. Once established, the Mecklenburgians imposed forced labour and the Finnish standard of living swiftly declined. There was even a proposal that the country should be sold to the Teutonic Order of Knights.

In a campaign to wrest control of the Swedish realm, a Swedish noble, **Grip**, acquired control of one Finnish province after another and by 1374 was in charge of the whole country. In doing this he was obliged to consider the welfare of the Finns and consequently living conditions improved. Another effect of Grip's actions was to underline Finland's position as an individual country – under the Swedish sovereign but distanced from Sweden's political offices.

A testament by Grip was intended to ensure that Finnish affairs would be managed by the Swedish nobility irrespective of the wishes of the monarch. The nobility, however, found themselves forced to look for assistance to Margrethe, Queen of Denmark and Norway. She agreed to come to the Swedes' aid provided they recognised her as sovereign over all the Swedish realm including Finland. This resulted in the **Kalmar Union** of 1397.

While the Finns were barely affected by the constitution of the Union, there was a hope that it would guarantee their safety against the Russians, whose expansionist policies were an increasing threat. Throughout the fifteenth century there were repeated skirmishes between Russians and Finns in the border lands and around the important Finnish Baltic trading centre of Viipuri (now Soviet Vyborg).

The election of King Charles VIII in 1438 caused a rift in the Union and serious strife between Sweden and Denmark. He was forced to abdicate in 1458 but his support in Finland was strong, and his successor, Christian I, sent an armed column to subdue Finnish unrest. While Turku Castle was under siege, the Danish noble **Erik Axelsson Tott**, already known and respected in the country, called a meeting of representatives from every Finnish estate where it was agreed that Christian I would be acknowledged as king of the Union.

Tott went on to take command of Viipuri Castle and was able to function almost independently of central government. He planned to make Viipuri the major centre for east–west trade. However, resources had to be diverted to strengthening the eastern defences. During the 1460s Novgorod was forced into Moscow's sphere of influence and finally absorbed altogether. This left Finland's eastern edge more exposed than ever before. Novgorod had long held claims on large sections of Karelia, and the border situation was further confused by the Finnish peasants who had drifted eastwards and settled in the disputed territories. Part of Tott's response to the dangers was to erect the fortress of **Olavinlinna** (in the present town of Savonlinna) in 1475, actually inside the land claimed by Russia.

Tott died in 1481 and **Sten Sture**, a Swedish regent, forced the remaining Axelssons to relinquish their familial domination of Finland. By 1487 Sture had control of the whole country, and appointed bailiffs of humble birth – instead of established aristocrats – to the Finnish castles in return for their surplus revenue. These monies were used to finance Sture's ascent through the Swedish nobility. As a result nothing was spent on maintaining the eastern defences.

Strengthened by an alliance with Denmark signed in 1493, Russia attacked Viipuri on November 30, 1495. The troops were repulsed by the technically inferior Finns, an achievement perceived as a miracle. After further battles it was agreed that the borders of the Treaty of Pähkinäsaari would remain. The Swedes drew up a bogus version of the treaty in which the border retained its fifteenth century position. It was this forgery which they used in negotiations with the Russians over the next hundred years.

Within Finland a largely Swedish-born nobility became established. Church services were conducted in Finnish although Swedish remained the language of commerce and officialdom. Because the bulk of the population were illiterate, any important deed had to be read to them. In the thirteenth and fourteenth centuries, any Finns who felt oppressed simply moved into the wild lands of the interior – out of earshot of church bells. Partly because the peasants still placed their faith in their ancient creeds, the **Reformation** was able to pass through Finland without bloodshed.

By the time Gustav Vasa took the Swedish throne in 1523, many villages were established in the disputed border regions. Almost every inhabitant spoke Finnish. but there was a roughly equal division between those communities who paid tax to the Swedish king and those who paid taxes to the Russian tsar. In the winter of 1555, a Russian advance into Karelia was quashed at Joutselkä by Finns using skis to travel speedily over the icy roads. The victory made the Finnish nobility confident of success in a full-scale war. While hesitant, Vasa finally agreed to their wishes: 12,000 troops from Sweden were dispatched to eastern Finland, and an offensive launched in the autumn of 1556. It failed, with the Russians reaching the gates of Viipuri, and Vasa retreating to the Åland Islands, asking for peace.

In 1556 Gustav Vasa made Finland a Swedish Grand Duchy and gave his son, Johan, the title Duke of Finland. It was rumoured that **Duke Johan** not only spoke Finnish but was an advocate of Finnish nationalism. These claims were exaggerated, but the duke was certainly pro-Finnish, surrounding himself with Finnish nobles and founding a chancery and an exchequer. He moved into Turku Castle and furnished it in splendour. The powers of his office, defined by the Articles of Arboga, were breached by his invasion of Livonia. As punishment he was sentenced to death by the Swedish Diet in 1563, although the king's power of pardon was acknowledged. Finland was divided between loyalty towards the friendly duke and the need to keep on good terms with the Swedish Crown, now held by Erik XIV. The Swedish forces sent to collect Johan laid siege to Turku castle for three weeks, executing thirty nobles before capturing the duke and imprisoning him.

The war between Sweden and Denmark over control of the Baltic took its toll on Erik. He became mentally unbalanced, slaying several prisoners who were being held for trial, and, in a moment of complete madness, released Johan from detention. The Swedish nobles were incensed by Erik's actions and rebelled against him – with the result that Johan became king in 1568.

In 1570 Swedish resources were stretched when hostilities again erupted with Russia, now ruled by the aggressive Tsar Ivan ("the Terrible") IV. The conflict was to last 25 years, a period known in Finland as **"the Long Wrath"**. It saw the introduction of a form of conscription instead of the reliance on mercenary soldiers, which had been the norm in other Swedish wars. Able-bodied men aged between 15 and 50 were rounded up by the local bailiff and about one in ten selected for military service. Russia occupied almost all of Estonia and made deep thrusts into southern Finland. Finally the Swedish-Finnish troops regained Estonia and made significant advances through Karelia, capturing an important eastern European trading route. The war was formally concluded by the **Treaty of Täyssinä** in 1595. Under its terms, Russia recognised the lands gained by Sweden and the eastern border was altered to reach up to the Arctic coast, enabling Finns to settle in the far north.

Sweden was established as the dominant force in the Baltic, but under Gustav II, who became king in 1611, Finland began to lose the special status it had previously enjoyed. Its administration was streamlined and centralised, causing many Finnish nobles to move to Stockholm. Civic orders had to be written rather than passed on orally, and many ambitious Finns gave themselves Swedish surnames. Finnish manpower supported Swedish efforts overseas – the soldiers gaining a reputation as wild and fearless fighters – but brought no direct benefit to Finland itself. Furthermore, the peasants were increasingly burdened by the taxes needed to support the Swedish wars with Poland, Prussia and Germany.

Conditions continued to decline until 1637, when **Per Brahe** was appointed governor-general. Against the prevailing mood of the time, he insisted that all officers should study Finnish, founded Turku University – the country's first – and instigated a successful programme to spread literacy among the Finnish people. After concluding his second term of office in 1654 he parted with the terse but accurate summary: "I was highly satisfied with this country and the country highly satisfied with me."

A terrible harvest in 1696 caused a **famine** which killed a third of the Finnish population. The fact that no aid came from Sweden intensified feelings of neglect and stirred up a minor bout of Finnish nationalism led by **Daniel Juslenius**. His book, *Aboa Vetus Et Nova*, published in 1700, claimed Finnish to be a founding language of the world and that Finns were descendants of the tribes of Israel.

In 1711 Viipuri fell to the Russians. Under their new tsar, Peter ("the Great"), the Russians quickly spread across the country, causing the nobility to flee to Stockholm and Swedish commanders to be more concerned with salvaging their army than saving Finland. In 1714, eight years of Russian occupation – **"the Great Wrath"** – began. Descriptions of the horrors of these times have been exaggerated, but nonetheless the events confirmed the Finns' long-time dread of their eastern neighbour. The Russians saw Finland simply as a springboard to attack Sweden, and lay waste to anything in it which the Swedes might attempt to regain.

Under the **Treaty of Uusikaupunki**, in 1721, the tsar gave back much of Finland but retained Viipuri, east Karelia, Estonia and Latvia, and thus control of the Baltic. Finland now had a new eastern border which was totally unprotected. Russian occupation was inevitable but would be less disastrous if entered into voluntarily. The Finnish peasants, with Swedish soldiers forcibly billeted on them, remained loyal to the king but with little faith in what he could do to protect them.

The aggressive policies of the Hats in the Swedish Diet led to the 1741 declaration of war on Russia. With barely an arm raised against them, Russian troops again occupied Finland – the start of **"the Lesser Wrath"** – until the **Treaty of Turku** in 1743. Under this, the Russians withdrew, ceded a section of Finland back to Sweden but moved their border west.

■ The Russian era (1809–1917)

In an attempt to force Sweden to join Napoleon's economic blockade, Russia, under Tsar Alexander I, attacked and occupied Finland in 1807. The **Treaty of Hamina**, signed in September, legally ceded all of the country to them. The tsar had needed a friendly country close to Napoleon's territory as a reliable ally in case of future hostilities between the two leaders. To gain Finnish favour, he had guaranteed beneficial terms at the Diet (based in Porvoo) in 1809 and subsequently Finland became an **autonomous Russian Grand Duchy**. There was no conscription and taxation was frozen at its current level, making it virtually nothing for years to come, while realignment of the northen section of the Finnish-Russian border gave additional land to Finland. Finns could freely occupy positions in the Russian Empire, although Russians were denied equal opportunities within Finland. The long period of peace which ensued saw a great improvement in Finnish wealth and well-being.

After returning Viipuri to Finland, the tsar declared Helsinki the **capital** in 1812, regarding Turku to be too close to Sweden for safety. The "Guards of Finland" helped crush the Polish rebellion and fought in the Russo-Turkish conflict. This, and the French and English attacks on Finnish harbours during the Crimean War, accentuated the bond between the two countries. Many Finns came to regard the tsar as their own monarch.

There was however an increasingly active **Finnish-language movement**. While a student leader, the future statesman **Johan Wilhelm Snellman** had met the tsar and demanded that Finnish replace Swedish as the country's official language. Snellman's slogan: "Swedes we are no longer, Russians we cannot become, we must be Finns" became the rallying cry of the **Fennomen**. The Swedish-speaking ruling class, feeling threatened, had Snellman removed from his university post and he retreated to Kuopio to publish newspapers espousing his beliefs. His opponents cited Finnish as the language of peasants, unfit for cultured use – a claim undermined by the work of a playwright, **Aleksis Kivi**, whose plays marked the beginning of the Finnish-language theatre. In 1835, the collection of Karelian folk tales, published in Finnish by **Elias Lönnrot** as the *Kalevala*, was the first written record of Finnish folklore, and became a literary focal-point for Finnish nationalism.

The liberal tsar Alexander II appointed Snellman to Turku University, from where he went on to become Minister of Finance. In 1858 Finnish was declared the official language of local government in areas where the majority of the population were Finnish speaking. And the Diet, convened in 1863 for the first time since the Russian takeover, finally gave native-tongued Finns equal status with Swedish speakers. The only opposition was from the **Svecomen** who sought not only the maintenance of the Swedish language but unification with Finland's westerly neighbour.

The increasingly powerful Pan-Slavist contingent in Russia was horrified by the growth of the Finnish timber industry and the rise of trade with the west. They were also unhappy with the special status of the Grand Duchy, considering the Finns an alien race who would contaminate the eastern empire by their links with the west. Tsar Alexander III was not swayed by these opinions but, after his assassination in 1894, Nicolas I came to power and instigated the **Russification process**. Russian was declared the official language, Finnish money was abolished and plans were laid to merge the Finnish army into the Russian army. To pass these measures the tsar drew up the unconstitutional **February Manifesto**.

Opposition came in varying forms. In 1899, a young composer called **Jean Sibelius** wrote *Finlandia*. The Russians banned all performances of it "under any name that indicates its patriotic character", causing Sibelius to publish it as *Opus 26 No.7*. The painter **Akseli Gallen-Kallela** ignored international art trends and depicted scenes from the *Kalevala* with his brush, as the poet **Eino Leino** did with his pen. Students skied to farms all over the country and collected half a million signatures against the Manifesto. Over a thousand of Europe's foremost intellectuals signed a document called *Pro-Finlandia*.

But these had no effect, and in 1901 the **Conscription Law** was introduced. This forced Finns to serve directly under the tsar in the Russian army. A programme of civil disobedience began, the leaders of which were soon obliged to go underground, where they titled themselves the *Kagel* – borrowing a name used by persecuted Russian Jews. The Finnish population became divided between the "compliants" (acquiescent to the Manifesto) and the "constitutionalists" (against the Manifesto), splitting families and even causing the rival sides do their shopping in different stores.

The stand against conscription was enough to make the Russians drop the scheme, but their grip was tightened in other ways. A peaceful demonstration in Helsinki was broken up by cossacks on horseback, and in April 1903 the tsar installed the tough **Bobrikov** as governor-general, giving him new and sweeping powers. The culmination of sporadic acts of violence came on June 16, 1904, when the Finnish civil servant **Eugen Schauman** climbed the Senate staircase and shot Bobrikov three times before turning the gun on himself. After staggering to his usual Senate seat, Bobrikov collapsed and died – and his assassin became a national hero.

In 1905, the Russians suffered defeat in their war with Japan and the general strike which broke out in their country spread to Finland, the Finnish labour movement being represented by the Social Democratic Party. The revolutionary spirit which was moving through Russia encour-

aged the conservative Finnish Senate to reach a compromise with the demands of the Social Democrats, and the result was a gigantic upheaval in the Finnish parliamentary system. In 1906, the country adopted a single-chamber parliament (the *Eduskunta*) elected by national suffrage – Finnish women being the first in Europe to get the vote. In the first election under the new system the Social Democrats won 80 seats out of the total of 200, making it the most left-wing legislature seen so far in Europe.

Any laws passed in Finland, however, still needed the ratification of the tsar, who now viewed Finland as a dangerous forum for leftist debate (the exiled Lenin met Stalin for the first time in Tampere). In 1910, Nicolas II removed the new parliament's powers and reinstated the Russification programme. Two years later the **Parity Act** gave Russians in Finland status equal to Finns, enabling them to hold seats in the Senate and posts in the civil service. The outspoken anti-tsarist parliamentary speaker, **P.E. Svinhufvud**, was exiled to Siberia for a second time.

As World War I commenced, Finland was obviously allied with Russia and endured a commercial blockade, food shortages and restrictions on civil liberties, but did not actually fight on the tsar's behalf. Germany promised Finland total autonomy in the event of victory for the kaiser and provided clandestine military training to about 2000 Finnish students – the *jäger* movement who reached Germany through Sweden and later fought against the Russians as a light infantry battalion on the Baltic front.

■ Towards Independence

When the tsar was overthrown in 1917, the Russian provisional government under Kerensky declared the measures taken against Finland null and void and restored the previous level of autonomy. Within Finland there was uncertainty over the country's constitutional bonds with Russia. The conservative view was that prerogative powers should be passed from the deposed ruler to the provisional government, while socialists held that the provisional government had no right to exercise power in Finland and that supreme authority should be passed to the *Eduskunta*.

Under the **Power Act**, the *Eduskunta* vested in itself supreme authority within Finland, leaving only control of foreign and military matters residing with the Russians. Kerensky refused to recognise the Power Act and dissolved the Finnish parliament, forcing a fresh election. This time a bigger poll returned a conservative majority.

The loss of their parliamentary majority and the bitterness felt towards the bourgeois-dominated Senate, who happily complied with Kerensky's demands, made the Social Democrats adopt a more militant line. Around the country there had been widespread labour disputes and violent confrontations between strikers and strike-breaking mobs hired by landowners. The Social Democrats sanctioned the formation of an armed workers' guard, soon to be called the **Red Guard**, in response to the growing **White Guard** – a right-wing private army operating in the virtual absence of a regular police force. A general strike was called on November 13 which forced the *Eduskunta* into reforms after just a few days. The strike was called off but a group of dissident Red Guards threatened to break from the Social Democrats and continue the action.

After the Bolsheviks took power in Russia, the conservative Finnish government became fearful of Soviet involvement in Finnish affairs and a *de facto* **statement of independence** was made. The socialists, by now totally excluded from government, declared their support for independence but insisted that it should be reached through negotiation with the Soviet Union. Instead, on December 6, a draft of an independent constitution drawn up by **K.J. Ståhlberg** was approved by the *Eduskunta*. After a delay of three weeks it was formally recognised by the Soviet leader, Lenin.

■ The Civil War

In asserting its new authority, the government repeatedly clashed with the labour movement. The Red Guard, who had reached an uneasy truce with the Social Democratic leadership, were involved in gunrunning between Viipuri and Petrograd, and efforts by the White Guard to halt it led to full-scale fighting. A vote passed by the *Eduskunta* on January 12, 1918, empowered the government to create a police force to restore law and order. On January 25, the White Guard was legitimised as the Civil Guard.

In Helsinki, a special committee of the Social Democrats took the decision to resist the Civil Guard and seize power, effectively pledging themselves to **civil war**. On January 27 and 28, a series of occupations enabled leftist committees to take control of the capital and the major towns of the south. Three government ministers who evaded capture fled to Vaasa and formed a rump administration. Meanwhile, a Finnish-born aristocrat, **C.G.E. Mannerheim**, who had served as a cavalry officer in the Russian army, arrived at the request of the government in Ostrobothnia, a region dominated by right-wing farmers, to train a force to fight the Reds.

Mannerheim, who had secured a 15 million markkaa loan from a Helsinki bank to finance his army, drew on the German-trained *jäger* for officers, while the Ostrobothnian farmers – seeking to protect their landowning privileges – along with a small number of Swedish volunteers, made up the troops. Their initial task was to "mop up" the Russian battalions remaining in western Finland, which had been posted there by the tsar to prevent German advancement in the world war, and which by now were politicised into Soviets. Mannerheim achieved this by the beginning of February, and his attention turned to the Reds.

The Whites were in control of Ostrobothnia, northern Finland and parts of Karelia, and were connected by a railway from Vaasa to Käkisalmi on Lake Ladoga. Although the Reds were numerically superior they were poorly equipped and poorly trained, and failed to break the enemy's line of communication. Tampere fell to the Whites in March. At the same time, a German force landed on the south coast, their assistance requested by White Finns in Berlin (although Mannerheim opposed their involvement). Surrounded, the leftists' resistance collapsed in April.

Throughout the conflict, the Social Democratic Party maintained a high level of unity. While containing revolutionary elements, it was led mainly by socialists seeking to retain parliamentary democracy and believing their fight was against a bourgeois force seeking to impose right-wing values on the newly independent state. Their arms, however, were supplied by the Soviet Union, causing the White taunt that the Reds were "aided by foreign bayonets". Many of the revolutionary socialists within the party fled to Russia after the civil war where they formed the Finnish Communist Party. The harsh treatment of the Reds who were captured – 8000 were executed and 80,000 were imprisoned in camps where more than 9000 died from hunger or disease – fired a resentment that would last for generations. The Whites regarded the war as one of liberation, ridding the country of Russians and the Bolshevik influence, and setting the course for an anti-Russian Finnish nationalism.

Mannerheim and the strongly pro-German *jäger* contingent were keen to continue east, to gain the whole of Karelia from the Russians, but the possibility of direct Finnish assistance to the Russian White Army, seeking to overthrow the Bolshevik government, came to nothing through the Russian Whites' refusal to guarantee recognition of Finland's independent status. Later that year, a provisional government of independent Karelia was set up in Uhtua. Its formation was masterminded by Red Finns, who ensured that its claims to make Karelia a totally independent region did not accord with the desires of the Finnish government. The provisional government's congress, held the following year, further confirmed a wish for separation from the Soviet Union and requested the removal of the Soviet troops who now held positions vacated by the Allies. This was agreed with a proviso that Soviet troops retained a right to be based in eastern Karelia. The collapse of the talks caused the provisional government and its supporters to flee to Finland as a Finnish battalion of the Soviet Red Army moved in and occupied the area. Subsequently the Karelian Workers' Commune, motivated by the Finnish Communists and backed by Soviet decree, was formed.

A few days later, the state of war which existed between Finland and Russia was formally ended by the **Treaty of Tartu**. The existence of the Karelian Workers' Commune gave the Soviet negotiators a pretext for refusing Finnish demands for Karelian self-determination, claiming the new set-up to be an expression of the Karelian people's wishes. The treaty was signed in an air of animosity. A bald settlement of border issues, it gave Finland the Petsamo area, a shoulder of land extending to the Arctic coast.

■ The Republic

The White success in the civil war led to a right-wing government with a pro-German majority, which wanted to establish Finland as a monarchy rather than the republic allowed for under the 1917 declaration of independence. Although twice defeated in the *Eduskunta*, Prime Minister **J.K. Paasikivi** evoked a clause in the Swedish Form of Government from 1772, making legal the election of a king. As a result, the Finnish Crown was offered to a German, Friedrich Karl, Prince of

Hessen. Immediately prior to German defeat in the world war, the prince declined the invitation. The victorious Allies insisted on a new Finnish government and a fresh general election if they were to recognise the nation's independent status. Since the country was now compelled to look to the Allies for future assistance, the request was complied with, sealing Finland's future as a republic. The first president was the liberal, Ståhlberg.

The termination of the monarchists' aims upset the unity of the right and paved the way for a succession of centrist governments. These were dominated by two parties, the National Progressives and the Agrarians. Through a period of rapidly increasing prosperity, numerous reforms were enacted. Farmers who rented land were given the opportunity to buy it with state aid, compulsory schooling was introduced, laws regarding religious freedom were passed and the provision of social services strengthened. As more farmers became independent producers, the Agrarians, claiming to represent the rural interests, drew away much of the Social Democrats' traditional support.

Finnish economic development halted abruptly following the world slump of the late 1920s. A series of strikes culminated in a dockworkers' dispute which began in May 1928 and continued for almost a year. It was settled by the intervention of the Minister for Social Affairs on terms perceived as a defeat for the strikers. The dispute was seen by the right as a communist-inspired attempt to ruin the Finnish export trade at a time when the Soviet Union had re-entered the world timber trade. It was also a symbolic ideological clash – a pointer to future events.

Moves to outlaw communist activity had been deemed an infringement of civil rights, but in 1929 the *Suomen Lukko* was formed to legally combat communism. It was swiftly succeeded by the more extreme and violent **Lapua Movement** (the name coming from the Ostrobothnian town, where a parade of communist youth had been brought to a bloody end by "White" farmers). The Lapuans rounded up suspected communists and communist sympathisers, and drove them to the Russian border, insisting that they walk across. Even the former president, Ståhlberg, was kidnapped and dumped at the eastern town of Joensuu. The Lapuans' actions were only half-heartedly condemned by the non-socialist parties, and in private they were supported. But when the

Lapuans began advocating a complete overthrow of the political system, much of the secret approval dried up.

The government obtained a two-thirds majority in the elections of October 1930 and amended the constitution to make communist activity illegal. This was expected to placate the Lapuans but instead they issued even more extreme demands, including the abolition of the Social Democrats. In 1932, a *coup d'état* was attempted by a Lapuan group who prevented a socialist member of parliament from addressing a meeting in Mäntsälä, 50km north of Helsinki. They refused to disperse, despite shots being fired by police, and sent for assistance from Lapuan bases around the country. The Lapuan leadership took up the cause and broadcasted demands for a new government. They were unsuccessful because of the loyalty of the troops who surrounded the town on the orders of the then Prime Minister, Svinhufvud. Following this, the Lapuans were outlawed, although the leaders received only minor punishments for their deeds. Several of them re-grouped as the Nazi-style Patriotic People's Movement. But unlike the parallel movements in Europe, there was little in Finland on which Nazism could focus mass hatred, and, despite winning a few parliamentary seats, it quickly declined into insignificance.

The Finnish economy recovered swiftly, and much international goodwill was generated when the country became the only nation to fully pay its war reparations to the USA after World War I. Finland joined the League of Nations hoping for a guarantee of its eastern border, but by 1935 the League's weakness was apparent and the Finns looked to traditionally neutral **Scandinavia** for protection as Europe moved toward war.

■ World War II

The Nazi-Soviet Non-Aggression Pact of August 1939 put Finland firmly into the Soviet sphere. Stalin had compelled Estonia, Latvia and Lithuania to allow Russian bases on their land, and in October was demanding a chunk of the Karelian isthmus from Finland to protect Leningrad, as well as a leasing of the Hanko peninsula on the Finnish Baltic coast. Russian troops were heading towards the Finnish border from Murmansk, and on November 30 the Karelian isthmus was attacked – an act which triggered the **Winter War**.

Stalin had had the tsarist military commanders executed, and his troops were led by young communists well-versed in ideology but ignorant of war strategy. Informed that the Finnish people would welcome them as liberators, the Soviet soldiers anticipated little resistance to their invasion. They expected to reach the Finnish west coast within ten days and therefore carried no overcoats, had little food, and camped each night in open fields. The Finns, although vastly outnumbered, were defending their homes and farms as well as their hard-won independence. Familiarity with the terrain enabled them to conceal themselves in the forests and attack through stealth. And they were prepared for the winter temperatures which were to plunge to minus 18°F. The Russians were slowly picked off and their camps frequently surrounded and destroyed.

While Finland gained the world's admiration, no practical help was forthcoming and it became a matter of time before Stalin launched a better-supplied, unstoppable advance. It came during February 1940 and the Finnish government was forced to ask for peace. This was granted under the **Treaty of Moscow**, signed in March by President **Kyösti Kallio**, who cursed "let the hand wither that signs such a paper" as his hand put pen to paper. The treaty ceded eleven percent of Finnish territory to the Soviet Union. There was a mass exodus from these areas, with nearly half a million people travelling west to the new boundaries of Finland. Kyösti Kallio was later paralysed on his right side.

The period immediately following the Winter War left Finland in a difficult position. Before the war, Finland had produced all its own food but was dependent on imported fertilizers. Supplies of grain, which had been coming from Russia, were halted as part of Soviet pressure for increased transit rights and access to the important nickel-producing mines in Petsamo. Finland became reliant on grain from Germany and British shipments to the Petsamo coast, which were interrupted when Germany invaded Norway. In return for providing arms, Germany was given transit rights through Finland. Legally, this required the troops to be constantly moving, but a permanent force became stationed at Rovaniemi.

The Finnish leadership knew that Germany was secretly preparing to attack the Soviet Union, and a broadcast from Berlin had spoken of a "united front" from Norway to Poland at a time when Finland was officially outside the Nazi sphere. Within Finland there was little support for the Nazis, but there was a fear of Soviet occupation. While Finland clung to its neutrality, refusing to fight unless attacked, it was drawn closer and closer to Germany. Soviet air raids on several Finnish towns in June 1941 finally led Finland into the world war on the side of the Nazis. The ensuing conflict with the Russians, fought with the primary purpose of regaining territory lost in the Winter War, became known as **the Continuation War**. The bulk of the land ceded under the Treaty of Moscow was recovered by the end of August. After this, Mannerheim, who commanded the Finnish troops, ignored Nazi encouragement to assist in their attack on Leningrad. A request from the British Prime Minister, Winston Churchill, that the Finns cease their advance, was also refused, although Mannerheim didn't cut the Murmansk railway which was moving Allied supplies. Even so, Britain was forced to acknowledge the predicament of their ally, the Soviet Union, and declared war on Finland in December 1941.

In 1943, the German defeat at Stalingrad, which made Allied victory almost inevitable, had a profound impact in Finland. Mannerheim called a meeting of inner-cabinet ministers and decided to seek a truce with the Soviet Union. The USA stepped forward as mediators but announced the peace terms set by Moscow too severe to be worthy of negotiation. Germany meanwhile had learned of the Finnish initiative and demanded an undertaking that Finland would not seek peace with Russia, threatening to withdraw supplies if it was not given. (The Germans were also unhappy with Finnish sympathy for Jews. Several hundred who had escaped from Central Europe were saved from the concentration camps by being granted Finnish citizenship.) Simultaneously, a Russian advance into Karelia made Finland dependent on German arms to launch a counter attack. An agreement with the Germans was signed by President **Risto Ryti** in June 1944 without the consent of the *Eduskunta*, thereby making the deed invalid when he ceased to be president.

Ryti resigned the presidency at the beginning of August and Mannerheim informed Germany that the agreement was no longer binding. A peace with the Soviet Union was signed in Moscow two weeks later. Under its terms, Finland was forced to give up the Pestamo region and the border was restored to its 1940 position. The Hanko peninsula was returned but instead the Porkkala peninsula, nearer to Helsinki, was to be leased to the Soviet Union for fifty years. There were stinging reparations. The Finns also had to drive the remaining Germans out of the country within two weeks. This was easily done in the south, but the bitter fighting which took place in Lappland caused the total destruction of many towns. It was further agreed that organisations disseminating anti-Soviet views within Finland would be dissolved and that Finland would accept an Allied Control Commission to oversee war trials.

■ The postwar period

After the war, the Communist Party was legalised and, along with militant socialists expelled from the Social Democratic Party, formed a broad leftist umbrella organisation – the **Finnish People's Democratic League**. Their efforts to absorb the Social Democrats were resisted by that party's moderate leadership, who regarded communism as "poison to the Finnish people". In the first peace-time poll, the Democratic League went to the electorate with a populist rather than revolutionary manifesto – something which was to characterise future Finnish communism. Both they and the Social Democrats attained approximately a quarter of the vote. Bolstered by two Social Democratic defections, the Democratic League narrowly become the largest party in the *Eduskunta*. The two of them, along with the Agrarian Party, formed an alliance ("The Big Three Agreement") which held the balance of power in a coalition government under the prime ministership of Paasikivi.

Strikes instigated by communist-controlled trade unions allowed the Social Democrats to accuse the Democratic League of seeking to undermine the production of machinery and other goods destined for the Soviet Union under the terms of the war reparation agreement, thereby creating a scenario for Soviet invasion. Charges of communist vote-rigging in trade union ballots helped the Social Democrats to gain control of the unions. The Democratic League won only 38 seats in the general election of 1948, and rejected the token offer of four posts in the new government, opting instead to stay in opposition. Their electoral campaign wasn't helped by the rumour – almost certainly groundless – that they were planning a Soviet-backed coup.

To ensure that the terms of the peace agreement were adhered to, the Soviet-dominated

Allied Control Commission stayed in Finland until 1947. Its presence engendered a tense atmosphere both on the Helsinki streets – there were several incidents of violence against Soviet officers – and in the numerous clashes with the Finnish government over the war trials. Unlike the Eastern European countries under full Soviet occupation, Finland was able to conduct its own trials, but had to satisfy the Commission that they were conducted properly. Delicate manoeuvring by the Chief of Justice, **Urho Kekkonen**, resulted in comparatively short prison sentences for the accused, the longest being ten years for Risto Ryti.

The uncertain relationship between Finland and the Soviet Union was resolved, to some extent, by the signing of the **Treaty of Friendship, Co-operation and Mutual Assistance** (FCMA) in 1948. It confirmed Finnish responsibility for its own defence and pledged the country not to join any alliance hostile to the Soviet Union. In the suspicious atmosphere of the Cold War, the treaty was perceived by the western powers to place Finland firmly under Soviet influence. The Soviet insistence that the treaty was a guarantee of neutrality was viewed as hypocritical while they were still leasing the Porkkala peninsula. When it became clear that Finland was not becoming a Soviet satellite and had full control over its internal affairs, the USA reinstated credit facilities – carefully structured to avoid financing anything which would be of help to the Soviets – and Finland was admitted to western financial institutions such as the IMF and World Bank.

The postwar economy was dominated by the reparations demand. Much of the bill was paid off in ships and machinery, which established engineering as a major industry. The escalating world demand for timber products boosted exports, but inflation soared and led to frequent wage disputes. In 1949 an attempt to enforce a piece-work rate in a pulp factory in Kemi culminated in two workers being shot by police, a state of emergency being declared in the town, and the arrest of communist leaders. Economic conflicts reached a climax in 1956 after right-wingers in the *Eduskunta* had blocked an annual extension of government controls on wages and prices. This caused a sharp rise in the cost of living and the trade unions demanded appropriate pay increases. A general strike followed, lasting for three weeks until the strikers' demands were

met. Any benefit, however, was quickly cancelled out by further price rises.

In 1957, a split occurred in the Social Democrats between urban and rural factions, the former seeking increased industrialistion and the streamlining of unprofitable farms, the latter pursuing high agricultural subsidies. At the annual party conference **Väinö Tanner** was elected chairman. His hopes for restoring unity were dashed by the pro-urban secretary Leskinen, who filled the party with his supporters. By 1959 the breakaway ruralists had set up the Small Farmers' Social Democratic Union and formed a new trade union organisation, causing a rift within the country's internal politics which was to have important repercussions in Finland's dealings with the Soviet Union. Although the government had no intention of changing their foreign policy, Tanner had a well-known antipathy to the Soviet Union. Coupled to this were a growing number of anti-Soviet newspaper editorials. These factors precipitated the **"night frost"** of 1958. The Soviet leader, Khruschev, suspended imports and deliveries of machinery, causing a rise in Finnish unemployment. Kekkonen, elected president in 1956, personally intervened in the crisis by meeting with Khruschev. This angered the Social Democrats, who accused Kekkonen of behaving undemocratically; meanwhile the Agrarians were lambasted for failing to stand up to Soviet pressure.

In 1960, Tanner was re-elected as chairman and the Social Democrats continued to attack Kekkonen. The Agrarians refused to enter government with the Social Democrats unless they changed their policies. As global relations worsened during 1961, the Soviet Union sent a note to Kekkonen requesting a meeting to discuss the section of the 1948 treaty dealing with defence of the Finnish-Soviet border. This was the precursor to the **"note crisis"**. The original note went unanswered, but the Finnish foreign secretary went to Moscow for exploratory talks with his opposite number. Assurances of Soviet confidence in Finnish foreign policy were given, but fears were expressed about the anti-Kekkonen alliance of conservatives and Social Democrats formed to contest the 1962 presidential election. Kekkonen again tried to defuse the crisis himself: using his constitutional powers he dissolved parliament early, forcing the election forward by several months and by so doing weakened the alliance. Kekkonen was re-elected and foreign policy remained unchanged. This was widely regarded as a personal victory for Kekkonen and a major turning point in relations with the Soviet Union. Through all subsequent administrations, the maintenance of the **Paasikivi-Kekkonen line** on foreign policy became a symbol of national unity.

Following Tanner's retirement from politics in 1963, the Social Democrats ended their stand against the established form of foreign policy, making possible their re-entry to government.

Throughout the early 1960s there was mounting dissatisfaction within the People's Democratic League towards the old pro-Moscow leadership. In 1965, a moderate non-communist was elected as the League's general-secretary, and two years later he became chairman; a similar change took place in the communist leadership of the trade unions. The new-look communists pledged their desire for a share in government. The election of May 1966 resulted in a "popular front" government dominated by the Social Democrats and the People's Democratic League, under the Prime Ministership of Rafael Paasio.

This brought to an end a twenty-year spell of centre-right governments in which the crucial pivot had been the Agrarian Party. In 1965, the Agrarians changed their name to the Centre Party, aiming to modernise their image and become more attractive to the urban electorate. A challenge to this new direction was mounted by the **Finnish Rural Party**, founded by a breakaway group of Agrarians in the late 1950s, who mounted an increasingly influential campaign on behalf of "the forgotten people" – farmers and smallholders in declining rural areas. In the election of 1970 they gained ten percent of the vote, but in subsequent years lost support through internal divisions.

The communists retained governmental posts until 1971, when they too were split – between the young "reformists" who advocated continued participation in government, and the older, hardline "purists" who were frustrated by the failure to implement socialist economic policies, and preferred to stay in opposition.

■ Modern Finland

Throughout the postwar years Finland has promoted itself vigorously as a **neutral country**. It joined the United Nations in 1955 and Finnish soldiers became an integral part of the UN Peace-Keeping Force. In 1969 preparations were started for the European Security Conference in Helsinki, and in 1972 the city was the venue for the **Strategic Arms Limitation Talks (SALT)**, underlining a Finnish role in mediation between the superpowers. But an attempt to have a clause to this effect inserted into the 1970 extension-signing of the FCMA Treaty was opposed by the Soviet Union, whose foreign secretary, Andrei Gromyko, had a year earlier defined Finland not as neutral but as a "peace-loving neighbour of the Soviet Union".

In 1971 the revelations of a Czech defector, General Sejna, suggesting that the Soviet army was equipped to take over Finland within 24 hours should Soviet defences be compromised, brought a fresh wave of uncertainty to relations with the eastern neighbour. As did the sudden withdrawal of the Soviet ambassador, allegedly for illicit scheming with the People's Democratic League.

The stature of Kekkonen as a world leader guaranteed continued support for his presidency. But his commitment to the Paasikivi-Kekkonen line ensured that nothing potentially upsetting to the Soviet Union was allowed to surface in Finnish politics, giving – some thought – the Soviet Union a covert influence on Finland's internal affairs. Opposition to Kekkonen was simply perceived as an attempt to undermine the Paasikivi-Kekkonen line. Equally, the unchallengable nature of Kekkonen's presidency was considered to be beyond his proper constitutional powers. A move in 1974 by an alliance of right-wingers and Social Democrats within the *Eduskunta* to transfer some of the presidential powers to parliament received a very hostile reaction, emphasising the almost inviolate position which Kekkonen enjoyed. Kekkonen was re-elected in 1978 although forced to stand down through illness in 1981. In 1982 the former Social Democrat Prime Minister **Mauno Koivisto** became president.

An understanding of the relationship between Finland and the Soviet Union has, since the end of the World War II and through the Cold War period, been dependent on assumptions about the Soviet attitude towards northern Europe. With the advent of nuclear weapons, the thought of a Soviet force needing to invade Finland to protect itself has long seemed laughable, although the Finnish army continue to practise manoeuvres designed for fighting a guerrilla war within Finland. A major change, at least in diplomatic terms, came in October 1989, when the

Soviet President, Gorbachev, on a state visit, toasted "neutral Finland" – the first acceptance by a Soviet leader of full Finnish neutrality.

Because Finland is heavily dependent on foreign trade, its well-being has closely mirrored world trends. The international financial boom of the 1960s enabled a string of social legislation to be passed and created a comparatively high standard of living for most Finns – albeit not on the same scale as the rest of Scandinavia. The global **recession** of the 1970s and early 1980s was most dramatically felt when a fall in the world market for pulp coincided with a steep increase in the price of oil. This brought about an economic crisis which forced Kekkonen to appoint an emergency centre-left government to deal with the immediate problems. Inflation has been brought down, but the recession continues to highlight the north-south divide within the country. Industry is heavily concentrated in the south, causing rural areas further north to experience high rates of unemployment and few prospects for economic growth – save through the rising levels of tourism. This is despite a number of improvement packages and the use of Finnish labour from impoverished Kainuu region in the building of the Soviet new town Kostamus.

The election of 1987 saw a break with the pattern of recent decades. Non-socialist parties made large gains, mainly at the expense of the Rural Party and Communists, while the Social Democrats lost just one seat – far fewer than anticipated. Initially it was hoped by the left that the slimness of the conservative majority in the new government would allow the Social Democratic Prime Minister Kalevi Sorsa to remain in office: in the event the National Coalition leader **Harri Holkeri** formed a cabinet. Although this represents a major change in domestic politics, the mechanisms of consensus government mean that any large-scale reforms are extremely unlikely.

Indeed, many Finns are becoming disillusioned with their system of government, chiefly over the time it takes for any new statutes to be introduced. The present government, too, is beginning to look increasingly inept – nowhere more so than in their lowering of the full-pension retirement age from 65 to 55. Nobody except the government, it seems, were surprised when thousands of 55–64-year-old Finns suddenly gave up their jobs, leaving a major gap in the labour field and putting an instant, massive financial burden on the state.

A BRIEF GUIDE TO FINNISH

Finnish has nothing in common with the other Scandinavian languages. It belongs to the Finno-Ugrian group, and its grammatical structure is complex: with fifteen cases alone to grapple with, it's initally a tricky language to learn, although once a basic vocabulary is attained things become less impenetrable; usefully, compared to other languages, there are very few actual words in Finnish – the majority of terms being compounded. English is widely spoken, particularly by young people and around the main towns. Swedish is a common second language and the first of the Finland-Swedes, found mainly in the western parts of the country.

Of the few available phrasebooks, *Finnish For Travellers* (Berlitz £2.95) is the most useful for practical purposes; the best Finnish-English dictionary is *The Standard Finnish Dictionary* (Holt, Rinehart and Winston; £22.50).

PRONUNCIATION

In Finnish, words are pronounced exactly as they are written, with the stress always on the first syllable: in a compound word the stress is on the first syllable of each part of the word. Each letter is pronounced individually, and doubling a letter lengthens the sound: double "kk"s are pronounced with two "k"-sounds and the double "aa" pronounced as long as the English "a" in "car". The letters b, c, f, q, w, x, z and å are only found in words derived from foreign languages, and are pronounced as in the language of origin.

a as in f**a**ther but shorter

d as in ri**d**ing but sometimes soft as to be barely heard

e between the e in p**e**n and the i in p**i**n.

g (only after 'n') as in si**ng**er

h as in **h**ot

i as in p**i**n

j like the y in **y**ellow

np like the m in **m**other

o like the aw in l**aw**

r is rolled

s as in **s**aid but with the tongue a little further back from the teeth

u as in b**u**ll

y like the French u in "s**u**r"

ä like the a in h**a**t

ö like the ur in F**ur** but without any "r"-sound.

BASICS

Do you speak English ?	*Puhutteko englantia ?*	Good evening	*hyvää iltaa*
Yes	*kyllä/joo*	Goodnight	*hyvää yötä*
no	*ei*	Goodbye	*hyvästi*
I don't understand	*En ymmärrä*	Yesterday	*eilen*
I understand	*Ymmärrän*	Today	*tänään*
Please	*olkaa hyvä*	Tomorrow	*huomenna*
Thank you	*kiitos*	Day after tomorrow	*ylihuomemnna*
Excuse me	*anteeksi*	In the morning	*aamulla/aamupäivällä*
Good morning	*hyvää huomenta*	In the afternoon	*iltapäivällä*
Good afternoon	*hyvää päivää*	In the evening	*illalla*

SOME SIGNS

Entrance	*Sisään*	Open	*Avoinna*	Police	*Poliisi*
Exit	*Ulos*	Closed	*Suljettu*	Hospital	*Sairaala*
Gentlemen	*Miehille/Miehet/Herrat*	Push	*Työnnä*	No Smoking	*Tupakointi kielletty*
Ladies	*Naisille/Naiset/Rouvat*	Pull	*Vedä*	No Entry	*Pääsy kielletty*
Hot	*Kuuma*	Arrival	*Saapuvat*	No Trespassing	*Läpikulku kielletty*
Cold	*Kylmä*	Departure	*Lähtevät*	No Camping	*Leiriytyminen kielletty*

QUESTIONS AND DIRECTIONS

Where's...?	*Missä on...?*	How much ?	*Kuinka paljon ?*
When ?	*Koska/million ?*	How much is that ?	*Paljonko se maksaa ?*
What ?	*Mikä/mitä ?*	I'd like	*Haluaisin*
Why ?	*Miksi ?*	Cheap	*Halpa*
How far is it to...?	*Kuinka pitkä matka on ...n ?*	Expensive	*Kallis*
Where can I get a	*Mistä lähtee saada juna ...n ?*	Good	*Hyvä*
train to...?		Bad	*Paha/Huono*
Train/bus/boat/ship	*Juna/bussi (or) linja-auto/*	Here	*Täällä*
	vene/laiva	There	*Siellä*
Where is the youth	*Missä on retkeilymaja ?*	Left	*Vasen*
hostel ?		Right	*Oikea*
Can we camp here ?	*Voimmeko leiriytyä tähän ?*	Go straight ahead	*Ajakaa suoraan eteenpäin*
Do you have	*Onko teillä mitään*	Is it near/far ?	*Onko se lähellä/kaukana ?*
anything better/	*parempaa/isompaa/*	Ticket/ticket office	*Lippu/matkalippu*
bigger/cheaper ?	*halvempaa ?*	Railway station/bus	*Rautatieasema/linja-*
It's too expensive	*Se on liian kallis*	station/bus stop	*autoasema/bussipysäkki*

NUMBERS

0	*nolla*	9	*yhdeksän*	18	*kahdeksantoista*	80	*kahdeksankymmentä*
1	*yksi*	10	*kymmenen*	19	*yhdeksäntoista*	90	*yhdeksänkymmentä*
2	*kaksi*	11	*yksitoista*	20	*kaksikymmentä*	100	*sata*
3	*kolme*	12	*kaksitoista*	21	*kaksikymmentäyksi*	101	*satayksi*
4	*neljä*	13	*kolmetoista*	30	*kolmekymmentä*	151	*sataviisikymmentäyksi*
5	*viisi*	14	*neljätoista*	40	*neljäkymmentä*	200	*kaksisataa*
6	*kuusi*	15	*viisitoista*	50	*viisikymmentä*	1000	*tuhat*
7	*seitsemän*	16	*kuusitoista*	60	*kuusikymmentä*		
8	*kahdeksan*	17	*seitsemäntoista*	70	*seitsmänkymmentä*		

DAYS AND MONTHS

Monday	*maanantai*	January	*tammikuu*	July	*heinäkuu*
Tuesday	*tiistai*	February	*helmikuu*	August	*elokuu*
Wednesday	*keskiviikko*	March	*maalisku*	September	*syyskuu*
Thursday	*torstai*	April	*huhtikuu*	October	*lokakuu*
Friday	*perjantai*	May	*toukokuu*	November	*marraskuu*
Saturday	*lauantai*	June	*kesäkuu*	December	*joulukuu*
Sunday	*sunnuntai*				

Days and months are never capitalised

GLOSSARY OF SWEDISH TERMS AND WORDS

Joki	River	*Museo*	Museum
Järvi	Lake	*Pankki*	Bank
Kauppahalli	Market hall	*Posti*	Post office
Kauppatori	Market square	*Puisto*	Park
Kaupungintalo	Town hall	*Rautatieasema*	Railway station
Katu	Street	*Sairaala*	Hospital
Keskusta	Town centre	*Taidemuseo*	Art museum
Kirkko	Church	*Tie*	Road
Kylä	Village	*Tori*	Square
Linna	Castle	*Torni*	Tower
Linja-autoasema	Bus station	*Tuomiokirkko*	Cathedral
Lipputoimisto	Ticket office	*Yliopisto*	University
Matkailutoimisto	Tourist Office		

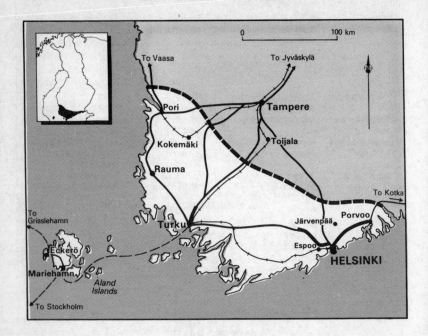

CHAPTER FOURTEEN

HELSINKI AND THE SOUTH

T
he southern coast of Finland makes up the most populated, industrialised and richest part of the country, with the densest concentration – not surprisingly – around the capital, **Helsinki**. A city of half a million people with the friendliness of a peasant village on market day, Helsinki's innovative architecture and batch of fine museums and galleries collectively expose the roots of the national character – while at night the pubs and clubs strip it bare. It may seem the perfect prelude to exploring the rest of Finland, and in the practical sense it is – being the hub of the country's road, rail, and air traffic routes. However, you should try to arrive in Helsinki *after* seeing the rest of the country. Only with some prior knowledge of Finland does the significance of the city as a symbol of Finnish self-determination become clear.

A couple of towns **around Helsinki** evince the change from ruralism to modernism even further. **Porvoo** sits placidly locked in the nineteenth century; the suburbs of **Espoo** form a showpiece of twentieth-century urban design. Further away, in the country's southeastern extremity, the only community of significant size and importance between Helsinki and the Soviet border is the shipping port of **Kotka** – not wildly appealing in itself but at the heart of a coastal region typified by historically intriguing small towns and villages, and a fair number of geological oddities.

Helsinki itself only became the capital in 1812, after Finland had been made a Russian Grand Duchy and Tsar Alexander I had deemed the existing capital, **Turku**, too close to Sweden for comfort. Today Turku, facing Stockholm across the Gulf of Bothnia, handles its demotion well. Both historically and visually, it's one of Finland's most enticing cities; indeed, the snootier elements of its Swedish-speaking contingent consider Åbo (the Swedish name for Turku) the real capital and Helsinki just an uncouth upstart.

Between Helsinki and Turku, along the whole southern coast, only small villages and a few slightly larger towns break the continuity of forests. Around Turku, though, things are more interesting, with the two most southerly of the Finland-Swedish communities: **Rauma**, with its unique dialect and well-preserved town centre; and the likeably downbeat **Pori**, a town that's gained notoriety from its annual jazz festival.

Where this corner of Finland meets the sea it splinters into an enormous archipelago, which includes the curious **Åland Islands** – a grouping of thousands of fragments of land, about half a dozen of which are inhabited, connected by small roadways skirting the sea. There's a tiny self-governing population here, Swedish-speaking but with a history distanced from both Sweden and Finland.

Much of the region is naturally most easily reached from Helsinki, from where there are frequent connections to Turku. Rauma and Pori are best reached by bus from Turku, and from Pori there are easy connections to Tampere and the Lake Region. Daily ferries also connect Turku to the Åland Islands.

HELSINKI

HELSINKI has a character quite different from the other Scandinavian capitals, and in many ways is closer in mood (and certainly in looks) to the major cities of Eastern Europe. For years an outpost of the Russian Empire, its very shape and form is derived from its powerful neighbour. Yet through this century the city has become a showcase of independent Finland, much of its impressive **architecture** drawing inspiration from the dawning of Finnish nationalism and the rise of the republic. Equally the **museums**, especially the National Museum and the Art Museum of the Ateneum, reveal the country's gradual assimilation of its own folklore and culture.

The streets have a youthful buzz, the short summer acknowledged by crowds strolling the boulevards, cruising the shopping arcades and socialising in the outdoor cafés and restaurants; everywhere there's prolific **street entertainment**. At night the pace picks up, with a great selection of pubs and clubs, free rock concerts in the numerous parks, and an impressive quota of fringe events. It's a pleasure just to be around, merging with the multitude and witnessing the activity.

Much of central Helsinki is a succession of compact granite blocks, interspersed with more characterful buildings, alongside waterways, green spaces and the glass-fronted office blocks and shopping centres similiar to what you'd find in any European capital. The city is hemmed in on three sides by water, and all the things you might want to see are within walking distance of one another – and certainly no more than a few minutes apart by tram or bus.

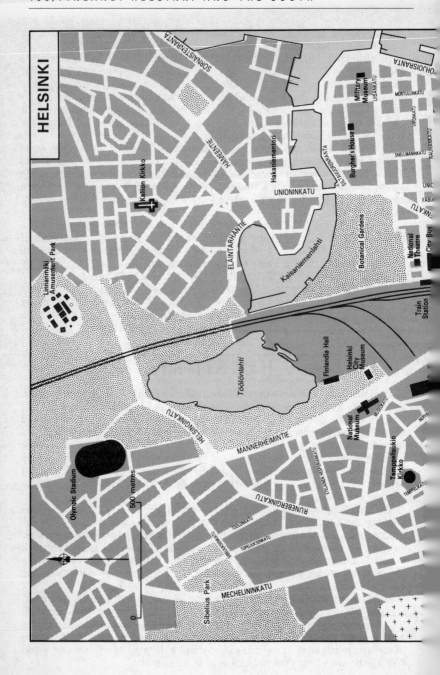

HELSINKI

Kallion Kirkko

Linnanmäki Amusement Park

SÖRNÄISTENRANTA

OHJOISRANTA

Military Museum

MERITULLINKATU

UISANKATU

VISOKATU

Burgher's House

SNELLMANINKATU

SILTAVUORENRANTA

RAUHANKATU

UNIONINKATU

Hakaniementori

UNIO

NKATU

FABI

Botanical Gardens

HÄMEENTIE

Kaisaniemenlahti

National Theatre

Cty Bus

ELÄINTARHANTIE

Train Station

Finlandia Hall

Töölönlahti

Helsinki City Museum

HELSINGINKATU

National Museum

MUSKONIA

Olympic Stadium

MANNERHEIMINTIE

Temppeliaukio Kirkko

TEMPPELIKATU

NERVA

500 metres

RUNEBERGINKATU

TOPELIUKSENKATU

BRIAVIRINGERDI

ETELINEN HESPERIANKATU

0

Sibelius Park

MECHELININKATU

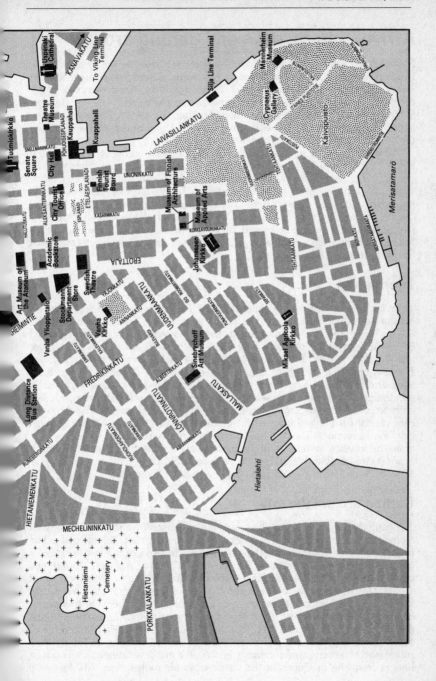

Arrival, information and getting around

However you arrive you'll be deposited somewhere close to the heart of town. Helsinki's airport, *Vantaa*, is 20km to the north, served by frequent **airport buses** (a thirty-minute journey; 15mk). These stop at the *Finnair* terminal under the *Inter-Continental Hotel*, halfway between the city centre and the Olympic Stadium, before continuing to the railway station. A cheaper, if slightly slower, airport connection is city bus #615; this costs 10mk and runs from the airport to the bus terminal beside the railway station.

The **ferry** lines, *Viking* and *Silja*, have their terminals on opposite sides of the South Harbour (docks known respectively as Katajanokka and Olympic) and disembarking passengers from either have a walk of less than a kilometre to the centre; the same applies if you're arriving from Tallinn, the Estonian vessel docking close to the *Silja Line* terminal. The **railway station** is right in the heart of the city centre, next door to one of the two city bus terminals, with all trams stopping immediately outside or around the corner in Mannerheimintie. Just across Mannerheimintie and a short way up Simonkatu is another city bus terminal and the **long-distance bus station**.

Information

The **City Tourist Office**, at Pohjoisesplanadi 19 (mid-May to mid-Sept Mon–Fri 8.30am–6pm, Sat 8.30am–1pm; rest of the year Mon 8.30am–4.30pm Tues–Fri 8.30am–4pm; ☎90/1693757 or 174088), has free street and transport maps, and the useful (and also free) tourist magazines – *Helsinki Today*, *Helsinki This Week*, and *Helsinki Guide*. It also stocks the essential, newspaper-like *Exploring Helsinki*, aimed at youngish, tight-budgeted travellers. If you're staying for a while and plan to see as much of the city and its museums as possible, consider purchasing a **Helsinki Card**. This gives unlimited travel on public transport, free entry to over forty museums and some substantial hotel discounts. The three-day card (110mk) is the best value, although there are also two-day (90mk) and one-day (65mk) versions. The card can be bought at the tourist office.

For information on the rest of the country, use the **Finnish Tourist Board** at Unioninkatu 26 (June–Aug Mon–Fri 9am–5pm, Sat 9am–1pm; rest of the year Mon–Fri 9am–1pm & 2–3.30pm) on the other side of Esplanadi.

Getting around the city

The central area and its immediate surround are linked by bus, tram and a small metro system in an integrated network. A single journey costs 6.50mk and unlimited transfers are allowed within one hour. A **multi-trip** ticket gives 10 rides for 51mk. A **tourist ticket** lasts one (40mk), three (65mk) or five days (85mk), and permits travel on buses and trams displaying double arrows (effectively all of them). This is, obviously, only a cost-cutter if used frequently. Single tickets are bought on board, others from the bus station or tourist office. On **buses** you enter at the front and must either buy or show your ticket. On **trams** get on at the front or back, and stamp your ticket in the machine. It's unlikely that you'll be asked to show your ticket except on some of the old vehicles on the #1 tram route, which have a seated conductor instead of a machine. **Metro** tickets can be bought from the machines in the stations. As for routes, tram #3T follows a figure-of-eight route around the city and if you're pushed for sightseeing time will take you past the most obvious attractions. **Taxis** have a basic charge of 10.50mk, with a further 5mk per km, plus a 5mk surcharge after 6pm and on weekends, and a 10mk surcharge after 10pm.

Finding somewhere to stay

There's plenty of **accommodation** in Helsinki, but by far the bulk of it is in mid-range hotels. Various discounts can reduce their cost but if they're still beyond your means there are a couple of cheaper summer hotels, several tourist hotels, and a few hostels. Wherever you stay, you should book as far ahead as possible: the various cut-price hotel deals get snapped up quickly, and hostel space is tight in summer. If you want a hotel or hostel bed but don't have anything planned ahead of arrival, you can book a room at the **Hotel Booking Centre** at the railway station (mid-May to mid-Sept Mon–Fri 9am–9pm, Sat 9am–7pm, Sun 10am–6pm; rest of the year Mon–Fri 9am–6pm).

Hostels

Though the staple accommodation option of budget travellers, Helsinki's **hostels** are not without drawbacks: curfews are common in dormitories, and there's often a limit on the length of stay imposed during the peak summer period.

Academica, Hietaniemenkatu 14 (☎90/440171). Hostel-type accommodation on production of an *IYHF* or student card. June to August only. Singles 155mk, doubles 180mk. See also "Hotels" below.

Nuorisotoimiston retkeilymaja, Porthaninkatu 2 (☎90/7099590). The hostel of the Helsinki Youth Office, and, by a couple of markkaa, the cheapest in town. One large dormitory for men and three smaller rooms for women. Open from mid-May to August. 2km from the centre and close to Hakaniemi metro station. Trams #1, #2, #3B and #7 stop nearby.

Stadionin retkeilymaja, in the Olympic Stadium (☎90/4960710). A 3km hike from the city centre; the hostel entrance is on the far side of the stadium complex. Open all year. A great venue for a youth hostel, but not serving very sporting quantities at breakfast and often crowded. Trams #3T, #4, #7 and #10 stop outside.

Vantaan retkeilymaja, in the Tikkurila Sports Ground, 18km from the centre (☎90/8393310). Take the train to Tikkurila, which runs four times an hour. Open all year.

Campsites

Of Helsinki's two **campsites**, only one makes a reasonable base if you're planning to spend time in the city. This is *Rastila* (☎90/316551), 13km to the east in Itäkeskus, at the end of the metro line and also served by buses #90, #90A, #90N and #96. It's open from mid-May to mid-September and there's always plenty of space. The other site is *Oittaa* (☎90/862585), about 30km to the west, which is open from June to mid-August; take a train to Espoo and then a bus.

Hotels and Tourist Hotels

Hotels in Helsinki are normally pretty expensive (450–600mk for an average double) but several top-notch business hotels drop their prices dramatically in the summer tourist season, and all hotels have reduced rates at weekends. To take advantage of these, it's essential to book as early as possible – either by phoning the hotel directly or making a reservation through a travel agent. However much you pay, it's unlikely that you'll leave any Helsinki hotel feeling ripped-off: service and amenities – such as the inclusive help-yourself breakfast – are usually excellent. If you're using a Helsinki Card, you can reduce costs a little by staying at one of the hotels which grant a special rate of 150–210mk to card holders, although these prices are per person per double room, so savings are hardly dramatic.

Though they lack the luxury of regular hotels, the city's **tourist hotels**, providing basic accommodation in private rooms without bathrooms, and usually inexpensive meals, can be a good value alternative to a regular hotel, especially for three or four people sharing.

Hotels

Academica, Hietaniemenkatu 14 (☎90/440171). A well-placed summer hotel, the cheapest doubles are 240mk. See also "Hostels" above.

Anna, Annankatu 1 (☎90/648011). Small and central, with a cosy atmosphere despite its past as a Christian mission. 360mk.

Finn, Kalevankatu 3b (☎90/640904). A modern, compact and peaceful place, virtually in the city centre. 300–380mk

Helka, Pohjoinen Rautatiekatu 23 (☎90/440581). Rather plain-looking exterior but very welcoming on the inside; slightly out of the centre but still within easy reach of everything. Usually 550mk, but offering weekend reductions.

Helsinki Hotel, Hallituskatu 12 (☎90/171401). The best aspect of this place is the location, a stone's throw from Senate Square in one of the prime central streets. Only worthwhile, though, if you get a weekend reduction on the usual price of 610mk.

Hesperia, Mannerheimintie 50 (☎90/43101). Swish and business orientated but extremely cosy, and with weekend reductions that cut prices to 550mk.

Hospiz, Vuorikatu 17 (☎90/170481). You can save money in this good quality hotel by getting a room without a bathroom – but do it early. 430mk, 380mk on weekends.

Klaus Kurki, Bulevardi 2–4 (☎90/602322). Very snug and situated perfectly for exploring the city. Weekend rates from 450mk.

Lord Hotel, Lönnrotinkatu 29 (☎90/680168). Designed as a mock-castle for those who really want – and can afford – to live like a lord. 700mk.

Marski, Mannerheimintie 10 (☎90/68061). With a jet-set international flavour and matching prices. The most advantageous deals are the weekend doubles for 500mk.

Marttahotelli, Uudenmaankatu 24 (☎90/646211). Recently refurbished in an enjoyable hi-tech way; doubles for 310mk in summer.

Metrocity Kaisaniemenkatu 7 (☎90/171146). Well-equipped rooms that can be good value at weekends; 400mk.

Satakuntalo, Lapinrinne 1 (☎90/6940331). Another handily-located summer hotel; doubles are 230mk, a further 70mk for an extra bed. Students get a fifty percent discount.

Torni, Yrjönkatu 26 (☎90/131131). On a clear day, the thirteenth floor bar here gives views all the way to Estonia, but the drinks are pricey and so are the rooms – even at the weekend rate of 640mk.

Ursula, Paasivuorenkatu 1 (☎90/750311). A bit out of the way, just north of the centre close to Hakaneimentori, but well-priced: 420mk, 350mk at weekends.

Tourist Hotels

Clairet, Itäinen Teatterikuja 3 (☎90/669707 or 656695). Fairly ramshackle and in need of a good dusting, but in a quiet street close to the rail and bus stations, and quite adequate for a night's rest. It also rents rooms cheaply by the day for those arriving in the city early and leaving later the same day. 230mk, extra bed 50mk.

Erottajanpuisto, Uudenmaakatu 9 (☎90/642169). Usefully-positioned, and especially good for several people together. Doubles 230mk, three sharing 270mk, four sharing 280mk.

Lönnrot, Lönnrotinkatu 16 (☎90/6932590). Close to the Old Church and everything central. Basic but quite endurable. 260mk.

Omapohja (☎90/666211). Downstairs from *Clairet*, and quite a bit tidier, complete with colour TVs and a microwave oven for use of guests. Doubles 280mk, three sharing 320mk.

The City

Following a devastating fire, and the city's appointment as Finland's capital in 1812, Helsinki was totally rebuilt in a style commensurate with its rank: a grid of wide streets and Neoclassical, Empire-style brick buildings, modelled on the then Russian capital, St. Petersburg. This forms the basis of the modern city, which divides into four fairly distinct portions. It's a tribute to the vision of planner Johan Ehrenström and architect Carl Engel that from **Senate Square to Esplanadi** the grandeur has endured, often quite dramatically. The square itself, with the gleaming Lutheran Cathedral in its centre, still forms the city's single most eye-catching feature; and, just a few blocks away, past the South Harbour and the waterside market, Esplanadi remains a handsome tree-lined avenue. Meeting one end of Esplanadi, the great artery of **Mannerheimintie**, the main route into the centre from the suburbs, carries traffic and trams past Finlandia Hall and the Olympic Stadium on one side, and the National Museum and the streets leading to Sibelius Park and the vast Hietaniemi Cemetery, on the other. The bulge of land that extends **south of Esplanadi** was and still is one of the most affluent sections of town. It is dotted by palatial embassies and wealthy dwellings, and rises into the rocky Kaivopuisto park, where the peace is disturbed only by the rumble of the trams and the summer rock concerts.

Along the seafront are old Mediterranean-style villas, which continue into the narrow streets of the exclusive Eira quarter. Divided by the waters of Kaisaniemenlahti, the districts of **Kruununhaka** and **Hakaniemi** contain what little is left of pre-seventeenth-century Helsinki – in the small area up the hill behind the cathedral, compressed between the botanical gardens and the bay; over the bridge is a large market place and the hill leading past the formidable Kallio kirkko towards the modern housing districts further north. Helsinki also has innumerable offshore islands, the biggest of which are **Suomenlinna** and **Seurasaari**. Each of these, despite their location just minutes away from the city centre, offers untrammelled nature and a rewarding crop of museums.

Senate Square to Esplanadi

Most of the streets which lead into **Senate Square** are fairly narrow and unremarkable, a fact which simply serves to increase the impact as the square comes into view and you're struck by the sudden burst of space, by the graceful symmetry of the buildings and most of all the exquisite form of the **Lutheran Cathedral** (Mon–Sat 9am–7pm, Sun noon–7pm), raised on granite steps which support it like a pedestal. Designed, like most of the other buildings on the square, by Engel, and overseen by him until his death in 1840, it was finally completed, with a few variations, in 1852. Among the post-Engel additions are the statues of the

Twelve Apostles that line the roof, which may seem familiar if you've visited Copenhagen; they're copies of Thorvaldsen's sculptures for Vor Frue Kirke. After the Neoclassical extravagances of the exterior, the spartan Lutheran interior comes as a disappointment; better is the gloomily atmospheric **crypt** (June–Aug daily 10am–4pm; entrance on Kirkkokatu), now often used for exhibitions – when it's likely there'll be an admission charge.

The buildings around the square contribute to the pervading sense of harmony, and although none are open to the public, some are of great historical significance. The **Government Palace** (*Valtioneuvosto*), known as the Senate House until independence and seating the Senate from 1822, consumes the entire eastern side. It was here that an angry Finnish civil servant became a national hero by assassinating a much-hated Russian governor-general in 1904; shortly after he killed himself. Opposite are the Ionic columns of **Helsinki University** (*Helsingin Yliopisto*), next door to which is the **University Library** (*Yliopiston kirjasto*), considered by many to be Engel's finest single building (students and bona-fide researchers are allowed in). Between Kirkkokatu and Rauhankatu is **The House of Scientific Estates** (*Säätytalo*), the seat of the Diet which governed the country until 1906, when it was abolished in favour of a single-chamber parliament elected by universal suffrage (at the time, Europe's most radical parliamentary reform). In the small park behind the Government Palace is the **House of Nobility** (*Ritarihuone*), where the upper crust of Helsinki society rubbed shoulders a hundred years ago. One place anyone can enter, although it's only worthwhile if you're keen on Finnish drama, is the **Theatre Museum**, just off the square at Aleksanterinkatu 12 (Tues–Sun noon–4pm, Wed until 6pm; 5mk), which has some small displays on two of the National Theatre's leading figures – Aleksis Kivi and Kaarlo Bergbom.

The square at the end of Aleksanterinkatu is overlooked by the red and green onion-shaped domes of the Russian Orthodox **Uspenski Cathedral** (June–Aug Tues–Fri 10am–4pm; rest of the year Tues & Thurs 9am–1pm, Wed 2–6pm) on Katajanokka, a wedge of land extending out to sea between the North and South Harbours and currently the scene of a dockland development programme, converting the area's old warehouses into pricey new restaurants and apartments for Helsinki's yuppies. In contrast to its Lutheran counterpart, the cathedral is drab outside but on the inside has a rich display of icons and other mesmerising adornments, incense mingling with the sound of Slavonic choirs.

Walking from here towards the South Harbour takes you past the **President's Palace**, noticeable only for its conspicuous uniformed guard, and the equally bland **City Hall**, used solely for administrative purposes. There's more colour and liveliness among the stalls of the modest-sized **kauppatori** (Mon–Sat 7am–2pm; evening market in summer Mon–Fri 3.30–8pm), along the waterfront, laden with fresh fruit and veg; around the edge of the harbour you can buy fresh fish directly from the boats moored there. The **kauppahalli** (Mon–Fri 8am–5pm, Sat 8am–2pm), a bit further along, is a good place for snacks and watching tourists contemplating the reindeer kebabs.

Across a mish-mash of tramlines from the South Harbour is **Esplanadi**. At the height of the Swedish/Finnish language conflict, which divided the nation during the mid-nineteenth century, this neat boulevard was where opposing factions demonstrated their allegiance – the Finns walking on the south side and the Swedes on the north. Nowadays it's dominated at lunchtime by office workers, later in the afternoon by buskers, and at night by couples strolling hand-in-hand along the central pathway seemingly oblivious to the whistles and leers of the young bucks occupying the seats. Musical accompaniment is provided free on summer evenings from the hut in the middle of the walk – expect anything from a Salvation Army band to rock groups. Entertainment of a more costly type lies at the far end of Esplanadi in the dreary off-white horseshoe of the **Swedish Theatre** building, its main entrance on Mannerheimintie.

Aleksanterinkatu runs parallel to Esplanadi, its Mannerheimintie end taken up by the brick constructivist exterior of the **Stockmann Department Store**, Europe's largest department store, selling everything from bubblegum to Persian rugs. The **Academic Bookstore** is part of *Stockmann*'s and has its own entrance on Aleksanterinkatu. There's an extensive collection of books (more titles here, in fact, than in any other bookstore in Europe), including many English-language paperbacks and a sizeable stock of foreign newspapers and magazines. On the fifth floor is the **Stockmann Museum** (Mon–Thurs noon–1pm; free), a small and surprisingly interesting history of the century-old enterprise. What you won't see in the museum is any reference to the popularity of the massive *Forum* shopping mall, directly across Mannerheimintie, which has been cutting into the *Stockmann* profits in recent years.

Opposite *Stockmann*'s main entrance is a statue by Felix Nylund, the *Three Smiths*, a commemoration of the workers of Finland who raised money to erect a building for the country's students. The building is the **Vanha Ylioppistalo** – the old Students' House – its main doors facing the statue. The Finnish Students' Union is based here, now owning some of the most expensive square metres of land in Finland and renting them out at considerable profit. In the Vanha, as it's usually known, is the **Vanhan Galleria** (during exhibitions 10am–6pm; free) a small gallery with frequent modern art events. The adjoining **Kirjakahvila** – the Book Café – has a similarly arty room, the **Kirjakahvilan Galleria** (Mon–Fri noon–7pm; free). It's worth becoming acquainted with the layout during the day, as the building contains a couple of lively bars which are well worth visiting at night (see "Drinking"). Taking a few strides further along Mannerheimintie brings you to the *Bio* cinema and, beside it, steps lead down into a little modern courtyard framed by burger joints and pizzerias, off which runs the entrance to **Tunneli**, an underground complex containing shops, the central metro station and a pedestrian subway to one of the city's most enjoyable structures – the railway station.

Erected in 1914, **Helsinki railway station** is often thought of as architect Eliel Saarinen's finest work. In response to criticism of his initial design, Saarinen jettisoned the original National Romantic features and opted for a style more akin to late Art Nouveau. Standing in front of the huge doors (so sturdy they always give the impression of being locked) it's hard to deny the feeling of strength and solidity which the station exudes. Yet the power is tempered by gentleness, a feeling symbolised by four muscular figures on the facade, each clasping a spherical glass lamp above the heads of passers-by. The interior details can be admired at leisure from either one of the station's two restaurants. Later, Saarinen was to emigrate to America; his son in turn became one of the best-known postwar American architects, his most famous creation being the *TWA* terminal building in New York.

Beside the station is the imposing granite form of the **National Theatre**, home of Finnish drama since 1872. "Finnish culture" was considered a contradiction in terms by the governing Swedish-speaking elite right up to the mid-nineteenth century, and it was later felt (quite rightly) to pose an anti-Russian, pro-nationalist threat to Finland's Tsarist masters. Finnish theatre was so politically hot during the Russification process that it had to be staged away from the capital, in the southwest coastal town of Pori. At the forefront of Finnish drama during its early years was Aleksis Kivi, who died insane and impoverished before being acknowledged as Finland's greatest playwright. He's remembered here by Wäinö Aaltonen's bronze sculpture. Interestingly, nobody knows for sure what Kivi actually looked like, and this imagined likeness, finished in 1939, came to be regarded as the true one.

Directly opposite the open square of the bus station is the **Art Museum of the Ateneum** (June–Aug Mon–Fri 9am–5pm, Wed until 8pm, Sat & Sun 11am–5pm; rest of the year daily 9am–5pm, Wed until 8pm; 5mk), however, for several years the building has been undergoing renovation. This is expected to be finished in 1991, until when the collection is housed at Kansakoulukatu 3 (same times), not far from the long-distance bus station. Chief among the museum's large collection of Finnish paintings is the stirring selection of Golden Age works from the late nineteenth century – a time when the spirit of nationalism was surging through the country and the movement towards independence gaining strength; indeed, the art of the period was a contributing factor in the growing awareness of Finnish culture, both inside and outside the country. Among the prime names of this era were Akseli Gallen-Kallela and Albert Edelfelt, particularly the former, who translated onto canvas many of the mythic scenes of the *Kalevala*, both of whom are extensively represented in the museum. Slightly later came Juho Rissanen with his moody and evocative studies of peasant life, and Hugo Simberg, responsible for the eerie *Death and the Peasant* and the powerful triptych *Boy Carrying a Garland*. Cast an eye, too, over the works of Helene Schjerfbeck, for a long time one of the country's most underrated artists but now enjoying an upsurge in popularity – and collectability.

The cultural importance of the early Finnish artists endows their work with a special passion which, perhaps inevitably, seems lacking in the museum's twentieth-century works, save for a brief glimmer of provocative expressionism from Tyko Sallinen and the November Group, who were working around 1917.

Along Mannerheimintie

Mannerheimintie is named after the military commander and statesman C.G.E. Mannerheim, who wielded considerable influence on Finnish affairs in the first half of the twentieth century. He's commemorated by a statue near the busy junction with Arkadiankatu, a structure on which the city's bird population have left their mark.

The section of Mannerheimintie from *Stockmann*'s northwards passes a number of outstanding buildings, though the first isn't one of them. The **Parliament Building** (guided tours July & Aug Mon–Fri 2pm, Sat 11am & noon, Sun noon & 1pm; rest of the year Sat & Sun only; free), with its pompous columns and choking air of solemnity, was the work of J.S. Sirén, completed in 1931. Intended to celebrate the new republic, its style was drawn from the revolutionary Neoclassicism that dominated public buildings from Fascist Italy to Nazi Germany, and its authoritarian features seem wildly out of place.

From here onwards things improve with the **National Museum** (May–Sept daily 11am–4pm, Tues also 6–9pm; rest of the year daily 11am–3pm, Tues also 6–9pm; 10mk), the design of which was the result of a turn-of-the-century competition won by the three Young Turks of Finnish architecture – Armas Lindgren, Herman Gesellius and Eliel Saarinen. With National Romanticism at its zenith, they steeped their plan in Finnish history, drawing on the country's legacy of medieval churches and granite castles (even though many of these were built under Swedish domination), culminating in a weighty but slender tower that gives the place a cathedral-like profile. The entrance is guarded by Emil Wikström's sculptured bear, the interior ceilings are decorated by Gallen-Kallela with scenes from the *Kalevala*.

The museum's contents are exhaustive, and unless you have limitless reserves of energy it's best to concentrate on a few specific sections. Beginning with prehistoric finds and leading through the turbulent Middle Ages to the present, the exhibits veer from the rather banal – the "world's oldest fishing net" (it looks like an old fishing net) – to the interior of a seventeenth-century manor house so effectively restored and laid out you could actually be back there waiting for the dinner guests to arrive. The ethnographic sections, exploring the characteristics of the nation's varied regions, are perhaps the most interesting and certainly worth a look if you're planning to visit the particular areas. The *Same* department is a good, if inevitably brief, introduction to the people of the far north.

Stylistically a far cry from the National Museum building but equally affecting, **Finlandia Hall** (guided tours when not in use, check at the city tourist office for the latest details), stands directly across Mannerheimintie, partially hidden by the roadside foliage. Designed by the country's premier architect, **Alvar Aalto**, a few years before his death in 1976, Finlandia was conceived as part of a grand plan to rearrange the entire centre of Helsinki. Previously, Eliel Saarinen had planned a traffic route from the northern suburbs into a new square in the city centre, to be called Vapaudenkatu (Freedom Street) in celebration of Finnish independence. Aalto plotted a continuation of this scheme, envisaging the removal of the rail-freight yards which would enable arrivals to be greeted with a fan-like terrace of new buildings reflected in the waters of Töölönlahti. Finlandia was to be the first of these, and only by looking across from the other side of Töölönlahti do you perceive the Hall's soft sensuality and the potential beauty of the greater concept. Inside the building, Aalto's characteristic wave pattern (the architect's surname, as it happens, means "wave") and asymmetry are present. From the walls and ceilings through to the lamps and vases, the place has a quiet and graceful air. But the view from the foyer is still the rail-freight yards, and the great plan for a future Helsinki is still being discussed.

Next door is the **Helsinki City Museum** (Sun–Fri noon–4pm; 5mk) set in *Villa Hakasalmi*, an Italian style Neoclassical villa built in the 1840s by a councillor and patron of the arts whose collection inspired the founding of the museum. It's refreshingly manageable after the all-encompassing National Museum, with a systematic record of the growth of the city using maps and diagrams showing, above all, the impact of Ehrenström's plan and Engel's architecture on what had previously been a small community living in ramshackle wooden houses.

From this point on, the decisive outline of the **Olympic Stadium** becomes visible. Originally intended for the 1940 Olympic Games, the stadium eventually staged the first postwar games, in 1952. From the **Stadium Tower** (Mon–Fri 9am–8pm, Sat & Sun 9am–6pm; 5mk) there's an unsurpassed view over the city and a chunk of the southern coast. If you're a stopwatch and spikes freak, ask at the tower's ticket office for directions to the **Sport Museum** (Mon–Fri 11am–5pm, Thurs until 7pm, Sat & Sun noon–4pm; 7mk), whose mind-numbing collection of track officials' shoes and swimming caps overshadows a worthy attempt to present sport as an integral part of Finnish culture. The nation's heroes, among them Keke Rosberg and Lasse Virén, are lauded to the skies. Outside, Wäinö Aaltonen's sculpture of Paavo Nurmi captures the champion runner of the Twenties in full-stride, and full-nudity – something that caused a stir when the sculpture was unveiled in 1952.

There's little of note north of the stadium, and you should cross Mannerheimintie and follow the streets off it, which lead to **Sibelius Park**, and Eila Hiltunen's monument to the composer made from 24 tons of steel tubes, like a big silver surrealist organ. Next to this, the unfortunate side-work is an irrefutably horrid sculpture of Sibelius' dismembered head. The shady and pleasant park is rudely cut by a main road called Mechelininkatu. Following this back toward the city centre brings you first to the small Islamic and Jewish cemeteries, and then to the expanse of tombs comprising **Hietaniemi Cemetery** (usually open until 10pm). A prowl among these is like a stroll through a "Who was Who" of Finland's last 150 years: Mannerheim, Engel and a host of former presidents are buried here; just inside the main entrance lies Alvar Aalto, his witty little tombstone consisting partly of a chopped Neoclassical column; behind it is the larger marker of Gallen-Kallela, his initials woven around a painter's palette. It's to the cemetery that local schoolkids head after skiving lessons during warm weather, not for a smoke behind the gravestones but to reach the **beaches** which line the bay just beyond the western walls. From these you can enjoy the best sunset in the city.

On the way back towards Mannerheimintie, at Lutherinkatu 3, just off Runeberginkatu, is **Temppeliaukio kirkko** (June–Aug daily 10am–8pm; rest of the year Wed–Mon 10am–8pm Tues 10am–12.45pm & 2.15–8pm). Brilliantly conceived by Timo and Tuomo Suomalainen and finished in 1969, the church is built inside a large lump of natural granite in the middle of an otherwise ordinary residential square. Try to see it from above if you can (even if you have to shin up a neighbouring drainpipe) because the copper dome which pokes through the rock makes the thing look like a ditched flying saucer. The odd combination of man-made and natural materials has made it a fixture on the tourist circuit, but even when crowded it's a thrill to be inside. Classical concerts frequently take place, the raw rock walls making for excellent acoustics – check the notice board at the entrance for details.

South of Esplanadi: Kaivopuisto and Eira

From the South Harbour it's a simple walk past the *Silja* terminal to Kaivopuisto, but it's more interesting to leave Esplanadi along Kasarmikatu for its small, offbeat museums. First of these is the **Museum of Medical History** (Tues & Fri noon–3pm, Thurs 4–7pm; 4mk) at nos. 11–13. Head through the courtyard and past the clinic and you'll find the museum in what was once an isolation ward, with an imposingly morbid selection of medieval folk cures, glass eyes, a mock-up of a leprosy patient's room (from a hospital which only closed in 1953) and some vicious-looking dental accessories. Nearby, at no. 24, the **Museum of Finnish Architecture** (Tues–Sun 10am–4pm, Wed until 7pm; free), is aimed at the serious fan, arranging architectural tours of less accessible buildings, both in Helsinki and around the country. Combined with an extensive archive, it's a useful resource for a nation with an important architectural heritage.

A block from Kasarmikatu is Korkeavuorenkatu and the excellent **Museum of Applied Arts** (Tues–Fri 11am–5pm, Sat & Sun 11am–4pm; 15mk) at no. 23, which traces the relationship between art and industry in Finnish history. There are full explanatory texts and period exhibits, from Karelianism – the representations of nature and peasant life from the Karelia region in eastern Finland which dominated Finnish art and design in the years just before and just after independence – to the modern movements, along with the postwar shift towards the more familiar, and less interesting, pan-Scandinavian styles.

Kasarmikatu ends close to the base of a hill, from which footpaths lead up to the Engel-designed **Astronomical Observatory**. Down on the other side and a few streets on is the large and rocky **Kaivopuisto** park. In the 1830s this was developed as a health resort, with a spa house that drew Russian nobility from St Petersburg to sample its waters. The building, another of Engel's works although greatly modified, can be found in the middle of the park's central avenue, today pulling the crowds as a restaurant.

Off a smaller avenue, Itäinen Puistotie, runs the circular Kallionlinnantie, which contains the house where Gustaf Mannerheim spent the later years of his life, now maintained as the **Mannerheim Museum** (Fri & Sat 11am–3pm, Sun 11am–4pm; 15mk). A Finnish-born Russian-trained military commander, Mannerheim was pro-Finnish but had a middle-class suspicion of the working classes: he led the right-wing Whites during the Civil War of 1918, and two decades later the Finnish campaigns in the Winter and Continuation Wars (for more on these see the "Military Museum" below). His influence in the political sphere was also considerable, including a brief spell as president. While acknowledging his importance, the regard that Finns have for him these days, naturally enough, depends on their own political viewpoint.

Ideology aside, the house is intriguing. The interior is left much as it was when the man died in 1951, and the clutter is astounding. During his travels Mannerheim raided flea markets at every opportunity, collecting a remarkable array of plunder – assorted furniture and antiques, ornaments and books from all over the globe. Upstairs is the camp-bed which Mannerheim found too comfortable ever to change, and in the wall is the vent inserted to keep the bedroom as airy as a field-tent.

If he had lived a few decades earlier, one of Mannerheim's Kallionlinnantie neighbours would have been Frederik Cygnaeus, art patron and Professor of Aesthetics at Helsinki University. In 1860 Cygnaeus built a summer house at no. 8, a lovely yellow-turreted affair, and filled it with an outstanding collection of art. Later he donated the lot to the nation and today it's displayed as the **Cygnaeus Gallery** (Wed–Sun 11am–4pm, Wed also 6–8pm; 6mk). Everything is beautifully laid out in the tiny rooms of the house, whole walls of work by the most influential of his contemporaries. The von Wright brothers (Ferdinand, Magnus and Wilhelm) are responsible for the most touching pieces – the characteristic bird and nature studies. Look out too for a strange portrait of Cygnaeus by Ekman, showing the man sprouting sinister wings from under his chin.

The edge of Kaivopuisto looks out across a sprinkling of little islands and the Suomenlinna fortress. Following one of the pathways leads down into Merikatu, on which lie several of the Art Nouveau villas lived in by the big noises of Finnish industry during the early part of the century. Easily the most extreme of these is no. 25, the *Enso-Gutzeit* villa, now portioned off into offices and with a lingering air of decay hanging over its decorative facade, making the squat little statues strewn around the garden seem quite indecent.

Inland from Merikatu, the curving alleys and tall elegant buildings of **Eira** are landmarked by the needle-like spire rising from the roof of **Mikael Agricola kirkko**, named after the translator of the first Finnish Bible but making no demands on your time. A hundred metres to the right of the church's entrance is the oddball **Post and Telecommunications Museum** at Tehtaankatu 21B (Tues–Fri noon–3pm, Wed until 6pm; 5mk), whose contents are a sprightly documentation of the Finnish postal service ranging from postal sleds and horns to unwieldy telephone exchanges and toytown uniforms. An additional incentive for the uncommitted are the free postcards with which you can stuff your pockets upon leaving. A few streets away, the twin-towered **Johannes kirkko** is again not worth a call in itself but functions as a handy navigation aid, being close to the junction of Merimenhenkatu and Yjrönkatu. Following the latter takes you past the partly-pedestrianised Iso Robertinkatu, before reaching Bulevardi and the square containing **Vanha kirkko** or Old Church. A humble wooden structure, and another example of Engel's work, this was the first Lutheran church to be erected after Helsinki became the Finnish capital, pre-dating Senate Square by some years but occupying a far less glamourous plot – a graveyard dating from 1710.

Heading left along Bulevardi leads to the wide Hietalahdentori, a concrete square which perks up with a daily morning flea market and in summer an evening market from 3.30–8pm. Across the road is the Sinebrychoff brewery, which bestows a distinctive aroma of hops to the locality, and finances the **Sinebrychoff Art Museum** at no. 40 (June–Aug Mon–Fri 9am–5pm, Wed until 8pm, Sat & Sun 11am–5pm; rest of the year same hours except Sat 9am–5pm; 5mk). This rather precious museum houses mostly seventeenth-century Flemish and Dutch paintings, including some excellent miniatures, delicately illustrated porcelain and refined period furniture.

Kruununhaka and Hakaniemi

North of Senate Square is the little district of **KRUUNUNHAKA**. Away from the general city hubbub, its closely-built blocks shield the narrow streets from the sunlight, evoking a forlorn and forgotten mood. At Kristianinkatu 12, the **Burgher's House** (Sun–Fri noon–4pm, Thurs until 8pm; 5mk) is a single storey wooden structure that's a vivid contrast to the tall granite dwellings around it and is an indication of how Helsinki looked when wood was still the predominant building material. The interior has been kitted out with furnishings of the mid-nineteenth century, the period when the city burgher did indeed reside here.

Kristianinkatu meets Maurinkatu at right-angles, a short way along which is the **Military Museum** (Sun–Fri 11am–3pm; 3mk), a rather formless selection of weapons, medals, and glorifications of armed-forces life, but with some excellent documentary photos of the Winter and Continuation Wars of 1939–1944. Finland was drawn into World War II through necessity rather than choice. When Soviet troops invaded eastern Finnish territories in November 1939, under the guise of protecting Leningrad, they were repelled by technically inferior but far more committed Finns. The legends of the "heroes in white" were born then, alluding to the Finnish soldiers and the camouflage used in the winter snows. Soon after, however, faced with possible starvation and a fresh Soviet advance, Finland joined the war on the Nazi side, mainly in order to continue resisting the threat from the east. For this reason, it's rare to find World War II spoken of as such in Finland, much more commonly it's divided into these separate conflicts. (For more on these wars, and their enormous ramifications for modern Finland, see "History").

Across the busy Unioninkatu, dividing Kruununhaka from the centre of the city, begin the pleasurably explorable **botanical gardens**, while a bridge over Kaisaniemenlahti heads directly into Hakaniemi and the wide Hakaniementori with its **kauppahalli** (Mon–Fri 8am–5pm, Sat 8am–2pm). Although Hakaniementori is surrounded by drab store-fronts and office blocks, the indoor market is about the liveliest in the city – mainly due to its position near a major junction for city buses and trams as well as a metro station. From the square you can see right up the hill to the impressive Art Deco brickwork of the **Kallio kirkko**, beyond which is the open green area partly consumed by **Linnanmäki amusement park** – the scene of several killings a few years back when its roundabouts and dodgems provided the backdrop for a bout of teenage gang warfare. Thankfully, things have quietened down since then.

Suomenlinna

Built by the Swedes in 1748 to protect Helsinki from seaborne attack, the fortress of **Suomenlinna** stands on five inter-connected islands that make a rewarding break from the city – even if you only want to laze around on the dunes, put here by the Russians with sand shipped in from Estonia after they'd wrested control of Finland and wanted to strengthen the new capital's defences. If you're feeling inquisitive, there are hour-long summer **guided walking tours** (15mk), beginning close to the ferry landing stage. Ferries leave for here from the South Harbour half-hourly. The tours are conducted in English at 12.30pm, but check timings at the information booth or the city tourist office.

Suomenlinna has a few museums, none particularly riveting, although the **Nordic Arts Centre** (May–Sept daily 11am–7pm; rest of the year daily 10am–6pm; free), with its small displays of contemporary arts from the Nordic countries, is worth a browse. Of the others, the **Ehrensvärd Museum** (early May–Sept daily 10am–5pm; rest of the year Sat & Sun 11am–3pm; 5mk) is in the residence used by the first commander of the fortress, Augustin Ehrensvärd. He oversaw the building of Suomenlinna and now lies in the elaborate tomb in the grounds; his personal effects remain inside the house alongside displays on the fort's construction. The **Armfelt Museum** (mid-May–Aug daily 11am–5.30pm, Sept Sat & Sun 11am–5.30pm; 5mk) contains the eighteenth- and nineteenth-century family heirlooms of the Armfelt clan who lived in the Joensuu Manor at Halikko. Finally, the **Coastal Defence Museum** (mid-May–Aug daily 11am–5pm; rest of the year Sat & Sun 11am–5pm; 5mk) records Suomenlinna's defensive actions and lets visitors clamber around the darkly claustrophobic World War I submarine *Vesikko*.

Seurasaari

A fifteen-minute tram (#4) or bus (#18, #24 or #36) ride from the city centre, **Seurasaari** is a small wooded island delightfully set in a sheltered bay. The three contrasting museums on the island or nearby make for a well-spent day. Access to the island proper is by bridge, at the southern end of Tamminiementie. The public transport stops are a few hundred metres to the north, at the junction of Tamminiementie and Meilahdentie, conveniently close to the **Helsinki City Art Museum** (Wed–Sun 11am–6.30pm; 5mk). Though one of the best collections of modern Finnish art, the museum is hardly a triumph of layout, with great clumps of stuff of differing styles thrown at the walls. But the good pieces shine through: Yrjö Saarinen's unflattering self-portrait, Viktor Dalbo's few strong works, and the paintings of Ellen Thesleff. There's also some worthwhile sculpture, an array of French work (mostly contemporaneous with the Finnish) and usually an up-to-date exhibition featuring industrial design and photography.

A few minutes' walk from the art museum, towards the Seurassari bridge, is the long driveway leading to the **Urho Kekkonen Museum** (May to mid-Sept daily 11am–4pm; rest of the year daily 11am–3pm; 10mk), the villa where the esteemed former president lived from 1956, and which had been the official home of all Finnish presidents since 1940. Whether they love him or loathe him, few Finns would deny the vital role Kekkonen played in Finnish history, most significantly in continuing the work of his predecessor, Paasikivi, in the establishment of Finnish neutrality and what became known as the "Paasikivi-Kekkonen line". He accomplished this largely through delicate negotiations with Soviet leaders, whose favour he would gain, so legend has it, by taking them to a sauna, narrowly averting major crises and seeing off the threat of a Soviet invasion on two separate occasions.

Kekkonen often conducted official business here rather than at the Presidential Palace in the city. Yet the feel of the place is far from institutional, with a light and very Finnish character, filled with birchwood furniture and with large windows giving peaceful views of surrounding trees, water and wildlife. The house was given to Kekkonen on his retirement from office, and he lived here for six years until his death in 1981. Close by, in another calm setting on Seurasaari itself across the bridge, is the **Open-Air Museum** (June–Aug daily 11am–5pm, Wed until 7pm; rest of the year Mon–Fri 9am–3pm, Sat & Sun 11am–5pm; 10mk), a collection of vernacular buildings assembled from all over Finland, connected up by way of the various pathways that stretch all around the island. There are better examples of traditional Finnish life elsewhere in the country, but if you're staying only in Helsinki this will give a good insight into how the country folk lived until surprisingly recently. The old-style church is a popular spot for city couples' weddings.

Aside from the museums and the scenery, people also come to Seurasaari to strip off. Sex-segregated **nudist beaches** line part of the western edge – also a popular offshore stop for the city's weekend yachtsmen, armed with binoculars.

Helsinki's other museums

Helsinki has a number of **other museums** outside the centre that don't easily fit into accounts of the city's various districts. All are within fairly easy reach with public transport, and sometimes a little legwork.

Co-operative Bank Museum

Arkadiankatu 23. *Bank hours*. Ask at reception and there may be a wait while they find some-one willing to give you a tour of this unsurprisingly neglected museum.

A collection of photos and documents relating to the history of the Co-operative Bank.

Gallen-Kallela Museum

Gallen-Kallelantie 27 on the little Tarvaspää peninsula. *Mid-May to Aug Tues–Thurs 10am–8pm Fri–Sun 10am–5pm; rest of the year Tues–Sat 10am–4pm, Sun 10am–5pm; 15mk.*

This museum is housed inside the Art Nouveau studio-home of Gallen-Kallela, where the infuential painter lived and worked from 1913, though it's a bit of an anti-climax, with neither atmosphere nor a decent display of the artist's work. There are a few old paints and brushes under dirty glass coverings in the studio, while in an upstairs room are the pickled remains of reptiles and frog-like animals collected by Gallen-Kallela's family. Inscribed into the floor is a declaration of Gallen-Kallela's: "I Shall Return". It's probably not worth the bother. Tram #4 from the city centre to the end of its route (on Saunalahdentie), then walk 2km along Munkkiniemi on the bay's edge, to a footbridge which leads over the water and towards the poorly signposted museum. Alternatively, bus #33 runs from the tram stop to the footbridge about every twenty minutes.

Hotel and Restaurant Museum

Inside the big *ALKO* factory at Itämerenkatu 23. *Tues–Fri noon–3pm; free.*

Although specifically designed for aficionados of the catering trade, the photos on the walls of the two rooms reveal a fascinating social history of Helsinki, showing hotel and restaurant life from both sides of the table, alongside a staggering selection of matchboxes, beermats emblazoned with the emblems of their establishments, and menus signed by the rich and infamous. Take tram #8 to the end of its route, or bus #20, #65a or #66a.

Kansallis-Osake-Pankki

Pohjoisesplanadi 29. *Bank hours.*

Ten cabinets of coins and bank notes throughout the ages and the world, with emphasis on Finnish/Swedish/Russian issues. On the ground floor as you enter and exactly as interesting as it sounds; allow about thirty seconds.

Photographic Museum of Finland

Vattuniemenkuja 4, on Lauttasaari. *June–Aug daily 11am–4pm, Sat & Sun 11am–3pm; rest of the year Mon–Fri 11am–5pm, Sat & Sun 11am–4pm; 5mk.*

Despite the grand title, a shabby herd of old cameras that suggest Finnish photography never really progressed beyond the watch-the-birdie stage. Amends are made by the innovative temporary collections of photos which regularly adorn the spacious gallery. Take bus #65A, #66A, #21 or #21V.

Union Bank of Finland Museum

Aleksanterinkatu 3 .*Bank hours*. Ask at reception, who will ring for a guide.

The most entertaining of Helsinki's three bank museums, with a late-nineteenth-century banking hall that's a riot of inlaid wood, carved desks, chandeliers and spidery ledgers. There's a fine collection, too, of wicked-looking typewriters, medieval contraptions and twisted keys.

Eating and drinking

Eating in Helsinki, as in the rest of the country, isn't cheap, but there is plenty of choice, and with careful planning plenty of ways to stretch out funds. Other than hotel all-you-can-eat **breakfast** tables (city hostel breakfasts tend to be strictly rationed), it's best to hold out until **lunch**, when many restaurants offer a cut-rate fixed-price menu or a help-yourself table, and in almost every pizzeria you'll get a pizza, coffee and all you can manage from the bread and salad bar for around 35mk. **Picnic food**, too, is a viable option. Use the markets and market halls at the South Harbour or Hakaniementori for fresh vegetables, meat and fish. Several supermarkets in Tunneli, by the railway station, stay open until 10pm.

Throughout the day, up until 5pm or 6pm, you can also take a coffee and pastry, or a fuller snack, for 10–25mk at one of the numerous **cafés**. The best cafés are stylish, atmospheric affairs dating from the turn of the century. Alternatives include myriad multinational hamburger joints and the slightly more unique *Grilli* roadside stands, which sell hot-dogs, sausages, and the like; if you're tempted, experts claim the *Jaskan Grilli*, in Töölönkatu behind the National Museum, to be the best of its kind in Finland.

As for **evening eating**, ethnic restaurants, principally Italian and Greek, are plentiful, and you should expect to pay 50–60mk each for dinner, provided you don't drink anything stronger than mineral water. There are also three vegetarian restaurants which charge about the same. Finnish restaurants, on the other hand, and those serving Russian specialities, can be terrifyingly expensive; expect to spend around 150mk each for a night of upmarket over-indulgence.

Mensas

If you're hungry and impoverished (and are, in theory at least, a student), you can get a full meal for 12–15mk from one of the **student mensas**, two of which are centrally located in the main university building at Aleksanterinkatu 5, and at Hallituskatu 11–13. One or the other will be open during the summer; both will be open during term time. The mensas can be cheaper still in the late afternoon, from 4–6pm, and are also usually open on Saturdays from 9am–1pm.

Cafés

Café Aalto, in the Academic Bookstore, Pohjoisesplanadi 39. Designed by the world famous Finnish architect, the interior of this cafeteria makes it worth sitting down to appreciate after a morning's book browsing.

Café Ekberg, Bulevardi 9. Nineteenth-century fixtures and a deliberately *fin-de-siécle* atmosphere, with starched waitresses bringing the most delicate of open sandwiches and pastries to green marble tables.

Café Eliel, on the ground floor of the railway station. An airy vaulted Art Nouveau interior with a good value self-service breakfast – and a roulette table.

Café Fazer, Kluuvikatu 3. Helsinki's best-known bakery, justly celebrated for its lighter-than-air pastries.

Kappeli, in Esplanadi Park. An elegant glasshouse with a relaxed form of self-service: you take what you want and tell the waitress later what you've had. The cellar is also a great spot for an evening drink – see *Kappelin Olutkellari*, under "Drinking".

Café Mini Succes, Korkeavourenkatu 2. Freshly baked bread, doughnuts and pastries every day.

Café Socis, Kaivokatu 12. Big, cosmopolitan and very beautiful – though also very expensive.

Café Ursula, Kaivopuisto. On the beach at the edge of the Kaivopuisto park, with a wonderful sea view from the outdoor terrace.

Restaurants

Ani, Telakkakatu 2. Turkish food at its best from the 35mk open-table laid out at lunchtime.

Aurinkotuuli, Lapinlahdenkatu 25a. A good range of vegetarian dishes, and prices to suit all but the tightest of budgets.

Golden Onion, Kanavaranta 3. A tastebud-thrilling though financially ruinous choice of six gourmet dishes, several based on traditional *Same* fare.

Green Way, Erottajankatu 11. Wholefood restaurant with a well-stocked fruitshake and juice bar.

La Havanna, Uudenmenkatu 9–11. Pioneering Cuban eaterie doing great things with seafood, but make sure you come at lunchtime – at night it's packed with boozers. See "Drinking".

Holvari, Yrjönkatu 15. Believe it or not, this place specialises in mushrooms, personally picked by the owner and providing the basis of tasty soups and stews.

Houne ja Keittiö, Huvilakatu 28. The name means literally "a room and a kitchen", and this tiny place is just that, producing fine home-cooked dishes from a small selection starting at a bargain 40mk. Closed at weekends.

Iso-Ankkuri, Pursimiehenkatu 16. Fairly downbeat and used mostly by local people, but with a nourishing, unextravagant menu.

Kannu, Punavuorenkatu 12. Much of the original interior, designed by Alvar Aalto, remains in this locals' haunt, where the staff will dish up delicious, down-to-earth food, though they only speak Finnish.

Kasakka, Meritullinkatu 13. Over the top spirit-of-the-Tsars atmosphere and great food, in this old-style Russian restaurant.

Kasvisravintola, Korkeavuorenkatu 3. Literally a "vegetable restaurant", and one of the oldest and best (though not the cheapest) in the country.

Katajanokan Kasino, Laivastokat 1. A gourmet and theme restaurant, in which you can feast on á la carte elk or reindeer in anything from a mock wartime bunker to the "Cabinet Room", decorated with markers to Finnish independence. A great place if someone else is paying.

Katarina, Aleksanterinkatu 22–24. An inspired if immensely costly mating of Finnish and French cuisines.

Kuu, Töölönkatu 27. Unpretentious place to quoff equally unpretentious inexpensive Finnish food.

Pasta Factory, Mastokatu 6. An intimate and discreetly stylish Italian food joint. Quite affordable.

Pizza No.1, Mannerheimintie 18, second floor of the *Forum*, shopping centre. Standard pizzas, but good deals at lunchtime and an entertaining selection of English cricket memorabilia on the walls.

Saslik, Neitsytpolku 12. Highly-rated for its Russian food, backed up with lush, Tsarist-period furnishings and live music.

Sea Horse, Kapteeninkatu 11. Serves a range of fairly inexpensive Finnish dishes, and is renowned for its Baltic sprats.

Drinking

Although never cheap, alcohol is not a dirty word, and **drinking**, especially beer, can be enjoyed in the city's many pub-like restaurants, which are where most Helsinki folk go to socialise. You'll find one on virtually every corner, but the pick of the bunch are listed below. Only the really swanky joints have a dress code, and they are usually too elitist – and expensive – to be worth bothering with anyway. Sundays to Thursdays are normally quiet; on Fridays and Saturdays on the other hand, it's best to arrive as early as possible to get a seat without having to queue. Most drinking dives also serve food, although the grub is seldom at its best in the evening (where it's good earlier in the day, we've included it under "Restaurants". If you want a drink but are feeling anti-social, or just very hard-up, the cheapest method, as ever, is to buy from an *ALKO* shop: the biggest and most central is at Hallituskatu 15.

Pubs

Angleterre, Fredrikinkatu 47. Utterly Finnish despite the flock wallpaper and Dickensian fixtures – good for a laugh and cultural disorientation.

Aseman Yläravintola, second floor of the railway station. Socially much more interesting than the *Eliel* restaurant downstairs (see "Cafés"), a lively and diverse place for a drink, surrounded by architect Saarinen's fabulous features. Don't risk it if you've a train to catch.

Ateljeebaari, Hotel Torni, Yrjönkatu 26. On the thirteenth floor of a plush hotel: great views, great posing – and the women's toilet has whole-wall windows. Drinks are pricey, though.

Bulevardia, Bulevardi 12. Many customers are technicians or singers from the neighbouring Opera House who swoop in after a concert. Join them for the Art Deco decor – matt-black furniture designed by Thirties architect Pauli Blomstedt, and burr birch walls.

Elite, Etläinen Hesperiankatu 22. Once the haunt of the city's artists, many of whom would settle the bill not with money but with paintings – a selection of which lines the walls. Especially good in summer, when you can drink on the terrace.

La Havanna, Uudenmenkatu 11. A Cuban restaurant, though there's much more boozing than dining in the evenings, and not much space to move as Latin American music fills the smoky air. A must. See also "Eating".

Juttutupa, Säästöpankinranta 6. The building was once HQ of the Social Democrats; they built it with a tower to allow their red flag to fly above the neighbouring church spires. The decision to take up arms, which culminated in the 1918 civil war, was made here and photos commemorate the fact. Apolitical entertainment is provided on Wednesdays, Fridays and Saturdays by an accordian and/or violin player, encouraging enjoyable singalongs.

Kappelin Olutkellari, in Esplanadi Park. The entrance is around the back of this distinctive multi-purpose building of glass and fancy ironwork (see also "Cafés" above). A garrulous and gloriously eclectic clientele.

Kirjakahvila, Mannerheimintie 3. This, the "Book Café", only serves coffee and tea, and it closes at weekends and at 10pm on weekdays. But would-be beatniks love the place for its small-scale literary and art events – and there's a reading room well-stocked with Finnish and foreign magazines. The building also contains the alcohol-equipped *Vanhann Kellari* and *Vanha Kavila*, see below.

Kosmos, Kalevankatu 3. This is where the big media cats – TV producers, PR people, the glitzier authors – hang out and engage in loud arguments as the night wears on. The wonderful interior is unchanged since the Twenties, but you'll only see it if you get past the extremely officious doorman.

Kultäinen Härkä, Uudenmenkatu 16–20. Load your plate from the inexpensive salad bar by day; drink and heckle the singer tinkling the piano by night.

No Name Irish Bar, Töölönkatu 2. Looks like an American cocktail bar and pulls an intriguing cross-section of Finns on the razzle.

Richard's Pub Rikhardinkatu 4. Close to the editorial offices of the major Helsinki newspapers. Usually contains a few hacks crying over lost scoops.

Salve, Hietaladenranta 11. Filled with nautical paraphernalia but no longer the seedy sailor's haunt that it was. Worth a call, to eat or drink, although the recently hiked-up prices suggest the place has ideas above its station.

St. Urho's Pub, Museokatu 10. One of the most popular student pubs – which accounts for the lengthy queue that forms from about 9pm on Fridays and Saturdays.

Vanhan Kahvia, Mannerheimintie 3. A self-service and therefore comparatively cheap bar. It fills quickly, so try to arrive early for a seat on the balcony overlooking the bustle of the streets below.

Vanhan Kellari, Mannerheimintie 3. Downstairs from the *Vanhan Kahvia* (see above), its underground setting and bench-style seating help promote a cosy and smoky atmosphere. Rumour has it that this is where the Helsinki beat-poets of the early Sixties drank, and where they now bring their children.

Nightlife: music, clubs and the cinema

Helsinki probably has a greater and more diverse number of ways to spend the evening than any other Scandinavian city; there is, for example, a steady diet of **live music**. Finnish rock bands, not helped by the awkward metre of their native language, often sound absurd on first hearing, but at least seeing them is relatively cheap at 20–35mk – around half the price of seeing a British or American band. The best gigs tend to be during term time, but in summer there are dozens of free events in the city parks, the biggest of which take place almost every Sunday in Kaivopuisto. Many bands also play on selected nights in one of the growing number of surprisingly hip **clubs and discos**, in which you can gyrate, pose or just drink into the small hours – admission is usually 20–30mk.

For up-to-the-minute details of **what's on**, read the entertainments page of *Helsingin Sanomat*, or the free fortnightly paper, *City*, found in record shops, book shops and department stores, which has listings covering rock and classical music, clubs, cinema, theatre, and opera. Or simply watch for posters on the streets. **Tickets** for most events can be bought at the venue or, for a small commission, at a couple of agencies: *Lippupalvelu*, Mannerheimintie 5 (Mon–Fri 9.30am–4.30pm, Sat 10am–2pm), and *Tiketti*, on the second floor of the *Forum* shopping centre, off Mannerheimintie (Mon–Fri 9am–5pm). Both of these are open slightly longers hour in winter.

Clubs and venues

Back to the USSR, Sturenkatu 4 (☎90/7708241). This place usually has something trendy and contemporary to dance to.

Berlin, Töölönkatu 3 (☎90/499002). Depending on the night, you'll find the latest acid and hip-hop sounds, heavy rock, or black music specials.

Disco Joy, Ratakatu 9 (☎90/646674). Reggae on Mondays, and calypso and Afro-beat sounds on Tuesdays.

Fokka, Kirjatyöntekijänkatu 10 (☎90/636667). DJs with assorted reggae and British indie-pop sounds on Fridays and Saturdays.

KY-Exit, Pohjoinen Rautatiekatu 21 (☎90/407238). Sometimes has visiting foreign bands, more often lively disco nights.

Lepakko-Klub, Porkkalankatu 1 (no phone). Doesn't sell alcohol, but youthful customers flock to see the live combos, who appear once or twice a week. The name, incidently, means "Bat Club".

Natsa, Kasarmikatu 40 (☎90/667297). On Wednesdays this club has a "Rock Sauna" night, showcasing new local bands.

New Botta, Museokatu 10 (☎90/446940), joined to St. Urho's Pub (see "Drinking" above). Vibrant dance music of various hues most nights.

Olutkellari, Merihotelli, John Stenbergin ranta 6 (☎90/708711). Acoustic blues on Mondays and Tuesdays.

Orfeus, Eerikinkatu 3 (☎90/640378). Free live jazz and blues on Thursdays, Friday and Saturdays.

Tavastia-Klubbi, Urho Kekkosenkatu 4–6 (☎90/6943401). A major showcase for Finnish and Swedish bands. Downstairs has the stage and self-service bar, while the balcony is waitress service.

Vanha Maestro, Fredrikinkatu 51–53 (☎90/644303). The place to go if you fancy some traditional Finnish dancing, and a legend among the country's enthusiasts of *humpa* – a truly Finnish dance, distantly related to the waltz and tango. Afternoon and evening sessions most days (entry 10–30mk).

Vanha Ylioppilastalo, Mannerheimintie 3 (☎90/176616). The main venue for leading indie bands from around the world; see also the Vanha bars under "Drinking".

Gay nightlife

The city's comparatively small amount of **gay activity** is largely organised by *SETA*, an umbrella organisation of sexual minority groups. They have a hand in the gay nightlife and are also behind the Gay Pride Days which take place each summer. Get the latest information by calling into the *SETA* office at Mäkelänkatu 36 A 5 (Mon–Fri 11am–noon & 2–6pm; ☎90/769642). They can be phoned between 6pm and 9pm on Wednesdays, Thursdays, Fridays and Sundays.

SETA arrange a **gay disco** night, *Triangle*, at *Berlin* (see live music listings) on Mondays. They also part-own *Gambrini* at Iso Roobertinkat 3 (Tues–Sun 7–1am; ☎90/644391) – a **gay bar/café** which is smaller and perhaps friendlier than *Berlin*; it's open to women only every other Saturday. Its entrance is through a courtyard, and straight friends of gays are welcome. The side bars of the *Vanhan Kellari* (see "Drinking", above) have also earned a reputation as a place where gay men and lesbians can imbibe at ease.

Cinema and Opera

Both the latest blockbusters and a good selection of fringe **films** are normally showing somewhere in Helsinki. A seat is usually 25–30mk, although some places offer a 12mk matinee show on Mondays; this isn't loudly advertised but discreetly indicated by handwritten notices outside the venue. Check the listings in *City* or pick up a copy of *Elokuva-Viikko*, a free weekly leaflet which lists the cinemas and their screenings. English-language films are shown with Finnish subtitles – there's no overdubbing. If you're at a loose end the three-screened *Nordia*, Yrjönkatu 36 (☎90/13119250), commonly has an excellent programe of new art house films and cult classics – and cheap prices.

Finally, if you've missed out on the Savonlinna **opera** festival (see *The Lake Region*), but want to find out why Finnish opera is raved about by those in the know, take your place at the *Finnish National Opera*, Bulevardi 23–25 (☎90/129255).

Listings

Airlines *British Airways*, Keskuskatu 7 (☎90/650677); *Finnair*, Mannerheimintie 102 (☎90/81881); *SAS*, Phojoisesplanadi 23 (☎90/177433).

Airport *Finnair* buses to Vantaa airport leave every 15–30 minutes from the railway station, calling at the *Finnair* terminal (☎90/410411) and at the *Inter-Continental Hotel* before continuing directly to the airport (☎90/8292451). The fare is 15mk and the journey time is thirty minutes. City bus #615, from stop no.12 by the railway station, goes to the airport more slowly but more cheaply, 10mk.

Books The *Academic Bookstore* at Pohjoisesplanadi 39 has several floors containing thousands of books in various languages on all subjects, including a large stock of English paperbacks.

Car Hire *Avis* Fredrikinkatu 67 (☎90/441155); *Budget* Frederikinkatu 61 (☎90/6945300); *Europcar/Inter-Rent* Hakaniemenranta 2–4 (☎90/7556133).

Chemists 24-hour pharmacy: *Yliopiston Apteeki*, Mannerheimintie 96 (☎90/415778).

Doctor ☎008.

Embassies *UK*, Uudenmaankatu 16–20 (☎90/647922); *USA*, Itäinen Puistotie 14 (☎90/171931); *Canada*, Pohjoisesplanadi 25B (☎90/171141). Citizens of *Australia* and *New Zealand* should contact the Australian Embassy in Stockholm, and those of *Ireland* the relevant authority in Amsterdam.

Emergencies ☎000.

Hitching *Radio City* on 96.2mhz has a phone-in (☎90/6941366) lift service each Thursday – and they speak English.

Hospital Casualty departments: Töölö Hospital, Töölönkatu 40. Helsinki University Central Hospital, Haartmaninkatu 4.

Late Shops The shops in Tunneli, the underground complex by the railway station, are open Mon–Sat 10am–10pm, Sun noon–10pm.

Launderettes At Punavuorenkatu 3 (Mon–Fri 7am–9pm, Sat & Sun 9am–9pm) and Mannerheimintie 93 (Mon–Thurs 9am–5pm, Fri 8am–1pm), but not cheap: 20–58mk.

Left Luggage At the long-distance bus station (Mon–Sat 7am–10pm, Sun 11am–7pm), or railway station (daily 6.15am–11.25pm).

Libraries The word is *kirjasto*; central branches are at Topeliuksenkatu 6 in Töölö, at Rikhardinkatu 3 near Esplanadi, and at Viides linja 11, close to Kallio kirkko (each Mon–Fri 9.30am–8pm, Sat 9.30am–3pm).

Lost Property Office (*Löytötavaratoimisto*) Sixth floor, Päivänteentie 12A (Mon–Fri 8am–3.15pm; ☎90/1893180).

Media There's a tourist-orientated "News in English" on ☎90/040. See also "What's On".

Money Exchange Outside banking hours at the airport 7am–11pm; and slightly more cheaply at Katajanokka harbour (where *Viking* and *Finnjet* dock) daily 9–11.30am & 3.45–6pm.

Peace Movement A number of peace organisations are based at The Peace Station, Pasila (north of the city centre).

Police Olavinkatu 1 (☎90/6940633).

Post Office The main office is at Mannerheimintie 11. Mon–Fri 9am–5pm; post restante at the rear door Mon–Fri 8am–10pm, Sun 11am–10pm. Stamps from post offices or the yellow machines in shops which take 1mk and 5mk coins.

Transport Information In Finnish only, for planes (☎90/821122 or 818500); long-distance buses (☎97004000 – very expensive); trains (☎90/659411); and city transport ☎90/765966.

What's On Tourist events: ☎90/058. Free, if limited, listings in: *Helsinki This Week* (covers a month), *Helsinki Today*, and *Helsinki Guide* (covers whole summer) from the city tourist office, hotels, youth hostels etc.

Women's Movement Although it's closed throughout July, the place to make contact is the Finnish feminists' union: *Naisasialiitto Unioni*, at Bulevardi 11A (☎90/642277), where there's also *Naistenhuone*, a women's bookshop-café (Mon–Fri 4–9pm, Sat noon–6pm, Sun 2–6pm).

AROUND HELSINKI

To be honest, there's little in Helsinki's outlying area that's worth venturing out for. But three places, all an easy day-trip from the city, merit a visit: the visionary suburbs of **Espoo**, the home of the composer, Sibelius, at **Järvenpää**, and the evocative old town of **Porvoo** – which also serves as an obvious access route to the underrated southeastern corner of the country.

The Espoo area

Lying west of Helsinki, the suburban area of **ESPOO** comprises several separate districts. The nearest, directly across the bay, is the "garden city" of **TAPIOLA**. In the 1950s Finnish urban planners attempted to blend new housing schemes with surrounding forests and hills, frequently only to be left with a compromise which turned ugly as expansion occured. Tapiola was the exception to this rule, built as a self-contained living area rather than a dormitory town, with alternating high and low buildings, abundant open areas, parks, fountains and swimming pools. Much praised by the architectural world on completion, it's still refreshing to wander through and admire the idea and its execution. In the very centre is Tapiontori, which contains a **tourist office** (May–Sept Mon–Fri 8am–5pm, Sat 10am–2pm; rest of the year Mon–Fri 8am–3pm, Thurs until 5.30pm; ☎90/467652), handling inquiries about the whole Espoo area.

Walking about 3km north of Tapiola, past the traffic-bearing Hagalundintie, brings you to the little peninsula of **Otaniemi** and a couple more notable architectural sites. One of these is the Alvar Aalto-designed campus of Helsinki University's technology faculty; the other – far more dramatic – is the *Dipoli* student union building on the same campus. Ever keen to harmonise the artificial with the natural, architects Reimi and Raili Pietilä here created a building which seems fused with the rocky crags above Laajalahti, the front of the structure daringly edging forward from the cliff face.

Though the town of Espoo has little to delay you, just beyond lies the absorbing **Hvitträsk** (June–Aug Mon–Fri 10am–8pm, Sat & Sun 10am–7pm; rest of the year daily 11am–6pm; 10mk), the studio home built and shared by Eliel Saarinen, Armas Lindgren and Herman Gesellius until 1904, when the partnership dissolved amid the acrimony caused by Saarinen's independent (and winning) design for Helsinki's railway station. Externally, it's an extended and romanticised version of the traditional Finnish log cabin, the leafy branches that creep around making the structure look like a mutant growth emerging from the forest. Inside are frescoes by Gallen-Kallela and changing exhibitions of Finnish art and handicrafts. Both Eliel Saarinen and his wife are buried in the grounds.

Buses run throughout the day from Helsinki to Tapiola but you usually need to specifically request them to stop there; check the details and times at the bus station ticket office or the city tourist office. To get from central Helsinki to Hvitträsk, take the local (line L) train to Louma and follow the signs for 2km.

Järvenpää

Thirty-eight kilometres north of Helsinki and easy to get to, with either a bus or train to **JÄRVENPÄÄ**, is **Ainola** – the house where Jean Sibelius lived from 1904 with his wife, Aino (sister of the artist Eero Järnefelt), after whom the place is named.

Though now regarded as one of the world's greatest composers, **Jean Sibelius**, born in Hämeenlinna in 1865, had no musical background whatsoever, and by the age of 19 was enrolled in a law course at Helsinki University. He had, however, developed a youthful passion for the violin and took a class at the capital's Institute of Music. Law was soon forgotten as Sibelius' real talents were recognised, and his musical studies took him to the cultural hotbeds of the day: Berlin and Vienna. Returning to Finland to teach at the Institute, Sibelius soon gained a government grant which enabled him to compose full-time, the first concert of his works taking place in 1892. His early pieces were inspired by the Finnish folk epic, the *Kalevala*, and by the nationalist sentiments of the times. Sibelius even incurred the wrath of the country's Russian rulers when in 1899 they banned performances of his rousing *Finlandia* under any name which suggested its patriotic sentiment; to circumvent this, the piece was published as "Opus 26 No. 7".

While the overtly nationalistic elements in Sibelius' work mellowed in later years, he continued composing with what's regarded as a very Finnish obsession with nature ("Other composers offer their public a cocktail," he said, "I offer mine pure spring water"). He is still highly revered in his own land, although he was also notorious for his bouts of heavy drinking, and a destructive quest for perfection which helped fuel suspicion that he completed, and destroyed, two symphonies during his final thirty years. This was an angst-ridden period when no new work appeared and which became known as "the silence from Järvenpää". Sibelius died in 1957, his best-known symphonies setting a standard almost impossible for younger Finnish composers to live up to.

The house is just the kind of home you'd expect for a man who would include representations of flapping swans' wings in his music if one happened to fly by while he was at work – a tranquil place, close to lakes and forests. Indeed, the wood-filled grounds are as atmospheric as the building (May–Sept Tues–Sun 10am–6pm, Wed noon–8pm), which is a place of pilgrimage for devotees: books, furnishings and a few paintings are all there is to see. His grave is in the grounds, marked by a marble stone inscribed simply with his name. For more tangible Sibelius memories, and more of his music, visit the Sibelius Museum in Turku (see "The Southwest").

Porvoo

One of the oldest towns on the south coast, **PORVOO**, 50km east of Helsinki, with its narrow cobbled streets lined by small wooden buildings, gives a sense of the Finnish life which predated the capital's bold squares and Neoclassical geometry. This, coupled with its elegant riverside setting and unhurried mood, means you're unlikely to be alone. Word of Porvoo's peaceful time-locked qualities have spread.

The Town

First stop should be the **tourist office** at Rauhankatu 20 (Mon–Fri 8am–4pm, Sat 10am–2pm; ☎915/140145 or 142741), over the road from the bus station, for a free map of the town. The immediate area is comparatively recent, but look in at the preserved **Johan Ludwig Runeberg House**, at Runeberginkatu 20 (May–Aug Mon–Sat 9.30am–4pm, Sun 10.30am–5pm; rest of the year Mon–Sat 10am–3pm, Sun 11am–4pm), where the man regarded as Finland's national poet lived from 1852 while a teacher at the town school. Despite writing in Swedish, he greatly aided the nation's sense of self-esteem, especially with *Tales of Ensign Ståhl*, which told of the people's struggles with Russia in the 1808–9 conflict. The first poem in the collection, *Our Land*, later provided the lyrics for the national anthem. Across the road, the **Walter Runeberg Gallery** (May–Aug Tues–Sat 9.30am–4pm, Sun 10.30am–5pm; rest of the year Tues–Sat 11am–4pm, Sun 11am–5pm) has a collection of sculpture by Runeberg's third son, one of Finland's more celebrated sculptors. Among many acclaimed works, he's responsible for the statue of his dad which stands in the centre of Helsinki's Esplanadi.

The old town (follow the signs for *Vanha Porvoo*) is built around the hill on the other side of Mannerheimkatu. Near the top, its outline partially obscured by vegetation, is the fifteenth-century **Tuomiokirkko** (May–Sept Mon–Sat 10am–6pm, Sun 2–5pm). It was here in 1809 that Alexander I proclaimed Finland a Russian Grand Duchy, himself Grand Duke, and convened the first Finnish Diet. This, and other aspects of the town's past, can be explored in the **Porvoo Museum** (May–Aug daily 11am–4pm; rest of the year Tues–Sat 11am–3pm, Sun noon–4pm) at the foot of the hill in the old town's main square. There are no singularly outstanding exhibits here, just a diverting selection of furnishings, musical instruments and general oddities, largely dating from the years of Russian rule. For on the spot advice, there's an **information counter** (mid-May to mid-Aug daily 10am–6pm; ☎915/130747) on the old square.

Practical details

Buses run all day from Helsinki to Porvoo, and a one-way trip costs around 20mk. Idling around the town is especially pleasant late in the day as the evening stillness descends, and conveniently the last bus back to the city departs around midnight. There's also a **boat**, the *J.L.Runeberg*, which sails from Helsinki's South Harbour on Wednesdays, Fridays and weekends in summer at 10am, arriving in Porvoo at 1.15pm and leaving two hours later; the one-way fare is 75mk.

If you've exhausted Helsinki, **spending a night** in Porvoo leaves you well-placed to continue into Finland's southeastern corner (see below). If possible, check accommodation details in Helsinki before reaching Porvoo, especially to discover any hotel bargains – rates in Porvoo are steep. There is, however, a **youth hostel**, open all year, at Linnankoskenkatu 1 (☎915/130012), and a **campsite** (☎915/141967 or ☎716422), open from June to August, 2km from the town centre.

THE SOUTHEAST

As it's some way from the major centres, foreign tourists tend to neglect the extreme **southeastern corner** of Finland; Finns, however, rate it highly, flocking here to make short boat-trips around the small islands and to explore the many small communities, which enticingly combine a genuine rustic flavour with sufficient places of minor interest to keep boredom at bay. For Finns, the region also stirs memories: its position on the Soviet border means it saw many battles during the Winter and Continuation Wars, and throughout medieval times it was variously under the control of Sweden and Russia. It's an intriguing if not exactly vital area, worth two or three days of travel – most of it by bus; railways are almost non-existent.

Lovissa, Ruotsinpyhtää, Pyhtää and Siltakylä

If Porvoo seems too tourist-infested, make the 40km journey east to **LOVISSA**, an eighteenth-century fishing village pleasantly free of Helsinki day-trippers. The village, whose 10,000-strong population divides into equal amounts of Finnish- and Swedish-speakers, is overlooked by the two very explorable old fortresses of Resen and Ungern. The **tourist office**, on the market square, can supply details of how to get to them; off the square, a row of prettily-preserved houses shows the way to the **district museum**, containing, besides the usual local hotch-potch, a fine stock of turn-of-the-century romantic postcards. Later on, if you have the cash, spend it on a slap-up meal at *Degerby Grille*, Sepänkuja 4; if you don't, poke your head around the restaurant's door anyway to marvel at the wonderfully-maintained ancient interior.

In the bay off Lovissa there's a less welcome modern sight – one of the country's **nuclear power stations**. Finland's balancing act between East and West has led to the country buying its nuclear hardware from both power blocs. This one has spent the last 25 years producing plutonium for (allegedly) Soviet nuclear weapons. The other, Western-backed, at Olkiluoti (near Rauma), is newer and is still the subject of much argument. The Finnish public are divided over the merits of nuclear power in general – the country takes about forty percent of its energy from nuclear sources, but the growing anti-nuclear movement is calling for a switch to hydroelectric power. Whatever the outcome of the debate, and whatever the state of the thaw in the Cold War, the view of a Soviet nuclear reactor so close to a picturesque Finnish coastal village is an unnerving one.

If you have the time, a couple of smaller settlements on the way to Kotka can comfortably consume half a day. In 1809, the Swedish-Russian border was drawn up in this area, splitting the region of Pyhtää in two. Some 20km from Lovissa is **RUOTSINPYHTÄÄ** (or Swedish Pyhtää), the local **tourist office** (☎915/78104) heroically positioned on the bridge over the inlet which once divided the two feuding empires. Historical quirks aside, the main attraction here, unappetising though it may at first sound, is the seventeenth-century **ironworks** – now turned into craft studios, with demonstrations of carpet-weaving, jewellery-making and painting. It's all quite enjoyable to stroll around on a sunny day. You should also visit the oddly octagonal-shaped **wooden church** (June–Sept daily noon–3pm; rest of the year Sun noon–4pm), to admire Helene Schjerfbeck's beautiful altarpiece. It was here, incidentally, using the contrast of the spacious mill-owners' houses and the cramped workers' cottages, that a Finnish TV company filmed a very popular soap opera: *Vihreän Kullanmaa* ("the Land of the Green Gold") – the nation's equivalent of *Dallas*.

The village of **PYHTÄÄ**, whose position on the Russian side of the border meant it retained its Finnish name, is a twenty-minute bus ride further east. There's a **stone church** here (June–Sept daily noon–3pm; rest of the year Sun noon–3pm), one of the oldest in the country, dated at around 1301. Its interior frescoes are primitive and strangely moving, discovered only recently when the Reformation-era whitewash was removed. From the quay on the other side of the village's sole street, there's a ferry service to the nearby islands, including Kaunissaari ("Beautiful Island"), where you can connect with an evening motor-boat straight on to Kotka.

The land route to Kotka takes you through **SILTAKYLÄ**, a small town significant only for the hills around it and its **tourist information counter** at the town hall, beside the main road. The hills afford great views over a dramatic legacy of the Ice Age: spooky Tolkein-esque forests and many miles of a red-granite stone known as *rapakivi* which is unique to southeast Finland, covered by a white moss. A number of marked hiking trails lead through the landscape, strewn with giant boulders, some as big as four-storey buildings and supporting their own little ecosystem of plant and tree-life. After a day's trek, you can reward your efforts with food and drink – or even a swim – at the not-too-pricey *Pyhtään Motelli* (☎952/31661), which despite its name is situated on the edge of Siltakylä.

Kotka

After the scattering of little communities east of Porvoo, **KOTKA**, a few kilometres on from Siltakylä, is immense by comparison, the only large town between Helsinki and the Soviet border. Rail and road connections bring you right into the compact centre, and the **tourist office** at Keskuskatu 5 (June–Aug Mon–Fri 8am–6pm, Sat 9am–1pm; rest of the year Mon–Fri 8am–4pm; ☎952/11736), will fill you in on local bus details – essential for continuing around the southeast.

Built on an island on the Gulf of Finland, **Kotka's past** reflects its closeness to the sea. Numerous battles have been fought off its shores, among them the Sweden-Russia confrontation of 1790 which was the largest battle ever seen in Nordic waters – almost 10,000 losing their lives. Sixty-odd years later, the British fleet virtually reduced Kotka to rubble during the Crimean war. In modern times the sea has been the basis of the town's prosperity: sitting at the end of the Kymi river with a deep water port harbour, the town makes a perfect cargo transit point – causing most locals to live in fear of a major accident occuring in the industrial section, or in the frieght yards. Only two roads link Kotka to the mainland and a speedy evacuation of its inhabitants would be almost impossible.

The town itself has little to delay you, it's more a place to eat and sleep than anything else. Only the eighteenth-century Orthodox **St. Nicolai Kirkko** (Tues–Sun noon–2pm) survived the British bombardment, and even that is not particularly interesting, although you should make a point of visiting the **Langinkoski Imperial Fishing Lodge** (summer 10am–8pm; winter by appointment ☎952/21050), off the main island, about 5km north of the town centre (take bus #20). It was here that Tsar Alexander III would relax in transit between Helsinki and St Petersburg; the wooden building, a gift to him from the Finnish Government, is most striking for its un-Tsar-like simplicity and the attractive setting in the woods near the fast-flowing Kymi river.

Practical details

As for **practical needs** in Kotka, grumbling stomachs can be quietened in *Kairo*, Satamakatu 7, an authentic seaman's restaurant, popular with Eastern bloc sailors, or in *Vanha Stuju*, at Kotkankatu 9, which has an inexpensive fish menu. The least costly **hotel** is *Ruotsinsalmi*, Kirkkokatu 14 (☎952/13440), which has doubles from 250mk, and there's choice of three **youth hostels**: the most central are *Uimaja retkeilymaja* inside the Sports Hall at Puistotie 9–11 (☎952/11603 or 11736), open all year, and *Retkeilymaja Koskisoppi* at Keisarinmajantie 4 (☎952/25555), open from mid-May to August. More scenically situated, overlooking a spectacular bay, is *Kärkisaariis retkeilymaja* (☎952/604215), open from May to September, 6km north of Kotka in Mussalo, where there's also an all-year **campsite** (☎952/604831) – take bus #20 from central Kotka. Beside the campsite is *Hotel Santalahti*: rooms here are 300mk per double, but anybody can drop in to use the cheapish **cafeteria**.

East of Kotka: Hamina, the Soviet border and around

Twenty-six kilometres east of Kotka is **HAMINA**, founded in 1653 and sporting a magnificently bizarre town plan, the main streets forming concentric circles around the centre. It was built this way to allow the incumbent Swedish forces to withstand attack – the town being the site of many Swedish-Russian battles. Besides the layout, however, there's not an awful lot to amuse in the town, although you can pick up suggestions and local information from the **tourist office**, at Frederikinkatu 4 (☎952/44320).

For anybody who isn't a Eastern bloc old-hand, it's the proximity of the **Soviet border**, just 38km away, that soon becomes the region's most intriguing aspect. There's a bus (running two–three times daily; details from the Hamina tourist office) which goes as far as **VIROLAHTI**, from where you might try to hitch the remaining 7km to **VAALIMA**. Aside from making a legal crossing of the border, this is as far as you can go, and all you can do is to ferret about for tacky momentoes in the souvenir shop at the *Aimoannas* restaurant, or send postcards endowed with a special border postage stamp.

Further, more absorbing, evidence of the border lies a few kilometres east of Virolahti, with the **Salpalinjan Bunkkerit**, or the Salpa Line Bunkers – fortifications which stretched from here to Lappland and were intended to protect Finland from Soviet attack during the run-up to the Winter War of 1939. Massive hunks of granite blocked the way of advancing tanks. These days Finnish war veterans are eager to show off the bunker's details and lead visitors to the seats (and controls) of ageing anti-tank guns.

The only other place to aim for in the vicinity (to reach it you'll need personal transport – no buses cover the route) is **YLÄMAA**, 27km north of Vaalima on the road to **LAPEENRANTA**. Here you'll come upon one of the world's two **spectrolite** mines. Spectrolite is a kind of feldspar, first discovered in Canada (where the only other mine is), although Finnish spectrolite is considered far superior. This can be appreciated in the mine shop's display of dazzlingly beautiful jewellery and watches made from the mineral, which vary in colour according to the angle of the light striking them. It's remarkable stuff, though unfortunately it doesn't come cheap.

THE SOUTHWEST

The area between Helsinki and the country's southwestern extremity is probably the blandest section of the whole country. By road or rail the view is much the same, endless forests interrupted only by modest-sized patches of water and virtually identical villages and small towns. Once at the southwestern corner, however, things change considerably, with islands and inlets around a jagged shoreline, and the distinctive Finland-Swedish coastal communities.

Turku

There is very little in Åbo which has entertained me in the survey, or can amuse you by the description. It is a wretched capital of a barbarous province. The houses are almost all of wood; and the archiepiscopal palace, which has not even a single storey, but may be called a sort of barrack, is composed of no better materials, except that it is painted red. I inquired if there was not any object in the university, meriting attention; but they assured me that it would be regarded as a piece of ridicule, to visit it on such an errand, there being nothing within its walls except a very small library, and a few philosophical instruments.

From *A Tour Round The Baltic* by Sir N.W. Wraxall, 1775.

TURKU (or Åbo as it's known in Swedish) was once the national capital, but it lost its status in 1812, and most of its buildings in a ferocious fire soon after – occurences which clearly improved the place. These days Turku is small and highly sociable – thanks to the boom-years under Swedish rule, and a high ration of students from its two universities, bristling with history and culture, and with a sparkling nightlife to boot.

Arrival, information and accommodation

The river Aura splits the city, its tree-lined banks forming a natural promenade as well as a useful landmark for finding your way around. The interesting older features, the cathedral and castle, are at opposite ends of the river, while the main museums are along its edge. Gleaming department stores, banks and

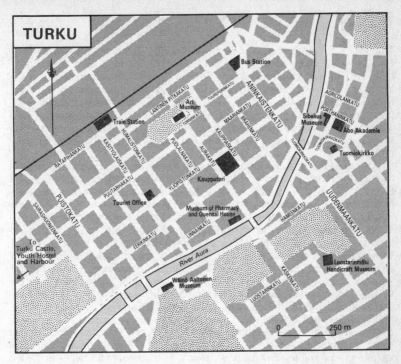

offices are on the northern side of the river in Turku's central grid, where you'll also find the **tourist office** (June–Aug Mon–Fri 8am–5pm; rest of the year Mon–Fri 8.30–4pm ☎921/336366), at Käsityöläiskatu 3. Close by is the **kauppatori** and the effervescent **kauppahalli** (Mon–Fri 8am–5pm, Sat 8am–2pm). Both the **railway station** and **bus station** are within easy walking distance of the river, just north of the centre.

If you turn up on a weekend having made an early reservation, there can be some good deals in Turku's mid-range **hotels**: around 340mk will get you a double in *Hotel Julia*, Eerikenkatu 4 (☎921/5013300), *Cumulus*, Eerikenkatu 28 (☎921/638211), or *Seurahuone*, Humalistonkatu 2 (☎921/637301). Their prices rise substantially during the week, when you'll be better off trying the less luxurious **tourist hotels**: *Aura*, Humalistonkatu 18 (☎921/311973); *Matkakievari*, Läntinen Pitkäkatu 8 (☎921/327208), or *Touristi-Aula*, Käsityöläiskatu 11 (☎921/334484) – each of which has doubles for 200–230mk, and further savings for three people sharing.

At the budget end of the market, Turku has two official **youth hostels**: at Linnankatu 39 (☎921/16578), open all year and within easy walking distance of the ferry harbour; and the student union-run *Kåren*, at Hämeenkatu 22 (☎921/320421), open from June to August. The nearest **campsite** (☎921/306649) is on the small island of Ruissalo, overlooking Turku harbour. It's open from June to August and takes about fifteen minutes to reach on bus #8. Ruissalo is a good place to visit anyway, for its two sandy beaches, a botanical garden sporting a host of rare and spectacular plants, and fine views to the archipelago.

The City

Though it's not much of a taster for the actual city, **Turku Art Museum** (Mon–Fri 10am–4pm, Thurs also 6–10pm, Sun 10am–6pm; 10mk), housed in a purpose-built Art Nouveau granite structure close to the railway station, is one of the better collections of Finnish art, with works by all the great names of the country's Golden Age – Gallen-Kallela, Edelfelt, Pekka Halonen, Simberg and others – plus a commendable stock of moderns; not least the wood sculptures of Kain Tapper and Mauno Hartman which stirred up heated debate during the Seventies when they were first shown on the merits of carefully shaped bits of wood being presented as art.

To get to grips with Turku itself, and its pivotal place in Finnish history, cut through the centre to the river, and the tree-framed space which, before the great fire of 1879, was the bustling heart of the community, and which is still over-looked by the **Tuomiokirkko** (June–Aug Mon–Fri 9am–7pm, Sat 10am–3pm, Sun 2.30–4.30pm; rest of the year Mon–Fri 10am–4pm, Sat 10am–3pm, Sun 2.30–4.30pm; free guided tours in English hourly). The cathedral, erected in the thirteenth century on the "Knoll of Sheep", a pre-Christian place of worship, was the base of the Christianisation process inflicted by the crusading Swedes on the pagan Finns, and grew larger over the centuries as the new religion became stronger and Swedish involvement in Finland escalated. The building, still the centre of the Finnish church, has been repeatedly ravaged by fire, although the thickness of the walls enabled many of the medieval features to survive. Of these, it's the tombs that catch the eye: Torsten Stålhandske, commander of the Finnish cavalry during the seventeenth-century Thirty Years' War, in which Sweden sought to protect its domination of the Baltic and the Finns confirmed their reputatation as wild and fearless fighters, lies in a deliriously ornate coffin (to the left as you enter), opposite a couple of Scots who fought alongside him, Samuel Cockburn and Patrick Ogilvie. A little further along, Karin Månsdotter, the commoner wife of the Swedish King Erik XIV with whom, in the mid-sixteenth century, she was imprisoned in Turku Castle, is as popular in death as she reputedly was in life, judging by the numbers who file past her simple black marble sarcophagus. The window behind it carries her stained-glass image – the only authentic likeness known.

For 5mk you can visit the **cathedral museum** upstairs (hours as cathedral), which gives a stronger insight into the cathedral's past. There's an assortment of ancient jugs, goblets, plates and spoons, though more absorbing are the collections of church textiles – funeral flags and the like – at the far end.

Immediately outside the cathedral is a statue to **Per Brahe**, governor-general of Finland from 1637 and the first Swedish officer to devote much attention to the welfare of the Finns, encouraging a literacy program and founding the country's first university. The site of this is within the nearby yellow Empire-style buildings, although the actual seat of learning was moved to Helsinki during the era of Russian rule. Next to these are the oldest portions of the **Åbo Akademi** – Finland's only remaining Swedish-language university, while the modern, Finnish-language, **Turku University** is at the other end of Henrikinkatu: these days both are notable as places to eat in rather than to view.

Back past the cathedral and across Piispankatu is the sleek low form of the **Sibelius Museum** (Tues–Sun 11am–3pm, Wed also 6–8pm; 10mk). Although Sibelius had no direct connection with Turku, this museum is a fitting tribute to him and his contribution to the emergence of an independent Finland. Chances are that the recorded strains of *Finlandia* will greet you as you enter: when not the venue for live concerts (which usually take place during the winter), the small but acoustically perfect concert area pumps out recorded requests from the great man's oeuvre; take your place beside dewy-eyed Finns for a lunchtime of Scandinavia's finest composer. Elsewhere, the Sibelius collection gathers family photo albums, original manuscripts of compositions, along with the great man's hat, walking stick and even a final half-smoked cigar. The exhibits cover the musical history of the country, from intricate musical boxes and the frail wooden *kantele* – the instrument strummed by peasants in the *Kalevala* – to the weighty keyboard instruments, housed downstairs.

On the other side of the cathedral from the Sibelius museum, you'll see a small hill topped by the wooden dome of the **Observatory and Maritime Museum** (May–Sept daily 10am–6pm; Oct–April daily 10am–3pm; 5mk). Although not worthy of too much time, this was designed – rather poorly – by Carl Engel, who had arrived in Turku seeking work in the days before his great plan for Helsinki made him famous. Originally the building was intended to serve the first Turku University as an observatory, but disputes between Engel and his assistants, and a misunderstanding of scientific requirements, eventually rendered the place useless for its intended purpose. To make things worse, the university moved to Helsinki, and the building was turned into a navigational school. Despite various nautical and astronomical odds and ends, the chief attraction is the great view over Turku and out to Åland archipelago from the top-floor windows.

Outside the observatory, the old water tower is a regular host of minor art exhibitions in summer. From there, head directly down the side of the hill to the far more engrossing **Luostarinmäki Handicrafts Museum** (May–Sept daily 10am–6pm; Oct–April daily 10am–3pm; 10mk), one of the best – and certainly the most authentic – open-air museum in Finland, and as true a record of old Turku as exists. Following a severe fire in 1775 rigorous restrictions were imposed on new buildings, but, due to a legal technicality, these didn't apply in this district. The wooden houses here were built by local working people in traditional style and they evolved naturally into a museum as descendants of the original owners died and bequeathed their inherited homes to the municipality. The unpaved streets run between tiny wooden houses which once had goats tethered to their chimneys to contain the turfed roofs. The chief inhabitants now are the museum volunteers who dress up in period attire and demonstrate the old handicrafts.

A short walk from the handicrafts museum, on the southern bank of the river, is another worthwhile indoor collection: the **Wäinö Aaltonen Museum** (Mon–Fri 10am–4pm & 6–8pm, Sat 10am–4pm, Sun 10am–6pm; 10mk). Unquestionably the best-known modern Finnish sculptor, Aaltonen, born in 1894, grew up close to Turku and studied for a time at the local art school. His first public show, in 1916, marked a turning point in the development of Finnish sculpture, introducing a freer, more individual style to a genre struggling to break from the restraints of the Neoclassical tradition and French realism. Aaltonen went on to totally dominate his field throughout the Twenties and Thirties and his influence is still felt today; the man's work turns up in every major town throughout the country, and even the parliament building in Helsinki was designed with special niches to hold some of his pieces. Much of his output celebrates the individuals who contributed to the growth of the Finnish republic, typically remembering them with enormous heads, or immense statues which resemble haulking chunks of socialist realism.

But Aaltonen, who died in 1966, really was an original, imaginative and sensitive sculptor, as the exhibits here show. There's also a roomful of his paintings, some of which perhaps show why he concentrated onsculpture.

Strolling back in the direction of the cathedral from the Aaltonen museum soon leaves you facing, on the other side of the river, a sign in the grass which spells out TURKU:ÅBO. Close to this is a wooden staircase running up to the front door of the **Museum of Pharmacy and Quensel House** (May–Sept daily 10am–6pm; Oct–April daily 10am–3pm; 5mk). Quensel was a court judge who moved to the house in 1694, and it became the home of Professor Josef Gustaf Pipping – the "father of Finnish medicine" – in 1785. Period furnishings remain, proving just how wealthy and stylish the life of the eighteenth-century bourgeoisie actually was. Many chemists' implements from around the country are on show, among them some memorable devices for drawing blood.

Turku Castle

Even if you don't fancy the low-key medical and social history, you should cross to the northern bank here and head along Linnankatu towards the mouth of the river, where you'll eventually see, oddly set among the present-day ferry terminals, the relatively featureless and unappetising exterior of **Turku Castle** (May–Sept daily 10am–6pm; Oct–April daily 10am–3pm; 10mk) – follow the signs for *Turun Linna*. Fight your dismay though, since the compact cobbled courtyards, maze-like corridors and darkened staircases make the castle a good place to wander – and to dwell on the fact that this was the seat of the government of the country for many centuries; much of Finland's (and a significant portion of Sweden's) medieval history took shape within these walls. Unless you're an expert on the period, you'll get a migraine trying to figure out the importance of everything that's here, and it's a sensible idea to buy one of the castle guide leaflets on sale at the entrance.

The castle probably went up around 1280, when the first bishop arrived from Sweden; gradual expansion through the following years accounts for the patchwork effect of its architecture – and the bewildering array of finds, rooms and displays. The major fortification was during the turbulent sixteenth century, instigated by Swedish ruler Gustavus Vasa for the protection of his son, whom he made Duke Johan, the first Duke of Finland. Johan pursued a lavish court life but exceeded his powers in attacking Livonia and was sentenced to death by the Stockholm Diet. Swedish efforts to seize Johan were successful only after a three week siege, and he was removed to Stockholm. The subsequent decision by the unbalanced Erik XIV to release Johan resulted not only in Johan becoming king himself, but also in poor Erik being imprisoned here – albeit a with full quota of servants and the best food and wine. The bare cell he occupied for a few weeks contrasts strongly with the splendour from Johan's time, and offers a cool reminder of shifting fortunes. There's a gloom-laden nineteenth-century painting here by Erik Johan Löfgren of Erik with his head on his queen's (Karin Månsdotter) lap, while the lady's eyes look askance to heaven.

Eating and drinking ... and travelling on

You'd need to be very fussy not to find somewhere to **eat** in Turku that's to your liking; walking around checking the lunchtime offers can turn up many bargains, while, among the usual plethora of pizzerias, *Italia*, Linnankatu 3, regularly produces sizeable portions for very affordable prices. With a bit more cash, and an appetite for traditional Finnish food, go to *Brahen Kellari*, Puolankatu 1, preferably at lunchtime when you can munch through three courses for a set-price of 78mk. Otherwise, try some of the drinking places listed below; or, if money's extremely tight, make for *Gadolinia*, a **student mensa** that's part of Åbo Akademi on Henrikenkatu – look for the sign saying "Rouka".

You might also eat at either of the two riverside restaurants, *Pinella*, in Porthaninkatupuisto, or *Samppalinna*, on Itäinen Rantakatu, though these do most business at night, when they're mainly used for **drinking**. Other popular imbibing venues are *Olavinkrouvi*, Hämeenkatu 30, drawing numerous students; *Pub Peltimies*, part of the *Rantasipi Hotel* at Pispulantie 7 (see also below); *Erik XIV* Eerikenkatu 6, which also serves decent food. Consider also the pair of recently-opened "English-style" pubs: *Hunter's Inn*, part of *Hotel Julia* but with its own entrance at Brahenkatu 3, and the *Green Dog*, Yliopistonkatu 29b, above which is the *Green Frog*, mostly frequented for its food.

For something more energetic than boozing to fill the nights, there are several **discos**. *Submarina*, in the *Marina Palace* hotel at Linnankatu 32, is the trendiest spot on a Saturday night for the latest hip-hop and house sounds; not far behind is *Rendez-Vous*, inside the *Rantasipi Hotel* at Pispalantie 7; more sedate, with a slightly older clientele, are *Kilta*, Humalistonkatu 8, and *Casablanca*, Eerikinkatu 30.

Travelling on . . .

Continuing from Turku **north along the coast**, there are direct bus services to the next main towns, RAUMA and PORI. To Pori by train takes virtually a whole day and involves going to Tampere and changing at least once, possibly three times. From **Turku Harbour** ferries sail through the vast archipelago to the ÅLAND ISLANDS, and on to Sweden. The harbour is 3km from the city centre and bus #1 covers the route frequently. There's also a daily sailing to the Åland Islands from NAANTALI, 16km from Turku; a direct bus links Turku to the Naantali docking stage. While pleasant enough, with its wooden buildings and slight passageways, Naantali isn't worth spending more than a few hours in. But useful, if you're staying overnight to catch a ferry, is its centrally placed **campsite** (✆92/751354), open from June to August.

Rauma and Pori

Small and largely unsung **RAUMA**, 90km north of Turku, is one of the oldest towns in the country, its eighteenth- and nineteenth-century buildings evoking a strong historic flavour. Strangely for the west coast, it's a mainly Finnish-speaking community, although the dialect is a studied and archaic one which many ordinary Finns find hard to understand. Such insularity perhaps goes back to the mid-sixteenth century, when the inhabitants were forced to move their seafaring skills to the newly founded Helsinki – making Rauma a ghost town for some time. The past is documented in the **History Museum** in the eighteenth-century town hall at Kauppakatu 13 (Tues–Fri 10am–4pm, Tues also 6–8pm, Sat 10am–2pm, Sun 11am–5pm; free). You should also investigate **Marela**, at Kauppakatu 24, a house preserved in the style of a rich shipowner's home from the turn of the century.

For practical information, there's a **tourist office** at Eteläkatu 7(June–Aug Mon–Fri 8am–5pm, Sat 10am–2pm; rest of the year Mon–Fri 8am–4pm; ☎938/224555). For stopping over, there's a combined **youth hostel** and **campsite** (☎938/224666), open from mid-May to August, a kilometre from the town centre.

Pori

Due to its yearly jazz festival, **PORI** has become one of the best-known towns in Finland. For two weeks each July its streets are full of music and the 10,000 people who come to hear it. Throughout the rest of the year Pori reverts to being a small, quiet industrial town with a worthy regional museum and a handful of architectural and historical oddities. The central section, despite its spacious grid-style streets, can be crossed on foot in about fifteen minutes.

In the centre of Pori, just around the corner from the tourist office (where visits can be arranged), in the centre of Pori, lies the **Pori Theatre**, at Hallituskatu 14. Built in 1884, and temporary home of the Finnish-language theatre during the period of Russification, when Finnish drama was too provocative to take place in a larger centre like Turku or Helsinki, the building has a striking Renaissance facade, and the tiny interior – seating just 300 – is heavy with the opulence induced by its frescoes and sculptured chandeliers. A bit further along Hallituskatu is another good stop – the **Satakunta Museum** (Tues, Thurs–Sat noon–4pm, Sun & Wed noon–6pm; free), its three well-stocked floors tracing the roots of both Pori and the surrounding Satakunta region. The town's life is chronicled here through medieval findings, late-nineteenth-century photos and shop-signs, and typical house interiors, alongside interesting memorabilia from the powerful labour movement of the Thirties.

Pori doesn't officially have a preserved **old town**, but if you walk away from the centre across Varvinkatu the tarmac disappears and the streets become dust and stone. The houses here are rundown wooden specimens from the middle of this century, and the compact district is a frozen image of decay. Pori's strangest item, however, is in the big Käppärä cemetery, a twenty-minute walk along Maantiekatu. In the cemetery's centre is the Gothic-arched **Juselius Mausoleum** (Mon–Fri noon–3pm, Sat 10am–2pm; free), erected in 1898 by a local businessman, F.A. Juselius, as a memorial to his daughter, Sigrid, who died aged eleven. The leading Finnish church architect of the time, Josef Steinbäck, was called on to design the thing, while Gallen-Kallela decorated the interior with some of his best large-scale paintings. The artwork was adversely affected by both fire and the local sea air, but has been restored by Gallen-Kallela's son from the original sketches enabling the structure to fulfil its purpose as powerfully, and as solemnly, as ever.

Practical details

It's a short walk from either the **bus station** – into Isolinnankatu and straight on – or the **railway station** – follow Rautatienpuistokatu – into the centre of town, where you'll find the **tourist office** at Antinkatu 5 (June–Aug Mon–Fri 8am–6pm, Sat 9am–1pm; rest of the year Mon–Fri 8am–4pm; ☎939/335780). The **youth hostel** at Korventie 52 (☎939/28400), open from mid-May to mid-August, is about 4km from the centre; buses #30, #31, #32, #40, #41 and #42 stop nearby. The **campsite** (☎939/410620), open from mid-June to August, is beside the Isomäki sports complex about 2km from central Pori; buses #7 and #8 both run to the nearby hospital (*sairaala*) from the town centre.

In the **evening** most people gravitate to the town centre and watch a procession of highly polished cars aimlessly meander up and down the main streets. Cafés and bars fall in and out of favour quite rapidly, although one of the most consistently popular is *Monttu*, at Antinkatu 15, which invites singers from the floor every Thursday. Check out also the all-year spin-off from the jazz festival, the *Jazz-Café*, at Eteläranta 6 on the banks of the Kokemäenjoki.

It's best to have accommodation fixed in advance if you're coming for the **jazz festival**, since hotels, the hostel and the campsite become very crowded – the tourist office endeavour to house as much of the overspill as possible in private homes or in local schools. As for tickets, advance booking forms can be obtained from Finnish Tourist offices outside the country. Also, during the course of the festival, there's a Festival Centre at Eteläranta 6, which sells tickets (50–200mk) and hands out programmes and information. Obviously the big names sell out well in advance.

The Åland Islands

The **Åland Islands**, all six thousand-plus of them, lie scattered between Finland's southwest coast and Sweden. Politically Finnish but culturally Swedish, the Ålands cling to a weird form of independence, with their own flag (a red and yellow cross on a blue background) and parliament. The currency is Finnish but the language is Swedish – which explains why the main and only sizeable town is more commonly known by the Swedish **MARIEHAMN** than the Finnish *Maarianhamina*.

The Ålands (in Finnish *Ahvenanmaa*) were in Swedish hands through the Middle Ages, but, coveted by the Russians on account of their strategic location on the Baltic, they became part of the Russian Grand Duchy of Finland in 1807. When Finland gained independence, the future of the Ålands was referred to the League of Nations (though not before several Åland leaders had been imprisoned in Helsinki on a charge of high treason). As a result, Finnish sovereignty was established in return for autonomy and a complete demilitarisation – the Ålanders now regard themselves as a shining example of Nordic cooperation, and living proof that a small state can run its own affairs while being part of a larger one.

The Ålands' ancient history is as interesting as the modern: many Roman coins have been found, there are scores of Viking burial mounds, and the remains of some of the oldest Finnish churches. The excellent **Åland Museum** (May–Aug daily 10am–4pm, Tues until 8pm; rest of the year Tues–Sun 11am–4pm, Tues also 6–8pm) in Mariehamn's Stadshusparken tells the full story, and is complemented by the ship-shaped **Åland Maritime Museum** (June–Aug daily 9am–5pm, rest of the year daily 10am–4pm), a kilometre away at the other end of Storagatan, celebrating the fact that, despite their insignificant size, the Åland's once had the world's largest fleet of wooden sailing ships.

Smaller local history museums in Åland's other communities reflect the surprisingly strong regional differences within the islands; it seems the only thing which is shared are the ubiquitous Åland maypoles – which stand most of the year – and the fact that specific sights generally take a back seat to the forms of nature. There are, however, several things worth making for. To the northeast of Mariehamn, in Tosarby Sund, are the remains of **Kastelholm**, a fourteenth-century fortress built to consolidate Swedish domination of the Baltic. Strutted through by numerous Swedish monarchs, it was mostly destroyed by fire in the mid-nineteenth century and is now being restored (and may still be closed when you visit). The Russians also set about building a fortress, **Bomarsund**, but before it could be completed the Crimean War broke out and an Anglo-French force stormed the infant castle, reducing it to rubble; just the scattered ramparts remain. Both would-be castles are on the same bus route from Mariehamn. Elsewhere you can trace the route of the old **post road**, the only mail link from Stockholm to what was then tsarist St Petersburg. To their long-lasting chagrin, Åland people were charged with seeing the safe-passage of the mail, including taking it across the frozen winter sea – and quite a few died in the process. The major remnant of these times is the nineteenth-century Carl Engel-designed **Post House** in **ECKERÖ**, at the islands' western extremity. Standing on the coast facing Sweden, the building was intended to instil fresh arrivals with awe at their first sight of the mighty Russian Empire. Despite retaining its grandeur, it now looks highly incongrous amid the tiny local community.

Having waded through the history, all that's left to say is that the Ålands have sea, sun, and beckoning terrain in unlimited quantities – which is precisely their appeal. Nowadays the Ålands' primary source of income is the summer tourists, especially Swedes on day trips to Mariehamn. Elsewhere the flat and thickly-forested islands contain plenty of secluded spots to search out and enjoy.

Practical details

Ferries from Finland and Sweden (for more see "Travel Details") stop in Mariehamn's West Harbour and there's a **tourist office** a few minutes' walk away at Storagatan 18 (June to mid-Aug daily 9am–6pm; rest of the year Mon–Sat 10am–4pm; ☎928/16575), which can provide the latest details regarding travel and accommodation. You're going to have a hard time finding **somewhere to stay** if you turn up in summer on spec and without a tent: there are no official youth hostels on the islands and, although there are a number of cheapish guest-houses, some of which offer hostel-type facilities, these fill quickly. If you're at a loose end in Mariehamn, try *Kronan* at Neptinigatan 52 (☎928/12617), or *Nyholms* at Södragatan 33 (☎928/13189). The wise option, though, is to camp: there are plentiful **campsites** (in isolated areas you should be able to camp rough with no problems) and a fairly thorough **bus service** covering the main islands. Cycling is a sound alternative to the buses, offering not only freedom but also bike hire rates slightly cheaper than on the mainland. Most of the islands not linked by road bridge can be reached by small and often free local ferries. If you're feeling lazy, or don't have much time, get a feel of the place by taking one of the **guided bus tours** which leave Mariehamn on most weekdays, costing 55–60mk, and last a few hours. Details from the tourist office.

travel details

Trains

From Helsinki to Espoo (30 daily; 30min); Luoma (30 daily; 37min); Turku (7 daily; 2hr 15min); Lahti (15 daily; 1hr 30min); Tampere (12 daily; 2hr 15min); Jyväskylä (7 daily; 4hr); Mikkeli (9 daily; 3hr 30min); Kuopio (7 daily; 5hr 30min); Kajaani (5 daily; 7hr 30min); Oulu (7 daily; 8hr 30min); Rovaniemi (4 daily; 10hr 30min).

From Turku to Tampere (6 daily; 2hr 30min).
From Pori to Tampere (7 daily; 2hr).

Buses

From Helsinki to Porvoo (18 daily; 1hr); Kotka (7–9 daily; 1hr 30min–2hr 10min); Turku (21 daily;

2hr 30min); Tampere (16 daily; 3hr); Lahti (26 daily; 1hr 30min); Mikkeli (8 daily; 4hr); Savonlinna (3 daily; 5hr 30min); Jyväskylä (8 daily; 5hr).

From Porvoo to Loviisa/Phytää/Kotka (8–10 daily; 40min/1hr/1hr 40min).

From Hamina to Virolahti (2–3 daily; 35–55 min).

From Turku to Rauma (10 daily; 1hr 30min); Pori (7 daily; 2hr).

From Rauma to Pori (4 daily; 45min).

From Mariehamn to Eckerö (5 daily; 45min); Bomarsund (5 daily; 30min); Kastelholm (5 daily; 30min).

Ferries

From Turku to Mariehamn (2 daily; 5hr 30min).

From Naantali to Mariehamn (1 daily; 7hr 30min).

International Trains

From Helsinki to Leningrad (2 daily; 10hr); Moscow (1 daily; 16hr 30min).

International Ferries

From Helsinki to Stockholm (2 daily; 15hr); Tallinn (May–Aug Fri–Wed 1 daily 3hr; rest of the year 2–4 weekly; 5hr).

From Turku to Stockholm (2 daily; 12hr).

CHAPTER FIFTEEN

THE LAKE REGION

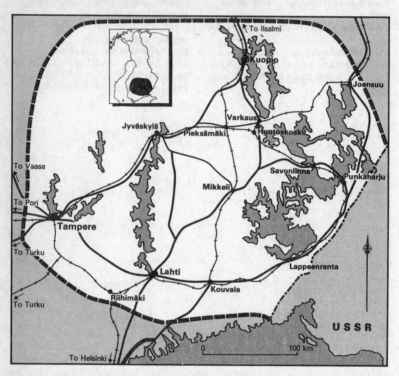

T he **Lake Region** is unique in Finland, if not in Scandinavia. Extensive
lake chains, chiefly the Päijanne and Saimaa systems, consume a third of
the country, particularly the chunk that bulges towards the USSR. Each
chain features countless bays, inlets and islands, while the dense
surrounding forests are interspersed by streaky ridges. The settlements that
flourished here began as papermills, which used natural waterways and purpose-
built canals to transport the timber to pulping-factories powered by gushing
rapids.

Wherever you go, water is never far away, further pacifying an already tranquil,
verdant landscape. Even **Tampere**, Finland's major industrial city, is likeable for
its lakeside setting as much as for its cultural delights. It's also the most accessible of the region's cities, being on the railway line between Helsinki and the
north. Also reachable from Helsinki, **Lahti** only fufills its promise as a winter
sports resort; during summertime the town is comparatively dull and lifeless.

Diminutive **Mikkeli** has far more character, and makes a good stopover en route to the atmospheric eastern part of the Lake Region, where slender ridges furred with conifers link the few sizeable landmasses. Its regional centre, **Savonlinna**, stretches delectably across several islands, and boasts a superbly-preserved medieval castle. To get a sense of Karelian culture visit **Joensuu** or the city of **Kuopio**, where many displaced Karelians settled after World War II. In the heart of the Lake Region lies **Jyväskylä**, whose wealth of buildings by Alvar Aalto draws modern architecture buffs to what is otherwise a typically sleepy town. Down-to-earth **Iisalmi** is effectively a bridge between the Lake Region and the rougher, less watery terrain further north.

Unless you want total solitude (which is easily attained), it's advisable to spend a few days in the larger towns and make shorter forrays to the smaller ones, leaving time to spare for exploring the thinly-populated areas. Although the western Lake Region is mostly well served by trains, connections to – and within – the eastern part are awkward and infrequent. With daily services between the main towns and less frequent ones to the villages, buses are handier for **getting around**. To really explore the countryside, it's necessary to hire a car or bicycle. Slow, expensive ferries link the main lakeside towns, while practically every community runs short pleasure cruises.

Tampere and around

"Here it was as natural to approve of the factories as in Mecca one would the mosques", wrote John Sykes of **TAMPERE** in the 1960s and you soon see what he meant. Although Tampere is Finland's biggest manufacturing centre and Scandinavia's largest inland city, it's a highly scenic one, with leafy avenues, sculpture-filled parks and two sizeable lakes. The factories which line the Tammerkoski rapids in the heart of the city actually accentuate its appeal, their chimneys standing as bold monuments to Tampere's past. Its rapid growth began just over a century ago, when Tsar Alexander I abolished taxes on local trade, encouraging the Scotsman James Finlayson to open a textile factory drawing labour from rural areas where traditional crafts were in decline. Metalwork and shoe factories soon followed, their owners paternally supplying culture to the workforce by promoting a vigorous local arts scene. Free outdoor rock and jazz concerts, lavish theatrical productions and one of the best modern art collections in Finland maintain such traditions to this day.

Arrival, information and getting around

Almost everything of consequence is within the central section, bordered on two sides by the lakes: Näsijärvi and Pyhäjärvi. The main streets run off either side of Hämeenkatu, which leads directly from the **railway station** across Hämeensilta – the bridge over Tammerkoski, famous for its weighty bronze sculptures by Wäino Aaltonen, representing four characters from local folklore. Although there's little call to use local **buses**, most routes begin from the terminal on Hämeenkatu. Tampere's **tourist office** (June–Aug Mon–Fri 8.30am–8pm, Sat 8.30am–6pm, Sun noon–6pm; rest of the year Mon–Fri 8.30am–4pm; ☎931/126652 or 126775) is on Hatanpään, to the left of the bridge, roughly four blocks from the railway station, where a smaller branch is open daily in summer from 1.30–8pm.

During summer both offices, most transport terminals and hotels sell the **Tampere Card** (40mk), valid for travel on all local buses and entry to most museums within a 24-hour period. You'll have to sweat through a fairly intensive sightseeing programme to make a big saving, but it can cut costs if well-used.

Finding somewhere to stay

Budget travellers are only fully catered for during the summer, when both the main **youth hostels** are open. *NNKY* (the Finnish YWCA, open to both sexes) stands opposite the cathedral at Tuomiokirkonkatu 12A (☎931/35900), while *Sorin retkeilymaja* is located at Sorinkatu 16 (☎931/131122). More official hostel lodgings can be found in the bigger, much more impersonal summer hotel, *Domus*, at Pellervonkatu 9 (☎931/550000), behind the Kaleva kirkko. *Uimahallinmaja*, centrally-located at Pirkankatu 10–12 (☎931/229460), 1km from the railway station, does dearer hostel beds for around 75mk, and also has the cheapest double hotel rooms in town (from 180mk).

Tampere's other **hotels** will typically set you back 350–500mk, although for about 300mk in summer, an early booking might get you some lakeside luxury at the *Rosendahl*, Pyynikinti 13 (☎931/112233), a couple of kilometres from the city centre. As usual, however, the least expensive option beside a lake is a **campsite**: *Härmälä* (☎931/651250), 5km to the south and accessible by bus #1, is open from June to late August.

The City

Hämeenkatu expires in front of the upwardly thrusting neo-Gothic **Aleksanterin kirkko** (May–Aug daily 10am–6pm; rest of the year daily 11am–5pm), perhaps the least interesting of the city's churches. To the left, following the line of greenery up the slender Hämeenpuisto, is the Tampere Workers' Theatre and, in the same building but with a separate entrance on Hallituskatu, the **Lenin Museum** (Tues–Sat 11am–3pm, Sun 11am–4pm; 10mk). After the abortive 1905 revolution in Russia, Lenin lived in Finland and attended the Tampere conferences, held in what is now the museum. It was here that he first encountered Stalin, although this is barely mentioned in either exhibition; one concentrates on Lenin himself, the other on his relationship with Finland. For a detailed explanation, borrow the English-language brochure from reception.

Turn right at the church and walk on for several blocks to reach the Amuri district, originally built to house Finlayson's workers. Some thirty homes have been preserved as the **Workers' Museum of Amuri** (May–Aug Tues–Sun noon–6pm; 10mk) at Makasiininkatu 12, a simple but affecting place which records the family life of working people over a hundred year period. In each home is a description of the inhabitants and their jobs, and authentic articles from the relevant periods – from beds and tables to family photos, newspapers and biscuit packets.

Just around the corner at Puutarhakatu 34 is the **Art Museum of Tampere** (daily 11am–7pm; 10mk), its bleak corridors providing an unhappy setting for mainly Finnish nineteenth-century paintings, including several of Ferdinand von Wright's ornithological studies. More interesting temporary exhibtions are often held in the basement, but if you're looking for older Finnish art, head instead for the far superior **Heikki Art Gallery**, a few minutes' walk away at Pirkankatu 6

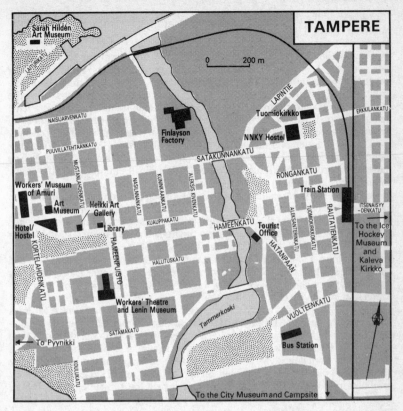

(Wed & Sun noon–3pm; 3mk). Kustaa Heikka was a gold and silversmith whose professional skills and business acumen made him a local big-shot around the turn of the century. The art collection he bequeathed to Tampere reflects Heikka's interest in traditional lifestyles; borrow a catalogue from reception, since most pieces are only identified by numbers. Amongst the most notable work (including sketches by Gallen-Kallela and Helene Schjerfbeck) are two of Heikka's own creations: a delicately wrought brooch marking the completion of his apprenticeship, and a finely detailed bracelet with which he celebrated becoming a master craftsmen.

Nearby stands the **Tampere Library** (Mon–Fri 9am–8pm, Sat 9am–3pm), an astounding feat of user-friendly modern architecture which should not be missed. The work of Reimi and Raili Pietilä (who also designed the epic Kalevala kirkko – see below), and finished in 1986, the library's curving walls evoke a warm, comfy feeling; believe it or not, the building's shape is inspired by a certain type of grouse (a stuffed specimen of which sits in the reception area). Strolling around is the best way to notice the many small, intriguing features, and will eventually lead you up to the top-floor café, which gives a good view of the cupola, deliberately set eleven degrees off the vertical – to match the off-centre pivot of the earth.

Just beyond the grid-planned central streets, the tremendous **Sara Hildén Art Museum** (daily 11am–6pm; 10mk), built on the shores of Näsijärvi, displays Tampere's premier modern art collection. There's a great start in the grounds with Rauni Liukko's *Ruuhkaratikka*, a replica rush-hour tram into which you can step and swap menacing expressions with the grotesque passengers: it's rather unnerving when they start to speak. In the main gallery, the paintings on the ground floor tend to be overshadowed by exhibits downstairs; amongst them the sculptures of Mauno Hertman, which examine Finnish traditions using a national material – wood. The most controversial piece is Edward Kienholz's comment on American decadence, *Regeneration*: a piano with a decaying woman draped over the keys, and its innards turned into a tadpole pool. Since the original tadpoles matured into frogs and hopped off, their place is now taken by goldfish. The museum is on the other side of Paasikiventie from Amuri (take a #16, or the summer-only #4 bus from the town centre or railway station).

Occupying the same waterside strip as the Hildén collection is **Särkänniemi**, a tourist complex incorporating a dolphinarium, aquarium, planetarium and observation tower. Seen from the tower, an unmistakeable part of Tampere's skyline, the city seems insignificant compared to the trees and lakes which stretch to the horizon. The rapids which cut through them can be identified from afar by the factory chimneys alongside. The tower is open 10am–8pm during summer, and charges 8mk admission; the other diversions cost 15–25mk apiece and are rarely uncrowded; to make a day of it, buy the 60mk Särkänniemi Passport (40mk in winter), valid for all sections of the complex.

Tampere's secondary artery, Satakunnankatu, runs from the centre to cross Tammerkoski near the **Finlayson factory**, which still bears its founder's name even though the plant has recently been turned over to crafts workshops. A little way on, the **Tuomiokirkko** stands in a grassy square, a picturesque cathedral in the National Romantic style, designed by Lars Sonck and finished in 1907 (daily 10am–6pm, guided tours 11am and 5pm). It's most remarkable for the gorily symbolic frescoes by Hugo Simberg – particularly the *Garden of Death*, where skeletons happily water plants, and *The Wounded Angel*, showing two boys carrying a bleeding angel through a Tampere landscape – which caused an ecclesiastical outcry when unveiled. So did the viper (a totem of evil) which he placed amongst the angel wings on the ceiling; Simberg retorted that evil could lurk anywhere – including a church.

After viewing the cathedral, you've more or less completed a circular trek around the city and seen all that the central part has to offer, except for the glittering *Koskikeskus* shopping mall near the station. To learn about Tampere's origins, take a pleasant walk along the shores of Pyhäjärvi to the **City Museum** (Tues–Sun noon–6pm; 10mk) on the Hatanpää peninsula. Its most interesting section deals with the early twentieth century – a turbulent time for both Tampere and Finland. As an industrial town with militant workers, Tampere instigated a general strike against the Russification of Finland: filling the streets with demonstrators and painting over the Cyrillic names on trilingual street signs. After independence it became a Social Democratic stronghold, ruthlessly suppressed by the bourgeois White Army in the civil war of 1918 – yet the municipal administration remains amongst the most left-wing in Finland.

On a totally different note, Itsenäisyydenkatu runs uphill behind the railway station to meet the vast concrete folds of the **Kaleva kirkko** (daily 10am–6pm, guided tours at 11am and 5pm). Built in 1966, it was a belated addition to the neighbouring **Kaleva estate**, which was heralded as an outstanding example of high-density housing in the Fifties. Though initially stunning, the church's interior lacks the subtlety of the city library, despite being designed by the same team – perhaps because Reimi and Raili Pietilä based their plan on a fish this time.

Continuing past the church, follow the signs for *Jäähalli* (Ice Hall) to the Ice Hockey Stadium just off Kekkosentie. Its **Ice Hockey Museum** (open during matches or by special request; ☎931/124200 or 155344; 10mk) naturally accords due honour to the local teams Ilves and Tappora, which have won more national championships than all of Finland's other teams combined. Other exhibits include a vast collection of hockey sticks from around the world, and a white puck used during the immediate postwar period, when matches were played on the blue ice of frozen lakes because artificial ice was unavailable.

Eating, drinking and nightlife

Several places in the Koskikeskus shopping mall on Rautatienkatu offer cheap lunchtime specials; aside from pizzerias, try the herring-laden open-table at *Sillakka*, for around 50mk. But as usual, the cheapest **places to eat** are the student mensas in the university at the end of Yliopistonkatu, just over the railway line from the city centre. Otherwise, check out *Frendi*, a music pub at Itensäisyydenkatu 3, with loud rock music downstairs, and substantial vegetarian pizzas (roughly 40mk) upstairs.

Numerous **supermarkets** are good for buying your own provisions. Try the big *Sokos* store at Hämeenkatu 21; *Anttila*, Puuthakatu 10; *Centrum*, Hämeenkatu 11; or *Forum*, Kuninkaankatu 21 – all of which are central. Slightly cheaper and further out are *City Market*, Sotilaankatu 11, and *Sokos Market* at Sammonkatu 73. There's also a large **kauppahalli** at Hämeenkatu 19 (Mon–Fri 8am–5pm, Sat 8am–2pm), and open-air markets at Laukontori (Mon–Fri 6am–2pm, Sat 6am–1pm), Keskustori (the first Monday of every month, 6am–6pm), and Tammelantori (Mon–Fri 6am–2pm, Sat 6am–1pm).

For news of **nightlife**, scan the free monthly magazine *City*. Generally, though, the liveliest spot is the student house, *Yo-talo*, at Kauppakatu 10, which often features live music; arrive early to avoid the queues. The only other place with regular (and listenable) live music is *Rock-Cabare*, part of *Oscar's Cabare*, at Kirkkokatu 10. If you just want a drink, consider the *Tillikka* theatre house by the bridge on Hämeenkatu, frequented by students and arty types; *Freetime*, in the Koskikeskus shopping centre; *Doris*, at Aleksi 20; and, if you're desperate for draught Guinness, *Salhojankadun*, on Itsenäisyydenkatu.

On warm nights many locals head for the Pyynikki area, a natural ridge on the edge of Tampere, beside Pyhäjärvi. Tickets for the **Pyynikki Summer Theatre** cost around 70mk, but it's worth trekking out just to look at the revolving auditorium which spins the audience around during performances, blending the surrounding woods, rocks and water into the show's scenery.

Around Tampere: Hämeenlinna, Hattula, and moving on

Half an hour from Tampere on the busy railway to Helsinki, **HÄMEENLINNA** is revered as the birthplace of Sibelius and Finland's oldest inland town. Though somewhat self-important, it's nonetheless worth a visit if you have time. The major attraction is **Hämeen linna** (May–Aug daily 10am–6pm; rest of the year daily 10am–3pm), a sturdy thirteenth-century castle from which the town takes its name. Next comes the **Sibelius Childhood Home** (May–Aug Mon–Sat 10am–3pm, Sun noon–4pm; rest of the year Mon–Fri 10am–2pm, Sun noon–4pm), at Hallituskatu 11, where the great composer was born; now reverentially restored to how it was during the first years of his life. A few blocks away at Viipuriintie 2, the **art museum** (Mon–Fri 10am–8pm, Sat & Sun noon–6pm) musters a mundane collection of minor works by major Finnish names, among them Järnefelt, Gallen-Kalella and Halonen.

Seeing all this won't take long, and any spare hours are better spent in the outlying area of **Hattula**, roughly 5km from Hämeenlinna's centre. The local **Hattulan kirkko** (June to mid-Aug daily 10am–6pm; May daily 9am–6pm; rest of the year daily noon–4pm) is probably the finest medieval church in Finland – outwardly plain, but totally covered inside by 180 sixteenth-century frescoes of biblical scenes. En route to here, a combined **youth hostel** and **campsite** (☎917/28560), open from May to mid-September, face Hämeenlinna across the river.

Moving on from Tampere

Lahti – the gateway to the eastern Lake Region – can be reached by direct bus from Tampere (several times daily), or by catching a train and changing at Hyvinkää.

Lahti

LAHTI doesn't know if it's a Lake Region town or a Helsinki suburb. The major transport junction between the Lake Region and the south, Lahti lacks any lake area atmosphere; its growth has all been this century (mostly since Alvar Aalto opened several furniture factories, which kept him going between architectural commissions) and local cultural life is diminished by the relative proximity of Helsinki. Lahti finds compensation for this by being a **winter sports** centre of international renown: three enormous ski-jumps hang over the town, and there's a feeling of biding time when summer grass rather than winter snow* covers their slopes. Unless you're here to ski, Lahti isn't a place you'll need or want to linger in – the town can easily be covered in a day.

Head first for the **observation platform** on the highest ski-jump (May–Sept 11am–6pm, Sat & Sun 10am–5pm), whose location is unmistakeable. From such a dizzying altitude the lakes and forests around Lahti stretch dreamily into the distance, and the large swimming pool directly below resembles a puddle (during wintertime it's frozen and is used as a landing zone).

The only structures matching the ski-jumps for height are the twin radio masts atop Radiomäki hill, between the railway station (a fifteen-minute walk away) and the town centre. Steep pathways wind uphill towards the **Broadcasting Museum** (Sun 1–4pm; free) inside the original transmitting station at the base of one of the masts. Here, two big rooms are packed with bulky Marconi valves, crystal sets, antiquated sound-effect discs, room-sized amplifiers and intriguing curios. Look out for the *Pikku Hitler* – the German-made "little Hitler", a wartime portable radio that forms an uncanny facsimile of the dictator's face.

---

* Ironically, what was to be Lahti's greatest moment, the hosting of the 1989 World Ski Championships, almost had to be cancelled because an exceptionally mild winter yielded insufficient snow. Emergency plans were made to transport snow from the far north, but an eleventh-hour snowfall saved the day.

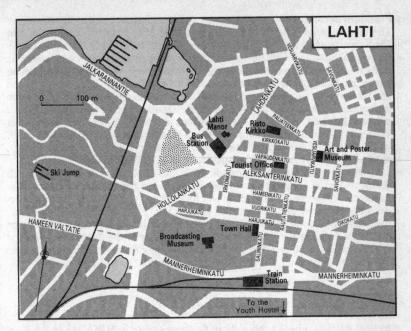

At Radiomäki's foot, the distinctive redbrick-work of Eliel Saarinen's **Town Hall** injects some style into the concrete blocks that make central Lahti dull and uniform. Built in 1912, many of its Art Nouveau features were considered immensely daring at the time, and although most of the originals were destroyed in the war, careful refurbishment has recreated much of Saarinen's design. Viewable during office hours, the interior is definitely worth seeing. Lahti's other notable building is at the far end of Mariankatu (cutting through the town centre from the town hall): **Risto kirkko** (daily 10am–3pm), whose white roof slopes down from the belltower in imaginative imitation of the local ski-jumps. Interestingly, this was the last church to be designed by Alvar Aalto: he died during its construction and the final work was overseen by his wife. Outside, Wäinö Aaltonen produced one of his most discreetly emotive sculptures to mark the war graves in the cemetery.

By now you've more or less exhausted Lahti, although Hämeenkatu, running parallel to (and far less hectic than) Aleksanterinkatu, contains a number of little art galleries owned by local artists and a few browsable secondhand book stores. The **Art Museum** (Tues–Sun noon–4pm, Wed also 6–8pm) just around the corner at Vesijärvenkatu 11 exhibits nineteenth- and twentieth-century works, most notably by Gallen-Kallela and Edelfelt; the adjacent **Poster Museum** (separate entrance at Vapaudenkatu 22; daily 11am–7pm) mounts temporary displays and a bi-annual international poster festival.

Finally, near the hazardous web-like junction by the bus station, the wooden nineteenth-century Lahti Manor hides behind a line of trees. Now a **Historical Museum** (Tues–Sun noon–4pm Tues also 6–8pm), it contains regional paraphernalia, numerous Finnish medals and coins, plus an unexpected hoard of French and Italian paintings and furniture.

Practical details

The **tourist office** is at Torikatu 3B (June–Aug Mon–Fri 8am–5pm, Sat & Sun 10am–2pm; rest of the year Mon–Fri 8am–4pm; ☎918/182580). Though the official **youth hostel** at Kivikatu 1 (☎918/26324) is open all year, it's a monotonous thirty-minute walk from the centre: go under the railway station tunnel, along Launeenkatu, right into Tapparakatu and through a housing estate. Buses #9 and #51 run between the hostel and the town centre although only the latter goes to the railway station. With distance in mind, it's worth trying two slightly dearer **private hostels**: *Patria* at Vesijärvenkatu 8 (☎918/23783), and *Yöpöllö* at Yrjönkatu 5 (☎918/20004), both near the railway station. About 4km to the north of Lahti is a lakeside **campsite** (☎918/306554), open from June to August, reached directly by bus from the bus station at the end of Aleksanterinkatu.

Low-priced **eating** options include *Grilli Serdika* at Hämeenkatu 21, which claims to be the cheapest steakhouse in Lahti, and the Italian takeaway, *Pikka Italia*, on the corner of Rauhankatu and Kirkkokatu. You'll also find large **supermarkets** clustered along Savonkatu. Though hardly remarkable for its nightlife, Lahti holds its own compared to smaller towns in the Lake Region. For an evening **drink**, try the lively *Marco Polo* belonging to the *Seurahuone Hotel* at Aleksanterinkatu 14, or *Jokeri*, slightly further along the street. The terrace-style café on Mariankatu offers more refined forms of social intercourse.

Mikkeli

In 1986 a Helsinki bank robber chose the main square in **MIKKELI** as the place to blow up himself, his car and his hostage. This, the most violent event seen in Finland for decades, was an echo of Mikkeli's blood-spattered past. In prehistoric times the surrounding plains were battlegrounds for feuding tribes from east and west. The Finnish Defence Force has a long association with Mikkeli, and it was from here that General Mannerheim conducted Finland's defence during the Winter War against the Soviet Union. Having missed out on industrial development because of its location on an awkward-to-reach extremity of the Saimaa lake transport system, Mikkeli still functions as a regional market town, with a disproportionately large and active *kauppatori*. Both the **railway and bus stations** are within a few minutes' walk of the centre, and the whole town can easily be explored on foot.

Most Finns who visit Mikkeli make a beeline for the office used by Mannerheim, which is preserved as the **Headquarters Museum** at Päämajakatu 1–3 (mid-May to Aug daily 11am–5pm; free), inside the local primary school. (It's easiest to use the entrance by the corner of Ristimäenkatu and Vuorikatu, following the *Päämajamuseo* signs). Although Mannerheim's desk – kept as it was, with his spectacles and favourite cigars close at hand – is the most striking exhibit, the fact that the Winter War of 1939 was waged and won from this room has made it a place of pilgrimage. Indeed, it was the volume of visitors wandering through the school seeking the actual spot of such crucial decision-making, that caused the office to be restored at all. A smaller adjacent room has photo displays and a guide who will run a short-slide show about Mannerheim's days in Mikkeli.

Mannerheim took his meals at the **Mikkeli Club**, a sort of cross between a speakeasy and a masonic lodge, which still exists in one part of the *Sokos* department store on the corner of Hallituskatu and Maaherrankatu. The club's walls are

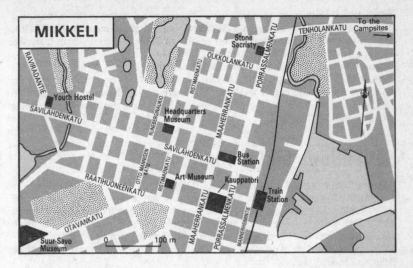

lined with photos of Mannerheim, although less prominence is given to the snaps of the Marshal riding with Hitler during the Fuhrer's birthday visit (kept in an unmarked folder usually lying on a side table). The club is not strictly open to the public but the **tourist office** (mid-June to mid-Aug Mon–Fri 8.30am–6pm, Sat 8.30am–2pm; rest of the year Mon–Fri 8.30am–4pm; ☎955/151544), virtually next door, will arrange for you to be shown around if you seem sufficiently interested.

The excellent **Art Museum** at Ristimäenkatu 5A (Tues, Fri & Sun noon–6pm, Sat noon–3pm; free), is also well worth a call, with some stimulating temporary exhibitions of the latest Finnish art, plus two permanent bequests. The *Martti Airio Collection* is a forceful selection of early twentieth-century Finnish impressionism and expressionism, hung in pleasingly ungallery-like fashion beside Rococo and Baroque furnishings. The museum's other benefactor was the sculptor, Johannes Haapsalo, who left all his 300 finished works and 1000 sketches to the museum.

Elsewhere, the regional **Suur-Savo Museum** at Otavankatu 11 (April–Sept Tues–Sun 11am–3pm; rest of the year Sun 11am–3pm & Wed 6–8pm) is rumoured not to have changed its exhibits for twenty years. Perhaps not surprisingly, the museum's prize-find is also its oldest: the *Tukkula matron* – a prehistoric dress rebuilt from threads. Considerably more interesting, if less numerous, relics can be found in the **Stone Sacristy** (mid-May to Aug daily 11am–5pm; free), a modest-sized Gothic structure on the site of a twelfth-century graveyard which bisects the main road, Porrassalmenkatu. The small interior room is a treasure trove of church implements from the Middle Ages; spare a thought for the 22 mummified nineteenth-century corpses that used to be on show but are now encased beneath the concrete floor.

Sleeping . . . and heading on

The **youth hostel** (☎955/366542), open from June to mid-August, is a simple fifteen-minute walk from the centre along Savilahdenkatu, and then right after crossing the river, into Raviradantie. Mikkeli's two **campsites** are *Visualahti*

(☎955/18281), 5km from town beside the dismal tourist centre of the same name, open all year (take bus #1 to the end of the line); and *Rauhaniemi* (☎955/11416), open from June to August, on the other side of the lake roughly 3km from the centre, accessible by bus #2M or #2T.

Travelling from **Mikkeli to Savonlinna** is easiest by bus. With the train it's necessary to change at PIEKSÄMÄKI, which adds an hour to the journey. However, the second leg is travelled in a titchy train whose windows provide great views of the forests and gaping lakes – in this part of the Lake Region, water is more common than land.

Savonlinna and around

Leisurely draped across islands, **SAVONLINNA** is one of the most relaxed towns in Finland. The significance of its woodworking industries (a key point on the Saimaa route) pales beside the revenue from tourism and its prestigious annual opera festival. Savonlinna is packed throughout the summer, but out of peak season its streets and beaches are uncluttered, and the town's easy-going mood – enhanced by the slow glide of pleasure craft from its harbour – make this a place to linger for several days.

The Town

The best locations for soaking up the atmosphere are the **harbour** and **kauppatori** at the end of Olavinkatu. Moored in the harbour is the **Salama Boat** (summer daily 9am–8pm; free), a steamship built in 1874 now maintained as a museum of the pioneering days of lake travel. Other than the plush period fittings of the passengers' area, the vessel isn't too interesting unless you're partial to boats and their innards. Instead, cast an eye over the grand **Seurahuone Hotel** facing the *kauppatori*. Erected in 1901, it burned down in 1947 when it was notorious as a speakeasy, selling "hard tea" laced with brandy and homebrewed *pirtu*, also known as "the tearful liquid" or "hot-stuff". While the forbidden pleasures are long gone and their current equivalents at the bar are forbiddingly expensive, you can still admire the reconstructed Forties decor with its Art Nouveau fripperies. Newspaper clippings related to the fire are hung on the wall.

Walking along Linnankatu, or better still around the sandy edge of Pihlajavesi, brings you to **Olavinlinna castle** (June to mid-Aug daily 9am–6pm; rest of the year daily 9am–3pm; 10mk), perched on a small island like some great seamonster emerged from the deep. Try to catch one of the **guided tours** on the hour, since the castle's excellent state of repair is matched by an intriguing history. Founded in 1475 (when Sweden ruled Finland) to guard the eastern marches, it witnessed a series of bloody conflicts, with ownership alternating between Sweden and Russia during the eighteenth century, until the Russians claimed permanent possession after the Peace of Turku in 1743. When Finland became a Tsarist Grand Duchy the fort was relegated to being the town gaol. The Russians added the Adjutent's Apartment which, with its bright yellow walls and carved windows, resembles a large portion of Emmenthal cheese. Also remarkable are the brick cubicles which jut outwards from the main living rooms – possibly the first WCs in Finland. There's a straight drop through the pan to the river several dozen metres below.

Savonlinna lacks any more inspiring buildings, though it's worth detouring to view the dainty **Pikkukirkko** (summer daily 10am–3pm) on Olavintori, the old main square. It's considerably more interesting than the **Tuomiokirkko** (May–Sept Mon–Fri 10am–4pm, Sun 9am–7pm), across the harbour bridge and up Papplinkatu. Rebuilt in an unattractive neo-Gothic way after being destroyed during World War I, the cathedral is something to pass on your way to enjoying the view from the hill on which it stands.

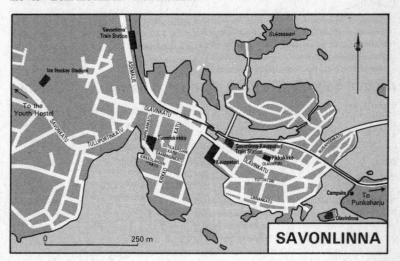

Practical details

Of the two **railway stations**, the larger *Savonlinna* is mainly used for freight, although passenger trains may stop there en route to the more central *Savonlinna-Kauppatori*, which is virtually next door to the **tourist office** at Olavinkatu 35 (June to mid-Aug daily 8am–10pm; May & mid-Aug–Sept daily 8am–6pm; rest of the year Mon–Fri 9am–4pm; ☎957/13492). The **bus station** is off the main island but within easy walking distance of the town centre.

The **private hostel** *Hospits*, Linnankatu 20 (☎957/22443), is by far the most central accommodation, and only marginally dearer than the official **youth hostels**. *Malakias*, Pihlajavedenkatu 6 (☎957/23283), 2km walk from the centre along Tulliportinkatu and then Savontie, is open from June to August; *Mertmalakias* at Otavankatu 8 (☎957/20685), open during June and July, is likewise 2km out; follow Olavinkatu and eventually turn left into Miekkoniemenkatu and Otavankatu. Alternatively, you could rent a **cabin** in the *Heinivesi* steamship tethered in the harbour; single beds go for upwards of 70mk, and the tourist office can supply details. The nearest **campsite** (☎957/537353), 6km from the centre at Vuohimäki, is open from June to August. You might be able to avoid the long journey by **camping rough** on Sulossaari island, which is often tolerated – but seek advice first. To get there, cross the small bridge behind Kauppatori station, and keep going.

Anything sold around the harbour is liable to be overpriced and under-nourishing, but you can find cheaper, better **food**. Try the pizza joints along

Olavinkatu; *Pata-Krouvi* at Kaartilantie 44, a thirty-minute walk from the centre (bus #2 stops outside it); or *Majakka*, Satamakatu 11, which offers good traditional Finnish nosh at lunchtime, from 50mk.

The *Tott Hotel*, on the corner of Tottinkatu near the harbour, has long been the focus for **nightlife**, although the finicky management often shuts the place down for alterations. If it's closed, the next best option is *Tamino*, the disco section of the *Seurahuone*; the *Hopeasalmi* boat-restaurant-bar in the harbour is another alternative.

Tickets for Savonlinna's international **opera festival** in July go on sale the previous November, and sell-out rapidly. The tourist office hold back a small number for most performances; otherwise try the opera office in the school building at Puistokatu 3.

Around Savonlinna: Punkaharju and Retretti Arts Centre

Locals believe that **Punkaharju Ridge** has the healthiest air in the world, super-oxygenated by abundant conifers. This narrow strip of land between the Puruvesi and Pihlalavesi lakes starts about 28km from town, with two roads and a railway somehow squeezed onto an area that's 7km long but hardly the width of a football pitch. With the water never more than a few metres away on either side, this is the Lake Region at its most breathtakingly beautiful.

The ridge runs into the town of PUNKAHARJU after passing the incredible **Retretti Arts Centre** (May–Sept daily 10am–8pm; rest of the year Tues–Thur & Sat & Sun 11am–7pm; 35mk, students 20mk). Devoted to the visual and performing arts, it's situated in man-made caves gouged into three-billion-year-old rock. In the large sculpture park outside, fibreglass human figures by Olavi Lanu are cunningly entwined with natural forms; branches turning into human limbs while innocent-looking boulders mutate into piles of torsos – or so it looks. The main exhibitions inside the caves are chosen to complement the rockface, and changed yearly. There are more weird pieces by Lanu, and underground streams whose gushings and bubblings underlie the piped music. By comparison, the Finnish paintings hung in a regular gallery upstairs can only seem ordinary.

Buses **from Savonlinna to Punkaharju** are less frequent than trains, whose schedules should be checked at the tourist office. Either way, you need to make a special request to be dropped at Retretti. In both cases the fare is around 18mk. It's more expensive but a lot more convenient to catch one of the special direct buses to Retretti, which run from the *Finnair* office near Savonlinna's *kauppatori*, more or less every half hour during the summer.

About 23km west of Savonlinna, the village of KERIMÄKI boasts the **Kerimäki kirkko** (June–Aug daily 9am–8pm), probably the largest wooden church in the world. With enough pews to seat 3000, its awesome proportions drastically eclipse the tiny village and make the church seem like an elaborate folly. There's usually a bus from Savonlinna to Kerimäki every half hour, costing roughly 15mk.

Varkaus, Valamo Monastery and Joensuu

Although Savonlinna is deep in the heart of the Lake Region with beautiful scenery all around, it's the jumping-off point for several still more striking places. The gateway to these is the small industrial town of Varkaus, easily reached by train (change at HUUTOKOSKI to meet the main service from the west) or more scenic buses routed via RANTASALMI. Even if you don't want to stay long in Varkaus, it makes a feasible base for continuing eastwards to the much bigger Joensuu – and the Valamo monastery.

Varkaus

VARKAUS resembles a large industrial sculpture set in the middle of a nature reserve. The sawmills and pulp factories of this diminutive but commercially important town sit amid gentle hills and dense forests, the chimneys and steel piping artily mirrored in the placid waters of the neighbouring lakes. Even the **Varkaus kirkko** (June–Aug Mon–Sat 9am–8pm, Sun noon–8pm) mimics their shape, for this was one of Finland's first Functional-style churches. It's on the corner of Ahlströminkatu and Savontie in what used to be the town centre, but nowadays contains little except for factories and the tourist office since the hub of daily life switched to Kauppakatu, straight ahead from the railway station which has the main shops and the **kauppatori**. At one end is a decrepit-looking water-tower with a rickety lift to an **observation platform** (summer Mon–Fri 8.30am–8pm, Sat 9am–5pm, Sun noon–7pm; free). None of the landscapes in the small **art museum** (Mon, Thur & Fri 9am–1pm, Tues & Wed 9am–7pm, Sun noon–7pm) here can compare with the view of town from the observation platform.

Varkaus expanded following the opening of the Taipale Canal in the 1860s, which made the town a main link in the Saimaa transport system. Although now replaced by a deeper waterway, the original canal can still be seen by following a footpath which begins close to the present canal's control tower (unmissable beside Taipaleentie) and runs about 100m through the woods. Crumbling bricks and a modest trickle of water are all that remain of the first canal, a poor tribute to the 227 workers who starved to death while building it (they're commemorated by a monument atop Varkausmäki hill overlooking town). By now there should also be a **canal museum** in a former warehouse between the old and new canals.

Practical details
The **tourist office** is in the old town centre at Ahlströminkatu 11 (June–Aug Mon–Fri 9am–6pm, Sat 9am–3pm; rest of the year Mon–Fri 9am–4.30pm; ✆972/292383). Varkaus's official **youth hostel** is at Kuparisepänkatu 5 (✆972/162882), open from June to early August, can be reached by buses #1, #3 or #5, or by walking along Jäppilantie and into Hasintie. There's also a privately run hostel, *Joutsenkulma*, at Käämeniementie 20 (✆972/614688), plus a lakeside **campsite** (✆972/26644), open from June to August.

Valamo Monastery

Direct trains and buses connect Varkaus and Joensuu, but you shouldn't miss seeing **VALAMO MONASTERY**, 60km northeast of Varkaus by route 23. The original Valamo Orthodox monastery, on an island in Lake Ladoga, was the spiritual headquarters of Karelia from the thirteenth century. In 1939, with Soviet attack imminent, the place was abandoned and rebuilt here, well inside the Finnish border and 4km off the main road. Most days it can be reached by a few direct buses from Varkaus, Joensuu or KUOPIO. Once there you can stay over at the monastery **hostel** (✆972/61911) for around 70mk, although it's often full during peak months. The chief attractions are the tranquillity of the remote setting, and the sight of the monks – and the many volunteer workers – going about their daily routines. If it's a bonanza of icons you crave it's far easier to head for the Orthodox Museum in Kuopio.

Joensuu

The capital of what was left of Finnish Karelia after the eastern half was ceded to the Soviet Union at the end of World War II, **JOENSUU** is small and sedate and lends itself to a couple of days of slow exploration. The town proper is across the short bridge opposite the **railway station**, though beside the bridge is an island, Illosaari, featuring the **Northern Karelia Museum** (Tues–Fri noon–4pm, Wed until 8pm, Sat 10am–4pm, Sun 10am–6pm). Located inside the **Karelian House** (*Karelia Talo*), it gives an entertaining, informative overview of Karelian culture from prehistory to recent times. It's a good place to get a feeling for the region, while more practical details can be gleaned from the **tourist office** (mid-June to mid-Aug Mon–Fri 8am–6pm, Sat 8am–2pm; rest of the year Mon–Fri 8am–4pm; ☎973/210362), at the town end of the bridge.

Considering the devastation caused by the war, Joensuu has a surprising number of nineteenth-century buildings, and in the old school house, at Kirkkokatu 23, is the **Art Museum**, worth entering if only to gaze at Edelfelt's finely-realised portrait, *The Parisienne*. Staying over in Joensuu is a good idea, and several budget options exist: of two **youth hostels**, the closest to the centre is *Joensuun Elli* at Länsikatu 18 (☎973/25927), open from June to August. Further out, but still within easy walking distance, is *Partiotalon* at Vanamokatu 25 (☎973/123381), open from June to August. There's also a **campsite** (☎973/201364), open from June to August, on the lakeside.

Moving on from Varkaus and Joensuu

If you decide to skip Joensuu in favour of heading north, direct buses are the best transport **from Varkaus to Kuopio**; going by train you'll need to check schedules to avoid being stranded for hours at Pieksämäki, waiting for a northbound connection. The same applies to the journey **from Joensuu to Kuopio**; travelling by train takes most of the day, with a delay changing at VIINIJÄRVI.

Kuopio

Superficially cosmopolitan with smart broad streets and modern buildings, **KUOPIO** is the only city in a vast expanse of countryside, and its earthy peasant heritage is always felt: traditional dress is common, sophistication is rare – and everything takes a backseat to unbridled revelry when the night comes.

The Town

All the sights are within the immediate central area, with one exception: the wonderful **Orthodox Church Museum** (May–Aug Tues–Sun 10am–4pm; rest of the year Mon–Fri 10am–2pm; 5mk) on the brow of the hill, the road to which begins at the junction of Asemakatu and Puistokatu. The museum houses many of the objects from the original **Valamo Monastery** (see above) and it's easy to

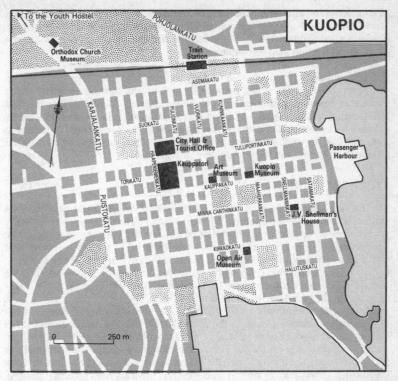

spend several hours wandering around the elaborate icons, gold-embossed bibles, gowns, prayer books and other extravagant objects.

On a more earthly plane, and back in the town centre, the block formed by Kirkkokatu and Kuninkaankatu contains the preserved wooden houses of the **Kuopio Open-Air Museum** (daily mid-May to mid-Sept 10am–5pm, Wed also 5 to 7pm; 3mk). The buildings, still in their original locations, have interiors decked out to show housing conditions of ordinary townspeople from the late eighteenth century to the 1930s. Typical present-day dwellings – blocks of flats – surround the place. A few streets away is another old house, **J.V.Snellman's Home** (summer daily 10am–5pm, Wed also 5–7pm; rest of the year Sat & Sun 10am–3pm; 2mk) by the corner of Snellmaninkatu and Minna Canthinkatu. Snellman domiciled himself here after the Swedish-speaking ruling class expelled him from his university post in 1843. He became head of the Kuopio elementary school and from this house continued his struggle to have Finnish granted the status of an official language. While it's small and worth seeing, the place is tainted with a slightly desperate pieces-of-floorboard-he-stood-on mentality, and it comes as a relief to step out into the nearby park, named after Snellman, with an entrance by the corner of Maaherrankatu and Minna Canthinkatu.

Culture and Kuopio are uneasy bedfellows, but the **Kuopio Art Museum** at Kauppakatu 35 (Mon–Sat 9am–4.30pm, Sun 11am–6pm; 2mk), marshals a decent selection of Finnish painting and sculpture, while further along the street at no.

23, the **Kuopio Museum** (summer Mon–Fri 9am–4pm, Sat 10am–6pm, Sun 11am–7pm; rest of the year closed Sat; 1mk) attempts to unravel local history. However, the building itself – a finely detailed reconstruction of a medieval castle – is more interesting than its contents.

Perhaps a better course is to simply hang around the passenger harbour at the end of Kauppakatu, from where a fleet of pleasure craft ferry holidaymakers up and down the lake, depositing them close to the small **harbour market** which doubles as an **evening market** each night from June to August. This is the best place to sample **kalakukko** – a kind of bread pie, baked with fish and pork inside it. While found around the country, Kuopio is kalakukko's traditional home and at least one stall here will be selling it, warm and wrapped in silver foil. A fist-sized piece will cost about 15mk.

Practical details

The **railway station** is at one end of Puijonkatu, which leads past the **bus station** and into the **kauppatori**. When the market's in progress there's nearly always some form of free entertainment on the covered stage overlooking it. The **kauppahalli** (Mon–Fri 8am–5pm, Sat 8am–1pm) adds a dash of colour and contrasts nicely with the uniform glass fronts of the encircling department stores. Opposite stands the nineteenth-century City Hall, around the side of which is the **tourist office** on Haapaniemenkatu (June–Aug Mon–Fri 8am–6pm, Sat 8am–2pm; rest of the year Mon–Fri 8am–4pm; ☎971/182584).

There's a large **campsite** (☎971/312244), open from May to mid-August, a few kilometres outside town close to the *Rauhalahti* hotel. The **youth hostel**, open June to mid-August, is more central at Taivaanpankontie 14B (☎971/222925), in the Puijonlaakso area on the far side of the motorway – a thirty-minute walk or take a bus to the University Hospital (*Yliopistollinen keskussairaala*), not far from the hostel. Even more central are several privately-run hostels: *Hospitsi*, Myllykatu 4 (☎971/114501); *Puijohovi*, Vuorikatu 35 (☎971/114943); and *Souvari*, Vuorikatu 42 (☎971/122144). For peace and seclusion, stay at *Jynkän* (☎971/312361), an official youth hostel 8km south of Kuopio in a quiet lakeside setting, open from May to mid-October; bus #20 runs there about twice an hour from the bus station.

Away from the harbourside market, **food** is less exotic and generally confined to the customary pizza places: *Restaurant Rosso*, Haapaniemenkatu 24–26, offers some sizeable pizzas with help-yourself salads, although the bland rock music blasting through the place doesn't help digestion; *Taverna Traviata*, Kirkkokatu 40, does cheapish **lunches**, as does *Henry's Pub*, Kauppakatu 18, which might repay a second visit in the evening, when drunken Finnish rock musicians are liable to burst in and instigate impromptu jam sessions. Other viable **nightlife** spots are *Kultainen Noutaja*, Vuorikatu 25; the *Kammari Pub*, Puijonkatu 19; and the mellow *Sampo*, at Kauppakatu 13.

Further out from central Kuopio, the upmarket *Hotel Rauhalahti*, 6.5km to the south, is prone to letting its hair down and staging some wild bashes on Fridays, often laying on free transport from the city. Check if anything's going on here since it's where the hard-core hedonists are likely to be.

Heading **on from Kuopio** there are two obvious choices. To the north, easily reached by bus or train, Iisalmi is a good bet if your ultimate destination is Kainuu or Oulu; the central Lake Region town of Jyväskylä is equally accessible.

Jyväskylä

JYVÄSKYLÄ is the most low-key and provincial of the main Lake Region towns, despite the industrial section which takes up one end and a big university which consumes the other. It also has more than its fair share of buildings by **Alvar Aalto**. The legendary architect grew up here and opened his first office in the town in 1923, and his handiwork – a collection of buildings spanning his entire career – has greatly shaped the place.

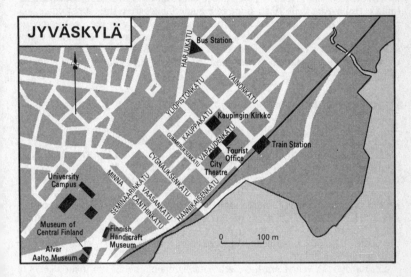

The Town

After some minor projects, Aalto left Jyväskylä in 1927 for fame, fortune and Helsinki, but returned in the 1950s to work on the teacher training college. By the 1970s this had grown into the **Jyväskylä University**, whose large campus halts traffic where the main road gives way to a series of public footpaths, leading to a park and sports ground. Although Aalto died before his ambitious plan for an Administration and Cultural Centre was complete, the scheme is still under construction along Vapaudenkatu. Across the road from the (perhaps intentionally) uninspiring police station – unveiled in 1970 – stands a **city theatre** resembling a scaled-down version of Helsinki's Finlandia (free guided tours at 2pm daily in summer from the tourist office).

The town's museums are clustered together on the hill running down from the university towards the edge of the lake, Jyväsjärvi. At the request of the town authorities rather than through vanity, Aalto built the **Alvar Aalto Museum** at Seminaarinkatu 7 (Tues noon–8pm, Wed–Sun noon–6pm; 5mk). The architect's best works are obviously on the streets, making this collection of plans, photos and models seem rather superfluous. But the Aalto-designed furniture makes partial amends, as does the **regional art gallery** downstairs, boasting a fair display of twentieth-century paintings. He also contributed to the exterior of the nearby **Museum of Central Finland** (Tues–Sun noon–7pm; 5mk), which contains an interesting display of Jyväskylä home interiors from the nineteenth century, plus photos of the locality at that time.

Walking back towards the town centre along Keskussairaalantie brings you to the **Finnish Handicraft Museum** beside the main road at Seminaarinkatu 32 (June–Aug daily noon–7pm; rest of the year Tues–Sun noon–7pm; 5mk). Preserved in its 1910 style, the building is a centre for research into the origins and development of all kinds of crafts, and the displays range from bell-making to spectrolite jewellery. Another place to see is the nineteenth-century **Kaupungin-kirkko** (June–Aug daily 10am–5pm, free guided tours from the tourist office, ask for the times), opposite the tourist office. The church was the centrepiece of Jyväskylä life a century ago, but declined in importance as the town gained new suburbs and other churches. Despite recent restoration – when the interior was repainted in its original pale yellow and pale green – the church looks authentically dingy.

Practical details

The **tourist office**, at Vapaudenkatu 38 (June–Aug Mon–Fri 8am–6pm, Sat & Sun 10am–6pm; rest of the year Mon–Fri 8am–4pm; ☎941/294083), can supply a useful free leaflet on the local buildings designed by Aalto. For **sleeping**, there are two **youth hostels** close together off Laajavuorentie, 4km from the centre. *Laajari* (☎941/253355) is a state-of-the-art affair linked to a winter sports centre (but open year-round), which has taken trade from the older, more basic *Pelastakaa Lapset* (☎941/241985), only open in the summer. The nearest **campsite** (☎941/624903), 2km north off the E4 – take Puistokatu and then continue along Taulumäentie – is open from June to August. In the other direction, 6km to the south, is another campsite, *Sippulanniemi* (☎941/241917), open from mid-May to mid-September.

Eating options veer from the pizza establishments along the main streets to the more upscale *Kissanviikset* (literally, "the Cat's Whiskers") at Puistokatu 3, which serves some sizeable and just about affordable fish dishes at lunchtime. The university often hosts events outside of term-time so it's worth checking the **student mensas**. The neighbourhood is also a focus for **nightlife**, such as there is. Two notable haunts are *Ilokivi*, Keskussairaalantie 2, often featuring art exhibitions and live bands; and *Ruthin ravintola*, Seminaarinkatu 19, where members of the philosophy and politics departments get down to chess and/or hard drinking. This gets more expensive after 6pm, when self-service is replaced by waitresses; the same applies to *Mörssäri*, at Voionmaankatu 32. However, there's self-service throughout the evening in the basement bar of *Alvari*, at Kauppakatu 30: a more central hangout whose easy-going atmosphere makes it popular with local **gays**; on Wednesdays there's a gay night at *Becker's Book Café*, Seminaarinkatu 28.

Iisalmi

The farmland around **IISALMI** makes a welcome break from pine forests and marks the centre of northern Savolax, a district that's regularly voted the least desirable place to live in public opinion polls. The reason for this is slightly mysterious; the modestly-sized town looks nice enough – but might be due to the locals' reputation for geniality mixed with low cunning. Whether this is innate, or a defensive reaction by country folk who've been pitchforked into urban life, is debatable.

Whatever the truth, two museums give a very good insight into local life. The **District Museum** (daily noon–8pm) on the shores of the Palosvirta river – cross the river from the centre of town and turn left – reveals the down-at-heel life of the peasantry; while the **Juhani Aho Museum** (summer daily 11am–3pm & 4–8pm) in Mansikkaniemi, 5km along the Kajaani road, shows how the other half lived. Aho was a major influence on Finnish literature as it emerged around the turn of the century, and the simple buildings filled with the author's possessions manage to convey the commitment of the artists who came together in the last years of Russian rule.

Aside from a few hotels, accommodation in the town is limited. However, the **tourist office** at Kauppakatu 14, (June–Aug Mon–Fri 8am–6pm, Sat 10am–2pm; rest of the year Mon–Fri 8am–3.30pm; ☎977/15011 or 22346) on the corner with the main street Pohjolankatu , can point you towards two summertime budget options on the outskirts: the privately-run *Runni* **hostel** (☎977/48201), and a **campsite** with cabins (☎977/49161).

travel details

Trains

From Tampere to Hämeenlinna (12 daily; 53min); Savonlinna (1 daily; 4hr); Oulu (6 daily; 5hr 15min); Pori (6 daily; 1hr 45min); Turku (7 daily; 2hr 15min); Helsinki (12 daily; 2hr 15min).
From Lahti to Mikkeli (9 daily; 2hr).
From Mikkeli to Savonlinna (usually 2 daily; duration depends on connection from Pieksämäki).
From Varkaus to Joensuu (2 daily; 1hr 45min).
From Kuopio to Jyväskylä (6 daily; 3hr 45min); Iisalmi (5 daily; 1hr); Kajaani (4 daily; 2hr 15min); Mikkeli (5 daily; 1hr 45min).
From Jyväskylä to Tampere (7 daily; 1hr 45min).

From Iisalmi to Kajaani (3 daily; 1hr); Oulu (3 daily; 3hr 30min).

Buses

From Tampere to Helsinki (5 daily; 2hr); Turku (5 daily; 2hr 30min); Pori (5 daily; 1hr 45min).
From Lahti to Mikkeli (6 daily; 2hr 15min); Savonlinna (2 daily; 3hr 45min).
From Mikkeli to Savonlinna (2 daily; 1hr 45min).
From Savonlinna to Varkaus (2 daily; 1hr 30min); Kuopio (3 daily; 3hr).
From Varkaus to Joensuu (2 daily; 2hr); Kuopio (8 daily; 1hr 15min).
From Joensuu to Kuopio (5 daily; 2hr 30min).
From Kuopio to Jyväskylä (3 daily; 2hr 15min).

CHAPTER SIXTEEN

OSTROBOTHNIA, KAINUU AND LAPPLAND

B etween them, these three regions take up nearly two-thirds of Finland, but unlike the populous south or the more industrialised sections of the Lake Region, they're predominantly rural, with small communities separated by long distances. Despite this, or perhaps because of it, each region has a very individual flavour and equally distinct people.

Living along the coast of **Ostrobothnia** are most of the country's Swedish-speaking Finland-Swedes, a modestly-sized section of the national population whose culture differs from that of either Swedes or Finns. Distance from war-time ravages has enabled the towns in this area to retain some of their old wooded form (and usually their Swedish name is used as often as the Finnish), while much of the region's affluence stems from the adjacent flat and fertile farmlands. The main reason you're likely to be here are the numerous ferry connections from Sweden: **Vaasa** and **Kokkola** are the chief entry points although there are lesser ones to the north and south. Overall, though, given the lack of exciting scenery – save for a few fishing settlements scattered along the jagged shoreline – and the social insularity of the place, you'd be generous to devote more than a couple of days to it. Even busy and expanding **Oulu**, the region's major city, has an off-putting anodyne quality, causing its best aspect to be the ease of transport in and out, although you could always drink your way into oblivion slightly further north at the border town of **Tornio**.

Kainuu is the thickly forested, thinly populated heart of Finland and – something perhaps felt more strongly here than anywhere else in the country – is traditionally peasant land. Over recent decades Kainuu has suffered a severe economic decline as wealth has become concentrated in the south. There's a surprising level of poverty in some parts, but this is being alleviated by the marketing of the area's strong natural appeal – woods, rivers, hills and wide stretches of barely-inhabited country. The only sizeable town, **Kajaani**, still retains venerable wooden buildings. It's a good base for wider explorations by foot, bike or canoe, and, since no railways serve the territory beyond, it's the hub of a bus network which connects the region's far-flung settlements. **Kuhmo**, east of Kajaani, is notable for the web of nature trails and hiking routes around it, while heading north through the twin villages of **Suomussalmi** and **Ämmänsaari** and on past **Kuusamo**, the landscapes become wilder: great gorges, river rapids and fells, visited by reindeer as often as people. Hikers here are well-catered for by a number of marked tracks in addition to totally uninhabited regions traversable only with map, compass and self-confidence. The villages have little to offer beyond accommodation and transport to and from the end-points of the hikes, so stay away if you're not a nature buff.

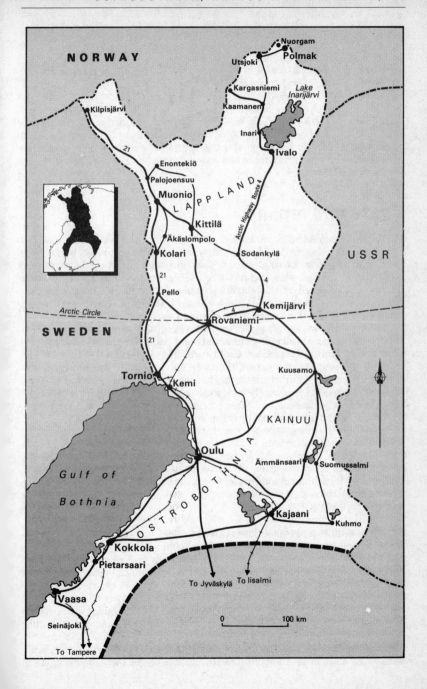

Much the same applies to **Lappland**, probably the most exciting place to hike in the world. **Rovaniemi**, the main stopover en route, can provide little except factual information on the area beyond, and trains to Kemijärvi (there are no services to points north), but it is the junction for the two major road routes into the **Arctic North**. Its wide open spaces are great for guided treks through gold-panning country and along the edges of the mountain chains, which continue far into Sweden and Norway. Elsewhere you can be totally isolated, gazing from barren fell-tops across to the Soviet Union. But while the Arctic settlements are small, and few and far between, the whole region is home to several thousand *Same*, who've lived in harmony with this special, often harsh environment for millenia. Discovering their culture and way of life can be as exciting as experiencing the Arctic North itself.

Vaasa and around

The lifeblood of **VAASA** is its harbour, through which the produce of southern Ostrobothnia's wheatfields is exported, and the lucrative tourist traffic from Sweden arrives. Years of steady income have given the town a staid, commercial countenance, and its wide avenues (the old centre was obliterated by fire a century ago) are lined by shipping offices, consulates, and a plethora of boozing venues aimed at Swedes from Sundsvall or Umeå, who come here to get smashed. It's yet another reason to get the first bus or ferry out.

Seventy-odd years ago Vaasa was briefly seat of the provisional government after the Reds (an alliance of Communists and Social Democrats who took up arms against Finland's repressive Civil Guard) had taken control of Helsinki and much of the south at the start of the Civil War in 1918: it was among Ostrobothnia's right-wing farmers that the bourgeois-dominated government drew most of its support. This barely endearing fact is recalled by the reliefs of the then President Svinhufvud and Mannerheim, who commanded the Civil Guard, on the front of the town hall and by the monument outside it.

Since then, it seems, little besides drunkenness has broken the peace. The apex of local cultural activity is the **Ostrobothnia Museum** (Mon–Fri noon–8pm, Sat & Sun 1–6pm) at Museokatu 3, which tells the story of the town and boasts an enjoyable collection of sixteenth- and seventeenth-century Dutch, Italian and Flemish art. Another way to pass the hours is to take the local bus which skirts across a ring of islands off the coast to reach the windswept little fishing village of BJÖRKÖBY.

Practical details and travel connections

If you have to stay overnight before moving on, **hostels** are your best bet. The official one at Palosaarentie 58 (☎961/117850), open year round, lies 3km from the centre; slightly nearer and dearer are *Oso*, Asemakatu 12 (☎961/114558), and *Vaasa*, Tiilitehtaankatu 31 (☎961/115778). In the summer months, there's the further option of the **campsite** (☎961/31015), which is 2km from the town centre but close to the ferry harbour. For local information use the **tourist office** (June–Aug Mon–Sat 8am–7pm, Sun 9am–7pm; rest of the year Mon–Sat 8am–4pm; ☎961/113853), inside the town hall.

Some **trains** from Vaasa (whose station is at the end of Hovioikeudenpuisto-kirkko) go straight to Tampere, but it's quicker to get there by changing at

SEINÄJOKI (which all trains from Vaasa pass through), on the main line between Helsinki and Oulu. A train for Jyväskylä leaves directly from the harbour following the arrival of the Sundsvall ferry.

There are numerous buses (but no trains) **south from Vaasa** to Pori and Turku (described in *Helsinki and the South*). On the way, some 70km south of Vaasa, is KASKÖ (in Swedish, KASKINEN), a small port receiving sailings from Gävle, and the neighbouring KRISTIINANKAUPUNKI (KRISTINESTAD), notable only for its still-surviving seventeenth-century layout; both settlements have direct rail links to Seinäjoki.

Travelling **north from Vaasa** to the major coastal city of Oulu involves a mildly scenic bus journey past fishing hamlets along the archipelago, and the small and still largely wooden towns of UUSIKAARLEPYY (NYKARLEBY) and PIETARSAARI (JAKOBSTAD). Aside from the **ferry from Skellefteå** in Sweden, which docks at Pietarsaari, there's no special reason to come here; if you arrive by boat, you'll need to take the bus to Kokkola to venture further into Finland.

Kokkola

Deep offshore waters have allowed **KOKKOLA** to industrialise its harbour, so that passengers steaming in from Skellefteå are greeted by views of a massive oil refinery. Aside from your first contact with the Finnish language, there's nothing quite so dramatic about arriving in Kokkola proper; there's usually a bus waiting to take passengers 5km from the harbour into town.

The ferry schedules make it difficult to avoid spending a night here: Kokkola has an official **youth hostel** at Vidnäsinkatu 2 (☎968/18274), open from late May to late August, and a couple of others: *Hansa*, Kustaa Aadolfinkatu 4 (☎968/ 12317), and *Touristi*, Isokatu 22 (☎968/26209). Another possibility is the **campsite** (☎968/14006), open from June to August, just across the town bypass from the centre.

For what it's worth, the **tourist office** at Kaarlenkatu 21 (Mon–Fri 9am–4pm; ☎968/311102), can point you towards the only remotely interesting local sight: the **English Park**, at one end of Isokatu, which contains a boat captured when the British fleet tried to land here in 1854, during the Crimean campaign. A much more welcome sight, though, is the **railway station** at Isokatu's other end. **Travelling on from Kokkola** is straightforward since the town is on the main rail line between Oulu and Helsinki.

Oulu

The spick-and-span streets of neatly-arranged **OULU** reflect the city's place as the national leader in computing and microchip industries. You feel you should wear a white lab coat when walking in them lest a speck of dust should escape, upset the scientific cleanliness, and cause the precise rows of glass and steel buildings to buckle and fall. Things were less clinical in the nineteenth century, when Oulu became a world centre for tar. The black stuff was brought by river from the forests of Kainuu, and the international demand for its use in ship- and road-building helped line the pockets of Oulu's merchants. Their affluence and quest for cultural refinement made the town a vibrant centre, not only for business but also for education and the arts. Today, a handsome series of islands, a couple of highly conspicuous old buildings, and the nightlife fuelled by the roaming fun-hungry students from the university, are the only things bringing colour into Oulu's otherwise pallid flesh-tones.

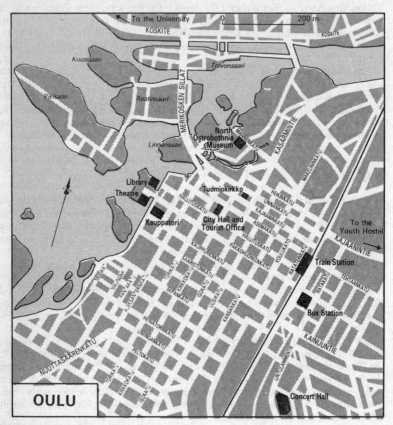

Arriving – and seeing the city

The platforms of the **railway station** feed into an underground walkway with two exits: one runs to the nearby **bus station** while the other leads into the compact city centre from which there's a few minutes' walk straight ahead to the **harbour** and the neighbouring **kauppatori** and **kauppahalli** (Mon–Sat 8am–4pm). Locally there's a joke about Oulu putting its buildings on water and its boats on land, which derives from the former steamship *Hailuoto*, sitting permanently landlocked in the marketplace serving traders as a café, overlooked by the sleekly modern **library** and **theatre**, rising on stilts from the waters of Rommakonselkä. The library, by the way, frequently stages **art and craft exhibitions**, worth dropping into if you have time.

A few minutes' walk away on Kirkkokatu, the **city hall** retains some of the Renaissance grandeur of the late nineteenth century, when it was built as a luxury hotel which symbolised the affluence and cosmoplitan make-up of the tar-rich town. A local newspaper called it "a model for the whole world. A Russian is building the floor, an Austrian is doing the painting, a German is making the bricks, an Englishman is preparing the electric lighting, the Swede is doing the masonry, the Norwegian is carving the relief and the Finn is doing all the drudgery." The present-day drudgery is performed by local government officials who've become accustomed to visitors stepping in to gawp at the wall-paintings and enclosed gardens which remain from the old days. While inside, venture up to the second floor where the Great Hall still has its intricate Viennese ceiling-paintings and voluminous chandeliers. The **tourist office** (July Mon–Sat 9am–6pm, Sun 10am–4pm, rest of the year Mon–Fri 9am–4pm; ☎981/241011) occupies the basement of the building, with its entrance on the Hallituskatu side.

Further along Kirkkokatu, the slight form of the **Tuomiokirkko** (summer daily 10am–7pm) seems outrageously anachronistic amidst the bulky blocks of modern Oulu. Stowed away inside the cathedral, but available for perusal on request, is a portrait of Johannes Messinius, the Swedish historian, supposedly painted by **Cornelius Arenditz** in 1612; restored and slightly faded, it's believed to be the oldest surviving oil painting in Finland, despite the efforts of the Russian cossacks who lacerated the canvas with their sabres in 1714. The small park outside the cathedral is a former cemetery, and bits of clothing and bone found under the floor of the seventeenth-century cellar of the *Franzen Café*, on the corner of Kirkkokatu and Linnankatu, are displayed around the café's walls – perfect for macabre ponderings over a snack.

Cross the small canal just north of the cathedral to reach Ainola Park, and continue along the footpath to find the **North Ostrobothnia Museum** (May to mid-Sept Mon, Tues & Thurs 11am–6pm, Wed 11am–8pm, Sat 11am–3pm, Sun noon–6pm; shorter hours the rest of the year). It's packed with tar-stained remnants from Oulu's past, a large regional collection, and a highly-viewable *Same* section. On a fine day skip the museum in favour of a picnic, and conserve your energies for exploring the four small islands across the mouth of Rommakonselkä, collectively known as **Koskikeskus**. The first island, LINNANSAARI, has the inconsequential remains of Oulu's sixteenth-century castle; next comes RAATINSAARI, followed by TOIVONSAARI, and the rapids which drive a power station designed by Alvar Aalto, with Twelve Fountains added by the architect to prettify the plant. PIKISAARI, the fourth island, is much the best to visit, and is reached by a short roadbridge from Raatinsaari. A number of tiny seventeenth-century wooden houses here have survived Oulu's many fires, and Pikisaari has become the stamping ground of local artists and trendies, with several **art galleries** and **craft shops**, and the *Kuusrock* **rock festival** in the third week of July.

Out from the city: the university and botanical gardens

The islands can also be glimpsed through the windows of buses #27, #32 and #33, all of which pass through Koskikeskus on the twenty-minute ride to the **university**. It's not a bad destination if you're at a loose end, if only for the opportunity to gorge in the student mensa. To work up an appetite, try finding the **Geological Museum** or the **Zoological Museum** (both Tues–Sun noon–4pm on request; admission free), secreted within the university's miles of corridors. The former is much as you'd expect, with a large collection of rare gems; the latter's best feature is the painstakingly hand-painted habitats created for each of the numerous specimens of stuffed Finnish wildlife.

Once you've ventured onto the campus you may as well take a look at the tropical and Mediterranean flora inside the two glass pyramidal structures which comprise the **Botanical Museum** (Tues–Fri 8am–3.30pm, Sat & Sun noon–3pm; free). Also keep an eye out for **Computerland** (*Tietomaa*), which is scheduled to relocate here from the city. A private enterprise founded to teach computer skills to top executives at vast expense, it has spawned a cheaper offshoot which allows members of the public to play with a wide range of computers for 30mk a day.

Sleeping, eating and moving on

Low-cost **accommodation** is unfortunately limited. The highly central *Turisti*, Asemaktu 24–26, offers the cheapest **hotel** bed, and provides hostel-type accommodation during summer, when it takes the overspill from the official **youth hostel** at Kajaanintie 36 (☎981/227707), a fifteen-minute walk from the railway and bus stations, open from June to August. Bus #5 can get you to the **campsite** (☎981/541541) with cabins on Mustassaari Island, 4km from town; nearby is the sliver of sand that locals call a beach.

Aside from university mensas and the cafés and pubs listed under nightlife, one of the best options for **eating** is the help-yourself salad bar at the Lapp restaurant *Samik* (Hallituskatu 14). The salads are generously laced with chunks of raw Baltic herring, while the lunchtime menu can be good value providing you avoid obvious budget-busters. Alternatively, load up in any of Oulu's pizzerias; the cheapest being *Iloinen tori* at Isokatu 18. For more class, venture into the Concert Hall on Lintulammentie, a little way south of the bus station. A coffee in the hall's café isn't cheap, but it does allow you to admire the gleaming Italian marble interior, with the bonus of live classical music during summer (Mon–Sat 12.30–1pm).

Oulu's **nightlife** revolves around numerous **cafés** and **pubs**, best of which is probably *Club Clementine* (often referred to simply as "*Ainola*") in the Ainola Park at Mannenkatu 1 – small and cosy with modest prices and an infectiously loud jukebox. Elsewhere, rapid alcoholic imbibing goes on amongst the technology students who frequent *Rattori-lupi*, at Asemakatu 32. There's a good bar and food on the lower level of *Jumpru*, Kauppurienkatu 6, which has the throbbing *Kaarlenholvi* disco upstairs. *Reidar*, a student bar/disco serving decent, cheapish food, connected to the summer youth hostel (see below), is at its best in term-time – but still worthy of investigation on Friday and Saturday. *Botnia*, Pakkahuonenkatu 30, can be worth trying if the others are dull, as can *Sarkka*, on Hallituskatu, for its incredibly diverse mix of punters. A number of these places regularly feature **live music** (check the notices outside them and around the city), as does *Café Adams*, on Pakkahuonenkatu, though it lacks a full alcohol licence.

If you're too lazy to cruise Oulu's night spots (mostly within walking distance of each another) but still want a diverse evening, make for *Hotel Cumulus* at Kajaaninkatu 17, where there are three spots to make merry: *Restaurant Madonna*, which offers reasonably priced food; *Pub Oliver*, which pulls mostly youngish people; and *Bar Tiffany*, where everybody meets to get tanked up, especially if there's a gig at the nearby *Rattori-lupi* (see above).

Despite its size, Oulu is little more than a stopover on the way somewhere else, but handy for **trains** in various directions. These run directly to KAJAANI in the east, or ROVANIEMI in the north, but if you want to cross overland into Sweden, the place to make for is TORNIO, 130km northwest of Oulu; doing so requires a change of train at KEMI. Although otherwise undistinguished, Kemi is where you can join a four-hour "cruise" on a genuine **arctic ice-breaker**, between December and May, which costs 520mk. Details from *Sampo Tours*, Pohjoistantakatu 5, in Kemi (☎9698/16548).

Tornio

Situated on the extreme northern tip of the Gulf of Bothnia, **TORNIO** makes a living by selling booze to fugitives from Sweden's harsh alcohol laws, and catering to Finns who are here to enjoy the beach, fish, or shooting the Tornionjoki Rapids. After the Swedish-Russian conflict of 1808–1809, the border between Sweden and Finland was drawn around Suensaari, an oval piece of land jutting from the Swedish side into the river, on which central Tornio now sits. With no formalities at the customs post on the bridge linking the two countries, the traffic in liver-damaged Swedes from nearby Haaparanta (in Swedish, Haparanda) is substantial. If you're **arriving by bus** the journey will terminate in Suensaari. From the **railway station** you'll need to walk across a bridge, immediately opposite, to get onto the island.

The dominant features of the town are its bars and restaurants, so numerous it seems pointless to list them. Simply stroll around Hallituskatu and Kauppakatu and drop into the ones with the most promising noises. Always lively are *Pub Tullin*, Hallituskatu 5, and *Aarninholvi*, Aarnintie 1, while everyone who sets foot in Tornio seems to visit *Pizzeria Dar Menga*, Kauppakatu 12–14, one of the cheapest spots for solid nourishment. Alternatively, you can buy a bag of salted and smoked whitefish along the banks of the rapids (roughly 12mk for a meal's worth).

If you're not into drinking and feel uneasy with the boozy atmosphere, try visiting the seventeenth-century **Tornionkirkko** (summer Mon–Fri 9am–5pm) on the edge of the town park, or climbing the **observation tower** (June–Aug daily 9am–10pm). Otherwise there's only the **district museum** (summer Thurs & Fri noon–7pm, Sat & Sun noon–5pm) near the corner of Torikatu and Keskikatu, or the possibility of some diversion suggested by the **tourist office** at Lukiokatu 10 (June to mid-Aug daily 8am–9pm; rest of the year Mon–Fri 8am–4pm; ☎9698/40048).

It might be slightly cheaper to join the drunken legions staggering back across the border to sleep in Haaparanta (see *The Bothnian Coast: Gävle to Haparanda*). Tornio itself has two **youth hostels**: one centrally placed at Kirkkotie 3 (☎980/41682), open from June to mid-August; the other beside a **campsite** on the banks of the mainland side of the river, both open from June to the end of September (☎9988/40146).

Kajaani

KAJAANI, 178km southeast of Oulu, could hardly be more of a contrast to the communities of the Bothnian coast. Though small and pastoral, the town's by far the biggest settlement in this very rural part of Finland, where trains and buses are rare and the pleasures of nature take precedence over anything else.

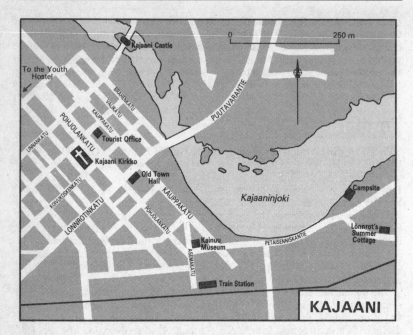

Obviously there's little daily bustle or nightlife, but the place offers some insight into Finnish life away from the more prosperous regions. Fittingly, it was in Kajaani that Elias Lönnrot wrote the final parts of the *Kalevala*, the nineteenth-century collection of Finnish folktales which extolled to the hilt the virtues of traditional peasant life.

From the **railway station**, Kauppakatu leads directly into Kajaani's miniscule centre, but by turning left into Asemakatu you can spot the decorative exterior of the **Kainuu Museum** (Tues & Thurs–Sat noon–3pm, Sun & Wed noon–6pm) at no. 4. Inside, an engrossingly ramshackle collection of local art and history actually says a lot about the down-to-earth qualities of the area. Bypassing this and heading straight for the centre, you'll find the **old town hall** (whose designer, Carl Engel, is famous for Helsinki's Senate Square) at the junction of Kauppakatu and Lönnrotinkatu. Slightly further on stands the dramatic **Kajaani kirkko**, whose wooden frame, weird turrets and angular arches were heralded as the epitome of neo-Gothic style when the church was completed in 1896. Resembling a leftover from a *Munsters* set, its spectral qualities are most intense by moonlight.

More historically significant, perhaps, but far less thrilling, is the ruined **Kajaani Castle**. Built in the seventeenth century to forestall a Russian attack, it later served as a prison where Johannes Messenius the troublesome Swede was incarcerated, among others. Although schemes to rebuild it are constantly bandied about, the castle was ruined so long ago that nobody's sure what it actually looked like, and the present heap of stones is only worth seeing if you're already idling along the riverside beside it.

Given the lack of other **evening** activities, idling is what you'll likely be doing if you stay here overnight. The problem of complete boredom is no less severe for the local youth, who've taken to lining the pavements of Kauppakatu in their hundreds, waiting for something to happen. The town authorities even created *Nuorisokahvila Majakki* at Kauppakatu 7: initially a café, it then became just a room with a record player to wean youngsters off the streets – with limited success.

About the only other way to pass the sunset hours is to take a quiet walk along the riverside footpath, from the corner of Ammakoskenkatu and Brahenkatu. On the route is the **open-air theatre**, and a chance to gaze at logs sliding blissfully towards destruction at the pulp mill up ahead. Following the river in the other direction leads to **Lönnrot's summer cottage**. Built by Elias for his wife, the small wooden structure now stands totally empty and in insignificant isolation; the only acknowledgement of its existence seems to be the name of the neighbouring *Elias Restaurant*: an odd outcome for a man whose lifework was so influential – and so revered.

Once arrived in Kajaani, you may well find yourself staying for the night. The official **youth hostel** at Oravatie 1–3 (☎986/25704), is on the far side of town from the railway station (from Pohjolankatu turn into Sissikatu and continue through the parks and a residential area) and open from June to August; though you might try the more central hostel, *Nevalainen*, at Pohjolankatu 4 (☎986/22254). The **campsite** (☎986/22703) is by the river not far from the Lönnrot Cottage, and is open from June to August. All practical details can be checked at the **tourist office** (mid-June to mid-Aug Mon–Fri 8am–8pm, Sat 9am–2pm; rest of the year Mon–Fri 8am–4pm; ☎986/155517) at Kirkkokatu 24.

Close to Kajaani . . . and beyond

There's a once-hourly bus from Kajaani to the preserved village of **PALTANIEMI**, 9km away on the shores of Oulujärvi, a nice place to camp if Kajaani feels like too much of a metropolis. In contrast to down-at-heel Kajaani, eighteenth-century Paltaniemi was home to Swedish-speaking aesthetes who were lured here by the importance of Kajaani Castle during the halcyon days of the Swedish Empire. Their transformation of Paltaniemi into something of a cultural hotbed seems incredible given the tiny size and placid setting of the place, but evidence of a refined pedigree isn't hard to find. Most obviously there's the **Paltaniemi kirkko**, built in 1726, a large church whose interior is deliberately chilled in order to preserve **frescoes** by Emmanuel Granberg, painted between 1778–81, which include a steamy vision of hell in the gruesome *Last Judgement*.

It's also fun to ferret around behind the pews, trying to decipher centuries-old graffiti. Even Tsar Alexander I paid a visit to Paltaniemi after Finland had become a Russian Grand Duchy, and his impromptu meal in a stable is reverentially commemorated in the **Tsar's Stable** by the Church. **Hövelö**, the cottage across the road, was the birthplace of **Eino Leino**, whose poems captured the increasingly assertive mood of Finland at the turn of the century. His life and the history of Kajaani Castle are the subject of a rather dull exhibition in the old dwelling.

Staying and moving on

The only place to stay is the **campsite** (☎986/475140) by the lake, open from June to August. Because it's located near the site of an old church which succumbed to shifting mud and slid into the water, campers occasionally find bones from the church cemetery poking through the ground. Buses provide the easiest way of **moving on** from Kajaani; the only rail-links are west to Oulu, and south to Joensuu or Iisalmi. The best direction for more rural delights is east towards KUHMO, where the scenery gets increasingly spectacular, especially around SOTKAMO (39km from Kajaani) and the acclaimed beauty spot of Vuokatti – a high pine-clad ridge commanding views all the way to the Soviet Union. The rolling hills make this Finland's premier ski-training area.

Kuhmo

With belts of forests, hills and lakes, and numerous nature walks and hikes within easy reach, **KUHMO** makes a fine base for exploring the countryside. The terrain is in some ways less dramatic than further north, but then again it's far less crowded.

You can get more details, and maps, of hiking routes and other practical information from the **tourist office** (June–Aug Mon–Fri 8am–6pm, Sat 9am–4pm; rest of the year Mon–Fri 8am–5pm; ☎986/561382) on the corner of Kainuuntie and Koulukatu. The tourist office can also pinpoint the whereabouts of the **Kuhmon Kulttuurikornitsa** (summer Mon–Thurs noon–7pm, Sun 3–8pm; winter Mon–Thur 10am–2pm & 3–6pm, Sun 3–6pm) which celebrates Karelia as a region in spite of the national and ideological boundaries imposed upon it. Most of the exhibits come from the Finnish-built Soviet new town, Kostamus, just across the border. When last spied the museum was behind the local fire station (on Torikatu), but there are plans for it to be incorporated into an elaborate **Kalevala Village** – a detailed mock-up of a traditional Karelian village and a surefire tourist puller as well as Kuhmo's only source of stimulation other than hiking.

HIKING ROUTES AROUND KUHMO

The local section of the **UKK hiking route** starts from the Kuhmo sports centre and winds 70km through forests and the Hiidenportti canyon; a northern section is planned that will continue to Suomussalmi. Several other hikes begin further out from Kuhmo and can be reached by buses from the town. **Elimyssalo**, to the east, is a 15km-track through a conservation area, and also to the east is **Kilpelänkankaan**, where a cycle path runs 3.5km across heathland, passing a number of Winter War memorials. To the north, **Sininenpolku** is a 12km hike over a ridge, past small lakes and rivers. In the northwest, **Iso-Palosenpolku** has two paths through a thickly-forested area, where there are overnight shelters. Additionally, several **canoeing routes** trace the course of the old tar-shipping routes between Kuhmo and Oulu.

Accommodation in Kuhmo ... and northwards to more hikes

For staying over in Kuhmo, there's a central **youth hostel** (☎986/561245), in the town school on the Sotkamo road. Other budget options are *Inn Seilonen* (☎986/50781) at Kontiokatu 17, and *Inn Tuuteli* (☎986/59343) at Kattilakoski 604; a double room in either costing around 200mk. The town **campsite** (☎986/50339), is just under 2km from the centre along Koulukatu, and is open from June to August.

Continuing northwards from Kuhmo leads only to more hiking-ripe lands, and if you need urbanity, nightlife and easy living now's the time to own up and duck out. If not, and your feet are itching to be tested over richly vegetated hills, gorges, river rapids, and hundreds of kilometres of untamed land, simply clamber on the bus for Suomussalmi.

Ämmänsaari and Suomussalmi . . . and around

Although separated by a lake, Kiantajärvi, **ÄMMÄNSAARI** and **SUOMUSSALMI** are really twin settlements. Ämmänsaari is on the main road, route 5, about 100km from Kajaani, while the smaller route 41 covers a similar distance to Suomussalmi from Kuhmo. The villages themselves are connected by a more or less hourly bus service. Ämmänsaari, the administrative centre for northern Kainuu, is a good place to gather details of hiking and accommodation in the wilds: contact the **tourist office** (summer Mon–Fri 8am–8pm, Sat noon–4pm, Sun noon–6pm; winter Mon–Fri 8am–5pm; ☎987/191243) in the town hall. You can stay overnight in Ämmänsaari at the **campsite** (☎987/12525), which is open from mid-June to August; or in Suomussalmi at the **youth hostel** (☎358/8715421) in the local school, open from June to early August. Buses from Ämmänsaari and Suomussalmi run to the main hiking areas in the province, usually on a daily basis.

To the east, something of the old Karelian culture can still be felt in the tiny villages of KUIVAJÄRVI and HIETAJÄRVI close to the Soviet border. Near Kuivajärvi is the **Saarisuo Nature Reserve**, where an 8km hiking trail traverses a protected forest and marshy areas, home to a wide variety of bird life. Adjacent is a youth hostel (☎358/8723179), open June to August.

Close to **HOSSA**, an old *Same* village on the road to Kuusamo, are eight hiking paths, graded according to difficulty, passing through pine forests and over ridges between limpid lakes. Dotted about are old tar pits, lumber camps, and a few of the traditional *laavu* shelters – crude slope-roofed huts open to the elements on one side, used by early lumber workers and based on a design by peasant hunters. All the hikes begin 8km from the village, which has a **campsite** (☎358/8732310) open all year, and a **holiday village** (☎357/8732322), both offering affordable cabins.

Just south of Hossa, at Ruhtinansalmi, is the **Martinselkonen Nature Reserve**, known locally as the "last wilderness". Rarely visited by tourists, the reserve has no marked paths or facilities, just a few disused barns remaining from the forestry which finished fifty years ago. Take local advice before venturing into it.

Kuusamo

KUUSAMO, 120km north of the twin villages, is a dull town organised around those who prefer to experience nature from the warm side of a hotel window. But it's also the starting point for the **Kuusamo Bear Circuit** (*Karhunkierros*), one of the most popular hiking routes in Finland: a 70km-trek weaving over the summit of Rukatunturi, dipping into canyons and across slender log suspension bridges over thrashing rapids. Herds of hikers are a far more common sight than bears, but the hike is still a good one – on and off the main track are several interesting shorter routes. From Kuusamo, take the bus to RISTIKALLION for the start of the hike. **On the hike**, wilderness huts are placed roughly at 10km intervals, though during peak months these are certain to be full. Fortunately there's no shortage of places to pitch your own tent, and about halfway along the complete route are two **campsites**, *Juuma* (☎989/45122) and *Jyrävä* (☎989/45136), both open from June to August. At the hike's end is a **youth hostel** (☎989/81104), open from June to September. For full details of local hiking and accommodation, call at the Kuusamo **tourist office** at Kaiterantie 22 (☎989/22131).

The tougher **Six Fells Hiking Route** starts south of SALLA, about 115km from Kuusamo. There's a daily bus from both towns to the Salla Tourist Centre, which marks the beginning of the trail. At the Centre is a **campsite** (☎9692/83524), open from mid-June to August. The 35km-hike includes some stiff climbs up the sides of spruce-covered fell-sides. From the bare summits you can enjoy spectacular views. NIEMELÄ, close to the road between Kuusamo and Salla, marks the end of the trail.

From Salla you can continue by bus directly to Ivalo in the Arctic North, or to KEMIJÄRVI to meet the train for Rovaniemi.

Rovaniemi and around

Relatively easy to reach by rail from Ostrobothnia or Kainuu, **ROVANIEMI** is touted as the capital of Lappland. An administrative centre just south of the Arctic Circle it may be, but tourists who arrive on day trips from Helsinki expecting sleighs and tents will be disappointed by a place that looks as Lappish as a palm tree. The wooden huts of old Rovaniemi were razed to the ground by departing Germans at the close of World War II, and the town was completely rebuilt during the late 1940s. Alvar Aalto's bold but impractical design has the roads forming the shape of reindeer antlers – which is fine if you're travelling by helicopter, but makes journeys on foot take far longer than they need to. Rovaniemi is a mess, and most visitors only use it as a short-term stopover, or to study Lapp culture. Aside from eating reindeer in any local restaurant, the best way to prepare yourself for what lies further north is to visit *Lapia* at Hallituskatu 11, past the **bus station** after you turn right into Ratakatu from the **railway station**.

Lapia

This Aalto-designed building contains a theatre and concert hall, and the fascinating **Museum of the Province of Lappland** (May–Aug Tues–Sat 10am–6pm; rest of the year Tues–Sat noon–4pm; 5mk). Its subject is the **Same** people, around 4000 of whom pursue a nomadic life in the Arctic, gradually retreating as "civilisation" encroaches from the south. The placing of genuine *Same* crafts and costumes side by side with the imitations sold in souvenir shops emphasises the misunderstanding and romanticising of their culture. Also demonstrated is the change in the use of hunting tools and clothing – anoraks and wellington boots have replaced traditional apparel – which has caused a young generation of *Same* to be plagued by rheumatism and foot trouble. On other walls are the stark, impressive paintings of Andreas Alariesto, a *Same* born in 1900, who devoted his retirement to depicting scenes from his native folklore.

The neighbouring **library** (June to mid-Aug Mon–Fri 11am–7pm, Sat 10am–4pm; rest of the year Mon–Fri 11am–8pm, Sat 10am–4pm) has a **Lappland Department**, at the bottom of the stairwell from the main lending section, with a staggering hoard of books in many languages covering every *Same*-related

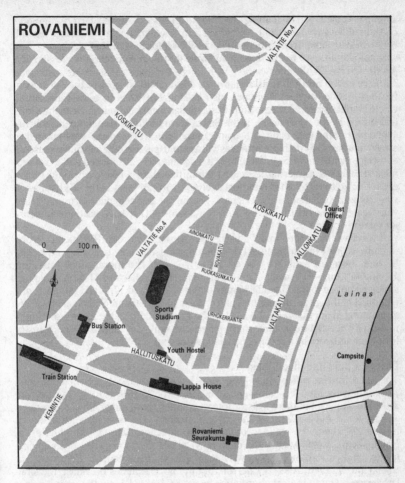

ROVANIEMI

KOSKIKATU

VALTATIE No.4

KOSKIKATU

Tourist Office

VALTATIE No.4

AINONKATU

ROVAKATU

AALLONKATU

RUOKASENKATU

0   100 m

Lainas

Sports Stadium

URHOKERRANTIE

VALTAKATU

Bus Station

Youth Hostel

HALLITUSKATU

Campsite

Train Station

Lappia House

KEMINTIE

Rovaniemi Seurakunta

subject, besides relevant magazine and newspaper articles. The constantly growing collection is already the largest of its kind, and probably the best place in the
world for undertaking research into the subject. (For more on the *Same*, see
Contexts.)

Other sights and the Artic Circle

Other points of interest in Rovaniemi are few. At Kirkkotie 1, **Rovaniemi
Seurakunta** (June to mid-Sept daily 9am–8pm), the parish church, repays a peek
on account of its jumbo-sized altar fresco, *Source of Life* by Lennart Segerstråle,
an odd work that pitches the struggle between good and evil into a Lappish
setting. About the only other thing meriting a look is the **J.Martinni Knife
Factory** (Mon–Fri 8am–3.30pm) at Marttinintie 6 in the industrial area, reached
by walking or bus #4. In the kingdom of the sharp edge the Martinni name reigns

supreme, and if you're looking for a knife the prices in the factory shop are cheaper than anywhere else – plus you can have your name inscribed on the blade. Prices range from a few markkaa to 300mk for the latest model.

Some people are lured to Rovaniemi solely for the dubious thrill of crossing the **Arctic Circle**. While the "circle" itself doesn't remain constant, its man-made markers – 8km north of town along route 4 – do. Bus #4 goes to the circle from the bus station, as does #8 which also calls at the stops in town with "Arctic Circle" emblazoned on them. Both buses depart roughly hourly. Near the circle and served by the same buses, is the **Santa Claus Village** (June–Aug daily 9am–10pm; rest of the year daily 9am–5pm). In the early 1960s, plans were mooted to create a monstrous Father Christmas village to capitalise on Lappland's seasonal association once and for all. Mercifully the scheme was abandoned and a compromise reached. Considering its tourist pitch, the place – inside a very large log cabin – is quite within the bounds of decency: you can meet Father Christmas all year round, contemplate the reindeer grazing in the adjoining farm and leave your name for a Christmas Card from Santa himself (I've been waiting four years for mine).

If you have more time to kill and the weather isn't too cold (Rovaniemi's prone to chilly snaps even in summer), two outdoor museums lie near each other just beyond town, accessible by buses #3 or #6. The **Ethnographical Museum Pöykkölä** (June–Aug daily 10am–5pm; 5mk) is a collection of farm buildings which belonged to the Pöykkölä family between 1640 and 1910, and form part of a potpourri of things pertaining to reindeer husbandry, salmon fishing and rural life in general. About 500m up the road is the **Lappish Forestry Museum** (June–mid-Sept Tues–Sat noon–6pm; 4mk) where the reality of unglamourous forestry life is remembered by a reconstructed lumber camp.

Practicalities and diversions

The main **tourist office** (June–Aug Mon–Fri 8am–7pm, Sat & Sun 10am–7pm; rest of the year Mon–Fri 8am–4pm; ☎960/16270 or 299279) is in the town centre at Aallonkatu 2C, but there's also a tourist counter (June–Aug daily 7.30am–noon & 2.30–6pm; ☎960/22218) at the railway station – the best place to make an immediate check on the accommodation situation. The **youth hostel** at Hallituskatu 16 (☎960/14644) is open all year but always crowded in summer – try to book in advance. Otherwise fall back on guesthouses: *Rovaniemi*, at Kosikkatu 27, about 70mk per person, but the price includes breakfast; the similarly-priced *Outa*, at Ukkoherrantie 16 (☎960/312474); or the more costly summer hotel *Ammatioppilaitoksen*, at Kairatie 75 (☎960/392652). The only other budget accommodation is the **campsite** (☎960/15304), on the far bank of Ounasjoki, facing town.

During the **evening** the few students of the Lappland University can usually be found socialising in *Lapinpaula* (often known by its nickname *Tupsu*) at Hallituskatu 24. *Sampo*, at Korkalonkatu 32, does some inexpensive **lunches** by day, but at night only plays host to very serious drinkers. Most of them are probably driven to booze by a lack of diversions, aside from watching logs floating downriver. The town is less dull if ROPS, the **Rovaniemi football team**, are playing at home. You'll hear the cheering all over town and be able see the game (without paying) through the gaps in the fencing – the stadium is on Pohiolankatu and the season runs through the summer. Despite their modest facilities, ROPS, aided by an English manager, are one of Finland's best teams.

The Arctic North

The least Finnish part of Finland*, **THE ARCTIC NORTH** is a long way from the great lake chains and endless forests. Much of it, in fact, lies beyond the tree-line and offers stark and often quite haunting terrain. It really belongs to the indigenous *Same* population, whose way of life, while seriously threatened from a number of sources – not least Chernobyl fallout (for more on this, see *Contexts*) – still exists in these high and uncompromising latitudes. Significantly, it's also a place where international boundaries fade, and you can easily travel a fair distance into Norway or Sweden before realising that you've entered them at all.

Hiking in the Arctic North: practical points

From a practical standpoint, the Arctic North is one hundred percent **hiking country**. You can look at the remarkable views through the window of a bus (the only form of public transport) but you can only begin to *know* it by travelling through it slowly, which means on foot. The rewards for making the physical effort are tremendous feelings of space and closeness to nature, the whole scene made more magical by the constant daylight which illuminates the region through the summer months (the only time of year when hiking is feasible).

Many graded hiking routes cover the more interesting parts of the region, and however experienced at hiking you are you'll meet plenty of challenges. Equally, a mere novice need have nothing to fear provided basic common sense is employed. Some hikes are very crowded: many people find this an intrusion into their contemplation of the natural spectacle – others enjoy the camaraderie. If you're seeking solitiude you'll find it, but you'll need at least the company of a reliable compass, a good quality tent – and emergency supplies.

We've assembled a broad introduction to the main hikes and the type of things you'll find on them under "Hiking Notes" below. Bear in mind that these aren't definitive accounts as conditions and details often change at short notice; you should always check these at the nearest Tourist Centre.

Basic rules and tips

Obviously you should observe the **basic rules** of hiking, and be aware of the delicate ecology of the region; don't go starting fires in any old place (most hikes have marked spots for this) or pitch your tent out of specified areas on marked routes. You should always check you have maps and spare supplies before embarking, and never aim to cover more ground than is comfortable. Bathe your feet daily to prevent blisters, and carry some form of mosquito repellent – the pesky creatures infest the region.

Accommodation

To be on the safe side, you really shouldn't go anywhere without a good-quality **tent**, although the majority of marked hikes have some form of basic shelter (see the details under "Hiking Accommodation" in *Finland Basics*), and always a

---

* Just as northern England ends at the Scottish border, so Finns and *Same* alike regard northern Finland as ending at the southern border of Lappland. Only for national administrative purposes are the two treated as one.

youth hostel and campsite (plus comfy hotels for those who can afford them) at both ends of the trail. These fill very quickly, however, and few things can be worse than having nowhere to relax after a long day's trek.

Public transport

Buses run far less frequently in the Arctic North than elsewhere in Finland, but they do run to schedules designed to deliver and collect hikers from either end of the trails. Just be sure to check timetables carefully (get the special northern bus timetable from the tourist office in Rovaniemi) and plan several days ahead. Forward planning applies equally to accommodation (above). On your way northwards, you'll almost certainly meet people returning from hikes, whose advice can be very useful.

Hiking Notes: the northeast and northwest

Basically the Arctic North divides into two sections, each linked by major bus routes from Rovaniemi. The **NORTHEAST** is generally flat and barren, giving views way across to the Soviet Union. Although it has its share of well-travelled routes, there are also great opportunites for lone exploration in the lands close to the Soviet border (unlike Norway or Sweden, this is one frontier that you *will* recognise, even from some distance). The Arctic Highway – route 4 – goes through this section linking the communities of **Ivalo**, **Inari**, **Utsjoki** and **Karigasniemi**. The **NORTHWEST** tends to be the busier of the two, and is a slightly more populous. There's higher ground here too, which becomes fully mountainous around the Norwegian border. The main route through it is route 21 connecting **Muonio** and **Kilpisjärvi**.

The Northeast

There's a daily bus from Kemijärvi (reachable by train from Rovaniemi) to **PYHÄTUNTURI**, and the beginning of the **Pyhätunturi and Luostotunturi hiking route**. The hike is 45km in length and rises from marshlands and pine woods to the summits of five fells. Five kilometres from the start is the waterfall of the Uhrikuru gorge, after which the track circles back for a short stretch, eventually continuing to Karhunjuomalampi (*The Bear's Pool*). Here there's a *päivätupa*, but the only other hut on the route is by the pool at Pyhälampi. Near the starting point is a **youth hostel** (☎9692/82713), open from February to mid-May, and a **campsite** (☎9692/52120), open from late June to late August. The hike ends at Luostotunturi, where – unusually – there's only a hotel (☎9693/44226) offering accommodation. A daily bus runs northward from here to SODANKYLÄ.

Beginning 30km south of Ivalo, the **Saariselkä** hiking area includes the uninhabited wilderness between the Arctic Highway and the Soviet border. There are pine moors and innumerable fells lacerated by crystal-clear streams and rivers – in fact, the highest of the fells are snow-covered all year. Recommended starting points are the hotel *Läänihovi* in Saariselkä, and the Saariselkä and Kiilopää Hiking Centres, all of which are close to the highway and served by passing buses. Marked routes stretch about 10km from the road, but to go beyond these you'll need a compass and a very good map. A network of both *autiotupa* and *varaustupa* lie scattered on the marked routes, though during the summer months they're invariably full and your own tent is a must. In Saariselkä there's a **campsite** (☎9697/81891), open all year.

IVALO is a mundane regional centre but possession of the north's biggest airport makes it a major tourist arrival point. The best advice is to bypass Ivalo and make straight for **INARI**, on the rocky shore of Inarijärvi. Here there's an open-air **Same Museum** (June & July daily 8am–10pm; Aug daily 8am–8pm; 7mk, students 3mk) with a fine gathering of log cabins and the utensils of *Same* existence. About 1km from the museum is the beginning of the 7km **Pielppajärvi Wilderness Church Hiking Trail**, leading to the isolated remains of a church built in 1752. Many travellers pass through Inari during the summer, so make a point of booking accommodation ahead of arrival. There's a **youth hostel** (☎9697/51244), open from June to September and during March and April, in the town's centre, and on the edge of the local forest is a **campsite** (☎9697/51106), open from June to mid-August.

A daily bus covers the 36km from Inari to the start of the **Lemmonjoki** hiking routes at NJURGALAHTI. In the 1940s this area witnessed a short-lived goldrush; a few panners still remain, ekeing out a meagre living. The hike is 55km long, but taking the twice-daily boat from Njugalahti to Kultasatama cuts 20km off the full distance. At Härkäkoski, the river is crossed by a small boat pulled by rope from bank to bank; the track then ascends through a pine forest to Morgamoja Kultala, the old gold-panning centre, where there's a big unlocked hut for the use of hikers. The **campsite** (☎9697/56101) is by the settlement of Menesjärvi, and open from June to August; at Lemmonjoki is a Holiday Village (☎9697/57103) with cabins, and a **guesthouse**, *Aslak Jomppanen* (☎9697/57101).

From Inari, the Arctic Highway continues to KAAMANEN, where there's a **campsite** (☎9697/11621) open all year. The highway then swings westwards while a smaller road continues due north to **UTSJOKI**, a small village which faces some of Finland's most desolate landscapes. It's also acknowledged as the best spot to watch the **Northern Lights** (see "Directory" in *Scandinavia Basics*) when the event is at its most spectacular during January and March. There's a local **campsite** (☎9697/61222), and 10km from Utsjoki is another site (☎9697/76103 or 21538), open from mid-June to mid-August, on the road to NUORGAM, a route which runs parallel to the Norwegian border. In Nuorgam itself is a further site (☎9697/61136), open all year, and a few kilometres on, within spitting distance of the border, is the village of POLMAK.

The end of the Finnish portion of the Arctic Highway is reached at KARIGASNIEMI, a tiny village with views of distant peaks and a bridge crossing the Karasjoki river into Norway. Here, there's a **youth hostel** (☎9697/61188), open all year, and two **campsites**: *Soarve Stohpu* (☎9697/61136) open from June to August, and *Tenorinne* (☎9697/61136) open from mid-June to August.

The Northwest

Buses from Rovaniemi connect with route 21 either at PELLO, or MUONIO. South of Muonio is the tiny but increasingly hiker-infested settlement of ÄKÄSLOMPOLO, on the upper slopes of Yllästunturi. Starting 4km from the village, the **Äkaslompolo-Olostunturi-Paalatunturi hiking route** crosses a line of fell summits with several unlocked huts and two cafés en route, and a youth hostel and campsite (both open from June to August; ☎9694/12238) by the starting point. From the eastern slopes of Äkäkero, the track leads to the road running to the *Äkäkero* hotel before descending towards the Äkäkasjärvi lake and a former grain mill, which contains one of the cafés. It then continues to the log-floating dam on Särkijoki, and on around Olostunturi to the Tourist Centre. After crossing the Muonio–Särkijärvi road, the track continues to the *Toras-Sieppi Holiday Village*, and to Pallas and the Pallas-Ounastunturi National Park, eventually ending at the *Pallastunturi* hotel, where an office has information and maps on all the local hikes. There are two **youth hostels** in the area: the small *Jerismaja* (☎9696/8505) at the foot of Pallastunturi, open from June to August; and *Pekonen* (☎9696/2237), open all year in Muonio, which also has a year-round **campsite** (☎9696/2001).

The Pallastunturi Tourist Centre marks the start of the **Pallas-Hetta** route which traverses part of the Pallas-Ounastunturi National Park. The highest point is the summit of Taivaskero, near the start, after which the route is fairly continuous fell plateau stretching for 64km. There are both *autiotupa* and *varastupa* along the route, and a sauna in the big hut at Haukkalinna. Close to the end you'll need to cross Ounasjärvi by boat. There's no **ferry service** at all between 11pm and 7am, but at other times, if the boat isn't there, you should raise the flag to indicate you want to cross. The end is the Hetta Tourist Centre by the village of ENONTEKIÖ, where there's a small **youth hostel** (☎9696/51106), open from mid-March to September, and a **campsite** (☎9696/15008), open all year.

Buses from Enontekiö link with the main route from Muonio to **KILPISJÄRVI**. The area around this border village contains several fells over 1000m high with stark tundra summits, highest of which is Halti (1328m) – take local advice before trying to climb it. Around Saana there are three hikes, each roughly 10km long. Two begin at the Kilpisjärvi Excursion Centre beside Kilpisjärvi (the lake which gives the village its name). The only way up (and down) Saana is by the steep north side which contains the main track, although another runs behind the fell to the northern shore of Saanijärvi, where there's a *päivätupa*. The third hike, from the Kilpisjärvi Tourist Hotel, is unmarked and crosses uninhabited country, so a good map and compass are vital.

Just north of the village is a 24km hike through the **Malla Nature Reserve**, starting and ending at Kilpisjärvi Excursion Centre, and including the **Three Countries Frontier** where Finland, Sweden and Norway meet. The track crosses by footbridge the rapids of Siilajärvi, after which a secondary track ascends to the top of Pikku Malla. The main route continues to Iso Malla. There's a steep and stony section immediately before the waterfalls of Kihtsekordsi, and then a reindeer fence marking the way down to an *autiotupa* beside the Kuokimajärvi lake. From here, a stone path leads to the cairn marking the three national borders. The **campsite** (☎9696/77771) here is open from mid-March to mid-May and mid-June to mid-September; nearby there's a private hostel, *Saana* (☎9696/77746).

travel details

Trains

From Vaasa to Kokkola (5 daily; 2hr 30min); Oulu (4 daily; 5hr 30min); Jyväskylä (2 daily; 5hr 30min, 2 more via Haapamäki); Tampere (4 daily; 2hr 30min); Helsinki (7 daily via Seinäjöki; 4hr 30min).

From Kokkola to Oulu (6 daily; 2hr 30min); Tampere (9 daily; 3hr 45min); Helsinki (9 daily; 4hr).

From Oulu to Kajaani (4 daily; 2hr 45min); Rovaniemi (5 daily; 3hr); Tornio (4 daily; 2hr 15min).

From Rovaniemi to Kemijärvi (1 daily; 1hr 15min).

Buses

From Vaasa to Pori (5 daily; 5hr 15min); Turku (6 daily; 6hr).

From Pietarsaari to Kokkola (4 daily; 40mins).
From Oulu to Kuusamo (6 daily; 4hr).
From Kajaani to Kuhmo (1 daily; 2hr direct, more by slower indirect routes); Ämmänsaari (1 daily; 1hr 45min direct, more by slower indirect routes); Kuusamo (1 daily; 4hr direct, more by slower indirect routes).
From Kuhmo to Suomussalmi (2 daily; 2hr 45min).
From Suomussalmi and Ämmänsaari to Hossa (1 daily; 1hr 30min); Kuusamo (3 daily; 2hr 45min).
From Kuusamo to Rukatunturi (2 daily; 50mins); Ristikallion (1 daily; 1hr 15min); Salla (2 daily; 3hr).
From Rovaniemi to Saariselkä (2 daily; 4hr 30min); Inari (2 daily; 6hr); Ivalo (3 daily; 5hr); Muonio (2 daily; 4hr); Pallastunturi (1 daily; 4hr 45min); Enontekiö (2 daily; 5hr 15min); Kilpisjärvi (2 daily; 7hr 45min).

From Inari to Kaamanen (6 daily; 1hr 45min); Utsjoki (2 daily; 3hr 45min); Karigasneimi (2 daily; 1hr 45 min).
From Utsjoki to Nuorgam (2 daily; 55min).
From Luosto to Sodankylä (1 daily; 40min).
From Tornio to Äkäslompolo (1 daily; 3hr 45min); Mournio (1 daily; 5hr 30min).
From Pallastunturi to Mournio (1 daily; 40min); Enontekiö (1 daily; 2hr 30min).
From Kolari to Äkäslompolo (1 daily; 55mins).

International Ferries

From Vaasa to Umeå (4 daily in summer; 4hr); Sundsvall (1 daily in winter; 8hr 30min); Örnsköldsvik (4 a week; 4hr 30min).
From Kokkola to Skellefteå (1 daily in summer; 5hr).
From Pietarsaari to Skellefteå (1 daily; 5hr).
From Kaskö to Gävle (1 daily; 10hr).

PART SIX

ICELAND

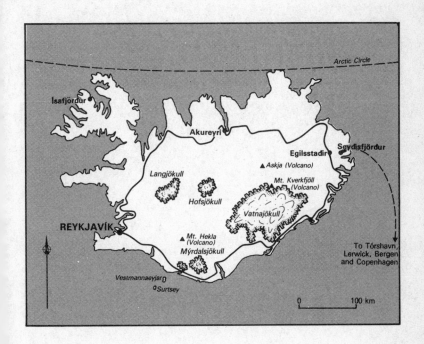

Arctic Circle

Ísafjörður

Akureyri

Egilsstadir Seydisfjördur

▲ Askja (Volcano)

Langjökull

Mt. Kverkfjöll
(Volcano)

Hofsjökull

Vatnajökull

REYKJAVÍK

▲ Mt. Hekla
(Volcano)

Mýrdalsjökull

To Tórshavn,
Lerwick, Bergen
and Copenhagen

Vestmannaeyjar

Surtsey

0   100 km

Introduction

Iceland is pure energy, raw and ardent.
—Magnús Magnússon

Iceland has a bad case of geological acne.
Desmond Bagley

Europe's second largest island, Iceland sits roughly midway between Scotland and Greenland, a few degrees south of the Arctic Circle. It holds the continent's largest ice-cap and straddles a rift of volcanic activity which influences everything you see. Geysers, hot pools, volcanoes, glaciers – nature is the dominant force in Iceland, and it continues to shape the lifestyles and culture of the people here as it has since the Settlement.

Perhaps not surprisingly – and despite an increasing cosmopolitanism – the Icelanders are an insular and self-reliant people; inventive too, not least in harnessing their land's natural energy to provide power. They've also taken advantage of the country's unique landscapes to encourage tourism: Icelandic airlines hold a near-monopoly on routes into the country and *Icelandair* promote short stopovers on their transatlantic routes. In season, at the more popular sites at least, the tourist numbers are remarkably high.

Nonetheless, it's difficult to imagine the emptiness of a country that is as large as England but has a population of just 250,000. Iceland has always been a tough place simply to survive and stay alive, and in many ways this still applies to modern travellers. It's not just the country's incredible expense and soaring inflation rate which make careful planning essential; public transport is infrequent, shops and supplies often long distances apart, and the weather can change dramatically within hours. Often, what looks like a substantial dot on a map turns out to be nothing more than a cluster of farmsteads, or even just a road junction.

But this is part of the country's charm. Because much of Iceland is so wild, myths, legends, and the legacy of the country's early literature are strongly felt. There's barely a piece of rock which wasn't previously a troll, hardly a cave or sheltered spot that wasn't some outlaw's hideout, and it's still possible to explore some of the Saga sites, such as those of *Laxdale Saga* and *Njal's Saga*, spotting places and things referred to in the old tales. The fact that everyone is known by their first name only heightens the feeling of being in a close-knit – if geographically far-spread – community.

■ Where to go

More than half the population live in or near **Reykjavík**, in the flat and fertile farmlands of the southwest; apart from the northern town of **Akureyri**, the rest reside in small fishing villages or in sheep farming hamlets in the valleys just inland. The **Ring Road** is the only major route, and sticking to it takes you right around the country and through much of the island's most viewable geological activity, including the dense concentration around the lake of **Mývatn**. Away from the Ring Road, the **Snæfellsnes peninsula** and the high, flat-topped mountains of **Vestfirðir** are rewarding and relatively accessible areas too. Just off the south coast, and easily reached by ferry, the islands of **Vestmannaeyjar** were propelled into world headlines by the 1973 volcanic eruption, and sport a dizzying four million birds on their cliffs. The desolate **interior**, on the other hand, except for guided tours, is best left to the experienced: there's nothing there beyond a few hydroelectric power stations and the ghosts of the early settlers who perished in its bleak, grey-sanded lava deserts.

■ When to go . . . and what to take

Though milder than you'd think, Icelandic weather is notoriously unpredictable. In **summer** there's a fair chance of bright and sunny days, and temperatures often reach 64°F, but these are interspersed with wet, foggy spells when the temperature can plummet to a chilly 50°F. Most budget accommodation is only open from late May to early September, and it's at these times, too, that buses run their fullest schedules. In the north, nights are light throughout June and July, and the **Midnight Sun** is visible for a couple of weeks; between late August and January the *aurora borealis* or **Northern Lights** can often be seen.

Winter temperatures fluctuate about 15°F either side of freezing point, and heavy snowfalls block many of the roads. There's little choice of accommodation other than the business hotels in Reykjavík and the other main towns, and hiking and camping are out of the question. However, a stay in the capital at this time gives an interesting view of the community without the summer crowds, and at Christmas its streets are bathed in the glow of candles burning behind every window. Daylight in mid-winter, however, is limited to a few hours.

Whenever you visit, **warm and waterproof clothing** is essential, and even if you don't plan any serious walking, a tough pair of shoes, or preferably hiking boots, are a must; rubber boots are useful in marshy areas and around rivers. Other invaluable **equipment** includes a first-aid kit: the sharp rocks and boulders can tear up your hands and knees, and even rip through boots. Lavafields generally lack recognisable features to aid navigation so always carry a compass (although magnetic rock can render it useless) and – for attracting attention in case of accident – a torch and whistle. A good quality sleeping bag is a must if you're using budget accommodation or camping. Sunglasses and sunscreen lotion are handy, especially on glaciers where the sun can dazzle and burn, and you should take a swimming costume for bathing in the many natural hot pools.

Getting There

Remoteness is one of Iceland's most appealing qualities, although this means that getting there can be harder – and more expensive – than reaching any other Scandinavian country. There's just one international ferry and only a handful of flights from the UK each week. In fact, depending on what you plan to do in Iceland, you could well save time and money by taking an inclusive package tour.

■ From the UK

Between late May and early September the Faroese-based *Smyril Line* **sails** from Lerwick in the Shetlands, via Tórshavn, to Seyðisfjörður – a service which also connects with Bergen in Norway, and Hanstholm in Denmark. The cheapest fares, with a couchette, run from £248 per person in high season (between late June and mid-August) down to £186 between late May and early September); sharing a two- or four-berth cabin costs £20–40 more. Students are entitled to a 25 percent discount; senior citizens qualify for similar reductions but only during low season. The trip to Iceland takes 34 hours from the Shetlands (even longer from Denmark or Norway), and it's as well to know that the return leg includes a three-day stop at Tórshavn, when

passengers are left to their own (potentially bankrupting) devices.

Flying to Iceland works out roughly the same in terms of cost, though it is of course a lot quicker. There are direct *Icelandair* flights from London (2hr 45min) and Glasgow (2hr) to Reykjavík's airport at Keflavík. Through April and May and from October to December, the cheapest return flight from London costs £214 (which must include one Saturday night stay and be for a trip of less than one month); during the peak summer months the lowest return fare is £318. If you're **under 23**, however, you qualify for a "youth fare" which gives around thirty percent off, more if you travel standby. Prices from Glasgow are roughly £30 less than this. Outside of high season especially, it's worth phoning *Icelandair* to check on any short-term discounts which may be on offer: winter fares, for example, are sometimes slashed for a short period to encourage skiing trips. Flying to Iceland also entails a £16 **departure tax**, which you have to pay when *buying* a ticket.

■ From Scandinavia/mainland Europe

Coming **from other parts of Europe**, *Icelandair* use Luxembourg as the hub of their route network and also operate flights from Paris, Amsterdam, Copenhagen, Stockholm, Gothenburg and Oslo. *Eagle Air* – owned, incidentally, by *Icelandair* – fly from Amsterdam, Brussels, Rome, Zürich and several major German cities. *SAS* have a weekly flight from Copenhagen, and *Lufthansa* have summer services to Iceland from Frankfurt and Munich.

AIRLINES AND OPERATORS

Arctic Experience, 29 Nork Way, Banstead, Surrey SM7 1PB (☎0737-362321).

Dick Phillips Whitehall House, Nenthead, Alston , Cumbria CA9 3PS (☎0498-81440).

Icelandair, 3rd Floor, 172 Tottenham Court Road, London W1 (☎071-388 5599).

Regent Holidays, 13 Small Street, Bristol BS1 1DE (☎0272-211711).

Scanscape Holidays, 197–199 City Road, London EC1 (☎071-251 2500).

Smyril Line, PO Box 5, Aberdeen (☎0224-572615).

Twickers World 22 Church Street, Twickenham, Middlesex (☎081-892 8371); 60 Marylebone Lane, London W1 (☎071-486 8371).

■ Package Tours

On shortish stays, it's wise to buy a flight and accommodation **inclusive deal** offered by one of several specialist operators. *Arctic Experience*, for example, put together seven nights accommodation in Reykjavík, inclusive of flights and transfers, for £332; and there are any number of operators offering longer, more adventurous trips which may include hiking, camping and minibus trips to otherwise inaccessible areas. Several also act as UK agents for (even more specialist) Icelandic tour operators, the best of whom – and the type of trips they organise – are listed on p.553.

Red Tape and Visas

Scandinavian citizens may enter Iceland without a passport; British and other EC citizens, Americans, Canadians, Australians and New Zealanders need both a passport and return ticket (a British Visitor's Passport will suffice). With these you can spend three months in any nine month period in Iceland – though this can be extended at a police station.

All other nationalities need a **visa**, obtainable for a small fee and valid for three months; again, extensions can be applied for at a police station. In many countries, you'll find that the Danish, or another Scandinavian embassy, handles Icelandic enquiries, but there is an **Icelandic embassy** in the UK at 1 Eaton Terrace, London SW1 (☎071-730 5131).

Health and Insurance

A reciprocal health arrangement exists between Iceland and the UK, meaning you won't have to pay for hospital (*sjúkrahús*) stays or spend more than Icelanders on prescriptions from a chemist (*apótek*). But in the case of emergency services – such as ambulances – you will have to pay. In a country where it's easy to be injured by ordinary hiking, it is strongly advisable to take out private health insurance before leaving (see *Basics* for details).

If you fall ill in a settlement outside of Reykjavík (the only place with a hospital) ask for help at a police station, youth hostel, hotel or shop – or knock at any door saying you need a doctor (*læknir*). Some large-scale maps of Iceland mark doctor's surgeries (*læknissetur*) with an encircled "L". Not all large towns have them – though, conversely, many small communities do.

Information and Maps

With much of Iceland so remote and seemingly cut-off from the outside world, it's a good idea to stock up on general information whenever you can – both before you get there and, once there, when you're in one of the few spots where tourist information is available. Also, in a country where travel through inhospitable, sparsely populated areas is inevitable, and often the reason for coming, good maps are essential if you're to see it all safely.

You can pick up free travel brochures and assorted information leaflets **before you leave** from the Iceland Tourist Board, who share the *Icelandair* offices in London (see above). **Once in Iceland**, assuming Reykjavík is your first stop, you should make a point of calling into the city's Tourist Information Centre (see "Arrival", Chapter Seventeen). Elsewhere, there are smaller tourist offices only in Ísafjörður, Akureyri and Egilsstaðir; in other places you'll need to rely on hotels and youth hostels, shops or even the nearest farmhouse for basic information.

Maps are vital, if only to trace your route from the inside of a bus. *Stanford's* in London (see *Basics* for address) stock the *Landmælingar Island* (the *Icelandic Geodetic Survey*) 1:500,000 map of the whole country (£7.95), which should be fine for general purposes. The same company also produces larger-scale regional plans that are better for more precise route planning. If you need something more detailed than these, particularly if you're hiking, visit the company's head office at Laugavegar 178, in Reykjavík; their shop is stocked with a very large assortment, including special editions for popular hiking areas. Costs vary but are generally 350–450kr per map.

Costs, Money and Banks

Far and away Scandinavia's most expensive country, Iceland is also, due to a combination of geographical isolation, geological turmoil and economic dependency on unpredictable fish stocks, subject to runaway inflation. Food, drink, accommodation and transportation each cost four or five times what you might be used to paying in the UK.

■ Prices and costs

Due to the rate of inflation – 25–50 percent most years – **prices** of many summer tourist services are seldom fixed much before May, and are usually expressed in US dollars. The *króna* figures we quote are the latest available but they are certain to have increased by the time you read them.

Costs can be devastating, although Iceland's greatest feature – its landscape – is free. By hitching and camping, either in the cheap official sites or freely in open country, and bringing most of your own food, it's possible to exist (barely) on around £15 per day. More realistically, staying in youth hostels or sleeping bag accommodation, and doing some local shopping, along with the occasional night in a hotel and meal in a restaurant, means spending £25–40 a day.

■ Money and banks

Icelandic currency is the *króna* (plural *krónur*), which comprises coins worth 50kr, 10kr, 5kr and 1kr, and notes to the value of 100kr, 500kr and 1000kr; you may also come across 10kr and 50kr notes, which are no longer printed but still legal tender. One *króna* is made up of 100 *aurar*, and 50 and 10 *aurar* coins are often given in change – though frankly they aren't worth the hole they'll make in your pocket. At time of writing the exchange rate was 100kr to £1.

While you can get Icelandic currency abroad, it's much less costly to carry sterling travellers cheques, which can be changed at almost any Icelandic bank, or at the airport on arrival. Remember, though, that **banks** (Mon–Fri 9.15am–4pm, Thurs until 6pm) are only found in the main towns, and while many hotels will also change money (at a poorer rate than the banks), many communities will have nowhere at all to change a travellers cheque, so plan ahead. Most major **credit cards** are accepted in restaurants and hotels, and in the bigger shops.

Communications

High-flying businesses in Reykjavík are equipped with every modern communications device, but ordinary forms of communication in Iceland are, by European standards, sluggish and awkward. This is due to the bizarre nature of the country: the uninhabitable interior is a major natural obstacle and most communities are so small

and isolated that it's simply not feasible for information to travel at speed. Equally, while Icelanders are credited with being among the best-informed people in the world, with a record consumption of newspapers and other reading material, there's a paucity of information in English, especially outside the larger settlements.

■ Post

If you want to post anything, do it when you're in a major settlement. Elsewhere, mail collections are infrequent, sometimes just once a week (ask locally for precise details), and severe weather can disrupt the service. The cost of sending anything under 20g to anywhere in Europe is currently 30kr, though inflation affects the mail as much as everything else. Buy stamps from **post offices** (Mon–Fri 9am–5pm, Sat 9am–noon) – again only found in the main towns and larger settlements. **Poste restante** is available at any named post office, and most youth hostels and hotels will hold mail in advance of your arrival; for obvious reasons, it's best to have your mail sent to a well-populated area.

■ Phones

Public phones are seldom seen anywhere other than the main towns. Instead there are usually pay phones at hotels, post offices, shops and service stations. Insert 5kr into the slot when the call is answered, and be ready with plenty more as the conversation continues. Some settlements are not linked to the national dialling system and have to be reached via the **operator** (☎02), who will also give general advice. Most youth hostel wardens will let you use their phone, provided, of course, that you pay. If you're stuck miles from anywhere and desperate to make a call, go to the nearest farmhouse – which will almost certainly have a phone you can use. The code for dialling Britain from Iceland is 90-44.

Media

Unless you understand Icelandic, none of Iceland's five daily **newspapers** are going to take long to digest. The best for listings, which should be fairly simple to decipher, is the top-selling daily, *Morgunblaðið*. For keeping up with world news, you'll find *Snæbjörn Jónsson & Co.*, in Lækjartorg, Reykjavík, sell **overseas newspapers** usually the day after issue; most UK dailies cost 100–150kr.

Icelandic **television** – which you probably won't see unless you're staying at a hotel – has two channels: Channel 1 is state-run and fills its schedules with a surprising number of BBC dramas and documentaries; Channel 2 is commercial, but like the state-run channel is legally required to screen a certain proportion of Icelandic-language programmes. The main **news** is on Channel 1 at 8pm; the eagerly-awaited weather forecast follows at around 8.30pm.

Getting Around

Iceland has no railway system, and buses are the main form of public transport, though even these are relatively infrequent. There's only one major road route, the Ring Road, which girdles the whole country, and other roads, especially those branching off to the more isolated settlements, are rarely tarmaced, and often stony and potholed.

Of the main alternatives, hitching is only occasionally a good bet, and cycling demands dedication, although well-planned ferry trips can sometimes cut out a dreary day's bus travel. You should also consider taking at least one guided tour – pricey, but a good (and sometimes the only) way of reaching inaccessible and spectacular parts of the country.

■ Buses

Like everything else in Iceland, bus travel isn't cheap, although discount tickets make things a little more affordable. Icelandic **buses** are operated by *BSÍ*, and will generally stop for passengers at any point along any road if waved down. The main Ring Road terminals are Reykjavík, Akureyri, Egilsstaðir and Höfn, between each of which there is a once-daily service; off the Ring Road, services are fairly frequent between major settlements in the southwest, but elsewhere may only run once or twice a week. Outside Reykjavík and Akureyri, hotel car parks usually double as the bus station, and information on the schedules can be found at the hotel reception desk. *BSÍ*'s *Leiðabók* contains the full timetables and fare details – 600kr from bus stations and tourist offices. As a broad guide to fares, the trip between Reykjavík and Akureyri costs 2000kr; between Akureyri and Egilsstaðir 1650kr.

You can buy tickets in advance, but it's more common to pay on the bus. If you're going to be doing a lot of travelling by bus, consider investing in one of two types of **discount ticket**, available either in Iceland or from Icelandic tourist offices abroad. These only work out marginally cheaper than standard fares but entitle the holder to a range of substantial additional discounts – ten percent off campsites and sleeping bag accommodation, seven nights' free hostel accommodation, 10–45 percent off *BSÍ* tours, and reduced-price ferry crossings. The **Full Circle Passport** (*Hringmiði*) enables travel in one direction around the Ring Road with no time restriction and costs £102. The **Omnibus Passport** (*Tímamiði*) is valid for all scheduled bus services in the country and is valid from as many weeks as you need up to four weeks; costs range from £115 for one week to £220 for four weeks.

■ Driving and hitching

Driving is obviously the most comfortable way of getting around Iceland, although **car hire** is very pricey. The charge for a small vehicle starts at around £30 a day, plus around £1 for every 20km and a stinging 25 percent sales tax. Also, most car hire companies insist that the car is returned to the place of hiring so you have to make a round trip. Bear in mind, too, that much of Iceland's terrain can only be traversed by four-wheel-drive vehicles.

Hitching can sometimes be viable and is certainly worth trying if you face a long wait between buses. It's not easy, however: Icelanders tend to travel long distances by air rather than road, there's little road freight transport, and Ring Road traffic is likely to be tourists too laden with luggage to have space for hitchhikers. Off the Ring Road, you may have to wait several hours just to see a car, although there's a good chance that the first one to appear will stop. Again, always carry a map and emergency supplies if you're heading into remote areas.

■ Planes

Flying is a common means of transport for Icelanders: even tiny communities have an airstrip, often the only connection with the outside world during the winter, though even in summer bad weather can delay many flights. Flying also has the effect of whizzing you over the most impressive landscapes too quickly. The main routings are between Reykjavík (the domestic airport), Ísafjörður, Akureyri, Egilsstaðir and Höfn. Fares aren't cheap – Reykjavík to Akureyri £46, for example – but *ISIC* card holders are entitled to a 25 percent reduction and there are a couple of discount deals: an **Air Rover** ticket which is valid for travel between the five centres in one direction and costs £130; and a **"Fly As You Please" Passport** which gives two return flights from Reykjavík to anywhere in the country or four flights between the five centres at a cost of £106. It's also possible to arrange an **Air/Bus Rover** ticket which combines air and bus travel on a wide selection of routes. Contact an *Icelandair* office for full details.

■ Ferries

Car ferries connect otherwise inaccessible points along the coast and offshore islands – and also break the monotony of road travel. Prices are roughly similar to buses. The main routes are Reykjavík–Akranes (400kr); Stykkishólmur–Brjánslækur (750kr); from Isafjörður around the Ísafjarðardjúp (a half-day round-trip; 900kr); and Þorlákshöfn–Heimaey (1000kr). Get details from the nearest tourist office, hotel or shop.

■ Hiking

Unless you stick to towns and guided tours, you're going to do some **hiking**. How easy this is depends on the terrain. Of the two lava types you'll come across, *Apalhraun* is the worst: it can lacerate anything less than the toughest boots, and is the cause of many a sprained or broken ankle, even in the lowlands where many of the older flows are covered by spongy moss. *Helluhraun*, the other kind, is easier on the foot, though still hazardous because of irregular gaps between the slabs sometimes concealed by vegetation.

Stick to **footpaths** if there are any. Stay outside any **fenced-off areas**: in many places the ground is very thin and can't bear much weight; typically this happens around sulphur springs, and the ground becomes coloured grey, white, blue or light yellow. Walking on the **glaciers** is dangerous too: always go with a guide and take proper equipment. Even simple **climbing** is more hazardous than you might anticipate: frost-shattering cracks the rock surface and pieces are likely to fall off if any weight is put on them.

■ Cycling

Long and short distance **cycling** is an unusual but feasible alternative: for 500kr a day you can hire bikes from youth hostels, tourist offices and most hotels – though the roads make the going slow and anything less than a mountain bike prone to constant breakdowns. There are no bike shops outside Reykjavík so carry plenty of spares and specialist tools. **Planning** is important: settlements of substance are often several days' cycle away and you should always carry enough food to sustain you, as well as a tent and the necessities for rough camping. You should, too, though it may seem obvious, arrange things so that you overnight somewhere with grass and water, and not in a desert, glacial outwash plain or on jagged lava. On the Ring Road, travel in an anti-clockwise direction to avoid heading continually into the wind, and wear walking boots and legwear with a padded bum to cushion the effect of several thousand bumps a day. If attacked by Arctic terns, as is quite likely, put your hand above your head and raise a finger. This causes them to dive at the finger rather than the head. An Arctic Skua attack is more difficult, and the only defence is to outpace them. When fed up with all this, flag down a bus, which will carry you and your bike.

■ Horse trekking

Horse trekking is an ideal way to see the Icelandic countryside, and any tourist office, hotel or hostel can give you details of local trekking centres. Interestingly, the Icelandic horse (and Icelandic horses, despite their small size, *are* horses, not ponies) is unique in having five gaits. In addition to walk, trot and canter, it will also "pace" and "tölt" – smooth fluid motions causing the creature to appear to be moving only from the hip down, and making riding extremely comfortable. Treks can vary from a few hours' hack for beginners to a fortnight's expedition across the interior for expert riders. If horses are your main interest, you can get more information on both the beasts themselves and riding holidays from the *Icelandic Horse Society of Great Britain*, Rosebank, Higher Merley Lane, Corfe Mullen, Dorset BH21 3EG (☎0202-86187).

■ Guided tours

Guided tours range from one-day coach excursions from Reykjavík to two-week-long specialist walking and bird-watching tours. The most popular **day trips** from Reykjavík – to Gullfoss, Geysir and Þingvellir – aren't really worthwhile unless you're severely pushed for time, since the sites can be easily reached on public transport. Others however, especially the more elaborate packages, are often the only way of getting to the

TOUR OPERATORS IN REYKJAVÍK

BSÍ, Umferðarmiðstöðinni, Vatnsmýrarvegut 10 (☎91/22300). Day trips from Reykjavík, Akureyri and Mývatn, which include crossing the interior over Sprengisandur or Kjölur (£68 each), a trip to Snæfellsnes, and a three-day jaunt to Kverkfjöll.

Ferðaskrifstofa Farfugla, Laufásvegur 41 (☎91/24950). Travel bureau of the Icelandic YHA, offering walking-based trips to remote spots with full board accommodation in their hostels. Prices are around £250 for a five-day "Highland Special" to over £700 for a five-day bird-watching tour of Snæfellsnes and Látrabjarg.

Ferðafélag Íslands, Öldugata 3 (☎91/19533). This is the Iceland Touring Club, who arrange extended hiking tours during the summer, often through uninhabited areas using their own FÍ huts for accommodation.

Guðmundur Jónasson Travel Bureau, Borgartún 34 (☎91/83222). Well-organised camping-based tours of the most scenic regions, inclusive of food and tent.

Saga Travel, Suðurgata 7 (☎91/624040). Mainstream and special-interest tours, including canoeing, fishing and glacier hiking.

Sagaland Travel, Laufásvegur 2 (☎91/27144). Interesting trips to some of the lesser known regions, and some good horse-riding tours.

Samvinn-travel, Austurstræti 12 (☎91/691010). Besides tours of the main areas, has a good range of specialist trips covering geology, flora and fauna, and even week-long "winter survival" exercises.

Útivist, Grófin 1 (☎91/14606 & 23732). Year-round hiking tours through many parts of the country on which you provide your own food and tent. Tickets must be bought at least a day in advance.

Utsýn Travel, Austurstræti 17 (☎91/26611 & 23638). Walking and cross-country skiing, single days and weekends.

remoter regions. Wherever you decide to go, you should book as early as possible, preferably before leaving home. Failing that, all Reykjavík travel agents can arrange trips. See the box for details of what's possible.

■ Independent travel through the Interior

Even by Icelandic standards, **independent travel through the interior** is a hair-raising undertaking, and should only be embarked upon with thorough planning and expert advice. Tracks are at best rough and marked only by stakes; at worst they're no more than the tyre-tracks of previous travellers. Only four-wheel-drive vehicles are able to withstand the buffeting and cross the numerous, dangerous, unbridged rivers. Take a good map, compass, full sets of tools and spares, extra warm clothing and food for a long unplanned stay; spare fuel is also essential – there is none in the interior and the state of the tracks makes consumption high. To deviate from the tracks is both stupid and illegal: it not only upsets the delicate ecological balance of the desert but can also mean a very long – and possibly fatal – wait if you break down or get stranded.

Remember, too, that the interior is **closed** (ie the entry roads are sealed-off, and there's strictly no admittance) for much of the year. On average it's only open for six weeks in the latter half of the summer.

Sleeping

Despite the new high-rise hotels which are springing up in Reykjavík, accommodation is far from abundant throughout Iceland, and what little there is, isn't cheap. If you're simply planning to take a tent to a quiet spot and stay there, you'll have no problems. More realistically, though, the crowds which descend on the established sights during the summer mean you must reserve a place to stay in the busy regions as early as possible. Hotels are extremely expensive, but guesthouses and the Edda hotels are dependable, affordable alternatives. Further down the budgetary scale are the youth hostels and the cleverly-engineered "sbacc" arrangement, which basically throws up any available space to impecunious, sleeping-bag carrying visitors.

■ Hotels, guesthouses and "Edda" hotels

Unless you work for a multinational conglomerate or are on a stopover deal (see "Getting There"), **hotels** (hótels) are likely to be way beyond your budget. Price start at 4000–5000kr for a double (a little less for a single), and rooms provide all the creature comforts you'd expect: private bathroom, colour TV, in-room phone, buffet breakfast and doting service. If you can afford it, a hotel room can be a welcoming place to return to after a hard day's hiking, though outside Reykjavík and Akureyri there's not much choice: most towns that have a hotel have just the one – and it's likely to be fully booked throughout the summer.

Cheaper than hotels, and often just as good, if lacking the luxuries, are **guesthouses** (*gestahús*) – family houses providing bed and breakfast-type accommodation for around 3000kr for a double, though these too are fairly scarce outside of the larger settlements, where you'll need to look for an **Edda hotel**. Similarly-priced, these often utilise the buildings of a state-run boarding school, which are otherwise unused throughout the summer.

■ Youth hostels and "*sbacc*"

At 900kr per person for members, 1250kr for others, and often with cooking facilities, **youth hostels** (*farfuglaheimilli*) are a good, inexpensive option, enabling you to cut costs on both sleeping and eating. The drawback is that there are only fifteen hostels in the whole country, and those on the Ring Road, particularly in the bigger towns, rarely have spare room if you turn up on spec during the summer. Nobody will be turned away and alternatives (often, on the coast, the local seamans' hostel) are suggested and arranged on the spot. But to be sure of a bed always phone ahead. Hostels off the Ring Road are seldom full, but it's still a good idea to check the situation before setting out. Unlike other Scandinavian hostels, you can use your own sleeping bag everywhere except at the old hostel in Reykjavík, which permits only sheet sleeping bags.

Where there are no youth hostels (and even in some places where there are), the staple budget option is **sleeping bag accommodation** (*svefn-poka gisting*) or "*sbacc*", provided by many Edda hotels, some guesthouses and even the odd hotel and community centre. Under this system, people can use their own sleeping bags on what might be anything from a large shared floor (mattresses usually provided) to a spartan private room. Reckon on paying 700–900kr per night.

■ Camping and the FÍ huts

Campsites (*Tjaldstvæði*) are the least costly option of all. Charges, per person and per tent, work out at about 600kr for two people sharing. Facilities are few, however, and apart from the sites at Reykjavík, Akureyri and Skaftafell National Park, there's not much more than a patch of grass and basic form of toilet. You can **camp rough** on any unfenced land out of sight of a settlement for free, and farmers will generally allow camping on their land if you ask first.

Ferðafélag Íslands, the Iceland Touring Club, have a number of **FÍ huts** (*FÍ kofi*) in the interior and other remote spots, for prices broadly akin to youth hostels. Most have water and mattresses, but you should bring your own cooking gear, Bear in mind that, although they can be used by anyone, members of the club have priority. Always check on a hut's existence and availability before setting off: some of those marked on maps may subsequently have closed. The nearest hotel, garage or shop should have up-to-date information; otherwise phone *Ferðafélag Íslands* direct.

Finally, if you're **completely stuck**, simply knock on the door of the nearest farmhouse: you'll usually be welcomed with open arms, given a bed and fed as well. Just be sure to offer a reasonable sum in return – say 500–700kr.

Food and Drink

Food and drink are wickedly expensive in Iceland, and even self-catering you can expect to spend a small fortune. That said, Icelandic cuisine – and for that matter, booze – features much that's unique, and worth sampling when you get the chance.

■ Food

If you are on a tight budget, bringing food from home can save a lot of money, though remember dairy products and uncooked meats are not allowed into the country, and there's a 10kg weight limit on imported food. Otherwise, stock up whenever you can at the major **supermarket** chains, *Hagkaup* and *Kaupfélagið*, which can be found in the main towns; elsewhere shops are both scarce and (even more) expensive. The only bargain on the shelves is the tasty *skyr*, a kind of thick yoghurt that comes in plain (25kr) and fruit-flavoured (40kr) varieties.

The delights of **Icelandic cuisine** include singed sheep heads, ram's testicles cooked in whey, and blood sausages (lamb's blood and internal organs mixed with flour and wrapped up in the animal's stomach lining). Fortunately perhaps, these tend to be festive specialities rather than staples, and more common Icelandic dishes consist of simple but carefully cooked

GLOSSARY OF ICELANDIC FOOD AND DRINK TERMS

Basics

Brauð	Bread	*Kaka*	Cake	*Samloka*	Sandwich
Deig	Pastry	*Kex*	Biscuits	*Súpa*	Soup
Hrísgrjón	Rice	*Mjólk*	Milk	*Sykur*	Sugar
Ís	Ice cream	*Pæ*	Pie	*Sælgæti*	Sweets
Kaffi	Coffee	*Ostur*	Cheese	*Te*	Tea

Meat (*Kjö*)

Kjúklingur	Chicken	*Skinka*	Ham	*Svínakjöts*	Pork
Nautavöðvi	Fillet of beef	*Steik*	Steak		

Fish (*Fiskur*)

Áll	Eel	*Lax*	Salmon	*Silungur*	Trout
Gedda	Pike	*Makríll*	Mackerel	*Þorskur*	Cod
Humar	Lobster	*Rækjur*	Shrimps	*Túnfiskur*	Tuna
Krydsíld	Pickled herring	*Sardínur*	Sardines	*Ýsa*	Haddock
		Síld	Herring		

Vegetables (*Grænmeti*)

Agúrka	Cucumber	*Kál*	Cabbage	*Spínet*	Spinach
Baunir	Beans	*Kartöflur*	Potatoes	*Spænskur*	Green pepper
Grænmeti baunir	Peas	*Laukur*	Onions		
		Maísstöng	Corn on the cob	*Sveppir*	Mushrooms
Gulrætur	Carrot			*Tómatur*	Tomatoes

Fruit (*Avöstur*)

Appelsína	Orange	*Greipaldin*	Grapefruit	*Plómur*	Plums
Aprikósa	Apricot	*Jarðarber*	Strawberries	*Rabarbari*	Rhubarb
Banani	Banana	*Kirsuber*	Cherries	*Sítróna*	Lemon
Epli	Apple	*Melóna*	Melon	*Vínber*	Grapes
Ferskja	Peach				

Drink

Appelsínusafi	Orange juice	*Greipaldinsafi*	Grapefruit juice	*Vatn*	Water
Bjór	Beer	*Límonaði*	Lemonade	*Vín*	Wine

lamb, or deliciously fresh cod, haddock or skate. **Vegetarians** who don't eat fish are in for a lean time, and may find themselves forced to become carnivores for the duration of their stay. You can eat most cheaply – 500–700kr a dish – in a **café** or cafeteria (*kaffitería*), usually open from morning until the early evening. These, along with **snackbars**, may also serve slices of pizza (about 300kr), burgers (450kr), and hot-dogs (150kr). To eat dinner out, you'll need a **restaurant** (*veitingastaður*) and at least 1000kr for a couple of courses. Outside Reykjavík and Akureyri, however, restaurants are quite rare, often only found in hotels. Indeed, one benefit of spending the extra money on a hotel or guesthouse is the inclusive – and usually substantial – **breakfast**, a meal surprisingly hard to find anywhere else.

■ **Drink**

Coffee costs around 100kr per cup, and is always fresh and served in all eateries. It's more widely drunk than the similarly-priced **tea**; if you ask for the latter make sure the water is boiling before it's added to the teabag. Coffee refills are often free; ask to be sure.

Iceland's **alcohol** laws are slowly catching up with the rest of the world. To much rejoicing, beer became legal on March 1, 1989, and is now available, along with spirits and wines, after 6pm at most restaurants and cafés – many of which mutate into bars – and at nightclubs. The bad news is the cost: 250kr for half a pint of beer, the same for a shot of spirits or a glass of wine. It's cheaper to buy booze from one of the state-run *ÁTVR* outlets, although these are only found in the main towns, or on arrival at Keflavík airport where the **duty-free shop** is open to both outgoing and incoming passengers (though there are plans to restrict it to departing passengers). This sells booze four times as cheap as inside the country.

Champion among the hard stuff is *Brennivín*, an Icelandic akvavit-type spirit which tastes like a pleasant blend of pernod and vodka but is enormously potent and takes effect rapidly. It's nicknamed "black death", partly for the colour of the bottle-label, and partly for the lethal hangover just a couple of measures can induce. A litre bottle at the airport costs about 450kr. Avoid bottles actually labelled "Black Death" – which are similar to the genuine article but five times as expensive.

You may be lucky enough to find a **Sveiteball**, a kind of country dance held in rural community halls every month or two during the winter and less often in summer. At these, people bring their own drink and gyrate to a live combo. The lack of rival attractions means everyone in the area turns up to have a good time and get drunk.

Work

Though once plentiful, work for foreigners in Iceland is nowadays virtually impossible to find. What's more, to work legally you should have an offer of a job before arriving in the country.

You can try asking your nearest Icelandic embassy for a list of employers who take on foreigners – though you'll most likely be told that none are looking for new staff – but steer clear of the unscrupulous employment-finding agencies in the UK who promise jobs. All they provide you with (for a fee) is an out-of-date list of Icelandic employers, many of whom barely have enough work for themselves. The only possibility, really, is to know somebody in Iceland who can find you a job by word of mouth. Once you do have a job, it's fairly easy to switch to another – most work is seasonal anyway – and move around different parts of the country.

The most lucrative form of work is on a **fishing boat**, but this is hard, often dangerous, and the vessels might be at sea for several days at a time. Working in a **fish factory** is less arduous but boring, and only a decent earner with the overtime which follows a good catch. **Hospital** work pays poorly but the fixed eight-hour day does leave time to explore the country. There is also sometimes work on **farms**, and in the nurseries of the southwest which produce fruit and vegetables.

Because rent and food costs are high it's a considerable advantage to get **accommodation** and **meals** included in your job. This is no problem on a farm or nursery, where you usually get a room in the house and eat with the family. People working in fish factories sometimes live in flats which are owned by the firm, often sharing with another person.

Geology

Geologically, Iceland is a young and volatile country. Lying on the North Atlantic Rift, at the margin of the European and American continental plates, it is actually being pulled apart by both continents, with the result that there's a volcanic zone crossing the country from the north central region to the south and west. Along this the earth's crust is very thin, and magma is able to force its way through at the weakest points, emerging on the surface as a volcanic eruption or, less violently, a lava flow, and bringing with it such phenomena as hot springs, geysers, fumaroles and solfataras.

■ Volcanoes

Of three kinds of volcano found in Iceland, the only completely extinct ones are **Shield Volcanoes**, formed when a very fluid lava emerges from a vent and flows in all directions. The resulting mountains are accumulations of lava from a succession of eruptions, tending to have a near-circular ground plan and a very shallow slope with a central crater. Examples are Skjaldbreiður, northeast of Þingvallavatn and Trölladyngja, north of Vatnjökull. **Fissure Volcanoes**, on the other hand, are sometimes still active. These occur where a fissure, which may be many kilometres long, opens and lava issues from points along it. Ash cones may form at the points of issue or the lava may flow clear and form a lavafield. An example is Laki, southwest of Vatnajökull.

The third kind of volcano, **Ash Volcanoes**, are formed when ash and larger particles are blown out of a vent and accumulate around it to form a cone. An example is Hverfjall at Mývatn. Ash can also be blown by wind across the surrounding lands and over great distances. An example is the layer of pumice dust on a large area of Ódáðahraun due to an eruption of this type at Askja.

■ Lavafields

There are two main types of lavafield, sometimes found together: **Apalhraun** is irregular blocks of sharp, spikey lava piled into thicknesses of several metres, caused by molten lava containing a high level of gas; **Helluhraun** comes in large and often smooth slabs but sometimes with rope-like or wave-like patterns on the surface. The slabs tend to lie at angles, with gaps and fissures between them.

Additionally, **volcanic ash** covers large areas, shattered by frost into small particles, creating wide deserts of grey gravel and sand.

■ Related phenomena

Pseudo Craters These have never produced lava themselves but were formed by hot lava flowing over wet ground causing the water to boil and come up through the lava as steam. The craters form around the escape holes. There are fine collections at Kirkjubæjarklaustur, and Skútustaðir at the southern end of Mývatn.

Fumeroles and Solfataras Found in high temperature zones, these occur when steam and gases escape through vents from the magma below the surface, sometimes at high pressure and with a lot of noise. Solfataras emit sulphurous gases, and deposits of sulphur – which are sometimes mined – accumulate around them in small cones. An example is Námaskar ð, east of Mývatn.

Hot Springs Concentrated mainly in volcanic areas, these are the result of water heated by contact with a hot lava mass below the ground. In some instances the water originates underground, in others it is rain or meltwater which percolates down through porous rocks on the surface. The temperature and rate of delivery can fluctuate wildly.

Geysers Hot springs which erupt periodically, sending jets of hot water into the air. The activity is thought to be the result of water under pressure being heated to over boiling point below the ground, but which, due to an obstruction of some kind or the weight of water above it, can only escape when the pressure becomes great enough for a passage to the surface to be forced.

■ Glaciers

Of Iceland's extant **glaciers**, Vatnajökull is the biggest, responsible for the wide sands along the southeastern coast, formed by the rocks torn from the mountain sides as the ice flows down the valley. These sands are carried by sea currents along the coast and form sand spits and lagoons. A prime example of these is off Höfn.

The glaciers are also the source of the great glacial rivers, or *jökulsa*, whose powerful waterfalls have carved deep gorges – such as those below Gullfoss, Dettifoss and Ásbyrgi. The flow of meltwater is highest during July and August, and the water is clouded due to dissolved minerals and particles of debris, which are carried and deposited at the river deltas as sand flats.

Occasionally glaciers can threaten the lowlands. An eruption under the ice or the sudden draining of a lake on the glacier will cause a *jökulhlaup* (glacier burst), causing water, ice and rock to slide at great speed onto the land below.

Directory

BRING . . . Food and film – both very expensive in Iceland.

CONTRACEPTIVES Condoms (*verja* or *smokkur*) can be bought from chemists. The Pill is available from chemists on prescription.

FISHING EQUIPMENT If you bring your own it has to be disinfected within seven days of arrival.

GAY LIFE Homosexual acts are legal in Iceland if the partners are over 18, but unlike the other Scandinavian countries, social acceptance is low and even in Reykjavík most gays have yet to come out. Indeed, openly gay adults have lost their jobs and sometimes have to relocate because of pressure from neighbours. Some Icelandic gays even move to other Nordic countries where they can enjoy a more relaxed lifestyle. There are a couple of gay bars in the capital, and a help organisation which it's worth contacting for details on the scene: *Samtokin·78*, Postbox 4166, 124 Reykjavík 4 (☎91/28539).

Another possible source of information is the *Leather and Motorbike Club*, MSC Iceland, Postbox 5521, 125 Reykjavík (☎91/62128).

LEAVING Buses leave *Hotel Loftleiðir* for Keflavik airport two hours before each flight.

POLICE AND THIEVES There is very little crime in Iceland, and what there is tends to be either company fraud or drunken driving. Police stations in the smaller communities are likely to be closed at evenings and weekends. Even the two Icelandic prisons let their inmates out for public holidays.

PUBLIC HOLIDAYS Most shops and museums are closed all day on January 1, Maundy Thursday in early April, Good Friday and Easter Monday, the first day of summer in late-ish April, May 1 (Labour Day), May 16 (Ascension Day), Whit Monday, June 17 (National Day), August 5 (shop and office workers' holiday), December 25, 26 and 31.

SHOPPING Shop hours are Mon–Thurs 9am–6pm, Fri 9am–7 or 8pm, Sat 9–11am or noon. These times apply to the larger shops in the main towns; shops in smaller communities keep shorter hours.

SWIMMING A national preoccupation. Most towns have geothermally heated baths (*sundlaug*) which cost about 50kr to use, and there are numerous naturally warm springs that are delightful for swimming. If you see no swimmers in one, take care to test the temperature – the water can sometimes be scalding.

WOOLLY JUMPERS The very warm but light Icelandic woollen jumpers can be bought in most towns for £35–40. The wool to knit your own, bought from a non-tourist shop, costs about £12.

History

Icelandic history has been recorded almost from its beginning. The nation's first historian, Ari Þorgilsson (1067–1148), was active within two centuries of the Settlement and learnt much of events from that time to his own through individual family histories. These he recorded in the *Íslendingabók* (Book of the Icelanders). Ari's immediate successor Snorri Sturluson (1178–1241), and many others, continued recording in this way. The result is a uniquely comprehensive history of the country and its people from the earliest days.

■ The Settlement

AD 860 is generally given as the date of Iceland's accidental discovery by two explorers: Nadod, a Swede, and later Garðar Svarsson, a Norwegian. Each was probably blown to Iceland by chance when sailing between Scandinavia and the western Nordic colonies in the British Isles. Yet they were not the first to set foot on the island: previously a few Irish hermit monks had arrived, seeking to escape worldly temptations. When exactly they came and where they went after the Scandinavians arrived remains a mystery, but some of the places they lived are recognisable by the element "pap" (meaning "father", as in priest) in the name.

About five years after Garðar's discovery, **Hrafn ("Raven") Flóki** became the first to spend a winter in the country. He and his household failed to store sufficient food for the bad weather and reached the brink of starvation. Flóki climbed a high mountain to look for signs of a thaw but could see only ice in all directions. This, it's said, is how the country got its name.

The first successful settler was the Norwegian **Ingólfur Arnarson**, who landed around 870 on the south coast at the present Ingólfshofði. As his ship approached, Ingólfur threw his seat pillars (an emblem of his high office) into the sea intending to settle – with the gods' blessing – wherever they were washed up. The pillars were eventually found at what's now Reykjavík and he made his home there in 874.

A stream of Norwegians followed in Ingólfur's wake, and they were delighted with the country. The land had never been grazed and the rivers and lakes teemed with fish. The *Landnamabók* (Book of Settlements) records more than 400 chieftains who arrived during this time, taking land for themselves and their followers. The first settlers were predominantly wealthy landlords driven to Iceland by the chronic shortage of land and political unrest in mainland Scandinavia; members of the Norwegian aristocracy preferred to emigrate rather than concede the power they wielded in their own neighbourhoods. They went to the British Isles as well as Iceland, sometimes picking up Celtic spouses, servants and slaves on the way. This is the root of the strong Celtic element in modern Icelanders.

Yet emigration from Norway to Iceland was made difficult. Would-be settlers faced stiff taxes on leaving and all kinds of restrictions when returning to Norway to trade. It was this which intensified opposition to establishing a monarchy in the new land and instead a commonwealth was formed – something unique in Europe during the Middle Ages. Despite this assertion of independence, there was a natural tendency to look for guidance from Norway in some matters, particularly in the legal sphere. **Úlfljótur** was sent to Norway to examine local governments and formulate a set of laws tailored to Iceland's needs. This led to the establishment of the **Alþing** – a kind of National Assembly held over two weeks each summer – in 930, with a set of laws based on the Gulaþing of southern Norway.

■ The Commonwealth: 930–1262

The early years of the Icelandic Commonwealth saw a flourishing of both material and intellectual life. The first of three distinct periods was the **Saga Age** (930–1030), so-called because of the Sagas, written much later, that detailed events of this period. During these years, the single most important event was the **conversion** of the Icelanders to Christianity. Many Icelanders travelling abroad had encountered Christianity and some had been baptised, though often as a matter of expediency rather than belief. King Olaf Tryggvason of Norway sent missionaries who were given aid by Icelandic Christians. The Alþing of 1000 was disrupted by Christians refusing to be bound by pagan laws, and it became clear that if national unity was to be preserved the entire population should have a common religion. The decision as to which creed should prevail rested with **Þorgeir of Ljósavatn**, a pagan who held the respect of both sides. The story goes that Þorgeir heard the respective arguments and retired to his bed for a day to ponder. He finally announced that the country would become Christian but that pagan worship would be allowed in private. His motivation for this decision is not clear, but fear of intervention from Norway if Christianity had been rejected may have been a strong factor.

Icelanders began westward exploration and in 986 Greenland was colonised by a group led by **Eirik Þorvaldson ("the Red")**. In 1000 his son, **Leif Eiriksson ("the Lucky")**, reached the North American coast, probably the present Labrador, calling it Vinland. An attempt at colonisation in Vinland led by Þorfinn Karlsefni in 1007 failed, but two colonies established on Greenland lasted until 1492, defeated eventually by the irregularity of trading ships from the east and worsening climatic conditions which drove the native inhabitants southwards, threatening the Scandinavian settlements. Icelanders traded with Norway and other countries along the Atlantic east coast and around the Mediterranean, and some joined Viking expeditions.

Politically and socially, the main event of the year was the Alþing. It was here that nationally important issues were discussed and disputes too complicated for the local courts were settled. Business and marriage deals were struck and the occasion served an important social function simply by bringing many people from around the country together. The chief officer at the Alþing was the **Lögsögumaður** (Law Speaker). Elected for a three-year term, he was expected to memorise and recite from the *Lögberg*, or Law Rock, to the assembly at Þingvellir, a different third of the laws each year. His was the final word in disputed points of law, although there was no executive body to enforce a settlement.

Many chieftains had established themselves as **goðar**. Initially heathen priests, they became the rough equivalent of modern-day solicitors, wielding secular as well as religious power. Everyone in the country gave allegiance to a *goði* in return for support and protection. This often took the form of aiding a successful litigant by ensuring the decision of the Alþing was adhered to, or, sometimes, helping resist it if a case had been lost. Powerful *goðar* were sometimes given gifts and even subtle bribes in return for their services. The country was divided into four sections, each with three or four courts presided over by local *goðar*. Sentences of the court ranged from a fine, paid to the injured party, to outlawry. If the victim of a crime thought that

only the death of his rival could satisfy his honour he might bypass the legal system and take action himself. This course often led to long and bitter feuds which later formed the basis of many of the Sagas.

The next period, known as the **Age of Peace** (1030–1200), saw these feuds lessen as laws became more firmly established. Immigration fell to a trickle and Iceland enjoyed a period of peace and prosperity, with an economy based on subsistence farming. Sheep and cattle were the prime forms of wealth while hay and a few cereals were the main agricultural products. Supplementing these were fishing, fowling and beachcombing. A landowner's right to flotsam on his particular stretch of shoreline was jealously guarded — driftwood was valuable due to the absence of native timber, and a stranded whale was a windfall of meat, oils and other products. Most household implements were made of wood, leather, metal or stone. Skins and woollens were the main exports. In return came finer textiles, foodstuffs and precious metals.

The adoption of Christianity had in turn stimulated learning and cultural life. Schools were established at **Oddi**, and in conjunction with the cathedrals at **Skálholt** and **Hólar**. Literacy spread and in 1117 the laws were written down. This was the beginning of the literary tradition which in the next century was to produce the Sagas, and the Eddaic and Skaldic poems.

The late twelfth century had seen a gradual shift in the balance of power between the *goðar*. Originally they were roughly equal, but by 1200 power had become concentrated in the hands of a few *goðar* whose families vied with each other for overall control. One of these families was the Sturlungs, the descendants of Sturla of Hvammur, and they gave their name to the period, the **Sturlung Age** (1200–1262). The political structure of the Commonwealth failed to provide curbs on the excesses of opposing factions. The rule of law collapsed and the rights of individuals were ignored as private armies roamed the country, seizing property and murdering anyone who attempted to stop them.

King Hákon of Norway took advantage of the economic and political instability and manipulated each side in turn, aiming to take eventual control of the country. By 1262 most of the heads of the leading families were dead. With the nation in turmoil, Icelanders brought the Commonwealth to an end, swearing allegiance to the Norwegian king in the hope that co-operation between the two countries would restore stability.

The decline: 1262–1550

From being a thriving and economically stable country, Iceland became a neglected backwater under a distant and largely indifferent government. Any promises of co-operation made by Norway turned out to be a front for domination. A new legal code (*Jónsbók*) was introduced in 1281, conferring absolute power on the Norwegian king and eroding the powers of the Alþing. The king was free to extract whatever level of taxes he liked from the increasingly impoverished population, and foreign officials took over the key ecclesiastical and secular posts. As if to presage the downturn, the Katla volcano erupted – the first in a succession of natural disasters which were to decimate the people and livestock through · succeeding centuries.

In 1380, the uniting of the Norwegian and Danish Crowns further isolated Iceland from its rulers. Trade with countries other than Norway and Denmark was forbidden despite a desperate need for supplies. Some non-Scandinavian traders did defy the ban and came to Iceland, but so too did foreign fisherman – most notably the British – and deprived the Icelanders still more.

Danish domination: 1550–1800

The growth of Danish dominance over Iceland (after Norway had become subject to Denmark) began with the imposition of the **Reformation**, in 1541 in the south and 1551 in the north. The slowness of the spread of the Reformation across the country was due to the vigorous opposition put up by **Jón Arason**, the last Catholic bishop of Hólar. He, with his sons and followers, almost succeeded in throwing the Danes out of Iceland altogether. But Arason was eventually declared an outlaw, captured, and taken to Skálholt where he and his son, Björk, were executed in 1550.

Danish power increased through seizure of Church property and that of any person opposing the new doctrine. Tenants were forced to provide labour and other services to the Crown without payment or compensation. New laws were created and capital punishment introduced for "crimes" such as heresy and adultery.

In 1602 the **Danish Trade Monopoly** was introduced. Under the terms of the Monopoly,

trading rights with Iceland were leased to a few shipping companies in Copenhagen. The Monopoly, combined with a spate of pirate attacks and the continuing natural disasters (especially the eruption of Laki in 1783), left the Icelandic people in a state of absolute poverty. But the greatest humiliation of all was suffered in 1800, when the Alþing was dissolved.

Towards independence: 1800–1944

The appalling standard of living endured under the Danes encouraged the **growth of nationalism**, which took much inspiration from the Romantic movement flourishing in Icelandic art. Many worked towards the goal of Icelandic independence, most notably **Jón Sigurðsson** (1811–1879), who is regarded as "the father of the Icelandic nation". Much of his time was spent in Copenhagen, having originally moved there as a student, agitating the Danish government into implementing reforms for Iceland. Free trade was restored in 1854 and Sigurðsson helped generate and organise business for Icelanders in Copenhagen.

The Alþing regained its powers as a consultative body in 1843 and a constitution was granted in 1874, making Iceland self-governing in domestic affairs. The **Act of Union**, passed in 1918, made Iceland a sovereign state under the Danish Crown. The Act was open for reconsideration at any time after 1940, but by then Denmark was occupied by the Nazis and the Alþing had assumed the duties normally effected by the monarch, declaring its intention to dissolve the Act of Union at the end of the war. The 133rd anniversary of Jón Sigurðsson's birth, June 17, 1944, was the day chosen to declare unilateral independence and officially proclaim the **Republic of Iceland** in a ceremony at Þingvellir.

Modern Iceland

In 1940 British troops had arrived in Iceland, uninvited but barely opposed, to prevent the Nazis gaining a strategic stronghold in the North Atlantic. In 1941 the British force left and was replaced by an American one. The foreign troops were stationed throughout the country, and their need for improved communications led to a sudden increase in employment for Icelanders through the construction of roads and airports, and in the provision of services. While the foreign governments agreed to employ Icelandic workers on rates of pay equal to those paid by Icelandic employers, the speed at which the work had to be carried out resulted in abundant and highly lucrative overtime being available. Iceland enjoyed a rapid economic boom and higher standards of living than ever before.

The Cold War and the US base

In 1946, after the war ended, the USA requested permission to keep three military bases in Iceland for 99 years. This was refused by the Alþing but after much heated debate it was agreed that they could use Keflavík airport as a staging post for transport aircraft, then being used for the Allied forces in Germany. In 1949 Iceland became one of the founder members of NATO, largely through American lobbying of the Icelandic parliament, overwhelming the general hostility toward such a move felt among Icelanders. As a condition of joining it was stated that under no circumstances were military forces to be based in Iceland during peacetime. In May 1951 a secret decision taken by the government allowed **US forces to be based at Keflavík**. This was only revealed to the Alþing in the autumn. The reason given was that Iceland was unable to defend itself and, as a consequence, peace-loving neighbours might be put at risk – possibly through a Soviet invasion of Iceland which would give their navy free access to the North Atlantic and a bridgehead to the USA.

The USA at this time was engaged in the Korean War and had conducted a scare campaign among Icelandic officials along classic Cold War propaganda lines – "Russian forces in Korea today, Russian forces in Iceland tomorrow". Following the end of the Korean War, the American forces remained in place.

Iceland's military importance to the USA continued through the Cold War: should the Soviet Navy launch an attack on the USA from its base on the Kola peninsula, went the thinking, its fleet would have to pass close to Iceland in doing so. In later years, Iceland became a part of the American "winnable nuclear war" strategy. After first-strike Cruise and Pershing missiles from Western Europe had wiped out Soviet land-based long-range weapons, the only remaining threat to the USA would be the Soviet submarines armed with sea-launched nuclear weapons operating in the North Atlantic. These could be tracked and destroyed from Keflavík. In 1979 Iceland became the only base outside the USA for AWACS (Airborne Warning And Control Systems) aircraft,

capable of monitoring ship and aeroplane movements over a vast area, and also able to function as a complete airborne command post – necessary if the Keflavík base was destroyed.

There has been frequent antagonism – ranging from arguments to fist-fights – between Icelanders and the personnel stationed at Keflavík, which has led to servicemen being restricted to just one evening per week away from the base. Because of its climate and lack of facilites Iceland is an extremely unpopular posting for the American services.

The Postwar Economy

Despite left-wing agitation against the continued existence of the NATO base, it's unlikely to be removed. This is largely because of the financial boost it gives to the **Icelandic economy**, constituting one of the few stable sources of revenue. The other is fishing. In a good year, the highly unpredictable fishing catch can account for ninety percent of the national income (most of the catch is made into fish oil or fish meal in the Icelandic factories which are the country's biggest employers). The importance of fishing led to the spate of so-called **Cod Wars** with Britain – and, to a lesser extent, West Germany. These disputes stemmed from an agreement between Denmark and Britain in 1901 which reduced Icelandic territorial fishing rights to within 6km of the coast, enabling the British fleets to fish in Icelandic fjords and bays. Since independence, the limits have been increased on several occasions. An extension to 93km during 1972 was eventually accepted by the British after a minor battle between two opposing skippers, but in 1975 a further extension to 370km led to a series of dangerous skirmishes between Icelandic gunboats and a British Navy frigate. The temporary agreement which resulted is still in force, and no British boat has fished within the limit since 1976.

Coal and peat had been the chief fuels through the early twentieth century, but reserves of both were exhausted by the late 1960s. Oil was increasingly in use until the steep price rise in 1973 plunged the Icelandic economy into crisis, and led to the instigation of a massive programme to harness the country's natural resources through the building of **hydroelectric power stations** and the utilisation of **geothermal energy**. One offshoot of this project has been an ambitious scheme to export power to the

UK, using an undersea cable. While agreed in principle, the technical details are still being examined. Should it prove workable, the undertaking is expected to provide a multi-million pound injection into the economy.

Natural resources have also been at the root of the country's fastest-growing industry – **tourism**. The national carrier *Icelandair* enjoys a near-monopoly on passenger flights into the country and has run huge advertising campaigns for its stopovers between Europe and the USA, while the hosting of the Reagan-Gorbachev summit in 1986 was a gigantic publicity bonanza for the country. Early the following year, the decrepit Keflavík air terminal was replaced by a large modern tourist complex – although the first view of Iceland for fresh arrivals is still a fleet of American military aircraft and hardware. There have been numerous new developments in Reykjavík over the last few years, including the siting of a branch of the American hotel chain, *Holiday Inn*, and an American-style shopping mall which includes the US-owned *Hard Rock Café*. At around the same time the state monopoly of broadcasting was ended, allowing a commercial television channel and a number of radio stations whose mass-market programming came to be regarded, by some, as an embrace of western consumer culture that in time would swamp all vestiges of Iceland's heritage.

The Political Present

Some years ago, dissatisfaction with modern Icelandic society began finding expression in the **Ásatrú**, a heathen sect reviving the pagan religion of the pre-Christian era. In 1972 it became officially recognised by the Icelandic government, under a law allowing complete religious freedom. The recognition empowered its leader, Sveinbjörn Beinteinsson, a well-known poet and *kvæðamaður* (a performer of epic verses in traditional style) to perform marriages, bury the dead and baptise children. A small amount of finance comes from the Church Fee, a sum paid by every Icelander to the denomination of their choice (or to the University if they don't have a religion). Ásatrú has several hundred paid-up members and a growing number of sympathisers.

Regular **domestic politics** reflect concern for the delicate state of the economy and the need to keep inflation to manageable levels: a rate of thirteen percent achieved in the mid-eighties was considered a success, the average over the previous ten years having been fifty percent. By western European standards all of Iceland's leading political parties are centrist or centre-right. In recent decades, each government had been a four-party coalition, until the 1987 election returned a tripartite government composed of the Independent, Progressive and Social Democratic parties. The new government pledged a series of reviews with the intention of reducing "unnecessary" expenditure.

In September 1988, after an economic downturn and subsequent rise in inflation, largely brought about by the slump in the world seafood market, Prime Minister Þorstein Pálsson ended the eighteen-month old government. After much wrangling, a new left-of-centre coalition government came into being, led by the leader of the centrist Progressive Party, Steingrímur Hermannsson, whose major concession to the left was to bring a few members of the People's Alliance into office.

The most radical force in Icelandic politics today is the dramatically successful **Women's Alliance**. After organising a one-day women's strike in 1975 which had great impact, as did a subsequent one exactly ten years later, they have gathered much support campaigning from a broadly Green and feminist-orientated platform. In the 1983 election the Women's Alliance won three parliamentary seats, and it doubled this figure four years later. Recent opinion polls suggest their popularity is growing quickly as more Icelanders – many having to take on two jobs just to pay their bills – become disillusioned with the apparent failure of traditional forms of government. Although offered a place in the new coalition, the Women's Alliance turned it down on the grounds that they, at present, are more effective in opposition. Their detractors used this to fuel their case that the Women's Alliance are idealists who couldn't stand the compromises necessary to govern. If current trends continue, the strength of this argument may soon be put to the test.

A BRIEF GUIDE TO ICELANDIC

Aided by a strong campaign for linguistic purity, Icelandic has changed little since the Settlement, making for an oddly archaic language when you examine it.

Modern inventions have been given names from existing Icelandic words: "computer" and "telephone" are *tolva* ("number prophetess") and *sími* ("the long thread") respectively, and even the late-opening food shop in Reykjavík is called *Kveld-úlfur* ("night-wolf"). Spoken Icelandic differs markedly from other Scandinavian tongues (with the exception of Faroese) although knowledge of another Scandinavian language is useful. Also, English is widely spoken and understood. Icelandic phrase books are hard to come by, and any Icelandic-English dictionary you come across will be imported from Iceland. It's far cheaper to buy both inside the country.

PRONUNCIATION

The Icelandic **alphabet** is as the English with the addition of ð, þ, æ, and ö. The letters a, e, i, o, u, and y may be accented.

þ (capital Þ)	like the "th" in "thin"		ll	as "dl" somewhere between the Welsh "ll" and the "tl" in "cutlery"
ð (capital Ð)	like the "th" in "that"			
a	as in "**ba**th"		o	as in "h**o**t"
á	as the ow in "n**ow**"		ó	as in "t**oe**"
e	as in "**e**lephant"		ö	as in "t**ur**n"
é	as in "y**e**t"		u	as in "t**ur**n"
hv	the "h" is sounded like a "k", the "v" more like a "u"		ú	as in "s**oo**n"
i	as in "h**i**t"		y	like the "i" in "h**i**t"
í	like the e in "**e**ach"		ý	like the e in "**e**ach"
j	as the "y" in **y**et		æ	as in "eye"

BASICS

Do you speak English ?	*Talarðu ensku ?*		Good morning/good afternoon	*goðan daginn*
Yes	*já*			
No	*nei*		Good evening	*gott kvöld*
I understand	*ég skil*		Good night	*goða nótt*
I don't understand	*ég skil ekki*		Today	*í dag*
Please	*viltu gera svo vel að*		Yesterday	*í gar*
Thank you	*takk*		Tomorrow	*á morgun*
Excuse me	*afsakið*		In the morning	*í fyrramálið*
Hello	*halló*		In the afternoon	*eftir hádegi*
Goodbye	*bless*		In the evening	*í kvöld*

QUESTIONS AND DIRECTIONS

I want . . .	*ég vil . . .*		Cheap/ expensive	*ódýrt/dýrt*
Where ?	*hvar ?*			
When ?	*hvenner ?*		Good/bad	*gott/vont*
How much/ many ?	*hvað mikið/hversu margir . . . ?*		I'm going to . . .	*ég er á fara til . . .*
			A ticket to . . .	*miða til . . .*
How?	*hevrnig ?*		Hitch-hiking	*ferðast á puttanum*
Why?	*hvers vegna ?*		Near	*nálægt*
What is . . . ?	*hvað er . . . ?*		Far	*langt í burtu*
Which is . . . ?	*hvot er . . . ?*		Left	*vinstri*
Here	*hérna*		Right	*hægri*
There	*þarna*		Straight on	*beint áfram*

SOME SIGNS

Danger/be careful	*Varúð*	Closed	*Lokað*
Camping is allowed	*Tjaldstæði*	Hot	*Heitt*
Camping is not allowed	*Tjaldstæði bönnuð*	Cold	*Kalt*
		One-way	*Einstefna*
Toilet	*Snyrting*	Hospital	*Sjúkrahús*
Woman	*Kona*	Police station	*Lögreglusstöd*
Man	*Maður*	Post office	*Pósthús*
Open	*Opið*	Bus station	*Umferðarmiðstöð*

NUMBERS

1	*einn*	10	*tíu*	19	*nítján*	80	*áttatíu*
2	*tveir*	11	*ellefu*	20	*tuttugu*	90	*nítíu*
3	*þrír*	12	*tólf*	21	*tuttuguogeinn*	100	*hundrað*
4	*fjórir*	13	*þrettán*	22	*tuttuguogtveir*	101	*hundrað og einn*
5	*fimm*	14	*fjórtán*	30	*þrjátíu*	200	*tvö hundrað*
6	*sex*	15	*fimmtán*	40	*fjörutíu*	300	*þrjú hundrað*
7	*sjö*	16	*sextán*	50	*fimmtíu*	500	*fimm hundrað*
8	*átta*	17	*saután*	60	*sextíu*	1000	*þúsund*
9	*níu*	18	*átján*	70	*sjötíu*		

DAYS AND MONTHS

Sunday	*sunnudagur*	January	*janúar*	July	*júlí*
Monday	*mánudagur*	February	*febrúar*	August	*aúgúst*
Tuesday	*þriðjudagur*	March	*marz*	September	*september*
Wednesday	*miðvikudagur*	April	*apríl*	October	*október*
Thursday	*fimmtudagur*	May	*maí*	November	*nóvember*
Friday	*föstudagur*	June	*júní*	December	*desember*
Saturday	*laugardagur*				

Days and months are never capitalised.

ICELANDIC NAMES

Icelanders take the forename of their father as the first part of their own surname, plus the Icelandic word for son or daughter. For example, a son of a man whose forename is Jón will have Jónsson as a surname. A daughter of the same man will have Jónsdóttir as a surname. Formally or informally, Icelanders are always addressed by their forename.

GLOSSARY OF ICELANDIC TERMS AND WORDS

Á	River	*Fjall*	Mountain	*Höfn*	Harbour	*Sandur*	Glacial sands
Borg	Rock (or "town" if used in place name)	*Fjörður*	Fjord	*Hraun*	Lavafield		
		Fljót	Large river	*Hver*	Hot spring	*Skarð*	Mountain pass
		Flói	Large bay	*Hvoll*	Hill		
Bjarg	Cliff	*Foss*	Waterfall	*Jökul*	Glacier	*Skógur*	Wood
Brekka	Slope	*Gígur*	Crater	*Klettur*	Rock	*Slétta*	Plain
Brú	Bridge	*Gil*	Gorge	*Laug*	Hot spring	*Staður*	Parish
Bær	Farm	*Gjá*	Fissure	*Lón*	Lagoon	*Strönd*	Coast
Dalur	Valley	*Heiði*	Moorland	*Lækur*	Stream	*Tindur*	Summit
Djúp	Long inlet (to a fjord)	*Hellir*	Cave	*Mörk*	Woodland	*Tjörn*	Small lake
		Hlið	Hillside	*Múli*	Headland	*Vatn*	Lake
Drangur	Rock column	*Hóll*	Rounded hill	*Mýri*	Marsh	*Vegur*	Road
Ey	Island	*Hólmur*	Small island	*Nes*	Headland	*Vík*	Bay
Eyri	Sand spit			*Núpur*	Peak	*Vogur*	Inlet
Fell	Hill	*Höfði*	Promontory	*Rif*	Reef	*Völlur*	Plain

CHAPTER SEVENTEEN

REYKJAVIK AND AROUND

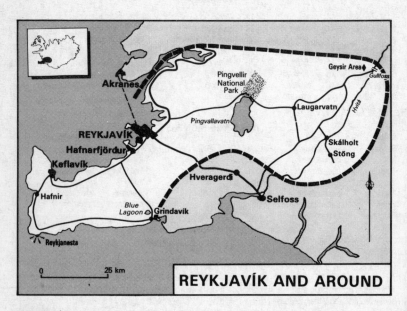

REYKJAVÍK AND AROUND

Labels on map: Akranes, Þingvellir National Park, Geysir Area, Gullfoss, REYKJAVÍK, Hafnarfjörður, Keflavík, Þingvallavatn, Laugarvatn, Hvítá, Skálholt, Stöng, Hafnir, Hveragerði, Blue Lagoon, Grindavík, Selfoss, Reykjanesta, 0 25 km

Reykjavík is the hub of Iceland's transport and communications, which means that it's virtually unavoidable on any trip. The city is not what brings most people to Iceland, but while here you should make the most of the world's most northerly capital. Its pleasures aren't so much in streetlife and nightlife but rather in the fresh blustery air, the views across the sea to glaciers and mountains – and the chance to unearth something of ordinary life in such a very individual and secluded society. And after seeing the rest of the country you'll probably find Reykjavík a throbbing urban metropolis.

The city also makes a good base for excursions, since **around Reykjavík** are three of Iceland's most visited places: the site of the old Alþing at **Þingvellir**, the water-spouts and waterfalls of **Geysir** and **Gullfoss**, and **Skálholt** church – all within simple reach by public transport or, more expensively, on day-long guided tours from the city. Also worthwhile is the less popular **Reykjanes peninsula**, a bleak lavafield that's as good an introduction as any to the stark scenery you'll find further into Iceland.

REYKJAVÍK

With concrete apartment blocks, more than one road and signs of life in the streets after 6pm, **REYKJAVÍK** is totally unrepresentative of the rest of Iceland, and most travellers view time spent here as time wasted. They are wrong. What the city lacks in scenery, it compensates for in other ways. The collections of the National Museum and the Árni Magnússon Institute, to name just a couple of the city's museums, unveil something of Iceland's stirring past; the outstanding work of sculptors Ásmundur Sveinsson and Einar Jónsson is everywhere, in the streets and the parks, as well as in two permanent exhibitions (indeed contemporary art has a high profile generally, in a feast of private galleries). And, perhaps more importantly, the atmosphere of the city is quite unique: even with all this activity, you can never forget that you're bang in the middle of the North Atlantic and the nearest neighbours are Greenland and the North Pole – an oddness which is at the core of Reykjavík's appeal.

Reykjavík's **origins** go back to the country's first settler, Ingólfur Arnarson, who arrived in the late ninth century, brought here by his high seat pillars – emblems of tribal chieftianship, tossed overboard from his boat – and settling, in pagan tradition, where they did. He named the place "smoky bay" mistakenly thinking that the distant plumes of steam issuing from boiling spring water were smoke caused by fire. It was a poor place to settle, however, the soil too infertile to support successful farming, and Reykjavík remained barely inhabited until the early-seventeenth-century sea-fishing boom, which brought Danish traders and a small shanty town to house their Icelandic labour force. Later, Skúli Magnússon, today regarded as the city's founder, used Reykjavík as a base to establish Icelandic-controlled industries, opening several mills and tanneries, and importing foreign craftspeople to pass on their skills. A municipal charter was granted in 1786 when the population totalled a mere 167 – and set the course for Reykjavík's acceptance as Iceland's capital. At the turn of the eighteenth century, the city replaced Skálholt as the national religious seat and gained the Lutheran Cathedral; eighty years later, with the opening of the new Alþing building, it became the base of the national parliament.

Since independence in 1944, expansion has been almost continuous. As a fishing harbour, a port for the produce of the fertile southwest's farms and a centre for a variety of small industries, Reykjavík provides employment for half the country's population. Recently there's been a substantial boom, too, in tourism. There are travel agents on every corner, and large expanses of land are currently being consumed by building sites throwing up hotels to service the bringers of the new wealth. The city has also pioneered the use of geothermal energy to provide low-cost heating – which is why you have to wait for the cold water instead of the hot when taking a shower, and why tap water always has a whiff of sulphur.

Arrival, information and getting around

International flights arrive at Keflavík airport, 48km from Reykjavík. Buses leave for the city twenty minutes after each flight arrival, and the 45-minute journey costs 350kr, payable on the bus in Icelandic or most major currencies. The bus stops at *Hotel Loftleiðir* and *Hotel Esja*, both about a 2-kilometre walk from the centre of Reykjavík.

Buses from elsewhere in Iceland finish their journeys at the *BSÍ* station, about a kilometre from the centre of town. This has a small tourist information booth, a cafeteria and left-luggage lockers. The **ferry** from Akranes docks in the harbour, a stone's throw from the city centre; **domestic flights** land at Reykjavík airport, about 2.5km from the centre, at the end of the #5 bus route.

There's a well-stocked **tourist information centre** at Ingólfsstræti 5 (June to mid-Sept Mon–Fri 8.30am–7pm, Sat 8.30am–4pm, Sun 10am–5pm; shorter hours rest of the year; ☎91/623045), where you can get maps, brochures, and general information on both Reykjavík and the rest of the country. This is by far the best source of up-to-date tourist information on Iceland, and if you're travelling independently you should check the fine points of your itinerary here, before you reach the remoter regions.

The city is easy to **get around** once you get used to the hills, which make its layout less than immediately obvious. The heart is still the low-lying old quarter between the harbour and the lake, busy with shoppers by day and with roaming adolescents, denied access by their age to bars and discos, by night. Most of the things to visit are within **walking** distance of here, although there is a thorough **city bus network**, whose services run roughly 7am to midnight Monday to Saturday, from 10am on Sunday, with a flat single-trip fare of 40kr, which must be paid in exact money to the driver when boarding. If you want to change buses ask for a transfer ticket, which is valid for 45 minutes. There are two terminals, both of which have offices (Mon–Fri 9am–6pm) issuing discount tickets – 24 for 600kr – and free route-maps and timetables. Discount tickets can also be bought on board, directly from drivers.

Finding a place to stay

All visitors to Iceland pass through Reykjavík at some point, which means, especially during the summer, finding a **bed** in the city is liable to be difficult and expensive. Most package tours include accommodation, as do *Icelandair* stopover deals. But if you're not travelling with either through the peak months, you should have at least the first night's stay arranged well in advance, through a travel agent.

Hotels

Reykjavík's **hotels** rarely skimp on comforts, but prices are high, often in excess of 7000kr for a double room in summer. Hotel rooms are slightly cheaper during the rest of the year, and in a few you can cut costs by taking a room without a bathroom. The rates given below are for double rooms in summer.

Hotel Borg, Pósthússtræti 11 (☎91/11440). The city's very first hotel, opened in the 1930s and reeking with historic atmosphere, despite its modernisation. 5250kr, or 8100kr with private bath.

Hotel City, Ránargata 4a (☎91/18650). A homely place, and one of the cheapest hotels. 3600kr.

Hotel Esja, Suðurlandsbraut 2 (☎91/82200). Big and impersonal, mainly housing Americans on stopovers. 7500kr.

Hotel Garður, Hringbraut (☎91/15656). Student rooms at the university campus available throughout the summer, but not exactly cheap. 5000kr. See also "Guesthouses and sbacc".

Hotel Geysir, Skipholt 27 (☎91/26210, 26477 or 623986). New, small and likeable, usefully placed for the major nightclubs but a fair walk from the city centre. 6250kr.

Hotel Lind, Rauðarástígur 18 (☎91/623350). Bright and modern. Good value at 6120kr.

Hotel Holt, Bergstaðastræti 37 (☎91/25700). The place to spend money if you have it – highly elegant, chocolate-on-the-pillow stuff. 7000kr.

Hotel Loftleiðir, Reykjavíurflugvöllur (☎91/22322). *Icelandair*'s biggest hotel; the rooms are adequate but the atmosphere dull and business-orientated. 7650kr.

Hotel Óðinsvé, Oðinstorg (☎91/25222). Stylish and relaxed, and within an easy trot of virtually everything. 5000kr, 7200kr with private bath.

Hotel Saga, Hagatorg (☎91/29900). Very international and usually packed with conference delegates dashing up to admire the view from the top-floor restaurant. 8600kr.

Guesthouses and sbacc

Generally offering rooms in ordinary houses and including breakfast, **guesthouses** can be half the cost of hotels; the best of them are listed below and are open all year. There are many more small, summer-only guesthouses, which tout for business with signs (in English) in their windows. Again, prices quoted below are for doubles. Only a couple of places in the city provide **sbacc** (sleeping bag accommodation), and this, not surprisingly due to its comparative cheapness, gets snapped up very quickly.

Family Guesthouse, Flókagata 1 (☎91/21155). One of the longest-established of the city's guesthouses, with nicely furnished rooms. But a couple of miles from the city centre. 3250kr.

Guesthouse Borgartún, Borgartún 34 (☎91/83222). Spacious and comfortable in what's otherwise an office building. 3500kr.

Hotel Garður, Hringbraut (☎91/15656). See "Hotels", above. Has some sbacc for 1500kr.

Salvation Army Guesthouse, Kirkjustræti 2 (☎91/13203). More a guesthouse than a dosshouse. A great location and inclusive breakfast make it an excellent low-cost option. 1800kr; 540kr for sbacc.

Townstar, Ránargata 10 (☎91/621804). In a quiet street close to the harbour. 2700kr.

Víkingur, Ránargata 12 (☎91/621290 & 623230). A nice house with small but fairly cosy rooms. 2700kr.

Youth hostels and camping

Providing the only genuine budget-priced sleeping in the city, the two **youth hostels** naturally get full very quickly, particularly in the peak summer period. The **campsite**, attached to the newer youth hostel, is inevitably the least scenic one in Iceland, but is nonetheless a reliable standby for those with tents.

The Old Youth Hostel, Laufásvegur 41 (☎91/24950). The pokiness makes it homely, but the summer crowds quickly fill the twelve-bedded dorms – and the bathrooms in the morning. It's essential to book in advance and also to tell the warden if you're arriving on a late flight. There's a small kitchen and the hostel is open all year. Midnight curfew; daytime lockout 11am–4pm. Sheet sleeping bags only.

The New Youth Hostel, Sundlaugavegur 34 (☎91/38110 & 24950). Close to the city sports ground and main swimming pool, a twenty-minute walk from the city centre. Though you should still reserve a place as early as you can, this is much less cramped than its older counterpart, with cooking and laundry facilities. The hostel is only open during the summer, as is the adjoining **City Campsite** (same phone numbers as the hostel). If you're travelling further afield in Iceland and intending to camp, you may as well save money by doing the same in Reykjavík. 630–750kr per tent.

The City

You'd be hard pushed to find a capital city much smaller than Reykjavík; a leisurely walk will take you around almost all of it in just an hour or two. Such smallness accounts for the city's lack of contrasting and well-defined areas: for simple convenience, we've divided the central portion into two sections separated by the lake, Tjörn, and the road, Lækjargata, which runs from the lake to Reykjavík's main square, Lækjartorg. Even the few things of note further out from the centre can be reached in a few minutes on public transport.

West of the Tjörn

The best place to get your first taste of Reykjavík is the area around **Lækjartorg**, along the pedestrianised **Austurstræti** – a general rallying-point for the city, where people stroll, strut and sit on the walls munching cakes and ice cream bought from snack stands. Consumed by makeshift clothing, jewellery and general bric-a-brac stalls on weekdays, Austurstræti is overlooked at one end by the playful blue and white facade of the *Morgunblaðið* newspaper building – the implication of its position being that the journalists need only to look through their windows to discover what's happening in the city.

The streets running left from Austurstræti lead into a small square, **Austurvóllur**, whose modest proportions and nondescript shops and offices belie its historical importance: this was the site of Ingólfur Arnarson's farm, and as such it marks the original centre of Reykjavík. Similarly, the elevated statue of the nineteenth-century independence campaigner, Jón Sigurðsson, in the middle of the square, faces two of the most important buildings in the country, though you'd never think so from looking at them. The **Alþinghusið** (Parliament House) is ordinary in the extreme, a slight stone building with the date "1881" etched into its dark frontage; the adjacent **Dómkirkjan** (daily except Wed & Sat 9am–5pm), is the Lutheran Cathedral, a wooden structure still partly shrouded by corrugated iron, that went up in 1785 after Christian VII of Denmark switched the seat of the Icelandic church here from Skálholt. The inside of the cathedral is as unremarkable as the outside, although Danish sculptor Bertel Thorvaldsen's elaborate font is worth a quick view.

Nearby, the junction of Aðalstræti and Hafnarstræti is marked by a number of shops specialising in sometimes tourist-aimed woollen products, and some of the city's spunkier clothes boutiques, while an adjacent courtyard contains **Hlaðvarpinn**, or the Women's Centre, an expanding complex that's home to a theatre, workshop, concert hall and an open-air market, which starts at noon on summer Saturdays. By day, the centre's opening hours are indeterminate – it's open when somebody's in – but specific evening events and the frequent exhibitions are listed in the free tourist magazines, or you can get the details at the tourist information centre. **Vesturgata**, which climbs uphill from the junction, is lined with tidy little dwellings, whose corrugated iron roofs, ranging in colour from a pallid two-tone green to bright blues and reds, have been carefully maintained by their owners – it's these houses you'll see on many postcards of "picturesque" Reykjavík. There's nothing specifically to see or do around here, but the lack of new hotels or milling tourists, and the trawler masts peeking over the roofs, make it one of the most atmospheric portions of the city.

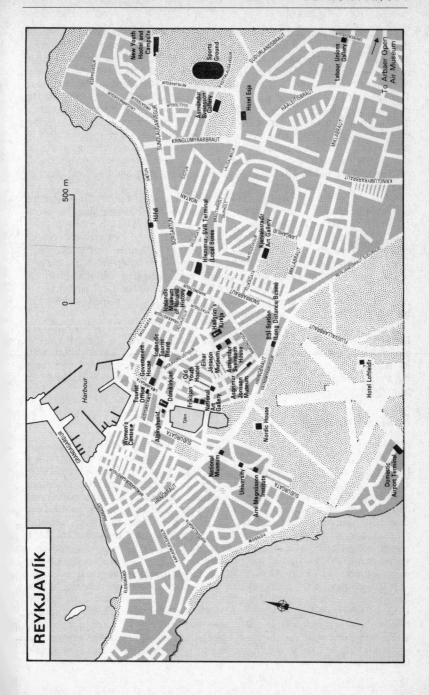

REYKJAVÍK

Harbour

500 m

New Youth Hostel and Campsite

Sports Ground

Labour Unions Gallery

To Arbaer Open Air Museum

Ásmundur Sveinsson Gallery

Hotel Esja

KRINGLUMÝRARBRAUT

HÁALEITISBRAUT

SUÐURLANDSBRAUT

SUNDLAUGAVEGUR

KLEPPSVEGUR

LAUGARÁSVEGUR

MIÐTÚN

Höfði

BORGARTÚN

SÆTÚN

NÓATÚN

Hlemmur, SVR Terminal Local Buses

Kjarvalsstaðir Art Gallery

LANGAHLÍÐ

MIKLABRAUT

KRINGLUMÝRARBRAUT

REYKJANESBRAUT

LJÓSHEIMAR

Icelandic Museum of Natural History

Hallgrím's Kirkja

BSÍ Station (Long Distance Buses)

SNORRABRAUT

Icelandic Tourist Board

Einar Jónsson Museum

Ásmundur Sveinsson House

Hotel Loftleiðir

Government House

SKÓLAVÖRÐUSTÍGUR

Old Youth Hostel

Ásgrímur Jónsson Museum

Fríkirkjan

HRINGBRAUT

Tourist Office

Dómkirkjan

Alþinghúsið

Town

National Art Gallery

Nordic House

Women's Centre

SUÐURGATA

National Museum

University

Árni Magnússon Institute

SUÐURGATA

Domestic Airport Terminal

HRINGBRAUT

ÆGISIÐA

GRANDAGARÐUR

ELDSGRANDI

Back down the hill, Tjarnargata leads around one edge of the **Tjörn** or Lake – a sizeable area of water populated by a variety of ducks whose precise demography is charted on noticeboards stationed at several points along the bank. At the far end, across the busy Hringbraut (the city's "ringroad"), is the entrance to the **National Museum** (mid-May to mid-Sept daily 1.30–4pm; rest of the year Tues, Thurs, Sat & Sun 1.30–4pm; free). Small but quite comprehensive, the museum gives an easily-digested summary of the country's past, including excavation finds from pagan places of worship and Viking graves, items from Bergþórshvoll, the farm where Njal of *Njal's Saga* lived (see p.608 for more). There's also an absorbing gathering of religious articles chiefly from the eleventh to thirteenth centuries, a weighty stock of craftworks of the sixteenth to nineteenth centuries and, fittingly, a room devoted to Jón Sigurðsson, with portraits and the furnishings of his home in Copenhagen.

A little further along Suðurgata is the country's biggest (in fact the only other one is a tiny affair in Akureyri) university, and the **Árni Magnússon Institute** (mid-June to mid-Sept Tues, Thurs & Sat 2–4pm; to visit at other times phone ☎91/25540; free), named after the man who during the seventeenth century collected and sent many old Icelandic manuscripts to Denmark for safekeeping. The works have been slowly returning to Iceland since independence and a few of the most important ones are displayed here, including the vital historical accounts, *Íslendingabók* and *Landnámabók*, and some of the fact-based fiction – *Njal's Saga*, the *Saga of Eirik the Red* and *Snorri's Saga* – that helped establish the high-flying cultural reputation Iceland once enjoyed.

Opposite the university, the Alvar Aalto-designed **Nordic House** (library Mon–Sat 1–7pm, Sun 2–5pm; display rooms daily 2–7pm) – buzzed over by aircraft landing at the nearby domestic airport – is devoted to Nordic culture, with an extensive library, temporary exhibitions and frequent evening activities ranging from classical concerts to talks. Check what's on from the posters inside, or from the free tourist magazines.

East of the Tjörn

A few minutes' walk from the Nordic House, on the eastern side of the Tjörn, is the **Fríkirkjan**, the Free Lutheran church, whose cute wooden tower is useful as a landmark to guide you to the neighbouring Íshúsið, or "Ice House". Once a storage place for the massive chunks of ice hewn in winter from the frozen lake and used to prevent fish stocks rotting, the building has been completely redesigned and enlarged and now houses the **National Art Gallery** (mid-May to mid-Sept daily 1.30–4pm; rest of the year Tues, Thurs, Sat & Sun 1.30–4pm; free). Icelandic art may lack worldwide recognition but it is much revered by Icelanders themselves; all the significant names are to be found here but – sadly and inexplicably – shown only in strictly rationed portions from the museum's enormous stock. Drop in, but expect to leave with your artistic appetite no more than whetted.

Walking from here back towards Lækjartorg, leaves you facing, across Bankastræti, a small unobtrusive white building which is in fact **Government House** (*Stjórnarráðið*) – another of Iceland's very parochial-looking public offices. Ignoring the odd minister who may emerge to catch a bus from Lækjartorg, turn right into the short Bankastræti and on into **Laugavegur**. This is the city's major commercial artery, and holds the main shops and a fair sprinkling of restaurants.

From the lower end of Laugavegur, Skólavöðustigir streaks steeply upwards to **Hallgrímskirkja** (tower mid-May to Aug Tues–Sat 10am–noon & 2–6pm; rest of the year Tues–Fri 10am–noon, Sat 2–5pm, Sun 2–4pm, closed Dec & Jan; 100kr), a modern structure whose neatly-composed space-shuttle-like form dominates the Reykjavík skyline. Work began on the church, named after a renowned seventeenth-century religious poet, immediately after World War II and still continues, the slow progress due to the task being carried out by a family firm – comprising one man and his son. Each year brings fresh rumours that the thing is about to be completed, but the church has yet to be formally opened. Opinions on the church's architectural style have split the city over the years, although nowadays most locals have grown to accept, rather than love, the thing. The tower has a viewing platform, but the cost is prohibitive – and you can see much the same for nothing from any piece of high ground in the city.

Leif Eiríksson, celebrated by a statue outside, keeps his back firmly to the church and his gaze towards Vinland. The heroic form of the statue is found in several others around the city, each of them the work of Einar Jónsson, who is remembered more officially by the building to Leif's left, which looks like three large adjoining cubes: the **Einar Jónsson Museum** (summer daily except Mon 1.30–4pm; rest of the year except Dec & Jan Sat & Sun 1.30–4pm; 100kr; garden daily 10am–6pm; free). Einar was Iceland's foremost modern sculptor, and this building was given to him as a studio and living space by the Icelandic government in 1923. He worked here, in an increasingly reclusive manner, until his death in 1954, when the building was given over to displaying more than a hundred of his works to the public. A specially-constructed group of rooms, connected by slim corridors and little staircases, takes the visitor through a chronological survey of Einar's career – and it's deep stuff. Jónsson claimed that his self-imposed isolation and total devotion to his work enabled him to achieve mystical states of creativity, and looking at the pieces exhibited here, many of them heavy with religious allegory, and all dripping with spiritual energy, it's a claim which doesn't seem far-fetched.

The work of another, equally-admired, modern Icelandic sculptor, Ásmundur Sveinsson, is featured a short walk away at Freyjugata 41, where the **Ásmundur Sveinsson House** (Mon–Fri 4–10pm, Sat & Sun 2–10pm) is a striking, if somewhat past its prime, functionalist building designed in 1933 by the sculptor with the architect Sigurður Gudmunsson. At the time, the combination of the building's uncompromising style and Ásmundur's array of sculptures in the garden caused many turned heads. But the sculptures have since gone (to the Sveinnson Gallery, see below), and the building now seems an integrated part of the cityscape, serving as the home of the Association of Icelandic Architects. There are often free exhibitions on architectural themes on the second floor; just walk in.

The streets between here and the Tjörn form one of the more affluent parts of the city, the houses often enlivened by the flourish of a turret or two. One of the best preserved of the older, less ostentatious abodes is the **Ásgrímur Jónsson Museum** at Bergstaðastræti 74 (June–Aug Sun–Fri 1–4pm; rest of the year Sun, Tues & Thurs 1.30–4pm; free), the former home of an artist who became a seminal figure in Icelandic painting. Born on a farm in southern Iceland, Ásgrímur begun drawing with chalk from a young age but had little experience of international art trends until he went, aged twenty, to Copenhagen in 1897. Six years later, having developed a style and adopted a subject matter which drew heavily from Icelandic folklore, he returned to Iceland and staged an influential exhibition, capturing the growing nationalistic mood of the country. The ground floor of the small house is kept as the artist left it when he died in 1952; upstairs, you'll find a selection of thirty or forty of his canvases, mostly touching – though occasionally violent – scenes of people and nature.

Another well-loved, but more recent, artist gave his name to the nearby **Kjarvalsstaðir Art Gallery** (daily 2–10pm; free; entrance in Flókagata), which has one of two large halls devoted to the work of Johannes Kjarval. Although they're something of an acquired taste, Kjarval's quasi-abstract depictions of Icelandic landscapes and emotion-charged portraits made him one of the country's most popular twentieth-century painters, and one who enjoyed at least some measure of acclaim overseas. The second gallery features some of the best temporary international exhibitions (and usually charges for admission).

More of a draw, perhaps, especially if you've already seen the sculptor's house, is the distinctively domed **Ásmundur Sveinsson Gallery** on Sigtún (June–Aug daily 10am–5pm; rest of the year Tues, Thurs, Sat & Sun 2–5pm), a twenty-minute walk away, close to the *Hotel Esja*. Sveinsson studied in Stockholm and Paris during the 1920s, returning to Iceland to develop the unique form of sculptural cubism infused with Icelandic myths and legends that you can view under the dome. Many more of his soft-edged, gently curving figures – monuments to the strength and resilience of the Icelandic people – which stood outside his house in Freyjugata (see above), now occupy the grounds of the gallery and can be seen at any time.

Leaving Sigtún by way of Kringlumýrarbraut and heading back to the city centre along Borgatún, takes you past the **Höfði**, venue of the Reagan-Gorbachev snap summit of 1986. The stocky white wooden structure, built early this century as the home of the legendary businessman/poet Einar Benediktsson (see "Þingvellir", below), stands in stately isolation on a grassy square beside the shore, and, apart from international summitry, enjoys a principal role as centre for the city's municipal functions. During the summit, the world's TV focused on the two leaders against a picturesque backdrop formed by the house and the sea immediately behind. This was no accident: the view in the other direction takes in some of the drabbest buildings in Reykjavík. Only one of these, at Hverfisgata 116, is of remote interest: the **Icelandic Museum of Natural History** (Tues, Thurs, Sat & Sun 1.30–4pm; free) – though if you're not eager for rocks, lava samples and various stuffed birds, there's little reason to loiter.

Out from the centre

There are only three places on the fringes of the city that are worth making for. The best of them, and a perfect destination on a calm, sunny day, is the historically-important island of **Viðey**, only a few minutes away by boat. Back on the mainland, the social history realistically documented in the **Árbær Open-Air Museum**, and the less enticing art collections of the **Labour Unions Gallery**, are a short bus ride (or a long walk) from the city centre.

Viðey

If you tire of the city and it's a fine day, make the short voyage to **Viðey**, a small island reached by ferry. Most Icelanders make the trip for a slap-up meal at the island's posh restaurant, but the real interest is the chance to view the restored eighteenth-century church and the remains of a thirteenth-century monastery which was an important seat of religious learning and – though its present-day serenity would suggest otherwise – a scene of bitter conflicts at the time of the Reformation. The island is also an ideal spot for a picnic and a stroll around the easy walking trails, with the striking blue slopes of Mount Esja across the sea on one side, and views of the city on the other. The ferry leaves from Sundhöfn, ten minutes' walk from the city campsite, at hourly intervals five times daily in summer, sailing only on weekends throughout the rest of the year. The return fare is 300kr.

The Árbær Open-Air Museum

On the eastern edge of Reykjavík, a gathering of diligently restored turf-roofed and corrugated iron buildings make up the **Árbær Open-Air Museum**, set up on the site of an ancient farm. The buildings, (which you can enter) and their contents, record the harshness of Icelandic farm-life, and show the immense changes which occurred as the national economy switched from agriculture to fishing and Reykjavík underwent rapid expansion. One item of note in the grounds is the only locomotive in Iceland, shipped in to aid the building of the harbour. The museum (admission 100kr) is open from June to August daily except Mon from 1.30pm to 6pm. Through the rest of the year, it can only be seen by appointment: phone ☎91/84412 between 9am and 10am. Get there with buses #1, #2, #3, #4, #5 or #17 from Lækjartorg, or #10 from Hlemmur.

The Labour Unions Gallery

The **Labour Unions Gallery** is a trade union art collection that includes a worthy permanent stock of Icelandic masters, backed-up by regular exhibitions of more contemporary fare. It's a rather dry place to while away a wet weekend evening. Check the listings in the tourist magazines for details. The gallery (free) is at Grensásvegur 16, and open from 2pm to 4pm, Tuesday to Friday, and on weekends from 2pm to 10pm. Take bus #3, #8, #9, #10, #11 or #12 from Hlemmur or #3, #6 or #7 from Lækjartorg.

Eating

As elsewhere in Iceland, anything edible in Reykjavík is expensive, although there are ways to reduce costs a little. Naturally, **self-catering** is the least costly of all. The best place to shop is the large *Hagkaup* store in the Kringlan Mall at the junction of Miklabraut and Kringlumýrarbraut. The only late-opening food store in the city is *Kveld-úlfur* at Freyjugata 15, open from 10am to 10pm daily except Sundays. For **coffee and snacks**, use one of the numerous cafés dotted around, many of which mutate into bars from 6pm, when they are able to serve alcohol – the pick of the bunch are listed under "Nightlife", below.

For full meals, many restaurants offer **lunch specials** from 11.30am to 2.30pm. These may either be set-dishes or (less often) help-yourself buffets costing from around 500kr. These are a fine way to initiate yourself into Icelandic cuisine. There are also a number of similarly-priced fast food outlets serving pizzas and burgers. If you can afford it, however, you really should have **dinner** in style at one of the small, atmospheric, and very high-quality restaurants, where you'll have to make a reservation, dress fairly smartly – and spend upwards of 5000kr for two. Most restaurants open for dinner around 6.30pm or 7pm and stay open until 11.30pm or midnight on Fridays and Saturdays, closing slightly earlier during the week. There are some ethnic restaurants around the city, though they're no cheaper than the Icelandic ones and are usually of a poorer standard.

Lunch and fast food

Brasserie Borg, Hotel Borg, Pósthússtræti. Often full of business people, but good value Icelandic dishes at lunchtime.

Gaukur á Stöng, Tryggvagata 22. Best known as a bar, but at lunchtime the soup and fish dishes are the cheapest and tastiest way to sample typical Icelandic fare.

Hard Rock Café, Kringlan Mall. A branch of the worldwide chain and expensive, but perfect for posing – and the t-shirts have great curiosity value back home.

Jertafaeði, Laugavegur 20b. Serving the only fully vegetarian meals in the country, most of the ingredients from geothermally heated greenhouses in south Iceland. Comparatively inexpensive too, with daily specials for around 500kr. Open weekdays, noon–2pm & 6–8pm.

Pizza Hut Suðurlandsbraut 2. Next door to *Hotel Esja*, the patrons of which tend to be the main customers. Dependable but unexciting; a standard pizza is around 600kr.

Potturinn og Pannan, Brautarholt 22. Fish and lamb dishes, and a welcomingly large salad bar. From 600kr.

Svarta Pannan, corner of Tryggvagata and Pósthússtræti. Slightly dingy-looking but a reliable fast-food outlet with fresh fish with chips for 500kr.

Tomma-Hamborgarar, Lækjartorg. Iceland's answer to the big American burger franchises (kept out of the country by law), this is the biggest of several branches around the city, and one of the few places where Reykjavík's adolescents can socialise.

Winnie's, Laugavegur 114. When all else fails, get a bag of chips (180kr) or a burger (300kr) here.

Dinner

Café Ópera, Lækjargata 6 (☎91/29499). Barbecued meats and a good selection of seafood make this an increasingly trendy place to wine and dine (see also "Nightlife").

Eldvagninn, Laugavegur 73 (☎91/622631). Dangerously expensive, but the menu, including some dishes cooked over an open-fire in front of the salivating diners, has inventive variations on traditional Icelandic recipes.

Fógetinn, Aðalsstræti 10 (☎91/16323). Above a popular bar (see below), and specialising in wildfowl, lamb and a wide range of seafood.

Hotel Holt, Bergstaðastræti 37 (☎91/25700). If you have a hankering to eat wild goose or reindeer steaks surrounded by some great Icelandic landscape paintings, this is the place. As posh as they come.

Naust, Vesturgata 6–8 (☎91/17759). Furnished in the style of a fishing boat, with plenty of top-notch Icelandic and international cuisine – and a special line in modern, lighter forms of traditional cookery.

Við Tjörnina, Templarasund 3 (☎91/18666). The chef's crafty variations on old-style fish recipes are rightly popular.

Nightlife

One of the biggest problems you'll have with Reykjavík's **nightlife** is finding it. Not only are things quieter during the summer than they are through the rest of the year, but much of the activity is confined to smallish places which you could easily walk right by without noticing at all. Also, very few people are out and about much before 10pm, after which time crowds seem to pour onto the streets and the nightspots fill rapidly. You'll need plenty of cash for even a few drinks, and going on to a disco or nightclub entails paying a steep admission fee. As you'd expect, things are liveliest on Friday and Saturday nights, when most places swing until 2am; closing time the rest of the week is around midnight – though discos, of course, stay open later.

Cafés and bars

The best spots to start socialising are **cafés and bars**, most of which double as non-alcoholic coffee and snack joints during the day, changing to more pubby venues after 6pm, when they start serving alcohol. Some bars are also attached to restaurants but you can always drink without eating.

Café Hressó on Lækjartorg at Austurstræti 18. The most central and one of the most enjoyable of Reykjavík's cafés. Good for coffee and snacks during the day.

Café 22, Laugavegur 22. Come in the early evening to get a table and stay late to soak up the Bohemian vibes of what is *the* place to be seen. There's a smaller, smokier bar upstairs.

Djúðpið, Hafnarstræti 15, in the celler of the Hornið restaurant. Fri & Sat only. A small bar pulling a mixed crowd and a good place to round off the night.

Duus-Hús, Fischersund 4, up an alley between Aðalstræti and Garðastræti. A sociable bar, and especially crowded when there's live music – anything from experimental jazz to retro-punk.

Fógetínn, Aðalsstræti 10. Fairly strait-laced, but worth a call on account of its siting in the oldest house in Reykjavík. There's a restaurant on the upper floor.

Gaukar á Stöng, Tryggvagata 22. Perhaps the closest thing to a typical watering-hole, this calls itself "Iceland's oldest pub" – true enough, since it's been plying liquor to the masses since 1985. See also "Lunch and fast food", above.

Geirsbúd, Vesturgata 6. Wine-sipping spot for Reykjavík's arty, media set. Sedate but interesting.

Kaffi Stræti, Lækjargata 1. The evocative nineteenth-century interior is the main draw, helping to turn what's a stylish café by day into an even more elegant bar by night.

Live music, clubs and discos

There's been a strong **rock music** network in Reykjavík for over a decade (see *Contexts*), though decent venues have always been thin on the ground, most gigs taking place in one of the city's gaping disco barns. Besides the local talent, a lot of British and American acts use *Icelandair* as a cheap way to cross the Atlantic and they often do a show here on the way. Find out what's new by calling into the *Gramm* record shop at Laugavegur 117 (☎91/12040).

The **club** scene is on the rise, with some inspired alternatives to the Sixties nostalgia and Top 40 fodder long proffered by the established **discos**. Club and disco admission is usually around 750kr. Don't expect to get in to a disco if you show up in full hiking gear, but otherwise the dress code is fairly lax; smartish casual attire should be fine.

Casablanca, Skúlagata 30 (☎91/1555). An appealing place, greatly improved of late, selecting the cream of UK and US club sounds and mixing them with a uniquely Icelandic fervour.

Hollywood, Ármúli 5 (☎91/83715 & 681585). Very popular chart-based disco, frequented by Reykjavík Casuals.

Hotel Borg, Pósthússtræti 11 (☎91/11440). Sometimes has live bands, but more frequently hosts a yuppie-orientated disco.

Hotel Ísland, Ármúli 9 (☎91/687111). Prone to Vegas-style spectaculars, though occasionally with more interesting fare.

Kjallari Keisaraus, Laugavegur 116 (☎91/10312). An enjoyable, compact basement with danceable music and a large bar at ground level. Free admission.

Leikhúskjallrinn, Hverfisgata (☎91/19636). In the cellar of the National Theatre, and popular with theatre-goers after the show. A pleasant place to unwind.

Tunglið, Lækjargata 2 (☎91/621625). By far the most fashionable club, despite its unpromising location in a disused cinema above the *Icelandair* office. Dress vivid. Fri & Sat only.

Theatre, classical music and cinema

Both major **theatre** productions and **classical concerts**, by the Icelandic Symphony Orchestra, are a rarity in summer, but throughout the rest of the year there are full programmes of both. Events are chiefly held at the *National Theatre* on Hverfisgata (☎91/11200), or the *Háskólabíó* on Hagatorg (☎91/22140). The tourist information centre will have full details. The **cinema** is a better bet if you've little money in your pocket and time on your hands: new international releases are screened with subtitles. Admission is generally 300kr; see any newspaper for full listings. More unusual is the **Volcano Show**, at Hellusundi 6a (☎91/13230), a two-hour set of films showing recent Icelandic eruptions from daringly close quarters. The screenings, which also include wildlife films, begin at 8pm daily throughout the summer, and have an English commentary nightly except Sundays and Mondays. There's also an extra screening at 6pm on Saturdays. Again, details from the tourist office.

Listings

Airlines *Icelandair (Flugleiðir)*, Lækjargata (international reservations ☎91/25100; domestic ☎91/26001; general enquiries ☎91/26622); *Eagle Air (Arnarflug)*, Lágmúli 7 (international reservations ☎91/84477; domestic ☎91/29577; general enquiries ☎91/29511); *SAS*, Laugavegur 3 (☎91/21199).

Banks and Exchange The main banks are *Landsbanki Íslands* Austurstræti 11 and *Utvegsbanki* Austurstræti 19. There's a branch of *Búnðarnbanki Íislands* inside the tourist information centre at Ingófstræti 5, which in summer is open Mon–Fri 10am–7pm & Sat 10am–2pm. The bigger hotels will change money, but at worse rates than banks.

Car Hire *ÁG*, Tangarhöða 8–12 (☎91/685544); *ÁS*, Skógarhlíð 12 (☎91/29090); *BĐJ* Skeifan 17 (☎91/618390); *E.G.* Borgertún 24 (☎91/24065); *Geysir* Borgartún 24 (☎91/11015); *Vík* Vatnesmýrarvegur 34 (☎91/25433).

Chemists *Ingólfs Apótek*, Hafnarstræti 5, and *Laugavegs Apótek*, Laugavegur 16, one of which will be open 24 hours.

Dental Treatment Call at Heilsuverndarstödin, Barónsstígur 47. Large fee payable on the spot.

Doctor Non-emergencies ☎696600.

Embassies and Consulates *UK*, Laufásvegur 49 (☎91/15883/4); *USA*, Laufásvegur 21 (☎91/29100); *Canada* (☎91/25355) Skúlagata 20. Irish, Australian and New Zealand nationals should use the British embassy.

Emergencies Fire and Ambulance (☎11100); Police (☎11166); Rescue (☎686068 & 27111); Doctor (weekdays ☎81200; nights and weekends ☎21230).

Hospital City Hospital at Sléttuvegur (☎81212). Casualty (☎696600).

Launderettes *Fönn* Skeifann 3; *Grýta* Nótatún 17; *Þvioð Sjálf Laundromat* Barónsstígur.

Left Luggage At the *BSÍ* station. Open in summer Mon–Fri 7.30am–9.30pm, Sat 7.30am–2pm, Sun 8am–2pm. Also at the youth hostels.

Library National Library at Hverfisgata 17, Mon–Fri 9am–5pm. City Library at Þingholtsstræti 29a, Mon–Fri 9am–9pm.

Lost Property Call at the Police Station, Hverfisgata 113.

Post The main post office is the Pósthúsið, on the corner of Pósthússtræti and Austurstræti; open Mon–Fri 9am–5pm, Sat 9am–noon. The post office at the BSÍ bus station is open Mon–Sat 2–7.30pm.

Public Transport Long distance bus information on ☎22300.

Swimming Pools *Sundlaugar* on Sundlaugarvegur, by the campsite and sports ground (Mon–Fri 7am–8.30pm, Sat 7.30am–5.30pm, Sun 8am–5.30pm); *Sundhölin,* at Barónsstígur (Mon–Fri 7am–8.30pm, Sat 7.30am–5.30pm, Sun 8am–2.30pm).

Taxis Best avoided on grounds of extreme cost. If you need one, call one of the following companies: *Borgarbíl* (☎22440); *BSR* (☎11720); *Bæjarleiðir* (☎33500); *Hreyfill* (☎685522).

What's On *Around Reykjavík* and *What's on in Reykjavík*, free from the tourist information centre, hotels, travel agents, etc., have monthly and fortnightly listings respectively. Both also provide general information about the city and country.

Woolly Jumpers Patterns in English are available in the large woolshops in the city. Wool at non-tourist prices can be bought in a dingy-looking shop on Laugavegur, on the right about 250m past Hlemmur as you walk away from the city centre.

Women's Movement Nothing as radical as other Scandinavian capitals, but phone or drop in to the Women's Centre at Vesturgata 3 (☎91/19055 & 19560) for information.

AROUND REYKJAVÍK

If you've only a few days in Iceland and don't want to stray far from the capital, some awareness of the severity of the countryside and the potent sense of Icelandic history which pervades it, can be found fairly close to the city. The national park of **Þingvellir** is a strikingly wide plain, appearing almost theatrically from behind barren lavafields and desolate peaks; more significantly, it was the scene of the early Icelandic – and Europe's first – parliament, still unspoilt and highly evocative. One of the more demonstrative aspects of Iceland's volatile geology can be viewed at the **Geysir area** – internationally famous because the gushing hot springs here have given their name to the phenomenon throughout the world. Nearby are the almost equally renowned "Golden Falls" of **Gullfoss**: a dynamic and spectacular waterfall which crashes into a large chasm. Less visually attractive, but important historically, is the church at **Skálholt**. Set in a moody landscape, it was a major religious centre and at the heart of national affairs during the medieval period. Less visited than any of these is the **Reykjanes peninsula**, Europe's largest bird sanctuary and home to the curious "blue lagoon", as well as a succession of ghostly, abandoned fishing settlements dotted along the mostly black and hostile-looking coastline.

You can see all of these, except Reykjanes, on a day-long guided coach tour from Reykjavík, although the first three places are easily (and much more cheaply) accessible by bus. You will, however, need several days to get to them all in this way (accommodation is available at each except Skálholt). Half-day organised tours run to the Reykjanes peninsula, which, except for the blue lagoon, is very difficult to penetrate significantly without your own wheels.

Þingvellir

Road 36 from Reykjavík runs through the barren heathlands of Mosfellsheiði towards the plain of **ÞINGVELLIR**, from 930 to 1798 the scene of the Alþing or National Assembly, where laws were made and ratified each June. As important as the legal function, however, was its place as a yearly social get-together for the whole population – a very scattered and isolated community. It's a major tourist attraction, but visitors are easily absorbed by the vast plain, fringed by tall peaks and a lake (Þingvallavatn), just as the early settlers – and the many thousands of modern Icelanders who celebrated the 1100th anniversary of the Settlement here in 1974 – must have been.

The sense of history is extremely strong, as is the power of nature itself. Þingvellir is situated bang on the mid-Atlantic rift, where the European and North American continental plates are pulling apart, causing the fissures which run across the plain and creating the gorges, the largest of which, Almannagjá – the Gorge of all Men – formed the main entrance to the Alþing. About halfway along the gorge, a flagpole marks the Lögberg – the Law Rock – on which the Law Speaker stood to address the assembly which filled the plain immediately in front of him, the wall of rock behind amplifying his voice. Close by are the remains of seventeenth- and eighteenth-century booths, which were inhabited by the participants in the Alþing, the floors and walls of which were dug into the rock and covered by temporary roofs.

Close to where the Öxará river crosses Almannagjá is the deep pool, **Drekkingarhylur**, used as a means of punishment for adultery, which remained a capital crime until the mid-nineteenth century: female adulterers were drowned here, while men who had committed the same crime were beheaded. On the far side of the river, on the plain itself, the white wooden **church** was built in 1859 and is, symbolically at least, perhaps Iceland's most important. Built on the site of a number of older churches, its bell was regarded as the country's only national possession during the years of Danish sovereignty, and it was here that the seeds of Icelandic independence were formally planted when the Danes handed over a measure of self-government to the Icelanders. Its graveyard holds the tombs of two of the most enduring national poets – Einar Benediktsson and Jónas Hallgrímson. Though from different eras, both of these are well-known national figures: Hallgrímsson's work romantically captures the great times of the Commonwealth (the halcyon centuries following the Settlement) along with Icelandic nature; Benediksson, a later writer, was a more robust figure, with what were, in the early twentieth century, high-flown notions of the Icelandic nation harnessing the country's natural resources to achieve self-sufficiency. He was also something of an entrepreneur, and is credited with having sold the Northern Lights to a gullible American businessman.

Because Þingvellir is a national park, camping is restricted to the **campsite**, beside the crossroads on Road 36, where the warden can also give advice on the many **walks** in the area – and the climbs up the nearby Ármannsfell and Burfell.

The Geysir area . . . and Gullfoss

From Þingvellir, Road 36 runs south and meets Road 365, which climbs fairly steeply until dropping towards **LAUGARVATN**, just before which it passes **Laugarvatnsvellir**, a cave inhabited until 1922 and thought to be haunted. The lake from which the village takes its name is fed by hot springs, which keep its waters warm enough for bathing – to the extent that those who found the waters of Öxará at Þingvellir too cold, came here instead to be baptised.

In the village there are two *Edda* hotels, one of which has **sbacc** (☎99/6118), but you may want to push on. Twenty-five kilometres further, Road 37, which branches off Road 36, enters the **Geysir area**. The most active part of the area is around **Stóri Geysir**, whose Anglicised form "Geyser" is the name given to the phenomenon worldwide. Stóri now lies dormant, but it regularly sent columns of scalding water up to a height of around 70m until the 1940s, when it either reached retirement age or became blocked by the garbage that tourists slung into its innards. Nowadays it does erupt, but not without artificial coaxing. One of the more recent chapters of Icelandic folklore tells of the American millionaire who brought some friends to Iceland by private plane just to see Geysir perform. Discovering that it didn't, a local was hired to stimulate activity by pouring 45kg of soap into its pool. The assembly waited . . . and waited. The millionaire and his party got bored and left. As soon as they were out of sight, Geysir acknowledged their departure with an eruption claimed by eye-witnesses to have been the greatest in living memory. Geysir is still stimulated like this during summer, usually on Saturday; the Reykjavík tourist information centre will have precise details.

If you want to see a genuine eruption, however, neighbouring **Strokkur**, or "Boy", obliges roughly every three minutes – though at just 30m or so it can't match the original for height. Immediately after a spurt, its water level drops deep within its pool, but shortly afterwards comes gurgling back towards the top to form a still surface that gradually begins to oscillate, building up to form a perfect dome just prior to shooting suddenly into the sky with rocket-like velocity. Visitors daringly inch closer to the pool's edge, trying to capture the moment of eruption on film, and then jump backwards to avoid the boiling fall-out.

Be careful as you tread around the edges of the geysers: they're surrounded by wafer-thin layers of fragile silicate, built up from the minerals dissolved in the waters. The same goes for the **still pools** (ie inactive geysers), the water in some of which is incredibly clear, in others incredibly blue, while one actually contains water of two colours, kept apart as if in defiance of nature. Have a look, too, at the **boiling mud pits**, hissing and bubbling close to the pools.

The park is best seen early or late in the day, when it's relatively free of trippers from Reykjavík, so it's worth considering bedding down at the nearby **guesthouse**, which has **sbacc** (☎99/6935), or at the **campsite** (☎99/6933). Information about either can be found at the roadside café facing the geysers.

Road 37 ends at **GULLFOSS**, 6km beyond Geysir, where the Hvítá negotiates a double fall, changing direction twice before crashing into a deep chasm. A sharp turn in the course of the river enables viewing from several angles and at very close quarters – sudden gusts of wind can leave onlookers drenched. There's a **campsite** by the car park, but the constant roar of the falls can make sleep difficult.

Skálholt and around

About 40km from the Geysir area, close to Road 35, **SKÁLHOLT** was Iceland's major religious seat and one of the leading educational centres of the country since the eleventh century. The first church here was built in 1002 by **Gizzur the White**, who a couple of years earlier had forced the country to accept Christianity through his high-handed tactics at the Alþing – the biggest single event of the Saga Age. Iceland was the first of the Scandinavian countries to be converted, and from the eleventh to the eighteenth centuries, Skálholt was the seat of the southern bishopric, as well as being the site of one of the country's most highly regarded schools and one of the largest centres of population. However, decades of natural disaster during the 1700s, coupled with Danish domination, reduced the Church's influence, and the cathedral was demolished and the bishopric and school transferred to Reykjavík. In the 1950s the present **church** (daily 10am–6pm) was erected, more as a memorial than a working church since the Church's base has remained in the capital. There's not much inside beyond a crypt (usually opened only on request) with artefacts from Skálholt's past, including the stone coffin of a thirteenth-century bishop, Páll, one of the great medieval Icelandic leaders – buried here with his crozier, which was found at Þingvellir. Outside the church, there's a monument to Jón Arasson, bishop of Hólar, a similarly powerful seat in the north of Iceland, who became a national hero for resisting the Danish-led Reformation. It was at Skálholt that he was beheaded in 1550. It's said that his body was then carried by horse back to Hólar via every major settlement in the country – and every single Icelander turned out to mourn as he passed.

Road 31 from Skálholt runs into the **Þjórsá valley**, once filled with wealthy farmsteads exploiting rich and fertile grasslands, most of which were buried under lava and ash following the eruption of Hekla in 1104. In 1939, one of the farms, at **Stöng**, was uncovered, and it gives an excellent impression of domestic life and conditions of the period. The building is made from the traditional materials, wood, stone and turf, and is filled with accurate reproductions of household goods and equipment which would have been in use at the time. It's a bit of a trek to get to unless you're really keen: without private transport you can only reach it on the Sprengisandur tour coach, which leaves Reykjavík four times a week (see p.616).

The Reykjanes peninsula

If you've arrived in Iceland by plane, you'll already have passed through some of the **Reykjanes peninsula**, the arm of land which stretches out south and west of Reykjavík. Until recently, the airport and the road from it to the capital were all most vistors saw of the peninsula, but these days more people are making a trip here, not least because a new guided tour is available from Reykjavík.

The chief draw is the so-called **blue lagoon** (*bláa lónið*), on Road 43, at which the scheduled local bus from Reykjavík will stop on request on its way to the dull town of GRINDAVÍK, a few kilometres south. A few years ago, quite unexpectedly, natural hot water used by a small geothermal power station here mixed with seawater which had passed through the porous rocks, creating a bright, turquoise-coloured, lagoon. Many Icelandic doctors prescribe a dip in these silicate-rich waters as a cure for skin disease – with a high rate of success. Even if you're in perfect health, there can be few stranger places in the world to bathe: steam from the power plant billows constantly over the lagoon, and the plants' steel tubing is a sci-fi-like addition to the otherwise stark surrounds. Be wary, though, of the lagoon's rough, rocky bottom, and the fact that some discharges from the plant are *very* hot (though chemically they are quite safe, such naturally-generated energy produces no dangerous waste). There's a small hut by the lagoon where you can hire costumes and towels if necessary; otherwise a relaxing swim costs 200kr.

The bumpy Road 425 heads west from Grindavík to loop around the tip of the peninsula. There's little specifically to see except a few ruined buildings (the local inhabitants moved away as near-shore fishing became uneconomic), a hazardous golfcourse, and, at the southern extremity, a path leading to the **lighthouse** at REYKJANESTA. There's nowhere better to watch the North Atlantic breakers crashing against the jagged shore. Further on, passing HAFNIR, the airport town of **KEFLAVÍK**, hardly merits a stop: besides the US military station here, the place is increasingly becoming a bland Reykjavík overspill community.

travel details

Buses
From Reykjavík to Akureyri (1 daily, extra daily service in summer Sun, Tues, Thur & Fri; 8hr); Akranes (Sun–Fri 2 daily, 1 on Sat; 1hr 45min); Borgarnes (Sun–Fri 6–8 daily, 3 on Sat; 2hr); Geysir via Hveragerði and Selfoss (in summer Tues & Wed, Fri 2 daily, otherwise 1 daily, in winter 4 weekly; 2hr 30min); Gullfoss via Laugarvatn and Geysir (summer Sun, Wed–Fri 2 daily, otherwise 1 daily, winter 1 daily except Wed; 2hr 40min); Gullfoss via Selfoss, Hveragerði, Laugarvatn and Geysir (Fri & Sun 2 daily, otherwise 1 daily, no Wed service in winter; 2hr 40min); Grindavík (2 daily in summer, otherwise 1 daily; 50min); Hellisandur via

Ólafsvík (Sat–Thur 1 daily, 2 on Fri; 4hr 15min); Höfn (summer 1 daily, otherwise 2–3 weekly; 9hr 30min); Hólmavík (Tues & Fri 1 daily; 6hr 30min); Ísafjörður (Tues & Thur 1 daily; 12hr); Reykholt (Mon–Fri 2 daily, Sat & Sun 1 daily; 2hr 30min); Selfoss via Hveragerði (usually 8 daily; 1hr); Stykkishólmur (Sun–Fri 1 daily, 2 on Sat; 4hr); Vík (Mon–Fri 2 daily, 1 daily Sat & Sun; 3hr 30min); Þingvellir (2–3 daily in Aug, otherwise 1 daily; 50min); Þorlákshöfn (2 daily; 1hr).

Ferries
From Reykjavík to Akranes (summer 5–6 daily, otherwise 4 daily; 1hr).

CHAPTER EIGHTEEN

NORTHWEST ICELAND: REYKJAVIK TO AKUREYRI

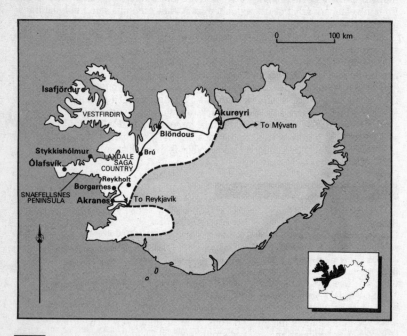

There's not much immediately north of Reykjavík that could be described as a destination in itself. Except for some shortish stops, it's best to follow the Ring Road for some way and then branch off into the more geologically distinct regions of the Northwest. You can actually get to **Akranes**, the first town of any size, most enjoyably by ferry, but the journey itself is likely to be more fun than the town. Further on, potent literary and historical connections make **Borgarnes**, and **Reykholt**, just inland from the Ring Road, of more interest, though neither are likely to detain you more than a night.

More of a pull is the **Snæfellsnes peninsula**, well away from the Ring Road but straightforward to reach by bus. At the end of the peninsula the cone-shaped glacier, **Snæfellsjökull** – from where Jules Verne's heroes descended towards the centre of the earth – tantalisingly reveals itself in the distance. The northern edge of the peninsula meets the mainland beside **Hvammsfjörður** and the lush landscapes which provided a backdrop for the events of *Laxdale Saga*. From here, there are two routes into the great jagged claw of land that makes up **Vestfirðir** – Iceland's northwest corner, also far off the Ring Road but again well connected by bus. High flat-topped mountains and long narrow fjords make Vestfirðir's landscapes unique in Iceland, and it's a place you should get to if you have the chance. The main roads through it meet at the small main town, **Ísafjörður**. Having made the detour, you can rejoin the Ring Road at **Brú**, from where the onward journey is enlivened by the broad fjords of the northern coast, though these are difficult to reach without your own transport. Further on, **Akureyri** is the chief centre of the north, and the biggest settlement in the country outside of Reykjavík.

Heading north: Akranes, Borgarnes and Reykholt

Immediately out of Reykjavík, the Ring Road skirts the towering form of Mount Esja, eventually following the edge of **Hvalfjörður**, a long, deep fjord that provided shelter during the last war to American supply convoys. The name means "whale fjord" and until recently tourist buses made the 45-minute journey from Reykjavík to the open-air whaling station at the fjord's head, allowing visitors to watch the grisly spectacle of a whale being sliced up. Iceland was catching whales up until the summer of 1989, the end of a four-year period of "scientific research whaling". Throughout this time there was immense opposition to the slaughter from various quarters, not least an international boycott of Icelandic seafood instigated by Greenpeace, and direct action when a Canadian craft sank two Icelandic whaling vessels and wrecked the processing plant here in November 1986. For the moment, Iceland has switched its energies to "non-lethal surveillance" of whales, a ploy which may well be a way of responding to international pressure without being seen to back down.

Akranes

On the far side of Hvalfjörður, the Ring Road veers sharply northward, while Road 51 continues on from the Akranes–Vegamot junction into **AKRANES**. This is one of the country's most prosperous centres, home to a thriving fishing and ship-repairing industry and Iceland's only cement factory (which uses crushed shells from the seabed rather than lime as raw material). It also has a tourist office and two campsites, although apart from the mountain, **Akrafjall**, which is good walking territory and has copious numbers of seabirds nesting on its crags, there's very little else to make you hang around.

Borgarnes

Back on the Ring Road, you come to **BORGARNES** which, unusually for a coastal town, is not dependent on fishing but is primarily a centre for the surrounding dairy farms. There's a **campsite** on the way into the town (by the *Esso* station) and a **mound** in the local park which is reputedly the burial place of Skallagrím Kveldulfsson, the father of Egil Skallagrímsson. A ninth-century pirate, thug and poet, Egil was the hero of *Egil's Saga*, and is commemorated

here by a statue of himself carrying his drowned son, Boðvar. A couple of kilometres outside the town on Road 54, the farm, **Borg**, was first settled by Skallagrím,
and was also home of Egil and, later, of the thirteenth-century writer and politician, Snorri Sturluson. The original farmhouse is no longer there but the unmistakeable rock – the borg – which gave the farm its name, survives.

Reykholt and around

There are further, more tangible memorials to **Snorri Sturluson** 18km inland
from Borgarnes on Road 50. Nestling in the valleys above Borgarfjörður,
REYKHOLT was once the great man's home, though it now consists of no more
than a school and a church. At the foot of the hillock on which the school stands,
the warm pool, **Snorralaugur**, is believed to be where Snorri would bathe and
receive visitors, and next to it are the restored remains of the tunnel thought to
have led to the cellar of Snorri's house, where he was assassinated in 1241.
Search out the Sturlung family plot in the churchyard, too, where Snorri is
reputed to be buried.

For accommodation in the area, in summer there's an *Edda* hotel with **sbacc**
(☎93/2560), in the Reykholt school; or you can follow Road 518 up the valley to
HÚSAFELL: an activity holiday centre with a number of self-catering cottages
and a **campsite** with full facilities. From the centre, a rough 10km track leads to
Surtshellir, a 1500m-long cave thought to have been a hideout of an eighteenth-
century outlaw, Eyvindur á Fjöllum. Another good base for exploration of the
area is the Varmaland **youth hostel** (☎93/5301 & 5303) on Road 527, about 5km
from the Ring Road. Further north on the Ring Road, there's another **campsite** at
Bifröst, at the foot of the crater **Grábrok**, which is itself reachable by climbing a
steep but well-defined path from the road.

The Snæfellsnes Peninsula

Keeping close to the coast, Road 54 from Borgarnes enters the **Mýrar district**, a
region of low-lying plains and bogs with a few small lakes. Directly ahead is the
mountain range which forms the spine of Snæfellsnes, and as the road turns west
you get a view of the oval-shaped crater of **Eldborg**, sitting conspicuously amid
the flatness of the **Eldborgarhraun** lavafield. To the east of Eldborg, **Fagrask-
ógarfjall** was the haunt of Grettir of *Grettir's Saga*: "a savage and dreadful place"
according to William Morris, who was here in 1871 – though these days it's
peaceful and very green. To the north, the caves of **Gullborgarhraun** are a maze
of intricate passageways containing coloured stalagmites and stalactites. Always
take care and get local advice before exploring them.

Before very long the road turns onto the **Snæfellsnes peninsula** proper, travelling along its southern flank between the mountains and the boggy tracts leading down to the sea. From here you can either pick your way over the mountains
to Stykkishólmur on the north coast by way of Road 56 (see p.588), or continue
on to **BÚÐIR**, around which there are fine walks through the local lavafields.
The nearest **sbacc** (☎93/9730) and **campsite** are at **LÝSUHÓLL** on Road 572,
which loops off Road 54 on the way to Búðir. From the turning for Búðir, Road 54
cuts north over to Ólafsvík (see p.596), but if you're aimimg to skirt around the
foot of Snæfellsjökull before climbing it, you should keep on the smaller road

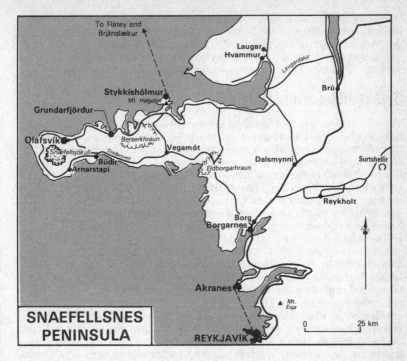

SNAEFELLSNES PENINSULA

0   25 km

which continues around the tip of the peninsula. It's possible to climb the glacier from **ARNASTAPI**, but while the shortest this is not the easiest route (Ólafsvík is, detailed below), and you should seek local advice before attempting the ascent. If you want to sleep on your options, there's a **campsite** and **sbacc** (☎93/5759) at the Arnarfell Community Centre.

Rounding the peninsula – and climbing the glacier

Rounding the peninsula gives views out to the rocky formations off the coast and the first sight of Vestfirðir's mountains. Caves are common in the cliffs along this stretch of coast, and some have blowholes issuing great bursts of spray, particularly during high winds. On the northern side of Snæfellsnes, the road passes the diminutive village of **HELLISSANDUR** – where there's a **campsite** and a little **nautical museum** opposite the service station – before reaching **ÓLAFSVÍK**, the largest town in Snæfellsnes and much the best place from which to climb **Snæfellsjökull**. There's a small local **museum** here too, in the Gamla Pakkhúsið – a timber warehouse built in 1841. At Ólafsbraut 19, there's a hotel with **sbacc** (☎93/6152) and a **campsite**, from where an easy-to-follow path leads all the way to the top of the glacier; allow about three hours for the assault.

Further along Road 57 are a few other accommodation options. The **GRUNDARFJÖRÐUR** community centre has sbacc (☎93/8763), and, a kilometre from the village, the *Kverna* farm (☎93/8813 & 8814) has limited **sbacc** and a **campsite**.

Heading on, a small bridge crosses Hraunsfjörður into the **Berserkjahraun**, a lavafield named after the two Berserkers who cleared a route through it during the Saga Age. Berserkers, periodically mentioned in the Sagas, were able to go into a trance which made them impervious to wounds and able to fight like madmen. They were much valued as warriors but given a wide berth socially.

Stykkishólmur and Helgafell

The road continues to the base of the **Þorsnes Promontory**, where Road 56 leads on to **STYKKISHÓLMUR**, an ancient town by Icelandic standards, established in the sixteenth century, and now renowned for its halibut and scallops. Inside the Gamla Húsið warehouse is a tiny **local museum** that's worth a look, while the hotel on the hill to the east of the harbour has **sbacc** (☎93/8330) and there's a **campsite** beside the road into town. **Boat trips** on the fjord can be arranged at the hotel, and on summer weekdays you can cross by **ferry** to BRJÁNSLÆKUR in Vestfirðir. Pick up information from the ferry office near the harbour (☎93/8120).

Five kilometres from Stykkishólmur, **Helgafell**, or "Holy Mountain," dwarfed by the neighbouring mountains, was in pagan times regarded as sacred. Early settlers here believed it was an entrance to Valhalla, into which they would go after their deaths. It's said that the major pagan god, Oðin, will grant three wishes to anyone climbing Helgafell for the first time, on the condition that they climb in silence and come down on the east side without looking back or speaking. This is not as simple as it sounds. The path up the west side is easy enough, but the eastern descent is steep and rocky and you have to pick your way carefully. The ascent, at least, is worth making though: at the top there are the ruins of a tiny thirteenth-century chapel, and striking views over the islands of Breiðafjörður and to the mountains of Vestfirðir. Guðrun Osvifursdóttir, heroine of *Laxdale Saga*, spent the last years of her life at the farm here and, 900 years on, people still decorate her grave – outside the nearby churchyard and marked by a headstone – with wild flowers.

Hvammsfjörður and Laxdale Saga country

There are more sites from the *Laxdale Saga* further north, around **BÚÐARDALUR** on Hvammsfjörður, on Road 60, where there's a hotel with **sbacc** (☎93/4322). Some of the Saga's characters lived along Laxárdalur, and although there are no remains of their homes, the rolling green landscapes are reminiscent of the most romantic of the old epics. At the valley's lower end was the farm of Hjarðarholt, established by one of the main characters in the Saga, Olafur Pá (Olaf the Peacock), and later taken over by his son Kjartan. In the Saga, Olaf moves his livestock from Goddastaðir, further up the valley, to Hjarðarholt and asks Höskuldur to watch the procession from his own farm. The first of Olaf's animals were arriving at Hjarðarholt while the last were still leaving Goddastaðir – a visual demonstration of wealth which can still be appreciated by standing at Höskuldsstaðir and looking at the distant hillside.

The other branch of Olaf's feud-torn family lived a little further north in the valleys which run down to **HVAMMUR**. This is one of the area's oldest settlements and was first occupied by **Unnur Djúpúðga** (Unn the Deep-Minded), the only woman recorded in the Book of Settlement as taking land on her own account – and to whom there's a small memorial erected by the University Women of Iceland. Beyond Hvammur, Road 60 runs through Svínadalur, which contains the gorge where Kjarten was ambushed and murdered.

Just out of Hvammur, Road 589 branches off towards **LAUGAR**, where the hot springs were a landmark on the main route from Vestfirðir to the south. There are some remains here of the old baths where Guðrun Osvifursdóttir had frequent meetings with Kjartan, with whom she had an intense affair, and the valley beyond was scene of Guðrun's early life. There's a **local history museum** in Laugar, along with a **campsite** and an *Edda hotel* with **sbacc** (☎93/4265).

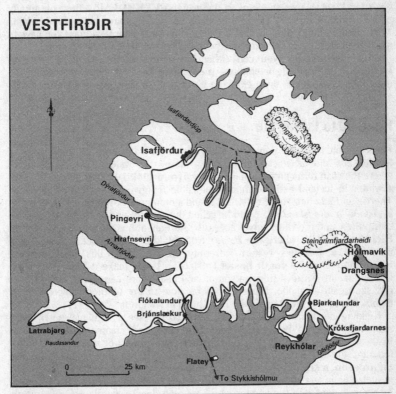

Vestfirðir

Vestfirðir, or the western fjords, is geologically the oldest part of Iceland and consequently it has none of the volcanic activity you'll find elsewhere. But its towering mountains and a coastline gnawed into rocky crags by the North Atlantic storms, make it a distinct corner of the country – and one that soon repays the effort you have to make to get here. Vestfirðir's roads are few and often far between (as are its settlements), sometimes inching over mountains but more often weaving around deep, sheer-sided fjords. Buses do serve the area, however, and two roads link this wild quarter to the Ring Road.

Gilsfjörður and the south

Gilsfjörður is the first fjord of Vestfirðir, though its main village **KRÓKSFJARÐARNES** is notable only for its shop (the only one for miles around) and a farm a few kilometres on which has **sbacc** (☎93/4762). About 20km on, the twin peaks of **Vaðalfjöll** rise from mundane hillsides, an extinct volcano whose outer layers have eroded away, leaving just this bare chimney. Leaving the road at **BJARKALUNDUR** (where there's a hotel with **sbacc**; ☎93/4762), it's a ninety-minute walk to the smaller of the two peaks. From Bjarkalundur, Road 807 gives lovely views over the fjord on the way to **REYKHÓLAR**, a tiny community based around a seaweed processing plant, which has **sbacc** in its school (☎93/4730). Bear in mind, though, that to catch a bus back from Reykhólar you have to notify the hotel staff in Bjarkalundur (who will tell the driver to collect you).

After Bjarkalundur, you can either cut across to the northern route **to Ísafjörður** on Road 61, or continue there along Road 60 – the latter much the most impressive route, often climbing into the mountains overlooking the fjords around Breiðafjörður.

Road 60 to Ísafjörður

Road 60 winds its way along the coast, each turn it takes giving fresh views of Snæfellsnes and its glacier, shimmering across the water. **FLÓKALUNDUR**, where the road turns north, is named after **Hrafn Flóki**, the first person to brave a winter in Iceland and the man responsible for giving the country its name. There's an *Edda* hotel here (☎94/2011) and a monument with the inscription "*. . . ok nefndu landið Ísland*" (". . . and he called the land Iceland"). There are also two **campsites**, and the village gives access by infrequent bus to the ferry terminal at **BRJÁNSLÆKUR**, where the *Baldur* from Stykkishólmur docks. About 30km from here, at Iceland's western extremity, are the "Bird Cliffs" of **Latrabjarg**, where there is also a **youth hostel** (☎94/575). If you make it here, don't leave without seeing **Rauðisandur**, a spit of land just before Látrabjarg, noted for its red sands and seal life. More details on how to get to these places can be obtained locally or by phoning the *Edda* hotel in Ísafjörður; (☎94/4111).

Heading north from Flókalundur, Road 60 crosses a high plateau of frost-shattered boulders before descending to **Dynjandi** (sometimes known as Fjallfoss), whose regularly widening cascade could almost be a carefully sculpted fountain. Further along Arnafjörður, **HRAFNSEYRI** was the birthplace of **Jón Sigurðsson**, a key figure in the nineteenth-century struggles that led eventually to Icelandic independence. There's a **museum** (mid-June to Aug daily 1–8pm or by arrangement with the curator who lives next door) recording his life, mostly with photographs, and a **chapel** with stained glass (unusual in Iceland) commemorating both Jón and Hrafn Sveinbjarnarson – after whom the tiny settlement is named. Hrafn was a twelth-century doctor, the first to return to Iceland to practice after being trained in Europe, and the grass mound just past the museum is thought to be the site of his boathouse.

Between Hrafnseyri and Þingeyri is one of the most hair-raising sections of road in the country. Approaching the mountains between Arnarfjörður and Dýrafjörður the road ahead appears to cling precariously to a vertical wall – though it's less terrifying once you get onto it, and the descent into **ÞINGEYRI** is comparatively comfortable. Local people often watch the sunset from the top of

Sandfell, an easily climbed hill behind the town, and there's **sbacc** in the school
(☎94/8235) on the other side of Dýrafjörður.

Ísafjörður

High mountains virtually enclosing **ÍSAFJÖRÐUR**, and a bend in the fjord that
denies views of the open sea, combine to lend a special feeling of remoteness to
Vestfirðir's main town – the regular buzz of small planes in and out of the airfield
is often the only reminder of the outside world. However, built largely on a curving sand-spit which provides exceptionally good shelter for oceangoing vessels,
there is a significant fishing industry here.

Practical details
Incoming buses pass the **tourist office** (☎94/3557) at Hafnarstræti 4 and terminate outside *Hotel Ísafjörður* in the town centre. There's an *Edda* Hotel on the edge
of town which has **sbacc** (☎94/4111), a **guesthouse** at Mánagata 4 (☎94/3043),
and a **Seamen's Hostel** (*Sjómannaheimilið*) by the harbour. The nearest **campsite** is 4km away in the sheltered valley of the Tunguá, along a path off Road 61.

The town and around
In town, along Aðalstræti and Suðurgata, you'll find some of Iceland's oldest
houses, some dating from the eighteenth century, one of which holds the
Vestfirðir Museum (usually 2–5pm). If the weather's good (local conditions are
unpredictable even by Icelandic standards) the **surrounding countryside** is a
powerful draw, but walking in the area is sadly limited because of the unstable
surface of the mountains: there are routes through the mountains but they
should only be attempted with proper equipment and advice – or with one of the
bus tours you can pick up in Ísafjörður. The ideal way, though, is **by air**: there
are regular sightseeing flights on offer, and less costly seats available most days
on the postal delivery plane; details from the hotel, tourist office or the *Ernir Air*
desk at the airfield. There's also the small **car ferry**, *Fagranes*, which makes a
once-weekly eleven-hour (return trip) voyage around Ísafjarðardjúp, calling at
several islands and some of the hamlets on either side – more or less the only
chance to see this part of Iceland, and allowing you to bypass a sizeable and relatively tedious chunk of Road 61.

Road 61 from Ísafjörður

After a circuitous negotiation of fjords, the road out of Ísafjörður rises away from
the coast and crosses **Steingrímsfjarðarheiði** – a bleak highland plateau marked
by rock ridges and a few small lakes. You can either branch off on Road 608 to
Bjarkalundur, or continue on Road 61 to **HÓLMAVÍK** – a small fishing village
with a **hotel** with **sbacc** (☎95/3185), and **camping** beside the *Kaupfelagið* shop.
From Hólmavík, there's a weekly bus to **DJÚPAVÍK** – a ghost village at the head
of a shadowy inlet, surrounded by towering rock buttresses and dominated by
the huge carcass of its old herring factory; most of the houses in the village have
fallen down and the picture of desolation is completed by the rusting hull of a
trawler beside the disused jetty.

    If you're keen to rejoin the Ring Road, though, Road 68 runs south from
Hólmavík to Brú, and gives views across to the tiny island of **Grímsey**. This was

formed, according to legend, when two trolls tried to separate Vestfirðir from the rest of the country but were turned by sunlight into what are now the Drangur rock formations just off DRANGSNES, on the other side of the water. During midsummer you can often see seals basking on the beaches. The road continues to BORÐEYRI, often mentioned in *Laxdale Saga* as a departure point for trips abroad. Once one of the country's largest communities, it now has the distinction of being Iceland's smallest town, with just thirty inhabitants.

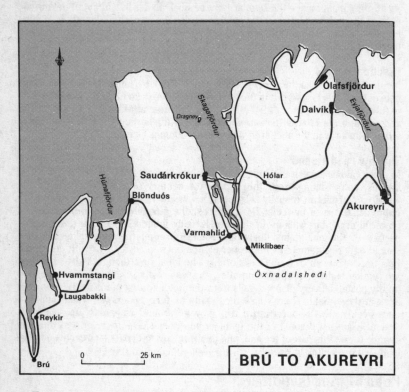

formed, according to legend, when two trolls tried to separate Vestfirðir from the rest of the country but were turned by sunlight into what are now the Drangur rock formations just off DRANGSNES, on the other side of the water. During midsummer you can often see seals basking on the beaches. The road continues to BORÐEYRI, often mentioned in *Laxdale Saga* as a departure point for trips abroad. Once one of the country's largest communities, it now has the distinction of being Iceland's smallest town, with just thirty inhabitants.

BRÚ TO AKUREYRI

Brú to Akureyri

The next stretch of the Ring Road is one of its least interesting. **BRÚ** exists primarily for its function as a road junction, and is about as fascinating as any other. Ten kilometres further along the fjord, **REYKIR** has an *Edda* hotel offering **sbacc** (☎95/1003 & 1004) and a **local history museum** (mid-June to Aug daily 10am–noon & 1–7pm). Road 72 branches off the Ring Road to **HVAMMSTANGI**, where the smaller Road 711 continues around the Vatnsnes promontory, passing some geothermal activity on the shore at Skarð – and, near Hindisvík, at the head of the promontory, a seal breeding ground where many of the creatures and their young can be seen during June and July.

Road 711 rejoins the Ring Road in **Víðidalur**, one of the area's most populated valleys, the focal point of which is **BLÖNDUÓSBÆR**, built on either side of the Blandá River. Not having a good harbour, the town is merely a service centre for the locality, although shrimping is boosting the economy. There's a hotel with all year **sbacc** (☎95/4126), and a **Museum of Handicrafts** (mid-June to Aug Tues, Wed & Thurs 4–6pm; ☎95/4310 & 4153 for visits at other times) in the Girls' College, assembled by Halldóra Bjarnardóttir, a turn-of-the-century women's rights campaigner. Part of Halldóra's platform was the elevation of domestic crafts like knitting and weaving to the status of art – an aim which seems more than justified looking at the exhibits here. Halldóra also happens to be the longest-lived Icelander ever known – 108 years old when she died in 1981.

Although awkward to get around by public transport, the area around **Skagafjörður** is worth exploring for a few days. The best base for this is **SAUÐÁRKRÓKUR**, about 30km east of Blöndóusbær, where there's a hotel with **sbacc** (☎95/5265), and a well-equipped **campsite**. From Sauðárkrókur there are **boat trips** (☎95/6503 & 75935) to the steep-sided, flat-topped island of **Drangey** – now a bird sanctuary, but once the hideout of Grettir the Strong, who stayed here for three years with his brother living off the birds and their eggs. Also known as Grettir Ásmundarson, a courageous but savage character of the Saga Age, he was outlawed for three years. The 7.5km of sea between the island and the mainland is known as **Grettir's Swim**, where the outlaw reputedly crossed to fetch fire (ie the glowing embers he spotted on the mainland after his own fire had been extinguished) and is still sometimes swum for sport.

Inland on the eastern side of Skagafjörður, accessible on Road 767, **HÓLAR** was very much the cultural capital of the north from the eleventh to the late eighteenth century. The country's first printing press was set up here in 1530 by Bishop Jón Arason (who was executed twenty years later at Skálholt for his resistance to the spread of the Reformation from the south, see p.582). The present **cathedral** (daily 2–6pm), built in the 1750s and one of the oldest buildings in the country, contains the bishop's sixteenth-century altarpiece. It's possible to **camp** in the nearby woods or arrange **sbacc** in the school (☎95/5962).

Back on the main easterly route, the Ring Road makes the steep ascent up the high moorland of **Öxnadalsheði**, where legend claims many of the victims of Sturlung Age battles are buried, close to the road at **MIKLIBÆR**. There are countless stories of the ghosts of lost travellers haunting the pass, and in winter it's one of the first in the country to become blocked. The government subsidises the highest farm, ensuring not only that it keeps going but also that help is available for anyone stranded.

Akureyri

If you're tired of hiking and tiny coastal settlements, **AKUREYRI**, Iceland's second town and commercial centre of the north, is a good place to relax in for a day or two. It's an unspectacular place in itself, but if you're doing much touring at all you're almost certain to find yourself here sooner or later.

The town's natural harbour, on the country's longest and deepest fjord, Eyjafjörður, wasn't put to full use until the seventeenth century, when the Danish trade monopoly brought merchants from Helsingør. From then on, the town pros-

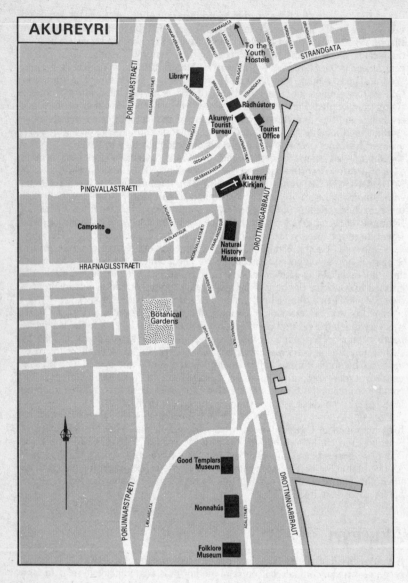

pered: in the late nineteenth century one of the country's first co-operatives was established here, and the Akureyri Co-operative Society (*KEA*) has since played a key role in the local economy. It's said that *KEA* own everything except the churches and the school – and certainly their logo is hard to ignore, plastered on everything from the fish factories to the main hotel and several supermarkets.

The Town

The town is hardly ostentatious, although you can't miss the dramatic **Akureyri Kirkján** (daily 9.30–11am & 2–3.30pm), at the junction of Hafnarstræti and Kaupvangsstræti, whose twin concrete towers (modelled on basalt columns) loom over the town with menace. Inside, there's a dazzling display of stained glass, the central panes of which are from the old Coventry Cathedral – removed, with remarkable foresight, at the start of World War II and sold to an Icelandic dealer who donated them to the then new Akureyri church. The church's other stained-glass windows depict scenes from national history on one side, and Icelandic legends on the other.

A narrow pathway from the top of the steps behind the church leads to **Sigurhæðir**, Eyrarlandsvegur 3 (mid-June to mid-Sept daily 2–4pm; 100kr), the former home of Matthías Jochumsson, poet and author of the national anthem, with a small and unexceptional collection of his furnishings, a few portraits and a little literature. Better to walk right by and head instead for the glorious **Botanical Gardens** at the end of Eyrarlandsvegur (Mon–Fri 8am–10pm, Sat & Sun 9am–10pm; free). Started in 1912 by a local woman, Margrjete Schiöth, the gardens are a rich display of plant life enclosed by the rarity (in Iceland) of fully-grown trees. Besides virtually every Icelandic species, there is an astonishing number of subtropical plants – defying nature by existing at all in these high latitudes.

Below the gardens is the oldest part of Akureyri, and of its many wooden buildings, several, along Aðalstræti, have been preserved and turned into museums. The first is probably the least interesting: the **Good Templars Museum** (Sun 2–5pm) at no. 46, which was where, in 1884, the first Icelandic Good Templars Order was founded – an occasion recorded inside with documents and photos. Further on, the **Nonnahús** (mid-June–Aug daily 2-4.30pm; 100kr) was the childhood home of Jón Sveinsson, author of the "Nonni" children's books, based on his experiences of growing up in North Iceland. Illustrations from some of the stories decorate the walls and numerous translations of the books are displayed. Dating from 1850, the house itself is the oldest in the town and still has its original furniture, giving a good indication of the living conditions of the time.

A few strides on is the **Folklore Museum** (daily June to mid-Sept 1.30–5pm; 100kr), set back from Aðalstræti behind a well-tended garden. The museum has a good assortment of farming and fishing items from Akureyri's past and supplements these with a glorious jumble of TV sets, typewriters, radiograms and some splendid art deco ashtrays. On the second floor, three local brothers contribute a photographic record of local social life through recent decades.

The **Museum of Natural History** (daily except Sat June to mid-Sept 11am–2pm; 100kr), back towards the town centre, contains a remarkably wide-ranging collection of both Icelandic and European fauna. The stuffed birds, with eggs, represent every nesting species in the country, and there's a good seashell collection to counter the truly revolting stock of pickled fish.

Practical details: arriving, sleeping and eating

Buses terminate opposite the little Ráðhústorg, over from which the **Akureyri Tourist Bureau** sell tickets for sightseeing tours in North Iceland, and the **tourist office** (mid-June to Sept Mon–Fri 10am–7pm, Sat & Sun 11am–1pm & 4–7pm), around the corner at Skipagata 13, has general and local information. There are also several banks around the square and the short pedestrianised section of Hafnarstræti contains the post office.

Akureyri has two **youth hostels**: the more central one is at Stórholt 1 (☎96/23657), about a ten-minute walk along Glerágata from the bus terminal, and is open all year. Or there's a newer hostel, *Lónsá* (☎96/25037), open from June to September – 5km north of the town and reachable with buses #8 or #9, leaving every fifteen minutes from Ráðhústorg. The **campsite** (☎96/23379) is just off Þórunnarstræti and gives nice views over the town. Three guesthouses offer sbacc: *Brauðstofan*, at Skólastigúr 5 (☎96/23648 & 21038); *Dalakofinn* Lyngholt 20 (☎96/23035); and *Eining*, Þingvallastræti 14 (☎96/24315).

For **eating**, there are a number of **cafeterias** clustered around the junction of Hafnarstræti and Kaupvangsstræti, and before travelling on to less populated areas it's sensible to stock up at one of the two large **supermarkets** – *Hagkaup* at Norðurgata 62 and the *KEA* store at Byggðavegur 98. On weekdays there's usually a morning market with fruit and veg on Ráðhústorg. There's not much nightlife, but the **library** on Brekkugata (Mon–Fri 1–7pm) can be a veritable haven on rainy afternoons, with numerous books in English about Iceland.

Around Akureyri

Akureyri also makes a handy base for minor jaunts in its vicinity. Road 82 runs along the western side of Eyjaförður, passing DALVÍK, on the way to OLAFSVÍK, an isolated little town walled in by mountains. Along the eastern side of the fjord, Road 83 leads to GRENIVÍK, first passing **Laufas** (Tues–Sun 10am–6pm), an old farm containing a small folk museum. It's worth seeing not so much for the exhibits, but for the fabulous herringbone arrangement of the turfs in the front walls.

A bit further out, about 30km along the Ring Road, is a better-known sight, the **GODAFOSS** waterfall. Although it's not the most spectacular of falls, the force and volume of the plunging water makes an impressive display, and its historical pedigree is impressive: almost a thousand years ago, it was into these swirling streams that Þorgeir of Ljósavatn, a pagan chieftain, hurled his heathen idols after his conversion to Christianity. His act gave the falls its name – waterfall of the gods. Buses (take any going east from Akureyri) generally stop for a few minutes at the nearby café.

travel details

Buses

From Akureyri to Egilsstaðir via Goðafoss & Reynihlið (summer 1 daily, otherwise 3 weekly); Húsavík (summer 1 daily, otherwise 5–6 weekly; 1hr 30min); Ólafsfjörður (summer Mon–Fri 1 daily, otherwise daily except Sat & Tues; 1hr 45min).

From Borgarnes to Akureyri (1 daily, in summer extra daily service on Sun, Tues, Thur & Fri; 6hr); Hólmavík (Tues & Fri 1 daily; 4hr 15min); Ísafjörður (Tues & Thur 1 daily; 10hr); Hellisandur via Ólafsvík (Sat–Thur 1 daily, 2 on Fri; 2hr 30min); Reykholt (Mon–Fri 2 daily; 1hr 30min); Stykkishólmur (Sun–Fri 1 daily, 2 on Sat; 2hr 15min).

From Ísafjörður to Borgarnes (summer Sun, Wed & Fri, 1 daily, otherwise Wed & Fri only; 10hr 15min); Látrabjarg (summer 1 on Sat; 3hr 30min); Reykjavík (summer Sun, Wed & Fri 1 daily, otherwise Wed & Fri only; 12hr).
From Hólmavík to Dragsnes (summer Wed, Sat & Sun 1 daily, otherwise Sat & Sun only; 1hr).

Ferries
From Akranes: to Reykjavík (summer 5–6 daily, otherwise 4 daily; 1hr).
From Stykkishólmur: to Brjánslækur via Flatey (Mon–Fri 2 daily; 4hr).
From Ísafjörður: Frequent trips around Ísafjarðardjúp and Jökulfirðir.

CHAPTER NINETEEN

THE EAST, SOUTH AND INTERIOR

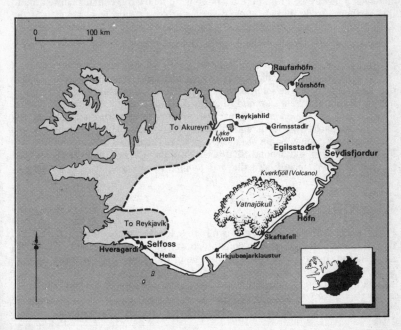

B eyond Reykjavík and the fjords of the northwest, the rest of Iceland is even more remote – a large area, much of which you'll pass through if you're sticking to the Ring Road. The route will certainly leave you with a good impression of Iceland's least-populated half, the **East**, separated by a great lava desert and the enormous Vatnajökull glacier from the West. Alternatively, striking off the Ring Road into areas rarely intruded upon by public transport, reveals hermit-like, seldom-visited communities. Once past Vatnajökull, you're heading into the scenically much duller **South**, for the most part perked up by only a few places of cultural interest. By contrast, there are five specific routes which penetrate the East and South by way of the mysterious, uninhabited **Interior**: each one takes in wide lavafields, passes close to glaciers and volcanoes, and can hardly fail to induce a sense of wonder at Iceland's unspoilt extremes.

THE EAST

Even by national norms, the communities of eastern Iceland are small and scattered, increasingly so the further you venture from the Ring Road. After **Mývatn**, a placid lake beside an astonishing collection of volcanic activity, comes the compellingly bleak **Búrfellshraun**, on the northern edge of Ódáðahraun, a huge lava desert skirted by the Ring Road (and traversable only by interior routes, see "The Interior"). On the other side of the Ring Road is the less forboding **Jökulsáargljúfur National Park**, with a colourful splash of flora (half the entire Icelandic stock of plant life, in fact), a collection of invitingly weird rock and cliff formations, and even a few trees. From here it's possible to follow the **coastal route** around the northern fjords: broad, often fairly featureless peninsulas, which face the Arctic Ocean and are only infrequently connected by public transport – something which contributes to their deep sense of isolation. The Ring Road, however, streaks directly on to **Egilsstaðir**, the largest town in the east but a place of few pleasures. A short distance from Egilsstaðir is **Seyðisfjörður**, the first village of the **East Fjords** (in Icelandic they're called Suðurfirði – the south fjords). It's also the docking place of the international ferry. The comparatively sizeable community of **Höfn** is the East's second Ring Road terminal, and it lies close to **Vatnajökull**, a vast and impenetrable glacier whose innumerable frozen tributaries flow slowly downwards from its uncharted heart – totally dominating everything in this corner of the country. Some of the best views of the glacier and its outflows, are from the hikes in and around **Skaftafell National Park**. This is always a busy place, but has terrain and views that are among the country's most spectacular.

Mývatn

From Goðafoss there's a choice of two routes. Road 85 to the north is the start of the **Akureyri to Egilsstaðir coastal route**, described on p.600. The area's major target, however, is 70km further along the Ring Road: **Mývatn**, a large, shallow lake, which is a favourite nesting place of many species of duck and other waterfowl and is surrounded by an electrifying proliferation of volcanic activity.

Practicals: information, sleeping . . . and shopping

Such is the variety of Mývatn, you could easily spend two or three days around the lake before you feel like moving on. The main base for exploration is **REYKJAHLÍÐ**, on the Ring Road at the northern end of the lake. Opposite the village's supermarket is a **tourist office** (☎96/44220) where you can pick up basic information and hire bikes – much the best way to reach the geological sights, most of which are on the eastern side of the lake, not far from Road 848 which runs close to the water's edge.

The deserved popularity of the area means **accommodation** can be in short supply. There's no problem if you're camping, but otherwise you should reserve space by phoning ahead. Reykjahlíð has two **campsites**, one behind the modern *Hotel Reynihlíð*, and the other on the waterside. On the southern edge of the village is the smaller hotel, *Reykjahlíð* (☎96/44142), which sometimes has **sbacc**. A more reliable spot for summertime **sbacc**, however, is the school at Skútustaðir, to the south of the lake, where there's also a **campsite** and supermarket.

The lake, the village . . . and moving on

There's a variety of natural quirks around the lake, and it's a simple business to see almost all of them in a day by bike; you'll need much longer to explore in depth or on foot. You might start with **Stóragjá**, a deep fissure immediately south of Reykjahíð, with a rope along its side that marks a pathway down to some warm pools where you can bathe. This is not something you'd want to do at **Grjótagjá**, a large fissure a little further from the lake – the water here is far too hot.

Dominating the skyline a few kilometres on is the massive ash cone of **Hverfjall**, estimated to have been formed about 2500 years ago in a single eruption which lasted only a day. The crater is roughly a kilometre wide, and climbing the steep but easy path up to its rim gives a commanding view across the lake. Between Hverfjall and the lake is **Dimmuborgir**, the "black castles", a maze-like collection of lava blocks which form erratic approximations of towers and arches. A track leads up from the road, and a well-defined path runs from the entrance, but it rapidly dissolves into less clear routes leading inside the labyrinth. The lure to delve deeper is powerful, but while Dimmuborgir covers quite a small area it's very easy to get lost; venture cautiously and with a compass when leaving the central path. Jutting into the lake is **Höfði**, a small, rocky and thickly vegetated piece of land inhabited by a large bird population, and where the reddish lava columns of **Klasar** can be seen rising out of the water.

The road swings around the southern end of Mývatn, passing many pseudo-craters and the small village of SKÚTUSTAÐIR before rejoining the Ring Road, which brings you back to Reykjahíð along the western side of the lake.

While you're in Reykjahíð, take the time to visit the local church, which is almost surrounded by lava from the **Mývatn Fires** of 1724–29, when the outpourings from Leirhnjúkur, 10km to the northeast, reached the lake. A carving on the pulpit depicts the church of the time being threatened by the flows. By some miracle the church wasn't harmed and, although it was later demolished, the foundations can still be seen.

The Ring Road moves **away from the lake** past a diatomite factory – the chief local employer – which feeds on the minute skeletons of diatoms (a kind of algae) accumulated on the lake bed. These were formerly used in the manufacture of dynamite, but now form part of a filtering process used in the chemical industry. The barren yellowish ridge immediately behind the diatomite plant and stretching for several kilometres is called **Námaskarð**. Solfataric activity is rife on both sides of the ridge, but the best place to see it is on the eastern side, where bubbling pits of mud and sulphur vents lace the air with noxious gases. The slopes are generally safe to walk on, but be sure to watch out for the light-coloured patches of ground where the crust is very thin and which may not yet have been fenced off.

Jökulsáargljúfur National Park

Soon after passing the track to Askja, the Ring Road reaches the suspension bridge spanning the narrowest point of the Jökulsá á Fjöllum. The structure is a rare man-made intrusion into the bleak handiwork of nature and a particularly welcome sight for lone hikers emerging from the wilderness. One such individual, Ted Edwards, described the sight of it as "a profound experience bordering on the religious," perhaps exaggerating slightly. A few kilometres away on the other side is GRÍMSSTAÐIR, which has a **campsite** (☎96/44292).

From a junction here, Road 864 runs north into the **Jökulsáargljúfur National Park**, a popular area with hikers but relatively uncrowded after the much better-known Mývatn. If you have a tent, a good map, and the inclination and energy, the park's certainly worth a go – but don't expect hotels and fully-equipped campsites.

Around the park

At the park's southern limit, about 30km from Grímsstaðir, is the most powerful waterfall in Europe, **Dettifoss**. The size and force of the Jökulsá á Fjöllum drives the falls, but they're less attractive than their reputation suggests. More eye-pleasing is another fall, **Hafragilsfoss**, about 5km downstream, thanks to the patterns formed by clear tributary waters merging with the glacial flood.

Still in the park, you can follow Road 864 25km north to **Ásbyrgi**, a horseshoe of high cliffs enclosing one of the rare instances of Icelandic woodland. Geologists consider it to have been the site of a huge waterfall; legends say that the formation was made by Oðin's horse, Sleipnir, stubbing a hoof on the ground while flying past. A **campsite** lies near the road, or you can pitch a tent inside the glades of the horseshoe. A further day's hike, along the track on the western side of the river, brings you to **Hlóðaklettar**. The noise of the river is distorted by a hollow in this huge rock, giving the illusion that the river flows through the rock itself. Camping is allowed nearby, but there are no facilities.

Akureyri to Egilsstaðir: the coastal route

Road 85 from just west of Goðafoss leads first to **HÚSAVÍK**, a fair-sized fishing village where there's a hotel (☎96/41220) which can arrange **sbacc**, and a **campsite**. The road continues across the cliffs of TJÖRNES, off which the uninhabited rocky island of Lundey can be seen, as can Flatey and the more distant Grimsey. A lighthouse atop a cliff marks the outpost of MÁNÁ, from which it's usually easy to pick out the Mánáreyjar, volcanic islands which haven't stirred since the nineteenth century. The road continues through the delta of the Jökulsá á Fjöllum beside newly-formed lakes, and passes Ásbyrgi, at the northern end of the Jökulsáargljúfur National Park (see above).

The road then turns north onto the wide, windswept peninsula of **Melrakkasletta**, where a few farms exist in spite of the inhospitable conditions. The only village on the western side is **KÓPASKER**, with a tiny harbour and a spit of modern houses, facing out across the northern headlands and the gentle curve of Öxarfjörður. A guesthouse (☎96/52121) does **sbacc**, and there's also a **campsite** here. Beyond Kópasker, the road curves around the headland, but it's possible to hike directly ahead to see **Rauðinúpur**, a flat-topped volcanic mountain rising like a sheer cliff from the sea. Once on the eastern coast, you can celebrate completing the circuit with the certificates issued in the hotel (☎96/51223) at RAUFARHÖFN, a declining fishing port, where **sbacc** is also available.

From here, the outlook becomes more hilly and the road ascends high heaths to connect the small villages at the heads of three expansive fjords. The first of

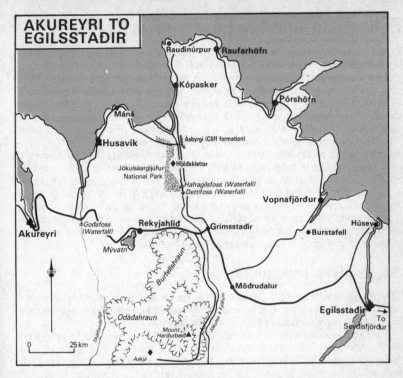

AKUREYRI TO EGILSSTADIR

Raudinúrpur · Raufarhöfn

Kópasker

Þórshöfn

Máná

Husavík

Ásbyrgi (Cliff formation)

Jökulsáargljúfur · Hljódaklettar
National Park

Hafragilsfoss (Waterfall)
Dettifoss (Waterfall)

Vopnafjördur

Godafoss · Rekjahlid · Grímsstadir · Húsey
(Waterfall)
Akureyri · Burstafell

Mývatn

Burfellshraun

Mödrudalur

Odádahraun · Egilsstadir →
To
0   25 km · Mount · Seydisfjördur
Herdurbeid

Askja

these is **ÞÓRSHÖFN**, where there's a **campsite**, and Road 869 which heads into the Langanes peninsula – a narrow strip of land with tall cliffs on either side. Continuing on Road 85 takes you to **VOPNAFJÖRÐUR**. There's a hotel here (☎97/32240) with **sbacc**, and a **campsite**, but otherwise the village is remarkable only for the fact that the 1988 Miss World, Linda Pétursdóttir, grew up here and once toiled in the local fish factory. Out of the village, the road climbs through a long valley and after 18km passes the **Burstafell museum** (summer only), a turf-gabled farmhouse that's decked out as a local museum, its interior well-stocked with domestic paraphernalia. Eight kilometres north of Möðrudalur, Road 85 rejoins the Ring Road.

Soon after Möðrudalur the Ring Road crosses **Möðrudalsfjallgurðar**, the highest pass of its entire circuit, and comes down into the long valley of **Jökuldalur**. Beside the road, the *Brúarás Hotel* (☎97/1046) has comfortable **sbacc**. A kilometre further on, a bridge crosses the river, beyond which Road 925 branches off towards the coast and the **Húsey youth hostel** (☎97/3010). The hostel is a working farm, and seals from a breeding colony on the coast are hunted from here, their skins cured and the meat eaten or sold at the hostel. If this doesn't put you off, the hostel is a good place to see an Icelandic farm in action and you're welcome to join in the daily tasks – though these may include sweeping up the seal entrails that are left lying around. You can usually be collected from the bridge if you phone in advance.

Egilsstaðir and the Eastern Fjords

EGILSSTAÐIR is the administrative centre and transport hub of eastern Iceland, but it has little to offer save for its **tourist office** (☎97/1510), bank and big super-market. Luckily this is the only terminus on the Ring Road where the bus sched-ules make it unnecessary to stay overnight: services to and from Akureyri and Höfn arrive in the early afternoon and depart a couple of hours later. Buses arrive at, and depart from, the hotel car park, from where the main amenities are a short walk down the hill. If you want to stop over anyway, the hotel (☎97/1500) arranges **sbacc**, and there's a **campsite** by the Ring Road.

Egilsstaðir is at the lower end of the long and narrow **Lagarfljót** lake, suppos-edly the home of the *Lagarfljótsormur*, a monster of the Scottish Loch Ness and Swedish Storsjön clan. A road rims the lake, but apart from a once-weekly organ-ised tour, there's a bus only as far as **HALLORMSSTAÐUR**, in the heart of Iceland's largest forest. Besides native birch and willow, imported species include deciduous and coniferous trees, planted and nurtured as a reafforestation experi-ment. It's a popular holiday spot for Icelanders, which means there's a **campsite** a kilometre into the woods and **sbacc** at the college (☎97/1761).

Seyðisfjörður and around

The villages which lie at the heads of the **fjords of the east coast** are very simi-lar in size and character. Insular and rarely visited by outsiders, they have few facilities but good measures of peace and tranquillity.

The only exception to this is **SEYÐISFJÖRÐUR**, where the *Smyril* ferry docks. After the nineteenth-century herring-boom, the town was set to become Iceland's biggest port, but the steep surrounding mountains made expansion impossible. It remains an active fishing and fish-processing centre, however, with past prosperity evidenced by a few elaborately carved Norwegian-style houses. You could do worse than to take a walk on the fjord-side paths, but there's nowhere specific to make for, and it'll take the best part of a day's trek before you even catch sight of the open sea. In the village is a **youth hostel** (☎97/2410), which is only busy on Wednesdays, the day before the ferry sails; the **campsite** is next door. During the week, there's one bus (Circle Passes are not valid and the fare is about 500kr) a day to Egilsstaðir. On Wednesday there's an extra bus which leaves at 3.30pm, an hour after the ferry arrives. The road between the two towns makes an attractive first impression of Iceland, its 25 kilometres rising over a high plateau where, even in late summer, snow remains and pools of meltwater seep into scores of little waterfalls.

It's possible to walk across the mountains from Seyðisfjörður south to the narrow and virtually deserted **Mjóifjörður**, although this should only be attempted by experienced hikers. Alternative ways in are the weekly bus from either Egilsstaðir or Neskaupstaður or a weekly ferry from Norðfjördur.

The Eastern Fjords

It's fairly straightforward to reach the succeeding fjords using buses from Egilsstaðir. Road 92 runs to ESKIFJÖRÐUR and NESKAUPSTAÐUR and prior to reaching them crosses a junction with Road 96 at BÚÐARYERI. This road connects the other fjord villages, after which it meets the Ring Road at Heydalir.

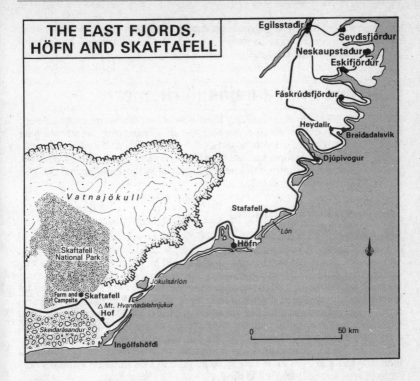

The Ring Road directly from Egilsstaðir runs due south over the high, rugged moorland of **Breiðdalsheiði** – where wild reindeer, descendants of a herd imported from Norway, can sometimes be spotted close to the road. Shortly after this the route swerves towards the coast and descends through the Breiðdalur valley, offering breathtaking views of the fjord below.

About 30km from the Heydalir junction is **BERUNES**, where there's a **youth hostel** in a former farmhouse, lying on a grassy strip between mountains and sea. There's a view straight across to the island of **Papey**, inhabited by Irish hermits before the Settlement and now a summer grazing ground for sheep. The town of **DJÚPIVOGUR** is directly across Berufjörður, close to the pyramidal mountain Búlandstindur. Berufjörður, according to *Njal's Saga*, is where the missionary Þangbrandur landed to begin the conversion of the Icelanders. Djúpivogur itself was once the main trading post of the east and enjoys a setting on a cove sheltered by rock ridges. The town has a **campsite** and a **hotel** (☎97/8887), which arranges **sbacc**, and also provides information on **boat trips** to Papey, and advice about climbing Búlandstindur and visiting the collection of zeoliths – colourful rock crystals which are only found in this area – belonging to a farmer at Teigarhorn.

The Ring Road continues along the coast and passes **Lón**, a lagoon enclosed by a long sandspit. From here, the coastal fringe broadens and is criss-crossed by innumerable glacial rivers. If your feet are itching for some adventurous hiking, a likely place to hole up is at **STAFAFELL**, actually little but a **youth hostel** (☎97/8717), which is a very good base for the **Lonsöræfi Highlands** – a rugged and mountainous but thickly vegetated area, cut by valleys and rapidly-flowing rivers, that is reachable with footpaths from the hostel. The Ring Road runs on to Höfn í Hornafirði, about 30km distant.

Höfn and the Vatnajökull Glacier

Road 99 stretches 5km off the Ring Road over a low, flat promontory between Skarðsfjörður and Hornafjörður, passing the local **campsite** before reaching **HÖFN** proper. There's a **youth hostel** (☎97/8736 & 8730) at Hafnarbraut 8, and, in the same street, a supermarket, bank and swimming pool. The *Hotel Höfn*, about a ten-minute walk from the hostel, functions as the bus terminal and also the local **tourist office** (☎97/8240).

The Town and the Glacier

Höfn actually began life elsewhere, and the town's unusual past is documented in the **local history museum** (daily in summer 2–6pm) by the side of the main road. It's inside one of two houses which arrived by barge in 1863 from a tiny trading post called Papós in Papafjörður. The settlement's shallow harbour had become inadequate for modern ships and the inhabitants were forced to travel on horseback twice a year to Reykjavík to do their shopping. This was too much, so they packed up and came here, from where Reykjavík could be reached by boat. Höfn itself remained small until the fishing boom of the 1950s and the establishment of a fish-freezing factory, still the largest local employer. The museum chronicles the life of the Höfn populace with a sizeable collection of household tools and furniture: but most visitors come here to pass the time when it's raining, and are pleased to flop out in the dry.

There really isn't much else to do. The place's saving grace is the view back towards the mighty Vatnajökull with its icy snouts reaching down. Unfortunately, day-long fogs have a tendency to drift in from the sea and smother the town's greatest asset. The size of the glacier makes it seem nearer than it really is – half a day can be consumed walking to its edge.

If you can't resist the lure of the ice, **guided glacier tours** are bookable from the hotel, or by phoning ☎97-8558. These trips are not cheap (around 2250kr for a half-day trip, 3600kr for a full day), but unless you're already a seasoned Arctic explorer they are an exceptional experience – and the only safe way to scale the glacier. You're driven to the edge of Skálafellsjökull and then have to scramble on foot over the melting edge of the ice-flow to a snowcat. Being on the glacier surface on a sunny day is remarkably warm, and the glare from the snow can be intense. There's a minor ski-run established here and the half-day tours only reach this point, giving memorable views across the neighbouring peaks and down to the speck of Höfn before turning back. On the full-day tour the snowcat penetrates further across the glacier, eventually reaching a mountain so remote it's never been named. On the return journey over the glacier's edge the day's meltwaters will have created little rivulets between the now highly slippery ridges, and it becomes easy to appreciate the dangers of the ice. In the 1920s, a plane crashed into Vatnajökull: the passengers who survived the crash didn't survive the glacier, and their bodies were unceremoniously regurgitated at the foot of the ice through subsequent years.

West to Skaftafell

The section of Ring Road west of Höfn was one of the last to be completed, running around Vatnajökull's icy spurs. Seventy kilometres from Höfn, beneath the stoutest of these spurs, is the glacial lake of **Jökulsárlón**. Buses usually stop for ten minutes here, allowing passengers to admire the ice blocks that have sheared from the glacier and float idly in the lake as if performing a slow ballet. The icebergs are predominantly white, but sometimes scarred black by moraine material, or tinted blue by sunlight reflected off the lake. You see all you need to see from the bank, but for a closer look there are **boat trips** on offer (500kr for twenty minutes). It's also possible to camp beside the lake, but there are no facilities and even in good weather the air is chilled. If the scenery seems oddly familiar, it's because it was used as a suitably dramatic backdrop in the James Bond film, *A View to a Kill*

The Ring Road continues between the glacier and the sea before curving inland by **HOF**. The hamlet stands at the foot of Iceland's highest mountain, **Hvannadalshnúkur**, and has a tiny nineteenth-century turf-church on the site of a pagan temple. **Sbacc** can be provided by the farmhouse *Austuehús* (☎97/8669). Due south of Hof, a series of sandbanks lead out to the rocky **INGÓLFSHÖFÐI**, where Ingólfur Arnarson, Iceland's first settler, landed and spent his first three winters. There's a monument to him erected in 1974 on the 1100th anniversary of his arrival. The Ring Road heads inland from here, passing **Svínafell**, which was the home of Flósi Þordarson, a major character in *Njal's Saga*.

Skaftafell National Park

Twenty-three kilometres from Svínafell, there's a short side-road to **Skaftafell National Park**. Even a barracks-like campsite and the usually high level of visitors can't destroy the beauty of this place. A huge variety of different landscapes packed into a comparatively small area make visiting a bit like taking a crash-course in Icelandic geology, with almost all the country's natural phenomena present in some form. The first priority, though, is finding somewhere to stay. Skaftafell is one of the busiest places in the country, and accommodation is restricted to the large **campsite** beside the entrance road, or very limited **sbacc** at the farm, *Bölti* (☎97/8626), a short way beyond.

The actual park is in a sheltered location, allowing rich patches of flowers and ferns to flourish, the lush vegetation made to look still lusher by the stark views – of powerful glaciers and wild moorlands – which surround. Through and around the park are marked **walks** of graded difficulty. If you're only staying a few hours, or just don't feel like exerting yourself unduly, the easiest is to **Bæjarstaðarskógar** in Morsárdalur, a small wood of rowans, willows and birches, close to a hot springs area ideal for bathing your feet – if not your whole body. Equally simple is the short stroll to **Svartifoss**, an overrated waterfall whose basalt columns inspired the architecture of the National Theatre in Reykjavík. More strenuous is the climb to the **Skorabrýr ridge** across Skaftafellsheiði, but the effort is rewarded with some awesome glacier views. It's also possible to climb the south face of the **Skaftafellsjökull** mountain, but only try if you're a dab hand with crampons and iceaxes.

THE SOUTH

The rare and impressive scenery near Vatnajökull recedes as you swing around Iceland's southeast corner, where the glacier's outwash plain causes a large chunk of the south coast, from Skaftafell to **Skógar**, to be flat and sandy, traversed by fast-flowing and often treacherous rivers. With the great exception of **Þórsmörk National Park**, some way inland, the south coast isn't very striking to look at, but interest is sustained through its historical and literary connections – nowhere more so than in **Njal's Saga country**, the main location of the Saga Age story of feuding dynasties that has become the most famous of Iceland's Sagas. The area also contains the first dash of greenery, a hint of the verdant farmlands further west. Indeed, you'll see little more than farmland from **Hella** to Reykjavík, although the infamous volcano of **Hekla** makes an inland detour from here worthwhile. Further on, **Selfoss** and **Hveragerði**, the latter with its geothermal activity, make reasonable overnight stays if you can't face continuing straight on to Reykjavík.

Because the Ring Road stays close to the coast, the early part of the route through the south has views across the sea to the beckoning outlines of the **Vestmannaeyjar** islands. A ferry from Þorlákshöfn runs to the only inhabited island in the group, **Heimaey**, where the population is proud of its distance from mainland life. Though you can't visit it, nearby **Surtsey**, a volcanic blob that rose from the sea just 25 years ago, is one of the world's newest islands.

Skaftafell to Skógar

Away from Skaftafell the Ring Road crosses the wide and shifting black sands of **Skeiðarársandur**, where high winds are known to whip up sandstorms violent enough to strip the paint from cars. A series of bridges carries the road over a network of turbulent rivers – the outflow from Skeidarárjökull, the glacier dominating the view to the north. It wasn't until the erection of these bridges in 1975 that the Ring Road was completed, and the unpredictability of the rivers and threat of flash floods caused by the occasional glacial burst still make this the most vulnerable stretch, liable to closure even in summer.

The immense square form of Lómagnúpur marks the end of the outwash area and a dramatic change in scenery. The road runs close to high green cliffs with scattered farms at their foot and waterfalls which crash to the ground in a single leap. Between here and Víĭ, this broken line of cliffs formed the coastline until the Ice Age glaciers melted and the land rose. From a layby about 25km onwards, an unsignposted path leads to an example of these cliffs, one with extraordinary hexagonal basalt columns.

Kirkjubæjarklaustur

The first village you reach is **KIRKJUBÆJARKLAUSTUR**, which has an *Edda* hotel with all year **sbacc** (☎99/7799), and a **campsite** a couple of kilometres away at Nýibær. Kirkjubæjarklaustur means "convent at the church farm" referring to the convent which stood here from 1186 until the Reformation. The Systrafoss mountain, behind the settlement, is named in memory of the nuns who lived here, as is Systrastapi, a great rock outcrop close to the village. According to legend, two nuns were buried on top of it after being executed; one for breaking her vow of chastity, the other for speaking ill of the Pope. The second was posthumously pardoned after the Reformation. Systrastapi can be climbed with the aid of chains fixed to its almost vertical sides. From the top there's a good view of some of the thousand-odd pseudo-craters formed by the eruption of Eldgjá in 950.

The village church is dedicated to a former pastor, **Jón Steingrímsson**. During the eruption of Laki in 1783, which produced the world's biggest-known lava flow from a single eruption, his now legendary "Fire Sermon" appeared to halt the molten rock, preventing it from engulfing Kirkjubæjarklaustur. Despite this, the devastation caused was catastrophic. Poisonous gases killed much of the country's livestock and the ruination of grazing and pasture land was the precursor to a famine which killed a quarter of the population.

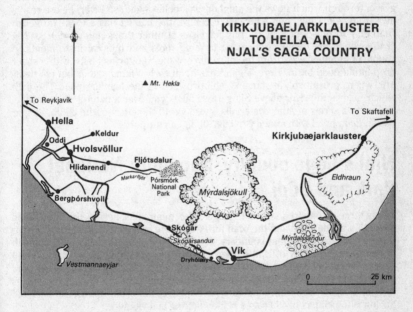

KIRKJUBAEJARKLAUSTER TO HELLA AND NJAL'S SAGA COUNTRY

Katla, Vík and Skógar

As you leave Kirkjubæjarklaustur, the dismal qualities of **Eldhraun**, part of the lavafield formed by the Laki eruption, are evident from the Ring Road, and the only brief relief is a small patch of pasture land which separates mournful Eldhraun from the miserable **Mýrdalssandur**, whose black sands are part of the outflow of Mýrdalsjökull. Beneath the glacier's hundreds of metres of ice is the **Katla volcano**, whose fourteen eruptions since the Settlement have been particularly destructive, mainly because of the speed with which rocks and other glacial debris have been carried by the great volumes of meltwater. An 1860 eruption swept a whole community – people, livestock, buildings and all – out into the sea.

For a closer look at the area, take Road 214 which runs to Kerlingardalur, a secluded valley in the hills on the western side of Mýrdalssandur, passing the *Reynisbrekka* **youth hostel** (☎99/7106 & 7234), from where there's easy walking and great views.

The landscape around **VÍK**, the next town on the Ring Road, is startlingly green and there's a tremendous view of the whole area from the top of Reynisfjall, at whose feet the place nestles. If you're feeling particularly adventurous, and the sea isn't too rough, you can hire a boat in Vík to go around the Reynisdrangar sea-stacks east of the town, and under the great arch of **Dyrhólaey**, the headland to the west. Dyrhólæy's flat top is a bird sanctuary with a number of puffins, fulmars and other species, and you can also reach it by land on Road 218, which branches from the Ring Road. In Vík, **sbacc** can be found at the Community Centre (☎99/7345) and there's a **campsite** close to the road.

Further west, the Ring Road crosses **Skógasandur**, a black carpet of sand and gravel through which flows the sulphorous-smelling Jökulsá River, before reaching **SKÓGAR**. Chiefly an educational centre, the hamlet has a **local museum** (mid-May to mid-Sept daily 5–7pm; for visits at other times phone ☎99/8842 & 8845) with lively demonstrations of farming tools and musical instruments. A couple of minutes' walk from the museum are the **Skógarfoss** falls, with a sheer drop into a deep basin. Here, legend has it, an early Viking settler hid his treasure, where presumably it remains, still drowned in the foaming pool. The path which follows the river above Skógarfoss takes you over a natural stone bridge, and on to a series of other waterfalls – well worth the effort of the climb. Skógar has an *Edda* hotel with **sbacc** (☎99/8870) and a **campsite**.

Njal's Saga country, Þórsmörk National Park and Oddi

Thirty-three kilometres west of Skógar, the mountains beside the Ring Road come to a sudden end and the road turns inland to cross the **Markarfljót**: a river that has been an important boundary since the time of the Settlement, and which is also the main artery of **Njal's Saga country**. Regarded as the most important of the Icelandic Sagas that detail the inter-family feuding of the tenth and eleventh centuries, *Njal's Saga* is a complex chronicle woven around the doings of **Njal Þórgeirsson** and his family. In the Saga, the brutal murder of Njal and his kin is the climax of 400 pages of bloodletting and violence.

The Saga sites ... and accommodation

Although there's little to acknowledge the fact, much of *Njal's Saga*'s action took place here, in and around the Markarfljót's wide valley, and Njal himself lived at **BERGÞÓRSHVOLL** in Landeyjar, a low-lying and boggy district near the mouths of the river. There are no remains of his home, which according to the Saga was burnt down with Njal and his family inside, probably in 1011. Bergþórshvoll has been excavated and many of the finds are in the National Museum in Reykjavík. Evidence of a fire at some date was also discovered, which perhaps bears out the account given in the Saga.

Gunnar Hamundarson, Njal's great friend, with whom his fate was entwined, lived in a more scenic spot overlooking the Markarfljót at **HLÍÐARENDI**, now a hamlet of three or four farms and a church. It can be reached on Road 261 branching off the Ring Road at HVOLSVÖLLUR. Hlíðarendi is at the lower end of a line of green hills which run up into the valley and contrast strongly with the grey mountains, topped by Eyjafjallajökull, on the opposite side. Rauðaskriður, the large rock in the middle of the valley where **Skarp-Heðinn Njalsson**, eldest son of Njall, waited to ambush Þrain Sigfússon, is clearly visible from Hlíðarendi. Such an outlook evoked one of the rare passages in Saga literature where the landscape is acknowledged, and in this case even influenced the course of events. Having been sentenced to three years' exile abroad, Gunnar takes a final look at his home before leaving and says:

How lovely the slopes are, more lovely than they have ever seemed to me before, golden cornfields and new-mown hay. I am going back home, and I will not go away.

Gunnar didn't go away and, for his love of the view (among other things), was murdered in his house soon after uttering these words.

The only Saga Age farm surviving almost intact is **Keldur** (daily 2–5pm or by local arrangement), on Road 264 which leaves the Ring Road 5km west of Hvolsvöllur. It was the home of **Ingjald Höskuldsson**, uncle of Njall's illegimate son, and parts of the farmhouse date back to around 1200, although it's been added to and modified over the centuries.

The village of Hvolsvöllur in itself is uninteresting, but it does have limited sbacc (☎99/8210) and a **campsite**, although a better option for accommodation is in the country beyond Hlíðarendi at the *Fljótsdalur* **youth hostel** (☎99/8498 & 8497). The hostel is often fully booked so you should phone ahead to check and to arrange to be picked up from the Ring Road. The warden, Dick Phillips, also runs walking tours throughout the country, and is a useful source of information on Iceland, as is his extensive collection of books.

Þórsmörk National Park

On the other side of the river from Fljótsdalur (get hiking directions from the hostel) lies **Þórsmörk National Park**, a sheltered valley hemmed in by glaciers and characterised by steep-sided gorges – with a network of walking trails offering eye-catching views across the richly-coloured vegetation. It's well away from the Ring Road and hard to reach: there are no scheduled buses although *BSÍ*, and other companies, run trips from Reykjavík. But the reward for getting here is some stunning scenery and comparatively few other people to have to share it with. Accommodation in the park is limited to very basic camping.

Oddi

Not mentioned in *Njal's Saga* but within easy reach if you're exploring the sites is **ODDI**, an ancient religious centre and seat of learning, on Road 266 from the Ring Road. Its name comes from the Old Norse word *oddr* meaning "spear point" – this supposedly being the place where a spear thrown from heaven struck earth, indicating where a church should be built. A school was established here during the eleventh century by **Sæmundur Sigfússon "the Learned"**.

Educated in Europe, reputedly at the Black School in Paris, Sæmundur became adept in sorcery. When the benefice of Oddi fell vacant, the king of Norway declared that the first claimant to get there could have it. To be sure of gaining the post, Sæmundur promised the Devil his soul in return for getting him there first. The Devil took the form of a seal and carried Sæmundur on his back across the sea from Norway. When they were in sight of Iceland, Sæmundur knocked out the Devil with a psalter, swam to safety and got the job. Sæmundur is held to be responsible for waking the volcano, Hekla, by tossing a closed box he had received from a jilted lover – a Saxon witch – into its crater. Interestingly, the first eruption of Hekla since the Settlement did indeed occur during Sæmundur's lifetime.

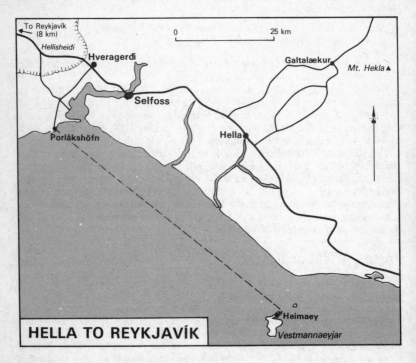

HELLA TO REYKJAVÍK

Hella to Reykjavík

HELLA, 13km beyond Oddi on the Ring Road, is not worth spending any time in except to buy supplies or as an unavoidable overnight stop. For this there's a hotel with **sbacc** (☎99/5928) and a **campsite** 200m from the Rangá bridge along a dusty track from the village. On the opposite side of the river from the campsite is a farm, Ægisíða, where several artificial caves – thought to have been inhabited by some of the Irish hermits who came here before the Settlement – are cut into the volcanic rock.

Mount Hekla

Otherwise the land immediately around Hella is largely flat and featureless, and the eye unfailingly comes to rest on the distant snow-topped outline of **Hekla**. A number of minor roads lead north from the Ring Road in the direction of the volcano, of which the main route is Road 26. Even experienced climbers shouldn't tackle Hekla without an expert guide, though the constant possibility of eruptions tends to deter people from the undertaking anyway. Hekla is the most active of Iceland's volcanoes and is traditionally regarded as the entrance to Hell. It was believed that by standing at its rim you could hear the anguished voices of the eternally damned souls below, crying out in Danish, and that its eruptions were caused by the Devil tormenting souls by tossing them up on his tail for a momentary cooling before they plunged back into the raging inferno. A sixteenth-century map of Iceland captioned the volcano: "Hekla, cursed with eternal fires and snow, vomits rocks with a hideous sound". The eruption of 1104 buried most of the nearby farms in ash, one of which was excavated in 1939 and is worth a quick look – though to get a clearer idea of twelfth-century life, you're better seeing the reconstruction near SKÁLHOLT, described on p.582. There are two **campsites** about 10km from Hekla, one by the farm Galtalækur, the other a little further south at Leirubakki, where you'll also find a **youth hostel** (☎99/5591).

Selfoss and Hveragerði

As the Ring Road draws close to Reykjavík, it passes through increasingly populous countryside and at **SELFOSS** civilisation begins to reassert itself. The town has a major dairy industry, a large supermarket and its **museum** (June–Aug daily 1–7pm, rest of the year Mon–Fri 1–9pm) boasts the country's biggest collection of stuffed animals. There is **sbacc** in the school (☎99/1765 & 1970), and a very well-equipped **campsite**.

HVERAGERÐI, 12km further on, is built in a geothermal area and greenhouses heated by natural energy have made the town a substantial fruit and vegetable producing centre. Even the souvenir shop here is a greenhouse, and doubles as a restaurant: it's called *Eden* and can hardly be missed. Geothermal activity is concentrated in the valley behind the town, where a geyser called Grýta sends up a boiling spurt about once an hour. There is a **youth hostel** at Hveramörk 4 (☎99/4700), next to which is a **campsite**.

From Hveragerði, the Ring Road ascends Hellisheiði and runs through a virtually unbroken lavafield for the remaining 40km to Reykjavík.

Vestmannaeyjar

The archipelago of **Vestmannaeyjar** – or the Westman Islands – comprises fifteen islands a few kilometres off the south coast. Of these, **Heimaey** is the only one that is inhabited, with just one settlement on the tiny island. It was to here that Ingólfur Arnarson pursued the slaves who had mutinied and killed his brother, Hjörleifur Hróðmarsson. Ingólfur caught the slaves and killed them, and because they had come from Britain the islands became known as the

"Westmenn's Isles"*. The present islanders have grown into a self-contained and resilient community that likes to consider itself independent of the mainland. There's even a Vestmannaeyjar "National Festival" staged over three days each August. Other than flying, the only way to get here is on the *Herjólfur* **ferry**, which crosses twice a day (once-daily outside of summer) from Þorlákshöfn on the mainland to Heimaey. Buses from Reykjavík connect directly with the sailings.

The islanders' powers of endurance have undergone two main tests. The first was in 1627 when Algerian pirates killed 40 of the 500 inhabitants and carried off a further 250 to be sold as slaves. The second was the **volcanic eruption of 1973** which began at 2am on January 23 with the appearance of a fissure nearly two kilometres long to the east of Heimaey, close to the long-dormant Helgafell. Molten lava gushed from about fifty separate craters and the 5000-strong population were evacuated on the first night to the mainland. The eruption, which continued until June 28, threatened to block the harbour and destroy the crucial fish-processing plants around it. Fortunately, the halting of the lava flow, by cooling with pumped seawater (the first stoppage of its kind), actually improved the harbour. Although the entrance had become narrower, it was now shielded from the strong easterly winds. Further protection from these winds was afforded by the crater of Eldfell, a volcano formed during the eruption, which enabled trees and other vegetation to be grown for the first time. The following summer saw the clearing away of the ash which had covered the town to a depth of two metres, and a return of the population, save for a few hundred who had lost their livelihoods and decided to stay on the mainland. The disruption caused to the fishing industry, however, was a contributing factor to the runaway inflation that afflicted the country's economy in the mid-1970s.

Around the island

Sailing into Heimaey's harbour, it's easy to pick out the newly-formed land, its greyness and the two brown humps which rise from it in strong contrast to the greenery on the rest of the island. Once ashore, it's hard to resist a walk along the otherwise unremarkable residential streets which disappear into a solid wall of lava at their eastern end. Several houses remain half-buried by the rock and close by are the shells of others, blitzed by lava bombs.

A short way up the hill from the harbour, on the corner of Kirkjuvegur and Birkihlíð, is a **tourist office** (Mon–Fri 9am–5pm, Sat & Sun 10am–2pm) where you can pick up a free map showing the town and the track that leads around the island and alongside the new lavafield. Heimaey is small enough to be leisurely explored in a day and all the peaks (the highest is Heimaklettur on the far side of the harbour) can be climbed fairly easily – although beware of loose surfaces. The track eastwards from the town leads over the edge of the lava and around Eldfell. A brief distance along it, a short path runs steeply upwards to a monument to **Jón Þorsteinsson**, a local priest who was killed during the Algerian pirate attack as he prayed in a cave. The original monument to him was buried beneath the lava but this replacement stands 100m directly above the site of his house, now deep within the rock. On **Eldfell**, the ground is warm to the touch, hot enough a few inches down to roast a potato and, at a depth of 20–30m, reaching 1000°C. Steam issues

---

* During these times, natives of the British Isles were known as "Westmenn" to distinguish them from the "Eastmenn" or Norwegians.

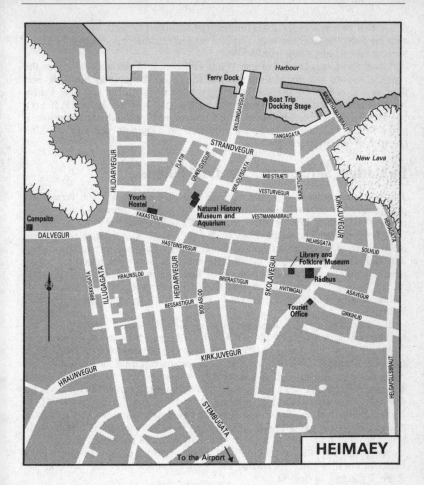

HEIMAEY

from the rock at several points and close by are the pipes of the heating system which utilises the natural energy to provide power for the town.

The new lavafield, **Kirkjubæjarhraun**, forms a tortured beach along the eastern coast. At its edge are near-vertical cliffs, formed when the molten lava was cooled by the cold Atlantic waters, and the generally desolate mood of the terrain is heightened by the crashing ocean waves. The force of the sea is sufficient to toss far ashore remnants of shipping lost in the area, and parts of the Belgian trawler *Pelagus*, which sank in 1982, can be seen.

Back in the town, the **Folklore Museum** (daily 1–3pm; free) inside the Rádhús, has an extensive collection dating from the Algerian invasion onwards, plus a comprehensive collection of Icelandic stamps and local art. There's also an enthralling archive of newspaper reports on the 1973 eruption and some outstanding photos. In the **Natural History Museum and Aquarium** (daily 11am–5pm) at Heiðarvegur 12, the stuffed creatures pale into insignificance beside the tanks of live fish, which include almost every type found off Iceland. The curator is a genuine fish-obsessive and watching him tenderly tickling his charges' bellies at feeding time makes a visit worthwhile.

A local sport, taught even to very young children, is to climb and swing on the ropes which are suspended from many of the cliffs. The technique was devised long ago to collect puffins and their eggs from nests on the cliff-face. **Puffin hunting** is still carried out and reaches a peak during July and August. Puffin is a special dish of Heimaey, but to eat it in a restaurant is prohibitively expensive. If you have the stomach for it, buying a puffin from a shop to cook yourself is far cheaper, about 100kr per bird.

Boat trips, Surtsey and practical details

The best way to see live puffins, and the rest of the immense and varied bird population that occupies the cliffs, is with the two-hour **boat trip** (for details phone ☎98/1616 & 1195 or ask at the tourist office) which leaves every evening from the harbour. The small vessel circles the island several times, visits caves hewn out by wave action and approaches **Surtsey** – an island formed by an eruption in 1963 where the evolution of plant and bird life on the otherwise barren rock is being scientifically observed. While this goes on (as it probably will indefinitely) visiting the island is prohibited. Whales are often seen to the east off Heimaey, although they are as easily spotted from the high ground around Eldfell as from a boat.

You'll need to spend at least one night on Heimaey if you come by ferry and want to stay more than a couple of hours: both the **youth hostel** at Faxastígur 38 (☎98/2915), and **campsite**, in Herjólfsdalur, are signposted from the harbour. As for **food**, it's a good idea to bring what supplies you can from the mainland, especially if you're staying over the weekend. Otherwise the best bet is *Bjössabar*, Bárustígur 11, which has a tasty variety of food to eat in or take away. It's to the campsite that many islanders relocate themselves during the course of the **National Festival**: in 1874 rough seas prevented a crossing to the mainland to attend the annual gathering at Þingvellir, so the Vestmannaeyjar people of the time stayed at home and held their own shindig. It has continued annually ever since, gaining a reputation for unbridled hedonism which causes Heimaey's population to swell to twice its normal size for the event's three-day duration. Get there, if you can, in August.

THE INTERIOR

Stark and desolate but at the same time charged with raw beauty, nothing you might see elsewhere in Iceland prepares you for **the Interior**. The very strength and unpredictability of nature means that the country's heart is desolate and entirely uninhabited, except for the ghosts of early pioneers who lost their way and perished in its uncharitable midsts. Much of the interior is only safely seen from a guided coach-tour, and even then it's a bumpy ride: there are no roads over what are mainly bleak grey lava deserts, just tracks marked by stakes, causing some hairy moments as dashing glacial rivers are forded. It's no surprise to learn that the first lunar astronauts came here to train for their landing on the moon.

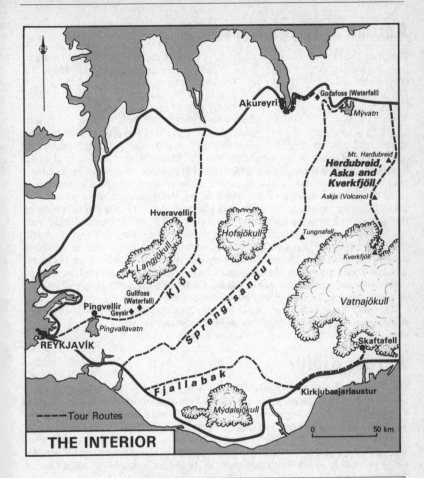

THE INTERIOR

- - - - Tour Routes

0   50 km

INTERIOR TOURS

Five tours penetrate Iceland's interior. Trips over **Sprengisandur** and **Kjölur** cross from Reykjavík to Akureyri or Mývatn, and from Akureyri to Reykjavík respectively. Trips to **Askja** leave from Mývatn, as do those to **Kverkfjöll** (also, though less frequently, from Egilsstaðir). The **Fjallabak** (Behind The Mountains) tour runs from Reykjavík to Skaftafell, or vice versa. All of these are one-day coach trips except the one to Kverkfjöll, which is a three-day tour by minibus including two nights' accommodation and a day walking on a glacier. All the tours except Fjallabak include a guide, although large parties tend to make the guides inaccessible – but this is not a problem with the smaller and more informal groups to Kverkfjöll. It's possible to leave or join any of the tours anywhere along their routes, and there's at least one FÍ hut and campsite on each.

Across Sprengisandur

Featuring the most desolate terrain found in Iceland, the **Sprengisandur** trip runs from Reykjavík, taking the Ring Road to Hella before turning inland and following the course of the Ytri-Rangá river. The coach passes within 10km of the foot of Hekla prior to reaching Þjorsárdalur and the reconstructed Saga Age farm at Stöng (described on p.582). This is easily missed unless the guide points it out. You stay longer at **Þórisvatn**, a lake whose waters find their outlet in the Þjórsá and feed a new hydroelectric power station. After this the tour climbs into the stony highlands between Hofsjökull and the western edge of Vatnajökull, which mark the beginning of Sprengisandur proper. This is where the fun begins, an incredible journey through mile after mile of grey sand, stones and rocks which have lain untouched for thousands of years. The enduring memory is of nothingness: the glaciers and mountains which fringe the desolation seem a long way away. Being part of a coachful of tourists obviously doesn't evoke the full power of the place, but is at least a safe way to gain an inkling of the perils of what was, during the times of horse travel, the major route between north and south Iceland.

Glacial rivers are periodically crossed and there's a stop for lunch at an FÍ hut deep in the heart of nowhere. Slowly, very slowly, the route gains traces of green and the coach pauses at the **Aldeyjarfoss waterfall**, high up in Barðardalur, before descending into the valley, whose scattered farms, after hours of looking at barren wastes, seem positively lively.

The road down from Barðardalur hits the Ring Road close to Goðafoss, where the coach turns left for Akureyri, or right for Mývatn.

Across Kjölur

From Akureyri, the **Kjölur** tour follows the Ring Road before turning off along the course of the Blandá River, passing a hydroelectric power station which is being built mostly underground. Once into the Interior, the outlook is similar to Sprengisandur – grey sand and stones. For much of its duration, the tour follows the line of a barbed-wire fence erected to keep the sheep from the west separate from the those of the east and restrict the spread of disease. Someone is actually employed solely to ride back and forth along the fence to check that it has not been breached.

Kjölur, the highest point on the tour, is a broad rocky pass between the massive ice-sheets of Langjökull and Hofsjökull. Hvítárvatn, at the foot of Langjökull, is where meltwater accumulates before flowing into the Hvítá and on towards Gullfoss. The tour pauses briefly at Gullfoss, as it does later at Geysir, before a teatime stop at Laugarvatn. There's another short stop at Þingvellir on the way to Reykjavík.

Fjallabak

This runs from Reykjavík through the uninhabited lands north of Mýrdalsjökull to Kirkjubæjarklaustur and Skaftafell, a trip which can also be made in the opposite direction. The route twists between mountains of green or earthy brown and there are two specific halts of 45–60 minutes. First off is at **Landmannalaugar**, said to have been the scene of many baptisms during the Conversion, and where the series of warm pools still provide good bathing. The second is for **Ófærufoss**, a waterfall spanned by a natural lava bridge. You rejoin the Ring Road 28km west of Kirkjubæjarklaustur, where the bus pauses briefly before continuing to Skaftafell.

Mount Herðubreið and Askja

The crown-like formation of the mountain of **Herðubreið** has earned it the nickname "Queen of the Icelandic Mountains". It lies in the desert of Ódáðahraun, north of Vatnajökull, and you can get within a few kilometres of it on a tour which leaves the Ring Road not far east of Mývatn, along a track leading eventually to Askja. Marked initially by wooden posts and tyre-tracks, the track subsequently hits a mass of jagged lava. Picking a tortuous route, it follows the course of the glacial river, Jökulsá á Fjöllum – in places up to a kilometre wide – until arriving at **HERÐUBREIÐARLINDIR**, an oasis of poor grass and small clear springs, where there's a **campsite** and **FÍ hut**.

The track then veers away from the river towards the Dyngjufjöll mountains, and **Askja**, the volcano responsible for creating the grim and forbidding surrounds. Its worst known eruption was in 1875, and the dust from it carried to mainland Scandinavia. Within the crater are two lakes, the deep and wide Öskjavatn and the smaller Víti – whose name means Hell. In 1839 Víti was described as "a complete devil's cauldron from which all living things fly; horses quake with mortal fear and can hardly stand when taken to the brink". It's quietened down a lot since then, and you can walk around the rim in about an hour or scramble down its steep sides, dotted with sulphur springs, to bathe in the opaque waters.

In 1986 a new bridge was opened across the Jökulsá á Fjöllum, allowing a route between Askja and Kverkfjöll further south. As yet the track is indistinct and not shown on maps, but assuming it survives it should become clearer with use.

Kverkfjöll

The main track to **Kverkfjöll** leaves the Ring Road 4km beyond Möðrudalur, crossing the undulating gravel and passing the occasional oasis. One of these is **Hvannalindir**, where the eighteenth-century outlaw, Eyvindur, fashioned a rough shelter using lava blocks around a hollow in the edge of the lavafield. The outlaw also built a sheep-pen with a covered passageway to the nearby stream, so the animals could drink without being spotted. Both can still be found but are well-concealed, as Eyvindur intended. Just before reaching Kverkfjöll, the track winds through a maze of ash hills to a **campsite** and **FÍ hut**, overlooking the braided streams of the Jökulsá á Fjöllum's upper reaches.

The river rises from hot springs under Vatnajökull and its heat forms an **ice cave**, whose opening is 5km from the FÍ hut. Some daylight penetrates a few metres into the cave but visibility rapidly diminishes in the thick damp fog which fills it. The walls and roof are sculpted by constantly dripping water, and the debris embedded in the ice gives a marbled effect. Not far from here the slopes of the glacier are climbable, but shouldn't be attempted without a guide.

Low white clouds hover overhead during the long hard slog, and once at the top these are revealed to be steam, issuing from deep fissures in the ice. Nearby sulphur springs, hissing like boiling kettles, prevent ice from forming in their immediate area, and the bare yellow earth is in stark contrast to the surroundings. The outstanding views from the glacier take in the entire expanse of Ódáðahraun, the Dyngjufjöll mountains, Herðubreið, and even the mountains of the distant northern coast.

travel details

Buses

From Egilsstaðir to Akureyri (summer Mon–Sat 1 daily, spring & autumn 3 weekly, winter none; 6hr); Breiðdalsvík (Mon–Fri 1 daily; 2hr 40min); Hallormsstaður (summer Mon–Fri 1 daily; 1hr); Höfn (summer 1 daily, autumn & spring Mon, Wed & Fri 1 daily, winter none; 5hr 15min); Neskaupstaður (summer Mon–Fri 1 daily, otherwise Sun–Fri 1 daily; 1hr 40min); Seyðisfjörður (summer Thur & Fri, Mon & Tues 1 daily, 3 on Wed, otherwise Mon–Fri 1 daily; 30min).

From Húsavík to Vopnafjörður via Raufarhöfn and Þórshöfn (summer Mon & Fri 1 daily; 4hr 45min); Mývatn (summer Mon & Tues, Thur & Fri 2 daily, 1 on Wed; 45min).

From Djúpivogur to Höfn (summer Sun & Tues–Fri 2 daily, otherwise 3 weekly; 1hr 45min).

From Höfn to Reykjavík via Skaftafell, Kirkjubæjarklaustur, Vík, Selfoss & Hveragerði, (summer 1 daily, winter two weekly; 10hr).

From Selfoss to Reykjavík (6–7 daily; 1hr 20min); Þorlákshöfn via Hveragerði (Mon–Thur 1 daily, 2 on Fri; 30min).

From Vík to Reykjavík via Hella, Hvolsvöllur & Selfoss (summer Mon–Sat 1 daily, 3hr 30min)

From Þorlákshöfn to Reykjavík via Hveragerði (2 daily, 3 on Sun; 1hr).

Ferries

From Þorlákshöfn: to Heimaey (summer 2 daily, rest of the year 1 daily; 3hr 45min).

International Ferry

From Seyðisfjörður: to Tórshavn, Lerwick, Bergen, Hanstholm (summer 1 weekly).

PART SEVEN

THE FAROE ISLANDS

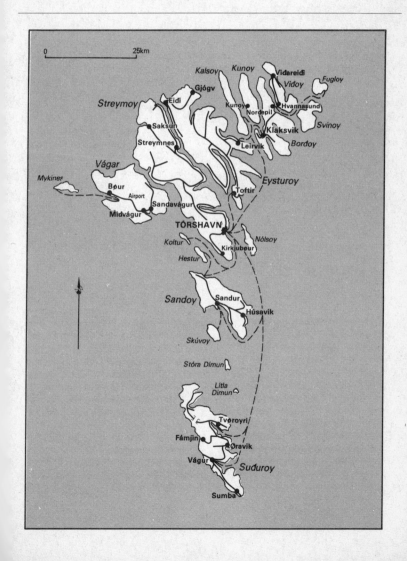

0   25km

Kalsoy   Kunoy   Viðareiði   Fugloy
Gjógv   Viðoy
Streymoy   Eiði
Kunoy   Nordepil   Hvannasund
Saksun   Svinoy
Streymnes   Klaksvik
Leirvík   Bordoy
Vágar
Mykines   Eysturoy
Bøur   Airport   Toftir
Midvágur   Sandavágur
TÓRSHAVN   Nólsoy
Koltur   Kirkjubøur
Hestur
Sandoy   Sandur
Húsavík
Skúvoy
Stóra Dimun
Litla Dimun
Tvøroyri
Fámjin   Øravík
Vágur   Suduroy
Sumba

Introduction

The Faroe Islands lie roughly halfway between Iceland and the Shetlands, a triangular grouping some 60 kilometres east to west and 90 kilometres north to south. They are volcanic islands – wild, wet and windy with no indigenous trees, few bushes and little farmland. But the original volcanic plateau has been eroded into an archipelago of fjords and mountains, covered in grasses and marsh plants, which gives the islands a distinct, austere beauty. There are millions of birds nesting on the cliffs and the seas are full of fish. It's a harsh, geographically isolated land, but a prosperous one, with a proud individual history and culture recently bolstered by the economic returns brought in by the fishing industry.

The **northern islands** are mountainous, the villages stuck on the steep slopes, their brightly painted houses contrasting with the grey-brown basalt behind and the deep blue of the sea in front. On the islands further **south**, the landscape is softer, with lower, gentler hills, larger expanses of farmland, and a treeless beauty which reveals the crisp, far-north patterns of colour and light on all but the dullest of days.

The **climate** is surprising. Lying in the main path of the Gulf Stream, the Faroes are mild in winter, cool in summer; the two main southern islands, Suduroy and Sandoy, have more sunny days than the northern islands and are generally slightly warmer. From December to March the average temperature is about 4.5°C (40°F), rising to an average of 11°C (52°F) during the summer; winter nights are long and North Atlantic storms can rage for days, cutting off some of the smaller islands. Throughout the year mist and rain are common, but weather changes are rapid, and there are nearly always different conditions prevailing on different islands.

Getting There

Surrounded by the turbulent seas of the North Atlantic, the Faroes have always been inaccessible, and getting there can still take time.

Flying is the obvious option, and there is a small airstrip on the western island of Vagar. Even so, variable weather conditions can make flight delays likely, if not regular. (The airlines will foot accommodation and food bills if you do get stuck.) *Danair* (the Danish airline, not the charter company) currently fly once daily Monday to Saturday from Copenhagen, and lay on extra summer flights Wednesday, Friday, Saturday and Sunday. The cheapest fare is around £200 return for a 14–28 day stay, but under 25s, groups and senior citizens qualify for concessions. *Icelandair* (see p.548 for address) have year-round Tuesday flights from Reykjavik and Egilsstadir, with extra summer flights on Thursdays and Saturdays, for around £185 return (concessions for under 21s); between May and September there are also Tuesday flights from Glasgow for around £140 return. Once you've landed, there's a connecting **airport bus-ferry-bus** service (£8–10) which runs into Tórshavn; the journey takes two hours.

By **sea** it's a far longer haul. Two ferry lines sail to the Faroes. From June to September the *Smyril* line (PO Box 5, Aberdeen; ☎0224-572615) connects Denmark, the Shetlands, the Faroes, Iceland and Norway. Fares are around £60 one-way with couchette from the Shetlands, £80 from Bergen in Norway; and there are big concessions for students under 28, children, groups and for travellers at the start or end of the sailing season. The total sailing-time between Denmark (Hanstholm) and Tórshavn is around 40 hours; the leg between the Shetlands and Tórshavn just over 13 hours. It's a continuous service and it's possible, if you wish, to simply stop over for 2 or 3 nights on your way to, say, Iceland. *Scandinavian Seaways* (see *Basics* for address) also sail once weekly during the summer from Esbjerg direct to Tórshavn, the journey taking around 35 hours; tickets cost a little over £100 one-way. Further details are available from the companies direct, the Danish Tourist Board in London or the **Faroese Tourist Board**, Skansaegur 1, 3800 Tórshavn, Faroe Islands.

Red Tape and Health

Scandinavians only need an ID card for entry to the Faroes; British, Irish and EC citizens require either a full or visitor's passport. All of these are allowed to stay for an unlimited period. US, Australian, New Zealand and Canadian visitors require a full passport but are only entitled to a maximum stay of three months. All other nationals should consult the Danish Embassy for visa regulations.

EC citizens are covered by a reciprocal agreement which entitles them to free **medical care** and a partial refund of dentists' and pharmacies' bills, though it's still worth taking out some form of **health insurance**. Other travellers should certainly take out insurance; see *Basics* for details of companies and costs.

Information and Maps

Before you leave, it's worth visiting the Danish Tourist Board in your home country (see *Basics*), who have bumph, useful booklets and timetables.

The best **map** you can buy outside the Faroes is the 1:100,000 plan of all the islands (£8.25) produced by the Danish cartographers, *Kort-og Matrykelstyrelsen* and available from *Stanford's* in London (again see *Basics* for their address). Once in the Faroes, there are **tourist offices** at Tórshavn and Klaksvik (in fact two in Tórshavn), and they have information on accommodation, eating and – such as there are – sights. The tourist office in Tórshavn also sells decent **maps** of the islands for around £3. Hours are erratic but the offices stay open until late during summer. In winter it's 9am–5pm, closed weekends.

Communications, Money and Costs

International calls have to be made from a hotel. The dialling code from the Faroes to Britain is 00944. Post offices (*Postverk Føroya*) are open shop hours (see "Directory"). Poste Restante is available at the post offices in Tórshavn and Klaksvik.

The Faroese **currency** is the *krone*, which has the same value as – and is interchangeable with – the Danish *krone*. **Banks** are open Monday–Friday 9.30am–4pm. As elsewhere in Scandinavia **prices** are high. Stick to youth hostels and self-catering and you can manage on around £12 a day. Start to eat out and the cost spirals: breakfasts cost about £4, lunches (the main meal) around £6 – though you can save on drinking, as alcohol is prohibited. Youth hostels (category 3 accommodation) cost £7 a night, while a bed in a category 2 hotel (the usual accommodation) averages around £15 single, £22 double.

Getting Around

Traditionally contact between Faroese villages was by boat. But in recent years the Faroese have undertaken a considerable road-building programme, linking villages by tunnels, causeways and bridges, and consequently transportation within the islands is far easier and more reliable than it used to be. The buses run to schedule and generally connect with inter-island ferries wherever necessary.

Transport costs for individual journeys are high. If you intend to travel around a lot, the Tórshavn bus station, on Gundalsvegur, sells a **bus pass** (valid 1 month, £40), which is good for all bus journeys on the islands. For **ferries**, on the first ferry you board (except the one to Suduroy which costs more), buy a **ten-journey card** (around £20): this is valid on all the ferries except the Suduroy service, and any round-trip costs two vouchers – though only one if you stay on the boat, which is what a lot of people do. Pick up, also, a bus and ferry **ferdaetlan** (timetable) and **route map** from the tourist office.

There's also a limited **helicopter** service linking most of the islands: an exhilarating way to get around and not as expensive as you might think – Tórshavn to Mykines costs around £20 one-way – though you have to book ahead.

Distances are short enough to make **hitching** easy, but it's rarely worthwhile as journeys often involve meeting ferries. **Walking** between villages by road is usually straightforward, and distances are again not vast. But the old walkways, marked by cairns, have deteriorated to make cross-country hikes sometimes difficult, even dangerous – a situation exacerbated by the inconsistent weather. Indeed, they should only be attempted in groups of at least two by experienced hikers, or wherever a guide is available; check with the tourist office for details.

Bicycles can be hired from *p/f Thomas Dam*, Niels Finsensgøta, Tórshavn, but be warned: the countryside is very hilly and in places there are very long and steep inclines that demand both stamina and excellent brakes. There is also the serious and very real danger of poisonous exhaust fumes overwhelming cyclists in the long tunnels. **Car hire** can usually be arranged but only at high rates – £25 per day is about average.

Sleeping

The Faroes have few tourists and, consequently, little accommodation, and at the cheap end of the market summertime pressure for beds can be intense. Details of places to stay are given throughout the guide and at many you'll need to reserve a bed in advance. If you want to be certain of your first night's accommodation in Tórshavn, reserve a room at the *Seamen's Home*, Tórsgøta 4, 3800 Tórshavn, by letter (see p.630); or, alternatively, head for the elastic gates of the youth hostel.

With the exception of Tórshavn (population 14,000) and Klaksvik (6000), the Faroese live in small villages. Many places offer some form of accommodation, but the more flexible – and forward-thinking – you can be, the better. Certainly if you want to stay on the smaller islands, take a **sleeping bag**, and, if you want to sleep out anywhere, a **tent**.

There are three **categories** of established accommodation: category 1, which covers plush hotels from around £35 per person per night; category 2, which includes more ordinary hotels and guesthouses for around £15 a night or £11 each in a double room; and category 3 – mostly youth hostels, normally (though not always) with dormitory accommodation for about £7 a night if you're an *IYHF* member, slightly more if you're not (see *Basics*).

There are other alternatives. Summer **cottages** booked through the tourist office are cheap for groups, but be sure to reserve them well in advance. **Private accommodation**, again booked through the tourist office, costs around the same as a category 2 hotel, but there's limited availability, concentrated almost entirely within Tórshavn. There are also seven official **campsites** spread around the main islands. If you are camping rough (and it's possible in most areas), ask before pitching a tent on any old piece of grass and bathing or washing in the nearest stream. Hay is a valuable winter fodder and the stream may be a village water supply.

Food and Drink

Few Faroese eat out and there are remarkably few restaurants on the islands. However, all category 2 accommodation provides basic Faroese food for about £10 a head, full-board, and in Tórshavn there are a couple of more expensive places to eat – the *Hotel Hafnia* and the *Hotel Borg*. If you eat a meal in either of them, be prepared to pay at least £20 per person.

As regards **what they serve**, you'll usually get some form of fish, mutton or poultry, with potatoes, at all the category 2 hotel restaurants; otherwise the only variation is the Danish *smørrebrød*. Despite improvements in communication with the outside world, **fresh vegetables** rarely make it onto the table and, amazingly enough, there are no **fresh fish** shops in the Faroes as most of the islanders still have easy access to the catches of friends, neighbours and relatives. If you want to try the fresh fish – and it is excellent – the *Borg* and *Hafnia* restaurants always serve fish, and you can also buy direct from the fish factories or, if you're around when they come in, the fishermen themselves: watch out for the small boats unloading on the quay, which they do more or less all day. The islanders' own favourite foods are **dried meats**, particularly puffin and mutton, and nearly everyone has their own meat-drying outhouse or *hjallur*. They're available from supermarkets, but are strong-smelling and something of an acquired taste.

Alcoholic drinks are *not* for sale in the Faroes as the islanders operate a system of public prohibition and private rationing. The easiest thing to do is to rely upon your duty-frees. Failing that, you can attempt the arduous task of getting onto the rationing books – the tourist office should be able to help.

Festivals

Despite the restricted sale of alcohol, there seems to be no shortage of the stuff during Olavsøka, the islands' principal festival, held annually on July 28–29.

The festival commemorates St Olav, king of Norway (killed on July 29, 1030), who was responsible for bringing Christianity to the islands and for the opening of the parliament. There are a variety of events, including rowing competitions in old-style Faroese boats, and both days end with hours of traditional **chain dancing** – a unique relic of the medieval ballad tradition in which the dancers provide their own music by singing ballads while adding simple complementary dance steps.

More controversial are the spontaneous celebrations that follow the **whale killings**. The whales travel in schools of between 50 and 1000 and cross the seas around the Faroes. If they come close enough to the islands, the Faroese attempt to drive the whales into a shallow fjord where they can be trapped and killed – a savage affair in which islanders of all ages join until the sea is blood-red. The whale-meat is divided up among the householders of the district, and was in the past an invaluable source of fresh meat and oil. Whale products are no longer necessary, but the whale-kill (*grindadráp*) still seems to many Faroese an important part of their heritage. To many outsiders, however, it is an unnecessary blood-letting.

Directory

BIRDS Lots of them, in hundreds of varieties. See *Contexts* for more details.

BOOKS The great figure of Faroese literature is William Heinesen. Most of his books are hard to get hold of outside the Faroes, but *Tower at the Edge of the World* and *Neils Peter* are worth reading if you can track them down. Heinesen conveys the small-town isolation of Tórshavn better than any other writer. The best history of the Faroes is John F. West's *Faroe, the Emergence of a Nation*. Also, if you can find a copy of Kenneth Williamson's wartime *The Atlantic Islands*, do so. It's an enthusiastic account of the islands by a British soldier who married a Faroese woman.

BOOKSHOPS *Nyggi Bokhandil*, near Ebenezer in Tórshavn, stocks the islands' best selection of books.

BRING . . . Heavy oilskins are useful for when it's wet (which is often) and, as a present for the prohibition-bound locals, whisky is hard to beat.

BUY . . . Faroese sweaters are still dirt cheap, and are the warmest you'll come across.

CONTRACEPTIVES Available, along with tampons and medicines, from the pharmacies in Tórshavn, Klaksvik and Tvøroyri.

EMERGENCIES Emergency wards at the hospitals in Tórshavn, Klaksvik and Tvøroyri. In more remote areas, doctors are supported by helicopters.

FISHING Fishing trips and angling are possible all year. Details from the tourist office.

FOOTBALL The Faroese have entered their national team for the 1992 European Championship for the first time. As there's no pitch up to scratch, their fixtures will be played in mainland Scandinavia – something, given Faroese prohibition, that will make the lager louts grateful.

LANGUAGE Faroese is the national language. Danish is widely spoken, as is some English.

LIBRARIES The best are in Tórshavn, where for a deposit you can take books out.

SHOPS Generally open Monday–Friday 9.30am–4.30pm, Saturday 9.30am–12.30pm.

SWIMMING BATHS At Tórshavn, Klaksvik, Vagur, Tvøroyri, Fuglafjørdur, Hestur and Sørvagur. Some have saunas too.

TIME One hour ahead of GMT.

WORK There is a labour shortage in the Faroes, and non-unionised seasonal work is still a possibility in the building and (more likely) the fishing industries. There are no employment agencies, so it's a matter of legging it around the fish-processing factories and asking. If you do fix yourself up, you then have to apply for a residence/work permit, which can create difficulties, as the Faroese have become far more reluctant to accept foreign workers since Denmark joined the EC.

History

The Faroes were first settled by Irish monks in search of a place of retreat, but they were soon supplanted by the first Norse settlers, who began to colonise the Faroes in the early part of the ninth century. In those days the islands were independent, but it wasn't long before they began to come within the orbit of the Norwegian kings, who by 1035 had made the payment of an annual tribute established practice. The Faroe Saga (*Faereyinga Saga*), written by Icelandic monks in the thirteenth century, records the rivalry and ritualised violence amongst these settlers as they struggled to survive in the harsh environment.

■ Christianity – and Danish Sovereignty

Christianity reached the Faroes in the eleventh century and rapidly overwhelmed its opponents. By 1100 a bishopric had been established at Kirkjubøur, and during the **Middle Ages** the Church became increasingly rich and powerful. By the sixteenth century over half the islands' farmland was in the hands of the Church. Paralleling the rise of the Church, the kings of Norway exercised control and collected tribute through loyal Faroese chiefs. Gradually these chiefs were replaced by royal appointees (bailiffs) who had a variety of powers including the raising of revenue and the control of trade. In 1380 Denmark and Norway were united under the Danish crown – a union which was to last until 1814 – and the Faroes came to be governed as a **Danish province**.

■ The Trade Monopoly

After the **Reformation** reached the Faroes (1535–40), church lands passed into royal ownership – even though the income the crown could secure was small and certainly not enough to compensate for the distances involved in administering the colony. Consequently, bailiffs were left with the responsibility of raising the necessary revenues, the king letting the islands operate as a virtual fiefdom. To encourage bailiffs to take the responsibility, they were given the **Faroese Trade Monopoly** – an arrangement which was to have a profound effect on the islands. When King Christian III granted the first formal contract to a Hamburg merchant in 1535

he began a trading system which was to last until 1856, with the Danish government assuming responsibility itself in 1709. All trade to and from the islands was handled by agents of the Monopoly based primarily at Tórshavn. Everything going out and coming in had to go through the agent's depots. In this way, under the aegis of the Crown, the Faroes established a largely peaceable society, settled in tiny villages dotted over the islands and based on subsistence agriculture.

The Trade Monopoly was a mixed blessing for the islands. On the one hand, it offered a valuable security in providing reserve food and fodder and guaranteed prices for a variety of Faroese goods. And it was, by and large, benevolently run and rarely did the islanders suffer famine. But it had its negative side too. The Monopoly Tariff put a premium on knitted goods and discouraged the development of fishing. It also hindered the arrival of new farming and fishing technology, discouraged the Faroese language in favour of Danish, and isolated the islanders from the outside world.

With the nineteenth-century expansion of international commerce, the Trade Monopoly became more and more anachronistic. In 1856 Tórshavn was still little more than a large village; also, ironically enough, the Faroese had no deep-sea fishing boats and almost no open-sea fishing experience. The more enterprising Faroese spearheaded **opposition** to the Monopoly, not least Paul Poulsen (**Nolsoyar Pall**), but population increases had already begun to force the islanders to do more fishing anyway, while a variety of technological improvements had started to change farming methods. Nonetheless, the **abolition** of the Crown Monopoly on January 1, 1856, marked a turning point in the islands' history, and the effective end of the subsistence economy.

■ Modern Faroe

Towards the end of the nineteenth century, the British fishing fleet turned to steam and sold off its old wooden fishing sloops. The Faroese bought large numbers and began to develop an offshore fishing industry, and agriculture became less and less important. It was difficult, though, for the Faroese to generate enough capital to modernise their fleet, and at the outbreak of **World War II** their ships were still largely wooden.

The British occupied the Faroes from 1940 to 1945 in an effort to secure the North Atlantic sea routes, and the Faroese were able to sell large quantities of fresh fish to Great Britain. They paid a heavy price for continuing to fish – 25 ships and 132 men – but were well rewarded and able to build up reserves of capital to invest in new ships after the war.

Since World War II the Faroese economy has revolved around the fortunes of the **fishing industry**. There have been booms and slumps, but the Faroese have learnt to invest shrewdly and have one of the most technologically advanced fleets in the world. In 1986 they had full employment – even a shortage of labour – and wages and fish prices continue to be high. The statistics support a picture of prosperity: 89 percent of the islanders live in their own homes; the traditional depopulation of the islands has ended; and by developing a comprehensive road system the Faroese administration have stopped the drift of the population to the towns.

The **political history** of the Faroes reflects this increasing prosperity and self-confidence. The local parliament (*Løgting*) has always enjoyed a large element of consensus, and the primary issue has traditionally been to define the relationship of the Faroes to Denmark. The principles of Faroese autonomy, within a general sphere of Danish influence, were defined in the **Home Rule Ordinance** of 1948, which remains in force, despite Denmark's membership of the EC and the Faroese insistence on a 150-mile fishing exclusion zone. The Ordinance has proved a flexible instrument of government, easily changed to suit new situations. Basically, the Faroes are autonomous except in the areas of defence and foreign policy – where the Danes have the final say and pay the bills.

In fact, the tendency since 1948 has been for the Faroese to assume more and more responsibility for their own affairs and to rely less and less on the Danes. The **language issue** illustrates this. Only in 1944 did Faroese (considered no more than a peasant dialect before) achieve equal status with Danish, but it is now considered the proper language of government.

A BRIEF GUIDE TO FAROESE

Faroese is an old Viking language, similar to Icelandic and West Norwegian. It's not an easy language to learn by any means, but few islanders speak more than the most basic English, and the following key words and phrases – given phonetically throughout – may come in handy. For more detailed reference, there is no Faroese phrasebook in print, although you might find the Faroese-English **dictionary** (published by *Mamsk-Svenska*) in some bookshops. A small **pronunciation guide** is available from bookshops in Tórshavn or if all else fails you could try the Danish Embassy cultural division (see *Basics*).

BASICS AND QUESTIONS

Good morning	*Góða morgun*	Welcome	*Vælkomin*
Good day/hello	*Góðan dagin*	How are you ?	*Hvussu hevur tú tað ?*
Good evening	*Gott kvøld*	How do you do ?	*Hvussu gongur ta tað ?*
Please	*Gerði so væl*	What is your name ?	*Hvussu eitur tú ?*
Thank you	*Túsund takk*	Where are you	*Hvar fert tú ?*
Pardon	*Orsaka*	going ?	
Sorry	*Fyrigevð*	What is the time ?	*Hvar er klokkan ?*

NUMBERS

1	*Eitt*	7	*Sjey*	20	*Tjúgu*		
2	*Tvey*	8	*Atta*	21	*Ein ogtjúgu*		
3	*Trý*	9	*Niggju*	100	*Hundrað*		
4	*Fýra*	10	*Tggju*	101	*Hundrað og eitt*		
5	*Fimm*	11	*Ellivu*	500	*Fimm hundrað*		
6	*Seks*	12	*Tólv*	1000	*Túsund*		

DAYS AND MONTHS

Sunday	*sunnudag*	January	*januar*	July	*juli*
Monday	*mánadag*	February	*februar*	August	*august*
Tuesday	*týsdag*	March	*mars*	September	*september*
Wednesday	*mikudag*	April	*april*	October	*oktober*
Thursday	*hósdag*	May	*mai*	November	*november*
Friday	*friggjadag*	June	*june*	December	*desember*
Saturday	*leygardag*				

(Days and months are never capitalised)

CHAPTER TWENTY

THE FAROE ISLANDS

Though technically still ruled from Copenhagen, the **Faroe Islands** are about as far away from the youthful Europeanism of the Danish capital as it's possible to get. They have a mild climate for somewhere so far north, but the landscape is for the most part bare and windswept, there are few hotels and even fewer restaurants – and alcohol, in these most puritanically Christian islands, is voluntarily prohibited. For all that, it's the very remoteness of the Faroes which makes up the islands' charm – along with a gruff warmth in the people (relatively unusual in Scandinavia) that can often turn first-time visitors into devotees.

Tórshavn, the capital, is a fast-growing small town, benefiting from the islands' recent prosperity. It's much the best base for exploring the central islands of the group – **Streymoy**, on which Tórshavn lies, and **Eysturoy** to the east. Both islands are well served by public transport and can be visited as a day trip. The other central islands, **Koltur**, **Hestur** and **Nólsoy**, are much smaller affairs grouped around the southern foot of Streymoy.

The northern islands include the wildest, most mountainous and, in an austere kind of way, most beautiful, areas of Faroe – as well as some of its most isolated villages. The area is lightly populated and, with the exception of the growing town of **Klaksvík**, has a tendency towards depopulation. The western islands are, by contrast, rather drab, especially **Vágar**; indeed, most people come to Vágar either for the airport or to visit neighbouring **Mykines**, an exposed and brooding island with an unforgettable approach. To the south, **Sandoy** is the flattest of the Faroe Islands, its hills curving gently up from wide valley bottoms. Life is much easier here: there's more arable land and the weather's a lot better than further north, something which has made Sandoy the traditional holiday spot for the northern Faroese, although its climate is hardly Mediterranean. Similarly, **Suduroy**, most southerly of the Faroes, has a good road system and is popular with hill walkers.

Tórshavn and the Central Islands

It's surprising that **Tórshavn** is the capital of the Faroes. In a country so dependent on the sea, the town has by no means the best natural harbour in the islands. Nevertheless, with a population of 14,000 its growth in the last 25 years has been dramatic, mirroring the Faroes' new prosperity.

The Town

Named after Thor, Norse god of war and agriculture, **TÓRSHAVN** spreads up the surrounding hills from its harbour, but its nucleus is still the old quarter, originally built on **Tinganes**, the rocky strip that now sticks out towards the middle of the harbour. Tinganes means "Assembly Headland", and, during the islands' period of independence (before 1035), the legislative body and supreme court –

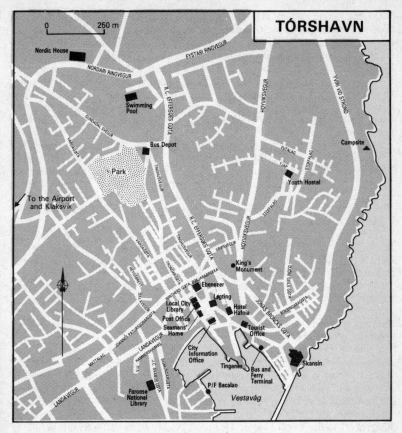

the *Althing* – met here. In the Middle Ages the *Althing* developed into a provincial court or *Løgting* of the king of Denmark, which would meet for the first time each year on St Olav's Day – a date, July 29, which retains its significance as the date of Tórshavn's main festival.

Nothing remains on Tinganes to indicate its medieval importance, but if you look at the headland from the side – from the docks to the east – it still gives the impression of a trading station, with its old warehouses and offices. On the inland side of the headland, and spreading west along **Grim Kamban's Gøta**, is the oldest part of Tórshavn: a lovely place to walk, with its huddled houses and twisting streets, evoking much of the atmosphere of the nineteenth-century town. It's worth studying some of the houses closely, not least the one towards the western end of Grim Kamban's Gøta – a decaying yellow and red wooden building with an elaborate carved roof in Norwegian style.

Further west around the harbour is most of the town's **industry**, principally a miniature shipyard and the fish factory, *P/F Bacalao*. "Bacalao" is the Spanish for cod, and the export of dried fish to the Mediterranean has long been the mainstay of the Faroese fishing industry.

On the other, eastern side of Tinganes are the docks and warehouses that cover the rocks known as **Krakusteinur** – crow's rocks. Annually and until well into the nineteenth century all male landowners had to submit to the *Løgting* a number of beaks from predatory birds, the idea being that this would protect the island's sheep, and it was here, on St Olav's Day, that the beaks were ceremonially burned. This "Beak Tax" was on a sliding scale (the rarer the bird, the more valuable the beak), and judging by the number of hooded crows left on the islands, the scheme couldn't have put much value on crows' beaks. On the other hand, a Faroese male received life exemption from the tax for the beak of a sea eagle, which is now extinct.

At the seaward end of the docks lies the small fortress of **Skansin**, originally a sixteenth-century fortification but destroyed when the French plundered Tórshavn in 1677. It was rebuilt a century later in its present star shape to accommodate an artillery battery and the first permanent Danish garrison; later it served as headquarters of the British when they occupied Faroe in the last war. Now, however, it's a neglected overgrown spot with uninteresting views, and little left to hint at any past importance.

Aarvegur runs inland from the docks, passing the stolid *Hotel Hafnia* on the left, and into Niels Finsen's Gøta and the semi-pedestrianised part of town. On the right is the *Løgting*, on the left the library, while nearby is **Ebenezer**, the central hall of the Plymouth Brethren. The Brethren were established here in 1865 by a Scottish missionary, and they still maintain close contacts with their British counterparts. Indeed, evangelical Christians of various denominations account for around twelve percent of the population of the Faroes, with the Brethren by far the largest group. This in mind, it's not difficult to understand the reasons behind voluntary prohibition.

Opposite Ebenezer is *Franz Restorff's Konditori*, a nice, cosy place to have a coffee amid some remaining small-town atmosphere. Further north still, off Hoydalsvegur, is Tórshavn's **main park**, or rather, tree plantation – which if you've spent a few days on treeless Faroese islands, can be a nice change. Beyond that, though, you've more or less exhausted Tórshavn. You could stroll up through the fast-developing suburbs and across the ring-road (Nordari Ringvegur) to the lavish **Nordic House**, a kind of Faroese Festival Hall built in 1983 to host concerts and the like, and from there look down on the whole town. But if you're content with the view of just the older part of town, the **King's Monument** is best. Erected in 1882, you can find the basalt obelisk commemorating Christian IX of Denmark's visit up towards the youth hostel, close to the junction of Effersøes Gøta and Hoyviksvegur.

Practical details

Orientation in Tórshavn couldn't be easier. The **airport bus** arrives at the "Central Bus Stop" (hardly a bus station), at the northern end of Havnargøta, where the **ferries** also arrive and depart. The **City Information Office** is nearby, and there's a **Tourist Office** at the harbour, both open until late in summer.

Apart from two very expensive, top-grade hotels – the *Hafnia* and the *Borg* – the best place to **sleep** is the *Seamen's Home* on Tórsgøta, which, like all seamen's homes (*sjomansheim*) in Faroe, is not restricted to sailors. It's friendly, relatively cheap and a good point for contacts. If you do stay and don't like traffic noise, try to get a room on the third or fourth floor – Tórsgøta is on the local adolescents' car run. Failing that, you can arrange **bed and breakfast** accommodation through the tourist office, or try the **youth hostel** at Tjarnardeild 7 (☎042/ 13414) – a basic spot open all year. It's a twenty-minute walk north from the harbour up Hoyviksvegur; or take bus #3 from the Central Bus Stop.

Eating choices are as wide as you'll find anywhere on the Faroes – which isn't saying much. Fast food snacks are sold all over the place but are nothing special and not particularly cheap. The *Hotel Hafnia* does a good buffet from Monday to Saturday for around 100kr, and the *Seamen's Home* provides good food all day, especially at lunchtime, for between 40kr and 50kr.

Around Streymoy

Even if you're only staying a short time, it's a good idea to get out of Tórshavn and see some of the rest of the island of **Streymoy**, on which the capital is situated. Only half an hour away by bus, **KIRKJUBØUR** was once, due to its copious supplies of seaweed (for fertiliser) and driftwood (for kindling and construction), the most important settlement on Faroe – effective capital and the site of the bishop's see in the Middle Ages. Bishop Erland, one of the most acquisitive of Faroe's medieval clerics, even attempted to build a stone **cathedral** here as a sign of his power and prestige. It was never completed, but most of what was built still stands – best the stone carving of Christ with the Virgin Mary and Mary Magdalen on the church's eastern wall, which was removed in 1905 for repair work to reveal a number of medieval relics in strangely perfect condition.

The white **Olav's church**, built in 1111 and restored in 1874 and 1966, is more complete, and served as the cathedral throughout the medieval period. The restoration work is, unfortunately, clumsy and the intricate wooden carvings of the interior have been transferred to Copenhagen. But one interesting feature remains: the bricked-up hole in the northern wall, which until leprosy died out in the mid-eighteenth century was used by lepers – who were not allowed into the church – to listen to Mass.

The old farmhouse next door, the **Roykstovan**, is also worth a look around, if only to get an idea of the traditional pattern of Faroese living – though it's hard to pick out which bits are medieval and which are modifications. The shape and structure are original, and the top floor follows the customary Faroese pattern of eating, sleeping and living in one large room. But the fanciful wooden carvings are twentieth-century imitation.

The area north of Tórshavn is a hilly region cut deeply by fjords. About an hour away from the capital by bus, **OYRARBAKKI** is a junction for the island's public transport. It's here you change for the (irregular) minibus to SAKSUN. Make sure the driver on the bus from Tórshavn to Oyrarbakki knows you want to make the connection to Saksun. He'll radio ahead if needs be. **SAKSUN** is a tiny village at the western end of Saksunadalur, a long and lovely valley that cuts right across Streymoy from east to west. For the last mile before the village the stream by the roadside runs through a deep ravine and into an almost circular pool of water, the *Pollur*. Further on, some 50m above sea level, there's a narrow path leading down to a beach.

In the village itself, the old farmhouse (*Duvugardur*) serves as a **museum** (afternoon admission only). Otherwise, it's the scenery that makes the journey worthwhile. If you want to **stay** in the area of Saksunadalur, there's the *Frahald* **youth hostel** in STREYMNES, the small village north across the bay from HALVIK, though you need to make reservations at the Tórshavn hostel.

Southeast from Oyrarbakki, changing buses at SKÁLABOTNUR, takes you down either the east or west coast of the best natural harbour in the Faroes, **SKALAFJORDUR** – a spectacular trip, although the string of settlements along the shoreline represents an unaesthetic industrial boom that'll probably make you want to stay on the bus. If you do get out, there's a friendly *Seaman's Home* at RUNAVIK, and from either STRENDUR or TOFTIR, at the southern end of Skalafjordur, there's a frequent **ferry** service back to Tórshavn that takes about half an hour.

Eysturoy

From Oyrarbakki there's a bus to **EIDI** on the northern coast of **Eysturoy**. Sandwiched between two hills, with a battered shoreline to the east and the precipitous end of Eysturoy to the west, Eidi enjoys a magnificent location. Walk down to the shoreline, past one of the most windswept football pitches in the world, and you get a glimpse of two **stacks** at the northern tip of the island – Risin and Kellingin. Faroese legend has these as the remains of a giant and giantess who were towing the Faroes north to Iceland when the rope broke, leaving the islands in the middle of the sea. While you're here, also have a look inside the village **church**, a late-nineteenth-century structure whose marvellous painted interior of creams, yellows, browns and blues dangles model sailing boats from its ceiling – a tradition, probably pre-Christian in origin, said to bring luck to local sailors.

There's a **hotel** nearby, the *Eidi* (category 1), perched on a ridge above the village, which is a nice place to spend a night or two. Just to the east, past the two highest mountains on the islands, is **GJÓGV** – a little tricky to get to and from in one day if you don't want to stay, but the scenery is worth the effort. It's a quiet village, dauntingly closed in by mountains and with a harbour set in a deep natural gorge. There's a new **youth hostel** (☎042/23171) here, open all year and with a top floor arranged like an old Faroese house – combined kitchen and living room with box-beds. You'll need to make a reservation in the summer.

Koltur, Hestur, Nólsoy

From Kirkjubøur you have a clear view of the islands of **Koltur** and **Hestur**, reached by ferry from Tórshavn. Frankly, there's little to draw you to either of these, but of the two, sugarloaf-shaped Koltur is of more interest, and overnight stays can be arranged at the City Information Office in Tórshavn.

It's the island of **Nólsoy** that makes the views out across the harbour from Tórshavn interesting, and it's easy to get to – there's a regular ferry service from the capital, taking thirty minutes. Even though it's so accessible, **NÓLSOY** village makes a striking comparison with Tórshavn. It's sedate, traditional and slow-moving, and entered, oddly enough, under an archway made from the jaw bones of a sperm whale. The nearby mountain can be reached by way of the small footbridge at the island's narrowest point – literally a few metres across – at the end of the village, to the left of which lie rounded basalt rocks thrown up by winter storms and to the right the bay. During easterly gales the greater part of the village can be drenched with spray, which perhaps explains why it isn't expanding, and certainly explains the numerous deep caves in the cliffs along the eastern shoreline. **Staying** in Nólsoy can be difficult, though it is apparently possible to arrange bed and breakfast; try the City Information Office in Tórshavn.

Klaksvik and the Northern Islands

KLAKSVIK, on the island of **Bordoy**, is the Faroes' second town, with a population of some 6000. It owes its size and prosperity to its development as a major fishing port, and sports some of the most technologically advanced ships in the world.

The quickest route from Tórshavn to Klaksvik is by **ferry** to TOFTIR, **bus** to LEIRVIK and then a second ferry into Klaksvik, each leg of the journey taking around thirty minutes. Once there, there are three places **to stay**, cheapest of which is the **youth hostel** (☎298/55403), open all year. The others are a sort of Christian **hostel** (*Soli Deo Gloria*), which is above the cafeteria, and the **Seamen's Home**, the large white building opposite the landing-point, a twenty-minute walk around the harbour. This last is the most expensive but easily the best option, with a friendly atmosphere, good food and usually places to spare. For further information ask at the Klaksvik **tourist office** (Mon–Fri 9am–5pm, Sat 9am–noon; ☎298/56939)

Unfortunately, Klaksvik is a rather dreary place, with little to see. There's a small **museum** (Tues & Thurs 2–4pm, Sun 4–6pm) in the early-nineteenth-century Danish Trade Monopoly house that includes a potpourri of old artefacts; and a large and rather drab-looking modern Lutheran **church** whose extravagant interior holds an altar fresco painted in 1901 by Joakim Skovgaard for the cathedral at Viborg in Denmark – and which somehow ended up being donated to the Klaksvik church. Hang around outside and look interested and the obliging custodian will appear and open up.

Out from Klaksvik: Bordoy and Vidoy

You can travel northeast by bus from Klaksvik to HARALDSSUND by way of a new causeway linking the two islands of **Bordoy** and **Kunoy**. Some 12km north of Haraldssund is what's left of the ruined village of **SKARD** – abandoned in 1913 after all the active men of the village lost their lives in an accident at sea. Across the fjord is what remains of the village of **SKÁLATOFTIR**, which was left for less dramatic reasons: life was just too hard.

NORDDEPIL, on Bordoy, is also a quick bus ride northeast from Klaksvik and is itself connected by a short causeway to the adjoining village of **HVANNASUND** on neighbouring **Vidoy** – a pleasant, if nondescript, place, in one of the harshest landscapes you can imagine, mountains rising on every side from turbulent seas. Near the causeway there's the friendly *Hotel Bella*, a simple affair run by Johan Peterson, which serves both as a **youth hostel** and category 2 **hotel** and is an excellent base for seeing the rest of the northern islands. Meals – good, straightforward Faroese cooking – are available by arrangement, but it's advisable to book in advance, as the hotel can get full with people waiting for the Fugloy ferry.

While you're up here, take the narrow road that goes north from Norddepil along the east side of Bordoy to MÚLI: a lovely walk with fine views. It does, however, end at Múli, and if you're tempted to keep on walking across the hills to the west, get a guide – it's dangerous. Just out of Norddepil, on the way, is the abandoned village of FOSSÁ, bought by an antiquarian society in Klaksvik to serve (eventually) as some sort of open-air museum. Right now it looks little more than an open-air field.

It's a 25-minute bus ride from Norddepil to **VIDAREIDI** on **Vidoy** – very much a traditional village, beautifully strung across the island between two huge hills. This, too, is a good place to stay. Most of the houses are old and the church on the western edge is framed by the sea and the hills of Bordoy. There's a surprisingly plush **hotel** with self-service restaurant, the *Hotel Nord*: open from June to September.

Kunoy and Kalsoy

One of Klaksvik's redeeming features is the view it gives across to the island of **Kunoy**. Between one and three ferries from Klaksvik daily do the round-trip to SYORADULAR, HUSAR (on Kalsoy) and KUNOY in about an hour and a half, during which time you get a good idea of the isolation of these three tiny villages and their dependency on the sea.

Alternatively, you can get off at either Syoradular or Husar and get a truck ride up to TRØLLANES at the northern tip of **Kalsoy**, the most mountainous of the Faroe Islands. It's a wild and windy spot, and until the road and its three tunnels were constructed, the hillside paths of Kalsoy were dangerous even for the islanders. Public transport both to Trøllanes and back can be erratic, so before you get on the ferry confirm connections at the Klaksvik **tourist office**. Also, if you intend to walk on Kalsoy, get some **detailed advice** – even if you are only keeping to the road and its tunnels.

Svinoy and Fugloy

The **ferry** to **Svinoy** and **Fugloy** leaves once or twice a day from Hvannasund. Svinoy has one small settlement of the same name and is a rather unremarkable island. Fugloy, on the other hand, is wild and hostile, a rocky outcrop with no sheltered harbour and two small villages – KIRKJA and HATTARVIK – connected by road. The views and bird cliffs make it a popular spot for school trips. There are no hotels on Fugloy, but Johan Peterson of the *Bella*, himself a native of the island, can arrange accommodation should you want it.

One thing you should bear in mind is that no matter how calm the waters of Hvannasund are, the ferry journey is not really designed for tourists and can be **rough**. In winter Fugloy can be cut off by sea for weeks on end and in summer the sheer swell of the ocean makes the boat bob like a cork. The length of the round-trip – anything from two to four-and-a-half hours – depends on which of the islands' landing spots they're calling at; check before you get on the boat. You can still get marooned on Fugloy. If you do, there's a helicopter service three times a week.

The Western Islands

If you come by air, **Vágar** is the first island you'll see – which is a pity as it's probably the dullest of the lot. Most of the island is uninhabited and presumably uninhabitable, and nearly all the settlements are on the main road that runs across the island past the airport. If you eliminate the expensive **airport hotel**, which seems as if it's been dropped there by mistake, there's only one place to **stay**: the *bed* *and breakfast* at **MIDVAGUR**, which should be booked through the tourist office in Tórshavn.

Midvagur itself is an unappealing village spread along the seashore. There's a small **museum** here, *Kalvalid*, in a house which apparently figured highly in the novel, *Barbara*, by Faroese novelist Jørgen Frantz Jacobsen. Midvagur's main claim to fame, though, was the disaster of March 1942 when a trawler from here, the *Nyggjaberg*, disappeared off Iceland with the loss of all hands – an event generally reckoned to be the Faroes' greatest wartime catastrophe.

From Midvagur you can walk east to the village of **SANDAVAGUR** – similar to Midvagur, and with a church built deliberately to rival the former's in style and size. Or you can walk or bus it to **SØRVÁGUR** and on to **BØUR**, a tiny village which huddles into the mountainside, sheltered from the full force of the sea, and gives good views of the sea stacks at Drangarnar (see below).

Mykines

Most people, if they're not using the airport, come to Vágar to go to **Mykines** – for which, from May to mid-August, **ferries** leave Sørvágur once or twice daily and take about an hour. It's usually a rough journey and even in the summer the ferries can be cancelled because of the difficulty of navigating the seas around the landing-point on Mykines. **Reservations** on ferries should be made in Tórshavn, where you can also, if you prefer, try and book a helicopter seat. As regards **staying**, there's no guesthouse on the island as such – though you can camp – but if you really want to stop over the Tórshavn tourist office should be able to help with private accommodation. It's worth knowing, however, that going on the Saturday morning ferry and returning in the afternoon leaves you with (just) enough time.

Mykines is something special. Looking down the fjord from Sørvágur it looks like a Walt Disney medieval island, the winds hurrying the clouds across the sky, changing its aspect as frequently as the light. Sometimes the island can seem sombre and threatening; at other times bright and inviting. As the ferry reaches the mouth of Søvágsfjordur, a series of dramatic views pan out both north and south. To the north are the cliffs of the western promontory of Vágar, while to the south rise the offshore stacks of Drangarnar – perhaps the most photographed view in the Faroes – followed by the small island of **Tindhólmur**. Amazingly enough, Tindhólmur was at one time inhabited.

The main **village**, on the west side of Mykines, is one of the most isolated places you'll ever visit – almost frighteningly exposed to the seas of the North Atlantic. Throughout the summer, the islanders share the island with thousands of birds, most prominently the **puffin**, whose burrows litter virtually all of the sea-cliffs. Until recently the puffins were an invaluable source of winter food for the isolated islanders, who would "harvest" an average of 30,000 birds each summer. Some fowling does continue, but it's a dangerous occupation and most of the islanders seem to prefer easier ways of making a living. One curious feature of fowling for puffin is the siting of the catching-places or *rók*, which have to remain the same generation after generation. For some reason, the puffins are not put off by the regular death tolls, but become wary and hard to catch if the *rók* are moved.

The Southern Islands

Ferries leave Tórshavn for **Sandoy** four times a day and take about an hour to reach SKOPUN, the village at the northern end of the island. It's a further twenty minutes by bus from here to the main settlement of **SANDUR**, where you'll find the island's only **hotel**, the cramped but cosy *Isansgardur* (category 2) – only open June–September and best booked in advance. The hotel is also the only place on the island where you can get a meal – an arrangement you must make with the family who run the hotel when you arrive.

Sandur strings out in an ungainly way up the valley. There's not much to the village, but nearby is **Lake Sandsvatn**, a favourite spot for autumn anglers when spawning sea trout struggle up the short stream that connects the lake to the sea. This same short stream cuts through sand dunes – the only ones in the Faroes – and across a beach of black basalt sand. Another walk starts at the post office near the hotel and takes you across the moorlands behind the southern cliffs. The track was originally laid to speed the movement of seaweed to the fields around Sandur and it takes you four miles west of the village to the uninhabited bay of Soltavik. Heading east, a few miles down the road is the village of **HÚSAVIK** – a beautiful spot where the sea rolls in from the Atlantic onto another black basalt beach. Húsavik was a Viking settlement that was destroyed by the Black Death in the middle of the fourteenth century and resettled some years later by the rich and powerful Gudrun of Shetland. Just off the main street are the remains of the foundations of a **medieval manor house**. Back in Sandur, a ferry makes the half-hour, frequently rough, journey to **Skuvoy** – a round-trip well worth making to see the puffins that fish off the northeastern cliffs.

Suduroy, Stora Dimun, Litla Dimun

To get to SUDUROY you have to go back to Tórshavn, from where it's a two-hour ferry journey (twice daily) to either TVØROYRI or VÁUR. On the way you pass the two tiny islands of **Stora Dimun** and **Litla Dimun**, to which there's no public ferry service but there are helicopters from Tórshavn. Incredibly, Stora Dimun is inhabited, but in the Middle Ages its isolation was considered sufficient for it to serve as a place of banishment. On the rocks near the landing-place it's said the last flightless and friendly Great Auk was killed and salted down for winter food. Litla Dimun, the smaller island of the two, was apparently once home to a herd of black-woolled sheep, brought by the Irish hermits who first settled Faroe – though these animals have since disappeared and the island is grazed by the hardier breeds which have replaced them over the years. It's said that the few that were left ran wild in the nineteenth century until rounded up and eaten by a hungry bunch of shipwrecked sailors – though that's a story that remains apocryphal.

As for **Suduroy**, it's much the most interesting of the southern islands. The ferry from Tórshavn docks at **TVØROYRI** and you can use the town as a conven-ient place to visit the north and central parts of the island. For **accommodation and food**, the cheapest option is the *Vid A Inn*, a simple guesthouse/youth hostel at the tiny village of ØRAVIK on the #700 bus route. It's south of Tvøroyri and doubles as a centre for walkers. Alternatively, there's the spick, span and convenient *Hotel Tvøroyri* overlooking the Tvøroyri harbour, or the *Hotel Bakkin* at VÁGUR, which serves more as a guesthouse for shipyard and fish-factory workers than it does for tourists. Failing that, there are houses or flats available for groups of four to six people; information from either of the Tórshavn tourist offices.

Tvøroyri itself has gradually taken over from the original Viking settlement of FRODBA, now just a few houses to the east, as the centre of activity on Trongisvagsfjodur. It's a pleasant enough town – or rather large village – and what activity there is takes place on the one long main road. If you want to head north by bus, the **buses** use the car park above the ferry terminal, though the timetable is a bit complicated; basically all buses go to SANDVIK.

HVALBA spreads right across Suduroy at a narrow isthmus, a wide hospitable shelf of land whose rocky, sea-battered old landing place, among the cliffs on the western side, is well worth a look. It was at Hvalba in 1629 that three Algerian pirate ships made a surprise attack, looted the village and took many of the inhabitants to be sold as slaves. The Faroese were too poor to raise the ransom money and the unfortunates were never seen again.

The next village north, **SANDVIK**, was the scene of even greater excitement. According to the Faroe Saga, Sigmund Bresterson, who had brought Christianity to the islands, was surprised by his pagan enemies on his farm at Skuvoy. To save his life Sigmund had to jump into the sea and swim for it. He managed the shore at Sandvik some ten miles away and collapsed on the beach. But, just to prove there's no justice in the world, the first person to find him, a local farmer aptly named "Thorgrim the Evil", immediately cut off his head.

The #700 bus from Tvøroyri heads south to the settlement of **VÁGUR**, a thriving shipbuilding centre and fishing port built along the side of a fjord. It has a rather fanciful Danish-style church and a sharply contoured rocky landing-point on the west side, sadly marred by the dumping of rubbish. The small stone memorial on the main road near the shipyard celebrates the launching (1804) of the first seagoing ship to be built and owned by the Faroese since the early Middle Ages – a tribute to the efforts of the Faroese hero **Nolsoyar Pall**, who led resistance to the Danish Trade Monopoly in the nineteenth century.

The #704 bus from Vágur will take you as far south as SUMBA, and the infrequent #706 to the southern tip of the island at AKRABERG: both journeys provide fine views. But you need to travel back to Tvøroyri to reach one of the nicest spots on the island, **FÁMJIN**, which can be reached by minibus #703 in about half an hour. It's a beautiful small village, ringed on its eastern side by a series of low-stepped hills that gradually merge up into the mountains at the centre of the island. The whole area is easily walked and is fringed by precipitous sea-cliffs – a lovely, isolated place that seems somehow forgotten.

PART EIGHT

THE
CONTEXTS

DANISH
FOOTBALL

On the eve of June 4, 1986, a strange hush descended over Denmark. Towns and villages across the country fell silent, and even in Copenhagen all humanity had deserted the normally teeming streets of Indre By. Across the city in Tivoli Gardens several thousand people had gathered, dressed from head to toe in Danish national colours and staring intently at an enormous TV screen relaying events happening 6000 miles away. Periodically they swigged heftily from bottles, jumped up and down, and filled the air with the cry: "We are red, we are white, we are Danish dynamite!"

It was the Danish national football team's opening match in the World Cup finals in Mexico, for which they had qualified for the first time ever. Until recently, football was a minor sport in Denmark: league games were attended by paltry crowds and badminton got more space on the sports pages. The *Dansk Boldspil-Union (DBU)* was founded in 1889 – the first football association on the European continent – but the game remained entirely amateur until 1978. Emphasis was placed on football for pleasure, clubs often fielding dozens of teams in different age-groups, from the under-10s upwards. Any player with sufficient talent who wanted to make a living from the game had to go to the professional leagues outside Denmark – a "foot-drain" which continued for several decades, with a number of Danish players becoming established with leading clubs around Europe. Because Danes playing professionally overseas were unable to turn out for the still-amateur national side, the country made no headway in international competitions. The rules were amended in 1971 to allow professionals to play for Denmark, but the club to whom the player was under contract could refuse to release him; and, beyond expenses, no payments could be made by the *DBU* to the player. The Danish team became infamous for its lack of commitment, a state of affairs epitomised by the player who arrived for an international fixture with Portugal equipped only with two right boots (Portugal won the game 5–0).

In 1978 the *DBU* adopted a semi-professional system, which enabled their clubs to have players under contract and financially compensate them for time spent training, and to seek commercial sponsorship. Although only about ten players were now able to support themselves from the domestic game, the new legislation caused standards to rise and stimulated public interest in the sport. Simultaneously there was wider TV coverage of the top games throughout Europe in which Danish players featured and a weekly live screening of a match from the English First Division.

Carlsberg began sponsorship of the national team in 1979 enabling the *DBU* to reward Danish international players with match fees and bonuses on a par with the rest of the world. Furthermore, a new clause written into the contracts of players leaving to play with foreign clubs guaranteed that they would be released for at least nine internationals each year. But the real reason for the rise of Danish international football was the appointment the same year of a new team manager, Sepp Piontek.

Piontek, a Polish-born former West German international, originally intended to build a Danish squad from players with Danish clubs but soon realised this was impossible. If real success was to be achieved, the bulk of the squad would have to consist of Danes playing abroad – who received a higher standard of training and regularly played at levels of pace and skill far higher than in the home league.

Piontek's eventual squad had undoubted individual skills: they were the most talented generation of players Denmark had ever produced, but the difficult task was to make them into a team. Despite some unspectacular early results – and failure to qualify for the 1982 World Cup – under Piontek's guidance Denmark slowly began to function as a cohesive unit. They enjoyed a run of outstanding international victories and reached the final stages of the 1984 European championships, in which the unfavoured Danes astonished the footballing world with a blend of innovative, exciting attacking play and stout defending. After a spectacular 5–0 trouncing of Yugoslavia they were beaten only on a penalty shoot-out after extra-time in the semi-final against Spain.

The next aim was qualification for the 1986 World Cup in Mexico. This was achieved in style, finishing top of a qualifying group which included the much fancied Soviet Union (whom Denmark defeated 4–2 in a memorable match in Copenhagen). All the Danes' home games drew capacity crowds and were watched by an estimated 3.6 million (more than half the population) live on television.

As kick-off time in Mexico drew nearer, soccer madness was erupting for the first time within Denmark. High Streets throughout the country draped their window displays in red and white (the national colours) and many carried photographs of the team. At international matches, home and away, support was provided by the "roligans" – self-styled non-violent hooligans, their nickname derived from the Danish word for peace.

Because of the seeding system used in the World Cup, Denmark were placed in the toughest of the first round groups and many outside the country thought they would struggle to reach the later stages. The first half of the opening game with Scotland was a dour affair with both sides testing each other (as well as the Mexican altitude) cautiously. There was no score by the interval. In the second half the Danes began to show a little of their attacking qualities and a goal was eventually forced which left them 1–0 victors. There was rejoicing in Tivoli, albeit muted – the game had not been a good one.

The mood turned to euphoria a few days later when Denmark played Uruguay. While largely an unknown quantity, Uruguay were expected by most pundits to do well. Denmark, however, surprised everyone and delivered a 6–1 thrashing, thereby ensuring a place in the next round. The following day the country was in ecstasy: on the streets people spontaneously burst into song (the one recorded by the team) and on television there were back-to-back reruns of the match. In the remaining group game – against old rivals, West Germany – Denmark played commandingly, containing the powerful Germans and finally coasting to a 2–0 win, and top place in their group.

By now there was serious talk of reaching the final, even of becoming World Champions*. In the next round (the start of the "sudden death" stage) Denmark were pitted against their bogey team of the European championships, Spain. Despite some reshuffling within their defence, necessary because of injuries, the Danes were still tipped to win. In the first

half they played some excellent football, frequently streaking forward from midfield with verve and guile, and they took the lead just before half-time, seemingly set to progress to the quarter-finals. But the Spaniards pulled level, and through the second half produced a display of inventive and skilful play that had previously been the preserve of the Danes. It surprised everybody, including the increasingly disorganised Danish defence, and the final score was 5–1 to Spain.

Returning to Denmark the players were naturally greeted as heroes, as were the few thousand *roligans* who had travelled to Mexico – easily spotted by their red and white sombreros. The euphoria of Mexico soon turned to despair, however, when Denmark suffered defeats in all three of their group matches during the 1988 European Championships in West Germany – a dismal performance equalled only by England.

More recently, Danish footballing fortunes have revived, and have included some outstanding victories – thrashings of Sweden and Brazil in friendlies, and a string of high quality results in the qualifying stages of the 1990 World Cup, including an accomplished 2–0 win in Bulgaria and a 7–2 trouncing of Greece. Despite these results, there was national anguish as Denmark failed to progress to the final stages of the competition by the narrowest of margins. This was a shame, since the blend of established names and talented new blood which Piontek had put together since Mexico was just beginning to pay dividends. As it was, Piontek resigned, ending an historic chapter in Danish soccer, and Richard Moeller Nielsen, coach of the Danish Olympic team, was appointed as his successor. Nielsen's first stab at major international glory will be the next European Championships – to be held in 1992.

---

* Denmark can claim to have won two previous World Championships. In 1959 a women's football club, Femina, was founded in Copenhagen and in 1970 it beat Italy 3–1 in an unofficial world championship decider. The following year another women's world championship was held in Mexico. In the final, watched by 110,000 people, Denmark beat the host nation 3–0, and the goals were scored by a 15-year-old schoolgirl, Susanne Augustesen, who went on to play professionally in Italy.

A VIEW OF NORWAY

Tolerance is a Scandinavian trait, it's claimed. Not so for *Caryl Phillips*, a black British writer who journeyed across Europe in 1984 and recorded his experiences, impressions, and the reactions to his colour, in his book *The European Tribe*. His account of his time in Norway, reprinted below, says much about the country and its fast-developing racism.

IN THE FALLING SNOW

By the time I reached Oslo's Fornebu airport I was tiring badly. I had spent the greater part of a year travelling, but I consoled myself with the thought that at least I would not have to endure the drudgery of a long queue at passport control. I had treated myself to Club class, and assumed therefore that I would disembark before most passengers. Ahead of me were two young American businessmen. They were swiftly processed with a smile. I stepped forward and presented myself. With one hand resting on my unopened passport, the customs officer fired a barrage of questions at me. How much money did I have? Where was I going to stay? Did I have a return ticket? Had I been to Norway before? Was I here on business? I threw down my return ticket and stared at her, my body barely able to contain my rage. "Stand to one side", she said. I stood to one side and watched as she dealt with each passenger in turn. There were no questions asked of them.

When everyone had gone through, she picked up my passport and ticket, and then left her counter. Five minutes later she reappeared in the company of a male officer. "How much money do you have?" he asked. I don't know. "How much money is in your bank account?" Which bank account? I asked. "Do you have any credit cards?" Yes. He nodded as though disappointed. "Please wait here." They both disappeared. On their return they found me looking down at the space between my feet, afraid of what I might say if I caught their eyes. "You can proceed now." I did not move. "Go on, you can proceed through customs control". I looked up and took both my passport and my ticket from the man. The sentence began from

the soles of my feet and travelled right up through my body. "You pair of fucking ignorant bastards." "Come with me, sir." I was instructed to reclaim my luggage, which were the only two pieces left on the revolving belt. In gaoler-like silence, they frogmarched me into the customs hall where I was searched. A middle-aged English woman who had witnessed the episode turned upon my escorts. "You should be ashamed", she said. At least it was clear to somebody else what was happening. The scene could not be dismissed as paranoia, or as a result of my having a "chip on my shoulder".

They ushered me into the chief's office. I stood and listened as the pair of them explained, in Norwegian, to the chief the reason for my presence. As they spoke all three of them kept glancing in my direction. Eventually, the case for the prosecution came to an end. The chief put down a sheaf of papers and came over to face me. "You must behave like a gentleman", he told me. "This", I assured him, "is how gentlemen behave when they meet arseholes." He asked me if I found it culturally difficult to deal with a woman customs officer. I burst out laughing. He suggested that I "leave now". Leave for where? "Oslo, or wherever you will be staying." I picked up my luggage, but had one final question for him. I asked if his staff would be treating Desmond Tutu, who was due to collect his Nobel Peace Prize in a week's time, in the same manner. "You may leave now."

Any ideas I had of a free and easy Scandinavia had already been destroyed. Like her neighbours Denmark and Sweden, Norway is now having to come to terms with people of different cultural backgrounds, and inevitably this is producing an unpleasant backlash. Out of a population of 4 million, Norway has 80,000 immigrants, 63,000 of whom are from Europe or the United States. This leaves 16,000 non-whites, mainly originating from Pakistan and the Middle East. The non-whites constitute only 0.35 percent of the population, yet a recent poll in the daily newspaper *Aftenposten* showed that 87 percent of Norwegians did not want any more immigrant workers to enter the country; 33 percent preferred not to see immigrant workers in the street; 52 percent wanted them to abandon their cultural traditions and adjust to Norwegian life; and 94 percent said they would not welcome an immigrant into their homes.

Norwegian resentment revolves around the usual fears of immigrant hygiene, unemployment, sexual fears, and displeasure at having to finance the social welfare support system that maintains some immigrants but far more Norwegians. Unfortunately, a similar bitterness exists in both Sweden and Denmark, where acts of racist violence are becoming more commonplace. Norwegian magazines, like *Innvandrer Informasjon*, which seeks to promote racial harmony by featuring articles illustrated with pictures of Africans in Scandinavian clogs, are no substitute for political will. It would appear that Ibsen's century-old observation (in *Ghosts*, 1881) of his fellow countrymen still holds true: "It isn't just what we have inherited from our father and mother that walks in us. It is all kinds of old and obsolete beliefs. They are not alive in us; but they remain in us none the less, and we can never rid ourselves of them."

In a way, I came to Norway to test my own sense of negritude. To see how many of "their" ideas about me, if any, I subconsciously believed. Under a volley of stares it is only natural to want eventually to recoil and retreat. In a masochistic fashion, I was testing their hostility. True, it is possible to feel this anywhere, but in Paris or New York, in London or Geneva, there is always likely to be another black person around the corner or across the road. Strength through unity in numbers is an essential factor in maintaining a sense of sanity as a black person in Europe. But, I asked myself, what happens 300 miles inside the Arctic Circle in mid-December, with nothing but reindeer and Lapps for many miles in any direction? I knew they would stare, for it is unlikely that many of them would have ever seen a black person before. Only then would I find out how much power, if any, was stored away in the historical battery that feeds my own sense of identity.

From the beginning my "experiment" went crucially wrong. I flew to Tromsø, a town about 200 miles inside the Arctic Circle where I hired a car. It began to snow quite heavily so I checked into a hotel, then decided to find a nightclub. The first person I met in the club was a Trinidadian woman. I had foolishly underestimated the extent of the Caribbean diaspora.

She was as shocked as I was, and anxious to strike up a conversation. I soon discovered that she was thirty-one, had three boys aged nine, eleven and fourteen, whose father was Norwegian and from whom she was now separated. She had met him in San Fernando, Trinidad when he was sailing through the Caribbean. Her move to Norway had caused a permanent breach with her parents and her life with him had recently fallen apart. She was drunk, and oblivious to the leering contempt with which other men in the club watched her. Then she remembered her children. They did not like her to go out at nights, so she urged me to speak to them on the telephone. My voice would prove that she had met a West Indian and justify her neglect.

Her phone call was brief, and she returned to confess that she was anxious to leave her children and have some fun on her own. When the eldest boy reached sixteen she would be free. "I'm still good-looking, aren't I?" she asked. "I can still have a life of my own, but you know, I love Tromsø more than anywhere. I hate Trinidad." She paused. "But I have my own life now." I asked her what she liked about Tromsø. "The nature" was her reply. I began to feel for the three boys waiting at home. Like a potter's wheel that has suddenly been jammed to a halt, West Indians have been flung out into history and tried to make good wherever they have landed. She was the saddest case I had come across. Defying everything that I know about the caring attitude of Caribbean women to motherhood, she was lost and ailing. As I made ready to leave the club she took my arm. Did I want to meet her children? They might be asleep if we stayed and had another drink or two, and that way I would be able to meet them in the morning. I suggested that she ask somebody else and left.

The next day I drove for hours. The snow lay thick, the landscape a chilled whitewashed canvas with no human beings, just a metal forest of rickety trees, and an odd mirror-glass lake breaking the monotony. Fifty miles northeast of Tromsø I stopped for petrol in a small town. It was mid-afternoon and pitch black. The ninety minutes of winter daylight had long since passed. Turning to face me, the woman attendant dropped the petrol pump in shock. Did she imagine that I was going to molest her? I picked up the pump and gave it back to her. She made some gesture to indicate that her hands were greasy. I smiled. From the car cassette player I heard Bob Marley singing "Redemption Song": "Emancipate yourself from mental slavery" did not refer to black people.

I arrived back in Oslo the day Bishop Desmond Tutu received his Nobel Peace Prize. On the television he talked about the need for moral action by the West with regard to South Africa, stating that a concerted and unified economic and political embargo was essential. He made the demand in the knowledge that the vested economic interests of the West would make such action unlikely. Norway trades openly and extensively with South Africa. Their lack of moral fortitude, and that of the rest of Western Europe, will inevitably help contribute to a bloody and protracted finale to this current chapter of South African history. Norway's presentation of a Peace Prize to Bishop Tutu seemed curious. Pontius Pilate washing his hands?

The following day I attended a "Desmond Tutu Celebration" in Oslo's "People's Hall". Organised by the Norwegian Trade Union movement, the festivities were attended by representatives from the church and state, the laureate and his family. Again he spoke passionately on the need for "economic pressure" and, naturally enough, he received a standing ovation. There then followed a series of performances that included a Norwegian "punk" band, a black American singer who delivered a barely recognisable version of Stevie Wonder's "I Just Called To Say I Love You", and a Scandinavian poet. Just when the evening seemed lost, seven blonde-haired Swedish schoolchildren strode on to the stage and proceeded to clap hands and, without accompaniment, sing a medley of African folk songs. Bishop Tutu and his family rushed to join them on stage. The spontaneity and vigour of their performance warmed an otherwise frosty evening. In this unexpected scene, there was, at last, hope.

After the celebrations I found myself sharing a table in an Oslo late bar with a drunk Norwegian. He complained to me that his fiancée had recently "run off" to do Third World aid work in Kenya, and was now refusing to come back. In a lilting and desperate voice, he asked me how black and white can grow to understand each other. I could only tell him the truth: in many ways, we already did but that a touch of mutual respect always helped. We shook hands on it. My ten minutes of solitary peace were soon disturbed by a drunk Eritrean "brother", who informed me that I must not stay in Europe too long as I would just get old and be pointed out as "an old nigger". He suggested that I go back to where I came from. He was "studying" in Norway. I asked him how long he had been here. "Fourteen years", but he was quick to explain that he had only stayed for so long because he knew how to deal with the white man. An hour later I watched as they carried him out. He was unconscious before his drunken body reached Norway's sub-zero streets.

© Caryl Phillips.
Reprinted by permission of Faber & Faber.

VIKING CUSTOMS AND RITUALS

Ibn Fadlan, a member of a diplomatic delegation sent from the Baghdad Caliphate to Bulgar on the Volga in 921–922 AD, was one of the most avid chroniclers of the Vikings. In the following extracts he details the habits and rituals of a tribe of Swedish Vikings, the Rus, who dealt in furs and slaves, the first noting with disgust the finer points of Viking personal hygiene, the second a sober eyewitness account of the rituals of a Viking ship burial.

HABITS AND RITUALS

I saw the Rus when they arrived on their trading mission and anchored at the River Atul (Volga). Never had I seen people of more perfect physique; they are tall as date-palms, and reddish in colour. They wear neither mantle nor coat, but each man carries a cape which covers one half of his body, leaving one hand free. Their swords are Frankish in pattern, broad, flat and fluted. Each man has (tattooed upon him) trees, figures and the like from the finger-nails to the neck. Each woman carries on her bosom a container made of iron, silver, copper or gold – its size and substance depending on her man's wealth. Attached to the container is a ring carrying her knife which is also tied to her bosom. Round her neck she wears gold or silver rings; when a man amasses 10,000 *dirhems* he makes his wife one gold ring; when he has 20,000 he makes two; and so the woman gets a new ring for every 10.000 *dirhems* her husband acquires, and often a woman has many of these rings. Their finest ornaments are green beads made from clay. They will go to any length to get hold of these; for one *dirhem* they procure one such bead and they string these into necklaces for their women.

They are the filthiest of god's creatures. They do not wash after discharging their natural functions, neither do they wash their hands after meals. They are as stray donkeys. They arrive from their distant lands and lay their ships alongside the banks of the Atul, which is a great river, and there they build big wooden houses on its shores. Ten or twenty of them may live together in one house, and each of them has a couch of his own where he sits and diverts himself with the pretty slave-girls whom he has brought along to offer for sale. He will make love with one of them in the presence of his comrades, sometimes this develops into a communal orgy and, if a customer should turn up to buy a girl, the Rus will not let her go till he has finished with her.

Every day they wash their faces and heads, all using the same water which is as filthy as can be imagined. This is how it is done. Every morning a girl brings her master a large bowl of water in which he washes his face and hands and hair, combing it also over the bowl, then blows his nose and spits into the water. No dirt is left on him which doesn't go into the water. When he has finished the girl takes the same bowl to his neighbour – who repeats the performance – until the bowl has gone round to the entire household. All have blown their noses, spat and washed their faces and hair in the water.

On anchoring their vessels, each man goes ashore carrying bread, meat, onions, milk, and *nabid* (probably a Scandinavian kind of beer), and these he takes to a large wooden stake with a face like that of a human being, surrounded by smaller figures, and behind them tall poles in the ground. Each man prostrates himself before the large post and recites: "O Lord, I have come from distant parts with so many girls, so many sable furs (and whatever other commodities he is carrying). I now bring you this offering". He then presents his gift and continues "Please send me a merchant who has many *dinars* and *dirhems*, and who will trade favourably with me without too much bartering". Then he retires. If, after this, business does not pick up quickly and go well, he returns to the statue to present further gifts. If results continue slow, he then presents gifts to the minor figures and begs their intercession, saying, "These are our Lord's wives, daughters and sons". Then he pleads before each figure in turn, begging them to intercede for him and humbling himself before them. Often trade picks up, and he says "My Lord has required my needs, and now it is my duty to repay him". Whereupon he sacrifices goats or cattle, some of which he distributes as alms. The rest he lays before the statues, large and small, and the heads of the beasts he plants upon the poles. After dark, of course, the dogs come and devour the lot – and the successful trader says, "My Lord is pleased with me, and has eaten my offerings".

If one of the Rus falls sick they put him in a tent by himself and leave bread and water for him. They do not visit him, however, or speak to him, especially if he is a serf. Should he recover he rejoins the others; if he dies they burn him. If he happens to be a serf, however, they leave him for the dogs and vultures to devour. If they catch a robber they hang him in a tree until he is torn to shreds by wind and weather . . .

THE BURIAL

. . . I had been told that when their chieftains died cremation was the least part of the their whole funeral procedure, and I was, therefore, very much interested to find out more about this. One day I heard that one of their leaders had died. They laid him forthwith in a grave which they covered up for ten days till they had finished cutting-out and sewing his costume. If the dead man is poor they make a little ship, put him in it, and burn it. If he is wealthy, however, they divide his property and goods into three parts: one for his family, one to pay for his costume, and one to make *nabid* which drink on the day when the slave woman of the dead man is killed and burnt together with her master. They are deeply addicted to *nabid*, drinking it night and day; and often one of them has been found dead with a beaker in his hand. When a chieftain among them has died, his family demands of his slave women and servants: "Which of you wishes to die with him?" Then one of them says: "I do"; and having said that the person concerned is forced to do so, and no backing out is possible. Even if she wished to she would not be allowed to. Those who are willing are mostly the slave women.

So when this man died they said to his slave women "Which of you wants to die with him?" One of them answered "I do". From that moment she was put in the constant care of two other women servants who took care of her to the extent of washing her feet with their own hands. They began to get things ready for the dead man, to cut his costume and so on, while every day the doomed woman drank and sang as though in anticipation of a joyous event.

When the day arrived on which the chieftain and his slave woman were going to be burnt, I went to the river where his ship was moored. It had been hauled ashore and four posts were made for it of birch and other wood. Further there was arranged around it what looked like a big store of wood. Then the ship was hauled near and placed on the wood. People now began to walk about talking in a language I could not understand, and the corpse still lay in the grave; they had not taken it out. They then produced a wooden bench, placed it on the ship, and covered it with carpets of Byzantine *dibag* (painted silk) and with cushions of Byzantine *dibag*. Then came an old woman whom they called "the Angel of Death", and she spread these cushions out over the bench. She was in charge of the whole affair from dressing the corpse to the killing of the slave woman. I noticed that she was an old giant-woman, a massive and grim figure. When they came to his grave they removed the earth from the wooden frame and they also took the frame away. They then divested the corpse of the clothes in which he had died. The body, I noticed, had turned black because of the intense frost. When they first put him in the grave, they had also given him beer, fruit, and a lute, all of which they now removed. Strangely enough the corpse did not smell, nor had anything about him changed save the colour of his flesh. They now proceeded to dress him in hose, and trousers, boots, coat, and a mantle of *dibag* adorned with gold buttons; put on his head a cap of *dibag* and sable fur; and carried him to the tent on the ship, where they put him on the blanket and supported him with cushions. They then produced *nabid*, fruit, and aromatic plants, and put these round his body; and they also brought bread, meat, and onions which they flung before him. Next they took a dog, cut it in half, and flung the pieces into the ship, and after this they took all his weapons and placed them beside him. Next they brought two horses and ran them about until they were in a sweat, after which they cut them to pieces with swords and flung their meat into the ship; this also happened to two cows. Then they produced a cock and a hen, killed them, and threw them in. Meanwhile the slave woman who wished to be killed walked up and down, going into one tent after the other, and the owner of each tent had sexual intercourse with her, saying: "Tell your master I did this out of love for him."

It was now Friday afternoon and they took the slave woman away to something which they had made resembling a doorframe. Then she placed her legs on the palms of the men and reached high enough to look over the frame, and she said something in a foreign language, after which they took her down. And they lifted her again and she did the same as the first time. Then they took her down and lifted her a third time and she did the same as the first and second times. Then they gave her a chicken and she cut its head off and threw it away; they took the hen and threw it into the ship. Then I asked the interpreter what she had done. He answered: "The first time they lifted her she said: "Look! I see my mother and father." The second time she said: "Look! I see all my dead relatives sitting around." The third time she said: "Look! I see my master in Paradise, and Paradise is beautiful and green and together with him are men and young boys. He calls me. Let me join him then!"

They now led her towards the ship. Then she took off two bracelets she was wearing and gave them to the old woman, "the Angel of Death", the one who was going to kill her. She next took off two anklets she was wearing and gave them to the daughters of that woman known by the name "the Angel of Death". They then led her to the ship but did not allow her inside the tent. Then a number of men carrying wooden shields and sticks arrived, and gave her a beaker with *nabid*. She sang over it and emptied it. The interpreter then said to me, "Now with that she is bidding farewell to all her women friends." Then she was given another beaker. She took it and sang a lengthy song; but the old woman told her to hurry and drink up and enter the tent where her master was. When I looked at her she seemed completely bewildered. She wanted to enter the tent and she put her head between it and the ship. Then the woman took her head and managed to get it inside the tent, and the woman herself followed. Then the men began to beat the shields with the wooden sticks, to deaden her shouts so that the other girls would not become afraid and shrink from dying with

their masters. Six men entered the tent and all of them had intercourse with her. Thereafter they laid her by the side of her dead master. Two held her hands and two her feet, and the woman called "the Angel of Death" put a cord round the girl's neck, doubled with an end at each side, and gave it to two men to pull. Then she advanced holding a small dagger with a broad blade and began to plunge it between the girl's ribs to and fro while the two men choked her with cord till she died.

The dead man's nearest kinsman now appeared. He took a piece of wood and ignited it. Then he walked backwards, his back towards the ship and his face towards the crowd, holding the piece of wood in one hand and the other hand on his buttock; and he was naked. In this way the wood was ignited which they had placed under the ship after they had laid the slave woman, whom they had killed, beside her master. Then people came with branches and wood; each brought a burning brand and threw it on the pyre, so that the fire took hold of the wood, then the ship, then the tent and the man and the slave woman and all. Thereafter a strong and terrible wind rose so that the flame stirred and the fire blazed still more.

I heard one of the Rus folk, standing by, say something to my interpreter, and when I inquired what he had said, my interpreter answered: "He said: "You Arabs are foolish." "Why?" I asked. "Well, because you throw those you love and honour to the ground where the earth and the maggots and fields devour them, whereas we, on the other hand, burn them up quickly and they go to Paradise that very moment." The man burst out laughing, and on being asked why, he said: "His Lord, out of love for him, has sent this wind to take him away within the hour!" And so it proved, for within that time the ship and the pyre, the girl and the corpse had all become ashes and then dust. On the spot where the ship stood after having been hauled ashore, they built something like a round mound. In the middle of it they raised a large post of birch-wood on which they wrote the names of the dead man and the king of the Rus, and then the crowd dispersed.

The above extract, translated by Karre Stov, was taken from The Vikings *by Johannes Brøndsted, and is reprinted by permission of Penguin Books.*

THE FINNISH SAUNA

Enshrined in the myths of the *Kalevala*), the sauna has played an integral part in Finnish life for centuries, the feelings of serenity (and incredible cleanliness) it induces thought to be an exorcism of all ills. The best way to understand its importance is to take one, preferably with Finnish friends, But if you don't get the chance, this description by John Sykes, taken from his book *Direction North – A View of Finland*, evokes much of the mood.

This particular sauna, just one of half a million (for a population of four and a half million) built in every corner of the country, was on a scale that befitted the paternalistic founder of the firm – that is to say, Lars's grandfather: who, with bible in his buttoned up frock-coat, might have been quite willing to see the then Russian masters of the country deal suitably with troublesome workers, but who equally for the meek, the obedient, the disciplined, had set up a range of amenities with the zeal of some pioneering Quaker. This sauna could be called his monument (as incongruous stylistically now as a London railway station but vast): a place in which to be cleansed through and through and issue forth a man of God. It had been renovated following an air raid during the last war; no one had dared dismantle it. Partly of timber, partly of concrete, it hummed from within like a Buddhist temple. The name of the founder, Henrik Stromfors, was still inscribed over its portal.

We had to wait our turn. In an outer chamber, rigged up now as a caféteria, we drank a slow premeditative tea, sinking naturally into silence. This was not the mean, barbed silence, nor the anxious overwhelmed-by-life silence, nor any of the silences drifting among Finns like a fog, but an inclusive, a friendly, a reverent silence gathering us properly into the occasion. It was my fifth sauna since arriving in Finland and I had noted variations in approach, some being more chatty than others – my welcoming sauna had been positively skittish: but in general the ground of the occasion was a sober, prayerful frame of mind. Man came here

to be renewed in heart through exercise of the body.

At last we entered, with an issue each of hand towel and birch whisk. We undressed and padded naked to the washroom beyond where were the sauna chambers. I remember, at school, we were constantly naked, scuffling and slipping under the showers, or racing dressing as we went, towards the library where the Quaker day began with prayer: but were we conscious of each other's shapes, of differences, except passingly? In later life when these differences had grown, when stomachs and chests have bulged and sagged, and hairs sprouted to a thick mat or thinned down long weedy legs, and faces are greyer, with cares and defeat, and chins have doubled, and the pubic region lost its pristine innocence, it is less easy to be so unaware. Usually, after all, one only sees one's own body, and the quite different body of the other sex, and one's children's bodies chiefly noted for whether they're toughening up – and maybe also there are moonlight occasions, in warm seas, when you all go bathing. I know a French acquaintance of mine regards the Finnish sauna as barbaric precisely for this: the trooping together of gross male bodies who wash themselves and loll in steam and beat themselves, all solemnly together – ch la la! When each could be at home in his apartment bathroom, gazing at his wife's shelf of perfumes, catching the good smell from the kitchen? As obscene, my acquaintance concludes, as Auschwitz.

He may have been unlucky. Finns have good bodies. They bring natural vigour to the sauna that the more urbanised men of the west could not do. Though they age also – though not so quickly, just because of this one remarkable institution.

So I entered with them, already a believer in the therapy we were to undergo.

In the dry chamber the thermometer reading was, roughly, one hundred and eighty degrees Fahrenheit. Not all the men were coming in here, some seemingly preferring the assault of the steam chamber without preparation. But Pekka's group had headed here, each of us leaving our whisk in a pail ready for the later stages. It was dark wooded, weak electric lit, a cell with steps to a ten-foot gallery with two facing wooden slatted benches, and wooden slats along the floor. I additionally carried a cool piece of wood, so as not to feel my bottom burned, and I perched on this like a fakir because it was too hot to put my feet down. Nobody else found it so. We sat there bunched together, waiting for the sweat to come. I blew on my arm – a trick I had observed to test the tinder-dryness of the air. Okay, as yet no discomfort: only the overall power of the cell to suck the moisture out of me into its low timbered hull. The light glimmered. The gloom fixed one. This was the door to purgatory, the moment to trust oneself to grace: for as soon as the sweat began to flow the later processes must unroll.

But no hurry. Nothing to be hurried. The cult must not be shorn of a minute.

Sweat. At last, patches of dampness beginning to bubble and trickle together, till suddenly one was afloat in moisture, slipping in ooze, oozing faster than the thirsty atmosphere could absorb. Ten men, oozing and glistening, and soulfully brooding the start of the sauna.

"Come." Pekka seemed always to be leader. We followed and picked up whisk and pail, and took a little warm water into the pail; and, a group of five, went next door, into the steam inferno. Again, a gallery with slatted benches, but in front of this, in front of the steps mounting to it, the brick-covered furnace, and enough space for three or four men to wet their whisks in the pails they carried, to make sure they were soft and whippy, then flick the whisks into the opening of the stove (each after a decent interval), straight in at the fiery stones, to raise a new hiss of steam.

Madness. Each time I experienced this panic, as my skin jumped and my heart raced and my breathing folded up before the attack of wet choking air. The temperature appeared to double itself; and, once on the platform, my pail between my feet, my first need was to hang my head, dumbly like the dumbest of beasts, to pause and discover if I was to endure. One waited for the next blast of steam with lungs seized up and suspended. Fish, eggs, vegetables, meat: any of these would be nicely cooked. How did man so cleverly survive?

Then, somehow, it was not so bad. Like the others I dipped my whisk in the pail and, starting at the extremities of arms and feet, gently and sedately whipped myself. A nice sensation and, not out of place in this sacrificial chamber.

Bring that evil blood to the surface! Sweat, ooze, gasp, smart, till the inner man shall win release from the aches and sloth of yesterday. More steam! Wilt! Be wrung through and through so that a right mind be forthcoming.

One soon got into the swing of the thing . . .

Alas! Thought too soon: some fellow penitent, or fellow priest, doused the furnace, so that an immense cloud of steam hissed forth as though to give us a flash of the Devil; and I for one was quickly descending, off that platform to ground-floor level.

I swear that the others were about to groan: but they somehow turned it into a laugh.

Another point regarding the sauna: the good humour it certainly gives rise to begins within the steam chamber.

Time anyway now for a wash, for a good rub down with soap and brush. This was rather better done in my experience, in the Turkish baths of the Middle East, where the practitioners in these more sybaritic temples knead the last dirt from one's pores; but no point in cavilling, there was also here an ancient toothy buxom matron, busy at the moment among the footballers, making sure they were soaped and soused and massaged free of any lingering pains. Left to oneself, there were hot and cold taps, before which one sat on a low stool, soaping the hollow of one's back with one's whisk: then showers, a deliriously heady experience as one alternated between extremes of temperature.

Then back into the steam once more.

At this point the country Finn would be preparing for the final challenge: to plunge straight from the hissing inferno into snow or icy lake (a practice he has followed for at least three centuries . . . he assures the visitor. . . without coming to harm); and I remembered that in 1940, while we were stationed at Joensuu ferrying the refugees westwards, we did try out that caper. We were invited to the sauna of a nearby farm, where the birch were already black and silver and the ice was puddled and the thrushes were flitting against a pale almond sky. We had been helping this farmer, in between shifts of ferrying the refugees, for the sheer pleasure of felling trees and feeling the good earth again, as the spring broke, with a rush of flooding water, over the northern country; so that suddenly he had said, through our interpreter . . . "Tomorrow I will heat the sauna for you". So, game for the experience, we had sweated and gasped in the smoky interior of a farmhouse sauna, then we had run for the snow! And rolled in it. The most extraordinary sight. And the most delicious experience! If memory rang true: one of life's best thrills. Which was why, returning to Finland now, I needed no preliminary conversion.

Sauna mad. It may seem banal for yet one more person to comment on the sauna; yet how to comment on the Finns if one doesn't?

On this occasion it had worked wonders with Pekka. After the final sluicing down, and a leisurely drying of oneself, and dressing, so that we each had a pink baby face staring out from our crusty clothes, he had lost his usual deployment of reserve and prejudice and broody involvement: to become dryly talkative and smiling. I was now fully introduced to his friends. They were gesturing the need for a drink. They were becoming unselfconsciously hearty. Pekka was emphasising a suggestion, with a beefy laugh, and now even in Swedish he told me it was agreed that we should dine together. On one side I was to have "the American", on the other a big doughy-faced man who spoke Swedish. "I do not speak Swedish," said Pekka in Swedish; "but my friend is our union organiser. He requires it. He can explain to you many things." He waved aside having said so much in a language he did not profess to use. A moment of making things easy for people. He smiled sagely, patted my shoulder — as though I were a "likely lad" (Yorkshire idiom) — and threw a patriarchal glance about the group. We had collected three more chaps in the sauna.

Eight all told.
Eight for dinner.

Reprinted by permission of Century Hutchinson Ltd.

THE SAME
AND
CHERNOBYL

It was in Scandinavia that evidence of what turned out to be the Chernobyl nuclear disaster first came to light; the fallout a nuclear power station worker had picked up on his boots on his way to work at Forsmark, 90 miles north of Stockholm, set alarm bells ringing at a routine check and prompted an emergency evacuation of the immediate area.

Scandinavia bore the brunt of much of the earliest and dirtiest fallout as clouds which had carried their load from the Ukraine dumped it in a broad belt across the northern half of the region. The worst contamination fell in heavy rainstorms around the Swedish coastal cities of Gävle and Sundsvall and on highland areas of what might be described as southern Lappland, on both sides of the Swedish-Norwegian border.

In Sweden, as in other countries, the reaction of the government was marked by uncertainty and confusion. The Radiation Protection Institute (SSI), with at least one eye to the Swedish nuclear industry's public relations, quickly put out a full colour brochure playing down any dangers, comparing Chernobyl favourably to natural sources of radiation and telling people to eat and drink as normal. Only pregnant women fond of berries, mushrooms and freshwater fish, and living in the contaminated areas – and "major consumers of reindeer meat", were advised to modify their diet somewhat.

While everyone in the worst affected areas was exposed to some threat, and to the anxiety of being unable to assess its magnitude, a number of circumstances make Chernobyl especially disastrous for the Same people, Arctic Scandinavia's aboriginal "major consumers of reindeer meat".

Among the oldest peoples of Europe, the Same are probably descended from the original inhabitants of much of Scandinavia and northern Russia. Now numbering about 40,000, they span the northernmost regions of Norway, Sweden, Finland and the Soviet Kola peninsula.

Reindeer, both wild and tame, have been at the centre of Same life and culture since the end of the Ice Age.

In summer, to escape the stinging flies, the herds move up onto the tundra above the treeline and graze on grass. In the winter, when they come down into the forests, they live entirely on the "reindeer lichen" they find under the snow. This lichen has no roots, takes all its moisture from the atmosphere, grows extremely slowly – and has a prodigious capacity to absorb and retain radioactive pollutants.

Originally the Same lived by herding wild deer, later keeping a few tame animals to draw sledges and provide milk, and only becoming herders to be able to pay the taxes imposed on them. Reindeer husbandry nowadays is largely geared to exporting meat as a cash crop to a "luxury market" of occasional individual consumers in southern Scandinavia, Germany, America and the Far East.

For the Same themselves, however, the meat is an important part of the ordinary daily diet. Wild game, fish, berries and fungi from the pine forests and birch woods – all exceptionally vulnerable to radioactive contamination – are also sources of food more important to the Same than to other Scandinavians. Thus the Same are particularly exposed to radioactivity, and the cost of replacing these traditionally free foods would be a considerable burden.

Added to this is the threat that contamination of reindeer meat would severely damage, if not destroy, the market on which the herders' future depends. Chernobyl was not the first time the Same had had to contend with fallout. Radioactive contamination of their herds was first detected in 1958 – the result of nuclear weapon testing in the atmosphere. It reached a peak in the mid-1960s, when meat in Sweden was found to contain ten times the maximum permitted level – and to account for 90 percent of the radioactive caesium in Same individuals. One group, the Skolt, living on the Finnish-Soviet border were found, owing to a diet poor in calcium, to be accumulating high doses of strontium 90, with a proportionately increasing risk of bone cancer. Research in Sweden and Finland then revealed the role of the "reindeer lichen", which could contain up to a hundred times as much radioactive caesium as other plants; and took ten years for the level to diminish by half.

This naturally led to fear over the safety of reindeer meat; a major setback to the *Same* economy, from which it had only recently recovered at the time of Chernobyl.

For a month following the disaster, *Same* organisations protested at the lack of clear information from the authorities. The Swedish Department of Food announced in early June that no reindeer in the provinces of Jämtland, Västerbotten, and Västernorland would be passed as fit for consumption; it was hoped that those in the more northerly province of Norbotten would be cleared by later tests.

Following the cancellation of the summer slaughter, the government promised full compensation to herders, but wrangles over the rate lasted for months and *Same* organisations were annoyed that the working party set up by the Ministry of Agriculture to draw up guidelines contained no *Same* representatives. In August, the government finally decided the slaughter would proceed at the normal rate and each carcass would be tested: all meat registering over 300 Becquerels per kilo would be condemned. As it turned out, virtually all the meat in the three worst affected areas exceeded this limit, much of it massively.

In Norbotten, previously thought to be a safe area, the *Same* were shocked to find that here too many animals were over the limit. "This is the beginning of the end", said Lars Pittsa, a *Same* spokesperson in Sörkaitum. "We thought our animals were clean, but a nightmare has come true. We need solace. What compensation is there for psychic suffering?"

The Swedish authorities had predicted that the levels of contamination in living animals would decline as the summer passed. The reverse proved to be the case: as the herds came down to the heaths and began to graze on the lichen, the levels rose sharply. Their herders were furious: it had been the authorities, unable to come up with a clear policy based on reliable information, who had made them postpone the summer slaughter, and many animals which would have cleared the limit then were now over it. The carcasses were added to the growing heaps awaiting processing into mink fodder.

Soon after, there were proposals from the authorities in both Sweden and Norway to raise the threshold of acceptable contamination. Once implemented, these measures came far too late to avoid serious damage to the market but did, as a matter of course, save the government much in compensation payments.

The *Same* continue to face a dilemma. Whatever radiation's true dangers, they cannot afford to ignore it, since they and their future generations are vulnerable to it. On the other hand, if the danger should be at all exaggerated, every degree of exaggeration drives an extra nail into the coffin of the reindeer economy. Perhaps a quarter of Sweden's *Same* are directly dependent on this way of life (many more benefit indirectly). But if something as central to the *Same* identity as reindeer herding were to vanish suddenly, it would be felt as a catastrophe by all *Same*, who, while trying to accommodate themselves in their own way to the changing world, have for centuries been resisting attempts by governments in distant capitals, big businesses, traders, farmers, miners, road-builders and hydroelectric engineers, to bully them off their land and out of existence as a distinctive culture.

The future may look bleak but there are optimists among the *Same*; one is Nikolaus Stenberg, Chairman of the National Federation of Swedish *Same*, who says: "I'm worried, but the *Same* culture won't die because of radioactivity. Chernobyl will have been an alarm clock. I believe people in general are now beginning to wake up. We must pay more attention to nature and to the environment, as the *Same* have been doing since time immemorial."

From an article by Louis Mackay, *originally published in the summer 1987 issue of END Journal; thanks to them for permission to reprint.*

ICELAND'S OTHER ROCK

"We filled the hall with plants. The idea was that they would send biological signals across space and communicate with plant-life in other galaxies. Yes, of course it was serious!" Recollections of a Þeyr gig in Reykjavík in 1981.

In the early 1980s two young Icelandic rock groups each released albums. Þeyr's *As Above...*, issued by the London-based Shout label in 1982, was packed with tumultuous, exciting and densely rhythmic music. The lyrics, sung in English, were frequently buried beneath the din, but plenty emerged to show the group weren't singing about moons in June or bird watching. The record was mysterious, intriguing and wild, and left you with a desire to know more. As did the accompanying press release, which at great length informed of the various philosophical, scientific and mathematical concepts woven into the group's music. Like the record, it was a demonstration of Þeyr's desire to disturb rock music's traditional forms. It also showed their pleasure at making people wonder if they were being wound up.

Purrkur Pillnikk's *Ekki een* had appeared the previous year. Its sleeve design alone was a simple but brilliant idea: showing the crazed figure from the horror movie, *Texas Chainsaw Massacre*, manically wielding an Icelandic sheep. The music, too, within narrow limits of both instrumentation and technical skills, was effective and challenging, the songs taut bursts of sound topped by wailing Icelandic vocals.

How could such things flourish in a country where everybody is off the streets by 10pm (where there *are* streets) and cultural activity is thought to have dried up at the end of the Saga Age? In fact it was these factors, and resistance to them, which enabled the likes of Þeyr and Purrkur Pillnikk to emerge: their very existence an act of defiance.

In mid-1970s Iceland, news of international contemporary music filtered through via imported British music papers and the radio of the NATO base at Keflavík, which broadcast mainly reactionary American rock. The base also accounted for the bulk of the live work available to Icelandic bands, and – like most Icelandic venues – expected them to play covers of American hits. In 1976 a radio show called *Afanga*, hosted by Ásmundur Jónsson and Guðni Rúnar, began playing punk records bought during the presenters' trips to London – the first airing in the country of such sounds. A few years later a cinema in Kópavogur was the unlikely setting for a series of Saturday afternoon gigs by Fræbblarnir (the Strangers): a rough and ready ensemble who swore a lot, had a guitarist with a mohican hair-do and played music which was slimy, unsophisticated, and – most importantly – original. Forced into arranging their own shows, the group were usually seen by a hard-core following of about 35 people, many of them from the Breiðholt area of Reykjavík – the most rundown and neglected part of the city.

While Fræbblarnir were influential on a small scale, much broader change came in 1980 with the release of an album called *Ísbjarnarblús* by Bubbi Morthens. Bubbi was from a family of migrant workers, who travel the country taking temporary work in the fishing industry and have long been considered Iceland's most oppressed people, and many of his songs dealt with the migrant workers' struggles. To hear a song on the radio about migrant workers was rare enough; to get it to number one in the singles chart, as Bubbi did, was unique; and he soon became Iceland's biggest pop star (which he still is, easily outselling Madonna). Another song of Bubbi's, *Radiation*, a criticism of the NATO base at Keflavík, did more to focus people's attention on the subject than the previous thirty-odd years of left-wing debate.

Simultaneously punk (by now also known by the cleaner soubriquet of "new wave") records from Britain and America were being imported and sold around the country, inspiring a rush of fresh creative activity. There was, however, hostility from many quarters: the Reykjavík city council rejected a proposed allocation of money for a youth centre, despite provision for this under a 1949 law; the former hippies who ran Reykjavík's nightclubs resisted booking punk bands on "taste" grounds; and *STEK*, the organisation responsible for collecting songwriters' royalties in Iceland, were also unkindly disposed to new bands – delaying payments which, with the soaring Icelandic inflation rate, meant that composers received only a fraction of the value of their original entitlement. On top of this was a massive (300 percent) import duty on musical equipment.

In spite of these obstacles, Þeyr and Purrkur Pillnikk had played in Europe and were gaining attention in the international music press. In 1981 a club, *NEFI*, opened in Reykjavík near the university, and gigs there began to pull crowds of 500, though there remained a nucleus of just thirty or so at the root of the movement. It was they who were to continue the philosophy of self-expression and disregard for prevailing fashions as New Romanticism – the trend for vapid music and dressing up – gained coverage in the British music papers and was adopted by many young Icelanders.

A film called *Rokk í Reykjavík*, shot during 1981 and 1982 by Freðrik Þor Freðriksson, captured many of the prime bands of the time. Viewed today, the film's a strange spectacle: Þeyr and Purrkur Pillnikk are the most galvanising contributors; Grýlurnar are a pleasant surprise. But the rest is full of odd moments: the guitarist in Sjálsfróun deliberately smashing his guitar after carefully disconnecting it from the amplifier; Q4U arguing for right-wing anarchism while playing in front of an Icelandic flag and a banner reading (in English) "Iceland Is The Only All White Paradise"; and the confessions of an adolescent glue-sniffer.

Even at the time of the film, however, the initial impetus was waning and – with a few exceptions – the general scene remained at a low ebb for several years. The pioneering bands split, their members moving into new projects of varying degrees of worth. The comparative stagnation wasn't helped by the fact that most venues had been acquired by Iceland's top (and more or less only) promoter, Ólafur Laufdal. His conservative booking policy and fly deals with *Icelandair* – whereby international stars use the airline between the USA and Europe, stop over in Reykjavík, stay for free at the *Hotel Borg*, which Ólafur owns, and appear at one of his clubs, usually the enormous *Hollywood*.*

But in 1987, with the release of the highly affecting single *Birthday*, the Sugarcubes struck a blow for musical originality not only in Iceland but internationally, too. Emotionally intense yet instilled with a sense of innocence and adventure, the disc (released by the small London-based One Little Indian label), topped the British · Independent chart for weeks, leading to television exposure and major features in the music press around Europe. The follow-up, the edgy *Cold Sweat*, continued the success, selling 22,000 copies in a single day.

While quite unique, the Sugarcubes are in many ways an extension of the ideas evolved by the earlier bands. Indeed, of the group's two vocalists one, Einar Benediktsson, was in Purrkur Pillnikk whilst the other, Björk Guðmundsdóttir – whose associative, quasi-surrealist lyrics are at the core of the group's sound – appeared (aged just 16) in *Rokk í Reykjavík* fronting a combo called Tappi Tíkarrass; like Einar, she was also was later in KUKL (see discography). The Sugarcubes' profound scope and imagination found fullest expression on the *Life's Too Good* album, released in May 1988, a refreshing antidote to the musical stagnation elsewhere in the world.

Just over a year later, their follow-up, *Here Today, Tomorrow Next Week!*, was a different matter: one critic dismissed the album as "Eurovision fodder" (perhaps not a bad notion given the standard of Iceland's previous entries into the song contest) and certainly the band's ideas seemed to have paled, possibly because of the tiredness induced by a year of touring before recording it. But the single lifted from the album, the haunting *Regina*, proved the Sugarcubes still have something to offer, and they look set to be a major influence on independent rock music throughout the world for some time to come.

---

* Beginning with a memorable Reykjavík gig by Led Zeppelin in 1972, a number of overseas artists have forged links with Iceland. To promote their 1978 *Black and White* album, the Stranglers arranged a gig at the Reykjavík Sports Centre and flew British journalists to it. The anarchist band, Crass, headlined a Peace Festival at the same Sports Centre in 1983, drawing 4500 people, with a further 1000 listening outside; the group have also lent their Southern Studios to a number of Icelandic bands (Purkurr Pillnikk recorded *Ekki een* there), and the Crass record label has released two albums by KUKL (see discography). The Fall have played in Iceland several times, recording part of their 1982 album, *Hex Induction Hour*, there, and Psychic TV's live double album, *Those Who Do Not*, was recorded in Reykjavík (part of the group's "world tour" which comprised four dates – in London, Berlin, New York and Reykjavík). Echo and The Bunnymen and Grace Jones have turned up to admire the scenery and use photos of it on their album covers, and two members of Killing Joke arrived after being told that northwest Iceland was the only place in the world safe from the effects of nuclear war.

SELECTED DISCOGRAPHY

ÞEYR

Útfrymi (Fálkinn/Eskvímó EF1). Their first single.
Iður til fóta (Eskvímó ESQ1). A ten-inch single.
As Above... (Shout LX 001). Their first – and last – album.
Mjötviður mær (Eskvímó ESQ2). Icelandic release of *As Above...*, with a couple of additional tracks and selected lyrics in Icelandic.

The Fourth Reich (Shout in England/MJÖT in Iceland). A twelve-inch EP, and their final record: dedicated to "the life and work of Wilhelm Reich who laid the foundation for paradise. His reward was punishment and death."

PURRKUR PILLNIKK

Tilf (Gramm 1). Their first single.
Ekki een (Gramm 3). Their first album.
No Time To Think (Gramm 9). A four-track EP, with English lyrics.

Googooplex (Gramm 6). Two twelve-inch EPs.
Maskínan (Gramm 10). Eighteen live tracks, some recorded during a British tour with The Fall.

BUBBI MORTHENS

Kona (Gramm 25). A slick, sensual album.
Blús Fyrir Rikka (Gramm 29). A double, mainly live, album of acoustic blues with Bubbi accompanying himself on a twelve-string guitar. All original songs in Icelandic, except Leadbelly's *Rock Island Line* and *Silver City Bound*, and Skip James' *Let Us Walk Together*.

Serbian Flower (MLR 63). Released by the Swedish label Mistlur, this is Bubbi's first English-language LP, and its accessible, articulate songs make it easy to see why he's so popular.
Bubbi & Megas (Gramm 40). Bubbi teams up with another Icelandic legend, the much-tattooed Megas (see below), for a thoroughly bizarre collection of crazed, pseudo-cabaret numbers.

OTHER ARTISTS

Das Kapital *Lili Marlene* (Gramm 20). Includes Bubbi Morthens; spirited and enjoyable.
Íkarus *Ras 5-20* (Gramm 18). Highly political, though the impact is lost on non Icelandic-speakers.
KUKL *Holidays In Europe – The Naughty Nought* (Crass) & *The Eye* (Crass 1984 1). Sometimes powerful, often overbearingly theatrical, their line-up includes former members of Þeyr and Purrkur Pillnikk, and subsequent members of the Sugarcubes.
Megas *Höfuðlausnir* (Gramm 36), Intriguing stuff from the undefinable Megas, here assisted by an all-star bunch of Icelandic instrumentalists, plus Björk of the Sugarcubes and Rose McDowall, of Strawberry Switchblade fame, on vocals.
S.H. Draumur. A chaotic but enjoyable trio who've released records, but are notable more for the cassettes they issue of unsung Icelandic bands

on their Erðanúmúsik label – and their English-language fanzine, *Gorilla Ice Cream*.
The Sugarcubes. The singles *Birthday* (12 tp 7) and *Cold Sweat* (12 tp 9), and the albums *Life's Too Good* and *Here Today, Tomorrow Next Week!*. Available in most record shops.
Various *Rokk í Reykjavík* (Hugrenningur). The double album soundtrack of the film. Very mixed, one or two great tracks and many terrible ones.
Vonbrigði *Kakófnía* (Gramm 14). The great hope of Icelandic music during 1983, though their gripping live shows were way ahead of their recordings.
Þorlákur Kristinson *The Boys From Chicago* (Gramm 15). Songs of the migrant worker situation in Iceland and political problems around the globe. The album lasts over an hour and the second side features the band Íkarus.

RECORD COMPANY ADDRESSES

Erðanúmúsik, Álfhólsvegur 302, 200 Kópavogur
Gramm, Laugavegur 17, 101 Reykjavík (see p.000).

Mjöt, Klapperstigur 28, Reykjavík.

WILDLIFE IN THE FAROES

Even to someone who doesn't know a blackbird from a buff-breasted sandpiper, the huge seabird colonies that breed on the Faroese cliffs every summer are one of nature's more inspiring sights. Literally millions of seabirds of all sorts – auks, terns, petrels, shearwaters and more – converge on the Faroes every year, both to breed and for the rich concentration of Lusitanic plankton that lives in the shallow waters around the islands, and which provides an abundant food source for them and their newly hatched young.

SEABIRDS

Breeding seabirds are probably the easiest of all birds to watch. Simply find yourself a suitable cliff, sit down, and let your senses take it all in, for the smell and sound of a colony is as striking as the sight. Each species has its own definite breeding niche on the cliff. At the top you'll find **Puffins**, unmistakeable with their brightly coloured bills and standing at the mouths of their breeding burrows. They are delightfully amusing birds, and ones which the Faroese have a long association with. Puffins used to be netted in huge numbers with *fleyg* nets, and still are to a lesser extent: dried puffin is an important winter food, and roasted or stewed fresh puffin is delicious – a bit like pigeon but better. The islanders know more about the bird's breeding biology than most scientists, and so are able to harvest puffins without affecting the overall population.

Below the puffins, on the vertical cliff faces, are **Guillemots**, a member of the auk family, who breed on narrow shelves, packed closely together – life for a guillemot chick is squashed and precarious. Elegant and neat, with their chocolate-brown backs and snowy-white breasts, they are appalling fliers and ungainly on land, like all the auks. But try to get above them when they are swimming underwater, and you'll see them in their true element: with bodies turned silvery by the air trapped under their oily feathers, they fly through the water in pursuit of their prey. **Razorbills** are a closely related species, distinguishable from guille-

mots by a blacker back and a thicker bill with a white line; they breed in smaller colonies and usually on the less vertical rocks at the top or the bottom of the cliff.

Scattered throughout the cliffs are **Fulmars**, a gull-sized member of the albatross family. They breed in huge numbers on the islands, and are one of the finest fliers of all birds, soaring along the cliffs on stiff, straight wings with scarcely a flap. Don't get too close to a nesting fulmar, though: one of their defence mechanisms is to spit an evil-smelling, indelible oil at would-be attackers, and they're accurate up to two metres. Another common seabird is the **Kittiwake**, the size of a small gull but pure white apart from black wingtips (it's said the melanin stops the wingtips from fraying). Kittiwakes nest in large colonies, usually on steep faces and in caves towards the bottom of the cliff, and are amongst the noisiest of seabirds. They're also unusual in that they build nests on the steep rock faces (auks lay straight onto the rock or in holes), which become a stinking mess of guano by the end of the summer.

Finally, in the rock jumbles at the bottom of cliffs, there's the final member of the auk family, the **Black Guillemot**. The rarest of the breeding auks, it has a deep-brown body with white wing patches, but its feet and the inside of its mouth are an incongruous bright crimson. **Shags** also breed at the bottom of the cliffs on most islands – large birds with glossy black plumage, an evil green eye, and a disconcerting hiss if you approach too closely.

Such a mass of seabirds is bound to attract predators. **Greater** and **Lesser Blackbacked Gulls** and **Herring Gulls** lurk around the edges of the colonies – quick to pounce on a fallen chick or an unguarded egg – and Skuas patrol offshore. The **Great Skua** is a mean brown bird the size of a large gull, while the **Arctic Skua** is slimmer and comes in three colour phases of brown and white. Both species use the same hunting technique, diving from the sky on auks returning with food to their nests. Usually they chase the unfortunate auk, forcing it to disgorge its food which they then eat; sometimes they drive the bird down to the sea and peck it to death.

At either end of the size scale are **Gannets** and **Terns**. Gannets are the largest seabirds in the North Atlantic, with a wingspan of nearly two metres. They're white with a yellow head and black wingtips, and fish by plummeting down on their prey from twenty metres or more – a dramatic sight. An ancient Faroese punishment for infidelity, apparently, was to send the erring husband for a swim under the Mykines gannetry with a herring tied to his head – an imaginative if unlikely punishment. **Arctic Terns** are much smaller and daintier, but use the same aerial dive as their fishing technique, often breeding in huge colonies in the inland valleys.

Nor does this teeming life stop at sunset. The petrels and shearwaters, having spent the day fishing way out at sea, return to their nesting burrows all over the islands as it gets dark. **Manx Shearwaters**, large seabirds which skim low over the waves shearing the water with their wingtips, gather just offshore in packs at dusk and make a terrific noise. There are two petrel species breeding on the islands: **Storm Petrels** and **Leach's Petrels**, both small, dusky black with a white rump and an eerie bat-like flight. Sit in the middle of a petrel colony at night and you'll be surrounded by darting black shapes, and the air will be full of weird bubbling cries as the birds – one in the nesting burrow, one in the air – call to each other.

OTHER SPECIES OF BIRDS

As you would expect from its small size and isolated position, the overall number of breeding species of birds in the Faroes is pretty low – less than sixty, of which about half are seabirds. But the interesting thing is to see how species have evolved to suit the environment. The **Redwing**, for example, is a handsome northern thrush, an adaptation of the song thrushes and blackbirds of mainland Europe, while the **Whimbrel** – a large brown wading bird with a decurved bill – replaces the more southerly Curlew.

Away from the sea-cliffs, there are a number of other habitats worth a visit. Almost any stretch of fresh water will be of interest, and may hold breeding ducks, waders, and possibly **Redthroated Divers**, a primitive water bird with a plaintive, spine-tingling cry. Marshland will have breeding waders, like the whimbrels mentioned above, and perhaps the delightful **Rednecked Phalarope**. These are usually extremely tame and, interestingly, the species' gender roles are reversed: females are larger and more brightly coloured than the males, hold territory, are polyandrous (ie have more than one mate), and it is the male that broods the eggs and rears the chicks. Finally, the upland fells hold more breeding waders, including a few pairs of **Purple Sandpipers** on their most southerly breeding ground.

WHEN TO GO; WHAT TO TAKE

Summer is best. Although all the breeding seabirds and waders return from their wintering grounds at different times, almost all of them are present and breeding between the end of May and mid-August, with the end of June and the beginning of July being the peak activity period. You get the advantage of the long summer nights then, too, as well as the added bonus of the national and exuberant festival of *Olafsaka* at the end of July.

A pair of **binoculars** is an enormous asset. To **photograph** birds you usually need expensive gear, but seabirds are tame enough to make this unnecessary; nonetheless, a telephoto is useful – say around 200mm. Any of the standard field **guides** gives you ample identification details. Ken Williamson's book *The Atlantic Islands* has lots of good bird information, and, although it doesn't cover the Faroes, *The Seabirds of Britain and Ireland* by Stanley Cramp *et al* (Collins o/p) is an excellent background read on seabird ecology before you go.

WHERE TO GO

Almost anywhere on the islands you'll find rolling hills within range of breeding waders. But you'll need to be a bit more selective to find the best stretches of open water, and not all islands have good seabird colonies.

Streymoy, the most-visited island, is probably not the best for birds, although there are some good seabird colonies on the northwestern cliffs. Saksum in the north of the island has one of the few colonies of Great Skuas on the islands. Walk through it if you want to know what it feels like to be dive-bombed. **Nolsoy**, just over the water from Tórshavn, is worth a visit if you want to see seabirds and you're short of time. The northern islands of **Kallsoy**, **Vidoy** and **Fugloy** have very large seabird colonies on their rugged northern cliffs.

Sandoy and its smaller neighbour **Skuvoy** are two of the best islands for birds, with excellent seabird colonies, Great Skuas breeding on Skuvoy, and waders, perhaps including Purple Sandpipers on both islands. Two lakes on Sandoy — Sandsvatn and Grothusvatn — have a good range of breeding waders and ducks, as well as divers and phalaropes.

Vägar is worth exploring for the lakes of Sorvagsvatn and Fjallavatn, and there's some very wild country especially in the west and north. Most sensible naturalists, however, use Vägar as a stepping-stone to **Mykines**, an island of extraordinary beauty and drama, and one of the best places to see seabirds in the whole of Europe. All the common auks are here, along with the only colony of Leach's Petrels in the Faroes, and also the only gannetry. The gannet colony dates back at least to 1673, and the Mykines people have a long and honourable association with them. Mykinesholmur — a small extension of the main island, connected by a narrow cliff path and a bridge — is the place to go for the gannets and many of the auks, and it also has a big concentration of petrels and shearwaters at night. There's nowhere to stay on the holm, unless you can persuade the lighthouse keeper to let you stay in the hut at the top of the steps, but it's only a short walk from the main village. Mykines also has its own species of mouse, rejoicing in the name of *Mus musculus mykinessiensis*, which has evolved a separate identity over the island's long isolation. Also, keep your eyes open on the boat trip from Sorvag to Mykines (or on any boat trip, for that matter) for **whales**, from the small pilot whale up to the large baleen whales, and even killer whales.

ONWARDS FROM SCANDINAVIA

Although there are some simple links into Western Europe, Scandinavia also makes a remarkably good starting point for travel into the USSR and parts of Eastern Europe. The Soviet Baltic Republics in particular are keen to forge tourist links with the Nordic countries, both to strengthen contact with the West and to boost their hard currency income. Enticing for totally different reasons is Greenland, a vast and mysterious ice-coated land that's becoming increasingly accessible, with direct connections from Reykjavík and Copenhagen.

THE USSR

In the age of *perestroika* and *glasnost* you'd think that travelling to the USSR would have become easy; in fact, it's still almost as hard (and just as expensive, upwards of £50 per day) as it ever was, and for the most part still ridden with bureaucratic restrictions. None of which should put you off visiting, however: from Finland, both travel and formalities are far simpler than from the UK – Finnish travel agents can provide Soviet **visas** (70Fmk) in a week to ten days and need only photocopies of the relevant sections of your passport to do so. Some cruises from Finland to the USSR are visa-free, although these are expensive and you only spend a fairly short time ashore.

Unless you've been formally invited to the USSR by friends, or are visiting some very off-the-beaten-track places, **independent travel** within the USSR is more trouble than it's worth. Your trip must be arranged through *Intourist*, and they'll insist on an exact (and they mean exact) itinerary. They will book you into the state-run tourist hotels, and provide tickets for transport, but they require pre-payment and an unchangeable booking made far in advance of travel – and you'll have to confirm your arrival at a police station in each town you visit. At least if you do travel this way, you'll be able to use one of the two daily trains from Helsinki to **Leningrad** (around 160Fmk), one of which continues to **Moscow** (around 290Fmk).

Package tours, which include full-board accommodation and sightseeing, work out cheaper than independent travel, and can be booked at much shorter notice (usually as long as it takes to process your visa) although Finnish tours to the USSR, especially in summer, often sell out quickly. Several Helsinki-based travel agencies – *Area Travel, Finnsov Tours, Kalevala Travel* – run trips to the Soviet Union, the brochures and addresses of which are available, outside Finland, from Finnish Tourist Board offices (see *Basics*); their Helsinki addresses are given below. Prices range from 1270Fmk for three days in Leningrad, to 3350Fmk for a week-long stay at a winter sports centre in the Georgian mountains.

It's possible to visit Leningrad for a day **without a visa** from Helsinki or Kotka with *Kristina Cruises*, though this is pricey, around 1000Fmk depending on the season. The same company runs cruises to Tallinn, Riga and Viipuri (also called Vyborg).

Of other packages, best value are those run by Copenhagen-based *Scandinavian Student Travel Service*, whose summer tours include accommodation in the spartan but cheap *Sputnik* hotels, normally reserved for young Soviet travellers, and meetings with Soviet youth. You can book tours either in Britain or Scandinavia, but the tours themselves begin in the Soviet Union, meaning you have to make your own way there – though there are sometimes connecting flights from Copenhagen and Stockholm. To join a tour you don't need to be a student but the over-35s need special confirmation from the *SSTS* head office. Prices vary from 2785DKr for a week split between Moscow and Leningrad, to 8515DKr for two weeks in Leningrad, Tashkent, Samarkand, Bukhara and Moscow. *SSTS* also offer a Trans-Siberian Railway trip from Helsinki to Yokohama, in **JAPAN**, for 9400DKr, which includes several stopovers and sightseeing tours.

THE BALTIC REPUBLICS

The easiest part of the USSR to reach from Scandinavia are the **Baltic Republics** of Estonia, Latvia and Lithuania. **ESTONIA**, especially, is quick and comparatively simple to reach from Scandinavia. Getting there is cheapest from Helsinki with *Saimaa Lines*, who offer an all-inclusive three-night stay in Tallinn, the capital, for around 1100Fmk (as little as 200mk

SCANDINAVIAN TOUR OPERATORS TO THE USSR

Area Travel, Kaisaniementkatu 13, 00100 Helsinki (☎90/18551).

Estline, tickets bookable in the UK through *Scandinavian Seaways* (see *Basics*) or contact PO Box 1215, 11182 Stockholm (☎08/6131 950).

Finnsov Tours, Eerkinkatu 3, 00100 Helsinki (☎90/6942011).

Kalevala, Mikonkatu 6C, 00100 Helsinki (☎90/602711).

Kristina Cruises, Tehtaankatu 25, 00150 Helsinki (☎90/629968).

Saimaa Lines, Pohjoinen Makasiinikatu 7, 00130 Helsinki (☎90/658733).

Scandinavian Student Travel Service, Hauchsvej 17, DK-1825 Copenhagen V (☎31/218500).

if you do it as a day-trip). From Stockholm, *Estline* run three times a week to Tallinn (around 600SKr return), and offer two-day stays without visas using accommodation on the boat for 800–900SKr per person. There's also a new scheduled air link – one of the few ways of flying into the USSR from the West without first landing at Leningrad or Moscow – to Tallinn from Stockholm with *SAS* (2440SKr return); *Aeroflot* are planning a rival service on the same route.

Estonia is particularly engrossing if you've spent time in Finland; the two countries have similar languages, a common ancestry, and histories that have largely run parallel – up until the Soviet annexation of Estonia in 1940. You'll spend most if not all of your time in **Tallinn**, a beautifully-maintained Hanseatic city with many museums and some fine old churches; this one of the few places in the USSR where you can wake to the sound of church bells. Going further afield in Estonia varies from being difficult to impossible, and is always expensive, unless you have Estonian friends with whom you can – not always legally – travel by car.

Wherever you are in Estonia, you can't forget that you're in an occupied country. These days there are many easily seen markers to the Estonians' struggle to regain their independence from the USSR – most obviously the blue, black and white Estonian flag banned by the Soviet authorities until a couple of years ago, and the number of people whose lapels carry the same thing in badge form. Yet while there is hope among Estonians for a future outside the Soviet Union, there's also a great deal of uncertainty and doubt engendered by political turmoil in Moscow, the shortages of

basic essentials – and the 30,000 Soviet troops stationed on Estonian soil.

Aside from a desire to assert their national cultures and regain independent statehood, the three Baltic countries do not have that much in common. Each has a distinct language and their pasts are less interwoven than you might expect. Religion is another difference. While Estonia and **LATVIA** are predominantly Lutheran, **LITHUANIA** is overwhelmingly Catholic (one of many common traits with neighbouring Poland). At present, the costly *Kristina Cruises* link from Helsinki is the only direct way to the Latvian capital of **Riga**, although a ferry from Norrköping in Sweden is due to begin a service to Riga in 1991. If you want to go on to **Vilnius** in Lithuania, you'll have to do so independently – at least for the time being.

NOTE: On March 11, 1990, the Supreme Soviet of Lithuania changed its name to the Supreme Council of Lithuania, and declared The Republic of Lithuania – dropping "Soviet Socialist" from the state's name – independent of the USSR. Though made in accordance with international law (and invoking the constitutional right of every Soviet Republic to "freely secede" from the Union), this act threw a spanner into the machinery of Soviet legislation and its full ramifications can, at present, only be guessed at. Estonia and Latvia, pursuing the same end along slightly different courses, are likely to make similar declarations in the near future. Frankly, anything can happen, but one effect of these changes may be to make travel to the Baltic Republics much easier, although obviously you should check the latest situation before embarking.

POLAND

Reaching **POLAND** directly is possible from Denmark, Sweden and Finland, the quickest and cheapest way being with the twice-weekly summer sailing from Rønne, on the Danish island of Bornholm, to Swinoujście (210DKr), a Polish port you can also reach one to two times daily from Ystad in Sweden (220SKr). The other links are to **Gdansk**: from Sweden, there's a direct sailing from Nynäshamn (380SKr), and one with *Polferries* from Helsinki (430Fmk).

At the time of writing, unless you're a Finn, Swede or Austrian you need a visa to enter Poland, obtainable most cheaply and with least hassle in western Europe. Compulsory currency exchange was recently abolished, and, within Poland, the **state tourist organisation**, *ORBIS*, have offices in the main hotels and elsewhere around the main cities, which can provide maps and information. *ALMATUR*, the Polish student travel service, also provide information, sell the *IUS* student card – which gives reductions on international train fares and entry to museums – and run the *ALMATUR Hotels*, which utilise the dormitory space vacated by students during the summer and are often the best-value places to stay in the cities (though you need to book ahead).

Travelling around Poland is inexpensive, but crowded and unreliable. Trains are best, divided between *expresowy*, expresses but few and far between and requiring a seat reservation; *pośpieszne*, more common and, by Polish standards, fast, but crowded; and the *osobowe* – incredibly slow, though very cheap, commuter trains. It's often a good move to avoid the crowds by travelling first class (half as much again on top of the ordinary fare) or by reserving a seat. Hitchhiking, uniquely, is officially encouraged and there's even a competition for the driver who gives most lifts, the winner determined using a system of dirt-cheap hitching coupons with which the traveller pays the driver. A *Rough Guide* to Poland is planned for publication in spring 1991.

GERMANY

Nothing could be simpler than ambling across southern Jutland (in Denmark) to **WEST GERMANY**. Trains depart several times a day from both Frederikshavn and Copenhagen for **Hamburg** (from around 640DKr), passing through most Danish mainline stations, and from Hamburg there are rail links to the rest of West Germany. There are also ferry connections between the southern Danish coast and islands, and West German towns, among them Fåborg to Gelting (40DKr), Bagenkop to Kiel (30DKr), and Gedser to Travemünde (30DKr); and it's also possible, if not particularly cheap, to sail with *Finnjet* from Helsinki to Travemünde, a 36-hour trip that costs around 350Fmk for deck passengers – though there are reduced rates for students and *Inter/EurRail* card holders. For more details, see the *Rough Guide: Germany* (Harrap-Columbus £8.95).

As yet, the only direct connection from Scandinavia into **EAST GERMANY**, is the two-hour ferry crossing from Gedser (in Denmark) to **Warnemünde** (48DKr). Since the country's political upheavals, entry requirements for western tourists into East Germany are in a state of flux – check the details when you're planning your trip.

GREENLAND

There are direct flights from both Reykjavík and Copenhagen to **GREENLAND**, and although it is possible to visit independently, you shouldn't attempt this without thorough planning. Shortest of the packages is *Icelandair's* summer four-times-a-week day-trip from Reykjavík to **Kulusuk**, a small island in the Angmagssalik fjord. This, however, is expensive – about £220 per person – and the total flying time of four hours means you only get about two hours on the ground. Also, the tiny Greenlandic community at **Kapdan**, on Kulusuk, is hardly typical, mainly due to the influx of tourists. It may be the only chance you get, though: tickets can be arranged through any *Icelandair* office or travel agent in Reykjavík, and are popular – book as early as possible.

Most longer tours centre on **Narssaq**, on the country's southern tip, or the capital **Nuuk** (formerly Godthåb), on the west coast. Options range from walking-based tours sleeping in mountain huts (£600 for a week from Reykjavík) to ten days of being towed on a sledge by huskies (£1750). Although independent since 1979, Greenland still uses Danish currency, and entry requirements are as for Denmark. There are no roads or railways and transport between the main centres of population has to be by aircraft or boat. General information can be obtained in advance from a Danish Tourist Board office (see *Basics*) or by writing to *Tusarliivik*, Postbox 1020, DK-3900 Nuuk, Greenland.

BOOKS

Books on Scandinavia in English are remarkably scant: surprisingly few travellers have written well (or indeed at all) about the region over the years, and historical or political works tend to concentrate almost exclusively on the Vikings.

However, Scandinavian literature is appearing more and more in translation – notably the Icelandic Sagas and selected modern novelists – and it's always worth picking up a turn-of-the-century Baedeker's *Norway and Sweden* (not to be confused with the modern, glossy Baedeker/AA guides), if only for the phrasebook, from which you can learn the Swedish and Norwegian for "Do you want to cheat me?", "When does the washerwoman come?" and "We must tie ourselves together with rope to cross this glacier."

Norvik Press are a good source of new translations of old and new Scandinavian writing; for their catalogue write to them at EUR/University of East Anglia, Norwich NR4 7TJ. For more obscure and out of print titles, try the *Travel Bookshop*, 13 Blenheim Crescent, London W11 (☎071-229 5260).

SCANDINAVIA

TRAVEL AND GENERAL

Jeremy Cherfas *The Hunting of Whale* (Bodley Head £12.95). Subtitled "A tragedy that must end", this is a convincing condemnation of whaling and all those involved in it. Norway, Iceland and the Faroe Islands take note.

Donald S. Connery *The Scandinavians* (Eyre & Spottiswood o/p). Worth hunting down for its gleefully opinionated views of the region and its peoples. It captures the Sixties' mood of

optimism perfectly, a time when "Scandinavianism" was fast becoming regarded as a blueprint for the world's future.

Julian Cremona and Robert Chote *Exploring Nature in the Wilds of Europe* (Ashford £8.95). Planning advice, camping and transport tips, wildlife- and plant-spotting – all contained in a weighty, general holiday guide, with substantial sections on Norway and Iceland.

Tom Cunliffe *Topsail and Battleaxe* (David & Charles £12.95). The intertwined stories of the tenth-century Vikings who sailed from Norway, past the Faroes and Iceland to North America, and the author's parallel trip in 1983 – made in a 75-year-old pilot cutter. Enthusiastically written, and nice photos.

Craig Evans *On Foot Through Europe: Scandinavia* (Quill £7.95). The authority on European hiking trails, this volume covers long-distance footpaths and national-park hiking. Packed with useful addresses, map and weather information.

Peter Lennon *Scandinavian Mountains* (West Col £11.95). Route-planning and in-depth coverage of the more demanding mountain trails.

John McCormick *Acid Earth* (Earthscan £2.95). Good for the background on the burning issue of acid rain, of which the Scandinavian countries are net recipients – especially from Britain.

Lawrence Millman *Last Places: A Journey in the North* (Deutsch £12.95). Up-to-date account of a journey around little-visited areas of the North Atlantic, including descriptions of Norway, the Faroes and Iceland.

Jane Smiley *The Greenlanders* (Fontana £4.50). A Tolkienesque novel, detailing the isolation and development of a fourteenth-century community in Greenland, cut off from mainstream Europe. A good, big holiday read, written in the style of the Sagas.

Mary Wollstonecraft *A Short Residence in Sweden, Norway and Denmark* (Penguin £3.95). A searching account of Wollstonecraft's three-month solo journey through southern Scandinavia in 1795. The same volume contains a short and classic biography of Wollstonecraft by her husband, William Godwin, shedding much light on the mind of an extraordinary woman undaunted by the prospect of travelling alone in what was then an unknown and sometimes dangerous land.

HISTORY, MYTHOLOGY AND ART

Johannes Brøndsted *The Vikings* (Penguin £5.99). Classic and immensely readable account of the Viking period, with valuable sections, too, on social and cultural life, art, religious beliefs and customs. Really, the best general guide available. See brief extract on p.646.

H.R. Ellis Davidson *The Gods and Myths of Northern Europe* (Penguin £3.95). A handy Saga companion, this is a Who's Who of Norse mythology, including some useful reviews of the more obscure gods. Displaces the classical deities and their world as the most relevant mythological framework for northern and western European culture.

T.K. Derry *A History of Scandinavia* (Allen and Unwin o/p). The standard historical tome, available in most libraries, though over-detailed for most tastes.

P.V. Glob *The Bog People* (Faber £5.95). A fascinating study of the various Iron Age bodies discovered preserved in full in northwestern European peat-bogs, most of which have been found in Denmark. Excellent, if ghoulish, photographs.

Gwyn Jones *A History of the Vikings* (OUP £6.95). Long-winded but probably the most up-to-date Viking history you can buy.

Neil Kent *The Triumph of Light and Nature: Nordic Art 1740–1940* (Thames & Hudson £20). Beautifully illustrated critical chronicle of Scandinavian art during its most influential periods. Highly recommended.

Ole Klindt-Jensen *A History of Scandinavian Archaeology* (Thames and Hudson £5.95). For dedicated burial-mound hunters and treasure-seeking enthusiasts.

Peter Limm *The Thirty Years' War* (Longman £2.95). A brief and accessible gallop through the period (1618–1648), containing some interesting, translated contemporary documents and a formidable bibliography for further reading.

F. Donald Logan *The Vikings in History* (Hutchinson £7.95). Scholarly – and radical – re-examination of the Vikings' impact on medieval Europe, indispensable for the Viking fan.

Geoffrey Parker *The Thirty Years' War* (RKP £8.95). One of the more recent accounts of this turbulent period, acknowledged as authoritative but a dry read.

HISTORY AND PHILOSOPHY

Inga Dahlsgård *Women in Denmark, Yesterday and Today* (DDS, the Danish Cultural Institute, 3 Douane Terrace, Edinburgh, £3.50) A refreshing presentation of Danish history from the point of view of its women.

W. Glyn Jones *Denmark: A Modern History* (Croom Helm £25). A valuable account of the present century (up until 1984), with a commendable outline of pre-twentieth-century Danish history. Strong on politics, useful on social history and the arts, but disappointingly brief on recent grassroots movements.

Stewart Oakley *The Story of Denmark* (Faber o/p). Good presentation of the complex medieval period, but decidedly scant on more recent times.

Roger Poole & Henrik Stangerup (eds.) *A Kierkegaard Reader* (Fourth Estate £7.95). By far the best and most accessible introduction to this notoriously "difficult" nineteenth-century Danish philosopher and writer. Besides a sparkling introductory essay, there are well-chosen selections from the great man's works, all entertaining and offering insights into Danish life.

LITERATURE AND BIOGRAPHY

Hans Christian Andersen (ed. Naomi Lewis) *The Fairy Tales of Hans Christian Andersen* (Puffin £1.95). Still the most internationally prominent figure of Danish literature, even if he often seems more tourist attraction than writer. Andersen's fairy tales are so widely translated and read that the full clout of their allegorical content is often overlooked: interestingly, his first collection of such tales (published in 1835) were condemned for their "violence and questionable morals," and it was some time before he achieved recognition in his own country. But Andersen didn't only write fairy tales. *A Visit to Germany, Italy and Malta, 1840–1841* (Peter Owen £12.50), inspired by a rough and hazardous journey through the lands of the Ottoman Empire in 1841, is the most enduring of his travel works. And his autobiography, *The Fairy Tale of My Life*, is a fine riposte to the numerous sycophantic biographies which have appeared since, with the author lashing out at those who gave him short shrift before his success. For more on Andersen, see p.91.

Steen Steensen Blicher *Diary of a Parish Clerk* (Hans Teitzel o/p); *Twelve Stories* (Kraus o/p). Blicher was a keen observer of Jutish life, writing stark, realistic tales in local dialect and gathering a seminal collection of Jutish folk-tales – published as *E Bindstouw* in 1842. For more on Blicher, see p.118.

Karen Blixen (Isak Dinesen) *Out of Africa* (Penguin £3.95); *Letters from Africa* (Picador £3.95); *Seven Gothic Tales* (Penguin £4.95). The haughty Danish aristocrat, Karen Blixen, was long celebrated in Denmark for her short stories, but it was only after the 1985 film of *Out of Africa* that she really became known abroad. *Out of Africa*, the account of her attempts to run a coffee farm in Kenya after divorce from her husband, is a lyrical and moving tale. But it's in *Seven Gothic Tales*, published in 1934, that Blixen's fiction was at its zenith: a flawlessly executed, weird, emotive work, full of twists in plot and strange, ambiguous characterisation. Several other titles by Blixen in translation are easily found, including *Winter's Tales* (Penguin £4.50) – essays with a stong Danish context. An acclaimed film of a Blixen story, *Babette's Feast*, was released in 1988, and is set in Jutland.

Poul Borum *Danish Literature: A Short Critical Guide* (DDS £4). A likeably opinionated rundown of Danish Literature from medieval times to the 1970s. DDS also publish *Out of Denmark: Danish Women Writers Today* (£7.50) – critical essays on Danish women writers, not least Karen Blixen.

Tove Ditlevsen *Early Spring* (The Women's Press £3.95). An autobiographical novel of growing up in the working-class Vesterbro district of Copenhagen during the 1930s. As an evocation of childhood and early adulthood, it's totally captivating, and provides an astute commentary on both the city and Danish society of the time.

Martin A. Hansen *The Liar* (Quartet £4.95). An engaging novel, showing why Hansen was one of Denmark's most perceptive – and popular – authors during the postwar period. Set in the 1950s, the story examines the inner thoughts of a lonely schoolteacher living on a small Danish island.

Annegret Heitmann (ed.) *No Man's Land* (Norvik Press £9.50). A recent anthology of the country's best-known modern women writers, a mix of poetry and prose, mostly dealing with women's issues but infused with a strong Danish outlook.

Judith Thurman *Isak Dinesen: The Life of Karen Blixen* (Penguin £4.95). The most penetrative biography of Blixen, with elucidating details of the farm period not found in the two "Africa" books.

Dea Trier Mørch *Winter's Child* (Serpent's Tail £4.95). A wonderfully lucid sketch of modern Denmark as seen through the eyes of several women in the maternity ward of a Copenhagen hospital. See also *Evening Star* (Serpent's Tail £4.95), which deals with the effect of old age and death on a Danish family.

NORWAY

TRAVEL AND GENERAL

Patrick Davis *An Experience of Norway* (David & Charles o/p). Dated – published in 1974 – but nonetheless reasonably entertaining account of a 4000-mile trip through Norway in a campervan.

John Douglas *The Arctic Highway* (David and Charles o/p). A blow-by-blow account of the E6 Arctic Highway (construction and travelling) between Mo-i-Rana and Kirkenes.

Thor Heyerdahl *The Kon-Tiki Expedition* (Unwin £3.95); *The Tigris Expedition* (Unwin £3.95); *The Ra Expeditions* (o/p); and *Fatu-Hiva* (o/p). Rattling good reads by Norway's most famous and adventurous modern explorer – see also p.172. Old Penguin editions of the out of print titles are also fairly easy to come by.

HISTORY AND SOCIOLOGY

T.K. Derry *A History of Modern Norway 1814–1972* (OUP o/p). More or less all there is available on the modern period, and stopping well short of more recent times.

Oddvar K. Hoidal *Quisling: A Study in Treason* (OUP £48). A long and comprehensive biography of the world's most famous traitor, Vidkun Quisling, the man presented in all his unpleasant fullness. The ludicrous price, sadly, means that few will ever dip into this volume.

Gwyn Jones *The Norse Atlantic Saga* (OUP £6.95). An excellent companion account of the (mainly Norwegian) discovery and settlement of Iceland, Greenland and North America, interspersed with extracts from the Sagas.

Francois Kersaudy *Norway 1940* (Collins £15). A short history of the Norwegian resistance – in 1940 – to the Nazi invasion of their country. A well-informed account, including coverage of the role of the British forces who helped the Norwegians in their fight.

Karen Larsen *A History of Norway* (Princeton University Press o/p). Enormous, comprehensive but dated – generally available in public libraries.

Magnús Magnússon and Hermann Palsson (trans.) *The Vinland Sagas: The Norse Discovery of America* (Penguin £2.95). This tells, in contemporary reportage, of the Viking Norwegians' "discovery" of North America in the tenth century.

Ronald G. Popplewell *Norway* (Ernest Benn o/p). A useful account of Norway and the Norwegians, with some succinct historical chapters. You should find it in public libraries.

Arne Selbyg *An Introduction to Norwegian Society* (OUP £20). Although an intelligent work, the price-tag puts this book out of reach to most general interest readers.

Arthur Spencer *The Norwegians* (David and Charles o/p). A good second best to the book above. Indiscriminately informative, offering an insight into how Norwegians live and work, from handicrafts to the social security system.

LITERATURE AND ART

Janet Garton & Henning Sehmsdorf *New Norwegian Plays* (Norvik Press £10.50). Four plays written between 1979 and 1983, including work by the feminist writer Bjørg Vik (see below) and a Brechtian analysis of Europe in the nuclear age by Edvard Hoem.

Knut Hamsun *Hunger* (Picador £3.95); *The Wanderer* (Picador £5.95); *Mysteries* (Picador £3.95); *The Women at the Pump* (Souvenir £5.95); *Wayfarers* (Souvenir £5.95); *Growth of the Soil* (Souvenir £5.95); *Pan* (Vision Press £4.95). Hamsun's novels are enjoying a resurgence of interest after a backlash initiated by his pro-Nazi sympathies during the last war. They're thoughtful, lyrical works on the whole, deliberately simple in style (as in *The Wanderer*), but with an underlying, sometimes sinister, ambivalence. The first volume of his letters (1878–1898) has just been published, too – *Selected Letters*, edited by Harald Næss and James McFarlane (Norvik Press £20).

Ebba Haslund *Nothing Happened* (Seal Press £5.95). First English translation of an early Norwegian novel dealing with lesbian love and friendship.

J.P. Hodin *Edvard Munch* (Thames & Hudson £4.95). The best introduction to Munch's life and work, with much interesting historical detail.

Henrik Ibsen *Ibsen Plays; One* to *Six* (Methuen £3.50–4.99 each). The key international figure of Norwegian literature, Ibsen was, like his Swedish counterpart Strindberg, a social dramatist, keen through his characters to portray contemporary society in all its forms and hypocrisies. Comparatively few of his plays are ever performed in Britain, though some – *A Doll's House*, *Hedda Gabler*, etc – are household names. All the major plays are contained in the six volume set and Methuen's Michael Meyer translations are superior in every way to the equivalent Penguin editions.

James McFarlane *Ibsen and Meaning* (Norvik Press £10.50). A new, critical study of Ibsen's work. Authoritative and thorough, though only for the real Ibsen fan.

Michael Meyer *Ibsen on File* (Methuen £3.95). The best brief introduction to Ibsen's work for the general reader. For more depth, Meyer's biography, *Ibsen* (Penguin £5.95), is invaluable, and a marvellous read to boot.

Sigbjørn Obstfelder *A Priest's Diary* (Norvik Press £7.50). The last, uncompleted work of a highly regarded Norwegian poet who died of consumption in 1900 aged 33. A moody, intense piece, it forms only a segment of an ambitious work that Obstfelder intended to be his life's major undertaking.

Cora Sandel *Alberta and Jacob; Alberta and Freedom; Alberta Alone* (The Women's Press £2.50 each). The celebrated *Alberta* trilogy follows the struggle of a young woman to prove herself in a hostile environment. With its depth of insight and contemporary detail, it ranks as a key work of twentieth-century Norwegian literature. Also published by The Women's Press are *Krane's Café* (£3.50), *The Leech* (£3.95) and *The Silken Thread* (£3.95). See also *Selected Short Stories* (Seal Press £7.95).

Amalie Skram *Betrayed* (Pandora £3.95). A psychological study of nineteenth-century sexual mores, concerning the marriage of a shy young bride to an older sea captain. It is autobiographical in tone and was considered shocking when first published.

Bjorg Vik *Aquarium of Women* (Norvik Press £7.50). A collection of nine, connected short stories by one of Norway's best-known feminist writers. Recommended.

SWEDEN

HISTORY AND POLITICS

Eric Elstob *Sweden: A Traveller's History* (Boydell Press £12.95). An introduction to Swedish history from the year dot, with useful chapters on art, architecture and cultural life.

Roland Huntford *The New Totalitarians* (Allen Lane o/p). A bitter attack on the Swedish character since medieval times. His argument is that Swedish society and its consensus welfare state, rather than a model of enlightenment, is a product of inadequacy and insecurity.

Stewart Oakley *The Story of Sweden* (Faber and Faber o/p). If you can get hold of a copy (from most libraries) this is a straightforward, historical narrative, ageing but fairly comprehensive.

Michael Roberts *The Early Vasas; A History of Sweden 1523-1611* (CUP o/p). This logical and general account of the period is complemented by his more recent *Gustavus Adolphus and the Rise of Sweden* (English University Press o/p) which, more briefly and enthusiastically, covers from 1612 to Gustavus' death in 1632.

LITERATURE

Gerd Brantenberg *The Daughters of Egalia* (Journeyman Press £14.95). A satirical swipe at Swedish relationships – by a Norwegian writer.

Stig Dagerman *The Games of Night* (Quartet £4.95). Intense short stories, including an autobiographical piece, by a prolific young writer who had written four novels, four plays, short stories and travel sketches by the time he was 26. He committed suicide in 1954 at the age of 31. This is some of the best of his work.

P.C. Jersild *A Living Soul* (Norvik Press £7.50). Latest English translation of one of Sweden's best novelists, it's a social satire based around the "experiences" of an artificially produced, bodiless human brain floating in liquid. Entertaining, provocative reading.

Sara Lidman *Naboth's Stone* (Norvik Press £9.50). A novel set in 1880s Västerbotten, in Sweden's far north, charting the lives of settlers and farmers as the industrial age – and the railway – approaches.

Michael Meyer *Strindberg on File* (Methuen £4.99). A useful brief account of Strindberg's life and work (see below), though for more stirring biography the same author's *Strindberg* (OUP £8.95) is the best and most approachable source.

Cynthia Ozick *The Messiah of Stockholm* (Andre Deutsch £9.95). Entertaining but slight story, set in Stockholm and concerning a group of non-Swedes who arrived as refugees during the last war, and their distance from ordinary Swedish life.

Irene Scobbie (ed.) *Aspects of Modern Swedish Literature* (Norvik Press £10.50). An account of the trends in Swedish literature since 1880, alongside studies – and translated quotations – of various authors.

Hjalmar Söderberg *Short Stories* (Norvik Press £7.50). Twenty six short stories from the stylish pen of Söderberg (1869–1941). Brief, ironic and eminently ripe for dipping into.

Maj Sjöwall & Per Wahlöö *The Terrorists* (Penguin o/p). Pacy police story with plenty of Swedish locational detail. A good read, one of several lively and aware contemporary detective novels by this team.

August Strindberg *Strindberg Plays: One* (including *The Father*, *Miss Julie* and *The Ghost Sonata*); *Strindberg Plays: Two* (*The Dance of Death*, *A Dream Play* and *The Stronger*) (Methuen both £3.95). *Motherly Love/Pariah/ The First Warning* (Amber Lane Press £3.95). *By the Open Sea* (Penguin £4.50). Strindberg is now seen as a pioneer in both his subject matter and style. His early plays were realistic in a manner not then expected of drama, and confronted themes – for example in *Miss Julie* and *The Father* – which weren't considered suitable viewing at all, examining with deep psychological analysis the roles of the sexes both in and out of marriage. Later plays were more expressionistic, influenced by a new religious zeal. A fantastically prolific writer, only a fraction of his sixty plays, twelve historical dramas, five novels, short stories, numerous autobiographical volumes and poetry has ever been translated into English.

FINLAND

TRAVEL AND GENERAL

John Sykes *Direction North - A View of Finland* (Hutchinson o/p). A perceptive and often amusing account of family life in mid-60s urban Finland. Sykes, who was a volunteer ambulance-driver during the Winter War, returns twenty years later to seek a soldier whose injuries he tended. See p.649 for an extract.

Nils-Aslak Valkeapää *Greetings From Lappland* (Zed Books £4.95). A compelling if somewhat histrionic account of the *Same's* modern struggles, in which the author – a noted *Same* poet – lays into the Finnish authorities for their anti-*Same* policies.

Philip Ward *Finnish Cities* (Oleander £6.95). The most up-to-date Finnish travelogue, but far from the best – sentimental and plodding.

HISTORY

Max Jacobsen *The Diplomacy of The Winter War* (CUP o/p). The definitive account of the complex manoeuvring behind this event, examining closely many of the conflicting strands in Finnish politics at the time.

Eino Jutikkala and Kauko Pirinen *A History of Finland* (Thames and Hudson o/p). Useful as a broad introduction, with handy coverage of events in Sweden and Russia which had direct bearing on Finland. But the post-Independence chapters are marred by the right-wing sympathies of the authors.

D.G.Kirby *Finland in the Twentieth Century – A History and Interpretation* (C.Hurst £16). By far the best insight into contemporary Finland and the re-shaping of the nation after Independence. Recommended.

Fred Singleton *A Short History of Finland* (CUP £7.95). A very readable and informative account of Finland's past, lacking the detail of most academic accounts but an excellent starting point for general readers.

LITERATURE

Tove Jansson The *Moomin* books (all published by Puffin £1.95 each). Enduring children's tales, and with evocative descriptions of Finnish nature.

Matti Joensuu *Harjunpää and the Stone Murders* (Gollancz Crime £8.95) The only one of the Harjunpää series, involving the Helsinki detective, Timo Harjunpää, to have been translated into English. It's set in contemporary Helsinki during a bout of teenage gang warfare, and cleverly reveals Finnish attitudes to city life.

Christer Kihlman *The Rise and Fall of Hlad Glab* (Peter Owen £12.95). Supremely evocative study of personal anguish set against a background of Finland's ascent from rural backwater to modern, prosperous nation. Kihlman's other titles in translation are *Sweet Prince* (Peter Owen o/p), a rambling tale of a successful modern Finn indulging in lengthy introspection of his life and relationships, and *All My Sons* (Peter Owen £11.95).

Väinö Linna *The Unknown Soldier* (Panther o/p). Using his experiences fighting in the Winter War, Linna triggered immense controversy with this book, depicting for the first time Finnish soldiers not as "heroes in white" but as men who drank and womanised.

Elias Lönnrot *Kalevala* (Athlone Press £10.95). A collection of previously oral folktales gathered over twenty years by Lönnrot, a rural doctor, and *the* classic tome of Finnish literature. Set in an unspecified point in the past, the plot centres around a state of war between the mythical region of Kalevala (probably northern Karelia) and Pohjola (possibly Lappland) over possession of a talisman called the *Sampo*. With its forests, lakes, saunas, and finely detailed descriptions of the domestic and social lives of village peasantry, the story is regarded as quintessentially Finnish, but it's not an easy read, due mainly to its length (some 22,750 lines), and the non-linear course of the plot. Its influence on Finnish literature is huge, and it was a lynchpin of the Finnish nationalist and language movements.

F.E.Sillanpää *Meek Heritage* (Eriksson o/p); *Fallen Asleep While Young* (Putnam o/p). With his near-mystical views on mankind and nature, Sillanpää dominated Finnish fiction through the early part of the twentieth century, and was awarded the Nobel Prize in 1939.

ICELAND

HISTORY AND TRAVEL

W.H.Auden and Louis MacNiece *Letters From Iceland* (Faber £3.95). Brilliant compilation of poems, spoofs, letters, and diary entries made on the pair's journey to Iceland in the 1930s.

Ted Edwards *Fight the Wild Island* (John Murray £11.95). Slightly flippant but an often gripping diary of the author's walk from east to west coasts – the first such journey known.

Magnús Magnússon *Iceland Saga* (Bodley Head £8.95). The greatest professional Icelander gives a solid account of Iceland's early history and the Sagas, though the book's clearly pitched at a MOR readership.

S.A.Magnússon *Northern Sphinx* (C.Hurst £6.95). A comprehensive account of Icelandic history and various aspects of society from the Settlement to the 1970s. Good as far as it goes, although it would benefit from deeper analysis of some of the issues.

William Morris *Icelandic Journals* (Centaur Press £18). Accounts of two trips to Iceland in 1871 and 1873 by the man who was instrumental in getting the Icelandic Sagas published in England. *Icelandic Jaunt* (£2.00), issued by the William Morris Society, is a study of both journeys.

Agnes Rothery *Iceland: Bastion of the North* (Andrew Melrose o/p). Bumptious but very readable observations of Icelandic life in the mid-twentieth century.

Paul Vander-Molen *Iceland Breakthrough* (Oxford Illustrated Press £12.95). Detailed account of a canoe and microlight aircraft navigation of the Jökulsá á Fjöllum. Stylewise a bit dry, but the photos are excellent.

EARLY LITERATURE

The Eddas Myths and legends from the remote past, the source of virtually all that is known about the religion and cosmology of pre-Christian Scandinavia. There are two main *Eddas*: the *Poetic*, or *Elder, Edda* (OUP £25), a collection of mythological and ethical poems thought to have been composed between the ninth and thirteenth centuries, and the *Prose*, or *Snorri's, Edda* (Dent £4.95) by Snorri Sturluson – a key figure in medieval Iceland as a writer, historian and politician, and sometimes credited as the author of *Egil's Saga*.

The Sagas *Njal's Saga; Egil's Saga Laxdaela Saga; King Harald's Saga* (all Penguin £3.95). A vast collection of historical, semi-fictitious stories (the above are merely the best-known) written anonymously between the twelfth and fourteenth centuries and describing events across several generations. The Sagas feature real people and tell of events which are known to have happened, but the plot is embroidered to suit the tales' heroic style. They reveal much about the Icelandic people during the formative years of the nation: arguments between individuals might spring from comparatively trivial disputes over horses or sheep, but due to a strict code of honour and revenge, every insult, whether real or imagined, had to be avenged, and minor arguments could develop into bloody family feuds. Plots are complex, the dialogue laconic, and the pared-down prose omits unnecessary detail. New characters are often introduced by tedious genealogies, necessary to explain the motivation behind their later actions. Personality is only revealed through speech, facial expressions and general demeanour, or the comments and gossip of others.

G.Turville-Petre *Origins of Icelandic Literature* (OUP o/p). An informative account of the early years of Icelandic writing, from pagan times to the mid-thirteenth century, when the greatest sagas were produced.

MODERN LITERATURE

Desmond Bagley *Running Blind* (Fontana £2.95). A thriller loaded with the author's usual Cold War spy chase clichés. But Icelandic landscapes feature prominently as bodies are hurled into fissures, cars are chased across the interior, and there's a final shoot-out at Geysir.

Gunnar Gunnarsson *Black Cliffs* (University of Wisconsin Press £14.95). One of Iceland's most prolific twentieth-century novelists, and a prominent writer throughout Scandinavia. Although Icelandic, he lived in Denmark and wrote about Iceland in Danish.

Halldor Laxness. *The Atom Station* (Methuen o/p). Clever satire of life in modern Reykjavík, the most famous work of an author who dominated Icelandic literature during the middle part of the twentieth century. His grand, epic works capture the essence of life in Iceland, and all are worth reading if you can find them. Look out also for *Christianity at Glacier*, an Icelandic film released in 1989, based on a Laxness story.

Agnar Thordarson *A Medal of Distinction* (Hippocrene £4.95). Ostensibly the tale of a man's struggle to live up to the expectations of society, it's heavy-going but worth seeking out – if only to exemplify the gloomy and introspective nature of much modern Icelandic fiction.

INDEX

HELP US UPDATE

We've gone to a lot of effort to ensure that this second edition of *The Rough Guide: Scandiinavia* is completely up-to-date and accurate. However, things do change – places get 'discovered', opening hours are notoriously fickle – and any suggestions, comments or corrections would be much appreciated.

We'll credit all contributions, and send a copy of the next edition (or any other Rough Guide if you prefer) for the best letters. Please write to:

Jules Brown and Mick Sinclair, The Rough Guides, 149 Kennington Lane, London SE11 4EZ.